THE OXFORD ENCYCLOPAEDIA OF
EUROPEAN COMMUNITY LAW

THE OXFORD ENCYCLOPAEDIA OF

EUROPEAN COMMUNITY LAW

VOLUME II

THE LAW OF THE INTERNAL MARKET

A. G. TOTH
Dr. Jur., Ph.D.
Emeritus Professor of European Law, University of Strathclyde

OXFORD
UNIVERSITY PRESS

OXFORD
UNIVERSITY PRESS

Great Clarendon Street, Oxford, OX2 6DP,
United Kingdom

Oxford University Press is a department of the University of Oxford.
It furthers the University's objective of excellence in research, scholarship,
and education by publishing worldwide. Oxford is a registered trade mark of
Oxford University Press in the UK and in certain other countries

First published 2005

Published in the United States of America by Oxford University Press
198 Madison Avenue, New York, NY 10016, United States of America

British Library Cataloguing in Publication Data
Data available

Library of Congress Cataloging in Publication Data
Data available

ISBN 978–0–19–825600–7

This book is dedicated to
the memory of my wife

LIST OF CONTRIBUTORS

Vanessa Edwards	Company law European Company European Economic Interest Grouping
Paul Farmer	Direct taxation
Inge Govaere	Intellectual property rights
Julian Hickey	Tax harmonization Value added tax (VAT)
Michael Lux	Classification of goods for customs purposes Common Customs Tariff (CCT) Community Customs Code (CC) Community customs territory Customs procedures Customs Union Customs value Origin of goods
Richard Lyal	Excise duties and similar taxes Taxation of goods (prohibition of discrimination)
Peter Oliver	Free movement of goods Goods Measures having equivalent effect to quantitative restrictions Quantitative restrictions
Akos Toth	Charges having equivalent effect to customs duties Equal pay (principle of) Equal treatment (principle of) Expulsion Freedom of establishment Freedom to provide services Free movement of capital Free movement of persons Official authority Public health Public policy Public security Public service Residence permit Right of entry and residence

	Right to leave Right to remain Social advantage State commercial monopoly Worker
Philippa Watson	Public procurement Social security

NOTES ON CONTRIBUTORS

Vanessa Edwards	Solicitor, Référendaire to Advocate General Jacobs, The Court of Justice of the European Communities.
Paul Farmer	Barrister, Pump Court Tax Chambers.
Inge Govaere	Professor of European Law, Ghent University, and Director of the European Legal Studies Department, College of Europe.
Julian Hickey	Fellow, School of Tax, Queen Mary, University of London.
Michael Lux	Head of Division, Customs Legislation and Control of the Application of Community Law, Taxation and Customs Union DG, European Commission.
Richard Lyal	Legal Adviser, European Commission.
Peter Oliver	Legal Adviser, European Commission.
Akos Toth	Emeritus Professor of European Law, University of Strathclyde.
Philippa Watson	Barrister, Essex Court Chambers, and Professor of Competition Law, Nottingham Law School.

PREFACE

At the time of writing Volume I of the *Encyclopaedia*, which dealt with *Institutional Law*, it was envisaged that Volume II would cover what is usually referred to as *Substantive Law*. During the period since the publication of Volume I, however, substantive Community law has expanded to such an extent that it has proved impracticable, indeed impossible, to cover this vast area in a single volume in the desired depth. It has therefore been decided to narrow down the scope of Volume II to those core areas of substantive law which are relevant to the creation and functioning of the internal market, namely, the four freedoms (free movement of goods, persons, services and capital, including the right of establishment); company law; customs law; intellectual property rights; public procurement; sex equality law; social security law; tax law; and areas closely related to these. As a result, contrary to the original plans, competition law and policy is not covered in this volume, but will be dealt with in Volume III.

There has also been a second reason for moving competition law to Volume III. The profound changes that have radically transformed competition law in recent years would have required a complete rewriting of the entries affected by the changes, which had already been drafted. This would have further delayed publication of Volume II, making a constant updating of the other parts necessary. Moreover, since some of the new competition rules became applicable only during 2004, after the cut-off date for this book, it was thought preferable to wait until they have been applied in practice and to see how they are interpreted by the Courts. Although competition law and the law of the internal market mutually complement each other, they are not inseparably interconnected. Each can be treated independently of the other so that the decision does not affect the contents of the present volume. Indeed, in official publications, like the *Bulletin of the European Union* and the *General Report*, they are dealt with under separate headings. The European Constitution also makes a clear distinction between them by placing the internal market within the shared competence of the Union and the Member States, while allocating the task of establishing the competition rules necessary for the functioning of the internal market to the exclusive competence of the Union (Articles I–13 and I–14).

It should be emphasized that Volume II, like Volume I, has been designed to form a complete, self-contained unit. Covering a distinct area of Community law, it can be used on its own, without the need to refer either to Volume I or to Volume III, which is in preparation. The purpose and general scheme of Volume II are the same as those of Volume I: to present Community law in the form of a work which contains legal definitions of its terms and concepts as they are used in the Treaties and acts of the institutions and, above all, as they have been interpreted in the extensive case-law of the European Court of Justice and the Court of First Instance. The entries are arranged in alphabetical order and have been drafted in such a way that a short and concise definition is followed by a longer and more detailed explanation, analysis, or description, putting the terms and concepts in the wider context of Community law as a whole.

There are, however, some notable differences between the two volumes, which necessarily follow from the different nature of their subject-matter. Volume I contains a fairly large number of relatively short entries. By contrast, the entries in Volume II are fewer in number but generally much longer. There are two reasons for this. The first is that while Volume I is based mainly on the Treaties and the case-law of the European Court of Justice, Volume II covers, in addition, a vast number of Community acts (regulations, directives, decisions, etc.) which make up a far larger proportion of substantive law than of institutional law.

The second reason has to do with the way in which the material is organized in Volume II. In this respect, a choice had to be made between two different solutions. The first was to treat each aspect or element of a complex term or concept as a separate (and consequently relatively short) entry. The second was to treat every aspect of a concept in a single continuous (and consequently relatively long) entry. As a general rule, the second solution was adopted, unless a term has acquired such a well-defined, self-contained meaning that it merited a separate entry.

The following three examples illustrate the point. First, the entry on the 'Free movement of persons' could have been divided into a number of short entries, each dealing in turn with different categories of persons, such as workers, students, Union citizens, and third-country nationals. However, since all of these are governed by certain common rules and principles, it was preferable to deal with them in one single, long entry. Secondly, it would have been possible to draft separate entries on the right of establishment of individuals and of companies, but again it was preferable to bring these together under the title 'Freedom of establishment'. This title also covers the mutual recognition of qualifications, because the case-law of the Court of Justice on the right of establishment, on recognition of qualifications, and the relevant secondary legislation (directives) are so much interwoven that a separate treatment of each seemed impracticable. Thirdly, the different forms of intellectual property rights, such as patents, trade marks, copyright, and other related rights, while having their own particular rules, are governed by common principles to such an extent that their discussion in a long, continuous entry seemed entirely justified. It is hoped that this general approach, which has been followed throughout the book, will be favourably received by readers. It provides a far more comprehensive overview of complex areas of the law than the opposite solution, which would have entailed repetition and fragmentation. Where, however, a term has acquired a distinct meaning, such as 'public policy', 'public security', 'public health', 'social advantage', 'worker', etc, it has been given a separate entry.

Since most of the entries are long and complex (which is in line with the nature of the book as an encyclopaedia), readers are assisted in three different ways in finding their way around the book. First, there is a detailed List of entries, which contains not only headings which have an actual entry, but also terms and concepts which do not have a separate entry but which are discussed under another entry, to which they are cross-referred. Thus, using the above examples, while 'Copyright and related rights', or 'Patent', or 'Trade mark' do not have a separate entry, they are all listed in the List of entries with cross-references to 'Intellectual property rights', where they are discussed. Likewise, 'Mutual recognition of qualifications' is included in the List of entries with a cross-reference to 'Freedom of establishment'. Such cross-reference-only headings appear also in the main body of the book in the relevant places. In addition, there are cross-references to related entries at the end of, and often within, each entry.

Secondly, the List of entries is followed by a detailed Table of contents, which shows the structure of (and thus the logic behind) each entry, with sub-headings and page references. This guides readers through the entry and directs them straight to the page where the relevant matter can be found. Thirdly, there is a very detailed Subject index at the end of the book.

The presentation of the material is the same as in Volume I. All relevant sources and authorities are fully cited, with the main emphasis being placed upon definitions and interpretations given by the Community Courts. Preliminary rulings are cited by the name of one party, direct actions by the names of both parties. Cases not yet reported at the time of proof-reading are cited in the text by volume and paragraph only (e.g. [2004] ECR I-0000, para 25), but the date of the judgment is given in the Table of cases. As mentioned above, the entries are concluded by extensive cross-references, and also by a list of further reading. Thus, as a work of reference, the book may be used on its own to obtain instant, comprehensive and up-to-date information on a point of Community law. Equally, since it contains full references to the sources, authorities and academic writings, it may serve as a basic research tool into an area of Community law.

The cut-off date for the book was set at 1 January 2004, but in most cases it has been possible to incorporate developments in legislation and case-law that occurred up to 1 July 2004, and in some cases even later.

Another difference between the first and the second volumes is that in producing Volume II, I have been able to benefit from the knowledge and expertise of a team of contributors who have undertaken the task of covering the more specialized subjects. I would like to express my grateful thanks to them not only for the professionalism and expertise with which they have performed that task and for the time and effort which they have devoted to the *Encyclopaedia* amidst their busy schedules, but also for their patience and understanding in repeatedly updating their contributions as required by successive delays in the production of the book. Although the volume is thus the result of team-work, each contributor is responsible only for the entries that he or she has contributed.

I wish to thank the British Academy for the award of a two-year Research Readership, which greatly facilitated preparation of the book. In this context, I am particularly grateful to The Right Hon The Lord Slynn of Hadley, former Advocate-General and Judge at the European Court of Justice and former Lord of Appeal in Ordinary, and to Mr Francis Jacobs,

Advocate-General at the European Court of Justice, for the support which they gave to my application for the Research Readership.

Last but not least, my thanks are due to the secretaries who typed the manuscript, and to the staff of Oxford University Press for the care and efficiency with which they have produced the book. I would particularly like to thank Christopher Rycroft, Katarina Wihlborg, Meg Zawadzki, and Geraldine Mangley for their useful advice and assistance in connection with the preparation of the volume.

My greatest debt is to my late wife, whose patience, support, and encouragement during the long period of writing have been as unfailing as on previous occasions.

Glasgow
14 February 2005

A G TOTH

CONTENTS—SUMMARY

LIST OF ENTRIES

CONTENTS

D

E

F

P

V

W

ABBREVIATIONS

ACP	African, Caribbean, and Pacific (States)
A.-G.	Advocate-General
Art.	Article
Bull. EC	*Bulletin of the European Communities*
Bull. EU	*Bulletin of the European Union*
CC	Community Customs Code
CCT	Common Customs Tariff
CFI	Court of First Instance
CLJ	*Cambridge Law Journal*
CML Rev.	*Common Market Law Review*
COM	Commission document
Comm.	Commission
Comp. Rep.	*Report on Competition Policy*
Dec.	Decision
Dir.	Directive
Doc.	Document
EAEC	European Atomic Energy Community
EBL Rev.	*European Business Law Review*
EC	European Community; Treaty establishing the EC
ECHR	European Convention on Human Rights
ECJ	European Court of Justice
ECLR	*European Competition Law Review*
ECR	European Court Reports
ECSC	European Coal and Steel Community; Treaty establishing the ECSC
EEA	European Economic Area
EEC	European Economic Community; Treaty establishing the EEC
EEIG	European Economic Interest Grouping
EFTA	European Free Trade Association
EHRR	European Human Rights Reports
EIPR	*European Intellectual Property Review*
ELJ	*European Law Journal*
EL Rev.	*European Law Review*
EMU	Economic and Monetary Union
EP	European Parliament
EU	European Union
Euratom	European Atomic Energy Community; Treaty establishing the Euratom
GATT	General Agreement on Tariffs and Trade
Gen. Rep. EC	*General Report on the Activities of the European Communities*
Gen. Rep. EU	*General Report on the Activities of the European Union*

ICLQ	*International and Comparative Law Quarterly*
IIC	*International Review of Industrial Property and Copyright*
JBL	*Journal of Business Law*
JHA	Justice and Home Affairs
JO	*Journal Officiel des Communautés Européennes*
JWTL	*Journal of World Trade Law*
LIEI	*Legal Issues of European Integration; Legal Issues of Economic Integration*
LQR	*Law Quarterly Review*
MLR	*Modern Law Review*
NLJ	*New Law Journal*
OCT	Overseas Countries and Territories
OJ	*Official Journal of the European Communities*
Rec.	Recommendation
Reg.	Regulation
Res.	Resolution
SEA	Single European Act
Sp. Edn.	*Special Edition of the OJ* (English edition)
Suppl.–*Bull. EC*	Supplement to the *Bulletin of the European Communities*
Suppl.–*Bull. EU*	Supplement to the *Bulletin of the European Union*
TEU	Treaty on European Union (Maastricht Treaty)
ToA	Treaty of Amsterdam
ToN	Treaty of Nice
TRIPS	Trade-Related Aspects of Intellectual Property Rights
VAT	Value added tax
WIPO	World Intellectual Property Organization
WTO	World Trade Organization
YEL	*Yearbook of European Law*
*	Designates entries in Volume I

TABLE OF CASES

European Court of Justice

Preliminary rulings are cited by the name of one party, direct actions by the names of both parties.

Alphabetical

Numerical

Court of First Instance

Alphabetical

Numerical

EFTA Court

European Court of Human Rights

TABLE OF COMMUNITY TREATIES

TABLE OF COMMUNITY ACTS

DECISIONS

DIRECTIVES

REGULATIONS

RECOMMENDATIONS

RESOLUTIONS

OTHER ACTS

TABLE OF INTERNATIONAL AGREEMENTS

TABLE OF UNITED KINGDOM LEGISLATION

TABLES OF EQUIVALENCES REFERRED TO IN ARTICLE 12 OF THE TREATY OF AMSTERDAM

A. Treaty on European Union

Previous numbering	*New numbering*
TITLE I	TITLE I
Article A	Article 1
Article B	Article 2
Article C	Article 3
Article D	Article 4
Article E	Article 5
Article F	Article 6
Article F.1*	Article 7
TITLE II	TITLE II
Article G	Article 8
TITLE III	TITLE III
Article H	Article 9
TITLE IV	TITLE IV
Article I	Article 10
TITLE V***	TITLE V
Article J.1	Article 11
Article J.2	Article 12
Article J.3	Article 13
Article J.4	Article 14
Article J.5	Article 15
Article J.6	Article 16
Article J.7	Article 17
Article J.8	Article 18
Article J.9	Article 19
Article J.10	Article 20
Article J.11	Article 21
Article J.12	Article 22
Article J.13	Article 23
Article J.14	Article 24
Article J.15	Article 25
Article J.16	Article 26
Article J.17	Article 27
Article J.18	Article 28
TITLE VI***	TITLE VI
Article K.1	Article 29
Article K.2	Article 30
Article K.3	Article 31
Article K.4	Article 32
Article K.5	Article 33
Article K.6	Article 34
Article K.7	Article 35
Article K.8	Article 36
Article K.9	Article 37
Article K.10	Article 38
Article K.11	Article 39
Article K.12	Article 40
Article K.13	Article 41
Article K.14	Article 42
TITLE VIa**	TITLE VII
Article K.15*	Article 43
Article K.16*	Article 44
Article K.17*	Article 45
TITLE VII	TITLE VIII
Article L	Article 46
Article M	Article 47
Article N	Article 48
Article O	Article 49
Article P	Article 50
Article Q	Article 51
Article R	Article 52
Article S	Article 53

* New Article introduced by the Treaty of Amsterdam
** New Title introduced by the Treaty of Amsterdam
*** Title restructured by the Treaty of Amsterdam

B. Treaty establishing the European Community

Previous numbering	*New numbering*
PART ONE	PART ONE
Article 1	Article 1
Article 2	Article 2
Article 3	Article 3
Article 3a	Article 4
Article 3b	Article 5
Article 3c*	Article 6
Article 4	Article 7
Article 4a	Article 8
Article 4b	Article 9
Article 5	Article 10
Article 5a*	Article 11
Article 6	Article 12
Article 6a*	Article 13
Article 7 (repealed)	—
Article 7a	Article 14
Article 7b (repealed)	—
Article 7c	Article 15
Article 7d*	Article 16
PART TWO	PART TWO
Article 8	Article 17
Article 8a	Article 18
Article 8b	Article 19
Article 8c	Article 20
Article 8d	Article 21
Article 8e	Article 22
PART THREE	PART THREE
TITLE I	TITLE I
Article 9	Article 23
Article 10	Article 24
Article 11 (repealed)	—
CHAPTER 1	CHAPTER 1
SECTION 1 (deleted)	—
Article 12	Article 25
Article 13 (repealed)	—
Article 14 (repealed)	—
Article 15 (repealed)	—
Article 16 (repealed)	—
Article 17 (repealed)	—
SECTION 2 (deleted)	—
Article 18 (repealed)	—
Article 19 (repealed)	—
Article 20 (repealed)	—
Article 21 (repealed)	—
Article 22 (repealed)	—
Article 23 (repealed)	—
Article 24 (repealed)	—
Article 25 (repealed)	—
Article 26 (repealed)	—
Article 27 (repealed)	—
Article 28	Article 26
Article 29	Article 27
CHAPTER 2	CHAPTER 2
Article 30	Article 28
Article 31 (repealed)	—
Article 32 (repealed)	—
Article 33 (repealed)	—
Article 34	Article 29
Article 35 (repealed)	—
Article 36	Article 30
Article 37	Article 31
TITLE II	TITLE II
Article 38	Article 32
Article 39	Article 33
Article 40	Article 34
Article 41	Article 35
Article 42	Article 36
Article 43	Article 37
Article 44 (repealed)	—
Article 45 (repealed)	—
Article 46	Article 38
Article 47 (repealed)	—
TITLE III	TITLE III
CHAPTER 1	CHAPTER 1
Article 48	Article 39
Article 49	Article 40
Article 50	Article 41
Article 51	Article 42

* New Article introduced by the Treaty of Amsterdam

Previous numbering	*New numbering*
CHAPTER 2	CHAPTER 2
Article 52	Article 43
Article 53 (repealed)	—
Article 54	Article 44
Article 55	Article 45
Article 56	Article 46
Article 57	Article 47
Article 58	Article 48
CHAPTER 3	CHAPTER 3
Article 59	Article 49
Article 60	Article 50
Article 61	Article 51
Article 62 (repealed)	—
Article 63	Article 52
Article 64	Article 53
Article 65	Article 54
Article 66	Article 55
CHAPTER 4	CHAPTER 4
Article 67(repealed)	—
Article 68 (repealed)	—
Article 69 (repealed)	—
Article 70 (repealed)	—
Article 71 (repealed)	—
Article 72 (repealed)	—
Article 73 (repealed)	—
Article 73a (repealed)	—
Article 73b	Article 56
Article 73c	Article 57
Article 73d	Article 58
Article 73e (repealed)	—
Article 73f	Article 59
Article 73g	Article 60
Article 73h (repealed)	—
TITLE IIIa**	TITLE IV
Article 73i*	Article 61
Article 73j*	Article 62
Article 73k*	Article 63
Article 73l*	Article 64
Article 73m*	Article 65
Article 73n*	Article 66
Article 73o*	Article 67
Article 73p*	Article 68
Article 73q*	Article 69
TITLE IV	TITLE V
Article 74	Article 70
Article 75	Article 71
Article 76	Article 72
Article 77	Article 73
Article 78	Article 74
Article 79	Article 75
Article 80	Article 76
Article 81	Article 77
Article 82	Article 78
Article 83	Article 79
Article 84	Article 80
TITLE V	TITLE VI
CHAPTER 1	CHAPTER 1
SECTION 1	SECTION 1
Article 85	Article 81
Article 86	Article 82
Article 87	Article 83
Article 88	Article 84
Article 89	Article 85
Article 90	Article 86
SECTION 2 (deleted)	—
Article 91 (repealed)	—
SECTION 3	SECTION 2
Article 92	Article 87
Article 93	Article 88
Article 94	Article 89
CHAPTER 2	CHAPTER 2
Article 95	Article 90
Article 96	Article 91
Article 97 (repealed)	—
Article 98	Article 92
Article 99	Article 93

* New Article introduced by the Treaty of Amsterdam
** New Title introduced by the Treaty of Amsterdam

Previous numbering	*New numbering*
CHAPTER 3	CHAPTER 3
Article 100	Article 94
Article 100a	Article 95
Article 100b (repealed)	—
Article 100c (repealed)	—
Article 100d (repealed)	—
Article 101	Article 96
Article 102	Article 97
TITLE VI	TITLE VII
CHAPTER 1	CHAPTER 1
Article 102a	Article 98
Article 103	Article 99
Article 103a	Article 100
Article 104	Article 101
Article 104a	Article 102
Article 104b	Article 103
Article 104c	Article 104
CHAPTER 2	CHAPTER 2
Article 105	Article 105
Article 105a	Article 106
Article 106	Article 107
Article 107	Article 108
Article 108	Article 109
Article 108a	Article 110
Article 109	Article 111
CHAPTER 3	CHAPTER 3
Article 109a	Article 112
Article 109b	Article 113
Article 109c	Article 114
Article 109d	Article 115
CHAPTER 4	CHAPTER 4
Article 109e	Article 116
Article 109f	Article 117
Article 109g	Article 118
Article 109h	Article 119
Article 109i	Article 120
Article 109j	Article 121
Article 109k	Article 122
Article 109l	Article 123
Article 109m	Article 124
TITLE VIa**	TITLE VIII
Article 109n*	Article 125
Article 109o*	Article 126
Article 109p*	Article 127
Article 109q*	Article 128
Article 109r*	Article 129
Article 109s*	Article 130
TITLE VII	TITLE IX
Article 110	Article 131
Article 111 (repealed)	—
Article 112	Article 132
Article 113	Article 133
Article 114 (repealed)	—
Article 115	Article 134
TITLE VIIa**	TITLE X
Article 116*	Article 135
TITLE VIII	TITLE XI
CHAPTER 1***	CHAPTER 1
Article 117	Article 136
Article 118	Article 137
Article 118a	Article 138
Article 118b	Article 139
Article 118c	Article 140
Article 119	Article 141
Article 119a	Article 142
Article 120	Article 143
Article 121	Article 144
Article 122	Article 145
CHAPTER 2	CHAPTER 2
Article 123	Article 146
Article 124	Article 147
Article 125	Article 148
CHAPTER 3	CHAPTER 3
Article 126	Article 149
Article 127	Article 150
TITLE IX	TITLE XII
Article 128	Article 151

* New Article introduced by the Treaty of Amsterdam
** New Title introduced by the Treaty of Amsterdam
*** Title restructured by the Treaty of Amsterdam

Previous numbering	*New numbering*
TITLE X	TITLE XIII
Article 129	Article 152
TITLE XI	TITLE XIV
Article 129a	Article 153
TITLE XII	TITLE XV
Article 129b	Article 154
Article 129c	Article 155
Article 129d	Article 156
TITLE XIII	TITLE XVI
Article 130	Article 157
TITLE XIV	TITLE XVII
Article 130a	Article 158
Article 130b	Article 159
Article 130c	Article 160
Article 130d	Article 161
Article 130e	Article 162
TITLE XV	TITLE XVIII
Article 130f	Article 163
Article 130g	Article 164
Article 130h	Article 165
Article 130i	Article 166
Article 130j	Article 167
Article 130k	Article 168
Article 130l	Article 169
Article 130m	Article 170
Article 130n	Article 171
Article 130o	Article 172
Article 130p	Article 173
Article 130q (repealed)	—
TITLE XVI	TITLE XIX
Article 130r	Article 174
Article 130s	Article 175
Article 130t	Article 176
TITLE XVII	TITLE XX
Article 130u	Article 177
Article 130v	Article 178
Article 130w	Article 179
Article 130x	Article 180
Article 130y	Article 181

Previous numbering	*New numbering*
PART FOUR	PART FOUR
Article 131	Article 182
Article 132	Article 183
Article 133	Article 184
Article 134	Article 185
Article 135	Article 186
Article 136	Article 187
Article 136a	Article 188
PART FIVE	PART FIVE
TITLE I	TITLE I
CHAPTER 1	CHAPTER 1
SECTION 1	SECTION 1
Article 137	Article 189
Article 138	Article 190
Article 138a	Article 191
Article 138b	Article 192
Article 138c	Article 193
Article 138d	Article 194
Article 138e	Article 195
Article 139	Article 196
Article 140	Article 197
Article 141	Article 198
Article 142	Article 199
Article 143	Article 200
Article 144	Article 201
SECTION 2	SECTION 2
Article 145	Article 202
Article 146	Article 203
Article 147	Article 204
Article 148	Article 205
Article 149 (repealed)	—
Article 150	Article 206
Article 151	Article 207
Article 152	Article 208
Article 153	Article 209
Article 154	Article 210
SECTION 3	SECTION 3
Article 155	Article 211
Article 156	Article 212
Article 157	Article 213
Article 158	Article 214
Article 159	Article 215
Article 160	Article 216

Previous numbering	New numbering
Article 161	Article 217
Article 162	Article 218
Article 163	Article 219
SECTION 4	SECTION 4
Article 164	Article 220
Article 165	Article 221
Article 166	Article 222
Article 167	Article 223
Article 168	Article 224
Article 168a	Article 225
Article 169	Article 226
Article 170	Article 227
Article 171	Article 228
Article 172	Article 229
Article 173	Article 230
Article 174	Article 231
Article 175	Article 232
Article 176	Article 233
Article 177	Article 234
Article 178	Article 235
Article 179	Article 236
Article 180	Article 237
Article 181	Article 238
Article 182	Article 239
Article 183	Article 240
Article 184	Article 241
Article 185	Article 242
Article 186	Article 243
Article 187	Article 244
Article 188	Article 245
SECTION 5	SECTION 5
Article 188a	Article 246
Article 188b	Article 247
Article 188c	Article 248
CHAPTER 2	CHAPTER 2
Article 189	Article 249
Article 189a	Article 250
Article 189b	Article 251
Article 189c	Article 252
Article 190	Article 253
Article 191	Article 254
Article 191a*	Article 255
Article 192	Article 256
CHAPTER 3	CHAPTER 3
Article 193	Article 257
Article 194	Article 258
Article 195	Article 259
Article 196	Article 260
Article 197	Article 261
Article 198	Article 262
CHAPTER 4	CHAPTER 4
Article 198a	Article 263
Article 198b	Article 264
Article 198c	Article 265
CHAPTER 5	CHAPTER 5
Article 198d	Article 266
Article 198e	Article 267
TITLE II	TITLE II
Article 199	Article 268
Article 200 (repealed)	—
Article 201	Article 269
Article 201a	Article 270
Article 202	Article 271
Article 203	Article 272
Article 204	Article 273
Article 205	Article 274
Article 205a	Article 275
Article 206	Article 276
Article 206a (repealed)	—
Article 207	Article 277
Article 208	Article 278
Article 209	Article 279
Article 209a	Article 280
PART SIX	PART SIX
Article 210	Article 281
Article 211	Article 282
Article 212*	Article 283
Article 213	Article 284
Article 213a*	Article 285
Article 213b*	Article 286
Article 214	Article 287
Article 215	Article 288
Article 216	Article 289
Article 217	Article 290

* New Article introduced by the Treaty of Amsterdam

Previous numbering	*New numbering*
Article 218*	Article 291
Article 219	Article 292
Article 220	Article 293
Article 221	Article 294
Article 222	Article 295
Article 223	Article 296
Article 224	Article 297
Article 225	Article 298
Article 226 (repealed)	—
Article 227	Article 299
Article 228	Article 300
Article 228a	Article 301
Article 229	Article 302
Article 230	Article 303
Article 231	Article 304
Article 232	Article 305
Article 233	Article 306
Article 234	Article 307
Article 235	Article 308
Article 236*	Article 309
Article 237 (repealed)	—
Article 238	Article 310
Article 239	Article 311
Article 240	Article 312
Article 241 (repealed)	—
Article 242 (repealed)	—
Article 243 (repealed)	—
Article 244 (repealed)	—
Article 245 (repealed)	—
Article 246 (repealed)	—
FINAL PROVISIONS	FINAL PROVISIONS
Article 247	Article 313
Article 248	Article 314

* New Article introduced by the Treaty of Amsterdam

AREA OF FREEDOM, SECURITY, AND JUSTICE
see FREE MOVEMENT OF PERSONS

A

C

CHARGES HAVING EQUIVALENT EFFECT TO CUSTOMS DUTIES

One of various measures applied by States in the context of international trade to the import and export of goods, either for the purpose of raising revenue or to afford protection to domestic products or industries. Since these charges present an obstacle to the free movement of goods between States, they are incompatible with the concept of a customs union. As the EC is based upon a customs union covering all trade in goods, charges having equivalent effect to customs duties on imports and exports are prohibited between Member States (Arts. 23 and 25 EC). These charges are also prohibited in respect of goods and products falling within the scope of application of the Euratom Treaty (Art. 93 Euratom). A similar prohibition applied under the ECSC Treaty (Art. 4(a) ECSC).

Arts. 23 and 25 EC prohibit charges having equivalent effect to customs duties only on imports and exports 'between Member States'. However, the ECJ has considerably extended the scope of these provisions by holding that they also prohibit charges levied on goods imported into, or exported from, a region of a Member State (as opposed to the whole territory of that State) when goods are coming from or going to another Member State or a country party to a free trade agreement with the Community, as well as charges levied on goods entering one region of the territory of a Member State solely from other regions of the same State and on goods despatched from one region solely to other regions of the same State. The reasoning of the Court has been that the principle of a customs union requires the free movement of goods generally within the union as a whole, and not only in inter-State trade. A charge levied at an internal regional frontier constitutes an obstacle to the free movement of goods, which is at least as serious as a charge levied at the external national frontier. The unity of the Community customs territory is undermined by the establishment of a regional customs frontier just the same, whether the products on which a charge is levied are domestic products or come from other Member States (Case C-163/90 *Legros* [1992] ECR I-4625 at pp. I-4665–7 and Cases C-363/93 etc. *Lancry* [1994] ECR I-3957 at pp. I-3989–92, both cases involving 'dock dues' (*octroi de mer*) levied on imports into the French overseas departments of Réunion and

Martinique; Cases C-485/93 etc. *Simitzi* [1995] ECR I-2655 at pp. I-2674–8, involving a communal tax on consumer goods entering or leaving the Dodecanese islands in Greece).

Under the EC Treaty, charges having equivalent effect to customs duties on imports were progressively eliminated during the transitional period and completely abolished, as between the original Member States, on 1 January 1970 (Art. 13(2) of the original EEC Treaty, repealed by the Treaty of Amsterdam (ToA), as interpreted by the ECJ in Case 94/74 *IGAV* [1975] ECR 699 at p. 711 and in subsequent cases). As between the Community as originally constituted and the Member States that acceded later, and between the latter Member States themselves, they were abolished in accordance with the respective Acts of Accession.

Although the EC Treaty is silent on this point, the ECJ held that in the context of trade with third countries, Member States were precluded, subsequent to the establishment of the Common Customs Tariff on 1 July 1968, from introducing, in a unilateral manner, new charges on goods imported directly from third countries and from raising the level of those in existence at that time. Both the unity of the Community customs territory and the uniformity of the common commercial policy would be seriously undermined if the Member Sates could unilaterally impose such charges. The reduction or elimination of the then existing charges was, however, a matter for the institutions of the Community (Cases 37/73 etc. *Diamantarbeiders II* [1973] ECR 1609 at pp. 1623–4; see also Case C-125/94 *Aprile I* [1995] ECR I-2919 at pp. I-2950–1). While in intra-Community trade the prohibition of charges having equivalent effect is unconditional and absolute, in trade with third countries it may be subject to exceptions and derogations. The reason is that in the latter case the abolition, maintenance, amendment, or introduction of these charges is determined, not by the need to establish free movement of goods within the Community, but by the requirements of the common commercial policy and by the requirements of their harmonization at the external frontiers of the Community (Case 70/77 *Simmenthal* [1978] ECR 1453 at pp. 1470–1).

Charges having equivalent effect to customs duties on exports were abolished, as between the original Member States, on 1 January 1962 (Art. 16 of the original EEC Treaty, repealed by the ToA, as interpreted by the ECJ in Case 18/71 *Eunomia* [1971] ECR 811 at p. 816 and in subsequent cases). As between the Community as originally constituted and the Member States which acceded later, and between the latter Member States themselves, they were abolished in accordance with the respective Acts of Accession.

1. Definition of charges having equivalent effect. In the system created by the EC Treaty, the prohibition of charges having equivalent effect to customs duties is necessarily complementary to the prohibition of customs duties themselves. The general intention has been to abolish not only measures that obviously take the form of the classic customs duty but also all those which, presented under other names or introduced by the indirect means of other procedures and imposed exclusively on imported or exported products, have, by altering their cost price, the same restrictive effect on the free movement of goods as customs duties (see e.g. Cases 2/62 etc. *Commission* v. *Luxembourg and Belgium* [1962] ECR 425 at p. 432).

Since the prohibition, together with customs duties, of all charges having equivalent effect constitutes a fundamental rule of the EC Treaty, the concept of these charges has been defined by the ECJ in the widest possible manner. Thus, in a consistent line of cases the Court has stated that

> Any pecuniary charge, however small and whatever its designation and mode of application, which is imposed unilaterally on domestic or foreign goods by reason of the fact that they cross a frontier, and which is not a customs duty in the strict sense, constitutes a charge having equivalent effect within the meaning of Articles 23 and 25 of the Treaty, even if it is not imposed for the benefit of the State, is not discriminatory or protective in effect and if the product on which the charge is imposed is not in competition with any domestic product (Case 24/68 *Commission* v. *Italy* [1969] ECR 193 at p. 201; Cases 2/69 etc. *Diamantarbeiders I* [1969] ECR 211 at p. 222; etc. See also the cases cited below).

When these conditions are fulfilled, it is immaterial whether the charge is applied at the time of the product's crossing the frontier or subsequently at the stage of its marketing or processing (Case 78/76 *Steinike und Weinlig* [1977] ECR 595 at p. 613). Where the prohibition of charges having equivalent effect to customs duties has been included in agricultural regulations or in bilateral or multilateral agreements concluded by the Community with third countries, it must be given the same scope and meaning as it has under the Treaty itself, whether applied to intra-Community trade or to trade with third countries (Case 24/68 *Commission* v. *Italy*, above, at p. 203; Case 34/73 *Variola* [1973] ECR 981 at pp. 988–9; Case C-125/94 *Aprile I*, above, at pp. I-2951–2).

2. Exceptions to the prohibition. Distinction between charges having equivalent effect and internal taxes. There are three exceptions to the rule prohibiting charges having equivalent effect to customs duties as defined above. First, a charge will not fall within that definition and will escape the prohibition if it constitutes payment for a specific service actually rendered to the importer or exporter and represents an amount proportionate to that service (Case 158/82 *Commission* v. *Denmark* [1983] ECR 3573 at p. 3586). However, this exception must be interpreted strictly and cannot lead to a circumvention of the general prohibition. Thus, the exception does not apply where the service benefits a wider class of persons or the economy as a whole, and not the imported or exported products specifically (see further point 3 below).

Secondly, subject to certain conditions, a charge is not prohibited if it is made for inspections carried out to fulfil obligations imposed by Community law (see further point 3(*e*) below).

Thirdly, financial charges and taxes within the general system of internal taxation applied systematically to categories of products in accordance with objective criteria irrespective of the origin of the products, are also not to be regarded as charges having equivalent effect even though, in the absence of identical or similar domestic products, they are borne only by imported products (Case 90/79 *Commission* v. *France* [1981] ECR 283 at pp. 301–2). Provided that the same duty is imposed on national products and identical imported products at the same marketing stage and that the chargeable event giving rise thereto is also identical in the case of both products, such charges and taxes fall to be governed by the tax provisions of the EC Treaty (Arts. 90 to 93) and thus escape the prohibition relating to customs duties (Arts. 25 to 27) (Case 132/78 *Denkavit* [1979] ECR 1923 at pp. 1923–35). This is because, as a matter of principle, one and the same scheme of taxation cannot, under the system of the Treaty, belong simultaneously to both of these categories. The reason is that charges having equivalent effect must be abolished, while Art. 90 only prohibits discrimination against imported products (see e.g. Case 25/67 *Eierkontor* [1968] ECR 207 at p. 220; Case 94/74 *IGAV*, above, at p. 710. See also Case 27/74 *Demag* [1974] ECR 1037 at pp. 1045–7, applying the same principle to exports).

Thus, even a discriminatory internal tax does not automatically constitute a charge having an effect equivalent to a customs duty. As the ECJ has held, 'a charge in the form of an internal tax may not be considered as a charge having an effect equivalent to a customs duty unless the detailed rules governing the levying of the charge, or its use if the charge in question is allocated to a particular use, are such that in fact it is imposed solely on imported products to the exclusion of domestic products' (Case 32/80 *Kortmann* [1981] ECR 251 at p. 269; see also Case 90/79 *Commission* v. *France*, above, at p. 301). In practice, distinguishing between charges having equivalent effect and internal taxes has given rise to problems and has generated a large body of case-law, but the Court has consistently made the distinction in the light of the criteria outlined above (of the more important and more recent cases, see the following: Case C-90/94 *Haahr Petroleum* [1997] ECR I-4085 at pp. I-4150–2; Case C-213/96 *Outokumpu* [1998] ECR I-1777 at pp. I-1807–9; Cases C-441/98 etc. *Kapniki Mikhailidis* [2000] ECR I-7145 at pp. I-7174–5; Case C-234/99 *Nygård* [2002] ECR I-3657 at pp. I-3686–93; Cases C-34/01 etc. *Enirisorse* [2003] ECR I-0000, paras. 53–62. With the exception of *Kapniki Mikhailidis*, in all of these cases the disputed charge was classified as an internal tax. *See further under* **Taxation of goods**).

Nevertheless, in deciding whether a given financial charge or duty falls within the one category or the other, the destination of the charge must also be taken into account. Thus, the ECJ has stated that when:

> a financial charge or duty is intended exclusively to support activities which specifically profit taxed domestic products, it can follow that the general duty levied according to the same criteria on the imported product and the domestic product nevertheless constitutes for the former a net supplementary tax burden, whilst for the latter it constitutes in reality a set-off against benefits or aids previously received. Consequently, a duty within the general system of internal taxation applying systematically to domestic and imported products according to the same criteria, can

nevertheless constitute a charge having an effect equivalent to customs duty on imports (Case 77/72 *Capolongo* [1973] ECR 611 at p. 623).

This can only happen, however, if the following three conditions are fulfilled. First, the charge has the sole purpose of financing activities for the specific advantage of the taxed domestic product; secondly, the taxed product and the domestic product benefiting from the tax are the same; and thirdly, the burden imposed on the domestic product is made good in full (ibid.; Case 77/76 *Cucchi* [1977] ECR 987 at p. 1006; Case 105/76 *Interzuccheri* [1977] ECR 1029 at p. 1042). In that case, the charge has an effect equivalent to a customs duty, and must be regarded as unlawful in its entirety. If, on the other hand, the advantages stemming from the use of the proceeds of the charge only partly offset the burden borne by the domestic product, the charge in question is an internal tax subject to Art. 90 EC and is prohibited only to the extent to which it discriminates against imported products, that is to say, to the extent to which it partially offsets the burden borne by the taxed domestic product. In that case, the charge levied on the imported product, being lawful in principle, simply has to be reduced proportionally (Cases C-78/90 etc. *Compagnie Commerciale de l'Ouest* [1992] ECR I-1847 at pp. I-1881–2; Case C-347/95 *UCAL* [1997] ECR I-4911 at p. I-4931). The criterion of whether the burden is offset requires financial equivalence, to be verified over a reference period, between the total amounts levied on domestic products in connection with the charge and the advantages afforded exclusively to those products. Any other parameter, such as the nature, scope, or indispensable character of those advantages, would not provide a sufficiently objective basis for determining whether a domestic fiscal measure is compatible with the Treaty (ibid.; Case C-266/91 *Celbi* [1993] ECR I-4337 at p. I-4363).

Similar principles apply to exports also. Thus:

an internal levy may have an effect equivalent to a customs duty on export when its application falls more heavily on export sales than on sales within the country, or when the levy is intended to fund activities likely to make internal marketing more profitable than exportation or in any way to give preferential treatment to the product intended for marketing within the country, to the detriment of that intended for export (Case 51/74 *Hulst* [1975] ECR 79 at p. 92).

3. Examples of charges having equivalent effect. Applying the above principles and definitions, the ECJ has declared, *inter alia*, the following charges to be charges having equivalent effect to customs duties prohibited by the Treaty:

(*a*) special import duties (Cases 2/62 etc. *Commission* v. *Luxembourg and Belgium*, above, at p. 435);

(*b*) administrative charges in consideration for specific services rendered where the only benefit obtained by the importer is the permission to market the imported products but the products themselves enjoy no direct or indirect advantage (Cases 52/65 etc. *Germany* v. *Commission* [1966] ECR 159 at p. 170; Case 229/87 *Commission* v. *Greece* [1988] ECR 6347 at pp. 6361–2);

(*c*) tax levied on the export of articles having an artistic, historic, archaeological or ethnographic value, for the purpose of ensuring the protection and safety of the national artistic, etc. heritage (Case 7/68 *Commission* v. *Italy* [1968] ECR 423 at p. 429);

(*d*) statistical levies where the statistical information obtained is beneficial to the economy as a whole and therefore constitutes an advantage too general to be regarded as a specific benefit actually conferred (see e.g. Case 24/68 *Commission* v. *Italy*, above, at p. 202);

(*e*) sanitary, phytosanitary, veterinary, and public health inspection fees imposed by Member States in the general interest on imported or exported products according to their own particular criteria, which are not comparable to the criteria applied to similar domestic products (see e.g. Case 29/72 *Marimex* [1972] ECR 1309 at pp. 1318–19; Case 87/75 *Bresciani* [1976] ECR 129 at pp. 137–9; Case 251/78 *Denkavit Futtermittel* [1979] ECR 3369 at p. 3394; etc.).

However, such fees may not be classified as charges having equivalent effect to customs duties if the following conditions are satisfied: the inspections in question are prescribed by Community law in the general interest of the Community or by an international agreement to which all the Member States are parties, such as the International Plant Protection Convention of 1951; the inspections are obligatory and uniform for all the products concerned in the Community; they promote the free movement of goods, in particular by removing the need for unilateral measures permitted under Art. 30 EC; and the fees do not exceed the actual costs of the inspections in respect of which they are charged (Case 46/76 *Bauhuis* [1977] ECR 5 at pp. 15 *et seq.*; Case 89/76 *Commission* v. *Netherlands* [1977] ECR 1355 at pp. 1363–5; Case 18/87 *Commission* v. *Germany* [1988] ECR 5427 at p. 544; etc.).

This last condition can be satisfied only if there is a direct link between the amount of the fee and the actual inspection. Such a link is present when the amount of the fee is calculated on the basis of the duration of the inspection, the number of persons required, the cost of materials, overheads or other similar factors, which does not preclude a fixed-rate assessment of inspection costs, such as, for example, a fixed hourly rate. However, there is no direct link when the calculation of the amount of the fee is based on the weight or invoice value of the products in question. Under a system of that kind, the fees must be regarded as charges having equivalent effect, and incompatible with Art. 25 EC (Case C-111/89 *Bakker Hillegom* [1990] ECR I-1735 at pp. I-1751–2). Likewise, fees for field inspections of plants charged only in respect of exported products, and not in respect of those intended for the home market, constitute charges having equivalent effect to customs duties on exports, even if those inspections are carried out to meet the requirements of international conventions affecting only exported products. The contrary is true only if the products intended for the home market derive no benefit from the inspections (ibid. at p. I-1753).

6 Health inspection charges are also not prohibited in the context of trade with third countries, provided that there is a sufficiently close connection

between the amount of those charges and the actual cost of the inspections (see e.g. Case 70/77 *Simmenthal*, above, at pp. 1470–1; Case 30/79 *Wigei* [1980] ECR 151 at pp. 163–7; Case 1/83 *IFG* [1984] ECR 349 at p. 367; etc.).

However, the fact that a measure adopted by a Member State is justified on one of the grounds laid down in Art. 30 EC does not in itself mean that a charge or fee imposed for carrying out that measure is compatible with the Treaty. In fact, the exemptions provided for in Art. 30 relate exclusively to quantitative restrictions or measures having equivalent effect and may not be extended to customs duties or to charges having equivalent effect which, as such, fall outside the scope of Art. 30 (Case 32/80 *Kortmann*, above, at p. 267; see also the *Marimex, Bauhuis*, and *Denkavit Futtermittel* cases cited above);

(*f*) unloading charges imposed solely on imported goods unloaded in the national ports, the income being devoted to the provision and maintenance of port installations (Case 34/73 *Variola*, above, at p. 989);

(*g*) charge relating to a mandatory quality control of exported products resulting in the issue of a certificate and in the affixing of a national export stamp, even if the recipient of the revenue is a body distinct from the State (Case 63/74 *Cadsky* [1975] ECR 281 at pp. 290–1);

(*h*) storage charges demanded solely in connection with the completion of customs formalities in intra-Community trade (Case 132/82 *Commission* v. *Belgium* [1983] ECR 1649 at p. 1660);

(*i*) dock dues (*octroi de mer*), proportional to the customs value of goods, levied on goods imported into the French overseas departments, whether coming from other Member States, from an EFTA State, from metropolitan France, or even from other French overseas departments (Case C-163/90 *Legros*, above, at pp. I-4665–9; Cases C-363/93 etc. *Lancry*, above, at pp. I-3989–92);

(*j*) an *ad valorem* charge (a communal tax on consumer goods) levied in the Greek Dodecanese islands on goods entering or leaving that region, whether coming from or going to other Member States or other parts of Greece (Cases C-485/93 etc. *Simitzi*, above, at pp. I-2674–8);

(*k*) a tax borne by manufacturers, importers, and persons making supplies in France of CB sets (transmitting-receiving sets operating on two-way channels) imported from other Member States and from non-member countries (Case C-109/98 *CRT France International* [1999] ECR I-2237 at pp. I-2272–4);

(*l*) an *ad valorem* charge on exported tobacco products, which is not levied on the same products when they are sold on the domestic market or imported from other Member States, even if the charge pursues a social objective (Cases C-441/98 etc. *Kapniki Mikhailidis*, above, at pp. I-7172–5);

(*m*) a mandatory contribution to a solidarity fund payable by all exporters of waste from Germany to other Member States (Case C-389/00 *Commision* v. *Germany* [2003] ECR I-2001, paras. 21–51).

4. Direct effect and enforcement. The ECJ has confirmed the direct effect of the original Art. 13(2) EEC, repealed by the ToA (abolition of charges on imports), as from 1 January 1970 (Case 33/70 *SACE* [1970] ECR 1213 at p. 1222 and subsequent cases, see in particular Case 94/74 *IGAV*, above, at p. 711), and of the original Art. 16 EEC, repealed by the ToA (abolition of charges on exports), as from 1 January 1962 (Case 18/71 *Eunomia*, above, at p. 816 and subsequent cases). The Court has stated that the direct effect of these provisions implies that, from the relevant dates, applications directed against national charges having an effect equivalent to customs duties or claims for repayment of such charges may be brought before the authorities and courts of Member States, even retroactively in respect of the period before that classification of those charges follows from an interpretation given by the Court under Art. 234 EC. The Member States are obliged in principle to repay charges levied in breach of Community law (see e.g. Cases C-441/98 etc. *Kapniki Mikhailidis*, above, at p. I-7176).

In the absence of Community rules, it is for the domestic legal system of each Member State to designate the courts and tribunals having jurisdiction in these matters and to lay down the detailed procedural rules governing actions brought for the repayment of charges paid but not owed, provided, first, that such rules are not less favourable than those governing similar domestic actions (principle of equivalence), and, second, that they do not make it virtually impossible or excessively difficult in practice to exercise the rights conferred by Community law (principle of effectiveness). The Court has held that it is compatible with Community law to lay down reasonable time-limits for bringing proceedings in the interests of legal certainty which protects both the taxpayer and the administration concerned. A time-limit of three years running from the date of the contested payment may be regarded as reasonable (see e.g. Case 61/79 *Denkavit Italiana* [1980] ECR 1205 at p. 1227; more recently Case C-228/96 *Aprile II* [1998] ECR I-7141 at pp. I-7172–4).

In accordance with national law, national courts may take account of the fact, where appropriate, that undertakings have been able to incorporate in their prices charges unduly levied and to pass them on, in whole or in part, to their purchasers. Thus, Community law does not preclude Member States from refusing repayment where this would entail unjust enrichment. However, it does preclude any presumption or rule of evidence which would shift to the trader concerned the burden of proving that the charges unduly paid have not been passed on to other persons (Cases C-441/98 etc. *Kapniki Mikhailidis*, above, at pp. I-7176–9).

See also **Common Customs Tariff, Customs Union, Free movement of goods, Goods, Taxation of goods.**

Further reading 1. BOOKS: Barnard, *The Substantive Law of the EU. The Four Freedoms* (2004), ch. 3; Craig and de Búrca, *EU Law. Text, Cases, and Materials*, 3rd edn. (2003), ch. 14; Wyatt and Dashwood, *European Union Law*, 4th edn. (2000), ch. 12.

2. ARTICLES: Barents, 'Charges of Equivalent Effect to Customs Duties' (1978) *CML Rev.* 415; Tinnion, 'Charges Having an Effect Equivalent to

Customs Duties' (1977) *EL Rev.* 359; Wooldridge and Plender, 'Charges Having an Effect Equivalent to Customs Duties: a Review of the Cases' (1978) *EL Rev.* 101.

▶ **CLASSIFICATION OF GOODS FOR CUSTOMS PURPOSES** is the method for finding the correct subheading in the customs tariff in order to establish the appropriate duty rate or any other trade measure applicable to the goods concerned.

Imported and exported goods have to be declared under the relevant subheading of the customs tariff in order to allow the customs authorities to establish whether customs duties and other taxes (such as value added tax, excise duty) are due and, if so, which amount is to be collected. Furthermore, the authorities have to ascertain whether or not other trade restrictions (e.g. on weapons, drugs, dangerous chemicals) apply, either generally or with respect to the country from which the goods are imported or to which they are to be exported (e.g. in case of embargoes for specific goods). The importer or exporter himself is, of course, also interested to know which duties and other restrictions are relevant. In order to create a link between import and export measures and the individual goods concerned, a customs nomenclature is used, i.e. a systematic classification (a list, arranged by codes) of goods (e.g. milk, heading 0401) or groups of products (e.g. toys and games, ch. 95) for which the measures applicable are indicated. The process of assigning goods to their place within the nomenclature (i.e. finding the correct tariff subheading) is called 'classification'. Most customs tariff nomenclatures are based on the Harmonized System, issued by the World Customs Organization (WCO) in Brussels (*see further under* **Common Customs Tariff (CCT)**).

I. International law

Since 1988 the nomenclature of the Community Customs Tariff—like those of most nations and customs unions—is based on the International Convention on the Harmonized Commodity Description and Coding System—HS (Council Dec. 87/369, *OJ* 1987 L198/1). This agreement provides a systematic and complete list of goods, supplemented by numerical codes ranged in four levels (2, 4, 5, and 6 digits), which is also used in the framework of bilateral and multilateral tariff negotiations (as in the framework of the WTO). It replaced the Convention on the Nomenclature for the Classification of Goods in Customs Tariffs concluded in 1950. The aims of the HS Convention that was established, like its predecessor, under the auspices of the Customs Co-operation Council (which has changed its title in the meantime to World Customs Organization—WCO), go far beyond the harmonization of customs tariff nomenclatures; it is notably intended to:

- facilitate the collection, comparison, and analysis of statistics, in particular those on international trade;
- reduce the expense incurred by redescribing, reclassifying, and record-

ing goods as they move from one classification system to another in the course of the international trade chain;

- to facilitate the standardization of trade documentation and the transmission of data;
- to provide for sufficiently detailed, accurate, and comparable data required for customs and statistical purposes by governments and trade interests, as well as for international and trade negotiations the interpretation of trade concessions;
- be used for the purposes of freight tariffs and transport statistics and to provide a close correlation with regard to production statistics.

According to Art. 3 of the HS Convention, Contracting Parties are obliged to:

- use in their nomenclature(s) for the customs tariff and for external trade statistics all the goods descriptions together with their complete numerical codes without addition or modification, except textual adaptations necessary for domestic law (e.g. 'truck' instead of 'lorry');
- apply the General Rules for the interpretation of the HS and all of the Section, Chapter, and Subheading Notes without modifying their scope;
- follow the numerical sequence of the HS;
- make publicly available their import and export trade statistics on the basis of the six-digit HS code or on a more detailed level, to the extent that publication is not precluded for exceptional reasons such as commercial confidentiality or national security.

Developing countries are allowed to use the nomenclature on a less detailed level (Art. 4). The nomenclature is regularly amended in order to adjust it to the needs of users and to changes in technology or patterns of international trade. The HS Committee establishes explanatory notes describing the scope of the different sections, chapters, headings, and subheadings as well as classification opinions indicating the correct classification of individual goods in order to give guidance for the interpretation of the HS and to settle disputes between Contracting Parties (Arts. 6 to 10).

If the validity of a Community regulation is challenged as being not in conformity with the HS Convention, the ECJ then considers such an argument (Case C-233/88 *Van de Kolk* [1990] ECR I-265 at pp. I-282–3).

II. Community law

1. The Treaty provisions. According to Art. 23 EC, the Community is based on a customs union that is implemented, in so far as relations with third countries are concerned, by means of a common customs tariff. Art. 25 EC deals with the prohibition of customs duties on goods traded between Member States and Art. 26 EC with the fixing of common duty rates with regard to trade with third countries. Art. 133 EC is to be used for changes of duty rates that are laid down in the framework of commercial policy. There is, however, no explicit mention of the customs tariff nomenclature in the Treaty. This lacuna has been closed by the argument that the authority for setting or changing a duty rate necessarily implies the power to define or amend the description of the goods to which the duty rate will apply. Consequently autonomous amendments (i.e. those enacted for internal reasons) of the nomenclature are to be based on Art. 26 EC, whereas Art. 133 EC applies for measures taken for commercial policy reasons. In Case 165/87 *Commission* v. *Council* [1988] ECR 5545 at pp. 5560–1, the ECJ justified the combined use of these Articles with regard to the approval of the HS Convention with the argument that the legal basis for the customs tariff nomenclature is to be found in these two Articles and that the nomenclature for external trade statistics, which is part of commercial policy, is to be set on the basis of Art. 133 EC. For the sake of completeness it has to be added that nomenclature (and duty rate) changes can also be based on:

- Art. 37 EC if they relate to an agricultural policy measure;
- Art. 187 EC if a tariff measure concerns the countries and territories dependent on a Member State; and
- Art. 310 EC if tariff preferences are granted in an association agreement.

The Euratom Treaty contains provisions relating to customs duties only with regard to the transitional period (see Arts. 94 and 95 Euratom). By virtue of Art. 305(2) EC, the EC provisions apply to Euratom goods in so far as their customs classification is concerned.

Art. 71 ECSC Treaty provided for a general responsibility of Member States with respect to commercial policy, whereas Art. 72 ECSC (minimum and maximum duties) and Art. 74 ECSC (anti-dumping and countervailing duties) empowered the Council or the Commission to take specific measures. Following Opinion 1/94 of the ECJ ([1994] ECR I-5267 at p. I-5396), most tariff measures concerning ECSC products, and consequently also nomenclature changes, were based on the EC Treaty provisions. Since the expiry of the ECSC Treaty on 24 June 2002, only the EC provisions apply to the former ECSC products.

2. Community nomenclatures for goods. The basic Community classification for customs purposes is set out in Council Reg. 2658/87 of 23 July 1987 on the tariff and statistical nomenclature and on the Common Customs Tariff (*OJ* 1987 L256/1, version for 2005 in *OJ* 2004 L327/1). As its title indicates, it is also used for the classification of goods in the framework of external trade statistics (Council Reg. 1172/95, *OJ* 1995 L118/10) and statistics on trade between Member States (Council Reg. 638/2004, *OJ* 2004 L102/1). Annex I of Reg. 2658/87, which is amended every year with effect from 1 January, lists goods in the Combined Nomenclature systematically in ca. 10,000 eight-digit subheadings on the basis of the ca. 5,000 six-digit subheadings of the Harmonized System (see section I above). For each of these subheadings the conventional (i.e. WTO bound) and—where applicable—the autonomous duty rate is indicated as well as any supplementary statistical unit to be declared besides the weight of the goods (e.g. number of pairs of shoes). The nomenclature contains, furthermore, General Rules,

Section, Chapter, Subheading, and Additional Notes aiming to assist in the classification of goods or in the determination of the applicable duty rate.

This regulation also provides the legal basis for the more detailed 'Taric' classification (this abbreviation is derived from French: *Tar*if *i*ntégré des *C*ommunautés européennes) which is amended, where necessary, daily and lists goods subject to import measures systematically in ca. 25,000 ten-digit subheadings on the basis of the above-mentioned Combined Nomenclature. For export measures and complex import measures four-digit additional codes are used. The Taric is held in an EC Commission database, which is available on the Internet (http://europa.eu.int/comm/taxation_customs/dds/en/tarhome.htm). Updates are transmitted to Member States' tariff databases that are used for customs clearance. Typical measures requiring a more detailed breakdown of the CN goods descriptions are:

- tariff suspensions and quotas;
- anti-dumping and countervailing duties;
- duties on agricultural components of processed agricultural goods;
- duty exemptions for pharmaceutical substances.

A further classification system, which is also based on the Combined Nomenclature and incorporated in the Taric is the Nomenclature for export refunds set out in Comm. Reg. 3846/87 (*OJ* 1987 L366/1, see version for 2004 in *OJ* 2003 L335/1). Four additional digits are used in order to identify all goods that may be subject to a specific amount of export refund. Whenever the refund mechanism requires amendments to this nomenclature, it is changed by means of a regulation.

A small number of import and export measures do not base their goods descriptions on the Combined Nomenclature and therefore escape traditional customs classification methods. These are, in particular,

- dual-use items subject to export controls (Council Reg. 1334/2000, *OJ* 2000 L159/1);
- endangered species subject to import and export controls (Council Reg. 338/97, *OJ* 1997 L61/1);
- dangerous chemicals subject to import and export controls (Council Reg. 304/2003, *OJ* 2003 L63/1);
- waste subject to import and export controls (Council Reg. 259/93, *OJ* 1993 L30/1).

For the purposes of production statistics the Community uses a special five-digit goods classification, based on the Central Product Classification (CPC) of the United Nations, which correlates closely to the Harmonized System and regroups the goods according to economic sectors of activity (Council Reg. 3924/91, *OJ* 1991 L371/1, see version for 2003 in *OJ* 2003 L57/1).

3. Implementing measures, sources of interpretation. In order to assist in the classification of goods in the Harmonized System, the World Customs Organization issues Explanatory Notes and Classification Opinions, which are not part of the HS Convention (see section I above), but are recognized by the ECJ as an important means for the interpretation of the nomenclature, provided they are compatible with the legal text (Case 14/70 *Bakels* [1970] ECR 1001 at p. 1004; and Case C-35/93 *Develop Dr. Eisbein* [1994] ECR I-2655 at p. I-2677).

Art. 9(1)(a) of Council Reg. 2658/87 (see point 2 above) authorizes the Commission, after seeking an opinion of the Customs Code Committee, to settle classification issues by way of a regulation which:

- either amends the Combined Nomenclature by introducing an Additional Note (e.g. Comm. Reg. 2509/97, *OJ* 1997 L345/44),
- or determines the tariff subheading to be applied to specific goods (e.g. Comm. Regs. 496/98 and 497/98, *OJ* 1998 L62/19 and 21).

Such regulations are recognized by the ECJ as long as they:

- respect the scope of the Common Customs Tariff subheadings (Case 37/75 *Bagusat* [1975] ECR 1339 at p. 1346);
- respect the Harmonized System and its interpretation by the WCO (Case 38/75 *Nederlandse Spoorwegen* [1975] ECR 1439 at p. 1450; and Case C-233/88 *Van de Kolk*, above, at p. I-281); and
- use objective, verifiable criteria corresponding to the State of technology and science and are economically practicable (Case C-265/89 *Vismans* [1990] ECR I-3411 at p. I-3433).

Though regulations have a legally binding effect only for the future, repayment claims (see Art. 236 Community Customs Code, Council Reg. 2913/92, *OJ* 1992 L302/1) can be based on the classification set out therein if a less favourable tariff subheading has been applied. The retrospective application of a less favourable tariff subheading is normally excluded because of the provisions on the protection of good faith (see Art. 220(2)(b) Community Customs Code).

Instead of settling classification issues by means of a regulation, the Commission may, after seeking an opinion of the Customs Code Committee, issue Explanatory Notes by virtue of Art. 9(1)(a) of Council Reg. 2658/87. They supplement the HS Explanatory Notes and are equally taken into account by the ECJ as long as they are in conformity with the scope of the Common Customs Tariff subheadings and any other relevant provisions of the nomenclature (Case 798/79 *Chem-Tec* [1980] ECR 2639 at p. 2646).

Art. 12 of the Community Customs Code—CC (Council Reg. 2913/92, *OJ* 1992 L302/1) authorizes Member States' customs authorities to issue binding tariff information, which is valid for a period of six years unless it is revoked or annulled or the nomenclature or its interpretation are changed in the meantime. The Customs Code protects importers and exporters from the collection of higher duties than those applicable for the subheading specified in the binding information during its validity and up to six months beyond, in so far as the interpretation of the nomenclature is concerned (Arts. 217(1)(a), 220(2) CC). It cannot, however, provide a protection against changes of the customs tariff (Case 90/77 *Stimming* v. *Commission* [1978] ECR 995 at p. 1008; and Case C-315/96 *Lopex* [1998] ECR I-317 at

p. I-342). Where the Commission finds that divergent binding tariff information exists in respect of the same type of goods it can adopt a decision requesting the Member State(s) concerned to withdraw the information considered incorrect (Art. 9 CC implementing provisions, Comm. Reg. 2454/93, *OJ* 1993 L253/1, see example in *OJ* 2003 L36/40). Binding tariff information issued by Member States can be consulted under http://europa.eu.int/comm/taxation_customs/common/databases/ebti/index_en.htm.

Finally, ECJ judgments are also a source of interpretation of the nomenclature given that the ECJ will normally decide a classification issue by reference to a previous case provided that the legal framework has not changed. National courts are bound by such judgments in that they cannot diverge from them without submitting the case to the ECJ (Cases 28/62 etc. *Da Costa & Schaake* [1963] ECR 65).

III. Classification principles

1. The rules of priority. The nomenclature of the Common Customs Tariff is based on the Harmonized System which is set out in an international Convention (see section I above). The Community is a Contracting Party to this agreement and therefore bound by it according to Art. 300(7) EC. Secondary Community law, such as Council Reg. 2658/87, has to respect the Convention and to be interpreted in the light of it (Case 38/75 *Nederlandse Spoorwegen*, above, at p. 1450; Case C-233/88 *Van de Kolk*, above, at p. I-281; Case C-61/94 *Commission* v. *Germany* [1996] ECR I-3989 at p. I-4021). The general rules for the interpretation of the nomenclature lead to the same result:

- According to rule 1, classification shall primarily be determined according to the terms of the headings and any relative section and chapter notes. All these provisions stem from the Harmonized System.
- Rule 6 stipulates that classification in the subheadings shall be determined according to the terms of those subheadings and any related subheading notes, on the understanding that only subheadings at the same level are comparable. Given that the subheadings may only be determined once the correct (four digit) heading has been established and that the six-digit subheadings (stemming from the Harmonized System) have to be determined before the (eight digit) Combined Nomenclature (CN) subheading may be sought, the Harmonized System, by virtue of this hierarchical structure, clearly has the priority over any further subdivisions created by the Community legislator.

The following rules apply with respect to the different parts of the nomenclature:

1. In principle, the four-digit headings and the section and chapter notes rank as top priority. In case of a contradiction between them, the more specific rule applies (e.g. heading 0507 covers 'ivory'; however note 3 to ch. 5 states that the teeth of all animals are to be regarded as 'ivory'; this definition determines the scope of heading 0507).

2. Some issues of a general nature (e.g. whether goods are to be classified in one or two headings, as a part or a complete product) are settled in the general rules; these rules can be applied immediately as long as the headings, section, or chapter notes do not provide a different solution for this type of problem (e.g. general rule 3(b) allows goods made up of different components to be classified as one article; however note 3(a) to ch. 62 does not allow classification of a jacket and trousers together as a 'suit' if their outer surface is not made from the same fabric).
3. If, according to the text of the headings, section, and chapter notes or according to the rules for mixtures (general rule 2(b)), goods seem to be classifiable under two or more headings (e.g. a mixture of different types of cereal, a combination between a radio and alarm clock), classification shall be effected as follows:
   (*a*) the heading with the most specific description shall be preferred to headings with a more general description, except where they refer only to a part of the materials or components (e.g. one type of cereal);
   (*b*) mixtures, composite goods, and goods put up in sets for retail sale are to be classified as if they consisted only of the material or component which gives them their essential character (e.g. the predominant type of cereal);
   (*c*) if both rules fail to give a result, the last in numerical order of the headings to be taken into consideration is applied (e.g. in the case of the combined radio/alarm clock, the heading for the clock [ch. 91] would prevail, if no essential character could be determined because both components are considered as equally important).
4. In cases where no heading is found, the heading appropriate to the goods to which they are most akin is applied.
5. Subsequently, the five-digit and then the six-digit HS subheading is to be determined taking into account the subheading notes and the general rules.
6. Following this, the eight-digit CN subheading has to be established taking into account the Community's additional notes and the general rules.
7. Specific Community measures may provide for further breakdowns of the CN subheadings which are either coded in ten-digit Taric subheadings or four-digit additional codes. The general rules apply at this finest level of detail, too.

2. Linguistic divergences. A textual interpretation is the starting point for any classification issue. General rules 1 and 6 confirm this by referring to the terms of the headings, subheadings, section, chapter, and subheading notes. This approach is the best guarantee:

- to treat importers and exporters in the same way irrespective of the place where the goods are declared;
- to avoid inconsistent statistical returns; and

- to maintain the coherence of the nomenclature which is used for many different purposes (such as customs and excise duties or export refunds).

The Combined Nomenclature is based on the Harmonized System. The two legally binding linguistic versions of this international classification system are English and French. For interpretation questions relating to the Harmonized System, these two versions are therefore authoritative (Cases 824/79 etc. *Folci* [1980] ECR 3053 at p. 3061; and Case C-143/96 *Knubben* [1997] ECR I-7039 at p. I-7051). If they lead to the same result, the issue is settled even if the other Community languages diverge. Where the two language versions diverge, the structure of the nomenclature and the purpose of the headings, subheadings, and notes as well as the general rules have to be considered (see above).

Interpretation questions outside the scope of the Harmonized System are to be settled on the basis of all Community languages. Where they diverge, the classification is not determined on the basis of the majority of converging versions but on the basis of the system and the purpose of the nomenclature (Case 816/79 *Mecke* [1980] ECR 3029 at p. 3041).

3. Classification criteria. In the interest of legal certainty and ease of verification by customs, the decisive criteria for the customs classification of goods must generally be their objective characteristics and properties, as defined by the wording of the headings, subheadings, notes, and general rules of the Common Customs Tariff; furthermore, the Explanatory Notes to the Harmonized System provide an important tool for safeguarding a uniform application of the nomenclature (consistent jurisprudence, see e.g. Case C-105/96 *Codiesel* [1997] ECR I-3465 at p. I-3486). With regard to animals and plants, the scientific species can also determine the classification where reference to it is made (Case C-38/95 *Foods Import* [1996] ECR I-6543 at p. I-6571). In the absence of any express provision, the same product cannot be classified in different headings of the Common Customs Tariff depending on whether they are used for the purposes of levying customs duties or for the application of the rules of the common organization of the market (Case 5/78 *Milchfutter* [1978] ECR 1597 at p. 1609; Case 158/78 *Biegi* [1979] ECR 1103 at p. 1121).

Given the large number of potential classification issues, only the following types of question are treated in more detail:

(*a*) how to determine whether two or more objects belonging together are classified as one or several goods;
(*b*) how to classify an article consisting of different materials or components, if a specific subheading exists for each of them;
(*c*) how to classify an article serving different purposes or uses, if a specific subheading exists for each of them.

(*a*) The nomenclature contains several specific rules with respect to components belonging together:

- According to general rule 2(a), unassembled or disassembled goods are to be classified like the complete goods (and not as 'parts'), even if the article is somewhat incomplete, provided they have already the essential character of the complete article (Case C-35/93 *Develop Dr. Eisbein*, above, at p. I-2676).
- Goods made up of different components and goods put up in sets for retail sale are, by virtue of general rule 3(b), to be classified as if they consisted only of the component that gives their essential character (e.g. an uninterruptible power supply consisting of a charger feeding power from networks and a battery that can operate independently for some time, Case C-105/96 *Codiesel*, above, at p. I-3488).
- Containers, specially shaped or fitted to contain specific articles, suitable for long-term use and presented with the articles for which they are intended are, by virtue of general rule 5(a), classified together with the articles for which they are intended, e.g. glass bottles for beer, including the plastic crates holding them (Case 357/87 *Schmid* [1988] ECR 6239 at p. 6260). Further examples are camera and gun cases but not however, a case made of gold.
- Other packing materials and packing containers presented with the goods therein are classified with the goods if they are of a kind normally used for packing such goods, e.g. a paper bag for sugar (general rule 5(b)).
- In the clothing area, the terms suit and ensemble are subject to very specific conditions if they are to be classified in one subheading (notes 3 and 7 and additional note 1 to ch. 61, notes 3 and 6 and additional note 1 to ch. 62). On the other hand, a pair of gloves or shoes is always classified together.
- Composite machines consisting of two or more machines fitted together and performing two or more complementary or alternative functions are classified according to the component performing the principal function (note 3 to section XVI). Separate or interconnected components of a machine intended to contribute to a clearly defined function are to be classified according to that function (note 4 to section XVI).
- Tools necessary for the assembly or maintenance of machines are classified together with the machines if imported with them (additional note 1 to section XVI).
- Machines imported in split consignments may, at the request of the declarant and subject to the conditions stipulated by the customs authorities (such as an assembly plan and a list of the contents of the various packages), be classified as the assembled machine (additional note 3 to section XVI).
- The classification of parts and units of automatic data processing machines is subjected to specific rules (note 5 to ch. 84, see Case C-11/93 *Siemens Nixdorf* [1994] ECR I-1945 at p. I-1960; Case C-121/95 *Vobis* [1996] ECR I-3047 at p. I-3067; and Cases T–133/98 etc. *Hewlett Packard* v. *Commission* [2001] ECR II-613 at p. II-628).

(*b*) For goods made up of different materials, a number of special rules have been created in order to simplify the classification. These include a definition of:

- seasoned meat, which is considered as such only if the seasoning is either visible to the naked eye or clearly distinguishable by taste (additional note 6a to ch. 2, Case C-233/88 *Van de Kolk*, above, at p. I-282);
- impregnated or coated fabrics, which are considered as such only if the impregnation or coating can be seen with the naked eye (note 2(a)(1) to ch. 59, Case 317/81 *Howe & Bainbridge* [1982] ECR 3257 at p. 3264);
- the cases in which sugar contained in fruit juices is to be considered as added sugar content (additional note 5 to ch. 20, Case C-219/89 *WeserGold* [1991] ECR I-1895 at p. I-1907);
- products to be classified as made of precious metal (such as gold) even if they consist only partly of such material (note 1 to ch. 71).

Where such specific rules do not exist, mixtures and goods made up of different materials are classified according to the material that gives them their essential character (general rule 3(b)). This material may be determined according to:

- the largest quantity (Cases 208/81 etc. *Palte & Haentjens* [1982] ECR 2511 at p. 2519);
- the highest value (Case 60/83 *Metro* [1984] ECR 671 at pp. 681–2);
- the function of the item as it is represented in one of the different materials (Case C-356/93 *Techmeda* [1994] ECR I-2371 at p. I-2387; and Case C-276/00 *Turbon* [2002] ECR I-1389 at p. 1423).

If none of the materials can be determined as giving the article its essential character, it is classified under the heading that occurs last in the numerical order among those which equally merit consideration (general rule 3(c)).

(*c*) Where the headings refer to the purpose or use of the goods, the typical, usual use is to be considered and not use that is theoretically possible but economically impracticable (Case C-395/93 *Neckermann* [1994] ECR I-4027 at p. I-4038; Case C-459/93 *Thyssen Haniel* [1995] ECR I-1381 at pp. I-1400–1). In certain cases the CCT gives a preference to a specific use of the import goods as compared to the other uses (e.g. tuna for the industrial manufacture of fish preparations, CN code 0303 41 11); in such cases the use of the product is normally subject to a surveillance by the customs authorities until the goods have been put to the prescribed end-use (Art. 82 Community Customs Code, *see further under* **Customs procedures**, section V.1). If such a surveillance is not stipulated, as in the case of pharmaceutical products, it has to be decided on the basis of the characteristics and properties of the goods, whether they serve the purpose set out under the relevant heading (e.g. the treatment or prevention of illness in the case of heading 3004) or whether they serve general purposes, such as food preparations under heading 2106 (Case C-405/95 *Bioforce* [1997] ECR I-2581 at p. I-2596; Case C-328/97 *Glob-Sped* [1998] ECR I-8357 at p. I-8381).

Where no specific rules exist, goods serving different purposes or uses are to be classified according to their main purpose or use (general rule 3(a) or (b), see Case C-395/93 *Neckermann*, above). If no main purpose or use can be established (e.g. because both functions are equally important) the item is classified under the heading that occurs last in numerical order among those which merit equal consideration (general rule 3(c), see Case C-67/95 *Rank Xerox* [1997] ECR I-5401 at p. I-5426).

IV. Classification disputes

Classification disputes typically arise in the following situations:

1. The importer declares the goods under one subheading but the customs authorities apply a different subheading, with a higher duty rate or some other type of restriction (e.g. the requirement of an import authorization).
2. The importer or exporter has applied for binding tariff information and he disagrees with the result of the information granted.
3. The importer or exporter has benefited from a favourable binding tariff information that is later revoked or becomes invalid because of a change of interpretation at Community or international level.
4. The importer or exporter has constantly, and with the approval of the local customs office, classified an article under a specific heading; a decision is subsequently taken at national or supranational level, to classify such articles elsewhere and the trader is faced with a claim for post-clearance recovery of import duties or for repayment of export refunds.
5. The importer or exporter finds out that his competitors in another Member State pay lower customs duties or receive higher export refunds because of a different classification.
6. The importer or exporter finds out that the customs authorities in a third country apply a more, or a less, favourable classification.

In those cases where a decision of Community customs authorities which relates to the application of customs legislation is involved, an appeal in accordance with Art. 243 Community Customs Code—CC (*see further under* **Customs procedures**, section VIII) can be lodged; if the classification dispute concerns export refunds (which are part of agricultural—and not customs—legislation), the national provisions on appeals apply instead of Art. 243 CC (Case C-334/95 *Krüger* [1997] ECR I-4517 at p. I-4551). This opens the way to the national courts and, eventually, to the ECJ by virtue of Art. 234 EC. Especially in the case of divergent application by Member States, a Member State or the Commission may raise the issue in the Customs Code Committee (Art. 249 CC). This can then lead to a classification regulation, new explanatory notes or a decision by the Commission that certain binding tariff information has to be withdrawn. Where the classification of third countries is involved, the issue may be raised by the Commission bilaterally or in the appropriate international forum, notably:

- in the Harmonized System Committee with a view to clarifying the HS Explanatory Notes or to issuing a classification opinion, provided the country concerned is a contracting party to the HS Convention,
- or—if a commitment of a preferential trade agreement is impaired—in the appropriate association or co-operation committee.

See also **Common Customs Tariff, Customs procedures.**

Further reading 1. Books: Berr and Trémeau, *Le droit douanier*, 5th edn. (2001), p. 105; Böhne, Möller, and Schumann, *Zolltarif* (2003); Lux and Reiser, *Das Harmonisierte System zur Bezeichnung und Codierung der Waren des internationalen Handels* (1986); Lux, *Guide to Community Customs Legislation* (2002), p. 73; id., *Das Zollrecht der EG* (2004), ch. III, p. 5; Lyons, *EC Customs Law* (2001), p. 111; Nassiet, *La réglementation douanière européenne* (1988), p. 44; Snyder, *International Trade and Customs Law of the European Union* (1998), p. 3; Walsh, *The Customs Code of the European Union* (1996), p. 46; Witte and Wolffgang (eds.), *Lehrbuch des Europäischen Zollrechts*, 4th edn. (2003), p. 366.

2. Articles: Dufour and Carli, 'La contribution de la commission de conciliation et d'expertise douanière à l'interprétation du droit communautaire' (1990) *Droit et pratique du commerce international* 441; Vander Schueren, 'Customs Classification: One of the Cornerstones of the Single European Market, but One which cannot be Exhaustively Regulated' (1991) *CML Rev.* 855; Vermulst, 'EC Customs Classification Rules: Should Ice Cream Melt?' (1994) 15 *Michigan Journal of International Law* 1241.

▶ **COMMON CUSTOMS TARIFF** (CCT) is the customs tariff of the European Community as stipulated in Art. 23 EC (*see also under* **Classification of goods for customs purposes**).

A 'tariff' is a list of prices or taxes or the factors allowing their calculation (e.g. the weight or the value of an article). Just as a freight tariff tells how much has to be paid for the transport of specific goods, a customs tariff sets out how much import or export duty has to be paid in case a specific article is imported into or exported from the territory concerned (such a territory is called 'customs territory'). In most cases, customs duties are levied on the value of the goods, which requires special rules on the value to be taken into account (*see further under* **Customs value**). In other cases, specific properties of the goods (such as their weight, number, or length) form the basis of the assessment. In modern customs legislation, customs duties are not due upon entry into or exit from the customs territory (except in the case of smuggling), but only when the goods are put in 'free circulation' or when the customs rules are infringed with regard to goods liable to import duties. This allows for the suspension of import duties in cases where the goods:

- only transit the territory;
- are stored in a customs warehouse or free zone, before a decision on

the final customs treatment of the goods (e.g. entry for free circulation, re-export) is taken;
- are processed before they are entered for free circulation or re-exported;
- are to be shown in trade fairs, pending a decision on their final customs treatment; or
- are temporarily used—like a car—before they are re-exported.

The suspension of duty liability

- avoids the need to tax goods which are eventually re-exported and do not therefore enter in competition on the home market (otherwise the duty would have to be refunded), and
- puts export goods incorporating imported components on the world market on an equal footing with other competitors in that the financial burden of import duties is relieved from goods which are re-exported after processing within the customs territory.

In such a system, the customs tariff has to be supplemented by rules determining the cases in which a customs debt is incurred, e.g. because of release for free circulation, unlawful introduction into the customs territory, unlawful removal from customs supervision (*see further under* **Customs procedures**, section VII).

The main purpose of a customs tariff is to make imported goods more expensive than those produced within the customs territory, in order to foster the production and the sale of locally made goods, thereby creating or maintaining investments and jobs within that territory (protective duties). Export duties are levied where scarce materials are to be prevented from being exported in order to avoid a shortage or, where the country has a monopoly with respect to a type of raw material, in order to maintain processing activities within the territory (in the latter case, this would be a trade barrier incompatible with WTO rules).

Other reasons for customs duties (and therefore the existence of a customs tariff) are:

- to collect revenue for the State budget (financial duties);
- to maintain a preferential margin towards partner countries with a preferential arrangement (the more customs duties are generally reduced, the more preferential trade arrangements lose their substance);
- to maintain customs duties as an object for international trade negotiations in order to improve the access to export markets;
- to combat dumping (i.e. the export of goods at lower than their normal value) and export subsidies, if imports of goods concerned in such practices harm the home industry;
- to enact countermeasures in cases of discrimination on export markets or non-compliance with international trade agreements (retaliation duties, see Council Reg. 2193/2003, *OJ* 2003 L328/3); or
- to protect the market against a sudden increase of imports that would create serious harm to producers on the home market (safeguard duties, see Comm. Reg. 1694/2002, *OJ* 2002 L261/1).

COMMON CUSTOMS TARIFF (CCT)

The customs duties that are to be levied where a customs debt is incurred, are to be found in the customs tariff which may constitute

- either one legal act, supplemented by annexes concerning special countries or transactions, or
- a multitude of legal acts, depending on the type of goods (e.g. agricultural v. industrial), the reason for the duty (e.g. anti-dumping duty v. tariff suspension) and the commercial policy pursued towards the country concerned (e.g. preferential v. normal duty).

The European Community calls its tariff the 'Common Customs Tariff'—CCT (see Art. 23 EC and Art. 1 of Council Reg. 2658/87, *OJ* 1987 L256/1) or 'Customs Tariff of the European Communities' (Art. 20(1)(3) Community Customs Code, Council Reg. 2913/92, *OJ* 1992 L302/1). The CCT is scattered over more than a hundred regulations as well as preferential agreements. However, the Commission has been charged by Art. 2 of Reg. 2658/87 to establish an integrated tariff called 'Taric' (derived from French: *Tar*if *i*ntégré des Communautés européennes), which sets out all tariff measures and commercial or agricultural policy restrictions on importation and exportation of specific goods. The Taric is not a legal act, but it provides the basis for the duty collection and the application of external trade restrictions by the customs administrations of the Member States. It can be consulted under http://europa.eu.int/comm/taxation_customs/common/databases/taric/index_en.htm.

I. International law

Customs tariffs create barriers in international trade. The advantage a country gains within its home market is a disadvantage for the other countries exporting to it, so the export markets of each country are negatively affected by customs tariffs. For centuries, countries have therefore negotiated trade agreements with the aim to expand the international exchange of goods under mutually advantageous arrangements. Since 1947 the General Agreement on Tariffs and Trade (GATT) provides a recognized legal framework for international trade relations. With the creation of the World Trade Organization (WTO) in 1994 these disciplines have been strengthened, notably by introducing an effective dispute settlement procedure. The Community is a contracting party to these agreements (Council Dec. 94/800/EC, *OJ* 1994 L336/1).

Art. I GATT obliges Contracting Parties to extend any advantage with respect to customs duties granted to products from one country immediately and unconditionally to like products from all other WTO Contracting Parties—general most-favoured-nation (MFN) treatment. In so far as the tariff concessions agreed under the WTO are concerned, WTO members are obliged to grant to the commerce of the other Contracting Parties treatment no less favourable than the bound duty rate provided for in the schedule of concessions (Art. II GATT). Such a binding agreement represents a maximum tariff.

The GATT rules provide, however, a variety of exceptions from MFN treatment, thus allowing bilateral or discriminatory treatment. These include:

- preferential treatment, as foreseen in Art. I(2)–(4) GATT and in an understanding of 1979 on 'Differential and More Favourable Treatment Reciprocity, and Fuller Participation of Developing Countries';
- preferential treatment within customs unions, free trade areas, and interim agreements leading to either (Art. XXIV GATT Understanding on the interpretation of Art. XXIV GATT, *OJ* 1994 L336/16);
- anti-dumping and countervailing duties (Arts. II(2)(6), VI, XVI GATT, Anti-dumping and Subsidies Codes, *OJ* 1994 L336/103 and 156);
- safeguard (Art. XIX GATT) and security measures (Art. XXI GATT); and
- countermeasures in case of nullification or impairment of a WTO obligation, such as a bound duty rate (Art. XXIII GATT).

Apart from stipulating MFN treatment and allowing certain exceptions from this principle, the GATT rules also oblige Contracting Parties

- to allow free transit through their territory (Art. V GATT);
- to limit the fees and charges related to imports and exports to the approximate cost of services rendered (Art. VIII GATT);
- to publish customs legislation, particularly when it is more burdensome than before the date of its entry into force (Art. X GATT);
- to administer tariff quotas in a non-discriminatory manner; an allocation of quotas among supplying countries is, however, feasible if due account is taken of their trade shares (Art. XIII GATT).

These rules set a framework for the establishment and management of WTO members' customs tariffs, and consequently also for the CCT. In its decision on the adoption of the WTO Agreement and its Annexes (the tariff schedule for the Community being one of them) the Council declared in the last recital that 'by its nature, the agreement establishing the World Trade Organization, including the Annexes thereto, is not susceptible to being directly invoked in Community or Member State courts'. This reflects, to some extent, the current jurisprudence of the ECJ (Cases 21/72 etc. *International Fruit Company* [1972] ECR 1219 at p. 1229; Case C-280/93 *Germany* v. *Council* [1994] ECR I-4973 at p. I-5072). In some cases the ECJ has, however, judged the compatibility of EC secondary legislation or its interpretation by a Member State on the basis of a WTO agreement, in particular when it aims at implementing WTO obligations, as in the case of the anti-dumping regulation (Case C-69/89 *Nakajima* v. *Council* [1991] ECR I-2069 at p. I-2178; Case C-61/94 *Commission* v. *Germany* [1996] ECR I-3989 at p. I-4013; Case C-76/00 P *Petrotrub* v. *Council* [2003] ECR I-79 at pp. I-141–2).

In so far as the nomenclature, i.e. the classification system, of the CCT is concerned, another international agreement sets out a precise framework, namely the International Convention on the Harmonized Commodity

Description and Coding System, in short the Harmonized System—HS (*see further under* **Classification of goods for customs purposes**, section I).

Taken together, both agreements cover important parts of the CCT, namely on the one hand, the description and classification of goods up to the six-digit-level, and on the other hand, the conventional duty rates attached to the eight-digit-subheadings as well as the tariff quotas agreed under the WTO. Nevertheless, the legislator of the CCT keeps a certain amount of autonomy, for example with respect to:

- the granting of duty suspensions, provided they are non-discriminatory and describe the goods on the basis of the HS;
- the conclusion of free trade or customs union agreements, as long as they respect Art. XXIV GATT; and
- the imposition of anti-dumping duties, provided Art. VI GATT and the Anti-dumping Code are respected, and the goods are described on the basis of the HS.

II. The Treaty provisions

Part Three of the EC Treaty ('Community policies') deals, under Title I ('Free movement of goods'), with the customs union. According to Art. 23 EC, the Community is based on a customs union which covers all trade in goods and involves the prohibition between Member States of customs duties on imports and exports and of all charges having equivalent effect, and the adoption of a Common Customs Tariff in trade with third countries (see also Art. 25). At first sight, it is surprising to find the objective of harmonizing Member States' customs tariffs towards third countries under the title 'Free movement of goods', which relates to trade between Member States. The internal market can, however, only function if, at its external frontiers, common rules are applied; otherwise third-country goods would enter the Union via the Member State with the most favourable conditions (e.g. a duty exemption) and could then benefit from the principle of free movement that applies both to goods made in a Member State and to import goods for which the formalities for entry into free circulation have been fulfilled (Art. 24 EC). More restrictive import rules in other Member States (e.g. a customs duty) could thus be circumvented. Consequently, the abolition of customs duties between Member States on 1 July 1968 was coupled with the introduction of the Common Customs Tariff (CCT) on the same date (see *Gen. Rep. EC* (1968), p. 21).

The dual nature of the CCT—being on the one hand the external protection of the internal market and on the other hand an instrument for commercial, industrial, agricultural, and other Community policies—means that the EC Treaty contains several legal bases for amending the CCT:

- Art. 26 EC allows autonomous changes,
- Art. 37 EC in conjunction with Art. 34 EC permits the establishment of common organizations of agricultural markets, which may include common rules for stabilizing imports or exports;

- commercial policy measures may, in accordance with Art. 133 EC, cover changes in tariff rates, the conclusion of tariff agreements, the granting of tariff preferences, as well as the introduction of duties combating dumping or subsidies or fixing safeguard or retaliation duties;
- Art. 187 EC is the legal basis for preferential tariff measures in relation to countries and territories dependent from a Member State, including Greenland (Case C-310/95 *Road Air* [1997] ECR I-2229 at p. I-2266);
- if the accession of a new Member State entails transitional tariff measures, they may be laid down in the Accession Treaty (Art. 49 TEU); and
- association agreements (Art. 310 EC) envisage usually a mutual or unilateral reduction of customs duties.

These provisions also apply with respect to goods covered by the Euratom Treaty, given that this Treaty deals with tariff measures only for the transitional period (Arts. 94 and 95 Euratom). In accordance with Art. 305(2) EC, this Treaty applies.

Since the expiry of the ECSC Treaty the coal and steel products formerly covered by that Treaty now fall under the rules of the EC Treaty. In the past, the legal situation with respect to ECSC products had created interpretation problems, given that:

- Art. 71 ECSC stated that 'the powers of the Governments of Member States in matters of commercial policy shall not be affected by this Treaty, save as otherwise provided therein', and
- Art. 305(1) EC stipulated that 'the provisions of this Treaty shall not affect the provisions of the Treaty establishing the European Coal and Steel Community, in particular as regards the rights and obligations of Member States, the powers of the institutions of that Community . . .'.

In its Opinion 1/94 ([1994] ECR I-5267 at p. I-5396) the ECJ had clarified that commercial policy measures, and in particular trade agreements, of a general nature (i.e. covering all types of goods) already fell under Community competence in accordance with Art. 133 EC. Only agreements specifically covering ECSC goods may have been based on the ECSC Treaty. Consequently, the ECSC Treaty provisions were only relevant for the CCT where:

- a tariff agreement was restricted to ECSC goods (e.g. the preferential agreement with Turkey, *OJ* 1996 L227/1), or
- the ECSC Treaty empowered a Community institution to take specific measures, as in the case of measures against dumping and subsidies (Art. 74 ECSC, see Comm. Dec. 2277/96, *OJ* 1996 L308/11, and Comm. Dec. 1889/98, *OJ* 1998 L245/3).

These special rules have now become obsolete.

III. Scope of the CCT

1. Goods versus services. Unlike the Community system of value added tax, the CCT taxes only goods, not services. Goods are, in principle, defined as material objects that can be brought over a border and be subject of trade (Case 7/68 *Commission* v. *Italy* [1968] ECR 423 at p. 642; Case 1/77 *Bosch* [1977] ECR 1473 at p. 1482; and Case C-2/90 *Commission* v. *Belgium* [1992] ECR I-4431 at p. I-4478). Electricity is also regarded as goods (Case 6/64 *Costa* [1964] ECR 585; Case C-393/92 *Almelo* [1994] ECR I-1477 at p. I-1516; and Case C-158/94 *Commission* v. *Italy* [1997] ECR I-5789 at p. I-5799).

Computer programs, licences, patents, music, and films are, in their own right, not subject to customs duties, but where such services or rights are incorporated in a material object, as in an architectural plan, a banknote, a record, tape, or disc, the question arises whether the duty covers only the value of the object or also the service it represents. The CCT and customs legislation provide differentiated answers to this question:

1. In a number of cases the CCT, or the system of duty relief (Council Reg. 918/83, *OJ* 1983 L105/1), provides for duty exemptions, so that the value of the service is automatically also exempted (e.g. books, newspapers, plans, magnetic tapes with data or instructions).
2. In other cases the duty depends on certain measurements, so that the value of the incorporated service is irrelevant (certain films of CN code 3706 90 99: €3.5/100 m, if the maximum *ad valorem* duty is not applied).
3. Where—as in the case of gramophone records—an *ad valorem* duty is fixed, the duty covers both the value of the object and of the service (the music), unless special rules apply. In cases where the service can be dissociated from the object, it is possible to exclude it from the customs value, e.g. the right to broadcast music (see Case 1/77 *Bosch*, above, and Case 135/77 *Bosch* [1978] ECR 855, *see further under* **Customs value**). With the rise of electronic media (and notably the Internet) a differentiated treatment of music, films and other data, according to whether they are incorporated in a material object or not, does create distortions for competing goods subject to customs duties. Further complications arise where an article is imported and later upgraded through the Internet. The origin of these problems lies, however, in the fact that the customs tariff and customs legislation deal only with goods and not with services; this is the heart of the current discussion on the Internet as a 'duty free area'.

2. *Res extra commercium.* The CCT is an instrument of economic, commercial, industrial, and agricultural policy. Corpses and foetuses are therefore not subjected to the customs tariff. Therapeutic substances of human origin are explicitly exempted through the system of duty relief (Council Reg. 918/83, *OJ* 1983 L105/1). The ECJ has added two further exceptions to the scope of the CCT that have subsequently been taken into account in

Art. 212 Community Customs Code (Council Reg. 2913/92, *OJ* 1992 L302/1), namely the unlawful importation of

- counterfeit currency (Case C-343/89 *Witzemann* [1990] ECR I-4477 at p. I-4494), and
- narcotic drugs and psychotrophic substances, if they are not to be used for medical or scientific purposes (Case 50/80 *Horvath* [1981] ECR 385 at p. 397; Case 221/81 *Wolf* [1982] ECR 3681 at p. 3707).

In all other cases of irregularity—such as theft before release for free circulation, importation without the required licence, or importation of counterfeit goods or smuggling—the duties of the CCT are to be applied (Case 186/82 *Esercizio Magazzini Generali* [1983] ECR 2951 at p. 2962; Case C-25/90 *Wünsche* [1991] ECR I-4939 at p. I-4954; Case C-3/97 *Goodwin and Unstead* [1998] ECR I-3257 at p. I-3271; Case C-455/98 *Tullihallitus* [2000] ECR I-4993 at p. I-5015).

IV. Secondary legislation

1. Elements of the CCT. The CCT is not contained in a single legal act but in more than one hundred regulations, decisions, or agreements. The duties and duty exemptions laid down therein can be classified by type of measure as:

- autonomous and conventional normal duties;
- autonomous tariff suspensions and tariff quotas;
- anti-dumping and countervailing duties;
- safeguard and retaliation duties;
- agricultural duties;
- autonomous and conventional preferential duties (including tariff quotas and ceilings); and
- exceptions from the CCT in favour of limited parts of the Community customs territory.

It should be noted that no customs duties are due in cases where Council Reg. 918/83 setting up a Community system of reliefs from customs duties (*OJ* 1983 L105/1) applies. This regulation covers cases such as:

- goods imported by reason of a transfer of residence by a person or company (for the interpretation of the term 'residence', see Case 127/86 *Ledoux* [1988] ECR 3741 at pp. 3757–8; Case C-297/89 *Ryborg* [1991] ECR I-1943 at pp. I-1973–4; and Case C-262/99 *Louloudakis* [2001] ECR I-5547 at pp. I-5592–3);
- consignments sent by a private individual to another private individual of a value not exceeding €45;
- goods contained in the personal luggage of travellers, provided such imports are of a non-commercial nature, and whose value does not exceed €175 per traveller; for tobacco, alcohol, perfume, and medicine, special thresholds apply (with regard to the scope of these arrangements see Case 158/80 *Rewe* [1981] ECR 1805 at p. 1830; with regard to the term 'non-commercial', see Case C-99/00 *Lyckeskog* [2002] ECR I-4839 at p. I-4888);

- goods used for certain educational, scientific, medical, or cultural purposes (with regard to the term 'scientific', see Case 236/83 *Universität Hamburg* [1984] ECR 3849; and Case 13/84 *Control Data Belgium* v. *Commission* [1987] ECR 275);
- goods for the benefit of handicapped persons or disaster victims;
- goods for trade or tourist promotion purposes; or
- fuel contained in the standard tanks of private and commercial motor vehicles and motor cycles (see Case C-247/97 *Schoonbroodt* [1998] ECR I-8095 at pp. I-8123–4).

The autonomous and conventional normal duties are set out in Council Reg. 2658/87 (*OJ* 1987 L256/1). The conventional rates are those agreed under the World Trade Organization (WTO). The autonomous rates are identified and applied only where they are lower than the conventional rates. The Community applies most-favoured-nation treatment (unlike some other countries) to all third countries, irrespective of whether they are WTO members, or have signed another agreement granting most-favoured-nation treatment or not, except where the Community has suspended the application of the conventional rate with regard to a specific country (see Council Reg. 1804/98, *OJ* 1998 L233/1). In the preliminary provisions of the tariff annex, this regulation also suspends customs duties in respect of goods to be used in the construction, repair, maintenance, or conversion of sea-going ships and drilling or production platforms. Furthermore, the conditions for granting certain goods favourable tariff treatment on account of their nature are laid down here.

In another provision a flat rate of 3.5% customs duty is stipulated for goods:

- contained in consignments sent by one private individual to another, or
- contained in travellers' personal luggage,

provided that such imports are not of a commercial nature and that the value of the goods does not exceed €350 per consignment or traveller. Tobacco products are excluded from this simplification, which applies in those cases where the threshold for duty relief (see above) is exceeded.

Another flat rate provision is contained in Art. 81 of the Community Customs Code (Council Reg. 2913/92, *OJ* 1992 L302/1); it allows the application of the highest rate of import duty applicable to a part of a consignment of goods falling within different tariff subheadings in cases where the drawing up of a detailed declaration would entail a burden of work and expense disproportionate to the import duties chargeable.

Autonomous tariff suspensions and quotas waive, for the period of validity of the measure, the application of the normal duty set out in Reg. 2658/87 with respect to specific goods, either for an unlimited quantity (suspension) or a limited quantity (quota). The duty may be suspended completely or partially. Their purpose is to enable Community enterprises to use raw materials, semi-finished goods, or components not available within the Community at a lower cost in order to improve their competitive capacity and, in particular, to create or maintain employment and to modernize their production process. Where import goods may be used both for direct consumption and for manufacture, the suspension is limited to the latter end-use, which is controlled by customs (*see further under* **Customs procedures**, section V.1). The Commission has published a communication on the rules governing autonomous tariff suspensions and quotas (*OJ* 1998 C128/2). The basic regulation for autonomous tariff suspensions is Council Reg. 1255/96 (*OJ* 1996 L158/1), and for autonomous tariff quotas Council Reg. 2505/96 (*OJ* 1996 L345/1). Such duties are applied *erga omnes* (i.e. with respect to goods coming from any third country).

Anti-dumping and countervailing duties are—like tariff suspensions—autonomous duties. They are, however, only applied with regard to goods originating in a specific country (*see further under* **Origin of goods**) and they impose an additional duty for such imports. Where a tariff suspension exists, it does not waive the anti-dumping or countervailing duty. Anti-dumping duties aim at combating price discrimination, i.e. selling at an export price that is lower than the price of the like product in the home market. If no market economy exists in the export country, the export price is compared with the price in a country with a market economy. Countervailing duties aim at offsetting export and other subsidies leading to an artificially low export price. In either case such duties can only be imposed, if:

- an investigation has been conducted (provisional duties may be imposed before);
- dumping or subsidies have been found;
- the Community producers have suffered or are threatened to suffer serious injury from the dumped or subsidized imports; and
- the measure is in the interest of the Community.

The rules for imposing:

- anti-dumping duties are set out in Council Reg. 384/96 (*OJ* 1996 L56/1) and
- countervailing duties in Council Reg. 2026/97 (*OJ* 1997 L288/1).

Agricultural duties are customs duties that are not set out in Reg. 2658/87 but either in the framework of a common market organization or in the trade rules for processed agricultural goods. The customs and agricultural regulations are complementary: Council Reg. 2658/87 sets, for example, the duty for durum wheat (CN code 1001 10 00) at €148/t; a footnote specifies, however, that the Community will apply a duty at a level and in a manner so that the duty-paid import price will not be greater than the effective intervention or support price increased by 55%. This duty is fixed in an agricultural regulation and changes constantly. The rate of €148/t constitutes, therefore, only the maximum tariff. In other cases, the duties set out in Reg. 2658/87 may be supplemented by additional agricultural duties or countervailing charges if certain conditions (e.g. increase of imports, decline in import prices) are met (see, for example, Comm. Reg. 1255/96, *OJ* 1996 L158/1). Given that Art. 23 EC stipulates a single common customs tariff (and not several customs tariffs for different economic sectors) and given that the rules for the common market apply also with respect to agricultural goods in so far as Arts. 33 to 38 EC do not provide for an exception (Art. 32(2) EC), agricultural duties laid down on the basis of Arts. 34 and 37 EC form part of the CCT. This is corroborated by Art. 20(3)(c) Community Customs Code (Council Reg. 2913/92, *OJ* 1992 L302/1), according to which the Customs Tariff of the EC also includes 'agricultural charges laid down under the common agricultural policy or under the specific arrangements applicable to certain goods resulting from the processing of agricultural products'.

Preferential duties are either contained in agreements with individual countries or groups of countries or are granted autonomously, on the basis of a Council regulation or decision, towards individual countries, groups of countries or territories dependent on a Member State or a third country. Given that a preferential duty is an exception from the most-favoured-nation principle, it can be granted only under certain conditions; without such rules, goods from any country could be imported via the country benefiting from preference and the purpose of preferential differentiation would fail. For imports of certain goods from certain countries (Turkey, Andorra, San Marino, Overseas Countries and Territories) it is, in principle, sufficient to prove that the goods have been in free circulation in the exporting country. This rule has been set on the assumption that the partner country applies customs duties with respect to third-country goods that are at least equivalent to those of the CCT. If third-country components have been used for the production of export goods, the duties must be collected before the document entitling preferential access can be issued (no drawback rule). In cases where the trading partner does not apply the anti-dumping and countervailing duties of the Community, such duties remain applicable when goods subject to such duties are imported via a country benefiting from preferences for goods that have been in free circulation there. In the other cases, preferential duties are only granted if the goods originate in the country or group of countries concerned. The use of Community components and—to some extent third-country components—is permitted (*see further under* **Origin of goods**).

Preferential agreements, since the latest enlargement of the Community in 2004, exist with the following countries or groups of countries:

- Europe Agreements with Bulgaria and Romania;
- the European Economic Area (EEA) with Iceland, Norway, and Liechtenstein; a separate agreement covers Switzerland;
- agreements with almost all Mediterranean countries: Algeria, Croatia, Egypt, Israel, Jordan, Lebanon, Macedonia, Morocco, Palestine, Syria, Tunisia, Turkey;
- the ACP countries: Angola, Antigua and Barbuda, Bahamas, Barbados, Belize, Benin, Botswana, Burkina Faso, Burundi, Cameroon, Cape Verde, Central African Republic, Chad, Comoros, Congo, Cook Islands, Côte d'Ivoire, Democratic Republic of Congo, Djibouti,

Dominica, Dominican Republic, Equatorial Guinea, Eritrea, Ethiopia, Fiji, Gabon, Gambia, Ghana, Grenada, Guinea, Guinea Bissau, Guyana, Haiti, Jamaica, Kenya, Kiribati, Lesotho, Liberia, Madagascar, Malawi, Mali, Marshall Islands, Mauritania, Mauritius, Micronesia, Mozambique, Namibia, Nauru, Niger, Nigeria, Niue, Palau, Papua New Guinea, Rwanda, Samoa, São Tomé and Príncipe, Senegal, Seychelles, Sierra Leone, Solomon Islands, Somalia, St Kitts and Nevis, St Lucia, St Vincent and the Grenadines, Sudan, Suriname, Swaziland, Tanzania, Timor Leste, Togo, Tonga, Trinidad and Tobago, Tuvalu, Uganda, Vanuatu, Western Samoa, Zambia, Zimbabwe;
- Andorra, San Marino, the Faeroe Islands;
- Chile, Mexico, South Africa.

Autonomous preferences are granted

- under the Generalized System of Preferences in favour of the following developing countries and territories: United Arab Emirates, Afghanistan, Antigua and Barbuda, Anguilla, Armenia, Netherlands Antilles, Angola, Antarctica, Argentina, American Samoa, Aruba, Azerbaijan, Barbados, Bangladesh, Burkina Faso, Bahrain, Burundi, Benin, Bermuda, Brunei Darussalam, Bolivia, Brazil, Bahamas, Bhutan, Bouvet Island, Botswana, Belarus, Belize, Cocos Islands, Democratic Republic of Congo, Central African Republic, Congo, Côte d'Ivoire, Cook Islands, Chile, Cameroon, People's Republic of China, Colombia, Costa Rica, Cuba, Cape Verde, Christmas Islands, Djibouti, Dominica, Dominican Republic, Algeria, Ecuador, Egypt, Eritrea, Ethiopia, Fiji, Falklands Islands, Federated States of Micronesia, Gabon, Grenada, Georgia, Ghana, Gibraltar, Greenland, Gambia, Guinea, Equatorial Guinea, South Georgia and South Sandwich Islands, Guatemala, Guam, Guinea-Bissau, Guyana, Heard Island and McDonald Islands, Honduras, Haiti, Indonesia, India, British Indian Ocean Territory, Iraq, Iran, Jamaica, Jordan, Kenya, Kyrgyzstan, Cambodia, Kiribati, Comoros, St Kitts and Nevis, Kuwait, Cayman Islands, Kazakhstan, Lao People's Democratic Republic, Lebanon, St Lucia, Sri Lanka, Liberia, Lesotho, Libyan Arab Jamarhiriya, Morocco, Moldova, Madagascar, Marshall Islands, Mali, Myanmar, Mongolia, Macao, Northern Mariana Islands, Mauritania, Montserrat, Mauritius, Maldives, Malawi, Mexico, Malaysia, Mozambique, Namibia, New Caledonia, Niger, Norfolk Island, Nigeria, Nicaragua, Nepal, Nauru, Niue Island, Oman, Panama, Peru, French Polynesia, Papua New Guinea, Philippines, Pakistan, St Pierre and Miquelon, Pitcairn, Palau, Paraguay, Qatar, Russian Federation, Rwanda, Saudi Arabia, Solomon Islands, Seychelles, Sudan, Saint Helena, Sierra Leone, Senegal, Somalia, Suriname, São Tomé and Príncipe, El Salvador, Syrian Arab Republic, Swaziland, Turks and Caicos Islands, Chad, French Southern Territories, Togo, Thailand, Tajikistan, Tokelau Islands, Turkmenistan, Tunisia, Tonga, Timor Leste, Trinidad and Tobago, Tuvalu, Tanzania, Ukraine, Uganda, United States Minor Outlying Islands, Uruguay, Uzbekistan,

St Vincent and Northern Grenadines, Venezuela, Virgin Islands (British), Virgin Islands (USA), Vietnam, Vanuatu, Wallis and Futuna, Samoa, Yemen, Mayotte, South Africa, Zambia, Zimbabwe, Council Reg. 2501/2001, *OJ* 2001 246/1, amended list in *OJ* 2003 L116/6);

- in favour of Ceuta and Melilla, Spanish territories on the African continent (Protocol No. 2 to the Act of Accession of 1985, *OJ* 1985 L302/400, and Council Reg. 2622/97, *OJ* 1997 L354/7);
- in favour of the Overseas Countries and Territories (OCT) dependent on a Member State (Council Dec. 2001/822, *OJ* 2001 L314/1 and L324/1):
  - — Denmark: Greenland;
  - — France: New Caledonia and Dependencies, French Polynesia, French Southern and Antarctic Territories, Wallis and Futuna Islands, Mayotte, Saint Pierre, and Miquelon;
  - — Netherlands: Aruba, Netherlands Antilles (Bonaire, Curaçao, Saba, Saint Eustatius, Saint Martin);
  - — United Kingdom: Anguilla, Cayman Islands, Falkland Islands, South Georgia and the Sandwich Islands, Montserrat, Pitcairn, Saint Helena and Dependencies, British Antarctic Territory, British Indian Ocean Territory, Turks and Caicos Islands, British Virgin Islands;
- in favour of Albania, Bosnia and Herzegovina, Macedonia, Montenegro, Kosovo, and Serbia (Council Reg. 2007/2000, *OJ* 2000 L240/1).

Certain areas of the Community customs territory are—because of their peripheral location—at a competitive disadvantage compared with the rest of this territory. Art. 299(2) EC calls for specific measures in favour of those areas. The Council has therefore granted tariff suspensions for certain imports into the Canary Islands and the free zone of Madeira (see, for example, Council Reg. 1454/2001, *OJ* 2001 L198/45, and Council Reg. 122/96, *OJ* 1996 L20/4).

Art. 20(4) Community Customs Code—CC (Council Reg. 2913/92, *OJ* 1992 L302/1) makes the application of preferential tariff measures (including autonomous tariff suspensions and tariff quotas) dependent on a request in the customs declaration; such an application may, however, also be made within the three-year period for a repayment claim (Art. 236 CC). In case of a tariff quota, the reduced duty rate will be granted only if, at the time the request is made, the amount of the quota is not yet exhausted (Art. 20(5) CC). Where the application of a preferential duty requires the presentation of a document (e.g. a certificate of origin), this document must be valid at the time of its presentation to customs.

2. Management of tariff quotas. Under Community legislation, tariff quotas are distributed among interested importers or exporters

- according to the first-come-first-served principle,
- or through licences granted by Member States' administrations and/or certificates issued by the export country,

- or—exceptionally—by invitation of tenders (e.g. Comm. Reg. 1032/98, *OJ* 1998 L148/3).

Where the first-come-first-served principle is stipulated, the following procedure applies (see Arts. 308a to 308c CCIP, Comm. Reg. 2453/93, *OJ* 1993 L253/1):

1. The goods are presented to customs and the declaration for release for free circulation is lodged, together with a request for the application of the tariff quota. If required, a security must be provided before the goods are released (Art. 248 CCIP).
2. If the request concerns a preferential tariff quota or a tariff quota requiring the presentation of another document (e.g. certificate of authenticity), the prescribed document has to be presented to customs.
3. Provided that the tariff quota is not yet exhausted, the customs office informs the EU Commission, via the national quota management centre, of the requested quantity.
4. The Commission attributes the requested quantities in the order of the dates at which the declaration for release for free circulation was accepted, until the tariff quota is exhausted, and informs the national quota management centre.
5. Once the customs office has received this information, the applicable duty is collected or—in the case of a duty exemption—duty free treatment is granted. Any security provided for this importation is released.

The State of exhaustion of such tariff quotas can be consulted under the following Internet address: http://europa.eu.int/comm/taxation_customs/common/databases/quota/index_en.

Under the licensing procedure, which is only used for certain agricultural products, the quantities are distributed as follows (see Comm. Reg. 1291/2000, *OJ* 2000 L152/1):

1. Importers or exporters apply for a licence at the national agricultural administration within the set deadline (such a modality is in conformity with Community law, Case C-369/95 *Somalfruit* [1997] ECR I-6619 at p. I-6651).
2. They submit any required documents, e.g. proof of importation or exportation of like products during the reference period (such a modality is in conformity with Community law, Case C-241/95 *Accrington Beef* [1996] ECR I-6699 at pp. I-6729–31).
3. The national administrations submit the requested quantities for which the stipulated proof has been presented to the EU Commission.
4. The Commission decides—normally by means of a regulation—to which extent the requests can be satisfied. Applicants have a right of appeal against such a regulation (Case C-354/87 *Weddel* v. *Commission* [1990] ECR I-3847 at p. I-3886; Case T-70/94 *Comafrica and Dole* v. *Commission* [1996] ECR II-1741 at p. II-1761), unless the definitive quantities are attributed by the national authorities (Cases

T-198/95 etc. *Comafrica and Dole* v. *Commission* [2001] ECR II-1975 at p. II-2018).

5. The national administrations issue import or export licences, normally against security in order to ensure that the licence is used (such a requirement is compatible with the principle of proportionality, see Case C-369/95 *Somalfruit*, above, at p. I-6647).
6. The security is released, once the goods have been released for free circulation or exported, or proof of *force majeure* has been submitted.

In attributing the tariff quotas, the Commission can rely on the information provided by Member States (Cases C-106/90 etc. *Emerald Meats* v. *Commission* [1993] ECR I-209 at p. I-303). If the Commission discovers discrepancies it can make the necessary corrections and the fact that other errors have not been discovered and corrected does not render such adaptations illegal (Case C-478/93 *Netherlands* v. *Commission* [1995] ECR I-3081 at p. I-3110). If the Commission has discovered errors and did not take any action for remedy, this can justify a waiver from post-clearance recovery in accordance with Art. 220(2)(b) Community Customs Code (Case T-42/96 *Eyckeler & Malt* v. *Commission* [1998] ECR II-401 at pp. II-445–51). Any method applied for the distribution of the quota among interested importers or exporters must avoid discrimination; this principle can be violated by the fact that certain operators need a licence and others do not (Case C-122/95 *Germany* v. *Council* [1998] ECR I-973 at p. I-1018; Cases C-364/95 etc. *T. Port* [1998] ECR I-1023 at p. I-1058).

On the other hand, no economic operator can claim a right to property in a market share that he has held in the past, since this constitutes only a momentary economic position exposed to the risks of changing circumstances (see Case 265/87 *Schräder* [1989] ECR 2237 at p. 2267; Case 5/88 *Wachauf* [1989] ECR 2609 at p. 2639; Case C-280/93 *Germany* v. *Council* [1994] ECR I-4973 at p. I-5065).

If a national administration has granted an import licence erroneously and the error could not be detected by the importer, this may justify a waiver from post-clearance recovery by virtue of Art. 220(2)(b) Community Customs Code (Council Reg. 2913/92, *OJ* 1992 L302/1; Case C-187/91 *Belovo* [1992] ECR I-4937 at p. I-4971).

The principles of the internal market do not allow the allocation of tariff quotas by Member States and restrictions on the movement of goods entered for free circulation under such quota (Case 218/82 *Commission* v. *Council* [1983] ECR 4063 at p. 4075; Case 51/87 *Commission* v. *Council* [1988] ECR 5459 at pp. 5480–1).

See also **Classification of goods for customs purposes, Customs procedures, Customs value, Freedom to provide services, Free movement of goods, Goods, Origin of goods.**

Further reading 1. Books: Berr and Trémeau, *Le droit douanier*, 5th edn. (2001), p. 82; Lasok and Cairns, *The Customs Law of the European Economic Community* (1983), p. 143; Lux, *Guide to Community Customs*

Legislation (2002), p. 73; id., *Das Zollrecht der EG* (2004), Ch. III; Lyons, *EC Customs Law* (2001), pp. 111 and 158; Nassiet, *La réglementation douanière européenne* (1988), p. 30; Müller, Khan, and Neumann, *EC Anti-Dumping Law—a Commentary on Regulation 384/96* (1998); O'Connor, *Tariff Rate Quotas in EC and GATT Law* (1997); Rom, *The Role of Tariff Quotas in Commercial Policy* (1979); Snyder, *International Trade and Customs Law of the European Union* (1998), p. 483; Van Bael and Bellis, *Anti-Dumping and other Trade Protection Laws of the EC*, 4th edn. (2004); Vermulst and Waer, *E.C. Anti-Dumping Law and Practice* (1996); Walsh, *The Customs Code of the European Union* (1996), p. 20.

2. ARTICLES: Cottier, 'Dispute Settlement in the World Trade Organization: Characteristics and Structural Implications for the European Union' (1998) *CML Rev.* 325; Van den Bossche and Marceau, 'Le système de règlement des differends de l'Organisation mondiale du commerce' (3/1988) *Revue du Marché Unique Européen* 29.

► **COMMUNITY CUSTOMS CODE (CC)** is laid down in Council Reg. 2913/92 (*OJ* 1992 L302/1), which, together with its implementing provisions—CCIP (Comm. Reg. 2454/93, *OJ* 1993 L253/1) contains the general rules and procedures that ensure the uniform implementation of tariff, agricultural, and commercial policy measures with regard to trade in goods between the Community and third countries. It secures a balance between the needs of customs authorities to ensure the correct application of customs and other trade-related legislation, on the one hand, and the right of traders to be treated fairly and with a minimum of formalities, on the other. The CC has been introduced with effect from 1 January 1994 following the inception of the single market; it therefore does not deal with trade in goods between Member States (except where the duties for import goods are suspended, or where Community goods are under customs supervision, e.g. because they have been declared for export).

I. International law

The World Customs Organization (WCO—formerly Customs Co-operation Council—CCC) is the most important body dealing with customs legislation on an international scale. It has issued the International Convention on the Simplification and Harmonization of Customs Procedures concluded on 18 May 1973 in Kyoto (Kyoto Convention, Council Dec. 75/199, *OJ* 1975 L100/1, see revised version in *OJ* 2003 L86/23). It contains standards and recommended practices for all aspects of customs legislation, including (the references concern the original version, given that the EC has not yet adopted any of the revised specific Annexes):

- formalities prior to the lodgement of the goods declaration (Annex A.1, *OJ* 1978 L160/14);
- clearance for home use (Annex B.1, *OJ* 1985 L87/9);
- exportation (Annex C.1, *OJ* 1985 L87/22);
- transit (Annex E.1, *OJ* 1977 L166/13);

- temporary admission (Annex E.5, *OJ* 1987 L362/2);
- inward processing (Annexes E.4, E.6, and E.7, *OJ* 1977 L166/25, 1988 L161/13, 1994 L331/11);
- processing for home use (Annex F.2, *OJ* 1986 L88/43);
- returned goods (Annex B.3, *OJ* 1980 L100/28);
- outward processing (Annex E.8, *OJ* 1977 L166/30);
- customs warehouses (Annex E.3, *OJ* 1975 L100/7);
- free zones (Annex F.1, *OJ* 1978 L160/21);
- origin rules (Annex D.1, *OJ* 1977 L166/3).

With respect to temporary importation, the Istanbul convention of 26 June 1990 (Council Dec. 93/329, *OJ* 1993 L130/1) sets out more stringent rules. The United Nations have also drafted international agreements in this area, notably on temporary importation of

- private road vehicles (Council Dec. 94/110, *OJ* 1994 L56/1);
- commercial road vehicles (Council Dec. 94/111, *OJ* 1994 L56/27);
- containers used in pools (Council Dec. 95/137, *OJ* 1995 L91/45).

The Customs Convention on the International Transport of Goods under Cover of TIR Carnets of 14 November 1975 (Council Reg. 2112/78, *OJ* 1978 L252/1) as well as the International Convention on Harmonization of Frontier Controls of Goods (Council Reg. 1262/84, *OJ* 1984 L126/1) have been concluded under the auspices of the Economic Commission for Europe (ECE), a regional organization of the United Nations.

Among the WTO agreements, those on customs valuation (*OJ* 1994 L336/119, *see further under* **Customs value**) and on origin (*OJ* 1994 L336/144, *see further under* **Origin of goods**) are of particular importance with respect to the CC. But, as a Court case has shown, also other agreements (like the International Dairy Arrangement, *OJ* 1994 L336/290) can have a bearing on the interpretation of the Community Customs Code (Case C-61/94 *Commission* v. *Germany* [1996] ECR I-3989 at p. I-4013).

Apart from such multilateral agreements, which are applied under the most-favoured-nation principle (*see further under* **Common Customs Tariff (CCT)**, section I), the Community has also concluded preferential agreements with specific rules, notably for the determination of origin entitling preferential access. These rules, as well as the decisions taken by the appropriate committees, are directly applicable where they are unconditional and sufficiently clear (Case 104/81 *Kupferberg* [1982] ECR 3641 at p. 3665; Case C-188/91 *Deutsche Shell* [1993] ECR I-363 at p. I-389). They take precedence over the autonomous rules of the CC.

II. The Treaty provisions

The EC Treaty does not contain specific provisions concerning general customs legislation [Art. 27 aiming at an approximation of Member States' legal and administrative provisions in respect of customs matters during the transitional phase was suppressed with the entry into force of the Amsterdam Treaty]. This reflects the opinion of those who drafted the EC Treaty that it would be sufficient for the functioning of the customs union to introduce and regulate a common customs tariff (Arts. 23 and 26 EC) and to develop a common commercial policy (Art. 133 EC). Already in 1973 the ECJ has however stated that the effective functioning of the customs union requires a large interpretation of Arts. 23, 26, and 133 EC in order to allow the Community institutions a consistent and coherent legislation on trade with third countries (Case 8/73 *Massey-Ferguson* [1973] ECR 897). Subsequently, the ECJ has confirmed that the residual competence provided for in Art. 308 EC is not to be used as a legal basis for customs legislation given that other Articles of the Treaty (notably Arts. 26 and 133 EC) allow the laying down of the arrangements for the importation of goods (Case 275/87 *Commission* v. *Council* [1989] ECR 259). Customs legislation can therefore be based on:

- Art. 26 EC where it relates to the autonomous application or non-application of customs duties (e.g. duty relief);
- Art. 133 EC for measures taken for commercial policy reasons (e.g. conclusion of an agreement relating to customs matters, such as the Kyoto Convention);
- Art. 95 EC for measures related to the internal market where none of the two preceding Articles applies.

The Community Customs Code has been based on all three of them together.

Art. 135 EC (inserted by the Amsterdam Treaty) allows the adoption of measures with the aim of strengthening the customs co-operation between Member States and between the latter and the Commission, provided such measures do not concern the application of national criminal law or the national administration of justice.

III. The scope and the objectives of the CC

The Community is a customs union. In relation to third countries this requires not only the introduction of a common customs tariff (Art. 23 EC), but also the creation of a single customs territory with common trade regulations, at least for a substantial part of trade with other countries (Art. XXIV(2) and (8) GATT). The Community Customs Code creates such common rules by setting a framework for all imports into and exports from the Community. Its rules apply to taxes, charges, levies, and duties created by Community provisions and collected by the Member States on behalf of the Community; they do not apply, therefore, to national taxes, charges, and duties even when they are levied in breach of Community law (Cases C-192/95 etc. *Comateb* [1997] ECR I-165 at p. I-187); nor is the CC applicable with regard to payments and repayments of export refunds, given that export refunds constitute the external aspect of the common pricing policy for Community agricultural products and cannot therefore be regarded as measures governed by customs rules (Case C-334/95 *Krüger* [1997] ECR I-4517 at p. I-4551). The CC is supplemented by Community and national implementing provisions.

The following subjects are regulated separately from the CC:

- the Common Customs Tariff (*see further under* **Common Customs Tariff (CCT)**);
- the system of duty relief (*see further under* **Common Customs Tariff (CCT)**, section IV.1);
- the procedures facilitating the issue of preferential certificates of origin and invoice declarations (*see further under* **Origin of goods**, section II.3);
- administrative assistance between EC customs administrations (Council Reg. 515/97, *OJ* 1997 L82/1, and the Agreement based on Art. 31 TEU, *OJ* 1998 C24/1);
- the mutual assistance for the recovery of claims concerning agricultural and customs duties (Council Dir. 76/308, *OJ* 1976 L73/18);
- the granting of export refunds for agricultural goods (Comm. Reg. 800/1999, *OJ* 1999 L102/11);
- the application of non-tariff commercial policy measures on importation or exportation, such as quantitative restrictions (e.g. with regard to textiles, Council Reg. 3030/93, *OJ* 1993 L275/1) or export controls for dual-use items (Council Reg. 1334/2000, *OJ* 2000 L159/1);
- the imposition of prohibitions and restrictions justified on grounds of public morality, public policy, or public security, the protection of health and life of humans, animals, or plants, the protection of national treasures possessing artistic, historic, or archaeological value or the protection of industrial and commercial property (e.g. the seizure of goods infringing intellectual property rights, Council Reg. 1383/2003, *OJ* 2003 L196/7);
- the collection of external trade statistics (Council Reg. 1172/95, *OJ* 1995 L118/10).

The last four points are referred to in Art. 1 CC, according to which this Code shall apply 'without prejudice to special rules laid down in other fields' regarding external trade. Such other fields are notably:

- the common agricultural policy;
- the common commercial policy;
- health, consumer protection, and environmental policy.

Nevertheless, the customs authorities are entitled or obliged to enforce such provisions on the occasion of an importation or exportation (Art. 58(2) CC).

International agreements that are directly applicable (e.g. the TIR Convention, preferential origin rules) take precedence over the CC.

The primary achievement of the Customs Code and its implementing provisions is that they codify in only two legal acts almost all Community customs legislation. This has brought about a level of transparency and simplification that can be fully appreciated only by those who, prior to 1994, had to apply or comply with over fifty legal texts spread across the *Official Journal*. The CC aims at securing a balance between the needs of the customs authorities in regard to ensuring the correct application of customs and other legislation related to external trade, on the one hand, and the right of traders to be treated fairly, on the other. In view of the paramount importance of external trade for the Community, the CC aims at keeping customs formalities and controls to the minimum required for maintaining security and compliance with regard to goods entering into or leaving the Community. The CC, being a balanced compromise between the different approaches and philosophies previously followed by Member States, serves as a model for countries trying to modernize their customs legislation or to create a customs union.

The procedural framework of the CC supports the commercial and agricultural policy, the collection of external trade statistics and provides the mechanisms for the charging of VAT and excise duties on import goods, as well as for discharging such taxes on exportation. Since the CC embodies concepts pertaining to general administrative law (e.g. annulment, repeal of a decision, protection of legitimate expectation in case of administrative errors, appeals) it has also played a part in creating a common European legal area.

The main challenge lying ahead is to ensure that the twenty-five national customs administrations in the enlarged Community act together as if they were one single administration (also with regard to computerized procedures) and that effective measures against security threats and fraud are taken. Legislative changes alone cannot achieve these aims and therefore the Customs 2007 action programme has been adopted by the European Parliament and the Council (Dec. 253/2003, *OJ* 2003 L36/1). It provides a framework for common actions aiming at a uniform application of Community customs law, the improvement and simplification of this legislation, the introduction of modern working methods, such as simplified procedures, including computerized clearance, risk analysis, audit techniques to check traders' records instead of individual consignments, as well as efficient measures against fraud. The simplification, rationalization, and computerization of the Community's customs procedures has also been called for by two Council Resolutions of 25 October 1996 (*OJ* 1996 C332/1) and 5 December 2003 (*OJ* 2003 C305/1). Trade facilitation through a simplification of customs legislation and procedures is a subject currently discussed in international fora, such as the World Customs Organization (WCO), the World Trade Organization (WTO), the Economic Commission for Europe (ECE), etc.

IV. The structure of the CC

The Community Customs Code is organized around eight titles, most of them being subdivided into chapters and sometimes also into sections.

Title I (General provisions):

- defines the material and territorial scope of the CC (with regard to the latter, *see further under* **Community customs territory**);
- provides definitions for the purposes of the CC;

- sets out the rights and obligations of traders and customs administrations (*see further under* **Customs procedures**, section III, **Classification of goods for customs purposes**, section II.3, and **Origin of goods**, section II.4);
- determines the method for converting values expressed in € for Member States using a national currency (Art. 18 CC); and
- provides a legal basis for simplifications to be laid down in the implementing provisions.

Title II (Factors on the basis of which import duties or export duties and the other measures prescribed in respect of trade in goods are applied):

- creates a link to the EC customs tariff and defines the term 'tariff classification' (*see further under* **Common Customs Tariff (CCT)** and **Classification of goods for customs purposes**);
- sets out the autonomous rules of origin (*see further under* **Origin of goods**);
- stipulates the rules for the determination of the customs value (*see further under* **Customs value**).

Title III (Provisions applicable to goods brought into the customs territory of the Community until they are assigned a customs-approved treatment or use) lays down obligations with regard to goods entering the EC customs territory and sets out the customs supervision of such goods (*see further under* **Customs procedures**, section IV).

Title IV (customs-approved treatment or use) contains the largest and most important part of the CC (*see further under* **Customs procedures**, sections V and VI). It:

- describes how goods are placed under a customs procedure under normal and simplified procedures;
- sets out the rules for the different customs procedures, i.e.
  — release for free circulation,
  — external transit,
  — customs warehousing,
  — inward processing,
  — processing under customs control,
  — temporary importation,
  — outward processing,
  — export, and
  — internal transit;
- defines the other types of customs-approved treatment or use, i.e.
  — free zones and free warehouses,
  — re-exportation, destruction, and abandonment.

Title V (Goods leaving the customs territory of the Community) calls for customs supervision of goods leaving the EC customs territory (*see further under* **Customs procedures**, section IV).

Title VI (Privileged operations):

- creates a link to the system of duty relief (*see further under* **Common Customs Tariff (CCT)**, section IV.1);
- exempts returned goods under certain conditions from import duties (*see further under* **Customs procedures**, section V.1); and
- provides for duty free treatment with regard to products of sea fishing (*see further under* **Customs procedures**, section V.1).

Title VII (Customs debt) links the customs tariff and the customs procedures with the duty to be paid (*see further under* **Customs procedures**, section VII). It:

- defines when and how security is to be provided for a customs debt;
- determines the conditions under which a customs debt is incurred;
- sets out how and when the customs debt is to be requested, paid, and extinguished;
- defines the cases in which duties are repaid or remitted.

Title VIII (Appeals) sets out some basic rules on the right to appeal against decisions taken by the customs authorities with regard to customs legislation (*see further under* **Customs procedures**, section VIII).

Title IX (Final provisions) sets out the role of the Customs Code Committee and defines the rules for the adoption of implementing provisions. Art. 250 CC stipulates the validity of decisions, measures, and findings of national customs authorities throughout the Community and Art. 251 CC repeals the regulations and directives superseded by the Community Customs Code. The regulation entered into force on 1 January 1994. It is applicable with regard to all imports or exports for which a customs declaration was lodged and accepted or a customs debt is incurred as of 1 January 1994 or later (Case C-261/96 *Conserchimica* [1997] ECR I-6177 at pp. I-6188–9; Case T-42/96 *Eyckeler & Malt* v. *Commission* [1998] ECR II-401 at p. II-419). The jurisprudence of the Court of Justice on provisions that have been taken over into the Customs Code remains applicable in so far as no changes of substance have occurred (Case C-48/98 *Söhl & Söhlke* [1999] ECR I-7877 at p. I-7937).

***See also* Classification of goods for customs purposes, Common Customs Tariff, Community customs territory, Customs procedures, Customs value, Origin of goods.**

Further reading: *see under* **Customs procedures.**

▶ **COMMUNITY CUSTOMS TERRITORY** is the customs territory of the European Community as defined in the Community Customs Code (*see further under* **Community Customs Code**).

The term 'customs territory' is defined in Art. XXIV(2) GATT to mean 'any territory with respect to which separate tariffs or other regulations of commerce are maintained for a substantial part of the trade of such territory with other territories'. A customs territory implies therefore a separated area with controls at its frontiers so that customs duties and any other trade restrictions can be applied on goods entering or leaving that territory; goods produced and consumed inside that territory are not subjected to such duties and restrictions.

I. The Treaty provisions

Art. 299 EC defines the territorial scope of the EC Treaty. In Art. 23 EC the Community is defined as a customs union. This could imply that the area in which the EC Treaty is applicable constitutes the Community customs territory. Such an interpretation would, however, fail to leave the necessary flexibility

- to exclude certain areas from the customs territory (e.g. the Canary Islands were until 1991 excluded from the customs territory, in order to allow them duty free access to world market goods), or
- to include certain areas belonging to a different country in the customs territory (e.g. the Principality of Monaco is a part of the Community customs territory; this avoids frontier controls at the entry and exit points to and from Monaco).

Also the original Art. 19 EEC referring to Member States' customs territories which, taken together, constitute the Community customs territory, seems to imply that a margin of discretion exists in that respect. The further advantage (or complication) of laying down the relevant territory in secondary legislation is that it can be defined differently for other purposes (e.g. the fiscal and the statistical territory).

The rules on free movement of goods between Member States (Arts. 23 to 31 EC) apply, however, with regard to the entire territory covered by the EC Treaty (with regard to a change of the territorial scope of the customs territory and the EC Treaty, see Case C-223/95 *Moksel* [1997] ECR I-2379 at p. I-2402).

II. Secondary legislation

According to Art. 3 Community Customs Code—CC (Council Reg. 2913/92, *OJ* 1992 L302/1) the Community customs territory comprises the territory of its Member States, from which the following areas are exempted:

- the Faeroe Islands and Greenland (Denmark);
- the Island of Heligoland and the territory of Büsingen (Germany);
- Ceuta and Melilla (Spain);
- the French overseas territories (New Caledonia, French Polynesia, French Southern and Antarctic Territories, Wallis and Futuna), Saint-Pierre and Miquelon, and Mayotte (France);
- Aruba and the Dutch Antilles (Netherlands);
- Livigno, Campione d'Italia and certain national waters of Lake Lugano (Italy).

The territory of the Principality of Monaco—though not part of the French territory—belongs also to the Community customs territory by virtue of a customs convention between France and Monaco. Likewise, the territory of the United Kingdom Sovereign Base Areas of Akrotiri and Dhekelia as defined in the Treaty concerning the Establishment of the Republic of Cyprus are part of the Community customs territory. The Channel Islands and the Isle of Man are part of the customs territory by virtue of Art. 299(6) EC and the Act of Accession of 1972 concerning the United Kingdom (see Court of Auditors Report, *OJ* 1993 C347/5 and 8).

Since Gibraltar is not mentioned in this context, it is not considered part of the Community customs territory, though the EC Treaty applies, in principle, with regard to Gibraltar (see Art. 299(4) EC: 'The provisions of this Treaty shall apply to the European territories for whose external relations a Member State is responsible'); Art. 28 of the Act of Accession of 1972 (*OJ* 1972 L73/20) excludes Gibraltar only from Community acts relating to agriculture and VAT (see Court of Auditors Report, *OJ* 1993 C347/22). Gibraltar benefits from preferences under the Generalised System of Preferences (*see further under* **Common Customs Tariff**, section IV.1).

Further areas in which Community customs legislation is not or not entirely applied include:

- the so-called 'free zones' of Gex and Haute Savoie (France), created by virtue of the Treaties of Vienna of 20 November 1815 and Turin of 16 March 1816 (see Court of Auditors Report, *OJ* 1993 C347/10);
- the so-called 'free zones' of Gorizia and Valle d'Aosta (Italy), in which customs duty exemptions are granted in favour of the population, trade, and industry (see Court of Auditors Report, *OJ* 1993 C347/11 and 12);
- the free zone of Trieste (Italy), in which some derogations from Community Customs legislation are granted pursuant to the Treaty of Paris concluded in 1947;
- Mount Athos (Greece), where certain customs privileges are granted to the inhabitants (see Court of Auditors Report, *OJ* 1993 C347/22);
- the exemption from customs duties on the French Islands of St Barthélémy and St Martin; and
- the UK Sovereign Base Areas of Akrotiri and Dhekelia in Cyprus by virtue of Protocol No. 3 to the Act of Accession of 2003 (*OJ* 2003 L236/33).

The territorial waters along and the airspace above the customs territory are also considered as a part of it. According to Art. 3 of the United Nations Convention on the Law of the Sea (*OJ* 1998 L179/4), every State has the right to establish the breadth of its territorial sea up to a limit not exceeding twelve nautical miles, measured from baselines determined in accordance with this Convention. The limits set by Member States in accordance with this Convention determine also the scope of the Community customs territory with regard to the sea.

In many countries free zones or so-called export processing zones are outside the customs territory. This is not so in the Community that defines control type I free zones in Arts. 166 to 168 CC as part of the customs territory, which are separated by an enclosure from the rest of it and in which certain specific rules apply (no need to present imported goods to the customs authorities, no need to lodge a customs declaration, simplifications for re-export and transhipments). The motive for this relatively restrictive approach has been to avoid trade distortions and trade diversions that could result from a proliferation of duty free zones and competition between Member States (as it exists in the area of indirect and direct taxes).

III. Customs union agreements

The Community has concluded several customs union agreements creating a common customs territory and stipulating duty free treatment for goods that have been put in free circulation in the partner country. Nevertheless, these agreements do not extend the Community customs territory beyond the boundaries of the EC. In those cases a common customs territory exists only by virtue of the agreements and under the stipulated rules. This means, for example, that the principle of free movement of goods without border controls and the need to prove the status of the goods does not apply to such transactions. Instead, goods circulating between the two parts of the customs union have to prove their privileged status through presentation of a document. Currently, such agreements are operational with

- Andorra, except for agricultural products pertaining to chs. 1 to 24 of the customs tariff (Council Dec. 90/680, *OJ* 1990 L374/13);
- San Marino, except for the former ECSC products (Council Dec. 92/561, *OJ* 1992 L359/13); and
- Turkey, except for agricultural and the former ECSC products (Association Council Dec. 1/95, *OJ* 1996 L35/1).

Furthermore, goods which have been in free circulation in the overseas countries and territories dependent on a Member State are, with certain exceptions, exempted from customs duties on importation into the EC (Council Dec. 2001/822, *OJ* 2001 L314/1 and L324/1).

IV. Customs v. statistical and fiscal territory

1. External trade statistics. The definition of the Community statistical territory used for statistics in external trade is identical with the Community customs territory; only the Island of Heligoland and Livigno are also included (Art. 3 of Council Reg. 1172/95, *OJ* 1995 L118/1).

2. VAT legislation. With respect to VAT there exists no common fiscal territory. In so far as Community rules have been adopted they apply to the fiscal territory of the Member States; certain parts are, however, excluded from EC VAT legislation (see Art. 3 of Council Dir. 77/388, *OJ* 1977 L145/1):

- the Island of Heligoland and Territory of Büsingen (Germany);
- the Canary Islands, Ceuta, and Melilla (Spain);
- Livigno, Campione d'Italia, and the Italian waters of Lake Lugano (Italy);
- Mount Athos (Greece);
- the Åland Islands (Finland);
- the overseas departments (France);
- the Channel Islands (United Kingdom).

Included are the Principality of Monaco and the Isle of Man, as well as the UK Sovereign Base Areas of Akrotiri and Dhekelia in Cyprus. The Act of Accession of 1972 concerning the United Kingdom (*OJ* 1972 L73/20) excludes Gibraltar from EU VAT legislation (Art. 28).

3. Excise duty legislation. According to EU excise duty legislation (applying to mineral oils, alcohol and alcoholic beverages, and manufactured tobacco), the territory of the Member States is in principle also the fiscal territory. Excluded are however (see Art. 2 of Dir. 92/129, *OJ* 1992 L76/1, and Protocol No. 2 to the Act of Accession of 1994 concerning Finland, *OJ* 1994 C241/352):

- the Island of Heligoland and Territory of Büsingen (Germany);
- the Canary Islands, Ceuta, and Melilla (Spain);
- Livigno, Campione d'Italia, and the Italian waters of Lake Lugano (Italy);
- Mount Athos (Greece);
- the Åland Island (Finland);
- the overseas departments (France).

Included are the Principality of Monaco, the Isle of Man, and the UK Sovereign Base Areas of Akrotiri and Dhekelia in Cypus.

4. Consequences with regard to indirect taxes. As a consequence of the lack of a common fiscal territory, commercial trade between Member States is treated in a similar way as exports (relief from VAT) and imports (VAT on intra-Community acquisition). Non-Community goods placed under external transit, temporary importation with total duty relief, any other suspensive procedure or placed in a free zone can pass from the import Member State to their final destination without being subjected to VAT formalities (see Art. 7(3) of Dir. 77/388). Similar principles apply with regard to excise duties (Council Dir. 92/12, *OJ* 1992 L76/1). For goods moving under excise duty suspension an accompanying administrative document is normally required (Comm. Reg. 2719/92, *OJ* 1992 L276/1) if they are not placed under a suspensive arrangement, such as external transit or customs warehousing. Special supervision is also required with regard to movements of goods from areas which are inside the customs but outside the fiscal territory (e.g. the Canary Islands) and vice versa.

See also **Common Customs Tariff, Community Customs Code, Customs procedures, Customs Union.**

Further reading 1. Books: Berr and Trémeau, *Le droit douanier*, 5th edn. (2001), p. 40; Communier, *Droit fiscal communautaire* (2001), pp. 265 and 356; Giffoni, *Droit douanier de la C.E. et aspects économiques, Commission des Communautés européennes* (1993), p. 66; Hine, *The Political Economy of European Trade: An Introduction to the Trade Policies of the EEC* (1985), p. 42; Lipsey, *The Theory of Customs Unions: A General Equilibrium Analysis* (1970); Lux, *Guide to Community Customs Legislation* (2002), p. 41; id., *Das Zollrecht der EG* (2004), ch. III; Lyons, *EC*

Customs Law (2001), p. 80; Robson, *The Economics of International Integration*, 3rd edn. (1987).

2. ARTICLE: Terra and Wattel, (2001) *European Tax Law* 238 and 290.

COMPANY LAW Company law is one of the few areas of private law directly referred to in the EC Treaty. Art. 43 EC prohibits restrictions on the freedom of establishment of nationals of a Member State in the territory of another Member State. Art. 44(1) EC requires the Council to act by means of directives in order to attain freedom of establishment as regards a particular activity. Art. 44(2)(g) EC requires the Council and the Commission to carry out the duties devolving upon them under Arts. 43 and 44(1) by co-ordinating to the necessary extent the safeguards which, for the protection of the interests of members and others, are required by the Member States of companies or firms within the meaning of the second paragraph of Art. 48 EC with a view to making such safeguards equivalent throughout the Communities. Art. 44(2)(g) is the cornerstone of a series of harmonizing directives that now cover much of the company law field.

Community legislation now regulates companies' disclosure and publicity requirements, the legality of pre-incorporation and *ultra vires* transactions and the nullity of companies (First Company Law Directive), the formation of public companies and the maintenance and alteration of their capital (Second Company Law Directive), mergers and divisions of public companies (Third and Sixth Company Law Directives), companies' annual and consolidated accounts (Fourth and Seventh Company Law Directives), the qualification of company auditors (Eighth Company Law Directive), disclosure by cross-frontier branches of companies (Eleventh Company Law Directive), single-member companies (Twelfth Company Law Directive), and takeover bids (Directive on Takeover Bids, adopted on 21 April 2004. These directives are considered below.

There are also pending proposals for company law directives on cross-border mergers of companies with share capital and the cross-border transfer of a company's seat or registered office (planned proposal for a Fourteenth Company Law Directive). These proposals are also considered briefly below. The draft Fifth Directive on the structure of public companies and the powers and obligations of their organs has now been formally abandoned, while the proposed Ninth Directive on groups never got beyond the draft stage.

Companies are also of course affected by the Treaty right of freedom of establishment (*see further under* **Freedom of establishment**, section V).

I. The First Directive

The First Company Law Directive (First Council Dir. 68/151 of 9 March 1968 on co-ordination of safeguards which, for the protection of the interest of members and others, are required by Member States of companies within the meaning of the second paragraph of Art. 48 of the Treaty, with a view to making such safeguards equivalent throughout the Community, *OJ Sp. Edn.* 1968 (I), p. 41) seeks to harmonize publicity requirements applying to companies, the circumstances in which company transactions will be valid and the rules relating to the nullity of companies. It extends to national forms of public and private companies limited by shares, together with a form of organization (e.g. *Kommanditgesellschaft auf Aktien, Société en commandite par actions*) which is a form of public company whose directors are personally liable for its debts (Art. 1). In July 2003, the Council adopted a directive amending the First Directive (*OJ* 2003 L221/13); the following summary takes account of those amendments.

In terms of substance, the main effects of the directive have been to impose a degree of co-ordination on national disclosure requirements and to create a European law of *ultra vires*, which blends elements from two incompatible theories of corporate representation into an uneasy compromise.

1. Disclosure. The directive requires the following information to be filed (including, as from 2005, by electronic means) in a central, commercial, or companies register and disclosed by publication in the national gazette (which may be electronic) appointed for that purpose, or other equally effective means decided on by the Member State concerned (Art. 3):

- the instrument of constitution and the statutes if separate, together with any amendment and the consolidation of each document as amended;
- the appointment, termination of office, and particulars of the persons who are 'authorized to represent the company' or who 'take part in the administration, supervision, or control of the company'; the details must show 'whether the persons authorized to represent the company may do so alone or must act jointly';
- at least annually, the amount of the issued capital, unless clear from an amendment to the statutes;
- the accounting documents for each financial year;
- any transfer of the company's seat;
- any declaration of nullity of a company by the courts and details of any liquidators, liquidation, winding up, and striking off (Art. 2).

The ECJ has held that, where the body authorized to represent a company may consist of one or several members, disclosure must be made not only of the scope of the authority to represent where there are several directors, but also, where there is only one director, of the fact that the latter represents the company alone, even if his authority to do so clearly flows from national law (Case 32/74 *Haaga* [1974] ECR 1201 at p. 1207).

Letters and order forms, whether paper or electronic, and company web sites, must give details of the register in which the company's file is kept, the company's number in that register, the legal form of the company, the location of its seat and, where appropriate, the fact that it is being wound up (Art. 4).

Member States are to provide for appropriate penalties for failure to disclose accounts and the omission of prescribed details from commercial documents (Art. 6). Some guidance as to the type of penalty required by Art. 6 has been provided by the ECJ. Under German law the penalty for failure to disclose the accounts of a GmbH was a fine, which could be imposed on application only by a member or creditor of the company, the central works council, or the company's works council. The ECJ ruled that the directive precluded a Member State from so restricting the rights to apply for imposition of the penalty for failure to disclose accounts (Case C-97/96 *Daihatsu-Händler* [1997] ECR I-6843 at pp. I-6864–5; Case C-191/95 *Commission* v. *Germany* [1998] ECR I-5449 at p. I-5504).

Documents and particulars subject to the disclosure requirement may moreover be relied on by the company against third parties only if they have been published as required, unless the company proves that the third party 'had knowledge thereof' (Art. 3(5)). In addition, third parties may always rely on any documents and particulars in respect of which the disclosure formalities have not been completed, save where non-disclosure causes them not to have effect (Art. 3(7)).

2. Pre-incorporation contracts. If, before a company being formed has acquired legal personality, action has been carried out in its name and the company does not assume the obligations arising from such action, the persons who acted shall, without limit, be jointly and severally liable therefor, unless otherwise agreed (Art. 7).

3. Irregular appointment of directors. Provided that the particulars of the persons who are authorized to represent the company have been completed, the company may not rely on any irregularity in their appointment as against third parties unless it proves that the third parties had knowledge thereof (Art. 8).

4. *Ultra vires* and directors' authority. A company is bound by acts done by the organs of the company that are not within its objects unless such acts exceed the powers which are or may be conferred by law on those organs. Member States may, however, provide that the company shall not be bound by acts outside its objects if it proves that the third party knew that the act was outside the objects or could not in view of the circumstances have been unaware of it; disclosure of the statutes shall not of itself be sufficient proof of this (Art. 9(1)). The ECJ has confirmed that Art. 9(1) does not apply where there is a conflict of interest between a member of an organ and the company he represented because of the former's personal circumstances, or to the question whether a third party was aware, or could not in the circumstances have been unaware, of such a conflict of interest. Such a situation accordingly remains subject to national law (Case C-104/96 *Rabobank* [1997] ECR I-7211 at p. I-7227).

Limits on the powers of the organs of a company that arise under its statutes or from a decision of the competent organs may never be relied on as against third parties even if they have been disclosed (Art. 9(2)). The principle of constructive notice cannot therefore apply to such limits, and third parties do not need to interpret the scope of limits which have been disclosed.

5. Nullity. Section III of the First Directive concerns the circumstances in which a company may be declared invalidly constituted and hence a nullity from its inception. In Member States that do not have a system of administrative judicial supervision of compliance with the legal requirements for forming a company, the instrument of constitution, company statutes, and any amendments thereto are to be drawn up and certified in due legal form (Art. 10).

Nullity must be ordered by decision of a court of law and only on the following grounds:

- failure to execute an instrument of constitution or comply with the rules of preventive control or the requisite legal formalities;
- unlawfulness or conflict with public policy of company's objects;
- failure to state in the instrument of constitution or the statutes the company's name, objects, or the amount of the individual and total capital subscription;
- failure to comply with national law requirements for minimum paid-up capital;
- incapacity of all the founder members;
- reduction of the number of founder members to less than two, contrary to the national law governing the company (Art. 11) (for single-member companies, see section VIII below).

Provisions of national law relating to nullity may not be interpreted in such a manner that the nullity of a company may be ordered on grounds other than those exhaustively listed in Art. 11 (Case C-106/89 *Marleasing* [1990] ECR I-4135 at p. I-4159).

Whether a declaration of nullity may be relied on as against third parties is governed by Art. 3, and where national law entitles a third party to challenge the decision he may do so only within six months of public notice thereof. Nullity shall, and dissolution may, entail the winding up of the company; it shall not of itself affect the validity of existing commitments involving the company. National law may provide for the consequences of nullity as between members; holders of unpaid or partly paid shares shall remain obliged to pay the unpaid balance to the extent that debts are owed to the company (Art. 12).

The rules on nullity in the directive do not apply where the acts involved were performed in the name of a company whose existence is not confirmed by the public register because the formalities for incorporation required by national law have not been completed (Case 136/87 *Ubbink Isolatie* [1988] ECR 4665 at pp. 4686–7).

II. The Second Directive

The Second Council Dir. 77/91 of 13 December 1976 on co-ordination of safeguards which, for the protection of interests of members and others, are required by the Member States of companies within the meaning of the second paragraph of Art. 48 of the Treaty, in respect of the formation of public limited liability companies and the maintenance and alteration of their capital, with a view to making such safeguards equivalent (*OJ* 1977 L26/1), applies to public limited companies and equivalent forms (Art. 1). The directive lays down a general principle, requiring Member States to ensure, for the purposes of its implementation, equal treatment of all shareholders in the same position (Art. 42). The remainder of the directive concerns the formation of public companies and the maintenance and alteration of their capital.

The Second Directive is undeniably of major importance, constituting a significant step towards company law harmonization in the EC. The provisions relating to financial assistance for the purchase by a company of its own shares and to redemption of shares were modelled on the existing United Kingdom legislation, and certain of the other provisions relating to the maintenance of capital reflected at least in part the pre-existing United Kingdom law. Many other provisions derived from continental legal systems, in particular those concerning minimum subscribed capital, the distinction between public and private companies, distributions, consideration for shares generally and in particular the valuation of non-cash consideration, pre-emptive rights, authorization for new issues, and the requirement to hold a meeting in the event of a serious loss of capital.

1. Formation of public companies. The directive requires public companies' names to comprise or include a description distinct from that required of other types of company (Art. 1).

The statutes or instrument of incorporation of a public company must disclose:

- its name and type;
- its object;
- its capital, both subscribed and, if relevant, authorized, both initially and on any change;
- 'in so far as they are not legally determined, the rules governing the number of and the procedure for appointing members of the bodies responsible for representing the company with regard to third parties, administration, management, supervision or control of the company and the allocation of power among those bodies';
- the duration of the company, unless indefinite (Art. 2).

In addition, the statutes or instrument of incorporation or a separate document published in accordance with the First Directive must disclose:

- the registered office;
- details of the issued share capital and classes thereof;
- the identity of the subscribers to the statutes or instrument of incorporation;
- the total amount or an estimate of the formation costs;
- any special advantage granted to promoters (Art. 3).

Where the laws of a Member State require a company to have authorization before starting business, they shall also provide for responsibility for liabilities incurred by or on behalf of a company before the grant or refusal of such authorization other than liabilities under contracts, which are conditional on the grant of authorization (Art. 4).

Where the laws of a Member State require a company to be formed by more than one member, the company shall not be automatically dissolved if the number of members or shareholders falls below the legal minimum (Art. 5) (for single-member companies, see section VIII below).

Member States must prescribe a minimum capital of not less than €25,000 to be subscribed before a company may be incorporated or obtain authorization to commence business (Art. 6). Shares issued for cash must be paid up by the time the company is incorporated or authorized to commence business as to at least 25% of their nominal value or, if none, their accountable par; non-cash consideration must be paid in full within five years of constitution (Art. 9). Member States may derogate from the first of these provisions to the extent necessary 'for the adoption or application of provisions designed to encourage the participation of employees, or other groups of persons defined by national law, in the capital of undertakings' (Art. 41). In order to fall within this derogation the practical application of the provisions in question must help to achieve the objective set out: thus the mere fact that a national rule provides for the hypothetical and ancillary possibility of transferring shares to employees is not sufficient (Cases C-19/90 etc. *Karella and Karellas* [1991] ECR I-2691 at pp. I-2719–20).

A report on consideration other than in cash is to be drawn up by independent experts appointed or approved by an administrative or judicial authority, describing the assets and the methods of evaluation used and stating whether the values so arrived at correspond to the nominal or accountable part value of, and where appropriate the premium on, the shares to be issued; the report is to be published in accordance with the First Directive (Art. 10). The valuation and disclosure provisions also apply to acquisitions by a company from subscribers to its statutes or instrument of incorporation within a period laid down by national law of at least two years after incorporation or authorization to commence business for a consideration that is not less than 10% of its subscribed capital, with the additional requirement of approval by the general meeting (Art. 11). This does not apply to acquisitions effected in the normal course of the company's business, at the instance or under the supervision of an administrative or judicial authority, or on a stock exchange.

Shareholders may not be released from the obligation to pay up their contributions (Art. 12). The subscribed capital may be formed only of assets capable of economic assessment and may not include an undertaking to perform work or supply services (Art. 7). Shares may not be issued at a price lower than their nominal value or, if none, their accountable par, subject to commission for those placing shares in the exercise of their profession (Art. 8).

A general meeting is required in the event of a serious loss of capital, 'serious loss' to be defined by national law at a figure not higher than half the subscribed capital. The meeting must be called within a period to be specified by national law and 'consider whether the company should be wound up or any other measures taken' (Art. 17).

2. Maintenance of capital. Except on a reduction of capital, no distribution (including the payment of dividends or interest on shares but excluding capitalization of reserves or 'bonus issues') may be made when the company's last annual accounts show that its net assets are, or following such a distribution would become, less than its subscribed capital (excluding any uncalled capital) and undistributable reserves. The amount of any distribution may not exceed the previous financial year's net profits plus any profits brought forward and distributable reserves, less any losses brought forward and sums placed to reserve in accordance with the law or the statutes (Art. 15). Any distribution made contrary to Art. 15 must be returned by the recipient if the company proves that he knew of its irregularity or could not in view of the circumstances have been unaware of it (Art. 16).

A company may not subscribe for its own shares, whether directly or through an intermediary or by means of a controlled company (Art. 18). Member States may however permit a company to acquire its own shares (other than by subscription), whether itself or through a nominee or by means of a controlled company, provided that certain conditions are satisfied (Art. 19) and subject to exceptions (Art. 20). Voting rights in respect of any shares so acquired must be suspended; if they are included among the assets shown in the balance sheet, an equivalent undistributable reserve must be included among liabilities and the company's annual report must contain specified minimum information as to the acquisitions (Art. 22). There are provisions for the disposal or cancellation of shares acquired in contravention of Arts. 19 or 20 or pursuant to an exemption (Arts. 20 and 21).

A company is prohibited from advancing funds, making loans, or providing security with a view to the acquisition of its own shares by a third party, unless (provided that the company's net assets do not as a result fall below the total of its subscribed capital and undistributable reserves) the company is a financial institution acting in the normal course of business or the transaction is done with a view to the acquisition of shares by or for employees or with a view to the acquisition by a fixed capital investment company of its shares at the investor's request (Art. 23). The acceptance by or on behalf of a company of its shares as security is assimilated to an acquisition for the purposes of Art. 23 (Art. 24).

Art. 24a, inserted by Dir. 92/101 (*OJ* 1992 L347/64), extends Arts. 18 to 24 to the subscription, acquisition, or holding of shares in a public company effected by another company under the public company's control. Where a public company 'directly or indirectly holds a majority of the voting rights' in or 'can directly or indirectly exercise a dominant influence on' a company within the meaning of the First Directive, or with a comparable legal form but governed by the law of a third country, the subscription, acquisition, or holding of shares in a public company by the controlled company is regarded as having been effected by the public company itself.

Any increase in capital must be decided on by the general meeting; it is for national law to prescribe the procedural requirements for the meeting. The decision of the meeting and the capital increase itself are required to be published in accordance with the First Directive (Art. 25(1)). An increase in subscribed capital up to a maximum amount may be authorized by the statutes or instrument of incorporation or by the duly published decision of the general meeting. Individual decisions to increase capital may then be taken by the body on whom the authority was conferred, normally the management organ. The authority may not be for more than five years, although it may be renewed by the general meeting (Art. 25(2)). Where there are several classes of shares, each class of shareholder 'whose rights are affected by the transaction' shall have the right to vote separately on decisions of the general meeting pursuant to either of the above provisions (Art. 25(3)). Member States may derogate from Art. 25 if necessary for the adoption or application of provisions 'designed to encourage the participation of employees, or other groups of persons defined by national law, in the capital of undertakings' (Art. 41(1); see Cases C-19/90 etc. *Karella and Karellas*, above, at pp. I-2719–20).

Art. 25(1) may be relied upon by individuals against the public authorities before national courts (*Karella and Karellas*, above, at pp. I-2716–17). Member States may not derogate from the provision in the case of companies in financial difficulties (ibid. at pp. I-2717–19). The directive continues to apply where ordinary reorganization measures are taken in order to ensure a company's survival, even if those measures meant that the shareholders and organs are temporarily divested of their powers (Case C-441/93 *Pafitis* [1996] ECR I-1347 at pp. I-1379–80).

Although Community law does not preclude national courts from applying national law in order to assess whether a Community law right is being abused, the ECJ has set limits on the scope of such national law as applied to the exercise of rights arising from Art. 25(1). Thus, a shareholder relying on Art. 25(1) cannot be deemed to be abusing the right arising therefrom merely because the increase in capital contested by him has resolved the company's financial difficulties and enured to his economic benefit, or because he has not exercised his preferential right under Art. 29(1) (see below) (Case C-367/96 *Kefalas* [1998] ECR I-2843 at pp. I-2870–1), or because he is a minority shareholder of a company subject to reorganization measures, or has benefited from reorganization of the company, or was among the shareholders who asked for the company to be placed under the scheme applicable to companies in serious difficulties, or has allowed a certain period of time to elapse before bringing his action (Case C-373/97 *Diamantis* [2000] ECR I-1705 at p. I-1737), since otherwise a shareholder of a company in financial crisis could never rely on Art. 25(1), thus altering the scope of that provision.

Shares issued for a consideration must be paid up to at least 25% of their nominal value or, if none, accountable par, plus the whole of any premium (Art. 26). Member States may derogate from Art. 26 if necessary for the adoption or application of provisions 'designed to encourage the participation of employees, or other groups of persons defined by national law, in the capital of undertakings' (Art. 41(1); see Cases C-19/90 etc. *Karella and Karellas*, above, at pp. I-2719–20).

Art. 27 contains provisions relating to the issue of shares for non-cash consideration on an increase in capital that are parallel to those contained in Arts. 9(2) and 19 in relation to the issue of shares at the time of formation, subject to derogations for mergers or takeovers. An increase in capital that is not fully subscribed may proceed only if the conditions of the issue so provide (Art. 28).

Shares to be issued for cash must be offered on a pre-emptive basis to shareholders in proportion to the capital represented by their shares (Art. 29(1)). Member States may exempt shares that carry a limited right to participate in distributions or the company's assets on liquidation and, where there are several classes of shares, may provide that new shares of one class shall be offered to shareholders of that class before shareholders of the other classes (Art. 29(2)). Where all a company's shares are registered, all the shareholders must be informed in writing; in other cases, publication in the national gazette designated for the purpose of the First Directive suffices (Art. 29(3)). Publication of an offer of subscription in daily newspapers does not constitute information given in writing to shareholders (Case C-441/93 *Pafitis*, above, at p. I-1381).

The statutes or instrument of incorporation may not restrict or withdraw the right of pre-emption but the general meeting may do so, provided that the administrative or management body justifies the proposed issue price to the meeting (Art. 29(4)). Member States may, however, provide that the statutes, the instrument of incorporation, or the general meeting may, for a renewable maximum period of five years, give the power to restrict or withdraw the right to the body empowered to decide on an increase in subscribed capital (Art. 29(5)).

Member States may derogate from Art. 29 if necessary for the adoption or application of provisions 'designed to encourage the participation of employees, or other groups of persons defined by national law, in the capital of undertakings' (Art. 41(1); see Cases C-19/90 etc. *Karella and Karellas*, above, at pp. I-2719–20).

The ECJ has held that Art. 29(1) and (5) are directly applicable (Case C-381/89 *Sindesmos Melon* [1992] ECR I-2111 at pp. I-2146–7). Art. 29 in terms applies only to issues of shares for cash and does not preclude Member States from extending its provisions to issues for non-cash consideration, or from subjecting a decision to withdraw the pre-emption right to a substantive review (Case C-42/95 *Siemens* [1996] ECR I-6017 at pp. I-6034–6).

The general meeting must approve any reduction in the subscribed capital, except under a court order (Art. 30). Where there are several classes of shares, the decision of the general meeting must be subject to a separate vote, at least for each class of shareholders whose rights are affected by the transaction (Art. 31). On a reduction in the subscribed capital, the minimum the creditors whose claims antedate publication of the decision to reduce capital shall be entitled to is at least the right to obtain security for claims that have not fallen due by the date of that publication; Member States may not set aside the right to security unless the creditor has adequate safeguards or the latter are not necessary in view of the company's assets (Art. 32(1)). Until the creditors have obtained satisfaction or a court has decided that their application should not be granted, the reduction is to be ineffective (Art. 32(2)).

Arts. 35 to 38 lay down a series of minimum conditions, concerning authorization, procedure, publication, and creditor and shareholder protection, for procedures analogous to a reduction of capital by way of redemption without reduction and by compulsory withdrawal of shares. Where Member States permit companies to issue redeemable shares, Art. 39 imposes a series of similar minimum conditions for redemption.

III. The Third and Sixth Directives

The Third Council Dir. 78/855 of 9 October 1978 based on Art. 44(2)(g) of the Treaty concerning mergers of public limited liability companies (*OJ* 1978 L295/36) and the Sixth Council Dir. 82/891 of 17 December 1982 based on Art. 44(2)(g) of the Treaty concerning the division of public limited liability companies (*OJ* 1982 L378/47) derive from a single proposal, originally intended to regulate both types of operation. Since they overlap to a large extent, it is convenient to deal with them together. The Third and Sixth Directives apply only to public limited companies as listed in Art. 1 of the Third Directive (Sixth Dir., Art. 1). The operations to which the Third and Sixth Directives apply are little used in the United Kingdom, and hence are relatively unfamiliar to lawyers from those jurisdictions.

The Third Directive applies:

(*a*) where one or more companies transfer all their assets and liabilities to another existing company, which issues shares (and, at its option, a cash payment not exceeding 10% of the nominal value of the shares so issued) to the shareholders of the transferring company or companies which are then dissolved ('merger by acquisition': Art. 3(1)) or

(*b*) where several companies transfer all their assets and liability to a company they have formed, which issues shares (and, at its option, a cash payment not exceeding 10% of the nominal value of the shares so issued) to the shareholders of the transferring companies, which are then dissolved ('merger by formation of new company': Art. 4(1)) or

(*c*) where one or more wholly owned subsidiaries transfer all their assets and liabilities to their parent and are then dissolved ('acquisition of subsidiary': Art. 24) or

(*d*) to operations analogous to the above where Member States permit such operations either with a threshold for cash consideration higher than 10% of the value of the shares issued or without all of the transferring companies thereby ceasing to exist ('analogous operations': Arts. 30 to 31).

The Sixth Directive applies:

(*a*) where a company transfers all its assets and liabilities to more than one other company, already existing ('division by acquisition': Art. 2(1)) and/or newly formed ('division by formation of new companies': Art. 21(1)), which issue shares (and, at its option, a cash payment not exceeding 10% of the nominal value of the shares so issued) to the shareholders of the transferring company which is then dissolved or

(*b*) to operations analogous to the above where Member States permit such operations either with a threshold for cash consideration higher than 10% of the value of the shares issued or without the company being divided ceasing to exist ('analogous operations': Arts. 24 to 25).

The Third and Sixth Directives lay down detailed rules to be followed on a merger or division, which may be summarized as follows:

(*a*) The boards of the companies involved must draw up written draft terms of the merger (Third Dir., Art. 5(1)) or division (Sixth Dir., Art. 3), setting out specified information; the draft terms must be published for each of the companies involved in accordance with the First Directive at least one month before the general meeting that is to decide on the operation (Third Dir., Art. 6; Sixth Dir., Art. 4). On a division under the supervision of a judicial authority, that authority may relieve the companies involved from the obligation to publish the draft terms in specified circumstances (Sixth Dir., Art. 23(2)(a)).

(*b*) Except in the case of the acquisition of a wholly owned subsidiary, two separate reports must be made on the draft terms.

First, the boards of each company involved must draw up a detailed written report explaining the draft terms and setting out prescribed information including the legal and economic grounds for the terms, in particular the share exchange ratio and, in the case of a division, the criterion determining the allocation of shares (Third Dir., Art. 9; Sixth Dir., Art. 7(1)). In the case of a division the board of the company being divided must inform both that company's general meeting when it is deciding on the draft terms and the boards of the recipient companies so that they can inform their general meetings of any material change in the assets and liabilities since the draft terms were prepared (Sixth Dir., Arts. 7(3) and 20(d)).

Secondly, one or more experts, acting on behalf of each of the merging companies or the companies involved in the division but independent of them, appointed or approved by a judicial or administrative authority, must examine the draft terms and draw up a written report to the shareholders (Third Dir., Art. 10(1); Sixth Dir., Art. 8(1)). The experts must, *inter alia*, state whether in their opinion the share exchange ratio is fair and reasonable and describe any special valuation difficulties that have arisen. Member States need not apply the relevant directive's requirements for management and experts' reports in a number of specified circumstances (Third Dir., Art. 28; Sixth Dir., Arts. 10 and 22(5)).

(*c*) The draft terms and any consequential alterations to the companies' statutes must be approved at the general meeting of each of the companies involved, by either (*i*) at least two thirds of the votes attaching either to the shares or to the subscribed capital represented, or (*ii*) a simple majority of such votes when at least half the subscribed capital is represented (Third Dir., Art. 7(1)(3); Sixth Dir., Art. 5(1)). In certain specified circumstances, a general meeting may be dispensed with. In the case of a merger or division by formation of a new company, that company's statutes must be approved at a general meeting of each of the companies that will cease to exist or of the company being divided (Third Dir., Art. 23(3); Sixth Dir., Art. 22(3)). Subject to specified exceptions, all shareholders must, at least one month before the general meeting, be entitled to inspect and to obtain on request free copies of (*a*) the draft terms, (*b*) the annual accounts and reports for the preceding three financial years of the companies involved and, in certain circumstances, a more recent accounting statement, and (*c*) the boards' and experts' reports (Third Dir., Art. 11(1); Sixth Dir., Art. 9(1)).

(*d*) Protection of the rights of the employees of each of the companies involved is to be regulated in accordance with Council Dir. 77/187 of 14 February 1977 on the approximation of the laws of the Member States relating to the safeguarding of employees' rights in the event of transfers of undertakings, businesses or parts of businesses (*OJ* 1977 L61/26) (Third Dir., Art. 12; Sixth Dir., Art. 11).

(*e*) Member States must provide for an adequate system of protection of the interests of creditors (including debenture-holders) of the companies involved whose claims antedate but have not fallen due by the publication of the draft terms (Third Dir., Art. 13; Sixth Dir., Art. 12). The protection may be different for the creditors of the different companies, but all creditors must at least be entitled to obtain adequate safeguards where the financial situation of the companies concerned makes such protection necessary and where they do not already have such safeguards. In the cases of divisions, there must in addition be joint and several liability of the recipient companies in so far as a creditor of the company to which the obligation has been transferred has not obtained satisfaction, and Member States may provide that the recipient companies shall in any event be jointly and severally liable for the obligations of the company being divided, in which case they need apply none of the foregoing specific provisions for the protection of creditors.

(*f*) Either the minutes of the general meetings that decide on the merger or division, together with any subsequent contract, or, where the operation need not be approved by general meetings, the draft terms, must be drawn up and certified in due legal form (Third Dir., Art.

16(1); Sixth Dir., Art. 14). The merger or division must be publicized in accordance with Art. 3 of the First Directive in respect of each of the companies involved (Third Dir., Art. 18(1); Sixth Dir., Art. 16(1)).

(*g*) The date on which a merger or division takes effect is to be determined by national law (Third Dir., Art. 17; Sixth Dir., Art. 15). *Ipso jure* and simultaneously the assets and liabilities are transferred, the shareholders are substituted, and the company being acquired or divided ceases to exist (Third Dir., Art. 19; Sixth Dir., Art. 17).

(*h*) Member States must lay down rules governing the civil liability towards the shareholders of the company being acquired or divided of (*i*) the members of its administrative or management bodies in respect of misconduct on their part in preparing and implementing the merger or division (Third Dir., Art. 20; Sixth Dir., Art. 18), and (*ii*) the experts responsible for drawing up on its behalf the experts' report in respect of misconduct on their part in the performance of their duties (Third Dir., Art. 21; Sixth Dir., Art. 18).

(*i*) The directives restrict the circumstances in which Member States may provide for the nullity of mergers, laying down a series of conditions to be observed (Third Dir., Art. 22; Sixth Dir., Art. 19).

IV. The Fourth Directive

The Fourth Council Dir. 78/660 of 25 July 1978 based on Art. 44(2)(g) of the Treaty on the annual accounts of certain types of companies (*OJ* 1978 L222/11) imposes certain common minimum reporting and disclosure requirements in the accounting field. Although the existence and number of options contained in the directive mean that accounts prepared in compliance with it can appear very different, the minimum information required to be given should enable the system that has been applied to be ascertained and the accounts interpreted accordingly, so that the objective of comparability has been attained.

The directive, which originally applied to public and private limited-liability companies of the same types as are covered by the First Directive, is also important in that it was the first company law directive to have a major impact on limited-liability companies in general, since the First Directive dealt with topics of limited relevance in practice (disclosure, validity of company obligations, and nullity) and the Second and Third (which was in fact adopted after the Fourth) Directives applied to public companies only. The scope of the directive was extended in 1990 by Dir. 90/605 (*OJ* 1990 L317/60) to encompass (*i*) partnerships, limited partnerships, and unlimited companies under various national names if all members with unlimited liability are limited-liability companies or, where not governed by the law of a Member State, have a comparable legal form, and (*ii*) unlimited-liability entities if all members with unlimited liability are themselves limited-liability entities.

The following commentary takes account of the substantial amendments made to the Fourth Directive by Dirs. 2001/65 (*OJ* 2001 L283/28) and 2003/51 (*OJ* 2003 L178/16). More generally, pursuant to Reg. 1606/2002 of the European Parliament and of the Council of 19 July 2002 on the application of international accounting standards (*OJ* 2002 L243/1) Member States may permit or require companies to prepare their annual accounts in conformity with international accounting standards.

1. The annual accounts. The Fourth Directive provides that the annual accounts are to comprise the balance sheet, the profit and loss account and the notes on the accounts; Member States may permit or require the inclusion of other statements in the annual accounts in addition to those documents (Art. 2(1)). Those documents are to constitute a composite whole and be drawn up clearly and in accordance with the provisions of the directive (Art. 2(1) and (2)). The annual accounts must 'give a true and fair view of the company's assets, liabilities, financial position and profit or loss' (Art. 2(3)). The ECJ has held that the principle of a true and fair view requires that account be taken of all elements, such as profits made, charges, products, risks, and losses, which actually relate to the financial year in question (Case C-234/94 *Tomberger* [1996] ECR I-3133 at p. I-3154) and that the accounts reflect the activities and transactions which they are supposed to describe and the accounting information be given in the form judged to be the soundest and most appropriate for satisfying third parties' needs for information, without harming the interests of the company (Case C-275/97 *DE + ES Bauunternehmung* [1999] ECR I-5331 at p. I-5358).

The directive prescribes the permitted formats for the balance sheet (two alternative layouts, horizontal and vertical, set out in Arts. 9 and 10 respectively) and the profit and loss account (four alternative layouts, set out in Arts. 23 to 26; two are in vertical form and two in horizontal form). Member States may:

(*a*) permit or require, for all or certain classes of company or for consolidated accounts, the presentation of amounts to have regard to the substance of the reported transaction or arrangement (Art. 4(6));
(*b*) prescribe special layouts for the annual accounts of investment companies and financial holding companies, provided that the layouts give a true and fair view of those companies' assets, liabilities, financial position, and profit or loss (Art. 5(1));
(*c*) permit or require all or certain classes of company to present balance-sheet items on the basis of a distinction between current and non-current items and to present a statement of their performance instead of the presentation of profit and loss items, provided that the information given is at least equivalent to that otherwise required (Arts. 10a and 22);
(*d*) permit small companies (i.e. those which on their balance-sheet date are within two of the following three criteria: balance-sheet total: €3.65m; net turnover: €7.3m; average number of employees during the financial year: 50) to draw up abridged balance sheets omitting a significant level of detail that would otherwise be required (Art. 11 as amended by Dir. 2003/38, *OJ* 2003 L120/22);

(*e*) permit medium-sized companies (i.e. those which on their balance-sheet date are within two of the following three criteria: balance-sheet total: €14.6m; net turnover: €29.2m; average number of employees during the financial year: 250) to avoid disclosure in the profit and loss account of the items (turnover and gross margins) making up gross profit by grouping certain items under the operating result (Arts. 12 and 27 as amended by Dir. 2003/38).

The directive requires disclosure in the balance sheet and profit-and-loss account of specified information about affiliated undertakings (defined in Art. 41 of the Seventh Dir. by reference to the group relationships set out in Arts. 1 and 12 of that directive and hence in effect as any subsidiary, fellow subsidiary, or parent undertaking as those terms are defined in the national implementing legislation) and participating interests (rights in the capital of other undertakings, which, by creating a durable link with those undertakings, are intended to contribute to the company's activities; a holding that exceeds a percentage fixed by the Member States which may not exceed 20% is presumed to constitute a participating interest: Art. 17 of the Fourth Dir.).

2. Valuation rules. The items shown in the annual accounts must be valued in accordance with the following general principles:

(*a*) the company must be presumed to be carrying on its business as a going concern;
(*b*) the methods of valuation must be applied consistently from one financial year to the next;
(*c*) valuation must be made on a prudent basis, and in particular:
- only profits made at the balance-sheet date may be included;
- account must be taken of all liabilities arising in the course of the financial year concerned or a previous one, even if such liabilities become apparent only between the date of the balance sheet and the date on which it is drawn up; Member States may additionally permit or require account to be taken of all foreseeable liabilities and potential losses arising in the course of the financial year concerned or of a previous one, even if such liabilities or losses become apparent only between those two dates; and
- account must be taken of all depreciation, whether the result of the financial year is a loss or a profit;

(*d*) account must be taken of income and charges relating to the financial year, irrespective of the date of receipt or payment thereof;
(*e*) the components of asset and liability items must be valued separately; and
(*f*) the opening balance sheet for each financial year must correspond to the closing balance sheet for the preceding financial year (Art. 31(1) and (1a)).

There is no guidance in the directive as to when a profit is to be regarded as 'made' for the purpose of Art. 31(1). The question arose in *Tomberger*, above, although the Court failed to give any genuine guidance on the issue.

In *DE + ES Bauunternehmung*, above, at p. 5361, the ECJ ruled that Art. 31(1) requires provision to be made for potential liabilities under warranties as obligations which arise in law before the balance-sheet date but whose effects will not become apparent until after that date, and that a single provision for all such potential liabilities must be made where a global valuation is the most appropriate way of ensuring that the expenditure to be shown under 'Liabilities' represents a true and fair view of its amount. Further guidance as to provisions and liabilities was given in a highly specific context in Case C-306/99 *BIAO* [2003] ECR I-1.

Departures from these principles may be permitted in exceptional cases; they must be disclosed in the notes to the accounts and the reasons for them given together with an assessment of their effect on the assets, liabilities, financial position, and profit or loss (Art. 31(2)). The exceptional cases referred to in Art. 31(2) are those in which separate valuation would not give the truest and fairest possible view of the actual financial position of the company concerned (*DE + ES Bauunternehmung*, above, at p. 5359).

Art. 32, which provides that the items shown in the annual accounts are to be valued in accordance with Arts. 34 to 42 based on the principle of purchase price or production costs, in effect adds another general principle, namely historical-cost accounting. Member States may however permit or require (*i*) valuation by the replacement value method for tangible fixed assets with limited useful economic lives and for stocks, (*ii*) valuation by other methods 'designed to take account of inflation for the items shown in annual accounts, including capital and reserves', subject to disclosure in the notes to the accounts, and (*iii*) revaluation of fixed assets (Art. 33(1)).

By way of derogation from Art. 32, Art. 42a (added by Dir. 2001/65) requires Member States to permit or require in respect of all or any class of companies valuation at fair value of financial instruments, including derivatives; Art. 42d requires certain disclosure in the notes on the accounts. The fair value is to be determined by reference to a market value where a reliable market can readily be identified or otherwise to generally accepted valuation models and techniques (Art. 42b). Changes in the value of such instruments are to be included in the profit-and-loss account or in certain circumstances directly in equity, in a fair value reserve (Art. 42c). Moreover, by virtue of Art. 42e (added by Dir. 2003/51) Member States may permit or require in respect of all companies or any classes of company or consolidated accounts the valuation of specified categories of assets other than financial instruments at amounts determined by reference to fair value, in which case Member States may permit or require that a change in the value is included in the profit-and-loss account.

To the extent that it was acquired for valuable consideration, goodwill must be shown as an asset on the balance sheet, and written off within a maximum period of five years. Member States may, however, permit companies to write goodwill off systematically over a longer period provided that that period does not exceed the useful economic life of the asset and is disclosed in the notes to the accounts together with supporting reasons (Art. 37(2)).

Art. 59 (as replaced by Art. 45 of the Seventh Dir.) lays down rules for the valuation of participating interests (as defined by Art. 17, see above) in the capital of undertakings over the operating and financial policies of which significant influence is exercised. An undertaking shall be presumed to exercise a significant influence over another undertaking where it has 20% or more of the shareholders' or members' voting rights in that undertaking. Member States may require or permit such an interest to be shown in the balance sheet either (*i*) at book value calculated in accordance with Arts. 31 to 42, or (*ii*) at the amount corresponding to the proportion of the capital and reserves represented by it. In either case, (*i*) the difference between these two values, calculated as at the date at which the method is applied for the first time, is to be disclosed separately in the balance sheet or in the notes to the accounts; (*ii*) the value or amount used is to be adjusted to reflect variations over the financial year in the proportion of capital and reserves represented and reduced by the amount of the dividends relating to the interest; and (*iii*) a positive difference, in so far as it cannot be related to any category of asset or liability, is to be dealt with in accordance with the rules applicable to goodwill.

3. The notes on the accounts. Art. 43(1) lists certain minimum information that must be disclosed in the notes on the accounts, without specifying any format or order. In addition, extensive information is required under other provisions of the directive, principally disclosure of departure from prescribed practice and use of concessions. There are various exemptions in Arts. 43 to 45.

4. The annual report. Art. 46 requires the annual report to include 'at least a fair review of the development of the company's business and of its position, together with a description of the principal risks and uncertainties that it faces'. The review is to be a balanced and comprehensive analysis of the development and performance of the company's business and of its position, consistent with the size and complexity of the business. Where necessary for an understanding of the company's development, performance, or position, the analysis must include non-financial key performance indicators, including information relating to environmental and employee matters. In addition, the report must give an indication of (*a*) any important events that have occurred since the end of the financial year; (*b*) the company's likely future development; (*c*) activities in the field of research and development; (*d*) the information concerning acquisitions of own shares prescribed by Art. 22(2) of the Second Directive; (*e*) the existence of branches of the company; and (*f*) certain information in relation to the use of financial instruments.

Member States may exempt small companies from the obligation to prepare annual reports, provided that the notes to the accounts give the above information concerning the acquisition by a company of its own shares (Art. 46(3), added by Dir. 90/604, *OJ* 1990 L317/57).

5. Publication of accounts. The 'annual accounts, duly approved, and the annual report, together with the opinion submitted by the person responsible for auditing the accounts' must be published in accordance with the First Directive (Art. 47(1)). It must also be possible to obtain a (paper or electronic) copy of all or part of the accounts and report upon request, at a price not exceeding its administrative cost (Art. 3(3) of the First Dir., and second subparagraph of Art. 47(1) of the Fourth Dir. as substituted by Art. 38(3) of the Seventh Dir.).

In the case of branches of companies from other Member States, Arts. 1(1), 2(1)(g), and 3 of the Eleventh Company Law Directive (Council Dir. 89/666 of 21 December 1989 concerning disclosure requirements in respect of branches opened in a Member State by certain types of company, *OJ* 1989 L395/36; see further section VII below) requires the accounting documents of the company as drawn up, audited, and disclosed pursuant to the law of the Member State by which the company is governed in accordance with the Fourth, Seventh, and Eighth Directives to be disclosed pursuant to the law of the Member State of the branch in accordance with Art. 3 of the First Directive. Where the company has opened more than one branch in a Member State, the disclosure may be made in the register of the branch of the company's choice, in which case the other branches must disclose the particulars of the branch register where disclosure was made (Art. 5).

In the case of branches of companies from third countries which are of a legal form comparable to the types of company to which the First Directive applies, the accounting documents of the company as drawn up, audited, and disclosed pursuant to the law of the State that governs the company are to be disclosed in accordance with the law of the Member State of the branch as laid down in Art. 3 of the First Directive (Arts. 7(1), 8(j), and 9(1)). Where those documents are not drawn up in accordance with or in a manner equivalent to the Fourth and Seventh Directives, Member States may require that accounting documents relating to the activities of the branch be drawn up and disclosed (Art. 9(1)).

6. Auditing. Art. 51 requires companies to have their annual accounts audited by one or more persons approved by Member States to carry out statutory audits on the basis of the Eighth Directive (see section VI below). The auditors must also express an opinion concerning the consistency or otherwise of the annual report with the annual accounts. Art. 51a, added by Dir. 2003/51, lists a number of items to be included in the auditors' report. Member States may exempt small companies from the audit requirement, in which case they must introduce appropriate sanctions for cases in which the annual accounts or annual reports of such companies are not drawn up in accordance with the directive.

Member States need not apply the provisions of the directive concerning auditing of the profit-and-loss account to companies which are parent undertakings as defined in the Seventh Directive provided that (*i*) the parent undertaking draws up consolidated accounts in accordance with the Seventh Directive; (*ii*) the exemption is disclosed in the notes to the parent undertaking's annual and consolidated accounts; and (*iii*) the profit or loss of the parent company is shown in its balance sheet (Art. 58 as inserted by Art. 44 of the Seventh Dir.).

V. The Seventh Directive

The Seventh Council Dir. 83/349 of 13 June 1983 based on Art. 44(2)(g) of the Treaty on consolidated accounts (*OJ* 1983 L193/1) complements the Fourth Directive, extending many of the latter's requirements to the consolidated accounts which it requires to be prepared in certain defined circumstances. Consolidation practice in the ten Member States at the time of adoption of the Seventh Directive diverged widely, with at one extreme the Netherlands, Denmark, the United Kingdom, and Ireland, where companies were required to draw up group accounts, and at the other Luxembourg and Greece, where there was no such obligation or convention. Within those Member States where consolidated accounts were prepared, there were significant differences in the relationship which triggered consolidation and the consolidation techniques used. The measure of harmonization introduced by the Seventh Directive was accordingly much needed.

The Seventh Directive contains provisions on the notes on the accounts, the annual report, auditing and publication of accounts that broadly reflect those of the Fourth Directive and are accordingly not further considered. More generally, for financial years starting in or after 1 January 2005, Member States may permit or require companies to prepare their consolidated accounts in conformity with international accounting standards; companies whose securities are admitted to trading on a regulated market of any Member State must so prepare consolidated accounts (Reg. 1606/2002).

1. Conditions for consolidation. The directive provides that a Member State must require an undertaking ('the parent undertaking') governed by its national law to draw up consolidated accounts and a consolidated annual report in the following circumstances:

(*a*) If the parent undertaking has a majority of the shareholders' or members' voting rights in another undertaking (Art. 1(1)(a)). The voting rights held by the parent undertaking are deemed to include the rights of any other subsidiary undertaking and those held on behalf of the parent undertaking or of another subsidiary undertaking (Art. 2(1)) but to exclude rights attaching to shares held by the parent or a subsidiary undertaking on behalf of any person not within the group (Art. 2(2)(a)) and rights attaching to shares held by the parent or a subsidiary undertaking by way of security (Art. 2(2)(b)).

(*b*) If the parent undertaking has the right to appoint or remove a majority of the members of the board of another undertaking of which it is shareholder or member (Art. 1(1)(b)). In determining whether the parent undertaking has such a right, the rules set out above for the calculation of voting rights apply.

(*c*) If the parent undertaking controls alone, pursuant to an agreement with other shareholders in or members of another undertaking of which it is shareholder or member, a majority of shareholders' or members' voting rights in that undertaking (Art. 1(1)(d)(bb)).

In addition, Member States may require consolidation in the following circumstances:

(*d*) If the parent undertaking has the right to exercise a dominant influence over another undertaking of which it is a shareholder or member, pursuant to a contract entered into with that undertaking or to a provision in its memorandum or articles of association (Art. 1(1)(c)).

(*e*) If the parent undertaking is a shareholder or member of another undertaking a majority of whose board who have held office from the beginning of the preceding financial year until the time when the consolidated accounts are drawn up have been appointed solely as a result of the exercise of the parent undertaking's voting rights (Art. 1(1)(d)(aa)). Member States may specify that in order for this definition to apply the parent undertaking's holding represents 20% or more of the shareholders' or members' voting rights.

(*f*) If the parent undertaking has the power to exercise, or actually exercises, dominant influence or control over another undertaking or the parent and another undertaking are managed on a unified basis by the parent undertaking (Art. 1(2)).

(*g*) In the case of undertakings with no parent/subsidiary relationship, if (*a*) the undertakings are managed on a unified basis pursuant to a contract concluded between them or provisions in their memorandum or articles of association, or (*b*) their bodies consist for the major part of the same persons in office during the financial year and until the consolidated accounts are drawn up (Art. 12(1)).

2. The undertakings to be consolidated. A parent undertaking and all of its subsidiary undertakings are to be consolidated where either the parent or one of more subsidiaries is established as one of the types of company listed in Art. 1 of the Fourth Directive as amended (broadly, public or private limited-liability companies and, since 1990, certain unlimited-liability entities) (Art. 4(1) as amended by Dir. 90/605) and regardless of where the registered offices of such subsidiary undertakings are situated (Art. 3(1)).

Member States may exempt a parent undertaking from the requirement to draw up consolidated accounts where it is not established as one of the listed types of company (Art. 4(2)).

3. Exemptions. The directive provides the following further exemptions from the requirement to draw up consolidated accounts, subject in some cases to additional disclosure requirements:

(*a*) Member States must exempt any parent undertaking governed by its national law that is also a subsidiary undertaking if its own parent undertaking is governed by the law of a Member State and either (*a*) that parent holds all its shares or (*b*) that parent holds 90% or more of its shares and the remaining shareholders have approved the exemption, provided in either case that the exempted undertaking and all its subsidiary undertakings are included in audited consolidated accounts for a larger group drawn up in accordance with the directive by an EC parent (Art. 7).

(*b*) Member States may extend the above exemption to cases where the shareholders in the exempted undertaking who own a minimum proportion (which Member States may fix at not more than 10% for public companies and not more than 20% for undertakings of other types) of its subscribed capital have not requested the preparation of consolidated accounts at least six months before the end of the financial year (Art. 8).

(*c*) Member States may exempt intermediate parents which themselves have a non-EC parent provided that the exempted undertaking and all its subsidiary undertakings are included in audited consolidated accounts for a larger group drawn up in accordance with the directive or in an equivalent manner (Art. 11(1)). There is no holding threshold as in the case of EC groups.

(*d*) Member States may also extend the optional exemption provided for in Art. 8 to intermediate parents with non-EC parents (Art. 11(2)).

(*e*) Member States may exempt small groups that do not include a listed company and satisfy two of the following three criteria on a parent undertaking's balance-sheet date in two successive financial years: balance sheet total: €14.6m; net turnover: €29.2m; average number of employees: 250 (Art. 27 of the Fourth Dir., as amended by Dir. 2003/38 and Reg. 1103/97, incorporated by Art. 6 of the Seventh Dir).

(*f*) Member States may exempt financial holding companies (defined in Art. 5 of the Fourth Dir. as companies whose sole object is to acquire and profitably manage holdings in other undertakings without involving themselves in their management) subject to certain conditions (Art. 5(1)).

(*g*) Member States may provide that an undertaking need not be included in consolidated accounts where:

- it is not material for the purpose of the true and fair view of the assets, liabilities, financial position, and profit or loss of the group to be given by the consolidated accounts; if two or more subsidiary undertakings are individually immaterial but taken together are material for that purpose, they must be included;
- severe long-term restrictions substantially hinder either its parent from exercising its rights over the assets or management of the subsidiary, or, in the case of a horizontal group, the exercise of unified management of the undertaking;
- the information necessary for the preparation of consolidated accounts cannot be obtained without disproportionate expense or undue delay;

- its shares are held exclusively with a view to their subsequent resale (Art. 13);

(*h*) Where the activities of one or more subsidiary undertakings are so different that their inclusion in the consolidated accounts would be incompatible with the requirement that those accounts give a true and fair view of the assets, liabilities, financial position, and profit or loss of the group, they must be excluded from the consolidation (Art. 14(1)).

(*i*) Member States may, for the purposes of giving a true and fair view, permit the omission from consolidation of 'any parent undertaking not carrying on any industrial or commercial activity which holds shares in a subsidiary undertaking on the basis of a joint arrangement with one or more undertakings not included in the consolidated accounts' (Art. 15).

4. The preparation of consolidated accounts. Consolidated accounts, defined as comprising the consolidated balance sheet, the consolidated profit-and-loss account and the notes on the accounts together with any other statements whose inclusion is permitted or required by Member States (Art. 16(1)), are required to be drawn up clearly and in accordance with the Seventh Directive (Art. 16(2)) and, more specifically, with the principles set out in Arts. 25 to 28 (Art. 24). The provisions of the Fourth Directive on the true and fair view, the layout of the accounts, and valuation are reflected *mutatis mutandis* in the Seventh Directive (Arts. 16(3)(4)(5), 17(1), and 29(1)). In addition:

- the methods of consolidation must be applied consistently from one financial year to the next; derogations may be permitted only in exceptional cases and must be disclosed in the notes to the accounts (Art. 25); and
- consolidated accounts must normally be drawn up as at the same date as the parent undertaking's annual accounts whereas subsidiary undertakings' accounts may be drawn up on the basis of a different financial year (Art. 27).

5. Consolidation techniques

(*a*) The requirement that the assets and liabilities of the consolidated undertakings be incorporated in full in the consolidated balance sheet (Art. 18) and their income and expenditure incorporated in full in the consolidated profit-and-loss account (Art. 22) is subject to the elimination of intra-group transactions (Art. 26). Derogations must be permitted where the amounts concerned are not material for the purpose of the true and fair view.

(*b*) In the case of subsidiary undertakings owned as to less than 100%, the requirement to incorporate in full their assets, liabilities, income, and expenditure still applies, and the minority interests are to be shown separately in the accounts (Arts. 21 and 23).

(*c*) The acquisition method of accounting is the principal method prescribed by the directive for calculating goodwill arising on consolidation (Art. 19): the book values of shares in consolidated undertakings are to be set off against the proportion that they represent of the capital and reserves of those undertakings, on the basis of book values as at first consolidation. The book values are, so far as possible, to be entered directly against those items in the consolidated balance sheet with values above or below their book values. The remaining difference is regarded as goodwill arising on consolidation, required to be shown as an asset on the consolidated balance sheet and, in general, dealt with in accordance with the Fourth Directive (see above) (Art. 30(1)). Member States may, however, permit goodwill arising on consolidation to be deducted 'immediately and clearly' from reserves (Art. 30(2)).

(*d*) Merger accounting is an alternative method of accounting for acquisitions that avoids accounting both for any premium (by way of the (undistributable) share premium account) on shares issued by the parent and for goodwill on consolidation. Member States may require or permit the book value of shares in a subsidiary undertaking to be set off in the consolidated accounts against the corresponding percentage of capital only (as opposed to capital and reserves) where (*i*) the parent holds at least 90% of the nominal value of the shares; (*ii*) that shareholding was obtained pursuant to an arrangement providing for the issue of shares by the parent; and (*iii*) any cash payment involved did not exceed 10% of the nominal value of the shares issued (Art. 20(1)).

6. Equity accounting. The directive lays down rules for the accounting treatment in consolidated accounts of certain holdings in associated undertakings. An associated undertaking is an undertaking that is not itself consolidated but over whose operating and financial policy a consolidated undertaking exercises a significant influence. Where a consolidated undertaking holds a 'participating interest' in an associated undertaking, that interest must in general be accounted for using what is known as the equity method, under which the investing company's balance sheet shows its investments in such interests at cost plus a share of undistributed profits (or less a share of losses) and the profit-and-loss account shows a share of the associated undertaking's earnings (Art. 33). 'Participating interest' is defined in the Fourth Directive (see above).

7. Joint ventures. Member States may permit or require proportional consolidation of joint ventures, namely undertakings managed jointly by a consolidated undertaking and one or more other undertakings not included in the consolidation (Art. 32(1)).

VI. The Eighth Directive

The Eighth Council Dir. 84/253 of 10 April 1984 based on Art. 44(2)(g) of the Treaty on the approval of persons responsible for carrying out the statutory audits of accounting documents (*OJ* 1984 L126/20) is an essential complement to the Fourth and Seventh Directives, which impose an audit requirement for both annual and consolidated accounts: the imposition of a Community-wide standard for the preparation and certification of company accounts would have limited effect if those required to audit the accounts had divergent qualifications and were not subject to equivalent requirements of independence and integrity. The Eighth Directive seeks to ensure that auditors in all Member States have equivalent minimum qualifications. It does not seek to go beyond that aim: in particular, it does not deal with the issue of auditors' liability, not currently regulated at Community level.

The directive covers the persons responsible for carrying out the statutory audits of the annual accounts of companies and firms or the consolidated accounts of bodies of undertakings and verifying that the annual reports are consistent with those accounts in so far as such audits and such verification are required by Community law (Art. 1(1)). The persons responsible for the statutory audit may be natural or legal persons or other types of company, firm, or partnership.

The authorities of the Member States may approve only (*a*) natural persons who satisfy at least the conditions laid down in Arts. 3 to 19 or (*b*) firms of auditors satisfying at least the following conditions (Art. 2(1)):

- the natural persons who actually carry out the audits on behalf of the firms must satisfy at least the conditions imposed in Arts. 3 to 19;
- a majority of the voting rights in the firm must be held by, *and* a majority of the members of the board must be, natural persons or firms of auditors who themselves satisfy at least the conditions imposed in Arts. 3 to 19;
- in either case, Member States may require such natural persons or firms of auditors themselves to be approved.

Approval may be granted only to persons of good repute who are not carrying on any activity which is incompatible, under the law of the Member State concerned, with the statutory auditing of annual accounts (Art. 3).

Natural persons may be approved only after having attained university entrance level, completed a course of theoretical instruction, undergone practical training, and passed an examination of professional competence of university final examination level organized or recognized by the State (Art. 4). The directive lays down requirements for the form and content of the theoretical, practical, and professional components (Arts. 6 to 8). Member States may, subject to conditions, approve persons who have obtained all or part of their qualifications in another State (whether a Member State or a third country) (Art. 11).

In certain defined circumstances Member States may approve auditors even if they do not fulfil the above conditions (Arts. 9 to 10). The directive also contains provisions to facilitate the continuing approval of those approved as auditors before it entered into force (Art. 12).

Member States must require persons approved as auditors, and natural persons who carry out audits on behalf of a firm of auditors, to carry out audits with professional integrity and not to carry out audits required by law if they are not independent (Arts. 23 to 25). Approved persons must be liable to appropriate sanctions for infringement of those provisions (Art. 26). Member States must ensure that the members and management of approved firms of auditors who do not personally fulfil the conditions for approval in a particular Member State do not intervene in the execution of audits in any way which jeopardizes the independence of the natural persons carrying out the audits on behalf of such firms (Art. 27).

The directive leaves to Member States the task of assessing in accordance with national law the independence and integrity of auditors practising within their territory; a Member State may require compliance with rules of professional practice, justified by the public interest, relating to the integrity and independence of auditors and applying to all persons practising as auditors within the territory of that State. Requirements relating to the existence of infrastructure within the national territory and the auditor's actual presence are not objectively necessary where the audit is carried out by an auditor who, while established and authorized to practise in another Member State, is temporarily in the service of a person authorized to practise as an auditor by the authorities of the Member State in which that audit is carried out (Case C-106/91 *Ramrath* [1992] ECR I-3351 at pp. I-3385–6; *see also under* **Freedom of establishment**, section IV.3).

Finally, the directive requires Member States to ensure that specified information concerning approved auditors is made available to the public (Art. 28).

The directive is complemented by Comm. Rec. 2001/256 of 15 November 2000 on quality assurance for the statutory audit in the European Union: minimum requirements (*OJ* 2001 L91/91), which essentially recommends that Member States take measures to ensure that all persons carrying out statutory audits are subjected to a quality assurance system and gives guidance on such a system, and Comm. Rec. 2002/590 of 16 May 2002 on statutory auditors' independence in the EU: a set of fundamental principles (*OJ* 2002 L191/22), which recommends that rules, standards, and/or regulation in the Member States should implement a prescribed set of fundamental principles designed to ensure statutory auditors' independence.

VII. The Eleventh Directive

The Eleventh Council Dir. 89/666 of 21 December 1989 concerning disclosure requirements in respect of branches opened in a Member State by certain types of company governed by the law of another State (*OJ* 1989 L395/36) seeks to stop a lacuna in the system of protection of third parties by the mandatory disclosure of certain information relating to companies. As has been seen, the First, Fourth, Seventh, and Eighth Directives impose a series of disclosure requirements on companies. Where a company incorporated in one Member State seeks to exercise its right of establishment by setting up a subsidiary in another Member State, that subsidiary, being a company, will be subject to those requirements in the Member State where it is incorporated. Where, however, a company establishes a branch rather than a subsidiary in another Member State, that branch, not being a corporate entity, will not be so subject. The Eleventh Directive aims to redress the balance by subjecting branches to certain of the disclosure requirements.

The directive concerns (*i*) branches opened in a Member State by a company which is governed by the law of another Member State and to which the First Directive applies (Art. 1(1)) and (*ii*) branches opened in a Member State by a company that is not governed by the law of another Member State but is of a legal form comparable with the types of company to which the First Directive applies (Art. 7(1)).

Documents and particulars relating to a branch must be disclosed pursuant to the law of the Member State of the branch in accordance with Art. 3 of the First Directive. Where there are conflicting disclosure requirements in respect of branch and company, those applying to the branch take precedence with regard to transactions carried out with the branch (Art. 1).

Disclosure is in general limited to information relating to the branch with a reference to the register of the company of which the branch is part, since the company is already required to make its own disclosure in that register; certain items relating to the company's winding-up and insolvency are, however, required to be disclosed in the State of the branch. The documents and particulars that must or may (at the Member State's option) be disclosed are listed in Art. 1 for branches of EC companies and in Art. 8 for branches of non-EC companies.

The Member State of the branch may require that the company's accounts and, if required to be disclosed, its statutes be published in another official language of the Community and that such translation be certified (Art. 4). A company with more than one branch in a Member State that does not have a single, central register for disclosure may decide in which register those documents may be disclosed; the other branch or branches must then simply disclose the particulars of that register and the number of the branch in that register (Art. 5). Member States must prescribe that letters and order forms used by a branch state the register in which its file is kept together with its number in that register (Arts. 6 and 10).

VIII. The Twelfth Directive

When the Twelfth Council Dir. 89/667 of 21 December 1989 on single-member private limited-liability companies (*OJ* 1989 L395/40) was adopted, the various Member States had widely different approaches to such companies. The directive sought to overcome the divergences between the laws of the Member States in this area by providing a legal instrument allowing the limitation of liability of the individual entrepreneur throughout the Community.

The directive provides that it is to apply to the laws, regulations, and administrative provisions of the Member States relating to listed types of company: the list that follows comprises those companies equivalent in each Member State to a private company (Art. 1). Member States may in addition allow single-member companies in the case of public limited companies, in which case the directive is to apply (Art. 6). A Member State need not however allow the formation of single-member companies where its legislation provides that an individual entrepreneur may set up an undertaking the liability of which is limited to a sum devoted to a stated activity, on condition that safeguards are laid down for such undertakings that are equivalent to those imposed by the directive or by any other Community provisions applicable to the companies referred to in Art. 1 (Art. 7).

A company 'may have a sole member when it is formed and also when all its shares come to be held by a single person' (Art. 2(1)). Thus, a single-member company may either be created as such *ab initio* or arise as a result of the concentration of all the shares in an existing company in the hands of a single shareholder. Member States may, pending co-ordination of national laws relating to groups, lay down special provisions or sanctions for cases where a natural person is the sole member of several companies or a single-member company or any other legal person is the sole member of a company (Art. 2(2)).

Where a company is incorporated as a single-member company, that fact will be apparent from the disclosure made in accordance with the First Directive. Art. 3 of the Twelfth Directive complements that provision with a requirement for disclosure where a company becomes a single-member company because all its shares come to be held by a single person. It requires that fact, together with the identity of the sole member, to be either disclosed in the companies register or equivalent or 'entered in a register kept by the company and accessible to the public'.

The sole member is to exercise the powers of the general meeting of the company and decisions taken by him in that capacity are to be recorded in minutes or drawn up in writing (Art. 4). Contracts between the sole member and his company as represented by him are to be recorded in minutes or drawn up in writing, although Member States need not apply that provision to 'current operations concluded under normal conditions' (Art. 5).

IX. The Directive on Takeover Bids

Agreement on a directive on takeover bids was finally reached in December 2003, fifteen years after the Commission's first proposal, albeit on a version so watered down that it was effectively disowned by Frits Bolkenstein, the Internal Market Commissioner responsible for presenting the final proposal (COM(2002) 534, *OJ* 2003 C45E/1). Dir. 2004/25 of the European Parliament and the Council was formally adopted on 21 April 2004 (*OJ* 2004 L142/12). It requires implementation by Member States by 20 May 2006.

1. Supervision and jurisdiction. The directive applies to takeover bids for listed companies incorporated in the European Union (Art. 1(1)). Each Member State is to designate an authority or authorities to supervise takeover bids; the authorities may be public or private bodies (Art. 4(1)). A takeover bid for a company whose voting securities are admitted to trading on a regulated market in the Member State of its incorporation is to be governed by the rules of, and subject to supervision in, that Member State. A takeover bid for a company whose voting securities are admitted to trading on a regulated market in a Member State other than that of its incorporation is to be subject to 'split jurisdiction': 'matters relating to company law' (including the threshold for control, the mandatory bid, and the taking of frustrating action by the board) and the provision of information to employees are to be governed by the law of the Member State of incorporation and supervised by that State's supervisory authority whereas other matters relating to the conduct of the bid, including consideration, contents of the offer document, and disclosure of the bid, are to be governed by the law of, and subject to supervision in, the Member State where the company's voting securities were first admitted to trading (Art. 4(2)).

In response to grave concerns expressed from the outset by the United Kingdom, the directive provides that it 'shall not affect the power which courts may have in a Member State to decline to hear legal proceedings and to decide whether or not such proceedings affect the outcome of a bid' (Art. 4(6)).

2. General principles. Member States are required to ensure that their implementing legislation complies with the following principles (Art. 3(1)):

(*a*) all holders of the same class of voting securities of a target company are to be afforded equivalent treatment and, where a person acquires control of a company, the other holders of voting securities (hereafter 'shareholders') are to be protected;
(*b*) shareholders are to have sufficient time and information to enable them to reach a properly informed decision on the bid; where it advises shareholders, the target's board is to give its views on the effects of the bid on employment and business location;
(*c*) the target's board is to act in the interests of the company as a whole and must not deny shareholders the opportunity to decide on the merits of the bid;
(*d*) false markets must not be created in the securities of any company involved in or concerned by the bid;
(*e*) an offeror must announce a bid only after ensuring that it can fulfil any cash consideration offered and taking all reasonable measures to secure the implementation of any other consideration;
(*f*) an offeree company must not be hindered in the conduct of its affairs for longer than is reasonable.

3. The mandatory offer and its acceptance. A natural or legal person who acquires control of a company, either alone or with persons acting in concert, must at the earliest opportunity make an offer to all shareholders at the highest price paid by him or persons acting in concert over a period of six to twelve months before the bid and during the course of the bid ('the equitable price') (Art. 5(1) and (4)). The obligation to make a bid does not apply to controlling holdings already in existence when the directive is implemented (tenth recital). 'Persons acting in concert' means persons co-operating on the basis of an agreement (whether express or tacit, oral or written) aimed at obtaining control of the target (Art. 2(1)(d)). It is for the Member States to determine the percentage of voting rights constituting control (Art. 5(3)). Member States may also authorize their supervisory authorities to adjust the price offered in circumstances and according to criteria that are clearly determined provided that the general principles are respected and any decision adjusting the price is substantiated and made public (Art. 5(4)). The consideration may be voting securities and/or cash; where however it does not consist of liquid voting securities admitted to trading on a regulated market it must include a cash alternative and where the offeror or persons acting in concert have over a period of six to twelve months before the bid and during the course of the bid purchased in cash securities carrying 5% of the voting rights, the offeror must offer a cash consideration at least as an alternative (Art. 5(5)).

The period of acceptance of the bid must be a prescribed period of between two and ten weeks from the date of publication of the offer document, discussed below. Member States may permit extension of the period on condition that the offeror gives at least two weeks' notice of its intention to close the bid and may authorize the supervisory authority to derogate from the prescribed period in order to allow the target company to call a general meeting to consider the bid (Art. 7(1) and (2)).

4. Information on the bid. Member States are to ensure that the decision to make a bid is made public without delay (Art. 6(1)) and in such a way as to ensure market transparency and integrity for the securities of all companies involved, in particular in order to prevent the publication or dissemination of false or misleading information (Art. 8(1)). The supervisory authority is to be informed of the bid (Art. 6(1)). The offeror must draw up and make public in good time an offer document containing the information necessary to enable the target shareholders to reach a properly informed decision (including certain information prescribed by the directive, such as the terms of the bid and the offeror's intentions concerning the future business of the target); the document is to be communicated to the supervisory authority before it is made public and to both companies' employees or their representatives when it is made public (Art. 6(2) and (3)). An offer document that, in accordance with national requirements, has been approved by the supervisory authority is to be recognized, subject to translation, in any other Member State on whose market the offeree's securities are admitted to trading (Art. 6(2)). The document and prescribed information must be readily and promptly available to the target shareholders at least in those Member States where its voting securities are traded on a regulated market and to the target's employees or their representatives (Art. 8(2)).

The target company's board must also draw up and make public, and communicate to employees or their representatives, a document setting out its opinion on the bid and reasons therefor, including employment issues. If that company's employee representatives have prepared a separate opinion which is received by the target board in good time, it must be appended to the board's document (Art. 9(5)).

5. Frustrating action by the target board. The directive's provisions attempting to restrict the right of the board of the target company to take action to frustrate a bid without shareholder approval were hotly contested by certain Member States and the compromise which resulted considerable weakens their impact by making them optional: Member States may decide not to require companies with their registered offices on their territory to apply the provisions (Art. 12(1)). Such companies however must have a reversible option (exercisable by the shareholders in a general meeting by the same majority required to amend the articles of association) to apply them (Art. 12(2)). In a further twist, Member States may exempt companies that apply the provisions from applying them if they are the target of an offer launched by a company which itself does not apply them (Art. 12(3)).

During a prescribed period—at least from the time it is informed of the decision to make a bid and until the result of the bid is made public or the bid lapses—the target company's board must obtain the prior authorization of the shareholders in general meeting before taking any action other than seeking alternative bids which may result in frustration of the bid (Art. 9(2)). The general meeting must also approve or confirm any decision taken before the beginning of the prescribed period and not yet partly or fully implemented which does not form part of the normal course of the company's business and whose implementation may frustrate the bid (Art. 9(3)). Member States may provide for such general meetings to be called at short notice of not less than two weeks (Art. 9(4)).

6. Disclosure of information. The directive requires Member States to ensure that listed companies publish in their annual reports, and the board presents to the annual general meeting an explanatory report on, detailed information on their capital structure and any defensive mechanisms including restrictions on the transfer of voting shares, restrictions on voting rights, shareholders' agreements known to the company that may result in either of such restrictions, rules governing the appointment and replacement of the board and the amendment of the articles of association, the board's power to issue or buy back shares, significant agreements that take effect, alter, or terminate upon a change of control, and agreements with directors or employees providing for compensation if their employment ceases because of a takeover bid (Art. 10(1), (2), and (3)).

7. Breakthrough provisions. Member States are required to ensure that, when a bid has been made public, any restrictions on the transfer of voting securities provided for in the target's articles, in contractual agreements between the target and its shareholders or in contractual agreements between the target's shareholders entered into after adoption of the directive, are not to apply *vis-à-vis* the bidder during the period for acceptance of the bid (Art. 11(1) and (2)). Moreover restrictions on voting rights provided for in the target's articles or in such agreements are not to have effect at the general meeting which decides on any defensive measures in accordance with Art. 9 and multiple voting securities are to carry one vote only at such general meeting (Art. 11(3)). Finally, where, following a bid, the offeror holds 75% of the voting capital, (*i*) any such restrictions on transfer or on voting and any extraordinary rights of shareholders in the target's articles concerning the appointment or removal of directors are not to apply, and (*ii*) multiple voting securities are to carry one vote only at the first general meeting called by the offeror after the bid has closed in order to amend the articles of association or to remove or appoint board members (Art. 11(4)). The offeror may convene such a general meeting on short notice of not less than two weeks (Art. 11(4)). 'Equitable compensation' must be provided, in accordance with national law, for any loss incurred by the holders of any such rights that are so disabled (Art. 11(5)). Art. 11 does not apply to 'golden shares' held by Member States in the target company and other special rights provided for in national law provided those shares or rights are compatible with the Treaty (Art. 11(5) and (6)).

Art. 11 was a major stumbling block during negotiation of the directive and compromise was only reached at the eleventh hour by making its provisions optional: Art. 12, described above, applies also to Art. 11.

8. Squeeze-out and sell-out. Where an offeror has acquired or firmly contracted to acquire at least 90% (or a higher threshold not exceeding 95% set by the Member State concerned) of the voting capital of the target, (*i*) he must be able to require the holders of the remaining voting securities to sell him those securities at a fair price (Art. 15(2)), and (*ii*) holders of the remaining voting securities must be able to require him to buy their securities at a fair price (Art. 16(2)). In both cases the right must be exercised within three months after the end of the period for acceptance of the bid and the price is to take the same form as the consideration offered in the bid or to consist of cash, although Member States may require cash to be offered at least as an alternative. In general the consideration offered in the bid is presumed to be fair (Arts. 15(5) and 16(3)).

9. Other rules and derogation. Member States are to lay down rules governing at least lapse, revision and irrevocability of bids, competing bids, and disclosure of the results of bids (Art. 13).

Provided that the general principles are respected, Member States may provide for derogations from the rules implementing the directive either generally, to take account of national circumstances, or by empowering their supervisory authorities to waive the rules to take account of either national or specific circumstances; in the latter case, a reasoned decision is required (Art. 4(5)).

X. Miscellaneous draft legislation

1. Proposed Directive on Cross-border Mergers. The proposal for a directive on cross-border mergers of companies with share capital (COM(2003) 703) complements the Third Directive on domestic mergers of public limited companies. The proposal started life as a draft Convention under Art. 293 EC, abandoned in 1980 because of resistance from Germany, which was concerned to ensure that the scope of the Convention—namely the required link between a company and a Member State—was defined so as to obviate any risk of international mergers being used by companies as a method of avoiding German worker-participation laws. In 1985 the Commission submitted a proposal for a Tenth Directive on cross-border mergers of public limited companies (COM(84) 727, *OJ* 1985 C23/11, Suppl. 3/85–*Bull. EC*), but progress was blocked by the European Parliament's failure to deliver its opinion on the proposal. In 2003 the Commission presented a fresh proposal, covering both public and private companies with share capital.

The proposed directive would set up a cross-border merger procedure whereby mergers—as defined in the Third and Sixth Directives, see above—would be governed in each Member State by the principles and rules applicable to domestic mergers, which would ensure protection for creditors, debenture holders, the holders of securities other than shares, minority shareholders, and employees.

With regard more specifically to employees' rights, the national law of the company created by the merger would apply. Where however at least one of the merging companies was subject to rules on employee participation whereas the merged company was not so subject, then the negotiation procedure provided for under the European Company Statute would apply, allowing for agreement on employee participation in the merged company. If agreement could not be reached, the pre-merger regime would be extended (Art. 14. *See further under* **European Company**).

2. The planned proposal for a Fourteenth Directive on the cross-border transfer of the registered office of a limited company. In 1997, the Commission issued a draft proposal for a Fourteenth Directive on the transfer of the registered office or *de facto* head office of a company from one Member State to another with a change in applicable law. Following two rounds of public consultation, it announced in 2004 that it was planning to produce instead a proposal for a directive on the cross-border transfer of the registered office of a limited company with acquisition of legal personality in the host State and without the need for dissolution. Further consultation was in progress at the time of going to press.

See also **European Company, European Economic Interest Grouping, Freedom of establishment.**

Further reading 1. Books: Andenas and Kenyon-Slade (eds.), *EC Financial Market Regulation and Company Law* (1993); id., *Corporate Law—The European Dimension* (1991); Butterworths' *Compendium of EC Company Law* (1990); Buxbaum and Hopt, *Legal Harmonization and the Business Enterprise* (1988); Buxbaum, Hertig, Hirsch, and Hopt (eds.), *European Business Law* (1991); Edwards, *EC Company Law* (1999); Dine and Hughes, *EC Company Law* (1991, loose-leaf update); Ernst and Whinney, *The Fourth Directive* (1979); Hopt and Wymeersch, *European Company and Financial Law* (1994); Karayanni, *Les sociétés d'une seule personne dans le droit des états membres de la Communauté européenne* (1992); Newman (ed.), *The Seventh Directive: Consolidated Accounts in the EEC*

(1984); Schmitthoff, *The Harmonisation of European Company Law* (1973); Stein, *Harmonization of European Company Laws* (1971); Villiers, *European Company Law—Towards Democracy?* (1998); Werlauff, *EU Company Law: Common Business Law of 28 States* (2003); Wooldridge, *Company Law in the United Kingdom and the European Community* (1991).

2. Articles and Papers: Andenas, 'Company Law Reform in the UK and European Harmonisation' in Rider (ed.), *The Corporate Dimension* (1998); Barbaso, 'The Harmonisation of Company Law with regard to Mergers and Divisions' (1984) *JBL* 176; Barker, 'The Seventh and Eighth Directives on Company Law' (1984) *Journal of the Irish Society for European Law* 65; Bellingwout, Clayton, and de Vallois, 'The Fourth Company Law Directive on the Annual Accounts of Limited Liability Companies' (1978) *Droit et pratique du commerce international* 405; Cooke, 'The Seventh Directive—An Accountant's Perspective' (1984) *EL Rev.* 143; Dine, 'The Community Company Law Harmonisation Programme' (1989) *EL Rev.* 322; id., 'The Harmonization of Company Law in the European Community' (1989) *YEL* 93; Feuillet, 'La huitième directive du Conseil des Communautés européennes et le commissariat aux comptes' (1984) *Revue des sociétés* 26; Gordon, 'European Community Company Law' in Folsom, Lake, and Nanda (eds.), *European Community Law After 1992* (1993); Morse, 'The Second Directive: Raising and Maintenance of Capital' (1977) *EL Rev.* 126; Nobes, 'The Harmonisation of Company Law Relating to the Published Accounts of Companies' (1980) *EL Rev.* 38; Pennington, 'Consolidated Accounts: the Seventh Directive' (1984) *The Company Lawyer* 63; Rajak, 'Proposal for a Fourteenth European Parliament and Council Directive on the Transfer of the Registered Office of a Company from One Member State to Another With a Change in Applicable Law' (2000) *EBL Rev.* 43; Schmitthoff, 'The Second EEC Directive on Company Law' (1978) *CML Rev.* 43; Schneebaum, 'The Company Law Harmonization Program of the European Community' (1982) *Law & Policy in International Business* 293; Van Hulle, 'The EEC Accounting Directives in Perspective: Problems of Harmonization' (1981) *CML Rev.* 121; Van Ommeslaghe, 'La Première Directive du Conseil du 9 mars 1968 en Matière de Sociétés' (1969) *Cahiers de droit européen* 495; Werlauff, 'The Development of Community Company Law' (1992) *EL Rev.* 207; id., 'Common European Company Law: Status 1998 (2)—The Background to Harmonisation, Disclosure, Capital etc.' (1998) *EBL Rev.* 210; id., 'Common European Company Law: Status 1998 (3)—Group, Company Structure, New Company Forms etc.' (1998) *EBL Rev.* 274; Wooldridge, 'The Harmonization of Company Law: The First and Second Directives of the Council of Ministers of the European Economic Community' (1978) *Acta Juridica* 327; id., 'The Third Directive and the Meaning of Mergers' (1980) *The Company Lawyer* 75; id., 'The EEC Council Seventh Directive on Consolidated Accounts' (1988) *ICLQ* 714; Wouters, 'European Company Law: Quo Vadis?' (2000) *CML Rev.* 257; Wymeersch 'Company Law in Europe and European Company Law' in

Reports for the 1st European Jurist Forum (2001) and (2001) *Zeitschrift für Schweizerisches Recht* 85.

3. Official Publications: Commission of the European Communities, 'The Fourth Company Law Directive—Implementation by Member States' (1987); id., 'Study on Transfer of the Head Office of a Company from one Member State to Another' (1993); id., 'Acts of the Conference on Company Law and the Single Market' (1998); id., 'Interpretative Communication concerning certain Articles of the Fourth and Seventh Council Directives on Accounting' (*OJ* 1998 C16/5); House of Lords, Select Committee on the European Communities, Session 1974–5, 24th Report, 'Second Directive'; Session 1975–6, 4th Report, 'Fourth Directive'; Session 1975–6, 20th Report, 'Third Directive'; Session 1979–80, 43rd Report, 'Sixth Directive'; Session 1976–7, 25th Report, 'Seventh Directive'; Session 1979–80, 12th Report, 'Eighth Directive'; Session 2002–3, 28th Report, 'Takeovers Directive'.

▶ **COPYRIGHT AND RELATED RIGHTS** *see* **INTELLECTUAL PROPERTY RIGHTS**

▶ **CUSTOMS DUTY** *see* **COMMON CUSTOMS TARIFF** *and* **CUSTOMS UNION**

▶ **CUSTOMS PROCEDURES** This term is understood here to cover all procedures relating to the import or export of goods into or out of the customs territory and—in so far as the customs rules apply—the movement of such goods within this territory. The purpose of customs procedures is to ensure that customs duties are collected where they are due and that any other stipulated trade restrictions are applied at importation or exportation (e.g. presentation of an authorization). Non-compliance with the procedural rules leads normally to a customs debt if the customs tariff sets a customs duty for the goods concerned; in case of compliance, a customs debt is incurred only when the goods are entered for free circulation (and in some cases of temporary importation) or—where export duties exist—when the goods are exported. Under the terms of the Community Customs Code–CC (Council Reg. 2913/92, *OJ* 1992 L302/1) and its implementing provisions–CCIP (Comm. Reg. 2454/93, *OJ* 1993 L253/1), only the following are defined as a customs procedure (Art. 4 No. 16 CC):

- release for free circulation;
- transit;
- customs warehousing;
- inward processing;
- processing under customs control;
- temporary importation;
- outward processing; and
- exportation.

Other rules leading to duty suspension or duty relief concern:

- temporary storage of import goods following their entry into the customs territory and their presentation to customs;
- entry into a free zone or free warehouse;
- re-exportation;
- destruction;
- abandonment to the Exchequer;
- special circumstances qualifying for duty relief;
- returned goods; and
- products of sea-fishing by Member State vessels and products obtained therefrom on board factory ships.

Where a customs debt is incurred, it has

- to be entered in the accounts of the customs authorities and to be communicated to the debtor (unless the debtor has entered the correct amount of duties in his customs declaration), and subsequently
- to be paid.

Payment of duties leads to the extinction of the customs debt. In certain cases (e.g. erroneous duty collection), a repayment of customs duties is possible.

Any person affected by a decision of the customs authorities has the right of appeal.

The scheme, shown in table form on the following page, classifies the different arrangements under the terms of the CC.

Goods are under customs supervision from the time of their entry into the customs territory, except where they enter directly into a control type I free zone. They remain under such supervision for as long as necessary to determine their status as Community goods or, in the case of non-Community goods, until their customs status is changed or they enter into a control type I free zone, free warehouse, are re-exported, or destroyed under customs supervision (Art. 37 CC). Goods declared for transit, export, outward processing, or leaving the customs territory without a customs declaration are equally subject to customs supervision (Arts. 59(2) and 183 CC).

I. International law

A number of international agreements have a direct impact on customs procedures, notably:

- Art. V GATT which guarantees freedom of transit through the customs territory;
- the Customs Convention on the International Transport of Goods under cover of TIR Carnets of 14 November 1975 (Council Reg. 2112/78, *OJ* 1978 L252/1);
- the Istanbul Convention of 26 June 1990 concerning temporary importation (Council Dec. 92/329, *OJ* 1993 L130/1), as well as several agreements on this subject concluded under the auspices of the United Nations (*see further under* **Community Customs Code (CC)**, section I).

Customs-approved treatment or use				Privileged operations
Customs procedures			Other	1. Duty relief (Reg. 918/83) 2. Returned goods 3. Products of sea-fishing by Member State vessels
customs procedures with economic impact	suspensive customs procedures	Other		
	1. External transit	1. Release for free circulation	1. Entry into a free zone/free warehouse	Customs debt
2. Customs warehousing		2. Exportation	2. Re-exportation	1. Security to cover a customs debt
3. Inward processing		3. Internal transit	3. Destruction	2. Entry in the accounts
suspension and drawback system	suspension system		4. Abandonment	3. Payment, extinction of customs debt
4. Processing under customs control				4. Repayment, remission of a customs duty/debt
5. Temporary importation				
6. Outward processing				Appeals

A general model for customs procedures is set out in the International Convention on the Simplification and Harmonisation of Customs Procedures of 18 May 1973, the Kyoto Convention (Council Dec. 75/199, *OJ* 1975 L100/1, revised version adopted by Council Dec. 2003/231, *OJ* 2003 L86/21).

In this context also belongs the Convention on Common Transit (Council Dec. 87/415, *OJ* 1987 L226/1), creating a transit procedure between the Community on the one hand and Iceland, Norway, and Switzerland (including Liechtenstein) on the other.

The TIR and the common transit agreements and the committees established by them create and manage rules that are directly applicable in the Community. The other agreements relating to customs procedures have been transposed in the Community Customs Code and its implementing provisions. The particular aspect of the common transit procedures lies in the fact that in this case the customs procedure starts or ends outside the customs territory of the Community. The scope of the Customs Code, however, does not go beyond the Community customs territory (San Marino and Andorra are an exception from this principle given that these countries have agreed to apply on their territory the CC with regard to the Community transit procedure). The same reasoning applies with regard to origin rules set out in international agreements; it is, in principle, the export country which is responsible for checking that the criteria for conferring preferential origin are met (Case 218/83 *Les Rapides Savoyards* [1984] ECR 3105 at pp. 3123–5).

II. The Treaty provisions

The EC Treaty does not contain specific provisions with regard to customs procedures. The drafters of the Treaty had focused on the basic elements of a customs union, namely the introduction of a common customs tariff coupled with the abolition of customs duties between Member States and had neglected the procedures leading to the collection of or waiver from the customs duties of the Common Customs Tariff. This lacuna has been closed by using the provisions on customs duties and commercial policy (Arts. 26 and 133 EC) and on the achievement of the internal market (Art. 95 EC) for legislation on customs procedures (*see further under* **Community Customs Code (CC)**, section II). Agreements concerning customs procedures are normally based on Art. 133 EC; if they are part of an association agreement Art. 310 EC is applicable.

III. General provisions

The material and territorial scope of the CC is defined as covering trade in goods between the Community customs territory and areas outside that territory (Arts. 1 to 3 CC, *see further under* **Community customs territory**).

Since goods normally do not enter into or exit from a customs territory of their own will (this may happen with regard to cattle), customs legislation fixes rights and obligations with regard to persons bringing goods into or out of the customs territory. The importer or exporter has, *inter alia*, the right

- to appoint a representative with regard to customs formalities (Art. 5 CC; he may, however, not be compelled to use a representative, see Case C-323/90 *Commission* v. *Portugal* [1992] ECR I-1887 at p. I-1906; Case C-119/92 *Commission* v. *Italy* [1994] ECR I-393 at pp. I-415–19);
- to receive a decision when a request had been made in accordance with the relevant provisions (Art. 6 CC);
- to request information on customs legislation; with regard to the tariff classification or the determination of the origin of specific goods, information that binds the customs authorities may be requested (Arts. 11 to 12 CC);
- that his confidential data are not disclosed by the customs authorities, except with his permission or in connection with legal proceedings or

on the basis of Community or national legislation allowing a disclosure (Art. 15 CC);

- to appeal against decisions taken by the customs authorities in the framework of customs legislation (Arts. 243 to 246 CC).

On the other hand, the importer or exporter is obliged

- to provide the customs authorities with all documents and information relating to international trade in goods (Art. 14 CC);
- to keep such documents for at least three calendar years, the period starting at the end of the year in which the relevant event took place (Art. 16 CC);
- to convey goods brought into and out of the Community customs territory by specific routes, to present and declare them to customs (Arts. 37 to 47 and 183 CC);
- to assign imported non-Community goods a customs-approved treatment or use within the set deadline (Arts. 48 and 49 CC) and to present and declare or notify goods before they are exported or re-exported from the Community customs territory (Arts. 161 and 182 CC).

The customs authorities are entitled

- to annul or revoke their decision if the applicant has provided incorrect or incomplete information or if one of the conditions laid down for the issue of the decision are no longer fulfilled (Arts. 8 to 10 CC);
- to carry out customs supervision and controls (Art. 4 Nos. 13, 14, Arts. 13, 37, 59(2), 78, 82, and 183 CC).

Though the Community customs territory is administered by twenty-five national customs administrations, the decisions, other measures, and findings of a Member State's customs authority have the same legal effect or conclusive force in the territory of any other Member State (Art. 250 CC).

IV. Supervision of goods entering or leaving the customs territory

The CC has a two-tier approach for customs supervision and customs-approved treatments or uses, in order to avoid traffic congestion at the frontier and to allow the involvement of a customs office close to the operator's premises.

On entry:

- goods have to be presented immediately to customs (Art. 40 CC) and a summary declaration has to be lodged (Arts. 43 and 44 CC), thus allowing the customs authorities to establish the Community or non-Community status (these terms are defined in Art. 4 Nos. 7 and 8 CC) of the goods; for Community goods customs supervision ends immediately after their status has been established (Art. 37(2) CC);
- non-Community goods presented to customs have the status of goods in temporary storage until such time as they are assigned a customs-approved treatment or use, at the choice of the person responsible for the goods (Arts. 48, 50, and 58 CC); where goods are to be placed under

a customs procedure, a customs declaration to that effect has to be lodged (Art. 59 CC); the importer can lodge immediately a customs declaration instead of a summary declaration (Art. 45 CC).

On exit:

- goods have normally to be presented and declared for exportation (in the case of non-Community goods this is called 're-exportation', Art. 182(1) CC) at the customs office responsible for the place where the exporter is established or where the goods are packed or loaded for export shipment (Arts. 161(5) and 182(3) CC); non-Community goods leaving a free zone are only subjected to a prior notification (Art. 182(3) CC);
- the exit of both Community and non-Community goods is supervised by the customs authorities and—where necessary—proof of exit is provided (Arts. 37(2), 183 CC, Art. 793 CCIP).

The aim of customs supervision is to ensure that

- any import or export duties (and, in case of importation, any national taxes such as VAT and excise duties) due are paid or secured;
- the payment of export refunds and the repayment or remission of import duties, VAT and excise duties is justified; and
- any import or export restrictions are applied whether based on commercial, environmental, health, cultural or security policy or imposed for the protection of industrial, commercial or intellectual property rights (Art. 4 No. 13, Art. 59(2) CC).

In order to ascertain whether such measures have to be applied to import or export goods, the customs authorities may examine the goods, take samples, verify the existence and authenticity of documents, audit the accounts and other records of those involved in the operations, inspect means of transport, luggage, and other goods carried by or on persons, carry out enquiries, and ask for information and the provision of documents, including data stored on electronic media (Art. 4 No. 14, Arts. 13, 14, 68, 78, and 168 CC). They may also ask for administrative assistance of the customs authorities of another Member State (Council Reg. 515/97, *OJ* 1997 L82/1).

The unlawful introduction of goods into the customs territory as well as the unlawful removal of goods from customs supervision or the infringement of the customs rules leads to a customs debt being incurred if the goods concerned are liable to import duties (Arts. 202 to 205 CC).

V. Customs procedures under the terms of the CC

The CC differentiates between customs procedures and other customs-approved treatments or uses (Art. 4 Nos. 15 and 16 CC). Customs procedures have certain common features, notably the following:

- goods are placed under a customs procedure by virtue of a declaration to that effect (Art. 4 No. 17, Art. 59 CC),

- the customs declaration (or the assignment to any other customs-approved treatment or use) has to be lodged within twenty days—or in the case of goods carried by sea—within forty-five days from the date the goods were first presented to customs and covered by a summary declaration (Art. 49 CC);
- the customs declaration (with regard to the necessary details of a customs declaration, see Case 378/87 *Top Hit* v. *Commission* [1989] ECR 1359 at p. 1386) can be made in writing on the single administrative document, a commercial or administrative document or by means of an entry in the records, or by using data-processing techniques, and in some cases by means of an oral declaration or any other act, such as passing the frontier without making a declaration (Arts. 61 to 77 CC);
- the customs declaration shall be accompanied by all the documents required for the procedure requested (e.g. invoice, certificate of origin, import authorization, transport document, Art. 62(2) CC); however, where a customs declaration is made by means of a data-processing technique, the customs authorities may allow that the documents are kept at their disposal (Art. 77(2) CC);
- whilst in principle any person who is able to present the goods or have them presented to customs may lodge a customs declaration, in the cases where the use of the procedure is subject to an authorization (see Case C-119/92 *Commission* v. *Italy* [1994] ECR I-393 at pp. I-415–18), only the authorization holder or his representative is entitled to submit the declaration; except for transit, temporary importation and occasional imports or exports, the declarant or his representative must be established in the Community (Art. 4 No. 18, Arts. 5(3) and 64 CC, see Case C-262/99 *Louloudakis* [2001] ECR I-5547 at pp. I-5592–3);
- goods subject to a customs declaration have to be presented to customs; this requirement may be waived under the local clearance procedure an with regard to authorized consignors and consignees (Art. 4 No. 19, Arts. 63, 76(1)(c) CC, Arts. 398 to 408a CCIP);
- the use of a customs procedure with economic impact (customs warehousing, inward and outward processing, processing under customs control, and temporary importation) and entry for free circulation under the end-use provisions is subject to an authorization issued by the customs authorities (Arts. 21 and 86 CC); the rights and obligations of the holder of such an authorization may be transferred to another person (Art. 90 CC);
- the placing of goods under a customs procedure which suspends the application of customs duties (external transit, customs warehousing, inward processing—suspension system, processing under customs control, temporary importation) may be—and in certain cases must be—made conditional upon the provision of a security (Arts. 88 and 94 CC);
- non-Community goods placed under a suspensive arrangement may be assigned any other customs-approved treatment or use (e.g. from customs warehousing to inward processing or re-exportation, Art. 89 CC); goods that have obtained the status of Community goods can change

their status back (and thus be assigned another customs-approved treatment or use) only under exceptional circumstances (Art. 83 CC).

Customs declarations complying with the conditions of the CC shall be accepted by the customs authorities; the date of acceptance of the customs declaration determines normally the customs duty and other restrictive trade measures to be applied where the goods are released for free circulation (Arts. 63, 67, and 214 CC). Where a customs debt is incurred for other reasons, the date of incurrence of the debt determines the duty rate and any other restrictions to be applied (Art. 214 CC). However, restrictions relating to the entry of goods into the Community are already applied at that moment (see Art. 509 CCIP).

After acceptance of the customs declaration, the customs authorities may verify it (Art. 68 CC) and will collect the duties where they are due; they may defer payment and ask for a security. Where no obstacles (such as bans, restrictions, or seizure) exist, the goods are subsequently released (Art. 4 No. 20, Arts. 73 to 75 CC).

Art. 76 CC provides for simplified procedures the details of which are set in the implementing provisions both in general provisions and with regard to individual procedures (see Case C-292/96 *Göritz Intransco International* [1998] ECR I-165 at p. I-179).

1. Release for free circulation. Art. 23 of the EC Treaty stipulates free circulation for Community goods throughout the EC. This principle applies not only to goods originating (i.e. made) in the Community but also to third-country goods that have been released for free circulation (Art. 24 EC). By this act goods from outside the customs territory (under the terms of the CC 'non-Community goods', see Art. 4 No. 8 CC) obtain the status of Community goods (Art. 4 No. 7, Art. 79 CC).

Release for free circulation is one of the various options for the customs treatment of import goods (Art. 58 CC). This option is exercised by means of a customs declaration to that effect (Arts. 59(1) and 61 CC). It entails (see Art. 79 CC):

- the collection of import duties where they are due according to the Common Customs Tariff and where no duty relief is applicable, as well as
- the application of commercial policy measures and any other formalities laid down in respect of the importation of such goods (e.g. health or safety requirements, payment of import VAT).

The rules on the customs debt enumerate release for free circulation of goods liable to import duties as a particular case in point (Art. 201(1)(a) CC; with regard to irregularities during the clearance procedure, see Case C-66/99 *Wandel* [2001] ECR I-873 at pp. I-930–4).

The CC provides for a number of special arrangements under which release for free circulation can be made under more favourable conditions:

- If Community goods have left the customs territory under the internal transit procedure, their status is maintained on their re-importation into the Community so that no customs duty needs to be paid (Art. 163 CC); under certain circumstances, the use of a status document is sufficient (Art. 164 CC, Arts. 313 to 336 CCIP).

- If the imported goods had previously been exported under the outward processing procedure, a partial or total duty relief can be granted (Arts. 151 to 153 CC).
- If the import goods are released for free circulation under the inward processing drawback system, the import duties can be repaid or remitted, if these goods or the products made from them are exported or placed under a suspensive arrangement (Art. 128 CC).
- No customs debt is incurred if Community goods are re-imported without having undergone processing during their stay outside the Community customs territory—relief for returned goods (Arts. 185 and 186 CC).
- Exempt from import duties are products of sea-fishing and other products taken from the territorial sea of a third country by a vessel registered or recorded in a Member State and flying the flag of that Member State, and products obtained from such goods on board factory-ships fulfilling the above-mentioned conditions when they are released for free circulation (Art. 188 CC).
- Sometimes a favourable tariff treatment depends on the nature of the goods, which has to be proved by certain means (e.g. a certificate, making the goods unfit for human consumption, marking of seeds, Art. 21 CC, Title II, Section F of the Preliminary Provisions to the Combined Nomenclature, see *OJ* 2004 L327/18).
- The customs tariff and the rules on duty relief (Council Reg. 918/83) make a favourable treatment in certain cases dependent on the end-use of the goods (e.g. processing of tuna fish, goods to be used for tests); as a consequence, the goods remain under customs supervision in spite of the fact that they have been released for free circulation (Art. 82 CC). In many cases the use of this procedure requires an authorization (Art. 291 CCIP, see Cases 248/88 etc. *Chimica del Friuli* [1989] ECR 2837).

The customs supervision for goods in free circulation under the end-use provisions ends when:

- the prescribed end-use has been achieved and any other conditions laid down for the preferential treatment cease to apply (Art. 82 CC);
- the goods are exported with the permission of the customs authorities (no customs debt is incurred, Art. 206(2) CC);
- the goods are destroyed under the supervision of the customs authorities (no customs debt is incurred, Art. 206(1) CC), any remaining waste and scrap are deemed to be non-Community goods (Art. 207 CC); if the waste and scrap are released for free circulation, any duty already paid on account of the end-use is deducted (Art. 208 CC); or
- the goods are put to another use other than the prescribed end-use and the normal duties are paid (the customs debt is incurred by virtue of Art. 204(1)(b) CC, any customs duty previously paid is deducted, Art. 208 CC).

Goods released for free circulation lose their status as Community goods where:

- the declaration is invalidated in accordance with Art. 66 CC;
- the import duties are repaid or remitted because the goods are exported or are given an equivalent customs-approved treatment or use, notably after inward processing, or in respect of goods which are defective or do not comply with the terms of the contract (Arts. 83, 238, 239 CC).

2. **Transit** aims at

- facilitating the transport of goods that are under customs supervision within the EC customs territory or between the Community and third countries with which transit agreements have been concluded;
- creating incentives for the accomplishment of customs formalities at a customs office close to the operator's premises rather than the office at the frontier;
- limiting customs formalities for goods only passing through the customs territory to the strict minimum, and avoiding the collection and subsequent repayment of import duties;
- allowing customs supervision of goods moving within the customs territory, and providing the necessary guarantees for the payment of customs duties and other taxes if the goods do not arrive at their destination.

Only in exceptional circumstances do Arts. 30 and 296 EC or secondary Community law allow the application of restrictions on goods in transit (e.g. in case of strategic material or counterfeit goods, see Case C-367/89 *Richardt* [1991] ECR I-4621 at p. I-4652; Case C-60/02 *X* [2004] ECR I-0000, OJ 2004 C47/7).

The CC distinguishes between:

- the external transit procedure (Art. 91 CC) allowing the movement from one point to another within the customs territory of
  - — non-Community goods, exempting them from customs duties, VAT, excise duties, and—in so far as such measures do not apply to entry into or exit from the Community—also from commercial policy measures, and
  - — Community goods subject to export refunds in so far as the transit procedure is stipulated (e.g. if such goods are moved to or through an EFTA country, Art. 340c(3)(a) CCIP), and
- the internal transit procedure (Art. 163 CC), allowing the movement of Community goods from one point to another within the customs territory passing through the territory of a third country (e.g. from Germany to Italy via Switzerland) without any change in their customs status; this procedure is also used where goods are moved to or from a territory where the Community VAT provisions do not apply, e.g. from the Canary Islands to the United Kingdom (Art. 340c(1) CCIP).

Non-Community goods placed under a suspensive customs procedure with economic impact may move under this procedure from one point to another within the customs territory without using the transit procedure (Art. 91(3) CC, Arts. 511 to 513 CCIP).

Besides the procedures provided for in the CC, also the international conventions concerning transit may be applied, if the movement begins or ends outside the Community, such as (Arts. 91(2) and 163(2) CC):

- the TIR Convention;
- the Istanbul Convention (ATA carnet);
- the Rhine Manifest;
- the NATO Treaty;
- postal traffic in accordance with the provisions of the Universal Postal Union.

Besides the transit procedures of the CC and the above-mentioned international conventions governing transit, the Convention on Common Transit (Council Dec. 87/415, *OJ* 1987 L226/1; see Case C-188/91 *Deutsche Shell* [1993] ECR I-363 at pp. I-387–90) allows transit through Iceland, Norway, Switzerland, and the Community; its aims are to:

- link different parts of the Community customs territory (e.g. from Germany to Italy via Switzerland);
- reduce frontier formalities with neighbouring countries and to promote economic integration;
- enhance customs co-operation and provide for mutual assistance, notably with regard to the recovery of debts.

As a result, the rules of the Community transit procedure and of the common transit are to a large extent identical (except for the territorial scope and with regard to presentation of the goods at the border which is no longer necessary within the internal market).

The CC implementing provisions set out special rules for transport by rail, air, sea, and pipeline (Arts. 412 to 450 CCIP). Postal traffic in transit is monitored through a postal label (Art. 462a Annexes 42 and 42b CCIP).

In those cases where customs duties are suspended, a customs debt can be incurred through:

- the unlawful removal from customs supervision, such as theft (Art. 203(1) CC), or
- the non-fulfilment of one of the obligations arising from the use of the transit procedure (Arts. 92 and 204(1)(a) CC).

Where several persons (such as the person illegally in possession of the goods, the carrier, or the principal, i.e. the person responsible under the procedure, see Art. 96 CC) are liable for the customs debt, they are jointly liable (Art. 213 CC). The Member State responsible for the collection of the customs duty, including cases in which the place where the customs debt and other charges incurred is unknown, is set out in Art. 215 CC and Arts. 450a to 450d, 455a, 457c CCIP. In any event, even if there are several reasons for the incurrence of a customs debt or several persons are liable, a customs debt has to be paid only once (Case 252/87 *Kiwall* [1988] ECR 4753 at p. 4766).

3. **Customs warehousing** is a customs procedure allowing the storage of:

- non-Community goods without subjecting them to import duties and commercial policy measures applicable at release for free circulation or exportation (Art. 98(1)(a) CC);
- non-Community goods with a view to discharge another suspensive arrangement (e.g. inward processing) and to respect at the same time any deadline for re-exportation (Art. 89 CC);
- Community goods in order to allow them to benefit already from measures requiring the export (e.g. export refunds, Art. 98(1)(b) CC);
- goods that have been released for free circulation and for which the import duties are to be repaid or remitted under the inward processing procedure (drawback system) or with regard to goods that are defective or fail to comply with the terms of the contract or other situations allowing repayment or remission on export or re-export of the goods (Arts. 83, 128, 238, and 239 CC).

The premises of a customs warehouse can also be used

- to store Community goods that are not placed under the customs warehousing procedure together with non-Community goods either to make optimum use of the storage facilities—common storage (e.g. a silo for rice) or to allow certain handling of the goods (e.g. installation of radios [Community goods] in cars [non-Community goods], Art. 106(1)(a) CC, Art. 534 CCIP);
- to process non-Community goods under the inward processing or processing under customs control procedure; the goods concerned can pass under simplified procedures from one procedure—including customs warehousing—to another (Art. 106(1)(b) and (c) CC, Arts. 277a, 278, and 535 CCIP);
- to process agricultural basic Community products with a view to obtain advance payment of export refunds in accordance with Council Reg. 565/80 (*OJ* 1980 L62/5, Art. 524 CCIP);
- to store goods that have been brought into the customs territory and are in temporary storage until such time as they are assigned a customs-approved treatment or use (Art. 50 CC, Art. 526(1) CCIP);
- to store goods for the purposes of a victualling warehouse in accordance with Art. 40 of Comm. Reg. 800/99 (*OJ* 1999 L102/11, Art. 526(4) CCIP).

Goods stored in a warehouse can therefore be either under the customs warehousing procedure or only placed there. In addition, it is possible to enter non-Community goods for the customs warehousing procedure without storing them in a customs warehouse, as long as the records show at all times the current stock of goods placed under the procedure (Art. 98(3) CC, Art. 534(2) and (3) CCIP).

Except where the customs authorities operate a customs warehouse, the operation of a customs warehouse and the use of the customs warehousing procedure require an authorization (Arts. 85 and 100 CC). As for any customs procedure, records have to be kept (Arts. 105 and 107 CC, Arts. 515 and 516 CCIP). The goods placed under the procedure may undergo usual forms of handling intended to preserve them, improve their appearance or marketable quality or prepare them for distribution or resale; the details are set out in the implementing provisions (Art. 109 CC, Art. 531 and Annex 72 CCIP, see Case 49/82 *Commission* v. *Netherlands* [1983] ECR 1195 at pp. 1206–7; Case 276/84 *Metelmann* [1985] ECR 4057 at p. 4066).

The customs authorities can permit the temporary removal of the goods from the customs warehouse, for example to show them to customers or to submit them to usual forms of handling (Art. 110 CC, Art. 532 CCIP). The goods remain under the procedure though they have left the customs warehouse.

The procedure can be discharged through any customs-approved treatment or use (see Art. 4 Nos. 15 and 16, and Art. 89 CC). When the goods are entered for free circulation or a customs debt is incurred for other reasons (e.g. theft or non-compliance, Art. 203 or 204 CC, see Cases 186/82 etc. *Magazzini Generali* [1983] ECR 2951 at p. 2962) the following costs can be excluded, if shown separately (Art. 112 CC):

- the cost of warehousing and preserving (see Case 38/77 *Enka* [1977] ECR 2203 at p. 2214);
- the increase in value incurred through usual forms of handling.

It is also possible to determine the nature of the goods (i.e. their classification in the customs tariff), their customs value and quantity already at the time they are placed under the customs warehousing procedure (Art. 112(3) CC); the duty rate and commercial policy measures applicable will, however, be those in force at the time when the declaration for release for free circulation is accepted (Arts. 67 and 214 CC, Art. 509 CCIP).

When goods are re-exported after having been placed under the customs warehousing procedure, a customs declaration has to be lodged (Art. 182(3) CC). The same applies where customs warehousing goods enter into a control type I free zone (Art. 170(2)(a) CC).

4. Inward processing. Whilst customs warehousing allows the storage of goods without payment of customs duties and any treatment of the goods is limited to certain handling intended to preserve them or to prepare them for distribution (Art. 109 CC), the inward processing procedure (which may take place at the premises of a customs warehouse, see point 3 above) is intended for import goods which are processed and then re-exported (Art. 114 CC).

The import duties are:

- either suspended (suspension system)
- or paid at release for free circulation, and repaid at the time the import goods or the products made therefrom are exported (drawback system).

Under the suspension system, also commercial policy measures relating to release for free circulation and re-exportation are suspended (under the drawback system, this is not possible, since it constitutes a special arrangement of release for free circulation under which all import formalities have to be fulfilled, Art. 79(2) CC). However, commercial policy measures set in an international agreement, which also create obligations with regard to products imported under inward processing, are not suspended (Case C-61/94 *Commission* v. *Germany* [1996] ECR I-3989 at p. I-4015); nor are measures pertaining to goods brought into or out of the EC customs territory irrespective of their customs status, such as embargoes (Art. 509 CCIP).

Art. XVI GATT prohibits export subventions; the exemption from or the repayment of import duties is however not considered as a subvention (see also Art. 1(1)(a)(ii) of the WTO Agreement on Subsidies and Countervailing Measures, *OJ* 1994 L336/156). Inward processing constitutes therefore one of the internationally recognized methods of export promotion; it allows Community producers to compete on world markets by using inputs at world market prices (tariff suspensions have the same effect, the difference being that also goods placed on the Community market benefit from the duty suspension).

In order to simplify the use of the system, also goods which are (re-)exported in the unaltered state can benefit from the suspension or drawback of import duties. This mitigates to some extent the fact that the CC does not provide for a general drawback system, under which customs duties would always be refunded when imported goods leave the customs territory (the other drawback cases admitted are set out in Arts. 238 and 239 CC).

The use of the inward processing procedure requires an authorization by the customs authorities (see Case C-291/91 *TVU* [1993] ECR I-579 at pp. I-595–6) and, in so far as the suspension system is concerned, a security may be imposed (Arts. 85 to 88, 116, and 117 CC). In the course of the authorization procedure, the customs authorities have the opportunity to examine whether the use of the procedure would adversely affect the essential interests of Community producers (Art. 117(c) CC, Arts. 502 to 504 CCIP). This is the corollary to the lifting of the external protection of the Community, which may have as a consequence that Community producers of goods equivalent to the import goods lose the opportunity to sell their products to the authorization holder. However, in many cases the economic conditions are deemed to be fulfilled so that no examination is necessary (Art. 539 and Annex 73 CCIP).

The use of the drawback system is more restricted in that it excludes goods (Art. 124 CC):

- subject to quantitative import restrictions;
- imported under a tariff quota;
- subject to an agricultural import or export licence;
- subject to export refunds.

The prior exportation facility (see below) is not admitted under the drawback system (Art. 126 CC).

The following types of facilitation can be authorized (Art. 115 CC, Arts. 545 and 546 CCIP):

- the use of equivalent Community raw materials from which the export products (called 'compensating products') are made and the use of a corresponding quantity of import goods (for which no import duties are paid) for consumption in the customs territory (Case C-103/96 *Eridania Beghin-Say* [1997] ECR I-1452 at pp. I-1483–4);
- the export of the products obtained from equivalent Community goods before importation of the raw materials (this procedure is called 'EX/IM'—exportation before importation, the provision of a security is obligatory);
- the release for free circulation of goods placed under the suspension system without customs declaration at the expiry of the period for discharge if the goods have not been assigned a customs-approved treatment or use before.

Whilst under the customs warehousing procedure normally no limit is fixed for the length of time the goods may remain under the procedure (Art. 108 CC), inward processing is authorized always under specification of the (re-) export period (Case C-325/96 *Fábrica de Queijo Eru Portuguesa* [1997] ECR I-7249 at p. I-7267); within this period (see Art. 507 CCIP), the goods may also be assigned to another customs-approved treatment or use, such as transit, customs warehousing or entry into a control type I free zone (Art. 118 CC). Furthermore, it is possible to enter the import goods or processed products for free circulation. Other reasons for the incurrence of a customs debt include:

- unlawful removal from customs supervision (e.g. through entering the goods on the market, Art. 203(1) CC);
- non-fulfilment of an obligation arising from the procedure (e.g. the non-respect of the period for re-exportation, Art. 204(1)(a) CC);
- non-compliance with a condition governing the placing of the goods under the procedure (e.g. the lack of a valid authorization, Art. 204(1)(b) CC);
- validation of documents enabling preferential treatment in a third country (application of the 'no drawback rule', Art. 216 CC).

As an exception from Art. 214(1) CC, according to which a customs debt shall be determined on the basis of the nature, quantity, and the value of the goods at the time when the customs debt is incurred, several special rules have been created with regard to inward processing, in order to be able to disregard the value added in the Community and the quantity or value of secondary products (such as waste) that are not exported together with the main product, the export of which is to be promoted (Arts. 121 and 122 CC). In order to offset the advantage of the suspension of import duties, compensatory interest normally has to be paid (Art. 214(3) CC, Art. 519 CCIP).

5. Processing under customs control. The Common Customs Tariff has been established according to the principle that raw materials and waste bear the lowest import duties or are duty free, semi-finished products bear higher duties, and finished products the highest. There are however a number of exceptions to this principle, since

- it cannot always be foreseen for which finished product a raw material or semi-finished product is going to be used;
- a finished product may be incorporated in another finished product;
- several GATT rounds have lead to the result that the import duties for certain semi-finished and finished products (e.g. microelectronic products) have been reduced or even abolished, whilst the duties for the raw materials have been maintained or reduced to a smaller extent;
- the duties for agricultural goods are generally high, whilst the duties for processed agricultural goods or industrial goods using agricultural components are normally lower.

If there were no correction mechanism, such duty disparities (they are also called 'tariff anomalies') would create incentives to process raw materials and semi-finished products outside the Community customs territory in order to benefit from the lower duty for the finished product. The same disadvantage would occur with regard to production processes where waste occurs which as such would be duty free or subject to a reduced duty (e.g. stripping of raw tobacco for which the duties are levied according to weight).

Processing under customs control allows for such cases to enter the import goods under a suspensive procedure (this meaning that the import duties and the commercial policy measures relating to release for free circulation are not yet applied), to process them and to declare them subsequently for free circulation. The import duties applied are in principle those due for the processed product (Art. 130 CC); if the import goods qualified for preferential treatment, a tariff preference can also be applied with regard to the processed product, provided that the preferential arrangement also covers the processed product (Art. 136 CC). Commercial policy measures (e.g. import authorization) are applied only, if both the processed product and the import good are subject to such measures (Art. 509(3) CCIP). Furthermore, the procedure can be used in order to adjust import goods to technical requirements for their release for free circulation (Art. 551(1) CCIP).

As the procedure can lead to a circumvention of the aims of customs and commercial policy measures, it is subjected to prior authorization and an examination of economic conditions (Arts. 131 to 134 CC, Arts. 502 to 504 CCIP), unless the need for such an examination is waived (Art. 552(1) and Annex 76 CCIP).

Like any suspensive arrangement, the procedure can be discharged with any new customs-approved treatment or use (Art. 89 CC and Case C-437/93 *Temic Telefunken* [1995] ECR I-1687 at pp. I-1704–5).

A customs debt can be incurred for the following reasons:

- release for free circulation (Art. 201(1)(a) CC); special rules for the calculation of the customs debt exist with regard to goods in the unaltered state or at an intermediate stage of processing (Art. 135 CC) and with regard to the customs value (Art. 551(3) CCIP);
- unlawful removal from customs supervision, e.g. theft or placing on the market without customs formalities (Arts. 134, 135, and 201(1)(a) CC);
- non-fulfilment of one of the obligations arising from the procedure, e.g. non-respect of the deadline for assigning the goods another customs-approved treatment or use (Arts. 135 and 204(1)(a) CC);
- non-compliance with a condition governing the placing of the goods under the procedure, e.g. lack of a valid authorization (Arts. 135 and 204(1)(b) CC).

6. Temporary importation is a customs procedure allowing the temporary use of non-Community goods with total or partial relief from import duties and a suspension of commercial policy measures, provided that the goods do not undergo changes, except maintenance operations and normal depreciation due to the use made of the goods (Art. 137 CC). The use of the procedure requires an authorization (Arts. 85 to 87, 138, and 139 CC) and the provision of a security, except for certain cases (Art. 581 and Annex 77 CCIP). The use of the procedure is, in principle, restricted to persons established outside the EC customs territory (see Art. 142 CC, and—with regard to the interpretation of the term 'residence' used in this context—Case 127/86 *Ledoux* [1988] ECR 3741 at p. 3757; Case C-297/89 *Ryborg* [1991] ECR I-1943 at p. I-1974; Case C-262/99 *Louloudakis*, above, at pp. I-5592–3). Where means of transport are temporarily imported, the rules for 'commercial use' are stricter than for 'private use' (see Arts. 555 to 562 CCIP).

The cases in which goods qualify for total relief from import duties are set out in the implementing provisions (Art. 141 CC, Arts. 555 to 578 CCIP). These cases coincide to a large extent with the privileges agreed under the Istanbul Convention (*OJ* 1993 L130/4). Covered are, *inter alia*:

- professional equipment;
- goods for display or use at exhibitions, fairs, etc.;
- teaching aids and scientific equipment;
- disaster relief materials;
- means of transport, pallets, and containers;
- personal effects imported by travellers (see Case C-210/91 *Commission* v. *Greece* [1992] ECR I-6735 at p. I-6750).

In situations not covered by these rules or where the conditions of these provisions are not fulfilled, temporary importation with partial relief may be granted (Art. 142 CC). In such cases, for each month the procedure is used, 3% of the import duties that would have been due under release for free circulation are to be charged, but no more than the total amount of duty liable in case of release for free circulation (Art. 143 CC). Since at the time the goods are placed under the procedure, the precise period of use is not yet known, the customs office enters the import duty in the accounts only once the procedure has been discharged and the amount of duty can be calculated (Art. 218(3) CC); the customs debt is however incurred already at the time the goods are placed under the procedure and this moment determines also the duty rate to be applied (Arts. 211(1)(b) and 214(1) CC).

Though the purpose of the procedure is to re-export the goods after their use (Art. 137 CC), the arrangement may be discharged with any new customs-approved treatment or use (Art. 89 CC). If the goods are released for free circulation or a customs debt is incurred for other reasons, compensatory interest is normally to be paid in order to offset the financial advantage created by the deferment of the date on which the customs duty is paid (Art. 214(3) CC, Art. 519 CCIP).

If a customs debt is incurred with regard to goods that have been placed under the temporary importation procedure, the amount already charged under the rules for partial relief is deducted (Art. 144 CC).

7. **Outward processing** fosters, like inward processing, globalization of production. Whilst under inward processing raw materials and semi-finished products are imported in order to be processed in the customs territory and subsequently be re-exported, under outward processing raw materials and semi-finished products are exported in order to be processed outside the customs territory and re-imported (Art. 145 CC). For the two countries involved in the operations, one of these procedures applies normally. It is even possible to combine both procedures in one country, namely if goods imported under inward processing are temporarily exported in order to undergo processing outside the customs territory. The goods can then be re-imported for further processing and subsequently be re-exported or put to any other customs-approved treatment or use (Art. 123 CC).

The main motives for outward processing are:

- to benefit from lower labour cost outside the Community;
- to benefit from a technology not available in the Community;
- to allow the repair of import goods by a foreign producer;
- to encourage producers in third countries to use Community components, since this lowers the import duty on the final product at re-importation into the Community.

The use of the procedure requires an authorization (Arts. 85 to 87, 147, and 148 CC). The procedure cannot be used for (Art. 146 CC):

- exports giving rise to repayment or remission of import duties;
- goods which have been released for free circulation under the end-use provisions, as long as they are still under these arrangements;
- exports giving rise to the granting of export refunds or other financial advantages under the common agricultural policy.

The authorization is normally granted to the person who arranges the processing operations to be carried out (Art. 147(1) CC). It is, however, possible to grant the authorization to another person if (Art. 147(2) CC):

- goods of Community origin are exported for processing and re-importation, and
- the sale of the export goods is promoted without adversely affecting the essential interests of Community producers of goods similar or identical to the re-import goods.

A typical case in point is the sale of tyres to a foreign car manufacturer who would otherwise use locally produced tyres.

The duty relief at release of the processed (re-imported) goods is normally calculated as follows (Art. 151 CC; see Case C-16/91 *Wacker* [1992] ECR I-6821 at pp. I-6844–5; and Case C-142/96 *Wacker* [1997] ECR I-4649 at pp. I-4666–7):

- as a first step, the amount of duties liable for the re-imported product is calculated according to the general rules;
- as a second step, the amount of duties is calculated for the temporarily exported goods, as if they had been imported from the processing country at the time the re-imported products are released for free circulation (this applies also with regard to agricultural duties, except where otherwise specified, see Case 118/79 *Knauf* [1980] ECR 1183 at pp. 1190–1; anti-dumping and countervailing duties cannot be deducted, Art. 590(1) CCIP); and
- as a third step, the fictitious duty for the export goods is deducted from the duty for the re-imported product.

This calculation method provides an advantage in all those cases where import duties exist for the goods that are to be processed outside the Community. If the temporary export goods are, however, duty free (as in the case of electronic components), there is no duty that can be deducted. An alternative method of duty relief has therefore been introduced that allows the charge of the duty on the valued added outside the customs territory (Art. 153 CC and Art. 591 CCIP). This method can also be used for goods that are repaired outside the customs territory (Art. 153 CC). If the goods are repaired free of charge because of an obligation arising from a guarantee or because of a manufacturing defect, the goods can be re-imported duty free (Art. 152 CC).

In cases of repair, it is also possible to export the defective article and to re-import an equivalent replacement product without this defect; the import may in such cases even take place before the export (Arts. 154 to 159 CC).

8. **Export** is the procedure for Community goods which are to be exported out of the customs territory for other purposes than outward processing. The export declaration must, in principle, be lodged at the customs office responsible for the place where the exporter is established or where the goods are packed or loaded for export shipment—customs office of export (Art. 161(5) CC). This allows the customs authorities to check whether the exit formalities are fulfilled (such as payment of export duties or presentation of an export authorization) on the traders' premises instead of at the frontier (see Case C-371/92 *Ellinika Dimitriaka* [1994] ECR I-2391

at p. I-2431). Subsequently, the goods and the declaration must be presented at the customs office of exit (Art. 793 CCIP). The procedure ends when the goods have left the customs territory. In certain cases, it is sufficient to present and declare the goods at the customs office of exit (Arts. 790, 791, 793(2), and 794 CCIP). Specific rules apply where Community goods are placed under the outward processing or the internal transit procedure and in certain other cases where goods, without being placed under a customs procedure, are under customs supervision (Arts. 161(2) and 164 CC, Arts. 313a to 336, 843 CCIP). Goods subject to export refunds must be declared and presented at the place where they are loaded for export shipment (Art. 5(7) of Comm. Reg. 800/1999, *OJ* 1999 L102/11).

For goods liable to export duties, a customs debt is incurred at the time when

- the customs declaration for export is accepted (Art. 209 CC), or
- the goods leave the customs territory where no customs declaration has been lodged (Art. 210 CC).

Where non-Community goods are brought out of the customs territory, the rules on re-exportation apply (see section VI.1 below).

VI. Other customs-approved treatments or uses

The CC distinguishes between 'customs procedures' and other 'customs-approved treatments or uses'. The main difference between these categories is that goods

- are normally placed under a customs procedure by means of a declaration to that effect (Art. 4 No. 17, Art. 59 CC), and
- can be assigned any other customs-approved treatment or use by a simple act, such as the bringing of goods into a control type I free zone or out of the customs territory (Arts. 169, 170, and 182(1) CC).

Art. 4 No. 15 CC lists the following as 'customs-approved treatments or uses' other than customs procedures:

- entry of goods into a free zone or free warehouse (though Art. 168a CC stipulates for control type II free zones the customs formalities of the customs warehousing procedure);
- re-exportation;
- destruction; and
- abandonment to the Exchequer.

1. Re-exportation covers the removal out of the customs territory of non-Community goods that have previously been brought into the customs territory and have not changed their customs status (Art. 182(1) CC). In so far as measures exist with regard to non-Community goods leaving the customs territory (e.g. authorization requirement—except for goods only transiting through the Community—for dual-use items in accordance with Council Reg. 1334/2000, *OJ* 2000 L159/1), they are to be applied before the exit from the customs territory. The application of certain export measures (e.g. export duties, quantitative restrictions) can be suspended (Art. 182(2)

CC). The CC stipulates a suspension of commercial policy measures for non-Community goods placed under/in:

- temporary storage (Art. 50 CC);
- external transit (Art. 91(1)(a) CC);
- customs warehousing (Art. 98(1)(a) CC);
- the inward processing suspension system (Art. 114(1)(a) CC);
- processing under customs control (Art. 130 CC);
- temporary importation (Art. 137 CC); and
- free zones and free warehouses (Art. 166 CC).

Such suspension does, however, not apply with regard to export restrictions covering goods leaving the customs territory irrespective of their customs status, such as political embargoes (see Art. 509 CCIP with regard to entry into the Community).

In order to facilitate customs supervision of goods leaving the customs territory (Art. 183 CC), they are subjected to the following formalities (Art. 182(3) CC):

- a customs declaration in accordance with the rules for export if the goods have been placed under a customs procedure with economic impact (customs warehousing, inward processing suspension system, processing under customs control, temporary importation), or
- a prior notification in the other cases (re-export from temporary storage, a control type I free zone, or a free warehouse). No re-export formalities are required where the goods are only transhipped through a free zone or where the goods only pass through the customs territory under a transit procedure.

2. Free zones and free warehouses. Under Community legislation (and in difference to many other countries) free zones are part of the customs territory. In such zones (see Art. 166 CC)

- non-Community goods are, in principle, considered as being outside the customs territory for the purposes of import duties; commercial policy measures, in so far as they do not relate to entry into or exit from the Community, are not applied;
- Community goods can already benefit from measures requiring export (e.g. export refunds, repayment of import duties under the inward processing drawback system, see also Art. 128(1) CC).

The same treatment is accorded to free warehouses, i.e. authorized premises in the customs territory.

As in the case of customs warehouses, the application of import duties and commercial policy measures is suspended (fiscal legislation also provides for a suspension of VAT and excise duties). Further advantages of free zones are that they allow:

- concentration of foreign trade through controllable channels;
- facilitation of customs supervision by isolating the free zone from the rest of the customs territory;

- concentration of staff as well as of storage and distribution facilities, thus creating economies for the country concerned and fostering regional development.

Apart from storage of the goods, the following activities can be performed in a free zone or free warehouse (Arts. 173 and 174 CC):

- usual forms of handling without authorization;
- inward processing under the conditions of that procedure (including the granting of an authorization, special rules are stipulated with regard to the examination of economic conditions in certain free zones);
- processing under customs control under the conditions of that procedure;
- the use of non-Community goods in accordance with the rules for temporary importation under the conditions of that procedure;
- destruction and, where national legislation provides for it, abandonment to the Exchequer.

In addition, non-Community goods can be released for free circulation, including under the provisions for end-use (Art. 82 CC).

Goods can be exported or re-exported from a free zone or free warehouse under the export procedure or the provisions on re-exportation (Art. 177 CC). Non-Community goods remaining on their means of transport or being transhipped (this may include a short-term storage) are or can be exempted from the notification requirement (Arts. 811 and 814 CCIP).

When goods are brought into another part of the Community customs territory, the rules on entry of goods into the customs territory (Arts. 37 to 57 CC) apply, except in the case of goods leaving by sea or air without being placed under a customs procedure. If a customs debt is incurred in respect of non-Community goods (e.g. because of release for free circulation), the value added in the free zone or free warehouse may be disregarded at the request of the declarant (Art. 178 CC).

Community legislation distinguishes between two types of free zones:

- control type I free zones, in which customs supervision is principally based on controls of a fence or wall around the zone, as well as the entry and exit points (Art. 168 CC, Art. 799(a) CCIP), and
- control type II free zones, in which customs checks and formalities are principally carried out and the customs debt is incurred according to the rules of the customs warehousing procedure (Art. 168a CC, Art. 799(b) CCIP).

Whilst goods brought into the customs territory are, from the time of their entry, subjected to customs supervision (Art. 37(1) CC) and must be conveyed without delay to the designated customs office or other place (Art. 38(1)(a) CC), goods in control type I free zones and free warehouses are exempted from such supervision (Art. 37(2) CC). Furthermore, goods brought into such a free zone directly

- by sea or air, or
- by land without passing through another part of the customs territory where the free zone adjoins the external frontier

are exempted from the obligation to be conveyed to the designated customs office or other place (Art. 38(1)(b) CC).

The main attraction of control type I free zones is the absence of customs formalities:

- on entry;
- for the storage, transport, and usual forms of handling of non-Community goods in the free zone; and
- on exit to third countries if the goods are only transhipped.

In exchange for the absence of customs formalities and the lack of customs supervision inside a control type I free zone or a free warehouse, their perimeter and entry and exit points are subjected to customs supervision (Art. 168 CC).

Apart from occasional checks by the customs authorities, goods entering into a control type I free zone need not be presented to customs, nor need a customs declaration be lodged (Art. 170(1) CC). Exceptions to this principle concern cases where (Art. 170(2) CC):

- a customs procedure is discharged,
- remission or repayment of import duties is sought,
- Community goods benefit from measures attached to export, such as export refunds.

Apart from such activities, consumption and use of non-Community goods or Community goods benefiting from export measures are prohibited (Art. 175 CC); in case of non-compliance, a customs debt is incurred (Art. 205 CC). Persons carrying out activities in a free zone or free warehouse must keep records in order to allow the customs authorities to identify the goods and their movements (Art. 176(1) CC). Transhipments and short-term storage (up to three days) in a free zone are exempted from this obligation (Art. 176(2) CC). The main disadvantage of control type I free zones concerns the treatment of Community goods: whilst it is normally assumed that goods in the customs territory have Community status, the burden of proof is reversed in such free zones (Art. 313 CCIP).

This disadvantage is avoided in control type II free zones where:

- non-Community goods or Community goods benefiting from export refunds are placed under the arrangements by means of a customs declaration, and
- other Community goods can be stored in the zone without a need to prove their status when they leave the zone.

A list of Community free zones of either type is published in *OJ* 2002 C50/16.

3. Destruction, abandonment. In certain cases imported goods turn out to be without use for the importer, for example because:

- they are defective and it would be too costly to send them back to the exporter (see Art. 238 CC), or
- the client of the importer refuses to take the merchandise and no other client can be found (in certain cases an invalidation of the customs declaration, and a repayment or remission of the duties is possible if the goods are re-exported, see Arts. 251(1b) and 900(1)(d) (i) CCIP).

In order to avoid payment of import duties, the goods can be destroyed or abandoned to the Exchequer, where national provisions to this effect exist (Art. 182 CC). If waste or scrap results from the destruction, it has to be assigned a customs-approved treatment or use (according to the Common Customs Tariff, most waste and scrap is, however, duty free, so that it can be entered for free circulation without payment of import duties).

VII. Customs debt, security

The Community Customs Tariff (*see further under* **Common Customs Tariff (CCT)**) defines the goods subject to import or export duties and the rate to be applied; under certain circumstances partial or total duty relief is granted (see section V.1 above). Wherever an import or export duty is due, the person obliged to pay the duty has to be established and the payment of the duty has to be secured. This is the purpose of the rules on customs debt and security (with regard to Member States' obligation to establish the Community's own resources, to collect them, to credit them to the Commission's account, and to take effective measures against fraud, see Case 68/88 *Commission* v. *Greece* [1989] ECR 2965 at pp. 2983–6; Case C-96/89 *Commission* v. *Netherlands* [1991] ECR I-2461 at pp. I-2493–7). The principle of legal certainty requires that rules imposing charges on the taxpayer be clear and precise so that he may know without ambiguity what are his rights and obligations and take steps accordingly (Case 169/80 *Gondrand* [1981] ECR 1931; Cases 92/87 etc. *Commission* v. *France and United Kingdom* [1989] ECR 405 at p. 443).

The CC distinguishes two types of situations under which a customs debt can be incurred:

- the placement of goods under a procedure or any other act in compliance with customs legislation which entails the payment of customs duties (release for free circulation, temporary importation with partial relief, exportation, validation of preferential export documents for goods under the inward processing procedure); in such cases, the debt is incurred at the time when the declaration is accepted or the preferential export document is validated; the debtor is the declarant, the person who provided information to him, and—in the event of indirect representation—the person on whose behalf the declaration is made (Arts. 201, 209, and 216 CC);
- non-compliance with customs legislation, such as the unlawful

introduction into or removal from the customs territory, the unlawful removal from customs supervision, the non-fulfilment of obligations or the non-compliance with certain conditions; in such cases the customs debt is incurred at the time the act of non-compliance has taken place; the debtor is the person who committed the act of non-compliance, but also those who participated or held the goods and were aware or should reasonably have been aware of the act of non-compliance and, where appropriate, also the person responsible for fulfilling the non-respected obligation (Arts. 202 to 205 and 210 CC).

Payment of a customs debt may also be requested from a guarantor who has undertaken to pay the secured amount of a customs debt (Arts. 193 and 195 CC). Though several grounds for a customs debt being incurred may exist, it has to be paid only once (Case 252/87 *Kiwall*, above, at p. 4766).

Under certain circumstances, in spite of non-compliance with customs legislation, no customs debt is incurred or it may be totally or partially waived or the duties may be repaid or remitted. This concerns cases where:

- it is established that the failure to fulfil one of the conditions or obligations relating to the outward processing procedure has no significant effect on the correct operation of the procedure (Art. 150(2) CC);
- it is established that the failure to fulfil one of the obligations arising from the temporary storage of goods or the use of a customs procedure or to comply with a condition governing the placing of goods under the procedure or concerning the end-use of the goods had no significant effect on the correct operation of the procedure in question (Art. 204(1) CC, Arts. 859 and 860 CCIP);
- the non-fulfilment of certain obligations results from the total destruction or irretrievable loss of the goods as a result of the actual nature of the goods or unforeseeable circumstances or *force majeure*, or as a consequence of authorization by the customs authorities (Art. 206(1) CC);
- counterfeit currency, narcotic drugs, or psychotropic substances are entered outside the economic circuit (Art. 212 CC, this is a consequence of Case 50/80 *Horvath* [1981] ECR 385 and Case C-343/89 *Witzemann* [1990] ECR I-4477 at pp. I-4495–6);
- a failure to comply with the conditions for favourable tariff treatment in accordance with Arts. 21 and 82, the rules for outward processing (Art. 145 CC) or duty relief (Arts. 184 to 187 CC) implies neither fraudulent dealing nor manifest negligence and the person concerned produces evidence that the other conditions for the application of favourable tariff treatment, relief or exemption have been satisfied (Art. 212a CC);
- in spite of the amount legally due no customs duty or a lower customs duty has been collected and a post clearance recovery is excluded because of binding tariff or origin information or because of an error on the part of the customs authorities which could not reasonably have been detected by the person liable for payment, as long as he has acted

in good faith and complied with all the provisions regarding the customs declaration (Art. 220 CC, Arts. 869 to 876a CCIP, see, for example, Case C-64/89 *Deutsche Fernsprecher* [1990] ECR I-2535 at p. I-2557; Case C-80/89 *Behn* [1990] ECR I-2659 at pp. I-2677–8; Case C-348/89 *Mecanarte* [1991] ECR I-3277 at pp. I-3306–8; Case C-47/95 *Olasagasti* [1996] ECR I-6579 at p. I-6605; Case C-251/00 *Ilumitrónica* [2002] ECR I-10433);

- special circumstances exist in which no deception or obvious negligence may be attributed to the person concerned (Art. 239 CC, Arts. 900 to 904 CCIP), for example because the legal situation was unclear (Case C-38/95 *Foods Import* [1996] ECR I-6543 at p. I-6575) or serious failures have been committed by the customs authorities or the Commission (Case T-42/96 *Eyckeler & Malt* v. *Commission* [1998] ECR II-401 at pp. II-445–51; Cases T–186/97 etc. *Kaufring* v. *Commission* [2001] ECR II-1337 at pp. II-1420–32).

A customs debt is extinguished (Arts. 233 and 234 CC):

- by payment of the duty;
- by remission (this is defined in Art. 235 CC as 'a decision to waive all or part of the amount of a customs debt or a decision to render void an entry in the accounts of all or part of an amount of import or export duty which has not been paid');
- by invalidation of the customs declaration (see Art. 66 CC, Art. 251 CCIP) or the formalities for preferential treatment in a third country (see Art. 216 CC);
- by seizure, destruction, irretrievable loss, or abandonment before the release of the goods (see Arts. 56, 57 and 75 CC).

Furthermore, no customs debt can be charged after the expiry of a period of three years from the date on which a customs debt was incurred, where no act that could give rise to criminal court proceedings is involved (Art. 221(3) and (4) CC, see Case C-273/90 *Meico-Fell* [1991] ECR I-5569 at p. I-5587).

Under certain conditions, duties may be repaid or remitted, notably because:

- such duties were not legally owed or should not have been entered in the accounts, for example because the amount exceeds that determined on the basis of binding tariff or origin information or because an error has occurred (Arts. 236 and 237 CC), not however in cases where the importer makes deliberately false declarations which lead to the determination of a duty higher than that which he should have paid (Case 328/85 *Deutsche Babcock* [1987] ECR 5119 at p. 5140);
- the goods were defective or did not comply with the terms of the import contract at the time the customs declaration was accepted, and the goods are exported again (Art. 238 CC);
- special circumstances existed in which no deception or obvious negligence may be attributed to the person concerned (Art. 239 CC, see Case 160/84 *Oryzomyli Kavallas* v. *Commission* [1986] ECR 1633 at pp. 1648–9; Cases C-121/91 etc. *CT Control* v. *Commission* [1993]

ECR I-3873 at pp. I-3910–14; Case C-446/93 *SEIM* [1996] ECR I-73 at pp. I-112–15).

Where a customs debt has been remitted or the corresponding amount of duty repaid in error, the original debt becomes payable again, once the previous decision has been revoked or amended (Art. 9 CC), and provided the provisions on the protection of good faith (Art. 220(2)(b) CC) do not apply (Art. 242 CC).

VIII. Appeals

Persons affected by a decision of customs authorities may lodge an appeal:

- initially before the customs authorities, unless national law gives direct access to a court (see Case C-1/99 *Kofisa* [2001] ECR I-207 at pp. I-242–4), and
- subsequently before an independent court (Art. 243 CC).

An appeal can also be lodged if the customs authorities have not decided within the deadlines upon an application for a decision (Art. 6 CC; this general provision on decisions, does however not fix a precise deadline). Appeals against decisions taken on the basis of criminal law are governed by national legislation (Art. 246 CC).

An appeal as such does not suspend the application of the disputed decision; the customs authorities shall, however, suspend implementation where they have good reason to believe that the decision is inconsistent with customs legislation or that irreparable damage is to be feared for the person concerned (Art. 244 CC). Normally, a security is required if duties are suspended, except where this would cause serious economic or social difficulties for the debtor (see Case C-130/95 *Giloy* [1997] ECR I-4291 at p. I-4306).

See also **Common Customs Tariff, Community Customs Code, Community customs territory.**

Further reading 1. Books: Berr and Trémeau, *Le droit douanier*, 5th edn. (2001), p. 172; Giffoni, *Droit douanier de la CE et aspects économiques* (1993); Lux, *Guide to Community Customs Legislation* (2002), p. 241; id., *Das Zollrecht der EG* (2004), chs. VIII to XVII; Lyons, *EC Customs Law* (2001), p. 291; Prahl, *Le droit douanier* (1997); Snyder, *International Trade and Customs Law of the European Union* (1998), p. 71; Walsh, *The Customs Code of the European Union* (1997); Witte and Wolffgang, *Lehrbuch des Europäischen Zollrechts*, 4th edn. (2003), p. 76.

2. Article: Lux, 'Free Zones in the European Community' (1999) *Journal of the Flagstaff Institute* 19.

► **CUSTOMS UNION** This term is defined as the joining together of several countries (or more precisely: customs territories) which undertake:

- to refrain from applying to one another customs duties and other trade restrictions, and
- to apply to countries outside the union a common external customs

tariff and a common system of other trade rules (e.g. with regard to quantitative import restrictions).

A customs union is a form of economic integration limited to trade in goods. A common or internal market includes also the abolition of barriers for the movement of persons, services, and capital between the members of the union and the introduction of common rules for such matters with regard to countries outside the union. A common or internal market is destined to eliminate also barriers on the movement of goods that exist for other motives than trade or economic policy, such as restrictions for the protection of the health of people, animals, and plants or the protection of intellectual property rights. Furthermore, it combats trade distortions and discrimination in areas such as competition, subsidies, or taxation.

A customs union also needs rules on how the revenue from customs duties is distributed to its members or transferred to a common institution, as well as a decision-making procedure for laying down common rules for its external protection. In case of divergent application of such rules or disputes between its members, a mechanism for resolving such issues must exist.

A free-trade area has as a common feature with a customs union the abolition of customs duties and other trade restrictions between its members; the difference being that the members of a free-trade area retain autonomy for laying down their external tariff and other trade measures towards countries not belonging to this area. In a free-trade area it is essential to limit the preferential treatment to goods produced or substantially processed in one or several of the member countries (originating goods, *see further under* **Origin of goods**), since otherwise goods from outside the area could be imported via the most liberal member and thus avoid the external protection of the other members of the free-trade area.

A customs union with a common system of external protection can afford free movement of goods between its members both for goods originating in a member country and for goods imported from a country outside the union once the customs duties and other trade formalities (which are common for all member countries) have been applied. Import goods for which the customs duties and other import formalities have not been applied can, of course, also move between the members of the union, but this would take place under a suspensive customs procedure (e.g. transit, inward processing) and the goods would remain under customs supervision (*see further under* **Customs procedures**, section V).

I. International law

Art. XXIV GATT stipulates minimum standards for customs unions and free-trade areas. A customs union is defined as the substitution of a single customs territory (*see further under* **Community customs territory**) for two or more customs territories so that:

- between the members of the union customs duties and other trade restrictions on economic grounds are eliminated with respect to substantially all the trade in goods originating in any member country, and

- with regard to countries outside the union substantially the same customs duties and other trade restrictions on economic grounds are applied.

This definition allows exceptions both for trade between the members and in respect of non-member countries. A further exception concerns agreements aiming at the formation of a customs union: the condition that substantially all the trade is covered by common rules need not be fulfilled immediately, as long as the contracting parties have agreed a plan and a schedule towards this aim within a reasonable length of time. A 'reasonable length of time' should exceed ten years only in exceptional cases (Understanding on Art. XXIV GATT, *OJ* 1994 L336/16).

In order to avoid that other WTO members suffer from the formation of a customs union, Art. XXI(5) GATT stipulates that the customs duties and other external trade restrictions of the union shall not on the whole be higher or more restrictive than the general incidence of such measures prior to the formation of the union. This evaluation shall be based upon an overall assessment of weighted average tariff rates and of customs duties collected, broken down for a previous representative period on a tariff-line basis and in values, quantities, and by origin (Understanding on Art. XXIV GATT, above).

The introduction of a common customs tariff and a common system for other trade restrictions may lead with regard to certain goods from certain countries to an increase of the customs duties or to a more restrictive trade regime. Art. XXIV(6) GATT provides therefore for a procedure allowing WTO members to maintain their advantages. This will normally be achieved through negotiations which must commence before the tariff concession is withdrawn or modified. In such negotiations due account will be taken of reductions on duties on the same tariff line made by other constituents of the customs union upon its formation (Understanding on Art. XXIV GATT, above). Should such reductions not be sufficient, the customs union has to offer compensation, which may take the form of duty reductions on other tariff lines. If within a reasonable period of time, no agreement is reached, the customs union may nevertheless modify or withdraw a concession agreed by one of its members; the affected WTO member is then free to withdraw substantially equivalent concessions previously agreed under the WTO rules. In this context the WTO dispute settlement procedure (*OJ* 1994 L336/234) may be invoked.

A free-trade area is defined in Art. XXIV GATT as an agreement between two or more countries which—albeit maintaining their separate customs territory and their autonomy for customs and commercial policy—undertake to eliminate customs duties and other trade restrictions on economic grounds on substantially all the trade between the constituent territories in products originating in such territories. A free-trade area may be created by an interim agreement, if it includes a plan and schedule for its formation within a reasonable length of time (normally no more than ten years, see Understanding on Art. XXIV GATT, above).

The obligation stipulated in Art. I GATT, according to which duty reductions granted to one country must be extended to any WTO member (most-favoured-nation treatment), does not apply with regard to preferences between members of a customs union, free-trade area, or an interim agreement leading to the formation of such a union or area.

II. The Treaty provisions

1. The EC Treaty. The EC is a customs union, as stated in Art. 23 EC. Nevertheless, the term 'customs union' is not defined in the Treaty, but taken for granted. This can be considered as an implicit reference to Art. XXIV GATT. Art. 23 EC emphasizes however two particularly important aspects of the EC customs union:

1. the prohibition between Member States of customs duties and charges having equivalent effect both on imports and exports (since the inception of the single market the terms 'import' and 'export' are normally reserved for trade with non-Member States; for intra-Community trade, terms like 'supplies' and 'acquisition' or 'dispatch of goods' are used);
2. the adoption of a common customs tariff in relations with third countries.

The plan and schedule for the formation of the customs union as required by Art. XXIV GATT has been set out in:

- Arts. 12 to 17 of the original EEC Treaty with regard to the abolition of customs duties and charges having equivalent effect between Member States;
- Arts. 18 to 26 EEC for the introduction of the common customs tariff;
- Arts. 30 to 35 EEC with regard to the abolition of quantitative restrictions and measures having equivalent effect; and
- Arts. 110 to 116 EEC for the introduction of a common commercial policy.

This overview shows that the founders of the EEC took great care to respect the GATT rules for customs unions. Furthermore, they expressed in Arts. 18 and 110 EEC [now Art. 131 EC] their intention to reduce barriers to international trade. With the entry into force of the Amsterdam Treaty, the transitional provisions covering the time until 31 December 1969 were repealed. The customs union between the original Member States was completed on 1 July 1968 (see Gen. Rep. EC (1968), p. 21).

2. The ECSC Treaty. While the EC Treaty juxtaposes the concepts of a 'common' or 'internal market' and a 'customs union', the ECSC Treaty only used the expression 'common market'. Art. 4 ECSC prohibited within the Community import and export duties or charges having equivalent effect, as well as quantitative restrictions. As with the EC Treaty, the principle of free intra-Community movement applied not only to products originating in the Member States, but also to goods from third countries that had been entered for free circulation in a Member State. Exceptions from this basic principle were allowed only in the cases specified in the Treaty (Case 36/83 *Mabanaft* [1984] ECR 2497 at pp. 2523–4).

Unlike the EC Treaty, the ECSC Treaty shared responsibility for regulating trade with third countries between the Community and the Member States:

- The Community could set minimum and maximum customs duties (Art. 72 ECSC), co-ordinate the administration and control of import and export licences (Art. 73(2) ECSC), and adopt protective measures against dumping, subsidies, or price undercutting, including quantitative restrictions (Art. 74 ECSC).
- The Member States remained responsible for the other aspects of commercial policy, taking into account international obligations, such as the GATT rules (Art. 71(1) and (2) ECSC). The Community could, however propose mutual assistance measures (Art. 71(3) ECSC), or invoke the general enabling clause of the Treaty, which allowed the adoption of measures necessary to attain one of the objectives of the Community (Art. 95 ECSC).

On the basis of these provisions and the subsequent entry into force of the EC Treaty, the ECJ concluded that:

- the ECSC was not a free-trade area, but more akin in its structure to the principle of a customs union (Case 36/83 *Mabanaft*, above, at p. 3523);
- Art. 133 EC empowered the Community to conclude commercial policy agreements for all types of goods, including ECSC products (Opinion 1/94 [1994] ECR I-5267 at p. I-5396);
- in the absence of specific rules for ECSC products customs legislation was to be based on the provisions of the EC Treaty (Case 239/84 *Gerlach* [1985] ECR 3507 at p. 3517; Case 328/85 *Deutsche Babcock* [1987] ECR 5119 at p. 5139).

Since the expiry of the ECSC Treaty on 24 July 2002, only the EC Treaty is applicable to the former ECSC goods.

3. The Euratom Treaty. Since the Euratom Treaty contains no specific provisions relating to the customs union for the time after the transitional period (see Arts. 93 to 95 Euratom), the relevant provisions of the EC Treaty apply also with respect to goods covered by the Treaty establishing the European Atomic Energy Community (Art. 305(2) EC).

III. Customs union and free-trade agreements concluded by the Community

Currently customs union agreements between the Community and a third country are operational with:

- Turkey (Dec. 1/95 of the EC–Turkey Association Council, *OJ* 1996 L35/1);
- Andorra (Council Dec. 90/680, *OJ* 1990 L374/13); and
- San Marino (Council Dec. 92/561, *OJ* 1992 L359/13).

The customs union with Turkey being the most important one, the common features and differences with the EC customs union will be summarized with regard to the EC–Turkey agreement:

- First of all, Turkey is not a member of the EC customs union; instead, Turkey forms a customs union with the EC. The rules in force in the EC are therefore as such not applicable in Turkey. The legal basis for the EC–Turkey customs union is the agreement between the two partners, including the decisions taken by the committees competent for managing the Agreement (see Case C-192/89 *Sevince* [1990] ECR I-3461 at pp. I-3502–4; Case C-188/91 *Deutsche Shell* [1993] ECR I-363 at p. I-389), and supplemented by parallel Turkish and EC legislation. Nevertheless, the customs tariff and the commercial policy measures of both partners are to a large extent identical with regard to the products covered by the customs union agreement. Where these rules are not the same (as in the area of anti-dumping duties), measures imposed for goods originating in specific countries can be applied even if such goods have been in free circulation in the partner country of the customs union.
- Progress achieved in the EC (such as the abolition of frontier controls for intra-Community movement of goods) is applied between the EC and Turkey only where this is provided for in the Agreement (this means, for example, that for Turkish goods their status has to be proved on entry into the Community and vice versa, whereas this formality has been abolished for goods dispatched from one EC Member State to another).
- The EC customs union relieves all types of goods that are in free circulation from internal barriers; the EC–Turkey customs union excludes the former ECSC goods and agricultural products from the free circulation principle; with respect to former ECSC goods and certain agricultural products, a free-trade agreement exists, according to which the origin in Turkey or the EC has to be proved.
- In so far as the EC–Turkey customs union stipulates the abolition of customs duties and charges having equivalent effect as well as quantitative restrictions and measures having equivalent effect, the interpretation of the corresponding prohibitions in intra-Community trade can be applied (see, with regard to a free-trade agreement, Case C-163/90 *Legros* [1992] ECR I-4625 at pp. I-4668–9), except where provisions of the single market go beyond the free trade agreed with a third country, as with regard to fiscal harmonization (Case C-312/91 *Metalsa* [1993] ECR I-3751 at p. I-3774).

Mutual free trade for most products originating in the partner countries has been agreed with:

- Iceland, Liechtenstein, and Norway under the European Economic Area Treaty;
- Switzerland and the Faeroe Islands;
- Bulgaria and Romania;

- Albania, Croatia, and Macedonia;
- almost all Mediterranean countries (Algeria, Egypt, Israel, Jordan, Lebanon, Morocco, Palestine, Syria, Tunisia);
- Chile, Mexico, and South Africa.

The current agreement with the ACP countries constitutes a unilateral free-trade area in that only ACP products are granted preferences (*see further under* **Common Customs Tariff (CCT)**, section IV.1).

The common features of the mutual free-trade areas can be summarized as follows:

- First of all, the partners of such an agreement are not members of the EC internal market, instead they mutually engage not to apply customs duties and charges with equivalent effect, quantitative restrictions, and measures having equivalent effect for the goods covered by the agreement. These principles are implemented through legislation on either side, and—in certain cases—decisions of the Association or Co-operation Council. With regard to the European Economic Area, most rules concerning the internal market and decisions of the ECJ are also applicable in Iceland, Liechtenstein, and Norway. Similar arrangements have been concluded with Switzerland.
- Whilst the EC internal market covers trade in all goods and irrespective of their origin in the Community or a third country, the free-trade arrangements exclude certain agricultural goods. Furthermore, only goods originating in one or several of the partner countries can benefit from the preference. The rules agreed allow, however, cumulating the use of components from and processing performed in the EC, the EEA, Switzerland, Bulgaria, Romania, and Turkey in order to confer preferential origin. A no-draw-back rule ensures that customs duties are paid on components from outside the interconnected preferential areas. This system is called 'pan-European cumulation'.
- Both the Community and its partners of the free-trade agreements maintain their own customs tariff and other commercial policy measures with regard to third countries. In order to allow for pan-European cumulation, partners of the EC must, however, conclude among each other free-trade agreements.
- The interpretation of the rules prohibiting customs duties and charges having equivalent effect as well as quantitative restrictions and measures having equivalent effect is, in principle, the same as within the EC, except where the rules of the single market go beyond those agreed with the relevant country.

See also **Common Customs Tariff, Community customs territory, Customs procedures, Origin of goods.**

Further reading 1. BOOKS: Dam, *The GATT: Law and International Economic Organization* (1970); Eeckhout, *The European Internal Market and International Trade* (1994); Jackson, *World Trade and the Law of the GATT: A Legal Analysis of the General Agreement on Tariffs and*

Trade (1969); Jackson, *The World Trading System: Law and Policy of International Economic Relations* (1989); Hilf, Jacobs, and Petersmann (eds.), *The European Community and GATT* (1986); Lipsey, *The Theory of Customs Unions: A General Equilibrium Analysis* (1970); Lux, *Guide to Community Customs Legislation* (2002), pp. 14 and 25; id., *Das Zollrecht der EG* (2004), chs. I and II; Lyons, *EC Customs Law* (2001), p. 21; Long, *Law and its Limitations in the GATT Unilateral System* (1985); Prieß and Berrisch, *WTO-Handbuch* (2003); Robson, *The Economics of International Integration*, 3rd edn. (1987).

2. ARTICLE: Devuyst, 'GATT Customs Union Provisions and the Uruguay Round: The European Community Experience' (1992) *Journal of World Trade* 15.

▶ **CUSTOMS VALUE** is the basis for calculating customs duties that are levied as a percentage of the value of imported goods. Such *ad valorem* duties have the following advantages:

- It corresponds to the principles of equity and free competition that a trader who negotiates a lower price than his competitors also pays lower duties and is not punished by the higher prices his competitors pay. From a consumer's point of view, it is also more equitable that those who can afford to acquire high priced goods pay higher duties.
- In case of inflation or deflation the duty follows automatically the rise or fall in prices, so that frequent adaptations of the customs tariff can be avoided.
- International trade negotiations are facilitated if only percentages (instead of duty rates linked to a national currency) are used. The same applies for the consultation of foreign customs tariffs. For the purposes of transparency and in order to avoid arbitrary valuation methods, internationally agreed valuation rules are needed, too.

The main disadvantages of *ad valorem* duties are the following:

- It is more difficult to determine the value of an article than, for example, applying a duty based on the weight of the good. The risk of fraud (e.g. through the use of false invoices) is also greater if the relevant criteria cannot be established on the basis of the characteristics of the article.
- In case of a recession the home market may need greater import protection (i.e. a higher duty). With falling prices the amount of import duties—and therefore the external protection—decreases however.
- In case of domestic inflation cheap imports could help to combat price increases. If, however, there is a rise in price of import goods, an *ad valorem* duty will inflate the price level even more.

Notably in order to be less exposed to the fluctuation of prices and to ensure a minimum protection, the common agricultural policy uses mainly duties based on weight (specific duties).

In theory, there are two options for establishing the value of goods. One can use either:

- the normal or 'national' value, i.e. the price normally paid on the market (this can either be the world market or the market of the import country), or
- the price actually paid for the import goods.

Both systems have been used worldwide and only with the conclusion of the GATT Tokyo Round in 1979 has the latter method been internationally recognized as a system that better follows commercial realities and makes duty collection less arbitrary than a theoretical or national value concept.

I. International law

Already during conferences held under the auspices of the League of Nations in Geneva in 1927 and 1930, trade negotiators were aware that duty concessions agreed between different countries could be hampered by arbitrary or protectionist valuation rules (e.g. by using the price in the import country instead of the actual price, as in the case of the American selling price system). In 1947 for the first time an international rule could be established with regard to valuation for customs purposes through the insertion of Art. VII GATT. It stipulates that the customs value should be based on the actual value of the imported or of like merchandise and should not be based on the value of merchandise of national origin or on arbitrary or fictitious values. The 'actual value' is defined as the price at which, at a time and place to be determined by the legislation of the import country, such or like merchandise is sold or offered for sale in the ordinary course of trade under fully competitive conditions. This definition allows in fact both a theoretical value concept (as long as it is not based on home market prices and is not arbitrary) and valuation based on the actual price. A protocol provided furthermore that contracting parties are not obliged to change their valuation legislation in force in 1947 if it is not in conformity with these rules (as the American selling price system). In 1949 the Convention on the valuation of goods for customs purposes was created under the auspices of the Customs Co-operation Council (now: World Customs Organization). This Convention was, *inter alia*, adopted by the founding members of the EC, and is still used by some developing countries that are not WTO members. The convention is not actively promoted any longer and countries party to it are few in number. According to Art. I of the Convention, the normal price is to be used for the establishment of the dutiable value, i.e.

- the price made under a contract of sale in respect of sale in respect of the imported goods,
- concluded in the open market,
- between a buyer and a seller independent of each other,
- at the time the goods become payable.

The price of the contract shall:

- be based on delivery of the goods to the buyer at the place of their introduction into the import country,

- include all selling expenses incidental to the sale and delivery at the place of introduction,
- exclude any taxes or duties on importation.

Following the adoption of the GATT Valuation Agreement (*OJ* 1980 L71/107) the Community has shifted its valuation rules from the normal value to a primarily 'transaction value' concept. The current version of this Agreement was adopted at the end of the Uruguay Round and is obligatory for all WTO members (*OJ* 1994 L336/119).

It stipulates six methods of valuation that have to be applied in hierarchical order (except for methods 4 and 5, which may be reversed at the request of the importer):

- step 1: the transaction value, i.e. the price actually paid or payable for the goods when sold for export to the country of importation, taking into account certain adjustments (Arts. 1 and 8);
- step 2: the transaction value of identical goods sold for export to the same country of importation and exported at or about the same time as the goods being valued (Arts. 2 and 8);
- step 3: the transaction value of similar goods sold for export to the same country of importation and exported at or about the same time as the goods being valued (Arts. 3 and 8);
- step 4: the deducted value, i.e. the unit price at which the imported goods or identical or similar imported goods are sold in the greatest aggregate quantity, at or about the time of the importation of the goods being valued, subject to deductions for
  - — commissions usually paid,
  - — the usual costs of transport, insurance, and associated costs,
  - — customs duties and other taxes payable on importation (Arts. 5 and 8);
- step 5: the computed value, i.e. the cost or value of materials and processing, an amount for usual profit, general, and other expenses (Arts. 6 and 8);
- step 6: a reasonable method consistent with the Agreement and on the basis of data available in the country of importation, excluding, *inter alia*, domestic selling prices and minimum values (Art. 7).

II. Community law

1. The Treaty provisions. According to Art. 23 EC, the Community is based on a customs union that is implemented, in so far as relations with third countries are concerned, by means of a common customs tariff. Furthermore, Art. 133 EC calls for a common commercial policy, which includes duty rates and trade agreements. A customs tariff with *ad valorem* duty rates cannot be implemented without provisions about how to establish the customs value. The rules on customs valuation are set out in an international trade agreement. Consequently, Art. 133 EC is the primary legal basis for Community legislation on the customs value (Council Reg. 1224/80, *OJ* 1980 L134/1, now superseded by the Customs Code, was based on this Article; Community competence in this matter was already confirmed in Case 8/73 *Massey-Ferguson* [1973] ECR 897 at p. 907).

2. Customs valuation rules. The Community provisions for the determination of the customs value are set out in Arts. 28 to 36 of the Customs Code—CC (Council Reg. 2913/92, *OJ* 1992 L302/1) and Arts. 141 to 181 and Annexes 23 to 29 of its implementing provisions—CCIP (Comm. Reg. 2454/93, *OJ* 1993 L253/1). They follow closely the WTO Valuation Agreement.

These valuation rules are applicable with regard to (see Art. 28 CC):

- the customs duties of the EC customs tariff (*see further under* **Common Customs Tariff (CCT)**);
- the determination of values in the context of origin rules, in so far as the value added or a minimum content of domestic products determines the origin (*see further under* **Origin of goods**);
- import or export quotas fixed according to the value of goods (see Council Reg. 520/94, *OJ* 1994 L66/1);
- external trade statistics (Council Reg. 1172/95, *OJ* 1995 L118/10).

Individual regulations may, however, determine special rules, i.e. in the area of anti-dumping or agricultural duties (see Case C-422/00 *Capespan* [2003] ECR I-597). Anti-dumping duties charging the difference between a minimum price and the—lower—export price are normally levied on the basis of the Community free-at-frontier price in order to avoid that costs being incurred on the Community territory and not shown separately from the price actually paid or payable (e.g. transport, insurance, handling of the goods) increase the price and thus reduce the amount of anti-dumping duty. Apart from this aspect, the customs valuation rules of the Customs Code can be applied in the absence of specific provisions in the anti-dumping regulation (Case C-93/96 *ICT* [1997] ECR I-2881 at p. I-2896).

The value established for customs purposes is also used with regard to the taxable amount of value added tax on importation; however, some special rules apply, notably in order to include the import duties and the transport cost inside the Community in the taxable amount (Art. 11(B) of Council Dir. 77/388, *OJ* 1977 L145/1).

3. The transaction value is the starting point for establishing the customs value (Arts. 29, 32, and 33 CC). Only when this value cannot be applied, recourse to other valuation methods is possible. The transaction value is defined as 'the price actually paid or payable for the goods when sold for export to the customs territory of the Community' (Art. 29(1) CC), adjusted by certain costs that have to be added (Art. 32 CC) or which may be deducted (Art. 33 CC). The 'price actually paid or payable' is the total payment made or to be made by the buyer to or for the benefit of the seller for the imported goods and includes all payments made or to be made as a condition of the sale; payments may be made by way of letters of credit or negotiable instrument and may be made directly or indirectly (Art. 30(3)(a) CC).

Amounts paid for certificates of authenticity are regarded as an integral and dutiable part of the contract for the value for customs purposes since they concern directly the imported good (Case C-219/88 *Malt* [1990] ECR I-1481 at pp. I-1500–1). This is not the case with regard to charges for export quota licences paid to another person than the seller since they are not directly linked to the imported goods, irrespective whether such transactions are legal in the export country or not (Case 7/83 *Ospig* [1984] ECR 609 at pp. 618–19; Case C-29/93 *Ospig* [1994] ECR I-1963 at p. I-1978). If, however, the seller himself is entitled to an export quota and increases his price because of that, this element is part of the 'price actually paid or payable' (Case C-340/93 *Thierschmidt* [1994] ECR I-3905 at p. I-3925). Weighing costs incurred by the buyer on his own account do not form part of the 'price actually paid or payable', since they cannot be regarded as of benefit to the seller (Case 65/85 *Van Houten* [1986] ECR 447 at p. 456). Marketing, warranty, and other activities undertaken by the buyer on his own account are in principle not considered to be an indirect payment to the seller (Art. 30(3)(b) CC).

The condition that the goods are 'sold for export to the customs territory of the Community' is deemed to be fulfilled when they are declared for free circulation in the Community. In the case of sequential (successive) sales before introduction into the EU the last sale is taken, except in cases where a declarant can prove that an earlier sale was in reality a sale intended for export to the EU. Prices resulting from sales after the sale by the exporter may be taken as a basis for valuation, even if buyer and seller are established in the Community (Art. 147(1) CCIP and Case C-11/89 *Unifert* [1990] ECR I-2275 at p. I-2292). A representative, even if he acts in his own name (Art. 5 CC), cannot be regarded as buyer, since he is not a party of the contract of sale and does not bear the financial risk of the transaction (Art. 147(3) CCIP and Case C-299/90 *Hepp* [1991] ECR I-4301 at p. I-4324).

Once the value declaration has been made and the goods have been released, the declarant can no longer correct his declaration with the argument that he could have declared a lower price (Case C-11/89 *Unifert*, above, at pp. I-2294–5; Case C-79/89 *Brown Boveri* [1991] ECR I-1853 at p. I-4891; Case C-379/00 *Overland Footwear* [2002] ECR I-11133). If the trader declares deliberately a price higher than that which he actually has to pay, he is not entitled to a refund (Case 328/85 *Deutsche Babcock* [1987] ECR 5119 at p. 5140), nor are the authorities obliged to apply this price with regard to other legislation, such as corporate taxation (Case 65/79 *Chatain* [1980] ECR 1345 at p. 1384).

Customs duties are only levied on goods, not on the provision of services or the transfer of rights (*see further under* **Common Customs Tariff (CCT)**, section III.1). However, royalties and licence fees related to the goods are part of the customs value (Art. 32(1)(c) CC, Arts. 157 to 162 CCIP). This applies even in cases where the owner of the licence is established in the Community and the patent or design has been developed there (Case C-116/89 *BayWa* [1991] ECR I-1095 at pp. I-1114–15). Where trade marks, patents, etc. are transferred independently from the imported article, their value is not part of the customs value (Case 1/77 *Bosch* [1977] ECR 1473 at p. 1482; Case 135/77 *Bosch* [1978] ECR 855 at p. 860).

The transaction value is, however, not recognized in the following cases (Art. 29(1)(a) to (d) CC):

- the seller imposes restrictions as to the disposal or the use of the goods other than legal or geographical restrictions, except where the value of the goods is not substantially affected thereby;
- the value of the goods cannot be determined because of some conditions or considerations related to the contract (e.g. barter trade);
- a part of the proceeds of any subsequent resale, disposal, or use of the goods by the buyer will accrue directly or indirectly to the seller and no appropriate adjustment can be made;
- the buyer and seller are related and the customs authorities have grounds for considering that the relationship influenced the price (the term 'related' is defined in Art. 143 CCIP) and the declarant cannot demonstrate that the price is 'at arms-length'.

Once it has been established that the transaction value can be used as the basis for the customs value, it is necessary to check whether certain costs incurred or certain services supplied by the buyer or certain proceeds accruing to the seller have to be added to the price actually paid or payable for the goods. Art. 32 CC contains an exclusive list of such elements to be added, provided they are not included in the price:

- general sales costs, such as commissions, except buying commissions (see Case C-11/89 *Unifert*, above; Case C-299/90 *Hepp*, above), the cost of containers (see Case C-17/89 *Olivetti* [1990] ECR I-2301 at p. I-2317) and packing;
- the value of goods and services supplied by the buyer, such as materials incorporated in the imported goods (if the materials have been temporarily exported under the outward processing procedure, the duty is calculated in accordance with Arts. 151 or 153 CC, *see further under* **Customs procedures**, section V.7, as well as Case C-16/91 *Wacker* [1992] ECR I-6821 at pp. I-6844–5; and Case C-142/96 *Wacker* [1997] ECR I-4649 at pp. I-4666–7), tools, dies, moulds used, and materials consumed in the production, as well as engineering, development, designs, plans, and sketches;
- royalties and licence fees related to the goods as a condition of sale (Case C-116/89 *BayWa*, above, at pp. I-1114–15), as well as the proceeds of any subsequent resale, disposal, or use of the goods that accrue to the seller;
- the cost of transport, insurance, loading, and handling, in so far as they relate to the transport of the goods to the place of introduction into the EC customs territory (this place is defined in Art. 163 CCIP), even if such costs are higher than usually (Case C-11/89 *Unifert*, above, at p. I-2297).

Certain costs, and in particular those which are incurred after the introduction of the goods into the EC customs territory, are excluded from the customs value, provided that they are shown separately from the price actually paid or payable (Art. 33 CC). This concerns:

- charges for the transport of goods after their arrival at the place of introduction into the EC customs territory; the amount of costs claimed for intra-Community transport may be checked by the customs authorities (Case 290/84 *Mainfrucht Obstverwertung* [1985] ECR 3909 at p. 3931);
- charges for activities undertaken after importation, such as construction, assembly, maintenance, or technical assistance;
- interests payable by the buyer and relating to the purchase of the imported goods, provided that the interest rate prevailing in the country concerned is not exceeded (Case C-21/91 *Wünsche* [1992] ECR I-3647 at pp. I-3665–6);
- charges for the right to reproduce imported goods in the Community;
- buying commissions, i.e. fees paid by an importer to his agent for the service of representing him in the purchase of the goods (see Art. 32(4) CC and Case C-11/89 *Unifert*, above, at p. I-2296; Case C-379/00 *Overland Footwear*, above);
- import duties and other charges due in the Community by reason of the importation or sale of the goods.

If a part of the goods have been lost or damaged before their entry into free circulation, a corresponding proportion can be deducted from the price actually paid or payable if the adjustment is made within twelve months following the date of acceptance of the declaration for free circulation (Art. 145 CCIP; see also Case 183/85 *Repenning* [1986] ECR 1873 at p. 1883; Case C-59/92 *Ebbe Sönnichsen* [1993] ECR I-2193 at p. I-2210).

4. The transaction value of identical goods. Where the transaction value cannot be used (e.g. because buyer and seller are related and the relationship has influenced the price, or because there is no sale), the customs value is determined according to the transaction value of identical goods sold for export to the Community and exported at or about the same time as the goods being valued (Art. 30(1)(a) CC). 'Identical goods' means goods produced in the same country, which are the same in all respects, including physical characteristics, quality, and reputation; minor differences in appearance are admitted (Art. 142(1)(c) CCIP). The term 'identical goods' does not include goods that incorporate or reflect engineering, development, artwork, design work, plans, and sketches for which no adjustments have been made because such elements were undertaken in the Community (Art. 142(2) CCIP). If the identical goods are sold at a different commercial level or in different quantities or differences in distances and modes of transport arise, adjustments shall be made; if two or more transaction values of identical goods are found, the lowest of such values is used (Art. 150 CCIP).

5. The transaction value of similar goods. Where the transaction value of identical goods is not available, the transaction value of similar goods sold for export to the Community and exported at or about the same time as the goods being valued is to be used (Art. 30(1)(b) CC). 'Similar goods' means goods produced in the same country, which, although not alike in all respects, have like characteristics and like component materials that enable them to perform the same functions and to be commercially interchangeable; the quality of the goods, their reputation, and the existence of a trade mark are among the factors to be considered in determining whether goods are similar (Art. 142(1)(d) CCIP). This term does not include goods that incorporate or reflect engineering, development, artwork, design work, plans, and sketches for which no adjustment has been made because such elements were undertaken in the Community (Art. 142(2) CCIP).

If the similar goods are sold at a different commercial level or in different quantities or differences in distances or modes of transport arise, adjustments shall be made; where more than one transaction value of similar goods is found, the lowest such values shall be used (Art. 151 CCIP).

6. The deductive method. Where the transaction value of similar goods is not available, the customs value is determined on the basis of the unit price at which identical or similar imported goods are sold within the Community in the greatest aggregate quantity to persons not related to the sellers (Art. 30(2)(c) CC). The declarant can however request that the computed value (see point 7 below) is used instead (Art. 30(1) CC).

Taken as a basis for the calculation can be the price of:

- the imported goods;
- identical goods; or
- similar goods (Art. 152(1) CCIP).

This method requires that such goods are sold in the Community. The unit price to be used is the price at which imported goods are sold in the greatest number of units at the first commercial level after importation to persons who are not related to the seller (Art. 152(3) CCIP). Deductions are made for:

- costs relating to the marketing of the goods in the Community or additions usually made for profit and expenses;
- the usual costs of transport and insurance and associated costs incurred within the Community;
- import duties and other charges payable in the Community by reason of the importation or sale of the goods;
- the value added by processing the goods in the Community (Art. 152(1) and (2) CCIP).

Prices of goods that have been processed in the Community can only be used at the request of the importer (Art. 152(2) CCIP).

7. The computed value. Where the unit price cannot be used or the importer does not want the application of this method, the customs value is determined on the basis of the computed value, consisting of the sum of:

- the cost or value of materials and processing employed in producing the imported goods;
- an amount for profit and general expenses equal to that usually reflected in sales of goods of the same class or kind as the goods being valued that are made by producers in the country of exportation for export to the Community;
- the cost or value of transport, loading and handling charges associated with the transport of the imported goods to the place of introduction into the customs territory of the Community (Art. 30(2)(d) CC).

The customs authorities may not require or compel any person not resident in the Community to produce for examination, or to allow access to, any account or other record for the purposes of determining the computed value. The producer of the goods can however supply such information and agree to such verification, provided that the authorities of the country concerned have been given sufficient advance notice and have not objected to the investigation (Art. 153(1) CCIP).

8. The fall-back method. Where the above-mentioned methods cannot be applied, the customs value shall be determined on the basis of data available in the Community using 'reasonable means', notably previously determined customs values which have been established according to the normal rules (Art. 31 CC, Annex 23 CCIP).

See also **Common Customs Tariff, Customs procedures, Origin of goods.**

Further reading 1. BOOKS: Berr and Trémeau, *Le droit douanier*, 5th edn. (2001), p. 127; Giffoni, *Droit douanier de la C.E. et aspects économiques* (1993), p. 132; Lux, *Guide to Community Customs Legislation* (2002), p. 187; id., *Das Zollrecht der EG* (2004), ch. V; Lyons, *EC Customs Law* (2001), p. 242; Müller-Eiselt, *E6-Zollrecht, Zollkodex/Zollwert* (loose-leaf); Sherman and Glashoff, *Customs Valuation: Commentary on the GATT Customs Valuation Code* (1988); Snyder, *International Trade and Customs Law of the European Union* (1998), p. 53; Walsh, *The Customs Code of the European Union* (1996), p. 27; Witte and Wolffgang (eds.), *Lehrbuch des Europäischen Zollrechts*, 4th edn. (2003), p. 402.

2. ARTICLE: Stobbe, 'Der Zollwert des Zollkodex' (1994) *Zeitschrift für Zölle und Verbrauchsteuern* 322 and 354; (1995) ibid. 9.

3. OFFICIAL PUBLICATION: Court of Auditors, 'Special Report No. 23/2000 concerning valuation of imported goods for customs purposes (customs valuation)' (*OJ* 2001 C84/1).

▶ **CUSTOMS WAREHOUSING *see* CUSTOMS PROCEDURES**

▶ **DESIGNATION OF ORIGIN** *see* **INTELLECTUAL PROPERTY RIGHTS**

▶ **DIRECT TAXATION** Whereas Art. 90 EC prohibits discriminatory taxation of products from other Member States and Art. 93 EC provides a specific legal basis for indirect tax harmonization, there are no equivalent provisions on direct taxation, i.e. the taxation of the income and capital of natural and legal persons. The EC Treaty merely provides, in Art. 293, that Member States shall, in so far as is necessary, enter into negotiations with each other with a view to securing the abolition of double taxation within the Community for the benefit of their nationals. Nevertheless, in so far as rules on direct taxation may 'directly affect the establishment or functioning of the common market', they may be the subject of approximating directives adopted under Art. 94 EC (fiscal provisions are excluded from the scope of Art. 95(1) EC by Art. 95(2) EC). The unanimity requirement under Art. 94 EC and Member States' reluctance to cede sovereignty in matters of direct taxation have severely impeded harmonizing initiatives. In the absence of harmonization, the case-law of the ECJ based on the Treaty freedoms articles has assumed growing importance.

I. Community measures on direct taxation

Despite the absence of a specific Treaty basis for direct tax measures the Commission, in February 1967, submitted to the Council a tax harmonization programme containing measures relating mainly to direct taxation, which were necessary for the establishment or functioning of the common market (Suppl.–*Bull. EC* 8–67) and from the late sixties onwards presented a series of harmonizing proposals, including a 1975 proposal on harmonization of systems of company taxation and of withholding taxes on dividends (*OJ* 1977 C253/2, withdrawn 2 April 1990) and a 1979 proposal on harmonization of income tax provisions with respect to freedom of movement for workers (*OJ* 1980 C21/6, withdrawn 9 September 1992).

However, it was not until 1990 that the first modest steps were taken towards removal of fiscal obstacles to the common market with the adoption of three specific measures aimed at eliminating tax disincentives to cross-border co-operation between companies established within the Community: the Merger and Parent-Subsidiary Directives and the Tax Arbitration Convention (concluded under Art. 293 EC). Despite initial optimism following the adoption of those instruments, little progress was made on two further related proposals, namely a proposal on arrangements for the taking account of losses incurred by permanent establishments and subsidiaries in other Member States (*OJ* 1991 C53/30, since withdrawn) and a proposal on a common system for interest and royalty payments made between parent and subsidiary companies in different Member States (*OJ* 1991 C53/26, since withdrawn). The Commission did however finally succeed in securing the adoption of a directive on interest and royalty payments by the Council in 2003 by re-presenting its proposal as part of a package aimed at combating harmful tax competition.

In 2001 the Commission published a Communication and detailed report on company taxation in the internal market reviewing progress to date and setting out a programme for further steps, including initiatives on transfer pricing, cross-border loss relief, tax treaties, and possible models for a single consolidated tax base (see 'Company taxation in the internal market', COM(2001) 582; 'An internal market without company tax obstacles—achievements, ongoing initiatives, and remaining challenges', COM(2003) 726).

The Council has not as yet adopted any measures dealing with tax obstacles to freedom of movement or investment for natural persons. The Commission has, however, issued guidance in the form of recommendations or communications, in particular in the light of case-law of the ECJ (see Comm. Rec. on the taxation of certain items of income received by non-residents in a Member State other than that in which they are resident, *OJ* 1994 L39/22; Comm. Communication on the elimination of tax obstacles to the cross-border provision of occupational pensions, *OJ* 2001 C165/4; Comm. Communication on dividend taxation of individuals in the internal market, COM(2003) 810).

1. Company taxation

(*a*). ***The Merger Directive.*** Dir. 90/434 establishes a common system of taxation applicable to mergers, divisions, transfers of assets, and exchanges of shares concerning companies of different Member States (*OJ* 1990 L225/1; see proposed amending directive, COM(2003) 613). The purpose of the directive is to remove disincentives to cross-border grouping or restructuring by deferring the tax charges that could otherwise arise immediately on the disposal of assets or shares as part of the aforementioned operations. At the same time the directive safeguards the financial interests of Member States by allowing Member States to collect tax when the assets or shares are disposed of subsequently.

The directive applies solely to operations involving companies from more than one Member State. 'Company from a Member State' means a company that takes one of a number of specified legal forms, is resident for tax purposes in a Member State, and is subject to one of the national corporation taxes listed (Art. 3 and Annex).

The directive applies to four categories of operation: mergers, divisions, transfers of assets, and share exchanges. A 'merger' means the transfer of all the assets and liabilities of one or more companies to another existing company, a newly formed company or the transferring company's parent company; a 'division' the transfer of all the assets and liabilities of a company to two or more existing or new companies. Save in the case of a merger with the transferring company's own parent company, the transfer is made in exchange for the issue of shares in the acquiring company (together in some cases with a limited cash payment) to the transferring company's shareholders. The notions of 'merger' and 'division' are based on those in the Third and Sixth Council Directives on company law, respectively (*OJ* 1978 L295/36; *OJ* 1982 L378/47); however, those directives apply solely to domestic mergers and divisions and as yet no directive has been adopted on the equivalent cross-border operations (see the draft Tenth Directive (*OJ* 1985 C23/11; *see further under* **Company law**). A 'transfer of assets' involves the transfer of one or more branches of a company's activity to another company in exchange for shares in the receiving company. An 'exchange of shares' covers the situation where a company acquires a holding in another company representing a majority of its voting rights in exchange for the issue of shares to the acquired company's shareholders (see Art. 2(a) to (d)).

Mergers, divisions, and asset transfers are liable under national systems to give rise to taxation of gains at the company level based on the difference between the real value of the transferred assets and liabilities and their value for tax purposes. The directive eliminates the tax charge on the occasion of such operations in respect of the transferred assets and liabilities. 'Transferred assets and liabilities' are limited to those that are effectively connected with a permanent establishment of the receiving company in the Member State of the transferring company. That proviso ensures that Member States retain the right to tax gains arising on the ultimate disposal of the transferred assets (double taxation conventions generally giving a Contracting State the right to tax that part of the profits of foreign enterprise which are attributable to a permanent establishment within its territory). Similarly, the tax exemption is conditional upon the receiving company's calculating any new depreciation and any gains or losses on the same basis as those applied by the transferring company; the tax history of the transferred assets and liabilities is therefore retained, ensuring that the relief granted on the occasion of the restructuring operation is one of deferral rather than permanent exemption. Provision is made for the transfer of properly constituted tax-free reserves, and carry-over of losses is provided for on the same terms as those applicable to domestic operations (see Arts. 4, 5, and 6).

Mergers, divisions, and share exchanges are also liable to give rise to taxation of gains realized by shareholders of the transferring or acquired company on the disposal or cancellation of their holdings. Under the directive such gains are exempt from immediate taxation but Member States retain the right to tax any gains arising on the ultimate disposal of the new shares as if they had been the old shares. Thus, any gain arising on the disposal is to be calculated by reference to the value that would have been used for calculating the gain on the cancellation of the old shares but for the directive (see Art. 8). The directive also contains provisions dealing with the situation in which a company of one Member State transfers a permanent establishment in a second Member State to a company of a third Member State (see Art. 10).

Member States may refuse the benefit of the directive where the operation has as its principal objective or as one of its principal objectives tax evasion or avoidance and may lay down a presumption to that effect where it is not carried out for valid commercial reasons. The competent national authorities are however obliged to consider each case on its merits and must not confine themselves to applying predetermined criteria automatically excluding certain categories of operation (see Art. 11; see also Case C-28/95 *Leur-Bloem* [1997] ECR I-4161 at p. I-4204).

(b). The Parent-Subsidiary Directive. Dir. 90/435 establishes a common system of taxation for parent companies and subsidiaries of different Member States (*OJ* 1990 L225/1, amended by Dir. 2003/123, *OJ* 2004 L7/41). Whereas the Merger Directive is directed at initial obstacles to cross-border co-operation arising from the restructuring operation itself, the Parent-Subsidiary Directive eliminates the more permanent disincentive arising from the double taxation of profits distributed by subsidiaries to their parent companies in another Member State.

The Directive requires:

(*a*) the Member State of a subsidiary company to abolish any withholding taxes on distributions of profits (notably dividend payments) made by the subsidiary company to its parent company in another Member State (subject to derogations for certain Member States); and

(*b*) the Member State of the parent company either to exempt profit distributions received by a parent company from a subsidiary of another Member State or, if it taxes the distribution, to grant a credit for the underlying company tax paid on the profits out of which the distribution is made (see Arts. 4 and 5).

The companies concerned must be a 'company of a Member State', a term defined in essentially the same way as the equivalent term in the Merger Directive (Art. 2 and Annex). 'Parent company' means a company that possesses a holding of at least 25% in the capital of another company or, if a Member State so chooses, 25% of its voting rights (the holding requirement to be progressively reduced to 10% by 1 January 2009 under Dir. 2003/123). Member States have the option of imposing a minimum two-year holding period as a requirement for gaining the benefit of the directive. Where a company complies with the holding period the benefit of the directive must be granted from the beginning of the holding period (Art. 3; see also Cases C-283/94 etc. *Denkavit* [1996] ECR I-5063).

The term 'withholding tax' covers any tax, irrespective of its classification under national law, where the chargeable event is the distribution of profits and the amount of the tax is directly related to the size of the distribution (see Case C-375/98 *Epson Europe* [2000] ECR I-4243 at pp. I-4274–5); Case C-294/99 *Athinaiki Zithopiia* [2001] ECR I-6797 at p. I-6826).

(c). The Arbitration Convention. The Convention on the elimination of double taxation in connection with the adjustment of profits of associated enterprises, concluded under Art. 293 EC, was signed on 23 July 1990 and came into force on 1 January 1995 in the twelve Member States (*OJ* 1990 L225/10; see also Convention on the Accession of Austria, Finland, and Sweden, *OJ* 1996 C26/1). Concluded for an initial time of five years, its period of validity was extended by a Protocol of 25 May 1999 (*OJ* 1999 C202/1). Unlike the Brussels Convention, it does not confer interpretative jurisdiction on the ECJ.

The Convention applies to all forms of tax on the income of individuals and corporations and is based on the arm's length principle of profit allocation advocated by the OECD. Where the financial arrangements made between associated enterprises in different Contracting States have the result that profits accrue to a firm other than the one to which they would have accrued had the firms been independent, the sums concerned may be included in the profits of the firm to which they would normally have accrued. Enterprises are associated where one participates directly or indirectly in the management, control, or capital of the other or where the same persons participate in the management, control, or capital of both (see Art. 4).

Where the tax authorities of a Contracting State intend to adjust the results of a firm on the ground that part of its profits have been transferred to a related firm contrary to the arm's length principle they must first inform the firm so that it can inform the related firm and the latter can inform the authorities of its Contracting State (Art. 5).

Where a firm considers that its results or those of a related firm have been adjusted in a manner that is inconsistent with the arm's length principle it may, within three years of the first notification of the action resulting in double taxation, submit its case to the competent authority of its State. The firm must inform the competent authority if other Contracting States may be concerned, and that authority must inform the competent authorities of those States. If no satisfactory unilateral solution is found, the competent authority of the first State must attempt to reach an agreement eliminating double taxation on the basis of the arm's length principle with the competent authority of any other State concerned. If no such agreement is reached within two years of the date on which the case was submitted the competent authorities concerned must appoint an advisory committee to give an opinion. The two-year time-limit is extended where one of the firms has also brought the case before a national court or tribunal or where it is waived with the consent of the firms concerned. The advisory committee, which comprises representatives of each authority and independent experts, must give its opinion within six months. Following the issue of the opinion the tax authorities must by common consent adopt a decision eliminating the double taxation. The authorities may depart from the opinion but are bound by it if they fail to agree on an alternative solution (Arts. 6 to 12).

(d). The Interest and Royalties Directive. Dir. 2003/49 establishes a common system of taxation applicable to interest and royalty payments made between associated companies of different Member States (*OJ* 2003 L157/49). Although finally adopted much later than the Parent-Subsidiary Directive on dividends, it serves similar aims to—and may be seen as complementing—that directive. The purpose of the directive is to eliminate double taxation of cross-border interest and royalty payments between associated companies However, whereas dividends are paid out of post-tax profits, interest and royalty payments are generally tax-deductible in the hands of the paying company. Consequently, while requiring the source State to exempt such payments from tax, it requires or allows it to impose a series of conditions aimed at ensuring that the payments are taxed (once) in another Member State (Art. 1). The source State may require the production of an attestation certifying compliance with the conditions (Art. 1(11)). The directive provides detailed definitions of the terms 'interest' and 'royalties' (Art. 2) and also of 'company', 'associated company', and 'permanent establishment' (Art. 3 and Annex). For budgetary reasons transitional rules are laid down for Greece, Spain, and Portugal (Art. 6). The directive was to be implemented in national law by 1 January 2004 (Art. 7).

2. Administrative co-operation between Member States. In 1977 the Council adopted a directive concerning mutual assistance by the competent authorities of Member States in the field of direct taxation (Dir. 77/799, *OJ* 1977 L336/15). The directive provides for exchange of information between competent authorities subject to various conditions and safeguards. More recently, the Council adopted Dir. 2001/44 extending the scope of Dir. 76/308 on mutual assistance for the recovery of certain claims so as to include claims relating to taxes on income and capital (*OJ* 2001 L175/17).

3. The package against harmful tax competition. In a paper entitled 'Taxation in the European Union' presented to the Council in April 1996, the Commission expressed the view that the removal of barriers within the single market made cross-border flows more sensitive to taxation and presented increased challenges for Member States to protect their revenues against erosion through tax competition. Central to the Commission's thinking was a distinction between fair tax competition between Member States (considered healthy) and harmful tax competition, which could indirectly penalize employment by producing a shift of taxation from more mobile factors and activities, such as capital and financial and other services, to less mobile activities such as labour. On 1 December 1997, Finance Ministers reached agreement on the principles of a package of three measures designed to tackle harmful tax competition in the European Union (see conclusions of the ECOFIN Council meeting on 1 December 1997, *OJ* 1998 C2/1). The package, which was finally adopted by the Council in June 2003, comprises a directive to ensure effective taxation of interest income from cross-border investment of savings by individuals (Dir. 2003/48, *OJ* 2003 L157/38), a Code of Conduct on business taxation, and the Interest and Royalties Directive (above).

Dir. 2003/48 introduces a system of information exchange between tax authorities concerning interest payments made by a paying agent in one Member State to individuals resident in another Member State. Under transitional arrangements Belgium, Luxembourg, and Austria are entitled to impose a withholding tax on such payments rather than exchange information. Although Member States are obliged to transpose the directive into national law by 1 January 2004, they are obliged to apply its provisions only from 1 January 2005 and provided that certain safeguards are met regarding the introduction of equivalent arrangements in certain third countries and dependent and associated territories.

The Code of Conduct is a political agreement requiring Member States to refrain from introducing and to amend laws or practices relating to business taxation that are deemed to be harmful in the light of the criteria laid down in the Code. The implementation of the Code was overseen by a Council working party known as the Code of Conduct Group. The scope of the Code, which is targeted primarily at preferential company tax regimes, overlaps to a significant extent with that of the Treaty rules on State aid. In 1998 the Commission published guidelines on the application of the State aid rules to measures relating to direct business taxation (*OJ* 1998 C384/3) and subsequently instituted State aid proceedings against a number of such measures (see Commission Report on the implementation of the Commission notice on the application of the State aid rules to measures relating to direct business taxation).

II. ECJ case-law concerning direct taxation

In a growing body of case-law, the ECJ has considered the compatibility of national rules on direct taxation with Arts. 39, 43, 49, and 56 EC. The ECJ has made it clear that such rules are no more sheltered from the application of the Treaty than any other category of national rules; and indeed the principles applied by the ECJ are largely the same as those applied to other rules—this entry merely notes features specific to this area of the case-law.

Tax law commonly distinguishes between taxpayers according to their residence or their place of establishment or investment. Generally speaking, a country taxes residents on their worldwide income but taxes non-residents solely on income from within its territory. This in turn leads to differences as between taxpayers in the arrangements for charging tax and for granting reliefs and deductions, e.g. differences in the rate of tax or basis of assessment, limits on refunds, deductions or reliefs, or procedural differences in the administration of the tax. For example, in the case of natural persons residents are often granted allowances to take account of their personal and family circumstances, whereas non-residents are taxed on an objective basis without such allowances.

As a matter of Community law, different treatment based on place of residence or place of establishment or investment, unless objectively justified, is liable to entail discrimination or other restriction contrary to one or more of the Treaty freedoms (see Case C-297/93 *Schumacker* [1995] ECR I-225 at p. I-259; Case C-264/96 *ICI* [1998] ECR I-4695 at pp. I-4721–2; Case C-200/98 *X and Y* [1999] ECR I-8261 at p. I-8286; Case C-141/99 *AMID* [2000] ECR I-11619 at p. I-11644; Case C-294/97 *Eurowings Luftverkehrs* [1999] ECR I-7447 at p. I-7474).

The ECJ examines arguments put forward by Member States to justify their tax rules critically and has rejected a number outright: the need in the absence of harmonization to take account of differences between national systems; the fact that a non-resident could have avoided the discrimination, e.g. by setting up a subsidiary company rather than a branch; the fact that a tax rule works to the advantage of taxpayers more often than not; the need to prevent loss of revenue or to protect the tax base; the need to compensate for lower taxes in other Member States in order to avoid distortions of competition; the fact that a rule corresponds to OECD guidance or generally accepted international practice such as the arm's length principle (see Case 270/83 *Commission* v. *France* [1986] ECR 273 at pp. 305–7; Case C-294/97 *Eurowings Luftverkehrs*, above, at p. I-7476; Case C-168/01 *Bosal Holding* [2003] ECR I-9409, para. 42; Case C-141/99 *AMID*, above, at p. I-11643; Case C-324/00 *Lankhorst-Hohorst* [2002] ECR I-11779, paras. 39–42).

It is in principle open to a Member State to contend that a difference in fiscal treatment corresponds to material differences in the situations of the non-resident and resident comparators. Any differences in situation must however be such as to justify the different treatment in the particular circumstances. In conducting its examination the ECJ takes account, where appropriate, of the treatment of the taxpayer under the tax laws of both (or all) the Member States concerned, including any relevant double taxation conventions. For example, a frontier worker's Member State of employment does not discriminate where it denies him the tax allowances granted to a resident taxpayer to take account of the latter's personal or family circumstances where the frontier worker's State of residence already grants him such allowances; if on the other hand, the frontier worker is unable to receive allowances in his State of residence because he has insufficient taxable income there, the Member State of employment discriminates by failing to grant allowances given to resident workers. The ECJ approaches the comparison of tax burdens on a tax-by-tax basis; thus, e.g. in one case the ECJ confined itself to a comparison of the annual taxation of the profits of a French company and a branch of a foreign company rather than considering whether the overall fiscal treatment of a branch was less favourable. Of particular importance for tax arrangements for groups of companies is the principle that different treatment of parent companies cannot be justified by differences in the tax situations of resident and non-resident subsidiaries (see Case 270/83 *Commission* v. *France*, above, at pp. 304–5; Case C-297/93 *Schumacker*, above, at pp. I-259–60; Case C-80/94 *Wielockx* [1995] ECR I-2508 at pp. I-2515–16; Case C-107/94 *Asscher* [1996] ECR I-3089 at pp. I-3125–6; Case C-391/97 *Gschwind* [1999] ECR I-5451 at pp. I-5487–90; Case C-141/99 *AMID*, above, at pp. I-11642–3; Case C-168/01 *Bosal Holding*, above, para. 39; see also Art. 58 EC which, although preserving the right of Member States to apply the relevant provisions of their tax laws that distinguish between taxpayers who are not in the same situation with regard to their place of residence or place of investment of their capital, provides that such provisions shall not constitute a means of arbitrary discrimination or a disguised restriction of the free movement of capital and payments).

In two related cases the ECJ held that a discriminatory provision of a Member State refusing a tax deduction for pension and insurance contributions paid to an insurer established in another Member State could be justified by the general interest in preserving the fiscal coherence of the first Member State's tax rules, in particular by the need to ensure that the tax deduction was matched by ultimate taxation of the benefits paid out under the relevant policy (see Case C-204/90 *Bachmann* [1992] ECR I-249; Case

C-300/90 *Commission* v. *Belgium* [1992] ECR I-305). In later cases, however, Member States' repeated attempts to rely on those authorities have failed. The ECJ has progressively restricted the scope of the fiscal coherence principle, in particular by requiring a strict and direct link between the benefit and the burden. No link is possible in the case of different taxes (e.g. corporate taxation and shareholder taxation) or different taxpayers (parent and subsidiary companies) (see Case C-80/94 *Wielockx*, above, at pp. I-2516–17; Case C-484/93 *Svensson and Gustavsson* [1995] ECR I-3955 at pp. I-3976–7; Case C-35/98 *Verkooijen* [2000] ECR I-4071 at pp. I-4132–3; Case C-168/01 *Bosal Holding*, above, paras. 30–1).

The ECJ, referring to the *Cassis de Dijon* case-law (Case 120/78 *Rewe* [1979] ECR 649), has held that the effectiveness of fiscal supervision also constitutes an overriding general interest requirement capable of justifying compliance rules. However, the ECJ examines closely the proportionality of such rules and in particular requires Member States to make use of mutual assistance instruments such as Dir. 77/799 (see Case C-205/95 *Futura Participations and Singer* [1997] ECR I-2471 at pp. I-2501–4).

The ECJ has also held that preventing tax avoidance constitutes a general interest requirement. Anti-avoidance measures must, however, be specifically targeted at wholly artificial arrangements; moreover, a situation will not necessarily entail tax avoidance if the taxpayer is in any event subject to the tax legislation of another Member State (Case C-324/00 *Lankhorst-Hohorst*, above, para. 37).

In practice there is considerable overlap between the above defences, in particular arguments based on comparability of situations and the general interests in fiscal coherence and preventing tax avoidance. However, neither the ECJ nor its Advocates-General have attempted to define the relationship between them. The ECJ's approach, having established a difference in treatment or other obstacle, is to consider in turn such arguments as are advanced on their merits.

Most countries have a network of bilateral tax conventions with other countries, which limit their taxing rights on a reciprocal basis with a view to eliminating or reducing double taxation. By virtue of the principle of the supremacy of Community law both primary and secondary Community law take precedence over conflicting provisions of double taxation conventions, including prior conventions, concluded between Member States. A Member State cannot therefore rely upon the provisions of such a convention in order to justify a discriminatory restriction. Moreover, since the rights conferred by the Treaty are unconditional, a Member State cannot make respect for them subject to the grant of reciprocal rights by another Member State under a double taxation convention (see Case 270/83 *Commission* v. *France*, above, at p. 307).

In the case of tax conventions concluded with non-member countries, the first paragraph of Art. 307 EC preserves, in accordance with principles of international law, rights and obligations arising from agreements concluded before the entry into force of the Treaty; however, it requires the relevant Member State(s) to take appropriate steps to eliminate any incompatibilities, imposing a duty on Member States to assist each other to that end and to adopt, where appropriate, a common attitude.

In the absence of harmonizing measures or a multilateral convention under Art. 293 EC Member States are competent, subject to compliance with the rules of the Treaty, to determine the criteria with a view to eliminating double taxation and to concluded bilateral conventions for that purpose. The use of nationality as such a criterion for the allocation of taxing powers does not of itself entail discrimination on grounds of nationality. Member States are nevertheless required to exercise their allocated tax powers in a manner consistent with Community law (see Case C-336/96 *Gilly* [1998] ECR I-2823 at pp. I-2833–6; Case C-307/97 *Saint-Gobain* [1999] ECR I-6181 at pp. I-6202–3; Case C-385/00 *De Groot* [2002] ECR I-11819, paras. 93–4).

See also **Company law, Freedom of establishment, Freedom to provide services, Free movement of capital, Free movement of persons, Tax harmonization.**

Further reading 1. BOOKS: Farmer and Lyal, *EC Tax Law* (1994), 2nd edn. (expected 2005); Pinto, *Tax Competition and EU Law* (2003); Terra and Wattel, *European Tax Law* (2001); Van Thiel, *Free Movement of Persons and Income Tax Law: The European Court in Search of Principles* (2002).

2. ARTICLE: Lyal, 'Non-Discrimination and Direct Tax in Community Law' (2003–2) *EC Tax Rev.* 68.

▶ **DUBLIN CONVENTION *see* FREE MOVEMENT OF PERSONS**

▶ **EQUAL PAY (PRINCIPLE OF)** Principle according to which men and women should receive equal pay for equal work or work of equal value. This principle is laid down in Art. 141 EC [Art. 119 of the original EEC Treaty], which has been described as the 'European translation' or counterpart of Convention No. 100 concerning equal remuneration for men and women workers for work of equal value, adopted by the International Labour Organization in 1951 (see Case 43/75 *Defrenne II* [1976] ECR 455 at p. 484 *per* A.-G. Trabucchi).

I. The legal framework

Since Art. 119 of the original EEC Treaty was substantially amended by the Treaty of Amsterdam (ToA) and renumbered Art. 141 EC, it is appropriate to discuss the two Articles separately in this section. It should be pointed out, however, that the case-law of the ECJ developed in relation to Art. 119 is fully valid today, and is applicable to Art. 141.

1. Article 119 of the original EEC Treaty. Already in Case 43/75 *Defrenne II*, above, at p. 472 (see also the opinion of A.-G. Trabucchi, ibid. at p. 485), the ECJ pointed out that in the context of the EC Treaty as a whole, Art. 119 [now Art. 141] pursues a double objective, which is both economic and social. In the economic field, it seeks to prevent any attempt at 'social dumping' by means of the use of female labour less well paid than male labour. Its aim is thus to avoid a situation in which undertakings established in Member States that have actually implemented the principle of equal pay suffer a competitive disadvantage in intra-Community competition as compared with undertakings established in Member States that have not yet eliminated pay discrimination against women. At the same time, being inserted in that section of the EC Treaty dealing with social policy (originally Title III, now Title XI, of Part Three of the Treaty), Art. 119 forms part of the social objectives of the Community, which is not merely an economic organization but is also intended to ensure social progress and the constant improvement of the living and working conditions of the peoples of Europe, as is emphasized by the preamble to the Treaty. Therefore, the Court concluded, the principle of equal pay forms part of the foundations of the Community and must be attained by raising the lowest salaries rather than by lowering the highest. In other cases, the Court has stressed that because of its fundamental importance, the meaning and scope of the principle cannot be determined by reference to rules or practices followed in the Member States but must be interpreted independently of those rules or practices in a uniform manner throughout the Community (Case C-7/93 *Beune* [1994] ECR I-4471 at p. I-4514).

In its subsequent case-law, the Court has more and more shifted the emphasis from the economic to the social objectives of Art. 119. Thus, it has repeatedly held that the right not to be discriminated against on grounds of sex is one of the fundamental human rights whose observance the Court has a duty to ensure (see Case 149/77 *Defrenne III* [1978] ECR 1365 at p. 1378; Cases 75/82 etc. *Razzouk and Beydoun* v. *Commission* [1984] ECR 1509 at

p. 1530; Case C-13/94 *P* [1996] ECR I-2143 at p. I-2165). This tendency has culminated in the recognition by the Court that where the two objectives are in conflict, the economic aim pursued by Art. 119, namely the elimination of distortions of competition between undertakings established in different Member States, must give way to the social aim pursued by the same Article, since the latter constitutes the expression of a fundamental human right (Case C-50/96 *Schröder* [2000] ECR I-743 at p. I-794).

Nevertheless, Art. 119 has a precisely defined scope in that it covers only one element of the employment relationship, namely, pay. In a series of cases, the ECJ has held that it is not possible to widen the scope of Art. 119 so as to include other conditions of employment, without jeopardizing its direct effect (for which, see below) and without intervening in an area of social policy that Arts. 117 and 118 of the original EEC Treaty reserved largely to the discretion of the Member States. Therefore, Art. 119 cannot be interpreted as prescribing, in addition to equal pay, equal treatment in respect of the other conditions of employment and working conditions applicable to men and women. Even the fact that the fixing of certain conditions of employment, such as a special age-limit for the termination of the employment relationship, may have pecuniary consequences that discriminate against women, is not sufficient to bring such conditions within the field of application of Art. 119. Equal treatment in respect of conditions of employment other than pay is ensured by a different set of rules of Community law (Case 149/77 *Defrenne III*, above, at p. 1377; see also Case 19/81 *Burton* [1982] ECR 555 at p. 575; Case 170/84 *Bilka* [1986] ECR 1607 at pp. 1629–30. *See further under* **Equal treatment**).

According to the original text of Art. 119, the principle of equal pay was to be fully and uniformly implemented in all the Member States by the end of the first stage of the transitional period, that is, by 1 January 1962. However, such full and uniform implementation did not take place, and by a Resolution adopted on 30 December 1961, the Member States extended the deadline to 31 December 1964. Several of the Member States failed to meet even this deadline.

To speed up the process, on 10 February 1975 the Council adopted Dir. 75/117 on the approximation of the laws of the Member States relating to the application of the principle of equal pay for men and women (*OJ* 1975 L45/19). The directive laid down both substantive and procedural provisions in implementation of Art. 119, and allowed the Member States a period of one year to comply with its terms (Art. 8. See further section VII below). Nevertheless, in Case 43/75 *Defrenne II*, above, at pp. 476–80, the ECJ held that neither the Resolution of 30 December 1961 nor Dir. 75/117 could modify the time-limit provided for by Art. 119. Consequently, the principle of equal pay became fully effective in the original Member States on 1 January 1962, and in the new Member States on the respective dates of the entry into force of the various Treaties of Accession.

In *Defrenne II*, the Court was confronted with the question whether Art. 119 produced direct effect in the sense that individuals could rely on the principle of equal pay before national courts independently of any national provision. This question arose in the context of an action brought by an air hostess against her employer, Sabena Airlines, for compensation on the grounds that as a female worker she suffered pay discrimination as compared with her male colleagues who carried out the same work as cabin stewards. To answer the question, the Court drew a distinction between, first, direct and overt discrimination, which 'may be identified solely with the aid of the criteria based on equal work and equal pay referred to by the article in question' and, secondly, indirect and disguised discrimination, which 'can only be identified by reference to more explicit implementing provisions of a Community or national character' (ibid. at p. 473). The Court pointed out that the complete implementation of Art. 119, by means of the elimination of all discrimination, direct or indirect, between men and women workers, not only in individual undertakings but also in entire branches of industry and even of the economic system as a whole, might in certain cases involve the elaboration of criteria whose implementation requires the adoption of appropriate Community and national measures.

The Court concluded that Art. 119 applies directly to all forms of discrimination falling within the first category, namely, those which may be identified solely with the aid of the criteria of equal work and equal pay referred to by Art. 119, without national or Community measures being required to define them with greater precision in order to permit their application. Among the forms of discrimination that may be thus judicially identified, the Court mentioned in particular those which have their origin in legislative provisions or in collective labour agreements, as well as cases where men and women receive unequal pay for equal work carried out in the same establishment or service, whether private or public. In such a situation, the national courts are in a position to establish all the facts enabling them to decide whether a woman receives less pay than a man engaged in the same work or work of equal value. As regards these forms of discrimination, Art. 119 is directly effective and may give rise to individual rights, which the national courts must protect (ibid. at pp. 473–4). Moreover, the Court added, 'since Article 119 is mandatory in nature, the prohibition on discrimination between men and women applies not only to the action of public authorities, but also extends to all agreements which are intended to regulate paid labour collectively, as well as to contracts between individuals' (ibid. at p. 476). In other words, Art. 119 can produce not only 'vertical' but also 'horizontal' direct effect.

The Court further considered that since Art. 119 imposed on the Member States 'a duty to bring about a specific result to be mandatorily achieved within a fixed period', it became directly effective in the above sense upon the expiry of that period, i.e. as from 1 January 1962. This direct effect could not be prejudiced either by the lack of implementation before that date or by the subsequent adoption of Dir. 75/117 (ibid. at pp. 475, 480). However, referring to 'important considerations of legal certainty affecting all the interests involved, both public and private', the Court found it impossible to reopen the question as regards the past. Therefore, it ruled that the direct effect of Art. 119 could not be relied on in order to support claims concerning pay periods prior to the date of its judgment (8 April 1976), except as regards those workers who had already brought legal proceedings or made an equivalent claim (ibid. at p. 481). Thus, while recognizing the direct effect of Art. 119 retroactively, in practice the Court restricted the possibility of invoking that effect to cases of discrimination taking place in the future.

The (horizontal) direct effect of Art. 119, relied on and confirmed in most of the cases to be discussed below, is of fundamental importance in the enforcement of the principle of equal pay. It means, in practice, that once pay discrimination on grounds of sex has been established, the national courts are bound to interpret and apply the relevant national legislative or administrative provisions in conformity with the requirements of Art. 119 and, where this is not possible, to set aside (disapply) any incompatible domestic provision acting, if necessary, of their own motion. This applies equally where the discriminatory provision is derived from a collective labour agreement or an individual contract of employment. In so doing, the national courts do not need to request or await the prior removal of the offending provision by collective bargaining or by any other constitutional procedure. Moreover, so long as measures for bringing about equal treatment have not been adopted, the national courts are required to apply to members of the disadvantaged group the same arrangements as those enjoyed by persons in the favoured group, this being the only proper way of complying with Art. 119. Finally, employees and their dependants may rely on the direct effect of Art. 119 not only against their employers (whether natural or legal persons) but also against the trustees and administrators of pension schemes, who are equally bound to observe the principle of equal pay (see e.g. Case 157/86 *Murphy* [1988] ECR 673 at p. 690; Case C-184/89 *Nimz* [1991] ECR I-297 at pp. I-320–1; Case C-200/91 *Coloroll* [1994] ECR I-4389 at pp. I-4411–14; Case C-128/93 *Fisscher* [1994] ECR I-4583 at p. I-4597; see further below).

2. Article 141 of the amended EC Treaty. Art. 119 of the original EEC Treaty underwent several changes as a result of successive Treaty amendments. First, without being formally amended in the Treaty itself, Art. 119 was in substance incorporated, with the addition of a new third paragraph, in the Agreement on Social Policy concluded between the Member States with the exception of the United Kingdom (see Art. 6), which Agreement was annexed to the Protocol on Social Policy, which in turn was annexed to the EC Treaty by the Treaty on European Union (TEU). Art. 6(3) of the Agreement, which was not applicable to the United Kingdom, enabled Member States to maintain or adopt measures providing for specific advantages in order to make it easier for women to pursue a vocational activity or to prevent or compensate for disadvantages in their professional careers (for an interpretation of this provision by the ECJ, see section IV below).

Secondly, as part of the wide-ranging changes introduced by the ToA into the social provisions of the EC Treaty, the Agreement on Social Policy was in substance incorporated in the EC Treaty (see Art. 2, point 22 ToA), although, curiously, the Protocol on Social Policy itself, to which the Agreement was annexed, was not repealed by the ToA (see also Case C-366/99 *Griesmar* [2001] ECR I-9383 at pp. I-9426–7). As a result of these changes and of the renumbering of the Treaty articles by the ToA, Arts. 117 to 122 of the EEC Treaty were replaced by Arts. 136 to 145 EC with effect from 1 May 1999, the date on which the ToA entered into force. From the same date, Art. 119 became Art. 141 EC, which added to the wording of Art. 119 a fourth paragraph reproducing, apart from some minor differences, Art. 6(3) of the Agreement on Social Policy. Art. 141 also added a new third paragraph to Art. 119, enabling the Council to adopt measures to ensure the application of the principle of equal opportunities and equal treatment of men and women in matters of employment and occupation, including the principle of equal pay for equal work or work of equal value. However, Art. 141 has not amended the first paragraph of Art. 119 (apart from some minor changes in wording), which lays down the principle of equal pay itself, nor the second paragraph, which defines the concept of 'pay'. For this reason, as pointed out above, the principles developed by the ECJ in its pre-Amsterdam case-law in relation to Art. 119 remain relevant and are fully taken into account in this entry. In the following discussion, Art. 119 will be referred to by its new number as Art. 141.

The ToA also inserted a new Art. 13 in the EC Treaty, which enables the Council to take 'appropriate action', within the limits of the Community's powers, to combat discrimination based on sex, racial, or ethnic origin, religion or belief, disability, age, or sexual orientation. A new second paragraph was added to Art. 13 by the Treaty of Nice (ToN), relating to the adoption of Community incentive measures by the Council to support Member State action in this area.

On the basis of Art. 13, the Council adopted two directives in 2000. The first is Dir. 2000/43 of 29 June 2000 implementing the principle of equal treatment between persons irrespective of racial or ethnic origin (*OJ* 2000 L180/22, rectified in *OJ* 2000 L199/86). The second is Dir. 2000/78 of 27 November 2000 establishing a general framework for equal treatment in employment and occupation (*OJ* 2000 L303/16). Dir. 2000/43 prohibits discrimination based on racial or ethnic origin (Arts. 1 and 2(1)). Dir. 2000/78 prohibits discrimination on the grounds of religion or belief, disability, age, or sexual orientation as regards employment and occupation (Arts. 1 and 2(1)). The scope of both directives is very broad and encompasses, amongst other things, employment and working conditions, including dismissals and pay (Art. 3(1)(c) of both directives). Dir. 2000/43 was to be implemented by the Member States by 19 July 2003; Dir. 2000/78 by 2 December 2003 (Arts. 16 and 18, respectively).

3. Conditions for the application of Article 141. Art. 141(1) can be relied on only by workers. However, the term 'worker' within the meaning of Art. 141(1) is not expressly defined in the Treaty. According to the Court, that term cannot be defined by reference to the legislation of the Member States but has a Community meaning, just as the term 'worker' within the meaning of Art. 39 EC dealing with the free movement of workers. Moreover, that term cannot be interpreted restrictively. For the purposes of both provisions, a worker is a person who, for a certain period of time, performs services for and under the direction of another person in return for which he receives remuneration (*see further under* **Worker**). Art. 141(2) defines 'pay' as a wage or salary that the worker receives from his employer in respect of this employment (see section II below). From this, the Court deduced that the authors of the Treaty did not intend that the term 'worker' within the meaning of Art. 141(1) should include independent providers of services who are not in a relationship of subordination with the person who receives the services. Once a person is a worker, the nature of his legal relationship with the other party to the employment relationship is irrelevant. Nevertheless, the Court added, the formal classification of someone as a self-employed person under national law does not exclude the possibility that that person must be classified as a worker for the purposes of Art. 141(1) if his independence is merely notional, thereby disguising an employment relationship within the meaning of that Article (Case C-256/01 *Allonby* [2004] ECR I-0000, paras. 43 and 62–72).

Generally, in order to be able to rely on Art. 141, a worker must show, first, that the remuneration or benefit in question constitutes 'pay' within the meaning of Art. 141; secondly, that he or she carries out 'equal work' or 'work of equal value'; and thirdly, that he or she suffers 'discrimination' based on sex in respect of that pay, which cannot be justified by objective factors. These three concepts are considered in turn in sections II, III, IV and V below. (See also the Commission's Memorandum on equal pay for work of equal value, adopted on 23 June 1994, COM(94) 6, *Bull. EU* 6–1994, p. 76 and the Commission's Code of practice on the implementation of equal pay, adopted on 17 July 1996, COM(96) 336, *Bull. EU* 7/8–1996, p. 87.)

II. The concept of pay

1. Definition of pay. It is clear that any remuneration or benefit is subject to the prohibition of discrimination on grounds of sex only in so far as it falls within the scope of the definition of 'pay' contained in Art. 141, as interpreted by the ECJ. According to Art. 141(2), 'pay' means:

> the ordinary basic or minimum wage or salary and any other consideration, whether in cash or in kind, which the worker receives directly or indirectly, in respect of his employment, from his employer.

According to the Court, this definition covers any consideration, 'whether immediate or future', whether paid during or after the termination of the employment relationship, and whether the worker receives it under a contract of employment, by virtue of legislative provisions or on a voluntary basis, provided that the worker receives it, albeit indirectly, in respect of his employment from his employer (see e.g. Case C-262/88 *Barber* [1990] ECR I-1889 at pp. I-1949–50; Case C-457/93 *Lewark* [1996] ECR I-243 at p. I-266, and the cases cited below). The Court has moreover held that Art. 1 of Dir. 75/117, which refers to the elimination of sex discrimination with regard to 'all aspects and conditions of remuneration', merely implements Art. 141 and in no way affects the concept of 'pay' as defined therein, but is based on that concept (Case 69/80 *Worringham and Humphreys* [1981] ECR 767 at p. 791; Case 96/80 *Jenkins* [1981] ECR 911 at p. 927). Thus, the only relevant provision in this respect is Art. 141.

In applying Art. 141, one difficult problem confronting the Court has been the question whether and, if so, under what circumstances contributions made to and benefits derived from social security schemes (in particular, retirement pensions) may fall within the definition of 'pay' contained in that Article. This question arose for the first time in Case 80/70 *Defrenne I* [1971] ECR 445 at p. 451, where the Court held that:

> Although consideration in the nature of social security benefits is not . . . in principle alien to the concept of pay, there cannot be brought within this concept, as defined in Art. 141, social security schemes or benefits, in particular retirement pensions, directly governed by legislation without any element of agreement within the undertaking or the occupational branch concerned, which are obligatorily applicable to general categories of workers. These schemes assure for the workers the benefit of a legal [i.e. statutory] scheme, to the financing of which workers, employers and possibly the public authorities contribute in a measure determined less by the employment relationship between the employer and the worker than by considerations of social policy. Accordingly, the part due from the employers in the financing of such schemes does not constitute a direct or indirect payment to the worker.

Moreover, the Court pointed out, the worker will normally receive the legally prescribed benefits not by reason of the employer's contribution but solely because the worker fulfils the statutory conditions laid down for the grant of benefits. The same considerations apply also to special schemes that, within the framework of the general system of social security established by legislation, relate in particular to certain categories of workers. The Court concluded that situations involving discrimination resulting from the application of such a statutory system are not subject to the requirements of Art. 141 (ibid. at pp. 451–2).

The principle laid down in *Defrenne I* that the concept of 'pay' does not cover generally applicable statutory social security schemes and benefits that do not involve any element of agreement has been consistently upheld in the case-law. Subsequently, the Court has developed a number of criteria to determine whether various schemes and benefits operated by employers fall within the statutory category and thus outside the scope of Art. 141 or may be classified as private occupational schemes covered by that provision. These criteria include the following: the statutory origin or nature of a (pension) scheme; negotiations between employers and employees' representatives; the fact that the employees' benefits supplement social security benefits; the manner in which the (pension) scheme is financed; its applicability to general categories of employees; and the relationship between the benefit and the employees' employment.

Thus, while the finding that a pension scheme is governed directly by statute is a strong indication that the benefits provided by the scheme are social security benefits, it is not sufficient to exclude the scheme from the scope of Art. 141, which covers all forms of direct discrimination including those of statutory origin (see *Defrenne II*, above). The Court normally looks beyond the statutory origin of a scheme and tends to give precedence to the criterion of whether there is an agreement between employers and employees. If so, or if the scheme is the result of a unilateral decision by the employer, it is likely to be governed by Art. 141. The same is true if the scheme is wholly financed by the employer, or by both the employer and the employees; if it supplements general social security benefits paid under legislation; and if it does not apply to 'general categories of workers' (i.e. if it only applies to a particular group of employees, such as civil servants).

Nevertheless, in doubtful or borderline cases the only possible decisive criterion is whether the benefit in question is paid to the worker by reason of the employment relationship between him and his present or former employer. If that is the case, the benefit may then be regarded as part of the remuneration and is therefore covered by Art. 141. Thus, considerations of social policy, of State organization, of ethics, or even the budgetary concerns that may have influenced the establishment of a statutory scheme cannot prevail if the benefit (pension) concerns only a particular category of workers, if it is directly related to the period of service completed, and if its amount is calculated by reference to the public servant's final salary. The pension paid by the public employer is in that case entirely comparable to that paid by a private employer to his former employees, and falls within the scope of Art. 141 (see, in general, Case C-7/93 *Beune*, above, at pp. I-4512–18 *per Curiam*, p. I-4484 *per* A.-G. Jacobs and the cases cited below).

2. Examples of pay. Using the above criteria, the Court has classified as 'pay' within the meaning of Art. 141 payments and benefits arising from schemes having the following characteristic features:

(*a*) A contribution to a retirement benefits scheme, whether occupational or statutory, which is paid by the employer in the name of the employee by means of an addition to the gross salary, where, although immediately deducted and paid into a pension fund, the contribution is included in the calculation of the gross salary and directly determines the calculation of other advantages linked to the salary, such as redundancy payments, unemployment benefits, family allowances, and credit facilities (Case 69/80 *Worringham and Humphreys*, above, at p. 790; Case 23/83 *Liefting* [1984] ECR 3225 at p. 3239). Where, however, a contribution to an occupational pension scheme, which is a substitute for a statutory scheme, is paid not by the employer but is deducted from the gross salary of the employee and results in a reduction in net pay without affecting gross pay on the basis of which the other salary-related benefits mentioned above are normally calculated, it cannot be regarded as part of the worker's 'pay' (Case 192/85 *Newstead* [1987] ECR 4753 at pp. 4782–3).

(*b*) Benefits paid to employees under an occupational pension scheme that, although adopted in accordance with legislation, is based on an agreement between employer and employees' representatives, has the effect of supplementing social benefits paid under generally applicable national legislation, and the benefits are financed entirely by the employer and the scheme forms an integral part of the contracts of employment (Case 170/84 *Bilka*, above, at pp. 1625–6; see also Case C-50/96 *Schröder*, above, at p. I-786).

(*c*) A retirement pension paid under a contracted-out private occupational scheme resulting either from an agreement between employer and employees or from a unilateral decision taken by the employer and financed entirely by the employer or by both employer and employees without any contribution being made by the public authorities that, although established in conformity with national legislation, is not compulsorily applicable to general categories of workers and is governed by its own rules. The fact that the contributions paid to the scheme and the benefits that it provides are in part a substitute for those of the general statutory scheme, or the fact that the scheme has been set up in the form of a trust and is administered by trustees who are technically independent of the employer, does not take the scheme out of the scope of Art. 141 (Case C-262/88 *Barber*, above, at pp. I-1951–2. For an analysis of, and distinction between, the different pension schemes figuring in the *Defrenne I, Worringham and Humphreys, Newstead, Bilka* and *Barber* cases, see the opinion of A.-G. Van Gerven, ibid. at pp. I-1918–22). Since the inclusion of occupational pensions within the concept of 'pay' with retroactive effect might have upset the financial balance of many contracted-out pension schemes (which frequently derogated from the principle of equal pay), the Court ruled that the direct effect of Art. 141 may not be relied upon in order to claim entitlement to such a pension with effect from a date prior to that of its judgment in *Barber* (17 May 1990), except in the case of workers who had before that date initiated legal proceedings or raised an equivalent claim (ibid. at p. I-1956. For the interpretation of this temporal limitation, see section IV.2(*f*) below).

(*d*) An additional payment (supplementary allowance) for workers who are made redundant at a particular age. Provided for by a collective agreement and thus being contractual in origin, the fact that the payment is subsequently made compulsory *erga omnes* by legislation and that it supplements a statutory social security benefit such as unemployment benefit is irrelevant (Case C-173/91 *Commission* v. *Belgium* [1993] ECR I-673 at pp. I-698–9. See also Case C-166/99 *Defreyn* [2000] ECR I-6155 at p. I-6184).

(*e*) A survivor's pension provided for by an occupational pension scheme set up by agreement between both sides of the industry concerned and funded wholly by employers and employees to the exclusion of any financial contribution from the public purse, even where the public authorities, at the request of the parties, declare the scheme compulsory for the whole of the industry and although, by definition, the pension is not paid to the employee but to his or her survivor (Case C-109/91 *Ten Oever* [1993] ECR I-4879 at pp. I-4942–4; Case C-200/91 *Coloroll*, above, at p. I-4410; see also Case C-147/95 *Evrenopoulos* [1997] ECR I-2057 at p. I-2081; Case C-50/99 *Podesta* [2000] ECR I-4039 at pp. I-4064–8).

(*f*) A bridging pension financed entirely by the employer and paid *ex gratia* to employees who are compelled on grounds of ill health to take early retirement before reaching the statutory retirement age (Case C-132/92 *Roberts* [1993] ECR I-5579 at pp. I-5600–1 and I-5603).

(*g*) A periodic pension derived from a defined-benefit/final salary occupational pension scheme (which provides employees reaching retirement age with a defined pension corresponding to a certain percentage of their final salary for each year of service), but not the funding arrangements chosen to secure the periodic payment of the pension, which remain outside the scope of Art. 141. In contributory schemes, the contributions made by the employees are an element of their pay since they are deducted directly from their salary, and the amount of those contributions must therefore be the same for all employees, male and female. This is not so in the case of the employer's contributions, which are necessary to ensure the adequacy of the funds. These contributions are higher for female employees than for male employees because women statistically have greater life expectancy than men. The ECJ has held that such inequality of employer's contributions, due to the use of actuarial factors differing according to sex, is not prohibited by Art. 141. Inequalities in the amounts of transfer benefits (transfer of acquired rights) and lump-sum options (conversion of part of the pension into capital), the value of which is lower for men than for women owing to the same actuarial factors, fall likewise outside the scope of Art. 141 (Case C-152/91 *Neath* [1993] ECR I-6935 at pp. I-6960–3; Case C-200/91 *Coloroll*, above, at pp. I-4423–6.

(*h*) Generally, all benefits payable to employees by an occupational pension scheme, irrespective of whether the scheme is contributory or non-contributory, but not including additional benefits stemming from additional voluntary contributions (Case C-200/91 *Coloroll*, above, at pp. I-4426–8).

(*i*) A (statutory) civil service pension that concerns only a particular category of employees (i.e. civil servants), is directly related to the period of service completed, and is calculated by reference to the civil servant's final salary (Case C-7/93 *Beune*, above, at pp. I-4512–19; Case C-366/99 *Griesmar*, above, at pp. I-9428–31; Case C-351/00 *Niemi* [2002] ECR I-7007, paras. 52, 56).

(*j*) The right to join an occupational pension scheme (Case 170/84 *Bilka*, above, at pp. 1626–7; Case C-57/93 *Vroege* [1994] ECR I-4541 at pp. I-4572–4; Case C-128/93 *Fisscher*, above, at pp. I-4592–3; Case C-435/93 *Dietz* [1996] ECR I-5223 at p. I-5251).

In addition, the Court has held that the concept of 'pay' within the meaning of Art. 141 also covers the following:

(*k*) Pay received by a worker while on sick leave (Case 171/88 *Rinner-Kühn* [1989] ECR 2743 at p. 2759; Case C-66/96 *Høj Pedersen* [1998] ECR I-7327 at pp. I-7369–70, I-7373).

(*l*) Pay received by a female worker while on maternity leave, whether under legislation, collective agreement, or an employment contract (Case C-342/93 *Gillespie* [1996] ECR I-475 at p. I-499; Case C-411/96 *Boyle* [1998] ECR I-6401 at p. I-6455; Case C-218/98 *Abdoulaye* [1999] ECR I-5723 at p. I-5747).

(*m*) An end-of-year or Christmas bonus, whether paid under legislation, collective agreement, or on a voluntary basis (Case C-281/97 *Krüger* [1999] ECR I-5127 at p. I-5146; Case C-333/97 *Lewen* [1999] ECR I-7243 at pp. I-7278–9).

(*n*) Family and marriage allowances (Case C-187/98 *Commission* v. *Greece* [1999] ECR I-7713 at p. I-7740).

(*o*) A supplement paid to the worker for performing duties at inconvenient hours (Case C-236/98 *JämO* [2000] ECR I-2189 at pp. I-2219–20) or duties of a particular kind (Case C-381/99 *Brunnhofer* [2001] ECR I-4961 at p. I-4990).

(*p*) Compensation paid by an employer to a worker on termination of the employment relationship due to redundancy or any other reason (i.e. a redundancy payment or severance grant), whether the payment is made under a contract of employment, by virtue of legislation, or on a voluntary (*ex gratia*) basis (Case C-262/88 *Barber*, above, at pp. I-1949–50; Case C-33/89 *Kowalska* [1990] ECR I-2591 at p. I-2611; Case C-249/97 *Gruber* [1999] ECR I-5295 at p. I-5324; see also Case C-220/02 *Österreichischer Gewerkschaftsbund* [2004] ECR I-0000, paras. 36–9).

(*q*) Compensation for unfair dismissal, even if it is a judicial award made on the basis of legislation (Case C-167/97 *Seymour-Smith and Perez* [1999] ECR I-623 at p. I-676).

(*r*) Compensation received from an employer in the form of paid leave or overtime pay for losses of earnings due to attendances at training courses for staff council members, even if it is paid by virtue of legislation (Case C-360/90 *Bötel* [1992] ECR I-3589 at p. I-3611; Case C-457/93 *Lewark*, above, at pp. I-266–7; Case C-278/93 *Freers and Speckmann* [1996] ECR I-1165 at p. I-1190).

(*s*) A practically automatic reclassification in a higher salary grade based on length of service (Case C-184/89 *Nimz*, above, at p. I-318); also a system for classifying workers converting from job-sharing to full-time employment, since it determines the progression of pay (Case C-243/95 *Hill and Stapleton* [1998] ECR I-3739 at p. I-3766); but not a mere placement on the list of candidates eligible for promotion to a higher grade and accordingly to a higher level of salary (Case C-1/95 *Gerster* [1997] ECR I-5253 at pp. I-5282–3).

(*t*) Special travel facilities and concessions granted by an employer to former employees, their spouses, or dependants, in respect of their employment, even if they are not based on a contractual obligation (Case 12/81 *Garland* [1982] ECR 359 at pp. 369–70; Case C-249/96 *Grant* [1998] ECR I-621 at p. I-642).

(*u*) Piece-work pay schemes in which pay depends entirely or in large measure on the individual output of each worker (Case C-400/93 *Royal Copenhagen* [1995] ECR I-1275 at p. I-1303).

III. The concept of equal work or work of equal value

The original text of Art. 119 EEC required that men and women should receive equal pay for 'equal work'. This narrow criterion of 'equal work' was extended by Dir. 75/117 in accordance with ILO Convention No. 100, mentioned earlier, Art. 2 of which lays down the principle of equal pay for 'work of equal value'. Thus, Art. 1 of Dir. 75/117 makes it clear that the concept of 'same work' or 'equal work' contained in Art. 119 also covers 'work to which equal value is attributed' (see Case 43/75 *Defrenne II*, above, at p. 473; Case 69/80 *Worringham and Humphreys*, above, at p. 791, and the cases cited below). Indeed, the ECJ has held that national legislation which lays down the principle of equal pay only in respect of the 'same work', without extending it to 'work of equal value', does not fulfil the requirements of Dir. 75/117 since it restricts the scope of that principle (Case 143/83 *Commission* v. *Denmark* [1985] ECR 427 at pp. 435–6). The Court has moreover held that Art. 119 requires the application of the principle of equal pay not only in the case of work of equal value but also where the lower-paid worker is engaged in work of higher value than that of the person with whom a comparison is to be made (Case 157/86 *Murphy*, above, at pp. 689–90).

These developments have been incorporated in the text of Art. 141(1) EC, replacing Art. 119, which now provides that:

> Each Member State shall ensure that the principle of equal pay for male and female workers for equal work or work of equal value is applied.

Moreover, in defining the concept of equal pay in more detail, Art. 141(2)(a) uses the term 'the same work', while Art. 141(2)(b) contains the term 'the same job' (see further section IV below). The case-law of the Court shows that all of these terms, i.e. 'the same work', 'the same job', and 'work of equal value', appearing in Art. 141 and Art. 1 of Dir. 75/117, are entirely qualitative in character in that they are exclusively concerned with the nature of the work actually performed (see Case C-381/99 *Brunnhofer*, above, at pp. I-4991–2). In this connection, the Court has repeatedly held that:

> in order to determine whether employees perform the same work or work to which equal value can be attributed, it is necessary to ascertain whether, taking account of a number of factors such as the nature of the work, the training requirements and the working conditions, those persons can be considered to be in a comparable situation (ibid. at p. I-4992. See also Case C-400/93 *Royal Copenhagen*, above, at p. I-1310 and the case cited immediately below).

Thus, where seemingly identical tasks (e.g. psychotherapy) are performed by different persons or groups of persons who do not have the same training or professional qualifications (e.g. psychologists and doctors employed as psychotherapists), it is necessary to ascertain whether, taking into account a number of factors such as the nature of the tasks actually assigned to each person or group respectively, the training requirements for the performance of those tasks and the actual working conditions, the different persons or groups in fact do the 'same work'. Accordingly, professional training is not only one of the factors that may be an objective justification for giving different pay for doing the same work (see section IV below), it is also one of the possible criteria for determining whether or not the same work is being performed. Where the same activities are carried out over a considerable length of time by persons the basis of whose qualification to exercise their profession is different, the term 'the same work' does not apply (Case C-309/97 *Angestelltenbetriebsrat der Wiener Gebietskrankenkasse* [1999] ECR I-2865 at pp. I-2916–17).

Likewise, the fact that different employees are classified in the same job category under the collective agreement applicable to their employment is not in itself sufficient for concluding that they perform the same work or work of equal value. Such a classification does not exclude the use of other evidence to support that conclusion. In any event, the general indications provided in a collective agreement must be corroborated by precise and concrete factors, such as those discussed above, based on the activities actually performed by the employees concerned (Case C-381/99 *Brunnhofer*, above, at pp. I-4992–3).

As regards job classification, Art. 1 of Dir. 75/117 provides that 'where a job classification system is used for determining pay, it must be based on the same criteria for both men and women and so drawn up as to exclude any discrimination on grounds of sex'. In Case 61/81 *Commission* v. *United Kingdom* [1982] ECR 2601 at pp. 2615–17, the Court found that while under the directive a job classification system was merely one of several methods for determining pay for work to which equal value is attributed, under the provisions of the United Kingdom legislation implementing the directive (the Equal Pay Act 1970 as amended by the Sex Discrimination Act 1975) the introduction of such a system was the sole method of achieving that result. However, the British legislation did not permit the introduction of a job classification system without the employer's consent. Consequently, workers were unable to have their work rated as being of equal value with comparable work if their employer refused to introduce a classification system. In the opinion of the Court, this state of affairs amounted to a denial of the very existence of a right to equal pay for work of equal value where no classification had been made, and was therefore plainly contrary to Dir. 75/117.

The Court also held that where there is a disagreement as to the application of the concept of 'work to which equal value is attributed', a worker must be entitled to claim before an appropriate authority that his work has the same value as other work and, if that is found to be the case, to have his rights under the Treaty and the directive acknowledged by a binding decision. Any other method is insufficient to achieve the aims of the directive. That is why Art. 6 of the directive itself requires the Member States to ensure that effective means are available to enforce the observance of the principle of equal pay (see further section VII below). By not adopting measures necessary to enable all employees to obtain recognition of equal value for work for which no job classification system existed, the Court concluded, the United Kingdom failed to fulfil its obligations under the Treaty.

In considering in more detail the criteria that may be used in a job classification system, in Case 237/85 *Rummler* [1986] ECR 2101 at p. 2114, the Court held that such criteria must not differ according to whether the work is carried out by a man or by a woman, and that the system as a whole must not be organized in such a manner that it has the practical effect of discriminating generally against workers of one sex. Accordingly, the Court considered that Dir. 75/117 does not prohibit the use of the criterion of muscle demand or muscular effort or that of the heaviness of the work (even if these criteria may tend to favour men who are generally stronger than women) if, in view of the nature of the tasks involved, the work to be performed does require the use of physical strength, so long as the system as a whole, by taking into account other criteria, precludes any discrimination on grounds of sex (ibid. at p. 2115). On the whole, the criteria governing pay-rate classification must ensure that work which is objectively the same attracts the same rate of pay whether it is performed by a man or a woman. The use of values reflecting the average performance of workers of one sex as a basis for determining the extent to which work makes demands or requires effort or whether it is heavy constitutes a form of sex discrimination contrary to the directive. To avoid discrimination, a job classification system must, so far as possible, take into account criteria for which workers of each sex may show particular aptitude (ibid. at pp. 2117–18).

IV. The concept of discrimination

1. Definition of discrimination. The principle of equal pay laid down in Art. 141(1) (see section III above) is defined in Art. 141(2), which provides that:

> Equal pay without discrimination based on sex means:
> (a) that pay for the same work at piece rates shall be calculated on the basis of the same unit of measurement;
> (b) that pay for work at time rates shall be the same for the same job.

Art. 1 of Dir. 75/117 further makes it clear that the principle of equal pay implies:

> for the same work or for work to which equal value is attributed, the elimination of all discrimination on grounds of sex with regard to all aspects and conditions of remuneration.

It is thus obvious that Art. 141 and Dir. 75/117 prohibit pay discrimination between men and women only in so far as it is based on the sex of the person concerned (see Case 96/80 *Jenkins*, above, at p. 925; Case C-381/99 *Brunnhofer*, above, at p. I-4991). In Case C-249/96 *Grant* [1998] ECR I-621 at pp. I-649–51, the ECJ confirmed that Community law, as it stood at the time of the judgment, did not cover discrimination based on sexual orientation. The Court held that the refusal by an employer to grant travel concessions to a person of the same sex with whom a worker had a stable relationship while granting such concessions to a worker's spouse or to a person of the opposite sex with whom a worker had a stable relationship outside marriage, did not constitute discrimination based on sex and therefore was not prohibited by Art. 141 or Dir. 75/117 since the employer's rules applied in the same way to male and female workers. Thus, travel concessions were refused to a male worker if he was living with a person of the same sex, just as they were refused to a female worker if she was living with a person of the same sex (ibid. at pp. I-646, I-652). Since, as Community law stood at the time, stable relationships between two persons of the same sex were not regarded as equivalent to marriages or stable relationships between persons of opposite sex, an employer was not required by Community law to treat the two situations in the same way (ibid. at p. I-648).

Similarly, in Cases C-122/99 P etc. *D and Sweden* v. *Council* [2001] ECR I-4319 at pp. I-4356–7, the Court held that, as the law stood at the material time, the relevant provisions of the Staff Regulations, which restricted the household allowance to married officials, did not discriminate on grounds of sex or sexual orientation contrary to Art. 141, since they applied equally to men and women. The Court again confirmed that the situation of an official who had registered a partnership between persons of the same sex in Sweden was not comparable, for the purposes of applying the Staff Regulations, to that of a married official even though under Swedish law a registered partnership had legal effects akin to those of marriage.

By contrast, inequality of treatment arises where a benefit that constitutes pay, such as a survivor's pension, cannot be awarded, not because it is restricted to married couples, but because a couple are unable to marry due to the fact that one partner's identity is the result of gender reassignment surgery and under the legislation of a Member State it is impossible for a transsexual to marry a person of the sex to which he or she belonged prior to such a surgery because, for the purposes of the registers of civil status, they belong to the same sex. Relying on judgments of the European Court of Human Rights, according to which United Kingdom legislation not admitting of legal recognition of transsexuals' new identity was in breach of their right to marry under Art. 12 of the ECHR (see judgments of 11 July 2002 in *Goodwin* v. *United Kingdom* and *I* v. *United Kingdom*), the ECJ held that such legislation was incompatible with Art. 141 since it deprived one of the couple of the benefit in question (Case C-117/01 *KB* [2004] ECR I-0000, paras. 28–36. For discrimination based on gender reassignment, see also Case C-13/94 *P* [1996] ECR I-2143, *discussed under* **Equal treatment**, section II.1(*b*)).

In both *Grant* and *D and Sweden* v. *Council* the Court made it clear that the scope of the provisions on non-discrimination could only be extended by legislative measures and not by means of judicial interpretation. As seen in section I above, such measures have been adopted in the form of Dirs. 2000/43 and 2000/78, the latter of which prohibits discrimination, amongst other things, on the ground of sexual orientation.

From the fact, mentioned above, that Art. 141 and Dir. 75/117 only prohibit discrimination based on sex it follows that a difference in pay between a man and a woman does not constitute discrimination contrary to those provisions if it may be explained by objectively justified factors unrelated to any discrimination on grounds of sex (of the many cases, see e.g. Case C-400/93 *Royal Copenhagen*, above, at p. I-1312; Case C-381/99 *Brunnhofer*, above, at pp. I-4988–9, I-4996, I-4997, I-5001, and the cases cited below). Although the scope of this principle is potentially very broad as it applies in cases of both direct and indirect discrimination (for the latter, see section V below), the legal criteria for establishing the existence of an objective justification for unequal treatment *prima facie* based on sex are not very clearly defined. The main reason is that this is primarily a question of fact that depends on the circumstances of each individual case. In preliminary ruling proceedings, through which most of the cases involving equal pay issues come before the ECJ, it is for the national court making the reference to establish the facts, i.e. whether, in the particular case before it, there are objective grounds unrelated to sex that may justify unequal treatment. The ECJ can only provide guidance in that respect (see Case 129/79 *Macarthys* [1980] ECR 1275 at p. 1289; Case 170/84 *Bilka*, above, at pp. 1627–8; Case C-381/99 *Brunnhofer*, above, at pp. I-4997–8). Thus, the ECJ has indicated that the grounds put forward by an employer to justify the inequality must correspond to a real need of the undertaking, be appropriate to achieving the objectives pursued and necessary to that end. The principle of proportionality must also be observed (ibid.).

In any case, only objective factors may justify unequal treatment. Thus, professional training is such a factor since it is objectively known at the time when the employee is appointed. It may therefore justify a difference in pay granted to employees doing the same work (see Case C-309/97 *Angestelltenbetriebsrat der Wiener Gebietskrankenkasse*, above, at p. I-2917; Case C-381/99 *Brunnhofer*, above, at p. I-5000). Where work is paid at piece rates, different individual output may also justify different pay if the unit of measurement is the same for both sexes (ibid. at pp. I-4998–9). However, where work is paid at time rates, circumstances linked to the person of an employee that cannot be determined objectively at the time of that person's appointment but come to light only during the actual performance of his or her duties, such as personal work capacity or the effectiveness or quality of the work actually done, cannot be relied on by the employer to justify the fixing, right from the start of the employment relationship, of pay different from that paid to a colleague of the other sex performing the same work. Individual work capacity and performance can only be taken into account to justify a difference in pay by moving the person concerned to a different post (ibid. at pp. I-4998–5003). Other factors capable of justifying unequal treatment will be mentioned below and in section V, in the context of the various situations involving discrimination to be discussed.

As seen in section I above, Art. 6(3) of the Agreement on Social Policy annexed to the Protocol on Social Policy, in turn annexed to the EC Treaty by the TEU, introduced a second justification for a difference in treatment on grounds of sex. It allows Member States to maintain or adopt measures providing for specific advantages in order to make it easier for women to pursue a vocational activity or to prevent or compensate for disadvantages in their professional careers (positive action). The ECJ has interpreted this provision as authorizing national measures intended to eliminate or reduce actual instances of inequality that result from the reality of social life and affect women in their professional life. Therefore, the national measures contemplated in Art. 6(3) must contribute to helping women conduct their professional life on an equal footing with men. The Court held that a French law that granted female civil servants who were mothers a service credit at the date of their retirement in order to increase the periods of service actually completed for the purposes of calculating their retirement pensions, was not covered by Art. 6(3) since it did not provide a remedy for the problems that women may have encountered in the course of their professional career. Art. 6(3) therefore could not justify the exclusion of male civil servants from entitlement to the credit in question (Case C-366/99 *Griesmar*, above, at pp. I-9438–9). Art. 6(3) has been incorporated, with some minor changes, in Art. 141(4) EC (the latter refers to the 'under-represented sex' instead of women).

Since the concept of 'pay' is inseparably linked to an employment relationship (see section II above), Art. 141 and Dir. 75/117 (just as Dir. 76/207 on equal treatment, see section VII below) prohibit only employment-related sex discrimination. They apply to men and women not generally but only in their capacity as workers (see Cases 48/88 etc. *Achterberg-te Riele* [1989] ECR 1963 at p. 1988. For a definition of the concept of 'worker', see section I.3 above).

As regards the method to be used for comparing the pay of male and female employees in order to verify compliance with the principle of equal pay, the ECJ has held that in the interests of transparency and effective judicial review, equal pay must be ensured not only on the basis of an overall assessment of all the consideration paid to employees but also in respect of each element of remuneration taken in isolation. Thus, where remuneration consists of a basic salary and a salary supplement, equal pay must be ensured in respect of each, taken separately (Case C-262/88 *Barber*, above, at pp. I-1953–4; Case C-236/98 *JämO*, above, at pp. I-2220–1, I-2223, I-2225; Case C-381/99 *Brunnhofer*, above, at pp. I-4990, I-5001).

In several cases, the ECJ has emphasized that the principle of equal pay set out in Art. 141 is a particular expression of the general principle of non-discrimination. According to that general principle, the concept of discrimination involves 'the application of different rules to comparable situations or the application of the same rule to different situations' (see the cases cited below). Therefore, for discrimination to occur, the male and female workers to whom Art. 141 applies must be in identical, or at least comparable, situations (Case C-381/99 *Brunnhofer*, above, at p. I-4991). Where that is not the case, unequal treatment in respect of pay does not constitute prohibited discrimination. Thus, for example, men and women are not in a comparable situation giving rise to discrimination in the following circumstances: between the ages of 60 and 65 with regard to receiving a bridging pension (Case C-132/92 *Roberts*, above, at pp. I-5604–5); where women are on maternity leave and men are actually at work (Case C-342/93 *Gillespie*, above, at p. I-499) or on sick leave (Case C-411/96 *Boyle*, above, at pp. I-6455–6); where women take parental leave and men perform military or civilian service (Case C-220/02 *Österreichischer Gewerkschaftsbund*, above, paras. 58–65); where the purpose of an advantage or benefit is to offset the occupational disadvantages inherent in maternity leave (Case C-218/98 *Abdoulaye*, above, at pp. I-5747–8), but not where its purpose is to offset the occupational disadvantages entailed in bringing up children, in which case male and female workers are in a comparable situation (Case C-366/99 *Griesmar*, above, at pp. I-9431–3, I-9436–7); they are also in comparable situations with regard to entitlement to a retirement pension with immediate effect in certain circumstances (Case C-206/00 *Mouflin* [2001] ECR I-10201 at pp. I-10233–4).

As discussed in section III above, being in a comparable situation also implies that the two groups compared (male and female workers) must carry out either the same work or at least work to which equal value is attributed. Subject to these conditions, Art. 141 prohibits any pay discrimination without exception, whatever the system or mechanism which gives rise to it, unless the difference in pay is justified by objective factors unrelated to sex (Case C-262/88 *Barber*, above, at p. I-1953; Case C-381/99 *Brunnhofer*, above, at pp. I-4988–9).

Although Art. 141(1) can be relied on only by workers, the applicability of that provision is not limited to situations in which men and women work for the same employer. It also covers discrimination arising directly from legislative provisions or collective labour agreements (see section I above). Thus, women may rely on statistics to show that a clause in State legislation is contrary to Art. 141(1) because it discriminates against female workers. In such a case, it is the legislature that is the sole source of the difference in treatment and the applicability of Art. 141(1) *vis-à-vis* an undertaking is not subject to the condition, discussed below, that the worker concerned can be compared with a worker of the other sex who is or has been employed by the same employer and who has received higher pay for equal work or work of equal value (Case C-256/01 *Allonby*, above, paras. 80–4). However, where the differences in pay cannot be attributed to a single source, Art. 141(1) does not apply. In that case, there is no body that is responsible for the inequality and that could restore equal treatment. In those circumstances, the work and the pay of the workers concerned cannot be compared on the basis of Art. 141(1) (Case C-320/00 *Lawrence* [2002] ECR I-7325, paras. 17–19; Case C-256/01 *Allonby*, above, paras. 43–50).

As seen in section I above, since Art. 141 is mandatory in nature, the prohibition of discrimination contained in it applies not only to the acts of public authorities but also to all collective agreements intended to regulate paid employment, to all contracts between private individuals and to unilateral action by an employer *vis-à-vis* his employers (Case 43/75 *Defrenne II*, above, at p. 476; Case C-200/91 *Coloroll*, above, at p. I-4412; Case C-333/97 *Lewen*, above, at p. I-7279). Moreover, the prohibition of discrimination applies not only to employers but also to bodies responsible for paying benefits falling within the scope of Art. 141, such as trustees and pension funds governed by national law, who/which are expressly charged with performing the employer's obligations, even where employees enjoy complete legal protection as against their employer (ibid. at p. I-4411; Case C-379/99 *Menauer* [2001] ECR I-7275 at pp. I-7300–1). Where discrimination has been suffered, equal treatment is to be achieved by placing the worker discriminated against in the same situation as that of the workers of the other sex, but the former cannot claim more favourable treatment (Case C-132/92 *Roberts*, above, at p. I-5607; Case C-128/93 *Fisscher*, above, at p. I-4598).

It should finally be mentioned that the principle of equal pay is not confined to situations in which men and women are contemporaneously doing equal work for the same employer. Thus, a woman may claim the same pay as that received by a man who previously did the same work for her employer (and vice versa). However, a worker cannot rely on Art. 141 in order to claim pay to which he or she would be entitled if he/she belonged to the other sex in the absence, at present or in the past, in the undertaking concerned, of workers of the other sex who perform or performed comparable work. In such a situation, the essential criterion for ascertaining that equal treatment exists in the matter of pay, namely the performance of the same work and receipt of the same pay, cannot be applied. This means that comparisons cannot be made with 'hypothetical' comparators because this would imply comparative studies of whole branches of industry and would require, as a prerequisite, the elaboration by the Community and national authorities of suitable criteria of assessment. This would take the situation outside the direct effect of Art. 141. Except where discrimination arises directly from legislation (see above), comparisons are confined to parallels that may be drawn on the basis of concrete appraisals of the work actually performed by workers of different sex within the same establishment or service. It follows that Art. 141 is not applicable to undertakings and pension schemes that have at all times had workers or members of only one sex (Case 129/79 *Macarthys*, above, at pp. 1288–90; Case C-200/91 *Coloroll*, above, at pp. I-4430–1).

2. Examples of direct discrimination. Applying these general considerations, the ECJ has established or indicated the existence of direct discrimination contrary to Art. 141 in the following main situations:

(*a*) Where a woman receives less pay than a man who previously carried out the same work in the same establishment (Case 129/79 *Macarthys*, above, at p. 1290).

(*b*) Where a male and a female employee performing the same work receive the same basic salary but the male employee receives a higher salary supplement than his female colleague, and the difference cannot be explained by objectively justified factors unrelated to sex (Case C-381/99 *Brunnhofer*, above, at pp. I-4982, I-4999–5003).

(*c*) Where the requirement to pay contributions to a retirement benefit scheme applies only to men and these contributions are paid by the employer by means of a deductible addition to the gross salary with the result that the gross salary of men, which is used to determine the amount of certain benefits and social advantages, is higher than that of women, even though after the deduction of the contributions their net salary is the same (Case 69/80 *Worringham and Humphreys*, above, at pp. 792–3. See also Case 23/83 *Liefting*, above, at pp. 3239–40).

(*d*) Where an employer provides special travel facilities for retired male employees but not for retired female employees (Case 12/81 *Garland*, above, at p. 370).

(*e*) Where collective agreements and arbitration awards make the grant of family and marriage allowances to married female workers subject to conditions that are not imposed on married male workers (Case C-187/98 *Commission* v. *Greece*, above, at pp. I-7735, I-7741, I-7743–4).

(*f*) Where retirement pensions paid under a contracted-out private occupational scheme are subject to an age condition that differs according to sex, even if the difference between the pensionable ages for men and women corresponds to that provided for by the national statutory pension scheme (i.e. higher for men, lower for women). The result of such discrimination is that within a certain age group a man made compulsorily redundant is entitled to claim only a deferred pension payable at the normal pensionable age while a woman of the same age and in the same position is entitled to an immediate retirement pension. This type of discrimination falls within the scope of the direct effect of Art. 141, and may therefore be brought before the national courts (Case C-262/88 *Barber*, above, at pp. I-1953–5).

As mentioned above, the Court imposed a temporal limitation on this direct effect (ibid. at p. I-1956, see section II.2(*c*) above), which was subsequently interpreted as meaning that the direct effect of Art. 141 may be relied on, for the purpose of claiming equal treatment in the matter of occupational pensions, only in relation to benefits payable in respect of periods of employment subsequent to 17 May 1990 (the date of the *Barber* judgment), subject to the exception in favour of workers or those claiming under them who had, before that date, initiated legal proceedings or raised an equivalent claim under the applicable national law (Case C-109/91 *Ten Oever*, above, at p. I-4945; see also e.g. Case C-110/91 *Moroni* [1993] ECR I-6591 at pp. I-6618–19; Case C-200/91 *Coloroll*, above, at pp. I-4417–18). The same temporal limitation applies to transfer benefits and lump-sum options (Case C-152/91 *Neath*, above, at p. I-6959), to survivors' pensions (Case C-200/91 *Coloroll*, above, at pp. I-4419–20), and to benefits not linked to the length of actual service (such as a lump-sum payment in the event of an employee's death during his employment), but only where the operative event occurred before 17 May 1990. After that date, such benefits must be granted in accordance with the principle of equal treatment without any need to distinguish between periods of service before and after the *Barber* judgment (ibid. at p. I-4420).

The above interpretation of the *Barber* judgment was essentially incorporated in the EC Treaty by Protocol No. 2 annexed to that Treaty by the TEU, which provides that:

For the purposes of Art. 141 of this Treaty, benefits under occupational social security schemes shall not be considered as remuneration if and in so far as they are attributable to periods of employment prior to 17 May 1990, except in the case of workers or those claiming under them who have before that date initiated legal proceedings or introduced an equivalent claim under the applicable national law (see also the *Beune, Vroege* and *Fisscher* cases at points (*h*) and (*k*) below and Case C-147/95 *Evrenopoulos*, above, at p. I-2086).

As a result of the *Barber* judgment, occupational pension schemes were required to achieve equal treatment as from 17 May 1990. As to the method to be used to achieve such equal treatment, the case-law of the Court distinguishes between three different situations.

First, as regards periods of employment completed between the date of the Court's judgment (17 May 1990) and the date of entry into force of measures adopted to bring about equal treatment, the only correct way of complying with Art. 141 is to grant to the persons in the disadvantaged class (in this case, men) the same advantages as those enjoyed by the persons in the favoured class (in this case, women). Consequently, during this period the pension rights of men must be calculated on the basis of the same retirement age as that for women, and employers and pension schemes are precluded from raising the retirement age for women to that for men, even if they are faced with financial difficulties.

Secondly, as regards periods of employment completed after the entry into force of measures taken to eliminate discrimination, Art. 141 merely requires that men and women should receive the same pay for the same work without imposing any specific level of pay. It does not therefore preclude equal treatment from being achieved by reducing the advantages of the persons previously favoured. Consequently, during this period equalization of retirement ages may be attained by raising the retirement age for women to that for men. However, such a step cannot be accompanied by measures, even if only transitional, designed to limit the adverse consequences which it may have for women, since this would amount to discrimination. For the same reasons, following equalization a pension scheme cannot maintain in favour of women a retirement age lower than that for men, even if such a difference is due to an election made by women, expressly or by implication, before the *Barber* judgment.

Thirdly, as regards periods of employment completed prior to the date of the *Barber* judgment (17 May 1990), that judgment excluded the application of Art. 141 so that employers and pension schemes are not required to ensure equal treatment for those periods. Consequently, Community law imposes no obligation that would justify retroactive reduction of the advantages enjoyed by the favoured class, i.e. the raising of the retirement age for women to that for men (Case C-200/91 *Coloroll*, above, at pp. I-4413–15; Case C-408/92 *Advel Systems* [1994] ECR I-4435 at pp. I-4465–9; Case C-28/93 *Van den Akker* [1994] ECR I-4527 at pp. I-4535–8).

Equalization of benefits in accordance with the above principles must be ensured by the national courts irrespective of any difficulties arising from the insufficiency of the funds held by the trustees of an occupational pension scheme or the inability of the employer to provide additional funds. The national courts must ensure correct implementation of Art. 141 by taking due account of the respective liabilities of employers and trustees under the rules of domestic law (Case C-200/91 *Coloroll*, above, at pp. I-4412–13 and I-4415–17).

(*g*) The principles stated in the *Barber* judgment (see point (*f*) above) are not limited to contracted-out occupational schemes and pensions paid following compulsory retirement on economic grounds. They also apply to supplementary schemes, and occupational pensions in general. Consequently, it is discrimination contrary to Art. 141 if under a supplementary occupational pension scheme a male employee is entitled to claim a company pension only at a higher age than a female employee in the same situation owing to the setting of different retirement ages for men and women. A male employee must be able to assert his right to payment of the company pension at the same age as his female counterpart and any reduction in the event of early departure from the service of the undertaking must be calculated on the basis of that age (Case C-110/91 *Moroni*, above, at pp. I-6616–17). Likewise, the principles laid down in the *Barber* judgment, and the limitation of its effects in time, apply to non-contracted-out occupational pension schemes (Case C-200/91 *Coloroll*, above, at pp. I-4421–3).

(*h*) Where the civil service pension of a married man is systematically lower than that of a married woman in the same position. In the absence of proper national implementation of Art. 141, disadvantaged married men must be treated in the same way and have the same rules applied to them as married women. Such a pension is subject to Protocol No. 2 on Art. 141, which extended the scope of the *Barber* judgment to all benefits payable under occupational social security schemes (Case C-7/93 *Beune*, above, at pp. I-4519–24).

(*i*) Where the award of a survivor's pension to a widower is subject to special conditions that are not applied to widows (Case C-147/95 *Evrenopoulos*, above, at pp. I-2082–3) or to a higher age-limit (65) than that which applies to widows (60) (Case C-50/99 *Podesta*, above, at pp. I-4068–9).

(*j*) Where additional redundancy payments provided for by a collective agreement are granted only to male workers aged between 60 and 65 but denied to female workers within the same age group (Case C-173/91 *Commission* v. *Belgium*, above, at p. I-699). Such payments constitute benefits under an occupational social security scheme within the meaning of the *Barber* Protocol and are subject to its temporal limitation (Case C-166/99 *Defreyn*, above, at pp. I-6185–6).

(*k*) Where an occupational pension scheme excludes women from membership. The ECJ has held that the limitation of the effects in time of the *Barber* judgment does not apply to the right to join an occupational pension scheme, nor to the right to payment of a retirement pension where the worker was excluded from membership of the scheme in breach of Art. 141. Consequently, the direct effect of Art. 141 can be relied on in order to enforce both of these rights retroactively as from 8 April 1976, the date of the *Defrenne II* judgment in which the Court held for the first time that Art.

141 has direct effect. Moreover, since Protocol No. 2 on Art. 141 is linked to the *Barber* judgment, it, too, relates only to benefits and does not, any more than *Barber*, affect the right to belong to an occupational scheme and the right to payment of a retirement pension where the worker was excluded from the occupational scheme in breach of Art. 141. These rights are governed by the judgment in Case 170/84 *Bilka*, above, at pp. 1626–7, which first dealt with this problem and which did not limit the temporal effects of its interpretation of Art. 141. While thus a female worker can claim retroactively to join an occupational pension scheme from which she had been wrongly excluded, together with the corresponding benefits, she cannot avoid paying the contributions relating to the period of membership concerned since she is only entitled to equal and not to more favourable treatment (Case C-7/93 *Beune*, above, at pp. I-4521–2; Case C-57/93 *Vroege*, above, at pp. I-4572–80; Case C-128/93 *Fisscher*, above, at pp. I-4592–601; Case C-435/93 *Dietz*, above, at pp. I-5253–7).

(*l*) Where a pregnant woman is deprived, before the beginning of her maternity leave, of her full pay when her incapacity for work is the result of a pathological condition connected with her pregnancy when all workers are entitled to receive full pay in the event of incapacity for work on grounds of illness. Such discrimination cannot be justified by the aim of sharing the costs connected with pregnancy between the pregnant worker, the employer, and society as a whole. This is not an objective factor unrelated to sex discrimination. There is no discrimination, however, where the pregnant woman's absence from work is not due to incapacity for work or to a pathological condition connected with pregnancy (Case C-66/96 *Høj Pedersen*, above, at pp. I-7370–2, I-7374).

(*m*) In contrast to point (l) above, the principle of equal pay neither requires that women should continue to receive full pay during maternity leave, nor lays down specific criteria for determining the amount of benefit payable to them during that period, provided that the amount is not set so low as to jeopardize the purpose of maternity leave. However, the principle of equal pay does require that women on maternity leave should receive any pay rise, even if backdated, awarded before or during that period (Case C-342/93 *Gillespie*, above, at pp. I-499–502; for taking account of any pay rise in the calculation of the maternity pay, see Case C-147/02 *Alabaster* [2004] ECR I-0000, paras. 49–50, 56).

V. The concept of indirect discrimination

1. Definition of indirect discrimination. If a rule or practice applies without distinction to male and female workers, there is no direct discrimination. Nevertheless, in certain circumstances it may still be necessary to examine whether such a rule or practice involves indirect discrimination, which is equally prohibited by Art. 141, as interpreted by the ECJ. Thus, in a number of cases the Court has said that:

> The principle of equal pay excludes not only the application of provisions leading to direct sex discrimination, but also the application of provisions which maintain different treatment between men and women at work as a result of the application of

criteria not based on sex where those differences of treatment are not attributable to objective factors unrelated to sex discrimination (Cases C-399/92 etc. *Helmig* [1994] ECR I-5727 at p. I-5753; see also the cases cited below).

To put it in another way, Art. 141 prohibits:

the application of any provision which, though formulated and applied in a manner which does not discriminate between men and women, entails *de facto* indirect discrimination because it places many more women than men at a disadvantage (ibid. at p. I-5752 *per* Commission), or

a national provision or a term of a collective agreement which applies independently of the sex of the workers, but actually affects a considerably higher percentage of women than men, unless that provision is justified by objective reasons unrelated to any discrimination on grounds of sex (Case C-281/97 *Krüger*, above, at pp. I-5147–8).

Thus, in simple terms, indirect discrimination arises where a legislative or contractual provision, albeit formulated in neutral terms, works to the disadvantage of far more women than men (or vice versa).

The concept of indirect discrimination, originally developed in the case-law of the ECJ, has been incorporated more recently in various Community directives. Thus, Art. 2(2) of Dir. 97/80 on the burden of proof (for which see further section VI below) provides that:

indirect discrimination shall exist where an apparently neutral provision, criterion or practice disadvantages a substantially higher proportion of the members of one sex unless that provision, criterion or practice is appropriate and necessary and can be justified by objective factors unrelated to sex (see also Art. 2(2) of Dir. 2002/73 of 23 September 2002 amending Dir. 76/207 on equal treatment, *OJ* 2002 L269/15).

The most frequent situation in which such indirect discrimination arises in practice is where an employer applies less favourable pay conditions to part-time workers than to full-time workers carrying out equal work and the former category comprises a considerably higher proportion of women than men. In Case 96/80 *Jenkins*, above, at pp. 925–6, the first case involving such a situation, the Court pointed out that since Art. 141 only prohibits discrimination based on sex, the fact that part-time work is paid at an hourly rate lower than pay for full-time work does not amount *per se* to prohibited discrimination provided that the hourly rates are applied to workers in each category without distinction based on sex. However, such inequality in pay will be contrary to Art. 141 if the category of part-time workers includes a much higher percentage of women than men, unless the pay policy of the employer may be explained by objective factors unrelated to sex, such as his intention to encourage full-time work on purely economic grounds and irrespective of the sex of the worker. In the absence of such justification, the difference in pay, although based on weekly working hours, is in reality an indirect way of reducing the level of pay of women who predominantly make up the category of part-time workers.

As seen in section I above, in Case 43/75 *Defrenne II*, above, at pp. 473–4, the Court restricted the direct effect of Art. 141 to cases of direct discrimination. However, in Case 96/80 *Jenkins*, above, at p. 927, the Court made it clear that the direct effect of Art. 141 also extends to situations where a national court is able to establish, solely with the aid of the criteria of equal work and equal pay referred to in that Article, and without the operation of Community or national measures, that indirect discrimination based on sex exists.

In subsequent cases, the Court has identified indirect discrimination in a variety of situations, whether related to part-time work or not, which will be discussed below. It appears from the Court's case-law that prohibited indirect discrimination exists only where the following three conditions are met.

First, there is a difference in pay between two groups of workers carrying out equal work or work of equal value.

Secondly, there is a substantially higher proportion of women than men in the disadvantaged group (or the other way round). The disparity between men and women must be evidenced by significant and valid statistical data, which cover enough individuals and do not illustrate purely fortuitous or short-term phenomena. Moreover, the disadvantaged worker and the other workers must be in an identical or similar situation.

Thirdly, the pay difference cannot be justified by objective factors unrelated to sex discrimination. Amongst other things, a Member State's social policy may constitute objective justification, provided that the *prima facie* discriminatory measure reflects a legitimate aim of social policy (e.g. the encouragement of recruitment of work force), is suitable and necessary for achieving that aim and the aim is unrelated to any discrimination based on sex. While social policy is essentially a matter for the Member States, the latter cannot use their discretion in this field to frustrate the implementation of a fundamental principle of Community law such as that of equal pay (see, in general, Case C-167/97 *Seymour-Smith and Perez*, above, at pp. I-681–6; Case C-249/97 *Gruber*, above, at pp. I-5325–6; Case C-333/97 *Lewen*, above, at pp. I-7281–5; Case C-50/96 *Schröder*, above, at p. I-786; Case C-236/98 *JämO*, above, at pp. I-2222–3; see also the cases discussed below).

2. Examples of indirect discrimination. Provided that the above conditions are satisfied, the ECJ has established or indicated the existence of indirect discrimination contrary to Art. 141 in the following main situations:

(*a*) Where legislation, collective agreement, or a contract of employment excludes part-time workers from an occupational pension scheme. Such a pay policy may be regarded as being objectively justified on economic grounds where it corresponds to a real need on the part of the employer, is appropriate to achieving the objective pursued (discouragement of part-time work), and is necessary to that end (Case 170/84 *Bilka*, above, at pp. 1626–9).

Periods of service completed by part-time workers who have suffered such indirect discrimination must be taken into account as from 8 April 1976, the date of the judgment in *Defrenne II* (which first established the direct effect of Art. 141), for the purposes of their retroactive membership of such a scheme and calculation of the additional benefits to which they are entitled. However, this time-limit does not preclude national provisions that are more favourable to part-time workers by entitling them to retroactive membership and the corresponding benefits even from a date earlier than that of the *Defrenne II* judgment. Although this might create the risk of distorting competition between undertakings in the various Member States (because some may have to pay retroactive benefits from an earlier date than others), nevertheless the social aim of eliminating sex discrimination must be given priority over the economic aim of ensuring undistorted competition (Case C-50/96 *Schröder*, above, at pp. I-786, I-790, I-792, I-794–5; see also Cases C-234/96 etc. *Vick and Conze* [2000] ECR I-799; Cases C-270/97 etc. *Sievers and Schrage* [2000] ECR I-929; Case C-246/96 *Magorrian and Cunningham* [1997] ECR I-7153 at p. I-7185. See section IV.2(*k*) above).

(*b*) Where national legislation permits employers to exclude part-time workers from the continued payment of wages in the event of illness, unless the Member State concerned can show that such legislation meets a legitimate aim of its social policy and that it is suitable and necessary for attaining that aim (Case 171/88 *Rinner-Kühn*, above, at pp. 2760–1).

(*c*) Where a collective agreement permits employers to exclude part-time workers from the payment of a severance grant on termination of their employment. In cases of indirect discrimination like this, Community law requires that the disadvantaged persons (part-time workers) should be treated in the same way and made subject to the same scheme, proportionately to the number of hours worked, as other workers, such scheme being, in the absence of correct transposition of Art. 141 into national law, the only valid point of reference (Case C-33/89 *Kowalska*, above, at pp. I-2611–13).

(*d*) The exclusion of persons in minor employment (i.e. one which involves a normal working week of less than fifteen hours) from a collective agreement providing for the grant of a special annual Christmas bonus equivalent to one month's salary (Case C-281/97 *Krüger*, above, at pp. I-5148–50).

(*e*) Where a collective agreement provides for the period of service of full-time workers to be taken fully into account for reclassification in a higher salary grade while only one-half of such period of service is taken into account in the case of part-time workers, unless the employer can prove that such a provision is justified by objective factors depending on the relationship between the nature of the duties performed and the experience gained by performing those duties during a certain number of working hours. A national court faced with such indirect discrimination is required to set aside the offending provision of the collective agreement and to apply to the disadvantaged persons the same arrangements as are applied to other workers (Case C-184/89 *Nimz*, above, at pp. I-319–21).

(*f*) Where job-sharing workers who convert to full-time employment are placed, on the full-time pay scale, at a level lower than that which they previously occupied on the pay scale applicable to job-sharing staff (Case C-243/95 *Hill and Stapleton*, above, at pp. I-3769–70, I-3772).

(*g*) Where national legislation provides for compensation to full-time workers for losses of earnings due to attending training courses for staff council members held during the full-time working hours, but does not provide for compensation to part-time workers who attend the same courses outside of their individual working hours. Such legislation is likely to deter part-time workers, preponderantly women, from serving on staff councils, thus making it more difficult for them to be represented by qualified staff council members. Such an indirect discrimination may only be justified by showing that it is both suitable and necessary for achieving a legitimate aim of social policy, which is not the case if that aim may be achieved by other means (Case C-360/90 *Bötel*, above, at pp. I-3612–14; Case C-457/93 *Lewark*, above, at pp. I-267–71; Case C-278/93 *Freers and Speckmann*, above, at pp. I-1190–3).

(*h*) It should be noted that there is discrimination between full-time and part-time workers only where the overall pay of the former is higher than that of the latter for the same number of hours worked. This is not the case, for example, where under a collective agreement both groups of workers are entitled to overtime supplements only for time worked in addition to the ordinary working hours fixed for full-time workers, but part-time workers are not entitled to the supplements for hours worked over and above their individual working hours but not exceeding the normal (full-time) working hours. In this situation, there is no discrimination contrary to Art. 141 since part-time workers do receive the same overall pay as full-time workers for the same number of hours worked (Cases C-399/92 etc. *Helmig*, above, at pp. I-5753–5). By contrast, there is discrimination where national legislation provides that teachers, part-time as well as full-time, do not receive any remuneration for additional hours worked over their regular monthly schedules when the additional work does not exceed three hours per month, if that legislation affects considerably more women than men and is not objectively justified. Although such an arrangement appears to be equal, it imposes a greater burden on part-time teachers then on full-time teachers since the unpaid additional hours represent a higher proportion of their monthly schedule (Case C-285/02 *Elsner-Lakeberg* [2004] ECR I-0000, paras. 17–19).

In addition to the above cases, the Court has identified indirect discrimination in the following situations not involving part-time work:

(*i*) Where an employer, although paying the same basic salary to employees in the same salary group, awards individual pay supplements calculated on the basis of criteria such as the employee's adaptability to variable hours and varying places of work, his training, or his length of service, and it appears that the application of these criteria systematically works to the disadvantage of female employees. Nevertheless, there is no discrimination contrary to Art. 141 if the employer is able to show that his salary practice is based on objectively justified economic factors unrelated to sex. Thus, the employer may justify the use of the above criteria by showing that they are of importance for the performance of the specific tasks which are entrusted to the employee (the criterion of length of service does not even have to be justified). If such a system of individual pay supplements is totally lacking in transparency and a female worker establishes, in relation to a relatively large number of employees, that the average pay for women is less than that for men, then it is for the employer to prove that his salary practice is not in fact discriminatory. Such a shift in the burden of proof from the employee alleging discrimination to the employer is necessary to ensure the effective enforcement of the principle of equal pay before national courts (Case 109/88 *Danfoss* [1989] ECR 3199 at pp. 3226–9; see also point (*j*) and section VI below).

(*j*) If the pay of one group of workers (e.g. speech therapists) is significantly lower than that of another group (e.g. pharmacists) working for the same employer and if the former group consists predominantly of women while the latter predominantly of men, there is a *prima facie* case of sex discrimination, at least where the jobs carried out by the two groups are of equal value and the pay differential is supported by significant statistics. In that case, the burden of proof shifts from the workers to the employer and it is for him to show that the difference in pay is based on objectively justified economic factors unrelated to sex. The fact that the respective rates of pay of the two groups were arrived at by collective bargaining processes which, although carried out by the same parties, are distinct, and, taken separately, have no discriminatory effect within either group, is not sufficient objective justification for the difference in pay. On the other hand, the state of the employment market, and in particular the shortage of applicants for a particular job and the need to attract them by higher pay, may constitute an objectively justified economic ground for all or part of the pay difference in question, subject to the principle of proportionality (Case C-127/92 *Enderby* [1993] ECR I-5535 at pp. I-5571–6). Any differences that might exist in the hours worked by the two groups whose pay is compared may also constitute objective justification for the difference in pay (Case C-236/98 *JämO*, above, at pp. I-2222–3, I-2225, involving a comparison between the salaries of midwives and clinical technicians. See also points (*i*) and (*k*) and section VI below).

(*k*) In contrast to point (*j*) above, in a piece-work pay scheme the mere finding that the average pay of one group of workers consisting predominantly of women is appreciably lower than the average pay of another group of workers consisting predominantly of men and carrying out work of equal value does not suffice to establish a *prima facie* case of sex discrimination. Such a pay differential may be due to a difference in individual output in which case it is not contrary to Art. 141. That provision only requires that the pay of the two groups is to be calculated on the basis of the same unit of measurement. However, where in a piece-work pay scheme individual pay consists of a variable element depending on output and a fixed element differing according to the group concerned, and it is not possible to identify the factors that determined the rates or units of measurement used to calculate the variable element, the objective of not depriving workers of any effective remedy may require the employer to bear the burden of proving that the differences are not due to sex discrimination. Needless to say that the two groups considered must be in a comparable situation and must cover a sufficiently large number of workers to ensure that the differences are not attributable to purely fortuitous or short-term factors or to differences in the individual output of the workers concerned (Case C-400/93 *Royal Copenhagen*, above, at pp. I-1305–11; see also section VI below).

(*l*) Where national legislation restricts the right not to be unfairly dismissed to employees who have been continuously employed for a minimum period of two years before dismissal and reliable and significant statistics indicate that a considerably smaller percentage of women than men is able to satisfy the condition of two years' employment, or if the statistical evidence reveals a lesser but persistent and relatively constant disparity between men and women over a long period. (The fact that 77.4% of men and 68.9% of women are able to fulfil that condition in a particular year does not indicate a sufficient disparity.) Such an apparently discriminatory rule is, however, not contrary to Art. 141 if the Member State concerned can show that it is objectively justified in that it reflects a legitimate aim of its social policy (such as the encouragement of recruitment of workforce), is necessary and suitable for achieving that aim, and the aim is unrelated to any discrimination based on sex (Case C-167/97 *Seymour-Smith and Perez*, above, at pp. I-681–6).

(*m*) Where, in certain circumstances, an employer refuses to award a Christmas bonus to workers on parenting leave, since female workers are likely to be on parenting leave when the bonus is awarded far more often than male workers (Case C-333/97 *Lewen*, above, at pp. I-7281–3).

(*n*) Where legislation imposes the requirement of being employed under a contract of employment as a precondition for membership of a pension scheme for teachers and a much lower percentage of women than of men is able to fulfil that requirement (Case C-256/01 *Allonby*, above, paras. 75–9).

VI. The burden of proof

In accordance with the normal rules of evidence, in principle the burden of proving the existence of sex discrimination in the matter of pay lies on the worker who, being the victim of such discrimination, brings legal proceedings against his employer. However, the ECJ has developed certain principles according to which the burden of proof may shift to the employer when this is necessary to avoid depriving workers of any effective means of enforcing the principle of equal pay. Thus, where an undertaking applies a system of pay with a mechanism for adding individual supplements to the basic salary, which is wholly lacking in transparency, it is for the employer to prove that this practice is not discriminatory if a female worker establishes, in relation to a relatively large number of employees, that the average pay for women is less than that for men. Under such a system, female workers are unable to compare the different components of their salary with those of the salary of their male colleagues belonging to the same salary group and can establish differences only in average pay. Therefore, in practice they would be deprived of any effective means of examining whether the principle of equal pay is being complied with if the employer did not have to indicate how the criteria concerning supplements are applied.

Similarly, where significant statistics disclose an appreciable difference in pay between two jobs of equal value, one of which is carried out almost exclusively by women and the other predominantly by men, so that there is a *prima facie* case of sex discrimination, Art. 141 requires the employer to show that that difference is based on objectively justified factors unrelated to sex (see Case 109/88 *Danfoss*, above, at pp. 3225–6; Case C-127/92 *Enderby*, above, at pp. I-5571–3; Case C-400/93 *Royal Copenhagen*, above, at pp. I-1306–8; see section V.2 (*i*), (*j*), and (*k*) above).

However, the above principles do not apply in cases of direct discrimination that arise from the inequality of the overall remuneration, or a precise component of it, paid by the employer to a male and a female employee. In such a case, the normal rules of evidence apply, which means that it is for the plaintiff to establish that the conditions giving rise to a presumption that there is unequal pay prohibited by Art. 141 are fulfilled. Thus, it is for the plaintiff to prove that the pay she receives is less than that of her chosen comparator, and that she does the same work as he, or work of equal value. In other words, she has to make out a *prima facie* case of discrimination that can be explained only by the difference in sex. The employer is not bound to show that the work of the two employees is different. However, once a *prima facie* case of discrimination has been established, it is then for the employer to prove that there is no breach of the principle of equal pay. Thus, he can show, *inter alia*, that the activities actually performed by the two employees are not comparable, or he can justify the difference in pay by objective factors unrelated to sex (see Case C-381/99 *Brunnhofer*, above, at pp. I-4994–6).

These principles have been incorporated in Council Dir. 97/80 of 15 December 1997 on the burden of proof in cases of discrimination based on sex (*OJ* 1998 L14/6). The directive was adopted on the basis of the Agreement on Social Policy annexed to the Protocol on Social Policy annexed to the EC Treaty by the TEU, and therefore initially did not apply to the United Kingdom. When the Agreement on Social Policy was incorporated in the EC Treaty by the ToA, Dir. 97/80 was extended to the United Kingdom by Council Dir. 98/52 of 13 July 1998 (*OJ* 1998 L205/66). Dir. 97/80 had to be implemented by the Member States by 1 January 2001, and by the United Kingdom by 22 July 2001 (Art. 7 of Dir. 97/80 and Art. 2 of Dir. 98/52).

Dir. 97/80 applies to the situations covered by Art. 141 EC and by Dir. 75/117 on equal pay, by Dir. 76/207 on equal treatment (see section VII below) and, in so far as discrimination based on sex is concerned, by Dir. 92/85 on the protection of pregnant workers and workers who have recently given birth or are breastfeeding (*OJ* 1992 L348/1) and by Dir. 96/34 on parental leave (*OJ* 1996 L145/4). It also applies to any civil or administrative procedure concerning the public or private sector that provides for means of redress under national law pursuant to these directives with the exception of out-of-court procedures, but it does not apply to criminal procedures, unless otherwise provided by the Member States (Art. 3 of Dir. 97/80). The directive applies to both direct and indirect discrimination based on sex (Art. 2(1)).

According to Art. 4 of the directive, Member States are required to ensure that, when persons who consider themselves wronged because the principle of equal treatment has not been applied to them establish, before a court or other competent authority, facts from which it may be presumed that there has been direct or indirect discrimination, it is for the respondent to prove that there has been no breach of the principle of equal treatment. This provision need not be applied to proceedings in which it is for the court or competent body to investigate the facts of the case. Member States are allowed to introduce rules of evidence that are more favourable to plaintiffs. They are to ensure that measures taken under the directive are brought to the attention of all the persons concerned by all appropriate means (Art. 5). Implementation of the directive may not lead to a reduction in the general level of protection of workers in the areas to which it applies (Art. 6).

VII. Directive 75/117

As mentioned previously, Art. 141 has been implemented by Dir. 75/117 of 10 February 1975 on the approximation of the laws of the Member States relating to the application of the principle of equal pay for men and women (the 'equal pay' directive; *OJ* 1975 L45/19). This directive must be compared with and distinguished from Dir. 76/207 of 9 February 1976 on the implementation of the principle of equal treatment for men and women as regards access to employment, vocational training and promotion, and working conditions (the 'equal treatment' directive; *OJ* 1976 L39/40).

On the one hand, the two directives are complementary in that they are intended to guarantee equal treatment of men and women in working life as a whole. Like Art. 141, they cover all types of employment, including employment in the public service (see Case 248/83 *Commission* v. *Germany* [1985] ECR 1459 at p. 1480).

On the other hand, the two directives have different scope of application and are, therefore, mutually exclusive. Dir. 75/117 concerns equal treatment in respect of pay only, while Dir. 76/207 concerns equal treatment as regards access to employment and conditions of employment other than pay. It follows that where a dispute concerns a benefit that constitutes 'pay' within the meaning of Art. 141, the case falls within the scope of Art. 141 and Dir. 75/117, and cannot be covered simultaneously by Dir. 76/207 as well (Case C-342/93 *Gillespie*, above, at p. I-501; Case C-249/96 *Grant*, above, at p. I-643; Case C-411/96 *Boyle*, above, at p. I-6455). Conversely, where the benefit in question does not constitute 'pay', the case is not covered by Art. 141 or Dir. 75/117, which has the same scope, but may be covered by Dir. 76/207 or one of the other directives implementing the principle of equal treatment in specific areas (i.e. Dir. 79/7 concerning equal treatment in social security, *OJ* 1979 L6/24, or Dir. 86/378 concerning equal treatment in occupational social security schemes, *OJ* 1986 L225/40, corrigendum in *OJ* 1986 L283/27, see Case 192/85 *Newstead*, above, at pp. 4783–23506). Nor can a case fall within the scope of Dir. 75/117 if it is covered by Dir. 76/207 (Case 19/81 *Burton*, above, at p. 575. *See further under* **Equal treatment**, section II.1(*d*)). Thus, for example, where an employee has been unfairly dismissed, the conditions determining whether he is entitled to obtain compensation fall within the scope of Art. 141, but the conditions determining whether he is entitled to obtain reinstatement or re-engagement fall within the scope of Dir. 76/207 (Case C-167/97 *Seymour-Smith and Perez*, above, at p. I-678).

The main purpose of Dir. 75/117 is to facilitate the practical application of the principle of equal pay, which it describes as an 'integral part of the establishment and functioning of the common market' (see the first and fourth recitals in the preamble). To that end, it provides further details concerning the material scope of Art. 141 (Art. 1) and lays down provisions to improve the legal protection of workers who suffer discrimination as regards pay (Arts. 2 to 7). Nevertheless, as the ECJ has emphasized in several cases, the directive in no way affects the concept of 'pay' or alters the content or scope of the principle of equal pay as defined in Art. 141. Therefore, terms such as 'pay' and 'the same work' used in both Art. 141 and the directive have the same meaning (Case C-381/99 *Brunnhofer*, above, at p. I-4988; see also Case 69/80 *Worringham and Humphreys*, above, at p. 791; Case 96/80 *Jenkins*, above, at p. 927; Case 192/85 *Newstead*, above, at p. 4784). It follows that where a question can be dealt with under Art. 141, which is usually the case, there is no need to resort to the directive (see e.g. Case 129/79 *Macarthys*, above, at p. 1290; Case C-262/88 *Barber*, above, at pp. I-1949–50), although in many cases the Court does refer to both Art. 141 and Art. 1 of Dir. 75/117 (see e.g. Case C-297/93 *Grau-Hupka* [1994] ECR I-5535 at p. I-5553; Case C-400/93 *Royal Copenhagen*, above, at pp. I-1303, I-1307–8; Case C-342/93 *Gillespie*, above, at pp. I-498–502).

While according to the established case-law of the Court a directive cannot produce 'horizontal' direct effect between individuals (see e.g. Case 152/84 *Marshall* [1986] ECR 723 at p. 749), and thus Dir. 75/117 cannot be relied on by an employee against a private employer before national courts, the principle of equal pay may still be enforced by virtue of the horizontal direct effect of Art. 141 itself. The scope of that direct effect cannot be restricted by Dir. 75/117 or by the various equal treatment directives mentioned above (Case 43/75 *Defrenne II*, above, at p. 480; Case C-110/91 *Moroni*, above, at p. I-6617, holding that Dir. 86/378 cannot prevent Art. 141 from being relied upon directly and immediately before national courts; see also Case C-7/93 *Beune*, above, at p. I-4523 to the same effect). Because of the direct effect of Art. 141 as discussed earlier, the Court has not found it necessary to pronounce on the direct effect of Dir. 75/117.

Art. 1 of Dir. 75/117, which contains substantive provisions, has already been considered in sections II to IV above. Art. 2 requires the Member States to introduce into their national legal systems 'such measures as are necessary to enable all employees who consider themselves wronged by failure to apply the principle of equal pay to pursue their claims by judicial process', after possible recourse to other competent authorities. That provision is reinforced by Art. 6 according to which the Member States are, in accordance with their national circumstances and legal systems, to take 'the measures necessary to ensure that the principle of equal pay is applied'. They are required to see that 'effective means are available to take care that this principle is observed'. Art. 2 is almost identical with Art. 6 of Dir. 76/207, which has been interpreted by the ECJ in a series of important judgments (*see further under* **Equal treatment**, section II.4).

It was a failure to adopt the measures referred to in Arts. 2 and 6 that led the Court to establish that the United Kingdom had failed to fulfil its obligations under the Treaty in Case 61/81 *Commission* v. *United Kingdom*, above, at pp. 2616–17 (see section III above). It was also the requirement of effective implementation of the principle of equal pay which underlies Art. 6, that caused the Court to reverse the rules on the burden of proof in special cases where a lack of transparency in the employer's pay policy would otherwise make it almost impossible for employees to prove pay discrimination before national courts.

As regards the procedure for enforcing the principle of equal pay before national courts, according to the ECJ's established case-law, in the absence of Community rules governing this matter it is for the domestic legal system of each Member State to designate the courts and tribunals having jurisdiction and to lay down the detailed procedural rules governing actions for safeguarding rights which individuals derive from Community law. However, such rules must not be less favourable than those governing similar domestic actions (the principle of equivalence) and must not render virtually impossible or excessively difficult the exercise of rights conferred by Community law (the principle of effectiveness). Thus, it is compatible with Community law for national rules to prescribe, in the interests of legal certainty, reasonable limitation periods for bringing proceedings. A national rule under which entitlement to arrears of remuneration or damages for breach of the principle of equal pay is restricted to a period of two years preceding the date of instituting proceedings is not contrary to Community law. The position is different, however, where the delay in bringing an action is due to the fact that the employer provided inaccurate or deliberately misleading information to the employee concerning the pay received by employees of the opposite sex (see Case C-326/96 *Levez* [1998] ECR I-7835 at pp. I-7864–8 and the cases cited therein).

It is also not contrary to Community law for a national procedural rule to require that a claim for membership of an occupational pension scheme, from which the right to pension benefits flows, must be brought within six months of the end of the employment to which the claim relates (Case C-78/98 *Preston* [2000] ECR I-3201 at pp. I-3256–7; but see also pp. I-3265–7 for the situation where there is a succession of short-term contracts concluded at regular intervals in the context of a stable employment relationship). By contrast, a procedural rule whereby the right to be admitted to such a scheme may have effect only from a date no earlier than two years before the institution of proceedings is incompatible with Community law as it deprives the persons concerned of the additional benefits under a scheme to which they are entitled to be affiliated. The object of such proceedings is not to obtain, with retroactive effect, arrears of benefits but to secure recognition of the right to retroactive membership of a scheme in order to obtain benefits in the future (ibid. at pp. I-3257–60; Case C-246/96 *Magorrian and Cunningham*, above, at pp. I-7187–8).

As regards the principle of equivalence, that principle requires that the national procedural rule in question be applied without distinction, whether the infringement alleged is of Community law or national law, where the purpose and cause of action are similar. The principle of equivalence would be infringed if a person relying on a right conferred by Community law were forced to incur additional costs and delay by comparison with a claimant whose action was based solely on domestic law (Case C-78/98 *Preston*, above, at pp. I-3262–4; Case C-326/96 *Levez*, above, at pp. I-7870–2).

Pursuant to Art. 3 of Dir. 75/117, Member States are to abolish all discrimination between men and women arising from laws, regulations, or administrative provisions which is contrary to the principle of equal pay. Under Art. 4, Member States must likewise ensure that provisions appearing in collective agreements, wage scales, wage agreements, or individual contracts of employment that are contrary to the principle of equal pay are or may be declared null and void or may be amended. This shows that collective agreements and individual contracts of employment, like laws, regulations, or administrative provisions, must observe the principle enshrined in Art. 141 (see e.g. Case C-127/92 *Enderby*, above, at p. I-5574). Employees must be protected against dismissal by the employer as a reaction to a complaint or legal proceedings aimed at enforcing the principle of equal pay (Art. 5). They must be made aware of the provisions adopted for implementation of the directive (Art. 7).

The Member States were required to implement Dir. 75/117 within one year of its notification (Art. 8). In Case 143/83 *Commission* v. *Denmark*, above, at pp. 434–6, the Court held that the relevant Danish legislation, which made equal pay compulsory only in cases where it was not already guaranteed under collective agreements, lacked the necessary 'clarity and precision' in that it did not unequivocally ensure that all workers, including workers who were not union members or were not covered by a collective agreement, were afforded the full protection provided for in the directive (see also Case C-187/98 *Commission* v. *Greece*, above, at pp. I-7741–4). By contrast, in Case 248/83 *Commission* v. *Germany*, above, at p. 1489, the Court found that the object of the directive, in particular as regards remuneration of public servants, had already been achieved in Germany at the time when the directive entered into force and that therefore no specific measure was required for its implementation.

***See also* Equality*, Equal treatment, Worker.**

Further reading 1. Books: *See under* **Equal treatment.**

2. Articles: Arnull, 'Article 119 and Equal Pay for Work of Equal Value' (1986) *EL Rev.* 200; Curtin, 'Occupational Pension Schemes and Article 119: Beyond the Fringe?' (1987) *CML Rev.* 215; Flynn, 'Equality between Men and Women in the Court of Justice' (1998) *YEL* 259; McGlynn and Farrelly, 'Equal Pay and the Protection of Women within Family Life' (1999) *EL Rev.* 202; Moore, '"Justice Doesn't Mean a Free Lunch": The

Application of the Principle of Equal Pay to Occupational Pension Schemes' (1995) *EL Rev.* 159; Whiteford, 'Lost in the Mists of Time: The ECJ and Occupational Pensions' (1995) *CML Rev.* 801; Zavvos, 'Pension Fund Liberalization and the Future of Retirement Financing in Europe' (1994) *CML Rev.* 609. *See also under* **Equal treatment.**

▶ **EQUAL TREATMENT (PRINCIPLE OF)** In a general sense, the principle of equal treatment entails the prohibition of all discrimination, direct or indirect, in law or in fact, on any ground whatsoever. This entry deals with the principle of equal treatment only in so far as it applies to men and women and prohibits any direct or indirect discrimination on grounds of sex in matters of employment and occupation (on the principle of equal treatment in general, *see further under* **Equality***; for the prohibition of discrimination on grounds of nationality, *see further under* **Freedom of establishment, Freedom to provide services, Free movement of persons**).

I. The legal framework

1. General principles of law and human rights. In Community law, the principle of equal treatment for men and women may be derived from two distinct sources. In the first place, it has an independent existence as one of the unwritten general principles of Community law and as a fundamental human right the observance of which the Court of Justice and the Court of First Instance have undertaken to ensure. Any measure adopted by the Community institutions in disregard of this principle is vitiated by illegality (see Case 149/77 *Defrenne III* [1978] ECR 1365 at p. 1378; Case T-45/90 *Speybrouck* v. *Parliament* [1992] ECR II-33 at p. II-46; more recently Case C-13/94 *P* [1996] ECR I-2143 at p. I-2165; Case C-25/02 *Rinke* [2003] ECR I-8349, paras. 25–8). Thus, in several staff cases the Court has held that in relations between the Community institutions and their employees the principle of equal treatment applies quite independently of any relevant written provisions of primary or secondary Community law, and may serve as a legal basis for the annulment of decisions of the institutions which, contrary to that principle, directly or indirectly discriminate between male and female officials (Case 20/71 *Sabbatini* v. *Parliament* [1972] ECR 345 at pp. 350–1; Case 21/74 *Airola* v. *Commission* [1975] ECR 221 at pp. 228–9; both cases involved indirect discrimination in respect of the payment of the expatriation allowance; Cases 75/82 etc. *Razzouk and Beydoun* v. *Commission* [1984] ECR 1509 at p. 1530, involving direct discrimination in regard to survivor's pension). On the other hand, where the employment relationship is governed by national law, the principle of equal treatment can only be enforced on the basis of written rules of Community law adopted in the matter (Case 149/77 *Defrenne III*, above, at pp. 1378–9, see further below), although as a fundamental principle of Community law it can play an important part in the interpretation and application of those written rules (Case C-13/94 *P*, above, at p. I-2165).

The principle of equal treatment is also recognized by the Charter of Fundamental Rights of the European Union (*OJ* 2000 C364/1). Art. 23

provides that 'Equality between men and women must be ensured in all areas, including employment, work and pay. The principle of equality shall not prevent the maintenance or adoption of measures providing for specific advantages in favour of the underrepresented sex' (see also Arts. 21(1) and 33(2)). The same principle is also enshrined in the Community Charter of the Fundamental Social Rights of Workers of 9 December 1989 (the 'Social Charter', point 16); in the European Social Charter of 1961; in Convention No. 111 of the International Labour Organization of 1958 concerning discrimination in respect of employment and occupation, to which the case-law of the Court occasionally refers (see e.g. the *Defrenne III* case, above); and in numerous other international agreements and conventions.

In the second place, the principle of equal treatment for men and women forms part of the social provisions and objectives of the EC Treaty and has been implemented by means of secondary legislation. In this respect, a distinction must be made between the original EEC Treaty and the EC Treaty as it is today, following a series of successive amendments.

2. The original EEC Treaty. In the original EEC Treaty, the social provisions were contained in Arts. 117 to 122, which made up Chapter 1 of Title III on social policy in Part Three of the Treaty. As interpreted by the Court of Justice, those social provisions fell into two distinct categories. First, Arts. 117 and 118 dealt, in general terms, with the conditions of employment and working conditions in the context of the harmonization of the social systems and social legislation of the Member States. According to the Court, those Articles were essentially in the nature of a programme in a field that the EEC Treaty reserved largely to the discretion of the Member States. Therefore, until the Community assumed responsibility in this area by means of adopting secondary legislation, the principle of equal treatment as regards conditions of employment and working conditions could not be enforced in respect of employment relationships governed by national law (Case 149/77 *Defrenne III*, above, at pp. 1376–9).

Secondly, Art. 119 [now Art. 141 EC] laid down the principle of equal pay for equal work, thus prohibiting discrimination between men and women as regards pay. In contrast to Arts. 117 and 118, Art. 119 constituted a binding legal rule that could, in certain circumstances, produce direct effect and was therefore enforceable before national courts. However, it had a precisely defined scope in that it covered only one element of the employment relationship, namely, pay. In a series of cases, the ECJ held that it was not possible to widen the scope of Art. 119 so as to include other conditions of employment, without jeopardizing its direct effect and without intervening in an area of social policy reserved to the Member States. Therefore, Art. 119 could not be interpreted as prescribing, in addition to equal pay, equal treatment in respect of the other conditions of employment and working conditions applicable to men and women. Even the fact that the fixing of certain conditions of employment, such as a special age-limit, might have pecuniary consequences was not sufficient to bring such conditions within the field of application of Art. 119 (ibid. at p. 1377; see further section II.1(*d*) below, and *see also under* **Equal pay**, section I.1).

As a result of the Court's case-law, which is still valid today, a clear distinction is to be made between the principle of equal pay, laid down in Art. 119 [Art. 141], and the principle of equal treatment in matters other than pay, although the two principles share the common feature that they prohibit only employment-related sex discrimination. They apply to men and women not generally but only in their capacity as workers (see Cases 48/88 etc. *Achterberg-te Riele* [1989] ECR 1963 at p. 1988). The importance of the distinction is that the principle of equal pay is governed by a stricter legal regime in that it is not subject to exceptions and may be enforced, both vertically and horizontally, that is, even between private individuals, directly on the basis of Art. 119 [141]. By contrast, the principle of equal treatment is subject to several exceptions and is not enforceable directly under any Treaty provision but only under one of the implementing directives which by their nature cannot give rise to 'horizontal' direct effect between individuals (i.e. between private employers and employees). As will be seen below, this distinction has created particular problems in certain situations, involving the difficult task of delimiting the respective scope of application of Art. 119 [141] on the one hand, and of the directives implementing the principle of equal treatment, on the other. As a general rule, it may be stated that where discrimination on grounds of sex concerns an aspect or element of the employment relationship which constitutes 'pay' as defined by the Court, it is covered by Art. 119 [141]; where it concerns any other condition of employment or working condition, it comes within the scope of one of the equal treatment directives.

3. The amended EC Treaty. The social provisions of the original EEC Treaty were amended on each of the four occasions when the EEC/EC Treaty itself was amended. The Single European Act (SEA) inserted new Arts. 118a and 118b. The Treaty on European Union (TEU) made a minor change to Art. 118a(2), added a Protocol on the interpretation of Art. 119, and, more importantly, contained an Agreement on Social Policy that was concluded between the Member States with the exception of the United Kingdom, and which was annexed to the Protocol on Social Policy, itself annexed to the EC Treaty. The Agreement on Social Policy, which was not binding on the United Kingdom, was in substance incorporated in the EC Treaty by the Treaty of Amsterdam (ToA, see Art. 2(22)), although, curiously, the Protocol on Social Policy itself, to which the Agreement was annexed, was not repealed by the ToA (see also Case C-366/99 *Griesmar* [2001] ECR I-9383 at pp. I-9426–7). As a result of these changes and of the renumbering of the Treaty articles by the ToA, Arts. 117 to 122 of the EEC Treaty were replaced by Arts. 136 to 145 EC with effect from 1 May 1999, the date on which the ToA entered into force. Art. 119 became Art. 141 and Title III of Part Three on social policy became Title XI on social policy, education, vocational training, and youth. The ToA also amended Arts. 2 and 3 of the EC Treaty and inserted a new Art. 13. Finally, the

Treaty of Nice (ToN) introduced amendments to Arts. 137, 139, and 144 EC.

Without going into a detailed discussion of these changes and of the social policy of the Community in general, it is sufficient to highlight only those provisions of the Treaty that have a direct bearing on the principle of equal treatment for men and women. The first striking feature of the amendments introduced over the years, and in particular by the ToA, is the increased importance that the Treaty now attaches to the principle of equal treatment. Thus, the promotion of equality between men and women is now listed as one of the tasks or objectives of the Community (Art. 2). Accordingly, the Community is required, in all the activities entrusted to it by the Treaty, to aim to eliminate inequalities, and to promote equality, between men and women (Art. 3(2)). Art. 13 authorizes the Council to take 'appropriate action' to combat discrimination based on sex, as well as on racial or ethnic origin, religion or belief, disability, age, or sexual orientation. With a view to achieving the objectives of its social policy, the Community is to support and complement the activities of the Member States, amongst other things, in the field of equality between men and women with regard to labour market opportunities and treatment at work (Art. 137(1)(i)). For the same purpose, the Commission is to encourage co-operation between the Member States in all areas of social policy (Art. 140).

Perhaps most importantly, the scope of Art. 141 [ex Art. 119], which, as seen above, was originally strictly limited to pay, has been extended to cover equal treatment as well. Art. 141(3) authorizes the Council to adopt measures to ensure the application of the principle of equal opportunities and equal treatment of men and women in matters of employment and occupation, including the principle of equal pay for equal work or work of equal value. Art. 141(4) encourages 'positive action' (or 'positive discrimination') by Member States. It provides that:

> With a view to ensuring full equality in practice between men and women in working life, the principle of equal treatment shall not prevent any Member State from maintaining or adopting measures providing for specific advantages in order to make it easier for the underrepresented sex to pursue a vocational activity or to prevent or compensate for disadvantages in professional careers.

Declaration No. 28 annexed to the ToA states specifically that when adopting measures referred to in Art. 141(4), Member States should, in the first instance, aim at improving the situation of women in working life (for an interpretation of Art. 141(4) by the ECJ, see section II.2(*c*) below).

The second striking feature of the amended provisions is the multiplicity of legal bases that are now available to the Community institutions to enact secondary legislation concerning the various aspects of equal treatment. It is perhaps surprising that the original EEC Treaty contained no specific provisions for this purpose, so that the directives on equal treatment, and even on equal pay, had to be adopted on the basis of the general harmonization and 'gap-filling' provisions, i.e. Art. 94 [ex Art. 100] and/or Art. 308 [ex Art. 235] (see point 4 below). By contrast, equal treatment legislation today may be based on Arts. 13, 137(2) [ex Art. 2(2) of the Agreement on Social Policy], 139(2) [ex Art. 4(2) of the same Agreement], under which the Council may implement agreements concluded at Community level by management and labour (the 'social partners'), and Art. 141(3). In fact, all of these legal bases have been used in the recent past (see point 4 below).

4. Secondary legislation. The measures that implement the principle of equal treatment in Community law may be divided into three broad categories. The first category comprises directives that are directly relevant to equal treatment between men and women. These are as follows:

- Council Dir. 76/207 of 9 February 1976 on the implementation of the principle of equal treatment for men and women as regards access to employment, vocational training and promotion, and working conditions (the 'equal treatment' directive, *OJ* 1976 L39/40; legal basis: Art. 308 [ex Art. 235]; see section II below);
- Council Dir. 79/7 of 19 December 1978 on the progressive implementation of the principle of equal treatment for men and women in matters of social security (*OJ* 1979 L6/24; legal basis: Art. 308 [ex Art. 235]; see section IV below);
- Council Dir. 86/378 of 24 July 1986 on the implementation of the principle of equal treatment for men and women in occupational social security schemes (*OJ* 1986 L225/40; corrigendum in *OJ* 1986 L283/27; legal basis: Arts. 94 and 308 [ex Arts. 100 and 235]), as amended by Council Dir. 96/97 of 20 December 1996 (*OJ* 1997 L46/20; legal basis: Art. 94 [ex Art. 100]; see section V below);
- Council Dir. 86/613 of 11 December 1986 on the application of the principle of equal treatment between men and women engaged in an activity, including agriculture, in a self-employed capacity, and on the protection of self-employed women during pregnancy and motherhood (*OJ* 1986 L359/56; legal basis: Arts. 94 and 308 [ex Arts. 100 and 235]; see section VI below);
- Dir. 2002/73 of the European Parliament and of the Council of 23 September 2002 amending Council Dir. 76/207 (*OJ* 2002 L269/15; legal basis Art. 141(3); see section III below).

The second category of measures includes directives that deal primarily with the protection of the health and safety of workers or with related matters, but which contain provisions which are relevant to the promotion of equality between men and women. These are as follows:

- Council Dir. 92/85 of 19 October 1992 relating to the safety and health at work of pregnant workers and workers who have recently given birth or are breastfeeding (*OJ* 1992 L348/1; legal basis: ex Art. 118a);
- Council Dir. 96/34 of 3 June 1996 on parental leave (*OJ* 1996 L145/4; legal basis: Art. 4(2) of the Agreement on Social Policy) and Council Dir. 97/75 of 15 December 1997 extending Dir. 96/34 to the United Kingdom (*OJ* 1998 L10/24; legal basis: Art. 94 [ex Art. 100]);

- Council Dir. 97/80 of 15 December 1997 on the burden of proof in cases of discrimination based on sex (*OJ* 1998 L14/6; legal basis: Art. 2(2) of the Agreement on Social Policy) and Council Dir. 98/52 of 13 July 1998 extending Dir. 97/80 to the United Kingdom (*OJ* 1998 L205/66; legal basis: Art. 94 [ex Art. 100]; see section II.7 below);
- Council Dir. 97/81 of 15 December 1997 on part-time work (*OJ* 1998 L14/9; legal basis: Art. 4(2) of the Agreement on Social Policy) and Council Dir. 98/23 of 7 April 1998 extending Dir. 97/81 to the United Kingdom (*OJ* 1998 L131/10; legal basis: Art. 94 [ex Art. 100]).

The third category of measures consists of directives and decisions which implement or promote the principle of equality in a general way. These include the following:

- Council Dir. 2000/43 of 29 June 2000 implementing the principle of equal treatment between persons irrespective of racial or ethnic origin (*OJ* 2000 L180/22; rectified in *OJ* 2000 L199/86; legal basis: Art. 13). The directive prohibits direct or indirect discrimination based on racial or ethnic origin (Arts. 1 and 2(1)). Its scope is very broad and encompasses, amongst other things, employment and working conditions, including dismissals and pay (Art. 3(1)(c)). It had to be implemented by the Member States by 19 July 2003 (Art. 16);
- Council Dir. 2000/78 of 27 November 2000 establishing a general framework for equal treatment in employment and occupation (*OJ* 2000 L303/16; legal basis: Art. 13). The directive prohibits direct or indirect discrimination on the grounds of religion or belief, disability, age, or sexual orientation as regards employment and occupation (Arts. 1 and 2(1)). Its scope is very broad and encompasses, amongst other things, employment and working conditions, including dismissals and pay (Art. 3(1)(c)). It had to be implemented by the Member States by 2 December 2003 (Art. 18);
- Council Dec. 2000/750 of 27 November 2000 establishing a Community action programme to combat discrimination (2001 to 2006) (*OJ* 2000 L303/23; legal basis: Art. 13);
- Proposal for a Council directive implementing the principle of equal treatment between women and men in the access to and supply of goods and services of 5 November 2003 (*OJ* 2004 C96/25; COM(2003) 657);
- Proposal for a European Parliament and Council directive on the implementation of the principle of equal opportunities and equal treatment between men and women in the field of employment and occupation of 21 April 2004 (COM(2004) 279).

In addition to the above directives, the Council and the Commission have adopted a number of legally non-binding measures for the promotion of equal treatment and equal opportunities for men and women. The most important of these are as follows:

- Council Res. of 21 January 1974 concerning a social action programme, particularly point 4 (*OJ* 1974 C13/1);

- Five Action Programmes on equal opportunities for men and women, each covering the period indicated: 1982–1985 (*OJ* 1982 C186/3); 1986–1990 (*OJ* 1986 C203/2); 1991–1995 (*OJ* 1991 C142/1); 1996–2000 (*OJ* 1995 L335/37); 2001–2005 (Council Dec. 2001/51 of 20 December 2000, *OJ* 2001 L17/22);
- Council Rec. 84/635 of 13 December 1984 on the promotion of positive action for women (*OJ* 1984 L331/34); Comm. Report of 13 June 1995 on the implementation of this recommendation (COM(95) 247);
- Council Conclusions of 26 May 1987 on protective legislation for women in the Member States of the European Community (*OJ* 1987 C178/4);
- Council Res. of 16 December 1988 on the reintegration and late integration of women into working life (*OJ* 1988 C333/1);
- Council Res. of 29 May 1990 on the protection of the dignity of women and men at work (*OJ* 1990 C157/3);
- Comm. Rec. 92/131 of 27 November 1991 on the protection of the dignity of women and men at work (*OJ* 1992 L49/1) and Council Declaration of 19 December 1991 on the implementation of this recommendation, including the code of practice to combat sexual harassment (*OJ* 1992 C27/1);
- Council Res. of 22 June 1994 on the promotion of equal opportunities for men and women through action by the European Structural Funds (*OJ* 1994 C231/1);
- Council and Member States Res. of 6 December 1994 on equal participation by women in an employment-intensive economic growth strategy within the European Union (*OJ* 1994 C368/3);
- Council Res. of 27 March 1995 on the balanced participation of men and women in decision-making (*OJ* 1995 C168/3) and Council Rec. 96/694 of 2 December 1996 on the same subject (*OJ* 1996 L319/11);
- Comm. Communication of 12 April 1995 on a (second) social action programme (1995–1997; COM(95) 134);
- Council and Member States Res. of 5 October 1995 on the image of women and men portrayed in advertising and the media (*OJ* 1995 C296/15);
- Comm. Communication of 21 February 1996 on incorporating equal opportunities for women and men into all Community policies and activities (COM(96) 67; see also COM(1998) 122);
- Comm. Communication of 25 November 1999 on certain measures to combat discrimination (COM(1999) 564; see also *565*, *566*, and *567*);
- Comm. Dec. 2000/407 of 19 June 2000 relating to gender balance within the committees and expert groups established by it (*OJ* 2000 L154/34) and Comm. Communication of 7 July 2000 relating thereto (*OJ* 2000 C203/4);
- Council and Member States Res. of 29 June 2000 on the balanced participation of women and men in family and working life (*OJ* 2000 C218/5);

- Comm. Reports (annual) on equal opportunities for women and men in the EU (COM(96) 650; COM(1998) 302; COM(1999) 106; COM(2000) 123; COM(2001) 179; COM(2002) 258; COM(2003) 98; COM(2004) 115).

In this entry, the principle of equal treatment will be considered mainly in the light of the directives falling into the first category mentioned above, although occasional references will be made to some of the other directives as and when necessary.

II. Directive 76/207 on equal treatment

As mentioned in section I above, the original EEC Treaty, pursuing primarily an economic objective, did not lay down in a legally binding form the principle of equal treatment, as opposed to the principle of equal pay. However, at the Paris Summit Conference of October 1972, the Heads of State or Government expressly confirmed that economic expansion was not an end in itself but should result in an improvement in the quality of life and the standard of living. Therefore, economic growth was to be accompanied by 'vigorous action' in the social field as well. Accordingly, the social action programme adopted in 1974 at the request of the Paris Summit (see Council Res. of 21 January 1974, cited in section I.4 above) set out a number of social objectives and priorities, including 'the undertaking of action to achieve equality between men and women as regards access to employment and vocational training and advancement and as regards working conditions, including pay' (point 4). It was to implement this part of the programme that Dir. 76/207 was adopted on the basis of Art. 308 [ex Art. 235] EC (see the first recital in the preamble). Its preamble links the directive to Art. 117 of the original EEC Treaty in stating that 'equal treatment for male and female workers constitutes one of the objectives of the Community, in so far as the harmonization of living and working conditions while maintaining their improvement are *inter alia* to be furthered' (third recital; see also the opinion of A.-G. Capotorti in Case 149/77 *Defrenne III*, above, at p. 1387).

The purpose and scope of the directive and the principle of equal treatment are defined in Arts. 1 and 2(1), while Art. 2(2), (3), and (4) contain certain exceptions to that principle. The directive imposes two kinds of obligations on the Member States. Arts. 3, 4, and 5 require them to abolish all forms of sex discrimination, while Art. 6 provides for the introduction of the necessary measures to enable individuals to pursue their claims arising from sex discrimination by judicial process. Finally, Art. 9 lays down rules for the implementation of the directive. These aspects are considered in turn below.

1. Purpose and scope. According to Art. 1(1), the purpose of Dir. 76/207 is to put into effect in the Member States the principle of equal treatment for men and women as regards three particular matters: access to employment, including promotion; access to vocational training; and working conditions, including dismissal. The directive is intended to bring about equality in substance rather than in form (Case C-342/01 *Merino Gómez* [2004] ECR I-0000, para. 37). Art. 1(2) excludes social security from the scope of the directive, leaving it to the Council to adopt further measures in that area. It was in implementation of this provision that the Council adopted Dirs. 79/7 and 86/378 (see sections IV and V below).

(*a*) ***Exclusion of social security.*** The ECJ has interpreted the scope and effect of the exception contained in Art. 1(2) in several cases. In Case 192/85 *Newstead* [1987] ECR 4753 at pp. 4784–6, the Court ruled that a social security benefit (e.g. survivors' pension) that is not covered by the special directives adopted by the Council in the matter (see Art. 3(2) of Dir. 79/7 and Art. 9(b) of Dir. 86/378) is, by virtue of the exception set out in Art. 1(2), not subject to the application of the principle of equal treatment. Nevertheless, in a series of cases the Court has held that, in view of the fundamental importance of that principle, Art. 1(2) must be interpreted strictly (see Case 151/84 *Roberts* [1986] ECR 703 at p. 721; Case 152/84 *Marshall I* [1986] ECR 723 at p. 746; Case 262/84 *Beets-Proper* [1986] ECR 773 at p. 792).

Therefore, because of the risk of detracting from the objective of Dir. 76/207, a scheme of benefits cannot be excluded from the scope of the directive solely because, formally, it is part of a national social security system. Such a scheme may come within the directive's scope of application if its subject-matter is access to employment, including vocational training and promotion, or working conditions. However, the directive does not become applicable to a social security scheme, such as supplementary allowance or income support, simply because the conditions of entitlement for receipt of benefits may be such as to affect the ability of a single parent to take up employment (Cases C-63/91 etc. *Jackson and Cresswell* [1992] ECR I-4737 at pp. I-4781–2). On the other hand, where the function of a benefit, such as family credit in the United Kingdom, is to keep low-paid workers in employment by supplementing their income and the benefit is thus linked to an employment relationship, it is concerned with both access to employment and working conditions and falls, therefore, within the scope of the directive. That is so even if, on account of a second function, that of meeting family expenses, the benefit in question is also covered by Reg. 1408/71 on social security (Case C-116/94 *Meyers* [1995] ECR I-2131 at pp. I-2150–2).

(*b*) ***Direct discrimination based on sex.*** Art. 2(1) defines the principle of equal treatment as meaning that 'there shall be no discrimination whatsoever on grounds of sex either directly or indirectly by reference in particular to marital or family status'. The principle is more specifically defined and implemented in relation to the three matters covered by the directive (access to employment, access to vocational training and working conditions) by Arts. 3, 4, and 5, respectively, which are considered in more detail below (see point 3).

As pointed out earlier, the directive prohibits only employment-related sex discrimination, although within its field of application the prohibition is comprehensive. It applies to all types of employment, including employment in the public service. The directive intends to guarantee equal treatment of men and women in working life as a whole and therefore does not allow the creation of new cases of discrimination by exempting certain groups from its provisions (Case 248/83 *Commission* v. *Germany* [1985] ECR 1459 at p. 1480). Its general application is inherent in the very nature of the principle that it lays down (Case C-1/95 *Gerster* [1997] ECR I-5253 at p. I-5281). National provisions governing admission to the practical training that is a necessary prerequisite of access to employment in the civil service thus fall within the scope of the directive (Case C-79/99 *Schnorbus* [2000] ECR I-10997 at p. I-11029).

In a series of cases, the Court has been confronted with the question whether the directive applies to the armed forces. The Court has recognized that it is for the Member States, which have to adopt appropriate measures to ensure their internal and external security, to take decisions on the organization of their armed forces. However, such decisions cannot fall entirely outside the scope of Community law. Although the Treaty allows derogations, on grounds of public security, from the rules relating to the free movement of goods, persons, services, and capital, there is no such general derogation on those grounds from the principle of equal treatment, which is of general application and applies to the public service. Thus, the directive is applicable to access to posts in the armed forces, and it is for the Court to verify whether the measures taken by the national authorities in that respect are justified by the requirements of public security and are appropriate and necessary for that purpose (Case C-273/97 *Sirdar* [1999] ECR I-7403 at pp. I-7439–40; Case C-285/98 *Kreil* [2000] ECR I-69 at pp. I-103–4; see further point 2(*a*) below). However, Community law does not govern the Member States' choices of military organization for the defence of their territory or of their essential interests, and therefore does not preclude compulsory military service being limited to men (Case C-186/01 *Dory* [2003] ECR I-2479, paras. 29–42).

It follows from the definition contained in Art. 2(1) that the directive prohibits discrimination only if it is based on the sex of the person concerned. Direct discrimination arises where a provision applies differently according to the sex of the persons in question (Case C-79/99 *Schnorbus*, above, at p. I-11030). Thus, for example, the rule that general medical training must include a certain number of periods of full-time training does not constitute direct discrimination, since it applies to male and female workers alike (Case C-25/02 *Rinke*, above, para. 32). Similarly, the provision of the Staff Regulations of Community Officials, which restricts the household allowance to married officials to the exclusion of registered partnerships, does not discriminate on grounds of sex since it is irrelevant whether the official is a man or a woman. Nor does it discriminate on grounds of sexual orientation since it is not the sex of the official's partner that determines whether the allowance is granted, but the legal nature of the ties between the official and the partner (Cases C-122/99 P etc. *D and Sweden* v. *Council* [2001] ECR I-4319 at p. I-4356).

Differences in treatment are not prohibited if they may be justified by objective factors unrelated to any discrimination based on sex. Thus, where access to employment (e.g. in the public service) is made subject to the 'aptitude' of the applicants, then it is based on an objective criterion of assessment and selection, which is entirely unconnected with the question of a person's sex. The use of such an objective criterion is not, in itself, contrary to the directive unless it is applied in practice in such a way as to lead to appointments based on sex discrimination (Case 248/83 *Commission* v. *Germany*, above, at pp. 1481–2). Moreover, the principle of equal treatment can apply only to persons in comparable situations (see below). Since the situation of a Community official who has registered a partnership between persons of the same sex (or of the opposite sex) is not comparable to that of a married official, the restriction of the household allowance to married officials cannot be regarded as being discriminatory on grounds of sex (Cases C-122/99 P etc. *D and Sweden* v. *Council*, above, at pp. I-4354–7).

In most cases, the test used by the Court to decide whether a measure such as a refusal of employment or dismissal involves direct discrimination on grounds of sex consists in establishing whether the fundamental reason for that measure applies without distinction to workers of both sexes or, conversely, to one sex only. The former situation does not, the latter situation does, involve discrimination. Thus, for example, if the reason for a refusal of employment or dismissal is pregnancy, then the measure constitutes direct discrimination on grounds of sex since it can apply to women alone. In that case the fact that there are no male candidates for a job and that therefore the employer has no choice between male and female candidates, makes no difference since his decision is still directly linked to the sex of the person concerned (Case C-177/88 *Dekker* [1990] ECR I-3941 at pp. I-3972–4; Case C-179/88 *HKF* [1990] ECR I-3979 at p. I-3998—'Hertz' case; Case C-320/01 *Busch* [2003] ECR I-2041, para. 39).

However, it must be remembered that according to the Court's consistent case-law, discrimination involves not only the application of different rules to comparable situations but also the application of the same rule to different situations. Thus, for example, a contractual term providing that an employer may dismiss workers of either sex after a certain number of weeks of continuous absence from work, although applying to men and women alike, will constitute direct discrimination on grounds of sex if applied in the same way to a pregnant woman who is unfit for work as a result of illness associated with her pregnancy and to a man who is ill and absent through incapacity for work for the same length of time, since the two workers are in different situations (Case C-394/96 *Brown* [1998] ECR I-4185 at pp. I-4234–5; see further point 3(*c*) below).

On the other hand, the dismissal of a female worker on account of repeated periods of sick leave, which are not attributable to pregnancy or confinement or on account of unavailability for work on non-medical grounds, does not constitute direct sex discrimination inasmuch as those reasons would lead also to the dismissal of a male worker in the same circumstances (Case C-179/88 *HKF*, above, at p. I-3999; Case C-421/92 *Habermann-Beltermann* [1994] ECR I-1657 at pp. I-1674–5; Case C-32/93

Webb [1994] ECR I-3567 at pp. I-3585–8. See further points 2 and 3 below). A national rule, the purpose of which is to promote positive action for women by providing that where male and female candidates for the same promotion are equally qualified women are automatically to be given priority in sectors where they are underrepresented, involves discrimination on grounds of sex contrary to the directive unless it falls within the exception set out in Art. 2(4) (Case C-450/93 *Kalanke* [1995] ECR I-3051 at p. I-3077; see further point 2 below).

In certain circumstances the test outlined above, according to which the decisive criterion is whether a measure applies without distinction to both sexes or to one sex only, may not be appropriate. Thus, in Case C-13/94 *P*, above, at pp. I-2164–6, the United Kingdom and the Commission argued that the dismissal of a transsexual for a reason related to his or her gender reassignment did not constitute sex discrimination, since the dismissal would have occurred irrespective of whether the person concerned had been a man or a woman prior to undergoing the operation. Therefore, the reason for dismissal applied without distinction to both sexes. However, the ECJ did not accept that argument. Pointing out that the directive is simply the expression of the general principle of equality, which is one of the fundamental principles of Community law, and that the right not to be discriminated against on grounds of sex is a fundamental human right, the Court said that the scope of the directive cannot be confined solely to discrimination based on the fact that a person is of one or other sex. In view of its purpose and the nature of the rights that it seeks to safeguard, the scope of the directive is also such as to apply to discrimination arising from the gender reassignment of the person concerned.

The Court emphasized that such discrimination is based, essentially if not exclusively, on the sex of the person in question. Dismissal on the grounds of gender reassignment involves unfavourable treatment by comparison with persons of the sex to which the transsexual was deemed to belong before undergoing the operation. To tolerate such discrimination, the Court said, would be tantamount to a failure to respect the dignity and freedom to which such a person is entitled, and which the Court has a duty to safeguard. Therefore, the Court concluded, dismissal for a reason related to gender reassignment is contrary to the directive.

On the face of it, the ruling of the Court has considerably extended the protection provided by the directive by bringing within its scope cases where a person suffers a disadvantage on account of sex but is not treated differently from the way in which he would have been treated had he belonged to the opposite sex at the material time. (In the present case, the person in question would have been dismissed for the same reason had he been a woman rather than a man prior to the operation.)

Clearly, this ruling cannot be explained by the traditional interpretation of the concept of discrimination between men and women. The only way to explain the decision is by taking the view that the Court has recognized the existence, if not of a third sex, at least of a third category of persons, that of transsexuals, as distinct from the categories of men and women (in this respect, see also the opinion of A.-G. Tesauro, ibid. at pp. I-2153 and I-2155, paras. 17 and 22). Indeed, the Court refers to the judgment of the European Court of Human Rights of 17 October 1986 in *Rees* v. *United Kingdom* (Series A, No. 106, 9 EHRR 56, para. 38), in which that Court recognized that 'transsexuals who have been operated upon . . . form a fairly well-defined and identifiable group'. The ECJ bases its decision on 'discrimination arising . . . from the gender reassignment' of transsexuals, not on discrimination against men or women. Consequently, the Court compares, not the treatment of men with that of women, but the treatment of a transsexual with that of 'persons of the sex to which he or she was deemed to belong before undergoing gender reassignment'. Interpreted in this way, the ruling has a fairly narrow scope by prohibiting sex discrimination only against transsexuals without in any way affecting the traditional concept of equal treatment of men and women.

(*c*) ***Indirect discrimination based on sex.*** Art. 2(1), in conjunction with Arts. 3, 4, and 5, prohibits not only direct but also indirect discrimination. According to the case-law of the ECJ, developed under both Art. 141 EC and Dir. 76/207:

> national provisions or rules relating to pay or social security benefits, access to employment and working conditions discriminate indirectly against women where, although worded in neutral terms, they work to the disadvantage of a much higher percentage of women than men, unless that difference in treatment is justified by objective factors unrelated to any discrimination on grounds of sex . . . Thus, once it is established that a measure adversely affects a much higher percentage of women than men, or vice versa, that measure will be presumed to constitute indirect discrimination on grounds of sex and it will be for the employer or the person who drafted that measure to demonstrate the contrary (Case C-226/98 *Jørgensen* [2000] ECR I-2447 at p. I-2479; see also e.g. Case C-189/91 *Kirsammer-Hack* [1993] ECR I-6185 at p. I-6221 and the cases cited below).

In practice, in most cases such indirect discrimination arises from measures that treat part-time employees less favourably than full-time employees because part-time employees as a rule comprise a considerably higher proportion of women than men. This was the position, for example, in Case C-1/95 *Gerster*, above, at pp. I-5284–7, where part-time employees, 87% of whom were women, could accrue length of service for purposes of promotion more slowly, and therefore could gain promotion later, than full-time employees; and also in Case C-100/95 *Kording* [1997] ECR I-5289 at pp. I-5297–300, where part-time employees, 92.4% of whom were women, had to work several years longer than full-time employees in order to gain exemption from the compulsory qualifying examination for tax advisers. By contrast, in Case C-189/91 *Kirsammer-Hack*, above, at p. I-6222, the disadvantageous measure, exclusion from the national system of protection against unfair dismissal, did not affect specifically part-time employees but all employees of certain undertakings, irrespective of whether they worked on a full-time or part-time basis, and did not therefore constitute indirect discrimination against women.

In order to establish indirect discrimination on grounds of sex, it must be shown that a measure in fact adversely affects a larger number of women than men (or vice versa). A situation may reveal a *prima facie* case of indirect discrimination only if the statistics describing that situation are valid, i.e. if they cover enough individuals, do not illustrate purely fortuitous or short-term phenomena, and appear, in general, to be significant (Case C-226/98 *Jørgensen*, above, at p. I-2480). The Court held that data showing that a provision of a scheme for the reorganization of medical practices in Denmark affected only 22 specialized medical practitioners, of whom 14 were women, out of a total of 1680, of whom 302 were women, could not be treated as significant (ibid.).

Once indirect discrimination has been established, it is necessary to determine whether the difference in treatment is justified by 'objective factors unrelated to any discrimination on grounds of sex' (in simple terms, by objective factors not related to sex). The burden of proving that such justification exists lies on the employer or the author of the measure in question. The Court has held that budgetary considerations cannot in themselves justify discrimination on grounds of sex. As regards justifications based on social policy, the Court has acknowledged that as Community law stands at present, social policy is a matter for the Member States, which enjoy a reasonable margin of discretion as regards social protection measures. If they meet a legitimate aim of social policy, are suitable and requisite for attaining that aim, and are therefore justified by reasons unrelated to discrimination on grounds of sex, such measures cannot be regarded as being contrary to the principle of equal treatment even if they affect far more women than men. It is for the national courts to determine whether an objective justification exists (ibid. at pp. I-2481–2, concerning reorganization of medical practices; see also Case C-322/98 *Kachelmann* [2000] ECR I-7505 at pp. I-7528–31, concerning dismissal on economic grounds; Case C-187/00 *Kutz-Bauer* [2003] ECR I-2741, paras. 48–63 and Case C-77/02 *Steinicke* [2003] ECR I-9027, paras. 53–74, both concerning part-time work for older employees).

Indirect discrimination may, of course, arise not only from measures that relate to part-time work but from any measure, which, although formulated in neutral terms, works to the disadvantage of one sex as compared with the other. Thus, Case C-79/99 *Schnorbus*, above, at pp. I-11030–3, involved a national provision that accorded priority admission to practical legal training for applicants who had completed compulsory military or civilian service. The Court held that while this rule did not constitute direct discrimination based on sex, it did amount to indirect discrimination in favour of men since under German law women were not required to do military or civilian service and therefore could not benefit from the priority. However, the Court accepted that the provision was objectively justified as it was intended to counterbalance disadvantages not faced by women, namely the delay resulting from the completion of compulsory military or civilian service, which affected only men. In Case C-25/02 *Rinke*, above, paras. 32–43, the Court found that the requirement that general medical training must include a certain number of periods of full-time training placed women at a particular disadvantage as compared with men, but was objectively justified by the need to ensure adequate preparation for the effective exercise of medical practice.

(*d*) ***The relationship between Dir. 76/207 and Art. 141 EC.*** Because the scope of Dir. 76/207 is limited to the principle of equal treatment, the question arises of its relationship to Art. 141 EC and Dir. 75/117 of 10 February 1975 on the approximation of the laws of the Member States relating to the application of the principle of equal pay for men and women (the 'equal pay' directive; *OJ* 1975 L45/19), which implemented Art. 141. This question has given rise to certain problems in practice. Initially, in Case 149/77 *Defrenne III*, above, at p. 1377, the ECJ expressed the view that Art. 141 concerns only pay discrimination and its scope cannot be extended to other conditions of employment, even where such conditions (e.g. a special age-limit) may have financial consequences. In line with this view, in Case 19/81 *Burton* [1982] ECR 555 at p. 575, the Court held that if a question of interpretation concerns not a particular benefit itself but the conditions of access to that benefit, then the matter is covered by Dir. 76/207 and not by Art. 141 or Dir. 75/117. (This case involved an alleged discrimination on account of different age conditions being set for men and women for payment of a voluntary redundancy benefit. The Court dealt with the case under Art. 5(1) of Dir. 76/207, see point 3(*c*) below).

By contrast, however, in Case 170/84 *Bilka* [1986] ECR 1607 at pp. 1623–7, the Court ruled that if a benefit, such as an occupational pension, constitutes 'pay' within the meaning of Art. 141, then the conditions of admission to that benefit (e.g. that it is available to full-time workers only, to the exclusion of part-time workers) are also governed by Art. 141. In other words, the Court established the principle that Art. 141 covers not only the benefits themselves paid (in that case) by an occupational pension scheme but also the right to join, and the conditions of joining, such a scheme. The *Bilka* ruling was followed in Case C-262/88 *Barber* [1990] ECR I-1889 at p. I-1953, where the Court held that Art. 141 prohibits not only any discrimination with regard to 'pay' itself, but also the imposition of a discriminatory age condition for the grant of a benefit which qualifies as pay within the meaning of Art. 141 (e.g. a pension paid under a contracted-out private occupational scheme). This principle has been applied subsequently in a number of cases to various types of benefits and conditions (*see further under* **Equal pay**). As a result of these developments, it may now be said that contrary to the earlier case-law, Art. 141 covers both a benefit which is part of 'pay' and the conditions governing access to it (for an attempt to reconcile the Court's rulings in *Defrenne III*, *Burton*, and *Bilka*, see the opinion of A.-G. Van Gerven in Case C-262/88 *Barber*, above, at pp. I-1922–8).

Nevertheless, conditions of employment that are not intimately linked to pay or to a benefit which qualifies as pay are still covered by Dir. 76/207 and not by Art. 141, even if they have financial consequences. Thus, in a series of more recent cases, the Court has upheld its ruling in *Defrenne III* and has confirmed that 'the fact that the fixing of certain working conditions may have pecuniary consequences is not sufficient to bring such conditions within the scope of Article 141, which is based on the close connection which exists between the nature of the services provided and the amount of remuneration' (Case C-167/97 *Seymour-Smith and Perez* [1999] ECR I-623 at pp. I-677–8, where the Court held that compensation for unfair dismissal constitutes a form of pay and falls under Art. 141, while reinstatement or re-engagement concern working conditions or access to employment and fall within the scope of Dir. 76/207; Case C-411/96 *Boyle* [1998] ECR I-6401 at pp. I-6457, I-6463, holding that maternity leave and annual leave constitute working conditions within the meaning of the directive; Case C-236/98 *JämO* [2000] ECR I-2189 at pp. I-2224–5, holding that reduction in working time relates to working conditions and falls under Dir. 76/207; Case C-476/99 *Lommers* [2002] ECR I-2891 at p. I-2933, holding that the making available to employees, by their employer, of nursery places is to be regarded as a working condition within the meaning of the directive; Case C-77/02 *Steinicke*, above, paras. 48–51, holding that a scheme of part-time work for older employees that is intended to reduce the normal working time concerns working conditions under the directive. By contrast, in Case C-281/97 *Krüger* [1999] ECR I-5127 at p. I-5146, the Court held that an end-of-year bonus paid by the employer was pay within the meaning of Art. 141).

The proper definition of the respective fields of application of the two sets of rules is important for two reasons. First, it seems that Art. 141 and Dir. 75/117 on the one hand, and Dir. 76/207 on the other, are mutually exclusive. Where a benefit constitutes pay and therefore falls within the scope of Art. 141 and Dir. 75/117, it cannot be covered by Dir. 76/207 as well, since that directive does not apply to pay (Case C-342/93 *Gillespie* [1996] ECR I-475 at p. I-501, dealing with maternity pay. In support of this view, the Court refers to the second recital in the preamble to Dir. 76/207. See also Case C-297/93 *Grau-Hupka* [1994] ECR I-5535 at p. I-5551. It is interesting to note that in his opinion in Case C-262/88 *Barber*, above, at p. I-1927, note 28, A.-G. Van Gerven expressed the view that Art. 141 and Dir. 76/207 are not mutually exclusive, and relied on the first recital of the same directive in support). Conversely, where a benefit does not constitute pay, the case is not covered by Art. 141 or Dir. 75/117, which has the same scope, but may be covered by Dir. 76/207 or one of the other directives implementing the principle of equal treatment (see Case 192/85 *Newstead*, above, at pp. 4783–6).

Secondly, Art. 141 can produce both vertical and horizontal direct effect. Therefore, if the person discriminated against is able to establish that his or her claim concerns 'pay' or a condition governing access thereto, the claim is enforceable in the national courts both against a Member State and against another private person, e.g. a private employer. It is almost certain that it has been this easier enforceability that has prompted the Court to interpret the concept of 'pay' in the broadest possible sense so as to allow the widest possible access to Art. 141. By contrast, while Dir. 76/207, or at least some of its provisions, may produce vertical direct effect, and may thus be relied on against a Member State, whether the State acts as employer or as public authority, it cannot produce horizontal direct effect. It may not impose obligations on individuals and is therefore not enforceable against a private person, e.g. a private employer, in the national courts (Case 152/84 *Marshall I*, above, at p. 749).

This does not mean, however, that the directive may never be relied on by a national court in proceedings between two persons governed by private law. According to a doctrine developed by the ECJ, a directive is binding on all the authorities of Member States, including the courts. In applying national law, regardless of whether the provisions in question were adopted before or after the directive, the national courts are required to interpret them, as far as possible, in the light of the wording and the purpose of the directive in order to achieve the result pursued by the latter. Therefore, since Dir. 76/207 has been transposed into national law, a national court may rely on it for the purposes of interpreting and applying the relevant provisions of national law. To that end, the national court may seek a preliminary ruling from the ECJ on the interpretation of the directive. Thus, while not having horizontal direct effect, Dir. 76/207 may still be considered by national courts in actions between private individuals (see Case 14/83 *Von Colson and Kamann* [1984] ECR 1891 at p. 1909; Case C-106/89 *Marleasing* [1990] ECR I-4135 at p. I-4159; Case C-421/92 *Habermann-Beltermann*, above, at p. I-1673; Case C-32/93 *Webb*, above, at p. I-3572 *per* A.-G. Tesauro).

In accordance with the general case-law of the ECJ on the direct effect of directives, in all cases in which a directive has been properly implemented its effects reach individuals through the implementing measures adopted by the Member States concerned. Therefore, where Dir. 76/207 has been correctly implemented, the question of its direct effect does not arise. On the other hand, where a Member State has failed to implement the directive correctly, individuals may rely on those of its provisions that are, so far as their subject-matter is concerned, unconditional and sufficiently precise, in order to avoid the application of any national legislation which is incompatible with the directive or which contains derogations going beyond the limits of the exceptions permitted by Art. 2(2), (3), or (4). While the Court has not found it necessary to rule on the direct effect of Art. 2(1) taken by itself, it has confirmed that Art. 2(1) can produce direct effect in conjunction with the substantive provisions which implement the principle of equal treatment in relation to specific matters, i.e. Arts. 3, 4, and 5 (see point 3 below and Case 152/84 *Marshall I*, above, at pp. 747–50; Case 222/84 *Johnston* [1986] ECR 1651 at pp. 1689–92).

2. Exceptions. Art. 2(2), (3) and (4) of Dir. 76/207 lay down three particular exceptions to the principle of equal treatment. Since the application of the principle is not subject to any general reservation or derogation on grounds of the protection of national security, public order, or public safety (apart from the possible application of Art. 297 EC which deals with a wholly exceptional situation), or on any other grounds, an act of direct sex discrimination may only be justified under one or more of these specific exceptions (Case 222/84 *Johnston*, above, at p. 1684; see also point 1(*b*) above). They are considered in turn below.

(*a*) ***Art. 2(2): sex as a determining factor.*** Art. 2(2) permits the Member States to exclude from the directive's field of application those occupational activities and, where appropriate, the training leading thereto, for which, by reason of their nature or the context in which they are carried out, the sex of the worker constitutes a determining factor. In several cases, the ECJ has emphasized that, being a derogation from an individual right guaranteed by the directive, Art. 2(2) must be interpreted strictly. In determining its scope of application, regard must be had to the principle of proportionality, which is one of the general principles of Community law. That principle requires that derogations must remain within the limits of what is appropriate and necessary for achieving the aim in view. Thus, the principle of equal treatment must be reconciled, as far as possible, with the requirements that are decisive for the carrying out of the specific activity in question (Case 222/84 *Johnston*, above, at pp. 1686–7; Case C-273/97 *Sirdar*, above, at p. I-7442; Case C-285/98 *Kreil*, above, at p. I-105).

In Case 165/82 *Commission* v. *United Kingdom* [1983] ECR 3431 at pp. 3447–8, the Court held that the exclusion from the prohibition of discrimination of employment in a private household and in small undertakings with not more than five employees by the United Kingdom Sex Discrimination Act 1975 went beyond the objective which might be lawfully pursued within the framework of Art. 2(2). On the other hand, the Court accepted that the exclusion of men, under the same Act, from access to the occupation of midwife and from training for that occupation did not exceed the scope of Art. 2(2) as it was justified by the need to respect the patient's sensitivities (ibid. at p. 3449).

In Case 222/84 *Johnston*, above, at pp. 1686–8, the Court recognized that for policing activities performed in situations where there are serious internal disturbances and frequent assassinations (i.e. in Northern Ireland) the sex of police officers constitutes a determining factor. A Member State (i.e. the United Kingdom) may therefore restrict such activities, and the training leading thereto, to men. In Case 318/86 *Commission* v. *France* [1988] ECR 3559 at pp. 3578–80, the Court likewise recognized that sex may be a determining factor for posts such as those of prison warders and head prison warders. The specific nature of those posts and the conditions under which warders carry out their activities may justify reserving such posts primarily for men in male prisons and primarily for women in female prisons. In Case C-273/97 *Sirdar*, above, at p. I-7443, the Court held that the exclusion of women from service in special combat units such as the Royal Marines in the United Kingdom may be justified under Art. 2(2) by reason of the nature of the activities in question and the context in which they are carried out. The Court said that the specific conditions for deployment of the assault units of which the Royal Marines are composed, and in particular the rule of 'interoperability' to which they are subject (i.e. the need for every Marine, irrespective of his specialization, to be capable of fighting in a commando unit), justified their composition remaining exclusively male. By contrast, in Case C-285/98 *Kreil*, above, at pp. I-106–7, the Court ruled that the total exclusion of women from all military posts involving the use of arms and allowing them access only to the medical and military-music services under German law was disproportionately broad in scope and therefore could not be justified under Art. 2(2).

The purpose of Art. 2(2) is not to oblige but to permit the Member States to exclude certain occupational activities from the scope of the directive. Member States are not required to exercise that power of derogation in a particular manner since the exceptions serve widely differing purposes and several of them are closely linked to the rules governing certain occupations. However, Art. 2(2) must be read in conjunction with Art. 9(2), which requires the Member States to assess periodically the activities referred to in Art. 2(2) in order to decide, in the light of social developments, whether there is justification for maintaining the exclusions in question (Case 222/84 *Johnston*, above, at p. 1687). They are also to notify the Commission of the results of that assessment. Thus, Art. 9(2) lays down a two-stage supervision: first, by the Member States themselves and, secondly, by the Commission on the basis of the notifications received. The purpose of this twofold supervision is to eliminate progressively existing exceptions which are no longer justified. The ECJ has held that it is primarily for the Member States to compile a complete and verifiable list, in whatever form, of the occupations and activities excluded from the application of the principle of equal treatment and to notify the results to the Commission. The Commission then has both the right and the duty to verify the application of Art. 2(2). Failure by a Member State to comply with this obligation may lead to a successful action by the Commission under Art. 226 (see Case 248/83 *Commission* v. *Germany*, above, at pp. 1484–7).

From a combined reading of Arts. 2(2) and 9(2), the Court concluded that the exceptions provided for in Art. 2(2) may relate only to specific activities, that they must be sufficiently transparent, and that in principle they must be capable of being adapted to social development. Transparency must be such as to enable both the Commission and the courts to exercise effective supervision and any persons adversely affected by discriminatory measures to defend their rights (ibid. at p. 1487; Case 318/86 *Commission* v. *France*, above, at pp. 3581–2, where the Court found that the French system of separate recruitment according to sex for appointment to certain corps in the prison service and in the national police force, under which the percentages of posts to be allotted to men and women respectively were fixed in advance, did not fulfil the first two requirements and was, therefore, contrary to Dir. 76/207).

(b) Art. 2(3): protection of women with regard to pregnancy and maternity. Art. 2(3) reserves to Member States the right to retain or introduce provisions concerning the protection of women, particularly as regards pregnancy and maternity. The ECJ has interpreted the scope of this exception in a series of cases, the earliest of which, Case 184/83 *Hofmann* [1984] ECR 3047 at p. 3075, contains the following standard definition, frequently referred to in subsequent cases:

> the directive recognizes the legitimacy, in terms of the principle of equal treatment, of protecting a woman's needs in two respects. First, it is legitimate to ensure the protection of a woman's biological condition during pregnancy and thereafter until such time as her physiological and mental functions have returned to normal after childbirth; secondly, it is legitimate to protect the special relationship between a woman and her child over the period which follows pregnancy and childbirth, by preventing that relationship from being disturbed by the multiple burdens which would result from the simultaneous pursuit of employment.

On this basis, the Court held that a measure such as a maternity leave granted to a woman on expiry of the statutory protective period, accompanied by the payment of an allowance, falls within the scope of Art. 2(3) as it seeks to protect a woman in connection with the effects of pregnancy and motherhood. That being its purpose, such leave may legitimately be reserved to the mother to the exclusion of any other person, including the father, since it is only the mother who may find herself subject to undesirable pressures to return to work prematurely. The directive, the Court pointed out, is not designed to settle questions concerned with the organization of the family, or to alter the division of responsibility between parents. It leaves Member States with a reasonable margin of discretion as to the social measures that they intend to adopt within their general system of social protection in order to guarantee, subject to the directive, the protection of women in connection with pregnancy and maternity, and to offset the disadvantages which women, by comparison with men, suffer with regard to the retention of employment. Therefore, the directive does not impose on Member States a requirement that they must, as an alternative, allow maternity leave to be granted to fathers, even where the parents so decide (ibid. at pp. 3075–6). It may be noted that Dir. 96/34 on parental leave, adopted subsequent to the Court's judgment (see section I.4 above), provides for an individual right to parental leave to be granted to all workers, both male and female, owing to the birth or adoption of a child.

In its subsequent case-law, the Court has frequently emphasized that, like Art. 2(2), Art. 2(3) must be interpreted strictly and that the express reference to pregnancy and maternity indicates that the sole purpose of Art. 2(3) is to protect a woman's biological condition and the special relationship which exists between a woman and her child. The exception therefore cannot cover legislation intended to protect women against risks and dangers that affect men and women in the same way. For the exception to apply, there must be a justified need for a difference in treatment. Thus, in Case 222/84 *Johnston*, above, at pp. 1688–9, the Court held that the total exclusion of women from service in the armed police force in Northern Ireland, imposed for reasons of public safety, was not justified by the concern to protect women since the risks and dangers to which women were exposed when performing their duties were not different from those to which men were also exposed when performing the same duties. For the same reasons, in Case C-285/98 *Kreil*, above, at p. I-107, the Court ruled that the total exclusion of women from all military posts involving the use of arms under German law was not one of the differences of treatment allowed by Art. 2(3) out of concern to protect women.

In Case 312/86 *Commission* v. *France* [1988] ECR 6315 at p. 6336, the Court found that French legislation which allowed in general terms any clause in collective agreements providing 'special rights for women' to remain in force could not be justified under Art. 2(3) because some of those 'special rights' related to the protection of women in their capacity as older workers or parents—categories to which both men and women might equally belong. Likewise, in Case C-345/89 *Stoeckel* [1991] ECR I-4047 at pp. I-4066–7, the Court held that the general prohibition of night-work by women under French law could not be justified on the grounds of protecting female workers since, whatever the disadvantages of night-work may be, the risks to which women are exposed when working at night are, in general, not inherently different from those to which men are exposed, except in the case of pregnancy or maternity. The fact that the risks of attack are greater at night than during the day makes no difference since they can be dealt with by the adoption of appropriate measures without undermining the principle of equal treatment. Where night-work is prohibited for both men and women, Art. 2(3) does not allow derogations from the prohibition which differ from one sex to the other and which are subject to more restrictive conditions in respect of women than in respect of men, unless such a difference is justified by the need to ensure the protection of women with regard to pregnancy and maternity (Case C-13/93 *Minne* [1994] ECR I-371 at pp. I-382–3).

On the other hand, statutory prohibition on night-time work during pregnancy is entirely compatible with Art. 2(3). However, compliance with such a prohibition may not render void an employment contract concluded for an indefinite period, or lead to its termination, on the ground that the prohibition prevents a pregnant employee from performing the night-time work for which she was engaged. The prohibition takes effect only for a limited period in relation to the total length of the contract, and to allow the contract to be terminated on account of the temporary inability of the pregnant employee to perform night-time work would be contrary to the objective pursued by Art. 2(3), and would deprive that provision of its effectiveness (Case C-421/92 *Habermann-Beltermann*, above, at pp. I-1675–7). Similarly, an employer cannot refuse to appoint a pregnant woman to a post for an indefinite period on the ground that a statutory prohibition imposed because of pregnancy temporarily prevents her from performing all of her duties during the pregnancy (Case C-207/98 *Mahlburg* [2000] ECR I-549 at pp. I-573–4). In general, the exercise of the rights conferred on women under Art. 2(3) cannot be the subject of unfavourable treatment regarding their access to employment or their working conditions. The result pursued by the directive is substantive, not formal, equality (Case C-136/95 *Thibault* [1998] ECR I-2011 at p. I-2035).

In other cases, the Court drew a clear distinction between pregnancy and illness, holding that while the dismissal of a female worker on account of pregnancy (or refusal to employ a pregnant woman) constitutes direct discrimination on grounds of sex; dismissal of a female worker on account of repeated periods of sick leave which are not attributable to pregnancy or confinement does not constitute such discrimination inasmuch as the periods of sick leave would lead to the dismissal of a male worker in the same circumstances. However, Art. 2(3) does not envisage the case of an illness attributable to pregnancy or confinement. Nevertheless, the Court held that if such illness occurs during the maternity leave granted under national law then, like pregnancy, it falls within the scope of Art. 2(3) and women are protected against dismissal due to absence. On the other hand, where an illness manifests itself after the maternity leave, there is no reason to distinguish an illness attributable to pregnancy or confinement from any other illness. Such a pathological condition is therefore covered by the general rules applicable in the event of illness. Since male and female workers are equally exposed to illness, there is no reason to afford special protection to women. If a woman is dismissed on account of absence due to illness in the same circumstances as a man then there is no direct discrimination on grounds of sex. In such a case, there is not even any reason to enquire whether women are absent owing to illness more often than men, and whether therefore there exists any indirect discrimination (Case C-179/88 *HKF*, above, at pp. I-3998–9—'Hertz' case; see also Case C-32/93 *Webb*, above, at pp. I-3586–7). Subsequently, the Court confirmed that the directive also precludes dismissal of a female worker at any time during her pregnancy for absences due to incapacity for work caused by an illness resulting from that pregnancy (Case C-394/96 *Brown*, above, at pp. I-4233–4; see further point 3(*c*) below).

(*c*) ***Art. 2(4): positive action for women.*** Art. 2(4) permits measures to promote equal opportunity for men and women, in particular by removing existing inequalities that affect women's opportunities in the areas covered by the directive. Referring to this provision, in 1984 the Council adopted a detailed recommendation on the promotion of positive action for women (Rec. 84/635, *OJ* 1984 L331/34). After pointing out the inadequacy of existing legal provisions on equal treatment for the elimination of all existing inequalities unless parallel action is taken by governments, both sides of industry and other bodies (third recital), the measure recommends Member States to adopt a positive action policy designed to eliminate inequalities affecting women in working life and to promote a better balance between the sexes in employment, thus counteracting the prejudicial effects on women which arise from social attitudes, behaviour, and structures (point 1).

The ECJ itself has interpreted Art. 2(4) strictly, just as it has interpreted Art. 2(2) and (3), holding that the exception in Art. 2(4) 'is specifically and exclusively designed to allow measures which, although discriminatory in appearance, are in fact intended to eliminate or reduce actual instances of inequality which may exist in the reality of social life' and that the granting of special rights to women in collective agreements does not fall within its scope. Thus, the Court has confirmed that the objective which Art. 2(4) aims to achieve is substantive (as opposed to formal) equality (Case 312/86 *Commission* v. *France*, above, at pp. 6336–7).

The Court relied on this interpretation in Case C-450/93 *Kalanke*, above, at pp. I-3077–8, which concerned the question whether the Bremen law on equal treatment for men and women in the public service was compatible with Art. 2(4). That law provided, in essence, that where candidates of different sexes shortlisted for an appointment or promotion were equally qualified, automatic priority was to be given to women in sectors where they were underrepresented. Underrepresentation was deemed to exist when women did not make up at least half of the staff in the individual pay brackets in the relevant personnel group within a department or in the function levels provided for in the organization chart. The purpose of the quota system was to help to overcome the disadvantages that women faced and which perpetuated past inequalities, and to enable women also to fill certain more senior posts in which they were traditionally underrepresented. The Court held that Art. 2(4) permits national measures relating to access to employment, including promotion, which give a specific advantage to women with a view to improving their ability to compete on the labour market and to pursue a career on an equal footing with men. However, national rules which guarantee women *absolute and unconditional priority* for appointment or promotion go beyond promoting equal opportunities and exceed the limits of the exception in Art. 2(4). Moreover, the Court added, in so far as it seeks to achieve equal representation of men and women in all grades and levels within a department, such a system 'substitutes for equality of opportunity as envisaged in Art. 2(4) the result which is only to be arrived at by providing such equality of opportunity' (ibid. at p. I-3078). Therefore, the Court concluded, the rules in question were incompatible with Art. 2(1) and (4) of the directive.

The ruling of the Court may seem somewhat harsh and legalistic at first sight, but it is submitted that it is perfectly in accordance with both the 'spirit' and the wording of Art. 2(4), interpreted in the light of the directive as a whole. Art. 2(4) allows measures to promote *equal opportunity* for, *not equal representation* of, men and women. The former is a means for achieving the latter. While 'positive measures' in favour of women are allowed for the purpose of enabling them to improve their chances of pursuing a suitable career, 'positive discrimination' in their favour is not permitted in the context of an actual appointment or promotion: they must compete with men on an equal footing. It is easy to see that a rigid quota system, such as that envisaged in the Bremen law in question, while promoting equal representation is *destroying* equal opportunity, i.e. that which Art. 2(4) is intended to achieve. It can attain only formal, not substantive, equality. The point of the Court's ruling is precisely that equal representation of men and women is to be arrived at, not by artificial quotas but by creating conditions in which both sexes have equal opportunity to perform to the best of their abilities (see also the opinion of A.-G. Tesauro, ibid. at pp. I-3057–67, especially at pp. I-3061 *et seq.*, and the opinion of A.-G. Jacobs in Case C-409/95 *Marschall* [1997] ECR I-6363 at pp. I-6374–5 and I-6379, paras. 32 and 47, where he expresses the view that the *Kalanke* ruling was entirely in accordance with the scheme of the directive, and describes criticisms of that ruling as 'misconceived').

On its part, the Commission clarified its interpretation of the *Kalanke* judgment by communications adopted on 27 March 1996 (COM(96) 88 and 93; *Bull. EU* 3–1996, p. 63). The Commission considers that the Court has not ruled out positive action in favour of women in general, but has condemned only one particular form of positive action: the rigid quota system under which there is no possibility of taking specific individual circumstances into account. Member States and employers are therefore free to avail themselves of a wide range of positive measures unaffected by the judgment, such as State subsidies granted to employers to encourage the employment of women in sectors where they are underrepresented; positive training-oriented action; vocational guidance; child care; and flexible quotas. In order to create a clear situation, the Commission put forward a proposal for the amendment of Art. 2(4) so as to indicate the kinds of positive action specifically permitted (*OJ* 1996 C179/8). These would include the giving of preference, as regards access to employment or promotion, to a member of either sex in cases where it is underrepresented, on condition that the employer always has the opportunity to take account of the particular circumstances of an individual case.

The Commission's interpretation of the *Kalanke* decision and proposal for amendment seem to have been vindicated by subsequent developments in the case-law. In Case C-409/95 *Marschall*, above, at pp. I-6392–3, the Court was asked to rule on the compatibility with Art. 2(4) of a law of the German *Land* of North Rhine-Westphalia which provided that, in sectors of the public service in which fewer women than men were employed in the relevant higher grade post in a career bracket, women had to be given priority where male and female candidates for promotion were equally qualified, unless 'reasons specific to an individual male candidate tilt the balance in his favour' (the 'saving clause'). The Court accepted the arguments of the *Land* and several governments that the mere fact that a male candidate and a female candidate are equally qualified does not mean that they have the same chances, because male candidates tend to be promoted in preference to female candidates particularly because of prejudices and stereotypes concerning the role and capacities of women in working life and their more frequent absence from work owing to pregnancy, childbirth, and breastfeeding. Thus, a national rule such as that in question may fall within the scope of Art. 2(4) if it can counteract the prejudicial effects of such attitudes and thus reduce actual instances of inequality, provided that it does not guarantee absolute and unconditional priority for women. The present case was distinguished from *Kalanke*, because the saving clause excluded such automatic priority.

The final ruling of the Court was that a national law such as that before it is not incompatible with Art. 2(1) and (4) of the directive, provided that in each individual case it provides for male candidates who are equally as qualified as the female candidates a guarantee that the candidatures will be the subject of an objective assessment that will take account of all criteria specific to the individual candidates and will override the priority accorded to female candidates where one or more of those criteria tilt the balance in favour of the male candidate, and such criteria do not discriminate against the female candidates.

In Case C-158/97 *Badeck* [2000] ECR I-1875 at p. I-1919, the Court summed up its rulings in *Kalanke* and *Marschall* by saying that a measure which is intended to give priority in promotion to women in sectors of the public service where they are underrepresented is compatible with Community law if it does not automatically and unconditionally give priority to women when women and men are equally qualified, and the candidatures are the subject of an objective assessment which takes account of the specific personal situations of all candidates. In the same case, the Court found that various provisions of the Law of the German *Land* of Hesse on equal rights for women and men satisfied this test and were therefore compatible with Art. 2(4) (ibid. at pp. I-1920–30). This was the case, in particular, where a provision reserved for women places, not in employment but in training with a view to obtaining qualifications with the prospect of subsequent access to trained occupations in the public service. By improving the chances of female candidates, such a provision was designed to eliminate the causes of women's reduced opportunities of access to employment and careers. It improved the ability of women to compete on the labour market and pursue a career on an equal footing with men (ibid. at p. I-1927). Relying in part on this ruling, in Case C-476/99 *Lommers*, above, at pp. I-2934–9, the Court held that Art. 2(4) did not preclude a scheme set up by the Netherlands Ministry of Agriculture to tackle extensive underrepresentation of women within it, under which a limited number of subsidized nursery places was reserved for female officials alone, provided that it allowed male officials who took care of their children by themselves to have access to the scheme on the same conditions as female officials.

In contrast to the *Kalanke, Marschall*, and *Badeck* cases, in Case C-407/98 *Abrahamsson and Anderson* [2000] ECR I-5539 at pp. I-5582–3, the Swedish legislation at issue automatically granted preference to candidates for a post in higher education belonging to the underrepresented sex if they were sufficiently qualified, even if they did not possess qualifications equal to those of other candidates of the opposite sex. The Court held that the result of such a legislation was that the selection of a candidate from among those who were sufficiently qualified was ultimately based on the mere fact of belonging to the underrepresented sex, and that this was so even if the merits of the candidate so selected were inferior to those of a candidate of the opposite sex. Moreover, candidatures were not subject to an objective assessment taking account of the specific personal situations of all the candidates. Such a method of selection was not permitted by Art. 2(4).

In some of the above cases, the Court had an opportunity to consider the relationship between Art. 2(4) of Dir. 76/207 and Art. 141(4) EC. The latter had its origin in Art. 6(3) of the Agreement on Social Policy and was inserted into the EC Treaty by the ToA, and also allows positive action or positive discrimination by Member States (see section I.3 above). The Court's view is that Art. 141(4) comes into operation only if a positive action measure is precluded by Art. 2(4) of the directive. Thus, the Court's practice is to examine such a measure under Art. 2(4) first (see Case C-158/97 *Badeck*, above, at p. I-1917; Case C-407/98 *Abrahamsson and Anderson*, above, at p. I-5579). This would seem to imply that Art. 141(4) is broader in scope, or less strict, than Art. 2(4). However, in the latter case the Court found that a measure prohibited by Art. 2(4) was also prohibited under Art. 141(4) as it was disproportionate to the aim pursued (ibid. at p. I-5583). It is therefore not clear in what respect the two provisions differ in their scope of application.

3. Substantive fields of application. Arts. 3, 4, and 5 of Dir. 76/207 define in more detail the scope of the principle of equal treatment laid down in Art. 2(1), with regard to the three areas covered by the directive: access to employment (Art. 3), access to vocational training (Art. 4), and working conditions (Art. 5). At the same time, they impose obligations on the Member States in almost identical terms relating to the abolition of all forms of sex discrimination. These obligations will be considered below, following a discussion of the three substantive fields of application.

(a) Access to employment. According to Art. 3(1), application of the principle of equal treatment means that 'there shall be no discrimination whatsoever on grounds of sex in the conditions, including selection criteria, for access to all jobs or posts, whatever the sector or branch of activity, and to all levels of the occupational hierarchy'. The ECJ has held that this provision, read in conjunction with Art. 2(1), is unconditional and sufficiently precise to produce direct effect for individuals as against an organ of the State, such as the Chief Constable of the Royal Ulster Constabulary, whether it acts as an employer or as public authority (Case 222/84 *Johnston*, above, at p. 1691).

In considering the circumstances in which a refusal to employ a woman may constitute direct discrimination on grounds of sex for the purposes of Art. 3(1), in Case C-177/88 *Dekker*, above, at pp. I-3972–4, the ECJ said that the answer depends on whether the fundamental reason for the refusal is one that applies without distinction to workers of either sex or, conversely, whether it applies exclusively to one sex. Where the reason is that the applicant is pregnant (and the employer would be financially unable to pay her the obligatory daily benefits during her maternity leave and at the same time employ a replacement) then the refusal constitutes direct sex discrimination since only women can be refused employment on grounds of pregnancy. Such discrimination cannot be justified by reference to the financial loss that the employer would suffer. Therefore, the Court ruled that an employer is in direct contravention of Arts. 2(1) and 3(1) of the directive if he refuses to enter into a contract of employment with a pregnant female candidate whom he considers to be suitable for the job where such refusal is based on the possible adverse consequences for him of employing a pregnant woman. The fact that there is no male candidate for the job and that therefore the employer has no choice between men and women makes no difference since his decision, being based on pregnancy, is still directly linked to the sex of the candidate. Likewise, an employer cannot refuse to appoint a pregnant woman to a post for an indefinite period on the ground that a statutory prohibition on employment attaching to the condition of pregnancy prevents her from being employed in that post from the outset and for the duration of the pregnancy (Case C-207/98 *Mahlburg*, above, at p. I-574).

Similarly, the termination or annulment of an employment contract on account of the employee's pregnancy concerns women alone and constitutes direct discrimination on grounds of sex. This is so even if the contract is for the performance of night-time work and there is a statutory prohibition on night-work during pregnancy. Since such a prohibition only temporarily prevents a pregnant employee from performing the night-time work for which she has been engaged, it would be contrary to Art. 2(1), read in conjunction with Arts. 3(1) and 5(1) of the directive, to allow the contract to be terminated or annulled if the contract is for an indefinite period (Case C-421/92 *Habermann-Beltermann*, above, at pp. I-1675–7).

The concept of 'access to employment' must be interpreted broadly. It is not only the conditions existing before an employment relationship comes into being that are relevant. A benefit such as family credit in the United Kingdom, the function of which is to keep poorly paid workers in employment, is concerned with access to employment since the prospect of receiving it encourages an unemployed worker to accept low-paid work. It therefore falls within the scope of the directive (Case C-116/94 *Meyers*, above, at pp. I-2151–2).

(*b*) ***Access to vocational training.*** Art. 4 provides for the application of the principle of equal treatment with regard to access to all types and to all levels of vocational guidance, vocational training, advanced vocational training, and retraining. This provision, too, has been found by the Court to be unconditional and sufficiently precise to produce direct effect for individuals in conjunction with Art. 2(1) as against a Member State (Case 222/84 *Johnston*, above, at p. 1691).

(*c*) ***Working conditions and dismissal.*** Pursuant to Art. 5(1), application of the principle of equal treatment with regard to working conditions, including the conditions governing dismissal, means that 'men and women shall be guaranteed the same conditions without discrimination on grounds of sex'. The ECJ has held that Art. 5 does not confer on the Member States the right to limit the application of the principle in its field of operation or to subject it to conditions. Art. 5(1) is therefore sufficiently precise and unconditional to be capable of being relied on by an individual before a national court against a State authority (but not against a private individual) in order to avoid the application of any national provision that does not conform to it, or in order to claim damages (Case 152/84 *Marshall I*, above, at pp. 749–50; see also Case C-345/89 *Stoeckel*, above, at p. I-4066). The

Court has defined the concept of State authority against which the directive may be invoked as 'any body, whatever its legal form, which has been made responsible, pursuant to a measure adopted by the State, for providing a public service under the control of the State and has for that purpose special powers beyond those which result from the normal rules applicable in relations between individuals' (Case C-188/89 *Foster* [1990] ECR I-3313 at p. I-3349).

In interpreting Art. 5(1), the ECJ has consistently held that the term 'dismissal' must be widely construed so as to include termination of the employment relationship between a worker and his employer whether it results from a voluntary redundancy scheme, from a mass redundancy caused by the closure of an undertaking's plant, from the compulsory dismissal of workers pursuant to an employer's general retirement policy, or from any other reason.

As already mentioned, in the earlier cases the Court's policy was to treat an age-limit for the termination of an employment relationship as falling within the term 'dismissal' and to examine it under Art. 5(1), even if the dismissal involved financial consequences, such as the grant of a retirement pension. In Case 19/81 *Burton*, above, at pp. 575–7, the Court had to consider the question whether the policy of the British Railways Board to pay a voluntary redundancy benefit only to workers who took voluntary early retirement within the five years preceding the minimum pensionable age fixed by the United Kingdom national social security legislation amounted to sex discrimination because that age was different for men and women (65 for men and 60 for women). Thus, men became eligible for the benefit at the age of 60 whereas women became eligible at the age of 55. The Court pointed out that because of the exception contained in Art. 7(1)(a) of Dir. 79/7 on equal treatment in social security matters, which permitted the Member States to exclude from the scope of the directive the determination of pensionable age for the purposes of granting old-age and retirement pensions (see section IV.5(*a*) below), the fixing of a different minimum pensionable age for social security purposes for men and women did not amount to discrimination prohibited by Community law. Since in this case the benefit in question was tied to the retirement scheme governed by the national social security legislation and was calculated in the same manner regardless of the sex of the worker, the different age conditions did not constitute sex discrimination within the meaning of Art. 5 of Dir. 76/207.

In Case 151/84 *Roberts*, above, at pp. 720–1, the Court pointed out that the exception contained in Art. 7(1)(a) of Dir. 79/7 concerned only the consequences that pensionable age had for social security benefits, while the present case was concerned with dismissal within the meaning of Art. 5 of Dir. 76/207. Therefore, a contractual provision that laid down a single age for the dismissal of men and women under a compulsory mass redundancy caused by the closure of a plant and involving the grant of an early retirement pension did not amount to sex discrimination under Art. 5 even though the normal retirement age was different for men and women.

In Case 152/84 *Marshall I*, above, at pp. 743–6, the most important of the group of cases dealing with discriminatory age conditions under Dir. 76/207, the Court was confronted with the question whether a general policy followed by a State authority (a regional Health Authority in the United Kingdom) involving the compulsory dismissal of a woman solely because she had attained the qualifying age for a State pension, which age, as seen above, was different for men and women, constituted discrimination on grounds of sex, contrary to the directive. The Court observed, in the first place, that the question did not concern access to a statutory or occupational retirement scheme, that is, the conditions for payment of an old-age or retirement pension, but the fixing of an age-limit with regard to the compulsory termination of employment. The question therefore related to the conditions governing 'dismissal' and fell to be considered under Art. 5(1) of Dir. 76/207. The Court then distinguished the case from *Burton*, which concerned access to a benefit that was tied to a national retirement scheme whose differential age conditions for men and women were exempted from the principle of equal treatment by Art. 7(1)(a) of Dir. 79/7. However, Art. 7(1)(a) concerned only the consequences that pensionable age had for social security benefits (for the grant of old-age and retirement pensions), whereas the present case was concerned with dismissal within the meaning of Art. 5 of Dir. 76/207. It therefore fell outside the ambit of the exception. Consequently, the Court's ruling was that a general policy involving the dismissal of a woman solely because she had attained the qualifying age for a State pension, which age was different for men and for women, did amount to sex discrimination contrary to Art. 5(1) of Dir. 76/207. Thus, in effect the Court confirmed that women are entitled to continue working beyond the qualifying age for an old-age pension, at least until the age at which men are supposed to retire. The Court gave a similar judgment in Case 262/84 *Beets-Proper*, above, at pp. 791–2.

In other cases the Court has confirmed that, just as a refusal to employ a pregnant woman is contrary to Art. 3(1) (see point (*a*) above), the dismissal of a female worker on account of pregnancy is contrary to Art. 5(1). On the other hand, Art. 5(1), in conjunction with Art. 2(1), does not preclude dismissals that are the result of absences from work due to an illness which is not attributable to pregnancy or confinement or to an illness that, although attributable to those conditions, manifests itself after the maternity leave. By contrast, if an illness attributable to pregnancy or confinement occurs during the maternity leave granted under national law (the length of which may vary from Member State to Member State) then, like pregnancy, it falls within the scope of Art. 2(3) and women are protected during the maternity leave against dismissal due to absence (Case C-179/88 *HKF*, above, at pp. I-3998–4000—'Hertz' case; Case C-421/92 *Habermann-Beltermann*, above, at pp. I-1675–7; see also point 2(*b*) above).

It should be mentioned that in Case C-400/95 *Larsson* [1997] ECR I-2757 at pp. I-2782–3, the Court held that the principle of equal treatment did not preclude account being taken of a woman's absence from work between the beginning of her pregnancy and the beginning of her maternity leave when calculating the period providing grounds for her dismissal under national law. The Court also held that, without prejudice to the provisions of national law adopted under Art. 2(3) of the directive, Arts. 5(1) and 2(1) did not preclude dismissals that were the result of absences due to an illness attributable to pregnancy or confinement, even where that illness arose during pregnancy and continued during and after maternity leave.

However, in Case C-394/96 *Brown*, above, at pp. I-4234–5, the Court expressly departed from the *Larsson* ruling and held that where a woman is absent owing to illness resulting from pregnancy or childbirth, and that illness arose during pregnancy and persisted during and after maternity leave, her absence not only during maternity leave but also during the period extending from the start of her pregnancy to the start of her maternity leave cannot be taken into account for computation of the period justifying her dismissal under national law. By contrast, her absence after maternity leave may be taken into account under the same conditions as a man's absence, of the same duration, through incapacity for work. The Court also ruled that Arts. 2(1) and 5(1) of the directive preclude dismissal of a female worker at any time during her pregnancy for absences due to incapacity for work caused by illness resulting from that pregnancy. This is so even if there is a contractual term allowing an employer to dismiss workers of either sex after a stipulated number of weeks of continuous absence. Such a contractual term, applying both to men and to women, would be applied here in the same way to different situations, since the situation of a pregnant worker who is unfit for work as a result of illness associated with her pregnancy is not the same as that of a male worker who is ill and absent through incapacity for work for the same length of time. Consequently, application of that contractual term in these circumstances constitutes direct discrimination on grounds of sex.

Community law now affords special protection to women during pregnancy and after childbirth by prohibiting dismissal during the period from the beginning of the pregnancy to the end of the maternity leave. This prohibition is not subject to any exception or derogation, save in exceptional cases not connected with pregnancy (Art. 10 of Dir. 92/85 of 19 October 1992 on the protection of pregnant workers, see section I.4 above. The directive had to be implemented by the Member States not later than 19 October 1994, see Art. 14). Women who are pregnant, have recently given birth, or are breastfeeding are entitled to a continuous period of maternity leave of at least fourteen weeks before and/or after confinement in accordance with national legislation, which must include compulsory maternity leave of at least two weeks (Art. 8. For an interpretation of this provision, together with Art. 5(1) of Dir. 76/207, see Case C-411/96 *Boyle*, above).

The Court has held that the prohibition of dismissal laid down in Art. 10 of Dir. 92/85 applies to both fixed-term employment contracts and to those concluded for an indefinite period. However, non-renewal of a fixed-term contract, when it comes to the end of its stipulated term, cannot be regarded as a dismissal prohibited by that provision. Nevertheless, where non-renewal of a fixed-term contract is motivated by the worker's state of pregnancy, it constitutes direct discrimination on grounds of sex, contrary to Arts. 2(1) and 3(1) of Dir. 76/207 (Case C-438/99 *Jiménez Melgar* [2001] ECR I-6915 at pp. I-6954–5). Likewise, Art. 5(1) of Dir. 76/207 prohibits dismissal on the ground of pregnancy of a worker recruited for a fixed period, even if the worker failed to inform the employer that she was pregnant although she was aware of this when the contract of employment was concluded and even if, because of her pregnancy, she was unable to work during a substantial part of the term of the contract (Case C-109/00 *Tele Danmark* [2001] ECR I-6993 at p. I-7026).

Referring to Dir. 92/85, in Case C-32/93 *Webb*, above, at pp. I-3585–8, the Court emphasized that dismissal of a pregnant woman recruited for an indefinite period cannot be justified by the fact that she is prevented by her pregnancy, on a purely temporary basis, from performing the work for which she was engaged. Even the fact that a woman was initially recruited to replace another woman during the latter's maternity leave but who was unable to do so because she was herself found to be pregnant shortly after her appointment, cannot justify her dismissal under Art. 5(1). The protection afforded by Community law cannot be dependent on whether the employee's presence at work during maternity is essential to the proper functioning of the undertaking in which she is employed.

In addition to prohibiting the dismissal of a woman on account of pregnancy, Art. 5(1) also precludes dismissal of a transsexual for a reason related to a gender reassignment (Case C-13/94 *P*, above, at p. I-2166; see also point 1(*b*) above).

Like the concept of 'access to employment' in Art. 3(1) and the concept of 'dismissal' in Art. 5(1), the concept of 'working conditions' in the same provision must be interpreted widely. Thus, in Case 163/82 *Commission* v. *Italy* [1983] ECR 3273 at p. 3288, the Court, following the view of the Commission and the opinion of A.-G. Rozès (ibid. at pp. 3297–8), accepted that the leave from work granted by Italian legislation to adoptive parents to settle the child in the family after adoption constituted 'working conditions' and had to be considered under Art. 5(1) rather than, as the Italian Government argued, being covered by the exception in Art. 2(3). The Court ruled that the fact that the adoptive father did not have the right, given to the adoptive mother, of maternity leave for the first three months following the actual entry of the child into the adoptive family (although after the three-month period the adoptive father had the same rights as the adoptive mother) was justified by the legitimate concern to assimilate as far as possible the conditions of entry of the adopted child into the family to those of the arrival of a newborn child during the delicate initial period. Therefore, the difference in treatment did not constitute discrimination within the meaning of the directive. In Case C-116/94 *Meyers*, above, at p. I-2152, the Court found that a benefit such as family credit, the purpose of which was to keep poorly paid workers in employment, was necessarily linked to an employment relationship and constituted a 'working condition' within the meaning of Art. 5(1). The Court said that to confine the concept of 'working conditions' solely to those conditions that are set out in the contract of employment or applied by the employer in respect of a worker's employment would remove situations directly covered by an employment relationship from the scope of the directive.

The right of employees to have their performances assessed each year and, consequently, to qualify for promotion, forms an integral part of their working conditions. It is therefore contrary to Arts. 2(3) and 5(1) to deprive a woman of that right and of the possibility of a promotion because she was absent from the undertaking on account of maternity leave (Case C-136/95 *Thibault*, above, at pp. I-2035–6). It is also contrary to Dirs. 76/207 and 92/85 for an employer to send home a woman who is pregnant, although not unfit for work, without paying her salary in full when he considers that he cannot provide work for her (Case C-66/96 *Høj Pedersen* [1998] ECR I-7327 at p. I-7376). Since annual leave is also part of the working conditions, a worker must be able to take her annual leave during a period other than the period of her maternity leave (Case C-342/01 *Merino Gómez*, above, paras. 36–41). Conditions of employment include the conditions applicable to employees returning to work following parental leave. Since the employer may not take the employee's pregnancy into consideration for the purpose of applying her working conditions, a female employee is not obliged to inform her employer that she is pregnant. An employer may not refuse, on account of pregnancy, to allow an employee to return to work before the end of her parental leave (just as an employer may not refuse to employ a woman, or dismiss her, or refuse to renew a fixed-term contract, on account of pregnancy) (Case C-320/01 *Busch*, above, paras. 38–47). A scheme of part-time work for older employees also involves working conditions (Case C-187/00 *Kutz-Bauer*, above, paras. 43–45. For a distinction between pay and conditions of employment, and further instances of the latter, see point 1(*d*) above).

The general prohibition of night-work by women, too, concerns working conditions. Not being justified by the exception in Art. 2(3), it falls within the scope of Art. 5(1). That provision is sufficiently precise to impose on the Member States the obligation not to lay down by legislation the principle that night-work by women is prohibited, even if that is subject to exceptions, where night-work by men is not prohibited (Case C-345/89 *Stoeckel*, above, at p. I-4067; see also point 2(*b*) above). Where night-work is prohibited for both men and women, Art. 5(1) does not allow a Member State to maintain derogations from the prohibition that differ according to sex and that are subject to more restrictive conditions in respect of women than in respect of men, if such a difference is not justified by the need to ensure the protection of women with regard to pregnancy and maternity. Nevertheless, in accordance with Art. 307(1) EC, Art. 5 of the directive cannot apply if the national provisions were adopted in order to comply with obligations arising under an international agreement concluded with non-member countries before the entry into force of the EEC Treaty, such as Convention No. 89 of the International Labour Organization of 9 July 1948 concerning night-work of women employed in industry (Case C-13/93 *Minne*, above, at pp. I-382–5;

see also Case C-158/91 *Levy* [1993] ECR I-4287 at pp. I-4306–7). Where a Member State denounced the Convention following the judgment in *Stoeckel*, prohibition of night-work by women became incompatible with Art. 5(1) where no such prohibition exists in relation to men (Case C-197/96 *Commission* v. *France* [1997] ECR I-1489 at pp. I-1500–1; Case C-207/96 *Commission* v. *Italy* [1997] ECR I-6869 at pp. I-6883–4).

(*d*) ***Common rules.*** Arts. 3, 4, and 5 impose three types of obligations on Member States concerning the abolition of all forms of sex discrimination in their respective fields of application. Thus, Member States are required to take the following measures:

(*i*) any laws, regulations, and administrative provisions contrary to the principle of equal treatment are to be abolished (Arts. 3(2)(a), 4(a), and 5(2)(a));

(*ii*) any provisions contrary to the principle of equal treatment that are included in collective agreements, individual contracts of employment, internal rules of undertakings, or in rules governing the independent occupations and professions are to be declared null and void or amended (Arts. 3(2)(b), 4(b), and 5(2)(b)). In Case 165/82 *Commission* v. *United Kingdom*, above, at pp. 3445–7, the Court found that the relevant United Kingdom legislation, the Sex Discrimination Act 1975, did not correctly implement this part of the directive, except in respect of individual contracts of employment. The Court could not accept the United Kingdom's argument to the effect that the fact that collective agreements were not legally binding in the United Kingdom removed them from the scope of the directive. The Court pointed out that the directive covers all collective agreements without distinction as to their binding force, the reason being that, even if they are not legally binding as between the parties, they have nevertheless important *de facto* consequences for the employment relationships to which they apply, particularly in so far as they determine the rights of the workers. Any clauses in such agreements that are incompatible with the obligations imposed by the directive must be rendered inoperative, eliminated, or amended. Similarly, in Case 312/86 *Commission* v. *France*, above, at pp. 6337–8, the Court could not accept the French Government's argument that collective negotiation was the only appropriate method of complying with this part of the directive. The Court found that the French legislation that left the removal of certain discriminatory conditions from collective agreements to the discretion of the two sides of industry working through collective negotiations, without laying down any time-limit, was not a proper implementation of the directive.

Relying on its established case-law, the Court has held that in the case of a breach of Dir. 76/207 by legislative provisions or by provisions of collective agreements introducing discrimination contrary to the directive, the national courts are required to set aside that discrimination, using all the means at their disposal, and in particular by treating the members of the disadvantaged class of persons in the same way as the members of the favoured class, and are not required to request or await the setting aside of the discriminatory provisions by the legislature, by collective negotiation or otherwise (Case C-187/00 *Kutz-Bauer*, above, paras. 72–5; Case C-77/02 *Steinicke*, above, para. 72);

(*iii*) laws, regulations, and administrative provisions that are contrary to the principle of equal treatment are to be revised when the 'concern for protection' which originally inspired them is no longer well founded; where similar provisions are included in collective agreements, labour and management are to carry out the necessary revision (Arts. 3(2)(c) and 5(2)(c)). The scope of the term 'concern for protection' is the same as that of the term 'protection of women' in Art. 2(3). Art. 2(3) therefore determines the scope of subparagraph (c) (Case 222/84 *Johnston*, above, at p. 1688; see also point 2(*b*) above). Art. 4 does not contain a similar provision. Instead, Art. 4(c) requires the Member States to ensure, without prejudice to the freedom granted to certain private training establishments, that vocational guidance, vocational training, advanced vocational training, and retraining are accessible on the basis of the same criteria and at the same levels without any discrimination on grounds of sex.

4. Remedies. Art. 6 of Dir. 76/207 requires Member States to introduce into their national legal systems the necessary measures to enable all persons who consider themselves wronged by discrimination to pursue their claims by judicial process. The meaning and scope of this provision have been interpreted by the ECJ in a series of important judgments. In Case 14/83 *Von Colson and Kamann*, above, at pp. 1907–9, as interpreted and confirmed in Case 222/84 *Johnston*, above, at pp. 1682–3 and 1692, and in Case C-271/91 *Marshall II* [1993] ECR I-4367 at pp. I-4407–11, the Court made it clear that Art. 6 does not prescribe any specific form of sanction for unlawful discrimination, but leaves Member States free to choose between the different solutions suitable for achieving the objective of the directive, depending on the different situations which may arise. However, since it is impossible to establish real equality of treatment without an appropriate system of sanctions, Art. 6 does imply that whatever measures Member States decide to adopt, those measures must satisfy two requirements. First, they must be sufficiently effective to achieve the objective of the directive, that is to say, to restore real equality of opportunity when it has not been observed, while having a real deterrent effect on the employer. Secondly, they must be such as to guarantee real and effective judicial protection before the national courts.

These requirements necessarily entail that the particular circumstances of each case of discrimination should be taken into account. Thus, in the event of a discriminatory refusal to employ a person contrary to Art. 3(1) of the directive, the measures adopted may require the employer to offer a post to the applicant discriminated against or to give him/her adequate financial compensation, backed up, where necessary, by a system of fines. However, Art. 6 does not require the imposition of an obligation upon the employer to conclude a contract of employment with the person concerned. In the event of a discriminatory dismissal contrary to Art. 5(1), the choice again may be between reinstating the victim of discrimination or granting him/her financial compensation for the loss and damage suffered.

Where a Member State chooses to penalize the breach of the prohibition of discrimination by the award of financial compensation, then in order to ensure that it is effective and has a deterrent effect, that compensation must be adequate. It must enable the loss and damage actually sustained as a result of discrimination to be made good in full in accordance with the applicable national rules. This includes an award of interest on the principal amount of compensation from the date of the unlawful discrimination to the date when compensation is actually paid in order to compensate for the loss sustained by the recipient as a result of the effluxion of time. The aim and effect of the compensation should be to restore real equality of treatment. It follows from these very strict requirements that national rules which limit reparation to an upper limit fixed *a priori* or to a purely nominal amount (such as, for example, the reimbursement only of expenses incurred in submitting an application for a post), or which exclude an award of interest, are not compatible with Art. 6 (see the *Von Colson and Kamann* and *Marshall II* cases). Subsequently, the Court made it clear that interest is only payable on the amount of compensation, but not on arrears of social security benefits whose payment was delayed because of prohibited sex discrimination (Case C-66/95 *Sutton* [1997] ECR I-2163 at pp. I-2188–9).

As regards the fixing of an upper limit for the compensation that may be obtained in the event of sex discrimination in the making of an appointment, the Court has distinguished between two situations. The first is where the employer can prove that, because the applicant appointed had superior qualifications, the unsuccessful applicant would not have obtained the post, even if there had been no discrimination in the selection process. In this case, the fixing of an upper limit (e.g. of three months' salary) is not contrary to Dir. 76/207. The second situation is where the applicant discriminated against would have obtained the post if the selection process had been carried out without discrimination. In this case, an upper limit (e.g. of three months' salary) cannot be imposed by domestic law. Similarly, domestic law cannot impose a ceiling of six months' salary on the aggregate amount of compensation that may be claimed by several applicants who have been discriminated against (Case C-180/95 *Draehmpaehl* [1997] ECR I-2195 at pp. I-2223–5).

It also follows from the requirement of an effective remedy that an employer's civil liability for a breach of the prohibition of discrimination is strict liability. Any breach of the prohibition must, in itself, be sufficient to make the employer fully liable, without there being any need to prove fault on his part and without it being possible for him to invoke any ground of exemption or justification that may be provided by national law (Case C-177/88 *Dekker*, above, at pp. I-3975–6; Case C-180/95 *Draehmpaehl*, above, at p. I-2220).

It follows from the foregoing that as far as sanctions for discrimination are concerned, Art. 6 does not contain any unconditional and sufficiently precise obligation which may be relied on by individuals in legal proceedings in order to obtain specific compensation under the directive, where that is not provided for or permitted under national law. In other words, in this respect Art. 6 cannot produce either vertical or horizontal direct effect. This does not mean, however, that Art. 6 can never be considered by national courts in proceedings brought by individuals. In the first place, national courts are required to interpret and apply national law, and in particular (but not only) the provisions adopted to implement Dir. 76/207, as far as possible, in conformity with the wording and the purpose of the directive (including Art. 6) in order to achieve the results pursued by it (Case 14/83 *Von Colson and Kamann*, above, at p. 1909; Case 79/83 *Harz* [1984] ECR 1921 at pp. 1940–3; Case C-106/89 *Marleasing*, above, at p. I-4159; Case C-185/97 *Coote* [1998] ECR I-5199 at p. I-5219).

In the second place, in Case C-271/91 *Marshall II*, above, at pp. I-4409–11, the Court pointed out that the fact that Member States may choose from different solutions in order to achieve the objectives of the directive cannot prevent individuals from relying on Art. 6 in a situation where the national authorities have no degree of discretion in applying the chosen solution. Thus, individuals should be able to enforce before national courts rights whose content can be determined sufficiently precisely on the basis of the provisions of the directive alone. In the instant case, the Court ruled that a person who has been injured as a result of discriminatory dismissal may rely on the combined provisions of Arts. 5 and 6 as against an authority of the State acting in its capacity as an employer in order to set aside a national provision that imposes limits on the amount of compensation recoverable by way of reparation. This ruling seems to be applicable not only in the case of discriminatory dismissal but also in the case of any discriminatory act that is contrary to the directive, provided that the national authorities have no discretion in implementing the offending national provision.

In the third place, the requirement of effective judicial protection laid down in Art. 6 has been interpreted by the Court as reflecting a general principle of law that underlies the constitutional traditions common to the Member States and which is also incorporated in Arts. 6 and 13 of the European Convention on Human Rights. As such, it must be taken into account in Community law. In the light of that principle, Art. 6 means that all persons who consider themselves wronged by sex discrimination must have the right to obtain an effective remedy in a competent national court against measures that are contrary to the principle of equal treatment. To that extent, Art. 6 is sufficiently precise and unconditional to be capable of being relied on by individuals as against a Member State which has not fully implemented it in its internal legal order. It is contrary to this principle of effective judicial control for a Member State to require that a certificate issued by the Executive stating that the conditions for derogating from the principle of equal treatment are satisfied in a particular case should be treated as conclusive evidence so as to exclude the exercise of any power of review by the courts (Case 222/84 *Johnston*, above, at pp. 1682–3 and

1692). On the basis of these considerations, the Court has held that Art. 6 requires Member States to ensure judicial protection for workers even after the employment relationship has ended, for example, where the employer, after the termination of the employment relationship, refuses to provide references as a reaction to legal proceedings brought to enforce compliance with the directive (Case C-185/97 *Coote*, above, at pp. I-5220–2; see also Art. 7 below). The Court has accepted that a general provision in a national Constitution to the effect that any person may bring proceedings to protect his rights and lawful interests without the need for any specific legislative measure satisfies the requirements of Art. 6 (Case 163/82 *Commission* v. *Italy*, above, at p. 3289; the Court was referring to Art. 24 of the Italian Constitution).

It should be noted that, as a final remedy, an individual wronged by sex discrimination may always rely on the principle of State liability, according to which a Member State is liable for loss and damage caused to individuals as a result of a breach of Community law for which the State can be held responsible, such as a failure by the State to implement Dir. 76/207 correctly in national law. According to the Court's established case-law, a Member State's obligation to make reparation for the loss and damage so caused is subject to three conditions: the rule of law infringed must be intended to confer rights on individuals; the breach must be sufficiently serious; and there must be a direct causal link between the breach of the State's obligation and the damage suffered by the injured party. While the right to reparation is based directly on Community law, the enforcement of that right takes place under the national law on liability, which must apply conditions that are not less favourable than those relating to similar domestic claims and are not so framed as to make it virtually impossible or excessively difficult to obtain reparation (see Cases C-6/90 etc. *Francovich* [1991] ECR I-5357 at pp. I-5414–6; Cases C-46/93 etc. *Brasserie du Pêcheur and Factortame* [1996] ECR I-1029 at p. I-1149; Case C-66/95 *Sutton*, above, at pp. I-2190–2, and the cases cited therein).

Apart from Art. 6, the directive contains two general provisions aimed at affording additional protection to workers. Art. 7 requires Member States to take the necessary measures to protect employees against dismissal ordered in retaliation for a complaint made within the undertaking or for legal proceedings brought to enforce compliance with the directive. The ECJ has held that the protection under Art. 7 cannot be limited solely to cases of dismissal, but must be available against any other measure that may effectively deter a worker from making use of the right to judicial protection, such as a refusal to provide references after the employment relationship has ended (Case C-185/97 *Coote*, above, at p. I-5222). According to Art. 8, measures adopted under the directive and those already in force must be brought to the attention of workers by all appropriate means, for example at the workplace.

5. Procedure. As regards the procedure for enforcing the principle of equal treatment before national courts, in the absence of Community rules governing the matter, it is for the domestic legal system of each Member State to designate the courts and tribunals having jurisdiction and to lay down the detailed procedural rules. Those rules must satisfy the two conditions outlined above: they must not be less favourable than those governing similar domestic actions (the principle of equivalence) and must not render virtually impossible or excessively difficult the exercise of rights conferred by Community law (the principle of effectiveness). Thus, it is compatible with Community law for national rules to prescribe, in the interests of legal certainty, reasonable limitation periods for bringing proceedings (see Case C-326/96 *Levez* [1998] ECR I-7835 at pp. I-7864–5 and the cases cited therein. See also point 7 below).

6. Implementation. According to Art. 9(1), Member States were required to implement the directive within thirty months of its notification, that is, by 14 August 1978 at the latest. By this date, Member States were obliged to abolish all discrimination in accordance with the provisions of Arts. 3, 4, and 5 (see point 3(*d*) above). However, the revision of discriminatory laws, regulations, and administrative provisions, which were inspired by outdated concepts of protection of women (see Arts. 3(2)(c) and 5(2)(c)) had to be completed within four years of notification, i.e. by 14 February 1980. Where the objective of the directive had already been achieved at the time when the directive entered into force, e.g. on account of a categorical affirmation by the Constitution of the equality of men and women before the law and the express exclusion of all discrimination on grounds of sex and the guarantee of equal access to employment in the public service for all nationals, in conjunction with the existing system of judicial remedies, no further legislative provisions were required for its implementation (Case 248/83 *Commission* v. *Germany*, above, at p. 1481, dealing with employment in the German public service and referring to the provisions of the German Basic Law). In addition to the periodical assessment of the occupational activities referred to in Art. 2(2) (see point 2(*a*) above), Member States are required to communicate to the Commission the text of laws, regulations, and administrative provisions that they adopt in the field covered by the directive (Art. 9(2) and(3)).

7. The burden of proof. In accordance with the normal rules of evidence, in principle the burden of proving the existence of sex discrimination lies on the worker who, being the victim of such discrimination, brings legal proceedings against his employer. However, the ECJ has developed certain principles, mainly in cases concerning equal pay, according to which the burden of proof may shift to the employer when this is necessary to avoid depriving workers of any effective means of enforcing the principle of equal pay (*see further under* **Equal pay**, section VI). In equal treatment cases, such a shift occurs in situations where a person can make out a *prima facie* case of indirect discrimination. As the Court has said in a number of cases:

once it is established that a measure adversely affects a much higher percentage of women than men, or vice versa, that measure will be presumed to constitute indirect discrimination on grounds of sex and it will be for the employer or the person who drafted that measure to demonstrate the contrary (Case C-226/98 *Jørgensen*, above, at p. I-2479; see also the cases cited at point 1(*c*) above).

Since indirect discrimination on grounds of sex can only be justified by objective factors unrelated to sex, the burden of proving that the difference in treatment is justified by such factors lies on the employer or the author of the measure in question.

The principles developed by the Court have been incorporated in Dir. 97/80 on the burden of proof, which was adopted on the basis of the Agreement on Social Policy and therefore initially did not apply to the United Kingdom. When the Agreement on Social Policy was incorporated in the EC Treaty by the ToA, Dir. 97/80 was extended to the United Kingdom by Dir. 98/52 (see section I.4 above). Dir. 97/80 had to be implemented by the Member States by 1 January 2001, and by the United Kingdom by 22 July 2001 (Art. 7 of Dir. 97/80 and Art. 2 of Dir. 98/52).

Dir. 97/80 applies to the situations covered by Art. 141 EC and by Dir. 75/117 on equal pay, by Dir. 76/207 on equal treatment and, in so far as discrimination based on sex is concerned, by Dir. 92/85 on the protection of pregnant workers, and by Dir. 96/34 on paternal leave (these are listed in section I.4 above). It also applies to any civil or administrative procedure concerning the public or private sector that provides for means of redress under national law pursuant to these directives with the exception of out-of-court procedures, but it does not apply to criminal procedures, unless otherwise provided by the Member States (Art. 3 of Dir. 97/80).

The directive applies to both direct and indirect discrimination based on sex (Art. 2(1)). According to Art. 2(2):

> indirect discrimination shall exist where an apparently neutral provision, criterion or practice disadvantages a substantially higher proportion of the members of one sex unless that provision, criterion or practice is appropriate and necessary and can be justified by objective factors unrelated to sex.

According to Art. 4, Member States are required to ensure that, when persons who consider themselves wronged because the principle of equal treatment has not been applied to them establish, before a court or other competent authority, facts from which it may be presumed that there has been direct or indirect discrimination, it is for the respondent to prove that there has been no breach of the principle of equal treatment. This provision need not be applied to proceedings in which it is for the court or competent body to investigate the facts of the case. Member States are allowed to introduce rules of evidence that are more favourable to plaintiffs. Implementation of the directive may not lead to a reduction in the general level of protection of workers in the areas to which it applies (Art. 6).

III. Directive 2002/73 amending Directive 76/207

Dir. 76/207 has been amended by Dir. 2002/73, which entered into force on 5 October 2002, but the Member States are not required to implement it until 5 October 2005 at the latest (Art. 2; see also section I.4 above). Since until that date Member States are free to apply the provisions of Dir. 76/207, it seems appropriate to discuss Dir. 2002/73 separately.

The amendment of Dir. 76/207 has been due to several reasons, such as the need to bring it into line with the rapidly evolving case-law; to include clear definitions of the concepts of direct and indirect discrimination; to bring sexual harassment within its scope; and to create independent bodies to promote equal treatment in the field of employment. Dir. 2002/73 accordingly incorporates the most important principles laid down by the Court of Justice, while retaining many features of Dir. 76/207. Since those principles and features have been covered in section II above, it is sufficient to highlight here only those provisions of Dir. 2002/73 that represent a significant change in the existing law.

When formulating laws and policies in the areas covered by the directive, Member States are required actively to take into account the objective of equality between men and women (Art. 1a). A new Art. 2(2) lays down the following definitions:

- direct discrimination: 'where one person is treated less favourably on grounds of sex than another is, has been or would be treated in a comparable situation';
- indirect discrimination: 'where an apparently neutral provision, criterion or practice would put persons of one sex at a particular disadvantage compared with persons of the other sex, unless that provision, criterion or practice is objectively justified by a legitimate aim, and the means of achieving that aim are appropriate and necessary';
- harassment: 'where an unwanted conduct related to the sex of a person occurs with the purpose or effect of violating the dignity of a person, and of creating an intimidating, hostile, degrading, humiliating or offensive environment';
- sexual harassment: 'where any form of unwanted verbal, non-verbal or physical conduct of a sexual nature occurs, with the purpose or effect of violating the dignity of a person, in particular when creating an intimidating, hostile, degrading, humiliating or offensive environment'.

Harassment and sexual harassment are deemed to be discrimination on the ground of sex and therefore prohibited (Art. 2(3)). Likewise, an instruction to discriminate against persons on grounds of sex is deemed to be discrimination within the meaning of the directive (Art. 2(4)). Member States are to encourage collective agreements or practice and employers to take measures to prevent all forms of discrimination on grounds of sex, in particular harassment and sexual harassment at the workplace (Art. 2(5)).

As regards remedies, Member States are to ensure that associations and organizations with a legitimate interest may engage, either on behalf or in support of the complainants, with his or her approval, in any judicial and/or administrative procedure provided for the enforcement of obligations under the directive (Art. 6(3)).

Member States are required to designate a body or bodies for the promotion, analysis, monitoring, and support of equal treatment of all persons without discrimination on the grounds of sex. These bodies may form part of national agencies charged with the defence of human rights or individuals' rights. The competences of these bodies must include the following activities: providing independent assistance to victims of discrimination in pursuing their complaints; conducting independent surveys, publishing independent reports, and making recommendations concerning discrimination (Art. 8a). Member States are to promote social dialogue between the social partners (i.e. management and labour) with a view to fostering equal treatment and to encourage the social partners to promote equality between men and women and to conclude agreements laying down anti-discrimination rules (Art. 8b). Member States are likewise to encourage dialogue with appropriate non-governmental organizations that have a legitimate interest in promoting equal treatment (Art. 8c). Member States are required to lay down effective sanctions against infringements of national rules implementing the directive (Art. 8d). They may introduce or maintain provisions that are more favourable than those laid down in the directive (Art. 8e).

IV. Directive 79/7 on equal treatment in social security

The need for Dir. 79/7 arose from Art. 1(2) of Dir. 76/207, which excluded matters of social security from the scope of the directive, leaving it to the Council to adopt the necessary provisions in that area at a later date (see section II.1 above). Accordingly, the purpose of Dir. 79/7 is the 'progressive implementation' of the principle of equal treatment for men and women in the field of social security and other elements of social protection (first recital in the preamble and Art. 1). Aiming at 'progressive implementation', the directive covers only statutory social security schemes, leaving it again to the Council to adopt further provisions with regard to private occupational schemes (second recital and Art. 3(3)). Such provisions were laid down in Dir. 86/378 (see section V below). Like Dir. 76/207, Dir. 79/7 is based on Art. 308 EC. Its structure is broadly similar to that of Dir. 76/207.

1. Personal scope. According to Art. 2, the directive applies to the 'working population' and to retired or invalided workers and self-employed persons. The term 'working population' is defined very broadly so as to include not only workers but also self-employed persons, workers and self-employed persons whose activity is interrupted by illness, accident, or involuntary unemployment, as well as persons seeking employment. According to the ECJ, this definition is based on the idea that a person whose work has been interrupted by one of the risks referred to in Art. 3(1)(a) (which defines the material scope of the directive, see point 2 below) belongs to the working population, even if he/she is not directly affected by that risk. Thus, a woman who has given up work solely because of the invalidity of her mother (which is one of the risks listed in Art. 3), in order to provide care for her, is to be regarded as a member of the working population and thus covered by the directive (Case 150/85 *Drake* [1986] ECR 1995 at p. 2009). Moreover, the concept of a 'worker' or 'working population' has the same broad Community meaning for the purposes of Art. 2 of Dir. 79/7 as it has for the purposes of Arts. 39, 42, or 141 EC. It thus encompasses workers in 'minor' employment whose income is lower than the minimum required for subsistence or who normally work only 18, 15, 12, or even 10 hours a week (Case C-317/93 *Nolte* [1995] ECR I-4625 at pp. I-4656–7; Case C-444/93 *Megner and Scheffel* [1995] ECR I-4741 at pp. I-4751–3; see also Case C-280/94 *Posthuma-van Damme and Oztürk* [1996] ECR I-179 at p. I-202).

On the other hand, it follows from Arts. 2 and 3, read in conjunction, that the directive does not apply to persons who have never been available for employment and are not seeking work or who have ceased to be available for a reason other than the materialization of one of the risks referred to by the directive. According to the Court, this interpretation is in conformity with the objectives of Community law and with the other provisions in the same field as Dir. 79/7, such as Art. 141 EC, Dir. 75/117 implementing Art. 141, and Dir. 76/207, which all implement equal treatment between men and women not generally but only in their capacity as workers (Cases 48/88 etc. *Achterberg-te Riele*, above, at p. 1988).

It follows from the foregoing that the directive does not apply to a person who has given up his or her occupational activity in order to attend to the upbringing of his or her children, since the interruption of employment due to the bringing up of children is not one of the risks listed in Art. 3(1)(a). Nevertheless, such a person may still be covered by the directive if he or she starts seeking employment but the search is interrupted by the materialization of one of those risks, such as illness. In order to be a member of the working population it is sufficient to be a person seeking employment, the reason why any previous employment has been terminated, or whether or not there has been any previous employment, being immaterial. However, the person concerned must prove that he or she was seeking employment when one of the relevant risks materialized, for example by showing registration with an employment agency, or the existence of job applications, or attendances at interviews, etc. Thus, the protection afforded by Dir. 79/7 to persons who have given up their occupation in order to attend to the upbringing of their children is available only to those who suffer incapacity for work while seeking employment. This situation clearly works to the disadvantage of women when they fall ill or suffer invalidity before starting to look for employment, since it is mainly women who give up work in order to devote themselves to the upbringing of their children. However, as the Court has pointed out, this simply follows from the fact that the directive aims only at the progressive implementation of the principle of equal treatment, leaving it to the Member States to regulate the acquisition of benefit entitlements following periods of interruption of employment due to the bringing up of children (Art. 7(1)(b); see point 5(*b*) below). Any resulting discrimination that may still exist in certain Member States can only be removed by further Community legislation (Case C-31/90 *Johnson I* [1991] ECR I-3723 at pp. I-3751–3).

On the basis of the above case-law, in Case C-77/95 *Züchner* [1996] ECR I-5689 at pp. I-5726–7, the Court came to the conclusion that to belong to the 'working population' within the meaning of Art. 2 presupposes being involved in an economic activity, that is to say, an activity undertaken in return for remuneration in the broad sense. Any other interpretation would have the effect of infinitely extending the scope of the directive, whereas the purpose of Art. 2 is precisely to delimit that scope. Therefore, the Court held that Art. 2 does not cover a person who undertakes, without payment, the care of a member of his or her family (e.g. of a handicapped spouse), even if such an activity requires training and competence and would otherwise have to be carried out by an outsider in return for remuneration, unless the person in question has, in order to do so, abandoned an occupational activity or interrupted efforts to find employment.

Since Art. 2 defines precisely the personal scope of the directive, that scope cannot be extended to persons not coming within it, on the ground that they are covered by a national statutory scheme which itself falls within the directive's material scope (Art. 3). Thus, the personal scope of the directive cannot vary according to its material scope (Cases C-87/90 etc. *Verholen* [1991] ECR I-3757 at pp. I-3789–90). Nevertheless, the right to rely on the provisions of the directive before a national court is not confined to individuals coming within its personal scope since the possibility cannot be ruled out that other persons may have a direct interest in ensuring that the principle of non-discrimination is observed as regards persons who are covered. Therefore, subject to the usual conditions of direct effect, an individual may rely on the directive in national legal proceedings if he suffers the effects of a discriminatory national provision through another person, who is not a party to the proceedings, provided that that other person himself falls within the scope of the directive (ibid. at pp. I-3790–1). A national court may, of course, examine of its own motion whether national rules are in conformity with the precise and unconditional provisions of the directive, once the period for its implementation has expired, even if the directive has not been invoked by individuals (ibid. at pp. I-3788–9. See also Case C-343/92 *De Weerd* [1994] ECR I-571 at pp. I-601–2).

2. Material scope. According to Art. 3(1), the directive applies to: (*a*) statutory schemes that provide protection against the following risks: sickness, invalidity, old age, accidents at work and occupational diseases, unemployment; and (*b*) social assistance, in so far as it is intended to supplement or replace those schemes.

The case-law of the Court lays down two main criteria that a benefit must meet in order to fall within the scope of the directive. First, it must constitute the whole or part of a statutory scheme providing protection against one of the specified risks or a form of social assistance having the same objective (Case 150/85 *Drake*, above, at p. 2009; see also the cases cited below). Secondly, although the way in which a benefit is paid is not decisive, the benefit must be directly and effectively linked to the protection provided against one of the risks listed in Art. 3(1) (Case C-243/90 *Smithson* [1992] ECR I-467 at p. I-489; see also the cases cited below). Thus, in Case 150/85 *Drake*, above, at p. 2010, the Court found that the fact that a benefit which formed part of a statutory invalidity scheme (an invalid care allowance) was paid, not directly to the disabled person but to a third party providing care for him, did not place the benefit outside the scope of the directive. The reasons were, first, that the payment of the benefit to a person who provided care still depended on the existence of invalidity inasmuch as the latter was an essential condition for such payment; and, secondly, that there was a clear economic link between the benefit and the disabled person, who derived an advantage from the fact that an allowance was paid to the person caring for him.

Similarly, in Case C-137/94 *Richardson* [1995] ECR I-3407 at pp. I-3427–9, the Court held that a system which exempted various categories of persons, in particular certain old people, from prescription charges fulfilled the above conditions and thus fell within the scope of the directive. First, the Court pointed out, it formed part of a statutory scheme. Secondly, it afforded direct and effective protection against the risk of sickness since the grant of the benefit was always conditional on materialization of the risk in question. Thirdly, a system of benefits could not be excluded from the scope of the directive simply because it did not strictly form part of national social security rules. The fact that in the United Kingdom the exemption from prescription charges was provided for in the National Health Service Act 1977 was therefore not decisive. For substantially similar reasons, in Case C-382/98 *Taylor* [1999] ECR I-8955 at pp. I-8979–82, the Court found that a winter fuel payment granted to elderly persons and protecting them against the risk of old age was covered by Art. 3(1).

By contrast, in Case C-243/90 *Smithson*, above, at p. I-490, the Court concluded that Art. 3(1) did not apply to a United Kingdom statutory scheme for housing benefit paid to persons whose real income was lower than a notional income in order to enable them to meet housing costs. Such a scheme was not amongst those referred to in Art. 3(1)(a), and the fact that some of the risks listed in that Article, such as old age, sickness, or invalidity, were taken into account in order to determine eligibility for a (higher) benefit was not sufficient to bring the scheme within the scope of the directive. Following this line, in Cases C-63/91 etc. *Jackson and Cresswell*, above, at pp. I-4779–80, the Court stated quite generally that Art. 3(1)(a) does not apply to a statutory scheme that, on certain conditions, provides persons with means below a legally defined limit with a special benefit, such as supplementary allowance or income support, designed to enable them to meet their needs. The fact that the recipient of the benefit is, as a matter of fact, in one of the situations envisaged by Art. 3(1)(a) does not suffice to bring that benefit within the field of application of the directive. This is particularly so where the law sets the amount of the theoretical needs of the person, which is used to determine the benefit, independently of any consideration relating to any of the risks listed in Art. 3(1)(a).

Similarly, in Case C-228/94 *Atkins* [1996] ECR I-3633 at pp. I-3662–7, the Court held that a statutory scheme under which concessionary fares on public passenger transport services were granted to various classes of persons, including certain elderly persons, was not covered by the directive. Such a scheme did not afford direct and effective protection against one of the risks listed in Art. 3(1)(a). Old age and invalidity were only two of the criteria that might be applied to define the classes of beneficiaries. The fact that in the given case a recipient had to be in one of the situations envisaged by Art. 3(1)(a) was not sufficient to bring the scheme within the scope of that provision. The Court further held that since the scheme was not covered by Art. 3(1)(a), it likewise could not be covered by Art. 3(1)(b) because the directive applied to social assistance only in so far as such assistance was intended to supplement or replace the schemes mentioned in Art. 3(1)(a). The Court could not accept the Commission's argument that the scope of the directive is wider than the scope of social security and social assistance in that it extends to social protection as a whole where measures of social protection, such as concessionary fares, benefit persons who are affected by one of the risks listed in Art. 3(1)(a). In this context, the Court pointed out that the reference in Art. 1 to 'other elements of social protection provided for in Article 3' is to be understood as a reference to provisions concerning social assistance, which generally fall outside the area of social security and that are clearly distinguished by the directive from the statutory schemes mentioned in Art. 3(1)(a). Even the provisions regarding social assistance do not fall within the directive's scope where such assistance is provided to persons who are in one of the situations specified in Art. 3(1)(a), but only where it is intended to supplement or replace the schemes referred to in that provision.

The question whether certain social security schemes, and in particular pension schemes, are covered by Art. 3(1)(a) (as statutory schemes providing protection against one of the listed risks, i.e. old age) or by Art. 141 EC (as forming part of 'pay'), or perhaps by both, has given rise to difficult problems in practice. The main problem is the definition of the mutual relationship between Dir. 79/7 and Art. 141 EC. The reason for the difficulty is that the Court has given a very wide interpretation to the concept of 'pay' in Art. 141, indicating that it also covers certain social security schemes. Dealing with the relationship between Dir. 86/378 on occupational schemes (see section V below) and Art. 141, in Case C-110/91 *Moroni* [1993] ECR I-6591 at p. I-6617, the Court made it clear that if it can be established that Art. 141 is applicable to a particular case, then there is no need to examine whether the directive is also applicable since its provisions cannot in any way restrict the scope of Art. 141. The same reasoning seems to be also valid for the relationship between Dir. 79/7 and Art. 141 (see the opinion of A.-G. Jacobs in Case C-7/93 *Beune* [1994] ECR I-4471 at p. I-4482).

In its case-law, the Court has developed a number of criteria for determining whether a pension scheme falls within the scope of Dir. 79/7 or of Art. 141 (see ibid. at pp. I-4510–19 *per Curiam*, pp. I-4484–5 *per* A.-G. Jacobs. For a detailed discussion of these criteria and the whole problem of defining the concept of 'pay', *see further under* **Equal pay**, section II). Basically, if a social security benefit, such as a retirement pension, is directly governed by statute to the exclusion of any element of negotiation and is obligatorily applicable to general categories of workers, then it is covered by Dir. 79/7. On the other hand, if it concerns only a particular category of employees, such as civil servants, is paid by reason and in the framework of the employment relationship and is directly related to the period of service, then it forms part of 'pay' and comes within the scope of Art. 141. It seems that in this latter case Dir. 79/7 is inapplicable since it applies only to those general social security schemes that are determined less by the employment relationship between the employer and the worker than by considerations of social policy. These general social security schemes are, in turn, excluded from the scope of Art. 141. It would thus seem to follow from the Court's case-law that Art. 141 and Dir. 79/7 are mutually exclusive. This view is supported by the opinion of A.-G. Jacobs in *Beune* (ibid. at pp. I-4490–1), and also by the ruling of the Court in which it held that since the pension scheme in question in that case was governed by Art. 141, there was no need to examine it from the point of view of Dir. 79/7 (ibid. at p. I-4519. See also Case 80/70 *Defrenne I* [1971] ECR 445 at p. 451).

Art. 3(2) excludes from the scope of the directive survivors' benefits as well as family benefits except those granted by way of increases of benefits due in respect of the risks referred to in Art. 3(1)(a). The Court has found that a family benefit such as a child-raising allowance does not provide direct and effective protection against one of the risks listed in Art. 3(1)(a) and therefore does not fall within the scope of the directive (Cases C-245/94 etc. *Hoever and Zachow* [1996] ECR I-4895 at p. I-4940). The Court has also held that in the absence of harmonization, the rules concerning survivors' benefits are a matter for provisions of national and international law in force in a given Member State. Therefore, Community law does not preclude a national court from interpreting Art. 26 of the International Covenant on Civil and Political Rights of 1966 as requiring equal treatment for men and women as regards survivors' benefits (Case C-337/91 *Van Gemert-Derks* [1993] ECR I-5435 at pp. I-5469–70).

3. Prohibition of discrimination. Art. 4 defines in more detail the scope of the principle of equal treatment laid down in Art. 1. According to Art. 4(1), that principle means that 'there shall be no discrimination whatsoever on ground of sex either directly or indirectly by reference in particular to marital or family status' as regards the following three matters:

(*a*) the scope of the statutory schemes listed in Art. 3(1)(a) and the conditions of access thereto. By virtue of this provision, women are entitled to claim benefits in respect of the various risks specified in Art. 3(1)(a) under the same conditions as men. Therefore, a national provision depriving women of the right to claim benefits that men in the same situation continue to receive constitutes discrimination within the meaning of Art. 4(1). Thus, the directive precludes a national rule that withdraws from widows who are unfit for work their benefits for incapacity for work on their being granted a widow's pension (unless that withdrawal results from a voluntary renunciation by the beneficiary), where the same rule is not applicable to widowers (Case C-337/91 *Van Gemert-Derks*, above, at pp. I-5471–2). Such a rule is, however, not precluded if, despite its wording, it is consistently applied by the national courts to both widows and widowers who are unfit for work (Case C-338/91 *Steenhorst-Neerings* [1993] ECR I-5475 at pp. I-5505–7). Discrimination contrary to Art. 4(1) also arises where under national legislation a benefit covered by Art. 3(1)(a) is not payable to a married woman who lives with or is maintained by her husband, although it is paid in corresponding circumstances to a married man (Case 150/85 *Drake*, above, at p. 2011); where a benefit is denied to women who have attained the age of 60 whereas men continue to receive it until the age of 65 (Case C-328/91 *Thomas* [1993] ECR I-1247 at pp. I-1271–2); or where women are exempt from prescription charges at the age of 60 whereas men are only exempt at the age of 65 (Case C-137/94 *Richardson*, above, at pp. I-3429–33);

(*b*) the obligation to contribute to statutory schemes and the calculation of contributions. This provision precludes national legislation that reserves to married women, widows, and students the possibility of being assimilated to persons not liable to pay any social security contributions without granting the same possibility of exemption from contributions to married men or widowers who otherwise satisfy the same conditions (Case C-373/89 *Rouvroy* [1990] ECR I-4243 at p. I-4262—'Integrity' case). Such inequality of treatment cannot be justified on the ground that the legislation in question is favourable to women since Dir. 79/7 requires the abolition of all sex discrimination without distinguishing between positive discrimination in favour of one sex and negative discrimination (ibid. at p. I-4254 *per* A.-G. Jacobs);

(*c*) the calculation of benefits including increases due in respect of a spouse and for dependants and the conditions governing the duration and retention of entitlement to benefits. As regards the calculation of benefits, the Court has held that this provision precludes national legislation which permits male and female workers to retire at identical ages from using a method for calculating the pension which is different according to sex, such difference being linked to the difference in pensionable age that existed under the previous legislation (Case C-154/92 *Van Cant* [1993] ECR I-3811 at p. I-3834). The Court has interpreted the term 'increases due in respect of a spouse and for dependants' as including any increases due in respect of spouses who are not dependants and, as regards other persons, in particular children, as requiring no proof of their actual dependency as a prior condition for equal treatment. Therefore, where married men automatically receive increases in social security benefits in respect of a spouse and children deemed to be dependants without having to prove actual dependency, married women in the same circumstances and without actual dependants are also entitled to those increases even if in some circumstances that will result in double payment of the increases (Case C-377/89 *Cotter and McDermott* [1991] ECR I-1155 at pp. I-1184–6; see also Case C-187/98 *Commission* v. *Greece* [1999] ECR I-7713 at pp. I-7740–4).

Art. 4 as a whole only applies within the scope *ratione personae* and *ratione materiae* of the directive. Therefore, only persons covered by Art. 2 (see point 1 above) and those affected through such persons may enjoy the protection of Art. 4 against prohibited discrimination, and only in respect of statutory schemes or social assistance referred to in Art. 3 (see point 2 above). However, where indivisible social security contributions relate to social security benefits that only partly come within the scope of Art. 3, the principle of equal treatment nevertheless applies to such contributions. The position is different where it is possible to apportion the contributions among the individual benefits (Cases 48/88 etc. *Achterberg-te Riele*, above, at p. 1989; Case C-373/89 *Rouvroy*, above, at pp. I-4261–2; Case C-343/92 *De Weerd*, above, at pp. I-601–2; see also Case C-328/91 *Thomas*, above, at pp. I-1271–2).

In a series of cases, the Court has stated that Art. 4(1) precludes, generally and unequivocally, all discrimination on grounds of sex. Therefore, notwithstanding the exceptions provided for in Art. 7 (see point 5 below) and the obligation imposed on Member States by Art. 5 (see below), Art. 4(1) is sufficiently precise and unconditional to produce direct effect as from 23 December 1984, the date by which the directive had to be implemented by the Member States in accordance with Art. 8. In the absence of full and correct implementation by that date, individuals may rely on Art. 4(1) before national courts in order to preclude the application of any national provision which is inconsistent with that article. Moreover, until such time as the necessary implementing measures have been adopted, women placed at a disadvantage by the maintenance of discrimination are entitled to be treated in the same manner, and to have the same rules applied to them, as men who are in the same situation, since where the directive has not been implemented correctly, those rules remain the only valid point of reference. Member States may not invoke their discretion with regard to the choice of methods for implementing the directive in order to deny all effect to Art. 4(1) (Case 71/85 *FNV* [1986] ECR 3855 at pp. 3875–7; Case 286/85 *McDermott and Cotter* [1987] ECR 1453 at pp. 1467–8; see also the cases cited below).

The Court has also emphasized in several cases that the directive does not contain any derogation from the principle of equal treatment in order to authorize the extension of the discriminatory effects of earlier provisions of national law beyond 23 December 1984. After that date, Member States may not maintain any inequalities of treatment that have their origin in such earlier laws by including transitional provisions in the legislation implementing the directive. Implementing measures adopted belatedly, i.e. after the expiry of the above deadline, must fully respect the rights which Art. 4(1) has conferred on individuals (Case 384/85 *Borrie Clarke* [1987] ECR 2865 at p. 2880; Case 80/87 *Dik* [1988] ECR 1601 at pp. 1615–17; Case C-377/89 *Cotter and McDermott*, above, at pp. I-1186–7; Case C-343/92 *De Weerd*, above, at pp. I-596–8; etc.).

In order to enable individuals effectively to protect the rights that they derive from the direct effect of Art. 4(1), the Court has held that a time-limit laid down by national law within which court proceedings must be initiated to enforce Art. 4(1) cannot begin to run until such time as the directive has been properly transposed into national law. Only then are individuals in a position to ascertain the full extent of their right. A defaulting Member State may not therefore rely on a person's delay in instituting proceedings against it so long as the directive has not been correctly implemented (Case C-208/90 *Emmott* [1991] ECR I-4269 at p. I-4299). By contrast, Community law does not preclude the application of a rule of national law that merely limits (e.g. to one year) the retroactive effect of successful claims made for the purpose of obtaining social security benefits under the directive, even where the directive has not been properly transposed into national law on the date of the claim (Case C-338/91 *Steenhorst-Neerings*, above, at pp. I-5503–4; Case C-410/92 *Johnson II* [1994] ECR I-5483 at p. I-5513).

Relying on these last two cases, subsequently the Court explained that the ruling in *Emmott* was justified only by the particular circumstances of that case, in which a time-bar had the result of depriving the plaintiff in the main proceedings of any opportunity whatsoever to rely on her right to equal treatment under the directive. However, the Court said, in general Community law does not prevent a Member State that has not properly transposed a directive from resisting actions brought pursuant to that directive by relying on a limitation period under national law (see Case C-231/96 *Edis* [1998] ECR I-4951 at pp. I-4993–4 and the two cases decided on the same day). Nevertheless, it is clear that *Emmott* and *Steenhorst-Neerings* dealt with two different situations. The former involved a rule of domestic law fixing mandatory time-limits for bringing proceedings, while the latter concerned a rule restricting the retroactive effect of successful claims for benefits (see the judgment of the Court in *Steenhorst-Neerings*, above). It is therefore difficult to see how the scope of *Emmott* could have been cut down by the rulings in *Steenhorst-Neerings* and *Johnson II*, as suggested by A.-G. Ruiz-Jarabo Colomer in *Edis* (above, at p. I-4973, para. 68).

Art. 4(1) prohibits not only direct but also indirect discrimination. Thus, the Court has consistently held that Art. 4(1):

> precludes the application of a national measure which, although formulated in neutral terms, works to the disadvantage of far more women than men, unless that measure is based on objectively justified factors unrelated to any discrimination on grounds of sex . . . That is the case where the measures chosen reflect a legitimate social policy aim of the Member State whose legislation is at issue, are appropriate to achieve that aim and are necessary in order to do so (Case C-343/92 *De Weerd*, above, at p. I-600; Case C-317/93 *Nolte*, above, at pp. I-4658–9; see also the cases cited below).

In this context, the Court has also pointed out that in the current state of Community law, social policy is a matter for the Member States. Dir. 79/7 has left intact the powers reserved by the Treaty to the Member States to define their social policy within the framework of close co-operation organized by the Commission. Consequently, it is for the Member States to choose the measures capable of achieving the aim of their social and employment policy and the way in which they are implemented. In exercising that competence, the Member States have a broad margin of discretion (ibid. at p. I-598 and at p. I-4660, respectively). For these reasons, Community law does not prevent Member States from taking measures, in order to control their social expenditure, which have the effect of withdrawing social security benefits from certain categories of persons or of reducing the number of persons eligible for a social security benefit, provided that those measures are compatible with the principle of equal treatment as defined in Art. 4(1) (Case C-343/92 *De Weerd*, above, at p. I-599; Case C-137/94 *Richardson*, above, at p. I-3432; Case C-280/94 *Posthuma-van Damme and Oztürk*, above, at pp. I-204–5).

The Court has applied these general principles to a variety of social security schemes and benefits, confirming that provisions which indirectly discriminated against persons of one or the other sex were nevertheless justified in the light of a Member State's social policy objectives, and were therefore not contrary to the prohibition in Art. 4(1) (see, in addition to the cases cited above, Case 30/85 *Teuling* [1987] ECR 2497 at pp. 2521–3; Case C-229/89 *Commission* v. *Belgium* [1991] ECR I-2205 at pp. I-2227–30; Case C-226/91 *Molenbroek* [1992] ECR I-5943 at pp. I-5968–70; Case C-444/93 *Megner and Scheffel*, above, at pp. I-4754–6; Case C-8/94 *Laperre* [1996] ECR I-273 at pp. I-294–6). Nevertheless, the Court has also made it clear that although budgetary considerations may influence a Member State's choice of social policy, they cannot themselves justify discrimination against one of the sexes (Case C-343/92 *De Weerd*, above, at p. I-600). Where indirect discrimination is not justified, the members of the group placed at a disadvantage, whether they are men or women, are entitled to be treated in the same manner, and to have the same rules applied to them, as members of the favoured group, just as in the case of direct discrimination (Case C-102/88 *Ruzius-Wilbrink* [1989] ECR 4311 at pp. 4332–3).

Art. 4(2) creates an exception to the principle of equal treatment by allowing the retention or introduction of provisions relating to the protection of women on the grounds of maternity. This exception is similar to that contained in Art. 2(3) of Dir. 76/207 (see section II.2(*b*) above), although it does not refer to pregnancy.

Art. 5 requires the Member States to take the measures necessary to ensure that any laws, regulations, and administrative provisions contrary to the principle of equal treatment are abolished. This provision corresponds to Arts. 3(2)(a), 4(a), and 5(2)(a) of Dir. 76/207 (see section II.3(*d*)(*i*) above). The ECJ has held that while Art. 5 leaves the Member States a discretion with regard to methods, it prescribes the precise result that is to be achieved, i.e. the abolition of any discriminatory provisions. Laying down an unconditional obligation, Art. 5 cannot prevent Art. 4(1) from having direct effect (Case 71/85 *FNV*, above, at p. 3876).

4. Remedies. Art. 6 provides that Member States are to introduce into their national legal systems the necessary measures to enable all persons who consider themselves wronged by discrimination to pursue their claims by judicial process. This provision is virtually identical with Art. 6 of Dir. 76/207, and therefore the case-law of the Court on the interpretation of that Article applies *mutatis mutandis*, in particular as regards the principle of effective judicial protection (see section II.4 above). In Case C-66/95 *Sutton*, above, at pp. I-2188–92, the Court held that Art. 6 of either directive does not require interest to be paid on arrears of a social security benefit when the delay in payment of the benefit is the result of sex discrimination. However, a Member State is required to make reparation for the loss and damage caused to an individual as a result of the breach of Community law, in accordance with the rules on State liability.

5. Exceptions. Art. 7(1) lays down five particular exceptions to the principle of equal treatment. It allows the Member States to exclude from the scope of the directive the following matters:

(*a*) 'the determination of pensionable age for the purposes of granting old-age and retirement pensions and the possible consequences thereof for other benefits'. In considering the scope and effects of this derogation, the Court has made it clear that, in view of the fundamental importance of the principle of equal treatment, it must be interpreted strictly (see Case 151/84 *Roberts*, above, at p. 721; Case 152/84 *Marshall I*, above, at p. 746; Case 262/84 *Beets-Proper*, above, at p. 792; Case C-328/91 *Thomas*, above, at p. I-1272). It authorizes only the following three forms of discrimination.

First, the setting of different statutory pensionable ages for men and women for the purposes of granting old-age and retirement pensions. It thus allows men and women to be treated unequally with respect to the moment at which they become entitled to a pension (Case C-9/91 *Equal Opportunities Commission* [1992] ECR I-4297 at pp. I-4336–7 and I-4339. See also Case 19/81 *Burton*, above, at p. 576 and the cases cited above. For the effect of different pensionable ages on 'dismissal' within the meaning of Art. 5(1) of Dir. 76/207, see section II.3(*c*) above).

Secondly, it authorizes other forms of discrimination that are necessarily linked to the above difference in pensionable age, such as the requirements (in the United Kingdom) that men must pay national insurance contributions for five years longer than women in order to be entitled to the same basic pension and that men must normally pay such contributions up to the pensionable age of 65, whereas women only up to the pensionable age of 60. Although these forms of discrimination are not expressly mentioned in Art. 7(1)(a), in Case C-9/91 *Equal Opportunities Commission*, above, at pp. I-4337–9, the Court held that they fall within the scope of the derogation because they are necessary in order to achieve the objectives of the directive and of Art. 7(1)(a). In particular, the maintenance of different contribution periods for men and women is essential to preserve the complex financial equilibrium of the pension system concerned; in their absence a different pensionable age for men and women, as envisaged by Art. 7(1)(a), would not be possible. This is because the financial equilibrium of the whole system is based on an obligation to contribute until pensionable ages that are different for men and women.

Thirdly, it allows the setting of different pensionable ages for men and women to produce discriminatory consequences for other benefits. However, forms of discrimination provided for in benefit schemes other than old-age and retirement pension schemes can be justified only if they are 'necessarily and objectively linked' to the difference in pensionable age. That is the position where such forms of discrimination are objectively necessary in order to avoid disturbing the financial equilibrium of the social security system or to ensure coherence between the retirement pension scheme and the other benefit schemes (Case C-328/91 *Thomas*, above, at pp. I-1273–5; Case C-92/94 *Graham* [1995] ECR I-2521 at pp. I-2552–3; Case C-137/94 *Richardson*, above, at p. I-3430).

Applying these strict criteria, the Court has found that the derogation laid down in Art. 7(1)(a) does not cover the following matters, which are consequently subject to the principle of equal treatment:

- legislation that denies women who have attained the (retirement) age of 60 entitlement to invalidity benefits, such as severe disablement allowance and invalid care allowance, whereas men continue to receive those benefits until the (retirement) age of 65 (Case C-328/91 *Thomas*, above, at pp. I-1273–5);
- legislation that exempts women from prescription charges at the age of 60 and men only at the age of 65 (Case C-137/94 *Richardson*, above, at pp. I-3431–3);
- a scheme under which winter fuel payment is made to women at the age of 60 and to men only at the age of 65 (Case C-382/98 *Taylor*, above, at pp. I-8982–4);
- an early old-age pension on account of incapacity for work for which the qualifying age differs according to sex (Case C-104/98 *Buchner* [2000] ECR I-3625 at p. I-3655).

By contrast, the derogation in Art. 7(1)(a) applies to the following:

- differences between the rates of invalidity pension payable to men and women from the time when they reach (the different) pensionable age and to difference between the qualifying dates for the grant of invalidity allowance that is paid in addition to invalidity pension and only to persons entitled to the latter (Case C-92/94 *Graham*, above, at pp. I-2553–6);
- a statutory early-retirement scheme under which the method of calculating early-retirement benefits differs according to sex (Case C-139/95 *Balestra* [1997] ECR I-549 at pp. I-578–82);
- a benefit payable to employees or former employees who have suffered a reduction in earnings following an accident at work or occupational disease, and thus designed to compensate for an impairment of earning capacity, which was introduced into national legislation after expiry of

the period prescribed for transposition of the directive and is subject to age conditions that differ according to sex (Case C-196/98 *Hepple* [2000] ECR I-3701 at pp. I-3736–40);

- an early old-age pension on account of unemployment which is subject to a different age condition according to sex (Case C-303/02 *Haackert* [2004] ECR I-0000, paras. 24–38).

The Court has also held that if national legislation has maintained a different pensionable age for male and female workers, the Member State concerned is entitled to calculate the amount of pension differently depending on the worker's sex (Cases C-377/96 etc. *De Vriendt* [1998] ECR I-2105 at p. I-2130; Case C-154/96 *Wolfs* [1998] ECR I-6173 at p. I-6193). On the other hand, if national legislation has abolished the difference in pensionable age, the Member State is not authorized to maintain a difference according to sex in the method of calculating the pension (Case C-154/92 *Van Cant*, above, at p. I-3834).

(*b*) 'advantages in respect of old-age pension schemes granted to persons who have brought up children'; and 'the acquisition of benefit entitlements following periods of interruption of employment due to the bringing up of children' (in this last respect, see Case C-31/90 *Johnson I*, above, at pp. I-3752–3 and point 1 above).

(*c*) 'the granting of old-age or invalidity benefit entitlements by virtue of the derived entitlements of a wife' (for an application of this exception, see Case C-165/91 *Van Munster* [1994] ECR I-4661 at pp. I-4693–4).

(*d*) 'the granting of increases of long-term invalidity, old-age, accidents at work, and occupational disease benefits for a dependent wife' (for an interpretation of this exception, see Case C-420/92 *Bramhill* [1994] ECR I-3191 at pp. I-3211–12).

(*e*) 'the consequences of the exercise, before the adoption of this directive, of a right of option not to acquire rights or incur obligations under a statutory scheme'.

According to the ECJ, all the above derogations reflect the progressive nature of the implementation of the principle of equal treatment. Their purpose is to allow Member States to maintain temporarily the advantages accorded to women with respect to retirement and other benefits in order to enable them progressively to adapt their pension systems without disrupting the complex financial equilibrium of those systems. The directive lays down no precise time-limit as to how long the derogations may be maintained but requires Member States periodically to examine them in order to ascertain, in the light of social developments, whether there is justification for continuing them (Art. 7(2)). Member States are to communicate to the Commission the provisions adopted in the field covered by the directive, including those adopted pursuant to Art. 7(2), and to inform it of their reasons for maintaining any existing exceptions and of the possibilities of reviewing them at a later date (Art. 8(2). See also Case C-9/91 *Equal Opportunities Commission*, above, at p. I-4337). Nevertheless, the Commission is under no obligation to approve or disapprove measures communicated to it under Art. 8(2), and its silence cannot constitute confirmation that any such measure is indeed covered by one of the exceptions (see Case C-137/94 *Richardson*, above, at pp. I-3434–5).

6. Implementation. According to Art. 8(1), Member States were required to implement the directive within six years of its notification, that is, by 23 December 1984 at the latest. Implementing measures adopted after the expiry of this period could be given retroactive effect as from the date of expiry, provided that the rights which the directive, and in particular Art. 4(1), confers on individuals as from that date were fully respected (Case 80/87 *Dik*, above, at p. 1617).

V. Directive 86/378 on equal treatment in occupational social security schemes

The need for Dir. 86/378 arose from Art. 3(3) of Dir. 79/7, which excluded private occupational schemes from the scope of Dir. 79/7, leaving it to the Council to adopt the necessary provisions in that area at a later date (see section IV above). Accordingly, the purpose of Dir. 86/378 is to implement the principle of equal treatment for men and women in occupational social security schemes (fourth and fifth recitals in the preamble and Art. 1). It is based on Arts. 94 and 308 EC. Its structure and many of its substantive provisions are broadly similar to those of Dir. 79/7. The directive was amended by Dir. 96/97 (see section I.4 above).

In defining the scope and importance of Dir. 86/378, account must be taken of the case-law of the Court of Justice developed partly before, but mainly after, the adoption of the directive. According to that case-law, occupational pensions for employees constitute 'pay' within the meaning of Art. 141 EC. Therefore, to the extent to which Art. 141 produces direct effect, all discrimination between men and women in occupational social security schemes in respect of pensions, including the right to join such schemes, is prohibited directly by that Article, without the need to rely on the equal treatment directives (see, in particular, Case C-262/88 *Barber*, above, at pp. I-1950–4; *see further under* **Equal pay**, section II).

This raises the question of the relationship between Art. 141 and Dir. 86/378 and whether the latter has now become redundant with regard to pensions. In dealing with that relationship, in Case C-110/91 *Moroni*, above, at p. I-6617, the Court referred to its established case-law according to which 'Article 141 applies directly to all forms of [direct and overt] discrimination which may be identified solely with the aid of the criteria of equal work and equal pay referred to by that article, without national or Community measures being required to define them with greater precision in order to permit their application'. Therefore, where with the aid of the constitutive elements of the pay in question and of the criteria laid down in Art. 141 discrimination may be directly identified, the effects of the directive become irrelevant because its provisions cannot in any way restrict the scope of Art. 141. Thus, the fact that Art. 8 of Dir. 86/378 required the Member States to implement the directive only by 1 January 1993 and enabled provisions of a pension scheme, which were previously applicable and were contrary to the principle of equal treatment, to be kept in force until that date, could not prevent Art. 141 from being relied on directly and immediately before national courts (see also Case C-7/93 *Beune*, above, at p. I-4523).

While the Court's case-law has considerably reduced the scope and importance of Dir. 86/378, it does not follow that Art. 141 completely excludes the application of the directive. It must be remembered that in dealing with the direct effect of Art. 141, in Case 43/75 *Defrenne II* [1976] ECR 455 at p. 473, the Court distinguished between 'direct and overt' discrimination, defined as in *Moroni* above, to which Art. 141 applies directly, and 'indirect and disguised' discrimination, which 'can only be identified by reference to more explicit implementing provisions of a Community or national character'. According to its preamble (second recital), Dir. 86/378 was meant to be precisely such an implementing provision aimed at defining 'more clearly' the scope of the principle of equal pay so as to make it applicable to cases of indirect and disguised discrimination. Therefore, the directive applies to types of indirect discrimination that are not caught by the direct effect of Art. 141.

The Court itself has recognized that the directive may apply to occupational pension schemes covered by Art. 141 and that, conversely, Art. 141 may apply to occupational social security schemes covered by the directive (Case C-262/88 *Barber*, above, at pp. I-1955–6; Case C-7/93 *Beune*, above, at p. I-4523 *per Curiam*, p. I-4491 *per* A.-G. Jacobs; Case C-147/95 *Evrenopoulos* [1997] ECR I-2057 at p. I-2081; Case C-50/99 *Podesta* [2000] ECR I-4039 at pp. I-4064–9; Case C-166/99 *Defreyn* [2000] ECR I-6155 at pp. I-6183–6). On the other hand, the directive does not apply to statutory schemes governed by Dir. 79/7 (Art. 2; see point 1 below). It thus seems that while Art. 141 and Dir. 79/7 are mutually exclusive (see section IV.2 above), Art. 141 and Dir. 86/378 are not. Nevertheless, the Court's jurisprudence developed in *Barber* and subsequent cases has invalidated some of the provisions of Dir. 86/378 (e.g. Arts. 8 and 9) in respect of employed persons. The purpose of the amendments introduced by Dir. 96/97 was precisely to adapt those provisions of Dir. 86/378 that were affected by the *Barber* case-law (see the preamble to Dir. 96/97, and in particular the last three recitals).

1. General scope. Dir. 86/378, as amended by Dir. 96/97, applies to 'occupational social security schemes'. These are defined as schemes not governed by Dir. 79/7 whose purpose is to provide workers, whether employees or self-employed, in an undertaking or group of undertakings, area of economic activity, occupational sector or group of sectors with benefits intended to supplement the benefits provided by statutory social security schemes or to replace them, whether membership of such schemes is compulsory or optional (Art. 2(1). For an interpretation of this provision, see the *Podesta* and *Defreyn* cases, cited immediately above). However, the directive does not apply to: individual contracts for self-employed workers; schemes for self-employed workers having only one member; in the case of salaried workers, insurance contracts to which the employer is not a party; optional provisions of occupational schemes offered to participants individually to guarantee them either additional benefits or a choice of date on which the normal benefits for self-employed workers will start, or a choice between several benefits; and occupational schemes in so far as benefits are financed by voluntary contributions paid by workers (Art. 2(2)). The directive allows employers to grant pension supplements in certain situations (Art. 2(3)).

2. Personal scope. The directive applies to members of the working population, including self-employed persons, persons whose activity is interrupted by illness, maternity, accident, or involuntary unemployment, and persons seeking employment, to retired and disabled workers and to those claiming under them, in accordance with national law and/or practice (Art. 3).

3. Material scope. The directive applies to: (*a*) occupational schemes that provide protection against the following risks: sickness, invalidity, old age (including early retirement), industrial accidents and occupational diseases, unemployment; and (*b*) occupational schemes which provide for other social benefits, in cash or in kind, and in particular survivors' benefits and family allowances, if such benefits are accorded to employed persons and thus constitute a consideration paid by the employer to the worker by reason of the latter's employment (Art. 4).

4. Prohibition of discrimination. Art. 5 defines in more detail the scope of the principle of equal treatment laid down in Art. 1. According to Art. 5(1), that principle means that 'there shall be no discrimination on the basis of sex, either directly or indirectly, by reference in particular to marital or family status' especially as regards the following three matters:

- the scope of the occupational schemes listed in Art. 4 and the conditions of access to them;
- the obligation to contribute to the schemes and the calculation of contributions; and
- the calculation of benefits, including supplementary benefits due in respect of a spouse or dependants, and the conditions governing the duration and retention of entitlement to benefits.

Art. 5(2) creates an exception to the principle of equal treatment by allowing the retention or introduction of provisions relating to the protection of women by reason of maternity.

Art. 6 lists a number of examples of provisions that are contrary to the principle of equal treatment. These include the setting of different conditions for men and women concerning, amongst others, participation in occupational schemes; reimbursement of contributions in certain circumstances; the granting and levels of benefits; retirement ages; workers' and employers' contributions; etc. Where the granting of benefits is left to the discretion of the scheme's management bodies, these must comply with the principle of equal treatment.

Art. 7 requires the Member States to take all necessary steps to ensure that discriminatory provisions in binding collective agreements, staff rules, or occupational schemes are or may be declared null and void or amended, and that schemes containing such provisions may not be approved or extended by administrative measures. Although under the original Art. 8(1) discriminatory provisions of occupational schemes were to be revised only by 1 January 1993, and under Art. 8(2) rights and obligations relating to a period of membership of such schemes prior to revision could be kept in force, as seen above, the ECJ has held that these provisions could not limit the scope of Art. 141 and could not prevent that Article, in so far as it applied to occupational schemes, from being relied on directly and immediately before national courts (see the *Moroni* and *Beune* cases, cited above, dealing with Art. 8(1) and (2), respectively). Art. 8 has been amended by Dir. 96/97 and is now applicable to occupational schemes for self-employed persons only.

5. Remedies. Member States are required to introduce into their national legal systems the necessary measures to enable all persons who consider themselves injured by discrimination to pursue their claims before the courts (Art. 10. For an interpretation by the ECJ of the almost identical Art. 6 of Dir. 76/207, see section II.4 above). Member States are to protect workers against dismissal ordered in retaliation for a complaint made within the undertaking or for legal proceedings brought to enforce compliance with the directive (Art. 11).

6. Exceptions. The original Art. 9 allows Member States to defer compulsory application of the principle of equal treatment with regard to determination of pensionable age for the granting of old-age or retirement pensions, and the possible implications for other benefits, either until the date on which such equality is achieved in statutory schemes or, at the latest, until such equality is required by a directive. Likewise, the principle of equal treatment need not be applied with regard to survivors' pensions until it is introduced in statutory schemes. By virtue of the amendments contained in Dir. 96/97, these exceptions now apply only to schemes for self-employed workers (this also follows from the Court's case-law). A newly inserted Art. 9a makes it possible for a flexible pensionable age to be applied to men and women under the same conditions.

7. Implementation. Member States were required to bring into force legislation necessary to comply with Dir. 86/378 at the latest three years after its notification, that is, by 30 July 1989 (Art. 12). However, discriminatory provisions of occupational schemes were to be revised by 1 January 1993 only (Art. 8(1), discussed above). Dir. 96/97 was to be implemented by 1 July 1997 with retroactive effect, as regards paid workers, to 17 May 1990 (the date of the *Barber* judgment), or to 8 April 1976 (the date of the *Defrenne II* judgment) in the case of workers who initiated legal proceedings before 17 May 1990. For Member States which acceded to the Community after 8 April 1976, that date is replaced by the date on which Art. 141 EC became applicable on their territory. For Member States whose accession took place after 17 May 1990 and who were on 1 January 1994 Contracting Parties to the Agreement on the European Economic Area, the date of 17 May 1990 is replaced by 1 January 1994 (Arts. 2 and 3 of Dir. 96/97).

VI. Directive 86/613 on equal treatment of the self-employed

The purpose of this directive, which was adopted on the basis of Arts. 94 and 308 EC, is to ensure the application in the Member States of the principle of equal treatment as between men and women engaged in an activity, including agriculture, in a self-employed capacity, or contributing to the pursuit of such an activity, as regards those aspects not covered by Dirs. 76/207 and 79/7 (Art. 1).

The directive applies to: (*a*) self-employed persons, i.e. those pursuing a gainful activity for their own account, including farmers and members of the liberal professions; and (*b*) their spouses, not being employees or partners, where they habitually participate in the activities of the self-employed person and perform the same or ancillary tasks (Art. 2). The directive thus aims to protect, in particular, wives of self-employed persons who do not enjoy protection under any other provision because they are neither paid employees nor self-employed persons working on their own, but contribute to their husbands' activities, and thus lack a clearly defined status.

According to Art. 3, the principle of equal treatment implies the prohibition of all discrimination on grounds of sex, either directly or indirectly, by reference in particular to marital or family status.

As regards self-employed persons, Member States are required to take the measures necessary to eliminate all provisions which are contrary to the principle of equal treatment as defined in Dir. 76/207, 'especially in respect of the establishment, equipment or extension of a business or the launching or extension of any other form of self-employed activity including financial facilities' (Art. 4). The ECJ has observed that where a discriminatory provision concerns a professional activity falling within the scope of Dir. 86/613, Art. 4 requires the combined interpretation of Dir. 86/613 and Dir. 76/207 (Case C-226/98 *Jørgensen*, above, at p. I-2478). Member States are to ensure that the conditions for the formation of a company between spouses are not more restrictive than the conditions for the formation of a company between unmarried persons (Art. 5). Member States must take measures to enable the spouses of self-employed persons referred to in Art. 2(b) who are not protected under the self-employed person's social security scheme to join a contributory social security scheme voluntarily, where such a scheme for self-employed persons exists (Art. 6).

While the above provisions (Arts. 4 to 6) impose obligations on the Member States, Arts. 7 and 8 are drafted in terms that imply mere recommendations rather than a duty to achieve concrete results. Under Art. 7, Member States 'shall undertake to examine' under what conditions recognition of the position of spouses 'may be encouraged' and, in the light of such examination, shall 'consider any appropriate steps for encouraging such recognition'. According to Art. 8, Member States 'shall undertake to examine' whether, and under what conditions, female self-employed workers and the wives of self-employed workers may, during interruptions in their occupational activity owing to pregnancy or motherhood, have access to services supplying temporary replacements or existing national social services, or be entitled to cash benefits under a social security scheme or under any other public social protection system. These are clearly the weakest provisions in the directive, unsuitable to achieve its objective of recognizing the professional status of wives working in family businesses and of conferring on them entitlement to replacement services or cash benefits during pregnancy or motherhood. Thus, the directive has so far produced insufficient results in practice (see the Commission's report of 16 September 1994 on the implementation of the directive (COM(94) 163; *Gen. Rep. EU* (1994), p. 200).

Art. 9 requires the Member States to provide adequate judicial remedies for persons suffering discrimination contrary to the directive. The measures adopted under the directive are to be brought to the attention of the relevant bodies representing self-employed persons (Art. 10). The directive was to be implemented by 30 June 1989. However, Art. 5 was to be complied with by 30 June 1991 (Art. 12).

See also **Equality*, Equal pay.**

Further reading 1. BOOKS: Barnard, *EC Employment Law*, 2nd edn. (2000), chs. 4 and 5; Bell, *Anti-Discrimination Law and the European Union* (2002); Craig and de Búrca, *EU Law. Text, Cases, and Materials*, 3rd edn. (2003), ch. 20; Dashwood and O'Leary, *The Principle of Equal Treatment in EC Law* (1997); Ellis, *EC Sex Equality Law*, 2nd edn. (1998); Hervey, *Justifications for Sex Discrimination in the EC* (1993); Hervey and O'Keeffe (eds.), *Sex Equality Law in the European Union* (1996); McCrudden (ed.), *Equality of Treatment between Women and Men in Social Security* (1994); Steiner, Woods, and Twigg-Flesner, *Textbook on EC Law*, 8th edn. (2003), ch. 24; Wyatt and Dashwood, *European Union Law*, 4th edn. (2000), ch. 27.

2. ARTICLES: Anagnostaras, 'Sex Equality and Compulsory Military Service: The Limits of National Sovereignty Over Matters of Army Organization' (2003) *EL Rev.* 713; Barnard, 'The Principle of Equality in the Community Context: P, Grant, Kalanke and Marschall: Four Uneasy Bedfellows?'(1998) *Cambridge Law Journal* 352; Barrett, 'Re-examining the Concept and Principle of Equality in EC Law' (2003) *YEL* 117; Bell and Waddington, 'Reflecting on Inequalities in the European Equality Law' (2003) *EL Rev.* 349; Brown, 'The Race Directive: Towards Equality for *All* the Peoples of Europe?' (2002) *YEL* 195; Burrows, 'Maternity Rights in Europe—An Embryonic Legal Regime' (1991) *YEL* 273; Caracciola di Torella and Masselot, 'Pregnancy, Maternity, and the Organization of Family Life: An Attempt to Classify the Case-Law of the Courts of Justice' (2001) *EL Rev.* 239; Connor, 'Community Discrimination Law: Temporal Limitations and Unlawful Conditions of Application Imposed by a Member State' (1999) *EL Rev.* 300; Curtin, 'Effective Sanctions and the Equal Treatment Directive: The Von Colson and Harz Cases' (1985) *CML Rev.*

505; Dougan, 'The Equal Treatment Directive: Retaliation, Remedies and Direct Effect' (1999) *EL Rev.* 664; Ellis, 'The Definition of Discrimination in European Community Sex Equality Law' (1994) *EL Rev.* 563; id., 'Recent Case-Law of the Court of Justice on the Equal Treatment of Women and Men' (1994) *CML Rev.* 43; id., 'Recent Developments in European Community Sex Equality Law' (1998) *CML Rev.* 379; id., 'The Recent Jurisprudence of the Court of Justice in the Field of Sex Equality' (2000) *CML Rev.* 1403; Fenwick and Hervey, 'Sex Equality in the Single Market: New Directions for the European Court of Justice' (1995) *CML Rev.* 443; Flynn, 'Equality between Men and Women in the Court of Justice' (1998) *YEL* 259; id., 'The Implications of Article 13 EC—After Amsterdam, Will Some Forms of Discrimination Be More Equal Than Others?' (1999) *CML Rev.* 1127; Koutrakos, 'EC Law and Equal Treatment in the Armed Forces' (2000) *EL Rev.* 433; Mancini and O'Leary, 'The New Frontiers of Sex Equality Law in the European Union' (1999) *EL Rev.* 331; McGlynn and Farrelly, 'Equal Pay and the Protection of Women within Family Life' (1999) *EL Rev.* 202; McInerney, 'Equal Treatment between Persons Irrespective of Racial or Ethnic Origin: A Comment' (2000) *EL Rev.* 317; Prechal, 'Combating Indirect Discrimination in Community Law Context' (1993/1) *LIEI* 81; Szyszczak, 'Positive Action after Kalanke' (1996) *MLR* 876; Waddington and Bell, 'More Equal than Others: Distinguishing European Union Equality Directives' (2001) *CML Rev.* 587; Whittle, 'The Framework Directive for Equal Treatment in Employment and Occupation: An Analysis from a Disability Rights Perspective' (2002) *EL Rev.* 303; Whittle and Bell, 'Between Social Policy and Union Citizenship: the Framework Directive on Equal Treatment in Employment' (2002) *EL Rev.* 677.

▶ **EUROPEAN CITIZENSHIP** *see* **FREE MOVEMENT OF PERSONS**

▶ **EUROPEAN COMPANY** The European Company statute has a long history: the idea of a uniform type of limited company that could be used throughout the Community without being subject to national law was first mooted in 1959 by Professor Sanders in an inaugural lecture at the Rotterdam School of Economics. Straddling frontiers, the European Company would enable a business to operate across borders without the administrative burdens involved in setting up and running subsidiaries, all of which typically remain subject to domestic law. Legislative progress has been exceptionally slow, primarily as a result of deadlock among the Member States over the provisions of the various proposals concerning employee participation. In October 2001, however, Reg. 2157/2001 on the statute for a European Company—SE (*OJ* 2001 L294/1) and its companion Dir. 2001/86 supplementing the statute for a European Company with regard to the involvement of employees (*OJ* 2001 L294/22) were finally adopted by the Council.

Many of the requirements of the regulation summarized below are expressed to be subject to requirements of the national law relating to public companies of the Member State in which the SE has its registered office ('national law'). Moreover, certain requirements of the regulation that merely duplicate provisions imposed on public companies by the company law directives are not repeated here (for these directives, *see further under* **Company law**).

The term SE, abbreviation for the linguistically neutral term Societas Europea, is used throughout this entry to denote a European Company. Unless otherwise indicated, in sections I, II, and IV article numbers refer to articles of the regulation; in section III they refer to articles of the directive.

I. Formation and capital

An SE may be set up within the Community in the form of a public company limited by shares (Art. 1). An SE may (*i*) be created by the merger (in accordance with the procedure laid down in Arts. 16 to 30, similar to that required by the Third Company Law Directive; *see further under* **Company law**, section III) of two or more public companies formed under the law of a Member State with their registered offices and head offices within the Community, provided that at least two of them are governed by the law of different Member States; (*ii*) be set up as a holding SE or subsidiary SE by two or more public or private companies formed under the law of a Member State with their registered offices and head offices within the Community, provided that at least two of them are governed by the law of different Member States or have for at least two years had a subsidiary governed by the law of another Member State or a branch situated in another Member State; or (*iii*) be created by the conversion of a public company formed under the law of a Member State with its registered office and head office within the Community if for at least two years it has had a subsidiary company governed by the law of another Member State (Art. 2).

Where an SE is formed by the conversion of a public company or by a merger, the existing rights and obligations of, respectively, the public company or the participating companies on terms and conditions of employment arising from national law, practice, and employment contracts or relationships are to be transferred to the SE (Arts. 29(4) and 37(9)).

An SE's registered office and head office must be located in the same Member State (Art. 7); its registered office may be transferred to another Member State without winding up or loss of legal personality (Art. 8). Every SE must be registered in the Member State where it has its registered office in a register designated in accordance with the First Company Law Directive (*see further under* **Company law**, section I); it may not be registered unless an agreement on arrangements for employee involvement pursuant to Art. 4 of the directive has been concluded, or a decision pursuant to Art. 3(6) of the directive has been taken, or the period for negotiations pursuant to Art. 5 of the directive has expired without an agreement having been concluded (Art. 12). An SE acquires legal personality from the date of registration (Art. 16). Notice of registration and of any transfer of registered office must be published in the *Official Journal* (Art. 14).

An SE must have a subscribed capital, expressed in euros, of at least €120,000 (Art. 4). SEs with registered offices in a Member State outside the

Eurozone do not have to express their capital in euros (Art. 67). An SE's capital and securities are to be governed by national law (Art. 5).

II. Management structure

An SE comprises a general meeting of shareholders and either a supervisory organ and management organ (two-tier system) or an administrative organ (one-tier system) depending on its statutes (Art. 38). Members of the organs are appointed for a period laid down in the statutes not exceeding six years (Art. 46). An SE's statutes may permit a company to be a member of an organ provided that this is permitted by national law (Art. 47) and must list the categories of transactions that require authorization of the management organ by the supervisory organ in the two-tier system or an express decision by the administrative organ in the one-tier system (Art. 48). Members of the organs are under a duty, even after they have ceased to hold office, not to divulge any information that they have concerning the SE the disclosure of which might be prejudicial to its interests (Art. 49). Members of all organs are to be liable, in accordance with national law, for loss or damage sustained by the SE following any breach on their part of the legal, statutory, or other obligations inherent in their duties (Art. 51).

1. Two-tier system. The management organ is responsible for managing the SE; its member(s) are appointed and removed by the supervisory organ, although a Member State may require or permit that members of the management organ be appointed and removed under the same conditions as for public companies with registered offices within its territory. No person may be a member of both the management and the supervisory organ (Art. 39). The supervisory organ supervises the work of the management organ; its members are appointed by the general meeting (Art. 40). The management organ must report to the supervisory organ at least once every three months on the progress and foreseeable development of the SE's business and must promptly pass to the supervisory organ any information on events likely to have an appreciable effect on the SE (Art. 41).

2. One-tier system. The administrative organ manages the SE; its member(s) are appointed by the general meeting (Art. 43). It must meet at least once every three months to discuss the progress and foreseeable development of the SE's business (Art. 44).

3. General meeting. The general meeting decides on matters for which it is given sole responsibility by the regulation, by legislation of the Member State in which the SE's registered office is situated, adopted in implementation of the directive, or by national law (Art. 52). An SE must hold a general meeting at least once each calendar year; general meetings may be convened at any time by the management organ, the administrative organ, or the supervisory organ (Art. 54) or by one or more shareholders holding at least 10% of the SE's subscribed capital (Art. 55). Decisions of the general meeting are taken by a majority of the votes validly cast (Art. 57); amendment of the SE's statutes requires a decision of the general meeting taken by a majority of at least two-thirds of the votes cast (Art. 59).

III. Employee involvement

Agreement on employee involvement in an SE proved particularly elusive. The compromise finally accepted aims to preserve existing rights unless the employees decide otherwise. As indicated, the principal employee involvement provisions are to be found in the directive, which requires arrangements for the involvement—but not necessarily the participation in management—of employees to be established in every SE in accordance with either the prescribed negotiating procedure or, in specified circumstances, standard rules set out in the Annex (Art. 1(2)). The importance attached to employee involvement is illustrated by Art. 11, which requires Member States to take appropriate measures to prevent the misuse of an SE for the purpose of depriving employees of rights to employee involvement or withholding such rights. Member States are moreover expressly required to ensure compliance with the directive by the management of local companies and establishments involved in the creation of an SE whose registered office is elsewhere (Art. 12).

Council Dir. 94/45 of 22 September 1994 on the establishment of a European Works Council or a procedure in Community-scale undertakings and Community-scale groups of undertakings for the purposes of informing and consulting employees (*OJ* 1994 L254/64) will not apply to an SE except where Art. 3(6) applies (see below).

1. Negotiating procedure. Where the management or administrative organs of the participating companies draw up a plan for the formation of an SE, they must, as soon as possible after publishing the draft terms of merger or creating a holding company or agreeing to form a subsidiary or to convert into an SE, take the necessary steps to start negotiations with the representatives of the companies' employees on arrangements for the involvement of employees in the SE (Art. 3(1)). For that purpose, a special negotiating body ('SNB') representative of the employees of the companies, subsidiaries, and establishments involved and made up of employee representatives and management in accordance with specified geographical and proportional criteria is to be established according to a prescribed procedure (Art. 3(2)).

The SNB and the competent organs of the participating companies are to determine by written agreement arrangements for the involvement of employees within the SE (Art. 3(3)); they are to negotiate in a spirit of co-operation with a view to reaching such agreement (Art. 4(1)). Negotiations are to start as soon as the SNB is established and may continue for six months; by joint agreement that period may be extended up to a total of one year (Art. 5). The legislation applicable to the negotiation procedure is that of the Member State in which the SE will have its registered office (Art. 6).

The SNB is to make decisions by an absolute majority of members representing an absolute majority of employees, except where the result of the negotiations would lead to a reduction in existing participation rights in which case a two-thirds majority of members representing a two-thirds majority of employees, including the votes of members representing employees employed in at least two Member States, is required in the following circumstances: (*i*) in the case of an SE to be established by merger, if participation covers at least 25% of the participating companies' total employees, and (*ii*) in the case of an SE to be established by the creation of a holding or subsidiary company, if participation covers at least 50% of the participating companies' total employees (Art. 3(4)). Except where an SE is to be established by conversion of a public company whose employees already have specified participation rights, the SNB may decide by the same majority either not to open negotiations or to terminate negotiations and to rely on the rules on information and consultation of employees in force in the Member State where the SE has employees (Art. 3(6)).

2. The agreement. The agreement is to cover, *inter alia*, (*i*) the composition, number of members and allocation of seats on the representative body which will be the discussion partner of the competent organ of the SE in connection with arrangements for the information and consultation of the employees of the SE and its subsidiaries and establishments, (*ii*) the functions and the procedure for the information and consultation of the representative body, and (*iii*) details of agreed arrangements for participation (Art. 4(2)). In the case of an SE established by conversion from an existing company, the agreement must provide for at least the same level of all elements of employee involvement as applied to the existing company (Art. 4(4)).

3. Default rules. Art. 7 requires Member States to lay down standard rules on employee involvement, which must satisfy the provisions set out in the Annex to the directive. Those standard rules apply where the parties so agree or where (*i*) no agreement on employee involvement has been reached, (*ii*) the competent organ of each participating company so accepts, (*iii*) the SNB has not taken the decision provided in Art. 3(6), and (*iv*) at least one of the companies involved in the formation of the SE was subject to specified rules on participation. In particular, the rules will apply (*a*) where an SE is established by conversion of an existing public company subject to national employee participation rules; (*b*) where an SE is established by merger, if participation covered either at least 25% of the participating companies' total employees or less than 25% thereof and the SNB so decides; or (*c*) where an SE is established as a holding or subsidiary company, if participation covered either at least 50% of the participating companies' total employees or less than 50% thereof and the SNB so decides (Art. 7(1) and (2)).

The all-important Nice compromise led to the inclusion of Art. 7(3), which permits Member States not to apply the default provisions in the case of an SE established by merger. However, an SE established by the merger of companies one or more of which was governed by participation rules may be registered in a Member State that has made use of this option only where an agreement pursuant to Art. 4 of the directive has been concluded (Art. 12(3) of the regulation).

The rules are somewhat complex and vary depending on the circumstances: they are in outline as follows.

Part 1 of the Annex concerns the composition of the body representative of the employees and sets out a number of rules for setting up the representative body similar to those applying to European Works Councils in accordance with the European Works Councils Directive (Dir. 94/45). The membership of the representative body reflects that of the SNB set up under Art. 3: in particular, one seat per Member State is to be allocated for every 10% (or fraction thereof) of the total EU workforce of the participating companies there employed (point (e)).

Pursuant to point (g) of the Annex, the representative body is to examine after four years whether to open negotiations for the conclusion of an agreement in accordance with Arts. 4 and 7, in which case the provisions of the directive are to apply with the representative body taking the place of the SNB, or to continue to apply the standard rules.

Part 2 of the Annex lays down standard rules for information and consultation. In essence, the rules require SE managers to provide regular reports on the basis of which the representative body is to be regularly consulted and informed. The reports are to cover the involved companies' structure, financial situation, the probable development of the business and of production and sales, current and probable employment trends, investments, management changes, mergers, divestments, potential closures, and layoffs.

With regard to participation, the rules in Part 3 of the Annex distinguish between SEs formed by conversion of an existing public company and those formed in other ways. In the former case, if the existing company was subject to national employee-participation rules before registration as an SE, all aspects of those rules are to continue to apply to the SE. For SEs established in other ways, the employees of the SE and its subsidiaries and establishments and/or their representative body are to be entitled to elect, appoint, recommend, or oppose the appointment of members of the SE's administrative or supervisory body representing the highest proportion in force in the companies concerned before registration as an SE. Where none of the companies participating in the formation of an SE was subject to participation before registration, there is no right to employee participation in the SE. That is essentially the case for participating companies subject to the law of Belgium, France, Ireland, Italy, Portugal, Spain, and the United Kingdom.

IV. Winding up, insolvency, and conversion

An SE is governed by national law as regards winding up, liquidation, insolvency, suspension of payments etc. (Art. 63).

If an SE no longer complies with the requirement that its registered office and head office are situated in the same Member State, the State in which its registered office is situated must take appropriate measures to oblige the SE to regularize its situation within a specified period, failing which it must ensure that the SE is liquidated (Art. 64).

An SE may be converted into a public company governed by national law in accordance with a prescribed procedure (Art. 66).

See also **Company law.**

Further reading 1. BOOKS: Tavares Da Costa and de Meester Dilreiro, *The European Company Statute* (2003); Werlauff, *SE—The Law of the European Company* (2003).

2. ARTICLES AND PAPERS: Ebert, 'The European Company on the Level Playing Field of the Community' (2003) *EBL Rev.* 183; Edwards, 'The European Company—Essential Tool or Eviscerated Dream?' (2003) *CML Rev.* 443; Hopt, 'The European Company (SE) under the Nice Compromise: Major Breakthrough or Small Coin for Europe?' (2000) *Euredia* 465; Teichmann, 'The European Company—A Challenge to Academics, Legislators and Practitioners' in Neville and Sørensen (eds.), *The Regulation of Companies* (2003); Wenz (ed.), '*Societas Europaea*: Flagship for European Company Law—Catalyst for EC Tax Law?' (2004) *European Taxation* 4; Werlauff, 'The SE Company: A New Common European Company from 8 October 2004' (2003) *EBL Rev.* 85.

▶ **EUROPEAN ECONOMIC AREA (EEA)** *see* **FREE MOVEMENT OF PERSONS**

▶ **EUROPEAN ECONOMIC INTEREST GROUPING** Council Reg. 2137/85 of 25 July 1985 on the European Economic Interest Grouping (EEIG) (*OJ* 1985 L199/1) seeks to provide a framework for effective co-operation across frontiers between natural persons, companies, firms, and other legal bodies by creating a Community legal instrument. The regulation is based on Art. 308 EC. As a legal concept, the EEIG falls somewhere between a partnership and a company; each EEIG will be governed in part by the regulation, in part by national law and in part by the terms of the contract of formation.

I. Formation, publicity, and official address

The purpose of an EEIG must be 'to facilitate or develop the economic activities of its members and to improve or increase the results of those activities' and not to make profits for itself; its activity must be related to, but not more than ancillary to, the economic activities of its members. It thus cannot, e.g. exercise any power of management over its members' activities or hold shares in a member undertaking; nor can it employ more than 500 persons or be a member of another EEIG (Art. 3). A Member State may, subject to judicial review, prohibit the carrying on of any activity in contravention of its public interest (Art. 38).

Members may be either (*a*) companies or firms within the meaning of Art. 48 EC and other legal bodies formed in accordance with the law of a Member State and with their registered office and central administration in the Community; where the body's national law does not require it to have a registered office, it suffices that its central administration is in the

Community; or (*b*) natural persons carrying on an activity or providing services in the Community (Art. 4(1)). At least two of the members must have their central administration or carry on their principal activities in different Member States (Art. 4(2)). Member States may restrict the number of members to twenty (Art. 4(3)).

Parties intending to form an EEIG must conclude a contract (Art. 1) which must include at least the EEIG's name (including 'EEIG' or the words in full), official address, objects, and duration (unless indefinite) and each member's name, business name, legal form, address, and number or place of registration if any (Art. 5); those particulars and other specified information must also be published in the official gazette of the Member State where it has its official address (Arts. 8. and 39(1)). Information so published may be relied on by the EEIG against third parties as under Art. 3(5) and (7) of the First Directive (Art. 9) (*see further under* **Company law**, section I.1).

The EEIG must be registered, and the formation contract and other specified information filed, at the registry designated by the Member State where it has its official address (Arts. 6 and 7); Member States must provide for appropriate sanctions for failure to comply (Art. 39(3)). The public must be able to inspect and obtain copies of the filed documents (Art. 39(1)). Notice of formation must also be published in the *Official Journal* (Art. 11). From the date of registration the EEIG has legal capacity; whether it has legal personality depends on national law (Art. 1).

An EEIG's official address must be in the Community and fixed either where it has its central administration or where one of its members has its central administration or principal activity, provided that the EEIG carries on an activity there (Art. 12). An EEIG may have an establishment in another Member State; the establishment must be registered and copies of the relevant documents filed in that State, with translations if required by the registry's practice (Art. 10). An EEIG's official address may be transferred within the Community (Art. 13). A procedure is prescribed where the transfer involves a change in the applicable law (Art. 14); otherwise, the decision to take is governed by the formation contract (Art. 13).

II. Management

An EEIG's organs are its members, acting collectively, and its manager(s), unless the formation contract provides for other organs (Art. 16). The manager(s) must be natural persons appointed in the contract or by decision of the members; Member States may however permit legal persons to be managers provided that they designate one or more natural persons, whose particulars must be filed (Art. 19). Only the members or a manager may represent an EEIG in dealings with third parties; each manager binds the EEIG even where he acts outside its objects unless the EEIG proves that the third party knew or could not in the circumstances have been unaware that the act was *ultra vires*; publication of particulars is not proof. No limitation on managers' powers may be relied on as against third parties, even if published, except for a duly published provision in the contract that the EEIG may be bound only by two or more managers acting jointly (Art. 20).

III. Members' rights and obligations

Each member has one vote unless the contract provides differently; it may not, however, give one member a majority of votes. A unanimous decision by the members is required for a number of specified circumstances. Otherwise the contract may provide for a quorum and a majority; in the absence of provision in the contract, decisions are taken unanimously (Art. 17).

An EEIG's profits are deemed to be the profits of its members and are to be apportioned amongst them in the proportion laid down in the contract or, if none, in equal shares. The same proportions apply to the contributions members are to contribute to make up any excess of expenditure over income (Art. 21). Profits or losses resulting from the activities of an EEIG are taxable only in the hands of its members (Art. 40). Members have unlimited joint and several liability for an EEIG's debts and other liabilities; a creditor may not however proceed against a member before liquidation of the EEIG unless he has first requested the EEIG to pay and payment has not been made within an appropriate period (Art. 24).

A member may, with the unanimous authorization of the other members, assign all or part of his participation to another member or to a third party and, subject to the contract, use his participation as security (Art. 22). Admission of a new member requires a unanimous decision of the members. A new member is liable for the EEIG's debts, etc. including (unless otherwise provided in the formation contract or instrument of admission) those preceding his membership (Art. 26).

Membership may cease by (*a*) withdrawal in accordance with the formation contract, with the unanimous consent of the other members or on just and proper grounds; (*b*) expulsion (ordered by a court on application by a majority of the members, unless the contract provides otherwise) on grounds specified in the contract or for serious failure in the member's obligations or for causing or threatening to cause serious disruption in the operation of the EEIG (Art. 27); (*c*) non-compliance with Art. 4(1) (see above); (*d*) death; (*e*) other grounds laid down by national law (Art. 28). Unless the contract provides otherwise, the EEIG continues to exist for the other members (Art. 30); the former member remains liable for five years after publication of the cesser of membership for the EEIG's debts, etc. arising out of its activities while he was a member (Arts. 34 and 37(1)).

IV. Nullity, winding up, and liquidation

Where the law applicable to the EEIG provides for nullity, the nullity must be established or declared by judicial decision; time must be allowed to permit the EEIG's affairs to be put in order where possible. The decision, which must be filed and published, may be relied on as against third parties in accordance with Art. 9 (see above), but does not affect the validity of existing liabilities. Nullity entails liquidation (Art. 15).

An EEIG may be wound up by unanimous (unless otherwise provided in the contract) decision of its members (Art. 31(1)). It must be wound up on expiry of the period (if any) fixed in the contract, the existence of any other cause for winding up there specified, the accomplishment of its purpose, the impossibility of pursuing it further (Art. 31(2)), or non-compliance with Art. 4(2) (see above) (Art. 31(3)). The court must, in general, order winding up in the case of infringement of Arts. 3, 12, or 31(3) (see above) or on just and proper grounds (Art. 32). The winding up of an EEIG entails its liquidation, which is governed by national law; the EEIG retains its legal capacity until the liquidation is concluded (Art. 35). Members remain liable for its debts for five years from publication of notice of conclusion of the liquidation (Art. 37(2)).

Further reading 1. BOOKS: Anderson, *European Economic Interest Groupings* (1990); Van Gerven and Aalders (eds.), *European Economic Interest Groupings* (1990).

2. ARTICLES AND PAPERS: Blouet, 'The Taxation of the European Economic Interest Grouping (EEIG)' (1991) *European Taxation* 2; Dine, 'The European Economic Interest Grouping and the European Company Statute: New Models for Company Law Harmonisation' in Andenas and Kenyon-Slade (eds.), *EC Financial Market Regulation and Company Law* (1993); Dine, 'The European Economic Interest Grouping (EEIG): Some Private International Law Issues' (1993) *The Company Lawyer* 10; Drury and Schießl, 'E.C. Competition Law Aspects of the European Economic Interest Grouping (EEIG)' (1994) *JBL* 217; Mackay, 'The European Economic Interest Grouping' in *Corporate Law—The European Dimension* (1991).

3. OFFICIAL PUBLICATIONS: House of Lords, Select Committee on the European Communities, Session 1983–4, 25th Report, 'European Economic Interest Grouping'.

▶ **EXCISE DUTIES AND SIMILAR TAXES** Taxes on the production, sale, or use of specific goods, often luxury or non-essential goods. They may be levied on the value of the goods (*ad valorem* duties) or on the basis of some other characteristic, such as volume or weight (specific duties). The main modern excise duties are those on alcoholic drinks, tobacco products, motor fuels, and motor vehicles.

High levels of excise duties discourage sales and hence imports of the product concerned; differences in the taxation of substitutable products affect consumers' choices between these products and hence distort competition between producers. The need for border tax adjustments where States apply different systems and rates of tax requires the retention of tax frontiers, making import and export more complicated and expensive. Accordingly, large variations in duties are considered to be inconsistent with the existence of a single market. However, differences in rates of tax reflect different choices by governments: excise duties are used by governments not only as a means of gathering revenue but also in order to influence their citizens' behaviour, often on grounds of health or energy policy. Harmonization is thus difficult and sensitive. Moreover, there can be no harmonization or indeed valid comparison of rates without harmonization of the structures of taxation: the manner in which goods are classified and defined for tax purposes, the basis of assessment and the type of tax. In addition, harmonization of structures is useful in itself, since differences in tax structures have significant effects on conditions of competition.

Harmonization of excise duty rates and structures was the object of discussions over several years. A package of directives was adopted in 1992 on the basis of proposals on minimum and target rates, which were presented as the minimum necessary for the elimination of tax frontiers. The measures adopted fell short of these proposals, so that considerable divergence remains.

I. General provisions

A harmonized framework is laid down in Council Dir. 92/12 of 25 February 1992 on the general arrangements for products subject to excise duty and on the holding, movement, and monitoring of such products (*OJ* 1992 L76/1), as amended by Dirs. 92/108 (*OJ* 1992 L390/124), 94/74 (*OJ* 1994 L365/46), 96/99 (*OJ* 1997 L8/12), 2000/44 (*OJ* 2000 L161/82), and 2000/47 (*OJ* 2000 L193/73), and Reg. 807/2003 (*OJ* 2003 L122/36). The 'products subject to excise duty' referred to in the title are mineral oils, alcoholic beverages, and manufactured tobacco. Member States may levy indirect taxes other than VAT on other products only if these taxes do not entail border controls. They may also impose taxes other than harmonized duties on products subject to excise duty so long as these taxes are levied for specific purposes and comply with the rules governing determination of the tax base and the calculation, charging, and monitoring of excise duties and VAT (for an illustration of the difference between these two rules, see Case C-437/97 *Evangelischer Krankenhausverein Wien* [2000] ECR I-1157). While the requirement that other taxes on excisable products comply with the rules on excise duty and VAT is a flexible one (see Case C-434/97 *Commission* v. *France* [2000] ECR I-1129 (social security tax on spirits)), it prevents Member States from imposing such taxes on goods exempt from excise duty (see Case C-346/97 *Braathens Sverige* [1999] ECR I-3419 (Swedish tax on aviation fuel in internal commercial transport); Case C-437/01 *Commission* v. *Italy* [2003] ECR I-9861 (Italian tax on lubricating oils)).

Products become subject to duty on their manufacture or their importation into the Community, and duty becomes chargeable on their release for consumption. While the manner in which duty is levied and collected remains a matter for national law, the same procedures must be applied to domestic products and those from other Member States (Case C-325/99 *Van de Water* [2001] ECR I-2729).

Where goods that have already been released for consumption are then held for commercial purposes in another Member State they are subject to duty in the second Member State, and the duty paid in the first State should be refunded (a destination system of taxation is thus retained). Products acquired by individuals for their own use are taxed in the country of purchase, and no duty is chargeable on their subsequent importation into another Member State. However, individuals may not make purchases abroad through agents and thus escape the rate of duty applicable in their home country (Case C-296/95 *EMU Tabac* [1998] ECR I-1605).

Dutiable products must be produced, processed, and held in a system of authorized tax warehouses until their release for consumption. This system, and the concomitant suspension of duty, extends to the stage of receipt of such goods by traders, so that products can be dispatched under suspension of duty from a warehouse in one Member State to a trader in another.

II. Tobacco

Previous legislation on the structure of duties, dating in part to 1972, was codified and replaced by Dir. 95/59 of 27 November 1995 on taxes other than turnover taxes that affect the consumption of manufactured tobacco (*OJ* 1995 L291/40); amended by Dirs. 1999/81 (*OJ* 1999 L211/47) and 2002/10 (*OJ* 2002 L46/26). It defines three main categories of tobacco products (cigarettes, cigars and cigarillos, and smoking tobacco). Manufacturers may set maximum retail prices freely. Cigarettes are subject to a combination of a proportional excise duty calculated on the maximum retail price and a specific excise duty calculated per unit; rates must be the same for all cigarettes.

Harmonization is to take place in stages. During the second stage, which has lasted since 1978, the specific component of the excise duty on cigarettes must be between 5% and 55% of the amount of the total tax burden (proportional and specific excise duty plus turnover tax) levied on cigarettes in the most popular price category. In the final stage the ratio between specific excise duty and the sum of proportional excise duty and turnover tax on cigarettes is to be uniform in all Member States. The rules for collecting duty are also to be harmonized at the final stage at the latest.

Rates of duty are the subject of two directives. Under Council Dir. 92/79 of 19 October 1992 on the approximation of taxes on cigarettes (*OJ* 1992 L316/8), amended by Dirs. 1999/81 (*OJ* 1999 L211/47) and 2002/10 (*OJ* 2002 L46/26), the minimum total excise duty (specific and *ad valorem* duty excluding VAT) is set at 57% of the retail price (including all taxes) of cigarettes in the price category most in demand, with a minimum of €60 per 1,000 cigarettes of that category (€64 from 1 July 2006). The 57% figure does not apply to those Member States which apply a high level of tax (at least €95 per 1,000 for cigarettes in the category most in demand, €101 from 1 July 2006).

Council Dir. 92/80 of 19 October 1992 on the approximation of taxes on manufactured tobacco other than cigarettes (*OJ* 1992 L316/10), amended by Dirs. 1999/81 (*OJ* 1999 L211/47) and 2002/10 (*OJ* 2002 L46/26), lays down minimum rates of duty for cigars and cigarillos, fine-cut tobacco intended for the rolling of cigarettes, and other smoking tobacco (snuff and chewing tobacco are omitted). A high degree of harmonization is considered less important for these products than it is for cigarettes. Member States may apply specific or *ad valorem* taxes or a mixture of both (there are nevertheless limits on their freedom of action—in Case C-365/98 *Brinkmann* [2000]

ECR I-4619 the Court considered that an *ad valorem* tax with a minimum amount was not a mixed system).

The minimum rates are expressed both as percentages and as amounts: for cigars and cigarillos, 5% of the retail price including taxes or €11 per 1,000 units or per kilogram; for fine-cut tobacco intended for rolling cigarettes, 33% or €29 per kilogram (36% or €32 from 1 July 2004); for other smoking tobacco, 20% or €20 per kilogram.

Under both directives, rates of duty are to be reviewed every four years.

III. Alcohol and alcoholic drinks

The taxation of alcoholic drinks is difficult to harmonize. Large differences in rates make it difficult to abolish frontier barriers without a risk of diversion of trade, yet attitudes to the proper level of rates vary. Rates are high in the northern countries of the Community, at least partly on health and moral grounds, and duties are a significant source of revenue, while many southern countries charge very low rates of duty.

Council Dir. 92/83 of 19 October 1992 on the harmonization of the structures of excise duties on alcohol and alcoholic beverages (*OJ* 1992 L316/21) defines several categories of drinks—beer, still and sparkling wine, other fermented beverages (still and sparkling), intermediate products, and ethyl alcohol.

Member States must apply excise duty to each of the categories of products, normally at a single rate for each category; they may apply separate rates to still and sparkling wine or other fermented beverages. They may apply reduced rates to beer and ethyl alcohol produced by small independent firms, to products with a low alcohol content, to intermediate products with an alcoholic strength not exceeding 15% and certain natural sweet wines. Denatured alcohol and alcohol used in the production of vinegar, medicines, and foodstuffs are exempted from duty; Member States may exempt alcohol used for scientific or medical purposes or in manufacturing processes.

For the calculation of tax on beer the Member States may choose one of two methods: a rate per hectolitre per degree Plato or a rate per hectolitre per degree (percentage point) of alcoholic strength by volume. Tax on wine and intermediate products is calculated by reference to the volume of the finished product, while tax on ethyl alcohol products is calculated per hectolitre of pure alcohol at 20°C.

Council Dir. 92/84 of 19 October 1992 on the approximation of rates of excise duty on alcoholic beverages (*OJ* 1992 L316/29) sets minimum rates. The minimum rate for beer is €0.748 per hectolitre per degree Plato or €1.87 per hectolitre per degree of alcohol of the finished product, while the minimum rate for both still and sparkling wine (and other fermented beverages) is €0.

The minimum rate for intermediate products is €45 per hectolitre of product. The minimum rate for alcohol and alcoholic drinks is €550 per hectolitre of pure alcohol content; however, Member States whose existing rate of duty does not exceed €1,000 may not reduce it, and Member States whose existing rate is more than €1,000 may not reduce it below that figure. Reduced rates are permitted in certain regions of Greece, Italy, and Portugal. Other derogations have been made under Art. 299 EC (provisions for certain remote territories): see, for example, Council Dec. 2002/166 on the reduced rate of excise duty on 'traditional' rum produced in French overseas departments (*OJ* 2002 L55/33).

Rates are to be reviewed every two years; however, no further proposals have been made.

In Case C-166/98 *Socridis* [1999] ECR I-3791, the validity of both directives was challenged on the ground that the difference in the taxation of beer and wine was contrary to the prohibition of discrimination in Art. 90 of the Treaty. The Court of Justice held that the different calculation methods and minimum rates set by the directives do not necessarily create discrimination. It remains for the Member States, in the exercise of their freedom of action, to ensure that there is no discrimination in the taxation of wine and beer.

IV. Mineral oils (petroleum products)

Excise duties on petroleum products bear most heavily on road fuel, and there is generally some link between those taxes and investment in transport infrastructure. Whereas taxes on tobacco or alcoholic drinks fall directly on the consumer, taxes on fuel affect industry and commerce, in the form of transport costs or production costs. Harmonization must therefore take into account not only possible deflection of trade but also possible effects on conditions of competition for businesses in different States. Varying levels of taxation also affect choices between energy sources and thus have repercussions for energy and environmental policy. For example, there is a contradiction between the desire to use tax to discourage consumption of petroleum products and the desire to apply a neutral system of taxation to all energy sources.

Council Dir. 92/81 of 19 October 1992 on the harmonization of the structures of duty on mineral oils (*OJ* 1992 L316/12), amended by Dirs. 92/108 (*OJ* 1992 L390/124) and 94/74 (*OJ* 1994 L365/46), covers a broad range of products. However, products other than those for which a rate is set in the rates directive, Dir. 92/82 (see below), are taxable only where they are intended for use as heating fuel or motor fuel; in such cases the rate of duty is to be that applied to the corresponding fuel referred to in the rates directive. Any other product intended for use as motor fuel or as an additive to motor fuels is to be taxed as motor fuel. Other hydrocarbons intended for use as heating fuel are taxable at the rate for the equivalent oil. Coal, peat and similar solid fuels, and natural gas are exempted from the latter rule, but they may be taxed by the Member States so long as no border formalities result.

Specific exemptions are laid down for products used for purposes other than as motor or heating fuels and for those used in commercial aviation and shipping or fishing in Community waters. Member States may establish exemptions or reduced rates in particular for products used in electricity generation or in combined heat and power plants, commercial navigation on inland waterways, rail transport, the development of 'environmentally-friendly' products, agriculture, and fisheries. The Council may authorize individual Member States to establish other derogations on specific public policy grounds.

Thus Council Dec. 2001/224, adopted pursuant to Art. 8(4) of the directive and replacing a series of earlier decisions, authorizes Member States to continue to apply a number of existing reduced rates or exemptions from excise duty to certain mineral oils when used for specific purposes (*OJ* 2001 L84/23). The most widespread exemptions or reductions are in favour of local public transport, air navigation, LPG, natural gas and methane used as motor fuel, navigation in private pleasure craft, and fuel used by the armed forces. There are also a large number of individual decisions authorizing specific derogations, for example in relation to biofuels.

Council Dir. 92/82 of 19 October 1992 on the approximation of the rates of excise duties on mineral oils (*OJ* 1992 L316/19) lays down minimum rates for leaded and unleaded petrol, diesel, heating oil, heavy fuel oil, liquid petroleum gas and methane, and kerosene. Different rates are set for diesel, LPG, and methane and kerosene depending on the use to which they are put, with a particularly low rate for use as heating fuel (€0 in the case of LPG and methane and kerosene). The rates are to be reviewed every two years.

A 1992 proposal for a directive introducing a tax on carbon dioxide emissions and energy found no agreement in the Council and was withdrawn in 2001. However, the concept of taxation related in part to emissions of carbon dioxide has been included in a proposal for a directive restructuring the taxation of energy products (*OJ* 1997 C139/14). The proposal consolidates and replaces Dirs. 92/81 and 92/82, and includes electricity in the scope of energy taxation. The text currently under discussion also incorporates what was originally a separate proposal envisaging reduced levels of excise duty for biofuels (*OJ* 2002 C103E/217).

V. Road tax, tolls, and user charges

There is a relationship between excise duties on motor fuels, national systems of road vehicle tax, and tolls and user charges. Varying levels of these charges are perceived to cause distortions in the conditions of competition for commercial road transport.

A judgment of the Court of Justice, which condemned as discriminatory a road use levy on heavy goods vehicles in Germany (C-195/90 *Commission* v. *Germany* [1992] ECR I-3141), gave additional impetus to harmonization in this area. A first directive, Dir. 93/89 (*OJ* 1993 L279/32), was annulled by the Court of Justice on procedural grounds (Case C-21/94 *Parliament* v. *Council* [1995] ECR I-1827).

It was replaced by Dir. 1999/62 of 17 June 1999 on the charging of heavy goods vehicles for the use of certain infrastructures (*OJ* 1999 L187/42). Vehicle taxes may be charged solely by the Member State of registration and are subject to minimum rates of tax for various categories of vehicle. Non-discriminatory tolls or user charges may be levied in respect of motorways and similar roads, bridges, tunnels, and mountain passes. Ceilings are set for user charges, with lower rates for less polluting vehicles. Two or more Member States may co-operate in a common system of user charges (six Member States—Belgium, Denmark, Germany, Luxembourg, the Netherlands, and Sweden—apply such a system). Tolls must be related to the cost of the infrastructures concerned.

► **EXPULSION** An act whereby a State orders a foreign national to leave its territory (also known as deportation). When applied by a Member State against the nationals of another Member State, expulsion is, in principle, incompatible with Community law as it negates the very right of free movement and residence conferred and guaranteed by the EC Treaty. As a derogation from one of the fundamental freedoms created by the Treaty, expulsion is normally only permissible in so far as it may be justified on grounds of public policy, public security, or public health, and provided that it is in accordance with the substantive and procedural provisions of Dir. 64/221 of 25 February 1964 on the co-ordination of special measures concerning the movement and residence of foreign nationals, which are justified on grounds of public policy, public security or public health (*OJ Sp. Edn.* 1963–4, p. 117. For a detailed discussion of this directive, *see further under* **Public policy**). It should be noted that Dir. 64/221 and many others concerning the movement and residence of persons will be repealed and replaced as from 30 April 2006 by Dir. 2004/38 of the European Parliament and of the Council of 29 April 2004 on the right of citizens of the Union and their family members to move and reside freely within the territory of the Member States (*OJ* 2004 L158/77, Art. 38. For a discussion of this directive, *see further under* **Right of entry and residence**, section VII).

According to Art. 3(1) and (2) of Dir. 64/221, measures taken on grounds of public policy or of public security must be based exclusively on the 'personal conduct' of the individual concerned. Previous criminal convictions cannot in themselves constitute grounds for the taking of such measures. The ECJ has interpreted the concept of 'personal conduct' as expressing the requirement that a deportation order may only be made for breaches of the peace and public security that might be committed by the individual affected, and that deportation of a Community national may not be ordered for the purpose of deterring other aliens, that is, as a general preventive measure (Case 67/74 *Bonsignore* [1975] ECR 297 at p. 307). When making a recommendation for deportation, a court must ensure that the directive is correctly applied, and must take account in particular of Art. 3 inasmuch as the mere existence of criminal convictions may not automatically constitute grounds for deportation measures (Case 30/77 *Bouchereau* [1977] ECR 1999 at p. 2011; Case 131/79 *Santillo* [1980] ECR 1585 at p. 1601).

On the basis of these considerations, in Case C-348/96 *Calfa* [1999] ECR I-11 at p. I-31, the Court held that the free movement provisions of the Treaty (Arts. 39, 43, and 49) and Art. 3 of the directive precluded legislation that required the national courts to order expulsion for life of nationals of other Member States found guilty of drug-related offences. The main concern of the Court was that under Greek legislation, from which the case arose, expulsion for life automatically followed a criminal conviction, without any account being taken of the personal conduct of the offender or of the danger that he represented for public policy. That expulsion for life is not permitted for any reason also follows from the right of the expelled person to apply for readmission after a reasonable time (see below).

Generally, a Member State may not expel a Community national from its territory by reason of conduct that, when attributable to its own nationals, does not give rise to punitive measures or other genuine and effective measures intended to combat such conduct (Cases 115/81 etc. *Adoui and Cornuaille* [1982] ECR 1665 at p. 1708; Case 249/86 *Commission* v. *Germany* [1989] ECR 1263 at p. 1292).

A mere failure to comply with the legal formalities concerning the entry, movement, and residence of foreign nationals, such as a failure to report to the police, to obtain a residence permit, or to register with a social security scheme, or the expiry of the identity card or passport used to enter the territory of the host State, cannot justify expulsion or temporary imprisonment for that purpose. In such circumstances, expulsion would constitute a penalty so disproportionate to the gravity of the infringement in question that it would virtually negate the right to free movement guaranteed by Community law (Case 48/75 *Royer* [1976] ECR 497 at p. 515; Case 118/75 *Watson and Belmann* [1976] ECR 1185 at p. 1199; Case 157/79 *Pieck* [1980] ECR 2171 at p. 2187; Case C-363/89 *Roux* [1991] ECR I-273 at p. I-291; Art. 3(3) of Dir. 64/221). For the same reasons, a Member State is not permitted to issue an expulsion order against a third-country national who is able to furnish proof of his identity and of his marriage to a national of a Member State on the sole ground that he entered the territory of the Member State concerned unlawfully or, where he entered the territory lawfully, that his visa expired before he applied for a residence permit (Case C-459/99 *MRAX* [2002] ECR I-6591, at pp. I-6664–5, I-6668).

Likewise, diseases or disabilities occurring after a first residence permit has been issued cannot give rise to expulsion (Art. 4(2) of Dir. 64/221). On the other hand, it is not contrary to Community law to order the expulsion of a Community national who entered the host State in order to seek employment if he has not found employment there after six months, unless he provides evidence that he is continuing the search and that he has genuine chances of being engaged (Case C-292/89 *Antonissen* [1991] ECR I-745 at p. I-779; but *see also under* Free movement of persons, section III.4(*b*)).

A person who has been expelled must be officially notified of the relevant decision, of the grounds upon which it is based, and of the period allowed for leaving the territory of the host State. Save in cases of urgency, this period cannot be less than fifteen days if the person has not yet been granted a residence permit and not less than one month in other cases (Arts. 6 and 7 of Dir. 64/221). The decision ordering expulsion cannot be executed, except in cases of urgency, until the person concerned has been able to complete the formalities necessary to avail himself of the remedies guaranteed by Arts. 8 and 9 of Dir. 64/221 (Case 48/75 *Royer*, above, at p. 517. For a detailed discussion of these remedies, *see further under* **Public policy**, section IV).

This does not mean that the person is entitled to remain in the host State throughout the proceedings initiated by him, although he must be able to obtain a fair hearing and to present his defence in full (Case 98/79 *Pecastaing* [1980] ECR 691 at pp. 713–14).

Since a decision prohibiting entry into a Member State of a national of another Member State cannot be of unlimited duration, a person who has been refused entry into or expelled from the territory of a Member State for reasons of public policy or public security has the right to re-apply for a fresh residence permit and is entitled to a new decision. The ECJ has held that such an application, when submitted after a reasonable period has elapsed, must be examined by the competent authority in the host State, which must consider, in particular, whether there has been a material change in the circumstances that justified the initial decision. However, where expulsion has been validly ordered under Community law and continues to be in force, the person has, under Community law, no right of entry into the host State during the examination of his further application (Cases 115/81 etc. *Adoui and Cornuaille*, above, at p. 1709; Cases C-65/95 etc. *Shingara and Radiom* [1997] ECR I-3343 at pp. I-3391–2).

See also **Free movement of persons, Public health, Public policy, Public security, Residence permit, Right of entry and residence.**

Further reading Doppelhammer, 'Expulsion: A Test Case for European Union Citizenship?' (1999) *EL Rev.* 621.

▶ **FREE CIRCULATION OF GOODS** *see* **CUSTOMS PROCEDURES**

▶ **FREEDOM OF ESTABLISHMENT** One of the fundamental freedoms forming the basis of the internal market, the purpose of which is to ensure the free movement of self-employed persons within the Community, as opposed to workers (i.e. employed persons) and providers and recipients of services, who are governed by different rules. (For the relationship between these three categories of persons and between the provisions of Community law applying to them, *see further under* **Freedom to provide services** and **Free movement of persons**).

According to Art. 43 EC, freedom of establishment includes the right, for nationals of a Member State, 'to take up and pursue activities as self-employed persons and to set up and manage undertakings, in particular companies or firms' in the territory of another Member State 'under the conditions laid down for its own nationals by the law of the country where such establishment is effected' (primary establishment). It also includes the right, for nationals of any Member State who are already established in any Member State, to set up agencies, branches, or subsidiaries in another Member State (secondary establishment). According to Art. 48 EC, companies or firms, as defined in that provision, are to be treated in the same way as natural persons who are nationals of Member States (see also e.g. Case 270/83 *Commission* v. *France* [1986] ECR 273 at pp. 302–3).

Although the primary objective of these provisions is to guarantee the right of establishment to foreign nationals and companies in, as well as their equal treatment with the nationals of, the host Member State, they also prohibit the Member State of origin from hindering the establishment in another Member State of its own nationals and companies, for example by preventing them from leaving the national territory in order to establish themselves elsewhere (Case 81/87 *Daily Mail* [1988] ECR 5483 at p. 5510), or by applying unfavourable tax measures that discourage them from setting up a primary or secondary establishment in another Member State (see e.g. Case C-264/96 *ICI* [1998] ECR I-4695 at pp. I-4721–2 *per Curiam*, pp. I-4704–5 *per* A.-G. Tesauro; Case C-251/98 *Baars* [2000] ECR I-2787 at p. I-2817). Art. 43 likewise prohibits a Member State from hindering the establishment in another Member State of nationals of Member States residing on its territory (ibid.).

Moreover, freedom of establishment is not confined to the right to create a single establishment within the Community. From the right to set up secondary establishments, i.e. agencies, branches, or subsidiaries, provided for in Art. 43, the ECJ has derived a general principle, applicable equally to the liberal professions, according to which the right of establishment includes freedom to set up and maintain more than one place of work or establishment in the Community. Thus, a natural or legal person may be established in more than one Member State. In the case of natural persons, and in particular in the case of members of the professions, this may be done by establishing a second professional base, and in the case of companies, by setting up agencies, branches, or subsidiaries (Case 107/83 *Klopp* [1984]

ECR 2971 at pp. 2989–90; Case C-55/94 *Gebhard* [1995] ECR I-4165 at pp. I-4194–5; Case C-53/95 *Kemmler* [1996] ECR I-703 at p. I-714; see further section IV below).

Finally, freedom of establishment includes the right not only to take up all types of self-employed activity, but also to pursue them in the broad sense of the term, and to have access to all the facilities which are necessary for that purpose, such as the renting or acquiring of business premises, property, housing, etc. (Case 197/84 *Steinhauser* [1985] ECR 1819 at p. 1827; see further section IV below).

For its part, the ECJ has defined the concept of establishment as involving 'the actual pursuit of an economic activity through a fixed establishment in another Member State for an indefinite period' (Case C-221/89 *Factortame II* [1991] ECR I-3905 at p. I-3965). This concept is a very broad one which, in the words of the Court, allows a Community national:

> to participate, on a stable and continuous basis, in the economic life of a Member State other than his State of origin and to profit therefrom, so contributing to economic and social interpenetration within the Community in the sphere of activities as self-employed persons (Case C-55/94 *Gebhard*, above, at p. I-4195).

It follows that a national of a Member State who pursues a professional activity on a stable and continuous basis in another Member State where he holds himself out from an established professional base to, amongst others, nationals of that State is covered by the provisions relating to the right of establishment and not by those relating to services (ibid. at pp. I-4195–6 and I-4198. For a distinction between establishment and services, *see further under* **Freedom to provide services**, section II.1).

From the definition cited above, the Court has deduced that the registration of a vessel does not necessarily involve establishment within the meaning of the Treaty, in particular where the vessel is not used to pursue an economic activity or where the applicant for registration is not established, and has no intention of becoming established, in the State concerned. However, where the vessel constitutes an instrument for pursuing an economic activity that involves a fixed establishment in another Member State, the registration of that vessel will be connected with the exercise of the freedom of establishment, and the conditions laid down for the registration must not form an obstacle to the exercise of that freedom or discriminate on grounds of nationality (Case C-221/89 *Factortame II*, above, at p. I-3965; see also Case C-246/89 *Commission* v. *United Kingdom* [1991] ECR I-4585 at p. I-4614). Later the Court extended this principle to the registration of aircraft (Case C-203/98 *Commission* v. *Belgium* [1999] ECR I-4899 at p. I-4910).

Subsequently, the Court has recognized that even the registration of a vessel not used in the context of an economic activity, such as a leisure craft, may fall within the scope of the Community provisions relating to freedom of movement (Arts. 39 and 43 EC). This is the case where the owner of the vessel exercises the right to pursue an employed or self-employed activity in the host State, or the right to reside there after having pursued such an activity. In these situations, the right to register a leisure craft is simply a corollary of the freedom of movement for persons (Case C-334/94 *Commission* v. *France* [1996] ECR I-1307 at p. I-1341).

Freedom of establishment must also be distinguished from the free movement of capital. Thus, the ECJ has held that as a general rule the acquisition by one or more natural persons residing in a Member State of shares in a company incorporated and established in another Member State is covered by the Treaty provisions on the free movement of capital, provided that the shareholding does not confer on those natural persons definite influence over the company's decisions and does not allow them to determine its activities. By contrast, where the acquisition involves all the shares in a company having its registered office in another Member State and the shareholding confers a definite influence over the company's decisions and allows the shareholders to determine its activities, it is the Treaty provisions on freedom of establishment that apply (Case C-251/98 *Baars*, above, at pp. I-2814–15 and Case C-208/00 *Überseering* [2002] ECR I-9919, para. 77. For the relationship between freedom of establishment and free movement of capital, *see further under* **Free movement of capital,** section VI).

I. The legal framework

The provisions of Community law governing the right of establishment fall into three distinct categories, which will be considered in turn below.

1. The Treaty provisions. The primary rules are laid down in Arts. 43 to 48 EC, which make up one of the three chapters dealing with the free movement of persons in Title III of Part Three of the EC Treaty, as amended by the Treaty on European Union (TEU) and the Treaty of Amsterdam (ToA) (the other two chapters deal with workers and services, respectively). Although in their application the chapters on establishment and services are mutually exclusive (see Case C-55/94 *Gebhard*, above, at pp. I-4193–4), there is a very close interrelationship between the three chapters since they all govern different aspects of the same basic freedom. In several cases, the ECJ has pointed out that they are based on the same principles both as regards entry into, residence, and the pursuit of an economic activity in the territory of the Member States by persons covered by Community law and as regards the prohibition of all discrimination against them on grounds of nationality (Case 48/75 *Royer* [1976] ECR 497 at p. 509; Case 118/75 *Watson and Belmann* [1976] ECR 1185 at pp. 1196–7, etc., as restated in Case C-107/94 *Asscher* [1996] ECR I-3089 at pp. I-3121–2).

In accordance with the Court's consistent case-law, Arts. 43 to 48 must be interpreted and applied in the light of Part One of the EC Treaty, which lays down the fundamental principles, objectives, and tasks of the Community. Of particular importance are Art. 2, which defines the tasks of the Community; Art. 3(1)(c), which provides for the creation of an internal market characterized by the abolition, as between Members States, of obstacles to the free movement of goods, persons, services, and capital (i.e. the four freedoms); and Art. 12, which prohibits any discrimination on grounds of nationality. In a number of cases, the Court has emphasized that Arts. 43 *et seq.* must be regarded as a specific implementation or application of these fundamental principles with regard to self-employed persons and companies, and that those provisions take precedence over any national rule that might conflict with them (see e.g. Case 118/75 *Watson and Belmann*, above, at p. 1198; Case 71/76 *Thieffry* [1977] ECR 765 at p. 776; Case 136/78 *Auerl* [1979] ECR 437 at p. 448).

The most important Treaty provision relating to the right of establishment is Art. 43, which, in the words of the ECJ, 'constitutes one of the fundamental legal provisions of the Community' (Case 197/84 *Steinhauser*, above, at p. 1826; see also, e.g. Case 270/83 *Commission* v. *France*, above, at p. 302). It lays down two important principles. First, that restrictions on the freedom of establishment are prohibited. According to the original (pre-Amsterdam) text of Art. 43 [Art. 52 EEC], such restrictions had to be abolished by progressive stages in the course of the transitional period, i.e. by 31 December 1969 at the latest. Secondly, that all nationals of Member States who establish themselves in another Member State must receive the same treatment as nationals of that State (the principle of national or equal treatment). Or, to put it in another way, that any discrimination on grounds of nationality resulting from the legislation of the host State must be abolished as constituting a restriction on freedom of establishment (ibid. at pp. 302–3. See further sections III and IV below).

The ECJ held that the original Art. 52 imposed an obligation to attain a precise result, i.e. the equal treatment of nationals and non-nationals, the fulfilment of which had to be made easier by, but not made dependent on, the implementation of a programme of progressive measures as envisaged in the original Arts. 54 and 57 [now Arts. 44 and 47] (see below). The fact that this progression had not been adhered to left the obligation itself intact beyond the end of the period provided for its fulfilment. Therefore, Art. 52 [now Art. 43] produced direct effect, in the sense of conferring enforceable rights on individuals, after the end of the transitional period despite the fact that the Council had failed to adopt in a particular sphere the directives provided for by Arts. 54 and 57 (Case 2/74 *Reyners* [1974] ECR 631 at pp. 651–2; see also Case 48/75 *Royer*, above, at p. 511; Case 118/75 *Watson and Belmann*, above, at p. 1197; Case 11/77 *Patrick* [1977] ECR 1199 at pp. 1204–5; Case 107/83 *Klopp*, above, at pp. 2987–8, etc. On the direct effect of Art. 52 [now Art. 43], see further section IV below).

Unlike Art. 49 on the freedom to provide services, which by virtue of Art. 51(1) is not applicable to transport services (the latter being governed by the provisions of the Title relating to transport), Art. 43 applies in the field of transport, including air transport. It applies to all companies, including airline companies, established in a Member State, even if their business in that State consists of services directed towards non-member countries (Case C-466/98 *Commission* v. *United Kingdom* [2002] ECR I-9427, paras. 39–43. See also the similar cases brought against seven other Member States and decided by the Court on the same day—'Open skies' cases).

The original Art. 53—repealed by the ToA—laid down a 'stand-still' provision by prohibiting Member States from introducing any new restrictions on the right of establishment as compared with those applying at the time when the Treaty entered into force. It also prohibited the revocation of liberalizing measures taken by the Member States in implementation of their obligations under Community law, e.g. in pursuance of a directive (Case 48/75 *Royer*, above, at pp. 517–19). It thus confirmed the irreversible nature of the liberalization achieved at any given time (Case 71/76 *Thieffry*, above, at p. 776). Art. 53 had direct effect since 1 January 1958, the date on which the Treaty came into force (Case 6/64 *Costa* [1964] ECR 585 at p. 596).

The original Art. 54(1)—deleted by the ToA—provided for the drawing up by the Council of a General Programme for the abolition of existing restrictions on freedom of establishment, setting out the general conditions under which, and the progressive stages by which, freedom of establishment was to be attained in the case of each type of activity during the transitional period. In order to implement this General Programme, Art. 54(2) required the Council to issue directives. Art. 54(3) specified a number of ways in which the Council and the Commission were to perform their task, for example by ensuring close co-operation between the competent authorities of the Member States and by adjusting administrative procedures and practices liable to hinder freedom of establishment. Art. 54(2) and (3) have been renumbered by the ToA as Art. 44(1) and (2), respectively.

In order to make it easier for persons to take up and pursue activities as self-employed persons, Art. 47 [ex Art. 57] makes the Council and Parliament responsible for issuing directives, first, for the mutual recognition of diplomas, certificates, and other evidence of formal qualifications and, secondly, for the co-ordination of the legal provisions of the Member States concerning the taking up and pursuit of activities as self-employed persons. This Article thus attempts to reconcile freedom of establishment with the application of national professional rules justified by the general good, such as rules relating to organization, qualifications, professional ethics, supervision, liability, etc. (see Case 71/76 *Thieffry*, above, at p. 776).

The General Programme and the directives provided for by the original Arts. 54 and 57 were intended to achieve a two-fold objective. First, to eliminate obstacles in the way of attaining freedom of establishment during the transitional period. Secondly, to introduce into the law of the Member States a set of provisions to facilitate the effective exercise of this freedom. While the General Programme was adopted by the Council on 18 December 1961 (see below), not all the directives needed to bring about freedom of establishment, as envisaged by Arts. 54 and 57, were issued by the end of the transitional period. Nevertheless, as seen above, in Case 2/74 *Reyners* the ECJ ruled that this fact could not prevent Art. 52 [now Art. 43] from having direct effect as from the end of that period (31 December 1969), since the attainment of freedom of establishment had to be made only easier by, but not made dependent on, the adoption of the directives. After the expiry of the transitional period, the Court said, the directives became superfluous with regard to implementing the rule on national (or equal) treatment, since this rule was henceforth sanctioned by Art. 52 [43] itself with direct effect. The Court, however, added that the directives had not lost all relevance since they still played an important part by making easier the effective exercise of the right of establishment (see also Case 11/77 *Patrick*, above, at p. 1205).

Arts. 45 and 46 lay down certain limitations on and exceptions to the right of establishment. According to Art. 45, Arts. 43 to 48 do not apply to activities connected, even occasionally, with the exercise of official authority. Art. 46 allows special treatment of foreign nationals justified on grounds of public policy, public security, or public health, and authorizes the Council to issue directives for the co-ordination of the relevant national provisions. These limitations and exceptions are considered under separate entries (*see further under* **Official authority, Public health, Public policy, Public security**).

Finally, Art. 48 defines the concept of 'companies or firms' and stipulates that they are to be treated in the same way as natural persons who are nationals of Member States (see further section V below).

It may be noted that in the absence of transitional provisions concerning the right of establishment in the Acts of Accession of 1972, 1979, 1985, 1994, and 2003, Arts. 43 to 48 and the various implementing measures entered into force with regard to the new Member States immediately upon their accession to the Community (see Case 11/77 *Patrick*, above, at p. 1205 concerning the Act of Accession of 1972). The only exception was Art. 221 of the Act of Accession of 1985, which allowed Portugal to maintain restrictions on the right of establishment for certain activities until 31 December 1988 and 31 December 1990, respectively.

The provisions of the Treaty on the right of establishment apply to the French overseas departments subject to Council Dec. 64/350 of 25 February 1964 (*OJ Sp. Edn.* 1963–4, p. 144) and to the overseas countries and territories (OCTs) subject to Council Dec. 2001/822 of 27 November 2001 on the association of the OCTs with the EC (*OJ* 2001 L314/1. Annex I A contains a list of the OCTs, which is slightly different from the list contained in Annex II to the EC Treaty. See also Arts. 183(5) and 299 EC). (For an interpretation by the ECJ of Art. 176 of Council Dec. 86/283 of 30 June 1986, *OJ* 1986 L175/1, which previously covered the right of establishment in OCTs, see Cases C-100/89 etc. *Kaefer and Procacci* [1990] ECR I-4647 at pp. I-4671–4 and Case C-263/88 *Commission* v. *France* [1990] ECR I-4611 at pp. I-4622–3. For the territorial scope of application of the EC Treaty, *see further under* **Free movement of persons**, section I.2(*c*).)

2. The General Programme. The second category of Community provisions relating to establishment consists of one single instrument: the General Programme for the abolition of restrictions on freedom of establishment, adopted by the Council on 18 December 1961 under Art. 54(1) of the original EEC Treaty (*OJ Sp. Edn.* 2nd Ser. (IX), p. 7). After defining the beneficiaries (see section II below), the General Programme lays down a timetable for the abolition of specified restrictions on freedom of establishment (see section IV below) and on entry and residence, in respect of a number of activities listed in five Annexes. The abolition of restrictions was usually to be either preceded, accompanied, or followed by the mutual recognition of the relevant qualifications and by the co-ordination of national provisions concerning the taking up and pursuit of these activities, as provided for by the original Art. 57 [now Art. 47] (see Title V of the General Programme).

The legal nature of the General Programme is not entirely clear. It is not one of the binding or non-binding measures listed in Art. 249 EC. Nevertheless, in a number of cases the ECJ has relied on the General Programme, holding that it provides 'useful guidance for the implementation of the relevant provisions of the Treaty' (Case 71/76 *Thieffry*, above, at p. 777; Case 197/84 *Steinhauser*, above, at p. 1827; Case 79/85 *Segers* [1986] ECR 2375 at p. 2388. See also the cases cited in section IV below).

3. The directives. The third category of provisions is made up of a large number of directives adopted for the implementation of Arts. 43 *et seq.* and of the General Programme, most (but not all) of which also apply to freedom to provide services. These directives may be divided into three broad groups.

First, directives concerning the entry and residence of nationals of other Member States and the members of their families. The most important of these, currently in force, are as follows:

- Council Dir. 64/221 of 25 February 1964 on the co-ordination of special measures concerning the movement and residence of foreign nationals which are justified on grounds of public policy, public security, or public health (*OJ Sp. Edn.* 1963–4, p. 117);
- Council Dir. 73/148 of 21 May 1973 on the abolition of restrictions on movement and residence within the Community for nationals of Member States with regard to establishment and the provision of services (*OJ* 1973 L172/14);
- Council Dir. 75/34 of 17 December 1974 concerning the right of nationals of a Member State to remain in the territory of another Member State after having pursued therein an activity in a self-employed capacity (*OJ* 1975 L14/10);
- Council Dir. 75/35 of 17 December 1974 extending the scope of Dir. 64/221 to include nationals of a Member State who exercise the right to remain in the territory of another Member State after having pursued therein an activity in a self-employed capacity (*OJ* 1975 L14/14);
- Dir. 2004/38 of the European Parliament and of the Council of 29 April 2004 on the right of citizens of the Union and their family members to move and reside freely within the territory of the Member States (*OJ* 2004 L158/77). The directive entered into force on 30 April 2004, and has to be implemented by the Member States by 30 April 2006. It will repeal and replace all of the above directives and some others from that date (Arts. 38, 40, and 41. *See further under* **Right of entry and residence**, section VII).

Since the rights guaranteed by these directives are the same as, or similar to, those enjoyed by workers, providers and recipients of services, and their family members, they are discussed in separate entries (*see further under*

Expulsion, Residence permit, Right of entry and residence, Right to leave, Right to remain).

Secondly, directives adopted for the implementation of the General Programme and designed to facilitate the effective exercise of the right of establishment (and freedom to provide services). These covered a wide range of industrial, commercial, and small craft activities, such as manufacturing and processing activities including agriculture; service activities including insurance, banking, stock exchanges and other securities markets, transport, real property, leisure, personnel, and other services; business activities; self-employed activities; medical and para-medical activities; and other activities. They provided either for liberalization or for transitional measures pending mutual recognition of qualifications and co-ordination of national provisions relating to the taking up and pursuit of those activities. Normally, they provided for the mutual recognition of occupational experience (rather than of formal qualifications) acquired in the Member State of origin. As seen above, in so far as these directives required the abolition of discrimination based on nationality, they were 'superseded' by the direct effect of Art. 43 after the end of the transitional period, although in other respects they still remained relevant (see, e.g. Cases C-330/90 etc. *López Brea* [1992] ECR I-323 at p. I-331 *per* A.-G. Jacobs). Thirty-five of these directives, adopted between 1963 and 1982, were repealed and replaced by Dir. 1999/42, which consolidated their main provisions into a single text (see further section IV.2(*b*) below).

Thirdly, directives adopted under Art. 47(1) and (2) for the mutual recognition of qualifications and for the co-ordination of national provisions concerning the taking up and pursuit of activities as self-employed persons, respectively. These directives include both 'sectoral' and 'general' mutual recognition directives (see further section IV.2(*a*) and (*b*) below).

Finally, it should be noted that in the field of freedom of establishment no general implementing regulation has been adopted similar to Reg. 1612/68, which gives effect to the rules of the Treaty concerning the free movement of workers (*OJ Sp. Edn.* 1968 (II), p. 475). However, the ECJ's case-law shows that many of the social rights provided for by Reg. 1612/68 in respect of workers and their families also apply to self-employed persons (see section III below).

II. Beneficiaries

The beneficiaries of the right of establishment may be divided into two groups: natural persons (individuals) and companies or firms, as defined in Art. 48, which are to be treated in the same way as natural persons. In this and the following two sections only natural persons are considered; the right of establishment of companies is discussed in section V.

As opposed to employed persons, whose position is governed by the Chapter on 'Workers' (Arts. 39 to 42), the beneficiaries of the right of establishment are self-employed persons. Although this concept is not defined by Art. 43 or the implementing legislation (except for the purposes of social security, see Art. 1(a) of Reg. 1408/71, *OJ Sp. Edn.* 1971 (II), p. 416, as amended, *see further under* **Social security**), it may generally be said that it includes such persons as professionals (lawyers, doctors, veterinary surgeons, accountants, etc.), businessmen, employers, company directors and managers, tradesmen, craftsmen, artists, writers, actors, etc., in so far as they do not carry out their activities in the context of an employment relationship, that is, they do not work for and under the direction of another person in return for remuneration (see e.g. Case C-107/94 *Asscher*, above, at p. I-3121, where the director and sole shareholder of a company was treated as a self-employed person, or Case C-53/95 *Kemmler*, above, at p. I-714, involving a self-employed lawyer established in two Member States. For the position of the family members of these beneficiaries, *see further under* **Right of entry and residence**, section II).

To benefit from the provisions of the Treaty concerning freedom of establishment, natural persons must be nationals of a Member State of the Community (Art. 43 EC; Case C-147/91 *Ferrer Laderer* [1992] ECR I-4097 at p. I-4115). For the purposes of setting up a primary establishment (chambers, surgery, office, workshop, company, etc.), this is the only requirement laid down by Community law. For the purposes of setting up a secondary establishment (an agency, branch, or subsidiary), there is the additional requirement that nationals of a Member State must be already established in the territory of a Member State (Art. 43; see also Title I of the General Programme). Nationals of third countries may benefit from the right of establishment under any relevant international agreement concluded by the Community with their country of origin (*see further under* **Free movement of persons**, section V).

Generally, the question whether an individual possesses the nationality of a Member State must be determined solely by reference to the national law of the Member State concerned (see the 'Declaration on Nationality of a Member State' annexed to the TEU). If a person is able to produce one of the documents required by Community law (a valid identity card or passport, see Arts. 3 and 6 of Dir. 73/148) to prove that he is a national of a Member State, other Member States are not entitled to dispute that status. Thus, they cannot prevent that person from exercising the freedom of establishment or any other basic freedom guaranteed by Community law, on grounds of their own domestic law (e.g. because the person is also a national of a non-Member State, the nationality of which takes precedence over the nationality of the Member State concerned under the legislation of the host State, see Case C-369/90 *Micheletti* [1992] ECR I-4239 at pp. I-4262–3). The fact that a person has dual nationality, being the national of both the host Member State and another Member State, may also not give rise to any restriction on freedom of establishment (Case 292/86 *Gullung* [1988] ECR 111 at p. 136). The time at which and the manner in which an individual acquires the nationality of a Member State (e.g. by naturalization) are irrelevant so long as he possesses that nationality when he wishes to exercise the right of establishment (Case 136/78 *Auer I*, above, at p. 450).

In accordance with the rules of public international law, the definition of the conditions governing the acquisition and loss of nationality by individuals falls within the competence of each Member State. However, the ECJ has pointed out that in exercising that competence, the Member States must have 'due regard' to Community law (Case C-369/90 *Micheletti*, above, at p. I-4262). Thus, the Court has stated, 'it is not permissible for a Member State to restrict the effects of the grant of the nationality of another Member State by imposing an additional condition for recognition of that nationality with a view to the exercise of the fundamental freedoms provided for in the Treaty' (Case C-148/02 *Garcia Avello* [2003] ECR I-11613, para. 28).

The same applies to the determination of the conditions for the grant of 'nationality' to ships, i.e. the conditions that must be fulfilled in order for a ship to be registered in the register of a Member State and granted the right to fly its flag, which right implies 'nationality'. Consequently, in defining these conditions, each Member State must comply with the prohibition of discrimination against the nationals of the other Member States on grounds of their nationality, which is a basic rule of Community law in general and of Art. 43 in particular. Therefore, the Court has held that it is contrary to Art. 43 for a Member State to stipulate as conditions for the registration of a fishing vessel in its register that the owners, charterers, managers, and operators of the vessel must be nationals of, and resident and domiciled in, that Member State or companies incorporated in that State. However, it is not contrary to Art. 43 to require that the vessel must be managed and its operations directed and controlled from within that Member State, since those requirements are inherent in the concept of establishment within the meaning of Art. 43, which implies a fixed establishment (Case C-221/89 *Factortame II*, above, at pp. I-3963–4 and I-3966–8; see also Case C-246/89 *Commission* v. *United Kingdom*, above, at pp. I-4612 and I-4615; Case C-334/94 *Commission* v. *France*, above, at pp. I-1339–41).

The actual wording of Art. 43(1) provides for the abolition of 'restrictions on the freedom of establishment of nationals of a Member State *in the territory of another Member State*' (emphasis added). According to Art. 43(2), freedom of establishment includes the right to take up activities as self-employed persons under the conditions laid down by the law of the host country 'for its own nationals'. A strict interpretation of these provisions would mean that the nationals of the host Member State could not be regarded, in their own country, as being beneficiaries of the various liberalization measures introduced under the Treaty, and that they would remain entirely subject to the provisions of their national legislation.

However, in Case 115/78 *Knoors* [1979] ECR 399 at pp. 409–11, the Court rejected such a narrow interpretation. The case involved a Netherlands national residing in Belgium who wished to establish himself in the Netherlands as a plumbing contractor on the basis of a trade qualification acquired in Belgium and recognized by a Community directive. The Court relied on Title I of the General Programme, which designates as beneficiaries the 'nationals of Member States' without any distinction as regards nationality or residence. The Court also pointed out that freedom of movement for persons, freedom of establishment and freedom to provide services, which are fundamental in the Community system, could not be fully realized if the Member States were able to refuse to grant the benefit of Community provisions to those of their nationals who have exercised one of those freedoms and have thereby acquired trade qualifications, recognized by a directive, in a Member State other than that whose nationality they possess. In particular, the Court stated that:

> Although it is true that the provisions of the Treaty relating to establishment and the provision of services cannot be applied to situations which are purely internal to a Member State, the position nevertheless remains that the reference in Article 43 to 'nationals of a Member State' who wish to establish themselves 'in the territory of another Member State' cannot be interpreted in such a way as to exclude from the benefit of Community law a given Member State's own nationals when the latter, owing to the fact that they have lawfully resided on the territory of another Member State and have there acquired a trade qualification which is recognized by the provisions of Community law, are, with regard to their State of origin, in a situation which may be assimilated to that of any other persons enjoying the rights and liberties guaranteed by the Treaty (ibid. at p. 410).

On the basis of the above considerations, the Court held that the nationals of all Member States must be able to rely on the liberalization measures laid down by a Community directive, provided that they come objectively within one of the situations defined by the directive, and that no differentiation of treatment on the basis of their residence or nationality is permitted. Thus, nationals of all Member States, including the host State, are beneficiaries of such measures and they may invoke the relevant directive even against the State whose nationality they possess. Nevertheless, the Court recognized the legitimate interests of Member States in preventing their nationals from attempting to evade the application of their national legislation as regards training for a trade, by making use of the freedoms created by the Treaty.

In subsequent cases, the Court has extended the *Knoors* principle to professional and vocational qualifications, holding that university and other diplomas obtained in another Member State and recognized by a Community directive may be relied on by individuals wishing to establish themselves in the Member State of which they are nationals (see Case 246/80 *Broekmeulen* [1981] ECR 2311 at pp. 2329–31, concerning a Netherlands national holding a Belgian diploma of medicine and wishing to establish himself in the Netherlands; Case 271/82 *Auer II* [1983] ECR 2727 at pp. 2744–5, concerning a French national holding an Italian diploma of veterinary medicine and intending to practise in France; Case C-61/89 *Bouchoucha* [1990] ECR I-3551 at pp. I-3567–8, involving a French national established in France but holding a diploma in osteopathy issued in the United Kingdom. In this last case, the diploma in question was not recognized by Community law and therefore the holder could not rely on it. See also Case C-19/92 *Kraus* [1993] ECR I-1663 at pp. I-1693–4, see section IV.2 below).

In the light of the Court's case-law, it may thus be generally stated that the rules of the Treaty on freedom of establishment and the provisions of the relevant secondary legislation may be relied on not only by a national of a Member State against another Member State in whose territory he seeks to establish himself or is already established, but also by a national of a Member State against his State of origin where he is (also) established if he is in a situation which can be assimilated to any of the situations envisaged by Community law, i.e., generally, once he has exercised the right to freedom of movement under the Treaty (Case C-147/91 *Ferrer Laderer*, above, at p. I-4115; Case C-107/94 *Asscher*, above, at pp. I-3122–3).

Moreover, Art. 43 may be relied on not only against laws and regulations enacted by Member States, but also against rules adopted by associations and organizations that do not form part of the State, e.g. national or local Bars, where such rules are designed to regulate, collectively, self-employment (and the provision of services). In several cases, the ECJ has pointed out that the abolition, as between Member States, of obstacles to freedom of movement for persons (whether they are workers, self-employed persons, or providers of services) would be compromised if the abolition of State barriers could be neutralized by obstacles resulting from the exercise of their legal autonomy by associations or organizations not governed by public law (Case C-309/99 *Wouters* [2002] ECR I-1577 at p. I-1694. The earlier cases referred to by the Court in its judgment involved workers and providers of services).

On the other hand, Arts. 43 *et seq.* do not apply to situations that are purely internal to a Member State, such as that of a national of a Member State who has never resided, worked, or acquired training/qualification in any other Member State. The reason is that there is no connecting factor between such situations and those envisaged by Community law (see e.g. Case 115/78 *Knoors*, above, at p. 410; Case 20/87 *Gauchard* [1987] ECR 4879 at p. 4896; Case 204/87 *Bekaert* [1988] ECR 2029 at p. 2039; Cases C-54/88 etc. *Nino* [1990] ECR I-3537 at p. I-3549).

A situation is not purely internal where a national of a Member State who is or intends to be established in his own country holds a trade, professional, or vocational qualification issued in another Member State (see above), or has already exercised freedom of movement and has previously been employed in another Member State as a worker (Case C-370/90 *Singh* [1992] ECR I-4265 at pp. I-4294–5). The fact alone that an individual resides in another Member State does not alter his situation as being purely internal to his State of origin if he has acquired his qualifications, has always carried on his professional activities and earns all or almost all of his income in the latter State (Case C-112/91 *Werner* [1993] ECR I-429 at p. I-470).

Although the Treaty provisions on the free movement of persons cannot be applied to activities that are confined in all respects within a single Member State, this is not the case with regard to harmonization directives, which may be applicable to purely internal situations. Nevertheless, a directive that merely requires the abolition of discrimination based on nationality but does not aim to harmonize or co-ordinate the conditions laid down by national law for access to and the pursuit of a certain occupation or profession, does not apply to purely internal situations (Cases C-330/90 etc. *López Brea*, above, at pp. I-336–8 *per Curiam*, pp. I-330–2 *per* A.-G. Jacobs, dealing with estate agents in Spain; Cases C-29/94 etc. *Aubertin* [1995] ECR I-301 at p. I-316, dealing with hairdressers in France).

III. Prohibition of discrimination

As seen in section I above, Art. 43 pursues a double objective. The first is the prohibition (originally the abolition) of restrictions on the freedom of establishment of Community nationals (Art. 43(1)). The second is the equal treatment of nationals and non-nationals as regards the taking up and pursuit of activities as self-employed persons (Art. 43(2)). The two objectives are closely connected as any discrimination on grounds of nationality at the same time constitutes a restriction on freedom of establishment and, conversely, most (although not all) restrictions arise from discriminatory treatment of foreign nationals (Case 136/78 *Auer I*, above, at pp. 448–9; Case 270/83 *Commission* v. *France*, above, at pp. 302–3). Prohibition of discrimination is considered here, prohibition of restrictions in the following section (on the concept of discrimination, *see also under* **Free movement of persons**, section I.4).

1. **Direct discrimination.** Art. 12 EC prohibits any direct discrimination on grounds of nationality within the whole field of application of the Treaty. In several cases, the ECJ has stressed that this rule is 'one of the fundamental legal provisions of the Community', which has been implemented in the special sphere of the right of establishment by Art. 43. The latter Article expresses the 'guiding principle' that, as regards the right of establishment, Member States must accord to nationals of other Member States the same treatment as they accord to their own nationals. Accordingly, discrimination occurs where the nationals of other Member States are put in a situation which, in law or in fact, is less advantageous than the situation of the nationals of the host Member State who are in similar circumstances. Discrimination is prohibited whether it results from laws, rules, regulations, or practices of the central Government, of regional or local authorities, of professional bodies, or of other private organizations of whatever nature, as long as it is based on the criterion of nationality (Case 2/74 *Reyners*, above, at pp. 650–1; Case 90/76 *Van Ameyde* [1977] ECR 1091 at pp. 1126–7; Case 197/84 *Steinhauser*, above, at pp. 1826–7; Case C-168/91 *Konstantinidis* [1993] ECR I-1191 at p. I-1218; see also the cases cited below).

Since Art. 12 is implemented in the field of the right of establishment by Art. 43, Art. 12 applies independently only to situations not covered by the latter Article (Case 63/86 *Commission* v. *Italy* [1988] ECR 29 at p. 52; Case 305/87 *Commission* v. *Greece* [1989] ECR 1461 at pp. 1476–7; Case C-1/93 *Halliburton Services* [1994] ECR I-1137 at p. I-1155). From the end of the transitional period, Art. 43 has been directly effective and thus the prohibition of discrimination may be invoked by individuals before national courts even in the absence of implementing directives in a particular area (see section I above, and in particular Case 2/74 *Reyners*, above, at pp. 651–2. The case concerned a Netherlands national who, although the holder of a Belgian law degree giving him the right to take up the profession of *avocat* in Belgium, was excluded from that profession by reason of his nationality. In the absence of any directive on the legal profession, he could rely on Art. 43 directly. See also Case 11/77 *Patrick*, above, at pp. 1204–5, etc.).

In the context of the right of establishment of individuals, the rule on non-discrimination or equal treatment means, in the first place, that nationals of all Member States must be guaranteed access to activities as self-employed persons on conditions defined by the legislation of the host Member State for its own nationals. Additional conditions related to nationality cannot be imposed. Thus, in a number of cases, the ECJ has held that a Member State which:

- subjects access to certain occupations by nationals of other Member States to a condition of reciprocity;
- makes the possession of its own nationality a condition for access to and exercise of certain professions and activities;
- permits only its own nationals to set up certain establishments or to take part in competitions for the award of licences to carry on certain businesses;
- restricts to its own nationals the possibility of obtaining recognition of foreign qualifications necessary for the pursuit of certain occupations;
- makes it more difficult for the nationals of other Member States to register as members of professional bodies where such registration is a precondition for and facilitates access to and exercise of the professions concerned;
- requires directors and managers of certain undertakings to reside within its territory;
- requires that only nationals of other Member States, not including its own nationals, reside within its territory in order to be entitled to the requisite authorization to take up and pursue certain activities

fails to fulfil its obligations under Art. 43 (Case 159/78 *Commission* v. *Italy* [1979] ECR 3247 at pp. 3263–4 (customs agents); Case 168/85 *Commission* v. *Italy* [1986] ECR 2945 at p. 2961 (journalists, pharmacists, tourist guides, etc.); Case 147/86 *Commission* v. *Greece* [1988] ECR 1637 at pp. 1655–6 (private teachers); Case 38/87 *Commission* v. *Greece* [1988] ECR 4415 at pp. 4429–31 (architects, civil engineers, surveyors, and lawyers); Case C-58/90 *Commission* v. *Italy* [1991] ECR I-4193 at p. I-4202 (health-care auxiliaries); Case C-375/92 *Commission* v. *Spain* [1994] ECR I-923 at p. I-940 (tourist guides and guide-interpreters); Case C-114/97 *Commission* v. *Spain* [1998] ECR I-6717 at pp. I-6744–5 (private security undertakings and staff); Case C-162/99 *Commission* v. *Italy* [2001] ECR I-541 at p. I-569 (dentists); Case C-263/99 *Commission* v. *Italy* [2001] ECR I-4195 at p. I-4212 (transport consultants)).

The same is also the case where a Member State:

- stipulates as conditions for the registration of a vessel in its national register (whether or not the vessel is used for the pursuit of an economic activity) that the owners, charterers, managers, and operators of the vessel must be nationals of, and/or resident, domiciled or established in, that Member State or companies incorporated in that State (Case C-221/89 *Factortame II*, above, at p. I-3967; Case C-246/89 *Commission* v. *United Kingdom*, above, at p. I-4615; Case C-334/94 *Commission* v. *France*, above, at pp. I-1340–1; subsequently the Court extended this principle to the registration of aircraft, see Case C-203/98 *Commission* v. *Belgium*, above, at p. I-4910), or

- requires nationals of other Member States who own fishing vessels registered in its register to set up a company governed by its law in order to obtain a fishing licence, if such a requirement is not imposed on its own nationals (Case C-93/89 *Commission* v. *Ireland* [1991] ECR I-4569 at p. I-4583).

Prohibited discrimination occurs also where a Member State stipulates that a certain activity (e.g. the activity of dealing in transferable securities) may be carried on only in the form of a company or firm whose registered office (i.e. principal establishment) is in its territory. Such a rule prevents dealers from other Member States from making use of certain forms of secondary establishment, such as a branch or agency, and thus discriminates against them by causing them to incur additional costs (i.e. the cost of setting up a new company) that its own dealers do not have to bear. Such a requirement may not be justified by the need for the effective supervision, control, and sanctioning of the activity in question, if these objectives can be achieved by less restrictive measures (Case C-101/94 *Commission* v. *Italy* [1996] ECR I-2691 at pp. I-2723–7).

However, the prohibition of discrimination is not confined to the specific rules concerning access to and pursuit of occupational activities. Discrimination is also prohibited in respect of the various general facilities which are of assistance in the pursuit of those activities, such as:

- the right to acquire, use or dispose of movable or immovable property in the territory of the host State;
- the right to obtain loans and to have access to the various forms of credit;
- the right to rent premises for business purposes and to participate in a tendering procedure for the allocation of public property for this purpose;
- the right to certain social benefits, such as childbirth and maternity allowances, special benefits for large families;
- taxation of income, etc.

Relying on Art. 44(2)(e) EC and on the General Programme, the ECJ has emphasized that these rights are the corollary of freedom of establishment. Therefore, the Court has said, a national of a Member State who wishes to pursue an activity as a self-employed person in another Member State must be able to obtain housing, even social housing, under the same conditions as the nationals of the host State, including the various financial facilities available for this purpose. Legislation which restricts the right to purchase or lease housing built or renovated with the help of public funds, and to obtain reduced-rate mortgage loans, to nationals of the host State or which in general makes the exercise of the right to purchase or use immovable property by nationals of other Member States subject to restrictions not imposed on local nationals, is contrary to the fundamental principle of non-discrimination laid down in Art. 43 (Case 63/86 *Commission* v. *Italy*, above, at pp. 52–3; Case 305/87 *Commission* v. *Greece*, above, at pp. 1478–9; see also Case 197/84 *Steinhauser*, above, at p. 1827 declaring the exclusion of foreign nationals from a tendering procedure for the allocation of public property used for business purposes to be contrary to Art. 43).

Discrimination in respect of other social benefits, such as childbirth and maternity allowances, special benefits for large families, is also prohibited under Art. 43 (Case C-111/91 *Commission* v. *Luxembourg* [1993] ECR I-817 at pp. I-844–5 and I-848; Case C-185/96 *Commission* v. *Greece* [1998] ECR I-6601 at pp. I-6623–4). Access to leisure activities is also regarded as a corollary to freedom of establishment, which must be available without discrimination (Case C-334/94 *Commission* v. *France*, above, at p. I-1341 concerning registration of a leisure craft. For other instances of prohibited discrimination, see e.g. Case C-34/98 *Commission* v. *France* [2000] ECR I-995; Case C-169/98 *Commission* v. *France* [2000] ECR I-1049).

2. Indirect discrimination. Art. 43 prohibits not only direct or overt discrimination based on nationality, but also all indirect (covert or disguised) forms of discrimination which, by the application of other criteria of differentiation, lead in fact to the same result, unless they are objectively justified. Thus, Title III (B) of the General Programme provides for the elimination of any requirements imposed by law or in practice in respect of the taking up or pursuit of an activity as a self-employed person where, although applicable irrespective of nationality, their effect is 'exclusively or principally, to hinder the taking up or pursuit of such activity by foreign nationals' (see also Case 71/76 *Thieffry*, above, at p. 777). Such covert discrimination often arises from legislation that, although applicable without distinction to all nationals, local and foreign, essentially favours the nationals of the host Member State by laying down conditions, e.g. a residence requirement, which can be more easily satisfied by them than by nationals of other Member States (see e.g. Case C-3/88 *Commission* v. *Italy* [1989] ECR 4035 at p. 4059 and Case C-272/91 *Commission* v. *Italy* [1994] ECR I-1409 at pp. I-1433–6, concerning Italian legislation restricting participation in certain contracts with the State to companies whose shares were in Italian public ownership; Case C-111/91 *Commission* v. *Luxembourg*, above, at pp. I-844–5 and I-848, concerning Luxembourg legislation imposing residence requirements for the grant of childbirth and maternity allowances; Case C-337/97 *Meeusen* [1999] ECR I-3289 at pp. I-3313, I-3315, concerning Netherlands legislation imposing a residence requirement for the grant of study finance only on the children of nationals of other Member States).

3. Tax discrimination. Discrimination, whether direct or indirect, is also prohibited in the field of taxation. As the ECJ has pointed out on a number of occasions, 'although direct taxation falls within the competence of the Member States, the latter must nonetheless exercise that competence consistently with Community law and therefore avoid any overt or covert discrimination by reason of nationality' (Case C-80/94 *Wielockx* [1995] ECR I-2493 at p. I-2514; see also the cases cited immediately below). Since in relation to direct taxes the situations of residents and non-residents in a Member State are not generally comparable, a difference in treatment between those two categories of taxpayers cannot in itself be regarded as discrimination within the meaning of the Treaty. However, a non-resident taxpayer, whether employed or self-employed, who receives all or almost all of his income in the State where he works or is established, is objectively in the same situation as regards income tax as a resident of that State who carries on the same activity there. Both are taxed in that State alone and their taxable income is the same. In such circumstances, a non-resident taxpayer must be given the same tax treatment in respect of deductions from his taxable income as a resident taxpayer (ibid. at pp. I-2515–16).

The application of a higher rate of income tax to non-residents than is applicable to residents pursuing the same activity constitutes prohibited indirect discrimination, unless objectively justified, even if the legislation applies irrespective of the nationality of the taxpayer. Such legislation is liable to act mainly to the detriment of nationals of other Member States, since non-residents are most frequently non-nationals (Case C-107/94 *Asscher*, above, at pp. I-3124–7). Tax discrimination is also prohibited where it is based not on the nationality or residence of taxpayers but on the seat of the companies of which they are shareholders (Case C-251/98 *Baars*, above, at p. I-2817, involving Netherlands legislation that granted to Community nationals residing in the Netherlands exemption from wealth tax in respect of assets invested in shares in companies established in the Netherlands, but denied that exemption to holders of shares in companies established in other Member States).

4. Objective justification. Discrimination is not contrary to the Treaty if it is 'objectively justified'. According to the Court's case-law, national rules that are directly discriminatory on grounds of nationality are compatible with Community law only if they can be brought within the scope of an express derogation, such as that contained in Art. 45 (exercise of official authority) or Art. 46 EC. The latter allows special (i.e. discriminatory) treatment of foreign nationals and companies on grounds of public policy, public security, or public health (but not on grounds of cultural policy). Economic aims cannot constitute grounds of public policy within the meaning of that provision (Case 352/85 *Bond van Adverteerders* [1988] ECR 2085 at pp. 2134–5; Case C-260/89 *ERT* [1991] ECR I-2925 at p. I-2960; Case C-288/89 *Gouda* [1991] ECR I-4007 at p. I-4040; etc. These cases concerned provision of services, but the principle is the same in the case of establishment), but the need to combat abuse and fraud can (Case 79/85

Segers, above, at p. 2388. *See further under* **Official authority, Public health, Public policy, Public security**).

National rules which are indirectly discriminatory, i.e. which apply without distinction to all nationals but essentially favour the nationals of the host Member State in some way, may be justified only by overriding reasons based on the general interest and if they are suitable for securing the attainment of the objective that they pursue and do not go beyond what is necessary to attain that objective (see in general Case C-55/94 *Gebhard*, above, at pp. I-4197–9; see section IV.3 below). Where it cannot be shown that 'indistinctly applicable' legislation puts exclusively or mainly foreign nationals at a disadvantage, or that such legislation was adopted for discriminatory purposes or otherwise produces discriminatory effects that are not objectively justified, there is no prohibited indirect discrimination (Case 143/87 *Stanton* [1988] ECR 3877 at pp. 3893–4; Case 221/85 *Commission* v. *Belgium* [1987] ECR 719 at p. 737; see also Case 182/83 *Fearon* [1984] ECR 3677 at pp. 3685–6, holding that Art. 43 does not prohibit a Member State from making exemption from compulsory acquisition of rural land subject to a requirement of residence on or near the land, if that requirement applies irrespective of nationality and is objectively justified).

Discriminatory tax legislation may be justified, in particular, on the following grounds: the need to safeguard the cohesion of the tax system (Case C-204/90 *Bachmann* [1992] ECR I-249 at pp. I-282–4; Case C-300/90 *Commission* v. *Belgium* [1992] ECR I-305 at pp. I-319–21); the prevention of tax evasion; and the effectiveness of fiscal supervision, but not on the ground of prevention of a reduction in tax revenue (see Case C-436/00 *X and Y II* [2002] ECR I-10829, paras. 50–1, and the cases cited therein and also the cases cited above in the context of discriminatory taxation, where the Court did not accept arguments based on these grounds).

5. Reverse discrimination. Since Art. 43 does not apply to purely internal situations (see section II above), it does not preclude 'reverse discrimination', i.e. the imposition by a Member State of stricter conditions on its own nationals who have never worked or resided abroad than on the nationals of other Member States. Thus, in the absence of harmonization or co-ordination measures at the Community level, it is not contrary to Art. 43 for a Member State to require its own nationals to hold a diploma as a condition for pursuing a certain occupation, while permitting nationals of other Member States to pursue the same occupation without holding such a diploma (Cases C-29/94 etc. *Aubertin*, above, at p. I-316, dealing with hairdressers in France; see also Cases C-330/90 etc. *López Brea*, above, at pp. I-336–8); nor to impose on its nationals a heavier tax burden if they do not reside in the national territory than if they do (Case C-112/91 *Werner*, above, at p. I-470).

6. Differences in national legislation. Arts. 12 and 43 are not concerned with any disparities in treatment that may result, between Member States, from differences in existing legislation. Therefore, they do not prohibit the application of stricter rules in one Member State than those applicable in another so long as those rules affect all persons in accordance with objective criteria and without regard to their nationality (Case C-177/94 *Perfili* [1996] ECR I-161 at pp. I-175–6).

IV. Prohibition of restrictions

1. Definition of restrictions. Title III (A) of the General Programme provides that, subject to the exceptions laid down in the Treaty, and in particular to Arts. 45 and 46, the following restrictions on freedom of establishment were to be eliminated in accordance with the timetable set out in Title IV: any measure, whether laid down by law or arising from administrative practice, which 'prohibits or hinders nationals of other Member States in their pursuit of an activity as a self-employed person by treating nationals of other Member States differently from nationals of the country concerned'. The Programme then goes on to provide a non-exhaustive list of such restrictive provisions and practices. They include those which, in respect of foreign nationals only:

- prohibit, or make subject to an authorization or to a period of prior residence or training in the host country, or make more costly through taxation or other financial burdens, the taking up or pursuit of an activity as a self-employed person (points (a) to (e));
- limit or hinder access to sources of supply, to distribution outlets, or to any necessary or useful vocational training (points (f) and (g));
- prohibit membership of companies or firms or restrict the rights arising from such membership (point (h));
- deny or restrict the right to participate in social security schemes (point (i); invoked by the ECJ in Case 79/85 *Segers*, above, at p. 2388; see further section V.2 below);
- grant less favourable treatment in the event of nationalization, expropriation or requisition (point (j); relied on by the ECJ in Case 182/83 *Fearon*, above, at p. 3685, dealing with compulsory acquisition of rural land in Ireland).

Similarly, in accordance with a second list, provisions and practices were also to be abolished that, in respect of foreign nationals only, exclude, limit, or impose conditions on the power to exercise rights normally attaching to the activity of a self-employed person, and in particular the power:

- to enter into contracts of various types, to submit tenders and to obtain licences or authorizations (points (a) to (c); relied on by the ECJ in Case 197/84 *Steinhauser*, above, at p. 1827, where a German national was excluded from a tendering procedure in France for the allocation of public property used for business purposes);
- to acquire, use, or dispose of movable or immovable property and intellectual property rights, and to borrow and have access to the various forms of credit (points (d) to (f); see also Art. 44(2)(e) EC which refers to the right of EC nationals to acquire and use land and buildings situated in the territory of another Member State. These provisions

were invoked by the ECJ in the above case and also in Case 63/86 *Commission* v. *Italy*, above, at pp. 52–3 and in Case 305/87 *Commission* v. *Greece*, above, at pp. 1478–9; both cases involved restrictions on the acquisition or use of immovable property by foreign nationals);

- to receive aids granted by the State; to be a party to legal or administrative proceedings and to join professional or trade organizations (points (g) to (i)).

It is apparent from the above provisions that the General Programme envisages solely the abolition of restrictions that result from measures or practices discriminating, directly or indirectly, against the nationals of other Member States (see also Cases C-330/90 etc. *López Brea*, above, at p. I-337 *per Curiam*, p. I-331 *per* A.-G. Jacobs). It is clear, however, as the case-law of the Court to be discussed below shows, that restrictions on the right of establishment prohibited by Art. 43 may also arise from non-discriminatory measures, i.e. those which apply to both nationals and non-nationals without distinction, where they have the effect of unjustifiably hindering the latter in the exercise of their right of establishment guaranteed by Art. 43 (see the opinions of A.-G. Van Gerven in Case C-340/89 *Vlassopoulou* [1991] ECR I-2357 at p. I-2370 and of A.-G. Jacobs in Case C-168/91 *Konstantinidis*, above, at p. I-1212. See also the argument put forward by the Commission, but rejected by A.-G. Lenz, in Case 221/85 *Commission* v. *Belgium*, above, at pp. 730–2 and 736. The case concerned Belgian legislation on the operation of clinical biology laboratories. The Court found that the legislation in question was not contrary to Art. 43, ibid. at p. 737). As the Court of Justice itself has pointed out:

> freedom of establishment is not completely ensured by the mere application of the rule of national treatment, as such application retains all obstacles other than those resulting from the non-possession of the nationality of the host State and, in particular, those resulting from the disparity of the conditions laid down by the different national laws for the acquisition of an appropriate professional qualification (Case 136/78 *Auer I*, above, at p. 449).

The reason is that the 'rule of national treatment', i.e. the requirement set out in Art. 43(2) that nationals of other Member States must be able to establish themselves 'under the conditions laid down for its own nationals by the law of the [host] country' has two sides. On the one hand, it guarantees that non-nationals are not placed at a disadvantage as compared with nationals. On the other, it also means that non-nationals must comply with the same rules and conditions as nationals as regards access to and pursuit of a trade or profession, which rules and conditions each Member State is free to lay down in the absence of Community provisions. These rules, even if applied without discrimination based on nationality, may produce an unjustified restriction on the movement of (self-employed) persons from one Member State to another and, if they do, they clearly fall within the scope of Art. 43(1). This prohibits *all* such restrictions, not only those which result from discriminatory measures.

It is therefore more correct to interpret the two paragraphs of Art. 43 as laying down two separate (although in practice closely connected) obligations, i.e. the abolition of restrictions on freedom of establishment and the equal treatment of nationals and non-nationals, rather than regarding the former as being part of, or automatically following from, the latter. It follows that national legislation may only be said to be fully compatible with Art. 43 if it satisfies both requirements. While the statement, sometimes made by the Court, that if national rules 'are compatible with Article 43 . . . they are also compatible with Article 12' (the general rule on non-discrimination) is certainly correct (see Case 90/76 *Van Ameyde*, above, at p. 1126; Case C-112/91 *Werner*, above, at p. I-471), the opposite formulation that 'any rules incompatible with [Art. 43] are also incompatible with Article 12' (see Case 305/87 *Commission* v. *Greece*, above, at p. 1476) does not seem to take account of the fact that Art. 43 has a wider scope than Art. 12. A non-discriminatory rule that nevertheless has a restrictive effect on freedom of establishment may be perfectly compatible with Art. 12 while being incompatible with Art. 43 (see the cases discussed below).

In this respect, there has been a noticeable development in the jurisprudence of the Court of Justice. While the earlier cases concentrated on the rule of equal treatment in Art. 43(2), implying that Art. 43 may be satisfied if non-nationals are treated in a non-discriminatory manner, in subsequent cases there has been a tendency to give more and more weight to the prohibition of restrictions laid down in Art. 43(1). This development is also reflected in the Court's approach to the direct effect of Art. 43. As seen in section I above, the early cases established the direct effect of the rule on national (or equal) treatment only. In the more recent case-law to be considered below, reference is made in general terms to the direct effect of Art. 43 as a whole, clearly including the requirement that restrictions must be eliminated. Art. 43(1) therefore seems to be capable of being relied on by individuals in certain circumstances as much as Art. 43(2).

The most frequent, and most serious, restrictions on the right of establishment that cannot be eliminated merely by the equal treatment of nationals and non-nationals (precisely because they result from such equal treatment) fall into two broad categories. The first is the requirement that anyone wishing to exercise a trade or profession must possess the relevant qualifications prescribed by the law of the host State. The second is the requirement that any such person must comply with the rules and conditions laid down by the host State that govern access to and pursuit of his chosen trade or profession. Those two types of restriction, and certain others, are considered in turn below.

2. Professional qualifications. With a view to ensuring complete freedom of establishment, Art. 47(1) provides for the adoption of directives by the Council and Parliament for the 'mutual recognition of diplomas, certificates and other evidence of formal qualifications' (hereafter referred to as 'qualifications'), while Art. 47(2) provides for directives for the co-ordination of national provisions concerning access to and pursuit of activities as self-employed persons. The purpose of these directives is 'to make it easier' for individuals to carry on such activities in the other Member States.

(*a*) ***Mutual recognition of qualifications: the 'sectoral' directives.*** The directives adopted by the Community institutions under the above provisions fall into two categories: 'sectoral' and 'general' directives. Initially, the institutions pursued a policy of harmonization and co-ordination on a sector-by-sector basis. Accordingly, they made recognition of qualifications dependent on the prior harmonization of the conditions on the basis of which they were awarded. Usually two directives were issued at a time in respect of a particular profession. One (the co-ordination directive) co-ordinated the national rules for taking up and pursuing the profession in question, and also harmonized the minimum conditions of the education and training (e.g. the minimum training periods, method and place of training, supervision, examinations, etc.) which had to be completed in order to obtain the necessary qualifications to practice that profession. The other (the recognition directive) provided for the compulsory recognition by all Member States of the qualifications awarded in accordance with the prescribed conditions (which qualifications were listed in the directive), since they had the same value irrespective of the Member State in which they were acquired. Recognition directives normally also included measures to facilitate the effective exercise of the right of establishment (and freedom to provide services). 'Sectoral' directives adopted by this method cover the following professions (where there are two directives, the first deals with recognition and the second with co-ordination and harmonization):

- doctors (Dir. 93/16, *OJ* 1993 L165/1);
- nurses responsible for general care (Dirs. 77/452 and 77/453, *OJ* 1977 L176/1 and 8);
- dental practitioners (Dirs.78/686 and 78/687, *OJ* 1978 L233/1 and 10);
- veterinary surgeons (Dirs. 78/1026 and 78/1027, *OJ* 1978 L362/1 and 7);
- midwives (Dirs. 80/154 and 80/155, *OJ* 1980 L33/1 and 8);
- architects (Dir. 85/384, *OJ* 1985 L223/15);
- pharmacists (Dirs. 85/433 and 85/432, *OJ* 1985 L253/37 and 34).

These directives (which were amended by Dir. 2001/19, see below) have created a system of automatic and unconditional recognition in that each Member State is obliged to recognize the diplomas, certificates, and other evidence of formal qualifications awarded to Community nationals, including its own nationals, by the other Member States in accordance with the conditions laid down in those directives. Thus, each Member State must give such qualifications, as far as the right to exercise the profession in question is concerned, the same effect in its territory as the qualifications that the Member State itself awards. The basis of this obligation is the mutual trust that Member States have in the adequacy of qualifications awarded by other Member States, such trust being based on a training system the standards of which were determined by mutual agreement. Thus, a diploma awarded under these directives amounts to a 'passport' enabling the holder to practice his profession throughout the European Community, without the qualification attested to by the diploma being open to challenge in the host State except in specific circumstances laid down by Community law (Case C-110/01 *Tennah-Durez* [2003] ECR I-6239, paras. 30–2, 57; see also Case C-232/99 *Commission* v. *Spain* [2002] ECR I-4235, at p. I–4277. Both cases concerned Dir. 93/16 relating to doctors).

The ECJ has held that since these directives impose on each Member State clear, complete, precise, and unconditional obligations that exclude the possibility of discretionary assessments, individuals may rely before the national courts on the direct effect of such directives if the latter have not been implemented by the prescribed date or have been only partially implemented (Case 271/82 *Auer II*, above, at p. 2744, where a French national was able to enforce his right to practise veterinary medicine in France by virtue of a university degree acquired in Italy, *after* the date by which the relevant directives should have been implemented by France, but he could not rely on those directives *before* that date, see Case 136/78 *Auer I*, above, at p. 451; see also Case 5/83 *Rienks* [1983] ECR 4233 at p. 4245 where a Netherlands national could enforce his right to practise veterinary medicine in Italy by virtue of a university degree obtained in the Netherlands).

Since the right to practise flows directly from the recognition of qualifications obtained in accordance with a Community directive, it cannot be made subject to requirements other than those laid down by the directive. Thus, the host Member State cannot require the possession of any additional qualification obtained in that State, which is not provided for by the directive, such as the completion of a period of additional training, even if such further requirement is also imposed on holders of similar qualifications awarded within that State (Case 246/80 *Broekmeulen*, above, at pp. 2329–31, concerning the practice of general medicine in the Netherlands. See also Case C-238/98 *Hocsman* [2000] ECR I-6623 at p. I-6654; Case C-110/01 *Tennah-Durez*, above, para. 30).

The sectoral directives only provide for the automatic recognition of qualifications awarded to nationals of Member States by the authorities of Member States, and not by third countries. While Member States are free, in accordance with their own rules and in respect of their own territory, to recognize qualifications awarded by non-Member States, such recognition does not bind the other Member States. This is so even if the holder is a Community national and the qualification has been recognized by a Member States as equivalent to one awarded in that Member State and mentioned in a directive (Case C-154/93 *Tawil-Albertini* [1994] ECR I-451 at p. I-463; Case C-319/92 *Haim I* [1994] ECR I-425 at pp. I-446–7, both concerning recognition of qualifications in dentistry). Nevertheless, when dealing with a non-Community qualification recognized by other Member States and examining whether the training requirements prescribed by the national rules are satisfied, the authorities of the host State must take into account any relevant professional experience acquired by the holder in the host State or in another Member State (ibid. at p. I-448; Case C-238/98 *Hocsman*, above, at pp. I-6651–2).

While, to be automatically recognized, a diploma must be awarded by a Member State, the training leading to the diploma may, in the absence of a provision in the relevant directive to the contrary, comprise training received partly or even mainly in a third country, provided that the competent authority of the Member State awarding the diploma is in a position to validate that training and to conclude on that basis that it meets the requirements laid down by the directive. Any certificate issued by the competent authority to that effect is binding on the authorities of the host State, which may reopen the matter of verification only in the case of serious doubts (Case C-110/01 *Tennah-Durez*, above, paras. 49–70, 81, dealing with the doctors' directive).

(*b*) ***Mutual recognition of qualifications: the 'general' directives.*** The great advantage of the sectoral directives is that, because of the automatic and unconditional nature of recognition of qualifications, they enable the persons concerned to know precisely and in advance if a particular diploma gives them the right to take up and pursue the corresponding profession in other Member States (see Case C-232/99 *Commission* v. *Spain*, above, at p. I-4277). On the other hand, the disadvantage of this system is that the prior harmonization and co-ordination of national rules in respect of each and every profession, on which the system is based, is a cumbersome and time-consuming process that yields only very slow results. To speed up the process, in 1974 the Council adopted a resolution (*OJ* 1974 C98/1), which called for a more 'flexible and qualitative approach' based on directives which resort 'as little as possible to the prescription of detailed training requirements'. Thus, the policy of 'sectoral' harmonization and co-ordination was to be replaced by a 'general system of mutual recognition' of qualifications.

The first directive based on this new approach was Council Dir. 89/48 of 21 December 1988 on a general system for the recognition of higher-education diplomas awarded on completion of professional education and training of at least three years' duration (*OJ* 1989 L19/16. The Member States had to implement the directive by 4 January 1991, see Art. 12. It was amended by Dir. 2001/19, see below). It sets out the circumstances in which a Member State is obliged to recognize diplomas issued by another Member State as equivalent to diplomas awarded in its own territory.

Dir. 89/48 differs from previous sectoral directives in several important respects (see *Bull. EC* 6–1988, p. 11). First, it is general in nature in that it applies to all regulated professions for which university-level training of at least three years is required and which are not covered by a specific sectoral directive. Second, recognition is based on the principle of mutual trust, without prior harmonization and co-ordination of the preparatory educational and training courses for the professions in question being necessary. The underlying rationale of the directive is that despite the differences in the national educational and training systems, the final qualifications giving access to similar professional activities are in practice broadly comparable in all the Member States. Therefore, a host Member State may not refuse entry to a regulated profession to a Community national who holds the qualifications necessary for the exercise of that profession in another Member State. As the fifth recital of the preamble states:

> any host Member State in which a profession is regulated is required to take account of qualifications acquired in another Member State and to determine whether those qualifications correspond to the qualifications which the Member State concerned requires.

Third, recognition is granted to the 'end product', i.e. to fully qualified professionals who have already received any professional training required in addition to their university diplomas. Fourth, where there are major differences between Member States in education and training or in the structure of a profession, the directive provides for compensatory mechanisms, i.e. either an adaptation period or an aptitude test. Since the authorities of the host State can thus exercise a certain degree of scrutiny and control over qualifications acquired in other Member States, Dir. 89/48, unlike the sectoral directives, does not lead to automatic and unconditional recognition of those qualifications (see Case C-110/01 *Tennah-Durez*, above, paras. 33–4; Case C-313/01 *Morgenbesser* [2003] ECR I-0000, para. 44).

The key provisions of Dir. 89/48 are Arts. 2, 3, and 4. Art. 2 defines its scope of application, both in positive and in negative terms. According to the first paragraph, the directive applies to 'any national of a Member State wishing to pursue a regulated profession in a host Member State in a self-employed capacity or as an employed person'. According to the second paragraph, the directive does not apply to professions that are the subject of a separate (i.e. sectoral) directive providing for the mutual recognition of diplomas. Moreover, according to the tenth recital in the preamble, the directive is not intended to amend rules, including those relating to professional ethics, applicable to persons pursuing a profession in a Member State, nor to exclude migrants from the application of those rules. It is confined to laying down appropriate arrangements to ensure that migrants comply with the professional rules of the host Member State.

Since the aim of the directive is to facilitate freedom of movement of persons and services within the Community, it applies only to nationals of a Member State who wish to pursue a regulated profession in another Member State. Consequently, it does not apply to 'purely internal' situations, i.e. those which have no connection with any of the situations governed by Community law but are confined in all respects within one Member State. Therefore, nationals of a Member State who have neither worked nor studied nor obtained a diploma in a Member State other than their country of origin may not rely on the rights conferred by the directive (Cases C-225/95 etc. *Kapasakalis* [1998] ECR I-4239 at pp. I-4249–50). On the other hand, the directive applies to employment in the public service (except where employment is covered by Art. 39(4) EC or by a separate sectoral directive), and public bodies are required to comply with its provisions (Case C-285/01

Burbaud [2003] ECR I-8219, paras. 39, 41; see also Case C-234/97 *Fernández de Bobadilla* [1999] ECR I-4773 at pp. I-4800, I-4803).

As seen above, the directive applies only to regulated professions. The ECJ has held that the definition of a regulated profession is a matter of Community law (ibid. at p. I-4800), and that whether or not a profession is regulated depends on the legal situation in the host Member State (Case C-164/94 *Aranitis* [1996] ECR I-135 at pp. I-154–6). The concept of a regulated profession is defined by Art. 1(c) and (d) of Dir. 89/48. According to the Court, the effect of those provisions is that where the conditions for taking up or pursuing a professional activity are directly or indirectly governed by legal provisions requiring possession of a diploma, that activity constitutes a regulated profession. Access to or pursuit of a profession must be regarded as directly governed by legal provisions where the laws, regulations, or administrative provisions of the host Member State create a system under which that professional activity is expressly reserved to those who fulfil certain conditions and access to it is prohibited to those who do not fulfil them. A profession is indirectly regulated where there is indirect legal control of access to or pursuit of that profession. Where a profession is not regulated in the host Member State, the provisions of the directive cannot be applied (Case C-164/94 *Aranitis*, above, at pp. I-154–8, holding that in the absence of relevant legal provisions the profession of geologist was not regulated in Germany, even though in practice only persons possessing a higher-education diploma as a rule sought and obtained employment in that profession; Case C-234/97 *Fernàndez de Bobadilla*, above, at pp. I-4800–2, holding that the terms of a collective agreement which in a general way governs the right to take up or pursue a profession may constitute 'laws, regulations or administrative provisions' for the purposes of Art. 1(d) of the directive; Case C-294/00 *Gräbner* [2002] ECR I-6515, at pp. I-6551–3, holding that the activity of 'Heilpraktiker'—lay health practitioner—as defined by German law was not a regulated profession in Austria; Case C-285/01 *Burbaud*, above, para. 45; Case C-313/01 *Morgenbesser*, above, paras. 46–52, holding that the activity of 'praticante-patrocinante'—a person undertaking the necessary period of practice for admission to the bar—was not a regulated profession in Italy separate from that of 'avvocato'—advocate).

A regulated profession also includes professional activities pursued by the members of certain professional associations or organizations of an essentially private character that are recognized by a Member State and fulfil certain conditions (Art. 1(d); see also the seventh recital in the preamble. The associations and organizations which satisfy the conditions of the directive are listed in the Annex).

If it is established that a situation falls within the scope of the directive, then Art. 3 becomes applicable. It provides that where, in a host Member State, access to or pursuit of a regulated profession is subject to possession of a diploma, the competent authority may not, on the grounds of inadequate qualifications, refuse to authorize a national of a Member State to take up or pursue that profession on the same conditions as apply to its own nationals: (a) if the applicant holds the diploma required in another Member State for the taking up or pursuit of the profession in question in its territory, provided that such diploma has been awarded in a Member State; or (b) if the applicant has pursued the profession in question full-time for two years during the previous ten years in another Member State which does not regulate that profession, and possesses evidence of one or more formal qualifications as specified by the directive.

The application of Art. 3(a) thus involves a comparison between the qualification required by the host Member State and the qualification held by the applicant. If the competent authority finds that both qualifications constitute diplomas within the meaning of the directive (see below) and that those diplomas are awarded on the completion of education and training that are equivalent in terms of both their duration and the matters that they cover, then the admission of the applicant to the profession in question cannot be made subject to the completion of additional training and the passing of further examinations. Nevertheless, the directive does no more than require the recognition of qualifications obtained in one Member State in order to allow their holder to apply for a job or to exercise a profession in another Member State. It does not concern the choice of selection and recruitment procedures for filling posts, and it does not create a right actually to be recruited or appointed, or to be exempted from such selection procedures (Case C-285/01 *Burbaud*, above, paras. 54–8, 91–3). The ECJ has held that Art. 3(a) has direct effect. It may be relied upon by individuals before a national court in order to have national provisions inconsistent with the directive disapplied (Case C-102/02 *Beuttenmüller* [2004] ECR I-0000, paras. 55, 57).

If the competent authority finds that the duration of the education and training completed by the applicant is at least one year less than that required in the host Member State, the applicant may be asked to provide evidence of professional experience in accordance with Art. 4(1)(a) of the directive. If there is a substantial difference between the matters covered by the applicant's education and training and those covered by the diploma required in the host Member State, or in the structure of a profession, the applicant may be asked to complete an adaptation period not exceeding three years or take an aptitude test in accordance with Art. 4(1)(b) (see ibid. paras. 55–6. For a definition of the concepts of 'adaptation period' and 'aptitude test', see Art. 1(f) and (g) of the directive, respectively, and Case C-145/99 *Commission* v. *Italy* [2002] ECR I-2235 at pp. I-2283–4, interpreting Art. 1(g)). Normally, the applicant is entitled to choose between the two options. However, where the practice of a profession requires precise knowledge of national law and involves provision of legal advice, the host Member State may stipulate which compensation mechanism should be applied. Nevertheless, the provisions of Art. 4(1)(a) and (b) may not be applied cumulatively (Art. 4(2)).

The concept of 'diploma' is defined by Art. 1(a) as any diploma, certificate, or other evidence of formal qualifications which: has been awarded in a Member State; shows that the holder has successfully completed a post-secondary course of at least three years' duration at a university or establishment of higher education and, where appropriate, that he has successfully completed the professional training required in addition to the post-secondary course; and shows that the holder has the professional qualifications required for the taking up or pursuit of a regulated profession in that Member State. It is thus clear that the directive applies only to fully qualified professionals who have already received any professional training which may be required in addition to a university degree or diploma (see Case C-313/01 *Morgenbesser*, above, paras. 54–5, where the Court held that the 'maitrise en droit' which the applicant obtained in France did not, in itself, constitute a 'diploma' for the purposes of the directive in the absence of the 'certificat d'aptitude a la profession d'avocat' (CAPA), which was the professional qualification required for access to the status of 'stagiaire' at the French Bar. The plaintiff was therefore unable to rely on Dir. 89/48 in order to obtain access to the profession of 'praticante' at the Genoa Bar in Italy. For an interpretation of the concept of diploma, see also Case C-285/01 *Burbaud*, above, paras. 46–52, where the Court held that confirmation of passing the final examination which led to permanent appointment to the French hospital public service was to be regarded as a diploma, even if it was not a formal document).

As seen above, both Art. 1(a) and Art. 3(a) provide for the recognition of diplomas which have been awarded in a Member State. Art. 1(a) further stipulates that the education and training leading to a diploma must be received 'mainly' in the Community. Nevertheless, diplomas awarded in a third country are also covered if the holder can show proof of three years' professional experience in a Member State which recognizes the diploma in question (see also Case C-110/01 *Tennah-Durez*, above, para. 66). By a recommendation adopted at the same time as Dir. 89/48, the Council urged the Member States to recognize diplomas awarded to Community nationals in third countries (Rec. 89/49 of 21 December 1988, *OJ* 1989 L19/24).

Where nationals of Member States fulfil the conditions for the taking up or pursuit of a regulated profession in a host Member State, they have the right to use the professional title of the host Member State corresponding to that profession (Art. 7(1)). They may also use their academic title deriving from their Member State of origin or the Member State from which they come, in the language of that State (Art. 7(2)).

The approach adopted in Dir. 89/48 was extended and complemented by Council Dir. 92/51 of 18 June 1992 on a second general system for the recognition of professional education and training to supplement Dir. 89/48 (*OJ* 1992 L209/25; corrigenda in *OJ* 1995 L17/20 and *OJ* 1995 L30/40. The Member States had to implement the directive by 18 June 1994, see Art. 17. It was amended on several occasions, most recently by Dir. 2001/19, see below). The aim of the directive is to facilitate the pursuit of all professional activities which in a host Member State are dependent on the completion of a certain level of education and training. Since the directive is complementary to the first general system set up by Dir. 89/48, it is based on the same principles and contains *mutatis mutandis* the same rules as the initial general system (see the fourth and fifth recitals in the preamble).

The directive applies to nationals of a Member State wishing to pursue a regulated profession in a host Member State in a self-employed capacity or as an employed person. It does not apply to professions which are the subject of a specific (sectoral) directive providing for the mutual recognition of diplomas, nor to activities covered by directives providing for the recognition of technical skills based on occupational experience, which are listed in Annex A (Art. 2. All but three of the latter directives have been repealed by Dir. 1999/42, see below). The definition of a regulated profession in Art. 1(e) and (f) is basically similar to that contained in Dir. 89/48 (see Case C-294/00 *Gräbner*, above, at pp. I-6551–3).

The directive covers two levels of education and training which are not covered by the first system, namely higher or post-secondary education and training of less than three years' duration and secondary education and training, possibly complemented by professional training or experience. It also applies to persons who have not obtained formal qualifications but have acquired professional experience.

Accordingly, in the first place the directive covers 'diplomas' awarded in a Member State which show that the holder has completed a post-secondary course (other than higher-education courses covered by Dir. 89/48) of at least one year's duration as well as any professional training that may be required, and which qualify the holder to take up a regulated profession in that Member State. The education and training must be received 'mainly' in the Community, but they may also be received outside the Community if they are provided in accordance with the rules of a Member State (see Case C-110/01 *Tennah-Durez*, above, para. 66). Third-country diplomas are also covered subject to the same conditions as under Dir. 89/48 (Art. 1(a)). By a resolution adopted at the same time as Dir. 92/51, the Council invited the Member States to recognize diplomas awarded to Community nationals in third countries (Res. of 18 June 1992, *OJ* 1992 C187/1).

Secondly, the directive covers 'certificates' awarded in a Member State which show that the holder has completed either a course of education or training other than the post-secondary courses referred to in Art. 1(a) above, or any probationary or professional practice required, after having followed a secondary course or a secondary course of a technical or vocational nature, and which qualify the holder to take up a regulated profession in that Member State (Art. 1(b)).

Thirdly, the directive covers 'attestations of competence', which either attest to education and training not forming part of a diploma or certificate within the meaning of Dir. 89/48 or Dir. 92/51, or show the personal qualities, aptitudes, or knowledge of the applicant which are essential for the pursuit of a profession, without proof of prior education and training being required (Art. 1(c)).

Arts. 3 and 4 of the directive correspond to Arts. 3 and 4 of Dir. 89/48 (see above). The ECJ has held that in the absence of implementing measures enacted within the period prescribed by Art. 17, a national of a Member State may rely on Art. 3(a) in the host State (Case C-102/02 *Beuttenmüller*, above, para. 67). Since Dirs. 89/48 and 92/51 together cover three different levels of education and training, Dir. 92/51 also lays down rules for determining under what conditions a person possessing a certain level of education and training may pursue a profession in another Member State where the qualifications for the same profession are regulated at a different level (Chapters III to VI). Where either directive provides for the recognition of a qualification, a Member State is not allowed to make recognition of that qualification subject to a condition of reciprocity (Case C-142/01 *Commission* v. *Italy* [2002] ECR I-4541, at p. I-4551).

Dirs. 89/48 and 92/51 do not apply to certain professional activities covered by the early directives adopted between 1963 and 1982 for the implementation of the General Programme. As seen in section I above, these directives covered a wide range of industrial, commercial, and small craft activities and provided either for liberalization or for transitional measures pending mutual recognition of qualifications. In order to improve and simplify the rules applying to these activities, the European Parliament and the Council adopted a third general system directive, Dir. 1999/42 of 7 June 1999 establishing a mechanism for recognition of qualifications in respect of the professional activities covered by the directives on liberalization and transitional measures and supplementing the general systems for the recognition of qualifications (*OJ* 1999 L201/77; corrigendum in *OJ* 2002 L23/48. The Member States had to implement the directive by 31 July 2001, see Art. 14). The directive consolidates into a single text the main provisions of the directives in question and repeals and replaces 35 liberalization and transitional measure directives listed in Annex B (Art. 11). Art. 3 incorporates the case-law of the ECJ, to be discussed below, by requiring a host Member State to take into account the knowledge and skills certified by any formal qualification awarded by another Member State. Art. 4 provides for the recognition of professional qualifications solely on the basis of professional experience acquired in another Member State over a reasonable and sufficiently recent period of time.

Dirs. 89/48 and 92/51 as well as all the sectoral directives listed above were amended by Dir. 2001/19 of the European Parliament and of the Council of 14 May 2001 (*OJ* 2001 L206/1. The Member States had to implement the directive by 1 January 2003, see Art. 16). The directive extends to Dir. 89/48 the concept of 'regulated education and training', introduced by Dir. 92/51. It incorporates into the general system directives the requirement, developed in the case-law of the ECJ to be discussed below, that the host Member State has to examine, before applying the compensation mechanisms, whether the professional experience acquired by the applicant since obtaining his qualification is sufficient to cover the knowledge which is lacking. It likewise incorporates into the sectoral directives the Court's case-law requiring Member States to take into account professional experience gained in a Member State when examining qualifications acquired in third countries and recognized by other Member States (see above). A right of appeal before national courts against a decision rejecting an application for recognition and in the case of failure to reach a decision within the prescribed period is also incorporated into the sectotal directives, in accordance with the Court's case-law (see below). Finally, in implementing the SLIM initiative ('Simpler legislation for the internal market', COM(96) 559), the directive simplifies the updating of the lists of qualifications eligible for automatic recognition under the sectoral directives.

In spite of the simplifications and improvements discussed above, recognition of professional qualifications is still covered at Community level by a large number of directives establishing a variety of unconnected recognition systems. Not only does this create unnecessary complexity, but it can also lead to situations that are not covered by any of the existing arrangements. To remedy these deficiencies, on 7 March 2002 the Commission submitted a Proposal for a directive of the European Parliament and of the Council on the recognition of professional qualifications (*OJ* 2002 C181E/183; COM(2002) 119; amended proposal: COM(2004) 317). The aim of the proposal is to rationalize, reorganize, and simplify the present rules by standardizing the principles applicable while maintaining the existing guarantees. The new directive will repeal and replace the twelve sectoral and three general system directives which apply at present, and consolidate their provisions into a single, consistent legal framework. Thus, the result will be a more uniform, transparent, and flexible regime of recognition of qualifications.

The draft directive applies to nationals of Members States wishing to practise a regulated profession in a host Member State on either a self-employed or employed basis (Art. 2). It lays down different rules for the free movement of services and freedom of establishment. In the case of services, a single system applies to all professions, basically allowing the free provision of services in another Member State by any provider legally established in a Member State for the purpose of practising the same professional activities there (Title II).

As regards establishment, the proposal retains the three existing recognition systems. First, the general system applies to all professions that are not covered by one or the other of the two specific systems and to all cases in which the applicant does not meet the conditions to benefit from a specific system. Thus, all situations will be covered, including those for which there are no provisions at present. This general system is based on the principle of mutual recognition without prior harmonization of the minimum training conditions, but subject to the right of the host Member State to impose a compensation measure in the form of an adaptation period of up to three years or an aptitude test if there are substantial differences between the training acquired by the migrant and the training required in the host State. Compensation measures must, however, be waived where the applicant's qualifications satisfy the accreditation criteria of 'common platforms' established by professional associations at European level and approved by the Commission. This will facilitate a more automatic recognition under the general system (Title III, Chapter I). Secondly, automatic recognition of qualifications based on professional experience acquired in another Member State over a reasonable and sufficiently recent period of time in the case of industrial, commercial, and small craft activities listed in Annex IV (Title III, Chapter II). Thirdly, automatic recognition of formal qualifications on the basis of co-ordination of the minimum training conditions in the case of the seven professions covered by the present sectoral directives, i.e. doctors, nurses responsible for general care, dental practitioners, veterinary surgeons, midwives, pharmacists, and architects (Title III, Chapter III). (See also the Commission's Proposal of 17 December 2003 for a decision of the European Parliament and of the Council on a single framework for the transparency of qualifications and competences (Europass, *OJ* 2004 C96/34; COM(2003) 796.)

(*c*) ***The legal profession.*** Separate mention must be made of the legal profession, which is not covered by any of the sectoral directives. Freedom to provide services by lawyers was already attained in 1977 under Council Dir. 77/249 (*OJ* 1977 L78/17), but this directive solely concerned provision of services and did not contain provisions for the mutual recognition of qualifications; nor did it deal with the right of establishment (*see further under* **Freedom to provide services**, section V.4). Lawyers wishing to practise their profession in another Member State by establishing themselves there on a permanent basis could normally do so only under the professional title used in that State. To be eligible to use that title, they first had to have their qualifications recognized in accordance with Dir. 89/48, which required the passing of an aptitude test or the completion of an adaptation period. Only very few Member States permitted lawyers from other Member States to practise under their home-country professional titles. The differences which existed between Member States in this respect led to distortion of competition between lawyers and also constituted an obstacle to their freedom of movement. To resolve these problems, on 16 February 1998, after four years of negotiations, the European Parliament and the Council adopted Dir. 98/5 to facilitate practice of the profession of lawyer on a permanent basis in a Member State other than that in which the qualification was obtained (*OJ* 1998 L77/36. The Member States had to implement the directive by 14 March 2000, see Art. 16).

The directive pursues three main objectives. First, to make it easier for lawyers to integrate into the profession in a host Member State as compared with the general system for the recognition of diplomas, by enabling them to practise there under their home-country professional titles on a permanent basis and to achieve full integration after a certain period of professional practice without passing an aptitude test or completing an adaptation period. Secondly, to eliminate the differences between Member States as regards legal practice under the home-country professional title. Thirdly, to meet the needs of consumers of legal services who, owing to the increasing trade flows resulting from the internal market, seek legal advice when carrying out cross-border transactions in which international law, Community law, and domestic law overlap (see the third to sixth recitals in the preamble).

According to Art. 1(1), the directive aims 'to facilitate practice of the profession of lawyer on a permanent basis in a self-employed or salaried capacity in a Member State other than that in which the professional qualification was obtained'. It does not cover provision of services by lawyers, which remains covered by Dir. 77/249 (Art. 1(4)). The term 'lawyer' means any person who is a national of a Member State and who is authorized to pursue his professional activities under one of the professional titles listed in Art. 1(2)(a). The directive thus applies only to lawyers fully qualified as such in their Member State of origin, and does not apply to persons who, although holders of a university law degree, have not yet acquired the professional qualification necessary to practise law (see Case C-313/01 *Morgenbesser*, above, para. 45). 'Home-country professional title' is defined as 'the professional title used in the Member State in which a lawyer acquired the right to use that title before practising the profession of lawyer in the host Member State' (Art. 1(2)(d)).

The directive enables lawyers to practise their profession in another Member State in two different ways: either under their home-country professional title (Art. 2) or under the professional title of the host Member State (Art. 10). There are considerable differences between the two situations. Whereas lawyers falling within the latter category may undertake all the activities open or reserved to the profession of lawyer by the host Member State, those falling within the former group may be forbidden to pursue certain activities and are subject to certain obligations, as discussed below (see also Case C-168/98 *Luxembourg* v. *Parliament and Council* [2000] ECR I-9131 at pp. I-9171–6). The two situations are considered in turn.

Under Art. 2, any lawyer is entitled to pursue on a permanent basis, in any other Member State, under his home-country professional title, the activities specified in Art. 5. The directive does not require any prior training in or assessment of knowledge of the law of the host Member State, nor the recognition of equivalence of qualifications, and the migrant lawyer has immediate access to the legal profession in the host State. According to Art. 5(1), a lawyer practising under his home-country professional title generally carries on the same professional activities as a lawyer practising under the relevant professional title used in the host Member State and may, *inter alia*, give advice on the law of his home Member State, on Community law, on international law and on the law of the host Member State. There are, however, certain restrictions. Thus, the host Member State may exclude such a lawyer from certain activities (Art. 5(2)) and may require him to work in conjunction with a local lawyer when representing or defending clients in legal proceedings (Art. 5(3)). Member States may also lay down specific rules for access to supreme courts, such as the use of specialist lawyers (ibid.).

A lawyer practising under his home-country professional title is also subject to certain obligations. Thus, he is required to practise under that title, which must be expressed in the official language of his home Member State in such a way as to avoid confusion with the professional title of the host Member State (Art. 4). He is subject to the rules of professional conduct both in his home Member State and in the host Member State, and may be required by the latter either to take out professional indemnity insurance or to become a member of a professional guarantee fund (Art. 6). If he fails to fulfil the obligations in force in the host Member State, the rules of disciplinary proceedings, penalties, and remedies provided for in that State apply to him. In addition, he may also be subject to disciplinary measures in his home Member State. The withdrawal by the competent authority in the home Member State of the authorization to practise automatically prohibits him from practising in the host Member State under his home-country professional title (Art. 7).

In addition to the above obligations, which arise from the directive, the ECJ has confirmed that a lawyer practising under his home-country professional title is also bound by the rules of professional conduct applicable to lawyers generally. These entail an obligation, breach of which may incur disciplinary sanctions, not to handle matters which the lawyer knows or ought to know he is not competent to handle. As the Court has pointed out:

> The [Community] legislature has not abolished the requirement that the lawyer concerned should know the national law applicable in the cases he handles, but has simply released him from the obligation to prove that knowledge in advance. It has thus allowed, in some circumstances, gradual assimilation of knowledge through practice, that assimilation being made easier by experience of other laws gained in the home Member State (Case C-168/98 *Luxembourg* v. *Parliament and Council*, above, at p. I-9176. The Court has derived this requirement in part from Article 3.1.3 of the Code of Professional Conduct adopted by the Council of the Bars and Law Societies of the European Union (CCBE), ibid. at p. I-9175).

The Court has explained that, with a view to making it easier for migrant lawyers to exercise the fundamental freedom of establishment, the Community legislature has chosen, in preference to a system of prior testing of qualification in the national law of the host Member State, an arrangement combining various measures, such as consumer information, restrictions on the right to practise, rules of professional conduct, compulsory insurance, and disciplinary measures. All of these rules, the Court has said, taken together, ensure an adequate level of consumer protection and the proper administration of justice (ibid. at pp. I-9172–6. In that case, Luxembourg challenged the validity of the directive on the grounds that it discriminated against the lawyers of the host Member State, prejudiced the public interest in consumer protection and in the proper administration of justice, was not adopted unanimously and contained insufficient and in part contradictory reasoning. The Court rejected all of these pleas and dismissed the action).

It is apparent from the foregoing that Dir. 98/5 differs from the previous sectoral directives in several respects. It is not based on the prior harmonization of training conditions throughout the Community, and it does not lead to automatic recognition of qualifications (see Case C-313/01 *Morgenbesser*, above, para. 44). In fact, it requires not the mutual recognition of the professional qualifications (which are not even examined by the host Member State) but the mutual recognition of the professional titles (i.e. of the authorization to practise) of migrant lawyers wishing to practise under their home-country professional title. This mechanism thus supplements that established by Dir. 89/48, which, as regards lawyers, is intended to authorize the unrestricted practice of the profession under the professional title of the host Member State (see Case C-168/98 *Luxembourg* v. *Parliament and Council*, above, at p. I-9179).

Nevertheless, Dir. 98/5 itself also contains provisions that allow migrant lawyers to practise their profession in a host Member State under the professional title of that Member State. Thus, according to Art. 10(1), a lawyer practising under his home-country professional title may be admitted to the profession of lawyer in the host Member State without having to meet the condition of an adaptation period or of an aptitude test laid down in Art. 4(1)(b) of Dir. 89/48, if he has, for a period of at least three years, effectively and regularly pursued an activity in the host Member State in the law of that State, including Community law. If he has effectively and regularly pursued a professional activity there for a period of at least three years but for a lesser period in the law of the host Member State, he may still obtain admission to the legal profession from the competent authority of that State subject to certain conditions, without having to meet the above-mentioned compensatory requirements (Art. 10(3)). In both cases, admission to the legal profession is subject to verification of the migrant lawyer's professional competence. Moreover, a lawyer practising under his home-country professional title in a host Member State may, at any time, apply to have his diploma recognized in accordance with Dir. 89/48 (Art. 10(2)). A lawyer who is admitted to the legal profession in the host Member State in accordance with these provisions is entitled to practise it under the professional title of the host Member State. In addition, he may also use his home-country professional title expressed in the official language of his home Member State (Art. 10(6). See also the fourteenth recital in the preamble).

The directive requires lawyers who wish to practise in a host Member State to register with the competent authority in that State (Art. 3). Decisions refusing registration and decisions imposing disciplinary measures are subject to judicial review (Art. 9). Joint practice in the host Member State is permitted subject to the conditions set out in Arts. 11 and 12.

(*d*) ***Mutual recognition of qualifications: the case-law of the Court of Justice.*** Although the directives discussed above cover a wide range of occupational and professional activities, situations have arisen, and continue to arise, which are not covered by any of those directives. In such situations the question is whether and in what conditions, in the absence of a (sectoral or general) directive on mutual recognition of qualifications, Community nationals can derive a right directly from Art. 43 EC to practise a profession in one Member State for the pursuit of which they have acquired the necessary qualification and/or professional experience in another Member State. In other words, does Art. 43 produce direct effect not only as regards the rule on equal treatment but also as regards the recognition of qualifications? As mentioned at the beginning of this section, in this respect there has been a remarkable development in the jurisprudence of the Court of Justice, which is considered below.

Initially, the Court formulated the basic principle of Community law as follows:

In the absence of harmonization of the conditions of access to a particular occupation or profession, the Member States are entitled to lay down the knowledge and qualifications needed in order to pursue it and to require the production of a diploma certifying that the holder has the relevant knowledge and qualifications (Case 222/86 *Heylens* [1987] ECR 4097 at p. 4116; Case C-340/89 *Vlassopoulou*, above, at p. I-2382; Case C-104/91 *Borrell* [1992] ECR I-3003 at p. I-3027).

Accordingly, the Court initially held that prior to the adoption of recognition and co-ordination directives governing a particular profession or, where they had been adopted, prior to the date by which the Member States were required to implement them, Community nationals could not rely on the direct effect of Art. 43 with a view to practising that profession in a Member State on any conditions other than those laid down by national legislation (Case 136/78 *Auer I*, above, at p. 451, involving a French national who was unable to enforce his right to practise veterinary medicine in France *prior to* the date by which the relevant directives should have been implemented since the French authorities did not recognize the equivalence of his Italian university degree in veterinary medicine to a French degree. However, he could enforce his right *after* that date on the basis of those directives, see Case 271/82 *Auer II*, above, at p. 2744). In other words, Member States were not required by Art. 43 to recognize a diploma or qualification obtained in another Member State that did not enjoy mutual recognition within the Community under the terms of a particular directive and did not satisfy the national requirements.

Nor did Art. 43 require the Member States, in the absence of harmonization at Community level, to allow persons to practise a profession with a qualification acquired in another Member State which was lower than that prescribed by national law (Case C-61/89 *Bouchoucha*, above, at pp. I-3567–8, where a French national could not rely on Art. 43 to practise osteopathy in France on the basis of a diploma issued in the United Kingdom as such a diploma was recognized neither by Community law nor by French law, was not covered by the directive on the mutual recognition of qualifications in medicine—the doctors' directive—and in France osteopathy could only be practised by qualified doctors. The Court also pointed out that France had a legitimate interest in preventing its nationals from evading the national rules by means of facilities created under the Treaty).

The position was, however, different where a 'foreign' qualification was recognized under the national law of the host Member Sate. Already in Case 71/76 *Thieffry*, above, at pp. 777–9, the Court ruled that in so far as Community law made no special provision for recognition of qualifications, freedom of establishment might be attained by measures enacted by the Member States, which were required by Art. 10 EC to facilitate the achievement of the Community's objectives. Consequently, the Court said, if freedom of establishment could be ensured in a Member State either under the laws and regulations in force or by virtue of the practices of the public administration or of professional bodies, a person subject to Community law could not be denied the practical benefit of that freedom solely because, for a particular profession, the directives provided for by Art. 47 had not yet been adopted. The national authorities and professional bodies were required to apply the relevant laws and practices in accordance with the rules on freedom of establishment. Therefore, the Court held, there was an unjustified restriction on that freedom where, in a Member State, admission to a particular profession was refused to a person covered by the Treaty who held a diploma obtained in his country of origin which had been recognized as an equivalent qualification by the competent authority of the host State and who furthermore had fulfilled the conditions regarding professional training in force in that State, solely by reason of the fact that he did not possess the national diploma corresponding to his diploma, which had been recognized as an equivalent qualification. The case concerned the admission to the Paris Bar of a Belgian advocate who was the holder of a Belgian diploma of Doctor of Laws, which had been recognized by a French university as equivalent to the French licenciate's degree in law, and who subsequently obtained a French qualifying certificate for the profession of advocate. In these circumstances, the Court held, demanding the possession of a French law degree constituted, even in the absence of the directives provided for in Art. 47, a restriction that was incompatible with Art. 43.

Subsequently, in Case 11/77 *Patrick*, above, at pp. 1205–6, the Court arrived at the same conclusion by relying on the direct effect of the rule on equal treatment contained in Art. 43. The Court said that in laying down that freedom of establishment should be attained at the end of the transitional period, Art. 43 imposed an obligation to attain a precise result, the fulfilment of which had to be made easier by, but not made dependent on, the implementation of a programme of progressive measures. The fact that this programme had not been adhered to left the obligation itself intact beyond the end of the transitional period. Consequently, the Court held, the fact that the mutual recognition directives envisaged by Art. 47(1) had not been adopted did not entitle a Member State to deny the practical benefit of freedom of establishment to Community nationals when that freedom could be ensured by virtue of the provisions of laws and regulations already in force in that Member State. Therefore, a national of a Member State who held a qualification recognized by the competent authorities of the host Member State as equivalent to the qualification required in that State enjoyed the right to be admitted to the relevant profession and to practise it under the same conditions as nationals of the host State without being required to satisfy any additional conditions (the case concerned a British national whose architect's certificate issued in the United Kingdom was recognized as equivalent to that required under French law).

Both of these cases were relied on in the next two cases, which represent a major and important development in the Court's jurisprudence. The first, Case 222/86 *Heylens*, above, at pp. 4116–8, concerned the free movement of workers and in particular the refusal by the French authorities to recognize the equivalence of a Belgian football-trainer's diploma. The second, Case C-340/89 *Vlassopoulou*, above, at pp. I-2382–5, concerned the refusal by the German authorities to grant admission as a 'Rechtsanwältin'—barrister or solicitor—in Germany to a Greek lawyer registered with the Athens Bar who besides her Greek diplomas also had a doctorate in law from a German university and was working with a firm of German lawyers under the responsibility of one of her colleagues. The refusal was based on the grounds that she did not have the required German qualifications and that Art. 43 EC did not give her the right to exercise her profession in Germany on the basis of her qualifications obtained in Greece. Since the judgment in the latter case incorporates the Court's relevant findings made in the former, only the latter case is discussed in detail below.

The importance of the *Vlassopoulou* case lies in the fact that in the absence of recognition and harmonization directives concerning the legal profession and because of the inapplicability of Dir. 89/48 to the facts of the case, the Court relied directly and exclusively on Art. 43 EC and established important principles regarding recognition of qualifications by way of interpretation of Art. 43. This case, and the subsequent line of authority based on it, therefore confirm the direct effect of Art. 43 as regards recognition of qualifications, which is an essential element of freedom of establishment.

Before the Court, the Italian and German Governments argued that in the absence of Community rules each Member State was entitled to make admission to a profession dependent on the fulfilment of non-discriminatory conditions laid down by national law. In response to this argument, the Court pointed out that:

> even if applied without any discrimination on the basis of nationality, national requirements concerning qualifications may have the effect of hindering nationals of the other Member States in the exercise of their right of establishment guaranteed to them by Art. 43 of the EC Treaty. That could be the case if the national rules in question took no account of the knowledge and qualifications already acquired by the person concerned in another Member State.
>
> Consequently, a Member State which receives a request to admit a person to a profession to which access, under national law, depends upon the possession of a diploma or a professional qualification must take into consideration the diplomas, certificates and other evidence of qualifications which the person concerned has acquired in order to exercise the same profession in another Member State by making a comparison between the specialized knowledge and abilities certified by those diplomas and the knowledge and qualifications required by the national rules (ibid. at pp. I-2383–4).

The Court then went on to say that the authorities of the host Member State must establish, on an objective basis, that the knowledge and qualifications certified by the foreign diploma are, if not identical, at least equivalent to those certified by the national diploma. That assessment of equivalence must be carried out exclusively in the light of the level of knowledge and qualifications that the holder can be assumed to possess on the basis of his diploma, having regard to the nature and duration of the studies and practical training involved. Objective differences between the two Member States relating to the profession in question and, in the case of the legal profession, differences between the national legal systems, may be taken into account. If there is an equivalence between the knowledge and qualifications certified by the foreign diploma and those required by the national provisions, the host State must recognize that diploma as fulfilling the national requirements. Where there is only partial equivalence, the authorities may require the person concerned to show that he has acquired the knowledge and qualifications that are lacking. The authorities must assess whether the knowledge acquired in the host Member State, either during a course of study or by way of practical experience, is sufficient to cover the difference. Professional experience acquired in the country of origin or in the host country must also be taken into account where completion of a period of preparation or training is a precondition for entry into the profession.

Finally, the procedure to be followed by the national authorities must satisfy the requirements of Community law concerning the availability of effective judicial remedies and the duty to state reasons. Thus, a decision refusing to recognize the equivalence of a foreign qualification must be capable of being challenged in judicial proceedings in which its legality under Community law can be reviewed, and the person concerned must be informed of the reasons on which the refusal is based.

Subsequently, the Court ruled that provided that the above procedure for assessing equivalence has been followed, Member States are not precluded by Community law from imposing criminal penalties in respect of the illegal pursuit by a national of another Member State of a regulated profession, in particular where the person concerned has failed to seek recognition of the equivalence of his qualifications or where such equivalence has not been recognized (Case C-104/91 *Borrell*, above, at pp. I-3030–1). Failure to establish a procedure for examining qualifications acquired in another Member State, as described above, amounts to an infringement of Community law, which may be subject to an action under Art. 226 EC (see Case C-375/92 *Commission* v. *Spain*, above, at pp. I-940–2, dealing with tourist guides and guide-interpreters).

The principles established by the Court in *Vlassopoulou* closely reflect the provisions of Dir. 89/48, which was adopted a few years earlier (see, in particular, the fifth recital in the preamble to the directive, cited above). In turn, the case-law of the Court on recognition of qualifications was incorporated in Dir. 2001/19, which amended the previous directives (see above and the third and sixth recitals in the preamble). This shows the close interaction between legislation and case-law in the development of this area of Community law.

The *Vlassopoulou* principle has been confirmed and applied to various situations in a long line of subsequent decisions (see below). According to the Court, those decisions are merely the expression in individual cases of a general principle, which is inherent in the fundamental freedoms of the Treaty (Case C-238/98 *Hocsman*, above, at p. I-6652; Case C-31/00 *Dreessen* [2002] ECR I-663, at p. I-686). This consistent case-law has qualified the principle, cited above, that in the absence of harmonization of a profession the Member States remain competent to define the exercise of that profession. While this is true, the Member States must, when exercising their powers in this area, respect the basic freedoms guaranteed by the Treaty (Case C-58/98 *Corsten* [2000] ECR I-7919 at p. I-7955; Case C-294/00 *Gräbner*, above, at p. I-6550).

The subsequent case-law has extended the scope of the *Vlassopoulou* principle quite considerably. Thus, when considering an application by a national of a Member State for admission to a profession, the authorities of the host Member State must take into account not only his diplomas, certificates, and other evidence of formal qualifications, but also his relevant professional experience, irrespective of whether those diplomas, qualifications, and experience were acquired in a Member State or in a third country (Case C-319/92 *Haim I*, above, at p. I-448; Case C-238/98 *Hocsman*, above, at pp. I-6651–2, I-6655–6; Case C-232/99 *Commission* v. *Spain*, above, at p. I-4276; Case C-313/01 *Morgenbesser*, above, para. 58). Moreover, the principle applies also to professional activities access to which in the host Member State is not subject by virtue of legal provisions to the possession of a diploma, and which are therefore not regulated for the purposes of Dirs. 89/48 and 92/51 (Case C-164/94 *Aranitis*, above, at pp. I-157–8; Case C-234/97 *Fernàndez de Bobadilla*, above, at pp. I-4803–4), or where the applicant's qualification does not constitute a 'diploma' for the purposes of Dir. 89/48 (Case C-313/01 *Morgenbesser*, above, paras. 54–72). Even in these situations the authorities of the host Member State must examine whether the whole of the academic and professional training and experience of the applicant obtained in that Member State or in his Member State of origin satisfies, even partially, the conditions for access to the activity concerned.

The *Vlassopoulou* principle was originally developed by the Court to deal with professions such as that of lawyer (at issue in that case) or estate agent (see Case C-104/91 *Borrell*, above, at pp. I-3027–9) for the practice of which there were no harmonization and mutual recognition directives in existence at the time. However, this does not mean that where a profession is covered by such directives the person concerned may not rely on the *Vlassopoulou* principle. The Court has held that the legal ambit of that principle cannot be reduced as a result of the adoption of directives on mutual recognition of qualifications. Therefore, the Member States must comply with their obligations as defined in *Vlassopoulou* even in a situation where a particular profession is covered by a mutual recognition directive but the holder of a diploma is unable to avail himself of the automatic recognition mechanism laid down by that directive for any reason, for example because his diploma was awarded in a third country or because his diploma was omitted by error from the list of qualifications covered by the directive (Case C-238/98 *Hocsman*, above, at pp. I-6654–7, involving a doctor whose diploma of specialist in urology, obtained in Spain, could not be recognized under the doctors' directive solely because his diploma in basic medicine was obtained in a third country; Case C-31/00 *Dreessen*, above, at pp. I-686–7, involving an architect whose diploma in engineering, obtained in Germany, could not be recognized under the architects' directive because by mistake it was not included amongst the diplomas listed in the directive).

There are situations which are not covered by any sectoral or general harmonization and mutual recognition directive, but to which the principles developed in *Vlassopoulou* can also not be applied, for example, because for some reason it is not possible to take account of existing qualifications. Such situations are covered directly by the relevant provisions of the Treaty, i.e. by Art. 39 (in the case of workers), Art. 43 (in the case of establishment), or Art. 49 (in the case of services). Those Articles require the removal of all restrictions on the basic freedoms. As the Court has said, 'all measures which are liable to prohibit, impede or render less attractive the exercise of those freedoms must be considered to be such restrictions' (Case C-294/00 *Gräbner*, above, at p. I-6553; see also Case C-19/92 *Kraus*, above, at p. I-1697; Case C-285/01 *Burbaud*, above, para. 95). Since national measures that prohibit the exercise of a profession recognized in another Member State, or render impossible or more difficult the recognition of a qualification obtained in another Member State, constitute restrictions contrary to the Treaty, they may be justified only if they fulfil the four conditions laid down by the Court in its case-law, namely, if they are applied in a non-discriminatory manner; are justified by overriding reasons based on the general interest; are suitable for securing the attainment of the objective that they pursue; and do not go beyond what is necessary in order to attain that objective (see Case C-294/00 *Gräbner*, above, at pp. I-6553–6, involving Austrian legislation prohibiting the exercise in Austria of the profession of 'Heilpraktiker', recognized in Germany, which profession was not regulated by harmonization at Community level; Case C-19/92 *Kraus*, above, at pp. I-1696–9, concerning the use in Germany by a German national, in the absence of harmonization of the relevant conditions by a directive, of a postgraduate academic title—LLM—acquired in the United Kingdom; Case C-285/01 *Burbaud*, above, paras. 95–112, concerning the admission to the French hospital public service of a Portuguese national with the qualification of hospital administrator acquired in Portugal. The four conditions were laid down in Case C-55/94 *Gebhard*, above, at pp. I-4197–9, see section IV.3 below).

To sum up, the question whether and to what extent a qualification acquired in one Member State must be recognized in another requires a three-stage investigation. First, it is necessary to examine whether the qualification in question is covered by a sectoral mutual recognition directive, including the lawyers' directive. If not, it must be examined, secondly, whether it comes within the scope of one of the general mutual recognition directives. Thirdly, if those directives do not apply, it is necessary to consider whether Arts. 39, 43, or 49 EC, as interpreted by the ECJ in *Vlassopoulou*, can be relied on. As a result of the automatic and unconditional effect of recognition under the sectoral directives, relying on those directives is generally more advantageous for the person concerned than is the application of Arts. 39, 43, or 49 EC, which do not ensure automatic recognition. Where the requirements of a sectoral directive are satisfied, mutual recognition of the qualification in question renders superfluous its recognition under the *Vlassopoulou* principle. However, that principle remains applicable in situations not covered by the directives on mutual recognition, even if the profession in question is covered by such directives (see Case C-234/97 *Fernàndez de Bobadilla*, above, at pp. I-4802–3; Case C-238/98 *Hocsman*, above, at pp. I-6654–5; Case C-232/99 *Commission* v. *Spain*, above, at p. I-4277; Case C-294/00 *Gräbner*, above, at pp. I-6550–1; Case C-313/01 *Morgenbesser*, above, paras. 43–4).

3. Professional rules. The basic principle of Community law concerning professional rules is the same as that concerning professional qualifications: in the absence of specific Community rules on the matter each Member State is free to regulate access to and pursuit of a particular trade or profession in its territory. This simply follows from Art. 43(2), which ensures freedom of establishment 'under the conditions laid down for its own nationals by the law of the country where such establishment is effected'. Where the taking-up of a specific activity is not subject to any rules in the host State, a national of any other Member State is entitled to establish himself and pursue that activity there. On the other hand, where access to and pursuit of an activity is subject to certain conditions in the host State, a national of another Member State intending to carry on that activity must in principle comply with those conditions (see Case C-55/94 *Gebhard*, above, at pp. I-4196–9; see further below). As the ECJ has stated, freedom of establishment must be reconciled with the application of national professional rules 'justified by the general good', in particular rules relating to professional bodies (organization and membership of, admission to, and registration with such bodies), professional ethics, supervision, liability, etc., provided that such rules are applied without discrimination on grounds of nationality (Case 71/76 *Thieffry*, above, at pp. 776–7; see also the cases cited above and below). The Court has confirmed and applied this basic principle in respect of a variety of trades and professions, such as the legal profession (ibid.; Case 107/83 *Klopp*, above, at p. 2989; Case 292/86 *Gullung*, above, at p. 139); veterinary profession (Case 271/82 *Auer*, above, at pp. 2744–5; Case 5/83 *Rienks*, above, at pp. 4245–6); medical and dental professions (Case 96/85 *Commission* v. *France* [1986] ECR 1475 at p. 1485; Case C-351/90 *Commission* v. *Luxembourg* [1992] ECR I-3945 at p. I-3962, also covering the veterinary profession; see also Cases 98/85 etc. *Bertini* [1986] ECR 1885 at pp. 1897–8 concerning the admission of students to medical faculties); clinical biology laboratory services (Case 221/85 *Commission* v. *Belgium*, above, at p. 737); wholesale and retail trade (Case 198/86 *Conradi* [1987] ECR 4469 at p. 4484); estate agents (Cases C-330/90 etc. *López Brea*, above, at p. I-338; Case C-147/91 *Ferrer Laderer*, above, at p. I-4115); auditors (Case C-106/91 *Ramrath* [1992] ECR I-3351 at pp. I-3384–6); maritime transport undertakings (Case C-379/92 *Peralta*, above, at p. I-3499); hairdressers (Cases C-29/94 etc. *Aubertin*, above, at p. I-316).

Thus, the Court has held that national laws that provide for compulsory registration with or membership of a professional body (e.g. a bar) are not incompatible with Community law provided that such registration is open to nationals of all Member States without discrimination. This requirement seeks to ensure the observance of moral and ethical principles and the disciplinary control of the activity of the persons concerned and thus pursues an objective worthy of protection. Member States may therefore prescribe such registration for nationals of other Member States wishing to establish themselves in their territory. Failure to register cannot, however, prevent a person from practising his profession and cannot give rise to criminal prosecution where registration is refused in breach of Community law, for example, because the national authorities wrongly refuse to recognize a qualification obtained in another Member State (Case 271/82 *Auer II*, above, at pp. 2744–5; Case 5/83 *Rienks*, above, at pp. 4245–6, both dealing with veterinary surgeons; Case 292/86 *Gullung*, above, at p. 140, concerning lawyers). The Court has also held that a prohibition of multi-disciplinary partnership between members of the Bar and accountants is not contrary to Art. 43 since it could reasonably be considered to be necessary for the proper practice of the legal profession, as organized in the Member State concerned (Case C-309/99 *Wouters*, above, at p. I-1695).

Nevertheless, Community law does impose certain limits on the power of the Member States to apply their rules of professional conduct to the nationals of other Member States. As the Court has stated:

> Nationals of a Member State who pursue their occupation in another Member State are obliged to comply with the rules which govern the pursuit of the occupation in question in that Member State . . . However, in so far as those rules have the effect of restricting freedom of movement for workers, the right of establishment and the freedom to provide services within the Community, they are compatible with the Treaty only if the restrictions which they entail are actually justified in view of the general obligations inherent in the proper practice of the professions in question and apply to nationals and foreigners alike. That is not the case where the restrictions are such as to create discrimination against practitioners established in other Member States or raise obstacles to access to the profession which go beyond what is necessary in order to achieve the intended goals (Case 96/85 *Commission* v. *France*, above, at pp. 1485–6).

The problem of restrictions of this latter type first arose in Case 107/83 *Klopp*, above, at pp. 2989–90, which concerned a German lawyer, a member of the Düsseldorf Bar, whose application for admission to the Paris Bar was rejected on the sole ground that under the French legislation and rules of professional conduct in force, an 'avocat' could establish chambers in one place only. The Paris Bar Council and the French Government argued that this rule was necessary to ensure the availability of the 'avocat' to both his clients and the court with which he is registered. Moreover, since the rule was applicable without distinction to French and foreign nationals, it was fully compatible with Art. 43(2). While the Court recognized that in the absence of any directive on freedom of establishment for lawyers each Member State was free to regulate the exercise of the legal profession in its territory, it also held that national legislation may not require a lawyer to have only one establishment throughout the Community territory. Such a requirement would be too restrictive. It would mean that a lawyer once established in a particular Member State would be able to enjoy the freedom of establishment in another Member State only at the price of giving up the establishment that he already had. That freedom of establishment was not confined to the right to create a single establishment within the Community was also shown by the fact, the Court pointed out, that Art. 43 enabled the setting up of agencies, branches, and subsidiaries by Community nationals already established in a Member State. This rule, the Court said, was 'a specific statement of a general principle, applicable equally to the liberal professions, according to which the right of establishment includes freedom to set up and maintain, subject to observance of the professional rules of conduct, more than one place of work within the Community' (ibid. at p. 2990).

However, the Court added, in view of the special nature of the legal profession, the second Member State must have the right to require that lawyers established in its territory should maintain sufficient contact with their clients and the judicial authorities (which was made possible by modern methods of transport and telecommunications) and should abide by the rules of the profession.

The final ruling of the Court was that even in the absence of any relevant directive, Arts. 43 *et seq.* prevented the authorities of a Member State from denying, on the basis of the national legislation and the rules of professional conduct in force, to a national of another Member State the right to enter and exercise the legal profession solely because he maintained chambers simultaneously in another Member State (ibid. at p. 2990). It is difficult to explain this ruling on the basis of Art. 43(2) alone or on the basis of the Court's previous case-law. The measure in question (the so-called 'single-surgery rule') was non-discriminatory, and in the absence of Community legislation its application to a German national could not have been incompatible with Art. 43(2). However, it appears that the Court derived its ruling from 'the scope of Article 43 of the Treaty as a directly applicable rule of Community law' (ibid. at p. 2988), without making a distinction between the first and the second paragraph of that Article. This seems to confirm the view put forward at the beginning of this section, first, that prohibited restrictions on the right of establishment may also arise from non-discriminatory measures when in some way they present an unjustified obstacle to the cross-border movement of persons, and secondly, that not only the second paragraph of Art. 43 can produce direct effect but also the first paragraph (the latter point was expressly confirmed in Case 143/87 *Stanton*, at p. 3894, see below. The Court refers to the direct effect of Art. 43 as a whole in virtually all subsequent cases and in the cases dealing with the establishment of companies, see section V below).

The principle laid down in *Klopp* has subsequently been applied to other professions. Thus, in Case 96/85 *Commission* v. *France*, above, at pp. 1486–7, the Court held that the French legislation prohibiting doctors and dentists established in another Member State from practising in France as an employee, as a principal in a practice or as a locum while maintaining their establishment in that other Member State was contrary to the rules of the Treaty on the free movement of persons (Arts. 39, 43, and 49 EC). The Court considered that such a prohibition (the 'single-surgery rule') was unduly restrictive and too absolute and general in nature to be justified by the need to ensure continuity of medical treatment or by the need of applying French rules of medical ethics in France (see also Case C-351/90 *Commission* v. *Luxembourg*, above, at p. I-3964, where the Court gave a similar ruling in respect of the Luxembourg 'single-surgery rule' concerning doctors, dentists, and veterinary surgeons). In Case C-162/99 *Commission* v. *Italy*, above, at p. I-566 and in Case C-145/99 *Commission* v. *Italy*, above, at pp. I-2277–8, the Court likewise held that the Italian rules requiring dentists and members of the bar, respectively, to reside in the district of their professional association or the judicial district of the court to which their bar was attached, was contrary to Art. 43 since it prevented dentists and lawyers established in other Member States from maintaining an establishment in Italy.

In Case 143/87 *Stanton*, above, at pp. 3893–5, the Court further extended the *Klopp* principle by holding that it applies not only to self-employed persons but also to persons who are employed in one Member State and wish, in addition, to work in another Member State in a self-employed capacity. The case concerned Belgian legislation under which a self-employed person was exempted from the payment of contributions to the Belgian social security scheme for self-employed persons if his principal occupation was employment in Belgium, but not if his principal occupation was employment in another Member State. The importance of this case is that although the Court established that the legislation in question did not discriminate on grounds of nationality, either directly or indirectly, the Court nevertheless found that it was contrary to Arts. 39 and 43 EC. The Court stated the main reasons for its finding thus:

> The provisions of the Treaty relating to the free movement of persons are . . . intended to facilitate the pursuit by Community citizens of occupational activities of all kinds throughout the Community, and preclude national legislation which might place Community citizens at a disadvantage when they wish to extend their activities beyond the territory of a single Member State (ibid. at p. 3894).

Moreover, since the contested legislation afforded no additional social protection to the persons concerned (because they were already affiliated to the social security scheme of the other Member State in which they pursued their principal employment), it was not objectively justified. Thus, the reason for the incompatibility of the legislation with Art. 43 was not its discriminatory treatment of foreign nationals but solely its restrictive effect upon the right of establishment in another Member State. The Court derived its ruling not from Art. 43(2) but from Art. 43(1), which it expressly described as 'a directly applicable rule of Community law' which the Member States were obliged to observe even though, in the absence of Community legislation on social security for self-employed persons at the material time, they retained competence to legislate in this field (ibid. at p. 3894; see also Cases 154/87 etc. *Wolf* [1988] ECR 3897 at pp. 3911–13 and Case C-53/95 *Kemmler*, above, at p. I-715. The latter involved a German national who was established as a lawyer both in Germany and in Belgium. He was required to pay contributions to the Belgian social security scheme for self-employed persons even though he was already covered by the German social security scheme. The Court held that this requirement was an unjustified impediment to freedom of establishment in more than one Member State since it afforded no additional social protection to him).

In Case C-106/91 *Ramrath*, above, at p. I-3382, the Court applied the *Klopp* principle to auditors, holding that a Member State may not prohibit a person from becoming established in its territory and practising as an auditor there on the grounds that that person is established and authorized to practise in another Member State. However, the Court was also confronted with the question whether such a person, although already authorized to practise as an auditor in another Member State, may be subjected in the host State to rules requiring permanent professional infrastructure for carrying out the work, actual presence in that State, supervision of compliance with the rules of professional conduct or, if he is an employee, that his principal employer be authorized to practise as an auditor within that State. The Court pointed out that in view of the special nature of certain professional activities, the imposition of specific requirements pursuant to the rules governing such activities is not incompatible with the Treaty. Nevertheless, the Court added, freedom of movement for persons may be restricted only by rules which are justified in the general interest and are applied to all persons pursuing those activities without discrimination, in so far as that interest is not already safeguarded by the rules to which the person is subject in the other Member State where he is established. In addition, such requirements must be objectively justified by the need to ensure compliance with professional rules of conduct and must be proportionate to the aim pursued. In the case of auditors, the Court held, requirements relating to permanent infrastructure, actual presence and supervision are justified unless compliance with the rules of professional conduct is already ensured through an auditor established and authorized in the host State in whose service the person concerned is employed. All the above considerations apply equally irrespective of whether the auditor who carries out audits in another Member State has the status of an employee, a self-employed person or a provider of services (ibid. at pp. I-3383–6).

Subsequently, the Court has summarized its case-law and has stated in general terms that national measures liable to hinder or make less attractive the exercise of fundamental freedoms guaranteed by the Treaty can be justified only if they fulfil four conditions: they must be applied in a non-discriminatory manner; they must be justified by overriding reasons based on the general interest; they must be suitable for securing the attainment of the objective which they pursue; and they must not go beyond what is necessary in order to attain that objective (Case C-55/94 *Gebhard*, above, at pp. I-4197–9; see also Case C-294/00 *Gräbner*, above, at pp. I-6553–4; Case C-424/97 *Haim II* [2000] ECR I-5123 at pp. I-5166–7, where the Court held that the requirement that a dentist must have the linguistic knowledge necessary for the exercise of his profession in the host Member State was justified by an overriding reason of general interest. *See further under* **Freedom to provide services**, section V.2).

4. Other restrictions. Certain restrictions on the right of establishment may also arise from rules other than those relating to professional qualification or professional conduct. As the ECJ has stated, 'Articles 43 and 49 of the Treaty require the elimination of restrictions on freedom of establishment and freedom to provide services respectively. All measures which prohibit, impede or render less attractive the exercise of such freedoms must be regarded as constituting such restrictions' (Case C-439/99 *Commission* v. *Italy* [2002] ECR I-305 at p. I-364; Case C-294/00 *Gräbner*, above, at p. I-6553). As seen in the previous section, an unjustified restriction may exist where a person established in two Member States is required to pay social security contributions in both (Case C-53/95 *Kemmler*, above, at p. I-715; see also Case 143/87 *Stanton*, above, at pp. 3893–5). Likewise, national rules relating to the issue and mutual recognition of driving licences constitute an obstacle to the free movement of persons (whether workers, self-employed persons, or providers of services) in that the possession of a driving licence duly recognized by the host State may affect the actual pursuit of a large number of occupations. Nevertheless, the Court has recognized that prior to the implementation of Dir. 91/439 as from 1 July 1996, which provides for the mutual recognition of driving licences issued by the Member States (*OJ* 1991 L237/1), such rules were not incompatible with Arts. 39, 43, and 49 unless they imposed disproportionately onerous requirements and penalties on the holders of driving licences obtained in other Member States (Case 16/78 *Choquet* [1978] ECR 2293 at pp. 2301–3; Case C-193/94 *Skanavi* [1996] ECR I-929 at pp. I-951–6).

Other examples of prohibited restrictions include national rules that, among other things, require the involvement of public authorities or local bodies in administrative appointments for trade-fair organizers (Case C-439/99 *Commission* v. *Italy*, above, at pp. I-369–72); national legislation that prohibits on pain of criminal penalties the activity of collecting bets, in particular bets on sporting events, without a licence or authorization from the host Member State, unless such legislation satisfies the four conditions discussed above (Case C-243/01 *Gambelli* [2003] ECR I-0000, paras. 46–9, 64–76); an administrative practice under which degrees awarded by a university of one Member State cannot be recognized in another Member State when the courses of preparation for those degrees are provided in the latter Member State by another educational establishment in accordance with an agreement made with the university (Case C-153/02 *Neri* [2003] ECR I-0000, paras. 39–44, 51); legislation under which a taxpayer wishing to transfer his tax residence outside the national territory, in exercise of the right of establishment, is subjected to disadvantageous tax treatment in comparison with a person who maintains his residence in the Member State of origin (Case C-9/02 *De Lasteyrie du Saillant* [2004] ECR I-0000, paras. 45–8, 58, 69).

On the other hand, the Court has held that national legislation on the closing of shops on Sundays and public holidays, applicable to all traders, does not aim to regulate the conditions of establishment of the undertakings concerned. Any restrictive effects that such legislation might have on freedom of establishment are too uncertain and indirect for them to be regarded as forming an obstacle to that freedom (Cases C-418/93 etc. *Semeraro Casa Uno* [1996] ECR I-2975 at p. I-3009).

V. Establishment of companies

1. The rules on establishment. Arts. 43 *et seq.* deal with companies in two different ways. First, Art. 43(2) grants natural persons who are nationals of a Member State the right 'to set up and manage undertakings, in particular companies or firms within the meaning of the second paragraph of Article 48', in the territory of another Member State 'under the conditions laid down for its own nationals by the law of the country where such establishment is effected' (primary establishment). Art. 43(1) prohibits restrictions 'on the setting-up of agencies, branches or subsidiaries by nationals of any Member State established in the territory of any Member State' (secondary establishment). These provisions are reinforced by Art. 294, which requires Member States to accord nationals of the other Member States 'the same treatment as their own nationals as regards participation in the capital of companies or firms within the meaning of Article 48'.

Secondly, Art. 48(1) extends the right of establishment in another Member State to companies themselves. It provides that:

> Companies or firms formed in accordance with the law of a Member State and having their registered office, central administration or principal place of business within the Community shall, for the purposes of this Chapter, be treated in the same way as natural persons who are nationals of Member States.

Art. 48(2) defines 'companies or firms' as 'companies or firms constituted under civil or commercial law, including co-operative societies, and other legal persons governed by public or private law, save for those which are non-profit-making'. Thus, non-profit-making companies are excluded from the provisions on the right of establishment (see Case C-70/95 *Sodemare* [1997] ECR I-3395 at p. I-3432). Although the reference to 'other legal persons' might suggest that an entity must possess full legal personality in order to benefit from the right of establishment, this is not necessarily so. While the ECJ has not yet directly ruled on this question, it seems that the decisive criterion is not the extent or degree of legal personality but the fact that the entity was validly constituted under national law (which is a mandatory requirement under Art. 48(1)). It can then enjoy freedom of establishment with whatever degree of legal personality it possesses according to its own legal system. This seems to follow also from the ruling of the Court in Case C-208/00 *Überseering*, above, para. 95, which makes it clear that the Member States are required to recognize the legal capacity (whatever it may be) 'which a company enjoys under the law of its State of incorporation' (see further below).

It may be noted that while non-EC nationals and companies do not enjoy the right of establishment under Community law, they may be able to form, or participate in the formation of, companies under the national law of a Member State. If such a company satisfies the conditions of Art. 48 it will benefit from freedom of establishment within the other Member States even though it is partly or wholly controlled from outside the Community. Nevertheless, according to Title I of the General Programme, where only the registered office of a company is situated within the Community, the activity of the company must show a 'real and continuous link' with the economy of a Member State, other than one of nationality, if the company wishes to set up a secondary establishment in the Community (see also Case C-208/00 *Überseering*, above, paras. 74–5).

It follows from Art. 48(1) that, like natural persons, companies enjoy the right of both primary and secondary establishment. A company incorporated in one Member State may set up a primary establishment in another Member State by transferring its activities and shares to a company newly incorporated there, if necessary after winding up in the first State, or by transferring its central management and control (i.e. the centre of administration or the real head office) to another Member State while maintaining its legal personality and its status as a company in the first State, where such moves are permitted by the laws of both States involved (see further below). A company may also exercise its right of primary establishment by taking part in the incorporation of a company in another Member State, and in that case Art. 294 EC ensures that it will receive the same treatment as nationals of that Member State as regards participation in the capital of the new company (see Case 81/87 *Daily Mail*, above, at p. 5511).

However, in the case of a company, the right of establishment is generally exercised by the setting up of secondary establishments in other Member States, i.e. agencies, branches, or subsidiaries, as is expressly provided for in Art. 43(1). A secondary establishment includes the opening of an investment management office in another Member State (ibid.), and the Court has held that an undertaking of one Member State that maintains a permanent presence in another 'comes within the scope of the provisions of the Treaty on the right of establishment, even if that presence does not take the form of a branch or agency, but consists merely of an office managed by the undertaking's own staff or by a person who is independent but authorized to act on a permanent basis for the undertaking, as would be the case with an agency' (Case 205/84 *Commission* v. *Germany* [1986] ECR 3755 at p. 3801—'Insurance' case).

Art. 48 requires companies properly set up within the Community to be treated 'in the same way as natural persons who are nationals of Member States'. It is clear, however, that companies cannot be treated in *exactly* the same way as natural persons in so far as cross-border movement is concerned. While, for example, natural persons can physically move from one

Member State to another without losing their identity, companies normally cannot or, at least, not with the same ease. Companies as legal persons depend for their existence on their law of incorporation and the extent to which they can change their residence, moving from one State to another, depends on the law of the State of incorporation and on that of the host State. As the ECJ has put it, 'unlike natural persons, companies are creatures of the law and, in the present state of Community law, creatures of national law. They exist only by virtue of the varying national legislation which determines their incorporation and functioning' (Case 81/87 *Daily Mail*, above, at p. 5511, see, however, the entry on *European Company*).

The legislation of the Member States varies as regards both the connecting factor between a company and the national territory and legal system which is required for the establishment of a company, and the circumstances in which a company, once established in a Member State, may transfer its seat to another State. In this respect, the Member States follow one or the other of two opposing principles. According to the 'incorporation principle', currently followed by six Member States (Denmark, Finland, Ireland, the Netherlands, Sweden, and the United Kingdom), the connecting factor is incorporation: the company is connected to the jurisdiction of the Member State in which it has been incorporated. It is the law of this State that governs the company, its organization and internal affairs, its legal personality and legal capacity, throughout the company's life. The company may carry on its activities in other States, including even the transfer of its seat, without losing its original status, legal personality, and legal capacity and without the need for reincorporation there.

According to the 'real seat principle', followed by the remaining nine Member States, the connecting factor is the real seat of the company: the company is connected to the jurisdiction of the Member State in which its real seat is. It is the law of this State that governs the company, its organization and internal affairs, its legal personality and legal capacity. If the company transfers its real seat to another State, it will lose its status, legal personality, and legal capacity in the State of origin and may have to be wound up. Depending on the legal system of the host State, it may have to reincorporate there. While, in the case of a transfer of seat, host Member States following the incorporation principle recognize foreign companies according to the rules applicable in the State of origin, those following the real seat principle refuse to do so and subject the foreign company to their own rules, requiring it to reincorporate. Otherwise the company will not have legal personality and legal capacity in the host State.

What the 'real seat' is, is not clearly defined. Often it is referred to as the 'corporate seat', 'real head office', '*siège réel*', 'central administration', or 'centre of management and control'. It is as much an economic concept as a legal one. It is normally the place where the company's central management and administration is located and where the decisions that are essential for the company's operations are taken. It is 'the economic centre of gravity of the undertaking', 'the place from which the company is actually run' (see

Case 81/87 *Daily Mail*, above, at p. 5501 *per* A.-G. Darmon, citing various authors).

These variations in national legislation clearly present an obstacle to freedom of establishment of companies, particularly when a company wishes to move from a Member State that follows the incorporation principle to another Member State which adheres to the real seat principle, or the other way round. That obstacle could be removed by harmonization at the Community level or by the conclusion of agreements between the Member States. However, none of the directives on the co-ordination of company law so far adopted under Art. 44(2)(g) EC (for which see below) deals with these differences. Art. 293 EC specifically provides for the conclusion of conventions between the Member States with a view to securing, *inter alia*, the mutual recognition of companies or firms and the retention of legal personality in the event of transfer of their seat from one country to another. On this basis, a Convention on the Mutual Recognition of Companies and Legal Persons was signed in 1968 (see Suppl.–*Bull. EC* 2–1969, p. 5), which in principle provides that companies formed under the law of one Contracting State shall be recognized in another as having the capacity accorded to them by the law of the first State. However, this Convention has not yet entered into force.

The EC Treaty itself has taken account of these differences in national legislation. Art. 48(1) provides that, in order to benefit from freedom of establishment, companies must fulfil two conditions. First, they must be formed in accordance with the law of a Member State. Secondly, they must have either their registered office, central administration, or principal place of business within the Community. Thus, in the case of companies, it is the location either of their registered office or central administration or principal place of business that constitutes the connecting factor with the legal system of a particular Member State in the same way as does nationality in the case of natural persons (Case 270/83 *Commission* v. *France*, above, at p. 304; Case C-212/97 *Centros* [1999] ECR I-1459 at p. I-1491; Case C-208/00 *Überseering*, above, para. 57). The Treaty places these three alternative connecting factors on the same footing, without giving priority to any one of them (Case 81/87 *Daily Mail*, above, at p. 5512). The Treaty does not make a choice between the incorporation and real seat theories. Nevertheless, the question still remains whether and to what extent the Treaty provisions on freedom of establishment may be relied on to remove the obstacles that the discrepancies between the various national company laws create for the establishment and free movement of companies within the Community. This question has been dealt with by the ECJ in a series of important cases, which will be considered below.

The first case to mention is Case 79/85 *Segers*, above, at pp. 2387–8. That case concerned a company that was formed in accordance with English law, had its registered office in London, but conducted all its business in the Netherlands through its Netherlands subsidiary. Its shareholders were Netherlands nationals. The Netherlands authorities refused to grant the director of the company sickness insurance benefits solely on the ground that the company was formed under the law of another Member State, where it also had its registered office, even though it did not conduct any business there. The Court held that since the company satisfied the conditions laid down by Art. 48(1) with regard to formation and connecting factors, it enjoyed the right of establishment and was entitled to the same treatment as national companies. The fact that it was formed in one Member State only for the purpose of establishing itself in another Member State, where it conducted its main, or even entire, business through an agency, branch, or subsidiary, was immaterial (as to the discriminatory treatment of the company's director, see further below).

The principle indicated in *Segers* was applied and taken to its logical conclusion in Case C-212/97 *Centros*, above, at pp. I-1490 *et seq*. In that case the company, Centros, was formed in England and Wales, where it had its registered office, but where it did not carry on any business. Its shareholders were Danish nationals living in Denmark. They wanted to set up a branch in Denmark, but the Danish authorities refused to register the branch on the grounds that the purpose of the branch was to enable Centros to carry on its entire business in Denmark while avoiding the formation of a company there, thus evading the application of Danish company law, which was more restrictive than English law so far as minimum paid-up share capital was concerned.

The Court noted, in the first place, that the situation fell within the scope of Community law. The fact that the company was formed in the United Kingdom for the purpose of avoiding Danish legislation did not mean that the setting-up by that British company of a branch in Denmark was not covered by the provisions on freedom of establishment. The refusal by a Member State to register a branch of a company having its registered office in another Member State constituted an obstacle to the exercise of that freedom (ibid. at p. I-1492).

In response to the argument of the Danish authorities that, since the sole purpose of forming the company in the United Kingdom was to circumvent the application of Danish law, refusal of registration was necessary in order to prevent an abuse of the right of establishment, the Court observed:

> The fact that a national of a Member State who wishes to set up a company chooses to form it in the Member State whose rules of company law seem to him the least restrictive and to set up branches in other Member States cannot, in itself, constitute an abuse of the right of establishment. The right to form a company in accordance with the law of a Member State and to set up branches in other Member States is inherent in the exercise, in a single market, of the freedom of establishment guaranteed by the Treaty . . .
>
> In addition, it is clear from paragraph 16 of *Segers* that the fact that a company does not conduct any business in the Member State in which it has its registered office and pursues its activities only in the Member State where its branch is established is not sufficient to prove the existence of abuse or fraudulent conduct which would entitle the latter Member State to deny that company the benefit of the provisions of Community law relating to the right of establishment (ibid. at pp. I-1493–4).

The fact that company law was not completely harmonized in the Community was of little importance. Moreover, the Court added, it was always open to the Council to achieve complete harmonization by using its powers under Art. 44(2)(g) EC (ibid.).

On the basis of these considerations, the Court concluded that the Danish practice was incompatible with Arts. 43 and 48 EC, and that it could not be justified by the need to protect creditors against the risk of insolvency of a company with inadequate capitalization. Such ground of justification was covered neither by Art. 46 EC nor by the Court's case-law relating to overriding reasons based on the general interest (ibid. at pp. I-1494–6; for the Court's case-law see Case C-55/94 *Gebhard*, above, at pp. I-4197–9, discussed in section IV.3).

The principles established in *Segers* and *Centros* were confirmed and applied in Case C-167/01 *Inspire Art* [2003] ECR I-10155. The case concerned the compatibility with Arts. 43 and 48 EC of the Netherlands Law on Formally Foreign Companies. According to that Law, 'formally foreign companies' are companies formed outside the Netherlands and having legal personality, which carry on their activities entirely or almost entirely in the Netherlands and do not have any real connection with the State in which they were formed (the so-called 'brass-plate' or 'letter-box' companies). The Law imposed a number of obligations on such companies relating, *inter alia*, to minimum capital and directors' liability. On the basis of the above cases, the Court held that the mandatory application of those obligations to branches of companies formed in other Member States had the effect of impeding the exercise by those companies of the freedom of establishment guaranteed by the Treaty. It subjected the creation of such branches to certain rules of national law on the formation of companies. The legislation was, therefore, incompatible with Arts. 43 and 48 EC, and could not be justified on grounds of protecting creditors, or combating abuse of freedom of establishment, or safeguarding fairness in business dealings or the efficiency of tax inspections, either under Art. 46 EC or under the Court's above-mentioned *Gebhard* case-law (ibid. paras. 95–105, 131–43).

While the above cases concerned the freedom to set up secondary establishments in other Member States, Case 81/87 *Daily Mail*, above, at pp. 5510–12, involved the entirely different question whether a company formed in accordance with the law of one Member State could transfer its registered office or its actual centre of administration to another Member State without losing its legal personality under the law of the Member State of incorporation. Daily Mail, a company incorporated under English law and having its registered office in London, wished to transfer its central management and control to the Netherlands, principally for tax reasons. It claimed that Arts. 43 and 48 EC gave it the right to do so without prior consent of the national authorities, which consent was required under United Kingdom tax legislation where the company sought to maintain its legal personality and status as a United Kingdom company.

Faced with the differences in national legislation concerning the required connecting factor and the question whether, and if so how, the registered office or real head office of a company incorporated under national law may be transferred from one Member State to another, the Court concluded that the Treaty regarded those differences as problems that were not resolved by the Treaty provisions on the right of establishment but would have to be dealt with by future legislation or conventions. Therefore, the Court held that in the present state of Community law, Arts. 43 and 48 could not be interpreted as conferring on a company incorporated under the law of a Member State and having its registered office there a right to transfer its central management and control and its central administration to another Member State while retaining its status as a company incorporated in the first Member State (ibid. at p. 5512). Nor could a company derive such a right from Art. 2 of Dir. 73/148 (see section I above), which expressly required the Member States to grant natural persons wishing to establish themselves in another Member State the right to leave their territory. The Court held that that directive governed solely the movement and residence of natural persons and that it could not be applied by analogy to legal persons (ibid. at p. 5513).

Finally, Case C-208/00 *Überseering*, above, paras. 52 *et seq.*, concerned yet another problem, namely, that of the legal status of a company which is incorporated in one Member State and is deemed to have moved its actual centre of administration to another Member State. Überseering was a company incorporated in the Netherlands and having its registered office there. Subsequently, two German nationals living in Germany acquired all the shares in it. When Überseering brought a legal action in Germany against a German company to enforce rights under a contract, the German courts dismissed its action on the grounds that as a result of the acquisition of its shares by German nationals Überseering had, according to German law, transferred its actual centre of administration to Germany and, as a company incorporated under Netherlands law, it did not have legal capacity under German law and consequently did not have the capacity to be a party to legal proceedings before German courts. Since German law follows the 'real seat principle', a company's legal capacity is determined by reference to German law, and a company incorporated in another State cannot possess such capacity unless it has been reincorporated in Germany (ibid. paras. 3–5). The ECJ was asked whether in these circumstances the freedom of establishment of companies (Arts. 43 and 48 EC) precluded Germany from denying the company in question legal capacity and therefore the capacity to bring legal proceedings before its courts, and required that such capacity be determined according to the law of the State of incorporation.

The Court started by saying that in a situation such as that described above, the rules which the host Member State applied to the company in question did not fall outside the scope of the Community provisions on freedom of establishment. Although the conventions that might be concluded under Art. 293 EC may, like the harmonizing directives under Art. 44 EC, facilitate the attainment of freedom of establishment, the exercise of that freedom could not be dependent upon the adoption of such conventions. Companies meeting the conditions set out in Art. 48 were able to exercise the right of establishment directly under Arts. 43 and 48, which had direct effect since the end of the transitional period, even in the absence of a convention on the mutual recognition of companies. Such a convention was not needed since recognition of those companies by any Member State in which they wished to establish themselves was a necessary precondition for the exercise of the right of establishment and therefore followed directly from the Treaty (paras. 52–60).

The Court then distinguished between *Daily Mail* and the present case. While *Daily Mail* concerned relations between a company and the Member State of incorporation in a situation where the company wished to *emigrate*, i.e. transfer its actual centre of administration to another Member State, the present case concerned an *immigration* situation, i.e. the recognition by one Member State of a company incorporated in another Member State, where that company was deemed by the host State to have moved its actual centre of administration to its territory (even although in fact Überseering never intended to transfer its seat to Germany, did not cease to be validly incorporated under Netherlands law, and did not lose its legal personality under that law). While the *Daily Mail* situation was covered by national law, in that case the Court did not recognize that a Member State had the power, in the *Überseering* situation, to subject a company's effective exercise in its territory of freedom of establishment to compliance with its domestic company law. Thus, Überseering could rely on that freedom in order to contest the refusal by German law to regard it as a legal person (ibid. paras. 61–77).

The Court next pointed out that as a company validly incorporated in the Netherlands and having its registered office there, Überseering was entitled under Arts. 43 and 48 to exercise its freedom of establishment in Germany as a Netherlands company. The fact that its shares were acquired by German nationals was of little importance since that had not caused Überseering to cease to be a legal person under Netherlands law. Its very existence was inseparable from its status as a company incorporated under that law. The requirement of reincorporation in Germany was therefore tantamount to outright negation of freedom of establishment. In those circumstances, the Court concluded, the refusal by Germany to recognize Überseering's legal capacity unless it was reincorporated under its law constituted a restriction on freedom of establishment which was, in principle, incompatible with Arts. 43 and 48 (ibid. paras. 78–82). It followed that in similar cases the host Member State was required to recognize the legal capacity which the foreign company enjoyed under the law of its State of incorporation (ibid. para. 95).

Finally, dealing with the question whether the restriction established could be justified, the Court pointed out that overriding reasons relating to the general interest, such as the protection of the interests of creditors, minority shareholders, employees, and even the taxation authorities, might, in certain circumstances and subject to certain conditions, justify restrictions on freedom of establishment. However, the Court added, such objectives could not justify denying the legal capacity of a company properly incorporated in another Member State in which it had its registered office.

Such a measure would be tantamount to an outright negation of the freedom of establishment (ibid. paras. 92–3).

The decisions of the Court considered above have generated much discussion and controversy amongst both legal practitioners and academic commentators (*see under **Further reading*** below). However, the questions raised may be narrowed down to two central issues. First, what is the effect of those decisions on the company laws of the Member States? Secondly, what is their impact upon freedom of establishment of companies under Community law? Before assessing the case-law, it should be pointed out that each ruling of the Court must be narrowly interpreted, strictly in the context of the case in which it was made. That drawing general conclusions can be wrong and misleading is shown by the fact that the Court itself rejected too broad interpretations of its decisions by Member States and private litigants alike (see, in particular, the *Überseering* and *Inspire Art* cases in which the Court did not accept arguments based on the *Daily Mail* and to some extent on the *Centros* decisions, and interpreted the *Daily Mail* ruling very strictly). It is also important to stress that, contrary to views expressed by some commentators, there is no contradiction or inconsistency between the five cases considered, provided that each decision is correctly interpreted. It is true that the Court has not so far had an opportunity to deal with every conceivable problem that may arise in this complex area of Community law (precisely because in each case it limited itself strictly to the given circumstances) so that certain questions remain unresolved (see below). However, all the decisions that have been made so far are underpinned by the same logic and thus form a coherent body of case-law aimed at achieving the same paramount objective, namely, the realization of complete freedom of establishment for companies.

As regards the first question, the effect of the cases on national company law should not be exaggerated. They affect each Member State's company law only as far as the intra-Community mobility of companies is concerned, and only to the extent strictly necessary to ensure freedom of establishment as guaranteed by the Treaty (see below). In relation to companies established within the national territory and in third countries, the Member States remain free to set the rules, subject to the already existing directives (as to the former companies, see *Daily Mail*). Far from attempting to harmonize company law through judicial decisions, the whole logic of the cases is that, on the contrary, freedom of establishment can be achieved without complete harmonization (see below). Where a problem cannot be resolved in the absence of harmonization, national law continues to apply (*Daily Mail*). Where a problem can be resolved under an existing harmonization directive, there is no need to resort to the Court's case-law (*Inspire Art*). In any case, the Court has expressly confirmed that harmonization of company law is a matter for the Community legislature (*Centros*). The case-law of the Court is moreover neutral in respect of the 'incorporation' and 'real seat' principles; it explicitly recognizes that the Treaty places those principles on an equal footing (*Daily Mail*).

As regards the second question, there can be no doubt whatsoever that the cases discussed have an enormously liberating effect on the mobility of companies in the internal market. It is no exaggeration to say that the Court has achieved more in this field over four years—between 1999 (*Centros*) and 2003 (*Inspire Art*)—than the Community legislature over the previous forty. Yet the Court has not used any revolutionary ideas. It simply applied the same logic as that which dictated its earlier decisions in other major areas of Community law. All the solutions adopted in these cases, however innovative they may seem, may be traced back to three fundamental principles of Community law, firmly established over the years in relation to other matters.

The first is the principle of direct effect. Since Arts. 43 and 48 have been directly effective since the end of the transitional period, freedom of establishment for companies can be derived directly from them. Harmonizing directives and conventions, while useful, are not an essential precondition for achieving that freedom (*Centros, Überseering*). This is exactly the same reasoning as that which the Court has used in relation to individuals, when deciding that equality of treatment and recognition of qualifications can be achieved by judicial interpretation of Art. 43 in the absence of harmonization by directives (see sections III and IV above). This reasoning puts companies in the same position as individuals, and is thus entirely in line with Art. 48 which requires that companies 'shall be treated in the same way as natural persons' (see above).

The second is the principle of mutual recognition. This principle is based on the *Cassis de Dijon* case (Case 120/78 *Rewe* [1979] ECR 649), and brings the free movement of companies in line with the free movement of goods. Once goods are lawfully produced and marketed in one Member State, they must in principle be recognized as being able to be marketed in any other Member State without being subject to additional controls, save in exceptional cases. Similarly, once a company is validly incorporated in one Member State and has its registered office there, its legal personality under the law of that State must be recognized by any other Member State to which it transfers its seat without being subject to the requirement of reincorporation (*Überseering*).

The third is the principle of primacy of Community law. Since freedom of establishment of companies is a rule of Community law, any rule of national company law that restricts that freedom or is in any way incompatible with it must not be applied to companies established within the Community. This is simply the application of a fundamental principle of Community law in the field of company law, just as the same principle applies in all branches of national law, whether it be constitutional law, criminal law, competition law, commercial law, etc. It follows that rules of national company law which in any way restrict the primary (*Überseering*) or secondary (*Seegers, Centros, Inspire Art*) establishment of Community companies may not be applied. From this point of view, there is no distinction between primary and secondary establishment: neither must be obstructed by provisions of national company law. It also follows that rules of national company law that do not interfere with the freedom of establishment continue to apply to primary or secondary establishments of Community companies, since these, like natural persons, must operate under the conditions laid down for its own nationals and companies by the law of the host Member State (Art. 43(2) EC; see below). National rules that are liable to hinder or make less attractive the exercise of freedom of establishment can be justified only under Art. 46 EC or if they fulfil the four conditions laid down by the Court in the *Gebhard* case-law. Whether a particular rule of national law relating to the formation, organization, operation, etc. of companies is incompatible with the freedom of establishment, can be decided only on a case-by-case basis.

Nevertheless, as mentioned above, the Court's case-law does not answer every conceivable question. Thus, for example, the *Überseering* case dealt exclusively with the situation where a company established in a Member State which follows the incorporation principle had moved, or was deemed to have moved, its actual centre of administration to a Member State which follows the real seat principle. The company in question had not lost its legal personality and its status as a validly incorporated company in the first State, so that recognition of its legal personality and capacity in the second State did not raise insuperable difficulties. It is, however, not clear what should happen in the opposite situation, namely, where a company established in a Member State which follows the real seat principle moves its centre of administration to a Member State which follows the incorporation principle (or to one which also follows the real seat principle). According to the law of the State of origin, in such a situation the company would lose its legal personality and its status as a company in the home State so that it could not continue its legal existence in the host State without reincorporation. According to *Daily Mail*, a company incorporated in one Member State does not even have the right under Community law to retain its legal personality and its status as a company when moving its centre of administration to another Member State. The case-law of the Court does not give an answer to the question whether in such a situation the host Member State is still required to recognize the legal personality of the company in question in spite of the fact that it has lost it under the law of its State of origin.

2. Prohibition of discrimination. While restrictions on the right of establishment of companies resulting from differences in national company law have not been fully eliminated, discriminatory treatment of foreign companies is strictly prohibited. As the ECJ has pointed out on several occasions, Arts. 43 and 48 EC 'guarantee nationals of Member States of the Community who have exercised their freedom of establishment and companies or firms which are assimilated to them the same treatment in the host Member State as that accorded to nationals of that Member State' (Case C-307/97 *Saint-Gobain* [1999] ECR I-6161 at p. I-6195; Case C-466/98 *Commission* v. *United Kingdom*, above, para. 45).

Discriminatory treatment of foreign companies most often arises in the field of taxation. With regard to taxation of companies, the same basic principle applies as in the case of taxation of individuals (see section III.3 above), namely, that 'although direct taxation falls within the competence of the Member States, the latter must none the less exercise that competence consistently with Community law and therefore avoid any overt or covert discrimination on grounds of nationality' (Case C-250/95 *Futura Participations and Singer* [1997] ECR I-2471 at p. I-2499; Case C-264/96 *ICI*, above, at p. I-4721; Case C-311/97 *Royal Bank of Scotland* [1999] ECR I-2651 at p. I-2671; etc.). As seen above, in the case of companies, 'nationality' is determined by the location either of their registered office or central administration or principal place of business, which are the factors that connect a company to the legal system of a particular Member State in the same way as does nationality in the case of natural persons. Therefore, in the case of companies, it is primarily discrimination based on the location of their registered office in the above-mentioned sense that is prohibited. As the Court has put it, 'acceptance of the proposition that the Member State in which a company seeks to establish itself [by setting up an agency, branch, or subsidiary] may freely apply to it a different treatment solely by reason of the fact that its registered office is situated in another Member State would deprive Article 48 of all meaning' (Case 270/83 *Commission* v. *France*, above, at p. 304; Case 79/85 *Segers*, above, at p. 2387). Thus, discrimination is prohibited even if the establishment is secondary.

On the basis of these considerations, in Case 270/83 *Commission* v. *France*, above, at pp. 303–7, the Court held that French tax legislation, which discriminated against branches and agencies in France of insurance companies whose registered office was in another Member State by comparison with companies whose registered office was in France, was contrary to Art. 43. The French tax system in question denied to such branches and agencies the benefit of shareholders' tax credits, which benefit was available to companies whose registered office was in France. The discrimination was made even more apparent by the fact that both forms of establishment were treated in the same way for the purposes of taxing their profits. The Court held that the fact that companies established in another Member State could have availed themselves of the tax credits by setting up a subsidiary in France instead of a branch or agency, could not justify different treatment. As the Court observed, Art. 43(1) 'expressly leaves traders free to choose the appropriate legal form in which to pursue their activities in another Member State and that freedom of choice must not be limited by discriminatory tax provisions' (ibid. at p. 305). The Court further held that neither the absence of harmonization of corporation tax nor the risk of tax avoidance could justify the difference of treatment. Art. 43 did not permit any derogation on such grounds. The rights conferred by Art. 43 were unconditional and could not be made subject to a requirement of reciprocity either.

In a number of subsequent cases, the Court has confirmed that discriminatory tax treatment of secondary establishments according to whether the seat of their parent company is located in the national territory or in another Member State is, unless objectively justified, contrary to Arts. 43 and 48. The grounds for justification are the same as in the case of individuals, as discussed in section III.4 above (Case C-250/95 *Futura Participations and Singer*, above, at pp. I-2499–504; Case C-311/97 *Royal Bank of Scotland*, above, at pp. I-2673–6; Cases C-397/98 etc. *Metallgesellschaft* [2001] ECR I-1727 at pp. I-1775–82; Case C-436/00 *X and Y II*, above, paras. 38–65; Case C-324/00 *Lankhorst-Hohorst* [2002] ECR I-11779, paras. 27–45).

Moreover, the Court has held that in the case of a double-taxation treaty concluded between a Member State and a non-member country, the national treatment principle requires the Member State that is party to the treaty to grant to permanent establishments of non-resident EC companies the advantages provided for by that treaty on the same conditions as those which apply to resident companies (Case C-307/97 *Saint-Gobain*, above, at p. I-6202). Subsequently, the Court applied this principle to the bilateral air transport agreements that eight Member States concluded with the United States. The effect of these agreements was that airlines established in each of those Member States but owned by another Member State or its nationals ('Community airlines') could always be excluded from the benefit of the agreement (i.e. from operating authorizations and technical permissions), while that benefit was assured to airlines established in and owned by the Member State which concluded the agreement or its nationals ('national airlines'). Consequently, Community airlines suffered discrimination that prevented them from benefiting from the treatment that the host Member State accorded to its own nationals. This constituted an infringement of Art. 43 EC, which could not be justified on grounds of public policy under Art. 46 (Case C-466/98 *Commission* v. *United Kingdom*, above, paras. 46–61; see also the similar cases brought by the Commission against Denmark, Sweden, Finland, Belgium, Luxembourg, Austria, and Germany and decided by the Court on the same day, Cases C-467/98, C-468/98, C-469/98, C-471/98, C-472/98, C-475/98, C-476/98 [2002] ECR I-9519, I-9575, I-9627, I-9681, I-9741, I-9797, I-9855—'Open skies' cases).

Differential tax treatment is prohibited not only when it is based on the seat of the parent company, but also when it is based on the location of subsidiaries. Thus, companies established in a Member State cannot be subjected to different tax treatment according to whether their subsidiaries are established in the national territory or in other Member States, unless such inequality of treatment is objectively justified (Case C-264/96 *ICI*, above, at pp. I-4721–5; Case C-200/98 *X and Y I* [1999] ECR I-8261 at p. I-8286; see also Case C-141/99 *AMID* [2000] ECR I-11619 at pp. I-11641–4).

In Case 79/85 *Segers*, above, at pp. 2387–9, the Court held that the requirement of equal treatment applies not only to companies but also to their employees who must have the right to be affiliated to a specific social security scheme of the host State. As the Court explained, discrimination against employees in connection with social security protection indirectly restricts the freedom of companies of another Member State to establish themselves through an agency, branch, or subsidiary in the host State. The Court relied on Title III (A) (i) of the General Programme, which requires the elimination of national provisions that deny or restrict the right of foreign nationals to participate in social security schemes, in particular sickness, accident, invalidity, or old-age insurance schemes, or the right to receive family allowances. Member States are therefore prohibited from excluding the director of a company from such schemes solely on the ground that the company was formed in accordance with the law of another Member State where it also had its registered office. Even the need to combat abuse and fraud, which may justify a difference of treatment in certain circumstances under Art. 46 EC, cannot justify such an exclusion.

Arts. 43 and 48 prohibit not only direct or overt discrimination by reason of the location of the registered office (seat) of a company but also all indirect or covert forms of discrimination that, by the use of other criteria of differentiation, such as that of fiscal residence, lead in fact to the same result. Thus, the Court has held that those provisions prevent national tax legislation from denying repayment supplement on overpaid tax to companies that are resident for tax purposes in another Member State whilst granting the supplement to companies that are resident for tax purposes in the Member State in question. Although applying independently of the registered office (seat) of a company, such legislation is liable to work to the disadvantage of companies having their registered office in other Member States because it is most often these companies that are resident for tax purposes outside the national territory (Case C-330/91 *Commerzbank* [1993] ECR I-4017 at pp. I-4043–4. See, however, Art. 58(1)(a) EC, inserted by the TEU, which in the context of the free movement of capital and payments allows differential tax treatment on the basis of residence, *see further under* **Free movement of capital**, section IV. For other instances of indirect or covert discrimination against companies established in other Member States, see Case C-1/93 *Halliburton Services*, above, at pp. I-1156–8 and Case C-254/97 *Baxter* [1999] ECR I-4809 at pp. I-4829–32, both involving differential tax treatment; Case C-3/88 *Commission* v. *Italy*, above, at p. 4059 and Case C-272/91 *Commission* v. *Italy*, above, at pp. I-1433–6, see section III.2 above).

3. **Non-discriminatory restrictions.** As in the case of individuals, prohibited restrictions on the right of establishment of companies may also arise from non-discriminatory measures. Thus, the Court has said that national measures constitute such a restriction if they are liable to place companies from other Member States in a less favourable factual or legal situation than companies from the State of establishment. Such a restriction, even if applied in a non-discriminatory manner, is contrary to Arts. 43 and 48 unless it is justified by overriding requirements in the general interest, such as the protection of industrial and commercial property, and satisfies the conditions laid down in the *Gebhard* case-law (Case C-255/97 *Pfeiffer Grosshandel* [1999] ECR I-2835 at pp. I-2860–2, where the Court held that a restraining order prohibiting the use of a trade name by companies established in another Member State where they lawfully used that name constituted a restriction on the right of establishment but was justified by the need to protect trade names against the risk of confusion). Legislation that restricts the grant of authorization to carry on certain activities to companies formed within the national territory is also contrary to Art. 43 since it prevents companies established in other Member States from carrying on

their activities through a branch or an agency. Such legislation cannot be justified under Arts. 45 and 46 EC (Case C-114/97 *Commission* v. *Spain*, above, at pp. I-6741–5, involving companies providing private security services).

Nevertheless, Art. 48 does not apply to situations that are purely internal to a Member State. Thus, a company formed and having its head office in a Member State where it pursues all its activities, cannot claim in the same State the benefits of the right of establishment granted to companies formed under the laws of the other Member States (see e.g. Case C-134/94 *Esso Española* [1995] ECR I-4223 at pp. I-4247–8). However, nationals of other Member States who have participated in the formation of such a company and have thereby exercised their right of establishment are entitled to equal treatment with the nationals of the host State (Case 182/83 *Fearon*, above, at pp. 3685–6, concerning compulsory acquisition of rural land in Ireland owned by an Irish company whose shareholders were British nationals; see also section III.4 above).

4. Company law directives. Finally, it should be noted that Art. 44 EC contains certain provisions that are designed to facilitate the establishment of companies by means of directives to be adopted by the Council and Parliament. Thus, Art. 44(2)(f) provides for the abolition of restrictions not only on the setting up of agencies, branches, and subsidiaries in other Member States but also on the transfer of personnel from the main establishment to managerial or supervisory posts in such secondary establishments (see also the last paragraph of Title III (A) of the General Programme). Art. 44(2)(g) requires the co-ordination of the safeguards that national company law provides for the protection of the interests of members of companies and others (e.g. creditors). The aim is to make such safeguards equivalent throughout the Community and thereby encourage dealing with foreign companies. A number of directives have been adopted under this provision (*see further under* **Company law**).

See also **Company law, Direct taxation, Expulsion, Freedom to provide services, Free movement of capital, Free movement of persons, Official authority, Public health, Public policy, Public security, Residence permit, Right of entry and residence, Right to leave, Right to remain, Social security.**

Further reading 1. Books: Adamson, *Free Movement and Establishment of Lawyers in Europe* (1991); Barnard, *EC Employment Law*, 2nd edn. (2000), ch. 3; id., *The Substantive Law of the EU. The Four Freedoms* (2004), part iii; Craig and de Búrca, *EU Law. Text, Cases, and Materials*, 3rd edn. (2003), ch. 18; Steiner, Woods, and Twigg-Flesner, *Textbook on EC Law*, 8th edn. (2003), ch. 16; Wyatt and Dashwood, *European Union Law*, 4th edn. (2000), ch. 15.

2. Articles: Biondi, 'In and Out of the Internal Market: Recent Developments on the Principle of Free Movement' (1999–2000) *YEL* 469; Bogusz, 'Regulating the Right of Establishment for Accession State Nationals: Reinforcing the "Buffer Zone" or Improving Labour Market Flexibility?'

(2002) *EL Rev.* 472; Cabral and Cunha, ' "Presumed Innocent": Companies and the Exercise of the Right of Establishment under Community Law' (2000) *EL Rev.* 157; Cath, 'Freedom of Establishment of Companies: A New Step Towards Completion of the Internal Market' (1986) *YEL* 247; Drury, 'Migrating Companies' (1999) *EL Rev.* 354; Dyrberg, 'Full Free Movement of Companies in the European Community at Last?' (2003) *EL Rev.* 528; Edward, 'Establishment and Services: An Analysis of the Insurance Cases' (1987) *EL Rev.* 231; Edwards, 'Secondary Establishment of Companies—The Case Law of the Court of Justice' (1998) *YEL* 221; Forwood and Clough, 'The Single European Act and Free Movement. Legal Implications of the Provisions for the Completion of the Internal Market' (1986) *EL Rev.* 383; Kaldellis, 'Freedom of Establishment v. Freedom to Provide Services: An Evaluation of Case-Law Developments in the Area of Indistinctly Applicable Rules' (2001) *LIEI* 23; Laslett, 'The Mutual Recognition of Diplomas, Certificates and Other Evidence of Formal Qualifications in the European Community' (1990/1) *LIEI* 1; Lasok, 'Freedom to Provide Insurance Services in the Light of the "Coinsurance Cases" '(1988) *MLR* 706; Lonbay, 'Picking Over the Bones: Rights of Establishment Reviewed' (1991) *EL Rev.* 507; id., 'Lawyers Bounding over the Borders: the Draft Directive on Lawyer's Establishment' (1996) *EL Rev.* 50; Looijestijn-Clearie, 'Centros Ltd—A Complete U-Turn in the Right of Establishment for Companies?' (2000) *ICLQ* 621; Marenco, 'The Notion of Restriction on the Freedom of Establishment and Provision of Services in the Case-Law of the Court' (1991) *YEL* 111; Micheler, 'Recognition of Companies Incorporated in Other EU Member States' (2003) *ICLQ* 521; Pertek, 'Free Movement of Professionals and Recognition of Higher-Education Diplomas' (1992) *YEL* 293; Roth, 'From *Centros* to *Ueberseering:* Free Movement of Companies, Private International Law, and Community Law' (2003) *ICLQ* 177; Siems, 'Convergence, Competition, *Centros* and Conflicts of Law: European Company Law in the 21st Century' (2002) *EL Rev.* 47; Skarlatos, 'European Lawyers' Right to Transnational Legal Practice in the European Community' (1991/1) *LIEI* 49; Tridimas, 'The Case-Law of the European Court of Justice on Corporate Entities' (1993) *YEL* 335; Wathelet, 'The Influence of Free Movement of Persons, Services and Capital on National Direct Taxation: Trends in the Case-Law of the Court of Justice' (2001) *YEL* 1; Wymeersch, 'The Transfer of the Company's Seat in European Company Law' (2003) *CML Rev.* 661; Wouters, 'Fiscal Barriers to Companies' Cross-Border Establishment in the Case-Law of the EC Court of Justice' (1994) *YEL* 73.

See also under **Free movement of persons.**

▶ **FREEDOM TO PROVIDE SERVICES** One of the four fundamental freedoms forming the basis of the internal market, the purpose of which is the liberalization within the Community of all gainful activity not covered by the other three freedoms, i.e. by the free movement of goods, persons, and capital (see Cases 286/82 etc. *Luisi and Carbone* [1984] ECR 377 at

p. 401; Art. 50(1) EC). Thus, the four freedoms should, in principle, encompass all economic activities falling within the scope of the European Community (see section II below).

Although the EC Treaty treats the free movement of services as a distinct 'freedom', it is clear that in most (even if not all) cases this freedom involves the cross-border movement of persons, just as freedom of movement for workers and freedom of establishment. There is thus a very close interrelationship between these three freedoms since they all pursue the same objective in the context of the realization of the internal market. They are often referred to together in the case-law of the ECJ as 'liberties which are fundamental in the Community system' (see e.g. Case 115/78 *Knoors* [1979] ECR 399 at p. 409). Their close relationship is also shown by the fact that they are dealt with in three consecutive chapters of Title III in Part Three of the EC Treaty, as amended by the Treaty on European Union (TEU) and the Treaty of Amsterdam (ToA): Chapter 1 dealing with workers (i.e. employed persons); Chapter 2 with the right of establishment (i.e. self-employed persons); and Chapter 3 with services (i.e. providers and recipients of services). Although in their application the chapters on establishment and services are mutually exclusive (see Case C-55/94 *Gebhard* [1995] ECR I-4165 at pp. I-4193–4), in several cases the ECJ has pointed out that the three chapters are based on the same principles both as regards entry into, residence, and the pursuit of an economic activity in the territory of the Member States by persons covered by Community law and as regards the prohibition of all discrimination against them on grounds of nationality (Case 48/75 *Royer* [1976] ECR 497 at p. 509; Case 118/75 *Watson and Belmann* [1976] ECR 1185 at pp. 1196–7; Case C-107/94 *Asscher* [1996] ECR I-3089 at pp. I-3121–2; etc. For the relationship between these provisions and between the three categories of persons, i.e. workers, self-employed persons, and providers/recipients of services, *see further under* **Free movement of persons** and **Freedom of establishment**).

Of the three freedoms concerning the movement of persons, freedom of establishment and freedom to provide services have particularly noticeable features in common since they are both intended to facilitate the cross-border movement of self-employed persons and companies. These two freedoms are not only based on common principles but are governed, to a large extent, by the same or similar provisions of primary and secondary Community law (see section I below). In certain situations, the borderline between their respective fields of application may become blurred with the result that it may be difficult to decide whether a particular economic activity involves establishment or provision of services (see section II below). Nevertheless, in spite of the common features, there are certain essential differences between the two types of activity that are reflected in the differences between some of the rules of Community law governing them. These differences in the legal regulation of establishment and the provision of services mainly concern the degree of control that Community law allows Member States to exercise over them (see section V below).

I. The legal framework

The provisions of Community law relating to freedom to provide services fall into three distinct categories, which will be considered in turn below.

1. The Treaty provisions. The primary rules are laid down in Arts. 49 to 55 EC. In accordance with the consistent case-law of the ECJ, these Articles must be interpreted and applied in the light of Part One of the EC Treaty, which sets out the fundamental principles, objectives, and tasks of the Community. Of particular importance are Art. 2, which defines the tasks of the Community; Art. 3(1)(c), which provides for the creation of an internal market characterized by the abolition, as between Member States, of obstacles to the free movement of goods, persons, services, and capital (i.e. the four freedoms); and Art. 12, which prohibits any discrimination on grounds of nationality. In its case-law, the Court has emphasized that Arts. 49 *et seq.* must be regarded as a specific implementation or application of these fundamental principles with regard to services, and that those provisions take precedence over any national rule which might conflict with them (see e.g. Case 36/74 *Walrave* [1974] ECR 1405 at pp. 1417–20; Case 118/75 *Watson and Belmann*, above, at p. 1198).

The most important Treaty provisions on freedom to provide services are Arts. 49 and 50, which are often referred to by the ECJ as 'fundamental Community provisions' (see e.g. Case C-49/89 *Corsica Ferries France* [1989] ECR 4441 at p. 4456). Art. 49(1) lays down the basic principle that restrictions on the freedom to provide cross-border services are prohibited in respect of nationals of Member States. According to the original (pre-Amsterdam) text of Art. 49 [Art. 59 EEC], such restrictions had to be progressively abolished during the transitional period, i.e. by 31 December 1969 at the latest. Art. 49(2) enables the Council to extend this freedom to third country nationals already established within the Community. Art. 50(1) and (2) define the concept of 'services' (see section II below), while Art. 50(3) allows a person providing a service temporarily to pursue his activity in the Member State where the service is provided, 'under the same conditions as are imposed by that State on its own nationals'.

The ECJ held that the original Art. 59 imposed an obligation to attain a precise result, the fulfilment of which had to be made easier by, but not made dependent on, the implementation of a programme of progressive measures as envisaged in the original Arts. 63 and 66 [now Arts. 52 and 55] (see below). The fact that this progression had not been adhered to left the obligation itself intact beyond the end of the transitional period. Therefore, 'the essential requirements' of Art. 59 [now Art. 49] became 'directly and unconditionally applicable' on the expiry of that period. Those essential requirements abolished all discrimination against the person providing the service by reason of his nationality or the fact that he is established in a Member State other than that in which the service is provided (Case 33/74 *Van Binsbergen* [1974] ECR 1299 at pp. 1311–12; Case 36/74 *Walrave*, above, at pp. 1420–1; Case 48/75 *Royer*, above, at p. 511; Cases 110/78 etc. *Van Wesemael* [1979] ECR 35 at p. 52; Case 279/80 *Webb* [1981] ECR

3305 at p. 3324; etc.). In other words, Art. 49 produces direct effect in the sense of conferring enforceable rights on individuals, and precludes the application by the national courts and administrative bodies of any conflicting provision of national law, whether legislative or administrative, including both general abstract rules and specific individual administrative decisions (Case C-224/97 *Ciola* [1999] ECR I-2517 at pp. I-2539–40).

Art. 51 [originally Art. 61] contains special rules concerning the provision of services in the transport, banking, and insurance sectors (see section II.4 below). The original Art. 62—repealed by the ToA—laid down a 'stand-still' provision by prohibiting Member States from introducing any new restrictions on the freedom to provide services. It also prohibited the revocation of liberalizing measures taken by the Member States in implementation of their obligations under Community law, e.g. in pursuance of a directive (Case 48/75 *Royer*, above, at pp. 517–19). Since, however, Art. 62 was complementary to the original Art. 59, it could not prohibit restrictions that did not fall within the scope of Art. 59 (Case C-159/90 *Grogan* [1991] ECR I-4685 at p. I-4741; Case C-109/92 *Wirth* [1993] ECR I-6447 at p. I-6470). Nor did Art. 62 apply to services in the transport sector, by virtue of the original Art. 61(1) (Case C-49/89 *Corsica Ferries France*, above, at p. 4457).

The original Art. 63(1)—deleted by the ToA—provided for the drawing up by the Council of a General Programme for the abolition of existing restrictions on freedom to provide services, setting out the general conditions under which, and the progressive stages by which, each type of service was to be liberalized during the transitional period. In order to implement this General Programme, Art. 63(2) required the Council to issue directives. Art. 63(3) specified certain services that had to be given priority in the process. Art. 63(2) and (3) have been renumbered by the ToA as Art. 52(1) and (2), respectively.

Under Art. 53 [ex Art. 64], Member States declare their readiness to undertake the liberalization of services beyond the extent required by the directives. According to Art. 54 [ex Art. 65], Member States are to apply existing restrictions, prior to their abolition, without discrimination on grounds of nationality or residence. Finally, Art. 55 [ex Art. 66] makes the provisions of Arts. 45 to 48, which concern the right of establishment, applicable to the provision of services. These Articles therefore regulate establishment and services in identical terms.

Art. 45 exempts from the application of the rules of the Treaty activities that are connected, even occasionally, with the exercise of official authority. Art. 46 allows special treatment of foreign nationals justified on grounds of public policy, public security or public health, and authorizes the Council to issue directives for the co-ordination of the relevant national provisions. These exemptions and derogations are considered under separate entries (*see further under* **Official authority, Public health, Public policy, Public security**).

In order to make it easier for persons to exercise their freedom to provide services, Art. 47 [ex Art. 57] makes the Council and Parliament responsible for issuing directives, first, for the mutual recognition of diplomas, certificates, and other evidence of formal qualifications and, secondly, for the coordination of the legal provisions of the Member States concerning the provision of services. The General Programme and the directives envisaged by the original Arts. 57 and 63 were intended to achieve several objectives. First, to abolish restrictions on freedom to provide services during the transitional period. Secondly, to introduce into the law of the Member States a set of provisions to facilitate the effective exercise of this freedom. Thirdly, to resolve the specific problems arising from the fact that since the provider of a service is not normally established on a permanent basis in the Member State where the service is performed, he may not be fully subject to the professional rules of conduct in force in that State.

While the General Programme was adopted by the Council on 18 December 1961 (see below), not all the directives needed to liberalize services were issued by the end of the transitional period. Nevertheless, as seen above, the ECJ ruled that this fact could not prevent Art. 59 [now Art. 49] from having direct effect as from the end of that period (31 December 1969) since the attainment of freedom to provide services was to be made only easier by, but not made dependent on, the adoption of the directives. After the expiry of the transitional period, the Court said, the directives became superfluous since the 'essential requirements' of Art. 59 [49], the abolition of all discrimination on grounds of nationality or residence, became directly and unconditionally applicable by virtue of Art. 59 [49] itself. Nevertheless, the Court added, the directives had not lost all relevance since they still played an important part by making easier the effective exercise of the freedoms created by the Treaty (Case 33/74 *Van Binsbergen*, above, at pp. 1311–12; Cases 110/78 etc. *Van Wesemael*, above, at p. 52; Case 279/80 *Webb*, above, at p. 3324. See also Case 2/74 *Reyners* [1974] ECR 631 at pp. 651–2, where the Court first laid down these principles in the context of the right of establishment).

Finally, Art. 48 stipulates that companies or firms, as defined in that Article, must be treated in the same way as natural persons who are nationals of Member States.

It may be noted that in the absence of transitional provisions concerning freedom to provide services in the Acts of Accession of 1972, 1979, 1985, and 1994, Arts. 49 to 55 and the various implementing measures entered into force with regard to the new Member States immediately upon their accession to the Community. The only exception was Art. 221 of the Act of Accession of 1985, which allowed Portugal to maintain restrictions on the freedom to provide services for certain activities until 31 December 1988 and 31 December 1990, respectively (see Case C-113/89 *Rush Portuguesa* [1990] ECR I-1417 at p. I-1442). The Act of Accession of 2003 contains transitional provisions on freedom to provide services, which are set out, separately in respect of each new Member State, in Annexes V to XIV to the Act (see Art. 24 of the Act, *OJ* 2003 L236/1).

The provisions of the Treaty relating to the liberalization of services apply to the overseas countries and territories (OCTs) subject to Council Dec. 2001/822 of 27 November 2001 on the association of the OCTs with the EC

(*OJ* 2001 L314/1. Annex I A contains a list of OCTs, which is slightly different from the list contained in Annex II to the EC Treaty. See also Art. 299 EC). (For an interpretation by the ECJ of Art. 176 of Council Dec. 86/283 of 30 June 1986, *OJ* 1986 L175/1, which previously covered the freedom to provide services in OCTs, see Cases C-100/89 etc. *Kaefer and Procacci* [1990] ECR I-4647 at pp. I-4671–4 and Case C-263/88 *Commission* v. *France* [1990] ECR I-4611 at pp. I-4622–3. For the territorial scope of application of the EC Treaty, *see further under* **Free movement of persons**, section I.2(*c*).)

2. The General Programme. The second category of Community provisions relating to services consists of one single instrument: the General Programme for the abolition of restrictions on freedom to provide services, adopted by the Council on 18 December 1961 under Art. 63(1) of the original EEC Treaty (*OJ Sp. Edn.* 2nd Ser. (IX), p. 3). The Programme is very similar to the other General Programme, adopted by the Council on the same date, which concerns the right of establishment (ibid. p. 7). After defining the beneficiaries (see section III below), the General Programme lays down a timetable for the abolition of specified restrictions on freedom to provide services (see section V below) and on entry, exit, and residence, in respect of a number of activities. The abolition of restrictions was usually to be either preceded, accompanied, or followed by the mutual recognition of the relevant qualifications and by the co-ordination of national provisions concerning the provision of services, as provided for by the original Art. 57 [now Art. 47] (see Title VI of the General Programme).

The legal nature of the General Programme is not entirely clear. It is not one of the binding or non-binding measures listed in Art. 249 EC. Nevertheless, in a number of cases the ECJ has relied on the General Programme, holding that it provides 'useful guidance' for the implementation of the provisions of the Treaty relating to the freedom to provide services (Case 63/86 *Commission* v. *Italy* [1988] ECR 29 at p. 52; see also the cases cited in section V below).

3. The directives. The third category of provisions is made up of a large number of directives adopted for the implementation of Arts. 49 *et seq.* and of the General Programme, most (but not all) of which also apply to freedom of establishment. These directives may be divided into three groups.

First, directives concerning the entry and residence of nationals of other Member States and the members of their families. These currently include the following:

- Council Dir. 64/221 of 25 February 1964 on the co-ordination of special measures concerning the movement and residence of foreign nationals which are justified on grounds of public policy, public security, or public health (*OJ Sp. Edn.* 1963–4, p. 117);
- Council Dir. 73/148 of 21 May 1973 on the abolition of restrictions on movement and residence within the Community for nationals of Member States with regard to establishment and the provision of services (*OJ* 1973 L172/14);

- Dir. 2004/38 of the European Parliament and of the Council of 29 April 2004 on the right of citizens of the Union and their family members to move and reside freely within the territory of the Member States (*OJ* 2004 L158/77). The directive entered into force on 30 April 2004, and has to be implemented by the Member States by 30 April 2006. It will repeal and replace the above directives and some others from that date (Arts. 38, 40, and 41. *See further under* **Right of entry and residence**, section VII).

Since the rights guaranteed by these directives are the same as, or similar to, those enjoyed by workers, self-employed persons, and their family members, they are discussed in separate entries (*see further under* **Expulsion, Residence permit, Right of entry and residence, Right to leave, Right to remain**).

Secondly, directives adopted for the implementation of the General Programme and designed to facilitate the effective exercise of the freedom to provide services (and the right of establishment). These covered a wide range of industrial, commercial, and small craft activities, such as manufacturing and processing activities including agriculture; service activities including insurance, banking, stock exchanges and other securities markets, transport, real property, leisure, personnel, and other services; business activities; self-employed activities; medical and para-medical activities; and other activities. They provided either for liberalization or for transitional measures pending mutual recognition of qualifications and co-ordination of national provisions relating to the taking up and pursuit of those activities. Normally, they provided for the mutual recognition of occupational experience (rather than of formal qualifications) acquired in the Member State of origin. As seen above, in so far as these directives required the abolition of discrimination based on nationality, they were 'superseded' by the direct effect of Art. 49 after the end of the transitional period, although in other respects they still remained relevant (see e.g. Cases C-330/90 etc. *López Brea* [1992] ECR I-323 at p. I-331 *per* A.-G. Jacobs). Thrity-five of these directives, adopted between 1963 and 1982, were repealed and replaced by Dir. 1999/42 (*OJ* 1999 L201/77; corrigendum in *OJ* 2002 L23/48), which consolidated their main provisions into a single text (*see further under* **Freedom of establishment**, section IV.2(*b*)).

Thirdly, directives adopted under Art. 47(1) and (2), in conjunction with Art. 55, for the mutual recognition of qualifications and for the co-ordination of national provisions concerning the provision of services, respectively. These directives include both 'sectoral' and 'general' mutual recognition directives. They are discussed under **Freedom of establishment**, section IV.2(*a*) and (*b*).

Finally, it should be noted that in the field of services no general implementing regulation has been adopted similar to Reg. 1612/68, which gives effect to the rules of the Treaty concerning the free movement of workers (*OJ Sp. Edn.* 1968 (II), p. 475). However, the ECJ's case-law shows that many of the social rights provided for by Reg. 1612/68 in respect of workers and their families also apply to providers and recipients of services (see section IV below).

4. Commission documents. Reference may also be made to certain recent documents produced by the Commission with regard to services such as, in particular, its Communication of 29 December 2000 entitled 'An internal market strategy for services' (COM(2000) 888; *Bull. EU* 12–2000, p. 47), aimed at making the free provision of services within the Community as simple as within an individual Member State and analysing the still existing barriers, and its Report of 30 July 2002 on 'The state of the internal market for services', presented under the first stage of the internal market strategy for services (COM(2002) 441; *Bull. EU* 7/8–2002, p. 20).

II. Definition of services

Arts. 49 and 50 define the concept of 'services' in a way that is both imprecise and incomplete. Many situations have arisen in practice in which, but for the broad interpretation given by the ECJ to these provisions, an activity could not have been classified as a 'service', but neither would it have been covered by the other basic freedoms. The whole jurisprudence of the Court in this area is characterized by a tendency to avoid any such lacunae in the law. The Court's intention has been to create a 'watertight' system in which any economic activity falling within the scope of Community law benefits from one or the other of the basic freedoms guaranteed by the Treaty. Indeed, the Court itself has expressly stated that the concept of services may not be interpreted restrictively (Cases C-51/96 etc. *Deliège* [2000] ECR I-2549 at p. I-2615). Nevertheless, in spite of the efforts of the Court, difficulties of classification may still arise, particularly between the provision of services and establishment, owing to the sometimes imperceptible transition from one to the other (see below).

Art. 49(1) provides for the abolition of restrictions on freedom to provide services within the Community 'in respect of nationals of Member States who are established in a State of the Community other than that of the person for whom the services are intended'. Art. 50(1) and (2) define the concept of 'services' as services that are 'normally provided for remuneration, in so far as they are not governed by the provisions relating to freedom of movement for goods, capital and persons', including, in particular, activities of an industrial or commercial character and activities of craftsmen and of the professions. Subject to Art. 51 (see point 4 below), the definition covers all types of services; the special nature of certain services does not remove them from the ambit of the above provisions (Case 279/80 *Webb*, above, at p. 3323). Thus, in a long line of decisions the Court has firmly established that freedom to provide services covers the field of social security; a medical service, whether provided within or outside a hospital environment, does not cease to be a provision of services within the meaning of the Treaty because it is paid for by a national health service or by a sickness insurance scheme providing benefits in kind rather than reimbursement. Although Community law does not detract from the power of the Member

States to organize their social security systems, nevertheless the Member States must comply with Community law, in particular with the rules on the fundamental freedoms, when exercising that power (Case C-158/96 *Kohll* [1998] ECR I-1931 at pp. I-1942–3; Case C-368/98 *Vanbraekel* [2001] ECR I-5363 at p. I-5400; Case C-157/99 *Geraets-Smits and Peerbooms* [2001] ECR I-5473 at pp. I-5526–9; Case C-385/99 *Müller-Fauré and Van Riet* [2003] ECR I-4509, paras. 39, 100, and 103. See further below).

Finally, Art. 50(3) makes it clear that, without prejudice to the right of establishment, 'the person providing a service may, in order to do so, temporarily pursue his activity in the State where the service is provided, under the same conditions as are imposed by that State on its own nationals'. By virtue of Art. 55, companies and other legal persons as defined in Art. 48 are also covered by the rules on services.

It follows from the above provisions that in order to fall within the scope of Arts. 49 *et seq.*, a service must satisfy the following three conditions. First, it must be an economic activity that is not covered by the Treaty provisions relating to the free movement of goods, capital, and persons (including the right of establishment). Secondly, it must normally be provided for remuneration. Thirdly, it must have a transnational (cross-border) element. These conditions are usually examined by the ECJ in that order. They are considered in more detail below.

1. The activity must not be covered by other Treaty provisions. In order to establish whether this condition is satisfied, services must be distinguished from the movement of goods, capital, and persons.

First, as regards the relationship between services and goods, in several cases the ECJ has held that activities which result directly in the manufacture of physical objects appearing in the Common Customs Tariff, such as the printing of newspapers or the production of video cassettes, are covered by the provisions on the free movement of goods (Arts. 23 and 28 *et seq.*) and therefore cannot be regarded as services (Case 18/84 *Commission* v. *France* [1985] ECR 1339 at p. 1347; Cases 60/84 etc. *Cinéthèque* [1985] ECR 2605 at p. 2623). Likewise, national legislation laying down rules for the conduct of the retail trade concerns the movement of goods, not of services (Case C-332/89 *Marchandise* [1991] ECR I-1027 at p. I-1042, employment of workers on Sundays; Case C-239/90 *Boscher* [1991] ECR I-2023 at p. I-2037, sale by public auction; Cases C-267/91 etc. *Keck and Mithouard* [1993] ECR I-6097 at p. I-6129, resale at a loss). Electricity constitutes goods and not services since the services needed for the import or export of electricity and its transmission and distribution merely constitute the means for supplying users with goods (Case C-158/94 *Commission* v. *Italy* [1997] ECR I-5789 at pp. I-5799–800). Similarly, waste, whether recyclable or not, is to be regarded as goods, even when non-recyclable and non-reusable waste, having no intrinsic commercial value, is sent abroad for the purposes of disposal or tipping, which is a service (Case C-2/90 *Commission* v. *Belgium* [1992] ECR I-4431 at pp. I-4478–9).

More problematic is the situation where goods are closely linked to, or are imported or exported for the purposes of, provision of services. Here the case-law of the Court has not been entirely consistent. In Case 155/73 *Sacchi* [1974] ECR 409 at p. 427, the Court held that while the transmission of television signals, including advertisements, fell within the scope of services, cross-border trade in material, sound recordings, films, apparatus, and other products used for television broadcasting was subject to the rules on the movement of goods. In Case C-412/93 *Leclerc-Siplec* [1995] ECR I-179 at pp. I-216–18, the Court considered restrictions on television advertising under the rules relating to goods, but in Cases C-34/95 etc. *De Agostini* [1997] ECR I-3843 at pp. I-3890–3 and in Case C-405/98 *Gourmet International Products* [2001] ECR I-1795 at pp. I-1822–9, the Court examined restrictions on television advertising and advertising in magazines, respectively, in relation to both goods and services.

In Case C-275/92 *Schindler* [1994] ECR I-1039 at pp. I-1088–9, the Court held that the importation into one Member State (the United Kingdom) of material objects such as advertisements, application forms, and tickets relating to a lottery organized in another Member State (Germany) was not covered by the provisions on the movement of goods. That activity was merely ancillary to the operation of the lottery itself and could not be considered independently of it. Lotteries were to be regarded as services within the meaning of the Treaty and not activities relating to goods. By contrast, in Case C-124/97 *Läärä* [1999] ECR I-6067 at pp. I-6113–15, the Court found that slot machines constituted goods capable of being imported and exported even although they were exclusively used for games of chance or gambling which, like lotteries, were services. The fact, the Court said, that an imported item was intended for the supply of a service did not in itself mean that it fell outside the rules regarding the free movement of goods. The Court confirmed this view in Case C-6/01 *Anomar* [2003] ECR I-8621, paras. 55–6, where it did not find it necessary to regard, by analogy with *Schindler*, the importation of slot machines as ancillary to their operation. The importation of gaming machines fell within the scope of the free movement of goods, while their operation was governed by the rules relating to services. Likewise, leasing constitutes a service. Although it implies the handing over of goods by the lessor to the lessee, the supply relates not to the goods themselves but to their use by the lessee, the goods in question remaining the property of the lessor (Case C-451/99 *Cura Anlagen* [2002] ECR I-3193 at p. I-3225; see also Case C-294/97 *Eurowings Luftverkehrs* [1999] ECR I-7447 at p. I-7473). Also, fishing rights or fishing permits form a provision of service and not a supply of goods (Case C-97/98 *Jägerskiöld* [1999] ECR I-7319 at pp. I-7344–5). While intellectual property rights may affect intra-Community trade in goods and services, they do not themselves constitute goods or services (ibid.).

Later the Court rationalized its practice by saying that where a national measure restricts both the free movement of goods and the freedom to provide services, the Court will in principle examine it in relation to only one of those two freedoms where, in the circumstances of the case, one of them is entirely secondary in relation to the other and may be considered together with it, as in *Schindler*. Where, however, it is difficult or impossible to determine which freedom should take priority because the two aspects are intimately linked, the restrictive measure must be examined simultaneously in the light of both Arts. 28 and 49 EC (Case C-390/99 *Canal Satélite Digital* [2002] ECR I-607 at pp. I-653–4, involving restrictions on the marketing in Spain, by providers of conditional-access television services, of digital satellite television decoders lawfully marketed in other Member States). While this practice seems reasonable, it is questionable whether it is strictly compatible with Art. 50(1), under which a 'service' cannot simultaneously be covered by the provisions relating to the other freedoms. (For the relationship between services and goods, *see also under* **Free movement of goods, Goods**).

Secondly, as regards the relationship between services and the movement of capital, the Court has encountered even more difficulties than in relation to goods. The case-law of the Court, including the opinions of the Advocates-General, is characterized by a certain degree of inconsistency, and it appears that the Court has so far failed to establish clear and coherent principles to define the dividing line between the two freedoms (*see further under* **Free movement of capital**, section VI).

Thirdly, the relationship between services and the movement of persons has two aspects. As regards the movement of workers, a distinction may be made on the basis that the latter always implies an employment relationship with an employer in the host Member State, while a service is carried out by a self-employed person or a company outside the framework of a contract of employment (see Case 36/74 *Walrave*, above, at p. 1419). Where an employer provides a service in another Member State by bringing his own workforce with him, as it often happens in the construction industry, the situation in the host State is governed by the rules on services and not by the rules on the movement of workers (see section V.3(*d*) below).

As regards the relationship between services and the right of establishment, the ECJ's starting point seems to be that the chapters of the Treaty governing each of these two freedoms are mutually exclusive, and that the provisions on services are subordinate to those on establishment (Case C-55/94 *Gebhard*, above, at pp. I-4193–4). This would imply, first, that one and the same person or activity cannot be covered by both chapters at the same time and, secondly, that it should always be possible to determine which chapter applies to a particular person or activity. The application of these principles in practice, however, is not always without difficulty.

According to the Court's case-law, the decisive factor in this respect is that under the Treaty the concept of establishment is broader than that of services, allowing a Community national to participate, on a stable and continuous basis, in the economic life of a Member State other than his State of origin. In contrast, where the provider of services moves to another Member State, Art. 50(3) envisages that he is to pursue his activities there on a *temporary basis*. According to the ECJ, the temporary nature of the activities in question must be determined in the light, not only of the duration of the provision of the service, but also of its regularity, periodical nature, or continuity. Therefore, in the case of services, the decisive criterion is the absence of stable and continuous participation by the provider in the economic life of the host Member State. Nevertheless, the temporary nature of the service does not mean that the provider may not equip himself with some form of infrastructure in the host State, such as an office, chambers or consulting rooms, if this is necessary for performing the service (ibid. at p. I-4195; Case C-131/01 *Commission* v. *Italy* [2003] ECR I-1659, paras. 22–3).

Thus, the concept of 'services' may cover services varying widely in nature, including services that are provided over an extended period, even over several years, where, for example, they involve the construction of a large building or the giving of advice or information with a greater or lesser degree of frequency or regularity over a long period. The Treaty provides no means of determining, in an abstract manner, the duration or frequency beyond which the supply of a service, or of identical or similar services, may no longer be regarded as a 'service' within the meaning of the Treaty (Case C-215/01 *Schnitzer* [2003] ECR I-0000, paras. 30–1).

On the basis of the above considerations, the Court has held that a national of a Member State who pursues a professional activity on a stable and continuous basis in another Member State where he holds himself out from an established professional base to, *inter alia*, nationals of that State, or who establishes his principal residence in another Member State in order to provide or receive services there for an indefinite period, or who has a stable and permanent establishment in two Member States, is covered by the chapter relating to the right of establishment, which excludes the application of the chapter on services (Case C-55/94 *Gebhard*, above, at pp. I-4195–6; Case 196/87 *Steymann* [1988] ECR 6159 at pp. 6173–4; Case C-53/95 *Kemmler* [1996] ECR I-703 at p. I-714; Case C-70/95 *Sodemare* [1997] ECR I-3395 at pp. I-3435–6). Similarly, the Court has ruled that an undertaking of a Member State that maintains a *permanent presence* in another Member State comes within the provisions on establishment and not those on services, even if that presence does not take the form of a branch or agency, but consists merely of an office managed by the undertaking's own staff or by a person who is independent but authorized to act on a *permanent basis* for the undertaking, as would be the case with an agency (Case 205/84 *Commission* v. *Germany* [1986] ECR 3755 at p. 3801—'Insurance' case).

On the other hand, in Case 39/75 *Coenen* [1975] ECR 1547 at p. 1555, the Court accepted that a Netherlands national who resided in Belgium but had a place of business (office) in the Netherlands for the purpose of carrying on the business of an insurance intermediary there, was in fact a provider of services in the Netherlands and covered by Art. 49. Presumably, in this case the Court regarded 'residence' in Belgium as being equivalent to 'establishment' there, and the 'office' in the Netherlands as not amounting to a 'permanent establishment' in that country. Similarly, in Case C-3/95 *Reisebüro Broede* [1996] ECR I-6511 at pp. I-6535–6, the Court held that the managing director of a debt-collecting company registered in France who resided in Germany and carried out debt-collection work there for a German client on several occasions, was covered by Art. 49 and not by Art. 43, in spite of her permanent presence in Germany, because the company had undertaken similar work both in France and in Germany for French and foreign clients. In Case C-215/01 *Schnitzer*, above, paras. 32–3, the Court ruled that the mere fact that an undertaking established in one Member State (Portugal) supplied identical or similar services in a repeated or regular manner over a long period of time (three years) in a second Member State (Germany), without having an infrastructure there, was not sufficient for it to be regarded as established in the second Member State.

The above cases show that the difference between establishment and the provision of services may often be one of degree rather than of substance, the decisive factor being the length, permanence, or frequency of stay in the State of destination. There is, however, no clear-cut definition at present of what, and under what circumstances, amounts to 'establishment', 'office', 'place of business', 'infrastructure', 'principal, permanent or temporary residence', particularly where a business activity is carried out partly from an office in one Member State and partly from home in another. All that may be said with certainty is that if an economic activity is pursued through a fixed establishment in another Member State for an indefinite period, it is governed by Arts. 43 *et seq.* (see Case C-221/89 *Factortame II* [1991] ECR I-3905 at p. I-3965). If, on the other hand, it involves only occasional visits to a Member State, each limited in time, from a fixed establishment or address in another Member State, it is covered by Arts. 49 *et seq*. Thus, the same type of activity may come within the scope of Arts. 39, 43, or 49, respectively, depending on the circumstances in which it is performed. This is illustrated, for example, in Case 147/86 *Commission* v. *Greece* [1988] ECR 1637 at pp. 1656–7, where the Court accepted that the setting up of coaching establishments and private music and dancing schools by the nationals of other Member States in Greece was covered by Art. 43; the giving of private music and dancing lessons at home on an occasional basis by Art. 49; while employment as director and teacher in such coaching establishments and private music and dancing schools fell within the scope of Art. 39. (For other instances where one and the same activity could potentially be covered by either Arts. 39, 43, or 49, see e.g. Case 48/75 *Royer*, above, at p. 509; Case 118/75 *Watson and Belmann*, above, at pp. 1196–7; Case C-106/91 *Ramrath* [1992] ECR I-3351 at p. I-3381.)

In its case-law, the Court has held that the following activities qualify as services within the meaning of Arts. 49 and 50, provided that the other two conditions are also met:

(*a*) ***The practice of sport*** in so far as it constitutes an economic activity within the meaning of Art. 2 EC, i.e. a remunerated service, as in the case of professional or semi-professional players (Case 36/74 *Walrave*, above, at p. 1417; Case 13/76 *Donà* [1976] ECR 1333 at p. 1340). In fact, sporting activities are capable of involving a number of separate, but closely related, services (e.g. between organizers, athletes, the public, television broadcasters, advertisers, sponsors), which may fall within the scope of Art. 49 even if some of those services are not paid for by those for whom they are performed (see Cases C-51/96 etc. *Deliège*, above, at pp. I-2616–17).

(*b*) ***Banking and insurance services,*** being services of a commercial character referred to in Art. 50(2)(b) (Case 15/78 *Koestler* [1978] ECR 1971 at p. 1979 (banking); Case 205/84 *Commission* v. *Germany*, above, at p. 3799 (insurance); Case C-484/93 *Svensson and Gustavsson* [1995] ECR I-3955 at pp. I-3975–6 (building loans); Case C-222/95 *Parodi* [1997] ECR I-3899 at p. I-3921 (mortgage loans); Case C-118/96 *Safir* [1998] ECR I-1897 at p. I-1926 (life assurance); Case C-136/00 *Danner* [2002] ECR I-8147, paras. 24–7 (pension insurance)).

(*c*) ***The broadcasting of television signals*** and their transmission by cable or satellite television, including the broadcasting of television advertisements (Case 155/73 *Sacchi*, above, at pp. 427–8, holding that televised commercial advertising, being a service, does not come under Art. 31 EC on State commercial monopolies, which applies to goods only; Case 52/79 *Debauve* [1980] ECR 833 at p. 855). The fact that the broadcasting body has established itself in another Member State for the purpose of avoiding the legislation of the receiving State does not alter the nature of its broadcasts as services (Case C-23/93 *TV10* [1994] ECR I-4795 at p. I-4831). In fact, the transmission, by cable network operators established in one Member State, of television programmes supplied by broadcasters established in other Member States and containing advertisements intended especially for the public in the receiving State, involves at least two separate services. The first is provided by the cable network operators to the broadcasters and consists of relaying to network subscribers the television programmes sent to them by the broadcasters. The second is provided by the broadcasters to advertisers established in the receiving State and consists of broadcasting advertisements prepared by the advertisers (see Case 352/85 *Bond van Adverteerders* [1988] ECR 2085 at pp. 2130–1).

(*d*) ***The showing of films,*** whether in a cinema or on television. In this case, the service is rendered by film producers to distributors by allowing them to make copies of their films and to organize public performances by using such copies (Case 262/81 *Coditel* [1982] ECR 3381 at pp. 3400–1; Case C-17/92 *Distribuidores Cinematográficos* [1993] ECR I-2239 at p. I-2271).

(*e*) ***The supply of manpower for hire or reward,*** provided that the staff remain in the employ of the supplying undertaking and no contract of employment is entered into with the user, notwithstanding that the employees may in certain circumstances be covered by the provisions of Arts. 39 to 42 EC and implementing regulations (Case 279/80 *Webb*, above, at p. 3323).

(*f*) ***The sale of travel by travel agents*** (Case 311/85 *VVR* [1987] ECR 3801 at p. 3831).

(*g*) ***The activities of a tourist guide.*** Where the guide is employed by a tour company, the service is provided by the tour company to tourists through its own guide. Where the tour company engages a self-employed tourist guide, the service is provided by the guide to the tour company. In either case, the service is of limited duration and is not governed by the provisions on the free movement of goods, persons, and capital but falls within Arts. 49 and 50 (Case C-154/89 *Commission* v. *France* [1991] ECR I-659 at p. I-684).

(*h*) ***The activities of patent agents*** as well as patent renewal services consisting of monitoring patents, advising the holders when renewal fees are due and paying those fees on their behalf (Case C-76/90 *Säger* [1991] ECR I-4221 at p. I-4241; Case C-131/01 *Commission* v. *Italy*, above, para. 25 (patent agents)).

(*i*) ***Medical and legal services,*** whether care is provided within or outside a hospital infrastructure, and whether the costs are paid by the patient, who subsequently receives reimbursement thereof, or by a national health service or a sickness insurance scheme (Case C-159/90 *Grogan*, above, at p. I-4739; Case C-158/96 *Kohll*, above, at p. I-1945; Case C-368/98 *Vanbraekel*, above, at pp. I-5399–400; Case C-157/99 *Geraets-Smits and Peerbooms*, above, at p. I-5528; Case C-385/99 *Müller-Fauré and Van Riet*, above, paras. 38–40, 103), and the ***services of a lawyer***, both being professional activities referred to in Art. 50(2)(d) (Case C-20/92 *Hubbard* [1993] ECR I-3777 at p. I-3794).

(*j*) ***Activities that enable people to participate in gambling in return for payment,*** such as lotteries (Case C-275/92 *Schindler*, above, at pp. I-1088–92); operation of gaming machines (Case C-124/97 *Läärä*, above, at pp. I-6113–15; Case C-6/01 *Anomar*, above, para. 56); betting on sporting events (Case C-67/98 *Zenatti* [1999] ECR I-7289 at pp. I-7311–13; Case C-243/01 *Gambelli* [2003] ECR I-0000, para. 52). In the case of lotteries, the service is rendered by the operator of the lottery to enable purchasers of tickets to participate in a game of chance with the hope of winning, and consists of the collection of stakes, the organization of draws and the paying out of prizes or winnings. In spite of the element of chance involved, lotteries have a profit-making, i.e. economic nature, which brings them within the scope of Arts. 49 and 50 (see the *Schindler* case above). However, games that are organized only on a small scale and for insignificant stakes, such as crosswords and puzzles published in magazines, do not constitute an economic activity in their own right and cannot be equated with lotteries (Case C-368/95 *Familiapress* [1997] ECR I-3689 at p. I-3716; see also the cases cited above).

(*k*) ***Offers of services*** without, at that stage, the existence of an identifiable recipient (Case C-384/93 *Alpine Investments* [1995] ECR I-1141 at p. I-1174, dealing with 'cold callings', i.e. contacting individuals by telephone without their prior consent in order to offer them financial services).

(*l*) ***Leasing.*** (Case C-294/97 *Eurowings Luftverkehrs*, above, at p. I-7473 (leasing of aircraft); Case C-451/99 *Cura Anlagen*, above, at p. I-3225 (leasing of motor vehicle)).

(*m*) ***The organization of professional training courses*** (Case C-55/98 *Vestergaard* [1999] ECR I-7641 at p. I-7665).

(*n*) ***The provision of advertising space in magazines*** (Case C-405/98 *Gourmet International Products*, above, at p. I-1828).

(*o*) ***The grant of fishing rights*** and the issue of fishing permits (Case C-97/98 *Jägerskiöld*, above, at p. I-7344).

2. The service must be provided for remuneration. Once it has been established that an activity qualifies as a 'service', it must then be shown that it is provided for remuneration and has a cross-border element. The concept of remuneration is not defined in Arts. 49 *et seq*. However, in Case 263/86 *Humbel* [1988] ECR 5365 at p. 5388 the Court stated that 'the essential characteristic of remuneration . . . lies in the fact that it constitutes consideration for the service in question, and is normally agreed upon between the provider and the recipient of the service'. In the same case, the Court held that that characteristic is absent in the case of courses provided under the national education system. In the first place, in establishing and maintaining such a system, the State is not engaged in a gainful activity but fulfils a social, cultural, and educational duty towards its own population. Secondly, as a general rule, the education system is funded from the public purse and not by students or their parents even if the latter must sometimes pay teaching or enrolment fees in order to make a certain contribution to the operating expenses of the system. Therefore, the Court held, courses taught at a university or institute of secondary or higher education that is financed essentially out of public funds do not constitute services for the purposes of Arts. 49 and 50 (see also Case C-109/92 *Wirth*, above, at pp. I-6468–70). Nevertheless, where an institute of education is financed mainly out of private funds, in particular by students or their parents, and seeks to make a commercial profit, then its object is to offer a service against remuneration. Courses provided by such an institute qualify as services within the meaning of the Treaty (ibid.). A contribution towards a compulsory insurance scheme set up by legislation does not constitute economic consideration (i.e. remuneration) for the benefits provided by the scheme but is in the nature of a charge imposed and fixed by the legislature and levied by the tax authority. Consequently, the benefits provided by such a scheme cannot be classified as services (Case C-355/00 *Freskot* [2003] ECR I-5263, paras. 55–9).

However, Art. 50 does not necessarily require that the remuneration be paid by those for whom the service is performed. Thus, in the case of transmission of television programmes by cable network operators, the Court has accepted that the fees that the operators charge their subscribers constitute remuneration for the service which the operators provide for the broadcasters in relaying their programmes, it being irrelevant that the broadcasters themselves generally do not pay for that service (Case 352/85

Bond van Adverteerders, above, at p. 2131, see point 1(*c*) above. The second service involved in this case, that provided by the broadcasters to advertisers, was paid for by the advertisers. See also Cases C-51/96 etc. *Deliège*, above, at pp. I-2616–17, concerning payments for services rendered in connection with international sporting competitions). Similarly, a medical service does not cease to be a provision of services because it is provided free of charge to the patient and is paid for by a national health service or by a sickness insurance scheme providing benefits in kind. It makes no difference whether the patient pays the costs incurred and subsequently receives reimbursement thereof or whether the sickness fund or the national budget pays the provider directly (Case C-157/99 *Geraets-Smits and Peerbooms*, above, at pp. I-5527–9; Case C-385/99 *Müller-Fauré and Van Riet*, above, para. 103, see point 1(*i*) above). Normally, however, the remuneration is paid by the recipient of the service. Thus, for example, in the case of films, the distributors pay back to the producers a part of their box-office takings (see Case C-17/92 *Distribuidores Cinematográficos*, above, at p. I-2271, see point 1(*d*) above). In the case of lotteries, the remuneration consists of the price of the lottery ticket (see Case C-275/92 *Schindler*, above, at p. I-1089, see point 1(*j*) above).

3. The service must have a cross-border element. This is the condition that brings a service within the scope of Community law. Thus, according to Art. 49(1), the provider must be 'established in a State of the Community other than that of the person for whom the services are intended'. This condition may be fulfilled in at least five different ways, which are discussed below.

(*a*) The provider of the service is established in State A and goes to State B, where the recipient is established or resident, to perform a service there (e.g. a doctor established in State A visits a patient in State B to perform an operation). This is the only situation expressly mentioned in Art. 50(3), which stipulates that 'the person providing a service may, in order to do so, temporarily pursue his activity in the State where the service is provided'.

(*b*) The recipient of the service is established or resident in State B and goes to State A, where the provider is established, to receive a service there. This situation is not expressly mentioned in Art. 50, but in Cases 286/82 etc. *Luisi and Carbone*, above, at p. 401, the Court held that it is a 'necessary corollary' of the previous one, and 'fulfils the objective of liberalizing all gainful activity not covered by the free movement of goods, persons and capital'. Referring to Dirs. 64/221 and 73/148 (see section I above), both of which recognize the right of entry and residence of persons going to another Member State as recipients of services, the Court stated that:

> the freedom to provide services includes the freedom, for the recipients of services, to go to another Member State in order to receive a service there, without being obstructed by restrictions, even in relation to payments and that tourists, persons receiving medical treatment and persons travelling for the purpose of education or business are to be regarded as recipients of services (ibid. at p. 403. See also Case 186/87 *Cowan* [1989] ECR 195 at pp. 220–1 and Case C-45/93 *Commission* v. *Spain* [1994] ECR I-911 at pp. I-918–20, both dealing with tourists as recipients of services, see section IV below).

(*c*) The provider and the recipient of the service are both established or resident in State A at the commencement of the service, but the recipient takes up residence in State B before the termination of the service (see Case 15/78 *Koestler*, above, at p. 1980, where certain banking services were provided by a bank established in France to a German national at the time resident in France, who moved to Germany before the termination of the contractual relations between the parties).

(*d*) The provider is established in State A and supplies his service to a recipient established in State B without moving there, for example by telephone (see Case C-384/93 *Alpine Investments*, above, at p. I-1174, involving 'cold calling', see point 1(*k*) above); by internet (see Case C-243/01 *Gambelli*, above, para. 54, involving placing bets abroad by internet, see point 1(*j*) above); by post (see Case C-275/92 *Schindler*, above, at p. I-1089, where lottery advertisements and application forms were sent by post from the Netherlands to the United Kingdom by a lottery operator established in Germany, see point 1(*j*) above); by television transmissions (see Case 352/85 *Bond van Adverteerders*, above, at p. 2131, see point 1(*c*) above); by providing advertising space in magazines (see Case C-405/98 *Gourmet International Products*, above, at p. I-1828, see point 1(*n*) above); or by any other means (see Case C-17/92 *Distribuidores Cinematográficos*, above, at p. I-2271, involving film producers and distributors as providers and recipients of services, respectively, established in different Member States, see point 1(*d*) above). This form of supply of services therefore does not involve any cross-frontier movement of persons.

(*e*) The provider and the recipient of the service are both established or resident in State A but the service is performed in State B. This situation is not envisaged by the Treaty, and *prima facie* seems to be incompatible with Art. 49(1), which, as seen above, requires that the provider and the recipient be established in two different Member States. However, the Court has said that the purpose of Art. 49(1) is to abolish restrictions on the freedom to provide services by persons who are not established in the State in which the service is to be provided. Consequently, the Court has held that Art. 49(1) applies not only where the provider of services and the recipient are established in different Member States, but also 'in all cases where a person providing services offers those services in a Member State other than that in which he is established, wherever the recipients of those services may be established' (Case C-154/89 *Commission* v. *France*, above, at p. I-685, where the providers of services, tour companies and self-employed tourist guides, and the recipients of those services, tourists and tour companies, respectively, were established or resident in the same Member State other than France, and the services were provided in France, see point 1(*g*) above. See also the similar Case C-180/89 *Commission* v. *Italy* [1991] ECR I-709 at p. I-721 and Case C-198/89 *Commission* v. *Greece* [1991] ECR I-727 at pp. I-738–9—'Tourist guides' cases. See further Case C-20/92 *Hubbard*, above, at p. I-3794, involving an English solicitor litigating in Germany for an English client; Case C-379/92 *Peralta* [1994] ECR I-3453 at p. I-3501 involving the master of an Italian tanker performing deliveries intended for other Member States; Case C-55/98 *Vestergaard*, above, at p. I-7665, involving a Danish national attending a tax training course organized by a Danish firm in Greece).

It follows from this third condition that the provisions of the Treaty on freedom to provide services cannot be applied to activities all the relevant elements of which are confined within a single Member State; in other words, which do not come within any of the situations envisaged by Community law ('purely internal situations', see Case 52/79 *Debauve*, above, at p. 855; Case C-41/90 *Höfner and Elser* [1991] ECR I-1979 at p. I-2020; Case C-60/91 *Batista Morais* [1992] ECR I-2085 at p. I-2105; etc.). However, a situation is not purely internal where a person provides cross-border services, even if he does not leave the Member State in which he is established (Case C-60/00 *Carpenter* [2002] ECR I-6279, at p. I-6318).

4. Services in special sectors. Certain sectors are exempted from the application of the general rules on the provision of services. Thus, according to Art. 51(1), 'Freedom to provide services in the field of transport shall be governed by the provisions of the Title relating to transport', i.e. by Arts. 70 to 80, and not by the provisions of the chapter on services. This rule has been interpreted by the ECJ to the effect that, in the transport sector, the objectives of Arts. 49 and 50 are to be achieved in the framework of the common transport policy referred to in Art. 70 and of the common rules and conditions that the Council was to lay down during the transitional period in accordance with the original Art. 75(1) and (2) [now, after amendment, Art. 71]. The Court held that by not adopting those rules and conditions, the Council failed to ensure freedom to provide services in the sphere of international transport and with regard to non-resident carriers (cabotage), in breach of its obligations under the Treaty. Nevertheless, that failure did not render Arts. 49 and 50 directly effective in the transport sector on the expiry of the transitional period (Case 13/83 *Parliament* v. *Council* [1985] ECR 1513 at pp. 1599–1601—'Common transport policy' case; see also Cases 209/84 etc. *Asjes* [1986] ECR 1425 at p. 1465; Case 4/88 *Lambregts Transportbedrijf* [1989] ECR 2583 at p. 2607, holding that Art. 71(1)(a) and (b) do not create enforceable individual rights).

Consequently, it was only as a result of the subsequent adoption by the Council of specific liberalization measures (regulations) in the various transport sectors that freedom to provide services in those sectors was attained. However, since those measures implement, with regard to transport, the principle of freedom to provide services as laid down in Arts. 49 and 50, they must be interpreted and applied in the light of those Articles and of the relevant case-law of the ECJ, as discussed in this entry (see, as regards maritime transport services: Case C-49/89 *Corsica Ferries France*, above, at pp. 4456–7 *per Curiam*, pp. 4447–9 *per* A.-G. Lenz; Case C-18/93 *Corsica Ferries Italia* [1994] ECR I-1783 at pp. I-1819–24; Case C-379/92 *Peralta*, above, at pp. I-3500–4; Case C-381/93 *Commission* v. *France* [1994] ECR I-5145 at pp. I-5167–70; Case C-205/99 *Analir* [2001] ECR I-1271 at pp. I-1309–13; as regards national road transport services: Case C-17/90

Wieger [1991] ECR I-5253 at pp. I-5282–3; as regards air transport services: Case C-361/98 *Italy* v. *Commission* [2001] ECR I-385 at pp. I-434–5; Case C-70/99 *Commission* v. *Portugal* [2001] ECR I-4845 at pp. I-4873–8; Case C-92/01 *Stylianakis* [2003] ECR I-1291, paras. 23–9).

A second exemption is contained in Art. 51(2), which provides that 'The liberalization of banking and insurance services connected with movements of capital shall be effected in step with the progressive liberalization of movement of capital'. Prior to the full liberalization of capital movements as from 1 January 1994 (see Art. 56 EC, inserted by the TEU), this provision meant in practice that where a particular banking or insurance service related to a capital movement which had not yet been liberalized, any restriction on that service could not constitute an infringement of Arts. 49 *et seq.* (see Case 267/86 *Van Eycke* [1988] ECR 4769 at p. 4793, dealing with savings deposits as capital movements; Case C-222/95 *Parodi*, above, at p. I-3919, concerning mortgage loans. *See further under* **Free movement of capital**).

III. Beneficiaries

The beneficiaries of freedom to provide services may be divided into two groups: natural persons (individuals) and companies or firms, which are to be treated in the same way as natural persons. To benefit from this freedom, natural persons must satisfy two requirements: they must be nationals of Member States and must be established within the Community (Art. 49(1); see also Title I of the General Programme. As to the requirement of nationality, *see further under* **Freedom of establishment**, section II). However, as seen above, the freedom to provide services benefits not only providers of services, who are normally self-employed persons (and therefore 'established' in the proper sense of the word), but also recipients of services such as, in particular, tourists, persons receiving medical treatment, and persons travelling for the purpose of education or business (see section II.3(*b*) above and the cases cited therein). These persons must likewise be nationals of Member States and established, or at least resident, in the Community (where the recipient is not a self-employed person, he cannot be 'established' properly speaking. For the position of the family members of these beneficiaries, *see further under* **Right of entry and residence**, section II). Nationals of third countries may benefit from freedom to provide services under a Council decision adopted under Art. 49(2) EC or under any relevant international agreement concluded by the Community with their country of origin (*see further under* **Free movement of persons**, section V).

'Companies or firms' are defined by Art. 48(2) (which, by virtue of Art. 55, also applies to services) as those 'constituted under civil or commercial law, including cooperative societies, and other legal persons governed by public or private law, save for those which are non-profit-making'. Thus, non-profit-making companies are excluded from the provisions on freedom to provide services (see Case C-70/95 *Sodemare*, above, at p. I-3432). To benefit from that freedom, companies must be formed in accordance with the law of a Member State and have their registered office, central administration, or principal place of business within the Community (Art. 48(1)). In addition, Title I of the General Programme also requires that, where only their registered office is situated within the Community, their activity must show 'a real and continuous link' with the economy of a Member State, other than one of nationality.

The beneficiaries of freedom to provide services comprise the nationals of *all* Member States, who may rely on that freedom not only against other Member States but also against the State of which they are nationals. This may happen in two different situations. First, a national of State A who is established in State B may rely on Arts. 49 *et seq.* or on any implementing directive with a view to providing services in the territory of State A. Thus, in Case 292/86 *Gullung* [1988] ECR 111 at p. 136, a lawyer of French and German nationality who was admitted to the legal profession in Germany, was able to rely on Dir. 77/249 concerning freedom to provide services by lawyers in order to supply services in France, provided that the conditions laid down in that directive were satisfied (see section V.4 below). Applying by analogy its earlier decision in Case 115/78 *Knoors* [1979] ECR 399 at pp. 409–11, where, in the context of the right of establishment, the Court first laid down the principle that an individual may rely on a directive even against his own State, the Court pointed out that freedom to provide services, being fundamental in the Community system, would not be fully realized if a Member State were able to exclude its own nationals from the enjoyment of that freedom within its own territory.

The second situation arises where restrictions on freedom to provide services are imposed not by the State of destination but by the State in which the provider is established. In several cases, the Court has held that that freedom may be relied on by an undertaking or an individual against the State in which it/he is established, if the services are provided to recipients established in another Member State and, more generally, whenever services are offered in a Member State other than the one in which the provider is established (see Case C-18/93 *Corsica Ferries Italia*, above, at p. I-1822; Case C-379/92 *Peralta*, above, at p. I-3501; Case C-381/93 *Commission* v. *France*, above, at p. I-5168; Case C-384/93 *Alpine Investments*, above, at p. I-1176; etc.).

Moreover, the provisions on freedom to provide services may be relied on not only against public authorities and laws enacted by Member States, but also against rules adopted by associations and organizations that do not form part of the State, e.g. sports associations, national or local Bars, etc., where such rules are designed to regulate gainful employment, self-employment, and the provisions of services in a collective manner. In several cases, the ECJ has pointed out that the abolition, as between Member States, of obstacles to freedom of movement for persons (whether they are workers, self-employed persons or providers of services) would be compromised if the abolition of State barriers could be neutralized by obstacles resulting from the exercise of their legal autonomy by associations or organizations not governed by public law (Cases C-51/96 etc. *Deliège*, above, at p. I-2614, involving rules laid down by sports associations; Case C-309/99 *Wouters*

[2002] ECR I-1577 at p. I-1694, involving regulations adopted by the Netherlands Bar; see also the cases cited in section IV.1 below).

IV. Prohibition of discrimination

Like Art. 43 in the field of establishment, Arts. 49 *et seq.* pursue a double objective. The first is the prohibition (originally the abolition) of restrictions on freedom to provide services within the Community (Art. 49(1)). The second is the equal treatment of nationals and non-nationals as providers or recipients of services (Arts. 50(3) and 54). However, as will be seen below, in the context of services the meaning and scope of these two objectives are not exactly the same as in the field of establishment, owing to the different nature of the two types of activity involved. Prohibition of discrimination is considered here, prohibition of restrictions in the following section (on the concept of discrimination, *see also under* **Free movement of persons**, section I.4).

1. Direct discrimination. Art. 12 EC prohibits any direct discrimination on grounds of nationality within the whole field of application of the Treaty. In several cases, the ECJ has emphasized that this rule is 'one of the fundamental legal provisions of the Community', which has been implemented in the special sphere of services by Arts. 49 *et seq.* The 'essential requirement' of Art. 49 is to 'abolish all discrimination against the person providing the service by reason of his nationality or the fact that he is established in a Member State other than that in which the service is to be provided' (Case 33/74 *Van Binsbergen*, above, at p. 1311; Cases 110/78 etc. *Van Wesemael*, above, at p. 52; Case 279/80 *Webb*, above, at p. 3324; etc. See also the cases cited below). Thus, Arts. 12, 49, 50, and 54 are intended 'to eliminate all measures which, in the field of . . . freedom to provide services, treat a national of another Member State more severely or place him in a situation less advantageous, from a legal or factual point of view, than that of one of the Member State's own nationals in the same circumstances' (Case 251/83 *Haug-Adrion* [1984] ECR 4277 at p. 4288). Nevertheless, a difference in treatment based exclusively on objective factors and objective criteria and not on nationality, place of residence, or establishment, or which is due to natural phenomena and not to human activity, cannot be regarded as discrimination (ibid.; Case 52/79 *Debauve*, above, at p. 858).

Discrimination is prohibited not only when it results from laws, rules, or practices of public authorities, but also when it arises from acts of professional bodies and private organizations of whatever nature, including the rules of sporting organizations and acts of private persons, as long as it is based on the criterion of nationality. However, the prohibition does not affect the composition of national sport teams, which is a matter of purely sporting interest and as such does not involve an economic activity (Case 36/74 *Walrave*, above, at pp. 1418–19; Case 13/76 *Donà*, above, at pp. 1339–41; Case 90/76 *Van Ameyde* [1977] ECR 1091 at p. 1127).

Since Art. 12 is implemented in the field of services by Art. 49, Art. 12 applies independently only to situations not covered by the latter Article

(Case 305/87 *Commission* v. *Greece* [1989] ECR 1461 at pp. 1476–7; Case C-55/98 *Vestergaard*, above, at pp. I-7664–5). As from the end of the transitional period, Arts. 49(1) and 50(3) have been directly effective and thus the prohibition of discrimination may be invoked by individuals before national courts even in the absence of implementing directives in a particular area (see section I above).

As in the context of the right of establishment, in the field of services the rule on non-discrimination or equal treatment means, in the first place, that nationals of all Member States must be guaranteed access to activities as self-employed persons on conditions defined by the legislation of the host Member State for its own nationals. Additional conditions related to nationality or residence cannot be imposed. In this respect, therefore, identical principles apply to both establishment and services, and the relevant case-law of the Court normally refers to both types of activity at the same time. Thus, in a number of cases, the Court has held that a Member State that:

- subjects access to certain occupations by nationals of other Member States to a condition of reciprocity;
- makes the possession of its own nationality a condition for access to and exercise of certain professions and activities;
- permits only its own nationals to take part in competitions for the award of licences to carry on certain businesses;
- restricts to its own nationals the possibility of obtaining recognition of foreign qualifications necessary for the pursuit of certain occupations;
- makes it more difficult for the nationals of other Member States to register as members of professional bodies where such registration is a precondition for and facilitates access to and exercise of the professions concerned;
- requires directors and managers of certain undertakings to reside within its territory

fails to fulfil its obligations under both Arts. 43 and 49 (see Case 168/85 *Commission* v. *Italy* [1986] ECR 2945 at p. 2961 (journalists, pharmacists, tourist guides, etc.); Case 147/86 *Commission* v. *Greece*, above, at p. 1656 (private teachers); Case 38/87 *Commission* v. *Greece* [1988] ECR 4415 at pp. 4429–31 (architects, civil engineers, surveyors, and lawyers); Case C-58/90 *Commission* v. *Italy* [1991] ECR I-4193 at p. I-4202 (health-care auxiliaries); Case C-375/92 *Commission* v. *Spain* [1994] ECR I-923 at p. I-940 (tourist guides and guide-interpreters); Case C-114/97 *Commission* v. *Spain* [1998] ECR I-6717 at pp. I-6744–5 (private security undertakings and staff); see also Case 13/76 *Donà*, above, at p. 1340 (professional football players)).

Prohibited discrimination occurs, moreover, whenever rules or practices favour national providers of services to the detriment of providers of the same services who are established in, or are nationals of, other Member States. Thus, in Case 352/85 *Bond van Adverteerders*, above, at pp. 2133–4, it was held that Netherlands legislation which prohibited the distribution by cable of television programmes transmitted from other

Member States that contained advertising or subtitles in Dutch, while permitting the broadcasting of advertisements on national television stations, discriminated against broadcasters established in other Member States. In Case C-260/89 *ERT* [1991] ECR I-2925 at pp. I-2959–61, the Court held that the concentration in the hands of a single television undertaking of the exclusive right both to broadcast its own programmes and to receive and retransmit programmes from other Member States gave that undertaking the possibility to favour its own programmes to the detriment of foreign programmes, and might lead to discrimination to the disadvantage of the latter, contrary to Art. 49. In Case C-17/92 *Distribuidores Cinematográficos*, above, at p. I-2272, the Court found that Spanish legislation which subjected the grant of licences for dubbing foreign films made outside the EC into one of the official national languages to the requirement that a Spanish film should be distributed, favoured Spanish film producers in relation to producers established in other Member States; had a protective effect in favour of the former and to the detriment of the latter; and was therefore discriminatory.

In Case C-20/92 *Hubbard*, above, at pp. I-3794–5, the Court ruled that the fact that a Member State (Germany) required payment of a security for the costs of legal proceedings brought by a lawyer established in another Member State (an English solicitor) on the sole ground that the lawyer was a national of another Member State, while its own nationals were not subject to such a requirement, constituted discrimination on grounds of nationality prohibited by Arts. 49 and 50. The Court also pointed out that, in accordance with its consistent case-law, the right to equal treatment could not be made dependent on the existence of reciprocal agreements between Member States. The subject-matter of the proceedings before the national court (in this case, the law of succession) did not justify any exception to the rule. In Case C-484/93 *Svensson and Gustavsson*, above, at pp. I-3976–8, it was held that a Luxembourg law which made the grant of a housing benefit (interest rate subsidy) subject to the requirement that the building loans were obtained from a credit institution established in Luxembourg discriminated against credit institutions established in other Member States, contrary to Art. 49(1) (for discrimination in the field of taxation, see below).

The principle of equal treatment applies not only to providers but also to recipients of services, including tourists, who under Art. 49 have the right to go to another Member State in order to enjoy those services under the same conditions as nationals. Thus, in Case 186/87 *Cowan*, above, at p. 221, which concerned the refusal by the French Treasury to pay compensation to a British citizen for physical injury that he suffered as a result of a violent assault during a brief stay in Paris as a tourist, on the grounds that such compensation was only available to French nationals or foreign nationals resident in France, the Court said:

> When Community law guarantees a natural person the freedom to go to another Member State the protection of that person from harm in the Member State in question, on the same basis as that of nationals and persons residing there, is a corollary of that freedom of movement. It follows that the prohibition of

discrimination is applicable to recipients of services within the meaning of the Treaty as regards protection against the risk of assault and the right to obtain financial compensation provided for by national law when that risk materializes. The fact that the compensation at issue is financed by the Public Treasury cannot alter the rules regarding the protection of the rights guaranteed by the Treaty.

The fact that the compensation in question was governed by the provisions of criminal legislation, which in principle fell outside the scope of the EC Treaty, made no difference since 'such legislative provisions may not discriminate against persons to whom Community law gives the right to equal treatment or restrict the fundamental freedoms guaranteed by Community law' (ibid. at p. 222).

The prohibition of discrimination is, moreover, not confined to the specific rules concerning access to and pursuit of occupational activities. Discrimination is also prohibited in respect of the various general facilities that are of assistance in the pursuit of those activities, and in respect of all the ancillary advantages that affect the conditions under which services are provided or received. These include the right to acquire, use, or dispose of movable and immovable property in the territory of the host State; the right to obtain loans and to have access to the various forms of credit; the right to rent premises for business purposes, etc. Relying on Art. 44(2)(e) EC and on the General Programmes, the ECJ has emphasized that these rights are the corollary of freedom to provide services. Therefore, the Court has said, a national of a Member State who wishes to pursue an activity as a self-employed person in another Member State must be able to obtain housing, even social housing, under the same conditions as the nationals of the host State, including the various financial facilities available for this purpose. Legislation which restricts the right to purchase or lease housing built or renovated with the help of public funds, and to obtain reduced-rate mortgage loans, to the nationals of the host State or which in general makes the exercise of the right to purchase or use immovable property by nationals of other Member States subject to restrictions not imposed on local nationals, is contrary to the fundamental principle of non-discrimination.

While the above considerations apply primarily to persons who exercise the right of establishment, they may also be relevant to providers of services. Although the latter retain their principal place of establishment in their State of origin, they may have to pursue their occupational activities in another Member State for such an extended period that they need to have permanent housing there, or other immovable property from which or in which to provide their services. They may also satisfy the conditions of a non-discriminatory nature for access to social housing. Therefore, the Court has pointed out, providers of services cannot be excluded from the benefit of national treatment in these matters (Case 63/86 *Commission* v. *Italy*, above, at pp. 52–3; Case 305/87 *Commission* v. *Greece*, above, at pp. 1478–9). Likewise, recipients of services are entitled to ancillary advantages that are connected with the services that they receive, on the same basis as nationals. Thus, in Case C-45/93 *Commission* v. *Spain*, above, at pp. I-919–20, the Court held that since visiting museums is one of the determining reasons for which tourists, as recipients of services, decide to go to another Member State, charging museum admission fees to non-resident nationals of other Member States while local nationals and residents benefit from free admission, entails discrimination within the meaning of Arts. 12 and 49 (see also Case C-388/01 *Commission* v. *Italy* [2003] ECR I-721, paras. 12–28, where the Court held that such discrimination could not be justified on purely economic grounds).

2. Indirect discrimination. Arts. 49 and 50(3) prohibit not only direct or overt discrimination based on nationality, but also all indirect (covert or disguised) forms of discrimination that, by the application of other criteria of differentiation, lead in fact to the same result, unless they are objectively justified. Thus, Title III (A) of the General Programme provides for the elimination, *inter alia*, of any requirements imposed by law or in practice in respect of the provision of services where, although applicable irrespective of nationality, their effect is 'exclusively or principally to hinder the provision of services by foreign nations' (see also Case 15/78 *Koestler*, above, at p. 1980). Such indirect discrimination often arises from legislation that, although applicable without distinction to all nationals, foreign or local, essentially favours the nationals of the host Member State by laying down conditions which can be more easily satisfied by them than by nationals of other Member States or which otherwise prove to be more onerous for the latter. This is the case, in particular, where a measure makes a distinction on the basis of residence, since such a measure is liable to operate mainly to the detriment of nationals of other Member States because non-residents are in the majority of cases non-nationals (see e.g. Case C-224/97 *Ciola*, above, at p. I-2536).

There is indirect discrimination also where the obligation to pay the employer's share of social security contributions is extended to employers established in another Member State who provide services in the first State by employing their own workforce there, and who are already liable under the legislation of the State of establishment for similar contributions in respect of the same workers and the same periods of employment. Clearly, such legislation, although indistinctly applicable, is economically more onerous for employers established in another Member State, who have to bear a heavier burden than those established in the first State. Such legislation cannot be considered to be objectively justified if the contributions do not entitle the workers to any additional social security benefits (Cases 62/81 etc. *Seco* [1982] ECR 223 at pp. 235–7; Case C-43/93 *Vander Elst* [1994] ECR I-3803 at p. I-3824). For other instances of indirect discrimination, see e.g. Case C-3/88 *Commission* v. *Italy* [1989] ECR 4035 at p. 4059 and Case C-272/91 *Commission* v. *Italy* [1994] ECR I-1409 at pp. I-1433–6 concerning Italian legislation restricting participation in certain contracts with the State to companies whose shares were in Italian public ownership; Case C-360/89 *Commission* v. *Italy* [1992] ECR I-3401 at pp. I-3418–19, involving Italian legislation reserving a proportion of public works to sub-contractors established in the region where the works were to be carried out and otherwise benefiting local undertakings; although the law applied without distinction to all companies, it essentially favoured undertakings established in Italy.

3. **Tax discrimination.** Discrimination, whether direct or indirect, is also prohibited in the field of taxation. As the ECJ has pointed out on a number of occasions, 'although direct taxation falls within the competence of the Member States, they must none the less exercise that competence consistently with Community law' (Case C-42/02 *Lindman* [2003] ECR I-0000, para. 18; see also the cases cited immediately below). Thus, the Court has held that national tax rules which treat providers of services differently depending on whether they are established in the territory of the Member State concerned or in another Member State, constitute discrimination prohibited by Art. 49 (Case C-390/96 *Lease Plan Luxembourg* [1998] ECR I-2553 at p. I-2582). In the context of leasing, the Court has stated that any legislation of a Member State which reserves a fiscal advantage to the majority of undertakings that lease goods from lessors established in that State whilst depriving those leasing from lessors established in another Member State of such an advantage gives rise to a difference of treatment based on the place of establishment of the provider of services, which is prohibited by Art. 49. Such a difference of treatment cannot be justified by the need to ensure the coherence of the tax system or by the fact that the lessor established in another Member State is there subject to lower taxation. Generally speaking, any tax advantage resulting for providers of services from the low taxation to which they are subject in the Member State in which they are established cannot be used by another Member State to justify less favourable tax treatment of recipients of those services established in the latter State (Case C-294/97 *Eurowings Luftverkehrs*, above, at pp. I-7473–6).

The same principle applies generally to all types of service, including insurance services. Case C-118/96 *Safir*, above, at pp. I-1925–9, concerned Swedish legislation that created different tax regimes for capital life assurance policies, depending on whether they were taken out with companies established in Sweden or with companies established elsewhere. In the latter case, taxation of savings resulting from such policies was generally higher than in the former case, and the legislation also contained a number of features that were liable to dissuade individuals from taking out policies with foreign companies and dissuade foreign companies from offering their services in Sweden. The Court held that the legislation was contrary to Art. 49 and could not be justified by the purely financial reasons put forward by Sweden. Similarly, in Case C-136/00 *Danner*, above, paras. 31, 36–8, 55–7, the Court found that Finnish tax legislation which restricted or disallowed the deductibility for income tax purposes of voluntary pension scheme contributions paid to pension providers in other Member States while allowing such contributions to be deducted when they were paid to institutions in Finland, was incompatible with Art. 49 if it did not at the same time preclude taxation of pensions paid by the above-mentioned pension providers.

Such legislation could not be justified by the need to ensure the coherence of the national tax system and the effectiveness of fiscal controls, and by the need to prevent tax evasion and the reduction of tax revenue (see also Case C-422/01 *Skandia and Ramstedt* [2003] ECR I-6817, concerning occupational pension insurance). Case C-42/02 *Lindman*, above, para. 27, involved Finnish legislation which discriminated against foreign lotteries in that winnings from lotteries organized in other Member States were treated as income of the winner chargeable to income tax, whereas winnings from lotteries conducted in Finland were not taxable income. Such discrimination fell within the prohibition laid down in Art. 49 (for another form of tax discrimination, see Case C-234/01 *Gerritse* [2003] ECR I-5933).

Tax discrimination is prohibited not only where it is based on the place of establishment of the service provider, but also where it is based on the place where the service is provided. Thus, in Case C-55/98 *Vestergaard*, above, at pp. I-7664–8, both the provider and the recipient of a service (a professional training course) were Danish nationals and residents, but the recipient (who attended the course) received a disadvantageous tax treatment because the service (the course) was provided in Greece and not in Denmark.

4. Differences in national legislation. Arts. 12 and 49 are not concerned with any disparities in treatment that may result, between Member States, from differences in existing legislation. Therefore, they do not prohibit the application of stricter rules in one Member State than those applicable in another so long as those rules affect all persons in accordance with objective criteria and without regard to their nationality (Case C-177/94 *Perfili* [1996] ECR I-161 at pp. I-175–6).

5. Differences between establishment and services. While the provisions of the Treaty on equal treatment are cast in similar terms in the context of both freedom of establishment and freedom to provide services, this does not mean that those provisions affect the beneficiaries of these freedoms in exactly the same way. Under Art. 43(2), freedom of establishment includes the right to pursue activities in another Member State 'under the conditions laid down for its own nationals by the law of the country where such establishment is effected'. Under Art. 50(3), the person providing a service may temporarily pursue his activities in the State where the service is provided 'under the same conditions as are imposed by that State on its own nationals'. While the former provision clearly prohibits discrimination against a person establishing himself in another Member State, it also means that such a person is subject to the laws, regulations, and supervision of the host country in the same way as the nationals of that country. This is a necessary consequence of the fact that his establishment in the host country is permanent and that, not normally being also established in his country of origin, he is not subject to the laws and supervision of the latter country.

While the principal aim of Art. 50(3) is likewise to enable providers of services to pursue their activities in the host Member State without suffering discrimination, the ECJ has made it clear in several cases that it does not follow from that provision that all national legislation applicable to nationals of the host State and usually applied to the permanent activities of persons established therein may be similarly applied in its entirety to the temporary activities of providers of services who are established in other Member States. These persons continue to be subject to the laws and control of their country of establishment. To oblige them to comply with requirements similar to those that they have already satisfied at home would place an extra burden on them not faced by the nationals of the host State. This would create an unnecessary and unjustified restriction on the free movement of services. In other words, a Member State cannot make the performance of services in its territory subject to observance of all the conditions required for establishment; this would deprive the provisions of the Treaty guaranteeing freedom to provide services of all practical effect (see Case 279/80 *Webb*, above, at p. 3324 *per Curiam*, p. 3332 *per* A.-G. Slynn; Case 205/84 *Commission* v. *Germany*, above, at p. 3802; Case C-154/89 *Commission* v. *France*, above, at p. I-685; Case C-294/89 *Commission* v. *France* [1991] ECR I-3591 at p. I-3613; Case C-288/89 *Gouda* [1991] ECR I-4007 at pp. I-4040–1 *per Curiam*, pp. I-4028–9 *per* A.-G. Tesauro; Case C-58/98 *Corsten* [2000] ECR I-7919 at pp. I-7958–60. See further section V below).

6. Derogations. Finally, it should be noted that according to the Court's consistent case-law, discriminatory national provisions, i.e. those that are not applicable to services without distinction according to their origin or the place of residence of the recipient or the place of performance, are compatible with Community law only if they can be brought within the scope of an express derogation, such as that contained in Art. 45 (exercise of official authority) or Art. 46 EC. The latter allows special (i.e. discriminatory) treatment of foreign nationals on grounds of public policy, public security, or public health (but not on grounds of cultural policy). Economic aims cannot constitute grounds of public policy within the meaning of that provision (Case 352/85 *Bond van Adverteerders*, above, at pp. 2134–5; Case C-260/89 *ERT*, above, at p. I-2960; Case C-288/89 *Gouda*, above, at p. I-4040; Case C-17/92 *Distribuidores Cinematográficos*, above, at pp. I-2272–3; Case C-224/97 *Ciola*, above, at p. I-2536. *See further under* **Official authority, Public health, Public policy, Public security**).

V. Prohibition of restrictions

1. Definition of restrictions. Title III (A) of the General Programme provides that, subject to the exceptions laid down in the Treaty, and in particular to Arts. 45, 46, and 51, and subject to the provisions concerning the free movement of goods, capital, and persons, the following restrictions on freedom to provide services were to be eliminated in accordance with the timetable set out in Title V, whether they affected the person providing the services directly, or indirectly through the recipient of the service or through the service itself: any measure, whether laid down by law or arising from administrative practices, which 'prohibits or hinders the person providing services in his pursuit of an activity as a self-employed person by treating him differently from nationals of the State concerned' (this provision was referred to by the ECJ in Case 15/78 *Koestler*, above, at p. 1980). The Programme then goes on to provide a non-exhaustive list of such restrictive provisions and practices. They include those which, in respect of foreign nationals only:

- prohibit, or make subject to an authorization or to a period of prior residence or training in the host country, or make more costly through taxation or other financial burdens, the provision of services (points (a) to (e));
- limit or hinder access to sources of supply or to distribution outlets (point (f));
- deny or restrict the right to participate in social security schemes (point (g));
- grant less favourable treatment in the event of nationalization, expropriation, or requisition (point (h)).

Similarly, provisions and practices were also to be abolished which, in respect of foreign nationals only, exclude, limit, or impose conditions on the power to exercise rights normally attaching to the provision of services, and in particular the power:

- to enter into contracts of various types, to submit tenders, and to obtain licences or authorizations (points (a) to (c));
- to acquire, use, or dispose of movable or immovable property and intellectual property rights, and to borrow and have access to the various forms of credit (points (d) to (f); see also Art. 44(2)(e) EC that refers to the right of EC nationals to acquire and use land and buildings situated in the territory of another Member State. These provisions were invoked by the ECJ in Case 63/86 *Commission* v. *Italy*, above, at pp. 52–3 and in Case 305/87 *Commission* v. *Greece*, above, at pp. 1478–9; both cases involved restrictions on the acquisition or use of immovable property by foreign nationals);
- to receive aids granted by the State and to be a party to legal proceedings (points (g) and (h)).

Title III (B) requires the abolition of any prohibition of, or hindrance to, the movement of the items, materials, tools, machinery, equipment, and other means to be supplied or employed in the course of the service. Title III (C) and (D) provide for the elimination of any prohibition of, or impediment to, the transfer of the funds needed to perform the service and of any restrictions in respect of payments for services, subject to the right of the Member States to verify the nature and genuineness of such transfers and payments and to prevent contravention of their laws (these provisions were relied on by the ECJ in Cases 286/82 etc. *Luisi and Carbone*, above, at p. 402). Finally, Title IV requires the Member States to accord to all beneficiaries, without distinction on grounds of nationality or residence, the most favourable treatment accorded under existing practices and agreements until all restrictions have been abolished.

It is apparent from the above provisions that the General Programme envisages solely the abolition of restrictions that result from measures or practices discriminating, directly or indirectly, against the nationals of other Member States (see also Cases C-330/90 etc. *López Brea*, above, at p. I-337 *per Curiam*, p. I-331 *per* A.-G. Jacobs). However, the ECJ and various Advocates-General have given a much broader interpretation to the concept of 'restrictions' which are prohibited under Arts. 49 and 50. A survey of the case-law of the Court, as it has gradually evolved over the years, shows that while discrimination on grounds of nationality or place of establishment always indicates the existence of a prohibited restriction, it is not an indispensable or exclusive element of such a restriction. Thus, already in Case 33/74 *Van Binsbergen*, above, at p. 1309, one of the earliest cases on services, the Court adopted a very broad definition by saying that:

> The restrictions to be abolished pursuant to Articles 49 and 50 include all requirements imposed on the person providing the service by reason *in particular* of his nationality or of the fact that he does not habitually reside in the State where the service is provided, which do not apply to persons established within the national territory *or which may prevent or otherwise obstruct the activities of the person providing the service* (emphasis added. A similar definition was adopted in Case 39/75 *Coenen*, above, at p. 1555).

Relying, *inter alia*, on this definition, in Case 279/80 *Webb*, above, at p. 3333 A.-G. Slynn expressed the opinion that:

> the abolition of the restrictions on the freedom to supply services within the Community entails more than the abolition of discrimination on the grounds of nationality or place of establishment and extends to the removal of *all obstacles* to the freedom to supply services across the Community's internal borders, save to the extent that they are preserved by Articles 45 to 48 and 55 (emphasis added).

In the same case, without as yet going so far as the Advocate-General, the Court acknowledged that a mechanical application of the rule on equal treatment laid down in Art. 50(3), which would require that the legislation of the host State be applied *in toto* to any person providing services, would not only fail to eliminate existing restrictions on freedom to provide services, but would be likely to reinforce them. The Court explained that the principal aim of Art. 50(3) is to protect the provider of the service against discrimination in favour of the nationals of the host State, but that it 'does not mean that all national legislation applicable to nationals of that State and usually applied to the *permanent activities* of undertakings established therein may be similarly applied in its entirety to the *temporary activities* of undertakings which are established in other Member States' (ibid. at p. 3324; emphasis added. The Court repeated this statement in many of the cases cited below).

In Case C-154/89 *Commission* v. *France*, above, at p. I-672—'Tourist guides' cases—A.-G. Lenz again stressed that 'as a matter of principle any impediment, in fact or in law, to the provision of services within the meaning of Article 49 may fall under the prohibition laid down in that provision . . .

without it being necessary to find discrimination'. The Court has echoed—but has not yet exactly repeated—this view by saying that:

> Articles 49 and 50 of the Treaty require not only the abolition of any discrimination against a person providing services on account of his nationality but also the abolition of any restriction on the freedom to provide services imposed on the ground that the person providing a service is established in a Member State other than the one in which the service is provided. In particular, the Member State cannot make the performance of the services in its territory subject to observance of all the conditions required for establishment; were it to do so the provisions securing freedom to provide services would be deprived of all practical effect (ibid. at p. I-685. See also Case 205/84 *Commission* v. *Germany*, above, at p. 3802; Case C-294/89 *Commission* v. *France*, above, at p. I-3613).

In Case C-288/89 *Gouda*, above, at pp. I-4040–1, the Court made explicit what had been implicitly present in its case-law, namely, that Art. 49 requires the abolition of two distinct types of restriction on freedom to provide services. In the first place, it entails the abolition of any discrimination against the provider of the service on account of his nationality or place of establishment. Secondly, it requires the elimination of restrictions, which, in the absence of harmonization of the rules applicable to services, may arise from the application of national rules that affect any person established in the national territory, to persons providing services established in another Member State, by reason of the fact that those persons already have to satisfy similar requirements embodied in the legislation of the Member State in which they are established (see also the opinion of A.-G. Tesauro, ibid. at pp. I-4028–9).

Finally, in Case C-76/90 *Säger*, above, decided on the same day as *Gouda*, the Court drew the logical conclusion from its previous case-law and settled the question whether Art. 49 extends to measures that do not involve either overt or covert discrimination. In his opinion, Advocate-General Jacobs cogently argued that Art. 49 prohibits all restrictions, including non-discriminatory ones, unless they are justified by the general interest. He rejected the parallel drawn by the United Kingdom between establishment and the supply of services, and suggested that services should rather be treated by analogy with goods. Accordingly, non-discriminatory restrictions on the provision of services should be treated in the same way as non-discriminatory restrictions on the free movement of goods under the *Cassis de Dijon* line of case-law (Case 120/78 *Rewe* [1979] ECR 649). Consequently, the principle should be that if an undertaking complies with the legislation of the State of establishment it may provide services to recipients in another Member State, even if the provision of such services would not normally be lawful under the laws of the latter State. Restrictions can only be imposed if they are justified by some requirement that is compatible with the aims of the Community. Such an approach is particularly appropriate, he said, when the service is provided by means of post or telecommunications without the supplier moving physically between Member States. He pointed out that if the scope of Art. 49 were to be restricted to discriminatory measures, Member States could adopt a variety of restrictions, so long as they were not discriminatory, which collectively might wholly frustrate the aims of Art. 49 and render impossible the attainment of a single market in services (ibid. at pp. I-4233–6. See also the opinion of A.-G. Tesauro in Case C-288/89 *Gouda*, above, at p. I-4028, to the same effect).

The Court followed the opinion of Advocate-General Jacobs and stated in categorical terms that:

> Article 49 of the Treaty requires not only the elimination of all discrimination against a person providing services on the ground of his nationality but also the abolition of any restriction, *even if it applies without distinction* to national providers of services and to those of other Member States, when it is liable to prohibit or otherwise impede the activities of a provider of services established in another Member State where he lawfully provides similar services (Case C-76/90 *Säger*, above, at p. I-4243, emphasis added).

In particular, the Court added in accordance with its previous case-law, a Member State may not make the provision of services in its territory subject to compliance with all the conditions required for establishment since this would deprive of all practical effectiveness the provisions of the Treaty that guarantee the freedom to provide services. Such a restriction is all the less permissible where the service is supplied without the supplier moving to the Member State of destination (ibid.).

In its subsequent case-law, the Court has repeatedly confirmed, sometimes expressly relying on the *Säger* formula, that national legislation may fall within the prohibition laid down in Art. 49 even if it is applicable generally and without distinction and does not aim to put the national market at an advantage over providers of services from other Member States, when it is liable to prohibit, impede, or render less advantageous the cross-border supply of services without objective justification or, in view of the objectives of the single market, makes the supply of services more difficult between Member States than purely within one Member State (see Case C-106/91 *Ramrath*, above, at p. I-3384; Case C-275/92 *Schindler*, above, at p. I-1093; Case C-43/93 *Vander Elst*, above, at pp. I-3823–5; Case C-381/93 *Commission* v. *France*, above, at p. I-5169; Case C-384/93 *Alpine Investments*, above, at pp. I-1176–7; etc.). The Court has moreover held that the prohibition in Art. 49 covers not only restrictions laid down by the State of destination but also those laid down by the State in which the provider of the service is established if the service is supplied in another Member State (ibid. at p. I-1176). Nevertheless, a measure does not constitute a restriction within the meaning of Art. 49 merely because other Member States apply less strict measures to providers of similar services established in their territory (ibid. at p. I-1175). Nor does a measure that is not directed at the providers of services (Case C-159/90 *Grogan*, above, at p. I-4740, where the prohibition on distributing information about clinics performing termination of pregnancy in other Member States was enforced in Ireland against student associations that had no links with the clinics as providers of those services).

2. Objective justification. It is clear from the foregoing that the Court has defined the concept of the 'restrictions' that are prohibited by Art. 49 very widely. At the same time, the Court has imposed certain important limitations on the scope of that prohibition. It has accepted that, having regard to the particular characteristics of certain types of services, specific requirements (restrictions) imposed on the provider, which result from the application of rules governing those types of activities, cannot be considered to be incompatible with the Treaty if they are objectively justified. However, the Court has made it clear that as a fundamental principle of the Treaty, the freedom to provide services may be restricted, apart from the express derogations listed in Art. 45 (official authority) and Art. 46 (public policy, public security, or public health) only by rules that fulfil a number of strictly defined conditions. Thus, national measures that restrict the freedom to provide services fall outside the prohibition laid down by Art. 49 only if they:

- are objectively justified by the 'general good' or, according to more recent terminology, by 'overriding reasons relating to the public interest';
- are applied in a non-discriminatory manner to all persons and undertakings operating in the State where the service is provided;
- are suitable for securing the attainment of the objective which they pursue;
- do not go beyond what is necessary in order to attain that objective; in other words, if it is not possible to attain the same result by less restrictive measures (the principle of proportionality); and
- the interest in question is not already protected by the rules to which the person providing the service is subject in the Member State where he is established (see, in particular, Case 33/74 *Van Binsbergen*, above, at p. 1309; Case 205/84 *Commission* v. *Germany*, above, at p. 3803; Case C-154/89 *Commission* v. *France*, above, at p. I-686; Case C-288/89 *Gouda*, above, at pp. I-4040–1; Case C-76/90 *Säger*, above, at p. I-4244; Case C-106/91 *Ramrath*, above, at pp. I-3384–5; Case C-3/95 *Reisebüro Broede*, above, at pp. I-6537–8 and the cases cited immediately below).

The 'overriding reasons relating to the public interest' that the Court has so far recognized include the following: professional rules (in particular, rules relating to organization, qualifications, professional ethics, supervision, and liability) intended to protect the recipients of the service in question; protection of intellectual property; protection of workers; consumer protection; fair trading; conservation and appreciation of the national archaeological, historical, artistic, and cultural heritage and the widest possible dissemination of knowledge thereof; cultural policy; the proper administration of justice (see Case C-288/89 *Gouda*, above, at pp. I-4041, I-4043, and the cases cited therein, above and below); limitation of gambling, prevention of crime and fraud, protection of morality, maintenance of public order (Case C-275/92 *Schindler*, above, at pp. I-1096–8; Case C-124/97 *Läärä*, above, at pp. I-6116–17; Case C-67/98 *Zenatti*, above, at p. I-7314; Case C-243/01

Gambelli, above, para. 63); protection of investor confidence in national financial markets (Case C-384/93 *Alpine Investments*, above, at pp. I-1179, I-1182); the risk of seriously undermining the financial balance of the social security system (Case C-158/96 *Kohll*, above, at p. I-1948; Case C-368/98 *Vanbraekel*, above, at p. I-5401; Case C-157/99 *Geraets-Smits and Peerbooms*, above, at p. I-5533; Case C-385/99 *Müller-Fauré and Van Riet*, above, para. 73); guaranteeing the quality of skilled trade work (Case C-58/98 *Corsten*, above, at p. I-7957); road safety (Case C-451/99 *Cura Anlagen*, above, at p. I-3235); social policy (Case C-355/00 *Freskot*, above, para. 69).

However, reasons of a purely economic nature, such as the reduction of tax revenue, cannot constitute overriding reasons in the public interest (Case C-158/96 *Kohll*, above, at p. I-1948; Case C-388/01 *Commission* v. *Italy*, above, para. 22; Case C-243/01 *Gambelli*, above, para. 61; etc.). Moreover, a Member State may invoke reasons of public interest to justify a national measure that is likely to restrict the freedom to provide services only if that measure is compatible with the fundamental rights protected by Community law (Case C-260/89 *ERT*, above, at p. I-2964; Case C-368/95 *Familiapress*, above, at p. I-3717; Case C-60/00 *Carpenter*, above, at p. I-6321). As to the requirement of proportionality, a measure cannot be regarded as necessary to achieve the aim pursued if it essentially duplicates controls that have already been carried out in the context of other procedures, either in the State where the service is provided or in another Member State (Case C-390/99 *Canal Satélite Digital*, above, at p. I-654).

The Court has also acknowledged that a Member State has the right to take measures to prevent the freedom guaranteed by Art. 49 from being used by a supplier of services for the purpose of avoiding the rules which would be applicable to him if he were established within that State, by providing services from the territory of another Member State. Such a situation may be subject to judicial control under the provisions relating to the right of establishment and not those concerning the supply of services (Case 33/74 *Van Binsbergen*, above, at p. 1309; Case 205/84 *Commission* v. *Germany*, above, at p. 3801; Case C-148/91 *Veronica* [1993] ECR I-487 at p. I-519; Case C-23/93 *TV10*, above, at p. I-4832).

To sum up, Art. 49 prohibits both restrictions which result from discriminatory measures and restrictions which apply without distinction to all providers of services. Discriminatory restrictions are compatible with Community law only if they can be brought within the scope of an express derogation, such as that contained in Art. 45 (exercise of official authority) or Art. 46 (derogation on grounds of public policy, public security, or public health). Non-discriminatory restrictions are compatible with Community law if they can be objectively justified by overriding reasons relating to the public interest and satisfy the other conditions laid down by the Court (see above). The justification required cannot be determined in the abstract; in each case it depends on the nature of the service and the nature of the restriction. The usual practice of the Court is to consider, first, whether a non-discriminatory measure has a restrictive effect on the freedom to provide services; secondly, if so, whether the restriction may be justified; and thirdly, if so, whether the public interest in question is already protected by the rules of the State where the service provider is established and whether the same result can be achieved by less restrictive rules (see e.g. Case C-272/94 *Guiot* [1996] ECR I-1905 at p. I-1921; Cases C-369/96 etc. *Arblade* [1999] ECR I-8453 at p. I-8515).

3. Examples of prohibited restrictions and objective justifications. The Court has identified a number of restrictions falling within the scope of Art. 49 and has recognized a number of overriding public interest considerations as justifying such restrictions. The most important of these restrictions and justifications are summarized below.

(*a*) ***The requirement to have a permanent establishment.*** The requirement that the person or undertaking providing the service must be habitually resident or must have a permanent establishment within the territory of the State in which the service is performed not only constitutes a restriction on the freedom to provide services but has been described by the Court as 'the very negation of that freedom'. It has the result of depriving Art. 49 of all effectiveness since the very purpose of that Article is to abolish restrictions on the freedom to supply services imposed on persons who are not established in the State where the service is to be supplied (this type of restriction has come before the Court in a large number of cases, see the cases cited below and Case 76/81 *Transporoute* [1982] ECR 417 at pp. 427–8).

However, in Case 33/74 *Van Binsbergen*, above, at pp. 1309–10 the Court accepted that such a requirement may be objectively justified by the need to ensure observance of rules of professional conduct connected, in particular, with the administration of justice and with respect for professional ethics, provided that these objectives cannot be achieved by less restrictive measures, such as having an address for service or a place of business in the host State (see also Case 39/75 *Coenen*, above, at pp. 1555–6. In both cases the Court held that the requirement of residence in the State of destination could not be justified in the given circumstances). In Case 205/84 *Commission* v. *Germany*, above, at pp. 3803–4 and 3809–11, the Court acknowledged that the requirement that Community insurance undertakings must have a permanent establishment within the Member State in which the insurance service is supplied, while amounting to a restriction under Art. 49, can in principle be justified by imperative reasons relating to the public interest, namely, by the protection of the consumer both as a policy-holder and as an insured person, provided that it constitutes a condition which is indispensable to the achievement of that objective. However, the Court concluded that in the circumstances of the case before it, the requirement of a permanent establishment did not constitute such an indispensable condition and was therefore incompatible with Arts. 49 and 50 (see also the similar Case 220/83 *Commission* v. *France* [1986] ECR 3663 at pp. 3708–10; Case 252/83 *Commission* v. *Denmark* [1986] ECR 3713 at pp. 3747–9; Case 206/84 *Commission* v. *Ireland* [1986] ECR 3817 at pp. 3848–51—'Insurance' cases; Case C-101/94 *Commission* v. *Italy* [1996] ECR I-2691 at pp. I-2727–8, concerning dealers in transferable securities; Case C-131/01

Commission v. *Italy*, above, paras. 40–8, concerning patent agents; etc.). In Case C-204/90 *Bachmann* [1992] ECR I-249 at pp. I-284–5, the Court held that Belgian legislation requiring an insurer to be established in Belgium as a condition for the eligibility of insured persons to benefit from the deduction of certain insurance contributions from total taxable income, although constituting a restriction within the meaning of Art. 49, was nevertheless justified by the need to preserve the cohesion of the applicable tax system (see also Case C-300/90 *Commission* v. *Belgium* [1992] ECR I-305 at p. I-321).

(b) The requirement to obtain a licence or authorization. The requirement that a person or undertaking must obtain a licence or authorization to provide a particular service generally constitutes a restriction within the meaning of Art. 49, but may be objectively justified on various grounds involving the public interest, depending on the nature of the service in question. In Cases 110/78 etc. *Van Wesemael*, above, at pp. 52–3, the Court held that the requirement that a fee-charging employment agency for entertainers established in another Member State must either obtain a licence or act through the holder of a licence in order to provide its services in Belgium may be justified by the need to ensure observance of the professional rules of conduct and to ensure the protection of the entertainer. However, the Court added, such a requirement is not justified when the service is provided by an employment agency that comes under the public administration of a Member State or by a person who already holds a licence in his State of establishment issued under conditions 'comparable' to those required by the host State and who is subject in the first State to proper supervision covering all his activities in any Member State.

In Case 279/80 *Webb*, above, at pp. 3325–6, the Court accepted that, owing to the particularly sensitive nature of the provision of manpower (temporary staff) both from the occupational and from the social point of view, Member States have the right to subject that activity to a system of licensing and to require a provider of such services established in another Member State to comply with that system even if he holds a licence issued in his State of establishment. However, in considering applications for licences and in granting them, the host State may not make any distinction based on the nationality of the provider of the services or his place of establishment, and must take into account the evidence and guarantees already furnished by him in his State of establishment. In Case C-279/00 *Commission* v. *Italy* [2002] ECR I-1425 at p. I-1457, the Court held that the requirement that all undertakings had to establish a guarantee in order to obtain a licence to carry on, in Italy, the business of providing temporary labour was contrary to Art. 49 because it precluded the taking into account of comparable obligations to which the provider was already subject in his Member State of establishment. Furthermore, the requirement that the guarantee had to be lodged with a credit institution having its registered office or a branch office in Italy also constituted discrimination against credit institutions established in other Member States, and was prohibited by Art. 49 (ibid. at pp. I-1458–9; see also Case C-439/99 *Commission* v. *Italy* [2002] ECR I-305 at pp. I-367–71, where the Court found a number of restrictions imposed on trade-fair organizers in Italy contrary to Art. 49, including the requirement of prior authorization).

In Case 205/84 *Commission* v. *Germany*, above, at pp. 3807–9, the Court acknowledged that the requirement that an insurance undertaking must be authorized in the State in which it provides its services is justified on grounds relating to the protection of the consumer both as a policy-holder and as an insured person. However, authorization must be granted to any undertaking meeting the prescribed conditions; those conditions may not duplicate equivalent statutory conditions that have already been satisfied in the State of establishment; and the supervisory authority of the host State must take into account supervision and verifications already carried out in the State of establishment. The Court also recognized that the above grounds for justification are not equally important in every sector of insurance and that there may be cases where, because of the nature of the risk insured and of the party seeking insurance, there is no need to protect the latter by the application of the mandatory rules of his national law. This is the case in the field of co-insurance taken out by large undertakings or groups of undertakings, which are in a position to assess and negotiate insurance policies proposed to them. Here, the considerations relating to consumer protection do not have the same force as in other areas, and do not justify the requirement of authorization (ibid. at pp. 3813–14; see also the other 'Insurance' cases cited under (*a*) above and Case C-222/95 *Parodi*, above, at pp. I-3921–6 concerning French legislation requiring authorization in order to supply banking services prior to the entry into force of the second banking directive).

In the 'Tourist guides' cases the Court ruled that the requirement laid down by a Member State that tourist guides travelling with a group of tourists from another Member State must be in possession of a licence that requires the acquisition of a specific qualification normally obtained by passing an examination, amounts to a restriction on the provision of services both by tour companies and by self-employed tourist guides. The Court accepted that the general interest in the proper appreciation and conservation of the historical, artistic, cultural, and archaeological heritage of a country and in consumer protection can constitute an overriding reason justifying a restriction. However, the Court said, a licence requirement for guiding tourists in places other than museums and historical monuments that may be visited only with a specialized professional guide, goes beyond what is necessary to safeguard that interest as it has the effect of reducing the number of tourist guides qualified to offer the service in question, to the disadvantage of both the tour operator and the tourists, and is therefore contrary to Art. 49 (Case C-154/89 *Commission* v. *France*, above, at pp. I-685–8; Case C-180/89 *Commission* v. *Italy*, above, at pp. I-722–5; Case C-198/89 *Commission* v. *Greece*, above, at pp. I-740–3. See also Case C-375/92 *Commission* v. *Spain*, above, at pp. I-942–3). In Case C-398/95 *SETTG* [1997] ECR I-3091 at pp. I-3119–21, the Court found that Greek legislation according to which tourist guides could only operate under a contract of employment was contrary to Art. 49 since it prevented those guides from working as self-employed persons and as providers of services. Such legislation could not be justified by the need to maintain industrial peace because that was a purely economic aim. In Case C-76/90 *Säger*, above, at pp. I-4243–5, the Court held that German legislation which made the provision of patent renewal services by an undertaking established in another Member State subject to the possession of an administrative licence, which might be issued only to persons having a specific professional qualification, such as lawyers or patent agents, constituted a restriction. Although in principle justifiable by the public interest in the protection of the recipients of the services in question, such a restriction was disproportionate to the objective pursued and was, therefore, incompatible with Art. 49.

The requirement for prior authorization may be imposed not only on providers, but also on recipients of services. For example, the assumption of costs, under a national social security system, incurred by recipients of hospital treatment provided in another Member State may be subject to prior authorization (see point (*j*) below). However, in both situations such a requirement is compatible with Community law only if it satisfies a number of conditions laid down by the ECJ. Thus, a system of prior administrative authorization cannot legitimize discretionary decisions taken by the national authorities that are liable to negate the effectiveness of provisions of Community law, in particular those relating to fundamental freedoms. Therefore, in order for such a system to be justified even though it derogates from the fundamental freedoms, it must be based on objective, non-discriminatory criteria which are known in advance to the persons concerned and which circumscribe the exercise of the national authorities' discretion, so that it is not used arbitrarily. Prior authorization is normally necessary only where a subsequent control would be too late to be genuinely effective and to achieve its purpose. Moreover, a prior authorization procedure must be easily accessible, must deal with the request for authorization objectively and impartially, within a reasonable time and subject to reasonable costs. Finally, refusals to grant authorization must be capable of being challenged in judicial or quasi-judicial proceedings (Case C-157/99 *Geraets-Smits and Peerbooms*, above, at p. I-5537; Case C-385/99 *Müller-Fauré and Van Riet*, above, paras. 83–5; Case C-390/99 *Canal Satélite Digital*, above, at pp. I-654–7).

(*c*) ***Prohibition of television advertising.*** Initially, the prohibition of television advertising on grounds of general interest was held not to constitute a restriction within the meaning of Art. 49 even where the prohibition extended to advertising originating in other Member States, if it applied without distinction to national and foreign television organizations (Case 52/79 *Debauve*, above, at pp. 856–7). Subsequently, the Court held that where the prohibition discriminates against broadcasters established in other Member States, it does entail a restriction contrary to Art. 49, which can only be justified by an express derogation such as that contained in Art. 46 EC (public policy), provided that it does not have an economic aim

(Case 352/85 *Bond van Adverteerders*, above, at pp. 2132–6). Non-discriminatory restrictions imposed on the transmission by cable of radio and television advertising originating in other Member States but intended specifically for the first State can in principle be justified by considerations of cultural policy aimed at safeguarding the freedom of expression, also protected by Art. 10 of the European Convention on Human Rights, and at creating a pluralist and non-commercial radio and television broadcasting system. Certain restrictions relating to the advertisements themselves (i.e. to their duration, frequency, presentation, the products involved, etc.) can also be justified by the need to protect consumers against excessive advertising and to maintain a certain level of programme quality. However, restrictions which are not objectively necessary in order to safeguard the above-mentioned general interests, or which have the effect of restricting competition from foreign broadcasters, are incompatible with Art. 49 (Case C-288/89 *Gouda*, above, at pp. I-4042–5. See also Case C-353/89 *Commission* v. *Netherlands* [1991] ECR I-4069 at pp. I-4095 *et seq.* and Case C-211/91 *Commission* v. *Belgium* [1992] ECR I-6757 at pp. I-6775–7; in both cases the Court established infringements of Art. 49. See also the two cases cited immediately below). A Member State is entitled to treat as a domestic broadcaster a radio and television organization that has established itself in another Member State in order to avoid the application of the law of the first State, when it provides services that are intended for the territory of the first State (Case C-148/91 *Veronica*, above, at pp. I-518–20; Case C-23/93 *TV10*, above, at pp. I-4832–4).

Following the co-ordination of national provisions concerning television broadcasting by Council Dir. 89/552 (*OJ* 1989 L298/23), as amended by Dir. 97/36 (*OJ* 1997 L202/60), Member States are required to ensure freedom to provide television broadcasting services, including advertising, in accordance with the terms of the directive. However, the ECJ has held that the directive has only partially co-ordinated national provisions on television advertising and sponsorship. Although the directive provides that the Member States are to ensure freedom of reception and are not to impede retransmission on their territory of television broadcasts coming from other Member States on grounds relating to television advertising and sponsorship, it does not have the effect of automatically and completely excluding the application of national rules aimed at consumer protection, provided that they do not involve secondary control of television broadcasts in addition to the control carried out by the broadcasting Member State. Consequently, where national legislation imposes prohibitions and restrictions on advertisers for the purpose of protecting consumers, application of such legislation to television broadcasts from other Member States cannot be considered to constitute an obstacle prohibited by the directive. However, in accordance with the Court's case-law discussed above, provisions that restrict the possibility for television broadcasters established in the broadcasting State to broadcast, for advertisers established in the receiving State, television advertising specifically directed at the public in the receiving State, involve a restriction on freedom to provide services. Such restriction may only be justified either under Art. 46 or on grounds of overriding requirements of public interest, such as fair trading and consumer protection (Cases C-34/95 etc. *De Agostini*, above, at pp. I-3888–9, I-3892–3. For an interpretation and application of Dir. 89/552 with regard to television advertising, see ibid. at pp. I-3886–9; Case C-412/93 *Leclerc-Siplec* [1995] ECR I-179 at pp. I-219–22; Case C-6/98 *ARD* [1999] ECR I-7599 at pp. I-7630–5, I-7637).

(*d*) ***Posting of workers abroad.*** Where an employer who is established in a Member State provides a service in another Member State (for example, in the construction industry) by bringing his own workforce with him, the requirement that he must obtain work permits for his workers in the host State, or must pay social security contributions for them, or draw up and retain certain social and labour documents in respect of them, is a restriction contrary to Art. 49 where the workers are nationals of the first Member State or, if nationals of a non-Member State, are lawfully resident and already possess work permits there, and where the employer is already liable to pay comparable contributions for the same workers and for the same period of work in the Member State where he is established, and already possesses the required documentation, and the contributions do not provide the workers with any real additional protection. Such workers, sent abroad temporarily, will return to their country of origin or residence after completion of their work and therefore do not seek access to the labour market in the host State. Nevertheless, Arts. 49 and 50 do not preclude the host State from imposing on such an employer the obligation to pay the workers deployed by him the minimum remuneration fixed by legislation or collective labour agreements applicable in that State, provided that the provisions in question are sufficiently precise and accessible; nor from enforcing those rules by appropriate means. Although such obligation constitutes a restriction on freedom to provide services, it is justified by an overriding reason relating to the public interest, namely, the protection of employees (Cases 62/81 etc. *Seco*, above, at pp. 235–7; Case C-113/89 *Rush Portuguesa*, above, at pp. I-1443–5; Case C-43/93 *Vander Elst*, above, at pp. I-3824–7; Case C-272/94 *Guiot*, above, at pp. I-1921–3; Cases C-369/96 etc. *Arblade*, above, at pp. I-8526–7; see also the cases cited below).

However, there are certain circumstances in which the application of the host Member State's rules on minimum wages to a service provider established in another Member State is neither necessary nor proportionate to the objective pursued, namely, the protection of posted workers. This is the case, for example, where the workers involved are employees of an undertaking established in a frontier region who carry out, on a part-time basis and for brief periods, a part of their work in the territory of several Member States. In that situation, the host Member State's objective of ensuring adequate welfare protection for employees is attained if all the workers concerned enjoy an equivalent position overall in relation to remuneration, taxation, and social security contributions in the host Member State and in the Member State of establishment (Case C-165/98 *Mazzoleni and ISA*

[2001] ECR I-2189 at pp. I-2223–5). Likewise, where the purpose of the minimum-wage legislation is to protect the domestic construction industry and to reduce unemployment in order to avoid social tension, then its application to a service provider established in another Member State cannot be justified. The aim of such legislation is not to protect posted workers, but to protect domestic businesses. This is a purely economic aim, which cannot justify a restriction on the freedom to provide services (Case C-164/99 *Portugaia Construções* [2002] ECR I-787 at pp. I-813–15).

Apart from its legislation on minimum wages, the host Member State may extend to a service provider established in another Member State rules that confer a genuine benefit on posted workers, adding significantly to their social protection. Thus, it may impose on such an employer national rules guaranteeing entitlement to paid leave for posted workers, provided that the workers do not enjoy an essentially similar level of protection under the law of the Member State of establishment and that the application of those rules is proportionate to the public interest objective pursued. The rules thus imposed may even provide for a longer period of paid leave than that provided for by Dir. 93/104 concerning certain aspects of the organization of working time (*OJ* 1993 L307/18, as amended by Dir. 2000/34, *OJ* 2000 L195, consolidated version: Dir. 2003/88, *OJ* 2003 L298) (Cases C-49/98 etc. *Finalarte* [2001] ECR I-7831 at pp. I-7903–5). The terms and conditions of employment that undertakings posting workers to another Member State must guarantee in accordance with the laws of the host State are laid down in Dir. 96/71 of 16 December 1996 concerning the posting of workers in the framework of the provision of services (*OJ* 1997 L18/1).

(*e*) ***Lotteries and gambling.*** National legislation that prohibits the holding of lotteries and, as a result, precludes lottery operators from other Member States from promoting their lotteries and selling their tickets, constitutes a restriction on the freedom to provide services. However, in so far as such legislation applies without discrimination on grounds of nationality, it may be justified by overriding public interest considerations of social policy, such as consumer protection, prevention of crime and fraud, protection of morality, and maintenance of order in society (Case C-275/92 *Schindler*, above, at pp. I-1093–8). The same considerations also apply to other forms of gambling, such as the operation of gaming machines (Case C-124/97 *Läärä*, above, at pp. I-6115–19, where the Court held that Finnish legislation that granted to a single public body exclusive rights to operate slot machines was not contrary to Art. 49; Case C-6/01 *Anomar*, above, paras. 65–75, 81, 88, where Portuguese legislation that authorized gambling solely in casinos in permanent or temporary gaming areas was found not to be contrary to Art. 49; the fact that other Member States laid down less restrictive rules was irrelevant) and betting on sporting events (Case C-67/98 *Zenatti*, above, at pp. I-7313–16 and Case C-243/01 *Gambelli*, above, paras. 56–76, both concerning Italian legislation on betting). However, to be compatible with Community law, such restrictions must be proportionate to the aims pursued. In so far as the authorities of a Member State encourage consumers to participate in lotteries, games of chance, and betting to the financial benefit of the public purse, they cannot invoke public order concerns in order to justify the restrictions (ibid. para. 69).

(*f*) ***Cold calling.*** The prohibition on 'cold calling', i.e. on making unsolicited telephone calls to potential clients established in other Member States in order to offer them certain financial services, is a restriction within the meaning of Art. 49. However, provided it is non-discriminatory, such prohibition may be justified by public interest considerations relating to the protection of investor confidence in the national financial markets and the maintenance of the good reputation of those markets (Case C-384/93 *Alpine Investments*, above, at pp. I-1175–82).

(*g*) ***Assignment of copyright.*** While the exclusive assignment of the copyright in a film for the whole territory of a Member State creates restrictions on the freedom of cable television companies to transmit that film on their network in that State having received it from a television broadcasting station established in another Member State which broadcast the film with the consent of the original owner of the copyright, such a restriction is justified by the need to protect intellectual property rights and is therefore not contrary to Art. 49 (Case 62/79 *Coditel I* [1980] ECR 881 at pp. 902–4).

(*h*) ***Test certificates.*** The legislation of a Member State whereby test certificates for vehicles registered in that State may not be issued by garages established in another Member State amounts to a restriction on freedom to provide services in that it may cause foreign garages loss of custom. However, such legislation is justified by the requirements of road safety, which constitute overriding reasons relating to the public interest (Case C-55/93 *Van Schaik*, above, at p. I-4858).

(*i*) ***Debt-collection.*** The rule that in a Member State an undertaking may carry out judicial debt-collection work for others only through the intermediary of a lawyer constitutes a restriction on freedom to provide services, but such a restriction is justified by the general interest, in particular by the need to ensure the protection of those to whom the service is provided and the sound administration of justice (Case C-3/95 *Reisebüro Broede*, above, at pp. I-6538–41).

(*j*) ***Social security rules.*** National social security rules under which reimbursement of the costs of medical treatment provided by a doctor established in another Member State is subject to prior authorization by the insured person's social security institution, and is denied in the absence of authorization, are contrary to Art. 49 where similar costs incurred in the State of insurance are not subject to that authorization. Such rules deter insured persons from approaching providers of medical services established in another Member State and constitute, for them and their patients, a barrier to freedom to provide services. However, such rules may be objectively justified by overriding reasons relating to the public interest, such as the risk of seriously undermining the financial balance of the social security system.

This justification cannot be invoked, however, where reimbursement is in accordance with the tariff of the State of insurance, because then it has no significant effect on the financing of the social security system. Such rules might also possibly be justified under Art. 46 EC, in conjunction with Art. 55 EC, which allow Member States to restrict the freedom to provide medical services on grounds of public health, in so far as this is necessary for maintaining a high level of health protection or treatment capacity and a balanced medical and hospital service open to all. Nevertheless, those provisions do not permit Member States to exclude the public health sector, as a sector of economic activity, from the fundamental freedoms of the Treaty (Case C-158/96 *Kohll*, above, at pp. I-1946–50, where the Court found that the requirement for prior authorization was not justified on any of the grounds put forward by Luxembourg. The case involved a Luxembourg national whose request for his daughter to receive treatment from an orthodontist established in Germany was not authorized).

Similarly, the fact that national legislation does not guarantee a person covered by its social insurance scheme, who has been authorized to receive hospital treatment in another Member State, a level of payment equivalent to that to which he would have been entitled if he had received such treatment in the Member State in which he is insured entails a restriction on freedom to provide services, which may possibly be justified on the grounds stated above (Case C-368/98 *Vanbraekel*, above, at pp. I-5400–3, where none of the grounds invoked could justify the restriction in question).

Nevertheless, the ECJ has accepted that, as regards the prior authorization requirement, there is a difference between medical services provided by practitioners in their surgeries or at the patient's home, and medical services provided within a hospital infrastructure. In the latter case, the number of hospitals, their geographical distribution, organization, and equipment, and the nature of the medical services which they offer, are matters which require careful planning. There is also a need to maintain a balanced range of high-quality hospital treatment, to control costs, and to prevent any wastage of financial, technical and human resources. For these reasons, the Court has recognized that the requirement that the assumption of costs, under a national social security system, of hospital treatment provided in another Member State must be subject to prior authorization is a measure that is both necessary and reasonable. Nevertheless, in order for a system of prior administrative authorization to be objectively justified, it must meet a number of strict requirements (see point (*b*) above), and the conditions attached to the grant of such authorization must also satisfy the principle of proportionality. Thus, the condition that the proposed treatment must be covered by the sickness insurance scheme of the Member State in which the patient is insured which requires that the treatment must be regarded as 'normal in the professional circles concerned' is acceptable, provided that the authorization cannot be refused on that ground where the treatment is sufficiently tried and tested by international medical science. Likewise, the condition that the proposed treatment must be medically necessary is also acceptable, provided that the authorization to receive treatment in another

Member State may be refused on that ground only if treatment which is the same or equally effective for the patient can be obtained without undue delay within the territory of the Member State in which the insured person's sickness fund is established (Case C-157/99 *Geraets-Smits and Peerbooms*, above, at pp. I-5530–43).

In its subsequent case-law, the Court has upheld the above distinction between hospital care and non-hospital care provided in a Member State other than that in which the insured person's sickness fund is established. In the case of hospital care, the requirement for prior authorization on the above-mentioned conditions is allowed, although a refusal to grant authorization solely on the ground that there are waiting lists for hospital treatment, without account being taken of the patient's medical condition, cannot be justified. In the case of non-hospital care, the requirement for prior authorization is contrary to Arts. 49 and 50, even when the national legislation provides for a system of benefits in kind under which insured persons are entitled not to reimbursement of costs, but to the treatment itself, which is provided free of charge (Case C-385/99 *Müller-Fauré and Van Riet*, above, paras. 40–4, 66–109; see also Case C-56/01 *Inizan* [2003] ECR I-12403, paras. 56–60).

Arts. 49 and 50 also preclude national rules under which reimbursement of expenditure incurred on board, lodging, travel, visitor's tax, and the making of a final medical report in connection with a health cure taken in another Member State is conditional on obtaining prior recognition of eligibility, which is given only where it is established that the proposed cure is absolutely necessary owing to the greatly increased prospects of success in that other Member State (Case C-8/02 *Leichtle* [2004] ECR I-0000, para. 51).

(*k*) ***Multi-disciplinary partnerships.*** Although a prohibition of multi-disciplinary partnership between members of the Bar and accountants constitutes a restriction on freedom to provide services, it may be justified on the ground that it is necessary for the proper practice of the legal profession, as organized in the Member State concerned (Case C-309/99 *Wouters*, above, at p. I-1695).

(*l*) ***Identity cards.*** The requirement that every staff member of a security firm or internal security service must carry an identification card issued by the Member State where the service is performed, in addition to the identity card or passport issued by the Member State of origin, is a restriction on freedom to provide that service as it is disproportionate in relation to the need to ensure the identification of the persons concerned (Case C-355/98 *Commission* v. *Belgium* [2000] ECR I-1221 at p. I-1248).

(*m*) ***Trades registers.*** The requirement imposed on an undertaking established in a Member State which wishes, as a provider of a service, to carry on a skilled trade activity in another Member State to be entered on the latter's trades register constitutes a restriction within the meaning of Art. 49. The objective of guaranteeing the quality of skilled trade work and of protecting those who have commissioned such work is an overriding reason relating to the public interest, which is capable of justifying such a restriction. However, this is not the case where the requirement of registration goes beyond what is necessary to attain that objective, namely, where it delays, complicates or renders more onerous the provision of the service in question, or where it gives rise to additional administrative expense or entails compulsory payment of subscriptions to the chamber of trades (Case C-58/98 *Corsten*, above, at pp. I-7956–60, involving an undertaking established in the Netherlands which contracted to lay composition floors in Germany; Case C-131/01 *Commission* v. *Italy*, above, paras. 27–33, involving patent agents providing services in Italy; Case C-215/01 *Schnitzer*, above, paras. 34–40, involving an undertaking established in Portugal which carried out plastering work in Germany; see also Case C-358/98 *Commission* v. *Italy* [2000] ECR I-1255 at pp. I-1271–3, involving cleansing undertakings providing services in Italy).

(*n*) ***Prohibition of advertising.*** A prohibition on the advertising of alcoholic beverages is a restriction within the meaning of Art. 49, but it may be justified by the protection of public health under Arts. 46 and 55, subject to the condition of proportionality (Case C-405/98 *Gourmet International Products*, above, at pp. I-1828–9).

(*o*) ***Tax on satellite dishes.*** A tax on satellite dishes that does not apply to the reception of television programmes transmitted by cable restricts the provision of services by television broadcasters whose programmes can only be received by satellite dishes, which is contrary to Art. 49 and cannot be justified by the need to protect the urban environment since that objective can be achieved by less restrictive measures (Case C-17/00 *De Coster* [2001] ECR I-9445 at pp. I-9500–2).

(*p*) ***Prohibition on infrastructure.*** A general prohibition that prevents a provider of services established in another Member State from equipping himself in the host Member State with an infrastructure (e.g. a principal or branch office, chambers, consulting rooms) necessary for the purposes of the services in question is incompatible with Art. 49 (Case C-145/99 *Commission* v. *Italy* [2002] ECR I-2235 at p. I-2276, concerning lawyers; Case C-298/99 *Commission* v. *Italy* [2002] ECR I-3129 at pp. I-3183–4, concerning architects).

(*q*) ***Registration of leased vehicles.*** Legislation requiring an undertaking established in a Member State which takes a lease of a vehicle registered in another Member State to register it in the first Member State and imposing on it conditions with which it is impossible or excessively difficult to comply and which restrict the cross-border provision of services, is contrary to Art. 49 (Case C-451/99 *Cura Anlagen*, above, at pp. I-3238–9).

(*r*) ***Respect for family life.*** Rules that prevent the spouse, who is a national of a third country, of a person who provides services in another Member State from residing with him in the Member State of establishment are liable detrimentally to affect that person's freedom to provide those services and are therefore contrary to Art. 49, read in the light of the fundamental right to respect for family life protected by Art. 8 of the European Convention on Human Rights (Case C-60/00 *Carpenter*, above at pp. I-6320–2).

(*s*) ***Prohibition of the practice of a profession.*** Legislation that prohibits the exercise in a Member State (Austria) of the profession of 'Heilpraktiker'—lay health practitioner—which is recognized in another Member State (Germany), by persons other than those with a doctor's qualification, constitutes a restriction on the freedom to provide services. Such restriction may be justified by an overriding reason relating to the public interest, such as the protection of public health referred to in Art. 46 (Case C-294/00 *Gräbner* [2002] ECR I-6515 at pp. I-6554–6, see also pp. I-6557–62).

(*t*) ***Compulsory insurance.*** A compulsory insurance scheme introduced in one Member State may constitute a restriction on the freedom of insurance companies established in other Member States to offer insurance services covering the same risks, although it may be justified by social policy objectives (Case C-355/00 *Freskot*, above, paras. 61–74).

(*u*) ***Professional rules and qualifications.*** The requirement that nationals of a Member State who pursue their profession in another Member State, whether as persons established there or as providers of services, must comply with the rules of the host State governing access to and pursuit of the profession in question, including rules concerning qualifications, is undoubtedly a major restriction on both freedom of establishment and freedom to provide services. In order to remove this restriction, Art. 47(1) EC, which applies to services by virtue of Art. 55, provides for the adoption of directives by the Council and Parliament for the 'mutual recognition of diplomas, certificates and other evidence of formal qualifications'. At the same time, Art. 47(2) provides for directives for the co-ordination of national provisions concerning access to and pursuit of activities as self-employed persons (see section I.3 above). Many of the directives adopted under these provisions apply equally to the right of establishment and freedom to provide services. Likewise, most of the principles developed by the ECJ in this respect in the context of the right of establishment apply also to services (for a detailed discussion of these directives and principles, *see further under* **Freedom of establishment**, section IV.2). Thus, the Court has made it clear that in so far as national professional rules have the effect of restricting the right of establishment and the freedom to provide services within the Community:

> they are compatible with the Treaty only if the restrictions which they entail are actually justified in view of the general obligations inherent in the proper practice of the professions in question and apply to nationals and foreigners alike. That is not the case where the restrictions are such as to create discrimination against practitioners established in other Member States or raise obstacles to access to the professions which go beyond what is necessary in order to achieve the intended goals (Case 96/85 *Commission* v. *France* [1986] ECR 1475 at pp. 1485–6).

In the same case, the Court held that French legislation prohibiting doctors and dentists established in another Member State from practising in France while maintaining their establishment in that other Member State was contrary to both Arts. 43 and 49 (and even to Art. 39). The Court considered that such a prohibition (the 'single-surgery rule') was unduly restrictive and too absolute and general in nature to be justified by the need to ensure continuity of medical treatment or by the need to apply French rules of medical ethics in France (ibid. at pp. 1486–7).

Case C-106/91 *Ramrath*, above, at pp. I-3383–6, involved national rules that made practice as an auditor by a person who was already authorized to practise that profession in another Member State subject to conditions relating to permanent infrastructure for carrying out the work, actual presence in the host State and supervision of compliance with the rules of professional conduct. The Court found that such rules and conditions were objectively justified by the public interest relating to the integrity and independence of auditors and therefore not contrary to Art. 49, unless compliance with them was already ensured through an auditor established and authorized in the host State in whose service the auditor in question was employed for the duration of the work. In Case C-375/92 *Commission* v. *Spain*, above, at pp. I-940–2, the Court applied also to services the rule developed earlier in the context of the right of establishment in Case C-340/89 *Vlassopoulou* [1991] ECR I-2357 at pp. I-2382–5, that a Member State which receives a request to admit a person to a profession to which access, under national law, depends on the possession of a diploma or a professional qualification must take into consideration the diplomas and qualifications that the applicant has acquired in order to exercise that profession in another Member State. In particular, the host State must make a comparison between the knowledge certified by those diplomas and the knowledge required by the national rules in accordance with a procedure which ensures that the assessment of the equivalence of qualifications is carried out on an objective basis and is subject to judicial review. Failure to establish such a procedure is contrary to both Art. 43 and 49 (as well as to Art. 39).

In contrast to rules regulating access to and pursuit of an occupation or profession, rules governing the selection of professional or semi-professional athletes for participation in high-level international sports competitions, which do not involve national teams competing against each other, do not in themselves constitute a restriction on freedom to provide services (Cases C-51/96 etc. *Deliège*, above, at pp. I-2618–20).

4. The legal profession. Separate mention must be made of the legal profession, in respect of which freedom to provide services was attained by Council Dir. 77/249 of 22 March 1977 (*OJ* 1977 L78/17, as amended by the successive Acts of Accession). The directive applies only to the provision of services by lawyers (Art. 1(1)). The term 'lawyer' covers any person entitled to pursue his professional activities in a Member State under one of the designations listed in Art. 1(2), which in the United Kingdom include advocates, barristers, and solicitors. Any such person must be recognized as a lawyer in each Member State for the purposes of the directive (Art. 2), including the Member State of which he is a national if he is authorized to practise as a lawyer in another Member State (Case 292/86 *Gullung*, above, at p. 136; Case C-294/89 *Commission* v. *France* [1991] ECR I-3591 at pp. I-3609–10). Since the directive does not require the mutual recognition of legal qualifications, a lawyer providing services must adopt the professional title used in the Member State in which he is established, expressed in the language of that State (Art. 3). The authorities of the host State may request such a person to establish his qualifications as a lawyer (Art. 7(1)).

Activities relating to the representation of a client in legal proceedings or before public authorities must be pursued in each Member State under the conditions laid down for lawyers established in that State, with the exception of any conditions requiring residence or registration with a professional organization in that State (Art. 4(1)). A lawyer pursuing these activities must observe the rules of professional conduct of the host State, without prejudice to his obligations in his State of origin (Art. 4(2)). Thus, apart from the exceptions expressly mentioned, all other conditions and rules in force in the host Member State may apply to the transfrontier provision of services by a lawyer, including the rules governing the reimbursement by the unsuccessful party of the fees of the lawyer of the successful party (Case C-289/02 *AMOK Verlags* [2003] ECR I-0000, paras. 30–1). A lawyer pursuing other activities generally remains subject to the conditions and rules of professional conduct of his State of establishment, and is required to respect the rules which govern the profession in the host State only in so far as those rules are capable of being observed by a lawyer who is not established in that State and in so far as their observance is objectively justified to ensure the proper exercise of a lawyer's activities, the standing of the profession and respect for the rules concerning incompatibility (Art. 4(4)).

In the event of non-compliance with the obligations in force in the host State, the competent authority of that State is to determine the consequences of such non-compliance in accordance with its own rules and procedures. The authority is required to notify the competent authority of the State of establishment of any decision taken (Art. 7(2)). The ECJ has interpreted the above provisions as meaning that members of the legal profession, when providing services, are required to comply with the rules relating to professional ethics in force in the host State. Consequently, a lawyer may not rely on Dir. 77/249 in order to provide services in another Member State in which he had been barred from access to the legal profession for reasons relating to dignity, good repute, and integrity (Case 292/86 *Gullung*, above, at pp. 137–8).

Art. 5 of the directive provides that 'for the pursuit of activities relating to the representation of a client in legal proceedings', a Member State may require a lawyer providing services (*a*) to be introduced, in accordance with local rules or customs, to the presiding judge and, where appropriate, to the President of the relevant Bar; and (*b*) 'to work in conjunction with a lawyer' who practises before the judicial authority in question and who would be answerable to that authority. In two important cases, the ECJ has had opportunity to define the precise scope of the obligation 'to work in conjunction with a lawyer' established in the host State. It has held that this obligation cannot be imposed when the lawyer providing services is acting before authorities or bodies that have no judicial function and when acting in legal proceedings in which the law of the host State does not make the assistance of or representation by a lawyer compulsory. Nor can the host State impose disproportionate requirements in respect of co-operation between the foreign and the local lawyer that go beyond what is necessary to attain the objectives of such co-operation (see Case 427/85 *Commission* v. *Germany* [1988] ECR 1123 at pp. 1157–67; Case C-294/89 *Commission* v. *France*, above, at pp. I-3610–15). Where national legislation requires the foreign lawyer to work in conjunction with a local lawyer, the successful party represented by the foreign lawyer is entitled to recover from the unsuccessful party the fees of both the foreign and the local lawyer (Case C-289/02 *AMOK Verlags*, above, para. 41).

5. **Proposed legislation.** In order to rationalize, reorganize, and simplify the present rules relating to the recognition of qualifications, on 7 March 2002 the Commission submitted a Proposal for a directive of the European Parliament and of the Council on the recognition of professional qualifications (*OJ* 2002 C181E/183; COM(2002) 119; amended proposal: COM(2004) 317). The draft directive lays down different rules for the free movement of services (Title II) and freedom of establishment (Title III). In the case of services, a single system will apply to all professions, basically allowing the free provision of services in another Member State by any provider legally established in a Member State for the purpose of practising the same professional activity there (Art. 5(1)). Where the service provider moves to the host Member State, the pursuit of a professional activity there for a period not exceeding sixteen weeks per year shall be presumed to constitute a 'provision of services', although the presumption does not preclude assessment on a case-by-case basis in the light of the duration, frequency, regularity, and continuity of the provision (Art. 5(2)). The service must be provided under the professional title of the Member State in which the provider is legally established (Art. 5(3)). The host Member State is to exempt service providers established in another Member State from the requirements that apply to professionals established in its territory relating to authorization by, registration with, or membership of a professional body and registration with a public social security body (Art. 6). Where the service provider moves to another Member State, he is required to inform the authorities of his State of establishment in advance (Art. 7), and is also to furnish the recipient of the services with the information prescribed by the directive (Art. 9).

On 13 January 2004, the Commission adopted a Proposal for a directive of the European Parliament and of the Council on services in the internal market (COM(2004) 2). The purpose of the directive is to provide a legal framework that will eliminate the obstacles to the freedom of establishment for service providers and the free movement of services between the Member States. The basic principle of the directive is that a service provider is subject only to the law of the Member State in which he is established. The proposal covers a wide variety of economic service activities, with exceptions such as financial services, transport, and electronic communications services and networks, which are already covered by Community legislation.

See also **Direct taxation, Expulsion, Freedom of establishment, Free movement of capital, Free movement of goods, Free movement of persons, Goods, Official authority, Public health, Public policy, Public security, Residence permit, Right of entry and residence, Right to leave, Right to remain, Social security.**

Further reading 1. BOOKS: Andenas and Roth (eds.), *Services and Free Movement in EU Law* (2003); Snell, *Goods and Services in EC Law* (2002).

2. ARTICLES AND PAPERS: Art, 'Legislative Lacunae, the Court of Justice and Freedom to Provide Services', in Curtin and O'Keeffe (eds.), *Constitutional Adjudication in European Community Law and National Law* (1992), p. 121; Bronkhorst, 'Lawyers' Freedom under the New Directive' (1977) *EL Rev.* 224; Cabral, 'Cross-Border Medical Care in the European Union—Bringing Down a First Wall' (1999) *EL Rev.* 387; Davis, 'Welfare as a Service' (2002) *LIEI* 27; Fernandez-Martin and O'Leary, 'Judicial Exceptions to the Free Provision of Services' (1995) *ELJ* 308; Giesen, 'Posting—Social Protection of Workers vs. Fundamental Freedoms?' (2003) *CML Rev.* 143; Gkoutzinis, 'Free Movement of Services in the EC Treaty and the Law of Contractual Obligations Relating to Banking and Financial Services' (2004) *CML Rev.* 119; Hatzopoulos, 'Recent Developments of the Case-Law of the ECJ in the Field of Services' (2000) *CML Rev.* 43; id., '*Killing* National Health and Insurance Systems but *Healing* Patients? The European Market for Health Care Services After the Judgments of the ECJ in *Vanbraekel* and *Peerbooms*' (2002) *CML Rev.* 683; Roth, 'The European Community's Law on Services: Harmonization' (1988) *CML Rev.* 35; Van der Woude and Mead, 'Free Movement of the Tourist in Community Law' (1988) *CML Rev.* 117; Van Empel, 'The Visible Hand in Invisible Trade' (1990/2) *LIEI* 23.

See also under **Freedom of establishment.**

► **FREE MOVEMENT OF CAPITAL** One of the four fundamental freedoms forming the basis of the internal market, which is, in practice, also a precondition for the effective exercise of the other three freedoms (free movement of goods, persons, and services), and in particular of the right of establishment (see Case 203/80 *Casati* [1981] ECR 2595 at p. 2614). However, under the provisions of the original EEC Treaty, the free movement of capital was treated differently from the other freedoms, until those provisions were replaced by the Treaty on European Union (TEU) and finally repealed by the Treaty of Amsterdam (ToA) (ibid.; see further section I below).

I. The legal framework

1. The original EEC Treaty. In the original EEC Treaty, the free movement of capital was governed by Arts. 67 to 73. Art. 67(1) differed from the corresponding provisions of the Treaty relating to the free movement of goods, persons, and services, which required the abolition of all restrictions on those freedoms by the end of the transitional period at the latest (in some respects even earlier). By contrast, Art. 67(1) imposed the obligation on the Member States to liberalize capital movements only 'to the extent necessary to ensure the proper functioning of the common market'. As the ECJ pointed out, the scope of that restriction, which remained in force even after the expiry of the transitional period, varied in time and depended on an assessment of the requirements of the common market. Such an assessment was entrusted to the Council, which was to issue the necessary directives under Art. 69 for the progressive implementation of Art. 67. As a result, Art. 67(1) did not have the effect of abolishing restrictions on movements of capital by the end of the transitional period. Their abolition was a matter for Council directives adopted on the basis of Art. 69 (Case 203/80 *Casati*, above, at pp. 2614–15; Cases 286/82 etc. *Luisi and Carbone* [1984] ECR 377 at p. 405; Case C-484/93 *Svensson and Gustavsson* [1995] ECR I-3955 at p. I-3974; see further below).

A second difference between Art. 67(1) and the other provisions of the Treaty dealing with the fundamental freedoms was that while the free movement of persons, freedom of establishment, and freedom to provide services applied to nationals of the Member States only, Art. 67(1) required the progressive abolition of all restrictions on the movement of capital 'belonging to persons resident in Member States', irrespective of their nationality. It also required the abolition of any discrimination 'based on the nationality or on the place of residence of the parties or on the place where such capital is invested'.

A third difference concerned the so-called 'standstill' provisions. While in respect of the free movement of goods, persons, and services the Treaty imposed a clear and unconditional obligation on the Member States not to introduce new restrictions or increase existing ones, Art. 71 only required the Member States to 'endeavour' to avoid introducing any new exchange restrictions on the movement of capital and current payments connected therewith, and to 'endeavour' not to make existing rules more restrictive. Because of this difference in the wording, the ECJ held that, in contrast with the other standstill provisions, Art. 71, like Art. 67(1), could not produce direct effect (Case 203/80 *Casati*, above, at p. 2616).

Closely connected with the free movement of capital was the need to liberalize the cross-border movement of payments, without which the fundamental Treaty freedoms could not have been effectively exercised. For this reason, Art. 106(1) of the original EEC Treaty, contained in the chapter on balance of payments, required each Member State to authorize, in the currency of the Member State in which the creditor or the beneficiary resided, any payments connected with the movement of goods, services, or capital, and any transfers of capital and earnings, 'to the extent that the movement of goods, services, capital and persons between Member States has been liberalized pursuant to this Treaty'. Art. 67(2) also provided that current payments connected with the movement of capital between Member States should be freed from all restrictions by the end of the first stage at the latest. The purpose of these provisions was to ensure that the necessary transfers of currency could be made both for the liberalization of capital movements and for the free movement of goods, persons, and services, without the restrictions applicable to capital movements themselves (see Case 7/78 *Thompson* [1978] ECR 2247 at p. 2274; Case 203/80 *Casati*, above, at p. 2616). Arts. 108 and 109 laid down special measures and procedures where a Member State was in difficulties or was seriously threatened with difficulties as regards its balance of payments. These provisions remained operative even after the free movement of capital had been fully achieved (see below).

Finally, Art. 61(2) EEC provided that the liberalization of banking and insurance services connected with movements of capital (such as, e.g. the granting of a mortgage loan by a bank established in one Member State to a borrower established in another Member State) should be effected in step with the progressive liberalization of movement of capital. This provision allowed Member States, where there had been no liberalization of capital movements, to retain measures designed to restrict those movements without thereby infringing the rules of the Treaty on the free movement of services (Case C-222/95 *Parodi* [1997] ECR I-3899 at p. I-3919).

Since the different freedoms were originally governed by different rules, it was necessary to distinguish between their respective scope of application. In Case 7/78 *Thompson*, above, at pp. 2274–5, the ECJ held that means of payment, such as coins that were legal tender in a Member State, were not to be regarded as goods falling within the scope of the rules on the free movement of goods. They fell within the scope of other provisions, i.e. those on the movement of capital or payments. By contrast, coins that were no longer legal tender and thus ceased to be means of payment, could be designated as goods falling within the scope of the free movement of goods. In Cases C-358/93 etc. *Bordessa* [1995] ECR I-361 at p. I-383, the Court likewise held that the physical transfer of assets (coins, banknotes, bearer cheques) fell not under the rules on movement of goods or services but under the rules on movement of capital or payments.

In Cases 286/82 etc. *Luisi and Carbone*, above, at p. 404, the Court distinguished between movement of capital and payments, saying that:

> current payments are transfers of foreign exchange which constitute the consideration within the context of an underlying transaction, whilst movements of capital are financial operations essentially concerned with the investment of the funds in question rather than remuneration for a service. For that reason movements of capital may themselves give rise to current payments, as is implied by Articles 67(2) and 106(1).
>
> The physical transfer of bank notes may not therefore be classified as a movement of capital where the transfer in question corresponds to an obligation to pay arising from a transaction involving the movement of goods or services.

Consequently, the Court concluded, payments in connection with the provision or receipt of services, such as tourism or travel for the purposes of business, education, or medical treatment, could not be classified as movements of capital, even where they were effected by means of the physical transfer of bank notes.

In the same cases, the Court further held that it followed from Art. 106(1) that, since in accordance with the Treaty restrictions on the freedom to provide services within the Community were to be abolished during the transitional period, as from the end of that period any restrictions on payments relating to the provision of services had also to be abolished (ibid.). Since restrictions on the free movement of goods and persons, including freedom of establishment, were also to be abolished by the end of the transitional period, it may be concluded that payments relating to those other freedoms were also liberalized at the end of the transitional period. In accordance with the Court's case-law on those other freedoms, this meant that Art. 106(1) became directly effective at the end of that period.

Nevertheless, the Court gave a narrow interpretation to Art. 106(1), holding that it obliged Member States to authorize the payments referred to only in the currency of the Member State in which the creditor or beneficiary resided. Payments made in the currency of a third country were not covered by that provision (ibid. at p. 405). Moreover, until the free movement of capital had been fully achieved, Member States retained the power to verify that transfers of foreign currency purportedly intended for liberalized payments were not in reality used for unauthorized movements of capital (ibid. at pp. 406–7. For other cases in which the Court interpreted Art. 106(1), see e.g. Case 203/80 *Casati*, above, at p. 2617 and Case 308/86 *Lambert* [1988] ECR 4369 at p. 4391, both holding that Art. 106(1) did not require the Member States to authorize the importation and exportation of bank notes since such transfers were not necessary for the free movement of goods because such method of payment was not in conformity with standard practice).

As mentioned above, the progressive abolition of restrictions on the movement of capital was to be attained by directives that the Council was to issue under Art. 69 EEC. The Council in fact adopted several directives (Dir. of 11 May 1960, *OJ Sp. Edn.* 1959–62, p. 49, as amended by Dir. 63/21, *OJ Sp. Edn.* 1963–4, p. 5 and by Dir. 86/566, *OJ* 1986 L332/22). These were all repealed and replaced by Dir. 88/361 of 24 June 1988 for the implementation of Art. 67 of the Treaty (*OJ* 1988 L178/5), which finally brought about the full liberalization of capital movements with effect from 1 July 1990 (subject to certain extensions granted to some of the Member States). Art. 1 of the directive required Member States to abolish restrictions on movements of capital taking place between persons resident in Member States. However, Art. 4 allowed Member States to take all requisite measures to prevent infringements of their laws and regulations, *inter alia*, in the field of taxation and prudential supervision of financial institutions, or to lay down procedures for the declaration of capital movements for purposes of administrative or statistical information. The ECJ held that Art. 1 laid down a precise and unconditional obligation for the Member States and did not require a specific implementing measure. Since application of the proviso in Art. 4 was amenable to judicial review, it did not prevent Art. 1 from conferring rights on individuals that they could rely on before national courts. Therefore, Art. 1 in conjunction with Art. 4 of the directive produced direct effect and rendered inapplicable any conflicting national rules (Cases C-358/93 etc. *Bordessa*, above, at p. I-387).

To facilitate application of the directive, capital movements were to be defined and classified in accordance with a Nomenclature contained in Annex I to the directive. According to its preamble, the Nomenclature was not intended to be an exhaustive list of the notion of capital movements, and therefore it was not to be interpreted as restricting the scope of the principle of full liberalization as set out in Art. 1.

2. The amended EC Treaty. With a view to establishing an Economic and Monetary Union (EMU), the TEU introduced major changes into the EEC Treaty, including the provisions relating to the free movement of capital and payments. The ToA made further amendments by renumbering all and repealing some of the relevant provisions. In so far as they affect capital and payments, these changes may be summarized as follows (for a more detailed discussion of the new provisions, see further sections II to V below).

The rules on the free movement of capital and payments were brought together in a single chapter, Chapter 4 of Title III in Part Three of the Treaty, whose title was changed from Capital to Capital and payments. Arts. 67 to 73 of the original EEC Treaty were replaced by Arts. 73b to 73g EC with effect from 1 January 1994, the beginning of the second stage of the EMU (Art. 73a EC). Arts. 67 to 73a, 73e and 73h were subsequently repealed by the ToA (see Art. 6, point 39), and Arts. 73b to 73g were renumbered Arts. 56 to 60.

The key provision now is Art. 56 [ex Art. 73b], which lays down the basic rule that within the framework of Chapter 4, all restrictions on the movement of capital and payments between Member States and between Member States and third countries shall be prohibited. Art. 57 [ex Art. 73c] allows the continuation of certain pre-1994 restrictions on the movement of capital to or from third countries. Art. 58 [ex Art. 73d] provides for exceptions to the prohibition set out in Art. 56 [ex Art. 73b]. Art. 59 [ex Art. 73f] enables the Council to take safeguard measures with regard to movements of capital to or from third countries in exceptional circumstances. Art. 60 [ex Art. 73g] authorizes the Council and the Member States to take urgent measures against third countries with regard to capital movements and payments in certain circumstances. The original Arts. 108 and 109, dealing with balance of payments difficulties, became Arts. 109h and 109i and were renumbered Arts. 119 and 120, respectively. Both Articles ceased to apply from the beginning of the third stage of the EMU, i.e. from 1 January 1999, but they continue to apply to a Member State with a derogation (Arts. 119(4) and 120(4) in conjunction with Art. 122(6)). Dir. 88/361 is still in force at the time of writing. In the following text, only the new numbering of the Treaty Articles will be used.

When dealing with cases involving the free movement of capital or payments, the ECJ usually carries out a three-stage investigation. First, the

Court examines whether the transaction in question falls within the definition of the concept of 'capital movement' or 'payment'. If so, the Court next considers whether the national law or practice complained of constitutes a restriction on, or obstacle to, free movement. If so, the Court finally determines whether such restriction may be justified on one of the grounds, or is covered by one of the exceptions, provided for by the Treaty. It is proposed to structure the discussion below in accordance with the Court's practice.

II. The concept of capital movements and payments

1. Definition of capital movements. Art. 56(1) EC provides that 'within the framework of the provisions set out in this Chapter, all restrictions on the movement of capital between Member States and between Member States and third countries shall be prohibited'.

The ECJ has held that this provision lays down a clear and unconditional prohibition for which no implementing measure is needed. Therefore, unlike the original Art. 67(1) EEC which it has replaced, Art. 56(1) EC is capable of conferring on individuals rights which they can rely on before national courts and renders inapplicable national rules inconsistent with it. The direct effect of Art. 56(1) is precluded neither by the exception provided for in Art. 57(1) in respect of non-member countries (since Art. 57(1) is precisely worded and grants no discretion to the Member States or the Community institutions regarding its application), nor by the exercise of the right reserved to Member States by Art. 58(1)(b) (because this provision is amenable to judicial review) (Cases C-163/94 etc. *Sanz de Lera* [1995] ECR I-4821 at pp. I-4841–3, confirming the direct effect of Art. 56(1) in conjunction with Arts. 57 and 58(1)(b). For Arts. 57 and 58, see further below).

It is, however, not quite clear whether the direct effect of Art. 56(1) is purely vertical (between the individual and the State), or whether that provision can also produce horizontal direct effect (between individuals *inter se*). Although there is no case-law on this point as yet, the better view seems to be that Art. 56(1) may be relied on by one private party against another (e.g. by an individual against a bank or other financial institution), since it prohibits in general terms 'all restrictions' on the movement of capital, irrespective of whether the restrictions have been imposed by a Member State or a private entity.

Art. 56(1) has not only brought the free movement of capital in line with the other Treaty freedoms, but has also extended the personal and territorial scope of application of the original Art. 67 EEC. It is no longer a requirement that the person to whom the capital belongs should be resident in a Member State. The movement of capital is ensured without any restrictions, irrespective of the nationality or residence of the person concerned. It is, moreover, ensured not only between Member States but also between Member States and third countries, although in this latter respect certain exceptions are allowed by Arts. 57, 59, and 60 (for which see section V below). As a result of Art. 56(1), a single market in capital has been created.

Art. 56(1) does not, however, define the concept of 'movement of capital'. In a long line of cases, the ECJ has held that inasmuch as Art. 56(1) substantially reproduces the contents of Art. 1 of Dir. 88/361, the Nomenclature annexed to that directive may be used for the purposes of defining the notion of capital movements, subject to the qualification that the list set out therein is not exhaustive (Case C-222/97 *Trummer and Mayer* [1999] ECR I-1661 at p. I-1678. This statement has been repeated in many of the cases cited below, more recently in Case C-367/98 *Commission* v. *Portugal* [2002] ECR I-4731 at p. I-4772). The Nomenclature and the attached explanatory notes indicate that capital movements include the following: direct investments; investments in real estate; operations in securities normally dealt in on the capital market; operations in units of collective investment undertakings; operations in securities and other instruments normally dealt in on the money market; operations in current and deposit accounts with financial institutions; credits related to commercial transactions or to the provision of services in which a resident is participating; financial loans and credits; sureties, other guarantees, and rights of pledge; transfers in performance of insurance contracts; personal capital movements; physical import and export of financial assets; other capital movements (including transfers of the moneys required for the provision of services).

The introduction to the Nomenclature further states that the capital movements listed are taken to cover all the operations necessary for the purposes of capital movements, i.e. the conclusion and performance of the transaction and related transfers, and should also include access for the economic operator to all the financial techniques available on the market approached for the purpose of carrying out the operation in question.

2. Examples of capital movements. Relying on the Nomenclature, the ECJ has confirmed that the following constitute capital movements within the meaning of Art. 1 of Dir. 88/361 and Art. 56(1) EC:

(*a*) loans and credits granted by non-residents to residents and vice versa (Case C-484/93 *Svensson and Gustavsson*, above, at p. I-3975; Case C-439/97 *Sandoz* [1999] ECR I-7041 at p. I-7071);

(*b*) the physical exports to third countries of coins, banknotes, and bearer cheques that do not represent payments for trade in goods or services (Cases C-163/94 etc. *Sanz de Lera*, above, at p. I-4836);

(*c*) the creation of a mortgage to secure a debt payable in the currency of another Member State, since such a mortgage is inextricably linked to the liquidation of an investment in real property, which is a capital movement (Case C-222/97 *Trummer and Mayer*, above, at pp. I-1678–9);

(*d*) investment in real estate (such as the purchase of immovable property) on the territory of a Member State by non-residents. This is closely linked to the right to acquire, use, or dispose of immovable property on the territory of another Member State, which is the corollary of freedom of establishment (Case C-302/97 *Konle* [1999] ECR I-3099 at p. I-3131; Case C-423/98 *Albore* [2000] ECR I-5965 at p. I-6001; Cases C-515/99 etc. *Reisch* [2002] ECR I-2157 at p. I-2204);

(*e*) direct foreign investments (Case C-54/99 *Église de Scientologie* [2000] ECR I-1335 at p. I-1360); direct investment in the form of participation in an undertaking in another Member State by means of a shareholding; in particular, participating effectively in the management of a company or in its control (Case C-367/98 *Commission* v. *Portugal*, above, at p. I-4772). However, the acquisition by natural persons of shares in a company established in another Member State is covered by the Treaty provisions on capital only if the shareholding does not confer on those persons definite influence over the company's decisions and does not allow them to determine its activities. By contrast, where the acquisition involves all the shares in a company established in another Member State and the shareholding confers a definite influence over the company's decisions and allows the shareholders to determine its activities, it is the Treaty provisions on establishment which apply (Case C-251/98 *Baars* [2000] ECR I-2787 at pp. I-2814–15; Case C-208/00 *Überseering* [2002] ECR I-9919, para. 77);

(*f*) acquisition on the capital market of securities issued in another Member State (Case C-478/98 *Commission* v. *Belgium* [2000] ECR I-7587 at pp. I-7619–20);

(*g*) receipt of dividends on shares in a company established in another Member State (Case C-35/98 *Verkooijen* [2000] ECR I-4071 at pp. I-4125–6);

(*h*) guarantees granted by non-residents to residents and vice versa (Case C-279/00 *Commission* v. *Italy* [2002] ECR I-1425 at p. I-1458);

(*i*) the transfer at undervalue of shares to a company established in another Member State in which the transferor has a holding (Case C-436/00 *X and Y II* [2002] ECR I-10829, para. 69).

3. Definition of payments. Art. 56(2) EC provides that 'within the framework of the provisions set out in this Chapter, all restrictions on payments between Member States and between Member States and third countries shall be prohibited'.

The ECJ has held that in order to ascertain the scope of Art. 56(2), it should be compared with the original Art. 106(1) EEC which it has replaced. Like Art. 106(1) EEC, Art. 56(2) 'is intended to enable a person liable to pay a sum of money *in the context of a supply of goods or services* to discharge that contractual obligation voluntarily without undue restriction and to enable the creditor freely to receive such a payment'. For this reason, the Court has said, Art. 56(2) is not applicable to a national procedural rule prohibiting the issue of a summary payment order to be served outside national territory. Such a rule does not constitute a restriction on the freedom to make payments (Case C-412/97 *ED* [1999] ECR I-3845 at pp. I-3881–2, emphasis added). Likewise, Art. 56(2) does not apply to the physical exports of coins, banknotes, and bearer cheques that do not represent payments for trade in goods or services. Such transfers constitute capital movements and cannot be regarded as payments within the meaning of Art. 56(2) (Cases C-163/94 etc. *Sanz de Lera*, above, at p. I-4836). Thus, the distinction made by the Court between these two concepts in its earlier, pre-TEU case-law remains applicable in the context of Art. 56 also (see Cases 286/82 etc. *Luisi and Carbone*, above, at p. 404, discussed in section I above). Such a distinction is still relevant today in spite of the fact that Art. 56(1) and (2) are drafted in identical terms. The reason is that Art. 56 must be applied 'within the framework of the provisions set out in this Chapter', and while some of those provisions (exceptions) apply to both capital movements and payments (Arts. 58 and 60), others apply to capital movements only, but not to payments (Arts. 57 and 59; see further sections IV and V below). This makes it necessary to distinguish between the two concepts, as the Court did in the *Sanz de Lera* case (see above).

Art. 56(2), like Art. 56(1), lays down a clear and unconditional prohibition for which no implementing measure is needed. In line with the case-law on Art. 56(1), Art. 56(2) must therefore be interpreted as producing at least vertical, and perhaps also horizontal, direct effect (see point 1 above). This is the more so as its predecessor, Art. 106(1) EEC, was also directly effective since the end of the transitional period (see section I above).

While thus there are several parallels between Art. 56(2) and Art. 106(1) EEC, the scope of application of the former is much broader, particularly since Art. 106(1) has been narrowly interpreted by the ECJ (see section I above). The main differences are, first, that Art. 56(2) has abolished 'all restrictions' on payments without regard to the residence of the beneficiary or the currency used; and, secondly, that it applies not only to payments between Member States but also to payments between Member States and third countries, although the latter are subject to certain exceptions set out in Art. 60 (for which see section V below).

III. Restrictions on capital movements and payments

1. Definition of restrictions. Art. 56 prohibits, in general terms 'all restrictions' on the movement of capital and payments. Accordingly, the ECJ has interpreted the concept of 'restrictions' in the broadest possible sense. In the first place, it includes measures that discriminate against nationals or residents of other Member States in respect of capital movements. Such discrimination is prohibited by Art. 56, unless it is justified on grounds permitted by the Treaty (Case C-302/97 *Konle*, above, at p. I-3131; Case C-439/97 *Sandoz*, above, at pp. I-7077–8; Case C-423/98 *Albore*, above, at pp. I-6001–2; see also the cases cited below). However, the prohibition goes beyond the mere elimination of unequal treatment, on grounds of nationality or residence, as between operators on the financial markets. Any measure taken by a Member State, even if it is non-discriminatory, which has the effect of impeding capital movements carried out in accordance with Community law or which is liable to dissuade its residents from obtaining loans or making investments in other Member States (or vice versa) and which, as a result, is such as to render the free movement of capital illusory, constitutes 'restriction' within the meaning of Art. 56 (Cases C-358/93 etc. *Bordessa*, above, at p. I-385; Case C-35/98 *Verkooijen*, above, at p. I-4127; Case C-478/98 *Commission* v. *Belgium*, above, at p. I-7620; Case C-367/98 *Commission* v. *Portugal*, above, at pp. I-4773–4; see also the cases cited below). However, to be caught by the prohibition, the restrictive measure must have a sufficient intra-Community (cross-border) element, i.e. it must affect the movement of capital between Member States (or between Member States and third countries). A restriction on the basis of the place of residence is sufficient (Case C-364/01 *Barbier* [2003] ECR I-0000, paras. 58–61). However, a purely internal measure is not covered by Art. 56 (Case C-478/98 *Commission* v. *Belgium*, above, at pp. I-7619–20 *per Curiam*, pp. I-7599–7600 *per* A.-G. Jacobs; Case C-436/00 *X and Y II*, above, para. 69).

2. Examples of restrictions. On the basis of the above considerations, the ECJ has held that the following measures taken by Member States constitute restrictions on capital movements and payments:

(*a*) the rule that recipients of building loans may obtain an interest rate subsidy from the State only if the bank granting the loan is established within national territory (Case C-484/93 *Svensson and Gustavsson*, above, at p. I-3975);
(*b*) the imposition of a stamp duty on loans contracted in another Member State (Case C-439/97 *Sandoz*, above, at pp. I-7074–5);
(*c*) a rule prohibiting registration of a mortgage in the currency of another Member State (Case C-222/97 *Trummer and Mayer*, above, at pp. I-1679–80; Case C-464/98 *Stefan* [2001] ECR I-173 at pp. I-202–3);
(*d*) generally, measures that are liable to dissuade or prevent residents from obtaining loans or making investments in other Member States, such as the prohibition of the acquisition by residents of securities of a loan issued abroad (Case C-478/98 *Commission* v. *Belgium*, above, at pp. I-7619–22);
(*e*) unfavourable tax treatment of share transfers to companies established in other Member States (Case C-436/00 *X and Y II*, above, paras. 70, 73);
(*f*) legislation which restricts exemption from income tax payable on dividends to dividends paid by companies established within national territory (Case C-35/98 *Verkooijen*, above, at pp. I-4126–7);
(*g*) the requirement that undertakings providing temporary labour which are established in other Member States must lodge a guarantee with a credit institution having its registered office or a branch office within national territory (Case C-279/00 *Commission* v. *Italy*, above, at p. I-1458);
(*h*) legislation whereby a Member State, on grounds relating to the defence of the national territory, exempts only its own nationals from the obligation to obtain authorization for purchase of real estate in an area of military importance (Case C-423/98 *Albore*, above, at p. I-6003);

(*i*) generally, any national law which makes a direct foreign investment subject to prior authorization (Case C-54/99 *Église de Scientologie*, above, at p. I-1360), whether the investment is made on national territory by non-residents or abroad by residents. This includes rules which require prior authorization for: (*i*) the export of currency to other Member States (Cases C-358/93 etc. *Bordessa*, above, at pp. I-385–7) or to third countries (Cases C-163/94 etc. *Sanz de Lera*, above, at pp. I-4837–9; (*ii*) the acquisiton of land (Case C-302/97 *Konle*, above, at p. I-3134; Cases C-515/99 etc. *Reisch*, above, at p. I-2204); or (*iii*) the acquisiton of shares in privatized undertakings in excess of a specified level (Case C-367/98 *Commission* v. *Portugal*, above, at pp. I-4773–4);

(*j*) a prohibition precluding investors from other Member States from acquiring more than a given number of shares in privatized undertakings (ibid. at pp. I-4772–3).

IV. Justifications for restrictions

Restrictions on capital movements and payments do not fall within the prohibition laid down in Art. 56 if they can be justified on grounds permitted by Community law. The grounds justifying restrictions are set out in Art. 58 or have been developed by the ECJ in its case-law.

Art. 58 consists of three paragraphs. The first paragraph is further subdivided into two parts, which will be considered in turn.

Art. 58(1)(a) provides that Art. 56 is to be without prejudice to the right of Member States 'to apply the relevant provisions of their tax law which distinguish between taxpayers who are not in the same situation with regard to their place of residence or with regard to the place where their capital is invested'. However, this provision is subject to certain limitations. According to Art. 58(3), the national provisions referred to in Art. 58(1)(a) are not to constitute a means of arbitrary discrimination or a disguised restriction on the free movement of capital and payments as defined in Art. 56. Declaration No. 7 annexed to the TEU further states that as regards capital movements and payments between Member States, Art. 58(1)(a) applies only with respect to national tax provisions which existed at the end of 1993.

The scope of the exception contained in Art. 58(1)(a), which in effect allows Member States to differentiate in their tax legislation between taxpayers according to their place of residence or the place where their capital is invested, may be defined in the light of the case-law which the ECJ developed before the entry into force of Art. 58 (1 January 1994) on the possibility of differential tax treatment of residents and non-residents. The basic principle is that although direct taxation falls within their competence, the Member States must nonetheless exercise that competence consistently with Community law and avoid any discrimination on grounds of nationality (see Case C-251/98 *Baars*, above, at p. I-2813; Case C-35/98 *Verkooijen*, above, at p. I-4126 and the cases cited therein). National tax provisions to which Art. 58(1)(a) refers can be compatible with Community law provided that they apply to situations which are not objectively comparable or can be justified by overriding reasons in the general interest, such as the need to ensure the cohesion of the tax system. However, aims of a purely economic nature cannot constitute an overriding reason in the general interest justifying a restriction of a fundamental freedom guaranteed by the Treaty (ibid. at pp. I-4129–30; see also Case C-367/98 *Commission* v. *Portugal*, above, at pp. I-4775–6).

On the basis of the above considerations, in Case C-35/98 *Verkooijen*, above, at pp. I-4131–4, the Court held that a Netherlands tax provision which made the grant of exemption from income tax payable on dividends subject to the condition that those dividends were paid by a company established in the Netherlands, was contrary to Art. 1(1) of Dir. 88/361 (the forerunner of Art. 56(1)). Such a provision could not be justified by the need to preserve the cohesion of the Netherlands tax system since there was no direct link between the grant of the income tax exemption to shareholders residing in the Netherlands and taxation of the profits of companies established in other Member States. They were two separate taxes levied on different taxpayers. Nor could the loss of tax revenue which would result from changing the system, being a purely economic consideration, be regarded as an overriding reason in the public interest justifying the restriction on the free movement of capital. In Case C-436/00 *X and Y II*, above, paras. 72–4, the Court based its judgment on similar considerations in holding that unfavourable tax treatment of certain share transfers to companies established in other Member States was contrary to Arts. 56 and 58.

Art. 58(1)(b) provides that Art. 56 is to be without prejudice to the right of Member States:

> to take all requisite measures to prevent infringements of national law and regulations, in particular in the field of taxation and the prudential supervision of financial institutions, or to lay down procedures for the declaration of capital movements for purposes of administrative or statistical information, or to take measures which are justified on grounds of public policy or public security.

Art. 58(1)(b), too, is subject to the proviso set out in Art. 58(3) that the national measures and procedures referred to are not to constitute a means of arbitrary discrimination or a disguised restriction on the free movement of capital and payments.

Art. 58(1)(b) essentially reproduces Art. 4(1) of Dir. 88/361, but also contains two additional grounds of justification: public policy and public security. In considering the scope of the two provisions, the ECJ has held that they permit Member States to take not only measures that are necessary to prevent infringements of national law in the field of taxation and to ensure effective fiscal supervision, but also other measures that are designed to prevent illegal activities of comparable seriousness, such as tax evasion, money laundering, drug trafficking, and terrorism. Thus, the fight against tax evasion and the effectiveness of fiscal supervision may be relied on under Art. 58(1)(b) to justify restrictions on the free movement of capital.

However, the national measures must be both necessary ('requisite') in order to uphold the objectives pursued and proportionate in the sense that the same objectives cannot be achieved by less restrictive measures. A general presumption of tax evasion or tax fraud cannot in itself justify a fiscal measure that obstructs free movement (Cases C-358/93 etc. *Bordessa*, above, at pp. I-384–5; Cases C-163/94 etc. *Sanz de Lera*, above, at p. I-4837; Case C-478/98 *Commission* v. *Belgium*, above, at pp. I-7625–6).

In its subsequent case-law, the Court further clarified the scope of the exception by saying that:

> The free movement of capital, as a fundamental principle of the Treaty, may be restricted only by national rules which are justified by reasons referred to in Article 58(1) of the Treaty or by overriding requirements of the general interest and which are applicable to all persons and undertakings pursuing an activity in the territory of the host Member State. Furthermore, in order to be so justified, the national legislation must be suitable for securing the objective which it pursues and must not go beyond what is necessary in order to attain it, so as to accord with the principle of proportionality (Case C-367/98 *Commission* v. *Portugal*, above, at p. I-4775; see also the related Case C-483/99 *Commission* v. *France* [2002] ECR I-4781 at p. I-4803 and Case C-503/99 *Commission* v. *Belgium* [2002] ECR I-4809 at p. I-4832).

In the light of these considerations, the Court has assessed the compatibility with Art. 56 of a wide range of national measures restrictive of the free movement of capital. Thus, in Case C-478/98 *Commission* v. *Belgium*, above, at pp. I-7622–7, the Court held that a Belgian law prohibiting Belgian residents from acquiring Eurobonds issued by Belgium on the Eurobond market could not be justified by the need to prevent tax evasion and ensure the effectiveness of fiscal supervision, nor by the need to preserve the coherence of the tax system, because the law did not comply with the principle of proportionality and there was no direct link between any fiscal advantage and a corresponding disadvantage which was to be preserved in order to ensure fiscal coherence. In Case C-439/97 *Sandoz*, above, at pp. I-7076–9, the Court found that Arts. 56(1) and 58(1)(b) and (3) did not preclude the imposition by Austria of a stamp duty on loans contracted in another Member State where the duty applied to all borrowers resident in Austria without distinction as to nationality or the place where the loan was contracted. However, a measure that discriminated between Austrian residents according to whether they took out a loan in Austria or in another Member State, by imposing a stamp duty in the latter case hut not in the former, could not be justified under Art. 58(1)(b).

In several cases, the Court has had to consider whether national rules that make various types of foreign investment conditional on prior authorization or a prior declaration can be compatible with Arts. 56(1) and 58(1)(b). In Cases C-358/93 etc. *Bordessa*, above, at pp. I-385–7, and Cases C-163/94 etc. *Sanz de Lera*, above, at pp. I-4837–9, which concerned the export of currency to other Member States and to third countries, respectively, the Court held that the requirement of prior authorization would subject the free movement of capital to the discretion of the administrative authorities and would thus render that freedom illusory. The same objective, namely, the effective supervision of capital movements to prevent infringements of national law, could be achieved by the less restrictive means of a prior declaration. The requirement of prior authorization therefore was not, while that of prior declaration was, compatible with Art. 58(1)(b).

The same question arose in Case C-302/97 *Konle*, above, at pp. I-3131, I-3134–7, and in Cases C-515/99 etc. *Reisch*, above, at pp. I-2203–7, which concerned Austrian legislation imposing an obligation to apply for administrative authorization prior to the acquisition of land. The acquirer had to show that the acquisition would not be used to create a secondary residence (except in certain circumstances). The Court first pointed out that although the system of property ownership continues to be a matter for each Member State under Art. 295 EC, that provision does not have the effect of exempting such a system from the fundamental rules of the Treaty. Therefore, national legislation that regulates the acquisition of land for the purposes of prohibiting, in the interests of regional planning, the establishment of secondary residences in certain areas must comply with the provisions of the Treaty on freedom of establishment and the free movement of capital. The Court recognized that restrictions on the creation of secondary residences in specific areas with a view to maintaining for planning purposes a permanent population and an economic activity independent of the tourist sector, coupled with concerns for the protection of the environment, may be regarded as an overriding objective in the public interest, which, if applied in a non-discriminatory manner and in accordance with the principle of proportionality, may justify restrictions on the free movement of capital. The Court also accepted that the requirement of a declaration or notification prior to the purchase of building plots, accompanied with other measures, was compatible with Community law. It provided the public authorities with all necessary means to prevent infringement of the legislation. However, the prior authorization procedure, with its inherent risks of discrimination and subjectivity, went beyond what was necessary to achieve the same objective and therefore constituted a restriction not justified under Art. 58(1)(b).

Subsequently, the Court recognized that if the purpose of legislation regulating the acquisition of land is to preserve agricultural communities and viable farms, then a system of prior authorization for transfer of property might be justified. In the absence of such authorization, the legislation could not achieve its objective of ensuring that land is used only for agricultural purposes. Any supervision subsequent to the transfer would be insufficient. However, the restriction imposed must be proportionate to the aim pursued. Thus, the requirement that the acquirer must himself farm the land and be resident on it would go beyond what is necessary and would be incompatible with the free movement of capital (Case C-452/01 *Ospelt* [2003] ECR I-9743, paras. 37–54).

Case C-367/98 *Commission* v. *Portugal*, Case C-483/99 *Commission* v. *France*, and Case C-503/99 *Commission* v. *Belgium*, all cited above, concerned certain restrictive measures adopted by the three defendant States in order to control widespread intra-Community investments generated by the process of privatizations. Those measures involved, broadly, the requirement of prior authorization for, or the exercise of a right of veto by public authorities in respect of, intra-Community investments in privatized undertakings, which had a restrictive effect on the latter. In its Communication on certain legal aspects concerning intra-EU investment adopted on 19 July 1997 (*OJ* 1997 C220/15), the Commission examined the compatibility of such measures with Community law. It concluded that discriminatory measures (i.e. those applied exclusively to investors from other Member States) were incompatible with Arts. 56 and 43 (right of establishment) of the Treaty unless justified on grounds of public policy, public security, or public health. Non-discriminatory measures (i.e. those applied to nationals and other EU investors alike) were permitted in so far as they were based on a set of objective and stable criteria which had been made public and could be justified by imperative requirements in the general interest, and also complied with the principle of proportionality (see the three cases cited above, at pp. I-4767–8, I-4796–7, and I-4824–5).

On its part, the Court accepted that certain concerns might justify the retention by Member States of a degree of influence within undertakings that were initially public and subsequently privatized, where those undertakings were involved in the provision of services in the public interest or strategic services. However, the Court added, those concerns did not entitle Member States to plead their own systems of property ownership under Art. 295 EC in order to justify obstacles to the exercise of the basic Treaty freedoms, resulting from their privileged position as shareholders in privatized undertakings (ibid. at pp. I-4774, I-4803, and I-4832).

The Court then examined the particular measures adopted by the three defendant States. The Portuguese legislation, which prohibited the acquisition by investors from other Member States of more than a given number of shares in certain privatized Portuguese undertakings, was plainly discriminatory and therefore contrary to Art. 56. The obligation to obtain prior authorization from the State for the acquisition of a holding in certain undertakings in excess of a specified level was also contrary to Art. 56 since it could not be justified on the purely economic grounds put forward by Portugal. To be compatible with Community law, the Court held, a scheme of prior administrative authorization must be proportionate to the aim pursued; must be based on objective, non-discriminatory criteria which are known in advance to the undertakings concerned; and all persons affected by it must have a legal remedy available to them (ibid. at pp. I-4772–3, I-4775–6).

The French legislation vested in the State a 'golden share' in a major French petroleum company whereby any holding of shares or voting rights that exceeded certain limits had to be authorized in advance by the relevant Minister and any decision to transfer the assets of certain subsidiaries of that company could be opposed by the State. The objective of the legislation was to safeguard supplies of petroleum products in the event of a crisis. The Court recognized that this objective fell within the ambit of a legitimate public interest inasmuch as public security was one of the grounds of justification referred to in Art. 58(1)(b). However, requirements of public security, as a derogation from the fundamental principle of the free movement of capital, had to be interpreted strictly. The French legislation left a wide discretionary power to the Minister concerned, the exercise of which was not qualified by any condition or subject to any precise, objective criteria. As a result, individuals could not ascertain the extent of their rights and obligations under Art. 56, which was contrary to the principle of legal certainty. Therefore, the legislation went beyond what was necessary to attain the objective pursued and was incompatible with Art. 56 (ibid. at pp. I-4801–2, I-4804–6).

The Belgian legislation differed from the French in that it was based on opposition *ex post facto* and no prior approval was required. The power to oppose any transfer of the strategic assets of the companies concerned was to be exercised on the basis of objective criteria which were subject to judicial review, thus observing the requirements of legal certainty. The legislation was therefore justified by the objective of guaranteeing energy supplies in the event of a crisis; there was no infringement of Art. 56 (ibid. at pp. I-4833–5. See also Case C-463/00 *Commission* v. *Spain* [2003] ECR I-4581 and Case C-98/01 *Commission* v. *United Kingdom* [2003] ECR I-4641, and the opinion of A.-G. Ruiz-Jarabo Colomer, paras. 29–40, criticizing the Court's judgments in the previous three cases. See also Case C-58/99 *Commission* v. *Italy* [2000] ECR I-3811 and the case discussed immediately below).

Case C-54/99 *Église de Scientologie*, above, at pp. I-1361–3, raised the question whether a system of prior authorization for direct foreign investments that are such as to represent a threat to public policy or public security might be justified on those two grounds, which are expressly mentioned in Art. 58(1)(b). Relying on its earlier case-law (*see further under* **Public policy, Public security**), the Court observed, first of all, that while Member States are still, in principle, free to determine the requirements of public policy and public security in the light of their national needs, those grounds must, as derogations from the fundamental principle of the free movement of capital, be interpreted strictly. Their scope cannot be determined unilaterally by each Member State without any control by the Community institutions. Thus, public policy and public security may be relied on only if there is a genuine and sufficiently serious threat to a fundamental interest of society. Moreover, those derogations must not be used so as to serve purely economic ends. Further, any person affected by a restrictive measure based on such a derogation must have access to legal redress. In particular, measures that restrict the free movement of capital may be justified on public policy and public security grounds only if they are necessary for the protection of the interests which they are intended to guarantee and only in so far as those objectives cannot be attained by less restrictive measures (the principle of proportionality).

The Court then went on to point out that its previous case-law does not mean that a system of prior authorization can never be justified, particularly where such authorization is necessary for the protection of public policy or public security. In the case of direct foreign investments, the difficulty in identifying and blocking capital once it has entered a Member State may make it necessary to prevent, at the outset, transactions that would adversely affect public policy or public security. Therefore, where direct foreign investments constitute a genuine and sufficiently serious threat to public policy and public security, a system of prior declaration may prove to be inadequate to counter such a threat.

In the present case, the problem with the French system in question was that prior authorization was required for every direct foreign investment which was 'such as to represent a threat to public policy [and] public security', without any more detailed definition. Thus, investors were given no indication whatever as to the specific circumstances in which prior authorization was required. Such lack of precision did not enable individuals to ascertain the extent of their rights and obligations arising from Art. 56, which was contrary to the principle of legal certainty. Therefore, the system could not be justified under Art. 58(1)(b).

Case C-423/98 *Albore*, above, at pp. I-6002–3, involved Italian legislation which, on grounds relating to the defence of the national territory, exempted only Italian nationals from the obligation to apply for an administrative authorization for any purchase of real estate situated within an area of military importance. The Court noted that although the concept of public security included the external security of a Member State, that concept could not justify derogations from the freedom of capital movements unless the principle of proportionality was observed (see above). In any case, Art. 58(3) excluded arbitrary discrimination or disguised restrictions on the free movement of capital. A mere reference to the requirements of defence of the national territory was not sufficient to justify discrimination on grounds of nationality against nationals of other Member States regarding access to immovable property. The position would be different only if non-discriminatory treatment of the nationals of all the Member States would expose the military interests of the Member State concerned to real, specific, and serious risks that could not be countered by less restrictive measures.

As seen above, national rules that restrict the free movement of capital may be justified not only on grounds referred to in Art. 58(1) but also by 'overriding reasons in the general interest'. Although the ECJ has laid down a number of conditions that must be satisfied before such reasons may be successfully invoked, in some cases it has interpreted the concept of general or public interest fairly broadly. Case C-148/91 *Veronica* [1993] ECR I-487 at pp. I-518–20 concerned the Dutch Media Law which prohibited a broadcasting organization established in the Netherlands from investing in a broadcasting company to be set up in another Member State for the purpose of providing commercial radio and television services directed towards the Netherlands, thereby evading certain obligations arising from the Dutch legislation. The law was designed to establish a pluralistic and non-commercial broadcasting system and thus formed part of a cultural policy intended to safeguard the freedom of expression of the various social, cultural, religious, and philosophical components existing in the Netherlands. The Court accepted that those cultural-policy objectives were related to the public interest which a Member State might legitimately pursue, and which justified the restrictions in question on the free movement of capital and the freedom to provide services.

V. Exceptions with respect to third countries

While Art. 56 prohibits restrictions on the movement of capital and payments both between Member States and between Member States and third countries, Arts. 57, 59, and 60 allow certain exceptions to the prohibition in respect of capital movements and payments between Member States and third countries.

Art. 57(1) authorizes the continued application to third countries of any restrictions that existed on 31 December 1993 under national or Community law adopted in respect of the movement of capital to or from third countries involving direct investment (including investment in real estate), establishment, the provision of financial services or the admission of securities to capital markets. This exception thus does not apply to payments. In Cases C-163/94 etc. *Sanz de Lera*, above, at pp. I-4839–41, the ECJ held that national rules which make the physical export of means of payment (coins, banknotes, or bearer cheques) conditional on prior authorization do not fall within the scope of the exception in Art. 57(1) because the export of such items cannot itself be regarded as a type of capital movement referred to in that provision. Nevertheless, since Art. 57(1) does allow certain restrictions, the Member States are entitled to verify, by means of a prior declaration, the nature and reality of the transactions in question to ensure that they are not used for the purposes of capital movements which may be lawfully restricted.

A further exception is provided for in Art. 57(2), under which the Council may adopt measures on the movement to or from third countries of capital falling within the categories referred to in Art. 57(1), even if such measures constitute 'a step back' in Community law as regards the liberalization of capital movement. In any case, the Council is only required to 'endeavour' to achieve the free movement of capital in relation to third countries 'to the greatest extent possible'.

Since the entry into force of the Agreement on the European Economic Area (EEA) (1 January 1994; in the case of Liechtenstein 1 May 1995), non-EU States party to that Agreement (Iceland, Liechtenstein, and Norway) cannot be regarded as 'third countries' for the purposes of Art. 57. Since that date, Member States may no longer invoke Art. 57(1) *vis-à-vis* such countries since the EEA Agreement itself contains provisions on the free movement of capital which have the same legal scope as that of Art. 56, to which they are identical in substance (Case C-452/01 *Ospelt*, above, paras. 30–2).

Under Art. 59, in exceptional circumstances the Council may take safeguard measures with regard to third countries for a period not exceeding six months where movements of capital to or from such countries cause, or threaten to cause, serious difficulties for the operation of the Economic and Monetary Union.

Finally, where it is decided in the framework of the common foreign and security policy that the Community should interrupt or reduce economic relations with one or more third countries, the Council may take the necessary urgent measures on the movement of capital and on payments as regards the third countries concerned. As long as the Council has not acted, a Member State may take unilateral measures for serious political reasons and on grounds of urgency (Art. 60 in conjunction with Art. 301).

VI. Relationship to other Treaty freedoms

It may, and in fact often does, happen that a national measure imposes restrictions which may affect, directly or indirectly, more than one of the four fundamental freedoms guaranteed by the Treaty. In such a situation it becomes necessary to decide with regard to which freedom the measure should be examined in order to establish its compatibility or incompatibility with Community law. This question was particularly important prior to the amendment of the rules on the free movement of capital by the TEU, since initially that freedom had a narrower scope than the other three freedoms. As seen in section I above, already in Case 7/78 *Thompson*, and later in Cases C-358/93 etc. *Bordessa*, the Court had clarified the relationship between the free movement of goods and free movement of capital and payments. The relationship between the free movement of persons (workers) and capital has not raised any problem before the Court. By contrast, the question of the relationship between the free movement of capital and the freedom to provide services, on the one hand, and the freedom of establishment, on the other, has not been satisfactorily resolved to date, in spite of the fact that it has given rise to copious case-law. This case-law is characterized by a certain degree of inconsistency (*a*) between the opinions of the various Advocates-General; (*b*) between the opinion of the Advocate-General and the judgment of the Court in some of the cases; and (*c*) between some of the Court's rulings in similar cases.

In particular, the Court has so far failed to develop clear principles for the determination of the dividing lines between the free movement of capital and freedom to provide services and between the free movement of capital and freedom of establishment, and of the order in which potentially overlapping freedoms should be examined, similar to the principles that it laid down in respect of the relationship between the freedoms of establishment and to provide services (see Case C-55/94 *Gebhard* [1995] ECR I-4165 at pp. I-4193–4, where the Court held that the chapters of the Treaty governing each of these two freedoms are mutually exclusive, and that the provisions on services are subordinate to those on establishment. *See further under* **Freedom of establishment, Freedom to provide services**). The question of the legal classification of a restriction has arisen in a number of cases, the most important of which are discussed below.

1. Freedom to provide services. First, as regards the relationship between the free movement of capital and the freedom to provide services, the problem of classification arose in Case C-204/90 *Bachmann* [1992] ECR I-249. The case concerned Belgian legislation that made the deductibility for income tax purposes of certain insurance contributions conditional upon those contributions being paid to an insurer established in Belgium. The Commission maintained that the legislation constituted discrimination based on 'the place where . . . capital is invested', and therefore it was contrary to Art. 67(1) EEC [replaced by Art. 56(1) EC]. If the Belgian law did not exist, more people would conclude insurance contracts with companies established in other Member States and the flow of capital from Belgium into those States would increase (ibid. at pp. I-273–4). A.-G. Mischo was not persuaded by this reasoning, holding that in the absence of a direct obstacle to the movement of capital the link between the contested legislation and the movement of capital was too tenuous and too indirect (ibid. at p. I-274). Following his opinion, the Court held that while the Belgian legislation was contrary to the free movement of persons and the freedom to provide services (although it could be justified by the need to preserve the cohesion of the tax system), it was not incompatible with the free movement of capital. The reason was that 'Article 67 does not prohibit restrictions which do not relate to the movement of capital but which result indirectly from restrictions on other fundamental freedoms'. In the present case, there was no restriction on capital movements, since the national provisions did not preclude the payment of contributions to insurers established in other Member States (ibid. at p. I-285).

The Court took a diametrically opposite approach in Case C-484/93 *Svensson and Gustavsson*, above, which involved a Luxembourg law under which a State interest rate subsidy on building loans was granted only where the loan was obtained from a credit institution established in Luxembourg, but was refused if the loan was raised in another Member State. Referring to the *Bachmann* case, with which the present case had an obvious parallel, A.-G. Elmer thought that the law in question, like the Belgian law in *Bachmann*, did not in itself mean that cross-border capital transactions were prevented or made more difficult, but only that it was economically less attractive to raise the loan abroad. Therefore, he suggested that the Luxembourg legislation should be examined not in relation to the free movement of capital but in relation to the provision of services ([1995] ECR I-3960). However, the Court held that the legislation concerned was liable to dissuade borrowers from approaching banks established in other Member States and therefore presented an obstacle to movements of capital such as bank loans (ibid. at p. I-3975).

Since the transactions in question (building loans) constituted services, the Court found it also necessary to ascertain whether the legislation was compatible with the provisions on freedom to provide services. As the legislation discriminated against credit institutions established in other Member States, the Court concluded that it was incompatible with *both* the free movement of capital *and* the freedom to provide services (ibid. at pp. I-3976–8). It may be noted that in the earlier Case C-148/91 *Veronica*, above, at pp. I-519–20, the Court also considered the national legislation involved (Dutch Media Law) from the point of view of both of these freedoms and held that it was contrary to neither.

The ruling of the Court in *Svensson and Gustavsson* was strongly criticized by A.-G. Tesauro in Case C-118/96 *Safir* [1998] ECR I-1897 at pp. I-1905–6, mainly on the grounds that it was inconsistent with the fact that the Treaty attributes residual value to the provisions on services in that services are covered by those provisions only 'in so far as they are not governed by the provisions relating to freedom of movement for goods, capital and persons' (Art. 50 EC). Moreover, the scope of the prohibition laid down in Art. 49 (services) on the one hand, and in Art. 56 (capital), on the other, is different in that the free movement of capital is subject to broader restrictions (Art. 58) than the freedom to provide services (Arts. 46 and 55). For these reasons, he argued, Arts. 49 and 56 should not be applied cumulatively but the compatibility with Community law of national legislation should be assessed *either* under Art. 49 *or* under Art. 56. If the legislation at issue *directly* restricts the transfer of capital, Art. 56 should apply; if it only *indirectly* restricts such transfer and primarily constitutes a non-monetary restriction on the freedom to provide services, then Art. 49 should apply. Both Articles should be applied together only where a national legislation restricts simultaneously, although from different angles, both freedoms (ibid. at pp. I-1903, I-1906–7).

The *Safir* case involved Swedish legislation which set up different tax regimes for savings in the form of capital life assurance depending on whether the policies were taken out with companies established in Sweden or with companies established elsewhere. In most cases, taxation was higher in the latter case. A.-G. Tesauro considered that since the legislation in question constituted an obstacle to the provision of cross-border insurance services but did not prevent or make more difficult capital movements, it fell within the scope of Art. 49 alone to the exclusion of Art. 56 (ibid. at p. I-1907). The Court held, without giving reasons, that since the legislation was incompatible with Art. 49, it was 'not necessary' to determine whether it was also incompatible with Art. 56 (ibid. at p. I-1929. See also Case C-136/00 *Danner* [2002] ECR I-8147, para. 58).

Both the Advocate-General and the Court took a similar approach in Case C-410/96 *Ambry* [1998] ECR I-7875. The case concerned a French law which provided that where a travel agency arranged (the obligatory) financial security with a credit institution or insurance company established in another Member State, the guarantor was required to conclude an additional agreement with a credit institution or insurance company established in France. A.-G. Mischo thought that the law at issue did not interfere with the cross-border movement of capital and payments, and proposed that it should be examined with regard to the freedom to provide services alone (ibid. at p. I-7881). The Court followed this approach and, having established that the law was incompatible with Art. 49, it held, again without giving reasons, that it was not necessary to examine whether it was also contrary to Art. 56 (ibid. at p. I-7904).

However, the next case, Case C-279/00 *Commission* v. *Italy*, above, represents a return to the *Svensson and Gustavsson* approach. Accepting both the Commission's complaint and the opinion of A.-G. Alber ([2002] ECR I-1443–4), the Court held that the contested Italian legislation, which required non-Italian undertakings providing temporary labour in Italy to lodge a guarantee with a credit institution having its registered office or a branch office on Italian territory, constituted a restriction on capital movements. It impeded such undertakings from using a guarantee lodged with a credit institution established in another Member State. At the same time, the legislation also constituted discrimination against such foreign credit institutions as service providers. Consequently, it was contrary to *both* Art. 49 *and* Art. 56 (ibid. at pp. I-1458–9; see also, to the same effect, Case C-334/02 *Commission* v. *France* [2004] ECR I-0000, para. 25).

2. Freedom of establishment. As regards, secondly, the relationship between the free movement of capital and freedom of establishment, this has given rise to even more problems and contradictions than the relationship between capital movements and provision of services. The first case to mention is Case C-302/97 *Konle*, above, which concerned Austrian legislation which made acquisition of land subject to prior administrative authorization. A.-G. La Pergola examined the legislation solely with regard to the freedom of establishment and, having concluded that it was incompatible with that freedom, found it unnecessary to consider whether it was also in conflict with the rules on free movement of capital (ibid. at p. I-3117). The Court took exactly the opposite approach. It started by noting that national legislation on the acquisition of land must comply with the provisions of the Treaty on *both* freedom of establishment *and* the free movement of capital. The former because the right to acquire, use, or dispose of immovable property on the territory of another Member State is the corollary of freedom of establishment. The latter because investments in real estate in another Member State constitute capital movements (ibid. at p. I-3131). However, having made this opening statement the Court continued, rather inconsistently, by scrutinizing the Austrian legislation solely with regard to the rules on capital movements. Having established its incompatibility with those rules, the Court concluded, without giving reasons, that there was no need to examine the legislation from the point of view of the right of establishment also (ibid. at p. I-3138).

The judgment of the Court in *Konle* was criticized by A.-G. Geelhoed in Cases C-515/99 etc. *Reisch*, above, which involved similar Austrian legislation. In the opinion of the Advocate-General, it was not at all self-evident why the Court dealt with that legislation in *Konle* exclusively under Art. 56 (capital). The aim of the Austrian law was to regulate the acquisition of land (building plots) for the purposes of restricting, in the interests of regional planning, the establishment of secondary residences in certain areas. Thus, the law concerned, in the first place, the *use* of land and not the transfer of capital that was necessary for its acquisition. Everyone was free to invest capital in buying property, only the buyer could not use his property for the purposes of a secondary residence. Therefore, the restrictive effect of the legislation on capital movements was only indirect or secondary; primarily it involved restrictions on services of a non-financial nature in so far as secondary residences were usually connected with the provision or receipt of services. Therefore, the Advocate-General proposed not to follow *Konle* but to deal with the legislation from the point of view of services in the first place ([2002] ECR I-2165–77). However, the Court did not accept his opinion but decided the case along the lines established in *Konle*. After pointing out again the close connection between freedom of establishment and the movement of capital ('the right to acquire . . . immovable property on the territory of another Member State, which is the corollary of freedom of establishment, . . . generates capital movements when it is exercised'), the Court assessed the Austrian legislation in the light of Arts. 56 to 60 (capital) alone (ibid. at pp. I-2203–7).

The *Konle* approach has been followed by the Court in several subsequent cases. Thus, in Case C-423/98 *Albore*, above, at p. I-6001, the Court again confirmed that 'whatever the reasons for it, the purchase of immovable property in a Member State by a non-resident constitutes an investment in real estate which falls within the category of capital movements between Member States'. The Court therefore examined the Italian legislation which required administrative authorization for purchase of real estate in areas of military importance from the point of view of the free movement of capital and, having established incompatibility, found it unnecessary to consider it with regard to the right of establishment also (ibid. at p. I-6004).

Case C-367/98 *Commission* v. *Portugal*, Case C-483/99 *Commission* v. *France*, and Case C-503/99 *Commission* v. *Belgium*, all cited above, concerned legislation that imposed various restrictions on the acquisition of shares in privatized undertakings. The Commission brought the three actions on the grounds that the legislation in question was contrary to both the freedom of establishment and the free movement of capital. A.-G. Ruiz-Jarabo Colomer thought that although the actions had to be considered in relation to both freedoms, only the freedom of establishment required in-depth examination ([2002] ECR I-4737). However, the Court took the opposite view and scrutinized the legislation exclusively with regard to the free movement of capital. Having found that the Portuguese and French legislation was contrary to Art. 56, the Court said:

> To the extent that the legislation in issue involves restrictions on freedom of establishment, such restrictions are a direct consequence of the obstacles to the free movement of capital considered above, to which they are inextricably linked. Consequently, since an infringement of Article 56 of the Treaty has been established, there is no need for a separate examination of the measures at issue in the light of the Treaty rules concerning freedom of establishment (ibid. at pp. I-4777, I-4806).

Since the Belgian legislation was justified on grounds of public security and therefore was not contrary to Art. 56, the Court dismissed the action in so far as it concerned the free movement of capital. With regard to establishment, the Court said that 'even if it were assumed' that the legislation might also constitute a restriction on freedom of establishment, such a restriction would also be justified on the same grounds. Without examining the matter any further, the Court dismissed the action also in so far as it concerned the right of establishment (ibid. at pp. I-4835–6).

These judgments were strongly criticized by A.-G. Ruiz-Jarabo Colomer in Case C-463/00 *Commission* v. *Spain*, above, and in Case C-98/01 *Commission* v. *United Kingdom*, above, which also concerned privatization legislation broadly similar to those involved in the cases against Portugal, France, and Belgium. The main thrust of his criticism was that in those cases the Court adopted an incorrect legal classification of the infringements in question. In his opinion, the 'natural and appropriate framework' within which to consider the various restrictions arising from the privatization laws was the freedom of establishment, not the free movement of capital. In each case, he pointed out, the defendant Member State sought to control the formation of the privatized company's corporate will, which had little to do with the free movement of capital. Contrary to the Court's finding, the resulting restriction of capital movements was incidental, in some respects even hypothetical or very tenuous, rather than inevitable (paras. 35–6 of the opinion). In spite of these criticisms, the Court followed the same line of reasoning and reached the same conclusions as in the cases against Portugal and France (paras. 84–6 and 49–52 of the judgments, respectively).

However, in a second group of cases, all concerning discriminatory tax treatment of companies or subsidiaries established in another Member State, the Court took exactly the opposite approach by assessing the contested legislation exclusively or primarily with regard to freedom of establishment and not the free movement of capital. In Case C-200/98 *X and Y I* [1999] ECR I-8261, Swedish legislation denied tax relief on intra-group transfers involving subsidiaries whose respective seats were in various other Member States. A.-G. Saggio expressed the opinion that such a legislation did not only impose restrictions on freedom of establishment but also constituted a restriction on the free movement of capital. It had the effect of dissuading Swedish companies from investing in subsidiaries established in other Member States because this would deprive them of the tax relief to which they would be entitled if all the members of the group were Swedish (ibid. at p. I-8274). The Court ruled that since the legislation in question was contrary to Arts. 43 to 48 (establishment), it was not necessary to examine whether it was also contrary to Arts. 56 to 58 (capital) (ibid. at p. I-8286).

In Case C-251/98 *Baars*, above, a Netherlands law exempted assets invested in shares from wealth tax but restricted that exemption to shares in companies established in the Netherlands. The Netherlands Government argued that this situation was covered solely by the provisions of the Treaty on the free movement of capital and not by those relating to freedom of establishment (ibid. at pp. I-2813–14). In his opinion, A.-G. Alber examined at length the respective scope of the two freedoms. He pointed out that there was a close relationship between them as shown by the reciprocal reservations contained in Art. 43(2) ('Freedom of establishment shall [be] . . . subject to the provisions of the chapter relating to capital') and in Art. 58(2) ('The provisions of this Chapter [on capital] shall be without prejudice to the applicability of restrictions on the right of establishment which are compatible with this Treaty'). However, those reservations did not exclude the possibility that the same activity might need protection under various chapters, and thus might fall simultaneously and concurrently within the scope of several fundamental freedoms. Therefore, in principle, the rules on capital and those on services and establishment should apply in parallel (ibid. at p. I-2792).

Then the Advocate-General put forward three criteria for deciding which freedom should be applied in a particular case. First, where the free movement of capital is *directly* restricted by a national measure so that only an *indirect* obstacle to establishment is created, only the rules on capital movements apply. Secondly, and conversely, where the right of establishment is directly restricted so that this restriction leads indirectly to a reduction of capital flows between Member States, only the rules on establishment apply. Thirdly, where there is direct intervention affecting both the free movement of capital and the right of establishment, both freedoms apply and the national measure must satisfy the requirements of both (ibid. at pp. I-2795–6. It may be noted that in Cases C-515/99 etc. *Reisch*, above, at pp. I-2174–5, A.-G. Geelhoed proposed that these three criteria should be applied also in determining the relationship between the free movement of capital and freedom to provide services). In the light of these criteria, A.-G. Alber concluded that the tax law in question was contrary to the freedom of establishment but did not directly affect the free movement of capital. Its effect on capital flows between Member States was indirect in that it rendered investment in a company established outside the Netherlands less attractive than investment within that country (ibid. at pp. I-2799–800). The Court held that since the legislation was contrary to Art. 43 (establishment), it was unnecessary to consider whether it was also contrary to Art. 56 (capital) (ibid. at p. I-2820; see also section II.2(*e*) above). The Court reached the same conclusion in Cases C-397/98 etc. *Metallgesellschaft* [2001] ECR I-1727 at p. I-1782, which dealt with a United Kingdom tax regime that benefited resident companies to the disadvantage of companies whose seat was in another Member State.

This line of authority was relied on by A.-G. Mischo in Case C-436/00 *X and Y II*, above, which involved Swedish legislation providing for unfavourable tax treatment of certain share transfers to companies established in other Member States. The Advocate-General opined that since the legislation infringed the freedom of establishment, it was not necessary to examine whether it also infringed the rules on the free movement of capital (paras. 44 and 74 of the opinion). However, the Court took yet again a different approach. First it stated that since the legislation at issue was only in part incompatible with the provisions on freedom of establishment, it had to be considered also with regard to the free movement of capital, but only to the extent that it involved a separate restriction on the latter which was not covered by the former (paras. 66–8 of the judgment). Then the Court found that the national legislation was liable to dissuade Swedish taxpayers from transferring shares to companies established in other Member States and that, therefore, it constituted, for those taxpayers, a restriction on free movement of capital, even although it did not actually prohibit such transfers (para. 70 of the judgment). Finally, the Court concluded that although in respect of a certain type of share transfer the Swedish legislation was not incompatible with Art. 43 (establishment), it was nonetheless contrary to Arts. 56 and 58 (capital) (para. 73 of the judgment).

3. Conclusions. It is apparent from this survey of the case-law that the Court has so far failed to establish clear and coherent principles as to which Treaty provisions to apply in situations in which a national measure simultaneously restricts more than one fundamental freedom. In some cases, the Court gives preference to the rules on services over those on capital, in spite of the fact that Art. 50 EC attributes residual importance to services ('Services shall be considered to be "services" within the meaning of this Treaty . . . in so far as they are not governed by the provisions relating to freedom of movement for goods, capital and persons'). In other cases, the Court examines the measure with regard to both sets of rules. Likewise, in some cases the Court restricts its considerations to the provisions on establishment, in others to the provisions on capital. In most cases, the Court gives no explanations as to why it starts with one set of rules rather than the other (even where the measure clearly falls within the scope of both), nor as to why, once the measure has been found to be contrary to one freedom, it is 'not necessary' to examine it with regard to the other. This may have good pragmatic reasons, but seems to be inconsistent with the principle, established in numerous cases, that in preliminary ruling procedures, whereby most cases involving the free movement of capital come before the Court, 'it is for the national courts alone to determine . . . both the need for a preliminary ruling . . . and the relevance of the questions which they refer to the Court' (see e.g. Cases C-515/99 etc. *Reisch*, above, at pp. I-2202–3). Given that in all but one of the cases discussed above the referring court asked for the interpretation of both sets of rules (i.e. those on capital and establishment or on capital and services), the Court at least should have given some explanation as to why it was unnecessary to comply with that request in full. It is true that in some cases the Court stated that the reason for not examining the contested measure with regard to one freedom was that the restriction on that freedom was indirect as it merely followed from restrictions which the measure imposed on another freedom. However, this still does not explain the Court's attitude in situations where the national measure imposes direct restrictions on two fundamental freedoms concurrently, and yet the Court examines it in relation to one of those only.

The view, also put forward by several Advocates-General, that a measure which directly restricts either freedom of establishment or freedom to provide services and only indirectly affects the free movement of capital (in the sense of making cross-border capital transactions economically less attractive but without preventing them) should be assessed only with regard to the first-mentioned freedoms, seems to be inconsistent with the wide definition of the concept of 'restrictions' on capital movements. As seen in section III above, any national measure will constitute a restriction on the free movement of capital which is liable to dissuade people from making investments in other Member States, and which is thus such as to render that freedom illusory, even if it does not actually prevent or prohibit the cross-border flow of capital. It follows that even an 'indirect' restriction is a restriction which is prohibited by Art. 56. This means that the distinction between 'direct' and 'indirect' restrictions, as put forward by some of the Advocates-General and the Court itself, is not compatible with Art. 56.

Two further factors support the view that the existing case-law is unsatisfactory. First, in view of the frequent disagreements between the Advocate-General and the Court as to the correct legal classification of a restriction, it is by no means certain that the Court always chooses the appropriate freedom as a starting point for its investigations. The failure of the Court to give adequate reasons for its choice often creates the impression that the choice is arbitrary. Secondly, as shown by the last-discussed case, the fact that a national measure is incompatible with one Treaty freedom does not necessarily mean that it is also incompatible with another, or vice versa. As a result of these factors, the practice of the Court not to scrutinize a national measure with regard to all the freedoms with which it might potentially be incompatible, and not to provide reasons for this, may create uncertainty in the minds of the national authorities, in the first place, of the legislatures, as well as of the Commission, as to whether or not the measure is also contrary to the other freedoms not considered, and as to what corrective action (e.g. legislative amendment) needs to be taken to ensure the measure's compatibility with Community law. All of these problems could be avoided were the Court to examine the contested legislation in relation to all the fundamental freedoms on which it may have direct or indirect, actual or potential, restrictive effects.

See also **Freedom of establishment, Freedom to provide services, Free movement of goods, Public policy, Public security.**

Further reading 1. BOOKS: Barnard, *The Substantive Law of the EU. The Four Freedoms* (2004), part iv; Craig and de Búrca, *EU Law. Text, Cases, and Materials*, 3rd edn. (2003), ch. 16; Mohamed, *European Community Law on the Free Movement of Capital and the EMU* (1998); Usher, *The Law of Money and Financial Services in the European Community*, 2nd edn. (2000).

2. ARTICLES: Flynn, 'Coming of Age: The Free Movement of Capital Case-Law 1993–2002' (2002) *CML Rev.* 773; Landsmeer, 'Movement of Capital and Other Freedoms' (2001) *LIEI* 57; Louis, 'Free Movement of Capital in the Community: The Casati Judgment' (1982) *CML Rev.* 443; id., 'Free Movement of Tourists and Freedom of Payments in the Community: The Luisi-Carbone Judgment' (1984) *CML Rev.* 625; Moloney, 'New Frontiers in EC Capital Markets Law: From Market Construction to Market

Regulation' (2003) *CML Rev.* 809; Oliver and Bache, 'Free Movement of Capital between the Member States: Recent Developments' (1989) *CML Rev.* 61; Peers, 'Free Movement of Capital: Learning Lessons or Slipping on Spilt Milk?' in Barnard and Scott (eds.), *The Law of the Single European Market* (2002), ch. 13; Szyszczak, 'Golden Shares and Market Governance' (2002) *LIEI* 255; Usher, 'Capital Movements and the Treaty on European Union' (1992) *YEL* 35; Wathelet, 'The Influence of Free Movement of Persons, Services and Capital on National Direct Taxation: Trends in the Case-Law of the Court of Justice' (2001) *YEL* 1.

▶ **FREE MOVEMENT OF GOODS** One of the four fundamental freedoms forming the basis of the internal market (for the others, *see further under* **Freedom of establishment, Freedom to provide services, Free movement of capital, Free movement of persons**). Together, these four freedoms liberalize all economic transactions between Member States, subject only to limited exceptions. However, with the exception of the free movement of capital, they do not apply in relations with third countries.

I. The legal framework

The provisions in the EC Treaty relating to the free movement of goods between Member States prohibit four distinct types of restriction on such movements: customs duties, charges having equivalent effect thereto, quantitative restrictions, and measures having equivalent effect (*see further under* the separate entries relating to each of those restrictions). The first two are governed by Art. 25 EC, while the second two are subject to Arts. 28 to 30 EC. Section II below ('Scope of application') is common to all of these; but sections III and IV ('Exceptions' and 'Community legislation') concern only quantitative restrictions and measures of equivalent effect.

Of particular importance in this context is Art. 14 EC, which was first inserted into the EC Treaty with effect from 1 July 1987 by the Single European Act (SEA). The first two paragraphs read as follows:

1. The Community shall adopt measures with the aim of progressively establishing the internal market over a period expiring on 31 December 1992, in accordance with the provisions of this Article and of Articles . . . 95 and without prejudice to the other provisions of this Treaty.

2. The internal market shall comprise an area without internal frontiers in which the free movement of goods, persons, services and capital is ensured in accordance with the provisions of this Treaty.

The free movement of goods has been described by the Court as 'one of the fundamental principles of the Treaty' (Case C-265/95 *Commission* v. *France* [1997] ECR I-6959 at p. I-6998 (violent action by farmers); see also Cases C-49/89 *Corsica Ferries France* [1989] ECR I-4441 at p. 4456 and C-205/89 *Commission* v. *Greece* [1991] ECR I-1361 at p. I-1377 (pasteurized butter)). It follows that the Treaty prohibitions on restrictions on inter-State trade are to be construed broadly, while the exceptions are to be construed narrowly (see sections III.1(*a*)(*i*) and III.2(*a*) below).

These prohibitions are complemented by a large body of Community legislation relating to goods, much of which is based on Art. 95 EC. That legislation will be considered in section IV below.

II. Scope of application

1. Material scope

(*a*) ***The movements concerned.*** Arts. 25 and 28 to 30 EC apply both to goods originating in the Community and to goods from third countries which have been put into free circulation in the Community. This is spelt out in Art. 23(2) EC (*see further under* **Customs procedures, Goods, Origin of goods**).

The Treaty provisions on the free movement of goods apply to all such movements, including: transit (the right of transit was itself held to constitute a general principle of Community law in Case 266/81 *SIOT* [1983] ECR 731 at p. 777); re-imports (Case 78/70 *Deutsche Grammophon* [1971] ECR 487); and parallel imports (Case 104/75 *De Peijper* [1976] ECR 613).

Moreover, it is well established that these provisions apply where goods are imported by a consumer rather than a commercial undertaking (Case 215/87 *Schumacher* [1989] ECR 617; Case C-362/88 *GB-INNO-BM* [1990] ECR I-667). In the latter case, the Court stated the proposition as follows: 'Free movement of goods concerns not only traders, but also individuals. It requires . . . that consumers resident in one Member State may travel freely to the territory of another Member State to shop under the same conditions as the local population.' Thus, it seems clear that no underlying commercial transaction need be shown at all; for instance, the individual who wishes to take his or her home-made jam to a relative in another Member State may rely on these Treaty provisions.

Until recently, it was considered to be axiomatic that the Treaty provisions on the free movement of goods apply exclusively to goods moving *between* Member States (see Arts. 3(1)(a) and (c), 14, 25, 28, and 29 EC). Accordingly, the Court has repeatedly held that these provisions do not preclude restrictions internal to a Member State (Cases 314/81 etc. *Waterkeyn* [1982] ECR 4337; Case 286/81 *Oosthoek's Uitgeversmaatschappij* [1982] ECR 4575; Case 355/85 *Cognet* [1986] ECR 3231). By the same token, reverse discrimination is tolerated (Case 355/85 *Driancourt* [1986] ECR 3231; Case 98/86 *Mathot* [1987] ECR 809). Two recent judgments (Cases C-363/93 etc. *Lancry* [1994] ECR I-3957; Cases C-321/94 etc. *Pistre* [1997] ECR I-2343) throw this previously well-established principle into doubt, but their implications are as yet unclear.

(*b*) ***Goods and services.*** Where a restriction on the movement of goods is merely ancillary to a restriction on services, then the matter is to be considered under Arts. 49 to 55 EC. Thus in Case C-275/92 *Schindler* [1994] ECR I-1039 a ban of the sale of German lottery tickets in the United Kingdom was held to constitute a restriction on services, the ticket being nothing more than proof that a service had been rendered (*see further under* **Freedom to provide services**). In contrast, in Case C-368/95 *Familiapress*

[1997] ECR I-3689 a restriction on granting prizes for crossword puzzles contained in newspapers was examined under Art. 28 EC, since the puzzles constituted an integral part of the newspapers.

Advertising is a clear example of the Court's approach to this matter: the economic activity itself is a service (Case 155/73 *Sacchi* [1974] ECR 409; Case 52/79 *Debauve* [1980] ECR 833), and yet an advertising restriction may in fact constitute a restriction on imports of goods. Thus, the Court has variously considered the lawfulness of advertising restrictions in relation to goods (Case 152/78 *Commission* v. *France* [1980] ECR 2299 (alcoholic drinks); Case C-362/88 *GB-INNO-BM*, above; Case C-412/93 *Leclerc-Siplec* [1995] ECR I-179), and to services (*Sacchi* and *Debauve*), depending on which aspect was predominant; and in Case C-34/95 *De Agostini* [1997] ECR I-3843 it examined certain Swedish restrictions on television advertising from the point of view both of Art. 28 and of Art. 49 EC.

2. Personal scope

(a) Who may rely on these provisions? The determining factor for the application of the Treaty provisions on the free movement of goods is the status of goods and not the nationality of their owner. This was made clear by the Court in Cases 2/69 etc. *Diamantarbeiders I* [1969] ECR 211, in the following terms:

> The Treaty prohibits any pecuniary charge on imports and exports between Member States, irrespective of the nationality of the traders who might be placed at a disadvantage by such measures. Thus, in applying these provisions, there is no justification for a distinction to be made according to whether the measures in question adversely affect certain Member States and their nationals, or all the citizens of the Community, or only the nationals of the Member State which was responsible for the measures in question.

While that case related to the prohibition on charges of equivalent effect in Art. 25 EC, this statement also holds good for Arts. 28 to 30 EC.

The only exception to this rule is that sanctions against a third country imposed pursuant to Arts. 297 or 301 EC may, in appropriate circumstances, take the form of a ban on nationals of that country trading within the Community. This will only occur in highly exceptional circumstances.

(b) Persons bound. The Treaty provisions on the free movement of goods are expressly addressed to the Member States. This covers all public authorities of the Member States, including the judiciary (Case 58/80 *Dansk Supermarked* [1981] ECR 181) and regional and local government (Case C-1/90 *Aragonesa de Publicidad* [1991] ECR I-4151; Case C-277/91 *Ligur Carni* [1993] ECR I-6621). Other bodies on which a Member State has conferred legislative or administrative powers are also to be regarded as part of the Member States for this purpose (Cases 266/87 etc. *Royal Pharmaceutical Society of Great Britain* [1989] ECR 1295). It is also helpful to have regard to the Court's case-law determining what bodies constitute part of the State for the purposes of bearing liability for the latter's failure to implement a directive properly or at all (Case 152/84 *Marshall* [1986] ECR

723; Case 222/84 *Johnston* [1986] ECR 1651; Case C-188/89 *Foster* [1990] ECR I-3313). In both contexts, the concept of the 'Member States' is to be construed broadly.

The question then arises whether these provisions also bind the Community institutions. In other words, can the Council or the Commission impose restrictions on movements of goods in inter-State trade, or authorize the Member States to do so? In a long series of cases, the Court has ruled that those institutions are indeed bound by those provisions, or at least by analogous principles (see e.g. Cases 80/77 etc. *Ramel* [1978] ECR 927; Case 218/82 *Commission* v. *Council* [1983] ECR 4063 (rum quotas); Case C-315/92 *Estée Lauder* [1994] ECR I-317; Case C-363/93 etc. *Lancry*, above, at p. 3994). Nevertheless, the Court has allowed the Council and the Commission greater leeway to impose restrictions than the Member States, by granting them a wider discretion to decide what is in the general interest (see e.g. Case 46/76 *Bauhuis* [1977] ECR 5; Case 37/83 *Rewe-Zentrale* [1984] ECR 1229 (phytosanitary directive); Case 15/83 *Denkavit Nederland* [1984] ECR 2171 (aid for processed skimmed milk)). As the Court put it in *Bauhuis*, the measures contested there were 'not prescribed by each Member State in order to protect some interest of its own but by the Council in the general interest of the Community'. Accordingly, the Court tends to apply a rebuttable presumption that restrictions imposed or authorized by the Community institutions are justified in the public interest, whereas it applies the contrary presumption to the Member States (see sections III.1(*a*)(*i*) and III.2(*a*) below).

Considerable discussion has centred on the question of whether private parties can be bound by the Treaty provisions on the free movement of goods. In other words, do these provisions have 'horizontal effect'? Today, it seems reasonably clear that this question should be answered in the negative, since the actions of private parties are caught instead by Arts. 81 and 82 EC, provided of course that the various conditions for the application of those provisions are fulfilled.

Indeed, the Court ruled to this effect in Cases 177/82 etc. *Van de Haar* [1984] ECR 1797, when it held that Art. 81 'belongs to the rules on competition which are addressed to undertakings and associations of undertakings and which are intended to maintain effective competition in the common market', whereas Art. 28 'belongs to the rules which seek to ensure the free movement of goods and to that end to eliminate measures taken by Member States'. Again, in Case 311/85 *Vereniging van Vlaamse Reisbureaus* [1987] ECR 3801 at p. 3830, it stated that Arts. 28 and 29 EC 'concern only public measures and not the conduct of undertakings'. More recently, A.-G. Lenz expressed the same view in Case C-265/95 *Commission* v. *France*, above, at p. I-6968 (violent action by farmers).

The counter-arguments nevertheless deserve consideration:

- In a number of cases, restrictions imposed by sporting organizations have been held to fall foul of Art. 39 EC on the free movement of workers (Case 36/74 *Walrave* [1974] ECR 1405; Case 13/76 *Donà* [1976] ECR 1333; Case C-415/93 *Bosman* [1995] ECR I-4921). More recently, this line of case-law has been extended beyond the field of sport (Case C-411/98 *Ferlini* [2000] ECR I-8081; Case C-309/99 *Wouters* [2002] ECR I-1577). Yet the rationale behind this line of case-law appears to be that the bodies concerned constitute quasi-public organizations in view of their extensive powers over the activity concerned.

- The Court's case-law on the unlawful exercise by private parties of their industrial property rights is sometimes cited as evidence that such parties are bound by the Treaty provisions on the free movement of goods. True, this case-law relates to Arts. 28 and 30 EC. However, in reality the exercise of industrial property rights merely constitutes reliance on measures adopted by Member States: without legislation, patent, trade mark, and copyright protection would simply not exist.
- In Case C-16/94 *Dubois* [1995] ECR I-2421 a contractual charge imposed by Garonor, a private company managing an international road station on customs forwarding agents, was held to constitute a charge of equivalent effect contrary to Art. 25 EC. This charge was intended to compensate Garonor for expenses that should have been borne by the French customs authorities; in particular, Garonor was making its premises available free of charge to customs officers for the latter's own use. In effect, those authorities had imposed a *de facto* charge of equivalent effect on Garonor, which that company sought to pass on to the forwarding agents. Consequently, this judgment cannot be taken to support the view that the Treaty provisions on the free movement of goods have horizontal effect.
- In Case 43/75 *Defrenne* [1976] ECR 455, judgments of national courts were held to constitute acts of Member States, so that Art. 141 EC was held to have horizontal effect (see also Case 14/83 *Von Colson and Kamann* [1984] ECR 1891 in relation to directives). There is some force in the argument that the same reasoning could be transposed to the Treaty provisions on the free movement of goods. Nevertheless, the clear wording of the Court's rulings in *Van de Haar* and *Vereniging van Vlaamse Reisbureaus* suggests that this is not so, since by their very nature the latter provisions do not lend themselves to such an interpretation.
- In Case C-281/98 *Angonese* [2000] ECR I-4139, it was held that a private party acting alone was bound to observe the provisions of Art. 39 EC. However, it would seem that the Court is prepared to take the free movement of natural persons further than the free movement of goods.

Thus it would seem to follow that, where an individual or private body boycotts certain imported goods, no breach of Art. 28 EC occurs. By the same token, an insurance company that refuses to insure imported cars would not fall foul of this provision. What is perhaps more worrying is that on this view dockers would not breach Community law by going on strike, thereby blocking imports.

At all events, in extreme cases, the Member State concerned will be liable under Art. 10 EC, read with the relevant provision relating to the free movement of goods, for failing to intervene to prevent interference with imports or exports by private individuals (see Case C-265/95 *Commission* v. *France*, above (violent action by farmers)).

3. Territorial scope. Plainly, Arts. 25 and 28 to 30 EC apply to all twenty-five Member States of the Community. The territorial scope of the Treaty is governed primarily by Art. 299 EC, read with the various Acts of Accession, including that which came into force on 1 May 2004 (*OJ* 2003 L236/1).

As regards the free movement of goods, account must also be taken of Art. 3 of Council Reg. 2913/92 establishing a Community Customs Code (*OJ* 1992 L302/1), as amended. That Article primarily reflects the provisions of the Treaties on the matter, as well as various agreements concluded between Member States and third countries. While the Court has yet to rule on the precise relationship between Art. 3 and the territorial scope of the Treaty as regards the free movement of goods, it seems clear that there is at the very least a rebuttable presumption that the two coincide.

Art. 299 EC contains a wholly new para. 2 introduced by the Treaty of Amsterdam (ToA), which begins with the following sentence: 'The provisions of this Treaty shall apply to the French overseas departments [namely French Guyana, Guadeloupe, Martinique, Réunion], the Azores, Madeira and the Canary Islands.' This sub-paragraph does not alter the status of these territories, as it stood prior to the entry into force of the ToA (see e.g. Case C-163/90 *Legros* [1992] ECR I-4625, Case C-363/93 etc. *Lancry*, above).

However, by the following sub-paragraph of Art. 299(2), the Council is granted exceptional new powers to adopt measures in favour of those islands, provided that it does not undermine 'the integrity and the coherence of the Community legal order, including the internal market and common policies'. The highly ambiguous nature of this wording need scarcely be pointed out.

Other territories that require special mention here are as follows:

- although the Faroe Islands are part of the Kingdom of Denmark, they are specifically excluded from the scope of the Treaty by Art. 299(6)(a) EC;
- Greenland, which is also part of Denmark, left the Community by a Treaty of March 1984 (*OJ* 1985 L29/1);
- while the Spanish enclaves of Ceuta and Melilla are within the Community, they are governed by the special provisions of Art. 25 of the Act of Accession of 1985 and the special Protocol thereto, which partly exclude the provisions on the free movement of goods; (but customs duties and charges of equivalent effect may not be levied on Community goods entering those territories; Case C-45/94 *Municipality of Ceuta* [1995] ECR I-4385). Both enclaves are outside the Community customs territory (Art. 1(2) of the Protocol and Art. 3 of the Community Customs Code);
- Gibraltar is within the Community, subject to certain exceptions spelt out in Art. 28 of the Act of Accession of 1972. However, Arts. 29 and

30 of the Act of Accession, read with Annexes I and II thereto, expressly excluded Gibraltar from the customs territory of the Community and assimilated it to a third country for these purposes (see now Art. 3 of the Community Customs Code). The amendments to Community legislation set out in the Annexes to an Act of Accession have Treaty status (Cases 31/86 etc. *LAISA* v. *Council* [1988] ECR 2285). Accordingly, it is clear that the provisions on the free movement of goods do not apply (see the answer to Written Question 1823/84, *OJ* 1985 L35/1 and Case C-30/01 *Commission* v. *United Kingdom* [2003] ECR I-9481 (Gibraltar));
- by virtue of Art. 299(6)(c) EC, the Treaty only applies to the Channel Islands and the Isle of Man 'to the extent necessary to ensure the implementation of the arrangements' set out in the Act of Accession of 1972. Art. 1(1) of the special Protocol to that Act, which relates to those territories, provides that 'the Community rules on customs matters and quantitative restrictions' apply to them. This language possibly covers all the provisions on the free movement of goods. In any event, Art. 3 of the Community Customs Code expressly includes these islands in the Community customs territory;
- the Treaty does not apply to the United Kingdom's sovereign base areas in Cyprus (Art. 299(6)(b) EC). Movements of goods between northern and southern Cyprus are governed by Protocol 10 to the Act of Accession of 2003 (*OJ* 2003 L236/955), as implemented by Council Reg. 866/2004 (*OJ* 2004 L161/128);
- despite being outside the Community, Monaco is within the latter's customs territory, pursuant to a convention between that principality and France (Art. 3(2) of the Community Customs Code); and
- finally, Art. 3 of the Community Customs Code excludes various small areas of Germany and Italy from the Community's customs territory, mainly by reason of certain treaties with Switzerland.

Moreover, Art. 3(3) of the Community Customs Code provides that 'the customs territory of the Community shall include the territorial waters, the inland maritime waters and the airspace' pertaining to the land comprising its customs territory. The continental shelf is not expressly mentioned (*see further under* **Community Customs Code, Community customs territory**).

Finally, it is settled law that the Treaty provisions on the free movement of goods prohibit restrictions of such movements into and out of part of the territory of a Member State, however small (Case C-21/88 *Du Pont de Nemours* [1990] ECR I-889; *Legros; Lancry; Municipality of Ceuta*, above; Case C-67/97 *Bluhme* [1998] ECR I-8033). These provisions are not subject to any *de minimis* rule (Cases 177/82 etc. *Van de Haar*; *Bluhme*, above).

4. Temporal scope. Under the EEC Treaty as it stood originally, various deadlines were fixed for the abolition of the various types of restriction on movements of goods between Member States. Unless they were caught by an exception clause, no such restrictions could be maintained beyond the end of the transitional period laid down in Art. 8 of the original EEC Treaty, namely 31 December 1969.

Moreover, each of the various Acts of Accession has extended the provisions on the free movement of goods to the new Member States, sometimes with transitional provisions. None of those transitional provisions is in force today.

III. Exceptions

1. Article 30 EC

(*a*) *General principles*

(*i*) *Narrow interpretation; burden of proof.* Art. 30, which allows restrictions on the free movement of goods on a number of grounds (see point (*b*) below) constitutes an exception to a fundamental freedom of Community law and must therefore be interpreted narrowly (Case 7/68 *Commission* v. *Italy* [1968] ECR 423 (works of art); Case 46/76 *Bauhuis*, above).

It follows, *inter alia*, that this Article, which refers in terms only to Arts. 28 and 29 EC, does not constitute an exception to the prohibition on customs duties and charges of equivalent effect enshrined in Art. 25 (Case 7/68 *Commission* v. *Italy*, above).

For the same reason, the burden of proving that a measure is justified falls on the Member State (Case 251/78 *Denkavit Futtermittel* [1980] ECR 3369). No doubt, if a private party were seeking to show that a measure was justified, then it would equally bear the burden of proof.

(*ii*) *Justification.* A measure cannot be saved under this provision merely because it relates to one of the grounds of justification set out in the first sentence. It must be 'justified' on such grounds within the meaning of that sentence, which means that it must be necessary to achieve that end (see e.g. Case 13/78 *Eggers* [1978] ECR 1935). Thus, if the aim in question can be achieved just as effectively by a measure that is less restrictive of inter-State trade, then the contested measure is not 'justified' (see e.g. Case 104/75 *De Peijper*, above). This principle of proportionality is rigorously applied by the Court, and most of the case-law relating to Art. 30 EC turns on the application of this principle. As a result, the Court is frequently called upon to grapple with complex scientific disputes, especially where public health is involved.

In this context, the Court has developed the principle whereby a Member State 'is not entitled to prevent the marketing of a product originating in another Member State which provides a level of protection . . . equivalent to that which the national rules are intended to ensure or establish' (Case 188/84 *Commission* v. *France* [1986] ECR 419 (wood-working machines)). Although there is no authority directly on the point, it seems clear from Art. 23(2) EC that this principle applies equally to goods originating in third countries and put into free circulation in the Community, assuming that they comply with the norms applicable in the Member State of transit.

Furthermore, it is well established that a restriction ceases to be justified once Community legislation relating to the matter in issue is in place, provided that it contains exhaustive guarantees (see e.g. Case 35/76 *Simmenthal* [1976] ECR 1871; Case 148/78 *Ratti* [1979] ECR 1629; Case C-5/94 *Hedley Lomas* [1996] ECR I-2553 (Ireland); Case C-1/96 *Compassion in World Farming* [1998] ECR I-1251). Whether the latter condition is fulfilled will depend on the precise wording of the Community instrument concerned (see further section IV.1 below).

(*iii*) *Arbitrary discrimination.* Art. 30 does not permit arbitrary discrimination or a disguised restriction on trade. Such discrimination may take the following forms:

- Discrimination against imports in favour of domestic products. Thus, a ban on imports of inflatable dolls into the United Kingdom could not be justified on public morality grounds, since the very same items could lawfully be manufactured and marketed within that Member State (Case 121/85 *Conegate* [1986] ECR 1007). Similarly, restrictions on advertising alcoholic drinks could not be justified on public health grounds when they fell more heavily on imports (Case 152/78 *Commission* v. *France* [1980] ECR 2299).
- By a parity of reasoning, where a restriction falls solely or more heavily on goods intended for export to the exclusion of products intended for the domestic market, arbitrary discrimination also occurs. For instance, in Case 53/76 *Bouhelier* [1977] ECR 197, a rule requiring that watches be accompanied by certificates of quality fell foul of the prohibition on arbitrary discrimination, since it applied exclusively to products intended for export.
- Discrimination between goods coming directly from the State of production on the one hand and indirect imports on the other is also caught by the concept of arbitrary discrimination (Case 8/74 *Dassonville* [1974] ECR 837).
- Less favourable treatment of parallel imports would also appear to constitute arbitrary discrimination (Case 104/75 *De Peijper*, above).
- Lastly, should Member State A favour goods from Member State B over those from Member State C, then that would no doubt also constitute arbitrary discrimination.

In each of these cases, where the difference of treatment is objectively justified, then no arbitrary discrimination occurs. This proposition is illustrated by the ruling in Case 4/75 *Rewe-Zentralfinanz* [1975] ECR 843, which concerned phytosanitary controls of imports of apples into Germany. The question arose as to whether the imposition of such controls constituted arbitrary discrimination, given that German apples were not subject to corresponding controls. The Court held in effect that this difference in treatment would be wholly lawful if it could be shown that imported products were more likely to be contaminated.

(*iv*) *Disguised restriction.* The requirement that a restriction must not constitute a disguised restriction on trade between Member States is obscure and plays little, if any, role in practice. In two relatively old rulings, the Court has held that a measure taken for improper or protectionist motives will fall within this limb and thus cannot be saved by Art. 30 (Case 34/79 *Henn and Darby* [1979] ECR 3795 and Case 40/82 *Commission* v. *United Kingdom* [1982] ECR 2793 (Newcastle disease)). Yet it is hard to believe that an act which is objectively warranted under one of the grounds of justification set out in that provision could be held to be unlawful merely because an improper motive was found. Rather, it would seem logical to treat such a motive as evidence that a measure is not objectively justified.

(*v*) *The European Convention on Human Rights.* The ECJ has held that Art. 30 EC is to be read in the light of the European Convention (Case C-368/95 *Familiapress*, above, and Case C-112/00 *Schmidberger* [2003] ECR I-5659). This ruling, which reverses that in Case C-61/84 *Cinéthèque* [1985] ECR 2605, is in line with the case-law relating to the corresponding exceptions to the free movement of persons (Case 36/75 *Rutili* [1975] ECR 1205) and services (Case C-260/89 *ERT* [1991] ECR I-2925).

(b) The grounds of justification

(*i*) *General.* It is settled law that Art. 30 EC is 'directed to eventualities of a non-economic kind' (Case 7/61 *Commission* v. *Italy* [1961] ECR 317; Case 288/83 *Commission* v. *Ireland* [1985] ECR 1761 (Cyprus potatoes); Case C-324/93 *Evans Medical* [1995] ECR I-563; Case C-265/95 *Commission* v. *France*, above). This rule is of the utmost importance, since otherwise any measure could be upheld on purely protectionist grounds and the principle of the free movement of goods would be wholly undermined. Consequently, the reduction of unemployment or inflation, controlling the balance of payments, and promoting investment cannot constitute valid grounds for imposing restrictions on imports or exports between Member States. Equally, the refusal to authorize the sale of a product can never be justified on the grounds that there is no demand for it (Case 174/82 *Sandoz* [1983] ECR 2445). By the same token, a restriction may not be justified on the basis of a 'Member State's wish to safeguard the survival of an undertaking' (*Evans Medical*).

(*ii*) *Public morality.* While the Court insists that it has jurisdiction to interpret and apply the concept of public morality, it has also stressed that: 'In principle, it is for each Member State to determine in accordance with its own scale of values and in the form selected by it the requirement of public morality in its territory' (Case 34/79 *Henn and Darby*, above). The European Convention on Human Rights and the related case-law from the European Commission and Court of Human Rights could be of considerable assistance to the ECJ in this regard.

As one might expect, the Court has acknowledged that a ban on imports of pornographic or obscene articles may be justified on these grounds (Case 34/79 *Henn and Darby*; Case 121/85 *Conegate*, above).

In relation to services, it was held in Case C-275/92 *Schindler*, above, that a ban on large-scale lotteries could be justified on such grounds. No doubt, this ruling may be transposed to the free movement of goods. However, in

Case C-368/95 *Familiapress*, above, the ECJ found that considerations of public morality could not justify a ban on newspapers holding crossword puzzles, where small prizes were awarded to competitors chosen by lot amongst the applicants who had filled in the puzzles correctly. The ban on such 'lotteries' could not be justified on this basis in view of their small scale.

(*iii*) *Public policy*. This ground of justification is less specific than the others, but it must nevertheless be construed just as narrowly. In this context, one should have regard to the statement in Case 30/77 *Bouchereau* [1977] ECR 1999 that 'recourse by a national authority to the concept of public policy presupposes . . . the existence . . . of a genuine and sufficiently serious threat to the requirements of public policy affecting one of the fundamental interests of society'. That case related to the free movement of workers, but there is no doubt that the principle enshrined in this passage is equally applicable here.

Indeed, instances of measures being held to fall under this exception are exceedingly rare. One such case was Case 7/78 *Thompson* [1978] ECR 2247, which concerned a ban on exporting British coins from the United Kingdom with a view to their being melted down or destroyed outside the country. This prohibition was held to be justified on public policy grounds, 'because it stems from the need to protect the right to mint coinage which is traditionally regarded as involving the fundamental interests of the State'.

Where serious or violent disturbances are likely or are threatened as a consequence of imports (or exports), that cannot in principle justify restrictions on such trade (Case C-265/95 *Commission* v. *France*, above). Admittedly, in that case the ECJ suggested that it may be otherwise where the Member State can show that it would be unable to cope with the ensuing public disorder by 'the means at its disposal' (para. 56 of the judgment).

(*iv*) *Public security*. This exception covers both internal security (e.g. the prevention and detection of crime and the regulation of traffic) and external security (the protection of the State and its population from external attack, see Case C-367/89 *Richardt* [1991] ECR 4621). In Case 72/83 *Campus Oil* [1984] ECR 2727, this ground of justification was held to cover the maintenance of essential oil supplies, since a country's economy as well as 'all its institutions, its essential public services and the survival of its inhabitants' depended upon it. Equally, in *Richardt* the ECJ found that appropriate restrictions on the import, export, and transit of goods which could be used by unfriendly third countries for strategic purposes would be justified on such grounds.

(*v*) *Public health*. 'Public health' refers to human health. This is by far the most important exception of all, both in terms of the number of relevant judgments and because it has been held to 'rank first among the property or interests protected' by Art. 30 EC (Case 104/75 *De Peijper*, above; Case C-322/01 *Deutscher Apothekerverband* [2003] ECR I-0000, para. 103).

In some cases, the Court has had little difficulty in ascertaining the spurious nature of public health arguments. Examples of such cases include:

- a minimum alcohol requirement (Case 120/78 *Rewe* [1979] ECR 649 (*Cassis de Dijon*));
- a ban on the importation of meat-based products manufactured in one Member State from animals slaughtered in another Member State (Case 153/78 *Commission* v. *Germany* [1979] ECR 2555);
- a prohibition on the importation and marketing of vinegar not based on wine (Case 788/79 *Gilli* [1980] ECR 2071);
- a ban on the sale of bread containing more than a prescribed percentage of dry matter (Case 130/80 *Kelderman* [1981] ECR 527); and
- the prohibition of harmless foodstuffs merely because they are of limited nutritional value (Case 216/84 *Commission* v. *France* [1988] ECR 793 (substitute milk powder); Case 274/87 *Commission* v. *Germany* [1989] ECR 229 (meat products)).

In a long series of other cases, genuine public health concerns have been in issue, but the Court has been called upon to grapple with the difficult question as to whether the contested measure was compatible with the principle of proportionality. In this regard, it has developed the following general principles:

- The authorities of a Member State are not at liberty to disregard controls and tests carried out by those of another Member State, or certificates made out by them (see e.g. Case 124/81 *Commission* v. *United Kingdom* [1983] ECR 203 (UHT milk); Case C-304/88 *Commission* v. *Belgium* [1990] ECR I-2801 (live cattle); Case 272/80 *Frans-Nederlandse Maatschappij voor Biologische Producten* [1981] ECR 3277). It follows that a total ban on imports, or even systematic import controls, will only be upheld in exceptional cases, since health certificates issued by the exporting Member State will generally suffice. However, this principle of mutual assistance does not preclude the importing State from questioning data supplied by another Member State.
- Where a product is widely thought to constitute a health hazard, a Member State may not impose a blanket prohibition on its use once and for all, but must be prepared to review the ban on the application of traders in the light of the latest scientific developments; it must also respond within a reasonable time to such applications. The *locus classicus* on this point is the well-known ruling in Case 178/84 *Commission* v. *Germany* [1987] ECR 1227 (beer), which related to the use of additives.
- Particular importance is to be attached to the data and opinions emanating from other international organizations such as the FAO and the World Health Organization, since they are regarded as both highly authoritative and neutral (see *Commission* v. *Germany* (beer)).

(*vi*) *Animal and plant health.* The protection of animal and plant health may itself be broken down into three subheadings, namely:

- the protection of rare or endangered species (see Case C-169/89 *Gourmetterie van den Burg* [1990] ECR I-3239);

- the prevention of animal and plant diseases (see Case 40/82 *Commission* v. *United Kingdom*, above (Newcastle disease); Case 74/82 *Commission* v. *Ireland* [1984] ECR 317 (Newcastle disease));
- animal welfare (Cases 141/81 etc. *Holdijk* [1982] ECR 1299; Case C-1/96 *Compassion in World Farming*, above).

This head of justification is governed by precisely the same principles as public health, with the obvious difference that the latter is more important, since it relates to human beings.

(*vii*) *National treasures possessing artistic, historic, or archaeological value.* There is a dearth of case-law on this head of justification. Thus there is no authority as to its scope or definition. However, guidance may be derived from the categories of items listed in Council Dir. 93/7 on the return of cultural objects unlawfully removed from the territory of another Member State (*OJ* 1993 L74/74) as amended by Council Dirs. 96/100 (*OJ* 1996 L60/59) and 2001/38 (*OJ* 2001 L187/43). The use of the word 'treasure' clearly indicates that the work or item must be of special importance or merit. On the other hand, it seems clear that an item may be regarded as a 'national' treasurer, even if it is only of value to a region of a Member State, and not its entire territory.

(*viii*) *Industrial and commercial property. See further under* **Intellectual property rights.**

2. The mandatory requirements

(*a*) ***General principles.*** In Case 120/78 *Rewe*, above (*Cassis de Dijon*), the Court added other grounds of justification not spelt out in Art. 30 EC, namely: the prevention of tax evasion, consumer protection, and the prevention of unfair competition. It described these additional grounds as 'mandatory requirements', although more recently it has come to prefer the term 'overriding requirements of general public importance' (see e.g. Case C-34/95 *De Agostini*, above). At all events, the ECJ subsequently added a number of other such grounds to the list, all of which will be considered below. Moreover, the categories are not closed.

The precise status of the mandatory requirements has long been a matter of controversy. The Court's traditional approach has been to regard the mandatory requirements as falling within Art. 28 EC rather than Art. 30 EC (see e.g. Case 113/80 *Commission* v. *Ireland* [1981] ECR 1625 (souvenirs); Case 177/83 *Kohl* [1984] ECR 3651; Case 207/83 *Commission* v. *United Kingdom* [1985] ECR 1201 (indications of origin)). At the same time, the Court has held that the mandatory requirements can only justify restrictions that apply in the same way to imports as to domestic products. The reason given by the Court for this approach has been that, as already mentioned, exceptions to the fundamental principle of the free movement of goods must be construed narrowly.

Yet it is by no means clear why this should be so, given that cases do arise occasionally in which measures falling exclusively or more heavily on imports are genuinely warranted. Moreover, it is noticeable that in reality the Court has found a number of such measures to be justified, often after some intellectual contorsions (see in particular Case C-2/90 *Commission* v. *Belgium* [1992] ECR I-4431 (Walloon waste), and also Case 113/80 *Commission* v. *Ireland*, above (souvenirs), and Case 207/83 *Commission* v. *United Kingdom*, above (indications of origin)). Accordingly, it is not surprising to find the Court appearing to reverse its traditional approach in some more recent cases (Case C-34/95 *De Agostini*, above; Case C-120/95 *Decker* [1998] ECR I-1831, and see paras. 89–90 of the opinion of A.-G. Jacobs in Case C-203/96 *Dusseldorp* [1998] ECR I-4075). However, this issue continues to be shrouded in uncertainty.

At all events, it is axiomatic that in all other respects the mandatory requirements are subject to the same principles as the heads of justification expressly set out in Art. 30 EC (see point III.1(*a*) above).

(b) The grounds of justification

(*i*) *The prevention of tax evasion.* There is a dearth of case-law on this exception, but see generally Case 13/77 *GB-INNO* [1977] ECR 2115; Case 823/79 *Carciati* [1980] ECR 2773; Case 134/83 *Abbink* [1984] ECR 4097.

(*ii*) *Consumer protection.* The Court has repeatedly held that a ban on the marketing of a product may not be justified on these grounds if the consumer will be adequately protected by a labelling requirement (Case 120/78 *Rewe*, above (*Cassis de Dijon*); Case 788/79 *Gilli*, above; Case 261/81 *Rau* [1982] ECR 3961).

Having said that, the requirement that goods be labelled in the language of the region concerned will not be justified on consumer protection grounds, where the information given in another language can easily be understood by consumers there (Case 27/80 *Fietje* [1980] ECR 3839; Case C-369/89 *Piageme* [1991] ECR I-2971). Equally, the possibility of using designs, symbols, or pictograms in lieu of words must also be taken into account (Case C-33/97 *Bigg's Continent Noord* [1999] ECR I-3175). Although this general principle was thrown into doubt for a time by the decision in Case C-51/93 *Meyhui* [1994] ECR I-3879, it was re-affirmed in *Bigg's* (see also the Commission's Communication on the same subject *OJ* 1993 C345/3).

The following specific restrictions have been upheld on consumer protection grounds:

- a ban on offering free gifts as a method of sales promotion (Case 286/81 *Oosthoek*, above);
- a prohibition on doorstep sales of language teaching materials (Case 382/87 *Buet* [1989] ECR 1235).

In contrast, the following measures have been held not to be justified under this head:

- restrictions on advertising special offers (Case C-362/88 *Confédération du Commerce Luxembourgeois* [1990] ECR I-667; Case C-126/91 *Rocher* [1993] ECR I-2361);

- abusive restrictions on the use of generic names such as 'beer' (Case 178/84 *Commission* v. *Germany*, above) or 'yoghurt' (Case 298/87 *SMANOR* [1988] ECR 4489);
- unwarranted bans on the name under which goods are sold. Thus a prohibition on marketing a cosmetic product under the name 'Clinique' has been held to be unlawful (Case C-135/92 *Estée Lauder* [1994] ECR I-317). The Court dismissed the argument of the Member State concerned (Germany) that this name gave the misleading impression that the product had therapeutic qualities.

Naturally, restrictions on the use of misleading names or labels will be justified on consumer protection grounds (Case 207/83 *Commission* v. *United Kingdom* [1985] ECR 1201 (origin marking); Case 178/84 *Commission* v. *Germany*, above; Case 298/87 *SMANOR*, above; Case C-135/92 *Estée Lauder*, above).

(*iii*) *The prevention of unfair competition.* This exception generally goes hand in hand with consumer protection: unfair competition is unlikely to arise unless there is a danger of the consumer being misled.

(*iv*) *The environment.* The protection of the environment was first recognized by the Court as a mandatory requirement in Case 302/86 *Commission* v. *Denmark* [1988] ECR 4607 (returnable bottles). In that case, the Court upheld Danish legislation requiring beer and soft beverages to be sold in reusable containers and to be made subject to a deposit. However, it found for the Commission as regards the Danish requirement that, subject to a limited exception, only containers conforming to types approved by the Danish authorities could be used; this restriction was held to be incompatible with the principle of proportionality.

In Case C-2/90 *Commission* v. *Belgium*, above (*Walloon waste*), an absolute ban on waste entering Wallonia was found to be justified on environmental grounds—save as regards material covered by Council Dir. 84/631 on the supervision and control within the European Community of the transfrontier shipment of hazardous waste (*OJ* 1984 L326/31). The paradoxical result is that the ban was upheld exclusively in relation to non-hazardous waste.

Another controversial ruling in this area was delivered in Case C-379/98 *PreussenElektra* [2001] ECR I-2099. There a scheme designed to promote the use of wind energy was upheld despite its manifestly discriminatory nature.

(*v*) *Working conditions.* In Case 155/80 *Oebel* [1981] ECR 1993, the improvement of working conditions was found to constitute a legitimate purpose of general interest, so that a ban on baking at night was compatible with Art. 28 EC. Similarly, in Case C-312/89 *Conforama* [1991] ECR I-997 and Case C-169/91 *Stoke-on-Trent* [1992] ECR I-6635, restrictions on Sunday trading were held to be justified on the same grounds.

(*vi*) *Maintaining diversity in the media.* In Case C-368/95 *Familiapress*, above, this was recognized as a new mandatory requirement. The Court found that a restriction on offering prizes in games, puzzles, or competitions in the press would be justified on these grounds, if this was necessary to protect small publishers who were unable to offer such prizes. This was for the national court to determine.

(*vii*) *Protection of fundamental rights.* In Case C-112/00 *Schmidberger*, above, the Court held that the protection of fundamental rights may itself justify restrictions on the free movement of goods, *in casu* the freedom of expression and the freedom of assembly. As A.-G. Jacobs pointed out, the right in question must be recognized as a fundamental right in Community law, not merely in national law.

(*viii*) *National or regional culture.* To judge by the case-law relating to the free provision of services (Case C-154/89 *Commission* v. *France* [1991] ECR I-649 (tourist guides)), it would seem that the protection of culture may be regarded as a mandatory requirement.

(*ix*) *Protection of social security systems.* In Case 238/82 *Duphar* [1984] ECR 523 at p. 541, the Court ruled that 'Community law does not detract from the powers of the Member States to organize their social security systems' (see also Case C-70/95 *Sodemare* [1997] ECR I-3395; Case C-120/95 *Decker*, above). Accordingly, in *Duphar* a scheme whereby excessively expensive pharmaceuticals were not covered by the social security fund was found to be lawful, provided that the following conditions were met: the exclusionary lists must be drawn up in accordance with objective criteria without reference to the origin of the products; they must be verifiable by any importer; and it must be possible to amend the lists whenever compliance with the specific criteria so required.

Curiously enough, in *Decker* the Court was more guarded about whether this aim was to be treated as a mandatory requirement at all, saying simply that it could not be 'excluded that the risk of seriously undermining the financial balance of the social security system may constitute an overriding reason in the general interest capable of justifying a barrier of that kind' (para. 39). It was not necessary to decide the point, since in any event the measure contested in the instant case—the refusal of the Luxembourg State sickness fund to grant a flat-rate sum in respect of the cost of spectacles merely because they had been purchased in other Member States without prior authorization—could not be justified on such grounds. The reason was that 'reimbursement at a flat rate of the cost of spectacles . . . purchased in other Member States has no effect on the financing or balance of the social security system' (para. 40).

(*x*) *Other possible grounds.* As already mentioned, the categories of mandatory requirement are not closed—but 'aims of a purely economic nature cannot justify a barrier to the fundamental principle of the free movement of goods' (Case C-120/95 *Decker*, above, para. 39 and Case C-203/96 *Dusseldorp*, above, para. 44). This long-standing principle has already been discussed at point III.1(*b*)(*i*) above.

The ruling in Case C-18/88 *GB-INNO-BM* [1991] ECR I-5941 at p. I-5983, which related to standards for telephone equipment, would appear to suggest that the 'protection of the public [telephone] network and its proper functioning' constitutes a mandatory requirement.

IV. Community legislation

1. Legal bases. The Council has adopted a vast body of legislation harmonizing the conditions under which goods are entitled to circulate within the Community.

The classic legal basis for such legislation is Art. 95 EC, which empowers the Council to adopt according to the procedure set out in Art. 251 EC 'the measures for the approximation of the provisions laid down by law, regulation and administrative action in Member States which have as their object the establishment and functioning of the internal market'. This provision is also stated to apply 'for the achievement of the objectives set out in Art. 14' (quoted in section I above) so that it is closely connected to the free movement of goods or the free provision of services, as the case may be (Case C-30/01 *Commission* v. *United Kingdom*, above (Gibraltar)).

Art. 95 has been interpreted widely by the Court to cover all measures designed to eliminate disparities in conditions of competition (Case C-300/89 *Commission* v. *Council* [1991] ECR I-2867 (titanium dioxide)). Community legislation that fulfils that condition and is therefore validly based on Art. 95 may also be applied to situations involving no interstate element (Case C-465/00 *Österreichischer Rundfunk* [2003] ECR I-4989).

However, in the celebrated ruling in Case C-376/98 *Germany* v. *Parliament and Council* [2000] ECR I-8419 (tobacco advertising), it was held that this provision does not 'vest in the Community legislature a general power to regulate the internal market'; legislation adopted under Art. 95 must contribute either to eliminating obstacles to the free movement of goods or to removing distortions of competition. Nor is Art. 95 the appropriate legal basis for legislation that is primarily concerned with some other purpose covered by another Treaty provision (e.g. Art. 175 in relation to the environment) (Case C-70/88 *Parliament* v. *Council* [1991] ECR I-4529).

Other provisions that may constitute the legal basis for legislation on the free movement of goods include the following:

- Art. 37 EC in relation to agriculture;
- Art. 152 EC that concerns public health. Para. 4(b) specifically provides that 'by way of derogation from Article 37, measures in the veterinary and phytosanitary fields which have as their direct objective the protection of public health' are to be enacted under this Article. However, in other respects the scope of this provision is somewhat limited, since Community action taken under it is merely intended to 'complement national policies' (para. 1). What is more, 'incentive measures designed to protect and improve public health' may not entail the 'harmonisation of the laws and regulations of the Member States' (para. 4(c)).

However, there is nothing to prevent the Community legislator from adopting more far-reaching health measures on the basis of other provisions of the Treaty;

- Art. 175 EC relating to the environment (see Case C-155/91 *Commission* v. *Council* [1993] ECR I-939 (waste); Case C-187/93 *Parliament* v. *Council* [1994] ECR I-2857 (waste); Case C-164/97 etc. *Parliament* v. *Council* [1999] ECR I-1139 (protection of forests)).

The choice of legal basis cannot depend on the whim of the institutions concerned, but must be based on objective factors which are amenable to judicial review (Case 45/86 *Commission* v. *Council* [1987] ECR 1493 (generalized tariff preferences); Case C-300/89 *Commission* v. *Council*, above; Cases C-164/97 etc. *Parliament* v. *Council*, above (protection of forests)).

2. Derogations under harmonizing legislation. A major exception to the rule that after harmonization the goods concerned may circulate freely is to be found in paras. 4 to 9 of Art. 95. In certain respects, these provisions differ markedly from the corresponding paragraphs of Art. 100a of the original EEC Treaty as they stood prior to the entry into force of the Treaty of Amsterdam. Para. 4 entitles a Member State, which 'deems it necessary to maintain national provisions on grounds of major needs referred to in Article 30, or relating to the protection of the environment or the working environment' after the adoption of a harmonizing measure, to notify the Commission of its measure as well as of its grounds for maintaining it. Para. 5 entitles a Member State to take similar action where it 'deems it necessary to introduce national provisions based on new scientific evidence relating to the protection of the environment or the working environment on grounds of a problem specific to that Member State arising after the adoption of the harmonisation measure'. The Member State is obliged to notify its measure in draft (see Case C-512/99 *Germany* v. *Commission* [2003] ECR I-845 and Case C-3/00 *Denmark* v. *Commission* [2003] ECR I-2643).

By virtue of para. 6, the Commission must then decide within six months whether to approve or reject the existing or envisaged provisions 'after having verified whether or not they are a means of arbitrary discrimination or a disguised restriction on trade between Member States and whether or not they shall constitute an obstacle to the functioning of the internal market' (see section III.1(*a*)(*iii*) and (*iv*) above).

It was held in Case C-319/97 *Kortas* [1999] ECR I-3143 that a directive having direct effect does not lose it when a Member State lodges a request for a derogation pursuant to these provisions.

Art. 176 EC should also be noted in this context, since it provides:

> The protective measures adopted pursuant to Article 175 shall not prevent any Member State from maintaining or introducing more stringent protective measures. Such measures must be compatible with this Treaty. They shall be notified to the Commission.

Plainly, the procedure laid down by this Article differs markedly from that of Art. 95 EC, especially as no provision is made for any approval or rejection by the Commission.

3. Types of harmonization. Total harmonization imposes a two-fold obligation on the Member States:

(1) to permit goods complying with the directive to be freely imported and marketed; and
(2) to prohibit the sale of goods not complying with the directive.

On the other hand, optional harmonization involves the first obligation only: each Member State is then free to allow the sale of goods not meeting the standards laid down in the directive. In that event, national norms will coexist with the Community standards. Small producers may then manufacture goods according to national norms, although this reduces the possibility of exporting their products.

By reason of its greater flexibility, optional harmonization has come to be preferred, although goods meeting the purely national standard can only circulate freely if the principles established pursuant to Art. 30 EC so permit.

4. Notification of national measures. A procedure for the provision of information in the field of technical standards and regulations was first laid down by Council Dir. 83/189 (*OJ* 1983 L109/8). That directive was amended on a number of occasions, prior to being replaced by Council Dir. 98/34 (*OJ* 1998 L204/37), a consolidating measure. That directive has in turn been amended by Council Dir. 98/48 (*OJ* 1998 L217/18).

Under Art. 8 of Dir. 98/34, each Member State is required to notify to the Commission draft technical regulations, which are then communicated to the other Member States. The regulations may not be adopted during a period of three months from the date of receipt by the Commission of the notification. Pursuant to Art. 9(3) and (4), a moratorium of twelve months shall apply where the Commission announces its intention to propose legislation on the matter or finds that an existing proposal relates to the same matter.

The Court has stressed that the aim of this scheme is to 'protect the free movement of goods, which is one of the foundations of the Community' (Case C-13/96 *Bic Benelux* [1997] ECR I-1753 at p. I-1776).

In a judgment that sent shock waves throughout the Community, the Court held that the corresponding provisions in Dir. 83/189 had direct effect so that technical regulations adopted by a Member States in breach of these Articles could not be applied to individuals (Case C-194/94 *CIA Security International* [1996] ECR I-2201). In view of the widespread failure of Member States to observe these provisions, it followed that very large numbers of such national regulations were invalid.

In the light of the far-reaching consequences of that ruling, the Court in Case C-226/97 *Lemmens* [1998] ECR I-3711 was at pains to preclude the abusive reliance on the directive, holding that 'While failure to notify technical regulations, which constitutes a defect in their adoption, renders such regulations inapplicable inasmuch as they hinder the use or marketing of a product which is not in conformity therewith, it does not have the effect of rendering unlawful any use of a product which is in conformity with regulations which have not been notified' (at pp. I-3735–6). Accordingly, where the authorities concerned had failed to notify in draft a new technical regulation for Breathalysers, the Court rejected the argument of a motorist charged with driving under the influence of alcohol that the results of a test carried out with a Breathalyser complying with the new standard must be disregarded.

The (highly complex) definition of the term 'technical regulation' is a broad one, including, *inter alia*, such instruments as 'administrative provisions, the observance of which is compulsory, *de jure* or *de facto*, in the case of marketing . . . or use in a Member State or a major part thereof' (Art. 1(11)). The Court in Case C-273/94 *Commission* v. *Netherlands* [1996] ECR I-31 ruled that even a measure that liberalizes existing national legislation may constitute a 'technical regulation'. Moreover, in Case C-13/96 *Bic Benelux*, above, the requirement that disposable razors bear a label stating that they were subject to an 'eco-tax' was likewise held to fall within the scope of this concept. In contrast, in Case C-33/97 *Bigg's Continent Noord*, above, a measure requiring labelling to be in a particular language was held not to constitute a 'technical regulation' in itself, but was found to be no more than an 'ancillary rule' necessary in order for the information on the label to be effectively communicated.

See also **Charges having equivalent effect to customs duties, Common Customs Tariff, Community Customs Code, Community customs territory, Customs procedures, Customs Union, Goods, Measures having equivalent effect to quantitative restrictions, Origin of goods, Quantitative restrictions.**

Further reading 1. BOOKS: Bermann, Goebel, Davey, and Fox, *Cases and Materials on European Union Law*, 2nd edn. (2002), ch. 13; Craig and de Búrca, *EU Law. Text, Cases, and Materials*, 3rd edn. (2003), chs. 14 and 15; Müller-Graff in *Kommentar zum EU-/ EG-Vertrag*, 6th edn. (2003), vol. I, p. 942; Oliver, *Free Movement of Goods in the European Community*, 4th edn. (2003); Vaulont in *Kommentar zum EU-/ EG-Vertrag, op. cit.*, vol. I, p. 805.

2. ARTICLES: Mortelmans, 'The Common Market, the Internal Market and the Single Market: What's in a Market?' (1998) *CML Rev.* 101; Oliver, 'Some Further Reflections on the Scope of Articles 28–30 (ex 30–36) EC' (1999) *CML Rev.* 783; Weatherill, 'Compulsory Notification of Draft Technical Regulations: the Contribution of Directive 83/189 to the Management of the Internal Market' (1996) *YEL* 129; id., 'Recent Case-Law Concerning the Free Movement of Goods: Mapping the Frontiers of Market Deregulation' (1999) *CML Rev.* 51.

▶ **FREE MOVEMENT OF PERSONS** One of the four fundamental freedoms forming the basis of the internal market (the other three being: free movement of goods, services, and capital). In the original EEC Treaty, these four freedoms appeared in Part Two under the title 'Foundations of the Community', which became Part Three of the EC Treaty entitled 'Community Policies' as a result of the amendments introduced by the Treaty on

European Union (TEU). In several cases, the ECJ has held that the object of this Part of the Treaty is 'to establish the basis of the common market, i.e. free movement of goods (Title I) and free movement of persons, services and capital (Title III)' within the Community (see Case 167/73 *Commission* v. *France* [1974] ECR 359 at p. 369; for other statements that the free movement of persons forms one of the foundations of the Community, see e.g. ibid. at p. 373; Case 139/85 *Kempf* [1986] ECR 1741 at p. 1750; Case C-292/89 *Antonissen* [1991] ECR I-745 at p. I-777).

Although the Euratom Treaty does not use the concept of basic 'freedoms' similar to those found in the EC Treaty, it does contain (more modest) provisions for facilitating the movement of persons in the specific sector to which it applies. Thus, Art. 96 of the Euratom Treaty requires the Member States to abolish all restrictions based on nationality affecting the right of nationals of any Member State to take skilled employment in the field of nuclear energy, subject to limitations justified on grounds of public policy, public security, or public health. This provision was implemented by Council Dir. of 5 March 1962 (*OJ Sp. Edn.* 1959–62, p. 245), which defines the concept of 'skilled employment' in the field of nuclear energy (Arts. 2 and 3 and the Annex) and provides for the automatic granting of authorizations required for the pursuit of such employment, on conditions not less liberal than those under the EC Treaty (Art. 4).

Since the EC Treaty is a *lex generalis* in relation to the Euratom Treaty, which is a *lex specialis*, its provisions relating to the free movement of workers and the measures adopted in implementation thereof apply to workers in the nuclear energy sector and to members of their families, in so far as their legal position is not governed by the special rules and implementing measure discussed above. Otherwise, the latter take precedence over the EC provisions and implementing measures (see Art. 305 EC; Art. 5 of the Dir. of 5 March 1962; Art. 42(1) of Reg. 1612/68 and Art. 11 of Dir. 68/360, see below). The ECSC Treaty also contained special provisions on the free movement of workers in the coal and steel industries, but that Treaty expired on 23 July 2002. This entry deals with the free movement of persons under the EC Treaty.

Freedom of movement for persons has three different aspects: economic, social, and political. Originally, it had a purely or predominantly economic significance in that it was seen as being complementary to the other freedoms, and in particular to the free movement of goods, which were necessary to establish a common market. It thus referred to or implied, primarily, an economic activity or, more precisely, an activity with an economic objective. It was a means to an end, the end being the full economic integration of the Member States. As the ECJ has put it, 'freedom of movement for persons is intended to contribute to the establishment of a common market, in which nationals of the Member States have opportunity to carry on their *economic activities* by establishing themselves or by providing services in any place within the territory of the Community' (Case 136/78 *Auer* [1979] ECR 437 at p. 448, emphasis added). It followed both from the very principle of freedom of movement for persons and from the position of the rules relating to that principle in the system of the Treaty as a whole that those rules 'guarantee only the free movement of persons *who pursue or are desirous of pursuing an economic activity*' (Case 53/81 *Levin* [1982] ECR 1035 at p. 1050, emphasis added. See further section I.2(*a*) below).

However, it has become clear that, while some of the rules and principles that are applicable to goods also apply to persons, persons cannot be equated with goods. They cannot be regarded as mere 'factors of production' or a 'source of labour' but must be viewed as human beings (see the opinions of A.-G. Trabucchi in Case 7/75 *Mr and Mrs F* [1975] ECR 679 at p. 696 and of A.-G. Jacobs in Case C-168/91 *Konstantinidis* [1993] ECR I-1191 at p. I-1205). They must be treated, not simply as instruments of integration but also (and perhaps even more so) as the beneficiaries of it. As the preamble to Reg. 1612/68 on freedom of movement for workers within the Community puts it, mobility of labour does not only serve the purpose of satisfying the requirements of the economics of the Member States, but is also 'one of the means by which the worker is guaranteed the possibility of improving his living and working conditions and promoting his *social advancement*' (third recital, emphasis added). Likewise, the 1976 action programme for migrant workers stresses the importance of the 'humanization of freedom of movement for workers' (Council Res. of 9 February 1976, *OJ* 1976 C34/2).

The social dimension of the Community and the social rights of persons (both employed and self-employed persons) have been given a more prominent place following the adoption of the Single European Act of 1986. The preamble to the Social Charter expressly states that in the context of the establishment of the single European market, 'the same importance must be attached to the social aspects as to the economic aspects' of the integration process (second recital in the preamble to the Community Charter of the Fundamental Social Rights of Workers adopted by the Heads of State or Government of the Member States, except the United Kingdom, on 9 December 1989, text in Rudden and Wyatt, *EU Treaties and Legislation*, 9th edn. (2004), p. 443). This view is supported by the case-law of the ECJ, which has consistently held that the Treaty aims at full economic *and social* integration (see e.g. Case 43/75 *Defrenne* [1976] ECR 455 at p. 472; Case 152/73 *Sotgiu* [1974] ECR 153 at p. 169 *per* A.-G. Mayras; Case 152/82 *Forcheri* [1983] ECR 2323 at p. 2335).

Apart from the economic and social aspects, the free movement of persons has acquired a wider, political importance. Already the preamble to Reg. 1612/68 states that 'freedom of movement constitutes a *fundamental right* of workers and their families' which should be exercised 'in freedom and dignity' (third and fifth recitals, emphasis added. These recitals are frequently relied on by the ECJ in interpreting and defining the scope of freedom of movement for persons). It thus refers to a right that, rather than being simply complementary to the other freedoms, can stand on its own; an objective to be achieved rather than a means of attaining a purely economic end. This idea has been further developed with the adoption of the concept of a 'People's Europe' (*see further under* **Committee on a People's Europe**

(**Adonnino Committee**)*) and with the creation of the internal market in which persons should be able to move freely whether or not in pursuit of an economic activity (see further section IV below). Thus, the free movement of persons has gradually assumed a constitutional significance going beyond the establishment of a common market. It has become the visible manifestation of an 'ever closer union among the peoples of Europe' to which the preamble to the EC Treaty refers.

This process has culminated in the Treaty on European Union (TEU), which expressly reaffirms the Member States' resolve 'to facilitate the free movement of persons' (eleventh recital in the preamble), and which has introduced the concept of the 'citizenship of the Union' (Art. 17 EC). It is now provided that 'Every citizen of the Union shall have the right to move and reside freely within the territory of the Member States . . .' (Art. 18(1) EC; see further section III below). This is nothing short of a constitutional guarantee of the freedom of movement for persons. In order to facilitate such movement, the Representatives of the Governments of the Member States decided that Member States should issue a uniform 'European Union Passport' to their nationals (Res. of 23 June 1981, *OJ* 1981 C241/1, as supplemented by Res. of 30 June 1982, *OJ* 1982 C179/1; Res. of 14 July 1986, *OJ* 1986 C185/1; Res. of 10 July 1995, *OJ* 1995 C200/1; and Res. of 17 October 2000, *OJ* 2000 C310/1).

A logical consequence of this development has been the gradual widening of the circle of 'persons' who are the beneficiaries of the right to free movement. Title III of Part Three of the EC Treaty secures freedom of movement for three categories of persons only: workers (i.e. employed persons, Arts. 39 to 42 EC), self-employed persons (under the title of 'Right of establishment', Arts. 43 to 48 EC), and persons providing services (Arts. 49 to 55 EC). As a result of the case-law of the ECJ, this latter category also includes recipients of services (Cases 286/82 etc. *Luisi and Carbone* [1984] ECR 377 at p. 403; Case 186/87 *Cowan* [1989] ECR 195 at pp. 220–1). Although basically each category is governed by a different set of rules, there are provisions that are common to workers and self-employed persons or providers of services; provisions that are common to self-employed persons and providers of services; and provisions that are common to all three categories. The latter provisions include, in particular, Art. 12 EC that prohibits discrimination on grounds of nationality 'within the scope of application of this Treaty', that is, in respect of any type of activity covered by the Treaty. They also include some of the rules relating to entry into and residence in the territory of Member States. One other feature that is common to all three categories of persons is that they are granted freedom of movement only for the purpose of carrying on an economic activity in another Member State. The above-cited Title III of Part Three of the EC Treaty does not recognize a general right of free movement available to anyone for any purpose; it only confers that right on 'economically active' persons (see further section I.2(*a*) below).

However, this situation has gradually changed over the years. For reasons explained above, new categories have been added to the original three, covering persons not engaged in any economic activity, such as persons of independent means (Dir. 90/364, *OJ* 1990 L180/26), retired persons (Dir. 90/365, *OJ* 1990 L180/28), students (Dir. 93/96, *OJ* 1993 L317/59), and 'citizens of the Union' in general (Art. 18(1) EC). These new categories will be considered in more detail below (see sections II, III, and IV).

It follows from the foregoing that in order to determine the precise legal position of a person with regard to his or her right to free movement, it is normally necessary, in the first place, to establish into which of the above categories he or she falls. However, in practice a clear-cut distinction between the three categories covered by Title III of Part Three (workers, self-employed persons, providers and recipients of services) may not always be easy or even necessary to make. One reason is that situations may arise in which the three categories interact, for example, where a person exercises or claims rights in his capacity as a self-employed person or provider of a service in one Member State, on the basis of his status or former status as a worker in another Member State (see e.g. Case 143/87 *Stanton* [1988] ECR 3877 at pp. 3894–5; Case C-106/91 *Ramrath* [1992] ECR I-3351 at pp. I-3381–3; Case C-370/90 *Singh* [1992] ECR I-4265 at pp. I-4291–5). The ECJ deals with such situations by referring generally to 'the provisions of the Treaty relating to the free movement of persons', saying that those provisions are intended:

> to facilitate the pursuit by Community citizens of occupational activities *of all kinds* throughout the Community, and preclude national legislation which might place Community citizens at a disadvantage when they wish to extend their activities beyond the territory of a single Member State (ibid. at p. 3894 (*Stanton*); p. I-3384 (*Ramrath*); p. I-4293 (*Singh*); Case C-18/95 *Terhoeve* [1999] ECR I-345 at p. I-389; emphasis added).

Therefore, once it is established that a person carries on, or intends to carry on, an economic activity in another Member State, the exact nature of the legal relationship under which such activity is carried out is in many situations without significance since Arts. 39, 43, and 49 EC afford the same legal protection and prohibit discrimination in the same terms (see e.g. Case 36/74 *Walrave* [1974] ECR 1405 at p. 1417 concerning pacemakers in cycling competitions; Case C-363/89 *Roux* [1991] ECR I-273 at p. I-293 concerning activities as a waitress; Case C-58/90 *Commission* v. *Italy* [1991] ECR I-4193 at pp. I-4201–2 concerning health-care auxiliaries; Case C-375/92 *Commission* v. *Spain* [1994] ECR I-923 at p. I-940 concerning tourist guides and guide-interpreters). As the ECJ has pointed out, a comparison of those provisions shows that they are based on the same principles both as regards entry into, residence, and the pursuit of an economic activity in the territory of the Member States by persons covered by Community law and as regards the prohibition of all discrimination against them on grounds of nationality (Case 48/75 *Royer* [1976] ECR 497 at p. 509; Case 118/75 *Watson and Belmann* [1976] ECR 1185 at pp. 1196–7; Case C-106/91 *Ramrath*, above, at pp. I-3381–2; etc., as restated in Case C-107/94 *Asscher* [1996] ECR I-3089 at pp. I-3121–2).

Nevertheless, since the particular rights that the different categories of persons enjoy under Community law differ, it is necessary to consider each category separately. Following an established division, this entry deals with workers (and certain other persons not covered by Title III of Part Three of the EC Treaty), while self-employed persons, providers and recipients of services are the subject of separate entries (*see further under* **Freedom of establishment** and **Freedom to provide services**, respectively). The position of third country nationals is also briefly discussed in this entry, irrespective of the category into which they fall (see sections I.2(*b*), IV and V below).

I. Workers

1. The legal framework. The rules of Community law governing the free movement of workers fall into three distinct categories. First, Part One of the EC Treaty lays down the fundamental principles, objectives, and tasks of the Community. These general provisions apply across the whole field of application of the Treaty and are thus relevant to the free movement of workers. Of particular importance is Art. 2, which states that the Community's tasks include, *inter alia*, the promotion of a 'harmonious . . . development of economic activities' throughout the Community; 'a high level of employment and of social protection'; 'the raising of the standard of living' and 'economic and social cohesion and solidarity' among Member States. For these purposes, Art. 3(1)(c) provides for an internal market characterized by the abolition, as between Member States, of obstacles to the free movement of goods, persons, services, and capital (i.e. the four freedoms). Art. 3(1)(d) provides for the adoption of measures concerning the entry and movement of persons. Art. 10 obliges the Member States to facilitate the achievement of the Community's tasks and to take all appropriate measures to fulfil their obligations arising from or under the Treaty.

Secondly, Chapter 1 of Title III of Part Three (Arts. 39 to 42) sets out the provisions specifically relating to workers. The most important of these is Art. 39, which states that freedom of movement for workers shall be secured within the Community (para. 1); prohibits discrimination based on nationality between workers of the Member States (para. 2); specifies four particular rights entailed by freedom of movement (para. 3); and lays down certain limitations on and exceptions to those rights (paras. 3 and 4) (see further section I.2(*a*) below). Art. 40 authorizes the Community institutions to adopt secondary legislation in the form of regulations and directives for the implementation of Art. 39. Art. 41 requires the Member States to encourage the exchange of young workers. Finally, Art. 42 enables the institutions to introduce such social security legislation as is necessary to provide freedom of movement for workers.

Thirdly, Art. 39 has been implemented by secondary legislation adopted by the Council, Parliament and the Commission. The most important pieces of this legislation currently in force are as follows:

- Council Reg. 1612/68 of 15 October 1968 on freedom of movement for workers within the Community (*OJ Sp. Edn.* 1968 (II), p. 475), as amended by Reg. 312/76 (*OJ* 1976 L39/2) and Reg. 2434/92 (*OJ* 1992 L245/1), and implemented by Comm. Dec. 93/569 (*OJ* 1993 L274/32);
- Council Dir. 68/360 of 15 October 1968 on the abolition of restrictions on movement and residence within the Community for workers of Member States and their families (*OJ Sp. Edn.* 1968 (II), p. 485);
- Comm. Reg. 1251/70 of 29 June 1970 on the right of workers to remain in the territory of a Member State after having been employed in that State (*OJ Sp. Edn.* 1970 (II), p. 402);
- Council Dir. 64/221 of 25 February 1964 on the co-ordination of special measures concerning the movement and residence of foreign nationals that are justified on grounds of public policy, public security or public health (*OJ Sp. Edn.* 1963–4, p. 117);
- Council Dir. 72/194 of 18 May 1972 extending to workers exercising the right to remain in the territory of a Member State the scope of Dir. 64/221 (*OJ Sp. Edn.* 1972 (II), p. 474);
- Dir. 2004/38 of the European Parliament and of the Council of 29 April 2004 on the right of citizens of the Union and their family members to move and reside freely within the territory of the Member States (*OJ* 2004 L158/77). The directive entered into force on 30 April 2004, and has to be implemented by the Member States by 30 April 2006. It will repeal and replace Arts. 10 and 11 of Reg. 1612/68 and Dirs. 68/360, 64/221, 72/194 and some others from that date (Arts. 38, 40, 41. *See further under* **Right of entry and residence**, section VII).

The three sets of provisions outlined above are in a hierarchical relationship to one another. This has important consequences for their interpretation and application. On top of the hierarchy are the fundamental principles, objectives, and tasks set out in Arts. 2, 3, and 12 EC, of which Art. 39 is a specific implementation with regard to workers (just as Arts. 43 and 49 implement those principles with regard to self-employed persons and providers and recipients of services, respectively). It follows that in determining the precise scope of application of Art. 39, the activities covered, the rights conferred, the prohibitions and limitations imposed by it, regard must be had, as the case may be, to Art. 2, 3, or 12 of the Treaty. Likewise, the obligation of the Member States to secure free movement arises from, and must be determined in the light of, Art. 10 (see e.g. Case 167/73 *Commission* v. *France*, above, at p. 369, referring to Art. 2; Case 36/74 *Walrave*, above, at p. 1417, referring to Arts. 2 and 12; Case 118/75 *Watson and Belmann*, above, at p. 1198, referring to Arts. 2 and 3(1)(c); Case 13/76 *Donà* [1976] ECR 1333 at pp. 1339–40, referring to Arts. 2 and 12; Case 53/81 *Levin*, above, at p. 1050, referring to Arts. 2 and 3; Case 222/86 *Heylens* [1987] ECR 4097 at pp. 4115–16, referring to Arts. 2, 3(1)(c), and 10; Case 196/87 *Steymann* [1988] ECR 6159 at p. 6172, referring to Art. 2. All of these cases will be further considered below).

In turn, the acts of secondary legislation listed above clarify and give effect to Art. 39, but cannot create new rights in favour of persons protected by Community law. The rights enjoyed by workers and other persons are conferred directly by the Treaty, while the regulations and directives only determine the scope and the detailed rules for the exercise of those rights. It follows that non-compliance with the legal formalities prescribed by the implementing regulations and directives, while capable of entailing legal consequences, in principle cannot affect the right to free movement itself, which is derived directly from the Treaty (see e.g. Case 48/75 *Royer*, above, at pp. 511–14; Case 118/75 *Watson and Belmann*, above, at p. 1197; Case 157/79 *Pieck* [1980] ECR 2171 at pp. 2183–4; Case C-419/92 *Scholz* [1994] ECR I-505 at p. I-520. See further below).

The hierarchical relationship is particularly relevant to the interpretation of Art. 39 and the implementing legislation. Since freedom of movement for workers constitutes a fundamental right and one of the foundations of the Community, that freedom must be interpreted broadly so as to achieve the basic objectives stated in Arts. 2, 3, and 12 of the Treaty, while the exceptions to and derogations from it must be given a strict interpretation. In the same way, provisions protecting Community nationals who exercise that fundamental freedom must be interpreted in their favour (see e.g. Case 152/82 *Forcheri*, above, at p. 2335; Case C-357/98 *Yiadom* [2000] ECR I-9265 at p. I-9297). These principles apply particularly to terms and concepts not defined by the above-mentioned provisions, such as 'worker' and 'activity as an employed person', which determine the sphere of application of that freedom. These terms and concepts must have an autonomous and uniform meaning throughout the Community, and must be defined in the light of the principles of the Community legal order (ibid.; see also, in particular, Case 53/81 *Levin*, above, at pp. 1048–9; Case 139/85 *Kempf*, above, at pp. 1750–1; Case 316/85 *Lebon* [1987] ECR 2811 at p. 2838; Case C-292/89 *Antonissen*, above, at p. I-777). Thus, the ECJ has expressly stated that Arts. 39 to 42 'are designed to establish the greatest possible freedom of movement for workers . . . In case of doubt [these] Articles and the measures taken in implementation of them must therefore be construed so as to avoid placing migrant workers in an unfavourable legal position' (Case 92/63 *Nonnenmacher* [1964] ECR 281 at p. 288; see also Case 44/65 *Hessische Knappschaft* [1965] ECR 965 at p. 971). Nevertheless, where a legal term in an implementing regulation is to be interpreted in the light of 'social developments', then the situation in the whole Community must be taken into account, not merely in one Member State, since such interpretation produces effects in all the Member States by virtue of the direct and general applicability of regulations. This may result in a narrow rather than broad interpretation (see Case 59/85 *Reed* [1986] ECR 1283 at p. 1300, interpreting the term 'spouse' in Art. 10 of Reg. 1612/68 as referring to a marital relationship only).

Moreover, Art. 39 and the implementing legislation must be interpreted not only in the light of the principles stated at the beginning of the EC Treaty, but also in the light of the general principles of Community law derived from the European Convention on Human Rights. Thus, in Case 36/75 *Rutili* [1975] ECR 1219 at p. 1232, in interpreting the concept of 'public policy' appearing in Dir. 64/221 and Reg. 1612/68, the Court referred to the general principle enshrined in Arts. 8, 9, 10, and 11 ECHR and in Art. 2 of the Fourth Protocol, that in the interests of national security or public safety, Member States may impose on the rights secured by those provisions only such restrictions as are necessary for the protection of those interests 'in a democratic society'. In Case 249/86 *Commission* v. *Germany* [1989] ECR 1263 at p. 1290, the Court interpreted Reg. 1612/68 in the light of the requirement of respect for family life set out in Art. 8 ECHR. In Case 222/86 *Heylens*, above, at p. 4117, the Court relied on Arts. 6 and 13 ECHR in support of a right to an effective judicial remedy before the national courts against any decision of a national authority refusing the benefit of free access to employment to a Community worker (see also Cases C-297/88 etc. *Dzodzi* [1990] ECR I-3763 at p. I-3800, where the Court interpreted Art. 9 of Dir. 64/221 in the light of Art. 6 ECHR and Art. 14 of the International Covenant on Civil and Political Rights of 1966).

Finally, it should be noted that the ECJ has interpreted Art. 39, Reg. 1612/68, and certain provisions of Dir. 64/221 as producing direct effect in the sense of conferring on individuals rights which they can enforce in the nationals courts. By virtue of the supremacy of Community law, these provisions take precedence over any national rules which are incompatible with them (Case 167/73 *Commission* v. *France*, above, at p. 371; Case C-19/92 *Kraus* [1993] ECR I-1663 at p. I-1696; Case 41/74 *Van Duyn* [1974] ECR 1337 at pp. 1346–7, 1349; Case 36/75 *Rutili*, above, at p. 1229; Case 118/75 *Watson and Belmann*, above, at pp. 1197–8; Case 13/76 *Donà*, above, at p. 1341; see also Case C-3/87 *Agegate* [1989] ECR 4459 at p. 4507 interpreting Arts. 55, 56, and 215, 216 of the Act of Accession of 1985, which laid down transitional provisions for the application of Art. 39 and Reg. 1612/68 to Spain and Portugal, respectively).

2. Scope of application. The scope of application of Art. 39 and of the secondary legislation implementing it may be determined from a material, personal, territorial, and temporal point of view. These are considered in turn below.

(*a*) ***Material scope.*** Broadly speaking, the material scope of Art. 39 is determined by two fundamental principles of Community law which Art. 39 is designed to implement with regard to workers: the principles of freedom of movement within the Community and of the prohibition of discrimination or equality of treatment with nationals (see e.g. Case 152/73 *Sotgiu*, above, at p. 162; Case 36/75 *Rutili*, above, at p. 1231). The first of these principles, freedom of movement, entails four particular rights, which are listed in Art. 39(3). These are as follows:

- the right to accept offers of employment actually made;
- the right to move freely within the territory of Member States for this purpose;

- the right to stay in a Member State for the purpose of employment in accordance with the legal provisions governing the employment of nationals of that State; and
- the right to remain in the territory of a Member State after having been employed in that State.

While these rules are primarily intended to secure the benefit of national treatment in the host Member State, in a number of cases the ECJ has held that they also preclude the Member State of origin from obstructing the freedom of its nationals to accept and pursue employment in another Member State. Therefore, in addition to the rights listed above, workers also have the right, which they derive directly from the Treaty, to leave their country of origin in order to pursue an economic activity in another Member State. Provisions that preclude or deter a worker from leaving his country of origin for that purpose constitute an obstacle to freedom of movement, even if they apply without regard to the nationality of the worker concerned. Such provisions are prohibited by Art. 39. They include the following:

- rules laid down by sporting associations that provide that a professional footballer may not be employed by a club of another Member State unless that club has paid to his former club a transfer fee. Such rules directly affect players' access to the employment market in other Member States and are thus capable of impeding freedom of movement for workers (Case C-415/93 *Bosman* [1995] ECR I-4921 at pp. I-5068–73);
- rules of sporting associations that prohibit a basketball club from fielding players from other Member States in championship matches if the players have been transferred after a specified date which is earlier than the date which applies to transfers from non-member countries, unless the rules are justified by objective reasons (Case C-176/96 *Lehtonen and Castors Braine* [2000] ECR I-2681 at pp. I-2732–5);
- national legislation relating to social security contributions that disadvantages workers who move to work in another Member State (Case C-18/95 *Terhoeve*, above, at pp. I-389–90; Case C-302/98 *Sehrer* [2000] ECR I-4585 at pp. I-4615–16);
- tax disadvantages suffered as a result of the worker taking up paid employment in another Member State (Case C-385/00 *De Groot* [2002] ECR I-11819, paras. 78–95; Case C-209/01 *Schilling* [2003] ECR I-0000, paras. 25–37);
- refusal to recognize periods of service completed in another Member State for the purposes of calculating a special length-of-service increment (Case C-224/01 *Köbler* [2003] ECR I-10239, paras. 70–6);
- measures that have the effect of preventing a migrant worker from benefiting from certain advantages provided by the employer, such as the use of a vehicle (Case C-232/01 *Van Lent* [2003] ECR I-11525, paras. 15–25).

By contrast, national provisions that deny a worker entitlement to compensation on termination of employment if he terminates his contract of employment himself in order to take up employment in another Member State are not contrary to Art. 39 (Case C-190/98 *Graf* [2000] ECR I-493 at pp. I-523–4).

In summary, it may thus be said that under Art. 39 freedom of movement entails, apart from the right to be employed, the right of entry and residence, the right to leave, and the right to remain.

According to a strict interpretation of Art. 39, workers are granted the right to move freely within the territory of Member States only for the purpose of accepting offers of employment actually made, and the right to stay in a Member State is granted only for the purpose of employment. The right to move and stay in order to *seek* employment is not expressly recognized. However, in Case C-292/89 *Antonissen*, above, at pp. I-776–9, the ECJ rejected such a narrow interpretation on the grounds that it would jeopardize the chances of workers to find employment in another Member State and, as a result, would make Art. 39 ineffective. The Court held that the list in Art. 39(3) is non-exhaustive, and that freedom of movement also entails the right to move freely within the territory of other Member States and to stay there for a 'reasonable time' for the purposes of seeking employment. A period of six months is generally not unreasonable, but after the expiry of that period the person concerned may be required to leave the territory if he has not found employment, unless he provides evidence that he is continuing to seek employment and that he has genuine chances of being engaged. Member States therefore cannot automatically require such persons to leave the national territory after the expiry of the 'reasonable period' (Case C-344/95 *Commission* v. *Belgium* [1997] ECR I-1035 at p. I-1053. See also Case 48/75 *Royer*, above, at p. 512, and Case C-171/91 *Tsiotras* [1993] ECR I-2925 at pp. I-2956–7).

Being one of the foundations of the common market, freedom of movement for workers encompasses the whole of the economic activities in the Community, including all modes of transport (inland, sea, and air transport, see Case 167/73 *Commission* v. *France*, above, at pp. 369–71). Likewise, while in the absence of harmonization at Community level Member Sates retain the power to organize their social security schemes, they must nevertheless comply with Community law when exercising that power. Thus, the fact that national rules concern the financing of social security does not exclude the application of Treaty rules, in particular those relating to freedom of movement for workers (Case C-18/95 *Terhoeve*, above, at p. I-388; Case C-302/98 *Sehrer*, above, at pp. I-4613–14). Therefore, when applying domestic law on social security, national courts must interpret it in the light of the aims of Arts. 39 to 42 EC and, as far as possible, in such a way as to avoid discouraging migrant workers from exercising their right to free movement. Certainly, the aims of those Articles would not be met if, through exercising their right to free movement, migrant workers were to lose social security advantages guaranteed to them by the laws of a Member State. This would constitute a barrier to the freedom enshrined in Art. 39.

Where application of domestic law in accordance with the requirements of Community law is not possible, the national courts must fully apply Community law and protect the rights conferred by it on individuals, if necessary disapplying any incompatible provision of domestic law (Case C-165/91 *Van Munster* [1994] ECR I-4661 at pp. I-4696–8; Case C-262/97 *Engelbrecht* [2000] ECR I-7321 at pp. I-7358, I-7361–3; Case C-135/99 *Elsen* [2000] ECR I-10409 at pp. I-10435–6. *See further under* **Social security**).

The second principle underlying Art. 39, equality of treatment, entails the abolition of any discrimination based on nationality between workers of the Member States as regards employment, remuneration, and other conditions of work and employment (Art. 39(2)).

The particular rights covered by Art. 39 will be considered in more detail below, following the structure of implementing Reg. 1612/68 (see sections I.3 to I.5). Rights that are common to workers, self-employed persons, providers and recipients of services are the subject of separate entries (*see further under* **Expulsion, Residence permit, Right of entry and residence, Right to leave, Right to remain**).

The material scope of application of Art. 39 and of the implementing legislation is subject to various limitations, exceptions, and derogations. These may be summarized as follows.

In the first place, the only basis for the various rights deriving from Art. 39, Reg. 1612/68, and the other implementing measures is a (present, past, or intended future) employment relationship (Case 197/86 *Brown* [1988] ECR 3205 at p. 3245; see also Case 48/75 *Royer*, above, at p. 512), although the employer need not be an undertaking (Case C-415/93 *Bosman*, above, at p. I-5063, where the employer was a football club). A purely hypothetical prospect of employment in another Member State is not sufficient (Case 180/83 *Moser* [1984] ECR 2539 at p. 2547). It follows that a person who is not and has never been employed in another Member State, has not received any offer of employment, and cannot be said to be looking for employment or to have a genuine chance of finding one after the expiry of a reasonable period (six months), cannot benefit from any of the rights connected with the freedom of movement for workers (Case C-171/91 *Tsiotras*, above, at pp. I-2956–8).

Secondly, as already mentioned, freedom of movement under Art. 39 applies only to persons who pursue or intend to pursue an economic activity (Case 53/81 *Levin*, above, at p. 1050; see also Case C-363/89 *Roux*, above, at p. I-290. The position is different under Art. 18(1) EC, which applies to citizens of the Union, see section III below). Thus, the ECJ has held that, having regard to the objectives of the Community, the practice of sport is subject to Community law only in so far as it constitutes an economic activity within the meaning of Art. 2 EC. Generally, an economic activity is one which has the character of gainful employment or remunerated service. Therefore, remunerated professional or semi-professional sportsmen (e.g. motor-cyclists and cyclists, footballers, basketball players) who are nationals of a Member State benefit in all the other Member States from the provisions of Community law concerning freedom of movement for persons or provision of services, including the prohibition of discrimination. Nevertheless, these provisions do not prevent the exclusion of foreign players from sport teams, in particular national teams, the formation of which is a question of purely sporting interest and as such has nothing to do with economic activity (Case 36/74 *Walrave*, above, at pp. 1417–18; Case 13/76 *Donà*, above, at p. 1340; Case C-415/93 *Bosman*, above, at pp. I-5063–4, I-5076; Case C-176/96 *Lehtonen and Castors Braine*, above, at pp. I-2730–2). Also, activities performed by members of a religious community as part of the community's commercial activities constitute economic activities, and therefore fall within the field of application of Community law, in so far as the services which the community provides to its members (taking care of their material needs, provision of pocket-money, etc., irrespective of the nature and extent of the work which they do) may be regarded as the indirect quid pro quo for genuine and effective work (Case 196/87 *Steymann*, above, at pp. 6172–3).

Thirdly, the provisions of the Treaty and secondary legislation on freedom of movement for workers cannot be applied to situations that are wholly internal to a Member State, in other words, where there is no factor connecting them to any of the situations envisaged by Community law. This follows from the very objective of Art. 39, which is to ensure the free movement of workers *within the common market*, that is to say, their movement *from one Member State to (and within) another*, and to prohibit discrimination against the nationals of *other* Member States. Consequently, Art. 39 does not preclude Member States from imposing restrictions, within their own territory, on the freedom of movement of their own nationals in implementation of their own domestic (criminal) law, on account of acts committed within the national territory, nor from discriminating against their own nationals. This is a purely domestic situation which falls outside the scope of the rules of Community law on freedom of movement for workers (Case 175/78 *Saunders* [1979] ECR 1129 at p. 1135; for a contrary view, see the opinion of A.-G. Warner, ibid. at p. 1143). It follows, generally, that a worker who has never resided or worked in another Member State in exercise of the right to free movement under Community law, cannot rely on Art. 39 and the implementing measures in order to prevent the application to him of the (for him unfavourable) legislation of his own country or to obtain a benefit from a (for him favourable) provision of Community law (see Cases 35/82 etc. *Morson and Jhanjan* [1982] ECR 3723 at p. 3736; Case 180/83 *Moser*, above, at pp. 2547–8; Case 298/84 *Iorio* [1986] ECR 247 at p. 255; Cases C-297/88 etc. *Dzodzi*, above, at pp. I-3791–2; Case C-299/95 *Kremzow* [1997] ECR I-2629 at p. I-2645; Cases C–64/96 etc. *Uecker and Jacquet* [1997] ECR I-3171 at pp. I-3189–90; etc.).

Conversely, a Community national who, irrespective of his place of residence and his nationality, has exercised the right to freedom of movement for workers and who is or has been employed in another Member State, falls within the scope of Art. 39, and enjoys the protection of Community law, even against the legislation of his own country. Thus, in Case C-370/90 *Singh*, above, at pp. I-4294–5, the Indian husband of a British national who, having been employed in Germany, returned to the United Kingdom as a self-employed person, could invoke his Community law right as a spouse to enter and reside in the United Kingdom. Similarly, in Case C-419/92 *Scholz*, above, at pp. I-521–2, an Italian national of German origin who had previously been employed in Germany could, on that basis, rely on the Community rule against discrimination when applying for a post in Italy. In Case C-336/96 *Gilly* [1998] ECR I-2793 at pp. I-2832–3, a German national who acquired French nationality by her marriage and who was working in Germany whilst residing in France, could rely on Art. 39 against France even although she retained her German nationality and was working in her State of origin. In Case C-18/95 *Terhoeve*, above, at p. I-386, a Netherlands national could invoke Art. 39 and Reg. 1612/68 against the Netherlands on the grounds that he was placed at a disadvantage because he worked in another Member State (see also Case C-302/98 *Sehrer*, above, at p. I-4614; Case C-385/00 *De Groot*, above, para. 80; Case C-209/01 *Schilling*, above, para. 27). This principle has been applied by the ECJ in a variety of situations, and has particularly important consequences for the right of entry and residence, the right to remain, and the Community law concept of discrimination. It is further discussed in those contexts (see the relevant entries and sections I.4 and I.5 below).

Fourthly, according to the express provisions of Art. 39(3), the rights listed in that paragraph (see above) are subject to limitations justified on grounds of public policy, public security or public health, and pursuant to Art. 39(4), Art. 39 does not apply to employment in the public service. These limitations are considered under separate entries (*see further under* **Public health, Public policy, Public security, Public service**).

Fifthly, in view of the special nature of certain professional activities, Member States retain the right to impose specific requirements (restrictions) on migrant workers in accordance with their rules governing such activities. However, the ECJ has emphasized that any measure that is likely to constitute an obstacle to freedom of movement for workers can be accepted only if it pursues a legitimate aim compatible with the Treaty; is objectively justified by pressing reasons of public interest; is applied in a non-discriminatory manner; is suitable for achieving the aim in question; and does not go beyond what is necessary for that purpose (see e.g. Case C-106/91 *Ramrath*, above, at pp. I-3384–5; Case C-415/93 *Bosman*, above, at p. I-5071; Case C-224/01 *Köbler*, above, para. 77. See further section I.3 below).

Sixthly, since the right of entry and residence is always connected with the concept of nationality, there is a residue of restrictions, other than those justified on grounds of public policy, public security, and public health, which apply to migrant workers even although they do not apply to workers of the host State. As A.-G. Trabucchi pointed out in Case 118/75 *Watson and Belmann*, above, at p. 1210, 'so long as there is no Community nationality, nationals of other Member States will always have a different status from that of a national of the State concerned even where he enjoys the right of free movement and residence on conditions of parity with such a national'. Thus, for example, foreign nationals may be subject to various control measures that do not apply to the nationals of the host State, such as the duty to report their presence to the authorities. In the above-cited case, the ECJ held that by creating the principle of freedom of movement for persons, involving the right of access to the territory of the Member States, Community law has not excluded the power of Member States to adopt control measures enabling the national authorities to have an exact knowledge of population movements affecting their territory. As long as such measures do not restrict freedom of movement itself and the right of persons protected by Community law to enter and reside in the territory of the Member States, the application of those measures, where it is based upon objective factors, cannot constitute 'discrimination on grounds of nationality' prohibited by Art. 12 EC (ibid. at pp. 1198–9. *See further under* **Expulsion, Right of entry and residence**).

(*b*) ***Personal scope.*** The personal scope of application of Art. 39 is determined by three interrelated concepts. First, Art. 39(1) itself secures freedom of movement for 'workers'. Secondly, Art. 1(1) of Reg. 1612/68 provides that 'any national of a Member State' shall have the right to take up an activity as an 'employed person' within the territory of another Member State. Also, Art. 47 of Reg. 1612/68 expressly provides that, subject to certain exceptions mainly related to workers' families, the regulation applies to the 'nationals' of the Member States. Thirdly, Arts. 10 to 12 of Reg. 1612/68 grant certain rights to members of workers' families even if they are not nationals of any Member State. Therefore, to fall within the scope of Art. 39, a person must be a 'worker' who is a 'national of a Member State', or a member of his family. (It may be noted that, unlike Arts. 43 and 49, which expressly refer to 'nationals of Member States' in the context of the right of establishment and freedom to provide services, Art. 39 itself does not lay down a nationality requirement. It only mentions 'workers' and 'workers of the Member States'. It is, however, accepted both in secondary legislation and in the Court's case-law that the workers to whom it refers must be nationals of the Member States.)

The concept of 'worker' or 'employed person' is not defined by Art. 39 or the implementing legislation (except for the purposes of social security, see Art. 1(a) of Reg. 1408/71, *OJ Sp. Edn.* 1971 (II), p. 416, as amended, *see further under* **Social security**). However, in a series of cases the ECJ has held that these terms have a Community meaning and must be defined in the light of the principles of the legal order of the Community (see e.g. Case 53/81 *Levin*, above, at p. 1049). Having an autonomous meaning, these concepts are dealt with in a separate entry (*see further under* **Worker**).

The concept of 'national of a Member State' is not defined either. In contrast with the term 'worker', 'nationality' is not a Community law concept since the Community as such does not have its own nationals. 'Citizenship of the Union', introduced by the TEU, is not a genuine citizenship or nationality as it is based on the nationality of a Member State (Art. 17(1) EC; see further section III below). In accordance with the rules of international law, the definition of the conditions governing the acquisition and loss of nationality by individuals falls within the competence of each Member State (see Case C-369/90 *Micheletti* [1992] ECR I-4239 at p. I-4262). A 'Declaration on Nationality of a Member State' annexed to the TEU accordingly states that wherever in the EC Treaty reference is made to nationals of the Member States, the question whether an individual possesses such nationality must be determined solely by reference to the national law of the Member State concerned. Member States may declare, for information, who are to be considered their nationals for Community purposes by way of a declaration lodged with the Presidency, and may amend any such declarations when necessary. Declarations of this kind must be taken into account for the purpose of determining the personal scope of the Treaty (see Case C-192/99 *Kaur* [2001] ECR I-1237 at pp. I-1265–7, interpreting the 1972 and 1982 Declarations whereby the United Kingdom defined the categories of persons who were to be regarded as its nationals for the purposes of Community law). It follows, therefore, that expressions such as 'Community nationals' or 'Community citizens' (as opposed to 'citizens of the Union'), often used in the case-law and academic writing, in fact mean nationals or citizens of the Member States of the Community. (On the question of nationality, *see also under* **Freedom of establishment**, section II. For the position of third country nationals, see section V below.)

Finally, as regards workers' families, those family members who, irrespective of their nationality, may enjoy rights under Art. 39 are defined in Arts. 10 to 12 of Reg. 1612/68 (see section I.5 below).

While the rights listed in Art. 39 are directly granted to workers and their families, the ECJ has held that employers may also rely on Art. 39 in order to employ, in the Member State in which they are established, workers who are nationals of other Member States. Otherwise, the Member States could easily circumvent the provisions of Art. 39 by imposing on employers restrictions which, if imposed directly on workers, would be contrary to Art. 39 (e.g. that an employer may appoint as manager only a person who is resident in the national territory, which constitutes indirect discrimination based on nationality, see section I.4(*c*) below) (Case C-350/96 *Clean Car Autoservice* [1998] ECR I-2521 at pp. I-2544–6).

(*c*) ***Territorial scope.*** Art. 39(1) provides that freedom of movement for workers shall be secured 'within the Community'. Art. 47 of Reg. 1612/68 stipulates that the regulation applies to the 'territories of the Member States'. This general rule must be understood in the light of Art. 299 EC and related provisions, which define the territorial scope of application of the EC Treaty. Regulations and other acts adopted by the institutions on the basis of the Treaty apply in principle to the same geographical area as the Treaty itself (Case C-214/94 *Boukhalfa* [1996] ECR I-2253 at p. I-2277). It follows from these provisions that the rules on freedom of movement for workers apply to:

- the territories of the Member States (Art. 299(1) as amended by Art. 19 of the Act of Accession of 2003; the rules apply to the whole of the national territory, not to any internal subdivision, see Case 36/75 *Rutili*, above, at p. 1234);

- the French overseas departments, the Azores, Madeira, and the Canary Islands, subject to specific measures to be adopted by the Council (Art. 299(2));
- the European territories for whose external relations a Member State is responsible (Art. 299(4); these include Gibraltar); and
- the Åland Islands, subject to Protocol No. 2 annexed to the Act of Accession of 1994 (Art. 299(5)).

On the other hand, those rules do not apply to:

- the overseas countries and territories (OCTs) originally listed in Annex IV to the EEC Treaty and currently listed in Annex II to the EC Treaty and in Annex I A to Council Dec. 2001/822 of 27 November 2001 on the association of the OCTs with the EC (*OJ* 2001 L314/1), which list is slightly different from the list contained in Annex II. OCTs are non-European countries and territories which have special relations with some of the Member States and to which special arrangements for association apply under Part Four (Arts. 182 to 188) of the Treaty (see Art. 299(3) in conjunction with Art. 186, which provides that freedom of movement for workers between the Member States and the OCTs is subject to the conclusion of agreements, but no such agreements have been concluded, see Cases C-100/89 etc. *Kaefer and Procacci* [1990] ECR I-4647 at p. I-4671);
- the Faeroe Islands (Art. 299(6)(a));
- the Sovereign Base Areas of the United Kingdom in Cyprus (Art. 299(6)(b));
- the Channel Islands and the Isle of Man (Art. 299(6)(c) in conjunction with Protocol No. 3 annexed to the Act of Accession of 1972, in particular Arts. 2 and 4 thereof, as interpreted by the ECJ in Case C-355/89 *Barr and Montrose Holdings* [1991] ECR I-3479 at pp. I-3502–4, see also the opinion of A.-G. Jacobs, ibid. at p. I-3494; and in Case C-171/96 *Pereira Roque* [1998] ECR I-4607); and
- Greenland (which withdrew from the Community in 1984 and now has the status of an OCT, see Art. 188).

Nevertheless, the scope of application of the rules on the free movement of workers is not restricted to activities that are carried out wholly within the territories of the Member States as defined above. Thus, in Case 36/74 *Walrave*, above, at p. 1420, the ECJ held that the rule on non-discrimination laid down in Arts. 12 and 39(2) EC and Reg. 1612/68 applies to all legal relationships which 'by reason either of the place where they are entered into or of the place where they take effect, can be located within the territory of the Community'. The Court indicated (although did not actually decide) that the rule on non-discrimination might be applied to legal relationships established in the context of the activities of an international sporting federation comprising many countries in addition to the Member States. Relying upon this decision, in Case 237/83 *Prodest* [1984] ECR 3153 at p. 3162, the Court ruled that activities temporarily carried on outside the territory of the Community do not exclude the application of the principle of non-discrimination as long as the employment relationship retains a sufficiently close link with that territory. That is the case where a national of a Member State who is employed by a company established in another Member State and is insured under the social security scheme of that State, is assigned to a temporary posting outside the Community while continuing to work on behalf of his employer. During this period of assignment, he is fully protected by the rules of Community law on non-discrimination. Generally, therefore, it may be said that a person pursuing occupational activities partially or temporarily outside the territory of the Community retains the status of worker employed in the territory of a Member State if the legal relationship of employment can be located within the territory of the Community or retains a sufficiently close link with that territory. That connection criterion also applies in the case of a national of a Member State who is permanently employed on board a ship flying the flag of another Member State (Case 9/88 *Lopes da Veiga* [1989] ECR 2989 at pp. 3009–10).

In Case C-214/94 *Boukhalfa*, above, at pp. I-2277–9, the Court again confirmed that Art. 299 EC, which defines the geographical application of the Treaty, does not preclude Community rules from having effects outside the territory of the Community. Thus, provisions of Community law may apply to professional activities pursued outside Community territory as long as the employment relationship retains a sufficiently close link with the Community or with the law of a Member State and thus with the relevant rules of Community law. The Court held that the prohibition of discrimination on grounds of nationality applied to a national of a Member State who was employed by another Member State in its embassy in a third country and whose contract of employment was governed by the legislation of the employing Member State.

(d) Temporal scope. Pursuant to Art. 48(1) of the original EEC Treaty [now Art. 39(1)], freedom of movement for workers was to be secured by the end of the transitional period at the latest, i.e. by 31 December 1969. However, with a view to ensuring the simultaneous completion of the main foundations of the Community, it was decided to bring this date forward so as to follow closely the establishment of the Customs Union on 1 July 1968, eighteen months earlier than required by the Treaty. For this purpose, Reg. 1612/68, which set up the definitive regime for the free movement of workers, was adopted on 15 October 1968 and entered into force for the six original Member States on the twentieth day after its publication on 19 October 1968. It replaced two earlier regulations, which implemented the first two stages of this process (Reg. 15, *JO* 1961, p. 1073 and Reg. 38/64, *JO* 1964, p. 965; see the second recital and Art. 48 of Reg. 1612/68).

With regard to Denmark, Ireland, and the United Kingdom, Art. 39 and the various implementing measures entered into force immediately upon their accession to the Community on 1 January 1973, there being no transitional provisions in this respect in the Act of Accession of 1972 (see Case

11/77 *Patrick* [1977] ECR 1199 at p. 1205, dealing with Art. 43, which was in the same position as Art. 39).

With regard to Greece, the application of the rules on the free movement of workers was subject to the transitional provisions laid down in Arts. 44 to 47 of the Act of Accession of 1979. According to Art. 45, Arts. 1 to 6 and 13 to 23 of Reg. 1612/68 (but not Art. 39 EC itself) became applicable only as from 1 January 1988, and Art. 11 only as from 1 January 1986 (for the interpretation of these provisions, see Case 77/82 *Peskeloglou* [1983] ECR 1085 at pp. 1093–5; Case 305/87 *Commission* v. *Greece* [1989] ECR 1461 at pp. 1477–8; Case C-171/91 *Tsiotras*, above, at p. I-2957).

With regard to Spain and Portugal, the application of the rules on the free movement of workers was also subject to transitional provisions, which were set out in Arts. 55 to 59 (Spain) and Arts. 215 to 219 (Portugal) of the Act of Accession of 1985. According to Arts. 56(1) and 216(1), as amended by Council Reg. 2194/91 (*OJ* 1991 L206/1), Arts. 1 to 6 of Reg. 1612/68 became applicable only as from 1 January 1992, and according to Arts. 57 and 217, Art. 11 of Reg. 1612/68 applied until 31 December 1990 under the special conditions laid down in those Articles (for the interpretation of these provisions, see Case C-3/87 *Agegate*, above, at pp. 4504–6 (Spain); Case 9/88 *Lopes da Veiga*, above, at pp. 3008–11; and Case C-113/89 *Rush Portuguesa* [1990] ECR I-1417 at pp. I-1443–5 (Portugal)).

As regards Austria, Finland, and Sweden, the only transitional measure concerning the free movement of persons was that these countries were allowed to maintain their existing legislation regarding secondary residences for five years from the date of accession (see Arts. 70, 87, and 114 of the Act of Accession of 1994. Denmark obtained a similar derogation, but on a permanent basis, in Protocol No. 1 to the TEU). Otherwise, the rules on the free movement of persons entered into force immediately upon their accession to the Community on 1 January 1995 (see Case C-195/98 *Österreichischer Gewerkschaftsbund* [2000] ECR I-10497 at p. I-10552). It may be noted, however, that all four Treaties of Accession contain Joint Declarations on the free movement of workers intended to deal with any special difficulties arising in this area, in accordance with the provisions of the Treaties and the relevant secondary legislation.

As regards the accession of the Czech Republic, Estonia, Cyprus, Latvia, Lithuania, Hungary, Malta, Poland, Slovenia, and Slovakia, the free movement of workers is subject to transitional provisions set out, separately in respect of each new Member State, in Annexes V to XIV to the Act of Accession of 2003 (see Art. 24 of the Act, *OJ* 2003 L236/1). Broadly speaking, until the end of the two-year period following the date of accession (1 May 2004), the fifteen old Member States may apply national measures or those resulting from bilateral agreements regulating access to their labour markets by nationals of the new Member States, with the exception of Cyprus and Malta whose nationals are not subject to restrictions. The fifteen Member Sates may continue to apply such measures until the end of the five-year period following the date of accession. Before the end of the two-year period, the Council is to review the functioning of the transitional provisions on the basis of a report from the Commission. A Member State maintaining national measures or those resulting from bilateral agreements at the end of the five-year period may, in case of serious disturbances of its labour market and after notifying the Commission, continue to apply those measures until the end of the seven-year period following the date of accession. Thus, complete freedom of movement for workers from the new Member States will be achieved only from 1 May 2011. While there are no automatic restrictions on the free movement of workers from the fifteen Member States to the new Member States, where the former have applied transitional measures, the latter may maintain in force equivalent measures. There are separate provisions for nationals of new Member States legally working in an old Member State at the date of accession, as well as for their family members. During the seven-year period following the date of accession, a Member State that is not applying transitional measures may request the Commission to authorize safeguard measures when it experiences serious disturbances on its labour market.

3. **Eligibility for employment.** The right of access to employment in another Member State is the most important aspect, indeed the raison d'être, of freedom of movement for workers. This right is directly conferred on workers by Art. 39(3) EC (see section I.2(*a*) above), but is defined in more detail and given effect by Arts. 1 to 6 of Reg. 1612/68 (see Case C-419/92 *Scholz*, above, at p. I-520). Art. 1 of Reg. 1612/68 lays down the basic principle as follows:

> 1. Any national of a Member State shall, irrespective of his place of residence, have the right to take up an activity as an employed person, and to pursue such activity, within the territory of another Member State in accordance with the provisions laid down by law, regulation or administrative action governing the employment of nationals of that State.
>
> 2. He shall, in particular, have the right to take up available employment in the territory of another Member State with the same priority as nationals of that State.

The effect of this provision is that, subject to the derogations laid down in Art. 39, a Member State cannot limit an activity as an employed person to its own nationals alone without infringing Community law (Case 13/76 *Donà*, above, at p. 1340; Case C-114/97 *Commission* v. *Spain* [1998] ECR I-6717 at pp. I-6741, I-6745, where a Spanish law which precluded nationals of other Member States from carrying on private security activities in Spain as employed persons was found to be contrary to Art. 39; see further section I.4 below). Access to employment in another Member State includes access to temporary and part-time employment, and cannot be refused on the grounds that the person concerned is already employed, and continues to be employed, in his country of origin (Case C-106/91 *Ramrath*, above, at p. I-3383).

It follows from the above provision that workers moving to another Member State for the purpose of employment are subject to the same rules regarding access to and pursuit of their occupation as the nationals of the host State. Thus, where access to and pursuit of an occupation or profession are governed by special rules, such as the rules relating to the medical, dental, veterinary, legal, etc. professions, the migrant worker must meet two requirements. First, he must possess the qualifications and diplomas necessary for the pursuit of that profession in accordance with the legislation of the host Member State. Secondly, he must comply with the specific rules governing the pursuit of the profession in question, such as the rules relating to professional conduct and practice, permanent infrastructure for the performance of work, actual presence in that Member State, supervision, liability, etc. In principle, these rules must be the same for the migrant worker and for the host State's own nationals (Case 131/85 *Gül* [1986] ECR 1573 at pp. 1588–93 dealing with doctors; Case 96/85 *Commission* v. *France* [1986] ECR 1475 at p. 1485 dealing with doctors and dentists; Case C-106/91 *Ramrath*, above, at pp. I-3383–6, dealing with auditors). Where the migrant worker continues to carry on his employment in his country of origin where he already satisfies the relevant professional rules, the considerations which the ECJ has developed in respect of self-employed persons and persons providing services will apply to him (ibid.; Case 143/87 *Stanton*, above, at p. 3894. *See further under* **Freedom of establishment**, section IV.3, **Freedom to provide services**, section V).

Where the conditions of access to a particular occupation have not yet been harmonized at the Community level, the Member States are entitled to lay down the qualifications needed to pursue that occupation and to require the production of a diploma certifying that the holder is in possession of those qualifications. In the case of a diploma obtained in another Member State, the authorities of the host State are required to assess, on an objective basis, whether it is equivalent to that prescribed, and to provide an effective judicial remedy against a final decision refusing to recognize equivalence (Case 222/86 *Heylens*, above, at pp. 4116–18; Case C-340/89 *Vlassopoulou* [1991] ECR I-2357 at pp. I-2382–5; Case C-58/90 *Commission* v. *Italy*, above, at p. I-4202; Case C-375/92 *Commission* v. *Spain*, above, at pp. I-940–2; *see further under* **Freedom of establishment**, section IV.2).

The power of the Member States to impose their own occupational and professional rules on migrant workers is, however, not unlimited. Thus, the ECJ has held that in so far as those rules have the effect of restricting freedom of movement for workers (or the right of establishment or the freedom to provide services), they are compatible with the Treaty only if the restrictions which they entail are justified by the need to ensure the proper practice of the professions in question and apply to nationals and non-nationals alike. That is not the case where the restrictions create discrimination against practitioners employed or established in other Member States or raise obstacles to access to the professions, which go beyond what is necessary in order to achieve the intended objectives. Accordingly, the Court found that the so-called 'single-surgery rule', whereby practitioners (doctors, dentists, veterinary surgeons) could have only one practice and consequently practitioners established in another Member State or working as employed persons there were prevented from establishing themselves in

France and Luxembourg or working there as employed persons while retaining their practice or employment in the other Member State, was unduly restrictive, discriminatory against foreign practitioners, and too absolute and general in nature to be objectively justified on public health grounds. It was therefore contrary to the rules on freedom of movement for persons (Case 96/85 *Commission* v. *France*, above, at pp. 1485–7; Case C-351/90 *Commission* v. *Luxembourg* [1992] ECR I-3945 at pp. I-3962–4; see also Case C-162/99 *Commission* v. *Italy* [2001] ECR I-541 at p. I-566, where Italian rules required dentists to reside in the district of their professional association, which prevented foreign dentists from setting up a second surgery in Italy).

The exercise in practice of the right of access to employment, guaranteed by Art. 1 of Reg. 1612/68, is facilitated in a number of ways by the regulation. Thus, Art. 2 provides that any national and any employer of any Member State may conclude and perform contracts of employment. This provision may be relied on by both workers and employers (see Case C-350/96 *Clean Car Autoservice*, above, at pp. I-2545–6). A national of a Member State seeking employment in another Member State must receive the same assistance there as that afforded by the employment offices in that State to their own nationals (Art. 5. In Case C-292/89 *Antonissen*, above, at p. I-777, the Court relied in part on this provision in support of the right to move to another Member State in search of employment). The engagement and recruitment of migrant workers must not depend on medical, vocational, or other criteria which are discriminatory, although an employer may request a migrant worker to undergo a vocational test (Art. 6).

Most importantly, Art. 3(1) ensures free access to employment by providing for the non-discriminatory treatment of migrant workers. It renders inapplicable national provisions laid down by law, regulation, or administrative action, or administrative practices, where they limit application for and offers of employment, or the right of foreign nationals to take up and pursue employment, or subject these to conditions not applicable in respect of the nationals of the host State; or where, although applicable irrespective of nationality, their exclusive or principal aim or effect is to keep nationals of other Member States away from the employment offered. These prohibited provisions or practices include those which prescribe a special recruitment procedure for foreign nationals; limit the advertising of vacancies; subject migrant workers' eligibility for employment to conditions of registration with employment offices; or impede their recruitment (Art. 3(2)). The ECJ has confirmed that Art. 3(1) prohibits not only discriminatory legal provisions but also discriminatory administrative practices since the concept of equal treatment presupposes not only that the same laws should be applied to nationals and to non-nationals, but also that those laws should be applied to both categories of persons in the same manner (Case 131/85 *Gül*, above, at p. 1591. For an infringement of Art. 3(1), see also Case C-123/94 *Commission* v. *Greece* [1995] ECR I-1457 at pp. I-1462–3). On the other hand, access to special employment and re-employment programmes, which are linked to unemployment, falls outside the scope of Art. 3(1) (Case C-278/94 *Commission* v. *Belgium* [1996] ECR I-4307 at p. I-4342).

The prohibition laid down in Art. 3(1) does not apply to rules requiring a particular linguistic knowledge by reason of the nature of the post to be filled. In Case C-379/87 *Groener* [1989] ECR 3967 at pp. 3993–4, the ECJ held that a permanent full-time post of lecturer in public vocational education institutions was a post of such a nature as to justify the requirement of an adequate knowledge of the Irish language, which was both the national language and the first official language of the Member State concerned. Such a requirement, the Court said, was justified by a policy of protecting and promoting the use of the national language as a means of expressing national identity and culture, provided that it did not encroach upon the free movement of workers, and was applied in a proportionate and non-discriminatory manner. Any requirement that the linguistic knowledge in question must have been acquired within the national territory was not permissible.

Art. 4 of the regulation reinforces the effect of the previous provisions by stipulating that any national law, regulation, or administrative action which restricts by number or percentage the employment of foreign nationals in any undertaking, branch of activity or region, or at a national level, shall not apply to nationals of the other Member States. When the granting of any benefit to undertakings is subject to a minimum percentage of national workers being employed, nationals of other Member States must be counted as national workers. The ECJ held that a French law that prescribed that a certain proportion of the crew of a ship must be of French nationality, and a Belgian law that reserved certain seamen's jobs, other than those of master and second master, to Belgian nationals, were contrary to Arts. 1 and 4 of Reg. 1612/68 (Case 167/73 *Commission* v. *France*, above, at p. 373; Case C-37/93 *Commission* v. *Belgium* [1993] ECR I-6295 at p. I-6302. France failed to comply with the above judgment, see Case C-334/94 *Commission* v. *France* [1996] ECR I-1307 at pp. I-1342–3).

Likewise, the Court has ruled that Art. 4 of the regulation and Art. 39 EC preclude the application of rules laid down by sporting associations under which football clubs may field only a limited number of professional players who are nationals of other Member States (Case C-415/93 *Bosman*, above, at pp. I-5073–8). On the other hand, Community law does not preclude a Member State from requiring, as a condition for authorizing one of its vessels to fish against its quotas, that 75% of the crew of the vessel in question must be nationals of the Member States of the Community (although it precludes a Member State from requiring, in the same circumstances, that 75% of the crew must reside ashore in that Member State, see Case C-3/87 *Agegate*, above, at pp. 4502–3; see also Case 223/86 *Pesca Valentia* [1988] ECR 83 at pp. 108–9).

4. Prohibition of discrimination. The principle of non-discrimination or equality of treatment is one of the fundamental principles of the Community legal system and as such applies to the whole range of matters covered by the

Treaties (on the principle of equality in general, *see further under* **Equality***). The prohibition of discrimination on grounds of nationality is merely a specific expression or application of that general principle (see ibid.). In the context of the free movement of persons, it is discrimination on grounds of nationality that is prohibited and is therefore considered below. Discrimination on grounds of sex or on other grounds is governed by different provisions of the Treaty and is the subject of separate entries (*see further under* **Equal pay, Equal treatment**).

Generally, discrimination may be defined as the application of different rules to comparable situations or the application of the same rule to different situations. Different treatment may be justified only if it is based on objective considerations independent of the nationality of the person concerned and is proportionate to the objective being legitimately pursued (see e.g. Case C-391/97 *Gschwind* [1999] ECR I-5451 at p. I-5487; Case C-411/98 *Ferlini* [2000] ECR I-8081 at p. I-8141; Case C-148/02 *Garcia Avello* [2003] ECR I-11613, para. 31). The question whether two categories of persons are in a comparable situation and must for that reason enjoy equal treatment is a question involving the interpretation of Community law. Consequently, the finding that two categories of persons are in a comparable situation from the point of view of national law does not preclude the possibility that those two categories are in a different position under Community law (Case C-466/00 *Kaba II* [2003] ECR I-2219, paras. 44–5).

(*a*) ***The scope of the prohibition of discrimination.*** In relation to the free movement of workers, discrimination is prohibited at three different levels (for the prohibition of discrimination in connection with citizenship of the Union, see section III below). First, Art. 12 EC provides that:

> Within the scope of application of this Treaty, and without prejudice to any special provisions contained therein, any discrimination on grounds of nationality shall be prohibited.
>
> The Council, acting in accordance with the procedure referred to in Article 251, may adopt rules designed to prohibit such discrimination.

Secondly, this general rule has been implemented, or given 'concrete form', in regard to workers by Art. 39; in regard to self-employed persons and the right of establishment by Art. 43; and in regard to persons providing or receiving services by Art. 49 (see e.g. Case 36/74 *Walrave*, above, at p. 1417; Case 13/76 *Donà*, above, at p. 1339; Case 59/85 *Reed*, above, at p. 1302; Case 186/87 *Cowan*, above, at p. 220; Case 305/87 *Commission* v. *Greece*, above, at p. 1476). In particular, Art. 39(2) provides that:

> freedom of movement [for workers] shall entail the abolition of any discrimination based on nationality between workers of the Member States as regards employment, remuneration and other conditions of work and employment.

The principle of equal treatment enshrined in this provision is not limited to access to employment, but also includes remuneration and other conditions of employment as well as any general facilities related thereto in the broadest possible sense. Thus, the Court has held that since access to leisure activities available in the host Member State is a corollary to freedom of movement, the registration by a migrant of a leisure craft in the host State falls within the scope of the Community provisions relating to that freedom. Therefore, legislation under which only the nationals of the host Member State may register in that State a leisure craft is contrary to the principle of non-discrimination (Case C-334/94 *Commission* v. *France*, above, at p. I-1341. See also Case C-90/96 *Petrie* [1997] ECR I-6527 at p. I-6556, holding that the principle covers the ineligibility of foreign-language assistants to be appointed to fill temporary teaching posts). As seen above, Art. 39 may be relied on not only by workers but also by employers in order to employ, in the Member State in which they are established, workers who are nationals of other Member States (Case C-350/96 *Clean Car Autoservice*, above, at p. I-2546).

Thirdly, Art. 39(2) has in turn been implemented by Reg. 1612/68, and in particular by the fifth and sixth recitals and Arts. 7 to 9 thereof.

Before considering these latter provisions in detail, it is necessary first of all to clarify the relationship between the three tiers of rules as well as the scope and the content of the prohibition of discrimination laid down in Arts. 12 and 39(2) EC.

The applicability of Art. 12 is subject to three (related) conditions. First, the prohibition may be invoked only in situations which are governed by Community law. As the ECJ has said in a number of cases, 'unequal treatment based on nationality must be regarded as discrimination prohibited by Article 12 of the Treaty *if it falls within the scope of the Treaty*' (Case 293/83 *Gravier* [1985] ECR 593 at p. 611, emphasis added. See also Case 152/82 *Forcheri*, above, at p. 2334; Cases 35/82 etc. *Morson and Jhanjan*, above, at p. 3736; Case 59/85 *Reed*, above, at p. 1302; Case C-85/96 *Martinez Sala* [1998] ECR I-2691 at pp. I-2724, I-2726; etc.). It follows that where unequal treatment is applied in relation to a matter that falls outside the scope of the EC Treaty, it does not constitute prohibited discrimination under Art. 12. Thus, in Case 39/86 *Lair* [1988] ECR 3161 at pp. 3194–5 and in Case 197/86 *Brown*, above, at pp. 3242–3, the Court held that since access to vocational training and to university studies fell within the scope of the EC Treaty, financial assistance granted by the Member States in respect of registration and tuition fees charged for access to education also fell within the scope of the Treaty and was, consequently, subject to the prohibition of discrimination. On the other hand, since education policy and social policy were not yet covered, or fully covered, by the Treaty, assistance given to students for maintenance and training fell outside the scope of the Treaty and hence of the rule on non-discrimination (see further section II below). Likewise, the prohibition of discrimination does not apply to the composition of sport teams, in particular national teams, which is a matter of purely sporting interest and, as such, is outside the field of application of the Treaty (Case 36/74 *Walrave*, above, at p. 1418; Case 13/76 *Donà*, above, at p. 1340. See also section I.2(*a*) above).

However, once national provisions fall within the scope of application of the Treaty, they are necessarily subject to the general prohibition of discrimination laid down in Art. 12, without there being any need to connect them with the specific provisions relating to free movement (Case C-43/95 *Data Delecta and Forsberg* [1996] ECR I-4661 at pp. I-4675–7, holding that Art. 12 precludes a Member State from requiring non-nationals to lodge security for the costs of court proceedings where no such requirement can be imposed on nationals and where the proceedings are concerned in a general way with the exercise of fundamental freedoms guaranteed by Community law).

Secondly, the general rule laid down in Art. 12 can only apply subject to 'any special provisions' contained in the Treaty. These special provisions include Arts. 39, 43, and 49 EC, which implement Art. 12 in regard to workers, self-employed persons, and persons providing or receiving services (see above), as well as the regulations and directives adopted for the implementation of those provisions (Case 186/87 *Cowan*, above, at p. 220; Case 8/77 *Sagulo, Brenca and Bakhouche* [1977] ECR 1495 at p. 1505). It follows that where these implementing provisions impose special obligations on migrant workers (such as the possession of a passport or an identity card), those workers cannot expect to be treated in the same way as the nationals of the host State. Such differential treatment does not amount to prohibited discrimination within the meaning of Art. 12 (ibid. at pp. 1505–6).

Thirdly, since Art. 12 has been implemented in the various areas of Community law by means of special provisions, it applies independently (autonomously) only to situations governed by Community law in regard to which the Treaty lays down no specific prohibition of discrimination. Art. 12 can therefore be infringed on its own only where there is no more specific rule on non-discrimination, such as Arts. 39, 43, or 49. Otherwise, any infringement of those specific rules entails infringement of Art. 12 itself. It follows that where a discriminatory treatment falls within the scope of Art. 39(2) and the relevant provisions of Reg. 1612/68 (for example, because it concerns 'workers' covered by those provisions), it must be considered under those provisions and not under Art. 12 (Case 305/87 *Commission* v. *Greece*, above, at pp. 1476–7 *per Curiam*, p. 1472 *per* A.-G. Jacobs; Case C-10/90 *Masgio* [1991] ECR I-1119 at p. I-1138; Case C-213/90 *ASTI* [1991] ECR I-3507 at p. I-3529; Case C-179/90 *Merci Convenzionali Porto di Genova* [1991] ECR I-5889 at p. I-5927; etc.).

By contrast, Art. 12 may be invoked in the case of discrimination against persons falling within the scope of Community law but not covered by a more specific provision, for example students (Case 293/83 *Gravier*, above, at p. 613; see further section II below); tourists as recipients of services (Case 186/87 *Cowan*, above, at pp. 220–1); owners of intellectual property rights, such as copyright and related rights (Cases C-92/92 etc. *Collins* [1993] ECR I-5145 at p. I-5180); EC officials (Case C-411/98 *Ferlini*, above, at pp. I-8139–40). In these cases, Art. 12 produces direct effect and may be relied on before a national court by the persons concerned as the basis for a claim that the court disapply discriminatory provisions of national law (Case 24/86

Blaizot [1988] ECR 379 at p. 407; Cases C-92/92 etc. *Collins*, above, at p. I-5182).

While the above principles clarify the relationship between Art. 12 and Art. 39(2), the relationship between Art. 39(2) and the implementing secondary legislation, and in particular the relevant provisions of Reg. 1612/68, remains somewhat unclear. Thus, in one case the Court applied the 'most specific' of these various provisions, which in that case was Art. 8 of Reg. 1612/68 (Case C-213/90 *ASTI*, above, at pp. I-3529–30). By contrast, in other cases the Court said that since Arts. 1 and 3 of Reg. 1612/68 'merely clarify and give effect to' Art. 39, the latter provision alone was relevant (Case C-419/92 *Scholz*, above, at p. I-520; Case C-90/96 *Petrie*, above, at p. I-6551; see also Case C-385/00 *De Groot*, above, para. 111, where the Court dealt with the question under Art. 39 and found it unnecessary to consider it also under Art. 7 of Reg. 1612/68). In yet other cases, the Court relied on all of those provisions together. Thus, it derived the right of a migrant worker to be accompanied by an unmarried companion from the combined effects of Arts. 12 and 39 EC and Art. 7(2) of Reg. 1612/68 (Case 59/85 *Reed*, above, at p. 1304), and the right of a migrant worker and self-employed person to register a leisure craft in the host Member State from Arts. 12, 39, and 43 EC, Art. 7 of Reg. 1251/70 and Art. 7 of Dir. 75/34 (Case C-334/94 *Commission* v. *France*, above, at p. I-1341. See also Case C-415/93 *Bosman*, above, at pp. I-5073–8, where the Court relied on both Art. 39(2) EC and Art. 4 of Reg. 1612/68). It seems that the scope of Art. 39(2) is wide enough to cover any discriminatory treatment of workers which is not otherwise covered by the specific provisions of Reg. 1612/68 (see above).

(*b*) ***Direct discrimination.*** In a number of cases, the Court has had opportunity to define in a comprehensive manner the content or substance of the prohibition of discrimination based directly on nationality. Thus, the Court has described it as 'the fundamental principle in the context of the rules on freedom of movement' (Case 249/83 *Hoeckx* [1985] ECR 973 at p. 989), which 'must be applied in every respect and in all circumstances governed by Community law to any person established in a Member State . . . for the purpose of employment' (Case 137/84 *Mutsch* [1985] ECR 2681 at p. 2695). Arts. 12 and 39, the Court has said, are intended to eliminate all measures of the Member States under which a worker who is a national of another Member State 'is subject to more severe treatment or is placed in an unfavourable situation in law or in fact as compared with the situation of a national in the same circumstances' (Case 222/86 *Heylens*, above, at pp. 4115–16; Case 251/83 *Haug-Adrion* [1984] ECR 4277 at p. 4288). In other words, Art. 12 requires that 'persons in a situation governed by Community law be placed on a completely equal footing with nationals of the Member State. In so far as this principle is applicable, it therefore precludes a Member State from making the grant of a right to such a person subject to the condition that he reside on the territory of that State—that condition is not imposed on the State's own nationals' (Case 186/87 *Cowan*, above, at pp. 219–20; see also Cases C-92/92 etc. *Collins*, above, at p. I-5181; Case C-43/95 *Data Delecta and Forsberg*, above, at p. I-4676, where the Court speaks of 'perfect equality of treatment' of nationals and non-nationals). The prohibition of discrimination is 'absolute' and 'general', and unequal treatment is prohibited even if it constitutes only an obstacle of secondary importance to the free movement of workers. Any national provision that is contrary to this prohibition must be repealed or amended (Case 167/73 *Commission* v. *France*, above, at p. 373). Moreover, the person discriminated against may seek compensation for the harm suffered before the competent national courts in accordance with the principles of Community law relating to State liability (Case C-90/96 *Petrie*, above, at p. I-6553).

The right to equal treatment is conferred directly by Community law and may not therefore be made subject to the issue of a certificate (e.g. a residence permit) to that effect by the authorities of the host Member State (Case 186/87 *Cowan*, above, at p. 220; Cases C-92/92 etc. *Collins*, above, at p. I-5182). Nor may the exercise of that right be made dependent on the existence of a reciprocal agreement or practice between the host State and the Member State of which the person concerned is a national (Case 186/87 *Cowan*, above, at p. 220). Thus, the Court has consistently held that a Member State which subjects access to certain occupations or professions by nationals of other Member States to a condition of reciprocity, or which restricts such access to its own nationals, contravenes the principle of equal treatment (see e.g. Case 307/84 *Commission* v. *France* [1986] ECR 1725 at p. 1739, concerning nurses in public hospitals; Case 168/85 *Commission* v. *Italy* [1986] ECR 2945 at p. 2961, concerning journalists, pharmacists, and various occupations in the field of tourism; Case C-58/90 *Commission* v. *Italy*, above, at p. I-4202, concerning health-care auxiliaries; Case C-179/90 *Merci Convenzionali Porto di Genova*, above, at p. I-5927, concerning dock workers; Case C-375/92 *Commission* v. *Spain*, above, at p. I-940, concerning tourist guides and guide-interpreters; Case C-114/97 *Commission* v. *Spain*, above, at pp. I-6741–5, concerning private security staff; Case C-162/99 *Commission* v. *Italy*, above, at p. I-569, concerning dentists). Moreover, when a Member State concludes a bilateral international agreement with a non-member country, for example on social security, the principle of equal treatment requires that Member State to grant nationals of other Member States the same advantages as those which its own nationals enjoy under the agreement, unless there are objective justifications for not doing so (Case C-55/00 *Gottardo* [2002] ECR I-413 at p. I-446).

The principle of non-discrimination set out in Art. 39 is drafted in general terms and is not specifically addressed to the Member States. Thus, the Court has held that discrimination based on nationality is prohibited not only when it is practised by the public authorities of the Member States, but also when it arises from rules or agreements of private organizations and employers regulating gainful employment in a collective manner. As the Court has explained, the abolition of obstacles to the free movement of persons between Member States would be compromised if State barriers could be replaced by obstacles resulting from the exercise of their legal autonomy by associations or organizations that are not governed by public law. Since working conditions in the various Member States are regulated sometimes by law or regulation and sometimes by agreements and other acts of private persons, limiting the scope of Art. 39 to acts of public authorities would create inequality in its application. Therefore, Arts. 12 and 39 must be taken into account by national courts also when assessing the validity or the effects of provisions inserted in the rules of private (e.g. sporting) organizations (Case 36/74 *Walrave*, above, at pp. 1418–19; Case 13/76 *Donà*, above, at p. 1341; Case C-415/93 *Bosman*, above, at pp. I-5065–7; see also Art. 7(4) of Reg. 1612/68, discussed below).

On the basis of these considerations, the Court has subsequently confirmed that the prohibition of discrimination on grounds of nationality laid down in Art. 39, just as the prohibition of discrimination on grounds of sex laid down in Art. 141, applies not only to collective agreements and rules of private organizations but also to contracts between private individuals (e.g. between a single employer and an employee). In other words, Art. 39(2) can produce 'horizontal' direct effect in this wider sense (Case C-281/98 *Angonese* [2000] ECR I-4139 at pp. I-4171–5, holding that Art. 39 prohibits an employer from accepting only one particular diploma as evidence of linguistic knowledge).

(*c*) ***Indirect discrimination.*** The rules relating to equality of treatment, whether laid down in Arts. 12 and 39(2) EC or in Art. 7 of Reg. 1612/68, prohibit not only direct or overt discrimination based on nationality, but also all indirect (covert or disguised) forms of discrimination which, by the application of other distinguishing criteria, lead in fact to the same result. The reason is that Community law strives to achieve equality of treatment both 'in fact and in law' (see the fifth recital in the preamble to Reg. 1612/68 and Case 152/73 *Sotgiu*, above, at p. 164). According to the ECJ:

> unless objectively justified and proportionate to its aim, a provision of national law must be regarded as indirectly discriminatory if it is intrinsically liable to affect migrant workers more than national workers and if there is a consequent risk that it will place the former at a particular disadvantage. It is not necessary in this respect to find that the provision in question does in practice affect a substantially higher proportion of migrant workers. It is sufficient that it is liable to have such an effect. Further, the reasons why a migrant worker chooses to make use of his freedom of movement within the Community are not to be taken into account in assessing whether a national provision is discriminatory (Case C-237/94 *O'Flynn* [1996] ECR I-2617 at pp. I-2638–9; see also Case C-278/94 *Commission* v. *Belgium*, above, at p. I-4337; Case C-57/96 *Meints* [1997] ECR I-6689 at p. I-6720).

In particular, national rules under which a distinction is drawn on the basis of origin or residence in that non-residents are denied certain benefits that are granted to persons residing within the national territory, are liable to operate mainly to the detriment of nationals of other Member States, as non-residents are in the majority of cases non-nationals (Case C-279/93 *Schumacker* [1995] ECR I-225 at p. I-259; see also e.g. Case C-350/96 *Clean Car Autoservice*, above, at p. I-2547). Such distinction may be tantamount, as regards its practical effect, to discrimination on grounds of nationality (Case 152/73 *Sotgiu*, above, at p. 164). In a number of cases, the ECJ has held that national provisions which, on the face of it, apply to all workers irrespective of nationality but which operate in practice to the disadvantage of the nationals of other Member States or contain conditions which may be more easily fulfilled by national workers than by migrant workers, are contrary to the rules on non-discrimination unless they are justified by objective considerations independent of the nationality of the workers concerned and proportionate to the legitimate aim pursued by the law (see point (*g*) below). Examples of indirect discrimination include the following:

- Case 152/73 *Sotgiu*, above, at pp. 164–5, where discrimination arose from the fact that the German Federal Post Office paid a lower separation allowance to workers whose residence was abroad;
- Case 33/88 *Allué I* [1989] ECR 1591 at p. 1610; Cases C-259/91 etc. *Allué II* [1993] ECR I-4309 at p. I-4335; Case C-272/92 *Spotti* [1993] ECR I-5185 at p. I-5207, where Italian and German law limited the duration of contracts of employment of foreign-language teaching assistants working at universities but there was no similar limitation in relation to other teachers. Although the law applied regardless of nationality, it indirectly discriminated against foreign nationals who made up the great majority of such assistants (see also Case C-90/96 *Petrie*, above, at p. I-6559; Case C-212/99 *Commission* v. *Italy* [2001] ECR I-4923 at pp. I-4954–9);
- Case C-27/91 *Le Manoir* [1991] ECR I-5531 at pp. I-5541–2, where French social security contributions in fact discriminated against trainee workers from other Member States;
- Case C-111/91 *Commission* v. *Luxembourg* [1993] ECR I-817 at pp. I-843, I-846, where the requirement that a mother must reside on Luxembourg territory for one year prior to the birth of her child in order to be entitled to childbirth and maternity allowances was found discriminatory because, although the requirement was imposed without regard to nationality, it was more easily satisfied by a Luxembourg national than by a national of another Member State;
- Case C-419/92 *Scholz*, above, at pp. I-521–2; Case C-15/96 *Schöning-Kougebetopoulou* [1998] ECR I-47 at p. I-68; Case C-187/96 *Commission* v. *Greece* [1998] ECR I-1095 at p. I-1117; Case C-195/98 *Österreichischer Gewerkschaftsbund*, above, at pp. I-10549–51, all holding that national rules under which previous periods of employment in the public service of another Member State may not be taken into consideration by the public authorities for purposes of recruiting, promotion, or determining salary or other benefits, constitute unjustified indirect discrimination contrary to Art. 39(2) and Art. 7(1) and (4) of Reg. 1612/68 (see also Case C-224/01 *Köbler*, above, paras. 71–7, where Austrian legislation that precluded, for the purpose of the grant of a special length-of-service increment, taking into account periods of

service completed by a university professor outside Austria was likewise found to be discriminatory);

- Case C-336/94 *Dafeki* [1997] ECR I-6761 at pp. I-6779–81, holding that a German law which accorded lower probative value to certificates of civil status issued by the authorities of other Member States than to certificates issued by the German authorities operated to the detriment of migrant workers who needed those certificates to determine entitlement to social security benefits;
- Case C-350/96 *Clean Car Autoservice*, above, at pp. I-2547–50, holding that a requirement that nationals of the other Member States must reside in Austria in order to be appointed managers of undertakings established there constituted indirect discrimination;
- Case C-35/97 *Commission* v. *France* [1998] ECR I-5325 at pp. I-5352–5, holding that France indirectly discriminated against frontier workers residing in Belgium by excluding them from qualifying for certain retirement benefits;
- Case C-274/96 *Bickel and Franz* [1998] ECR I-7637 at pp. I-7656–9, where Italian rules restricted the right to have criminal proceedings conducted in German to German-speaking Italian nationals who were residents of the Province of Bolzano. Thus, German-speaking nationals of other Member States travelling or staying in that Province were put at a disadvantage in that they could not use German in such proceedings, and this amounted to prohibited discrimination;
- Case C-411/98 *Ferlini*, above, at pp. I-8142–4, where the application by Luxembourg health-care providers to EC officials of higher fees than those applicable to Luxembourg residents affiliated to the national social security scheme constituted indirect discrimination on grounds of nationality;
- Case C-138/02 *Collins* [2004] ECR I-0000, paras. 53–4, 65–6, where under United Kingdom legislation nationals of other Member States seeking employment in the United Kingdom who were not workers and had no right of residence could claim a jobseeker's allowance only if they were habitually resident in the United Kingdom. The residence requirement constituted indirect discrimination.

(d) Tax discrimination. Discrimination, whether direct or indirect, is also prohibited in the field of taxation. As the ECJ has said on a number of occasions, 'although direct taxation falls within the competence of the Member States, the latter must none the less exercise that competence consistently with Community law and therefore avoid any overt or covert discrimination by reason of nationality' (Case C-391/97 *Gschwind*, above, at p. I-5487; see also the cases cited below). The Court has pointed out that the principle of equal treatment with regard to remuneration, expressly provided for in Art. 39(2) EC, would be rendered ineffective if it could be undermined by discriminatory national provisions on income tax. That is why Art. 7(2) of Reg. 1612/68 provides that migrant workers are to enjoy in the territory of the host Member State the same tax advantages as national workers (Case C-175/88 *Biehl* [1990] ECR I-1779 at p. I-1792; see also point (*h*) below). Therefore, Art. 39(2) does not allow a Member State, as regards the collection of direct taxes, to treat a national of another Member State employed in its territory less favourably than one of its own nationals in the same situation (Case C-279/93 *Schumacker*, above, at p. I-258).

In the field of taxation, discrimination most frequently arises from the different treatment of residents and non-residents. Tax benefits granted only to residents of a Member State may, in certain circumstances, constitute indirect discrimination on grounds of nationality (see point (*c*) above). However, in several cases the Court has emphasized that as far as direct taxes are concerned, the situations of residents and of non-residents are not, as a rule, comparable, since income received in the territory of a Member State by a non-resident is in most cases only a part of his total income, which is concentrated at his place of residence. Moreover, a non-resident's personal ability to pay tax, determined by reference to his aggregate income and his personal and family circumstances, is easier to assess at the place where his personal and financial interests are centred, which in general is the place where he has his usual abode. Accordingly, international tax law recognizes that in principle the overall taxation of taxpayers, taking account of their personal and family circumstances, is a matter for the State of residence. Consequently, the fact that a Member State does not grant to a non-resident certain tax benefits which it grants to a resident is not, as a rule, discriminatory since those two categories of taxpayer are not in a comparable situation both from the point of view of the source of their income and their personal ability to pay tax or their personal and family circumstances. It follows that Art. 39(2) does not in principle preclude national rules under which a non-resident worker is taxed more heavily on his income than a resident in a similar employment (Case C-279/93 *Schumacker*, above, at pp. I-259–60; Case C-391/97 *Gschwind*, above, at pp. I-5487–8).

It follows from the foregoing that there can be tax discrimination between residents and non-residents only if, notwithstanding their residence in different Member States, it can be established that the two categories of taxpayer are in a comparable situation. This is the case where the non-resident receives no significant income in the State of his residence and obtains all or almost all of his taxable income from work performed in the State of employment. In those circumstances, the State of his residence is not in a position to grant him the benefits resulting from the taking into account of his personal and family circumstances because the tax payable there is insufficient to enable it to do so. There is no objective difference between the situations of such a non-resident and a resident engaged in comparable employment, such as to justify different tax treatment. In the case of a non-resident who receives all or almost all of his family income in a Member State other than that of his residence, discrimination arises from the fact that his personal and family circumstances are taken into account neither in the State of residence nor in the State of employment. Such discrimination cannot be objectively justified, and the Community principle of equal treatment requires that in the State of employment his personal and family circumstances be taken into account in the same way as those of resident nationals and that the same tax benefits should be granted to him (Case C-279/93 *Schumacker*, above, at pp. I-261–3, involving a Belgian national who resided in Belgium with his family but was working in Germany, where he was taxed more heavily than a resident worker performing the same work).

The position is different where a large proportion (nearly 42%) of the total income of a non-resident worker and his non-resident wife is received in their State of residence, enabling that State to take into account his personal and family circumstances. The situation of such a married couple is not comparable to that of a resident married couple, with the result that Art. 39(2) does not require that they receive the same tax treatment (Case C-391/97 *Gschwind*, above, at pp. I-5489–90, involving a Netherlands national living with his wife in the Netherlands but working in Germany while his wife was employed in the Netherlands. See also Case C-336/96 *Gilly*, above, at p. I-2840, where the income of a French resident received in Germany was taxed, together with the income of her husband, in France, where she received the relevant tax advantages, so that the German tax authorities were not obliged to take account of her personal and family circumstances).

Other examples of tax discrimination include the following:

- Case C-175/88 *Biehl*, above, at pp. I-1793–4 and Case C-151/94 *Commission* v. *Luxembourg* [1995] ECR I-3685 at p. I-3707, where a Luxembourg tax law made refund of excess amounts of income tax deducted conditional upon permanent residence in Luxembourg. Although the law applied irrespective of nationality, in practice it worked against the nationals of other Member States because they were more likely to leave the country or take up residence there during the course of the tax year.
- Case C-204/90 *Bachmann* [1992] ECR I-249 at p. I-279 and Case C-300/90 *Commission* v. *Belgium* [1992] ECR I-305 at p. I-317, where a Belgian tax law made the deduction from taxable income of sickness and invalidity insurance contributions and pension and life assurance contributions conditional upon those contributions being paid in Belgium to insurance companies established in Belgium. Although the law was discriminatory as it operated to the detriment of foreign nationals, the Court accepted that it was objectively justified by the need to ensure the cohesion of the Belgian tax system and that therefore it was not contrary to Art. 39 or Art. 7 of Reg. 1612/68. The reason was that under the Belgian rules there was a connection between the deductibility of contributions and the liability to tax of sums payable by the insurers under pension and life assurance contracts. The loss of revenue resulting from the deduction of contributions from taxable income was offset by the taxation of pensions, annuities, or capital sums payable by the insurers, which was difficult or almost impossible to ensure if the insurers were established outside Belgium (ibid. at pp. I-282–4 and I-319–21, respectively).

- Case C-87/99 *Zurstrassen* [2000] ECR I-3337 at pp. I-3362–4, where indirect discrimination arose from the fact that the entitlement of married couples to joint assessment to tax was subject to the condition that both spouses had to be resident in Luxembourg. Luxembourg nationals could satisfy that condition more easily than nationals of other Member States who often resided in Luxembourg in order to work there, while their spouses and families lived outside the country. This case involved a Belgian national who was employed and resided in Luxembourg, while his wife and their children lived in Belgium. Almost the entire income of the family (98%) derived from his earned income in Luxembourg, where he was treated as a single taxpayer without dependants. In these circumstances, Luxembourg was the only State that could take account of his personal and family circumstances.
- Case C-385/00 *De Groot*, above, paras. 81–95, 110, 114–15, where a Netherlands national who resided in the Netherlands and received part of his income there suffered a tax disadvantage in his State of residence as a result of having also been employed in other Member States during the tax year. Thus, as a consequence of his exercise of his right to freedom of movement, he lost part of his tax-free allowance and of his personal tax advantages. In other words, he received a lesser tax advantage than he would have received had he been employed only in the Netherlands. The Court held that the national rules in question were contrary to Art. 39 as they were liable to discourage workers from taking up employment in other Member States. The Court added that while Community law lays down no specific requirement with regard to the way in which the State of residence must take into account the personal and family circumstances of a worker who receives income in that State and in other Member States, nevertheless the method used must not constitute discrimination, either direct or indirect, on grounds of nationality, or an obstacle to the exercise of a fundamental freedom guaranteed by the Treaty.
- Case C-209/01 *Schilling*, above, paras. 29–44, holding that Community officials must not suffer tax discrimination in their Member State of origin on account of the fact that they reside in Luxembourg.

It may be noted that although the abolition of double taxation within the Community is one of the objectives of the Treaty, no unifying or harmonizing measure has yet been adopted at Community level for that purpose, apart from the Convention of 23 July 1990 on the elimination of double taxation in connection with the adjustment of profits of associated enterprises (*OJ* 1990 L225/10). Nor have the Member States yet concluded any multilateral convention to that effect under Art. 293 EC. On the other hand, the Member States have concluded many bilateral conventions with a view to eliminating double taxation, based on the model conventions on income and wealth tax drawn up by the Organisation for Economic Co-operation and Development (OECD) (see Case C-336/96 *Gilly*, above, at p. I-2833). The Court has held that any unfavourable consequences entailed for taxpayers by the application of such bilateral conventions (e.g. a tax credit mechanism), which are the result of the differences between the tax scales of the Member States concerned, are not incompatible with Art. 39 EC (ibid. at pp. I-2839–40).

(*e*) ***Absence of discrimination.*** Unequal treatment does not always constitute prohibited discrimination under Community law. In the first place, as seen above, unequal treatment of persons whose situations are not comparable is not discrimination. Secondly, the general prohibition laid down in Arts. 12 and 39(2) EC and Art. 7 of Reg. 1612/68 does not apply to disparities in treatment that may result for Community nationals from divergences existing between the laws of the various Member States. Non-discrimination cannot be equated with prior harmonization of national laws. Therefore, the fact that one Member State applies stricter legislation in a certain area than other Member States cannot be regarded as prohibited discrimination, even if this detrimentally affects the competitiveness of undertakings established in that State, so long as the law is applied equally to every person subject to it, in accordance with objective criteria and without regard to their nationality. The only purpose of the prohibition set out in Art. 12 is to avoid the existence within one and the same Member State of different rules, or the different application of the same rules, depending upon the nationality of those subject to them (Case 14/68 *Wilhelm* [1969] ECR 1 at p. 16 *per Curiam*, p. 29 *per* A.-G. Roemer; Case 223/86 *Pesca Valentia*, above, at p. 109; Cases C-92/92 etc. *Collins*, above, at p. I-5181; Case C-92/02 *Kristiansen* [2003] ECR I-0000, para. 38; etc.).

Thirdly, since Art. 12 EC is concerned only with discrimination on grounds of nationality, it does not normally prohibit discrimination between the nationals of the same Member State (Case 223/86 *Pesca Valentia*, above, at p. 109). Nor does it prohibit discrimination between Community nationals and nationals of third countries (ibid.; Case C-3/87 *Agegate*, above, at pp. 4501–2; in both cases the Court held that it was not contrary to Art. 12 for a Member State to require a minimum proportion—75%—of the crews of its fishing vessels to be Community nationals). It follows that Art. 12 normally only prohibits discrimination between the nationals of the Member States of the Community (see, however, section III.4(*a*) below).

(*f*) ***Reverse discrimination.*** Since the purpose of Art. 39 is to ensure the free movement of workers within the Community, i.e. between the Member States, Art. 39(2) only prohibits discrimination by a Member State *against workers from other Member States* who wish to pursue their activities in the first State. It does not prohibit discrimination by a Member State *against its own nationals* ('reverse discrimination'). As the Court has held in a consistent line of cases, the mere fact that, under the legislation of a Member State, a foreign worker is in a more favourable situation than a national of the host State is not sufficient to confer on that national the benefit of the Community rules on the free movement of workers and on non-discrimination if all the circumstances of his situation are confined within the Member State of which he is a national (i.e. he is employed in that State by an employer established there and has never exercised the right of freedom of movement within the Community). Such a situation is purely internal to a Member State, to which the provisions of Community law cannot be applied (Case 44/84 *Hurd* [1986] ECR 29 at p. 85; Case C-332/90 *Steen I* [1992] ECR I-341 at pp. I-356–7; Case C-379/92 *Peralta* [1994] ECR I-3453 at pp. I-3497–8. See also section I.2(*a*) above and the cases cited therein).

Any discrimination that nationals of a Member State may suffer under the law of their own State falls within the scope of national law and must be dealt with within the framework of the internal legal system (Cases C-64/96 etc. *Uecker and Jacquet*, above, at p. I-3190). It follows that Community law does not preclude a national court from assessing the compatibility with the Constitution of a domestic law that discriminates against national workers by treating them less favourably than workers from other Member States. Therefore, where reverse discrimination is unconstitutional, it may be eliminated under national law (Case C-132/93 *Steen II* [1994] ECR I-2715 at p. I-2724). It may also be incompatible with fundamental human rights (see the opinion of A.-G. Van Gerven in Case C-206/91 *Koua Poirrez* [1992] ECR I-6685 at pp. I-6698–700).

It may be noted that the fact that the Court's case-law allows reverse discrimination has been criticized on the grounds that this is incompatible with the realization of the single European market. It is, however, submitted that reverse discrimination has no effect on the single market because it does not hinder the free movement of persons between Member States. Since reverse discrimination is the direct result of the exercise of sovereign powers by Member States over their own nationals in areas not covered by Community law, the possibility for it will necessarily remain so long as a single Union citizenship has not completely replaced Member State nationality. It is therefore a single citizenship rather than a single market that can provide a remedy.

(*g*) ***Objective justification.*** According to the Court's case-law, national rules that are directly discriminatory on grounds of nationality cannot be justified (Case C-85/96 *Martinez Sala*, above, at p. I-2726), and are compatible with Community law only if they can be brought within the scope of an express derogation, such as that contained in Art. 39(3) (derogation on grounds of public policy, public security, or public health) or Art. 39(4) EC (derogation in relation to employment in the public service), and are proportionate to the aim pursued (*see further under* **Public health, Public policy, Public security, Public service**).

National rules that are indirectly discriminatory may be justified by objective considerations independent of the nationality of the worker concerned, and in particular if they pursue a legitimate aim compatible with the Treaty, are justified by pressing reasons of public interest, are appropriate for ensuring the achievement of the aim in question and do not go beyond what is necessary for that purpose, in other words, are proportionate to the legitimate aim pursued (Case C-19/92 *Kraus*, above, at p. I-1697; Case C-415/93 *Bosman*, above, at p. I-5071; Case C-224/01 *Köbler*, above, para.

77; Case C-350/96 *Clean Car Autoservice*, above, at p. I-2547; see also the cases cited below).

Thus, in several of the cases discussed above the Court accepted that although discrimination did exist, it might in certain circumstances be justified for objective reasons. Examples include the following:

- Case 152/73 *Sotgiu*, above, at p.165, where the Court indicated that the lower separation allowance might be justified by objective differences between the situations of workers living in Germany and those whose residence was abroad;
- Case C-204/90 *Bachmann*, above, at pp. I-282–4 and Case C-300/90 *Commission* v. *Belgium*, above, at pp. I-319–21, where the Court found that the discriminatory provisions of the Belgian tax law were justified by the need to safeguard the cohesion of the tax system. It should be noted, however, that although this justification has been invoked by Member States in a large number of cases, involving not only the free movement of workers but also the right of establishment and freedom to provide services, it has almost never been successful because the Member States could not prove the existence of a direct link, in the case of one and the same taxpayer, between the grant of a tax advantage and the offsetting of that advantage by a fiscal levy, both of which related to the same tax (see e.g. Case C-279/93 *Schumacker*, above, at pp. I-261–2; Case C-209/01 *Schilling*, above, paras. 41–3, and most of the tax discrimination cases discussed above). Also, the Court's case-law shows that detrimental tax treatment contrary to a fundamental freedom cannot be justified by the existence of other tax advantages (see Case C-385/00 *De Groot*, above, para. 97 and the cases cited therein);
- Cases C-259/91 etc. *Allué II*, above, at p. I-4334, and Case C-272/92 *Spotti*, above, at p. I-5207, where the Court indicated that the duration of contracts of employment of foreign-language teaching assistants could be limited to a specific period where this was justified for objective reasons (see also Case C-90/96 *Petrie*, above, at pp. I-6557–9);
- Case 118/75 *Watson and Belmann*, above, at p. 1199, where the Court accepted that national rules concerning the control of foreign nationals (e.g. the requirement to report their presence to the authorities) did not constitute prohibited discrimination where they were based on objective factors such as the need to have an exact knowledge of population movements;
- Case 251/83 *Haug-Adrion*, above, at pp. 4288–9, where the Court held that the refusal of a no-claims bonus to insured persons resident in another Member State who owned a vehicle registered under customs plates did not involve discrimination as it was based exclusively on objective actuarial factors and on the objective criterion of registration under customs plates;
- Case C-274/96 *Bickel and Franz*, above, at pp. I-7658–9, where the Court accepted that the protection of ethno-cultural minority in the use of a particular language might constitute a legitimate aim, although it

did not justify discrimination in the circumstances of the case (see point (*c*) above);

- Case C-138/02 *Collins*, above, paras. 65–73, where the Court held that it was legitimate for a Member State to grant a jobseeker's allowance only where a genuine link existed between the person seeking work and the employment market, and to lay down a residence requirement for that purpose, provided that the period of residence was not disproportionately long.

It should be noted that the finding that discrimination is objectively justified is different from the finding that there is no discrimination because the situations involved are not comparable (see Case C-466/00 *Kaba II*, above, para. 55 and point (*e*) above).

(*h*) ***Prohibition of discrimination under Reg. 1612/68.*** Having considered the scope and the content of the prohibition of discrimination under Arts. 12 and 39(2) EC, it is now appropriate to turn to the relevant provisions of Reg. 1612/68 (fifth and sixth recitals in the preamble and Arts. 7 to 9).

Art. 7(1) of Reg. 1612/68 states the general rule that a worker who is a national of a Member State may not, in another Member State, be treated differently from national workers by reason of his nationality in respect of 'any conditions of employment and work', in particular as regards remuneration, dismissal, and should he become unemployed, reinstatement or re-employment. The sixth recital further stipulates that all nationals of Member States must have the same priority as regards employment as is enjoyed by national workers. The provision concerning conditions of dismissal may be invoked by a worker even when he is no longer in an employment relationship (Case C-35/97 *Commission* v. *France*, above, at p. I-5352).

Art. 7(1), and in particular the term 'any conditions of employment and work', has been interpreted very broadly by the ECJ. Thus, the Court has said that the aim of Art. 7 is to ensure equality of treatment 'with regard to all statutory or contractual provisions determining the position [of workers] and in particular their financial rights' (Case 152/73 *Sotgiu*, above, at p. 163). Therefore, the Court has held that the 'conditions of employment and work' include a separation allowance, paid in addition to wages to workers allocated to posts away from their place of residence, whether the payment is made by virtue of a statutory or contractual obligation or merely at the option of the employer (ibid. at pp. 163–4). Those conditions also include any special protection, in particular against dismissal, which the legislation of a Member State accords, on specific social grounds, to certain fixed categories of workers such as those who have suffered a serious industrial accident (Case 44/72 *Marsman* [1972] ECR 1243 at p. 1248). They further include provisions that entitle a worker to have the period of his military service taken into account in the calculation of his seniority in his place of work (Case 15/69 *Ugliola* [1969] ECR 363 at pp. 369–70). Art. 7(1) extends to measures provided by national legislation for the rehabilitation of handicapped workers themselves, but not of their children, to whom Art. 12

applies (Case 76/72 *S* [1973] ECR 457 at pp. 463–4). Finally, Art. 7(1) covers conditions for promotion on grounds of seniority (Case C-15/96 *Schöning-Kougebetopoulou*, above, at pp. I-68–9) and the grant of a special length-of-service increment (Case C-224/01 *Köbler*, above, paras. 77–88, 102–3). In respect of all these matters, migrant workers must be treated in the same way as the workers of the host State.

Art. 7(2) of the regulation provides that migrant workers shall enjoy the same 'social and tax advantages' as national workers. The provision also applies to the descendants of the migrant worker who are dependent on him (Case C-337/97 *Meeusen* [1999] ECR I-3289 at p. I-3313). The term 'social advantage' has been interpreted by the ECJ extremely broadly in a voluminous body of case-law. It has acquired a very specific meaning, which is dealt with in a separate entry (*see further under* **Social advantage**). As regards 'tax advantage', the purpose of the provision is to ensure that the principle of equal treatment with regard to remuneration is not undermined by discriminatory national provisions on income tax (Case C-175/88 *Biehl*, above, at p. I-1792; Case C-279/93 *Schumacker*, above, at pp. I-257–8. As seen above, in both cases the Court found the national tax laws in question to be discriminatory. See also Case C-300/90 *Commission* v. *Belgium*, above, at pp. I-320–1, where the Court held that the Belgian tax law concerned, although discriminatory in nature, did not infringe Art. 7(2) as it was justified by the need to preserve the cohesion of the applicable tax system).

Art. 7(3) ensures access for migrant workers to training in vocational schools and retraining centres under the same conditions as apply to national workers. In Case 39/86 *Lair*, above, at pp. 3197–8 and in Case 197/86 *Brown*, above, at p. 3242, the ECJ held that the fact that an educational institution provides some vocational training is not sufficient for it to be regarded as a 'vocational school' for the purposes of Art. 7(3). The term 'vocational school' has a narrower meaning and refers solely to establishments that provide only instruction either alternating with or closely linked to employment, particularly during apprenticeship. That is not the case as far as universities are concerned. Therefore universities, even if they provide vocational training, cannot be regarded as 'vocational schools' within the meaning of Art. 7(3) (for a definition of vocational training, see section II below).

Art. 7(4) renders null and void any clause of a collective or individual agreement or of any other collective regulation concerning eligibility for employment, employment, remuneration, and other conditions of work or dismissal in so far as it lays down or authorizes discriminatory conditions in respect of migrant workers. In Case 36/74 *Walrave*, above, at p. 1419, the Court referred to this provision in holding that the prohibition of discrimination extends to agreements and rules which do not emanate from public authorities (see above). Where a discriminatory clause in a collective agreement (e.g. one which provides for promotion on grounds of seniority but which takes no account of periods of comparable employment previously completed in the public service of another Member State) is rendered null and void by virtue of Art. 7(4), the national courts do not have to wait for that clause to be abolished by collective negotiation or by some other procedure, but must apply to the members of the group disadvantaged by the discrimination the same rules as those applicable to the other workers (Case C-15/96 *Schöning-Kougebetopoulou*, above, at pp. I-69–70).

Under Art. 8(1), migrant workers are to enjoy equality of treatment as regards membership of trade unions and the exercise of rights relating thereto, including the right to vote and to be eligible for the administration or management posts of a trade union. The ECJ has held that this provision applies not only to trade union organizations in the strict sense but also to bodies that, while not being in law trade unions, perform similar functions as regards the defence and representation of workers' interests. Therefore, Art. 8(1) precludes national legislation refusing foreign workers the right to vote and to stand as candidates for membership in elections organized by an occupational guild to which they are compulsorily affiliated, to which they must pay contributions, which is responsible for defending their interests and which performs a consultative function in the legislative field (Case C-213/90 *ASTI*, above, at pp. I-3530–1; Case C-118/92 *Commission* v. *Luxembourg* [1994] ECR I-1891 at p. I-1899).

Nevertheless, under Art. 8(1) migrant workers may be excluded from taking part in the management of bodies governed by public law and from holding an office governed by public law. As interpreted by the Court, this provision is not intended to debar migrant workers from certain posts, but merely permits them to be debarred in some circumstances from certain activities which involve their participation in the exercise of powers conferred by public law, such as those involving the presence of trade union representatives on the boards of administration of bodies governed by public law with powers in the economic sphere (Case 149/79 *Commission* v. *Belgium* [1980] ECR 3881 at p. 3902; Case C-213/90 *ASTI*, above, at p. I-3531). Finally, Art. 8(1) ensures to migrant workers the right of eligibility for workers' representative bodies in the undertaking.

Pursuant to Art. 9(1), migrant workers are to enjoy all the rights and benefits accorded to national workers in matters of housing, including ownership of the housing they need. Under Art. 9(2), they may put their names down on housing lists in the region in which they are employed and are to enjoy the benefits thereof with the same right and priority as nationals. In Case 305/87 *Commission* v. *Greece*, above, at p. 1478, the Court pointed out that access to housing and ownership of property, provided for in Art. 9, was the corollary of freedom of movement for workers and was therefore covered by the prohibition of discrimination. Therefore, the Court found that various provisions of Greek law prohibiting, restricting, or making subject to conditions not imposed on Greek nationals the acquisition of rights in immovable property in certain areas in Greece by workers who were nationals of other Member States, constituted an obstacle to freedom of movement and was for that reason contrary to Art. 39 EC.

5. Workers' families. Freedom of movement for workers can only be fully achieved if workers have the right, guaranteed by Community law, to be accompanied by the members of their families, and if the latter are entitled to the same advantages as the families of national workers. The third recital in the preamble to Reg. 1612/68 expressly states that freedom of movement constitutes a fundamental right not only for workers but also for their families, while the fifth recital requires that obstacles to the mobility of workers should be eliminated, in particular as regards 'the worker's right to be joined by his family' and 'the conditions for the integration of that family into the host country'. In its entire case-law relating to workers' families, the ECJ has construed the relevant provisions of Reg. 1612/68 (Arts. 10 to 12) in the light of these recitals so as to achieve those fundamental objectives. Thus, time and again, the Court has pointed out that those provisions cannot be interpreted restrictively (see e.g. Case 267/83 *Diatta* [1985] ECR 567 at p. 589); that they must be interpreted 'in the context of the overall structure and purpose of that regulation', taking into account, 'first, the importance for the worker, from a human point of view, of having his entire family with him and, secondly, the importance, from all points of view, of the integration of the worker and his family into the host Member State without any difference in treatment in relation to nationals of that State' (Case 249/86 *Commission* v. *Germany*, above, at p. 1290). Equality of treatment in respect of the advantages that are granted to the members of a worker's family 'contributes to the integration of migrant workers in the working environment of the host country in accordance with the objectives of the free movement of workers' (Case 316/85 *Lebon*, above, at p. 2836). Moreover, Arts. 10 to 12 of Reg. 1612/68 must also be interpreted in the light of the requirement of respect for family life set out in Art. 8 of the European Convention on Human Rights, which is one of the fundamental rights recognized by Community law (Case 249/86 *Commission* v. *Germany*, above, at p. 1290).

Art. 10(1) of the regulation specifies that, irrespective of their nationality, the following have the right to 'install themselves' with a worker who is a national of one Member State and who is employed in the territory of another Member State:

(*a*) his spouse and their descendants who are under the age of 21 years or are dependants;
(*b*) dependent relatives in the ascending line of the worker and his spouse.

Under Art. 10(2), Member States are required to facilitate the admission of any member of the family not coming within the above provisions if dependent on the worker or living under his roof in the country from where he comes.

The right to 'install themselves' referred to in Art. 10(1) means the right to enter and reside in the territory of a Member State (see e.g. Case 48/75 *Royer*, above, at p. 509). Under Art. 10(1)(a), this right is granted, apart from the spouse, both to the descendants of the worker and to those of his spouse, of whatever nationality. As the ECJ has pointed out, to give a restrictive interpretation to that provision to the effect that only the children common to the migrant worker and his spouse have the right to install themselves with them would run counter to the aim of the regulation (Case C-413/99 *Baumbast and R* [2002] ECR I-7091, para. 57). The worker must be a national of one Member State and employed in the territory of another Member State. It follows that Community law does not grant the right of entry and residence to the non-EC national spouse and dependent relatives of a worker who is employed within the territory of the Member State of which he is a national and who has never exercised the right to freedom of movement within the Community. This is a purely internal situation, which falls outside the scope of application of Community law (Cases 35/82 etc. *Morson and Jhanjan*, above, at pp. 3736–7, where nationals of Suriname were lawfully refused permission to enter and reside in the Netherlands where their children, of whom they were dependants, were employed. The children were Netherlands nationals but had never been employed in another Member State. See also Cases C-297/88 etc. *Dzodzi*, above, at pp. I-3791–2 and sections I.2(*a*) and I.4 above. If the spouse and relatives are Community nationals, they have a right of entry and residence in their own right).

However, once a national of a Member State has exercised the right to freedom of movement or establishment by taking up employment or self-employment in another Member State, the position is different. Then he has the right, upon returning to the Member State of which he is a national in order to pursue an activity as an employed or self-employed person, to be accompanied by his spouse who is a national of a non-Member State. In this situation, the spouse will exercise the right of entry and residence not under national law but under Community law as the spouse of a migrant worker and must enjoy at least the same rights as would be granted to him or her if his or her spouse entered and resided in another Member State. Nevertheless, Arts. 39 and 43 EC do not prevent Member States from applying to foreign spouses of their own nationals rules on entry and residence more favourable than those provided for by Community law. Nor are the Member States prohibited from taking the measures necessary to prevent any abuse of the rights and facilities created by the Treaty (Case C-370/90 *Singh*, above, at pp. I-4293–5, where the Indian husband of a British national who had been employed in Germany, could successfully rely on Community law to obtain leave to enter and reside in the United Kingdom where they had lived before). However, Art. 39 cannot benefit a child whose father is a national of a non-member country and whose mother, although a national of a Member State, is not an employed person (Case 238/83 *Meade* [1984] ECR 2631 at p. 2638, involving a father of United States nationality and a mother of British nationality, both resident in France).

Reg. 1612/68 covers only freedom of movement within the Community, but is silent on the question whether a national of a non-Member State, who is the spouse of a national of a Member State, has the right of access to the territory of the Community. The Court has held that in order to benefit from the rights provided for in Art. 10 of Reg. 1612/68, such a spouse must be lawfully resident in a Member State when he moves to another Member

State or returns to the first Member State together with his spouse. If he is not, he has no right under Art. 10 to install himself with his spouse in another Member State, and if he is not lawfully resident in that other Member State, he has no right to return to the first Member State with his spouse. Moreover, Art. 10 is not applicable where the national of a Member State and the national of a non-Member State have entered into a marriage of convenience in order to circumvent the provisions of Community law relating to the latter's right of entry and residence. On the other hand, where the marriage is genuine, the fact that the spouses installed themselves in another Member State in order to take advantage of rights conferred by Community law when they return to their State of origin is not relevant to an assessment of their legal situation in the latter State. If, upon their return, the spouse who is a non-Member State national cannot enjoy the rights provided for in Art. 10 because he has not resided lawfully on the territory of a Member State, the authorities of the first State must none the less have regard to the right to respect for family life under Art. 8 of the European Convention on Human Rights, provided that the marriage is genuine (Case C-109/01 *Akrich* [2003] ECR I-9607, paras. 46–61).

The ECJ has held that the term 'spouse' in Art. 10(1) refers to a marital relationship only. Therefore, the unmarried companion, even in a stable relationship, of a migrant worker cannot be treated as his 'spouse' for the purposes of that provision (Case 59/85 *Reed*, above, at pp. 1300–1, but *see also under* **Social advantage**). On the other hand, the Court has also held that an existing marital relationship cannot be regarded as being dissolved so long as it has not been terminated by the competent authority. There is no requirement under Art. 10(1) that the spouse (or the children or the other members of the family) must live permanently with the worker under the same roof in order to qualify for a right of residence. Consequently, the marital relationship does not come to an end merely because the spouses live separately, even where they intend to divorce at a later date (Case 267/83 *Diatta*, above, at pp. 589–90, involving a woman of Senegalese nationality married to a French national residing and working in Berlin; see also Case C-413/99 *Baumbast and R*, above, para. 62, concerning children living separately from their father).

While, therefore, separation does not deprive the spouse of the right of residence acquired *before* separation (as in *Diatta*, see above), it is still unclear whether a right of entry and residence can arise under Art. 10(1) *following* separation but before divorce. It is also uncertain how divorce affects the rights of the former spouse under Art. 10(1). It seems that following divorce Community law does not confer a right of residence on the former spouse who is a third country national, except where such a right is necessary to enable that spouse to look after his or her children during their studies in the host Member State (Case C-413/99 *Baumbast and R*, above, paras. 68–75, where the Court derived this right from Art. 12 of Reg. 1612/68, see below). Divorce does not affect the rights of the children acquired under Arts. 10 and 12 of the regulation (ibid. paras. 60–3; see further below).

As regards the concept of a 'dependent' relative, the ECJ has held that the status of a 'dependent member of a worker's family' is the result of a purely factual situation. The person having that status is a member of the family who is supported by the worker, and there is no need to determine the reasons for recourse to the worker's support (i.e. whether the person concerned is objectively in need of such support), or to inquire whether the person is able to support himself by taking up paid employment (Case 316/85 *Lebon*, above, at p. 2838). However, such dependent members of the family qualify only indirectly, through the worker, for the equal treatment accorded by Community law to the worker himself. Thus, children lose their entitlement to Community rights once they reach the age of 21, are no longer dependent on the worker and do not have the status of workers (ibid. at pp. 2836–7; Case C-85/96 *Martinez Sala*, above, at p. I-2719; Case C-131/96 *Mora Romero* [1997] ECR I-3659 at pp. I-3681–2, where the child of a worker could not benefit from equal treatment because his father died before his country of origin acceded to the Community).

Art. 10(3) of the regulation requires the migrant worker to provide housing for his family that is considered as normal for national workers in the region where he is employed. However, this provision must not give rise to discrimination between national and migrant workers. The Court has interpreted this requirement as applying only at the time of the arrival of members of the family in the host State, but once the family has been brought together, the position of the migrant worker cannot be different in regard to housing from that of a national worker. Therefore, a Member State cannot make renewal of the residence permit of members of the family conditional upon their living in appropriate housing, not only at the time of their arrival but for the entire duration of their residence. Non-renewal of the residence permit on the grounds that housing has become unsuitable, for example because of the birth of a child, would amount to a severe sanction that would lead to discrimination against the migrant and his family (Case 249/86 *Commission* v. *Germany*, above, at pp. 1290–3).

Art. 11 grants the spouse of the migrant worker as well as those of his children who are under the age of 21 years or dependent on him the right to take up any activity as an employed person throughout the territory of the host State, even if they are not nationals of any Member State. Thus, the spouse has the right to pursue any occupation, including those which are subject to administrative authorization and to special legal rules governing their exercise such as the medical profession, subject to the same conditions as nationals of the host State. He must have the same qualifications and diplomas and must observe the same professional rules as national workers. He is entitled to have his qualifications and diplomas recognized under the same conditions as apply to Community nationals, even if he is a national of a non-member country. For this purpose, he can rely on national law or on any relevant Community directive or on international agreements. Generally speaking, the spouse is entitled to the same non-discriminatory 'national treatment' as the worker and may rely on the provisions of Reg. 1612/68 (e.g. on Art. 3(1)), irrespective of his nationality (Case 131/85 *Gül*, above, at pp. 1588–93, where a doctor of Cypriot nationality with medical qualifications from the University of Istanbul could successfully rely on Art. 11 in order to practise medicine as an employed person in Germany on the basis that his British wife was working there and that his qualifications were recognized as equivalent).

The same rules apply to the migrant worker's children. Once the child has engaged in an activity as an employed person he may, as a Community worker, rely on the provisions of the Treaty and of Reg. 1612/68 relating to equality of treatment (Case 235/87 *Matteucci* [1988] ECR 5589 at p. 5609). The spouse and child may take up employment throughout the territory of the host State, even at a place away from the residence of the migrant worker. Nevertheless, Art. 11 cannot serve as a legal basis for a right of residence independent of that provided for in Art. 10 (Case 267/83 *Diatta*, above, at p. 590). Nor can Art. 11 be relied on by a national of a non-member country married to a worker having the nationality of a Member State when that worker has never exercised the right to freedom of movement within the Community (Cases C-64/96 etc. *Uecker and Jacquet*, above, at p. I-3190).

It must be noted that Art. 11 does not expressly allow the spouse and the dependent children to take up self-employed activity in the host State. This is in strange contrast with the position of the spouses and dependent children of migrants not involved in any economic activity, such as persons of independent means, retired persons, and students, who are granted the right to take up any employed *or* self-employed activity anywhere in the host State, even if they are not nationals of a Member State (see Art. 2(2) of Dir. 90/364, Dir. 90/365, and Dir. 93/96, respectively, *OJ* 1990 L180/26, *OJ* 1990 L180/28, *OJ* 1993 L317/59; *see further under* **Right of entry and residence**). This obviously creates discrimination against the members of the families of workers, particularly where they are third-country nationals. (If these family members are nationals of a Member State, then they may pursue activities as employed or self-employed persons in their own right, independently of Art. 11.) There seems to be no reason why this anomalous situation should be maintained, particularly as it disadvantages those who should be the primary beneficiaries of the right to free movement, namely, the economically active.

According to Art. 12, the children of a migrant worker who is or has been employed in another Member State must be admitted to the host State's general educational, apprenticeship, and vocational training courses under the same conditions as the nationals of that State, if the children are residing in its territory. Member States are to encourage all efforts to enable such children to attend these courses under the best possible conditions. The ECJ has interpreted these provisions extremely generously so as to achieve one of the principal objectives of Reg. 1612/68, namely, the integration of the migrant worker's family in the society of the host Member State (see Case C-308/89 *Di Leo* [1990] ECR I-4185 at p. I-4208; Case C-413/99 *Baumbast and R*, above, paras. 50, 59). Therefore, in a consistent line of cases the Court has held that the national treatment required by Art. 12 applies not only to admission to education, but also to general measures intended to facilitate educational attendance, such as educational grants, whether emanating from the central, regional, or local authorities. Although educational and training policy is not as such within Community competence and therefore national authorities are free to determine the conditions under which education is provided, those conditions must nevertheless be applied without discrimination between the children of national workers and those of migrant workers (Case 9/74 *Casagrande* [1974] ECR 773 at pp. 778–80; Case 68/74 *Alaimo* [1975] ECR 109 at pp. 113–14; see also the cases cited below).

The status of a child of a Community worker implies, the Court has said, that such children are entitled to financial assistance granted to cover the costs of students' education and maintenance (including the costs of access to education, the maintenance costs of the student and of his dependants, the costs of purchasing books and other educational materials, the costs of health insurance, etc.) under the same conditions as apply to the host country's own nationals. Such assistance constitutes a 'social advantage' within the meaning of Art. 7(2) of Reg. 1612/68, for which both migrant workers themselves and their children are eligible under the same conditions as nationals, even when the children arrived in the host country before the age at which they had to attend school. Moreover, the child retains his entitlement even when his parents return to their country of origin and the child remains in or returns to the host State in order to continue his studies, which he cannot pursue in his own country of origin because his diplomas are not recognized there (Cases 389/87 etc. *Echternach and Moritz* [1989] ECR 723 at pp. 760–2, 764–5). The enjoyment of these benefits, conferred directly by Community law, may not be made subject to the grant of a residence permit (ibid. at pp. 762–3).

In its subsequent case-law, the Court has further clarified and extended the rights of the children of migrant workers. Thus, in Case C-413/99 *Baumbast and R*, above, paras. 53–5, the Court rejected a restrictive interpretation of its ruling in *Echternach and Moritz* (see immediately above), according to which children could continue their education in the host Member State after the departure of their parents *only* where they cannot do so in their Member State of origin. Such a narrow interpretation, the Court said, would be contrary to both the letter and spirit of Art. 12. Thus, the Court has confirmed that children who installed themselves in the host Member State during the exercise by their parents of rights of residence as migrant workers are entitled to reside there in order to attend general educational courses, and that the fact that the parents have later divorced, the fact that only one parent is a national of a Member State and that parent has ceased to be a migrant worker in the host Member State and the fact that the children are not themselves nationals of a Member State are irrelevant in this regard (ibid. paras. 56–63).

The Court has moreover held that where children have the right to reside in the host Member State in order to attend general educational courses pursuant to Art. 12, the parent who is the primary carer of those children is entitled to reside with them in order to facilitate the exercise of that right, even if he or she is not a national of a Member State, even if the parents have meanwhile divorced and even if the parent who is a national of a Member State has ceased to be a migrant worker in the host State (ibid. paras. 68–75).

The principle of equal treatment laid down in Art. 12 extends to all forms of education, whether vocational or general, including university courses and advanced vocational training at a technical college (Cases 389/87 etc. *Echternach and Moritz*, above, at p. 763). It also extends to educational arrangements provided for handicapped children to enable them to realize or improve their aptitude for work (Case 76/72 *S*, above, at p. 464). Moreover, Art. 12 is not confined to education or training within the host Member State. The right to equal treatment implies that any educational grant provided by a Member State to its own nationals in respect of education or training abroad, must be available, under the same conditions, to children of migrant workers who wish to pursue their studies in another country, including the country of which they are nationals (Case C-308/89 *Di Leo*, above, at pp. I-4208–9, referring to Case 235/87 *Matteucci*, above, at pp. 5611–12, where the Court first established this principle in the context of 'social advantage' under Art. 7(2) of the regulation, for which *see further under* **Social advantage** and section II below). Finally, the Court has decided that the definition of 'child' for the purposes of Art. 12 is not subject to the conditions of age or dependency laid down in Arts. 10(1) and 11. Consequently, the benefits of Art. 12 (e.g. financial assistance) may be claimed by children who are older than 21 years of age and are no longer dependants of their parents (Case C-7/94 *Gaal* [1995] ECR I-1031 at pp. I-1047–9).

The application of Art. 12 is, however, subject to certain limitations. In the first place, Art. 12 imposes obligations only on the Member State in which the migrant worker resides. It does not preclude a Member State from applying discriminatory conditions to children of migrant workers residing in another Member State even when the nationals of that other Member State are treated in the same way as the first State's own nationals (Case 263/86 *Humbel* [1988] ECR 5365 at p. 5389, where the child of a French father working and residing in Luxembourg could be required to pay an enrolment fee—'minerval'—as a condition for admission to ordinary secondary education in Belgium, even where Belgian and Luxembourg nationals were not required to pay the fee in question. The position is different in the case of vocational training, see section II below). Secondly, to enjoy equal treatment, the child himself must reside in the host State, although this does not exclude the possibility of him pursuing studies in another country (Case C-308/89 *Di Leo*, above, at p. I-4208). Thirdly, although the entitlement to equality of treatment continues even when the parent is deceased or has left the host country (Case 42/87 *Commission* v. *Belgium* [1988] ECR 5445 at p. 5456; Cases 389/87 etc. *Echternach and Moritz*, above, at p. 761), it can only benefit a child who has lived with his parents or either one of them in that country whilst at least one of his parents resided there as a worker.

Art. 12 cannot create rights for a child who was born after the worker ceased to work and reside in the host State (Case 197/86 *Brown*, above, at p. 3246).

The objectives pursued by Art. 12 are further promoted by Council Dir. 77/486 on the education of the children of migrant workers (*OJ* 1977 L199/32). This requires Member States to provide free tuition to children covered by Art. 12 for whom school attendance is compulsory under the laws of the host State, including the teaching of the official language of that State. Member States are also to promote the teaching of the mother tongue and culture of the children's country of origin.

6. Vacancy clearance and exchange of information. To promote freedom of movement for workers, Part II of Reg. 1612/68, as amended by Reg. 2434/92, lays down provisions for developing close co-operation between the employment services of the Member States and between those services and the Commission with a view to exchanging job vacancies and applications at Community level as well as exchanging information concerning living and working conditions and the state of the labour market (Arts. 13 and 14). A machinery for vacancy clearance has been set up (Arts. 15 to 18), and measures have been introduced for controlling the balance of the labour market and for dealing with serious disturbances thereon threatening the level of employment or the standard of living (Arts. 19 and 20). A European Office for Co-ordinating the Clearance of Vacancies and Applications for Employment (known as the European Co-ordination Office) has been established within the Commission. Its general task is to promote vacancy clearance at Community level and to assist the national employment services (Arts. 21 to 23). Two Committees have also been created. The Advisory Committee is responsible for assisting the Commission in matters concerning the freedom of movement of workers and their employment, and for co-ordinating the employment policies of the Member States at Community level (Arts. 24 to 31). The Technical Committee's task is to assist the Commission in respect of all technical work and measures for giving effect to the regulation (Arts. 32 to 37). By Dec. 93/569, adopted under Art. 44 of the regulation, the Commission has set up a European network of services, designated EURES (European Employment Services) with responsibility for developing the exchange of information and co-operation provided for in Part II of the regulation. It has replaced the earlier SEDOC system (European system for the international clearing of vacancies and applications for employment).

II. Students

Students make up a separate category of persons, whose status differs both from that of workers and from that of other economically inactive persons. For a long time, it was not clear whether students enjoyed the right, under Community law, to move to and reside in another Member State for the purposes of education, which is not an economic activity. It was also not certain whether they benefited from the rules on equal treatment with nationals in respect of access to education and training and related matters, such as the payment of tuition fees and entitlement to educational grants. It was only if a student was himself a worker or the child of a migrant worker that he enjoyed these rights because then he was covered by Art. 39 EC and the relevant provisions of Reg. 1612/68 (in particular, Arts. 7 or 12, see sections I.4 and I.5 above).

The legal status of students has been clarified by the ECJ in a series of successive cases, which may be broadly divided into two groups. The first group, which came before the Court first, concerned the compatibility with Community law of discriminatory enrolment and tuition fees charged to foreign students attending educational courses. The second group raised the question whether students from other Member States were entitled to educational grants, in particular maintenance and training grants, awarded by the host State to its own students. The two groups of cases are considered in turn below.

1. Tuition fees. The first case to reach the Court was Case 152/82 *Forcheri*, above, at pp. 2335–6, where the Court established the principle that although educational and vocational training policy as such had not been allocated to the competence of the Community, access to courses of instruction fell within the scope of the Treaty, and was therefore covered by the non-discrimination provisions of Art. 12. In arriving at this conclusion, the Court relied on Art. 128 of the original EEC Treaty [now Art. 150 EC, as amended by the TEU], which enabled the Council to lay down general principles for implementing a common vocational training policy, and on Council Dec. 63/266 of 2 April 1963 implementing Art. 128 *(OJ Sp. Edn.* 1963–4, p. 25). On this basis, the Court held that if a Member State organizes educational courses relating 'in particular' to vocational training, the requirement that a national of another Member State 'lawfully established' in the first State should pay an enrolment fee which is not payable by the nationals of the host State in order to take part in such courses, constitutes discrimination by reason of nationality, which is prohibited by Art. 12 EC.

This case involved the wife of an official of the Commission working in Brussels, both of whom were of Italian nationality. She was already resident in Belgium (this was presumably what the Court meant by the words 'lawfully established') when attending a course at an institution of non-university further education, which mostly trained social workers. She was required to pay a supplementary enrolment fee ('minerval'), not payable by Belgian nationals. Not being a worker or the child of a migrant worker, she was not covered by Reg. 1612/68. This was probably the reason why the Court relied on Art. 12 EC.

The principle established in *Forcheri* was applied and further clarified in Case 293/83 *Gravier*, above, at pp. 611–13, which involved a student of French nationality, whose parents resided in France and who went to Belgium for the sole purpose of studying strip cartoon art in Liège. She was clearly not covered by Reg. 1612/68, and her position was different from that of Mrs Forcheri in that she was not 'lawfully established' in Belgium. She was charged the same enrolment fee ('minerval') as Mrs Forcheri, which was not payable by Belgian nationals. The Court held that such unequal treatment based on nationality had to be regarded as discrimination prohibited by Art. 12 if it fell within the scope of the Treaty. The Court pointed out that the common vocational training policy referred to in Art. 128 EEC, an indispensible element of the activities of the Community, was being gradually established. Access to vocational training, the Court said, was likely to promote the free movement of persons throughout the Community by enabling them to obtain a qualification in the Member State where they intended to work or whose vocational training programmes best suited their particular needs. Therefore, the conditions of access to vocational training did fall within the scope of the Treaty. Consequently, the imposition on students who were nationals of other Member States of a charge, a registration fee or the 'minerval' as a condition of access to vocational training, where the same fee was not imposed on students who were nationals of the host State, constituted discrimination prohibited by Art. 12. Thus, the Court extended the *Forcheri* principle to foreign students who were not 'established' in the host State but went there for the purpose of education.

Relying on Art. 128 EEC (as it then was) and on the various measures adopted for its implementation, the Court then defined the concept of 'vocational training' by saying that:

> any form of education which prepares for a qualification for a particular profession, trade or employment or which provides the necessary training and skills for such a profession, trade or employment is vocational training, whatever the age and the level of training of the pupils or students, and even if the training programme includes an element of general education (ibid. at p. 614).

This definition, the Court said, included courses in strip cartoon art provided by an institution of higher education, which was the subject-matter of the case before it (ibid.).

In Case 309/85 *Barra* [1988] ECR 355 at pp. 376–7, the Court confirmed that its interpretation of Art. 12 EC in *Gravier* had retroactive effect, i.e. that it also covered applications for admission to vocational training courses made prior to the date of that judgment (13 February 1985), and that students from other Member States who had unduly paid a supplementary enrolment fee had a right to repayment even if they did not bring legal proceedings before that date.

The concept of vocational training was further clarified, and considerably extended, in Case 24/86 *Blaizot*, above, at pp. 403–5, where the Court was confronted with the question whether university studies in veterinary medicine constituted vocational training. The Court first pointed out that neither the provisions of the original EEC Treaty, in particular Art. 128, nor the objectives which they sought to achieve, i.e. the promotion of the free movement of persons, justified a narrow interpretation which would exclude all university education, on account of its very nature, from the definition of vocational training. Because of the significant variations amongst the Member States as to the nature of university studies, the complete exclusion of university education would result in unequal application of Community law in different Member States. The Court then stated that university studies might fall within the scope of vocational training:

> not only where the final academic examination directly provides the required qualification for a particular profession, trade or employment but also in so far as the studies in question provide specific training and skills, that is to say where a student needs the knowledge so acquired for the pursuit of a profession, trade or employment, even if no legislative or administrative provisions make the acquisition of that knowledge a prerequisite for that purpose (ibid. at p. 404).

In general, the Court pointed out, university studies fulfil these criteria. The only exceptions are certain courses of study that, because of their particular nature, are intended for students wishing to improve their general knowledge rather than prepare themselves for an occupation. The fact that in certain cases university education is divided into two stages—such as the 'candidature' and the 'doctorat' in Belgium—is irrelevant. Since access to the second stage, leading to the final diploma or degree, is conditional upon completion of the first stage, the two stages together must be regarded as a single unit and it is not possible to make a distinction between one stage that does not constitute vocational training and a second that does. The whole course must be regarded as vocational.

In this particular case, the Court ruled that university studies in veterinary medicine fell within the scope of 'vocational training' and that, consequently, a supplementary enrolment fee charged solely to students who were nationals of other Member States and wished to enrol for such studies constituted discrimination prohibited by Art. 12 EC (ibid. at p. 405). However, since this was the first case in which the Court recognized that university education might constitute vocational training, the Court found it necessary to restrict the effect of the judgment to future cases only, except where students had already brought legal proceedings prior to the date of the judgment (2 February 1988) for recovery of enrolment fees improperly charged (ibid. at p. 407).

The finding of the Court in *Blaizot* concerning multi-stage educational programmes was further clarified in Case 263/86 *Humbel*, above, at p. 5387. In that case, the Court held that the various years of a study programme cannot be assessed individually but must be considered within the framework of the programme as a whole, in the light of its purpose. Thus, a year of study which does not in itself meet the definition of vocational training may nevertheless still constitute vocational training if it is an integral part of a programme that forms a coherent and indivisible body of instruction qualifying as vocational training.

In the same case (at p. 5389), the Court confirmed the principle laid down in *Gravier* that the prohibition of discrimination contained in Art. 12 EC always applies to vocational training, irrespective of the country of residence of the student and of his parents. Finally, the Court established that students cannot be regarded as recipients of services (and consequently cannot claim a right to free movement and equality of treatment on that basis) because courses provided as part of the national educational system and financed out of public funds do not constitute 'services' within the meaning of Art. 49 EC (ibid. at pp. 5387–8). By contrast, private education provided for remuneration and profit may be regarded as a 'service', and students receiving such education are entitled to all the rights enjoyed by recipients of services (*see further under* **Freedom to provide services**, section II.2).

Subsequently, the ECJ has held that national legislation which imposes a quota on the number of foreign students who may be taken into account for the purposes of financing vocational education and which has the effect of excluding students who are nationals of other Member States from such education once the quota is reached, constitutes discrimination prohibited by Art. 12 EC and Art. 12 of Reg. 1612/68 (Case 42/87 *Commission* v. *Belgium*, above, at pp. 5455–6. See also Case C-47/93 *Commission* v. *Belgium* [1994] ECR I-1593 at pp. I-1608–9, where the Court held that by failing to exempt from the 'minerval' nationals of other Member States, and by applying various discriminatory measures to them, Belgium failed to fulfil its obligations under Arts. 10 and 12 EC).

The scope of vocational training was one of the issues raised in Case 242/87 *Commission* v. *Council* [1989] ECR 1425 at pp. 1455–8, which concerned the question whether the Erasmus programme (European Community action scheme for the mobility of university students) could be adopted on the sole basis of the original Art. 128 EEC and implementing Dec. 63/266 relating to vocational training (the Commission's view), or whether it had to be based, in addition, on Art. 235 EEC [now Art. 308 EC] also (the Council's view). Relying on its case-law discussed above, the Court held that, in general, the studies to which the programme applied fell within the sphere of vocational training, and that only in exceptional cases would the planned action involve university studies which, because of their particular nature, were outside that sphere. The mere possibility of such exceptional cases could not justify the conclusion that the Council was not empowered to adopt the scheme under Art. 128 (ibid. at p. 1456). However, since the programme also included certain aspects falling within the sphere of scientific research, it exceeded the scope of vocational training. Therefore, the Court concluded, the Council was bound to base the programme on Art. 235 [now Art. 308] as well (ibid. at p. 1458). This decision thus makes it clear that the concept of vocational training does not include research.

2. Maintenance grants. The second group of cases started with Case 39/86 *Lair*, above, at pp. 3194–201 and Case 197/86 *Brown*, above, at pp. 3241–6, which were decided by the Court on the same day. In essence, they both raised the question whether students who were nationals of other Member States were entitled to financial assistance given by a Member State to its own nationals for the purpose of university studies. The Court made a distinction between assistance intended to cover registration and other fees, in particular tuition fees, charged for access to education, and assistance given to students for maintenance and training. Referring to its previous case-law discussed above, the Court held that since access to vocational training (which included most types of university studies) fell within the scope of the EC Treaty, assistance granted to cover registration and tuition fees also fell within its scope and was subject to the prohibition of discrimination under Art. 12. On the other hand, at that stage in the development of Community law, assistance given for maintenance and training fell in principle outside the scope of the EC Treaty and was therefore not covered by the rule on non-discrimination laid down in Art. 12. This kind of assistance was a matter of educational policy and social policy, which had not yet been brought, or fully brought, within Community competence (*Lair*, at pp. 3194–5; *Brown*, at pp. 3242–3). As a result, students from other Member States were entitled to grants covering registration and tuition fees charged by universities, under the same conditions as students who were nationals of the host State, but they were not entitled to grants awarded in respect of maintenance and training.

However, the Court went on to say that maintenance and training grants awarded for university studies leading to a professional qualification (i.e. studies which qualified as vocational training) constituted a 'social advantage' within the meaning of Art. 7(2) of Reg. 1612/68, because they enabled a worker to improve his professional qualifications and promote his social advancement. Therefore, a migrant worker who took up university studies in the host State was entitled to such grants in the same way as national workers (*Lair*, at pp. 3196–8; *Brown*, at p. 3245. *See also under* **Social advantage**).

The ruling of the Court in the above cases must be read in the light of its more recent case-law. Case C-184/99 *Grzelczyk* [2001] ECR I-6193 at pp. I-6241–6 raised the question whether a student of French nationality who attended a university course in physical education in Belgium and who was not a 'worker' for the purposes of Community law, was entitled in Belgium to a minimum subsistence allowance (called '*minimex*'), which was a non-contributory social benefit and which under Belgian law was available to foreign nationals to whom Reg. 1612/68 applied. The Court first pointed out that since its ruling in *Lair* and *Brown*, three important changes occurred in this area of the law. First, the TEU introduced citizenship of the European Union into the EC Treaty; secondly, it added to Title XI of Part Three of the Treaty a new Chapter 3 devoted to education and vocational training (Arts. 149 and 150); and thirdly, the Council adopted Dir. 93/96 on the right of residence for students (*OJ* 1993 L317/59). These changes had to be taken into account.

Since in the present case the *minimex* was available to students of Belgian nationality who were not 'workers', the only bar to its being granted to Mr Grzelczyk was the fact that he was not of Belgian nationality. This was discrimination on grounds of nationality, which was prohibited by Art. 12 if it fell within the scope of application of the Treaty. Art. 12 had to be read in conjunction with the provisions concerning citizenship of the Union, in particular with Art. 18(1), which granted to every citizen the right to move and reside freely within the territory of the Member States, subject to such limitations and conditions as were expressly provided for. Every citizen of the Union was entitled to rely on Art. 12 once he had exercised the right to freedom of movement conferred by Art. 18(1), which fact brought his situation within the scope of Community law. The fact that a Union citizen moved to another Member State to pursue university studies could not deprive him of the right to rely on the prohibition of discrimination laid down in Art. 12. Therefore, a student had to be treated in the host Member State in the same way as a national of that State. It followed that entitlement to the *minimex* could not be made conditional on the non-national student falling within the scope of Reg. 1612/68 when no such condition applied to the nationals of the host State.

Grzelczyk was followed by Case C-224/98 *D'Hoop* [2002] ECR I-6191 at pp. I-6222–5, which involved a student of Belgian nationality who was not entitled to receive an unemployment benefit in Belgium, known as 'tideover allowance', normally available to young people seeking their first employment after completing their studies, for the sole reason that she completed her secondary education in France and not in Belgium. Ms D'Hoop could not rely on Art. 39 EC or Reg. 1612/68 because she was neither a worker nor a family member of a migrant worker. However, the Court held that as a citizen of the Union who had exercised the freedom of movement and residence by studying in France, Ms D'Hoop fell within the personal and material scope of the Treaty and was therefore entitled to the same treatment in law as that accorded to other Belgian nationals who were in the same situation.

It would be incompatible with the right of freedom of movement, the Court said, if a citizen of the Union were to receive less favourable treatment in the Member State of which she was a national than she would enjoy if she had not availed herself of the opportunities offered by the Treaty in relation to freedom of movement. Those opportunities could not be fully effective if a national of a Member State could be deterred from availing herself of them by obstacles raised on her return to her country of origin by legislation penalizing the fact that she had used them. Ms D'Hoop was in fact disadvantaged simply because she had exercised her freedom to move in order to study in another Member State. That freedom, the Court pointed out, was particularly important in the field of education since the objectives of the Community now included a contribution to education and training of quality (Art. 3(1)(q) EC) aimed, *inter alia*, at encouraging mobility of students and teachers (Art. 149(2) EC). Such inequality of treatment was contrary to the status of citizen of the Union and could not be justified by objective considerations independent of nationality (for the increased importance of education in post-Maastricht Community law, see also the opinion of A.-G. Geelhoed, ibid. at pp. I-6205–6).

At first sight, it would seem to follow from the ruling in *Grzelczyk* that the distinction made in *Lair* and *Brown* between financial assistance intended to cover registration and tuition fees and assistance given for maintenance and training is no longer relevant: a student who is a citizen of the Union must be treated in the host Member State *in every respect* in exactly the same way as a national student. However, by virtue of Art. 18(1), this general rule is subject to the 'limitations and conditions' laid down by Community law, which in the case of students means the limitations and conditions specified in Dir. 93/96 (see Case C-184/99 *Grzelczyk*, above, at pp. I-6244–6). Among other things, the directive requires that when moving to another Member State, students must have sufficient resources to avoid becoming a burden on the social assistance system of the host State and must be covered by full sickness insurance (Art. 1). Most importantly, Art. 3 expressly stipulates that the directive does not establish any entitlement to payment of maintenance grants by the host Member State. Therefore, although such entitlement would arise as a result of the requirement of equal treatment under Arts. 12 and 18(1), as interpreted by the Court, it is excluded by the directive. The case-law of the Court, to be considered below, thus continues to be relevant (for a discussion of the right of free movement of Union citizens, see section III below; for the right of residence for students, *see further under* **Right of entry and residence**, section V).

The result of the Court's case-law and of Dir. 93/96 is that while a student from another Member State is not entitled to maintenance and training grants in his capacity as a 'student', he may be so entitled if he has already acquired the status of 'worker' in the host State by having been employed there prior to the commencement of his studies. This raises the further question whether a migrant worker can retain his status as a worker, on which the 'social advantage' provided for in Art. 7(2) of Reg. 1612/68 depends, when he gives up or interrupts his previous employment or, if unemployed, his search for employment, in order to pursue full-time studies in the host State. In relation to this question, the Court came to the conclusion that he can, provided that there is some continuity or relationship between the previous occupational activity and the course of study in question. Such continuity is, however, not necessary where a migrant has involuntarily become unemployed and is obliged by conditions on the job market to undertake occupational retraining in another field of activity. A migrant is not necessarily voluntarily unemployed solely because his contract of employment, which was concluded from the outset for a fixed term, has expired. The Court did not specify in detail how close the relationship between the purpose of the studies and the previous employment must be. It did, however, refer to 'current developments in careers', pointing out that continuous careers are less common than has been formerly the case. Occupational activities, the Court added, are therefore occasionally interrupted by periods of training or retraining (*Lair*, at pp. 3198–200; Case C-413/01 *Ninni-Orasche* [2003] ECR I-0000, paras. 41–8). The Court gave more guidance in this respect in subsequent cases, which are considered below.

While a student may claim a maintenance grant in another Member State only in his capacity as a worker, the host State cannot make the payment of the grant conditional upon the completion of a minimum period of prior employment within its territory (*Lair*, at p. 3201, where the host State, Germany, required a five-year period of prior employment). Nevertheless, a very short period of occupational activity is not covered by Community law, where it is clear that a prospective student has entered a Member State for the sole purpose of taking advantage of the student assistance system in that State (ibid.). Whether a student qualifies as a worker must be decided in accordance with the rules of Community law (*see further under* **Worker**). The Court has held that a national of a Member State who has entered into an employment relationship in the host State for a period of eight months with a view to subsequently undertaking university studies there in the same field of activity and who would not have been employed by his employer if he had not already been accepted for admission to university is to be regarded as a worker within the meaning of Art. 7(2) of Reg. 1612/68 (*Brown*, at p. 3244). However, since in this situation the prospective student has acquired the status of worker exclusively as a result of his being accepted for admission to university, the employment relationship, which is the only basis for his entitlement to a grant, is merely ancillary to the studies to be financed by it. In these circumstances, he is not entitled to a maintenance grant (ibid. at pp. 3245–6).

In subsequent cases, the ECJ has established that migrant workers are entitled to a grant under Art. 7(2) of Reg. 1612/68 not only where the education or training is provided in the territory of the host State, but also where it is provided in another Member State. Thus, the Court has held that where a Member State gives its own national workers the opportunity of pursuing education or training in another Member State and offers a scholarship (a maintenance grant) for that purpose, it cannot refuse to grant the same opportunity and scholarship to a migrant worker, even if the scholarship is based on a bilateral agreement between the two Member States involved which limits eligibility to the nationals of the Contracting Parties (Case 235/87 *Matteucci*, above, at pp. 5611–12, where an Italian national working in Belgium successfully relied on Art. 7(2) to obtain a scholarship to study in Berlin on the basis of a bilateral Cultural Agreement concluded between Belgium and Germany). The same principle applies also where the migrant worker intends to study in the Member State of which he is a national (Case C-308/89 *Di Leo*, above, at pp. I-4208–9; Case C-3/90 *Bernini* [1992] ECR I-1071 at p. I-1106).

The principles discussed above have been applied, and considerably extended in favour of the migrant, in two important cases decided on the same day: Case C-357/89 *Raulin* [1992] ECR I-1027 at pp. I-1059–67 and Case C-3/90 *Bernini*, above, at pp. I-1104–8. The Court held that in assessing, for the purposes of an educational grant, whether a person is a worker and whether there is a relationship between his employment and the subject-matter of the studies in question, account must be taken of *all* the occupational activities (not only the last one) which the person has pursued in the host Member State, regardless of whether or not they were interrupted by periods of training, retraining, or readaptation. In that context, all relevant factors must be considered, such as the nature and the diversity of the activities pursued and the duration of the period (if any) between the end of those activities and the commencement of the studies. If there is such a relationship, the person retains his status as a worker, even if he has voluntarily given up his employment in order to take up full-time studies, and even if there is a certain lapse of time between the employment and the studies. However, previous activities carried on in Member States other than the host State cannot be taken into account (*Raulin*, at p. I-1061; *Bernini*, at p. I-1106).

In the absence of the requisite link between employment and the studies, the person does not retain his status as a worker, except in the case of involuntary unemployment (*Raulin*, at p. I-1062). If the person has not acquired or has not retained the status of worker, he is entitled, under Art. 12 EC, to that part of the financial assistance granted by the host Member State to its own nationals that is intended to cover enrolment fees and other costs of access to the course. Where a grant scheme does not distinguish between enrolment and maintenance costs, it is for the national courts to determine what proportion of the grant is intended to cover the former (ibid. at pp. I-1062–4).

Most importantly, the Court ruled that a national of a Member State who has been admitted to a course of vocational training in another Member State derives from Community law a right of entry into and residence in that State. Such a right follows from, and is corollary to, the right to non-discriminatory access to vocational training. In its absence, the latter right would be illusory. Since the right of residence is derived directly from the Treaty, its exercise cannot be made conditional on the issue of a residence permit. Nor may the host State require possession of a residence permit as a prerequisite for study finance. Nevertheless, because of its corollary nature, the right of residence may be limited in time to the duration of the course and granted only for the purpose of the course. It may also be made subject to conditions deriving from the 'legitimate interests' of the host State, such as the covering by the student of maintenance costs and health insurance, to which the principle of non-discriminatory access to education does not apply (*Raulin*, at pp. I-1064–7). Presumably, the concept of 'legitimate interests' would also entitle the host State to impose limitations on the right of residence on grounds of public policy, public security, or public health, referred to in Art. 39(3) EC. This decision of the Court is fully in line with Dir. 93/96 on the right of residence for students (which replaced the almost identical original Dir. 90/366) although, like that directive, it extends that right only to students attending a vocational training course in another Member State. The right of entry and residence of other students seems to be governed by Dir. 90/364 on a general right of residence (*see further under* **Right of entry and residence**. See also Case C-295/90 *Parliament* v. *Council* [1992] ECR I-4193 at p. I-4234).

The Court further established that assistance for vocational education and maintenance granted by a Member State to the children of national workers constitutes for a migrant worker a 'social advantage' within the meaning of Art. 7(2) of Reg. 1612/68, but only where the worker continues to support his child. In that case, the child, as an indirect beneficiary, has an independent right to obtain such study finance on the basis of Art. 7(2), if under national law it is granted directly to the student. In that situation, the requirement may not be imposed on the child of the migrant worker that he should reside within the host State, if such a requirement is not imposed on the children of national workers (*Bernini*, at pp. I-1106–8).

3. **Summary.** As a result of the jurisprudence of the ECJ discussed above, the position of migrant students has in most, although not all, respects been assimilated to that of home students. As citizens of the European Union, students are covered by the principle of equal treatment, although the legal basis of that treatment varies according to their individual circumstances. It may be one (ore more) of the following four provisions: Art. 12 EC in conjunction with Art. 18(1) EC, Arts. 7(2), (3), or 12 of Reg. 1612/68. In the light of the foregoing discussion, the legal status of students who are Community nationals and therefore citizens of the Union may be summarized as follows:

(*a*) A student who is not a migrant worker nor the child of a migrant worker must be admitted to vocational training courses in another Member State under the same conditions as home students. He must be charged the same registration and tuition fees and is entitled to the same financial assistance covering such fees as home students. However, he is not entitled to maintenance grants and his right of residence in the host Member State is subject to certain conditions. He must be treated, even in the Member State of which he is a national, in the same way as all other citizens of the Union who are in the same situation. His position is governed by Arts. 12 and 18(1) EC and Dir. 93/96. Vocational training is widely defined and includes most, but not all, university courses but does not include basic general education and research.

(*b*) A student who is a migrant worker must be admitted to vocational training courses, and is entitled to receive for that purpose maintenance and training grants, under the same conditions as students of the host Member State, even if the course is provided in another Member State, provided that there is some continuity or relationship between his previous employment and the course, although this is not required where he is involuntarily unemployed. His position is covered by Art. 7(2) of Reg. 1612/68, and he enjoys entitlement to a grant as a 'social advantage'. A migrant worker must also have access to training in vocational schools and retraining centres under the same conditions as national workers under Art. 7(3) of Reg. 1612/68, but this provision does not apply to university studies.

(*c*) A student who is the child of a migrant worker must be admitted to the host Member State's educational, apprenticeship, and vocational training courses, and is entitled to financial assistance covering both registration and tuition fees and maintenance and training costs, under the same conditions as home students. He is entitled to these benefits even if the course is provided in another Member State. For this purpose, he can rely either on Art. 12 or on Art. 7(2) of Reg.

1612/68. Art. 12 applies to all forms of education, whether general or vocational, and irrespective of the age of the student and of whether or not he is dependent on his parents. Art. 7(2) applies only to vocational courses and may be relied on only where the child is supported by (i.e. dependent on) the worker, but it gives the child an independent right to obtain study finance. Under Art. 12, the child must reside in the host State, whereas under Art. 7(2) such a requirement may not be imposed if it is not imposed on home students. It follows from Arts. 10 and 11 of Reg. 1612/68 that the nationality of the child is irrelevant.

(*d*) The spouse of a migrant worker is not covered by Art. 12 of Reg. 1612/68, but is covered by Arts. 12 and 18(1) EC if he is a citizen of the Union and is then in the same position as students in group (*a*) above. It would seem that he is also covered by Art. 7(2) of Reg. 1612/68 and, if so, is in the same position as the child of the worker provided that he is dependent on the worker, but this point has not yet been decided by the Court. If the spouse is a worker himself, he is in the same position as students in group (*b*) above, irrespective of his nationality (see Art. 11 of Reg. 1612/68).

(*e*) Students who are enrolled for a vocational training course in another Member State enjoy the right of entry and residence in accordance with Dir. 93/96. Students attending non-vocational courses seem to be covered by Dir. 90/364.

(*f*) Generally, students cannot be regarded as recipients of services and are, therefore, not covered by Arts. 49 to 55 EC, except where they receive private education provided for remuneration and profit.

III. Citizens of the Union

1. The concept of Union citizenship. It has been seen previously that the original EEC Treaty granted the right to freedom of movement only to 'economically active' persons, that is, to workers, self-employed persons, and providers and recipients of services who were nationals of the Member States. This situation has changed as a result of two parallel, although legally distinct, developments.

The first was the Single European Act of 1986 (SEA), which inserted a new Art. 14 into the EC Treaty. This provides for the establishment of the internal market, which is defined as 'an area without internal frontiers in which the free movement of goods, persons, services and capital is ensured in accordance with the provisions of this Treaty'. The Article refers to the free movement of 'persons' in general, irrespective of their nationality and also irrespective of whether or not they are engaged in an economic activity. The implementation of this Article in the wider context of the internal market and of the establishment of an area of freedom, security, and justice is considered in section IV below.

To ensure the free movement of persons referred to in Art. 14, at least as far as Community nationals were concerned, the Council adopted three directives which extended the right of residence to persons who did not enjoy this right under other provisions of Community law because they were not economically active, that is, to persons of independent means (Dir. 90/364, *OJ* 1990 L180/26), retired persons (Dir. 90/365, *OJ* 1990 L180/28), and students (Dir. 93/96, *OJ* 1993 L317/59). Their position is discussed in a separate entry (*see further under* **Right of entry and residence**).

The second development was the Treaty on European Union of 1992 (TEU), which reaffirmed the resolve of the Member States 'to facilitate the free movement of persons' (eleventh recital in the preamble), and which expressly stated that one of the objectives of the Union was 'to strengthen the protection of the rights and interests of the nationals of its Member States through the introduction of a citizenship of the Union' (Art. 2, third indent; see also the ninth recital in the preamble, which refers to the establishment of 'a citizenship common to nationals of their countries'). Accordingly, the TEU inserted a new Part Two in the EC Treaty on 'Citizenship of the Union' (Arts. 17 to 22).

For the purposes of this entry, the key provisions of Part Two are Arts. 17 and 18. Art. 17(1) establishes citizenship of the Union and provides that 'Every person holding the nationality of a Member State shall be a citizen of the Union'. Thus, citizenship does not create a direct link between the individual and the Union; it creates an indirect connection through the nationality of a Member State. This is made clear in the last sentence of Art. 17(1), which states that 'Citizenship of the Union shall complement and not replace national citizenship'.

As will be seen below, the co-existence of national and Union citizenship has important consequences in that it gives rise to (or at least explains) the fact that in spite of Union citizenship being common to all nationals of the Member States (see the ninth recital above), it still does not create absolute equality between them. There is a residue of rights, mainly relating to entry and residence, which are so closely connected with 'national citizenship' (i.e. with nationality) that they remain particular to the nationals of each Member State and are not embraced by the concept of Union citizenship. It also follows from Art. 17(1) that acquisition and loss of Union citizenship is automatic and does not depend on the will of the individual: anyone who is a national of a Member State is, by virtue of that fact, a Union citizen, and anyone who is not a Member State national cannot acquire citizenship of the Union. Conversely, an individual cannot renounce the latter without first losing his or her nationality. Since, as seen in section I.2(*b*) above, it is for each Member State to define who its nationals are, the Union has no power to determine who are to be considered its citizens.

Art. 17(2) states that citizens of the Union enjoy the rights conferred by the Treaty and are subject to the duties imposed thereby. As discussed below, this provision has been used by the ECJ very effectively to give substance to the concept of citizenship.

Art. 18(1) lays down the fundamental rule that:

> Every citizen of the Union shall have the right to move and reside freely within the territory of the Member States, subject to the limitations and conditions laid down in this Treaty and by the measures adopted to give it effect.

This provision has been incorporated almost word for word, but without reference to limitations and conditions, in Art. 45(1) of the EU Charter of Fundamental Rights.

Art. 18(2), as amended by the Treaty of Nice (ToN), enables the Council to adopt provisions with a view to facilitating the exercise of the rights of free movement and residence. However, by virtue of Art. 18(3), this does not apply to provisions on passports, identity cards, residence permits, or any other such document or to provisions on social security or social protection. In addition, under Art. 22 the Council may adopt provisions to strengthen or to add to the rights laid down in Part Two, which it may recommend to the Member States for adoption in accordance with their respective constitutional requirements.

The remaining Articles in Part Two confer various additional rights on Union citizens, such as:

- the right to vote and to stand as a candidate in municipal elections in the Member State in which they reside (Art. 19(1); implemented by Dir. 94/80, *OJ* 1994 L368/38, as amended by Dir. 96/30, *OJ* 1996 L122/14);
- the right to vote and to stand as a candidate in elections to the European Parliament in the Member State in which they reside (Art. 19(2); implemented by Dir. 93/109, *OJ* 1993 L329/34);
- the right to diplomatic or consular protection in third countries (Art. 20; implemented by Dec. 95/553, *OJ* 1995 L314/73);
- the right to petition the European Parliament (Art. 21(1) in conjunction with Art. 194);
- the right to apply to the Ombudsman (Art. 21(2) in conjunction with Art. 195);
- the right to write to the Community institutions and to have an answer (Art. 21(3)).

These additional rights are not discussed further in this entry.

The main question to be considered below is to what extent has the introduction of the concept of citizenship of the Union, and in particular Arts. 17 and 18, enhanced the individual's right to move and reside freely within the Community as compared with the situation as it existed previously. In particular, has Art. 18(1) created a new and independent right of movement and residence in addition to that which already existed under Arts. 39 to 55 EC and the three directives mentioned above? If so, who are the beneficiaries of this new right? What is the relationship between Art. 18(1) and those other provisions? If not, what is the purpose of citizenship? What are the 'limitations and conditions' to which this right is subject by virtue of Art. 18(1)? Can Art. 18(1) produce direct effect? What are the 'rights conferred by this Treaty' which citizens are to enjoy under Art. 17(2)?

2. The opinions of the Advocates-General. Before turning to the rulings of the ECJ for an answer, it is worth examining briefly, and by no means exhaustively, some of the opinions put forward by various

Advocates-General on these questions. These opinions are considered broadly in chronological order.

In Case C-214/94 *Boukhalfa*, above, at pp. I-2271–2, A.-G. Leger dealt briefly with the consequences of Union citizenship for the equal treatment of Community nationals, even before the Court had an opportunity to give a ruling on the subject. He said that:

> If all the conclusions inherent in the concept [of citizenship] are drawn, every citizen of the Union must, whatever his nationality, enjoy exactly the same rights and be subject to the same obligations. Taken to its ultimate conclusion, the concept should lead to citizens of the Union being treated absolutely equally, irrespective of their nationality. Such equal treatment should be manifested in the same way as among nationals of one and the same State.

In Cases C-65/95 etc. *Shingara and Radiom* [1997] ECR I-3343 at p. I-3354, A.-G. Ruiz-Jarabo Colomer expressed the view that the creation of citizenship of the Union with the corollary of freedom of movement represents 'a considerable qualitative step forward' in that 'it separates that freedom from its functional or instrumental elements (the link with an economic activity or attainment of the internal market) and raises it to the level of a genuinely independent right inherent in the political status of the citizens of the Union'.

In Case C-85/96 *Martinez Sala*, above, at pp. I-2700–6, A.-G. La Pergola put forward a long and detailed analysis of the legal effects of the citizenship provisions. He was of the opinion that once Art. 18(1) has entered into force, the right of residence of a Union citizen who does not have the status of worker can no longer be considered to have been created by Dir. 90/364. The right to move and reside freely throughout the whole Union is now enshrined in an act of primary law, Art. 18(1), which extracted the 'kernel' from the other freedoms of movement. The existence of that right does not depend on whether or not it has been made subject to limitations under other provisions of primary or secondary Community law. The limitations provided for in Art. 18(1) concern the actual exercise but not the existence of the right. The right of movement and residence is not simply a derived right but a new and 'primary' right, inseparably linked to Union citizenship which is conferred directly on the individual, who is now formally recognized as a subject of law. Citizenship is the fundamental legal status guaranteed to every citizen without distinction by the legal order of the Community and of the Union. Consequently, nationality as a discriminatory factor ceases to be relevant and is prohibited. Citizenship of the Union falls within the scope of application of the Treaty and is therefore covered by the general prohibition of discrimination on grounds of nationality, but it cannot be indiscriminately superimposed on national citizenship. There are certain rights that are reserved to national citizens because they constitute an exclusive privilege associated with their nationality. But apart from these rights, nationals of any Member State enjoy equality of treatment in any Member State by virtue of their new legal status of common Union citizenship and regardless of any status or standing as users of the market.

These views were developed further in Case C-356/98 *Kaba I* [2000] ECR

I-2623 at pp. I-2655–62, where A.-G. La Pergola elaborated on the distinction made in the previous case between Union citizenship and national citizenship. He referred to Art. 17(1) EC according to which the former only complements but does not replace the latter. Therefore, he argued, national citizenship retains its own special features, including those deriving from public international law (e.g. that an individual cannot be expelled from, or denied admission to, the State of which he or she is a national). Consequently, the prohibition of discrimination does not mean that Union citizens who are the nationals of one Member State must be placed on an unqualified equal footing with nationals of another Member State in the matter of residence. The 'right of abode' that derives from nationality or similar status is not the same as the 'right of residence' that arises from Union citizenship. Once granted, the former is usually not subject to any temporal limitation or other conditions. By contrast, the latter is subject to the 'limitations and conditions' referred to in Art. 18(1). In the opinion of the Advocate-General, these 'limitations and conditions' are those which are laid down in the pre-existing provisions, such as Arts. 39 to 55 EC and the relevant secondary legislation, including the residence directives. The result is that *freedom of residence is still linked to the exercise of an economic activity or to the availability of sufficient resources*. On this basis, the Advocate-General concluded that Art. 18(1) 'does not, in itself, constitute a considerable qualitative step forward' (ibid. at p. I-2659).

By contrast, in his opinion in Case C-274/96 *Bickel and Franz*, above, at pp. I-7644–5, A.-G. Jacobs stressed the unifying effect of Union citizenship. In his words, 'The notion of citizenship of the Union implies a commonality of rights and obligations uniting Union citizens by a common bond transcending Member State nationality. The introduction of that notion was largely inspired by the concern to bring the Union closer to its citizens and to give expression to its character as more than a purely economic union'. It would be difficult to explain to a citizen, he pointed out, how, despite Arts. 12, 17, and 18 of the Treaty, a Member State could be allowed to discriminate against him on grounds of his nationality. 'Freedom from discrimination on grounds of nationality is the most fundamental right conferred by the Treaty and must be seen as a basic ingredient of Union citizenship'. Therefore, when a citizen exercises his right to move and reside within the territory of another Member State, his situation falls within the scope of the Treaty and consequently the rule on non-discrimination applies, even in criminal proceedings.

In Case C-378/97 *Wijsenbeek* [1999] ECR I-6207 at pp. I-6238–43, A.-G. Cosmas rejected the view that Art. 18(1) EC has no autonomous regulatory scope and that it is no more than a general declaration, which simply recapitulates in a non-binding manner the contents of other provisions of primary and secondary Community law on the free movement of persons. On the contrary, Art. 18(1) has introduced a new regime of freedom of movement, which differs from the previous regime not only because it extends the category of persons benefiting from this freedom to persons not pursuing economic activities, but also because it enshrines a right of a different kind, a true right of free movement that is independent of the economic objectives of the common market. Thus, freedom of movement now constitutes a goal in itself, and is inherent in the fact of being a citizen of the Union. The Advocate-General then put forward convincing arguments for the proposition that Art. 18(1) produces direct effect, which is not precluded by the 'limitations and conditions' to which it refers. In any case, he said, such limitations and conditions may be imposed only if they are justified and do not affect the very essence of the right of free movement and residence. The view that Union citizenship has created an original right of residence has also been endorsed by A.-G. Alber (see Case C-184/99 *Grzelczyk*, above, at p. I-6227).

In his opinion in Case C-413/99 *Baumbast and R*, above, paras. 103–15, A.-G. Geelhoed fully agreed with A.-G. Cosmas' view (see above) that Art. 18(1) has direct effect. He relied on the clear and unconditional wording of the first part of Art. 18(1), as well as on the scheme of the EC Treaty and the legislation adopted under it. In his view, Art. 18(1) subsumes under a single denominator the rights to move and to reside created by the Treaty and secondary legislation under two separate regimes, in favour of economically active and economically non-active citizens. For the latter, those rights, laid down previously in directives, now acquire the status of Treaty rights. The particular importance of Art. 18(1) is that in the absence of a single general and all-embracing set of rules concerning the exercise of those rights, any citizen who is not entitled to them under other provisions of Community law can now rely directly on Art. 18(1). However, that does not mean that Art. 18(1) has established an unrestricted right of movement and residence in favour of these citizens. The conditions and limitations imposed by other provisions of Community law, such as for example Arts. 39 to 55 EC, must be applied by analogy to persons who derive their rights directly from Art. 18(1). Those other provisions therefore determine the scope of Art. 18(1).

3. Action by the Community institutions. The Community institutions have taken full account of the importance of citizenship for free movement and residence. On 29 April 2004, the European Parliament and the Council adopted Dir. 2004/38 on the right of citizens of the Union and their family members to move and reside freely within the territory of the Member States (see section I.1 above). The preamble to the directive acknowledges that 'citizenship of the Union confers on every citizen of the Union a primary and individual right to move and reside freely within the territory of the Member States'. It further states that Union citizenship is 'the fundamental status of nationals of the Member States when they exercise their right of free movement and residence'. The purpose of the directive is to facilitate the exercise of this right by codifying and reviewing the existing legislation dealing separately with workers, self-employed persons, students, and other inactive persons and by replacing this sector-by-sector, piecemeal approach by a single, unified legislative act (see the first four recitals in the preamble).

The Explanatory Memorandum of the Commission of 15 April 2003 (COM(2003) 199) refers to the 'new legal and political environment resulting from the introduction of the concept of Union citizenship' and explains that the basic concept underlying the new directive is that 'Union citizens should, *mutatis mutandis*, be able to move between and reside in Member States in similar conditions to nationals of a Member State moving around or changing their place of residence in their own country' (Introduction, point 1.1. For the directive itself, *see further under* **Right of entry and residence**, section VII).

4. The case-law of the Court of Justice. Initially, the Court took a rather cautious and somewhat inconsistent approach to Union citizenship. In its early case-law, the Court tended to concentrate on one aspect of citizenship only, namely, the prohibition of discrimination on grounds of nationality. It was only in its more recent decisions that the Court finally gave full effect to the second, equally important aspect, that is, the right of Union citizens to move and reside freely within the territory of the Member States. Since these two aspects raise different issues, they are considered separately below.

(*a*) ***Prohibition of discrimination.*** When dealing with the question of discrimination in the context of citizenship, the Court follows the same general approach as in the case of workers, self-employed persons, and providers or recipients of services (see section I.4(*a*) above). The first step is always to establish into which category a person falls. The Court's general tenet is that Art. 18(1), like Art. 12, 'finds specific expression' in Arts. 39, 43, and 49 in relation to workers, self-employed persons, and providers or recipients of services, respectively. Therefore, where a Community national falls within the scope of one of those provisions, his position is governed by those Articles and not by Art. 18(1) (see Case C-100/01 *Oteiza Olazabal* [2002] ECR I-10981, para. 26, concerning workers; Case C-193/94 *Skanavi* [1996] ECR I-929 at p. I-951, concerning self-employed persons; Case C-92/01 *Stylianakis* [2003] ECR I-1291, paras. 18–20, concerning providers and recipients of services). Conversely, if the person concerned does not have the status of worker (or of one of the other categories), his position must be considered under the provisions on European citizenship (see Case C-85/96 *Martinez Sala*, above, at p. I-2725; Case C-184/99 *Grzelczyk*, above, at pp. I-6237–8; Case C-224/98 *D'Hoop*, above, at pp. I-6220 *et seq.*).

Where the latter is the case, the next step is to examine whether there is a sufficient connection between the person in question and Community law to justify its application. As the Court has pointed out, 'citizenship of the Union, established by Article 17 of the EC Treaty, is not intended to extend the scope *ratione materiae* of the Treaty also to internal situations which have no link with Community law . . . Any discrimination which nationals of a Member State may suffer under the law of that State fall within the scope of that law and must therefore be dealt with within the framework of the internal legal system of that State' (Cases C-64/96 etc. *Uecker and Jacquet*, above, at p. I-3190; see also Case C-148/02 *Garcia Avello*, above, para. 26. See, however, the *D'Hoop* and *Pusa* cases, discussed below).

When this second condition is also satisfied, the general prohibition of discrimination laid down in Art. 12 may be applicable, since there is no specific non-discrimination provision in the Treaty which could be applied to a citizen of the Union. However, for Art. 12 to be applicable, two further conditions must be met: the person concerned must fall within the personal and material scope of application of the Treaty.

Those conditions were examined by the Court for the first time in Case C-85/96 *Martinez Sala*, above, at pp. I-2724–6. The case involved a woman of Spanish nationality residing in Germany, whose application for child-raising allowance was rejected by the German authorities on the ground that she did not have a formal residence permit. The Court first pointed out that this amounted to unequal treatment since German nationals were not required to produce a similar document to receive the same benefit. Such unequal treatment constituted discrimination prohibited by Art. 12 provided that it fell within the personal and material scope of application of the Treaty. As a family benefit and a social advantage, the allowance clearly fell within the material scope of Community law. As regards its personal scope, if Mrs Martinez Sala had the status of worker (which was not clear from the facts of the case), the unequal treatment would be prohibited by Arts. 39 and 42 and the relevant secondary legislation. If she was not a worker, the Court said, then 'as a national of a Member State lawfully residing in the territory of another Member State', she came within the personal scope of the provisions of the Treaty on European citizenship. As a Union citizen, she could rely on Art. 17(2), which attached to the status of citizen the rights and duties laid down by the Treaty, including the right set out in Art. 12 not to suffer discrimination on grounds of nationality within the scope of application of the Treaty.

Thus, the Court confirmed, for the first time, that a citizen of the Union lawfully resident in the host Member State could rely on Art. 12 in all situations that fell within the material scope of Community law and was therefore protected against discrimination on grounds of nationality. This was the first major breakthrough in the area of citizenship. On the other hand, the Court avoided dealing with the second, equally important question, i.e. whether, as a citizen of the Union, Mrs Martinez Sala could rely on Art. 18(1) in order to claim a new right of residence, namely, to reside in Germany. The Court said that it was not necessary to answer this question because she had already been authorized to reside there under German domestic law.

While this case is of great importance, it has a somewhat limited scope, both in a material and in a personal sense, in that the situation of Mrs Martinez Sala fell within the scope of the Treaty only on the narrow grounds that the child-raising allowance was covered by Community law and that she was 'lawfully resident' in another Member State. In Case C-274/96 *Bickel and Franz*, above, at p. I-7655, the Court considerably extended the scope of application of Art. 12. The case raised the question whether an Austrian lorry driver and a German tourist were entitled to use the German language in criminal proceedings in the Province of Bolzano in Italy on the grounds that German-speaking Italian nationals living in that province had a right to do so. The Court pointed out that as recipients of services, both persons were free to visit and move around in the host Member State under Art. 49, independently of other freedoms guaranteed by the Treaty. *Furthermore*, the Court added, pursuant to Art. 18(1), every citizen of the Union had the right to move and reside freely within the Member States. The exercise of that right was enhanced if the citizens of the Union were able to use a given language in judicial proceedings on the same footing as the nationals of the host State. Consequently, the Court concluded, in exercising that right in another Member State Mr Bickel and Mr Franz were in principle entitled, under Art. 12, to treatment no less favourable than that accorded to nationals of the host State so far as the use of languages was concerned.

The principles underlying the ruling in *Bickel and Franz* were restated in more general terms in subsequent cases. In Case C-184/99 *Grzelczyk*, above, at pp. I-6242–3, a French student studying in Belgium was discriminated against on the ground of his nationality by not being granted a minimum subsistence allowance called the '*minimex*' (for further details of the case, see section II.2 above). The Court said that within the scope of application of the Treaty, such discrimination was, in principle, prohibited by Art. 12. In the present case, Art. 12 had to be read in conjunction with the provisions concerning citizenship of the Union in order to determine its scope of application, since Mr Grzelczyk's position as a student was not covered by any other, more specific, provision of the Treaty. Then the Court made the following general statement, repeated in the cases cited below:

> Union citizenship is destined to be the fundamental status of nationals of the Member States, enabling those who find themselves in the same situation to enjoy the same treatment in law irrespective of their nationality, subject to such exceptions as are expressly provided for.

A citizen of the Union, lawfully resident in a host Member State, thus can rely on Art. 12 in all situations that fall within the material scope of Community law. Those situations include, the Court stated, those involving the exercise of the fundamental freedoms guaranteed by the Treaty *and* those involving the exercise of the right to move and reside freely in another Member State, as conferred by Art. 18(1) (see also the cases cited below).

This case thus confirms, in general terms, that to bring a situation within the material scope of Community law, and therefore within the scope of Art. 12, it is sufficient that a citizen has exercised his freedom of movement, whether under Arts. 39, 43, and 49, *or* under Art. 18(1). To benefit from the prohibition of discrimination, it is no longer necessary to be an economically active person. Art. 18(1) provides an alternative legal basis of equal value for that.

While *Grzelczyk* provided a generalized definition of the material scope of application of Community law for the purposes of Art. 12, it still restricted the personal scope of Art. 12 to citizens of the Union 'lawfully resident in the territory of a host Member State'. However, the requirement of lawful residence in another Member State is unduly restrictive as it may not cover certain situations, for example, where a citizen is visiting another Member

State on a temporary basis but without residing there (as in *Bickel and Franz*), or where a citizen is resident, not in another Member State but in the Member State of which he is a national, where he suffers discrimination (see the *D'Hoop* case discussed below). Moreover, as will be seen under point (*b*) below, the requirement is superfluous since every citizen has a right to be a 'lawful resident' in another Member State, subject to the limitations and conditions to which Art. 18(1) refers.

The situation mentioned above arose in Case C-224/98 *D'Hoop*, above, at pp. I-6222–3, where a student of Belgian nationality was refused certain unemployment benefits, known as 'tideover allowances', not in another Member State but in Belgium (where she resided) on the ground that she had completed her secondary education in France (for further details of the case, see section II.2 above). Dealing with the personal scope of the citizenship provisions, the Court said that Art. 17 conferred the status of citizen of the Union on every person holding the nationality of a Member State. Since Ms D'Hoop possessed the nationality of Belgium, she enjoyed that status. Simply as a citizen of the Union, she had to be granted in *all* Member States (including her own) the same treatment in law as that accorded to the nationals of those Member States who were in the same situation. Therefore, the Court said, it would be incompatible with the right of freedom of movement if a citizen were to receive in the Member State of which she was a national less favourable treatment than she would enjoy if she had not availed herself of the right to free movement (in this case, the right to study in France). Such a citizen would, in effect, be penalized just because she had exercised her right of free movement. Thus, the requirement of lawful residence in another Member State was irrelevant. The Court also extended the temporal scope of application of the citizenship provisions by holding that those provisions became applicable as soon as the TEU entered into force (1 November 1993) and had to be applied to the present effects of situations that had arisen before that date (ibid. at p. I-6222).

The *D'Hoop* case shows that the citizenship provisions prohibit not only the different treatment of nationals of different Member States, but also the different treatment of the nationals of the same Member State, provided that they fall within the scope of Community law by virtue of the fact that they have exercised the right to free movement. Those provisions can therefore be invoked by citizens not only against other Member States, but also against the Member State of which they are nationals.

The above principles were confirmed by the Court in Case C-224/02 *Pusa* [2004] ECR I-0000, paras. 16–21, where the effect of the Finnish law on enforcement was that Finnish nationals residing in Finland were treated differently from Finnish nationals who, upon retirement, took up residence in another Member State, the latter being placed at a disadvantage. Referring to *D'Hoop*, the Court stated in general terms:

> National legislation which places at a disadvantage certain of its nationals simply because they have exercised their freedom to move and to reside in another Member State would give rise to inequality of treatment, contrary to the principles which underpin the status of citizen of the Union, that is, the guarantee of the same

treatment in law in the exercise of the citizen's freedom to move . . . Such legislation could be justified only if it were based on objective considerations independent of the nationality of the persons concerned and proportionate to the legitimate aim of the national provisions (ibid. para. 20).

In Case C-138/02 *Collins*, above, paras. 58, 61–4, the Court considerably extended the scope of the principle of equal treatment. In fact, the Court reinterpreted some of its earlier case-law decided under the non-discrimination provision of Art. 39(2), holding that in view of the establishment of citizenship of the Union it was no longer possible to exclude from the scope of Art. 39(2), read in conjunction with Art. 12 as interpreted in the cases discussed above, a benefit of a financial nature such as a job-seeker's allowance intended to facilitate access to employment in the labour market of a Member State.

This case marks a departure from the previous case-law in many respects. First, it goes against the established principle that Arts. 12 and 18(1) cannot be applied to situations that are covered by a more specific non-discrimination provision such as Art. 39(2) (see above). Secondly, the Court applied the citizenship provisions to enhance the rights of economically active persons (on the perfectly logical ground that they are also citizens of the Union), while previously those provisions were used in relation to the economically inactive (with the possible exception of *Bickel and Franz*, where the Court applied both Art. 49 and Art. 18(1)). Thirdly, the case shows that the Court is willing to revise its earlier decisions in order to bring its case-law in line with the development of Community law in general (a trend started with *Grzelczyk* in respect of student maintenance grants). This approach opens up new possibilities for giving real substance to the concept of citizenship.

Nevertheless, the principle of equal treatment applies only where the persons involved are in the same situation. Thus, as the Court has stated, the Member States are entitled to rely on any objective difference there may be between their own nationals and those of other Member States, for example when they lay down the conditions under which leave to remain indefinitely in their territory is to be granted to the spouses of such persons. Since, for the purposes of permanent residence, nationals and migrant workers are not in the same situation, Member States are entitled to require the spouses of migrants to be resident for a longer period than that required for the spouses of persons who already enjoy an unconditional right of residence, before granting the same right to them. Such a difference in treatment does not constitute discrimination, even although both migrants and nationals are citizens of the Union (Case C-356/98 *Kaba I*, above, at pp. I-2677–8; see also Case C-466/00 *Kaba II*, above, paras. 43–56, where the Court upheld its ruling in the previous case. See also Case C-148/02 *Garcia Avello*, above, paras. 20–45, confirming that the children of a Spanish father and a Belgian mother, resident in Belgium and having dual Belgian and Spanish nationality, could rely on Arts. 12 and 17 to avoid discrimination on grounds of nationality under the Belgian rules governing their surname since they were not in the same situation as persons having only Belgian nationality). These cases illustrate that, contrary to the opinions of some of the Advocates-General, European citizenship cannot create absolute equality between the nationals of the various Member States as long as national citizenship continues to coexist with it. Perfect equality can only be achieved when European citizenship *replaces*, and not merely *complements*, national citizenship.

(*b*) ***Right of movement and residence.*** As noted above, in *Martinez Sala* the Court evaded the question whether Art. 18(1) could give rise to a new and independent right of residence in another Member State. In subsequent cases, the Court tended to put the emphasis on the 'limitations and conditions' to which Art. 18(1) refers, rather than on the right which it confers on citizens. Thus, in Case C-378/97 *Wijsenbeek*, above, at pp. I-6264–6, the Court gave a negative answer to the question whether Art. 14 or Art. 18(1) allowed a person, whether or not a citizen of the Union, to enter the territory of a Member State by an internal Community frontier without establishing his nationality by presenting his passport. Referring to the 'limitations and conditions' mentioned in Art. 18(1), the Court held that even if under Art. 18(1) nationals of the Member States did have a right to move freely within the territory of the Member States, in the absence of common or harmonized rules on controls at external frontiers and on immigration, visa, and asylum policy, the Member States retained the right to carry out identity checks at the Community's internal frontiers. They could require persons to present a valid identity card or passport, as provided for by Dirs. 68/360, 73/148, 90/364, 90/365, and 93/96, in order to establish whether the person concerned was a national of a Member State having the right to free movement. Moreover, the Member States were free to impose penalties for breach of such an obligation, provided that the penalties were not so disproportionate as to create an obstacle to free movement, such as a term of imprisonment (see also section IV.I below).

In Case C-356/98 *Kaba I*, above, at pp. I-2676–7, the Court expressly stated that the right of nationals of a Member State to reside in another Member State was not unconditional. That situation derived, first, from the provisions on the free movement of persons contained in Title III of Part Three of the Treaty (Arts. 39 to 55) and the relevant secondary legislation and, second, from the provisions of Part Two of the Treaty, and more particularly from Art. 18(1), which expressly referred to the limitations and conditions 'laid down in the Treaty and by the measures adopted to give it effect'. Accordingly, the Court continued, Member States were entitled to rely on any objective difference between their own nationals and those of other Member States in order to apply different treatment to them (see further under point (*a*) above).

It seems to follow from these cases and from others (in particular *Grzelczyk* and *Baumbast and R*, to be discussed below) that the 'limitations and conditions' to which Art. 18(1) refers are those which apply to the free movement of workers, self-employed persons, providers and recipients of services under Arts. 39 to 55 and the implementing legislation, and to the right of residence of economically inactive persons under the three residence directives. Nevertheless, those limitations and conditions, being derogations from a fundamental freedom, must be interpreted strictly and applied in accordance with the principle of proportionality (Case C-357/98 *Yiadom*, above, at p. I-9297; see also *Baumbast and R* below). Moreover, the Member States must avoid adopting provisions that are disadvantageous to citizens who have exercised their right of free movement and residence guaranteed by Art. 18(1), causing them to lose certain social security benefits or other advantages as a result of transferring their residence to another Member State (Case C-135/99 *Elsen*, above, at pp. I-10435–6; Case C-224/02 *Pusa*, above, paras. 31–2).

In Case C-413/99 *Baumbast and R*, above, paras. 76–94, the Court finally gave full effect to the right of Union citizens to move and reside freely within the territory of the Member States, as provided for by Art. 18(1). Mr Baumbast, a German national, worked and resided with his family in the United Kingdom between 1990 and 1993. Subsequently, he was employed by German companies outside the European Union. In 1995, the United Kingdom authorities refused to renew his residence permit on the grounds that he was neither a worker nor a person having a general right of residence under Dir. 90/364. The question before the ECJ was whether, although no longer a migrant worker, Mr Baumbast, as a citizen of the Union, nevertheless enjoyed a right of residence in the United Kingdom by direct application of Art. 18(1). The United Kingdom and German Governments as well as the Commission argued that a right of residence could not be derived directly from Art. 18(1), because the limitations and conditions referred to therein showed that it was not intended to be a free-standing provision. In their opinion, that right was still linked either to an economic activity or to sufficient resources (paras. 78–9).

The Court did not accept those arguments. First, it pointed out that although before the TEU entered into force the right of residence had been subject to the condition that the person concerned was carrying on an economic activity within the meaning of Arts. 39, 43, and 49 EC, this was no longer the case. Under Art. 17(1), every national of a Member State is a citizen of the Union with the consequence that Union citizenship has become the fundamental status of Member State nationals. Moreover, the Court added, the TEU does not require that citizens of the Union pursue a professional or trade activity, whether as an employed or self-employed person, in order to enjoy the rights provided in Part Two of the EC Treaty. Consequently, citizens cannot be deprived of those rights when their economic activity in a host Member State comes to an end (paras. 81–3).

Then the Court confirmed in unequivocal terms that:

> the right to reside within the territory of the Member States under Art. 18(1) EC . . . is conferred directly on every citizen of the Union by a clear and precise provision of the EC Treaty. *Purely as a national of a Member State, and consequently a citizen of the Union, Mr Baumbast therefore has the right to rely on Article 18(1) EC* (para. 84, emphasis added).

Although the right of movement and residence is subject to limitations and conditions, the application of those limitations and conditions is in turn subject to judicial review. Consequently, referring to its established case-law, the Court concluded that any limitations and conditions imposed on that right do not prevent Art. 18(1) from conferring on individuals rights which are enforceable by them and which the national courts must protect (para. 86). In other words, Art. 18(1) has direct effect.

In any case, the Court pointed out, the limitations and conditions referred to (for example those imposed by the three residence directives) must be applied in compliance with the limits imposed by Community law and in accordance with the general principles of that law, in particular the principle of proportionality. Accordingly, any national measure which limits the right of movement and residence must be necessary and appropriate to attain the objective pursued (para. 91; *see further under* **Right of entry and residence**, section III).

Thus, in *Baumbast and R* the Court settled the long-standing dispute by confirming that Art. 18(1) has created a new and independent right to free movement and residence, which may be relied on by anyone who is a citizen of the Union.

In summary, it may be concluded that to benefit from the citizenship provisions as regards equal treatment, free movement and residence, only two conditions must be met. First, a person must be a citizen of the Union, which brings him within the personal scope of application of the Treaty. His involvement in any economic activity is no longer relevant. Secondly, he must have exercised the right to move to another Member State, which brings him within the material scope of application of the Treaty. The reason for his movement is also irrelevant. To enjoy equal treatment, he must be in the same situation as the Union citizen with whom he is compared.

IV. Free movement of persons, the internal market, and the area of freedom, security, and justice

1. The internal market. As seen in section III.1 above, long before the TEU created the concept of European citizenship, the Single European Act of 1986 (SEA) inserted a new Art. 14 into the EC Treaty, which required the Community to adopt measures with the aim of 'progressively establishing the internal market' by 31 December 1992. Art. 14(2) defined the internal market as comprising 'an area without internal frontiers in which the free movement of goods, persons, services and capital is ensured in accordance with the provisions of this Treaty'.

The precise meaning and scope of this provision had been the subject of much debate and controversy. Contradictory interpretations were put forward not only by academic commentators but primarily by the Member States and the Community institutions themselves. As regards, in particular, the free movement of persons, Art. 14 gave rise to the following four problems.

First, what meaning was to be attributed to the word 'persons'? Did it refer to nationals of the Member States only, whether or not they were economically active? Or did it include nationals of non-member countries and stateless persons who were long-term lawful residents in a Member State? Or did it embrace, in addition to the first two categories, all third-country nationals who had lawfully entered the territory of the Community via any Member State for whatever purpose and duration? The view of the Commission was that 'any interpretation of Article 14 that confined its effects to Community nationals only would deprive that Article of any practical effect' (*Gen. Rep. EC* (1992), p. 66).

Secondly, what was the meaning of the term: an area 'without internal frontiers'? Did it mean a mere simplification (or relaxation) of control procedures at the internal frontiers or their complete abolition? In the latter case, did it imply, in the case of persons, a complete abolition of passport controls? The Commission's 1985 White Paper 'Completing the Internal Market' (COM(85) 310, para. 27, p. 9), which initiated the whole single market project, stated that 'our objective is not merely to simplify existing procedures, but to do away with internal frontier controls in their entirety'. The Commission and the European Parliament repeatedly expressed the view that Art. 14 imposed on the Community and also on the Member States an obligation which could only be met if *all controls* on persons at internal frontiers were abolished (*Bull. EC* 5-1992, pp. 16–17; *Gen. Rep. EC* (1992), p. 66; *Gen. Rep. EC* (1993), pp. 48–9; *Bull. EU* 7/8–1995, p. 8; EP Res. of 19 November 1992, *OJ* 1992 C337/211, point 1). Since this result had not been achieved by 31 December 1992, as required by Art. 14, on 18 November 1993 the European Parliament brought an action against the Commission on the basis of Art. 232 EC for failing to put forward the necessary proposals for achieving freedom of movement for persons (Case C-445/93 *Parliament* v. *Commission, OJ* 1994 C1/12).

In 1995 the Commission adopted a set of three proposals for directives. The first provided for the elimination of systematic controls by 31 December 1996 on all persons, whatever their nationality, crossing any internal frontier by air, land, and sea (*OJ* 1995 C289/16; amended proposal in *OJ* 1997 C140/21). The abolition of controls was to be accompanied by essential 'flanking' measures relating to visas, asylum, immigration, the European information system, and, in particular, the strengthening of controls at the Community's external frontiers. The second proposal stipulated that third-country nationals holding a residence permit or a visa issued by a Member State could travel throughout the Community without further formalities (*OJ* 1995 C306/5; amended proposal in *OJ* 1997 C139/6. Both proposals were based on Art. 100 [now Art. 94] EC). The third proposal sought to amend Dirs. 68/360 and 73/148 by deleting any requirement for Community nationals to produce a valid identity document when crossing internal borders (*OJ* 1995 C307/18. The proposal was based on Arts. 49, 54(2), and 63(2) [now Arts. 40, 44(1), and 52(1)] EC) (see also *Bull. EU* 7/8–1995, p. 8; *Gen. Rep. EU* (1995), pp. 11, 381). Following these proposals, the Parliament withdrew its action against the Commission (Order of the Court of 11 July 1996, unpublished).

As mentioned above, the rationale behind these proposals was that the abolition of border controls could not be limited to Community nationals but had to be extended to all persons who were already within the Community, since to distinguish between nationals and non-nationals when crossing borders would inevitably have required the retention of some form of checks. Controls over third-country nationals were to be carried out at the Community's external frontiers. However, the above proposals were never adopted by the Council, the main reason being the failure to adopt the proposed Convention on controls on persons crossing external frontiers (see below). Thus, controls at the internal frontiers were maintained for all nationals.

The third problem arose from the requirement that the free movement of persons in the internal market was to be ensured 'in accordance with the provisions of this Treaty'. Taken literally, this would have meant that all the restrictions allowed under the Treaty (for example, on grounds of public policy, public security, and public health) would continue to be permitted, which would make genuine 'free' movement impossible.

Finally, the fourth problem was whether Art. 14 could produce direct effect. Could an individual enforce a right to move freely (i.e. without border controls) between Member States after the expiry of the deadline of 31 December 1992? This question was clouded by two declarations annexed to the SEA. According to the 'Declaration on Article 8a of the EEC Treaty' [now Art. 14 EC], that Article expressed the 'political will' of the Member States to take before that deadline the decisions necessary to complete the internal market. Moreover, the Declaration stated that 'setting the date of 31 December 1992 does not create an automatic legal effect'. The Declaration thus implied that Art. 14 did not impose a binding legal obligation on the Member States. The 'General Declaration on Articles 13 to 19 of the SEA' (which Articles relate to the internal market and include what is today Art. 14 EC) formally stated that these Articles did not affect the right of Member States to take such measures as they considered necessary to control immigration from third countries and to combat terrorism, crime, the traffic in drugs, and illicit trading in works of art and antiques. Even although, strictly speaking, these declarations could not have binding legal effect, they indicated the ambivalent attitude of the Member States towards the single market project and the lack of a clear conferment of competence on the Community institutions to adopt all the rules necessary to ensure the free movement of persons.

The question of the direct effect of Art. 14 came before the ECJ in Case C-378/97 *Wijsenbeek*, above, at pp. I-6264–5 (see section III.4(*b*) above), where the Court held that Art. 14 could not be interpreted as meaning that, in the absence of measures adopted by the Council before 31 December 1992 requiring the Member States to abolish controls of persons at the internal frontiers of the Community, that obligation automatically arose from the expiry of that period. Such an obligation presupposed harmonization of the laws of the Member States governing the crossing of the external borders of the Community, immigration, the grant of visas, asylum, and the exchange of information on those questions. In the absence of common rules or harmonized laws on controls at the external frontiers and on the other matters, the Member States retained the right to carry out identity checks at the internal frontiers of the Community even if nationals of the Member States did have an unconditional right under Art. 14 or Art. 18(1) EC to move freely within the territory of the Member States. Such checks were necessary to establish whether the persons concerned were Member State nationals, thus having the right to move freely within the Community, or third country nationals, not having that right (see also the detailed analysis of the scope and binding nature of Art. 14 by A.-G. Cosmas, ibid. at pp. I-6223–38).

2. Co-operation in the fields of justice and home affairs. Since, as mentioned above, the free movement of persons was not achieved by 31 December 1992, as required by Art. 14, the TEU included new provisions and, in fact, adopted an entirely new approach in order to attain that objective. The tenth recital in the preamble reaffirmed the intention of the Member States to facilitate the free movement of persons by including provisions on justice and home affairs (JHA) in the Treaty (see also Art. 2, fourth indent). These provisions were inserted under Title VI, which formed the 'third pillar' of the TEU. Together with Title V on a common foreign and security policy (the 'second pillar'), Title VI introduced into EU law the method of intergovernmental co-operation as opposed to the 'Community method', which characterized the three original Treaties, now forming Titles II, III, and IV of the TEU, respectively (the 'first pillar'). In particular, Art. K.1 [now Art. 29, as amended] listed nine areas in which the Member States were to co-operate for the purposes of achieving the free movement of persons. These included asylum policy; rules governing the crossing by persons of the external borders of the Member States; immigration policy and policy regarding third-country nationals, including conditions of entry, movement, residence, employment, and family reunion of such nationals in the Member States and combating any unauthorized form thereof; combating drug addiction and international fraud; judicial co-operation in civil and criminal matters; customs and police co-operation. Strangely, however, visa policy was allocated to the first pillar under Art. 100c of the EC Treaty (subsequently repealed by the Treaty of Amsterdam).

To say the least, intergovernmental co-operation on the free movement of persons did not prove to be very successful, and produced only few tangible results. Most of the measures were adopted in the form of 'soft law' (resolutions, recommendations, conclusions), while those adopted in the form of 'joint position' and 'joint action' had ill-defined legal effects. While the Council could also 'draw up' conventions, it had no power to bring them into force; it could only recommend them to the Member States for adoption in accordance with their respective constitutional requirements (Art. K.3 [now Art. 31, as amended]). Of the measures adopted under Title VI (JHA) concerning the free movement of persons (but excluding judicial, police, and customs co-operation), the following may be mentioned:

- Commission communication of 23 February 1994 to the Council and Parliament on immigration and asylum policies (COM(94) 23);
- Council conclusions of 20 June 1994 on the Commission communication on immigration and asylum policies (see above) (*OJ* 1996 C274/49);
- Council Res. of 20 June 1994 on limitation on admission of third-country nationals to the territory of the Member States for employment (*OJ* 1996 C274/3);
- Council Res. of 30 November 1994 relating to the limitations on the admission of third-country nationals to the territory of the Member States for the purpose of pursuing activities as self-employed persons (*OJ* 1996 C274/7);
- Council Res. of 30 November 1994 on the admission of third-country nationals to the territory of the Member States for study purposes (*OJ* 1996 C274/10);
- Council Dec. 94/795 of 30 November 1994 on a joint action concerning travel facilities for school pupils from third countries resident in a Member State (*OJ* 1994 L327/1);
- Council Res. of 20 June 1995 on minimum guarantees for asylum procedures (*OJ* 1996 C274/13);
- Council Dec. of 22 December 1995 on monitoring the implementation of instruments already adopted concerning admission of third-country nationals (*OJ* 1996 C11/1);
- Joint Position 96/196 of 4 March 1996 on the harmonized application of the definition of the term 'refugee' in Art. 1 of the Geneva Convention of 28 July 1951 relating to the status of refugees (*OJ* 1996 L63/2);
- Joint Action 96/197 of 4 March 1996 on airport transit arrangements (*OJ* 1996 L63/8);
- Council Rec. of 4 March 1996 relating to local consular co-operation regarding visas (*OJ* 1996 C80/1);
- Council Res. of 4 March 1996 on the status of third-country nationals residing on a long-term basis in the territory of the Member States (*OJ* 1996 C80/2);
- Council Rec. of 27 September 1996 on combating the illegal employment of third-country nationals (*OJ* 1996 C304/1);
- Joint Action 97/11 of 16 December 1996 concerning a uniform format for residence permits (*OJ* 1997 L7/1); replaced by Reg. 1030/2002, see point 5(*a*)(*iv*) below;
- Council Dec. 97/420 of 26 June 1997 on monitoring the implementation of instruments adopted concerning asylum (*OJ* 1997 L178/6);
- Council Res. of 4 December 1997 on measures to be adopted on the combating of marriages of convenience (*OJ* 1997 C382/1);
- Council Dec. 98/701 of 3 December 1998 on common standards relating to filling in the uniform format for residence permits (*OJ* 1998 L333/8).

Two regulations concerning visas were adopted under the first pillar, under Art. 100c EC:

- Council Reg. 1683/95 of 29 May 1995 laying down a uniform format for visas (*OJ* 1995 L164/1); amended by Reg. 334/2002, see point 5(*a*)(*i*) below;
- Council Reg. 574/1999 of 12 March 1999 determining the third countries whose nationals must be in possession of visas when crossing the external borders of the Member States (*OJ* 1999 L72/2); replaced by Reg. 539/2001, see point 5(*a*)(*i*) below. Reg. 574/1999 itself replaced Council Reg. 2317/95 of 25 September 1995 on the same subject (*OJ* 1995 L234/1), which was annulled by the ECJ in Case C-392/95 *Parliament* v. *Council* [1997] ECR I-3213 because Parliament was not consulted a second time.

On the other hand, the proposed Convention on controls on persons crossing the external frontiers of the Member States, on which the abolition of controls at the internal frontiers depended, was never adopted (see the Commission's proposal of 10 December 1993, *OJ* 1994 C11/6). Nor was the proposed Convention on rules for the admission of third-country nationals to the Member States (see the Commission's proposal of 30 July 1997, *OJ* 1997 C337/9).

3. The Schengen Agreements. Wishing to speed up the process of removing the obstacles to the free movement of persons, on 14 June 1985 Belgium, Germany, France, Luxembourg, and the Netherlands concluded at Schengen an Agreement on the gradual abolition of checks at their common borders (*OJ* 2000 L239/13). The Agreement had two main objectives. First, the relaxation with immediate effect for nationals of the EC Member States of the formalities to be complied with when crossing the common borders between the Contracting Parties. Secondly, the abolition of the internal border controls on all persons at a later stage.

This second objective was the subject of the Convention implementing the Schengen Agreement, signed by the same five States at Schengen on 19 June 1990 (*OJ* 2000 L239/19). The Convention provided for the abolition of controls on all persons, regardless of nationality, when crossing the common (internal) borders of the Contracting Parties by land, air, or sea, although border checks could be carried out for a limited period where public policy or national security so required. Controls were transferred to the external borders and the rules on the crossing of those borders were reinforced. The Convention established a common policy with respect to non-EC nationals covering such matters as asylum; common visas up to three months; rules on entry into and movement within the Schengen area not exceeding three months; and expulsion. A series of supporting and compensatory measures were also introduced, dealing with such matters as the necessary adaptation of the infrastructures (airports, seaports); fight against illegal immigration, terrorism, smuggling, and organized crime; an information system; judicial, administrative, and police co-operation, etc. An Executive Committee was set up to oversee the implementation of the Convention. The ultimate purpose of the Convention was to create an area without internal frontiers in which all persons, whatever their nationality, would be able to move freely.

Thus, the Convention aimed to achieve amongst the Contracting Parties that which the Community was unable to achieve under Art. 14 EC. Nevertheless, in spite of this clearly Community-related objective, and in spite of cross-references in the preamble to the EC Treaty, the SEA, and the internal market, the Convention (and the original Agreement) did not form part of EC or EU law, but were concluded under public international law and binding on the Contracting Parties only. Between 1990 and 1996, Italy, Spain, Portugal, Greece, Austria, Denmark, Finland, and Sweden acceded to the Schengen Agreement and implementing Convention (for the Accession Agreements, see *OJ* 2000 L239), leaving only Ireland and the United Kingdom as non-signatories. The incorporation of the Schengen *acquis* in EU law is considered under point 5(*b*) below.

4. The Dublin Convention. The Convention determining the State responsible for examining applications for asylum lodged in one of the Member States of the European Communities was signed in Dublin on 15 June 1990 and came into force on 1 September 1997 (*OJ* 1997 C254/1 and C-268/1; see also *Bull. EC* 6–1990, p. 154; *Gen. Rep. EU* (1997), p. 361; Council conclusions on the practical implementation of the Convention, *OJ* 1997 C191). The purpose of the Convention is to guarantee adequate protection to refugees in accordance with the terms of the Geneva Convention of 28 July 1951, as amended by the New York Protocol of 31 January 1967, relating to the status of refugees. To this end, a single Member State is responsible for examining an asylum application. The aim is to avoid the possibility that asylum seekers are sent from one Member State to another without any of these States accepting competence to deal with the application, whilst also avoiding the possibility of multiple asylum applications. Although the Convention constitutes a significant step in the development of co-operation between the Member States in immigration matters and is an essential element of the internal market project, to which reference is made in its preamble, it is, like the Schengen Agreements, not part of EC or EU law but is based on public international law. However, it has since been incorporated into the Community framework (see point 5(*a*)(*ii*) below).

5. An area of freedom, security, and justice. The SEA entered into force on 1 July 1987, but ten years later the internal market was still not completed with regard to the movement of persons. The main reasons were the failure to abolish internal border controls and the failure to agree on a common policy on the entry, movement, and residence of third-country nationals. To deal with these matters, and thus finally to accomplish the task set by the SEA, the Treaty of Amsterdam (ToA), which was signed on 2 October 1997 and entered into force on 1 May 1999, introduced radical changes into the TEU and the EC Treaty concerning the free movement of persons. At the heart of these changes was the creation of an 'area of freedom, security and justice', which features prominently in both the EU and EC Treaties, and of which the free movement of persons forms an integral and inseparable component.

This is expressed in various new provisions of the Treaties. Thus, a new eleventh recital inserted in the preamble to the TEU states the resolve of the Member States 'to facilitate the free movement of persons, while ensuring the safety and security of their peoples, by establishing an area of freedom security and justice, in accordance with the provisions of this Treaty'. The amended Art. 2 TEU, fourth indent, expressly confirms that one of the objectives of the Union is:

> to maintain and develop the Union as an area of freedom, security and justice, in which the free movement of persons is assured in conjunction with appropriate measures with respect to external border controls, asylum, immigration and the prevention and combating of crime.

To achieve this objective, the amended Art. 3(1)(d) of the EC Treaty stipulates that the activities of the Community are to include 'measures concerning the entry and movement of persons as provided for in Title IV'. Title IV, to be discussed below, in turn envisages the free movement of persons in accordance with Art. 14 as one of the prerequisites for the establishment of an area of freedom, security, and justice (Art. 61(a)). This idea is echoed in the first recital in the preamble to the Schengen Protocol (see point (*b*) below), which emphasizes that the Schengen Agreements and related measures are aimed at enhancing European integration and, in particular, 'at enabling the European Union to develop more rapidly into an area of freedom, security and justice'.

These three concepts are, of course, closely interlinked. As the Council and the Commission have put it, 'Freedom in the sense of free movement of people within the European Union remains a fundamental objective of the Treaty, and one to which the flanking measures associated with the concepts of security and justice must make their essential contribution' ('Action plan of the Council and the Commission on how best to implement the provisions of the Treaty of Amsterdam on an area of freedom, security and justice' adopted on 3 December 1998, point 6, *OJ* 1999 C19/1).

The ToA aims to attain the free movement of persons by the combination of two, closely interrelated means. The first is the transfer of all matters relating to the free movement of persons, including judicial co-operation in civil matters, from the intergovernmental third pillar (JHA) to the Community first pillar. This has been achieved by the insertion of an entirely new Title IV into Part Three of the EC Treaty having the title 'Visas, asylum, immigration and other policies related to free movement of persons' (Arts. 61 to 69 EC). In this way, this whole area has become an integral part of Community law, in principle governed by the substantive, institutional, procedural, and jurisdictional rules of the EC Treaty (although there are certain exceptions). As a result of this transfer of competences to the European Community, the truncated third pillar, renamed 'Provisions on police and judicial cooperation in criminal matters' (Title VI of the TEU), continues to cover only co-operation between the police forces, customs, judicial, and other competent authorities of the Member States in criminal matters and the (limited) approximation of rules of criminal law. The objective of this remodelled intergovernmental third pillar is 'to provide citizens with a high level of safety within an area of freedom, security and justice' (Art. 29 TEU, as amended by the Treaty of Nice of 2001 (ToN)). The second method of achieving freedom of movement for persons consists in the integration of the Schengen Agreements and related measures (the so-called 'Schengen *acquis*') into the framework of the European Union. These two major innovations introduced by the ToA are considered in more detail below.

(a) Title IV: Visas, asylum, immigration, and other policies related to free movement of persons (Arts. 61 to 69 EC). Art. 61 EC establishes a clear link between the free movement of persons in the internal market and the area of freedom, security, and justice by providing that, in order to establish progressively the latter, the Council is to adopt:

- within five years after the entry into force of the ToA, measures aimed at ensuring the free movement of persons in accordance with Art. 14, in conjunction with directly related flanking measures with respect to external border controls, asylum and immigration; and measures to prevent and combat crime under the third pillar;
- other measures in the fields of asylum, immigration, and safeguarding the rights of nationals of third countries;
- measures in the field of judicial co-operation in civil matters;
- measures to strengthen administrative co-operation;
- measures in the field of police and judicial co-operation in criminal matters under the third pillar, aimed at a high level of security by preventing and combating crime within the Union.

These tasks are further detailed in Arts. 62 to 66. As far as the free movement of persons is concerned, and leaving aside judicial co-operation, the Council was required to adopt the following measures within the above-mentioned five-year period following 1 May 1999:

- measures with a view to ensuring, *in compliance with Art. 14, the absence of any controls on persons, be they citizens of the Union or nationals of third countries*, when crossing internal borders (Art. 62(1), emphasis added). This provision clearly shows that the Commission and the Parliament were correct in maintaining that the realization of the internal market required the abolition of all controls on all persons, without regard to nationality;
- measures on the crossing of the external borders of the Member States, including rules on carrying out checks on persons at such borders and rules on visas for intended stay of no more than three months, the latter rules to include the list of third countries whose nationals must be in possession of visas when crossing the external borders and those whose nationals are exempt from that requirement; the procedures and conditions for issuing visas by Member States; a uniform format for visas; and rules on a uniform visa (Art. 62(2));

- measures setting out the conditions under which nationals of third countries are free to travel within the territory of the Member States during a period of no more than three months (Art. 62(3));
- measures on asylum, in accordance with the Geneva Convention of 28 July 1951 and the Protocol of 31 January 1967 relating to the status of refugees and other relevant treaties, covering the following matters: criteria and mechanisms for determining which Member State is responsible for considering an asylum application submitted by a third-country national in one of the Member States; minimum standards on the reception of asylum seekers, on the qualification of third-country nationals as refugees, and on procedures for granting or withdrawing refugee status (Art. 63(1));
- measures on refugees and displaced persons, including minimum standards for giving temporary protection to displaced persons from third countries and measures promoting a balance of effort between Member States in receiving refugees and displaced persons and bearing the consequences thereof (Art. 63(2));
- measures on immigration policy in the following areas: conditions of entry and residence and procedures for the issue by Member States of long-term visas and residence permits, including those for the purpose of family reunion; illegal immigration and illegal residence, including repatriation of illegal residents (Art. 63(3));
- measures defining the rights and conditions under which nationals of third countries who are legally resident in a Member State may reside in other Member States (Art. 63(4)).
- measures to ensure administrative co-operation between the Member States and between the Member States and the Commission (Art. 66; the adoption of these measures was not subject to the five-year period).

Art. 67, as amended by the ToN, lays the procedures which the Council was to follow during, and is to follow after, the transitional period of five years in adopting the above-mentioned measures. In an emergency situation characterized by a sudden inflow of third-country nationals, the Council is authorized to adopt provisional measures of a duration not exceeding six months for the benefit of the Member States concerned (Art. 64(2)). The jurisdiction of the ECJ over Title IV is governed by Art. 68. The application of Title IV is subject to the derogations granted to the United Kingdom, Ireland, and Denmark by Protocols annexed to the EU and EC Treaties (Art. 69; see point (*c*) below). As a result of these Protocols, the measures listed below do not apply to those three Member States, unless they have expressed their intention to participate in their adoption or have accepted them after their adoption.

The implementation of the above provisions by the institutions during the five-year period produced a large body of secondary legislation, which was adopted in accordance with the 'Action plan of the Council and the Commission on how best to implement the provisions of the Treaty of

Amsterdam on an area of freedom, security and justice' of 3 December 1998 (*OJ* 1999 C19/1). The work was complicated by the fact that account had to be taken of the already existing third-pillar legislation (see point 2 above), and it also had to be decided which measures should be replaced by more effective ones (for example, those regarded as 'soft law'). The aim was to ensure maximum continuity. Account had also to be taken of the Schengen *acquis*, now part of EC and EU law (see point (*b*) below); and many of the newly adopted measures were designed to build upon, supplement, amend or replace provisions of the Schengen Agreements and related measures (see generally the Action Plan referred to above).

An important step in the process of implementation was the special meeting of the European Council at Tampere on 15 and 16 October 1999, which was devoted to justice and home affairs and which laid down a number of policy guidelines and priorities for the institutions (*Bull. EU* 10–1999, p. 7). These emphasized the need to create a common European asylum system and migration policy (including combating illegal immigration) and, in particular, the need to ensure fair treatment of third-country nationals. Thus, the legal status of third-country nationals should be approximated to that of Member States' nationals. A person, who has resided legally in a Member State for a period of time to be determined and who holds a long-term residence permit, should be granted in that Member State a set of uniform rights which are as near as possible to those enjoyed by Union citizens, e.g. the right to reside, receive education, work as an employee or self-employed person, enjoy equal treatment with local citizens, and the possibility of obtaining the nationality of the receiving Member State (see the Conclusions of the Presidency, ibid. point 21). The right of third-country nationals to reside in another Member State for the purpose of work, study, or other purposes, is also an essential element of the internal market. These objectives have since been implemented by the Council (see Dir. 2003/109 and its preamble, point (*iv*) below).

The most important measures implementing Arts. 61 to 63 and 66 EC are listed below.

(*i*) *Visas (Art. 62(2)(b)):*

- Council Reg. 1683/95 of 29 May 1995 laying down a uniform format for visas (*OJ* 1995 L164/1), as amended by Reg. 334/2002 (*OJ* 2002 L53/7);
- Council Reg. 539/2001 of 15 March 2001 listing the third countries whose nationals must be in possession of visas when crossing the external borders and those whose nationals are exempt from that requirement (*OJ* 2001 L81/1), as amended by Reg. 2414/2001 (*OJ* 2001 L327/1) and by Reg. 453/2003 (*OJ* 2003 L69/10); replacing Reg. 574/1999, see point 2 above;
- Council Reg. 415/2003 of 27 February 2003 on the issue of visas at the border, including the issue of such visas to seamen in transit (*OJ* 2003 L64/1).

(*ii*) *Asylum (Art. 63(1)):*

- Council Dec. 2001/258 of 15 March 2001 on the conclusion of the Agreement between the European Community and Iceland and Norway concerning the criteria and mechanisms for establishing the State responsible for examining a request for asylum lodged in a Member State or in Iceland or Norway (*OJ* 2001 L93/38);
- Council Reg. 343/2003 of 18 February 2003 establishing the criteria and mechanisms for determining the Member State responsible for examining an asylum application lodged in one of the Member States by a third-country national (*OJ* 2003 L50/1), incorporating the Dublin Convention of 1990 into the Community framework;
- Comm. Reg. 1560/2003 of 2 September 2003 laying down detailed rules for the application of Council Reg. 343/2003 (above) (*OJ* 2003 L222/3);
- Council Dir. 2003/9 of 27 January 2003 laying down minimum standards for the reception of asylum seekers (*OJ* 2003 L31/18);
- Council Dir. 2004/83 of 29 April 2004 on minimum standards for the qualification and status of third-country nationals or stateless persons as refugees or as persons who otherwise need international protection and the content of the protection granted (*OJ* 2004 L304/12).

(*iii*) *Refugees and displaced persons (Art. 63(2)):*

- Council Dir. 2001/55 of 20 July 2001 on minimum standards for giving temporary protection in the event of mass influx of displaced persons and on measures promoting a balance of efforts between Member States in receiving such persons and bearing the consequences thereof (*OJ* 2001 L212/12);
- Comm. Dec. 2003/690 of 2 October 2003 on the request by Ireland to accept Council Dir. 2001/55 (above) (*OJ* 2003 L251/23).

(*iv*) *Immigration policy (Art. 63(3) and (4)):*

- Council Reg. 1091/2001 of 28 May 2001 on freedom of movement with a long-stay visa (*OJ* 2001 L150/4) (visas for stays exceeding three months are national visas issued by the Member States in accordance with their national laws);
- Council Dir. 2001/40 of 28 May 2001 on the mutual recognition of decisions on the expulsion of third-country nationals (*OJ* 2001 L149/34);
- Council Dec. 2004/191 of 23 February 2004 setting out the criteria and practical arrangements for the compensation of the financial imbalances resulting from the application of Dir. 2001/40 (above) (*OJ* 2004 L60/55);
- Council Dir. 2001/51 of 28 June 2001 supplementing the provisions of Art. 26 of the Convention implementing the Schengen Agreement of 14 June 1985 (*OJ* 2001 L187/45);

- Council Reg. 1030/2002 of 13 June 2002 laying down a uniform format for residence permits for third-country nationals (*OJ* 2002 L157/1), replacing Joint Action 97/11, see point 2 above;
- Council Dir. 2002/90 of 28 November 2002 defining the facilitation of unauthorized entry, transit, and residence (*OJ* 2002 L328/17);
- Council Dir. 2003/86 of 22 September 2003 on the right to family reunification (*OJ* 2003 L251/12);
- Council Dir. 2003/109 of 25 November 2003 concerning the status of third-country nationals who are long-term residents (*OJ* 2004 L16/44), to be implemented by the Member States by 23 January 2006;
- Council Dir. 2003/110 of 25 November 2003 on assistance in cases of transit for the purposes of removal by air (*OJ* 2003 L321/26).

(*v*) *Administrative co-operation (Art. 66):*

- Council Dec. 2002/463 of 13 June 2002 adopting an action programme for administrative co-operation in the fields of external borders, visas, asylum, and immigration (ARGO programme) (*OJ* 2002 L161/11).

When the five-year period referred to in Arts. 61 to 63 expired on 1 May 2004, not all the measures required to establish an area of freedom, security, and justice were adopted by the Council, although the Commission had presented the main proposals called for at Tampere. In its Communication of 2 June 2004 entitled 'Area of freedom, security and justice: Assessment of the Tampere programme and future orientations' (COM(2004) 401; see also Press Release IP/04/702), the Commission explains that although considerable progress had been made in most areas, still much remains to be done (see also Commission documents SEC(2004) 693, which includes an assessment by sector, and SEC(2004) 680, which contains the implementation 'Scoreboard'). The original ambition had been limited by legal and institutional constraints, particularly by the unanimity requirement for adopting Council decisions during the five-year period, laid down in Art. 67(1). The Commission urges the Council to take advantage of Art. 67(2), which offers the possibility of changing over to the co-decision procedure after 1 May 2004 (see also Declaration No. 5 annexed to the ToN). The Communication outlines the results achieved and the priorities for the future. It proposes the development of a second programme of measures to be adopted in the period 2004 to 2009.

The most important Commission proposals concerning the free movement of persons (and leaving aside judicial co-operation) which still awaited adoption by the Council on 1 May 2004 relate to the following matters:

- directive on the conditions of entry and residence of third-country nationals for the purpose of paid employment and self-employment (COM(2001) 386; *OJ* 2001 C332E/248);
- directive on the conditions in which third-country nationals have the freedom to travel in the territory of Member States for periods not exceeding three months (COM(2001) 388; *OJ* 2001 C270E/244);

- directive on minimum standards on procedures for granting and withdrawing refugee status (COM(2002) 326; *OJ* 2002 C291E/143);
- directive on conditions of entry and residence of third-country nationals for the purposes of studies, vocational training, or voluntary service (COM(2002) 548; *OJ* 2003 C45E/18);
- regulation establishing a European Agency for the management of operational co-operation at the external borders of the Member States of the European Union (COM(2003) 687); adopted on 26 October 2004 as Council Reg. 2007/2004 (*OJ* 2004 L349/1).

(*b*) ***The Schengen Agreements.*** The second innovation of the ToA was the incorporation of the Schengen Agreements and related measures in EU law. This was achieved by the Protocol integrating the Schengen *acquis* into the framework of the European Union, annexed to the EU and EC Treaties (the 'Schengen Protocol'). An Annex to the Protocol defines the Schengen *acquis* as comprising the following instruments (see also point 3 above):

- the Schengen Agreement of 14 June 1985;
- the Implementing Convention of 19 June 1990;
- the Protocols and Agreements whereby the other eight Member States of the European Union acceded to the Schengen Agreement and Convention;
- decisions, declarations, and acts adopted by the Schengen Executive Committee and other organs for the implementation of the Convention (all published in *OJ* 2000 L239).

Art. 1 of the Protocol authorized the thirteen Member States that were signatories to the Schengen Agreements (i.e. all the then Member States of the EU, with the exception of the United Kingdom and Ireland) to establish 'closer co-operation' among themselves within the scope of those Agreements and related provisions, such co-operation to be conducted within the institutional and legal framework of the EU and with respect for the relevant provisions of the TEU and EC Treaty. For this purpose, from the date of entry into force of the ToA (1 May 1999), the Schengen *acquis*, including the decisions of the Executive Committee, became immediately applicable to the thirteen Member States within the Union/Community framework, and the Council was substituted for the Executive Committee (Art. 2(1), but subject to Art. 2(2)).

The Council was given the task of adopting any necessary implementing measures and of determining the legal basis in the Treaties for each of the provisions or decisions which constituted the Schengen *acquis* (ibid.). Since these provisions and decisions concerned the free movement of persons and related flanking measures, their legal basis fell either within the new Title IV of Part Three of the EC Treaty (see point (*a*) above), or within the amended third pillar (Title VI of the TEU). The relevant provisions of these Treaties became also applicable to proposals and initiatives to build upon the

Schengen *acquis* (Art. 5(1). The legal bases were determined by Council Decs. 1999/435 and 1999/436 of 20 May 1999, *OJ* 1999 L176/1 and L176/17, respectively). Following the determination of the legal bases, the provisions and decisions in question (with the exception of those relating to the maintenance of law and order and the safeguarding of internal security) came within the jurisdiction of the ECJ to be exercised in accordance with the relevant applicable provisions of the Treaties (Art. 2(1)).

Since the United Kingdom and Ireland were not parties to the Schengen Agreements, they did not become bound by the Schengen *acquis* as incorporated in the Treaties. However, they were granted the right to request at any time to take part 'in some or all' of the provisions of this *acquis*. The Council is to decide upon such request with the unanimity of the thirteen Schengen Member States and of the applicant State (Art. 4, the so-called 'opt-in' clause). Both the United Kingdom and Ireland have since made and been granted such a request (see Council Dec. 2000/365 of 29 May 2000, *OJ* 2000 L131/43 concerning the United Kingdom and Council Dec. 2002/192 of 28 February 2002, *OJ* 2002 L64/20 concerning Ireland).

The position of Denmark is more complex. As a signatory to the Schengen Agreements, it continues to participate in those parts of the *acquis* which have been incorporated in Title IV of Part Three of the EC Treaty, but *only under international law*, as before the ToA, and *not under EC law* (see also point (*c*)(*iii*) below). On the other hand, it participates within the framework of the intergovernmental third pillar in those parts of the *acquis* which have been incorporated in Title VI of the TEU. In other words, Denmark participates in these parts within the framework of the EU, and not merely under international law (Art. 3).

While three Member States of the EU do not fully participate in the Schengen *acquis*, two non-member countries, Iceland and Norway, have been allowed to be associated with the implementation, application, and development of the *acquis* (Art. 6(1)). For this purpose, they concluded an Agreement with the EU Council on 18 May 1999 (*OJ* 1999 L176/36, approved by Council Dec. 1999/439 of 17 May 1999, ibid. L176/35; see also the Agreement in the form of Exchange of Letters, ibid. L176/53 and Council Dec. 1999/437 of 17 May 1999, ibid. L176/31). The reason for accepting Iceland and Norway into the Schengen *acquis* was to ensure the preservation of the Nordic Passport Union between the five Nordic States within the framework of wider European co-operation on the free movement of persons, after three of them (Denmark, Finland, and Sweden) acceded to the EU (see the preamble to the Agreement and the Conclusions of the Presidency of the Amsterdam European Council of 16 and 17 June 1997, *Bull. EU* 6–1997, p. 8). The rights and obligations between Ireland and the United Kingdom, on the one hand, and Iceland and Norway, on the other, in the field of the Schengen *acquis* are laid down in a separate Agreement concluded by the Council on 30 June 1999 on the basis of Art. 6(2) of the Protocol (see also Council Dec. 2000/777 of 1 December 2000 on the application of the Schengen *acquis* in Denmark, Finland, and Sweden, and in Iceland and Norway, *OJ* 2000 L309/24).

Art. 8 of the Protocol states that the Schengen *acquis* and the measures taken within its scope must be accepted in full by all new Member States acceding to the Union. Accordingly, Art. 3(1) of the Act of Accession of 2003 (see section I.2(*d*) above) provides that the provisions of the Schengen *acquis* and the acts building upon it or otherwise related to it, listed in Annex I to the Act, are to be binding on and applicable in the new Member States from the date of accession (1 May 2004). The provisions of the *acquis* not listed in Annex I are also binding on the new Member States from the date of accession but are to apply in them only from a date to be determined by a Council decision. The Agreements concluded by the Council under Art. 6 of the Schengen Protocol are binding on the new Member States from the date of accession (Art. 3(3)).

(*c*) ***Derogations.*** The impact of the breakthrough achieved by the ToA in the area of free movement of persons is considerably lessened by the various derogations ('opt-outs') granted to the United Kingdom, Ireland, and Denmark. These are laid down in the following four Protocols annexed to the EU and EC Treaties:

- Protocol on the application of certain aspects of Art. 7a [now Art. 14] of the EC Treaty to the United Kingdom and to Ireland (the 'Article 14 Protocol');
- Protocol on the position of the United Kingdom and Ireland (the 'Anglo-Irish Protocol');
- Protocol on the position of Denmark (the 'Danish Protocol');
- the Schengen Protocol.

These are considered in more detail below.

(*i*) *The Article 14 Protocol* entitles the United Kingdom, notwithstanding Art. 14 EC and any other provision of EC or EU law, to exercise at its frontiers with other Member States such controls on persons seeking to enter the UK as it may consider necessary for the purpose of verifying their right to enter the UK under Community law and the Agreement on the European Economic Area (EEA, for which see section V.1 below) (Art. 1). The Protocol further enables the UK and Ireland to continue to make arrangements for the movement of persons between their territories in the context of their Common Travel Area, while fully respecting the right of entry of persons governed by Community law or the EEA Agreement. As long as they maintain such special arrangements, the above provisions derogating from Art. 14 apply to Ireland under the same terms and conditions as for the UK (Art. 2).

On the basis of reciprocity, the other Member States are in turn entitled to exercise at their frontiers or at any point of entry similar controls for the same purposes on persons coming from the UK or from Ireland (Art. 3). Declaration No. 4 by Ireland makes it clear that its participation in the Article 14 Protocol reflects its wish to maintain its Common Travel Area with the UK in order to maximize freedom of movement into and out of Ireland.

(*ii*) *The Anglo-Irish Protocol* provides that, subject to Art. 3, the UK and Ireland 'shall not take part' in the adoption by the Council of proposed measures pursuant to Title IV of Part Three of the EC Treaty (Art. 1). However, under Art. 3(1) the United Kingdom or Ireland may notify the President of the Council in writing, within three months after a proposal or initiative has been presented to the Council pursuant to Title IV, that it wishes to take part in the adoption and application of 'any such proposed measure', whereupon 'that State shall be entitled to do so'. Thus, the UK and Ireland, while in principle excluded from the application of Title IV, have been granted an automatic right to opt into any measure (selected at will) prior to its adoption, and the exercise of this right 'to pick and choose' is not subject to any decision, consent, or approval by the Council. The only concession made in favour of the other Member States is that if a measure cannot be adopted within a 'reasonable time' with the UK or Ireland taking part, the Council may adopt such measure in accordance with Art. 1 without the participation of the two countries (Art. 3(2)). This is a safeguard provision the purpose of which is to prevent the two outsider States from slowing down or blocking Community legislation by abusing their right to opt in. A measure adopted under these provisions is binding upon all Member States that took part in its adoption. Where the UK and/or Ireland do not exercise their right to opt in, they cannot participate in the voting within the Council (Arts. 1 and 3(1)). Ireland has indicated its intention to exercise its opt-in right under Art. 3 to the maximum extent compatible with the maintenance of the Common Travel Area with the UK (Declaration No. 4, referred to above).

After the adoption of a measure by the Council under Title IV, the UK or Ireland may 'at any time' notify its intention to the Council and to the Commission that it wishes to accept that measure, although it no longer has an automatic right to do so. Ultimately, it is for the Commission to decide on the notification within four months, after giving an opinion to the Council within three months (Art. 4 in conjunction with Art. 11a EC, inserted by the ToA and replacing the former Art. 11(3)).

The legal effect of the derogation is that none of the provisions of Title IV, no measure adopted under it, no international agreement concluded by the Community pursuant to it, and no decision of the ECJ interpreting any such provision or measure is binding upon or applicable in the UK or Ireland, unless either country has exercised its right to opt in under Arts. 3 or 4. Moreover, no such provision, measure, or decision affects in any way the competences, rights, and obligations of those States or the *acquis communautaire* nor forms part of Community law as they apply to the UK or Ireland (Art. 2). This means that, since Title IV is indispensable to the establishment of an area of freedom, security, and justice, by opting out of Title IV and of the Schengen *acquis*, the UK and Ireland (and Denmark as well, see point (*iii*) below) have excluded themselves from the area of freedom, security, and justice, in spite of the fact that the creation of that area is now a major objective of the European Union *as a whole*, and not only of the remaining Member States (see point 5 above).

Where the UK or Ireland is bound by a measure as a result of opting in under Arts. 3 or 4, the relevant provisions of the EC Treaty, including Art. 68 on the jurisdiction of the ECJ, will apply to that State in relation to that measure (Art. 6). Ireland, but not the UK, has a right to notify the President of the Council that it no longer wishes to be covered by the Protocol. In that case, the normal Treaty provisions will apply to Ireland (Art. 8).

(*iii*) *The Danish Protocol.* Arts. 1 and 2 of the Danish Protocol are in substance identical with Arts. 1 and 2 of the Anglo-Irish Protocol (see point (*ii*) above). As a consequence, Denmark does not participate in the adoption by the Council of measures under Title IV, and is not bound by that Title or by any measure, international agreement, or ECJ decision adopted under or in relation to it. In this respect, Denmark is in the same position as the UK and Ireland. The only difference is that Arts. 1 and 2 of the Danish Protocol do not apply to measures which were already within the scope of the EC Treaty when the ToA was signed, namely, those determining the third countries whose nationals must be in possession of a visa when crossing the external borders of the Member States and those relating to a uniform format for visas, which measures are binding on Denmark (Art. 4). Such measures (regulations) had already been adopted in 1995 under Art. 100c EC (see point 2 above. Art. 100c was repealed by the ToA, see ibid.).

On the other hand, unlike the UK and Ireland, Denmark is not given the right to take part in the adoption of measures under Title IV. Denmark may, however, decide within a period of six months after the Council has decided on a proposal or initiative to build upon the Schengen *acquis* under Title IV whether it will implement this decision in its national law. If it decides to do so, this decision will create an obligation *under international law* between Denmark and the other Schengen Member States, as well as the UK or Ireland if they also participate (Art. 5(1)). This also shows the international law nature of Denmark's participation in the provisions of the *acquis* falling within the scope of Title IV (see also point (*b*) above). In the case of a negative decision by Denmark, the Schengen Member States will consider what appropriate measures to take (Art. 5(2)).

Another derogation is contained in Art. 6 in respect of Arts. 13(1) and 17 TEU (common foreign and security policy). Art. 6 allows Denmark not to participate in the elaboration, adoption, and implementation of decisions and actions of the Union that have defence implications, nor to contribute to the financing of operational expenditure arising from such measures.

Finally, at any time Denmark may inform the other Member States that it no longer wishes to avail itself of 'all or part' of the Protocol. In that case, Denmark will apply 'in full' all relevant measures in force taken within the framework of the European Union (Art. 7). It seems that a unilateral act by Denmark is sufficient for this purpose. No decision, consent, or approval by the other Member States or the Council is necessary.

(*iv*) *The Schengen Protocol.* This is discussed under point (*b*) above.

V. Nationals of third countries

For the purposes of exercising freedom of movement within the European Community, nationals of third countries may be divided into three broad categories. The first comprises family members of EC nationals. Irrespective of their nationality, such family members enjoy certain rights of entry, residence, and employment in the Community in accordance with the relevant provisions of Community law (*see further* section I.5 above and *under* **Right of entry and residence**). These rights take precedence over, and normally exclude, any rights that a third-country national might also enjoy as a person belonging to one of the other two categories.

The second category includes nationals of third countries with which the Community has concluded international agreements containing provisions on the movement of persons and services. The right of these nationals to enter, move, and reside in the territory of the Member States of the Community and to carry on an activity there as a worker or self-employed person or to provide and receive a service is determined by or under such agreements (see further below).

The third category covers nationals of all third countries with which no such agreements have been concluded. The status of these persons with regard to freedom of movement and residence in the Community is governed by the provisions of primary and secondary Community law considered in section IV above. As seen, the EU is gradually establishing a common visas, asylum, and immigration policy in the broader context of the internal market and of an area of freedom, security, and justice, partly under the EC Treaty and partly under the intergovernmental third pillar (Title VI TEU). The ultimate objective is to approximate the legal status of third-country nationals to that of Member States' nationals and to ensure that a person who has resided legally in a Member State for a longer period of time, normally five years, should be granted a set of uniform rights which are as near as possible to those enjoyed by the citizens of the Union. While much progress has been made in this area, the full integration of third-country nationals in the economic, political, social, and cultural life of the Union still requires a considerable amount of further legislation.

The provisions of the most important international agreements concluded by the Community with third countries, which relate to the free movement of persons (whether workers, self-employed persons, or providers of services) are summarized below.

1. Agreement on the European Economic Area (EEA). The Agreement was originally concluded between the European Communities (EEC and ECSC), their Member States, and Austria, Finland, Iceland, Liechtenstein, Norway, Sweden, and Switzerland (the EFTA States). It was signed on 2 May 1992 and entered into force on 1 January 1994, with the exception of Switzerland, which failed to ratify it, and Liechtenstein, where it entered into force only on 1 May 1995 (text in *OJ* 1994 L1/3). Because of the accession of Austria,

Finland, and Sweden to the European Union on 1 January 1995, the Agreement now applies, apart from the Community and its Member States, only to Iceland, Liechtenstein, and Norway ('EEA EFTA States') (see *Gen. Rep. EU* (1995), p. 315). On 14 October 2003, an Agreement was signed between the three EEA EFTA States, the Community, its Member States, and the ten Acceding States on the participation of the latter in the EEA ('EEA Enlargement Agreement'), together with four related Agreements. As a result, the EEA Agreement applies to the ten new Member States from 1 May 2004 (Council Dec. 2004/368 of 30 March 2004, *OJ* 2004 L130/1). The aim of the Agreement is to promote a continuous and balanced strengthening of trade and economic relations between the Contracting Parties with a view to creating a homogeneous European Economic Area (Art. 1(1)). In effect, the Agreement extends the internal market to the EEA EFTA States.

The free movement of persons, services, and capital is covered by Part III of the Agreement, which in substance incorporates the corresponding provisions of the EC Treaty and related secondary legislation, as listed in various Annexes, subject to a number of adaptations. Art. 28 and Annex V provide for the free movement of workers among EC Member States and EEA EFTA States. Freedom of establishment, including the right to take up and pursue self-employed activities and to set up and manage undertakings, in particular companies or firms, is guaranteed by Art. 31 and Annexes VIII to XI to 'nationals of an EC Member State or an EEA EFTA State in the territory of any other of these States'. This also applies to the setting up of agencies, branches, or subsidiaries by nationals of the States mentioned established in the territory of any of those States. Freedom to provide services within the territory of the Contracting States is granted by Art. 36 and Annexes IX to XI to nationals of EC Member States and EEA EFTA States who are established in one of those States other than that of the person for whom the services are intended. There are provisions on social security for workers and self-employed persons (Art. 29 and Annex VI) and on the mutual recognition of diplomas (Art. 30 and Annex VII).

2. Agreement establishing an Association between the EC and Turkey (1963) and Additional Protocol (1970) (*OJ* 1973 C113/2 and C113/17). The Agreement, whose aim is to strengthen trade and economic relations between the Parties (Art. 2(1)), itself contains only very general provisions on freedom of movement. Art. 9 prohibits discrimination on grounds of nationality in accordance with the principle laid down in Art. 12 EC. According to Art. 12, the Contracting Parties 'agree to be guided' by Arts. 39 to 41 EC for the purpose of progressively securing freedom of movement for workers between them. Likewise, under Arts. 13 and 14, the Parties 'agree to be guided' by Arts. 43 to 46 and 48 EC, and by Arts. 45, 46, and 48 to 54 EC, respectively, for the purpose of abolishing restrictions on freedom of establishment and on freedom to provide services between them. To ensure the implementation and the progressive development of the Association, an Association Council is set up, with power to take decisions in cases provided for in the Agreement (Arts. 6 and 22).

More detailed provisions are contained in the Additional Protocol. Under Art. 36, freedom of movement for workers between the Member States of the EC and Turkey is to be secured by progressive stages between the end of the twelfth and the twenty-second year after the entry into force of the Agreement. The Association Council is to decide on the rules necessary to that end. Arts. 37 to 40 lay down further provisions concerning non-discrimination on grounds of nationality between Turkish and Community nationals as regards conditions of work and remuneration; extension of work and residence permits; social security measures; and exchange of young workers. Art. 41(1) prohibits the introduction of any new restrictions on the freedom of establishment and the freedom to provide services between the Parties, while Art. 41(2) authorizes the Association Council to determine the timetable and rules for the progressive abolition of any existing restrictions.

In Case 12/86 *Demirel* [1987] ECR 3719 at pp. 3753–4, the ECJ held that Art. 12 of the Agreement and Art. 36 of the Additional Protocol essentially serve to set out a programme and that they are not sufficiently precise and unconditional to be capable of governing directly the movement of workers. They do not, therefore, have direct effect in the Member States. The same applies also to Art. 7 of the Agreement, which provides in very general terms that the Contracting Parties are to take all appropriate measures to ensure the fulfilment of the obligations arising from the Agreement. It is not possible to infer from Art. 7 a prohibition on the introduction of further restrictions on family reunification of Turkish workers (ibid.). For the same reasons as Art. 12, Art. 13 of the Agreement also does not have direct effect (Case C-37/98 *Savas* [2000] ECR I-2927 at pp. I-2960–2). Neither does Art. 41(2) of the Additional Protocol (ibid.). By contrast, Art. 41(1) (see above), laying down clearly, precisely, and unconditionally an unequivocal 'standstill' clause, does produce direct effect on which individuals can rely before national courts (ibid. at pp. I-2962–4).

Art. 12 of the Agreement and Art. 36 of the Additional Protocol have been implemented, in turn, by Decs. 2/76 and 1/80 of the Association Council (both unpublished). Dec. 2/76 constituted a first stage in securing freedom of movement for workers between the Community and Turkey, which lasted for four years as from 1 December 1976. Dec. 1/80 constituted a further stage, and has been applicable since 1 December 1980. As from that date, its relevant provisions replaced the corresponding, less favourable, provisions of Dec. 2/76 (see Case C-434/93 *Bozkurt* [1995] ECR I-1475 at p. I-1499). In Case C-192/89 *Sevince* [1990] ECR I-3461 at pp. I-3500–1, the ECJ confirmed that it has jurisdiction to interpret both decisions under Art. 234 EC. It also established that Art. 2(1)(b) of Dec. 2/76 and all three indents of the corresponding Art. 6(1) of Dec. 1/80 (see below), as well as Art. 7 of Dec. 2/76 and Art. 13 of Dec. 1/80, which contain a 'standstill' clause prohibiting the Parties from introducing new restrictions on access to employment of legally resident and employed workers, have direct effect in the Member States (ibid. at pp. I-3501–4; see also Case C-355/93 *Eroglu* [1994] ECR I-5113 at pp. I-5137–8).

The Court has moreover consistently inferred from the wording of Art. 12 of the Agreement and Art. 36 of the Additional Protocol, as well as from the objective of Dec. 1/80, that the principles enshrined in Arts. 39 to 41 EC must be extended, so far as possible, to Turkish nationals who enjoy the rights conferred by Dec. 1/80 (see Case C-434/93 *Bozkurt*, above, at p. I-1501; Case C-340/97 *Nazli* [2000] ECR I-957 at p. I-990, and the cases cited therein). Nevertheless, in contrast to nationals of the Member States, Turkish workers are not entitled to move freely within the Community but benefit from the rights conferred by that decision only in the host Member State whose territory they have lawfully entered (Case C-171/95 *Tetik* [1997] ECR I-329 at p. I-350).

Dec. 1/80 does not affect the competence of the Member States to regulate both the entry into their territories of Turkish nationals and the conditions under which they may take up their first employment. It merely confers certain rights on Turkish workers who are already integrated into the labour force of a Member State (Case C-237/91 *Kus* [1992] ECR I-6781 at p. I-6815). The most important of those rights are set out in Arts. 6 and 7 of the decision. According to Art. 6(1), a Turkish worker duly registered as belonging to the labour force of a Member State is entitled in that Member State, after one year's legal employment, to the renewal of his permit to work for the same employer; after three years, to respond to another offer of employment for the same occupation; and after four years of legal employment, to free access to any paid employment of his choice. As mentioned above, Art. 6(1) has direct effect in the Member States.

In several cases, the Court has interpreted the meaning of the term 'legal employment' (see also Art. 6(2)). Thus, in Case C-192/89 *Sevince*, above, at pp. I-3505–6, it held that that term presupposes a stable and secure situation as a member of the labour force (see also Case C-237/91 *Kus*, above, at pp. I-6812–15; Case C-355/93 *Eroglu*, above, at pp. I-5138–9). Moreover, although Art. 6(1) only deals with the right to employment and does not expressly confer the right of residence, the ECJ has repeatedly pointed out that those two aspects are closely linked since the right of residence is indispensable to access to employment. Therefore, a Turkish worker who fulfils the requirements of Art. 6(1) may rely directly on that provision in order to obtain the renewal not only of his work permit but also of his residence permit. Where 'legal employment' is established, a right of residence will necessarily follow. Otherwise, the right granted to the worker with regard to employment would be deprived of any effect (Case C-192/89 *Sevince*, above, at p. I-3505; Case C-237/91 *Kus*, above, at pp. I-6816–18). However, in the absence of any specific provision conferring on Turkish workers a right to remain in the territory of a Member State after working there, the right of residence, as a mere corollary of legal employment, ceases to exist when legal employment itself comes to an end, for example, because the person concerned retires or becomes totally and permanently incapacitated for work (Case C-434/93 *Bozkurt*, above, at pp. I-1502–6).

Art. 7 of Dec. 1/80 grants certain rights to the members of the family of a

Turkish worker covered by Art. 6 who have been authorized to join him. According to Art. 7(1), such family members are entitled to respond to any offer of employment after they have been legally resident in the host State for at least three years, and they enjoy free access to any paid employment of their choice after five years. Under Art. 7(2), children of Turkish workers who have completed a course of vocational training in the host country may respond to any offer of employment, provided that one of their parents has been legally employed there for at least three years. The ECJ has held that, like Art. 6(1), Art. 7(1) and (2) have direct effect in the Member States and that they imply a right of residence for family members (Case C-355/93 *Eroglu*, above, at pp. I-5140–2; Case C-351/95 *Kadiman* [1997] ECR I-2133 at p. I-2153). Nevertheless, the Member States retain the power to authorize family members to join the worker legally employed in their territories, and to subject their right of residence to certain conditions, for example, that they must actually live with the worker in the same household for a period of three years. Such a requirement might be necessary to prevent an abuse of the rights granted by Art. 7(1) by entering into sham marriages (ibid. at pp. I-2154–7).

The remaining provisions of Dec. 1/80 may be summarized as follows. Under Art. 8, Turkish workers may be given priority where a position cannot be filled by a Community worker. According to Art. 9, Turkish children residing legally in a Member State with parents who are or have been legally employed there are to be admitted to courses of general education, apprenticeship, and vocational training as the children of nationals of the host State. Art. 10(1) prohibits Member States from discriminating, on the basis of nationality, against Turkish workers belonging to their labour force as regards remuneration and other conditions of work. The ECJ has held that Art. 10(1), which merely implements the general principle of non-discrimination laid down in Art. 9 of the Association Agreement (see above), has direct effect in the Member States on which Turkish nationals may rely before the courts of those States (Case C-171/01 *Wahlergruppe Gemeinsam* [2003] ECR I-4301, paras. 57–67). Art. 12 allows a Member State or Turkey to refrain temporarily from automatically applying Arts. 6 and 7. Art. 13 contains a 'standstill' clause which has direct effect in the Member States (see above).

According to Art. 14(1), the provisions relating to the free movement of workers apply subject to limitations justified on grounds of public policy, public security, or public health. The Court has held that in determining the scope of this exception, reference should be made to the interpretation given to the same exception under the EC Treaty since Art. 14(1) is formulated in almost identical terms to Art. 39(3) EC (Case C-340/97 *Nazli*, above, at p. I-990). Arts. 17 and 18 contain provisions on the social and cultural advancement of Turkish workers and the vocational training of young workers. According to Art. 11, nationals of the Member States duly registered as belonging to the labour force in Turkey, and family members authorized to join them, are to enjoy the rights and advantages granted under Arts. 6, 7, 9, and 10 of the decision.

Finally, it should be mentioned that Dec. 3/80 of the Association Council adopted on 19 September 1980 (*OJ* 1983 C110/60) co-ordinates the social security schemes of the Member States with a view to giving Turkish workers who are or have been employed in one or more Member States of the Community and their family members and survivors the right to benefits in the traditional branches of social security (*see further under* **Social security**).

3. Co-operation Agreements between the EC and Algeria, Morocco, and Tunisia (1976) (*OJ* 1978 L263/2, L264/2 and L265/2). The objective of the Agreements is to promote overall co-operation between the Contracting Parties with a view to contributing to the economic and social development of Algeria, Morocco, and Tunisia but without aiming at their association with, or future accession to, the Community (Art. 1 of each Agreement). All three Agreements contain identical provisions on co-operation in the field of labour (Arts. 38 to 41, 40 to 43, and 39 to 42, respectively). While the right to free movement is not recognized, each Member State of the Community is required to accord to workers of Algerian, Moroccan, and Tunisian nationality employed in its territory treatment which is free from any discrimination based on nationality, as regards working conditions or remuneration, in relation to its own nationals. The three countries are to accord the same treatment to workers who are nationals of a Member State and employed in their territories (Arts. 38, 40, 39, respectively). Workers of Algerian, Moroccan, and Tunisian nationality and any members of their families living with them are to enjoy, in the field of social security, non-discriminatory treatment on grounds of nationality in relation to nationals of the Member States in which they are employed (Arts. 39(1), 41(1), 40(1), respectively).

The ECJ has held that the above provisions, far from being purely programmatic in nature, establish, in the field of working conditions, remuneration, and social security, a principle (i.e. that of non-discrimination) which is capable of governing the legal situation of individuals. Therefore, those Articles have direct effect in the Member States without the need for the adoption of implementing measures by the Co-operation Council (Case C-18/90 *Kziber* [1991] ECR I-199 at pp. I-225–7; Case C-58/93 *Yousfi* [1994] ECR I-1353 at pp. I-1368–9, both relating to Art. 41(1) of the EC–Morocco Agreement; Case C-103/94 *Krid* [1995] ECR I-719 at p. I-736, relating to Art. 39(1) of the EC–Algeria Agreement; Case C-416/96 *Eddline El-Yassini* [1999] ECR I-1209 at pp. I-1237–8, relating to Art. 40(1) of the EC–Morocco Agreement).

The Court has also established that the term 'social security' used in the above-cited provisions of the Agreements must be deemed to have the same meaning as the identical term used in Reg. 1408/71 on social security within the Community (*see under* **Social security**). Finally, the concept of 'worker', as it appears in the Agreements, encompasses both active workers and those who have left the labour market after reaching pensionable age or after becoming the victims of one of the risks conferring entitlement to allowances under other social security branches (see the first three cases cited above, at pp. I-227–8, I-1370–2, and I-737–41, respectively. On the non-discriminatory treatment of Moroccan workers, see also Case C-43/93 *Vander Elst* [1994] ECR I-3803 at p. I-3826).

4. Europe (Association) Agreements between the EC and the Central and East European countries. Europe Agreements were concluded with the following countries: Hungary, Poland, Romania, Bulgaria, Slovakia, Czech Republic, Estonia, Latvia, Lithuania, and Slovenia (*OJ* 1993 L347/2, L348/2; *OJ* 1994 L357/2, L358/2, L359/2, L360/2; *OJ* 1998 L68/3, L26/3, L51/3; *OJ* 1999 L51/3; *Gen. Rep. EU* (1995), p. 323 and (1996), p. 307). Separate Association Agreements were concluded with Turkey (1963, see point 2 above), and with Malta (1970) and Cyprus (1972). In their essential parts, the Europe Agreements are drafted in similar terms and are valid indefinitely. They all contain provisions on the movement of workers, establishment, and supply of services. Their purpose was to prepare the political, economic, social, and cultural integration of the countries of Central and Eastern Europe into the Community, the ultimate objective being their accession to the European Union. With the exception of Bulgaria and Romania (and Turkey), all the other countries in fact acceded to the Union on 1 May 2004, from which date their relationship with the Union is governed by the EU and EC Treaties in accordance with the Act of Accession of 2003 (see section I.2(*d*) above). Bulgaria and Romania are expected to join the Union in 2007.

5. ACP–EC Partnership Agreement (Cotonou Agreement). The Partnership Agreement between the Members of the African, Caribbean and Pacific (ACP) Group of States and the European Community and its Member States was signed in Cotonou (Benin) on 23 June 2000 (*OJ* 2000 L317/3) and entered into force on 1 April 2003 (*OJ* 2003 L83/69), although it was partially applicable for a transitional period since August 2000. The Agreement, concluded for twenty years, is successor to the Fourth Lomé Convention, which expired on 29 February 2000. The Agreement combines substantial political dialogue between the partners with innovative forms of economic and commercial co-operation and new development co-operation mechanisms. It enshrines respect for human rights, democratic principles, the rule of law, and good governance.

Art. 13 deals with migration and reaffirms the Parties' obligations and commitments under international law to respect human rights and to eliminate all forms of discrimination based particularly on origin, sex, race, language, and religion (Art. 13(1)). It provides for fair treatment of third-country nationals who reside legally on the Parties' territories, including granting them rights and obligations comparable to those of their citizens (Art. 13(2)). The treatment accorded by each EC Member State to workers of ACP countries legally employed in its territory is to be free from any discrimination based on nationality, as regards working conditions, remuneration, and dismissal, relative to its own nationals. In return, each ACP State is to accord comparable non-discriminatory treatment to workers who are nationals of an EC Member State (Art. 13(3)). Provisions are made for the training of ACP nationals and their vocational integration in their countries of origin (Art. 13(4)), as well as for the return and readmission of illegal immigrants (Art. 13(5)).

See also **Direct taxation, Equality*, Equal pay, Equal treatment, Expulsion, Freedom of establishment, Freedom to provide services, Public health, Public policy, Public security, Public service, Residence permit, Right of entry and residence, Right to leave, Right to remain, Social advantage, Social security, Worker.**

Further reading 1. BOOKS: Barnard, *EC Employment Law*, 2nd edn. (2000), ch. 3; id., *The Substantive Law of the EU. The Four Freedoms* (2004), part iii; Craig and de Búrca, *EU Law. Text, Cases, and Materials*, 3rd edn. (2003), ch. 17; Den Boer (ed.), *Schengen's Final Days? The Incorporation of Schengen into the New TEU, External Borders and Information Systems* (1998); Green, Hartley, and Usher, *The Legal Foundations of the Single European Market* (1991), part ii; Guild (ed.), *The Legal Framework and Social Consequences of Free Movement of Persons in the European Union* (1999); id., *Immigration Law in the European Community* (2001); Guild and Harlow (eds.), *Implementing Amsterdam: Immigration and Asylum Rights in EC Law* (2001); Hailbronner, *Immigration and Asylum Law and Policy of the European Union* (2000); Handoll, *Free Movement of Persons in the European Union* (1995); Marinho, *The Dublin Convention on Asylum: Its Essence, Implementation and Prospects* (1999); O'Keeffe and Twomey, *Legal Issues of the Amsterdam Treaty* (1999), chs. 16–23; O'Leary, *The Evolving Concept of Community Citizenship. From the Free Movement of Persons to Union Citizenship* (1996); Schermers *et al.* (eds.), *Free Movement of Persons in Europe* (1991); Staples, *Legal Status of Third Country Nationals Resident in the EU* (1999); Steiner, Woods, and Twigg-Flesner, *Textbook on EC Law*, 8th edn. (2003), chs. 8, 15, and 18; Weiss and Wooldridge, *Free Movement of Persons within the European Community* (2002); Wyatt and Dashwood, *European Union Law*, 4th edn. (2000), chs. 14, 16, and 17.

2. ARTICLES AND PAPERS: Arts, 'ACP-EU Relations in a New Era: The Cotonou Agreement' (2003) *CML Rev.* 95; Barrett, 'Family Matters: European Community Law and Third-Country Family Members' (2003) *CML Rev.* 369; Bernard, 'Discrimination and Free Movement in EC Law' (1996) *ICLQ* 82; Cannizzaro, 'Producing "Reverse Discrimination" through the Exercise of EC Competences' (1997) *YEL* 29; Caracciolo di Torella and Masselot, 'Under Construction: EU Family Law' (2004) *EL Rev.* 32; Castro Oliveira, 'Workers and Other Persons: Step-by-Step from Movement to Citizenship—Case Law 1995–2001' (2002) *CML Rev.* 77; Cholewinski, 'The Protection of the Right of Economic Migrants to Family Reunion in Europe' (1994) *ICLQ* 568; Costello, 'Market Access All Areas?—The Treatment of Non-Discriminatory Barriers to the Free Movement of Workers' (2000) *LIEI* 267; Cremona, 'Citizens of Third Countries: Movement and Employment of Migrant Workers Within the European Union' (1995/2) *LIEI* 87;

Daniele, 'Non-Discriminatory Restrictions on the Free Movement of Persons' (1997) *EL Rev.* 191; Fennelly, 'The Area of "Freedom, Security and Justice" and the European Court of Justice—A Personal View' (2000) *ICLQ* 1; Forwood and Clough, 'The Single European Act and Free Movement—Legal Implications of the Provisions for the Completion of the Internal Market' (1986) *EL Rev.* 383; Greenwod, 'Nationality and the Limits of the Free Movement of Persons in Community Law' (1987) *YEL* 185; Guild, 'Seeking Asylum: Storm Clouds Between International Commitments and EU Legislative Measures' (2004) *EL Rev.* 198; Hailbronner, 'Visa Regulations and Third-Country Nationals in EC Law' (1994) *CML Rev.* 969; Hailbronner and Thiery, 'Schengen II and Dublin: Responsibility for Asylum Applications in Europe' (1997) *CML Rev.* 957; Hailbronner, 'European Immigration and Asylum Law under the Amsterdam Treaty' (1998) *CML Rev.* 1047; Hall, 'Determining the Scope *Ratione Personae* of European Citizenship: Customary International Law Prevails for Now' (2001) *LIEI* 355; Hedemann-Robinson, 'Third-Country Nationals, European Union Citizenship, and Free Movement of Persons: A Time for Bridges Rather Then Divisions' (1996) *YEL* 321; id., 'From Object to Subject?: Non-EC Nationals and the Draft Proposal of the Commission for a Council Act Establishing the Rules for the Admission of Third-Country Nationals to the Member States' (1998) *YEL* 289; id., 'An Overview of Recent Legal Developments at Community Level in relation to Third-Country Nationals Resident within the European Union, with Particular Reference to the Case Law of the European Court of Justice' (2001) *CML Rev.* 525; Hilson, 'Discrimination in Community Free Movement Law' (1999) *EL Rev.* 445; Jacqueson, 'Union Citizenship and the Court of Justice: Something New under the Sun? Towards Social Citizenship' (2002) *EL Rev.* 260; Johnson and O'Keeffe, 'From Discrimination to Obstacles to Free Movement: Recent Developments concerning the Free Movement of Workers 1989–1994' (1994) *CML Rev.* 1313; Kuiper, 'Some Legal Problems Associated with the Communitarization of Policy on Visas, Asylum and Immigration under the Amsterdam Treaty and Incorporation of the Schengen *acquis*' (2000) *CML Rev.* 345; Nic Shuibhne, 'Free Movement of Persons and the Wholly Internal Rule: Time to Move on?' (2002) *CML Rev.* 731; O'Keeffe, 'The Schengen Convention: A Suitable Model for European Integration' (1991) *YEL* 185; id., 'The Free Movement of Persons and the Single Market' (1992) *EL Rev.* 3; id., 'The Emergence of a European Immigration Policy' (1995) *EL Rev.* 20; id., 'Recasting the Third Pillar' (1995) *CML Rev.* 893; O'Leary, 'Nationality Law and Community Citizenship: A Tale of Two Uneasy Bedfellows' (1992) *YEL* 353; Papagianni, 'Free Movement of Persons in the Light of the New Title IV TEC: From Intergovernmentalism Towards a Community Policy' (2002) *YEL* 107; Peers, 'Towards Equality: Actual and Potential Rights of Third-Country Nationals in the European Union' (1996) *CML Rev.* 7; id., 'Building Fortress Europe: The Development of EU Migration Law' (1998) *CML Rev.* 1235; id., 'Dazed and Confused: Family Members' Residence Rights and the Court of Justice' (2001) *EL Rev.* 76; Phuong, 'Enlarging "Fortress Europe": EU Accession, Asylum, and

Immigration in Candidate Countries' (2003) *ICLQ* 641; Pickup, 'Reverse Discrimination and Freedom of Movement for Workers' (1986) *CML Rev.* 135; Reich and Harbacevica, 'Citizenship and Family on Trial: A Fairly Optimistic Overview of Recent Court Practice with regard to Free Movement of Persons' (2003) *CML Rev.* 615; Schermers, 'The Effect of the Date 31 December 1992' (1991) *CML Rev.* 275; Schutte, 'Schengen: Its Meaning for the Free Movement of Persons in Europe' (1991) *CML Rev.* 549; Toner, 'Passport Controls at "Internal Borders" between Member States' (2000) *EL Rev.* 415; Toth, 'The Legal Status of the Declarations Annexed to the Single European Act' (1986) *CML Rev.* 803; id., 'The Legal Effects of the Protocols Relating to the United Kingdom, Ireland and Denmark', in Heukels, Blokker and Brus (eds.), *The European Union After Amsterdam. A Legal Analysis* (1998), p. 227; Wagner, 'The Integration of Schengen into the Framework of the European Union' (1998/2) *LIEI* 1; Wathelet, 'The Influence of Free Movement of Persons, Services and Capital on National Direct Taxation: Trends in the Case Law of the Court of Justice' (2001) *YEL* 1.

3. OFFICIAL PUBLICATIONS: House of Lords, Select Committee on the European Communities, Session 1998–9, 7th Report, 'Schengen and the United Kingdom's Border Controls' (1999); id., Session 2000, 5th Report, 'UK Participation in the Schengen *Acquis*' (2000).

▶ **FREE TRADE AGREEMENTS AND AREA** *see* **CUSTOMS UNION**

▶ **FREE ZONES AND WAREHOUSES** *see* **CUSTOMS PROCEDURES**

▶ **FRONTIER WORKER** *see* **RESIDENCE PERMIT** *and* **WORKER**

▶ GENERAL AGREEMENT ON TARIFFS AND TRADE (GATT) *see* COMMON CUSTOMS TARIFF, CUSTOMS UNION, *and* CUSTOMS VALUE

G

▶ GENERALISED SYSTEM OF PREFERENCES *see* COMMON CUSTOMS TARIFF

▶ **GOODS** Title I of Part Three of the EC Treaty is entitled 'Free movement of goods' and comprises Arts. 23 to 31. Logic suggests that the concept of 'goods' must be the same for all the provisions on the free movement of goods *between* Member States (i.e. Arts. 25 and 28 to 30 EC), in view of the very close link between those provisions (*see further under* **Charges having equivalent effect to customs duties, Measures having an equivalent effect to quantitative restrictions, Quantitative restrictions**).

In contrast, it is now established that in exceptional cases this concept may not correspond to the list of goods covered by the Community's tariff nomenclature and thus subject to the Common Customs Tariff (CCT) on their introduction into the Community from third countries (see below). This is despite the fact that Council Reg. 2658/87 on the tariff and statistical nomenclature and on the CCT (*OJ* 1987 L256/1), as last amended by Comm. Reg. 2344/2003 (*OJ* 2003 L346/40), is based in part on Art. 26, which falls within the same Title.

I. The concept of goods

While the EC Treaty speaks both of 'goods' and 'products' (see Arts. 23 and 24), it seems clear that the meaning of the two terms is identical; indeed, the German text uses the same term (*Waren*) throughout. Moreover, although Arts. 25 and 28 to 30 EC speak only of 'imports' and 'exports', it is plain that imports and exports of 'goods' are meant.

The Treaty does not define the concept of 'goods'. The *locus classicus* on this point is the Court's definition of this term as covering 'products which can be valued in money and which are capable, as such, of forming the subject of commercial transactions' (Case 7/68 *Commission* v. *Italy* [1968] ECR 423). Accordingly, the Court held in that case that art treasures fell within this concept. On the basis of the same definition, waste has also been held to constitute 'goods', even if it cannot viably be recycled and thus has a negative value (Case C-2/90 *Commission* v. *Belgium* [1992] ECR I-4431). Yet, despite the Court's consistent reference to the definition in *Commission* v. *Italy*, it has been authoritatively suggested that this is not to be regarded as exhaustive (see the opinion of A.-G. Fennelly in Case C-97/98 *Jägerskiöld* [1999] ECR I-7319 at p. I-7328).

As the Advocate-General also stated in the latter opinion, the concept of 'goods' applies only to tangibles, with one notable exception: it has also been held to extend to electricity (Case C-393/92 *Almelo* [1994] ECR I-1477 at p. I-1516).

In *Almelo*, the fact that electricity is listed in the CCT was taken as an indication that that commodity is to be regarded as 'goods'. However, the ruling in Case 7/78 *Thompson* [1978] ECR 2247 shows that this circumstance is not itself decisive: in that judgment coins and banknotes which were legal tender were held not to fall within this concept, despite appearing in the CCT (*see further under* **Common Customs Tariff, Customs Union**). Conversely, if an item is not listed in the Community's tariff nomenclature, it might nevertheless qualify as 'goods'.

At all events, it is clear that the concept of 'goods' does not extend to matters that are caught by the other freedoms enshrined in the EC Treaty. Thus, television signals have been found not to constitute 'goods' (Case 155/73 *Sacchi* [1974] ECR 409); and this applies equally to television advertisements (Case 52/79 *Debauve* [1980] ECR 833). The rationale behind this rule is that sending such signals is instead to be regarded as the provision of services for the purposes of the Treaty. The same reasoning would no doubt apply to communication by telephone, fax, e-mail, etc.—although related tangible items such as fax paper undoubtedly qualify as 'goods'. By the same token, coins and banknotes that are legal tender anywhere in the world fall outside this concept, as do cheques (*Thompson* and Cases C-358/93 etc. *Bordessa* [1995] ECR I-361 at p. I-383); these are to be regarded as current payments or capital, as the case may be (*see further under* **Freedom to provide services**, section II.1 and **Free movement of capital**, sections I and II).

There can be no doubt that one other category of tangibles also fails to qualify as 'goods': live human beings. They are of course caught instead by the Treaty provisions on the free movement of persons. But what of body parts, human corpses, and foetuses? In principle, there appears to be no reason to exclude them from the scope of the concept of 'goods'. Indeed, that view would appear to be confirmed by Case C-203/99 *Veedfald* [2001] ECR I-3569, from which it would seem that a human kidney donated for transplant constitutes a 'product' for the purposes of Council Dir. 85/374 on liability for defective products (*OJ* 1985 L210/29, subsequently amended). Moreover, human hair is expressly mentioned in the CCT. On the other hand, the Commission has stated that foetuses are not to be regarded as goods, albeit without giving any reasons (Written Question 442/85, *OJ* 1985 C263/19).

The position may therefore be summarized as follows: the concept of 'goods' in the Treaty covers all, or virtually all, tangibles other than (*i*) coins and banknotes which are legal tender in any country in the world, (*ii*) bearer cheques, and (*iii*) live human beings and electricity also constitutes 'goods'.

II. Goods in free circulation

Art. 23(2) provides that the provisions on the free movement of goods apply not only to goods originating in the Community, but also to products from third countries which have been put into free circulation in the Community. The latter category of goods is thus assimilated to Community goods (Case 41/76 *Donckerwolcke* [1976] ECR 1921 at p. 1933 and Case 288/83 *Commission* v. *Ireland* [1985] ECR 1761 (Cyprus potatoes)) (*see further under* **Customs procedures**, section V.1, **Origin of goods**).

III. Agricultural products

Finally, the provisions on the free movement of goods are fully applicable to agricultural products within the meaning of Art. 32(3) EC read with Annex I thereto. This is so whether a common market organization exists (e.g. Case 177/78 *McCarren* [1979] ECR 2161), or not (e.g. Case 48/74 *Charmasson* [1974] ECR 1383; Case 232/78 *Commission* v. *France* [1979] ECR 2729 (lamb); Case 194/85 *Commission* v. *Greece* [1988] ECR 1037 (bananas)). In any event, the overwhelming majority of agricultural products are now subject to a common market organization, the most important exception being the potato.

See also **Charges having equivalent effect to customs duties, Common Customs Tariff, Customs procedures, Customs Union, Freedom to provide services, Free movement of capital, Free movement of goods, Measures having equivalent effect to quantitative restrictions, Origin of goods, Quantitative restrictions.**

Further reading Bermann, Goebel, Davey, and Fox, *Cases and Materials on European Union Law*, 2nd edn. (2002), ch. 13; Müller-Graff in *Kommentar zum EU-/EG-Vertrag*, 6th edn. (2003) Vol. I, p. 1052; Oliver, *Free Movement of Goods in the European Community*, 4th edn. (2003), ch. 2.

I

▶ **INDUSTRIAL DESIGN** *see* **INTELLECTUAL PROPERTY RIGHTS**

▶ **INTELLECTUAL PROPERTY RIGHTS** Temporary exclusive rights on creations of the intellect that are granted by law. The term 'intellectual property rights' has two distinct meanings. It may be used in a restrictive sense to refer essentially to copyright and related rights. Often it is used in a broad sense to cover not only intellectual property rights *strictu sensu* but also industrial property rights, such as patents and utility models, and commercial property rights, such as trade marks (see further section V below). Art. 30 EC expressly mentions only the protection of industrial and commercial property. Specifically with respect to the economic rights, as opposed to the moral rights, inherent in copyright the ECJ has clarified that 'in the application of Article 30 of the Treaty there is no reason to make a distinction between copyright and other industrial and commercial property rights' (Cases 55/80 etc. *Musik-Vertrieb Membran* [1981] ECR 147 at p. 162). Intellectual property rights pose a specific problem for the internal market, in particular with respect to the rules on the free movement of goods and competition, as they are based on the principles of exclusivity and territoriality.

I. Characteristics and function

Intellectual property is to be distinguished from tangible or corporeal property, although it will often be attached to the latter (Case C-97/98 *Jägerskiöld* [1999] ECR I-7319). In the absence of legal protection intellectual property might be freely appropriated at little or no cost. This is not likely to induce creative activity and entails that the results of any such activity, where it does take place, will mostly be kept as secret as possible. In order to provide an incentive to invest time and money in research and development, temporary exclusive rights are granted on the basis of the principle of territoriality. The underlying rationale is to make it possible for the right-owner to obtain a reward for the creative effort in exchange for publicising the results from which others can then also profit, be it in the form of licences or for their own research. Or, specifically for trade marks, to indicate the commercial origin of products so that goodwill can be created (see further sections III.2 and V.2 below).

The principle of exclusivity implies that the right-owner may prohibit certain acts of third parties, which would be lawful in the absence of intellectual property protection, such as the manufacture, importation, and distribution of infringing products. This of necessity will have implications for the competitive market structure as third parties may be precluded from a part of the market to which they would otherwise have free access. Certain temporary restrictions on competition should, nonetheless, be tolerated in order to enhance competition in the long run in the public interest. Whether or not the right-owner has the possibility effectively to restrict competition will be largely dependent on the type of intellectual property right as well as on whether or not substitutable products, which do not infringe the exclusive right, are on, or may enter, the market.

Patent protection is the most likely to confer market power. Upon fulfilment of stringent conditions for protectability and registration, a temporary exclusive right is given on the invention of a new industrial product or process. Competition from substitute products will not necessarily be excluded but in exceptional cases, namely where there are no other products that do not infringe the exclusive right, the patent may give rise to a legal monopoly. Copyright is very different, in that it confers a temporary exclusive right on the original form in which ideas are expressed. The idea-expression dichotomy inherent in copyright law is based on the principle that ideas, information, and facts should be freely available and thus not made the subject of exclusive rights. As it is only the unauthorized reproduction of the original manner in which the ideas are expressed that is protected, a legal monopoly is less likely to occur. A third party may bring competing substitute products on the market using the same ideas, as long as the original manner of expression is not copied. Moreover, in principle no copyright infringement should be established if the third party comes to the same form of expression independently from the protected work. Industrial design rights borrow features from both patent and copyright protection. They essentially confer a temporary exclusive right on the new and/or original manner in which a technical or functional product is shaped. Contrary to patents, industrial designs relate to the external and visible features of products rather than to the way in which they function. The main difference with copyright is that the creative output protected by industrial designs serves to compete better in the market and, ultimately, to sell a functional product. Industrial design protection is not at all meant to confer a monopoly position in the market. To the contrary the objective is to encourage innovation in the aesthetic field which should lead to an increase in consumer choice, as industrial designs are an important factor of non-price, especially inter-brand, competition. Trade marks are very different still as they, in essence, merely confer exclusivity on a distinctive brand name and do not relate to the products to which the protected signs are affixed. Similar products may be marketed under a different trade mark. Through the use of his exclusive right, the proprietor of a trade mark can only prevent the unauthorized affixing of the protected, or a confusingly similar, trade mark to the same, or similar, products. As such they do not, of themselves, lead to a monopoly position although well-known brands may, of course, confer a certain degree of market power. Contrary to the other intellectual property rights, the duration of trade mark protection may be unlimited.

The principle of territoriality inherent in all types of intellectual property rights implies that the exclusive right is geographically limited to the territory of the State granting the protection. One may not invoke the exclusive right granted in one Member State to prohibit certain acts of third parties in another Member State. On the other hand one may, in principle, invoke intellectual property protection in order to prohibit the importation of infringing products from another Member State. This applies regardless of whether the goods were put on that market by a third party or by the right-owner, although in the latter case the principle of exhaustion, or a similar principle, may be invoked (see section III below).

Intellectual property rights of necessity pose specific problems in terms of the rules on the free movement of goods, services, and competition in the European Union. The enforcement of exclusive rights based on the principle of territoriality inevitably partitions the market whereas, in essence, it will also lead to a restriction of competition, be it inter-brand or intra-brand. Intellectual property protection is usually granted by national law. As a result, the scope and conditions of intellectual property protection may vary from one Member State to another. This is a further complicating factor when considered from the internal market perspective, but less so where EC harmonization measures have been adopted or Community exclusive rights introduced (see further sections II.5 and V below).

II. The legal framework

Intellectual property rights were initially expressly mentioned only in Art. 30 EC. Since the Treaty of Amsterdam a reference is also made in Art. 133 EC relating to the common commercial policy of the EC. From the beginning, it was clear that the protection of intellectual property rights could be invoked as an exception to the rules on the free movement of goods. For a long time, it was less certain whether, and to what extent, also other rules applied to intellectual property rights. Whereas the link between those exclusive rights and the rules on competition was already established early on by the ECJ, the application of basic principles and of other fundamental rules, in particular the rules on the freedom to provide services, was for long not so evident.

1. Principle of non-discrimination. It was not until the 1990s that the ECJ clarified that the principle of non-discrimination based on nationality as laid down in Art. 12 EC applies to intellectual property rights. It did so with respect to national copyright legislation, which discriminated against nationals of other Member States as regards the means of enforcing rights related to copyright. The fact that the different treatment was due to the non-adherence to relevant intellectual property conventions by a Member State was to no avail. This precedent is all the more important as the ECJ acknowledged that intellectual property protection comes within the scope of Art. 12 EC, without the need to establish a link with the rules on the free movement of goods or other rules. As a result, intellectual property owners who are nationals of an EC Member State should be able to obtain and enforce intellectual property rights under the same conditions as the nationals of the Member State where protection is sought (Cases C-92/92 etc. *Collins* [1993] ECR I-5145). Later on the ECJ clarified that Art. 12 EC might be invoked successfully also after the death of the author, even if this occurred before the entry into force of the EC Treaty in the Member State of which he was a national, by those claiming under him. It confirmed that the principle of non-discrimination based on nationality may not be restricted by the application of another criterion ensuing from intellectual property conventions, such as a country of origin criterion (Case C-360/00 *Ricordi* [2002] ECR I-5089) (see also section II.6 below).

2. Free movement of goods. The protection of intellectual property rights is one of the few expressly stated exceptions to the fundamental rules on the free movement of goods. The fact that, besides Art. 133 EC, Art. 30 EC is the only mention of intellectual property rights in the whole EC Treaty does not imply that the Member States retain an exclusive competence in the matter. Similarly to the other objectives mentioned, it only permits national intellectual property law to derogate from the principle of the free movement of goods to the extent to which such derogation is, and continues to be, justified for the attainment of this higher objective (Case C-350/92 *Spain* v. *Council* [1995] ECR I-1985 at p. I-2011). Neither can Art. 295 EC be interpreted 'as reserving to the national legislature, in relation to industrial and commercial property, the power to adopt measures which would adversely affect the principle of free movement of goods within the common market as provided for and regulated by the Treaty' (ibid.; Case C-30/90 *Commission* v. *United Kingdom* [1992] ECR I-829 at p. I-865).

Intellectual property rights thus come within the scope of Arts. 28 to 30 EC. Although the rules on the free movement of goods are directed to Member States, specifically with respect to intellectual property rights the ECJ has introduced the so-called existence/exercise dichotomy, which was first developed in the framework of the rules on competition (see further section II.4 below). This implies that, in the absence of harmonization, in principle the existence of an intellectual property right will not be affected by the provisions of the EC Treaty but the exercise of it by the right-owner may be struck down. As such it is not so much the content of the national intellectual property law as the way in which the intellectual property owner uses his exclusive rights that will determine whether Art. 30 EC may successfully be invoked. In this respect, the ECJ generally holds that derogation from the rules on the free movement of goods may only be admitted to the extent that such derogation is justified to safeguard the specific subject-matter of intellectual property. On these grounds and in spite of the express wording of Art. 30 EC, the ECJ has ruled that design rights could not be invoked in one Member State in order to prevent the mere transit of infringing products which are lawfully marketed in both the Member States of export and destination (Case C-23/99 *Commission* v. *France* [2000] ECR I-7653) (see further section III below. *See further under* **Free movement of goods**).

3. Freedom to provide services. In the rules on services no provision similar to the exception of Art. 30 EC, relating to intellectual property rights, is to be found. A textual interpretation of Arts. 49 to 55 EC would therefore imply that the rules on services are fully applicable to intellectual property rights. Having regard to the detrimental consequences which such a reasoning would have for the right-owners, as well as to the objectives similar to the rules on the free movement of goods, this reasoning was first impliedly (Case 62/79 *Coditel I* [1980] ECR 881) then expressly rejected by the ECJ. The ECJ clarified that 'the distinction, implicit in Art. 30 EC, between the existence of a right conferred by the legislation of a Member State in regard to the protection of artistic and intellectual property, which cannot be affected by the provisions of the Treaty, and the exercise of such right, which might constitute a disguised restriction on trade between Member States, also applies where that right is exercised in the context of the movement of services' (Case 262/81 *Coditel II* [1982] ECR 3381 at p. 3401. See also e.g. Case C-255/97 *Pfeiffer* [1999] ECR I-2835 at p. I-2861; Case C-97/98 *Jägerskiöld*, above). The existence/exercise dichotomy is thus applied by analogy to services, although the definition of the specific subject-matter may be influenced by the fact that it concerns an application of the rules on the provision of services rather than goods (see further section III below. *See further under* **Freedom to provide services**).

4. Competition rules. The Treaty rules on competition do not mention intellectual property rights. This may seem surprising, considering that the applicability of competition rules to those exclusive rights is a question of fundamental importance. In the absence of an express exception for intellectual property rights, Arts. 81 to 82 EC are, in principle, fully applicable to intellectual property rights. The rules on competition are very different from the rules on the free movement of goods and services as they are directed to anti-competitive behaviour of undertakings rather than to Member States. Reasoning by analogy was already early on firmly rejected by the ECJ when it held that 'Art. 30 EC . . . cannot limit the field of application of Art. 81 EC' (Cases 56/64 etc. *Consten and Grundig* v. *Commission* [1966] ECR 299 at p. 345). Art. 30 EC was, nonetheless, indirectly taken into account by the ECJ by further ruling that the grant of those rights could not be affected by the competition rules, only their exercise.

It was in the context of the application of the rules on competition that the ECJ for the first time introduced the existence/exercise dichotomy, which was later on transposed to the rules on the free movement of goods (see point 2 above). For the purpose of the application of the competition rules to intellectual property rights the ECJ introduced a further distinction. It clarified that 'the exercise of such rights cannot of itself fall either under Art. 81(1) EC, in the absence of any agreement, decision or concerted practice prohibited by this provision, or under Art. 82 EC, in the absence of any abuse of a dominant position' (Case 24/67 *Parke, Davis* [1968] ECR 55 at p. 73). This implies that the ECJ makes a triple distinction under the competition rules. Only the abuse of intellectual property rights may be curtailed by virtue of the competition rules, whereas the existence and the normal use may not. The main question is how to distinguish between normal use as opposed to abuse (see further section IV below).

5. Secondary legislation. Because they confer exclusive rights, intellectual property rights of necessity pose problems in terms of the application of the competition rules (see point 4 above). In order to clarify the relation with Art. 81 EC, the EC Commission has issued a block exemption for technology licensing agreements, which replaces the prior block exemptions for patents and for know-how licensing agreements.

(*a*) ***Need for harmonization.*** Intellectual property rights potentially have a major effect on the functioning of the internal market. They may be used, in principle, to prohibit the importation of infringing goods coming from other Member States. The market may thus be partitioned regardless of whether or not the products were legitimately marketed in the Member State of export, for instance in the absence of parallel intellectual property protection. The question is whether, and to what extent, harmonization measures can remedy this situation. Two elements need to be distinguished in this respect. The ECJ has consistently held that, in the absence of harmonization or approximation, it is up to the Member States to determine the conditions and procedures for obtaining intellectual property protection (see e.g. Case 341/87 *EMI Electrola* [1989] ECR 79 at p. 96. This is subject to the principle of non-discrimination, see point 1 above). Harmonization measures can be used to eliminate disparities in intellectual property legislation in order to prevent different competitive conditions prevailing in different Member States in spite of the internal market objective. Another major, and distinct, problem for the internal market arises because of the principle of territoriality inherent in intellectual property rights (see also section I above). The ECJ has pointed out that, in the absence of unification, the national character of intellectual property rights is capable of jeopardizing the internal market objective (Case 24/67 *Parke, Davis*, above, at p. 71).

(*b*) ***Need for unification.*** The difference between harmonization and unification is especially relevant with respect to intellectual property rights. Harmonization or approximation may create a more uniform or transparent system with respect to the conditions and procedures for obtaining protection but it leaves the national character of intellectual property rights, including the principle of territoriality, intact. The national principle of territoriality may be curtailed partially by virtue of an express reference to the principle of exhaustion in the harmonization measure, as is the case for instance in the Community trade mark directive (see further section V.2 below). Even so, the intellectual property owner is still entitled to oppose the importation of infringing products that were lawfully marketed in another Member State by a third party without his consent. This may be the case where, for instance, the intellectual property owner did not register his exclusive right or failed duly to renew his registration in the Member State of exportation. This implies that harmonization does not, of itself, prevent an intellectual property owner from successfully invoking Art. 30 EC in order to restrict the importation of infringing goods that were lawfully marketed in another Member State. Only unification of intellectual property law, in the sense that a Community exclusive right replaces the bundle of national exclusive rights, extends the principle of territoriality to the whole Community market and renders the application of Art. 30 EC void. The theoretical feasibility of such a construction is illustrated by the regulation on the Community trade mark and the regulation on the Community designs (see further sections V.2 and V.3 below). At the same time, the continued co-existence of national trade marks and industrial designs, albeit subject to harmonization, shows the reluctance of the Member States totally to transfer certain areas of intellectual property protection to the sole Community level.

(*c*) ***Legal basis.*** Having clarified that intellectual property rights do not fall within the sole competence of the Member States (see point 2 above), the ECJ has consistently held that 'at the level of internal legislation, the Community is competent, in the field of intellectual property, to harmonize national laws pursuant to Art. 94 and 95 EC and may use Art. 308 EC as the basis for creating new rights superimposed on national rights, as it did in Council Regulation 40/94 of 20 December 1993 on the Community Trade Mark (*OJ* 1994 L11/1)' (Case C-350/92 *Spain* v. *Council*, above, at p. I-2021; Opinion 1/94 *World Trade Organization* [1994] ECR I-5267 at p. I-5405; Case C-377/98 *Netherlands* v. *Parliament and Council* [2001] ECR I-7079 at p. I-7157). The ECJ further confirmed that Art. 95 EC, rather than Art. 94 EC, is the legal basis for harmonization measures to the extent that disparities in intellectual property legislation are liable to hinder the free movement of goods within the Community (Case C-350/92 *Spain* v. *Council*, above, at p. I-2014). Art. 95 EC may also be used to eliminate 'the emergence of future obstacles to trade resulting from multifarious development of national laws provided that the emergence of such obstacles is likely and the measure in question is designed to prevent them' (Case C-377/98 *Netherlands* v. *Parliament and Council*, above, at p. I-7155). Art. 308 EC may only be used to create new Community intellectual property rights superimposed on national rights. As such, it could not constitute the legal basis for Council Reg. 1768/92 of 18 June 1992 concerning the creation of a supplementary protection certificate for medicinal products, nor for Council Dir. 98/44 on the legal protection for biotechnological inventions, which do not create such a new right (respectively Case C-350/92 *Spain* v. *Council*, above, at p. I-2013; Case C-377/98 *Netherlands* v. *Parliament and Council*, above, at p. I-7157–8).

(*d*) ***External harmonization.*** A major problem with respect to harmonization, and *a fortiori* unification, of intellectual property legislation seems to be the reluctance of the Member States to limit their sovereignty in the matter by transferring legislative initiative to the Community level. This is illustrated by the fact that harmonization is achieved, in particular, with respect to those new matters for which a solution had not already been adopted in national law as well as trade marks (see further section V below). Community harmonization is thus far from complete, in spite of the fact that already in 1959, three working groups were established to study the feasibility of harmonizing national patent, trade mark, and industrial design law. The Member States seem to be more willing to align their intellectual property legislation by virtue of external harmonization, such as in the framework of the Agreement on the World Trade Organization (WTO) and the World Intellectual Property Organization (WIPO). Agreements concluded under the auspices of those international organisations, such as the Agreement on Trade-Related Aspects of Intellectual Property Rights

(TRIPS Agreement) annexed to the WTO, do not necessarily entail a transfer of competence to the Community (see further point 6 below). The ECJ has firmly rejected the argument that the existence of external harmonization would prevent further recourse to Community harmonization measures, in the following terms:

The purpose of harmonisation is to reduce the obstacles, whatever their origin, to the operation of the internal market which differences between the situations in the Member States represent. If divergences are the result of interpretation which is contrary, or may prove contrary, to the terms of international legal instruments to which the Member States are parties, there is nothing to prevent recourse to the adoption of a Directive as a means of ensuring a uniform interpretation of such terms by the Member States (Case C-377/98 *Netherlands* v. *Parliament and Council*, above, at p. I-7156).

(*e*) ***Method of interpretation.*** Where Community harmonization has been achieved, the method of interpretation of such measures in the field of intellectual property protection is, in principle, no different from that for other secondary legislation. The ECJ has consistently held that 'where Community directives provide for the harmonisation of measures necessary to ensure the protection of interests referred to in Art. 30 of the Treaty, any national measure relating thereto must be assessed in relation to the provisions of that directive and not Arts. 28 to 30 of the Treaty'. The Court has added that 'like any secondary legislation, however, the directive must be interpreted in the light of the Treaty rules on the free movement of goods and in particular Art. 30 EC' (Cases C-427/93 etc. *Bristol-Myers Squibb* [1996] ECR I-3457 at p. I-3527). One should not, however, forget to take into account the external harmonization measures in the field of intellectual property. The ECJ has, for instance, drawn attention to the fact that the Agreement on the European Economic Area (EEA, *OJ* 1994 L1/482–3) has amended secondary legislation specifically with respect to the trade mark directive (Case C-355/96 *Silhouette* [1998] ECR I-4799 at p. I-4825). The rules on intellectual property rights should also be applied, as far as possible, in the light of the wording and purpose of relevant provisions of the TRIPS Agreement (Case C-53/96 *Hermès* [1998] ECR I-3603 at pp. I-3647–8; Cases C-300/98 etc. *Dior* [2000] ECR I-11307). This is so even if the proceedings were already pending at the time of entry into force of the TRIPS Agreement in both the Member State concerned and the Community, to the extent that the infringement of intellectual property rights continues beyond that date (Case C-89/99 *Groeneveld* [2001] ECR I-5851) (see further point 6 below).

6. International agreements. International agreements are all the more important in the field of intellectual property rights because of the partial nature of Community harmonization. They may lead to external harmonization, including third countries, where internal harmonization among the Member States failed. An example is the accession to the Paris Act of the Berne Convention for the Protection of Literary and Artistic Works and the Rome Convention for the Protection of Performers, Producers of

Phonograms and Broadcasting Organisations, within the framework of WIPO. With the insertion of an obligation to adhere to specified intellectual property conventions by 1 January 1995 in the EEA (Art. 5 of Protocol 28 combined with Art. 65(2) EEA) this objective became legally binding on the Member States (Case C-13/00 *Commission* v. *Ireland* [2002] ECR I-2943). Another and very important example is constituted by the TRIPS Agreement, in the framework of the WTO, which was signed by both the EC and the Member States. As the ECJ succinctly stated, 'suffice it to say . . . that the harmonisation achieved within the Community in certain areas covered by TRIPS is only partial and that, in other areas, no harmonisation has been envisaged' (Opinion 1/94 *World Trade Organization*, above, at p. I-5418). With respect to the impact of such international agreements on EC law, a distinction should be made between the intellectual property conventions concluded only by the Member States and the agreements concluded also by the EC.

(*a*) ***Intellectual property conventions concluded by the Member States.*** The ECJ has clearly stated that it 'is common ground that, as a rule, the lawfulness of a Community instrument does not depend on its conformity with an international agreement to which the Community is not a party, such as the EPC' (Case C-377/98 *Netherlands* v. *Parliament and Council*, above, at p. I-7164). Intellectual property conventions concluded by all or most of the Member States, in particular in the framework of WIPO, are nonetheless often invoked by EC institutions. Especially in order to give guidance on matters of interpretation or to settle certain controversial issues (e.g. Case C-9/93 *Ideal Standard* [1994] ECR I-2789, at pp. I-2800–2 with respect to the principle of independence of trade marks). In case of incompatibility with Member States' obligations under EC law priority will usually need to be given to the latter (e.g. Case C-235/89 *Commission* v. *Italy* [1992] ECR I-777 at p. I-826; Case C-30/90 *Commission* v. *United Kingdom*, above, at p. I-867, concerning the grant of compulsory licences enabled by the Paris Convention but contrary to EC law). The ECJ clarified that in the relation between Member States the Berne Convention, which was signed before the EC Treaty, could not be successfully invoked to escape the application of the EC Treaty in so far as the rights of third countries were not involved (Cases C-241/91 P etc. *RTE and ITP* v. *Commission* [1995] ECR I-743 at p. I-832—'*Magill' case*). This seems to imply that intellectual property rights do not constitute an exception to the application of Art. 307 EC concerning prior Treaty obligations of Member States. The ECJ also confirmed that intellectual property conventions signed by the Member States after they adhered to the EC Treaty may not run counter to the latter (Cases C-241/91 P etc. *Magill*, above, at p. I-832; Case C-3/91 *Exportur* [1992] ECR I-5529 at p. I-5556). The importance of this should not be underestimated in particular since the ECJ ruled that the principle of non-discrimination, as laid down in Art. 12 EC, applies to intellectual property rights (Cases C-92/92 etc. *Collins*, above; Case C-360/00 *Ricordi*, above). Non-discrimination based on nationality is thus the rule in so far as nationals of the Member States are concerned regardless of whether or not relevant intellectual property conventions, on which national laws are often modelled, allow for a reciprocity requirement to be imposed or call for the application of different criteria, such as the country of origin (see also point 1 above).

(*b*) ***Agreements concluded also by the EC.*** The situation is different with respect to agreements dealing with intellectual property rights and which are concluded also by the EC, such as the EEA and the TRIPS Agreement. Such agreements form an integral part of EC law so that, in principle, they may not conflict with the EC Treaty. The ECJ has assumed jurisdiction to interpret the provisions of those agreements in spite of their mixed nature (see in particular Case C-13/00 *Commission* v. *Ireland*, above; Case C-53/96 *Hermès*, above; Cases C-300/98 etc. *Dior*, above; Case C-89/99 *Groeneveld*, above). Such international agreements take precedence over and may amend secondary EC intellectual property legislation (Case C-355/96 *Silhouette*, above, at p. I-4832; Case C-377/98 *Netherlands* v. *Parliament and Council*, above, at pp. I-7164–5). This is best illustrated by the extension of the principle of Community exhaustion as laid down in the trade mark directive to include the EEA signatory countries. The principle of regional exhaustion was introduced by virtue of Art. 65(2), in conjunction with Annex XVII, point 4, of the EEA Agreement. The aim of the EEA is to extend the internal market to include the EEA countries on the basis of the principle of homogeneity. The EEA Agreement, as well as the subsequent decisions of the EEA Joint Committee, will systematically modify Community harmonization measures with respect to intellectual property rights in order to extend their scope to include the EEA countries (e.g. *OJ* 1997 L316/21).

(*c*) ***The TRIPS Agreement.*** The major importance of the TRIPS Agreement lies in the fact that it provides a set of minimum standards of protection and enforcement of intellectual property rights which has to be implemented by all WTO members (Art. 1(1) TRIPS). It thus leads to world wide harmonization, as well as providing for dispute settlement. The scope of the TRIPS Agreement is vast. Not only does it stipulate that border measures need to be adopted against the importation of counterfeit products. It lays down detailed minimum standards concerning the availability, scope, and use of copyright and related rights, trade marks, geographical indications, industrial designs, patents, and lay-out designs of integrated circuits. As well as detailed rules concerning their enforcement relating, for instance, to fair and equitable procedures, evidence, injunctions, damages, remedies, and provisional measures. The TRIPS Agreement does not require the adoption of the principle of international exhaustion. It merely provides that if the principle of exhaustion is adopted, then the principles of national treatment and most-favoured-nation treatment may be invoked in dispute settlement (Art. 6 TRIPS). One of the stated aims of the TRIPS Agreement is further to establish a mutually supportive relationship between the WTO and the WIPO (see the preamble of TRIPS). This is essentially done through a system of cross-references to existing intellectual property conventions, integrating substantial parts of, for instance, the Berne and Paris Conventions (Arts. 2 and 9 TRIPS). An Agreement was also concluded between the WIPO and the WTO, on 22 December 1995, with a view to establishing appropriate arrangements for co-operation between them (http://www.wipo.int/clea/docs/en/wo/wo030en.htm).

The potential impact of the TRIPS Agreement on EC law and, in particular, on the relations between Member States can hardly be overestimated but is highly complex. The ECJ has consistently adopted a method of TRIPS-conform interpretation (see e.g. Case C-200/96 *Metronome Musik* [1998] ECR I-1953 at p. I-1980; Case C-316/95 *Generics* [1997] ECR I-3929 at p. I-3962; Case C-53/96 *Hermès*, above, at p. I-3647; Case C-89/99 *Groeneveld*, above). The question of interpretation is nonetheless to be distinguished from the question of direct effect of the TRIPS Agreement. The ECJ has ruled that the TRIPS Agreement, as annexed to the WTO Agreement, does not lend itself to direct effect by virtue of EC law whereas it might do so by virtue of national law to the extent that it is invoked with respect to a field which is not yet covered by EC measures. In the words of the ECJ:

> For the same reasons as those set out by the Court in paragraphs 42 to 46 of the judgment in *Portugal* v. *Council* (Case C-149/96 [1999] ECR I-8395), the provisions of TRIPs, an annex to the WTO Agreement, are not such as to create rights upon which individuals may rely directly before the courts by virtue of Community law.
>
> In a field to which TRIPs applies and in respect of which the Community has already legislated, as is the case with the field of trade marks, it follows from the judgment in *Hermès*, in particular in para. 28 thereof, that the judicial authorities of the Member States are required by virtue of Community law, when called upon to apply national rules with a view to ordering provisional measures for the protection of rights falling within such a field, to do so as far as possible in the light of the wording and purpose of Art. 50 of TRIPs.
>
> On the other hand, in a field in respect of which the Community has not yet legislated and which consequently falls within the competence of the Member States, the protection of intellectual property rights, and measures adopted for that purpose by the judicial authorities, do not fall within the scope of Community law. Accordingly, Community law neither requires nor forbids that the legal order of a Member State should accord to individuals the right to rely directly on the rule laid down by Art. 50(6) of TRIPs or that it should oblige the courts to apply that rule of their own motion (Cases C-300/98 etc. *Dior*, above, at pp. I-11360–1).

At the same time, as mentioned above, the ECJ will not hesitate to assume jurisdiction and give an interpretation of provisions of TRIPS, including Art. 50 TRIPS, which should apply uniformly throughout the EC (see e.g. Cases C-300/98 etc. *Dior*, above, at p. I-11364; Case C-53/96 *Hermès*, above, at pp. I-3653–4; Case C-89/99 *Groeneveld*, above).

III. Intellectual property rights and the free movement of goods

The protection of intellectual property and the realization of the internal market are two potentially conflicting objectives (see section I above). The difficult task of reconciling or finding an acceptable balance between those two important objectives is mainly incumbent on the ECJ, in particular since only few harmonization measures have been taken so far (see section II.5 above and section V below). The ECJ has introduced three crucial concepts to delineate between the normal use and misuse of intellectual property rights under the rules on the free movement of goods, and by analogy services, which will be considered in turn below.

1. The existence/exercise dichotomy implies that, in the absence of harmonization, national legislation laying down conditions and procedures for granting intellectual property rights will not, in principle, be subject to scrutiny (see e.g. Case 144/81 *Keurkoop* [1982] ECR 2853 at p. 2871). It is rather the manner in which the intellectual property owner uses his exclusive right that will be held to be incompatible with the rules on the free movement of goods or services. This basic principle is derived from the application of the competition rules to anti-competitive behaviour of intellectual property owners (see sections II.3 and II.4 above). A major problem is that it is not always easy to state clearly where the existence of a right ends and where the exercise begins. It is above all a theoretical distinction, as the existence of a right is essentially constituted by the different ways in which it can be exercised.

The existence/exercise dichotomy is not absolute. National legislation on intellectual property rights may be subject to scrutiny by the ECJ, in particular under the proviso laid down in the second sentence of Art. 30 EC, if it appears to arbitrarily discriminate against imports coming from other Member States. The following national rules were held to be unjustifiably discriminatory and therefore incompatible with Arts. 28 to 30 EC:

- A local manufacturing clause with respect to patents, to the extent that only manufacture in the national territory by the patent holder or with his consent were taken into account to determine whether or not to grant a compulsory licence. The national rules expressly stipulated that the importation of goods would not be considered as 'working' the patent. This was found to be contrary to Art. 28 EC in so far as it discriminates against imports coming from other Member States (Case C-235/89 *Commission* v. *Italy*, above; Case C-30/90 *Commission* v. *United Kingdom*, above).
- The possibility under patents endorsed 'licences of right' to impose, as one of the terms, 'a prohibition on importing the product covered by the patent with the result that while an undertaking which manufactures the product in the national territory is certain of obtaining a licence, the same is not true of an importer'. Similarly, the possibility to obtain an injunction against a third party who imports the products from another Member States where they were manufactured without the consent of the patent owner, whereas no injunction may be granted

against an infringer who manufactures the product in the national territory provided that he takes a licence of right, was found to unduly discriminate against imports coming from other Member States (Case 434/85 *Allen and Hanburys* [1988] ECR 1245).

- A national provision requiring the competent national authority 'to refuse a licence (of right) to import from another country when the patentee works the patent by manufacture in the United Kingdom but to grant a licence (of right) to import from a third country where the patentee works the patent by importation of products manufactured in other Member States'. Although this relates to imports from third countries, it was held to be discriminatory because the patentee is discouraged from importing his products from other Member States rather than manufacturing them domestically (Case C-191/90 *Generics (UK)* [1992] ECR I-5335).

The following national rules were equally subject to scrutiny by the ECJ but, in the end, were held not to infringe Art. 30 EC:

- Granting patents by virtue of the principle of relative novelty (fifty-year rule), as opposed to absolute novelty. The ECJ held that the national rule did not constitute arbitrary discrimination since no distinction was made between the Member States according to the place where the invention was originally filed, nor according to the nationality of the applicant. In the given circumstances there was no disguised restriction on trade either, as the justification for the rule of relative novelty was essentially to reward the rediscovery of an old and unused invention (Case 35/87 *Thetford* [1988] ECR 3585 at pp. 3606–7).
- Industrial design protection for car bodywork components. The ECJ ruled that this was not contrary to Art. 30 EC as these exclusive rights could be invoked against both persons who manufacture spare parts within the national territory and those who import them from other Member States. Furthermore, the national rules were not intended to favour national products over products originating in other Member States (Case 53/87 *Maxicar* [1988] ECR 6039 at p. 6072)
- Rental and lending rights. The possibility for the author to prohibit the hiring out of a video-cassette without his consent, also when imported from other Member States where it can be freely rented out, was not held to be arbitrary discrimination. More importantly, the ECJ for the first time scrutinized and upheld a national rule also under the first sentence of Art. 30 EC. It held that 'by authorising the collection of royalties only on sales to private individuals and to persons hiring out video-cassettes, it is impossible to guarantee to makers of films a remuneration which reflects the number of occasions on which the video-cassettes are actually hired out and which secures them a satisfactory share of the rental market. That explains why . . . certain national laws have recently provided specific protection of the right to hire out video-cassettes. Laws of that kind are therefore clearly justified on grounds of the protection of industrial and commercial property

pursuant to Article 30 of the Treaty' (Case 158/86 *Warner Brothers* [1988] ECR 2605 at p. 2629). The same reasoning applies to rental and lending rights for, *inter alia*, sound recordings (Case C-200/96 *Metronome Musik*, above, at p. I-1977; Case C-61/97 *Egmont Film* [1998] ECR I-5171 at pp. I-5194–5).

Except for these few cases, the ECJ usually proceeds on the basis of the existence/exercise dichotomy with respect to the various types of intellectual property rights. One major exception is geographical indications and designations of origin. The ECJ scrutinizes national legislation upon fulfilment of the specific function of denominations of origin, which it has held to be to safeguard that the product concerned comes from a well-defined geographical area and presents certain specific features (see e.g. Case C-47/90 *Delhaize* [1992] ECR I-3669; Case C-3/91 *Exportur*, above; Case C-388/95 *Belgium* v. *Spain* [2000] ECR I-3123; Case C-325/00 *Commission* v. *Germany* [2002] ECR I-9977; Case C-6/02 *Commission* v. *France* [2003] ECR I-2389; Case C-108/01 *Consorzio del Prosciutto di Parma* [2003] ECR I-5121). Also bilateral conventions concluded between Member States concerning designations of origin will be subject to legal scrutiny, in particular under Arts. 29 and 30 EC (Case C-87/97 *Gorgonzola* [1999] ECR I-1301; Case C-469/00 *Ravil* [2003] ECR I-5053).

2. The concept of specific subject-matter was introduced by the ECJ to delineate between normal use as opposed to misuse of intellectual property rights under Art. 30 EC. The ECJ has consistently held that derogation from the rules on the free movement of goods, and by analogy services, may only be admitted to the extent that such derogation is justified to safeguard the specific subject-matter of intellectual property rights (Case 78/70 *Deutsche Grammophon* [1971] ECR 487 at p. 500). The importance of this concept is best illustrated by the fact that the principle of exhaustion of rights may be invoked as soon as the specific subject-matter is held to be fulfilled (see point 3 below). With respect to patents, industrial designs, and to some extent copyright the ECJ has given a similar definition of the concept of specific subject-matter. The specificity of trade marks and performance rights have led the ECJ gradually to elaborate a different definition for each of those rights. They will be considered in turn below.

(*a*) ***Patents.*** 'The specific subject-matter of the industrial property is the guarantee that the patentee, to reward the creative effort of the inventor, has the exclusive right to use an invention with a view to manufacturing industrial products and putting them into circulation for the first time, either directly or by the grant of licences to third parties, as well as the right to oppose infringements' (Case 15/74 *Centrafarm* [1974] ECR 1147 at p. 1162). Initially it was thought that the reference to the 'reward for the creative effort' was the crucial element in this definition. The so-called 'reward theory' was soon to be replaced by the 'consent theory'. The ECJ clarified that the decisive element in the concept of specific subject-matter is whether or not the right-owner has consented to putting the products on the

EC market rather than whether or not he has obtained a reward for his creative effort. It is the exclusive right to put the product on the market for the first time that gives him the possibility, 'by allowing him a monopoly in exploiting his product, to obtain the reward for his creative effort without, however, guaranteeing that he will obtain such a reward in all circumstances' (Case 187/80 *Merck I* [1981] ECR 2063 at p. 2081).

The monopoly of first exploitation of the product includes the right to oppose the use of samples of medicinal products, manufactured in accordance with a patented process, for the purpose of obtaining a marketing authorization in so far as those samples are used without the direct or indirect consent of the patentee (Case C-316/95 *Generics*, above, at p. I-3962). A moratorium imposed by the national court, prohibiting the infringer from marketing such a product for a specified period after the expiry of the patent in order to prevent him from deriving any unfair profit from his infringement, is not considered to be a disproportionate form of reparation under EC law (ibid. at pp. I-3963–4).

(*b*) ***Industrial design rights.*** The specific subject-matter of industrial design rights is defined in a similar way to patents, although the ECJ seems here to have acknowledged the primarily prohibitive nature of intellectual property rights. It has held that '. . . the right of the proprietor of a protected design to prevent third parties from manufacturing and selling or importing, without its consent, products incorporating the design constitutes the very subject-matter of his exclusive right' (Case 238/87 *Volvo* [1988] ECR 6211 at p. 6236; Case 53/87 *Maxicar*, above, at p. 6071).

Intra-Community transit, i.e. the transportation of goods from one Member State to another across the territory of one or more Member States, is not covered by the specific subject-matter of industrial designs. The ECJ has clarified that the concept of 'putting into circulation' does not refer to the physical transportation of goods. It refers rather to the marketing of protected goods and the authorization given to a third party to use the appearance of the original design, which normally gives rise to the payment of fees to the proprietor of the right (Case C-23/99 *Commission* v. *France*, above) (see also section V below).

(*c*) ***Copyright and performance rights.*** Similarly as for patents, the specific subject-matter of copyright is, in essence, constituted by the exclusive right to first market the protected product in the EC. The consent of the author is thereby the most important criterion (see e.g. Cases 55/80 etc. *Musik-Vertrieb Membran*, above; Case 58/80 *Dansk Supermarked* [1981] ECR 181). A distinction nonetheless needs to be made between distribution rights and performance rights. With respect to the latter, which relate to the rules on services rather than goods (see section II.3 above), the ECJ has acknowledged that 'the right of a copyright owner and his assigns to require fees for any showing of a film is part of the essential function of copyright in this type of artistic and literary work' (Case 62/79 *Coditel I*, above, at p. 903) and should thus be fully upheld under EC law (see also point 3 below).

(*d*) ***Trade marks.*** Similarly as for performance rights, the ECJ has taken the essential function of trade marks into account when gradually elaborating upon the concept of specific subject-matter. As the function of trade marks is to guarantee the origin of the product to the consumer, the ECJ has acknowledged early on that it should offer protection not only against the use of the same, but also of confusingly similar trade marks (see e.g. Case 119/75 *Terrapin* [1976] ECR 1039; Case C-317/91 *Renault* [1993] ECR I-6227; Case C-255/97 *Pfeiffer*, above, at p. I-2861). Faced with the practice of repackaging and reaffixing trade marks by third parties of products which were put on the EC market by the trade mark proprietors, in particular for the sake of facilitating parallel importation, the ECJ has further clarified the subject-matter of trade marks. It has held:

> In relation to trade marks, the specific subject-matter is in particular to guarantee to the proprietor of the trade mark that he has the exclusive right to use that trade mark for the purpose of putting a product into circulation for the first time and therefore to protect him against competitors wishing to take advantage of the status and reputation of the trade mark by selling products illegally bearing that trade mark.
>
> In order to answer the question whether that exclusive right involves the right to prevent the trade mark being affixed by a third person after the product has been repackaged, regard must be had to the essential function of the trade mark, which is to guarantee the identity of the origin of the trade marked product to the consumer or ultimate user, by enabling him without any possibility of confusion to distinguish that product from products which have another origin.
>
> This guarantee of origin means that the consumer or ultimate user can be certain that a trade marked product which is sold to him has not been subject at a previous stage of marketing to interference by a third person, without authorisation of the proprietor of the trade mark, such as to affect the original condition of the product.
>
> The right attributed to the proprietor of preventing any use of the trade mark which is likely to impair the guarantee of origin so understood is therefore part of the specific subject-matter of the trade marked right (Case 102/77 *Hoffman-La Roche* [1978] ECR 1139 at p. 1164).

The ECJ has specified that in order to establish whether a trade mark distinguishes the goods or services concerned as originating from a particular undertaking 'regard must be had both to the ordinary use of trade marks as a badge of origin in the sectors concerned and to the perception of the relevant public' (Case C-104/01 *Libertel* [2003] ECR I-3793, para. 62). The perception of the relevant public, which is composed of average consumers, reasonable well-informed and reasonably observant and circumspect, is not necessarily the same when it concerns a word or a figurative mark or a sign which forms part of the look of the goods, such as a colour *per se* (ibid.) (see section V.2 below).

The use of trade marks will always be held to be contrary to Art. 30 EC if it contributes to the artificial partitioning of the EC market (see point 4 below).

3. The principle of Community exhaustion of intellectual property rights was introduced by the ECJ to counter the potentially negative effect of the principle of territoriality on the internal market (Case 78/70 *Deutsche Grammophon*, above). It implies that an intellectual property right may no longer be invoked to prohibit the (parallel) importation and sale of otherwise infringing goods, once the specific subject-matter, as defined by the ECJ, is held to be fulfilled (see point 2 above).

(*a*) ***Scope.*** The application of the principle of exhaustion is stringently linked to the internal market objective. The ECJ explained that allowing the common market to be partitioned through the invocation of national provisions by individuals would be contrary to the essential purpose of the EC Treaty, which is to unite the national markets into one single market (Case 78/70 *Deutsche Grammophon*, above, at p. 500). The principle of exhaustion, as introduced by the ECJ, therefore only applies in a Community context. Up till now, the ECJ has refused to extend the principle of Community exhaustion to include third countries by virtue of case-law. It held that provisions similar to Arts. 28 etc. in a free trade agreement should not necessarily be interpreted in the same way as the EC Treaty provisions, in particular in so far as the principle of exhaustion is concerned, as the content, objective, and formulation of the agreement concerned is different from that of the EC Treaty (Case 270/80 *Polydor* [1982] ECR 329).

The principle of regional exhaustion has been expressly written into the EEA Agreement, thereby extending the scope of this principle to include the signatory EFTA countries (see section II.6 above). This seems to be fully in accordance with the reasoning of the ECJ as the aim of the EEA is precisely to extend the internal market to those countries. The principle of Community exhaustion is now also systematically written into EC harmonization measures, such as Art. 7 of the trade mark directive 89/104 (as amended by the EEA Agreement). The ECJ has also interpreted the latter provision in the light of the internal market objective of ensuring uniformity. It ruled that the lack of an express reference to the principle of international exhaustion in the final text of Dir. 89/104 implies that Member States are no longer free to apply, or not, this principle (Case C-355/96 *Silhouette*, above). According to the ECJ, the provision should thus be interpreted in the sense that it only allows for trade marks to be exhausted in case the proprietor consented to putting the products on the EEA market for the first time or consented to import products coming from third countries into the EEA. This ruling is not without criticism. It gives a different interpretation of Art. 7 of Dir. 89/104 than the one given by the EFTA Court (Case E-2/97 *Mag Instruments* of 3 December 1997) (On the issue of international exhaustion of trade marks, see further section V.2 below).

(*b*) ***Criteria.*** The principle of Community exhaustion is mostly applied by the ECJ on the basis of a straightforward application of the consent-theory (see section II.2 above). As soon as the right-owner consented to putting the products on the market in the Member State of exportation, he may no longer invoke his exclusive right in another Member State to oppose importation. The ECJ has clarified that the principle of exhaustion applies even in the absence of parallel patent protection in the Member State of exportation. According to the ECJ it is up to the patent owner to decide, in the light of all the circumstances, under what conditions he wants to market his products. This includes the possibility to market the products in a Member State where he does not benefit from patent protection. If he decides to do so, then he must bear the consequences of his choice, in particular in view of the free movement of goods in the EC (Case 187/80 *Merck I*, above). This heavily criticized ruling was subsequently reiterated by the ECJ, albeit with a minor modification. Whereas the principle of exhaustion continues to apply even in the absence of parallel protection, this will not be the case if the patent owner 'can prove that he is under a genuine, existing legal obligation to market the product in that Member State' (Cases C-267/95 etc. *Merck II* [1996] ECR I-6285 at p. I-6392).

The emphasis placed on the consent to market the products, rather than on the possibility to obtain a reward for the creative effort, has led the ECJ to reject, off-hand, arguments relating to the existence of price differences resulting from government measures to control the price of the product in the Member State of exportation. The reasoning of the ECJ can be summarized as follows. Member States cannot justify the maintenance or introduction of measures, which are contrary to the rules on the free movement of goods. Therefore, neither can the latter be relied upon by individuals in order to counter the effect of factors in other Member States that are likely to distort competition. It is the task of the Community authorities to eliminate such obstacles through harmonization of national measures. As such, the maintenance of artificial price levels in the Member State of exportation cannot successfully be invoked by individuals as a justification for using their exclusive rights in the Member State of importation in order to prohibit parallel importation, or to charge additional royalties (Case 15/74 *Centrafarm*, above, at pp. 1164–5; Cases 57/80 etc. *Musik-Vertrieb Membran*, above).

Conversely, the ECJ has clarified that the existence of parallel protection and receiving a reward for the creative effort is not, of itself, sufficient to trigger the application of the principle of exhaustion. It did so with respect to patents worked under a compulsory licence in the Member State of exportation. The ECJ held that the patent owner could not be deemed to have consented to the placing of the products on the market by the third party. It was irrelevant whether or not he received a fair return under the system of compulsory licences (Case 19/84 *Pharmon* [1985] ECR 2281).

(*c*) ***Exhaustion and performance rights.*** The ECJ has acknowledged that the consent theory cannot as such apply to performance rights (Case 62/79 *Coditel I*, above, at p. 903). Performances of literary and artistic works, such as films or sound-recordings, may be repeated infinitely and fees may be asked for each showing (see also point 2 above). In the *Tournier* case, the ECJ was faced for the first time with the situation whereby both distribution rights and performance rights related to one and the same literary and artistic work, namely sound-recordings. It answered the question of whether or not the consent theory was to be applied, in the following way:

> It is true that the present case raises the specific question of the distinction between the conditions applicable to those two situations, in so far as sound-recordings are products covered by the provisions on the free movement of goods contained in Articles 28 *et seq.* of the Treaty but are also capable of being used for public performance of the musical work in question. In such circumstances, the requirements relating to the free movement of goods and the freedom to provide services and those derived from the observance of copyright must be reconciled in such a way that the copyright owners, or the societies empowered to act as their agents, may invoke their exclusive rights in order to require the payment of royalties for music played in public by means of a sound-recording, even though the marketing of that recording cannot give rise to the charging of any royalty in the country where the music is played in public (Case 395/87 *Tournier* [1989] ECR 2521 at p. 2571).

It was thus clarified that consent to putting the products on the market for the first time may entail the exhaustion of sale or distribution rights whereas it leaves the performance rights, and similarly the rental and lending rights, on the same products undisturbed (see also Case 158/86 *Warner Brothers*, above; Case C-200/96 *Metronome Musik*, above, at p. I-1977; Case C-61/97 *Egmont Film*, above, at pp. I-5194–5).

4. Specific issues relating to the Community exhaustion of trade marks. Trade marks pose a specific problem for the internal market. They relate to most products whereas they may easily be invoked to try and prevent parallel importation. The ECJ has unequivocally stated that 'trade mark rights are not intended to allow their owners to partition national markets and thus promote the retention of price differences which may exist between Member States' (see e.g. Cases C-71/94 *Eurim-Pharm* [1996] ECR I-3603 at p. I-3618; Case C-349/95 *Loendersloot* [1997] ECR I-6227 at p. I-6253). In order to minimize the potentially negative effect on the internal market, the ECJ has consistently held, similarly as for the other types of intellectual property rights, that a trade mark proprietor may no longer use his exclusive right to oppose the importation or marketing of a product which was put on the market in another Member State by him or with his consent (see e.g. Case 16/74 *Winthrop* [1974] ECR 1183 at pp. 1194–5; Cases C-427/93 etc. *Bristol-Myers Squibb*, above, at p. I-3528; Case C-349/95 *Loendersloot*, above, at p. I-6253). This approach needed to be refined in view of specific problems that were brought to the attention of the ECJ, such as trade marks with a common origin, the re-packaging of products whereby trade marks are reaffixed without the consent of the trade mark proprietor, and the practice of marketing products under differentiated trade marks. The ECJ endeavoured to gradually seek an appropriate balance between the need to respect the rights of the trade mark proprietor and the need to safeguard the internal market objective, thereby taking into account the essential function of trade marks. The ECJ usually stipulates that, even if the use of trade marks seemingly comes within the specific subject-matter of trade marks (see section III.2 above), the exercise will nonetheless be prohibited under Art. 30 EC if it contributes to the artificial partitioning of the markets between Member States.

(*a*) ***Common origin of trade marks.*** The ECJ has been confronted with a few cases whereby a trade mark originally belonged to the same owner in different Member States but was subsequently divided, so that one and the same trade mark on the same product in the end belonged to different proprietors in different Member States. This situation may be the intended result of voluntary trade mark assignments or may be due to government interference. The first cases brought before the ECJ concerned the latter in the form of trade mark division due to expropriation of enemy property. The question arose to what extent the proprietor in one Member State could invoke his trade mark in order to prevent the importation of products, put on the market by the other proprietor but bearing the same trade mark, without infringing the rules on the free movement of goods. Initially the ECJ introduced the so-called 'theory of common origin', meaning that the trade mark right was held to be exhausted due to the common origin of the trade mark (Case 192/73 *HAG I* [1974] ECR 731). This theory was heavily criticized because it failed to take the function of trade marks into account. As trade marks are meant to guarantee the commercial rather than the historical origin of the product, the ECJ later on expressly overturned the theory of common origin by holding that 'for the trade mark to be able to fulfil its role, it must offer a guarantee that all goods bearing it have been produced under the control of a single undertaking which is accountable for their quality' (Case C-10/89 *HAG II* [1990] ECR I-3711 at p. I-3758).

The ECJ subsequently clarified that this ruling also applies to voluntary assignments of trade marks. Each trade mark proprietor will be able to oppose the importation of goods bearing the trade mark affixed by another proprietor regardless of whether the splitting of the trade mark, which was originally held by the same owner, was due to an act of government or to a contractual assignment. The ECJ explained that:

> the consent implicit in any assignment is not the consent required for the application of the doctrine of exhaustion of rights. For that, the owner of the right in the importing State must, directly or indirectly, be able to determine the products to which the trade mark may be affixed in the exporting State and control their quality. That power is lost if, by assignment, control over the trade mark is surrendered to a third party having no economic links with the assignor (Case C-9/93 *Ideal Standard* [1994] ECR I-2789 at p. I-2850).

The ECJ took care to distinguish between trade mark assignments and trade mark licences, by pointing out that the licensor can control the quality of the products by inserting a provision to that effect in the licensing agreement (ibid. at p. I-2848). Both trade mark assignments and such provisions in trade mark licences may, however, under certain circumstances be contrary to the rules on competition (see section IV.1 below).

(*b*) ***Repackaging and reaffixing of trade marks.*** Often cases concern not straightforward parallel importation, but repackaging and the reaffixing of trade marks. In order to allow for parallel importation effectively to take place, it is sometimes necessary to repackage the products, not in the least so as to comply with the requirements of the Member State of importation. The question is whether and under what conditions a parallel importer may reaffix the trade mark without the consent of the proprietor. The ECJ clarified that, in case of repackaging by an importer, the trade mark proprietor may, in principle, oppose the affixing of the trade mark to the new packaging without his consent, as this is in conformity with the specific subject-matter (see point 2 above). In certain circumstances, however, the exclusive right to affix a trade mark to a product will be regarded as exhausted so as to allow an importer to market, under that trade mark, products which were put on the market in another Member State by the trade mark proprietor or with his consent (Cases C-427/93 etc. *Bristol-Myers Squibb*, above, at p. I-3529). Invocation of this exclusive right by the trade mark proprietor will, in particular, not be allowed if four conditions are fulfilled: 1. the use of the trade mark contributes to the artificial partitioning of the market; 2. the repackaging cannot adversely affect the original condition of the product; 3. the proprietor of the trade mark received prior notice of the marketing of the repackaged product; 4. it is stated on the new packaging by whom the products have been repackaged (Case 102/77 *Hoffman-La Roche*, above, at pp. 1164–5). These conditions were held to be fulfilled in a case whereby the importer had replaced the external wrapping by a transparent wrapping so that the internal packaging, which was left intact, and the trade mark were visible. It was furthermore indicated on the external wrapping that the product was manufactured by the subsidiary of the trade mark proprietor and repackaged by the importer (Case 1/81 *Pfizer* [1981] ECR 2913). Other cases, in particular concerning pharmaceutical products, were less clear-cut and have led the ECJ to further clarify the four conditions. They will be considered in turn below.

(*i*) *The use of the trade mark contributes to the artificial partitioning of the EC market.* The concept of 'artificial partitioning of the market' as used by the ECJ in this context does not imply that it is necessary to demonstrate that the trade mark proprietor deliberately sought to partition the market. The ECJ held that 'by stating that the partitioning in question must be artificial, the Court's intention was to stress that the owner of a trade mark may always rely on his right as owner to oppose the marketing of repackaged products when such action is justified by the need to safeguard the essential function of the trade mark, in which case the resultant partitioning could not be regarded as artificial'. The crucial element is whether the repackaging undertaken by the importer is necessary in order to market the product in the Member State of importation (Cases C-427/93 etc. *Bristol-Myers Squibb*, above, at pp. I-3535–6; Cases C-71/94 etc. *Eurim-Pharm*, above, at pp. I-3622–3; Case C-232/94 *Pharma* [1996] ECR I-3671 at pp. I-3685–6). The assessment to be made by the national court is different in a case concerning relabelling rather than repackaging. With respect to the latter, 'the national courts must consider whether circumstances in the markets of their own States make repackaging objectively necessary'. Whereas in case of relabelling they must assess whether this is 'necessary to protect the sources of supply of the parallel trade and to enable the products to be marketed on the various markets of the Member States for which they are intended' (Case C-349/95 *Loendersloot*, above, at p. I-6257). If the answer is negative, then the possibility for the trade mark proprietor to oppose the marketing of the repackaged or relabelled products under the same trade mark should remain unaffected.

The ECJ gave the following examples with respect to repackaging:

Repackaging will be held to be necessary when the size of the packet used by the owner in the Member State where the importer purchased the product cannot be marketed in the Member State of importation by reason, in particular:

- of a rule authorising packaging only of a certain size or a national practice to the same effect;
- sickness insurance rules making the reimbursement of medical expenses depend on the size of the packaging;
- well-established medical prescription practices based on standard sizes recommended by professional groups and sickness insurance institutions.

It is not sufficient for the trade mark proprietor to point to the fact that many different sizes of packaging are used in the Member State of importation whereas one of those sizes is also marketed in the Member State of exportation. The ECJ pointed out that 'partitioning of the markets would exist if the importer were able to sell the product in only part of his market' (Cases C-427/93 etc. *Bristol-Myers Squibb*, above, at pp. I-3534–5; Cases C-71/94 etc. *Eurim-Pharm*, above, at p. I-3622; Case C-232/94 *Pharma*, above, at p. I-3685).

Repackaging will not be necessary and may thus be opposed by the trade mark proprietor where the repackaging is done by the parallel importer solely in view of securing a commercial advantage (Case C-443/99 *Paranova* [2002] ECR I-3703; Case C-143/00 *Boehringer* [2002] ECR I-3759). It may also be opposed if the importer is able to achieve packaging which may be marketed in the Member State of importation by:

- affixing new labels in the language of the Member State of importation to the external or internal packaging (Cases C-427/93 etc. *Bristol-Myers Squibb*, above; Cases C-71/94 etc. *Eurim-Pharm*, above; Case C-232/94 *Pharma*, above). Labelling as a better alternative to repackaging or to reaffixing trade marks remains conditional on the relabelled product having an effective access to the market. In this respect, the ECJ has accepted that there might be such a strong resistance from a significant portion of the consumers to relabelled pharmaceutical products that it constitutes a hindrance to effective market access (Case C-443/99 *Paranova*, above; Case C-143/00 *Boehringer*, above);
- adding user instructions or information in that language;

- replacing an additional article not capable of gaining approval in the Member State of importation with another that has obtained approval (Cases C-427/93 etc. *Bristol-Myers Squibb*, above; Cases C-71/94 etc. *Eurim-Pharm*, above; Case C-232/94 *Pharma*, above).

With respect to relabelling by the parallel importer, the ECJ made the following clarifications:

- the removal of the word 'pure' and the official importer's name on the label may not be opposed by the trade mark proprietor to the extent that this is necessary to comply with the rules on labelling in force in the Member State of importation;
- the removal of identification numbers may be opposed by the trade mark proprietor to the extent that the application of identification numbers is necessary to comply with legal obligations (such as Dir. 89/396 on indications or marks identifying the lot to which a foodstuff belongs, *OJ* 1989 L186/21), or to realize other legitimate objectives such as the recall of faulty products and measures to combat counterfeiting. The ECJ specified that this does not prevent the parallel importer from invoking the rules on competition in case the trade mark proprietor uses the identification numbers in order to facilitate the detection of weaknesses in his sales organization and thus to combat parallel trade in his products (Case C-349/95 *Loendersloot*, above, at pp. I-6258–9).

The ECJ has indicated that any relabelling should be proportional, in the sense that the relabelling must use those 'means which make parallel trade feasible while causing as little prejudice as possible to the specific subject-matter of the trade mark right' (ibid. at p. I-6260). For example, if the affixing of a sticker with additional information would suffice to comply with the rules on labelling in force in the Member State of importation, then it is not necessary to remove and reaffix or replace the original labels.

(*ii*) *The repackaging cannot adversely affect the original condition of the product.* This refers to the condition of the product inside the packaging (Cases C-427/93 etc. *Bristol-Myers Squibb*, above, at p. I-3536; Cases C-71/94 etc. *Eurim-Pharm*, above, at p. I-3623, Case C-232/94, *Pharma*, above, at p. I-3686). Regard should be had to the nature of the product and the method of repackaging to determine whether there is a risk that the product will be exposed to tampering or to influences affecting its original condition (Case 102/77 *Hoffman-La Roche*, above, at pp. 1164–5; Cases C-427/93 etc. *Bristol-Myers Squibb*, above, at p. I-3536; Cases C-71/93 etc. *Eurim-Pharm*, above, at p. I-3623; Case C-232/94, *Pharma*, above, at p. I-3686).

The ECJ gave the following examples with respect to pharmaceutical products:

It will not necessarily be considered to affect the original condition and thus cannot be opposed, as such, by the trade mark proprietor:

- if, in case of originally double packaging, the repackaging affects only the external layer but leaves the inner packaging intact (ibid.);

- if the repackaging is carried out under the supervision of a public authority so as to ensure that the product remains intact (ibid.);
- the mere removal of blister packs, flasks, phials, ampoules or inhalers from their original external packaging and replacement in new external packaging. A hypothetical risk of isolated error, such as ensuing from the grouping together of blisters from different production batches with different use-by dates, was not accepted by the ECJ to be adversely affecting the condition of the product (Cases C-427/93 etc. *Bristol-Myers Squibb*, above, at p. I-3536; Case C-232/94 *Pharma*, above, at p. I-3687). It is for the national court to determine whether the cutting of blister packs or the reprinting of batch numbers is effected in such a way as to exclude any real risk of affecting the original condition of the product. This will be presumed to be the case where the operations were authorized and supervised by a public authority (Cases C-71/94 etc. *Eurim-Pharm*, above, at p. I-3624);
- the fixing of self-stick labels to flasks, phials, ampoules or inhalers (Cases C-427/93 etc. *Bristol-Myers Squibb*, above, at p. I-3536; Cases C-71/94 etc. *Eurim-Pharm*, above, at p. I-3624);
- the addition of new user instructions or information in the language of the Member State of importation to the packaging. Additional information provided by the importer should not contradict information provided by the trade mark proprietor in the Member State of importation (Cases C-71/94 etc. *Eurim-Pharm*, above, at p. I-3625; Case C-232/94 *Pharma*, above, at p. 3688);
- the insertion of an extra article from a source other than the trade mark proprietor (Cases C-427/93 etc. *Bristol-Myers Squibb*, above, at p. I-3536).

The ECJ made it clear that such practices may, nonetheless, indirectly affect the original condition and, if so, may be opposed by the trade mark proprietor, where:

- 'the external or inner packaging of the repackaged product, or a new set of user instructions or information, omits certain important information or gives inaccurate information concerning the nature, composition, effect, use or storage of the product' (ibid.; Cases C-71/94 etc. *Eurim-Pharm*, above, at p. I-3625; Case C-232/94 *Pharma*, above, at p. I-3688);
- 'an extra article inserted into the packaging by the importer and designed for the ingestion and dosage of the product does not comply with the method of use and the doses envisaged by the manufacturer' (Cases C-427/93 etc. *Bristol-Myers Squibb*, above, at p. I-3536);
- 'the packaging of the repackaged product is not such as to give the product adequate protection' (Cases C-71/94 etc. *Eurim-Pharm*, above, at p. I-3625).

It is for the national court to assess whether this is so, in particular by making a comparison with the product marketed by the trade mark proprietor in the Member State of importation (ibid.).

(*iii*) *The proprietor of the trade mark received prior notice of the marketing of the repackaged product.* Besides the prior notification, the trade mark proprietor may require that he also receives a specimen of the repackaged product before it goes on sale. The ECJ has pointed out that such a requirement allows him a better protection against counterfeiting. It also enables him to check whether the original condition of the product is not directly or indirectly affected by the repackaging and the presentation of the product does not damage the reputation of the trade mark (Cases C-427/93 etc. *Bristol-Myers Squibb*, above, at p. I-3541; Cases C-71/94 etc. *Eurim-Pharm*, above, at p. I-3628; Case C-232/94, *Pharma*, above, at pp. I-3690–1).

The purpose of those requirements is to safeguard the legitimate interests of the trade mark proprietors. The trade mark proprietor may oppose the marketing of the repackaged product in case of failure to give prior notification by the parallel importer himself, even if he was duly notified by other sources. As to the period of notice to be given, the ECJ considers that a reasonable time should be allowed for the proprietor to be able to react whilst giving regard also to the interests of the parallel importer in marketing his products as soon as possible. The ECJ forwards a period of fifteen working days prior notice, on a purely indicative basis, where a sample of the repackaged product is supplied by the parallel importer simultaneously with giving the prior notice (Case C-143/00 *Boehringer*, above).

(*iv*) *It is stated on the new packaging by whom the products have been repackaged.* This indication must clearly be stated on the external packaging. It is not necessary to expressly indicate that the product was repackaged without the authorization of the trade mark proprietor (Cases C-427/93 etc. *Bristol-Myers Squibb*, above, at p. I-3539; Cases C-71/94 etc. *Eurim-Pharm*, above, at p. I-3626; Case C-232/94 *Pharma*, above, at p. I-3689). A clear indication may be required as to who manufactured the product, so as not to induce the consumer in error as to who is the owner of the trade mark (Case 1/81 *Pfizer*, above, at pp. 2926–7; Cases C-427/93 etc. *Bristol-Myers Squibb*, above, at p. I-3540; Cases C-71/94 etc. *Eurim-Pharm*, above, at p. I-3627; Case C-232/94 *Pharma*, above, at p. I-3689). If an extra article is included from a source other than the trade mark proprietor, then the importer should take care to dispel any impression that the trade mark proprietor is responsible for it by indicating the origin of this extra article in an appropriate manner (Cases C-427/93 etc. *Bristol-Myers Squibb*, above, at p. I-3540). It is for the national court to assess whether the statement is printed 'in such a way as to be understood by a person with normal eyesight, exercising a normal degree of attentiveness' (Cases C-427/93 etc. *Bristol-Myers Squibb*, above, at p. I-3539; Cases C-71/94 etc. *Eurim-Pharm*, above, at p. I-3626; Case C-232/94, *Pharma*, above, at p. I-3689).

Such a statement on the package will not prevent a trade mark proprietor from successfully invoking his exclusive right to oppose the marketing of the product in case of an inappropriate presentation of the repackaged product, which may damage the reputation of the trade mark. Regard should be had to the nature of the product and the market for which it is intended. For instance, defective, poor quality, or untidy packaging of pharmaceutical products could undermine consumer confidence in a product and damage the reputation of the trade mark. This will not necessarily be so when the product is sold to hospitals as, according to the ECJ, the presentation of the product is of less importance to professionals (Cases C-427/93 etc. *Bristol-Myers Squibb*, above, at p. I-3540; Cases C-71/94 etc. *Eurim-Pharm*, above, at p. I-3627; Case C-232/94, *Pharma*, above, at p. I-3690). The national court should also take into account whether the trade mark proprietor has a particular interest in protecting a luxury image of his products as well as whether or not the products enjoy a considerable reputation (Case C-349/95 *Loendersloot*, above, at p. I-6256).

Besides the application of the Treaty rules on the free movement of goods to trade marks, due attention should be paid also to the first trade mark directive and the way in which its provisions are interpreted by the ECJ (see section V.2 below).

(*c*) ***Marketing products under differentiated trade marks.*** In the current state of EC law, the practice of marketing a product under different trade marks in different Member States will not, of itself, be held to be contrary to the rules on the free movement of goods, in spite of the potentially prejudicial effect on the internal market. A different question is to what extent a parallel importer may, without the consent of the trade mark proprietor, replace the original trade mark by the one normally used in the Member State of importation. The ECJ clarified in this respect that the guarantee of origin function of trade marks implies that only the trade mark proprietor may confer an identity upon the product by affixing the mark. A trade mark owner who markets his products in different Member States under different trade marks can, therefore, invoke his exclusive right to prohibit the importation of products that were marketed with his consent in another Member State, but to which a third party has affixed the trade mark of the Member State of importation without his consent; unless it were to be established, by the national court, that the practice of using differentiated trade marks was introduced in order to artificially partition the EC market (Case 3/78 *American Home Products* [1978] ECR 1823). The application of the latter condition does not require national courts to assess evidence of an intention to artificially partition the market. Similarly as for reaffixing the trade mark after repackaging (see above), the replacement of the trade mark must be objectively necessary. The ECJ more specifically stated that 'this condition of necessity is satisfied if, in a specific case, the prohibition imposed on the importer against replacing the trade mark hinders effective access to the markets of the importing Member State'. This would be the case where the marketing of products under the trade mark used in the Member State of exportation would be prevented by rules or practices in the Member State of importation, for instance on the grounds that it might mislead the consumers. Conversely, the ECJ specified that 'the condition of necessity will not be satisfied if replacement of the trade mark is explicable solely by the parallel importer's attempt to secure a commercial advantage' (Case C-379/97 *Upjohn* [1999] ECR I-6927 at p. I-6969).

IV. Intellectual property rights and competition law

Intellectual property rights are inherently temporary exclusive rights that may restrict competition in the short run in order to enhance competition in the long run (see section I above). This natural potential for tension between the application of intellectual property rights and competition rules already early on raised the difficult issue of where to draw the line between what is to be considered as a normal use, as opposed to an abuse, of those exclusive rights. The ECJ clarified from the very beginning that whereas the competition rules should be fully applicable to intellectual property rights, the essence or the normal use of the latter may, nonetheless, not be curtailed in order to safeguard competition in the market (see section II.4 above). Instead of giving a definition of these crucial concepts, the ECJ has very much followed a case-by-case approach. This will be considered in turn under Arts. 81 and 82 EC.

1. The relationship between Article 81 EC and intellectual property rights seems to be rather simple at first. It is apparent that Art. 81(1) EC cannot apply to the mere unilateral enforcement of an intellectual property right (see section II.4 above). The latter is a legal right which is granted by national law and not an agreement or a concerted practice. As such it does not, of itself, fulfil the basic requirements of that provision (see e.g. Case 24/67 *Parke, Davis*, above; Case 78/70 *Deutsche Grammophon*, above; Case 144/81 *Keurkoop*, above; Case 51/75 *EMI Records* [1976] ECR 811). Neither can agreements or concerted practices between undertakings which are held to belong to the same concern, as a parent company and subsidiary, come under Art. 81 EC if the following conditions are fulfilled: they form an economic unit; the subsidiary cannot determine freely its behaviour in the market; and the agreement concerns merely the internal allocation of tasks (Case 15/74 *Centrafarm*, above, at p. 1167). The latter condition was later on successfully challenged before the Courts (Case C-73/95 P *Viho* v. *Commission* [1996] ECR I-5457; Case T-198/98 *Micro Leader* v. *Commission* [1999] ECR II-3989 at p. II-4004). Also agreements of a minor importance will not be considered to infringe Art. 81 EC.

The difficulty arises when neither of those circumstances is applicable to a given case, so that the exercise of the exclusive right needs to be assessed upon its proper merits in the light of Art. 81 EC. The ECJ has held that the exercise of intellectual property rights will fall foul of Art. 81(1) EC 'each time it manifests itself as the subject, the means or the result of an agreement (or a concerted practice) which, by preventing imports from other Member States of products lawfully distributed there, has as its effect the partitioning of the market' (Case 78/70 *Deutsche Grammophon*, above, at p. 499), or 'where they serve to give effect to an agreement, decision or concerted practice which may have as its object or effect the prevention, restriction or distortion of competition in the market' (Case

262/81 *Coditel II*, above, at p. 3401). This implies that not only a licensing agreement, but also a concerted practice (see e.g. Cases 110/88 etc. *Lucazeau* [1989] ECR 2811) as well as an agreement whereby the exclusive right is assigned to a third party or created in its own right, might be held to be contrary to Art. 81 EC if its object or effect is to restrict intra-Community trade or to distort competition. Whether this will be held to be so is very much a case-by-case appraisal, as the following examples show:

- An agreement whereby one party was given the right to register a trade mark in a particular Member State whereas the trade mark was internationally registered in the name of the other party was held to be contrary to Art. 81 EC. The ECJ clarified that the application of Art. 81 EC is not precluded merely by the fact that the exclusive right may originate in legal or factual circumstances other than a contested agreement or concerted practice, such as the registration of a trade mark in conformity with national procedures (Cases 56/64 etc. *Consten and Grundig* v. *Commission*, above).
- Trade mark delimitation agreements may be lawful if they serve to delimit the spheres within which the respective trade marks may be used and are intended to avoid confusion and conflict between them. They will be considered to be contrary to Art. 81 EC if the aim is to divide the market or to restrict competition otherwise (Case 35/83 *BAT* v. *Commission* [1985] ECR 363 at p. 385).
- The combination of different trade mark assignments of national trade marks concerning the same product might be contrary to Art. 81 EC if it results in barriers being resurrected between Member States (Case 40/70 *Sirena* [1971] ECR 69 at pp. 82–3). With respect to trade mark assignments, the ECJ subsequently clarified that:

  > where undertakings independently of each other make trade mark assignments following a market-sharing agreement, the prohibition of anti-competitive agreements under Article 81 applies and assignments which give effect to that agreement are consequently void. However, . . . that rule and the accompanying sanction cannot be applied mechanically to every assignment. Before a trade mark assignment can be treated as giving effect to an agreement prohibited under Article 81 EC, it is necessary to analyse the context, the commitments underlying the assignment, the intention of the parties and the considerations for the assignment (Case C-9/93 *Ideal-Standard*, above, at p. I-2855).

- An agreement concerning trade marks between traders established inside and outside the EC whereby the Community market as a whole would be isolated might be contrary to Art. 81 EC. In particular if the trader outside the EC has subsidiaries inside the EC which could have used the trade mark if it were not for the contested agreement (Case 51/75 *EMI Records*, above, at p. 848).
- Reciprocal representation contracts between copyright collecting societies will not, as such, be held to be contrary to Art. 81 EC. Unless those contracts or a concerted practice confer exclusivity because the

collecting societies undertook not to grant access to their musical repertoires to anyone established outside their territory (Cases 110/88 etc. *Lucazeau*, above, at pp. 2828–9; Case 395/87 *Tournier*, above, at p. 2574).

- The practice whereby copyright collecting societies refuse consumers authorization with respect to only the foreign repertoire will not necessarily be contrary to Art. 81 EC. It is up to the national court to appreciate whether this is necessary to attain the legitimate objectives of those collecting societies (Case 395/87 *Tournier*, above, at p. 2575).
- An agreement conferring an exclusive right to exhibit a film for a specific period in a Member State is not necessarily contrary to Art. 81 EC. The ECJ held that the exercise of the exclusivity thus conferred should not be 'subject to a situation in the economic or legal sphere the object or effect of which is to prevent or restrict the distribution of films or to distort competition within the cinematographic market, regard being had to the specific characteristics of that market' (Case 262/81 *Coditel II*, above, at p. 3402).
- The practice whereby 'persons simultaneously or successively file the same design in various Member States in order to divide up the markets within the Community among themselves' may be contrary to Art. 81 EC (Case 144/81 *Keurkoop*, above, at p. 2873).
- The grant of an open exclusive licence with respect to plant breeder's rights is not, of itself, incompatible with Art. 81 EC, in particular where such a licence is needed in order to accept the risk of cultivating and marketing that product by an undertaking in other Member States. The ECJ stated that any other result 'would be damaging to the dissemination of a new technology and would prejudice competition in the Community between the new product and existing products' (Case 258/78 *Nungesser* [1982] ECR 2015 at p. 2069).
- On the other hand, exclusive licences that confer absolute territorial protection are contrary to Art. 81 EC (Cases 56/64 etc. *Consten and Grundig* v. *Commission*, above; Case 258/78 *Nungesser*, above, at p. 2070).
- The contractual obligation to pay royalties for an indeterminate period, including after the expiry of the patent, is not contrary to Art. 81 EC, unless the licensee is not given the possibility to terminate the agreement with reasonable notice or his freedom of action after the termination is restricted (Case 320/87 *Ottung* [1989] ECR 1177 at p. 1199).
- The contractual obligation to submit unprotected products, to which the protected product is to be fixed, to the licensor's approval is contrary to Art. 81 EC. Quality controls may be imposed on patented products provided that the quality and safety criteria are agreed upon in advance on the basis of objectively identifiable criteria (Case 193/83 *Windsurfing International* v. *Commission* [1986] ECR 611 at p. 655).
- A clause providing for the sales tie-in of unprotected products is

contrary to Art. 81 EC (Case 193/83 *Windsurfing International* v. *Commission*, above, at pp. 656–7).

- A non-competition clause, whereby the licensee is prohibited from manufacturing and marketing products after the expiry of the agreement as well as the patent is contrary to Art. 81 EC (Case 320/87 *Ottung*, above, at p. 1199).
- The insertion in an agreement of conditions, which unduly restrict the licensee's competitiveness *vis-à-vis* the licensor, will be contrary to Art. 81 EC. Examples are the obligation to affix notices to the unprotected product stating that they are licensed by the licensor and a no-challenge clause with respect to trade marks (Case 193/83 *Windsurfing International* v. *Commission*, above, at pp. 659–62).
- Whereas the ECJ has acknowledged that 'it is in the public interest to eliminate any obstacle to economic activity which may arise where a patent was granted in error' (Case 193/83 *Windsurfing International* v. *Commission*, above, at p. 663), it later on held that:

> a no-challenge clause in a patent licensing agreement may, depending on the legal and economic context, restrict competition within the meaning of Art. 81 of the EEC Treaty. Such a clause does not, however, restrict competition when the agreement in which it is contained granted a free licence and the licensee does not, therefore, suffer the competitive disadvantage involved in the payment of royalties or when the licence was granted subject to the payment of royalties but relates to a technically outdated process which the undertaking accepting the no-challenge clause did not use (Case 65/86 *Bayer* [1988] ECR 5249 at p. 5287).

The fact that restrictive practices took place before the EC Treaty came into force, for instance prior to the accession of a Member State to the European Union, does not suffice to escape the application of Art. 81 EC. The ECJ has held that, for this provision to apply, 'it is both necessary and sufficient that they continue their effects after that date' (Case 40/70 *Sirena*, above, at p. 83). This will not be held to be the case with respect to trade mark assignments if the effects thereof do not exceed those that constitute the normal exercise of the trade mark right (Case 51/75 *EMI Records*, above, at p. 849).

The difficulty of applying Art. 81 EC to intellectual property rights is illustrated by the radical shift in approach taken with respect to the granting of exemptions under Art. 81(3) EC by the Commission over the years. The initial communication of the Commission, the so-called 'Christmas message', indicated that the Commission would consider most of the possible provisions in patent licences not to be contrary to Art. 81(1), and thus not needing an exemption, as they are just an extension of the right of prohibition contained in the patentee's exclusive right (*JO* 1962 C139/2922). Subsequent to the *Consten and Grundig* case (see above), which made it clear that also vertical agreements may be caught by Art. 81(1) EC, the Commission gradually changed its approach to patent licences in the sense that now it would consider certain provisions, such as those conferring exclusivity, as *per se* prohibited and not meriting an exemption under Art. 81(3) EC. This approach again was departed from after the *Nungesser* judgment (see above), in which the ECJ clarified that open exclusive licences do not necessarily fall foul of Art. 81(1) EC. In the end, the Commission acquired enough experience with intellectual property licences so as to allow it to enact block exemptions with respect to both patent licensing agreements and know how agreements. These block exemptions have now been replaced by a single block exemption for technology transfer agreements.

2. **The relationship between Article 82 EC and intellectual property rights** is a complex one. As neither an agreement nor a concerted practice needs to be established, the mere unilateral enforcement of this exclusive right by an intellectual property owner may, in principle, suffice for this provision to apply. The ECJ has consistently held that the exercise of intellectual property rights will not be contrary to Art. 82 EC, unless it is established that there is a dominant position on the EC market or a substantial part thereof, which is abused, and whereby intra-Community trade is affected (see e.g. Case 24/67 *Parke, Davis*, above; Case 78/70 *Deutsche Grammophon*, above. See also section II.4 above). Considering the special competitive position that intellectual property rights confer (see section I above), the crucial issue is under what circumstances these conditions will be held to be fulfilled.

Intellectual property rights confer a certain degree of market power as they allow the right-owner to prohibit the marketing of infringing goods (see section I above). The ECJ has clarified that the use of the exclusive right to prohibit the importation of infringing goods, which is allowed under Art. 30 EC, does not automatically imply that the right-owner has a dominant position in the market (see e.g. Case 40/70 *Sirena*, above, at p. 83), nor does the exercise of the right to distribute the protected product (Case 78/70 *Deutsche Grammophon*, above, at p. 501). In order to concluded that there is a dominant position in the market, it needs to be established, in each case, whether the intellectual property owner can impede the maintenance of effective competition in a substantial part of the relevant market (see e.g. Case 78/70 *Deutsche Grammophon*, above, at p. 501; Case 51/75 *EMI Records*, above, at p. 849).

A further requirement is that the dominant position is abused. The ECJ has indicated that for Art. 82 EC to apply, an additional element to the normal use of the intellectual property right in accordance with Art. 30 EC is needed (see e.g. Case 102/77 *Hoffman-La Roche*, above, at p. 1167; Case 402/85 *Basset* [1987] ECR 1747 at p. 1769). The main question is what additional element is needed for the exercise of intellectual property rights by an undertaking in a dominant position to be qualified as abusive. The fact that the enforcement of intellectual property rights leads to the elimination of competition is not, of itself, sufficient to establish an abuse under Art. 82 EC. The ECJ clarified that 'the mere fact of securing a benefit of an exclusive right granted by law, the effect of which is to enable the manufacture and sale of protected products by unauthorized third parties to be prevented, cannot be regarded as an abusive method of eliminating competition' (Case 53/87 *Maxicar*, above, at p. 6072). This case concerned the elimination of competition in the after-sales market of replacement parts. In a later case, concerning the invocation of copyright in order to prevent the creation of a derivative market in a new product, the ECJ specified that 'the exercise of an exclusive right by the proprietor may, in exceptional circumstances, involve abusive conduct' (Cases C-241/91 P etc. *Magill*, above, at p. I-823).

The main issue is what exceptional circumstances might justify the application of Art. 82 EC. In the absence of clear criteria, establishing abusive conduct by intellectual property owners is very much a case-by-case appraisal, as the following examples of the case-law of the ECJ illustrate:

- Higher prices in themselves are not proof of an abuse, although they might be indicative of an abuse of a dominant position if they cannot be justified by objective criteria (Case 78/70 *Deutsche Grammophon*, above, at p. 501; Case 40/70 *Sirena*, above, at p. 84).
- As the principle of international exhaustion of trade marks does not apply in the EC, by analogy it is considered lawful to enforce copyright in order to prevent the importation into the Community of products coming from third states. Factual evidence of lower prices on the third market and excessive prices on the Community market may, nonetheless, point to an abuse of a dominant position (Case T-198/98 *Micro Leader* v. *Commission*, above, at pp. II-4010–1).
- Charging a supplementary mechanical reproduction fee, which is lawful under Art. 30 EC, is not of itself contrary to Art. 82 EC unless unfair conditions are imposed (Case 402/85 *Basset*, above, at p. 1769).
- Imposing unfair conditions, such as the imposition on its members, by an undertaking entrusted with the exploitation of copyright, of obligations which are not necessary to attain its objectives is contrary to Art. 82 EC (Case 127/73 *BRT* [1974] ECR 313 at p. 318).
- The imposition of higher royalties in one Member State as compared to another which is not justifiable on objective grounds is contrary to Art. 82 EC (Case 395/87 *Tournier*, above, at p. 2579; Cases 110/88 etc. *Lucazeau*, above, at pp. 2833–4).
- An arbitrary refusal to deliver spare parts to independent repairers, the fixing of prices for spare parts at an unfair level, or a decision no longer to produce spare parts for a particular model although many cars of that model remain in circulation were given as examples of abusive behaviour (Case 238/87 *Volvo*, above, at p. 6235; Case 53/87 *Maxicar*, above, at p. 6073).
- The acquisition of an exclusive licence by an undertaking in a dominant position, having regard to the effect on the structure of competition in the relevant market. Art. 82 EC may apply to such as case even though the exclusive licence benefits from an exemption under Art. 81(3) EC (Case T-51/89 *Tetra Pak I* v. *Commission* [1990] ECR II-309).
- The tie-in of unprotected products, so as to eliminate competition in the related market for unprotected products, and discriminatory sales policies are contrary to Art. 82 EC (Case C-53/92 P *Hilti* v. *Commission* [1994] ECR I-667).

- The refusal to grant a voluntary licence will not necessarily amount to an abuse of a dominant position. The ECJ held that:

  an obligation imposed upon the proprietor of a protected design to grant third parties, even in return for a reasonable royalty, a licence for the supply of products incorporating the design would lead to the proprietor thereof being deprived of the substance of his exclusive right, and that a refusal to grant such a licence cannot in itself constitute an abuse of a dominant position (Case 238/87 *Volvo*, above, at p. 6235).

- On the other hand, the ECJ subsequently held that the Commission may impose obligatory licences, on the basis of Art. 3 of Reg. 17, in the following way:

  In the present case, after finding that the refusal to provide undertakings such as Magill with the basic information contained in television programme listings was an abuse of a dominant position, the Commission was entitled under Article 3, in order to ensure that its decision was effective, to require the appellants to provide that information. As the Court of First Instance rightly found, the imposition of that obligation—with the possibility of making the authorisation of publication dependent on certain conditions, including payment of royalties—was the only way of bringing the infringement to an end (Cases C-241/91 P etc. *Magill*, above, at p. I-834).

As such it seems that, in exceptional circumstances, an affirmative action obligation may be imposed on intellectual property owners, in spite of the initial indications to the contrary given by the ECJ. The crucial issue remains the definition of exceptional circumstances that might trigger Art. 82 EC. The following were held to constitute such exceptional circumstances:

- the reliance on copyright to prevent the appearance of a new product on the market,
- for which there was a potential consumer demand,
- and the reservation to the copyright owners of the secondary market of weekly television guides by excluding all competition on the market (Cases C-241/91 P etc. *Magill*, above).

In a later case, which was not specifically related to intellectual property rights but concerned the refusal of a media undertaking holding a dominant position in the territory of a Member State to include a rival daily newspaper of another undertaking in the same Member State in its newspaper home-delivery scheme, the ECJ indicated that the following conditions would need to be fulfilled: all competition on the part of the person requesting the service is eliminated in the daily newspaper market; the refusal is incapable of being objectively justified; the service in itself is indispensable to carry on that person's business inasmuch as there is no actual or potential substitute in existence for that home-delivery scheme (Case C-7/97 *Bronner* [1998] ECR I-7791 at pp. I-7830–1). A pending question is whether the conditions regarded as constituting exceptional circumstances in *Magill* and *Bronner* are concurrent or non-cumulative (Case C-481/01 P(R) *NDC Health* v. *IMS Health and Commission* [2002] ECR I-3401).

V. Intellectual property rights and harmonization measures

Community harmonization with respect to intellectual property rights is far from complete. Up till now, harmonization has been achieved in particular for trade marks and industrial designs and with respect to those new matters for which a solution had not already been adopted in most national laws (see also section II.5 above). Also measures to be taken at the external Community border, in order to protect the Community market against counterfeit products coming from third countries, have been gradually elaborated upon. Whereas at an earlier stage the Community measures only concerned trade mark counterfeiting, Council Reg. 3295/94 of 22 December 1994 laying down measures to prohibit the release for free circulation, export, re-export, or entry for a suspensive procedure of counterfeit and pirated goods extended the scope to include other types of intellectual property rights, except for patents (*OJ* 1994 L341/8; as implemented *OJ* 1995 L133/2). Reg. 3295/94 was later on amended by Council Reg. 241/1999 of 25 January 1999 to include patents and supplementary protection certificates for medicinal and plant protection products, as well as appropriate provisions to take into account the Community Trade Mark (*OJ* 1999 L27/1). Such autonomous measures on cross-border trade aspects of intellectual property rights are validly adopted by the Community on the basis of Art. 133 EC, the common commercial policy (Opinion 1/94 *WTO*, above; Case C-383/98 *Polo/Lauren* [2000] ECR I-2519).

The ECJ has held that Reg. 3295/94 is 'expressly designed to apply to goods passing through Community territory from a non-member country destined for another non-member country'. It considered that external transit is not totally devoid of effect on the internal market as there is a risk that such goods may be fraudulently brought on to the Community market (Case C-383/98 *Polo/Lauren*, above, at p. I-2543). A similar reasoning does not apply in the context of internal transit (see section III.2(*b*) above). With respect to the latter, the ECJ has ruled that 'considerations concerning the effectiveness of Regulation 3295/94 cannot justify a breach of the rules of the Treaty relating to the free movement of goods within the Community' (Case C-23/99 *Commission* v. *France*, above, at p. I-7685).

The ECJ has underlined the essential role attributed to the right-owner by Reg. 3295/94. Arts. 3 and 4 make it clear that detention of goods by the customs authorities is, in principle, subject to an application on his part He must also refer the case to a competent authority for a final judgment. Effective application of the regulation is directly dependent on the information supplied to the right-owner. Consequently, Art. 6(1) on the protection of personal data, commercial and industrial secrecy, and professional and administrative confidentiality 'cannot, in those circumstances, be understood as precluding the disclosure to the holder of the right of information which he needs in order to safeguard his interests', such as the identity of the declarant or the consignee of the goods. Pursuant to Arts. 6(2) and 9(3) unlawful use of that information may give rise to liability of the right-owner (Case C-223/98 *Adidas* [1999] ECR I-7081).

The Commission has currently tabled a proposal for a Council regulation concerning customs actions against goods suspected of infringing certain intellectual property rights and the measures to be taken against goods found to have infringed such rights (COM(2003) 20). A proposal has also been elaborated for a directive on measures and procedures to ensure the enforcement of intellectual property rights (COM(2003) 46). The aim is to eliminate obstacles between the national systems of penalties applicable to infringements of intellectual property rights. This is complementary to the other harmonization measures that have been taken over the years and which focused on the harmonization of national substantive laws or the creation of a unitary intellectual property right on Community level. Those harmonization measures and the interpretation given by the ECJ, are considered in turn below (on the method of interpretation of secondary legislation, see section II.5 above. On the implications of the EEA, see section II.6 above).

1. Patents. The proposals of the working groups on patents, established in 1959 to study the feasibility of patent harmonization in the Community, have not led to Community harmonization measures in the proper sense of the word. They do, however, lie at the basis of the 1973 Munich Convention on the European Patent and the 1975 and 1989 Community Patent Convention (*OJ* 1976 L17/1, as amended by *OJ* 1989 L401/1). The objective of the latter was not only to introduce a common application procedure but also to harmonize substantive patent laws of the Member States of the EC. It has never entered into force. This unsuccessful initiative is to be replaced by Community harmonization measures.

(*a*) ***The Community patent.*** The Commission has tabled a proposal for a Council regulation on the Community patent (COM(2000) 412; see also the Commission Working Document and proposals on the planned Community patent jurisdiction (COM(2002) 480; COM(2003) 827; COM(2003) 828). The Community patent will basically be a European patent in the sense of the Munich Convention so that accession of the EC to the latter is required. The Community patent will have a unitary and autonomous character. It will have equal effect throughout the EC and may only be granted, transferred, revoked, or allowed to lapse in respect of the whole EC territory. The objective is not to totally replace national patents. The possibility to obtain a national patent rather than a Community patent will continue to exist but simultaneous protection will be prohibited in principle.

(*b*) ***Council Reg. 1768/92 of 18 June 1992 on the supplementary protection certificate for pharmaceutical products*** (*OJ* 1992 L182/1) was the first Community harmonization measure adopted with respect to patents. The objective of the regulation is to allow for the duration of protection conferred by the patent to be extended in the case of medicinal products for which a marketing authorization was granted, having regard to the long period needed to obtain that authorization. The period of effective protection under the patent is considered to be insufficient to cover the investment put into research and development of medicinal products. It is pointed out that, as medicinal products are the result of long and costly research, they will not continue to be developed in the EC unless sufficient protection is provided to encourage such research (second and third recitals). The ECJ has ruled that this harmonization measure was validly adopted on the basis of Art. 95 EC as it is intended to prevent the heterogeneous development of national laws in this respect and, hence, to safeguard the functioning of the internal market (Case C-350/92 *Spain* v. *Council*, above, at pp. I-2014–15). The ECJ has given the following interpretation of certain provisions of the regulation:

- In the absence of Community harmonization of patent law, the criteria for determining whether or not a product is protected by a basic patent and the extent of such patent protection, in particular in connection with Art. 3(a) of the regulation, must be determined in the light of the non-Community rules that govern that patent (Case C-392/97 *Farmitalia* [1999] ECR I-5553).
- Under Art. 3(b) of the regulation, where a product in the form referred to in the basic patent authorization is protected by a basic patent in force, the supplementary certificate is capable of covering the product, as a medicinal product, in any of the forms enjoying the protection of the basic patent (ibid.).
- Under Art. 3(b) of the regulation, the grant of the certificate is conditional upon a valid authorization to place the product on the market as a medicinal product having been granted in the Member State where the application is submitted and at the date of that application. The need to fulfil this condition is not precluded by the wording of Art. 19 of the regulation (Case C-110/95 *Yamanouchi Pharmaceutical* [1997] ECR I-3251 at pp. I-3275–7).
- Under Art. 3(c) of the regulation only one certificate may be issued for each basic patent. The ECJ has clarified that, where a medicinal product is protected by a number of basic patents in force, each holder of a basic patent may receive a supplementary certificate. According to Art. 13 of the regulation, the duration of such certificates is, however, to be calculated uniformly on the basis of the date of the first authorization to put the product on the Community market (Case C-181/95 *Biogen* [1997] ECR I-357 at p. I-396).
- Art. 8(1)(b) of the regulation stipulates that an application for a certificate must contain a copy of the marketing authorization for the medicinal product. The ECJ has held that, where the basic patent and the marketing authorization are held by different persons, the regulation does not require the holder of the marketing authorization to provide the basic patent holder with a copy of it. This may, however, be inherent in their contractual relationship (Case C-181/95 *Biogen*, above, at pp. I-397–8). In case the patent holder cannot provide a copy of that authorization, his application for a certificate may not be refused on

that basis alone, as the simple co-operation between national authorities can remedy this. The ECJ has held that the purpose of Art. 8(1)(b) of the regulation is 'to identify the product and verify that the time-limit for submitting an application and, where applicable, the duration of the supplementary protection are observed. It is therefore a formal requirement whose purpose is to demonstrate the existence of an authorization to place the product on the market as a medicinal product' (ibid. at pp. I-399–400).

(*c*) ***Dir. 98/44 of the European Parliament and of the Council of 6 July 1998 on the legal protection of biotechnological inventions*** was finally adopted on 6 July 1998, after a long debate and several amended proposals (*OJ* 1998 L213/13). The granting of legal protection to biotechnological inventions proved to be a highly controversial issue. The European Parliament had rejected an earlier version of the text in spite of the fact that it had been approved by the Conciliation Committee (*OJ* 1995 C68/26). The objective of the directive, as finally adopted, is 'limited to laying down certain principles as they apply to the patentability of biological material as such, such principles being intended in particular to determine the difference between inventions and discoveries with regard to the patentability of certain elements of human origin, to the scope of protection conferred by a patent on a biotechnological invention, to the right to use a deposit mechanism in addition to written descriptions and lastly to the option of obtaining non-exclusive compulsory licences in respect of interdependence between plant varieties and inventions, and conversely' (thirteenth recital), in order to ensure that the functioning of the internal market is not unduly distorted by the uncoordinated development of national laws in this respect (seventh recital).

Plant varieties are excluded from protection under this directive, as they are the subject of specific harmonization measures (see point 5 below). Art. 4 of the directive specifies that a patent may nonetheless be granted for an invention if its technical feasibility is not confined to a particular plant variety. The ECJ has ruled out an inconsistency in this respect by pointing out that 'it follows that a genetic modification of a specific plant variety is not patentable but a modification of a wider scope, concerning, for example, a species, may be' (Case C-377/98 *Netherlands* v. *Parliament and Council*, above, at p. I-7162).

This directive is subject to constant monitoring (Art. 16 of the directive). A report had to be made, within two years of the entry into force of the directive, assessing the implications for basic genetic engineering research or failure to publish, or late publication, of papers on potentially patentable subjects (COM(2002) 2). A report should also be presented annually on the development and implications of patent law in the field of biotechnology and genetic engineering (see e.g. COM(2002) 545). Furthermore, the Commission is to submit a report every five years on problems encountered in relation to international agreements on human rights to which the Member States have acceded.

The ECJ has firmly rejected a request for annulment of the directive (see also section II.5 above). It confirmed the validity of Art. 95 EC as the legal basis and expressly ruled that the principle of subsidiarity was not breached (Case C-377/98 *Netherlands* v. *Parliament and Council*, above). The ECJ also came to the conclusion that, as regards living matter of human origin, Arts. 5 and 6 of the directive frame 'the law on patents in a manner sufficiently rigorous to ensure that the human body effectively remains unavailable and inalienable and that human dignity is thus safeguarded' (ibid. at p. I-7170). The implementation of the biotechnology directive proves to be as cumbersome as its adoption. Three years after the implementation deadline the Commission decided to refer eight Member States to the ECJ for failure to implement the directive (IP/03/991 of 10 July 2003).

(*d*) ***Proposals.*** The Commission has tabled an amended proposal for a directive of the European Parliament and of the Council approximating the legal arrangements for the protection of inventions by utility model (COM(1999) 309 final/2). The objective is to grant exclusive protection for a technical invention, upon registration and for a maximum duration of ten years only. A more recent Commission proposal concerns a directive of the European Parliament and of the Council on the patentability of computer-implemented inventions (COM(2002) 92). The idea is that legal protection would be granted in a complementary manner by both patents and copyright in respect of the same program (see Dir. 91/250 on the legal protection of computer programs, point 4 below).

2. Trade marks. The working group on trade marks, established in 1959 to study the feasibility of trade mark harmonization in the Community, has by far been the most successful. Its proposals lay at the basis of Council Reg. 40/94 of 20 December 1993 on the Community trade mark (*OJ* 1994 L11/1, as amended in order to implement the TRIPS Agreement by Council Reg. 3288/94 of 23 December 1994, *OJ* 1994 L349/83; and implemented by Comm. Reg. 2868/95, *OJ* 1995 L303/1. For the application of Art. 29(5) of the regulation concerning priority claims in respect to Taiwan, see the terms of the agreement as related in Commission Communication of 5 November 1998, *OJ* 1998 C351/3). Council Reg. 40/94 was further amended by Council Reg. 1992/2003 of 27 October 2003 to give effect to the accession of the European Community to the Protocol relating to the Madrid Agreement concerning the international registration of marks adopted at Madrid on 27 June 1989 (*OJ* 2003 L296/1); see also Council Dec. of 27 October 2003 approving the accession of the European Community to the Protocol relating to the Madrid Agreement concerning the international registration of marks, adopted at Madrid on 27 June 1989 (*OJ* 2003 L296/20), as well as the Protocol relating to the Madrid Agreement concerning the international registration of marks, adopted at Madrid on 27 June 1989 (*OJ* 2003 L296/22). Council Reg. 40/94 in turn stands as an example for the other Community intellectual property rights.

(*a*) ***The Community trade mark.*** The ambitious objective of Council Reg.

40/94 on the Community trade mark is to render trade mark protection in the Community uniform and to eliminate obstacles to intra-Community trade posed by the principle of territoriality inherent in trade marks (see the preamble of the regulation, above). This is done through the introduction of the Community trade mark based on the principle of the unitary character. The latter means, in principle, that a Community trade mark 'shall have equal effect throughout the Community: it shall not be registered, transferred or surrendered or be the subject of a decision revoking the rights of the proprietor or declaring it invalid, nor shall its use be prohibited, save in respect of the whole Community' (Art. 1(2) of the regulation). Specialized Community institutions are established, in particular the Office for Harmonisation in the Internal Market (Trade Marks and Designs) (OHIM), with legal, administrative, and financial autonomy (see also Comm. Reg. 216/96 of 5 February 1996 laying down the rules of procedure of the Boards of Appeal of the OHIM, *OJ* 1996 L28/11). The Community trade mark is governed by Community law, the uniform interpretation of which is safeguarded by the ECJ. On this basis, the ECJ will also interpret the relevant provisions of the TRIPS Agreement which apply to Community trade marks as well as national marks (Case C-53/96 *Hermes*, above, at p. I-3648. See also section II.6 above). Under Arts. 91 and 143(2) of the regulation, Member States are required to designate a limited number of national courts as 'Community trade mark courts'. The latter are to act as specialized courts to hear cases arising from Community trade marks and to ensure that proprietors of those rights enjoy the same level of protection and legal certainty throughout the EU.

Under Art. 63 of the regulation, actions may be brought on appeals against decisions of the Boards of Appeal of the OHIM. The Court of First Instance has the power to annul or alter the contested decision of the OHIM. An appeal against a decision of the CFI may, in turn, be lodged before the ECJ on points of law (see e.g. Case C-248/97 P(R) *Chaves Fonseca Ferrao* v. *OHIM* [1997] ECR I-4729; Case C-383/99 P *Procter & Gamble* v. *OHIM* [2001] ECR I-6251; Case C-104/00 P *DKV* v. *OHIM* [2002] ECR I-7561). Many of the cases brought against the OHIM concern a refusal by the OHIM to register a Community trade mark on the basis of Arts. 7 or 8 of the regulation. Those provisions are to be interpreted in a similar way as the similar provisions of trade mark Dir. 89/104 (see below). The legality of decisions of the Boards of Appeal is to be assessed purely by reference to Reg. 40/94, as interpreted by the Community Courts, and not the Office's practice in earlier decisions. There is also no provision in Reg. 40/94 which requires the OHIM to come to the same conclusion as reached by national authorities in similar circumstances. Registrations already made in Member States are only one of the factors which may be taken into consideration for the purpose of registering a Community trade mark, without being given decisive weight (see e.g. Case C-104/00 P *DKV* v. *OHIM*, above, para. 39; Case T-32/00 *Messe München* v. *OHIM* [2000] ECR II-3829; Case T-24/00 *Sunrider* v. *OHIM* [2001] ECR II-449).

The Commission has tabled proposals to improve Reg. 40/94

(COM(2002) 767). Among others it is proposed to make the Community trade mark accessible to all without any requirement of reciprocity, equivalence, or nationality and to abolish the search system which is considered to be costly and complex (COM(2002) 754). The Commission has also identified the need to bring the provisions on professional representation before the OHIM into line with the principles of freedom of establishment and provisions of services (COM(2002) 766).

(*b*) ***Trade mark Dir. 89/104.*** The Community trade mark does not totally replace national trade marks. National trade mark legislation remains in force, albeit subject to approximation. The stated objective of the First Council Dir. 89/104 of 21 December 1988 to approximate the laws of the Member States relating to trade marks is limited to approximating those national provisions of law which most directly affect the functioning of the internal market (see the preamble to the directive, *OJ* 1989 L40/1, as amended by the EEA, *OJ* 1994 L1/482). The entry into force of this directive, which is the only one so far, was delayed in order to align it to that of the Community trade mark regulation (Council Dec. 92/10, *OJ* 1992 L6/35). For instance, the trade mark directive endeavours to render the conditions for obtaining and continuing to hold a registered trade mark identical in all Member States. As the aim is not to undertake a full-scale harmonization, the Member States remain free to determine, *inter alia*, the procedures for, and the effect of, revocation or invalidity of national trade marks. The ECJ has given the following interpretation of certain provisions of the directive, which mostly find their counterpart also in the Community trade mark regulation:

(*i*) *Art. 2 of the directive is similar to Art. 4 of Reg. 40/94.* It provides that any sign may constitute a trade mark, provided that it is capable of being represented graphically and is capable of distinguishing the goods or services of one undertaking from those of other undertakings. It also gives a non-exhaustive list of examples of such signs (see e.g. Case C-383/99 P *Procter & Gamble* v. *OHIM*, above). Art. 2 makes no distinction between different categories of trade marks. The same criteria therefore apply to three-dimensional trade marks (Case C-299/99 *Philips* [2002] ECR I-5475; Cases C-53/01 etc. *Linde* [2003] ECR I-3161). The ECJ has interpreted Art. 2 'as meaning that a trade mark may consist of a sign which is not in itself capable of being perceived visually, provided that it can be represented graphically, particularly by means of images, lines or characters, and that the representation is clear, precise, self-contained, easily accessible, intelligible, durable and objective'. Those requirements of graphic representability are not satisfied by a chemical formula, a description in written words, a deposit of an odour sample, or by a combination of those elements in respect of an olfactory sign (Case C-273/00 *Sieckmann* [2002] ECR I-11737). It cannot be excluded offhand that a colour '*per se*' satisfies the conditions of Art. 2. In particular a combination of a sample of a colour with a description in words of that colour might constitute a graphic representation. A deficiency in terms of lack of precision or durability might further be remedied by adding a colour designation from an internationally recognized identification code (Case C-104/01 *Libertel*, above).

(*ii*) *Art. 3(1) of the directive is similar to Art. 7(1) of Reg. 40/94* and lays down the grounds for refusal or invalidity. The ECJ has consistently held that the various grounds for refusing registration must be interpreted in the light of the public interest underlying each of them (Case C-299/99 *Philips*, above). The various absolute grounds for refusal are connected with lack of distinctiveness, descriptiveness, and customary usage and have their own sphere of application. Those grounds are applicable separately but may also apply cumulatively (Case T-345/99 *Harbinger* v. *OHIM* [2000] ECR II-3525 at pp. II-3537–8). For a registration to be refused it is sufficient that one of the grounds listed applies (Case C-104/00 P *DKV* v. *OHIM*, above). In order to safeguard the unitary character of the Community trade mark, Art. 7(2) of Reg. 40/94 stipulates that 'para. 1 shall apply notwithstanding that the grounds of non-registrability obtain in only part of the Community'. As a consequence, in order to be accepted for registration as a Community trade mark, a sign must possess a distinctive character throughout the EC (Case C-104/00 P *DKV* v. *OHIM*, above, para. 40; Case T-91/99 *Ford* v. *OHIM* [2000] ECR II-1925 at p. II-1937).

Art. 3(1)(b) of the directive lists trade marks that are devoid of any distinctive character. In assessing the potential distinctiveness of a given colour as a trade mark, the ECJ has ruled that 'regard must be had to the general interest in not unduly restricting the availability of colours for the other traders who offer for sale goods or services of the same type as those in respect of which registration is sought' (Case C-104/01 *Libertel*, above, para. 55). A stricter test should not be applied when assessing distinctiveness of a three-dimensional shape than for other types of trade marks (see e.g. Cases C-53/01 etc. *Linde*, above, para. 49; Cases T-324/01 etc. *Axions* v. *OHIM* [2003] ECR II-1897, para. 32).

Art. 3(1)(c) of the directive provides that trade marks which consist exclusively of signs or indications which may serve, in trade, to designate the kind, quality, quantity, intended purpose, value, geographical origin, or the time of production of the goods or of rendering the service, or other characteristics of the goods or service, should not be registered or, if registered, are liable to be declared invalid. The ECJ has held that Art. 3(1)(c) of the directive pursues an aim of public interest, namely that those descriptive signs and indications of geographical origin may be freely used by all, including as collective marks or as part of complex or graphic marks (Cases C-108/97 etc. *WSC* [1999] ECR I-2779 at pp. I-2823–4; Cases C-53/01 etc. *Linde*, above, para. 73). Similarly, a sign must be refused registration as a Community trade mark by virtue of Art. 7(1)(c) of Reg. 40/94 if at least one of its possible meanings designates a characteristic of the goods or services concerned (Case C-191/01 P *OHIM* v. *Wrigley* [2003] ECR I-0000, para. 32). Specifically with respect to geographical names, this provision should be interpreted as meaning that:

it does not prohibit the registration of geographical names as trade marks solely where the names designate places which are, in the mind of the relevant class of persons, currently associated with the category of goods in question; it also applies to geographical names which are liable to be used in the future by the undertakings concerned as an indication of the geographical origin of that category of goods;

where there is currently no association in the mind of the relevant class of persons between the geographical name and the category of goods in question, the competent authority must assess whether it is reasonable to assume that such a name is, in the mind of the relevant class of persons, capable of designating the geographical origin of that category of goods;

in making that assessment, particular consideration should be given to the degree of familiarity amongst the relevant class of persons with the geographical name in question, with the characteristics of the place designated by that name, and with the category of goods concerned;

it is not necessary for the goods to be manufactured in the geographical location in order for them to be associated with it (Cases C-108/97 etc. *WSC*, above, at p. I-2826).

Art. 3(1)(d) deals with signs or marks that have become customary in the current language or in the *bona fide* and established practice of the trade. The ECJ interprets this provision in the light of the essential function of trade marks as reflected in Art. 2 of the directive. It ruled that the provision only precludes to register a trade mark if the signs or indications of which the mark is exclusively composed have become customary. It is thereby immaterial whether the signs or indications in question describe the properties or characteristics of those goods or services (Case C-517/99 *Merz* [2001] ECR I-6959).

Art. 3(1)(e) excludes from protection those signs which consist exclusively of a shape, which results from the nature of the goods themselves, which is necessary to obtain a technical result, or which gives substantial value to goods. The ECJ has acknowledged that this provision is in the public interest, namely that a shape whose essential characteristics perform a technical function and were chosen to fulfil that function may be freely used by all. The fact that the technical result may be achieved by other shapes is to no avail (Case C-299/99 *Philips*, above, at pp. I-5517–8). Three-dimensional shapes which are not refused registration on the basis of Art. 3(1)(e) may still be refused if they fall under one of the other categories of Art. 3(1)(b) to (d) (Cases C-53/01 etc. *Linde*, above, para. 68).

(iii) Art. 3(3) of the directive is similar to Art. 7(3) of Reg. 40/94 (see e.g. Case T-91/99 *Ford* v. *OHIM*, above). A major exception to the application of Art. 3(1)(b), (c), or (d) of the directive is the case whereby the trade mark has acquired a distinctive character following use made of it before the application for registration. The appraisal of the distinctive character following the use made of the trade mark, similarly as for distinctive character which is a requirement to register the trade mark following Art. 3(1)(b) of

the directive, implies that the competent authority or the national court must 'make an overall assessment of the evidence that the mark has come to identify the product concerned as originating from a particular undertaking, and thus to distinguish that product from goods of other undertakings'. Distinctiveness cannot be shown to exist merely by reference to general and abstract data, such as predetermined percentages (Cases C-108/97 etc. *WSC*, above, at p. I-2829; Case C-517/99 *Merz*, above; Case C-299/99 *Philips*, above). The examination must refer to the actual situation and take account of all the relevant circumstances of the case. This may, *inter alia*, include the fact that registration for a colour '*per se*' is sought for a large number of goods or services (Case C-104/01 *Libertel*, above). It also implies that regard must be had to the specific nature of the geographical name in question whereas other factors which may be taken into account include the market share held by the mark; how intensive, geographically wide-spread, and long-standing use of the mark has been; the amount invested by the undertaking in promoting the mark; the proportion of the relevant class of persons who, because of the mark, identify goods as originating from a particular undertaking; statements from chambers of commerce and industry or other trade and professional associations; or opinion polls in this respect (Cases C-108/97 etc. *WSC*, above, at p. I-2830).

(iv) Art. 4(1)(b) of Dir. 89/104 is in essence the same as Art. 8(1)(b) of Reg. 40/94, so that the provisions are interpreted in a similar manner (see e.g. Case T-99/01 *Mystery Drinks* v. *OHIM* [2003] ECR II-43; Case T-156/01 *Laboratorios RTB* v. *OHIM* [2003] ECR II-2789). It is stipulated that, in case of conflict with an earlier right, a trade mark will not be registered or be declared invalid if both the trade marks and the products or services are identical or similar, so that there is 'a likelihood of confusion on the part of the public, which includes the likelihood of association with the earlier trade mark'. Specifically in so far as the Community trade mark is concerned, the relevant public in relation to which likelihood of confusion must be assessed is composed of average consumers in the Member States where the earlier marks are registered (see e.g. Case T-388/00 *Institut für Lernsysteme* v. *OHIM* [2002] ECR II-4301 at p. II-4324; Case T-129/01 *Alejandro* v. *OHIM* [2003] ECR II-2251, para. 41).

A provision in substantially similar terms is also to be found in Art. 5(1) of the directive. A similar interpretation should therefore be given of the concepts used (Case C-342/97 *Lloyd Schuhfabrik Meyer* [1999] ECR I-3819). Art. 5(1) of the directive carries out a complete harmonization and defines the rights of the trade mark proprietor to oppose the use of the trade mark by third parties in the course of trade in the EC (see e.g. Case C-206/01 *Arsenal* [2002] ECR I-10273, para. 43). Art. 5(2) enables Member States to offer more extensive protection to trade marks with a reputation. Pursuant to Art. 5(5), national provisions offering reinforced protection of a trade mark's distinctive character or reputation against uses of a sign other than for the purpose of distinguishing goods or services are to remain unaffected, as they are not covered by EC harmonization (Case C-23/01 *Robelco* [2002] ECR I-10913, para. 30–1).

The ECJ clarified that the concept of likelihood of association serves to define the scope of the concept of likelihood of confusion on the part of the public and is not an alternative to it (Case C-251/95 *Sabel* [1997] ECR I-6191 at p. I-6223; Case C-425/98 *Marca Mode* [2000] ECR I-4861 at p. I-4892). Whether or not there is likelihood of confusion on the part of the public needs to be appreciated globally, whereby its perception by the average consumer plays a decisive role (ibid.; see also Case C-342/97 *Lloyd Schuhfabrik Meyer*, above, at pp. I-3841–2). The ECJ held, in particular, that 'that global appreciation of the visual, aural or conceptual similarity of the trade marks in question, must be based on the overall impression given by the marks, bearing in mind, in particular, their distinctive and dominant components', so that 'the more distinctive the earlier mark, the greater will be the likelihood of confusion' (Case C-251/95 *Sabel*, above, at p. I-6224). The ECJ has acknowledged that the mere aural similarity between trade marks might possibly create a likelihood of confusion (Case C-342/97 *Lloyd Schuhfabrik Meyer*, above). The perception of marks in the mind of the average consumer plays a crucial role in the global assessment of the likelihood of confusion. The average consumer is deemed to be reasonably well informed, observant, and circumspect. The ECJ has underlined that the average consumer normally perceives a mark as a whole and does not analyse the various details. He only rarely has a change to make a direct comparison between different marks and mostly relies on the imperfect picture kept in his mind. His level of attention is also likely to vary according to the category of goods and services in question. It is apparent that the concept of distinctiveness is to be interpreted as clarified by the ECJ in the *WSC* case in relation to Art. 3 of the directive (see above) (Case C-342/97 *Lloyd Schuhfabrik Meyer*, above, at pp. I-3840–1).

The appreciation as to whether or not there exists likelihood of confusion on the part of the public may be different according to whether the mark enjoys a reputation with the public or is not especially well known (see also Case C-39/97 *Canon* [1998] ECR I-5507 at p. I-5534). It does not suffice that the public might make an association between trade marks, because of their analogous semantic content, for there to be likelihood of confusion in the sense of Art. 4(1)(b) of the directive (Case C-251/95 *Sabel*, above, at p. I-6225). It remains necessary to prove that there exists a similarity between the products or services concerned, even in case of well-known trade marks. Regard should thereby be had to their respective nature, destination, usage, as well as to their competitive or complementary character (Case C-39/97 *Canon*, above, at p. I-5534). The global assessment nonetheless entails that there may be some interdependence between the relevant factors, so that 'a lesser degree of similarity between the goods or services may be offset by a greater degree of similarity between the trade marks, and vice versa' (Case C-342/97 *Lloyd Schuhfabrik Meyer*, above, at p. I-3839). It is apparent that 'the more similar the goods or services covered and the more distinctive the earlier mark, the greater will be the likelihood of confusion' (ibid. at p. I-3842). The reputation of a mark, where demonstrated, is an element that, *inter alia*, may have a certain importance. The reputation may confer a highly distinctive character to the mark thus giving it a broader protection than marks with a less distinctive character. The reputation of a mark does not, however, give grounds 'for presuming the existence of a likelihood of confusion simply because of the existence of a likelihood of association in the strict sense' (Case C-425/98 *Marca Mode*, above, at p. I-4894). Accordingly, where there is no likelihood of confusion, Art. 5(1)(b) of the Directive cannot be invoked to protect a mark with a reputation against impairment of the distinctive character or repute of the mark (Case C-292/00 *Davidoff II* [2003] ECR I-389, paras. 28–9).

The risk of confusion relates to the fact that the public may be let to believe that the products or services come from one particular undertaking, or from undertakings economically linked to it. The exercise of the exclusive rights under Art. 5(1) of the directive is reserved to those cases where the use of the trade mark by third parties is liable to affect the essential function of trade marks of guaranteeing the origin of products to consumers (Case C-206/01 *Arsenal*, above, para. 51). A trade mark proprietor may not rely on his exclusive right, if it is clear that the trade mark is merely used for purely descriptive purposes in the course of trade, namely to denote the particular characteristics of a product, and is not perceived as an indicative of the undertaking of origin (Case C-2/00 *Hölterhoff* [2002] ECR I-4187). This is different where the use of the trade mark is not intended for purely descriptive purposes and may create the impression that there is a material link between the goods and the trade mark proprietor. It is immaterial that the use of the mark is perceived as a badge of support for, loyalty, or affiliation to, the trade mark proprietor (Case C-206/01 *Arsenal*, above, para. 51). Pointing to the fact that there is no confusion on the part of the public with respect to the place of production of the products does not suffice as it does not exclude the risk of confusion as to the origin of the products or services (Case C-39/97 *Canon*, above, at pp. I-5534–5).

(*v*) *Genuine use requirement.* Pursuant to Arts. 10(1) and 12(1) of the directive, if the trade mark is not put to genuine use in the Member State in connection with the goods or services in respect to which it registered during an non-interrupted period of five years, it shall be liable to revocation, unless there are proper reasons for non-use. The concept of genuine use is also to be found in Arts. 15 and 50 of Reg. 40/94 as a prerequisite for the Community trade mark. The ECJ has interpreted this concept in the light of the provisions of the Paris Convention for the Protection of Industrial Property, as meaning that:

> there is 'genuine use' of a trade mark where the mark is used in accordance with its essential function, which is to guarantee the identity of the origin of the goods or services for which it is registered, in order to create or preserve an outlet for those goods or services; genuine use does not include token use for the sole purpose of preserving the rights conferred by the mark. When assessing whether use of the trade mark is genuine, regard must be had to all the facts and circumstances relevant to establishing whether the commercial exploitation of the mark is real, particularly

whether such use is viewed as warranted in the economic sector concerned and to maintain or create a share in the market for goods or services protected by the mark, the nature of those goods or services, the characteristics of the market and the scale and frequency of use of the mark. The fact that a mark is not used for goods newly available on the market but for goods that were sold in the past does not mean that its use is not genuine, if the proprietor makes actual use of the same mark for component parts that are integral to the make-up or structure of such goods, or for goods or services directly connected with the goods previously sold and intended to meet the needs of customers of those goods (Case C-40/01 *Ansul* [2003] ECR I-2439, para. 43).

Art. 12(2)(b) of the directive leaves it up to the Member State to determine whether and to what extent the use of a revoked trade mark must be prohibited. This includes the possibility to prohibit the importation of products, lawfully marketed in another Member State, but bearing a trade mark that the trade mark proprietor was specifically prohibited from using in the Member State of importation on the basis that it was held to be liable to mislead the consumers (Case C-313/94 *Graffione* [1996] ECR I-6039 at p. I-6061).

(*vi*) *The principle of Community exhaustion,* as first introduced by virtue of case-law (see section III.3), is expressly written into Art. 7 of the trade mark directive. It reads as follows, under the heading 'Exhaustion of the rights conferred by a trade mark':

1. The trade mark shall not entitle the proprietor to prohibit its use in relation to goods which have been put on the market in the Community under that trade mark by the proprietor or with his consent.

2. Paragraph 1 shall not apply where there exist legitimate reasons for the proprietor to oppose further commercialisation of the goods, especially where the condition of the goods is changed or impaired after they have been put on the market.

The purpose of Art. 7(1) of the directive is 'to make possible the further marketing of an individual item of a product bearing a trade mark that has been put on the market with the consent of the trade mark proprietor and to prevent him from opposing such marketing' (Case C-173/98 *Sebago* [1999] ECR I-4103 at p. I-4122; Case C-337/95 *Kruidvat* [1997] ECR I-6013 at p. I-6047; Case C-63/97 *BMW* [1999] ECR I-905 at p. I-946). On this basis, the ECJ has made the following clarifications:

- The concept of consent, under Art. 7(1) of the directive, necessarily relates to each individual item in respect of which the principle of exhaustion is invoked. The right of the trade mark proprietor to oppose the importation of individual items of the product which were put on the market without his consent is not exhausted, otherwise trade mark protection would be devoid of its substance (Case C-173/98 *Sebago*, above, at pp. I-4121–2).
- Art. 7(1) of the directive requires that the goods have been put on the market in the Community 'under that mark'. It does not apply where the proprietor marketed his products under differentiated trade marks

and the parallel importer replaces the original trade mark with a different one. The latter case is determined by Arts. 28 and 30 EC (Case C-379/97 *Upjohn*, above, at p. I-6965) (see section III.4(*c*) above).

- The principle of exhaustion under Art. 7(1) of the directive is applicable where the importer has repackaged the product and reaffixed the original trade mark without the consent of the trade mark proprietor (Cases C-427/93 etc. *Bristol-Myers Squibb*, above, at pp. I-3529–30). With respect to repackaged goods, the main question is when this may be opposed on the basis of Art. 7(2) of the directive. The ECJ has held that the use of the word 'especially' in Art. 7(2) of the directive shows that the case expressly envisaged there is given only as an example. The provision should be interpreted 'as meaning that a trade mark proprietor may rely on its trade mark rights in order to prevent a parallel importer from repackaging pharmaceutical products unless the exercise of those rights contributes to artificial partitioning of the markets between Member States' (Case C-143/00 *Boehringer*, above, para. 35). With respect to the latter concept the case-law of the ECJ under Art. 30 EC, in particular the four criteria as first laid down in the *Hoffman-La Roche* case and subsequently elaborated upon, must be taken as the basis for an assessment (Cases C-427/93 etc. *Bristol-Myers Squibb*, above, at p. I-3531) (see section III.4(*b*) above). As such the ECJ has, for instance, held that 'the mere addition on the label of information does not constitute a legitimate reason within the meaning of Art. 7(2) of the Trade Mark Directive, provided that the label so altered does not omit important information or give inaccurate information and its presentation is not liable to damage the reputation of the trade mark and that of its owner' (Case C-352/95 *Phyteron International* [1997] ECR I-1729 at pp. I-1748–9).
- The use of the trade mark for advertising purposes, in particular in order to attract attention to further commercialization, including for repair and maintenance work, is exhausted in the same way as the right of resale. This in spite of the fact that Art. 5(3)(d) of the directive provides that the trade mark proprietor may prohibit the use of the trade mark in advertising by third parties. If not, the further commercialization of products 'would be made considerably more difficult and the purpose of "exhaustion of rights" rule laid down in Art. 7 would thus be undermined' (Case C-337/95 *Kruidvat*, above, at p. I-6047; Case C-63/97 *BMW*, above).
- The damage done to the reputation of a trade mark might in principle be a legitimate reason, within the meaning of Art. 7(2) of the directive, which renders the principle of exhaustion inapplicable. A balance therefore needs to be struck between the legitimate interests of the trade mark proprietor and those of the reseller. The ECJ indicated that:

> the fact that a reseller, who habitually markets articles of the same kind but not necessarily of the same quality, uses for trade-marked goods the modes of advertising which are customary in his trade sector, even if they are not the same

> as those used by the trade mark owner himself or by his approved retailers, does not constitute a legitimate reason, within the meaning of Article 7(2) of the Directive, allowing the owner to oppose that advertising, unless it is established that, given the specific circumstances of the case, the use of the trade mark in the reseller's advertising seriously damages the reputation of the trade mark. For example, such damage could occur if, in an advertising leaflet distributed by him, the reseller did not take care to avoid putting the trade mark in a context which might seriously detract from the image which the trade mark owner has succeeded in creating around his trade mark (Case C-337/95 *Kruidvat*, above, at pp. I-6049–50).

Art. 7 of the directive was subsequently amended by the EEA, replacing the principle of Community exhaustion by the so-called principle of regional exhaustion. One of the conditions for the principle of exhaustion to apply is, therefore, that the product was put on the EEA market by the trade mark proprietor or with his consent (Case C-355/96 *Silhouette*, above, at pp. I-4825, I-4829; see also section II.6 above). It is irrelevant that the product was manufactured in a non-member country as long as it was imported and put on the market in the EEA by the trade mark proprietor or with his consent, including by another company in the same group as the proprietor of the trade mark (Case C-352/95 *Phyteron International*, above, at p. I-1748).

(vii) The question of international exhaustion. A crucial question is whether, and to what extent, the principle of exhaustion should apply to products that were put on the market of a non-member State by the trade mark proprietor or with his consent, in case of direct importation from the non-member country. The directive does not provide for the principle of international exhaustion. Contrary to the interpretation given by the EFTA Court, the ECJ held that the silence of the trade mark directive in this respect does not imply that the Member States remain free to adopt, or even to maintain, this principle in their national trade mark legislation (Case C-355/96 *Silhouette*, above, at p. I-4829; Case C-173/98 *Sebago*, above, para. 17, as opposed to Case E-2/97 *Mag Instruments*, above). According to the ECJ:

> Articles 5 to 7 of the Directive must be construed as embodying a complete harmonization of the rules relating to the rights conferred by a trade mark' . . . 'Accordingly, the Directive cannot be interpreted as leaving it open to the Member States to provide in their domestic law for the exhaustion of the rights conferred by a trade mark in respect of products put on the market in non-member countries. This, moreover, is the only interpretation which is fully capable of ensuring that the purpose of the Directive is achieved, namely to safeguard the functioning of the internal market. A situation in which some Member States could provide for international exhaustion while others provided for Community exhaustion only would inevitably give rise to barriers to the free movement of goods and the freedom to provide services' (Case C-355/96 *Silhouette*, above, at p. I-4831).

In the current state of EC law, the trade mark proprietor may thus control the initial marketing, in the EEA, of products which were put by him, or with his consent, on the market outside the EEA. The proprietor's consent to import such products into the EEA should be positively expressed. This might be implied 'where it follows from facts and circumstances prior to, simultaneous with or subsequent to the placing of the goods on the market outside the EEA which, in the view of the national court, unequivocally demonstrate that the proprietor has renounced his right to oppose the placing of the goods on the market within the EEA'. Implied consent may not be inferred from the mere silence of the trade mark proprietor, for instance from the fact that the proprietor has not communicated his intention to oppose importation into the EEA to all subsequent purchasers of the goods; from the lack of a stated warning to this effect on the goods; or from the absence of a contractual reservation when transferring ownership of the products bearing the trade mark. The fact that the trader importing the goods into the EEA was ignorant of the opposition of the trade mark proprietor is irrelevant. It is for the trader alleging consent to import into the EEA to prove it rather than for the trade mark proprietor to prove the contrary (Cases C-414/99 etc. *Davidoff I* [2001] ECR I-8691). This is different from the question relating to the burden of proving where the trade marked goods were first put on the market, in or outside the EEA, which may be incumbent on the trade mark proprietor (Case C-244/00 *Van Doren* [2003] ECR I-3051).

The right to oppose the importation of products put on the market outside the EEA by the trade mark proprietor or with his consent does not follow from Art. 7(1) but rather from Art. 5, which lays down the exclusive rights conferred by a trade mark. As directives do not have horizontal direct effect an individual could in any case not rely solely on Art. 7(1) of the directive in order to oppose the importation of products coming from countries outside the EEA (Case C-355/96 *Silhouette*, above, at pp. I-4833–4).

The principle of exhaustion might always be extended to include third countries through the conclusion of international agreements by the Community authorities (Case C-355/96 *Silhouette*, above, at p. I-4832). It is noteworthy to point out that the issue of international exhaustion of trade marks remains a controversial and much debated one in the Community, even after those judgments by the ECJ, so that it may well be the subject of further legislative initiative in the future.

3. Industrial designs. The working group established in 1959 to study the feasibility of harmonizing national laws on industrial designs indicated in its report of 1962 that the differences in the national design law of the six original Member States were so important that harmonization seemed unlikely. It was indicated that a solution could perhaps consist in the introduction of an independent Community system for the protection of industrial designs, which would co-exist with the national systems. The Commission eventually followed up this suggestion and, similarly as for trade marks (see point 2 above), in 1993 submitted proposals for both a Council regulation on the Community design (*OJ* 1993 C29/20) and a directive on the legal protection of designs (*OJ* 1993 C345/14). Those proposals proved to be highly controversial, in particular with respect to the legal protection of spare parts. The directive was finally adopted in 1998 whereas it took another three years to agree on the regulation on the Community design.

(*a*) ***Dir. 98/71 of the European Parliament and of the Council of 13 October 1998 on the legal protection of designs*** (*OJ* 1998 L289/28) was the first harmonization measure adopted. It lays down a definition of the concept of design, including both the whole or a part of product (Art. 1(a) of the directive), and stipulates for instance that a design will be protected by a registered design right to the extent that it is new and has individual character (Art. 3(2) of the directive). The directive does not aim at obtaining a full-scale harmonization of industrial design law. For instance, provisions on sanctions, remedies, and enforcement are left to national law (fifth recital). Furthermore, the lack of agreement on the so-called spare parts issue has led to the adoption of the directive whilst expressly leaving this question open. Member States may therefore in a first stage continue to apply their national laws in that respect (nineteenth recital). This non-solution should be subject to evaluation three years after the implementation of the directive and should lead to a new proposal for revision, in particular with respect to the spare parts issue, one year later (Art. 18 of the directive).

(*b*) ***Council Reg. 6/2002 of 12 December 2001 on Community designs*** (*OJ* 2002 L3/1) set up a unified system for Community designs with unitary character and equal effect throughout the territory of the EC. The substantive provisions on design law in both the directive and the regulation should be aligned (ninth recital to the regulation). Two forms of protection are granted. A short-term unregistered Community design may be obtained for a period of three years as from the date on which the design was first made available to the public in the EC (Art. 11 of the regulation). The registered Community design gives rise to five years of protection renewable up to a total of twenty-five years from the date of filing (Art. 12 of the regulation). Similarly as for the Community trade marks, under Art. 2 of this regulation a crucial role is attributed to the Office for Harmonisation in the Internal Market (Trade Marks and Designs) (see point 2 above). Comm. Reg. 2245/2002 of 21 October 2002 implementing Council Reg. 6/2002 on Community designs aims to ensure the smooth and efficient operation of design proceedings before the OHIM (*OJ* 2002 L341/28). Comm. Reg. 2246/2002 of 16 December 2002 more specifically lays down the rules and amounts for payment of fees to the OHIM (*OJ* 2002 L341/54).

The spare parts controversy is still not settled with the regulation. Reference is made to the obligation to make an evaluation as written into Dir. 98/71 so that 'under these circumstances, it is appropriate not to confer any protection as a Community design for a design which is applied to or incorporated in a product which constitutes a component part of a complex product upon whose appearance the design is dependent and which is used for the purpose of the repair of a complex product so as to restore its original appearance, until the Council has decided its policy on this issue on the basis of a Commission proposal' (thirteenth recital to the regulation).

4. Copyright and related rights. It was not until 1988 that Community harmonization of certain aspects of copyright was seriously considered (see the Commission's Green Paper on copyright and the challenge of technology: copyright issues requiring immediate action, COM(88) 172). Even then, the Commission held that a sufficient level of harmonization of traditional aspects of copyright protection could be obtained within the framework of the traditional intellectual property conventions, in particular the Berne Convention, provided that these were concluded by all Member States (see section II.6 above). Community harmonization was thought to be necessary mainly with respect to new technologies, such as computer programs, and for specific rights, such as rental and lending rights. Subsequent to certain cases before the ECJ, which exposed the potential implications for the internal market of differences in duration of copyright protection (Case 341/87 *EMI Electrola*, above), the Commission saw the need also to harmonize the duration of copyright protection in the Community.

(*a*) ***Council Dir. 91/250 of 14 May 1991 on the legal protection of computer programs*** stipulates that Member States should protect computer programs, under copyright law, as literary and artistic works in the meaning of the Berne Convention for the Protection of Literary and Artistic Works (Art. 1 of the directive, *OJ* 1991 L122/42, as amended, *OJ* 1993 L290/9). It further establishes who and what should be protected, the exclusive rights on which protected persons should be able to rely in order to authorize or prohibit certain acts and for how long the protection should apply. In its Report on the implementation and effects of Dir. 91/250, the Commission considers that the objectives of the directive have been achieved, whereas also the effects on the software industry are satisfactory, so that there appears to be no need for amendments to this copyright directive (COM(2000) 199). The Commission has now proposed to introduce complementary patent protection for computer-implemented inventions (see point 1 above).

(*b*) ***Council Dir. 92/100 of 19 November 1992 on rental right and lending right and on certain rights related to copyright in the field of intellectual property*** is 'limited to establishing that Member States provide rights with respect to rental and lending for certain groups of right holders and further to establishing the rights of fixation, reproduction, distribution, broadcasting and communication to the public for certain groups of right holders in the field of related rights protection (see the preamble to the directive, *OJ* 1992 L346/61, as amended by Dir. 93/98, see below). Art. 1 of the directive stipulates that rental and lending rights will not be exhausted because of any sale or other act of distribution. The ECJ has held that this provision is valid. The distinction made between those rights in Art. 1 and distribution rights in Art. 9 of the directive is justified, in particular having regard to the case-law of the ECJ under Art. 30 EC (see section III.3 above) (Case C-200/96 *Metronome Musik*, above, at p. I-1978). As such, it is not contrary to the directive for an owner of the exclusive rental right to prohibit the rental of a cinematographic work in one Member State whereas it was authorized in another (Case C-61/97 *Egmont Film*, above). The directive does not lay down the criteria for establishing what constitutes an equitable remuneration when a phonogram is broadcast. The ECJ has clarified that it is therefore for each Member State to determine those criteria in order to achieve a proper balance between the interests of performing artists and producers in obtaining remuneration for the broadcast and the interests of third parties in being able to broadcast the phonogram on reasonable terms (Case C-245/00 *SENA* [2003] ECR I-1251). Although the directive only lays down a minimal harmonization, the implementation is not without problems (see e.g. the Commission's Report on the public lending right in the European Union (COM(2002) 502; Case C-433/02 *Commission* v. *Belgium* [2003] ECR I-12191).

(*c*) ***Council Dir. 93/83 of 27 September 1993 on the co-ordination of certain rules concerning copyright and rights related to copyright applicable to satellite broadcasting and cable retransmission*** (*OJ* 1993 L248/15) is complementary to Council Dir. 89/552 of 3 October 1989 on the co-ordination of certain provisions laid down by law, regulation, or administrative action in Member States concerning the pursuit of television broadcasting activities (*OJ* 1989 L298/23). The aim is to supplement the latter, which establishes a legal framework for the creation of a single audiovisual area, by defining the rights of copyright owners in a uniform manner throughout the Community. The directive only provides for a minimum degree of harmonization in the field of copyright and related rights. This has led the ECJ to conclude that 'the question whether the reception by a hotel establishment of satellite or terrestrial television signals and their distribution by cable to the various rooms of that hotel is an "act of communication to the public" or "reception by the public" is not governed by the directive, and must consequently be decided in accordance with national law' (Case C-293/98 *Egeda* [2000] ECR I-629 at p. I-662).

(*d*) ***Council Dir. 93/98 of 29 October 1993 harmonizing the term of protection of copyright and certain related rights*** uniformly fixes the duration of copyright protection at seventy years after the death of the author (Art. 1 of the directive, *OJ* 1993 L290/9). The term of protection for rights of performers and of producers of phonograms is, in principle, set at fifty years (Art. 3 of the directive). The objective is to avoid situations whereby rights have expired in some Member States but are still protected in others (second recital to the directive). The implementation of the directive by 1 July 1995 meant an extension of the duration of protection in most Member States. This entailed that certain rights on works, which had already fallen into the public domain in certain Member States, were revived. Art. 10(3) of the directive provides that this should not be to the prejudice of any acts of exploitation lawfully performed by third parties before the 'revival' of the right. It is up to the Member Sates to lay down the necessary provisions to protect the acquired rights of third parties. The ECJ has interpreted this as being 'measures which the Member States are obliged to adopt, but whose detail is left to the discretion of the Member States, provided, however, that they do not have the overall effect of preventing the application of the new terms of protection on the date laid down by the directive' (Case C-60/98

Butterfly Music [1999] ECR I-3939 at p. I-3939). To hold that a national law, which lays down a limited period in which sound-recordings may be distributed by third parties who had been able to reproduce and market them before the original rights had been revived, was not contrary to the directive.

(*e*) ***Dir. 96/9 of the European Parliament and of the Council of 11 March 1996 on the legal protection of databases*** concerns the copyright and sui generis protection to be granted by national law to any collection or compilation of independent works, data, or other materials arranged in a systematic or methodical way and individually accessible by electronic or other means, to the exclusion of computer programs used in the making or operation of databases accessible by electronic means (Art. 1 of the directive, *OJ* 1996 L77/20, as last amended by Dec. 2003/239, *OJ* 2003 L89/11).

(*f*) ***Council Dec. 2000/278 on the approval, on behalf of the European Community, of the WIPO Copyright Treaty and the WIPO Performances and Phonograms Treaty*** (*OJ* 2000 L89/6) was adopted on 16 March 2000. This important decision of principle allows for the Commission to negotiate in the Assemblies of the WCT and the WPPT on behalf of the EC on all matters within the latter's sphere of competence (Art. 2 of the decision). The WCT and the WPPT thus become integral part of Community law, in spite of the fact that also the Member States still need to approve the WCT and the WPPT (see section II.6 above).

(*g*) ***Dir. 2001/29 of the European Parliament and of the Council of 22 May 2001 on the harmonization of certain aspects of copyright and related rights in the information society*** is complementary to the other harmonization measures in the field of copyright and related rights (*OJ* 2001 L167/10).The objective is not so much to introduce new concepts for the protection of intellectual property as to adapt and supplement the existing laws to respond adequately to new economic realities created by the technological development, such as new forms of exploitation (fifth recital to the directive). Liability for activities in the network environment concerning not only copyright but also for instance trade mark infringements are addressed horizontally in Dir. 2000/31 on electronic commerce (*OJ* 2000 L178/1).

(*h*) ***Dir. 2001/84 of the European Parliament and of the Council of 27 September 2001 on the resale right for the benefit of the author of an original work of art*** is 'intended to ensure that authors of graphic and plastic works of art share in the economic success of their original works of art' (third recital, *OJ* 2001 L272/32). The resale right is defined in Art. 1 of the directive as 'an inalienable right, which cannot be waived, even in advance, to receive a royalty based on the sale price obtained for any resale of the work, subsequent to the first transfer of the work by the author', whenever art market professionals are involved in the resale. The term of protection is aligned to that of copyright and related rights pursuant to Dir. 93/98, namely seventy years after the death of the author.

5. **Other harmonization measures** relating to the protection of intellectual property rights include the following:

(*a*) ***Council Dir. 87/54 of 16 December 1986 on the legal protection of topographies of semiconductor products*** (*OJ* 1987 L24/36). The objective is limited to establishing certain basic principles, in particular 'provisions specifying whom and what should be protected, the exclusive rights on which protected persons should be able to rely to authorize or prohibit certain acts, exceptions to these rights and for how long protection should last' (see the preamble to the directive). Member States remain free to extend, or not, the protection to persons outside the Community for as long as no Community decisions have been taken. Due regard should be had in particular to Council Decs. 90/510 and 90/511 on the extension of the legal protection of topographies of semiconductor products to persons from certain territories and countries (*OJ* 1990 L285/29 and 31, as implemented, *OJ* 1990 L307/21, and further amendments. For the extension to persons from the United States and certain territories, see *OJ* 1993 L11/20, as amended, *OJ* 1993 L246/31. For the extension to persons from Canada, see *OJ* 1994 L284/61). See also Council Dec. 94/824 of 22 December 1994 on the extension of the legal protection of topographies of semiconductor products to persons from a Member of the World Trade Organization (*OJ* 1994 L349/201) and Council Dec. 96/644 in respect of persons from the Isle of Man, which will apply until the Isle of Man is bound by the TRIPS Agreement (*OJ* 1996 L293/18).

(*b*) ***Council Reg. 2100/94 of 27 July 1994 on Community plant variety rights*** (*OJ* 1994 L227/1, as amended, *OJ* 1995 L258/3. For the implementing rules concerning the agricultural exemption provided for in Art. 14(3), see Comm. Reg. 1768/95, *OJ* 1995 L173/14, as amended, *OJ* 1998 L328/6). The objective is to introduce a Community regime for the protection of plant varieties, which co-exists with national regimes, allowing for the grant of an industrial property right valid throughout the Community. A Community Plant Variety Office, with legal personality, is set up in order to carry out the implementation and application of the Community regime (see the Commission implementing regulations regarding fees and procedures before this Office, *OJ* 1995 L121/31 and 37, respectively). An appeal may be lodged before the ECJ against decisions of the Community Plant Variety Office, or its Boards of Appeal, on similar grounds as with respect to decisions taken by the OHIM or its Boards of Appeal (Council Reg. 2506/95 amending Reg. 2100/94 on Community plant variety rights, *OJ* 1995 L258/3). An extension of the terms of protection under the Community plant variety right, specifically for potatoes, is laid down by Council Reg. 2470/96 (*OJ* 1996 L335/10). Furthermore, similarly as was done in relation to patents for medicinal products (see point 1 above), the duration of effective protection for plant protection products has been extended by virtue of Reg. 1610/96 of the European Parliament and of the Council of 23 July 1996 concerning the creation of a supplementary protection certificate for plant protection products (*OJ* 1996 L198/30).

Art. 14(1) of Reg. 2100/94 seeks to strike a balance between the protection of the rights of the plant variety holder and the public interest in safeguarding agricultural production. By way of exception it authorizes a farmer to use, on his own holding, the product of the harvest obtained by planting, also on his own holding, propagating material from a protected Community plant variety right, in the case of plant species listed in Art. 14(2). According to Art. 14(3), the authorization is subject to certain conditions to be fulfilled by the farmer, such as the payment of an equitable remuneration to the plant variety holder and the provision of relevant information on the plant variety holder's request. The ECJ has held that the conditions of Art. 14(3) may not be imposed on all farmers as this would go beyond what is necessary in order to safeguard the legitimate interests of both the breeder and the farmer. Information may therefore not be requested from farmers who never planted propagating material from a variety covered by a Community plant variety right belonging to one of the species listed in Art. 14(2), or 'where there is no indication that the farmer has used or will use, for propagating purposes in the field, on his own holding, the product of the harvest obtained by planting, on his own holding, propagating material of a variety other than a hybrid or synthetic variety which is covered by that right and belongs to one of the agricultural species listed in Art. 14(2) of Regulation 2100/94' (Case C-305/00 *Schulin* [2003] ECR I-3525, para. 72).

(*c*) ***Council Reg. 2081/92 of 14 July 1992 on the protection of geographical indications and designations of origin for agricultural products and foodstuffs*** (*OJ* 1992 L208/1, as amended). The objective is to lay down a more uniform approach to geographical indications and designations of origin, in a way that fair competition is ensured between producers of products bearing such indications and the credibility of the products enhanced in the consumer's eyes (seventh recital to the regulation). Its scope is limited to certain agricultural products and foodstuffs for which a link between product or foodstuff characteristics and geographical origin exists, including wines and spirits (eighth recital; see also Case C-388/95 *Belgium* v. *Spain*, above), although it could be enlarged to include also other products (ninth recital).

The ECJ has succinctly stated that it is 'clear from Regulation 2081/92 that the protection of designations of origin and of geographical indications presupposes registration, which in turn requires that the products in question fulfil the conditions laid down by the regulation, in particular those relating to the direct link between the quality or characteristics of the product for which authorization is sought and its specific geographical origin' (Cases C-321/94 etc. *Pistre* [1997] ECR I-2343, at p. I-2371). Domestic legislation, which granted protection to a description, such as mountain, which is quite general in character and whereby no such direct link could be established, was therefore held to be too remote from the regulation to be precluded by the regulation but was found to be contrary to Arts. 28 to 30

EC (ibid. at p. I-2372). The ECJ confirmed that the simple geographical indications of source whereby there is no link between the characteristics of the product and its geographical provenance do not fall within the scope of the regulation. National legislation which prohibits the potentially misleading use of a geographical indication of source, in the case of which there is no such link, is therefore not precluded by the regulation (Case C-312/98 *Schutzverband* [2000] ECR I-9187).

Registration must be done at Community level under the procedure laid down in the regulation and may not be granted for names that have become generic (Art. 3 of the regulation). According to Art. 4 of the regulation, eligibility to use a protected designation of origin (PDO) or a protected geographical indication (PGI) is subject to the product's compliance with a specification. The specification contains the detailed definition of the protected product drawn up by the producers concerned. An application for registration of the specification as a PDO is made to the Commission through the intermediary of the Member State either under the ordinary procedure (Arts. 5 to 7) or under the simplified procedure of Art. 17. The latter does not require publication of the conditions in the specification in the *Official Journal* of the EC. The ECJ has stressed that the specification constitutes the instrument which determines the extent of uniform protection to be given under the regulation. It 'determines both the extent of the obligations to be complied with for the purposes of using the PDO and, as a corollary, the extent of the right protected against third parties by the effect of registration of the PDO, which lays down at Community level the rules set out or referred to in the specification' (Case C-108/01 *Consorzio del Prosciutto di Parma*, above, para. 47; Case C-469/00 *Ravil*, above, para. 80). Art. 4 of the regulation does not preclude the application of special technical rules to operations leading to different presentations on the market of the same product. The ECJ has interpreted this in the sense that it does not preclude the insertion of a condition in the specification that operations such as the slicing and packaging of Parma ham, or the grating and packaging of Grana Padano cheese, should take place in the region of production. To the extent that under the simplified procedure of Art. 17 of the regulation such a condition was not brought to the knowledge of third parties by adequate publicity in Community legislation, the principle of legal certainty may nonetheless prevent it from being relied on against economic operators (respectively Case C-108/01 *Consorzio del Prosciutto di Parma*, above; Case C-469/00 *Ravil*, above).

Once a registration has been requested in accordance with Art. 17 of the regulation, a Member State may no longer alter the designation of origin by adopting provisions of national law and protect that designation at national level (Cases C-129/97 etc. *Chiciak and Fol* [1998] ECR I-3315). The ECJ has recalled that Art. 17(3) of the regulation only permits Member States to maintain the national protection of a name until such time as a decision has been taken on its registration as a name protected at EC level (Case C-87/97 *Gorgonzola*, above). As to the conditions for registration, the ECJ has rejected the argument that the simplified procedure of Art. 17 is conditional on the application for registration being uncontroversial at national level. Neither were amendments to the original application for registration after expiry of the six months time-limit held to render the simplified procedure unlawful (Case C-269/99 *Kühne* [2001] ECR I-9517).

Conversely, the ECJ has stressed that, 'in the context of procedures for registration of a name of a product under the basic regulation, account must be taken of the existence of products which are legally on the market and have therefore been legally marketed under that name in Member States other than the State of origin by which registration is applied for' (Cases C-289/96 etc. *Denmark, Germany and France* v. *Commission* [1999] ECR I-1593 at p. I-1541—'Feta' case). On this basis, it for instance annulled Comm. Reg. 1107/96 of 12 June 1996 on the registration of geographical indications and designations of origin under the procedure laid down in Art. 17 of Council Reg. 2081/92 (*OJ* 1996 L148/1) to the extent that it registered 'Feta' as a protected designation of origin (ibid.). The name 'Feta' of the said Annex was subsequently deleted by Comm. Reg. 1070/1999 amending the Annex to Reg. 1107/1996 (*OJ* 1999 L130/8). Taking into account the reasoning of the ECJ, the Commission proceeded to an analysis of the actual situation in the Member States with respect to the name 'Feta'. This led to the adoption of Comm. Reg. 1829/2002 of 14 October 2002 amending the Annex to Reg. 1107/96 with regard to the name 'Feta' (*OJ* 2002 L277/10). Art. 1 thereof stipulates that the name 'Feta' shall be included in the register provided for in Art. 6(3) of Reg. 2081/92 as a protected designation of origin (PDO) and shall be added to part A of the Annex to Reg. 1107/96 under the heading 'Cheeses', 'Greece'. With respect to compound designation of origin, the ECJ held that the absence of a footnote in the Annex to Comm. Reg. 1107/96 does not necessarily imply that each of its constituent part is protected (Cases C-129/97 etc. *Chiciak and Fol*, above).

The ECJ clarified the relationship between names registered under the regulation and trade mark law, which is specifically governed by Art. 14 of Reg. 2081/92. It first of all rejected an interpretation of the concept of evocation in Art. 13(1) of the regulation in the light of its case-law on trade marks. According to the ECJ this concept of evocation 'covers a situation where the term used to designate a product incorporates part of a protected designation, so that when the consumer is confronted with the name of the product, the image triggered in his mind is that of the product whose designation is protected', even where 'there is no likelihood of confusion between the products concerned and even where no Community protection extends to parts of that designation which are echoed in the term or terms at issue' (Case C-87/97 *Gorgonzola*, above, at p. I-1333). As to the continued use of an earlier trade mark which is allowed under Art. 14(2) of the regulation, the ECJ stated that it is for the national court to assess whether the trade mark was registered in good faith before the date of application for registration of the designation of origin and is not liable to be declared invalid or revoked pursuant to the provision of the trade mark Dir. 89/104 (Case C-87/97 *Gorgonzola*, above). The continued use of an earlier trade mark is to be distinguished from the system of derogations, provided for by Art. 13(2) of the regulation, in order to allow the continued use of an earlier name for a limited time and under certain conditions (ibid.). With respect to the latter the ECJ has ruled that when a Member State applies to register a name as a PDO under the simplified procedure, this presupposes that products which do not comply with the specification for that name cannot be marketed legally on its territory. The derogation for continued use of an earlier name under Art. 13(2) of the regulation can therefore only apply to products not originating in the Member State of the PDO (Case C-66/00 *Bigi* [2002] ECR I-5917).

See also **Freedom to provide services, Free movement of goods.**

Further reading 1. Books: Anderman, *EC Competition Law & Intellectual Property Rights. The Regulation of Innovation* (2000); Arnold, *Performer's Rights*, 2nd edn. (1997); Cornish, *Intellectual Property*, 4th edn. (1999); Drahos (ed.), *Intellectual Property* (1999); Franzosi, *European Community Trademark* (1997); Garnett *et al.* (eds.), *Copinger & Skone James on Copyright*, Supplement to the 14th edn. (2002); Gastinel *et al.*, *The Legal Aspects of the Community Trade Mark* (2001); Govaere, *The Use and Abuse of Intellectual Property Rights in EC Law* (1996); Groves *et al.*, *Intellectual Property and the Internal Market of the European Community* (1993); Hays, *Parallel Importation under European Union Law* (2003); Jongen *et al.* (eds.), *Copyright Software Protection in the EC* (1994); Kamstra *et al.*, *Patents on Biotechnological Inventions: The European Directive* (2001); Van der Kooij, *Introduction to the EC Regulation on Plant* (1997); id., *The Community Trade Mark Regulation: An Article by Article Guide* (2000); Llewelyn *et al.*, *European Plant Intellectual Property* (2003); Mclean, *EC Intellectual Property Law* (1998); Reinbothe *et al.*, *The EC Directive on Rental and Lending Rights and on Piracy* (1993); Musker, *Community Design Law: Principles and Practice* (2002); Sterling, *Intellectual Property and Market Freedom* (1997); Tritton, *Intellectual Property in Europe*, 2nd edn. (2002); Wilkof, *Trade Mark Licensing* (1995).

2. Articles: Alexander, 'Exhaustion of Trade Mark Rights in the European Economic Area' (1999) *EL Rev.* 56; Cohen Jehoram, 'European Copyright Law: Ever More Horizontal' (2001) *IIC* 532; Cornish, 'Trade Marks: Portcullis for the EEA?' (1998) *EIPR* 172; Davis, 'To Protect or to Serve?: European Trade Mark Law and the Decline of the Public Interest' (2003) *EIPR* 180; Dworkin *et al.*, 'Phil Collins and the Term Directive' (1994) *EIPR* 187; Firth, 'Aspects of Design Protection in Europe' (1993) *EIPR* 42; Flynn, 'Intellectual Property and Antitrust: EC Attitudes' (1992) *EIPR* 49; Forrester, 'Software Licensing in the Light of the Current EC Competition Law Considerations' (1992) *ECLR* 5; Galiardi, 'Trade Mark Assignments under EC Law' (1998) *EIPR* 371; Govaere, 'The Quest for a Master Key to Control Parallel Imports' (2002) *Cambridge Yearbook of European Legal Studies* 191; Hart, 'The Copyright in the Information Society Directive: An Overview' (2002) *EIPR* 58; Koutrakos, 'In Search of a Common Vocabulary in Free Movement of Goods: The Example of Repackaging Pharmaceuticals'

(2003) *EL Rev.* 53; Kur, 'The Green Paper's Design Approach—What's Wrong With It?' (1993) *EIPR* 374; Reindl, 'The Magic of Magill: TV Program Guides as a Limit of Copyright Law?' (1993) *IIC* 60; Schmidt, 'Article 82's "Exceptional Circumstances" that Restrict Intellectual Property Rights' (2002) *ECLR* 210; Ullrich, 'Patent Protection in Europe: Integrating Europe into the Community or the Community into Europe?' (2002) *EL Rev.* 433; Urlesberger, '"Legitimate reasons" for the Proprietor of a Trade Mark Registered in the EU to Oppose Further Dealings in the Goods After They Have Been Put on the Market for the First Time' (1999) *CML Rev.* 1195; Vinje, 'Magill: its Impact on the Information Technology Industry' (1992) *EIPR* 397; Würtenberger, 'Risk of Confusion and Criteria to Determine the Same in European Community Trade Mark Law' (2002) *EIPR* 20; Zarpellon, 'The Scope of the Exhaustion Regime for Trade Mark Rights' (2001) *ECLR* 382.

▶ **INTERNAL MARKET *see* CUSTOMS UNION, FREE MOVEMENT OF GOODS, FREE MOVEMENT OF PERSONS, INTELLECTUAL PROPERTY RIGHTS, PUBLIC PROCUREMENT, *and* TAX HARMONIZATION**

▶ **INWARD PROCESSING *see* CUSTOMS PROCEDURES**

J

▶ **JUSTICE AND HOME AFFAIRS (JHA)** *see* **FREE MOVEMENT OF PERSONS**

K

▶ **KYOTO CONVENTION** *see* **COMMUNITY CUSTOMS CODE** *and* **ORIGIN OF GOODS**

M

▶ **MEASURES HAVING EQUIVALENT EFFECT TO QUANTITATIVE RESTRICTIONS** Art. 28 EC prohibits quantitative restrictions on imports and measures of equivalent effect between Member States, while Art. 29 EC prohibits the same restrictions when imposed on exports between Member States. In exceptional cases, quantitative restrictions may fall under the various safeguard clauses, particularly Art. 30 EC (*see further under* **Free movement of goods**, section III).

While the definition of quantitative restrictions on both imports and exports is narrow (*see further under* **Quantitative restrictions**), the concept of measures of equivalent effect on imports is very broad. In contrast, the corresponding concept relating to exports covers a relatively limited class of measure. Accordingly, import and export restrictions will be examined separately below.

First, however, it should be pointed out that there are certain principles which apply both to measures of equivalent effect on imports and those on exports. For instance:

- neither concept applies exclusively to binding measures. Thus recommendations or other non-binding acts emanating from the State may be caught (Case C-249/81 *Commission* v. *Ireland* [1982] ECR 4005 ('Buy Irish' campaign));

- since the ruling in Cases 177/82 etc. *Van de Haar* [1984] ECR 1797, it has been axiomatic that no *de minimis* rule applies. This principle has been re-affirmed recently in Case C-67/97 *Bluhme* [1998] ECR I-8033, in which a ban on keeping certain species of bee on a tiny island in Denmark was held to constitute a measure of equivalent effect within the meaning of Art. 28 EC.

As to other points common to the two concepts, *see further under* **Free movement of goods.**

I. Measures of equivalent effect to quantitative restrictions on imports

1. The classic definition: *Dassonville*. The classic definition is that laid down in Case 8/74 *Dassonville* [1974] ECR 837 at p. 852, according to which:

> All trading rules enacted by Member States, which are capable of hindering, directly or indirectly, actually or potentially, intra-Community trade are to be considered as measures having an effect equivalent to quantitative restrictions.

This definition, which is manifestly extremely wide, has been repeated with minor variations in all the subsequent cases on the subject. The word 'trading' is generally omitted.

2. Potential restrictions. As is clear from the *Dassonville* judgment, even potential or indirect restrictions on imports from other Member States will constitute measures of equivalent effect. Accordingly, where such a potential or indirect effect is established, there is no need to show—by statistical means or otherwise—that imports have actually been restricted.

This is clearly illustrated by the recent ruling in Case C-184/96 *Commission* v. *France* [1998] ECR I-6197 ('foie gras'). In that case, the Commission alleged that France had infringed Art. 28 by laying down standards for goods sold under the trade description 'foie gras'. The defendant argued that the infringement was purely hypothetical and theoretical, since this product was only produced in very small quantities in other Member States, those States had no specific requirements of their own and products from those States generally complied with the French standards in any event. While A.-G. La Pergola accepted this argument, the Court dismissed it in the following terms:

> Article 28 applies . . . not only to the actual effects but also to the potential effects of legislation. It cannot be considered inapplicable simply because at the present time there are no actual cases with a connection to another Member State.

In a separate development, the Court has held in a series of cases that measures fell outside Art. 28 on the grounds that they were indistinctly applicable and that the possibility of their effecting imports was too 'uncertain and indirect' (e.g. Case C-69/88 *Krantz* [1990] ECR I-583; Case C-379/92 *Peralta* [1994] ECR I-3453; Case C-96/94 *Centro Servizi*

Spediporto [1995] ECR I-2883; Case C-134/94 *Esso Española* [1995] ECR I-4223; Case C-266/96 *Corsica Ferries* [1998] ECR I-3949). Thus, in *Peralta*, where the captain of an Italian vessel was charged with discharging caustic soda at sea, he maintained that the ban on this practice constituted an unlawful restriction on imports of that product into Italy; and the Court dismissed this contention on the grounds that the effect on imports was too 'uncertain and indirect'. While the terminology used by the Court is not entirely clear, the better view is that in each case the Court, applying the *Dassonville* formula, has found that the contested measure did not even constitute a potential or indirect restriction on imports.

3. The relationship with other Treaty provisions. Read literally, the *Dassonville* definition is so wide as to embrace restrictions covered by other more specific prohibitions or rules in the EC Treaty, such as Art. 25 EC banning customs duties and charges of equivalent effect; Arts. 87 to 89 EC relating to State aids; and Art. 90 EC prohibiting discriminatory internal taxation. However, each provision in the Treaty is always to be read in the context of the Treaty as a whole. Accordingly, in Case 74/76 *Iannelli* [1977] ECR 557 at p. 574 the Court held:

> However wide the field of application of Article 28 may be, it nevertheless does not include obstacles to trade covered by other provisions of the Treaty.
>
> In fact, since the legal consequences of the application or of a possible infringement of these various provisions have to be determined having regard to their particular purpose in the context of all the objectives of the Treaty, they may be of a different kind and this implies that their respective fields of application must be distinguished, except in those cases which may fall simultaneously within the field of application of two or more provisions of Community law.
>
> Thus obstacles which are of a fiscal nature or have equivalent effect and are covered by Articles 23 to 25 and 90 of the Treaty do not fall within the prohibition in Article 28.

As to Arts. 23, 25, and 90 EC, this ruling has been confirmed on a number of occasions, see Cases C-78/90 etc. *Compagnie Commerciale de l'Ouest* [1992] ECR I-1847; Case C-228/98 *Dounias* [2000] ECR I-577; Case C-383/01 *De Danske Bilimportører* [2003] ECR I-6065.

As the *Iannelli* judgment itself shows, however, the relationship between Art. 28 EC and the provisions on State aids is fraught with difficulty; and unfortunately the subsequent case-law has not laid this problem to rest (see e.g. Case C-249/81 *Commission* v. *Ireland*, above ('Buy Irish' campaign); Case C-21/88 *Du Pont de Nemours* [1990] ECR I-889). In *Iannelli*, the Court reasoned that, while Art. 28 EC must not be construed so widely as to treat an aid as such as constituting a measure of equivalent effect, that provision does apply to a condition of a State aid, which is severable from the aid itself. It is unclear whether this test is still good law in the light of the subsequent rulings. At all events, one should take good note of the Court's statement in *Du Pont de Nemours* (at p. I-922) that Art. 87 'may in no case be used to frustrate the rules of the Treaty on the free movement of goods'.

4. *Cassis de Dijon.* Can a measure constitute a measure of equivalent effect within the meaning of Art. 28 EC even if it does not discriminate against imports? Moreover, what is meant by 'discrimination' in this context? These are questions which have been the source of constant debate for more than thirty years, and this controversy has still not abated.

The starting point must be the language of Art. 28 EC itself, which speaks of 'restrictions' but does not mention the word 'discrimination'. However, that consideration alone does not suffice to dispose of the matter, given that in construing provisions of the Treaty one must have regard to their purpose as well as the literal meaning of the words used.

The first judgment to shed light on these matters was the Court's celebrated ruling in Case 120/78 *Rewe* [1979] ECR 649, generally known as *Cassis de Dijon*. The measure in issue there was held to constitute a measure of equivalent effect within the meaning of Art. 28 EC, even though it applied in the same way to domestic goods as to imports from other Member States (i.e. it was 'indistinctly applicable'). That case concerned a provision of German law laying down a minimum alcohol content for various categories of beverage. The product concerned, a blackcurrant based drink produced in France, contained a lower level of alcohol than that prescribed by the German provision; and it could therefore not be sold in Germany unless extra alcohol was added. Consequently, this rule amounted to a very real restriction on imports, even though it applied in precisely the same way to drinks manufactured in Germany. Accordingly, the Court found that this measure fell foul of Art. 28 EC.

A number of judgments followed in which other indistinctly applicable restrictions of a similar nature were held to contravene that provision. This was the case, for instance, with: an Italian ban on the sale of all vinegar not based on wine (Case 788/79 *Gilli* [1980] ECR 2071 at p. 2078); a prohibition on the sale of substitute milk powder or 'coffee whitener' (Case 216/84 *Commission* v. *France* [1988] ECR 793); a ban on the sale of pasta made wholly or partly from soft wheat (Case 90/86 *Zoni* [1988] ECR 4285); and a prohibition on the sale of any drink under the name 'beer' unless it was made exclusively with certain permitted ingredients including barley, malt, and hops, but excluding rice and maize (Case 178/84 *Commission* v. *Germany* [1987] ECR 1227).

Even in these judgments, it was still not clear to what extent discrimination against imports was a relevant criterion. It was argued by some that this case-law merely showed that a measure might fall within the concept of measures of equivalent effect under Art. 28 EC, although it did not discriminate against imports *on its face*. After all, the restrictions concerned in these cases entailed *de facto* discrimination against imports.

At all events, in the late 1980s a body of case-law developed in which various import restrictions were held to fall within the scope of Art. 28 EC despite not involving *any form* of discrimination against imports. This trend started with Cases 60/84 etc. *Cinéthèque* [1985] ECR 2605, which concerned a prohibition on the sale or rental of video cassettes within one year of the film in question being authorized for showing in cinemas. A whole series of such cases followed, perhaps the best known being Case C-145/88 *Torfaen Borough Council* [1989] ECR 3851, which related to restrictions on Sunday trading. A further ruling of this kind was that in Case C-271/92 *Laboratoire de Prothèses Oculaires* [1993] ECR I-2899, which concerned a French legislative provision that reserved to qualified opticians the right to sell contact lenses.

In these cases, the effect on imports was merely accidental and of an ancillary nature. Indeed, it became increasingly clear that reliance on Art. 28 EC with respect to measures of this kind was abusive, and the Court therefore decided to recast the scope of that provision in its landmark judgment in Cases C-267/91 etc. *Keck and Mithouard* [1993] ECR I-6097 by partially reversing its earlier case-law.

5. *Keck* and its aftermath. In *Keck*, the Court sought to re-set proper bounds to the scope of Art. 28, stating:

14. In view of the increasing tendency of traders to invoke Article 28 of the Treaty as a means of challenging any rules whose effect is to limit their commercial freedom even where such rules are not aimed at products from other Member States, the Court considers it necessary to re-examine and clarify its case-law on this matter.

15. In *Cassis de Dijon* (Case 120/78 *Rewe* [1978] ECR 649) it was held that, in the absence of harmonisation of legislation, measures of equivalent effect prohibited by Article 28 include obstacles to the free movement of goods where they are the consequence of applying rules that lay down requirements to be met by goods (such as requirements as to designation, form, size, weight, composition, presentation, labelling, packaging) to goods from other Member States where they are lawfully manufactured and marketed, even if those rules apply without distinction to all products unless their application can be justified by a public interest objective taking precedence over the free movement of goods.

16. However, contrary to what has previously been decided, the application to products from other Member States of national provisions restricting or prohibiting certain selling arrangements is not such as to hinder directly or indirectly, actually or potentially, trade between Member States within the meaning of the *Dassonville* judgment (Case 8/74 [1974] ECR 837), provided that those provisions apply to all affected traders operating within the national territory and provided that they affect in the same manner, in law and in fact, the marketing of domestic products and of those from other Member States.

Thus it divided import restrictions into two categories, namely:

- measures relating to the inherent characteristics of goods 'such as requirements as to designation, form, size, weight, composition, presentation, labelling, packaging'; and
- so-called 'selling arrangements'.

As regards the first category, which includes measures such as that in issue in *Cassis de Dijon* itself, the Court upheld its earlier case-law. Import restrictions falling within this category (frequently referred to now as 'product-bound' measures) were held to be subject to the same rules as before: such restrictions may constitute measures of equivalent effect even if no element of discrimination is present.

In contrast, the Court reversed its previous position as regards the second category: 'selling arrangements' were held to fall within Art. 28 only if they were shown to discriminate against imports either in fact or in law. Non-discriminatory measures relating to 'selling arrangements' were found not to be 'by nature such as to prevent . . . access to the market' of the Member State concerned.

Examples of measures held to be 'product-bound' include: a ban on the sale of a cosmetic product under the name 'Clinique', this being a restriction as to the designation of the product (Case C-315/92 *Estée Lauder* [1994] ECR I-317); and a prohibition on the sale of ice-cream bars with wrapping papers bearing the symbols '+ 10%' (Case C-470/93 *Mars* [1995] ECR I-1923).

As to the concept of 'selling arrangements', which the Court had not attempted to define in *Keck* itself, this has now been held to cover the following categories of measure:

- restrictions on when goods may be sold (Cases C-69/93 etc. *Punto Casa* [1994] ECR I-2355 and Cases C-401/92 etc. *Tankstation 't Heukske* [1994] ECR I-2199, which both concerned Sunday trading restrictions);
- restrictions on where or by whom goods may be sold (Case C-391/92 *Commission* v. *Greece* [1995] ECR I-1621, where an indistinctly applicable rule that processed milk for infants could only be sold in pharmacies was held to fall outside the scope of Art. 28 EC);
- advertising restrictions (Case C-292/92 *Hünermund* [1993] ECR I-6787; Case C-412/93 *Leclerc-Siplec* [1995] ECR I-179);
- price controls (Case C-63/94 *Belgapom* [1995] ECR I-2467).

The Court has persistently adhered to its distinction between product-bound measures and 'selling arrangements', and has done much to clarify its ruling in *Keck*. It now seems plain that the two categories of measure are mutually exclusive, although this was not obvious from that judgment itself. Similarly, *all* types of 'selling arrangements' would now appear to fall within the second category, despite the fact that the ruling in *Keck* speaks only of 'certain selling arrangements'. Moreover, when any doubt exists as to whether a measure is 'product-bound' or relates to a 'selling arrangement', the Court tends to incline towards the former (as in *Mars* and Case C-368/95 *Vereinigte Familiapress* [1997] ECR I-3689).

However, some areas of uncertainty still persist.

First, it is plain that some measures—such as import controls and discrimination in the award of public contracts—cannot reasonably be described either as 'product-bound' or as 'selling arrangements'. To what extent discrimination must be shown before measures of this sort are to be regarded as falling within Art. 28 is unclear. In any case it is necessarily present in the two examples given here.

Second, it is by no means clear what is meant by the requirement in para. 16 of *Keck* that the provisions concerned must 'apply to all affected traders operating within the national territory'. The Court has referred to it on occasion (Case C-34/95 *De Agostini* [1997] ECR I-3483 and Case C-322/01 *Deutscher Apothekerverband* [2003] ECR I-0000, para. 69), albeit without in any way clarifying it. In these circumstances, it would be premature to conclude that this requirement is redundant.

Third, the concept of *de jure* or *de facto* discrimination in relation to 'selling arrangements' is not entirely clear. In *Commission* v. *Greece* above (processed milk for infants), the Court found that a measure was not to be regarded as discriminatory merely because the product concerned was not produced in the defendant State. However, since then the Court's interpretation of the concept of discrimination in this context has been strikingly broad (see Case C-34/95 *De Agostini*, above; Case C-405/98 *Gourmet International Products* [2001] ECR I-1795; Case C-254/98 *TK-Heimdienst* [2000] ECR I-151; Case C-322/01 *Deutscher Apothekerverband*, above, paras. 70–4).

6. **Examples.** Examples of measures of equivalent effect include:

- import licences, even if they are granted automatically (Cases 51/71 etc. *International Fruit Company* [1971] ECR 1107);
- import inspections and controls (Case 4/75 *Rewe-Zentralfinanz* [1975] ECR 843; Case 35/76 *Simmenthal* [1976] ECR 1871);
- measures restricting the use made of imported products (Case 119/78 *Peureux II* [1979] ECR 975; Case 72/83 *Campus Oil* [1984] ECR 2727);
- prohibitions on the sale of goods having particular ingredients (*Cassis de Dijon; Gilli; Commission* v. *France* (substitute milk powder)) or a particular presentation (Case 261/81 *Rau* [1982] ECR 3961) or labelling (Case 27/80 *Fietje* [1980] ECR 3839 (language requirements) and *Mars*) or bearing a given generic or commercial name (*Commission* v. *Germany* (beer) and *Estée Lauder*);
- discrimination in the award of public supply contracts (Case 45/87 *Commission* v. *Ireland* [1988] ECR 4929 (Dundalk water mains); *Du Pont de Nemours*; Case C-243/89 *Commission* v. *Denmark* [1993] ECR I-3353 (Great Belt)) (*see further under* **Public Procurement**);
- measures requiring or encouraging the use of domestic products in preference to imports (*Commission* v. *Ireland* ('Buy Irish'));
- measures requiring importers to appoint a representative in the territory of the importing State (Case 155/82 *Commission* v. *Belgium* [1983] ECR 531 (pesticides); Case 247/81 *Commission* v. *Germany* [1984] ECR 1111 (pharmaceuticals));
- discriminatory restrictions on advertising and promotion (Case 152/78 *Commission* v. *France* [1980] ECR 2299 (alcoholic drinks); Case C-320/93 *Ortscheit* [1994] ECR I-5243; *Leclerc-Siplec; De Agostini*);

- discriminatory restrictions on the time at which goods may be sold (*Punto Casa*);
- discriminatory rules as to where, or by whom, goods may be sold (*Commission* v. *Greece* (processed milk for infants));
- discriminatory price controls (Case 229/83 *Leclerc* [1985] ECR 1 (books) and *Belgapom*); and
- origin marking requirements (Case 207/83 *Commission* v. *United Kingdom* [1985] ECR 1201).

This list in no way purports to be exhaustive: the Court has delivered several hundred judgments in this area of the law, and it would be impossible to consider that case-law fully here. In any event, the categories of measures of equivalent effect are not closed.

7. The timetable for abolition. For the six original Member States, the prohibition in Art. 28 EC on measures of equivalent effect became applicable on 1 January 1970, at the end of the transitional period. However, that prohibition applied prior to that date with respect to restrictions falling under either (*i*) a common organization of the agricultural market, or (*ii*) one of the Commission directives adopted pursuant to former Art. 33(7) of the original EEC Treaty (repealed by the Treaty of Amsterdam), which specifically empowered the Commission to address such directives to the Member States.

In addition, each of the various Acts of Accession has made provision for the abolition of such measures by, and with respect to, the acceding States.

II. Measures of equivalent effect to quantitative restrictions on exports

1. The definition. The Court's first ruling on this point is to be found in Case 15/79 *Groenveld* [1979] ECR 3409 where it held that Art. 29:

> concerns national measures which have as their specific object or effect the restriction of patterns of exports and thereby the establishment of a difference between the domestic trade of a Member State and its export trade in such a way as to provide a particular advantage for national production or for the domestic market of the State in question at the expense of the production or of the trade of other Member States.

This formula is the Court's standard definition of measures of equivalent effect under Art. 29, although the Court frequently omits the final limb ('at the expense of the production or of the trade of other Member States'), as in Case 155/80 *Oebel* [1981] ECR 1993 at p. 2009; Case C-47/90 *Delhaize* [1992] ECR I-3669 at p. I-3708; Case C-203/96 *Chemische Afvalstoffen Dusseldorp* [1998] ECR I-4075 at p. I-4126. However, the final limb of the *Groenveld* test is reproduced in Case C-9/89 *Spain* v. *Council* [1990] ECR I-1383 at p. I-1411; Case C-339/89 *Alsthom Atlantique* [1991] ECR I-107 at p. I–124.

In either event, despite the unduly cumbersome wording of this definition, it is plain that the Court seeks to limit the scope of Art. 29 EC to measures that discriminate against goods intended for export as against those destined for the home market of the Member State concerned, or which are intended to do so. Thus this provision is plainly far narrower in scope than Art. 28 EC.

The rationale behind this approach is that, if Art. 29 EC were to extend to all barriers to exports regardless of discrimination or protective intent, it would cover a large number of restrictions on production such as planning regulations for factories, which are far removed from inter-State trade. This would surely be exorbitant. Furthermore, States rarely have any incentive to restrict exports, except of course when a commodity is in short supply (as in Case 68/76 *Commission* v. *France* [1977] ECR 515 (export licences for potatoes)). Export restrictions—especially those applicable at the production rather the marketing stage—are thus of a fundamentally different nature from import restrictions.

Accordingly, indistinctly applicable restrictions on production or marketing have been held to fall outside the scope of Art. 29 EC. As an example of the former, one might refer to *Oebel*, where an indistinctly applicable ban on night baking was held to fall outside that provision; and Cases 141/81 etc. *Holdijk* [1982] ECR I-1299, where the Court ruled to the same effect with regard to minimum standards for enclosures for fattening calves. As to restrictions on marketing, in *Alsthom Atlantique* an indistinctly applicable provision imposing liability for latent defects on the vendor was also held not to constitute a measure of equivalent effect on exports.

Having said that, there are signs that the Court might be prepared to broaden its definition of this concept somewhat. Thus, a number of Advocates-General have criticized the current test as being too narrow (see e.g. A.-G. Capotorti in *Oebel* at p. 2016; and A.-G. Gulmann in *Delhaize* at p. I-3699). No doubt, this explains why, in Case C-388/95 *Belgium* v. *Spain* [2000] ECR I-3123 ('Rioja'), the Court recently came up with another formula, saying that Art. 29 applied to measures which have 'the effect of specifically restricting patterns of exports . . . and thereby of establishing a difference of treatment between trade within a Member State and its export trade'. This formula, which curiously omits any reference to the object of the measure, has been confirmed in Case C-108/01 *Consorzio del Prosciutto di Parma* [2003] ECR I-5121.

2. Examples. The following is a selection of measures which have been held to constitute measures of equivalent effect within the meaning of Art. 29 EC:

- a system of export licences (Case 68/76 *Commission* v. *France*, above);
- the requirement that exports of a particular category of goods be accompanied by a quality certificate, which was not required for goods of the same type placed on the domestic market (Case 53/76 *Bouhelier* [1977] ECR 197; Case 237/82 *Jongeneel Kaas* [1984] ECR 483);
- local bottling requirements (*Delhaize*, above);
- a restriction on the export of waste for reprocessing (*Chemische Afvalstoffen Dusseldorp*, above), (although it would be more accurate to describe that particular measure as a quantitative restriction pure and simple).

3. The timetable for abolition. Art. 34(2) of the original EEC Treaty prohibited measures of equivalent effect to quantitative restrictions on exports with effect from 1 January 1962.

In addition, each of the various Acts of Accession has made specific provision for the abolition of such measures by, and with respect to, the acceding States.

See also **Free movement of goods, Goods, Quantitative restrictions**

Further reading 1. BOOKS: Bermann, Goebel, Davey, and Fox, *Cases and Materials on European Union Law*, 2nd edn. (2002), ch. 13; Craig and de Burca, *EU Law. Text, Cases, and Materials*, 3rd edn. (2003), ch. 15; Müller-Graff in *Kommentar zum EU-/EG-Vertrag*, 6th edn. (2003), vol. I, p. 970 *et seq*.; Oliver, *Free Movement of Goods in the European Community*, 4th edn. (2003), chs. 6 and 7.

2. ARTICLES: Gormley, 'Reasoning Renounced? The Remarkable Judgment in *Keck and Mithouard*' (1994) *EBL Rev.*; Oliver, 'Some Further Reflections on the Scope of Articles 28–30 (ex 30–36) EC' (1999) *CML Rev.* 783; Reich, 'The "November Revolution" of the European Court of Justice: *Keck, Meng* and *Audi* Revisited' (1994) *CML Rev.* 459; Weatherill, 'After *Keck*: Some Thoughts on how to Clarify the Clarification' (1996) *CML Rev.* 885.

▶ **MUTUAL RECOGNITION OF QUALIFICATIONS *see* FREEDOM OF ESTABLISHMENT**

O

OFFICIAL AUTHORITY According to Art. 45(1) EC, the provisions of the Treaty on freedom of establishment (Arts. 43 to 48) do not apply to activities which in a Member State are connected, even occasionally, with the exercise of 'official authority'. By virtue of Art. 55 EC, the same exception applies also to the provisions on freedom to provide services (Arts. 49 to 55). However, neither the Treaty itself nor any act of secondary legislation defines the concept of 'official authority'. In Case 2/74 *Reyners* [1974] ECR 631 at pp. 664–5, A.-G. Mayras put forward the following definition:

> Official authority is that which arises from the sovereignty and majesty of the State; for him who exercises it, it implies the power of enjoying the prerogatives outside the general law, privileges of official power and powers of coercion over citizens. Connexion with the exercise of this authority can therefore arise only from the State itself, either directly or by delegation to certain persons who may even be unconnected with the public administration (for a similar definition proposed by the Commission, see ibid. at p. 640).

The Advocate-General then compared Art. 45(1) with Art. 39(4), which allows Member States to restrict the admission of foreign workers to certain activities in the public service which involve the exercise of powers of the State. The objective of Art. 45(1) is very similar: it excludes the nationals of other Member States from self-employed activities the pursuit of which would enable them to enjoy similar privileges (ibid. at p. 665. For Art. 39(4), *see further under* **Public service**).

In *Reyners*, which involved the interpretation of the concept of official authority in the context of the legal profession, and in subsequent cases, the ECJ stated that since it derogates from the fundamental rules of freedom of establishment and freedom to provide services, Art. 45(1) must be interpreted narrowly, in a manner that limits its scope to what is strictly necessary to achieve the objective for which it was inserted in the Treaty. This objective is to enable Member States to exclude non-nationals from taking up functions involving the exercise of official authority, which functions are connected with one of the activities of self-employed persons provided for in Arts. 43 and 49. This need is fully satisfied, the Court said, when the exclusion of non-nationals is restricted to those activities which, taken on their own, constitute a 'direct and specific connexion with the exercise of official authority'. An extension of the exception provided for by Art. 45(1) to a whole profession, such as the legal profession, would be possible only in cases where 'such activities were linked with that profession in such a way that freedom of establishment would result in imposing on the Member State concerned the obligation to allow the exercise, even occasionally, by non-nationals of functions appertaining to official authority' (ibid. at p. 654). On the other hand, such extension is not possible when, within the framework of an independent profession, the activities connected with the exercise of official authority are separable from the professional activity in question taken as a whole (ibid.; see also the cases cited below).

Where the practice of a particular profession (e.g. the legal profession) is not subject to harmonization directives, it remains governed by the national laws of the Member States. The possible application of Art. 45(1) must then be assessed separately in respect of each Member State in the light of the national legislation applicable to the organization and the practice of that profession. However, that assessment must take account of the Community character of the limits imposed by Art. 45(1) on the exceptions which it permits, in order to prevent the effectiveness of the fundamental freedoms from being undermined by unilateral national provisions. Generally, professional activities involving contacts, even regular and organic contacts, with the courts, including even compulsory co-operation in their functioning, do not constitute, in themselves, connection with the exercise of official authority. In the context of the profession of *avocat*, in particular, the Court pointed out that the most typical activities of this profession, such as consultation and legal assistance and also the representation and defence of parties in court, even when their performance is compulsory or is a legal monopoly, cannot be considered as involving in themselves a 'direct and specific connexion with the exercise of official authority' since they leave the discretion of judicial authority and the free exercise of judicial power intact. Therefore, neither the profession of *avocat* as a whole nor its most typical activities are exempt from the rules of the Treaty on establishment and services on the basis of Art. 45(1) (ibid. at pp. 654–6).

Following the principles established in *Reyners*, in its subsequent case-law the Court confirmed that the following activities are also not connected with the exercise of official authority and are therefore not covered by the derogation contained in Art. 45(1):

- private teaching activities, which are subject to supervision by the official authorities (Case 147/86 *Commission* v. *Greece* [1988] ECR 1637 at pp. 1654–5);
- the design, programming, and operation of data-processing systems for the public authorities, which activities are of a purely technical nature (Case C-3/88 *Commission* v. *Italy* [1989] ECR 4035 at p. 4060);
- the design, installation, and operation of a lottery computerization system for the public administration, which are likewise of a technical nature (Case C-272/91 *Commission* v. *Italy* [1994] ECR I-1409 at pp. I-1434–6);
- the activities of a traffic accident expert whose reports are not binding on the courts and leave the discretion of the judicial authority and the free exercise of judicial power intact (Case C-306/89 *Commission* v. *Greece* [1991] ECR I-5863 at p. I-5883);
- the activities of an approved insurance commissioner who plays only an auxiliary and preparatory role delegated to him *vis-à-vis* the Insurance Inspectorate, which itself exercises official authority by taking the final decision (Case C-42/92 *Thijssen* [1993] ECR I-4047 at p. I-4073);
- the activities of private security undertakings and private security staff since such undertakings and staff are not vested with powers of constraints (Case C-114/97 *Commission* v. *Spain* [1998] ECR I-6717 at pp. I-6742–3);

- activities which are confined to within a single Member State and which therefore do not have any connecting link with one of the situations envisaged by Community law in the area of freedom of establishment and freedom to provide services ('purely internal situations') (Case C-108/98 *RI.SAN.* [1999] ECR I-5219 at pp. I-5246–7).

See also **Freedom of establishment, Freedom to provide services, Public service.**

▶ ORIGIN OF GOODS Where legislation provides for different treatment of goods imported from or exported to specific countries (or groups of countries), this requires rules determining whether the country-specific treatment can be accorded or not. In theory the following concepts are available for such a determination:

- the country from which the goods have been imported or to which they will be exported (country of provenance or destination);
- the country in which the goods have been or will be in free circulation (market country); or
- the country in which the goods have been produced or underwent their last substantial transformation (country of origin).

These concepts overlap of course: goods produced in a specific country are normally in free circulation there and will be exported from there, but this may also be different, e.g. if the goods are:

- produced under a suspensive customs procedure such as inward processing (then they are not in free circulation); or
- exported from a different country than that in which they were produced.

This example shows already that the concept of provenance or destination—at least in isolation—is normally not a useful option, if a specific country is to be given a more favourable or less favourable treatment than other countries: such a measure could easily be circumvented by shipping the goods:

- first to the country benefiting from a more favourable treatment (e.g. duty free treatment, a higher export refund) and subsequently to their final destination; or
- first to a country not affected by an unfavourable measure (e.g. an anti-dumping duty, a quantitative restriction) and from there to the final destination.

A concept which is inherent in the goods (instead of using their physical location before export) provides less opportunities for circumvention. This is why the origin of goods (i.e. the place where they were wholly obtained or underwent their last substantial transformation) is largely used for customs and external trade purposes, wherever goods coming from or destined for different countries are treated in a distinct manner.

Examples for such measures are:

- preferential customs duties;
- anti-dumping duties;
- quantitative restrictions at import or export;
- export refunds;
- government procurement;
- labelling requirements (made in).

In other words: if all countries were treated equally in external trade, there would be no need for origin rules nor the alternative concepts (except for the collection of trade statistics and trade promotion purposes). In this context, Art. I GATT is relevant, which allows exemptions from most-favoured-nation treatment (i.e. equal treatment), to which all WTO members are entitled, only under specific conditions (*see further under* **Common Customs Tariff** (**CCT**), section I).

The origin concept is often combined with other concepts:

- In order to reduce the risk of fraud, goods benefiting from preferential tariff treatment must be transported directly from the country of origin (direct transport rule).
- For the same reason, goods benefiting from a more favourable export refund according to the destination country must not only have left the Community but also have entered into the market of the import country (i.e. they must have been put in free circulation there).
- The export of arms and dual-use items to a country exempted from restrictions is nevertheless prohibited if the exporter knows that the final destination is a country to which a restriction applies. In this context it is irrelevant whether such an item was produced in the Community or not.
- Where the Community has entered into a customs union with another country (Andorra, San Marino, Turkey) the same customs tariff is applied *vis-à-vis* third countries. In such cases any product which is in free circulation in either part of the customs union can enter into the other part without paying customs duties; the origin of the goods is therefore irrelevant in this context (this is, of course, also true for movements inside the Community). However, in so far as there are no common rules (e.g. anti-dumping duties with regard to the customs union EC–Turkey), the origin of the goods can play a role.

The determination of the origin is easy in cases where goods have been entirely produced in one country without using any inputs from other countries (e.g. extraction of minerals, harvesting of wheat, hatching of birds). Where more than one country has been involved in the production, the following alternative methods are available for determining the country of origin, especially in case of preferential origin:

- customs criteria: a change of the tariff heading (e.g. making flour [heading 1101] out of wheat [heading 1001]); or

- industrial criteria: a list of processing operations conferring origin (e.g. manufacture of fish conserves from fresh fish) or not being sufficient for conferring origin (e.g. manufacture of shirts from parts of shirts); or
- economic criteria: a percentage of the value that must be added or that may be used as foreign input (e.g. manufacture of cameras in which the value of the imported materials used does not exceed 40% of the ex-works price).

These methods may also be combined (e.g. change of tariff headings plus a maximum value of foreign inputs). Where no detailed rules are set out, it is also possible to use a general clause, such as the country 'in which the goods underwent their last substantial processing'. The Community applies all these methods (the last one only with regard to non-preferential origin) and makes also a distinction between preferential and non-preferential origin rules. With regard to preferential rules of origin, a further distinction has to be made, namely:

- whether they have been set out in a preferential Agreement (e.g. the Euro–Mediterranean Agreement with Tunisia)
- or whether they have been set autonomously (e.g. with regard to the Generalised System of Preferences—GSP).

Non-preferential rules of origin are thus far only fixed autonomously, given that no detailed international rules have been agreed yet.

I. International law

Art. IX GATT deals with laws and regulations relating to marks of origin on imported products. The rules should allow the marking of such products without seriously damaging them, materially reducing their value or unreasonably increasing their cost. According to Arts. 22 and 23 of the Agreement on Trade-Related Aspects of Intellectual Property Rights (*OJ* 1994 L336/213), WTO members take actions against misleading indications of origin.

The possible content of origin rules is set out in Annex D.1 (Annex K of the revised version) of the International Convention on the Simplification and Harmonization of Customs Procedures—the Kyoto Convention (Council Dec. 77/415, *OJ* 1977 L166/3, and Council Dec. 2003/231, *OJ* 2003 L86/21). According to this Convention the country of origin is the country:

- in which the goods have been wholly obtained or produced; or
- where two or more countries have taken part in the production—the country in which the goods underwent sufficient manufacturing or processing (substantial transformation criterion).

In order to determine whether substantial transformation has taken place, one or several of the following criteria may be used in customs legislation:

- a change of the tariff heading (possibly combined with a list of cases where this method does not apply);

- a list of those processes or workings which confer or do not confer the origin;
- a minimum percentage of added value.

These rules are supplemented by provisions on origin certificates (Annex D.2, Annex K of the revised version) and customs co-operation for *a posteriori* controls of origin certificates (Annex D.3, not adopted by the EC).

This Convention sets out a framework for origin rules but does not harmonize them with regard to individual types of goods, since it not only leaves a choice between three different criteria to express substantial transformation, but also does not provide for a uniform application of those criteria.

During the Uruguay Round it was recognized that a greater harmonization is necessary in order to facilitate international trade and to avoid that rights under the WTO Agreements are jeopardized through restrictive origin rules. The Agreement on Rules of Origin (Council Dec. 94/800, *OJ* 1994 L336/144) stipulates that rules of origin shall be harmonized and lays down an ambitious work programme with the aim to establish a common international system of origin rules, to be applied with regard to all non preferential commercial policy instruments such as:

- most-favoured-nation treatment;
- anti-dumping and countervailing duties;
- safeguard measures;
- origin marks;
- discriminatory tariff quotas and quantitative restrictions;
- trade statistics; and
- public procurement.

During the transition period until this harmonization will be completed, certain disciplines are to be respected, notably:

- the use of objective, transparent, and non-discriminatory criteria;
- the obligation to deliver upon request within 150 days binding origin information;
- the publication of origin rules and the possibility of a judicial review.

The scope of this harmonization is limited to non-preferential rules of origin. With regard to preferential rules of origin, different rules may be applied, but the Agreement lays down a set of disciplines which have to be respected (see Annex II to the Agreement).

II. Community law

1. The Treaty provisions. According to Art. 23 EC, the Community is based on a customs union which is implemented, in so far as relations with third countries are concerned, by means of a common customs tariff. Furthermore, Art. 133 EC calls for a common commercial policy and Art. 187 or Art. 310 EC form the legal basis for the association of dependent or independent countries or territories. Though these Articles do not explicitly mention origin rules, such provisions are to be based on them depending on whether they are set:

- autonomously or in a trade agreement (Art. 133 EC; Council Reg. 802/68, *OJ* 1968 L148/1, laying down autonomous origin rules, now superseded by the Customs Code, was based, *inter alia*, on Art. 133 EC);
- autonomously *vis-à-vis* the dependent countries or territories (Art. 187 EC); or
- in an association agreement (Art. 310 EC).

In the framework of the common agricultural policy specific origin rules may be laid down (Art. 37 EC).

2. Non-preferential origin rules. The non-preferential origin rules of the Community are set out in Arts. 22 to 26 of the Customs Code—CC (Council Reg. 2913/92, *OJ* 1992 L302/1) and Arts. 35 to 65 and Annexes 9 to 13 of its implementing provisions—CCIP (Comm. Reg. 2454/93, *OJ* 1993 L253/1). They apply, *inter alia*, to anti-dumping and retaliatory duties, quantitative restrictions, surveillance of imports from specific countries, and trade statistics, not however to origin marks for commercial purposes. With regard to normal customs duties which are levied according to the most-favoured-nation principle (*erga omnes* duties), the origin is irrelevant, except for the purposes of external trade statistics.

In accordance with the relevant international agreements (see section I above), the Customs Code sets out the criteria for:

- goods wholly obtained or produced in a country (Art. 23 CC); and
- goods whose production involved more than one country (Art. 24 CC).

The first case (production in one country) covers:

- mineral products extracted from the soil;
- vegetable products harvested;
- animals born and raised as well as the products derived therefrom (e.g. eggs);
- products of hunting and fishing;
- products taken from the sea by vessels registered in the country concerned and flying the flag of that country (with regard to the interpretation of the words 'taken from the sea', see Case 100/84 *Commission* v. *United Kingdom* [1985] ECR 1169 at p. 1182);
- products taken from the seabed and subsoil, provided that the country has the exclusive right of exploitation;
- waste and scrap derived from manufacturing operations and used articles;
- goods produced from the above-mentioned goods.

In cases where the territorial scope of the customs territory changes after the time the goods have been produced, this does not change their origin (Case C-223/95 *Moksel* [1997] ECR I-2379 at p. I-2401).

In the case of production in more than one country the origin of the goods is determined according to the country where they underwent their last substantial processing or working, provided that:

- this operation is economically justified;
- the undertaking is equipped for that purpose; and
- the operation results in the manufacture of a new product or represents an important stage of manufacture.

In order to clarify the scope of these terms, the Commission may, after seeking the opinion of the Customs Code Committee, adopt implementing provisions (Arts. 247 and 247a CC) on the basis of objective and non-discriminating criteria (see Case 34/78 *Yoshida* [1979] ECR 115 at p. 133; Case 162/82 *Cousin* [1983] ECR 1101 at p. 1119). Such provisions have been adopted notably with regard to:

- textiles (Arts. 36 to 38 and Annexes 9 and 10 CCIP);
- spare parts (Arts. 41 to 46 CCIP);
- the definition of the terms 'value', 'ex-works price', and 'value acquired as a result of assembly operations' (Art. 40 CCIP); and
- individual goods for which specific criteria have been determined (Annex 11 CCIP).

Where such rules do not exist or their interpretation leaves doubts or their validity is challenged, the question may be referred under Art. 234 EC to the European Court of Justice which has ruled, *inter alia*, on the interpretation of the terms:

- 'substantial processing or working' (Case 49/76 *Gesellschaft für Überseehandel* [1977] ECR 41 at p. 53);
- 'last substantial processing or working' (Case 34/78 *Yoshida*, above, at p. 136; Case C-26/88 *Brother International* [1989] ECR 4253 at p. 4280);
- 'manufacture of a new product or representing an important stage of manufacture' (Case 49/76 *Gesellschaft für Überseehandel*, above; Case 93/83 *Zentrag* [1984] ECR 1095 at p. 1106).

Particularly in the case of assembly operations where technical criteria alone do not allow the determination of the processes to be regarded as 'substantial', the value added may be used as a subsidiary criterion (Case 26/88 *Brother International*, above).

Art. 25 CC contains an anti-circumvention rule allowing operations to be disregarded whose sole object is to circumvent measures applicable to a specific country. In cases where the assembly has been transferred during or shortly after the introduction of a restrictive measure (e.g. an anti-dumping duty) from one country (subject to the measure) to another country (which is not affected by the measure) the manufacturer concerned must prove that there were reasonable grounds, other than avoiding the consequences of the measure in question, for carrying out the assembly operations in the country from which the goods were originally exported (Case 26/88 *Brother International*, above, at p. 4282).

In certain cases the presentation of a document proving the origin may be stipulated by law or may be requested by the customs authorities (Art. 26 CC). Specific legislation has been enacted, for example, for textile products subject to quantitative restrictions (Council Reg. 1541/98, *OJ* 1998 L202/11). The general provisions relating to universal certificates of origin and their verification are set out in Arts. 47 to 65 and Annexes 12 and 13 CCIP.

3. Preferential origin rules. Preferences are an exception from the most-favoured-nation principle (Art. I GATT), which are allowed under the WTO rules notably in the context of:

- the Generalised System of Preferences (GSP) for developing countries;
- agreements setting up a free-trade area in accordance with Art. XXIV GATT;
- agreements setting up a customs union in accordance with Art. XXIV GATT (*see further under* **Common Customs Tariff (CCT)**, sections I and IV.1(*e*)).

The principal aim of preferences is:

- either to foster the economic development by requiring that certain processes must be performed in the countries concerned; or
- to promote economic integration between certain countries or groups of countries by privileging materials produced in the zone.

The means of ensuring that only goods from the privileged countries can benefit, are preferential origin rules (where a customs union has been agreed, as in the case of Turkey, it is sufficient to prove that the goods have been in free circulation in the export country). If least developed countries cannot fulfil the requirements of a preferential origin rule (e.g. production of garments from yarn, because there is not sufficient yarn production), less restrictive rules may be enacted (e.g. Comm. Reg. 1713/97, *OJ* 1997 L 242/1). In accordance with the way the preferences have been set, the origin rules are either laid down in an international agreement or autonomously by the Community. Art. 27 Customs Code—CC (Council Reg. 2913/92, *OJ* 1992 L302/1) reflects this dual approach by referring:

- to the relevant agreements in cases where goods are covered by a preferential agreement; and
- to the Customs Code Implementing Provisions—CCIP (Comm. Reg. 2454/93, *OJ* 1993 L302/1) in cases where the Community has adopted unilaterally preferential tariff measures (in fact some autonomous origin rules are set outside this framework, as in the case of the preferences in favour of the countries and territories dependent on a Member State, see *OJ* 2001 L314/35).

The main difference between autonomous and conventional origin rules is that the former can be changed unilaterally by the Community whereas with regard to the latter Agreement between the Contracting Parties is required apart from exceptional circumstances (with regard to a unilateral suspension of trade concessions see Case C-162/96 *Racke* [1998] ECR I-3655 at pp. I-3706–8).

(*a*) ***Autonomous rules.*** Arts. 66 to 123 and Annexes 14 to 22 CCIP contain the origin rules for autonomous preferences with regard to:

- developing countries benefiting from the Generalised System of Preferences (GSP), and
- Albania, Bosnia and Herzegovina, the Kosovo, Montenegro, and Serbia.

For goods wholly obtained in a country the rules are largely identical with the provisions for the non-preferential origin. For products of sea fishing the requirements are however stricter in so far as:

- the vessel must not only be registered in and fly the flag of the country concerned, but
- the vessel must also for at least 50% be owned by nationals of the beneficiary country, and
- the captain and officers as well as 75% of the crew must be nationals of the beneficiary country.

If in the production of the exported goods non-originating materials have been used, the processing requirements conferring origin vary from product to product; the most important rules are:

- a change of the tariff heading in the production process to apply to non-originating materials;
- the exclusive use of originating products (e.g. canned fish);
- the type of manufacturing (e.g. garments from yarn);
- a minimum value to be added in the beneficiary country in the process of manufacture.

The ECJ has confirmed that it is the responsibility of the political institutions of the Community to decide whether a change of tariff heading is sufficient to confer origin or whether other and more restrictive rules are to be applied (Case 385/85 *S. R. Industries* [1986] ECR 2929 at p. 2942).

Certain processes are however considered as insufficient to confer the status of originating products, such as:

- operations ensuring the preservation of products during transport and storage;
- simple operations, such as washing, painting, cutting up, or placing in bottles, flasks, bags, boxes;
- the affixing of marks and labels;
- simple mixing or assembly of products;
- the slaughter of animals.

Where goods from the Community are incorporated in the final product, they are considered as materials originating in the beneficiary country (bilateral cumulation or donor's content). Certain groups of countries may also use materials from other members of the group as if they originate in the exporting country (regional cumulation, for GSP). A tolerance rule (5%) allows the use of non-originating materials (it does, in principle, not apply to textiles).

In order to qualify for preferential treatment, the goods must not only fulfil the requirements of the origin rules but also:

- have been transported directly from the exporting beneficiary country to the Community, for which evidence has to be supplied (see Case T-195/97 *Kia Motors Nederland* v. *Commission* [1998] ECR II-2907 at pp. II-2921–2); transhipment and temporary warehousing under customs surveillance are however possible;
- a valid certificate of origin (form A or EUR.1) or, where applicable, an invoice declaration must be presented; and
- in accordance with Art. 20(4) CC the declarant has to request the application of the preference.

Certificates of origin may be returned to the authorities of the export country for verification with the possible result that a certificate is declared invalid or that the authorities do not reply. In such a case the preference is not granted; the ECJ considers this as a normal trade risk which the importer has to accept (Case 827/79 *Ciro Acampora* [1980] ECR 3731 at p. 3745; Cases 98/83 etc. *Van Gend & Loos* v. *Commission* [1984] ECR 3763 at p. 3779). If the certificate form A or the EUR.1 movement certificate has been issued for another country than the Community, it is not valid in the EC; in certain cases it is however possible to issue retrospectively a certificate for imports into the Community (Case C-368/92 *Solange Chiffre* [1994] ECR I-605 at p. I-622). Non-compliance with the origin rules by the export country or a lack of administrative co-operation may lead to a withdrawal of autonomous preferences (see Art. 26(1)(e) of Council Reg. 2501/2001, *OJ* 2001 L346/1).

Products originating in the countries and territories dependent on a Member State are exempted from customs duties by virtue of Art. 184 EC (that this Article covers only originating products has been confirmed by the ECJ in Case C-310/95 *Road Air* [1997] ECR I-2229 at pp. I-2263–4). However, the Council has extended preferential treatment also to goods in free circulation in these countries and territories (Council Dec. 2001/822, *OJ* 2001 L314/1, and L 324/1), provided:

- in the export country the normal duties of the Community have at least been paid;
- the duties have not been repaid or remitted; and
- an export certificate is presented.

Agricultural products and goods subject to quantitative restrictions or anti-dumping duties on importation into the Community are excluded. The origin rules are largely identical with those applicable to ACP countries.

(*b*) ***Agreements.*** Preferential agreements exist at present with the following countries or groups of countries:

- the European Economic Area (EEA) comprising Iceland, Norway, and Liechtenstein; separate agreements cover Switzerland and the Faeroe Islands;
- Europe Agreements with Bulgaria and Romania; a further agreement covers Croatia and Macedonia;
- Mediterranean Agreements with Algeria, Egypt, Israel, Jordan, Lebanon, Morocco, Palestine, Syria, and Tunisia;
- the ACP countries (for these countries, *see further under* **Common Customs Tariff (CCT)**, section IV.1);
- Chile, Mexico, and South Africa;
- the Customs Union Agreements with Andorra, San Marino, and Turkey which use origin rules only for certain products excluded from the principle of free circulation and in order to allow cumulation with certain other preferential partners of the EC.

Further agreements are currently under negotiation (e.g. with the Mercosur and the Gulf countries).

The origin rules of these agreements are currently not identical. Efforts are however being made to achieve harmonization. Nevertheless the following common principles exist: origin is conferred

- for goods wholly obtained in the country or group of countries concerned; and
- with regard to products for which non-originating materials have been used, by sufficient working and processing, as defined in the relevant protocol of origin.

Originally, the basic rule used by the Community has been a change of the (four-digit) tariff heading; this rule was supplemented or replaced in certain cases by specific provisions (see for example Art. 3, Annexes II and III of the origin protocol with Egypt, *OJ* 1978 L266/30). Whilst this rule is still maintained in the Euro–Mediterranean Agreements (see for example Art. 7 and Annex II of the origin protocol with Tunisia, *OJ* 1998 L97/69), in the EEA and the Europe Agreements with Bulgaria and Rumania this concept has been abandoned in favour of a product-by-product (or group of products) list setting out the required processing (see Art. 5 and Annex II of the EEA origin protocol, *OJ* 2003 L137/48). Criteria used include:

- manufacture from materials wholly obtained in the preferential area (e.g. meat and fish);
- a change of tariff heading (e.g. production of oil from nuts);
- specific processes (e.g. cutting of marble, provided its thickness exceeds 25 cm);
- a certain value added (e.g. manufacture of aluminium sulphate in which the value of all the materials used does not exceed 50% of the ex-works price of the product);

- the use of certain materials and/or processes (e.g. either sewing together articles of apparel or manufacturing them from yarn).

Origin rules may be supplemented by explanatory notes (see for example *OJ* 2002 C228/6).

As in the case of autonomous preferences, special provisions exist with regard to:

- a *de minimis* (tolerance) rule for non-originating components (normally 10%, but not for textiles);
- simple operations not conferring origin (like simple preservation, loading, affixing of marks, etc.);
- the use of power and fuel, plant, equipment, machines, and tools in the production process;
- accessories, spare parts, and tools dispatched with the export good;
- sets which may contain up to 15% non-originating components.

Given the globalization of production, it is important to establish in which country or area processing may take place in compliance with the origin rules:

- The territoriality principle requires that all conditions stipulated for conferring origin must have been met without interruption within the relevant preferential country or area (e.g. the EEA). If originating products are exported from the beneficiary country or area, they are considered on their return as non-originating unless it can be proved that the returned goods are identical with those previously exported and have not undergone any operation beyond those necessary for their preservation (see Case C-207/91 *Eurim-Pharm* [1993] ECR I-3723 at pp. I-3745–6).
- The rule of direct transport aims at ensuring that no manipulation or processing has taken place outside the preferential area; transhipment and temporary warehousing under customs surveillance are however possible.
- Countries or areas benefiting from preferences may be interlinked through cumulation rules, so that materials processed in another country or area linked to the Community by a preferential agreement can be taken into account.

The following types of cumulation can be distinguished.

(*i*) *Bilateral cumulation* operates between the two partners of the agreement for originating materials (e.g. integrated circuits are assembled in Bulgaria from microchips originating in the EC and other materials originating in Bulgaria; the integrated circuits are considered as originating in Bulgaria and entitled to the preference on importation to the EC, even though the assembly operation in Bulgaria alone is not considered as a process conferring origin, given that no change of tariff heading occurs).

(*ii*) *Diagonal cumulation* allows several countries or areas linked to each other by agreements to use materials originating in any other of the countries concerned (e.g. television receivers are assembled in Romania from components originating in Bulgaria, Romania, and the EC; the television receivers are entitled to preferential treatment on importation into the EC, even though the components originating in Romania and the operations performed there are not sufficient to confer origin).

(*iii*) *Full cumulation* allows the taking into account of all processing of a product within the interrelated free-trade area, without the materials being used necessarily having to originate in one of the partner countries or areas; in other words: all stages of processing within the zone can be counted together (e.g. US cotton fibre is spun into yarn in the EC and woven into cotton fabric in Norway; the double transformation required for textiles has been partially performed inside the EC and partially in the territory of a preferential partner of the EC; under the rules for full cumulation all these processes are counted together and preferential treatment is granted to the cotton fabric on importation into the EC).

In the context of using materials from different countries the no-draw back rule is important; it aims to ensure that customs duties applicable to non-originating materials are paid, if preferential treatment is to be granted. Art. 216 Customs Code stipulates therefore that a customs debt is incurred on import goods for which on exportation a document enabling preferential treatment (e.g. EUR.1, declaration on the invoice) is validated. Without such a rule (which is also contained in preferential agreements, e.g. Art. 14 of the EEA origin protocol, *OJ* 2003 L137/48), a manufacturer in Bulgaria for example, could benefit from EU preferences for the export of finished products that contain materials from Asia for which no duty has been paid (e.g. imports under inward processing). However, a manufacturer in the Community having used the like non-originating materials must pay customs duties (unless the customs tariff provides for duty exemption) on the imported materials, if he wants to put his product on the Community market. The no-drawback rule therefore ensures a level playing field for economic operators within the zone. The effects of divergent import duties can, however, not be compensated by this rule (in some cases countries with higher duty rates are allowed to recover only a lower flat rate duty in case of preferential export after inward processing).

The origin has to be proved:

- either by a certificate EUR.1 issued by the competent authorities in the export country; or
- by an invoice declaration, which may be used in cases where the value of the goods is below a certain threshold and in cases where an exporter has been authorized for this procedure by the authorities of the export country.

Administrative procedures ensure a control of such documents which is in principle to be performed in the export country. This administrative co-operation between the import and the export country has been the subject of a number of ECJ decisions, e.g. with regard to:

- the assessment of the elements used in determining the origin of a product, which is, in principle, the responsibility of the customs authorities in the export country who apply their customs legislation to components imported from third countries (Case 218/83 *Les Rapides Savoyards* [1984] ECR 3105 at p. 3124);
- the impossibility to provide a certificate EUR.1 and the principle of *force majeure* (Case C-12/92 *Huygen* [1993] ECR I-6381 at pp. I-6415–6; Case C-334/93 *Bonapharma* [1995] ECR I-319 at p. I-339);
- the issuing of false certificates of origin, which as such cannot be regarded as *force majeure* (Cases 98/83 etc. *Van Gend & Loos* v. *Commission*, above, at p. 3779; Case C-446/93 *SEIM* [1996] ECR I-73 at p. I-113);
- the issuing of a certificate EUR.1 by an authority that is not recognized in the Community (Case C-432/92 *Anastasiou* [1994] ECR I-3087 at pp. I-3131–5);
- the consequences for the recovery of a customs debt, if the authorities issuing a certificate EUR.1 have committed an error (Cases C-153/94 etc. *Faeroe Seafood* [1996] ECR I-2465 at pp. I-2540–5);
- the recovery of a customs debt, if the authorities who had issued a certificate EUR.1 declare it invalid after a verification (Case C-446/93 *SEIM*, above, at p. I-113; Case C-97/95 *Pascoal & Filhos* [1997] ECR I-4209 at pp. I-4256–8);
- the use of forged certificates and the question whether this may constitute special circumstances justifying a remission of customs duties if the Commission was aware of fraud in this area (Case T-42/96 *Eyckeler & Malt* v. *Commission* [1998] ECR II-401; this case does not concern a certificate of origin but a certificate of authenticity, nevertheless the situations are comparable); if however the competent authorities have been lead to an error by wrong declarations of the exporter, this as such does not justify a waiver of customs duties (Case C-348/89 *Mecanarte* [1991] ECR I-3277 at p. I-3307; Cases C-153/94 etc. *Faroe Seafood*, above, at p. I-2541; Cases T-10/97 etc. *Unifrigo* v. *Commission* [1998] ECR II-2231 at p. II-2249).

4. Binding origin information (BOI). As a consequence of the WTO Agreement on rules of origin (see section I above), the Community has introduced with effect from 1 January 1997 into Art. 12 of the Customs Code the possibility for importers and exporters to obtain from the competent customs authorities binding origin information (Council and Parliament Reg. 82/97, *OJ* 1997 L17/1). Such information may be requested both for non-preferential and for preferential origin rules. The information issued is valid for three years, unless:

- a regulation or an agreement becomes applicable according to which the BOI no longer conforms to the law;
- explanatory notes or opinions are published by the EC or in the framework of the WTO Agreement, with which the BOI is not compatible;
- a judgment of the ECJ has been rendered and the BOI is not compatible with it;
- the BOI has been revoked or amended by the issuing authority.

In certain cases a BOI which has become invalid may subsequently be invoked for a maximum of six months if the importer or exporter has concluded a binding contract for the purchase or sale of the goods in question while the BOI was still valid.

5. **Protection of geographical indications and designations of origin.** Apart from customs legislation, the protection of origin indications has also been harmonized on Community level with regard to agricultural products and foodstuffs (Council Reg. 2081/92, *OJ* 1992 L208/1; see Cases C-321/94 etc. *Pistre* [1997] ECR I-2343; and Cases C-129/97 etc. *Chiciak and Fol* [1998] ECR I-3315). Specific rules exist with regard to:

- wine (Council Reg. 1493/1999, *OJ* 1999 L179/1);
- spirit drinks (Council Reg. 1576/89, *OJ* 1989 L160/1); and
- natural mineral waters (Council Dir. 80/777, *OJ* 1980 L229/1).

Furthermore, marketing standards may also contain rules on the indication of the origin, e.g. with regard to olive oil (Comm. Reg. 2815/98, *OJ* 1998 L349/56; see Case C-99/99 *Italy* v. *Commission* [2000] ECR I-11535).

Products infringing Community or national rules on origin marks may be withheld or seized and confiscated by customs (Council Reg. 1383/2003, *OJ* 2003 L196/7).

See also **Common Customs Tariff.**

Further reading 1. BOOKS: Berr and Trémeau, *Le droit douanier*, 5th edn. (2001), p. 112; Dehousse and Vincent, *Les règles d'origine de la Communauté européenne* (1999); Duric, *Die Freihandelsabkommen EG/EFTA* (1991), p. 125; Giffoni, *Droit douanier de la C.E. at aspects économiques* (1993), p. 99; Kaufmann, *Ursprungsregeln* (1996); Kirchhoff, *Zollpräferenzen und Vertrauensschutz* (2002); Lasok and Cairns, *The Customs Law of the European Economic Community* (1983), p. 172; Lux, *Guide to Community Customs Legislation* (2002), p. 145; id., *Das Zollrecht der EG* (2004), ch. IV; Lyons, *EC Customs Law* (2001), p. 194; Möller and Schumann, *Warenursprung und Präferenzen* (2002); Nassiet, *La réglementation douanière européenne* (1988), p. 70; Snyder, *International Trade and Customs Law of the European Union* (1998), p. 22; Vermulst, Waer, and Bourgeois, *Rules of Origin in International Trade (A Comparative Study)* (1994); Walsh, *The Customs Code of the European Union* (1996), p. 80; Witte and Wolffgang, *Lehrbuch des Europäischen Zollrechts*, 4th edn. (2003), p. 440; Wolffgang (ed.), *Management mit Zollpräferenzen* (1998); Zaimis, *EC Rules of Origin* (1992).

2. ARTICLES: Cremona, 'Annotation to Case C-432/92' (1996) *CML Rev.* 125; Forrester, 'EEC Customs Law: Rules of Origin and Preferential Treatment' (1980) *EL Rev.* 173; Feenstra, 'Rules of Origin and Textile Products: Recent Case-law of the Court of Justice' (1985) *CML Rev.* 533; McNamara and Vermulst, 'Special Trade Law Issues in the EC for Assembly Products' (1994) *Journal of World Trade* 83; Stobbe, 'Die Präferenzmaßnahmen des Zollkodex' (1997) *Zeitschrift für Zölle und Verbrauchsteuern* 38, 80, and 114; Oliver, 'Annotation to Case C-310/95' (1998) *CML Rev.* 747; Pethke, 'Strukturmerkmale des präferentiellen Ursprungsrechts' (1998) *Zeitschrift für Zölle und Verbrauchsteuern* 153 and 192; Vander Schueren, 'Annotation to Case 26/88' (1990) *CML Rev.* 341; Vermulst and Waer, 'European Community Rules of Origin as Commercial Policy Instruments?' (1990) *Journal of World Trade* 55.

3. OFFICIAL PUBLICATIONS: Court of Auditors, 'Annual Report Concerning the Financial Year 1989' (*OJ* 1990 C313/36); European Commission, 'Communication on the Management of Preferential Tariff Arrangements' (COM(97) 402, 23 July 1997); European Commission, 'Green Paper on the Future of Rules of Origin in Preferential Trade Arrangements' (COM(2003) 787, 18 December 2003).

▶ **OUTWARD PROCESSING *see* CUSTOMS PROCEDURES**

P

▶ **PATENT** *see* **INTELLECTUAL PROPERTY RIGHTS**

▶ **PLANT VARIETY RIGHTS** *see* **INTELLECTUAL PROPERTY RIGHTS**

▶ **PREFERENTIAL TRADE AGREEMENTS** *see* **COMMON CUSTOMS TARIFF**

▶ **PUBLIC HEALTH** One of the grounds on which the Member States may derogate from certain provisions of Community law (other, closely related grounds for derogations include public policy and public security). Thus, under Art. 96(1) Euratom, the Member States may impose limitations, on grounds of public policy, public security, or public health, on the right of nationals of other Member States to take skilled employment in the field of nuclear energy (a similar derogation existed under Art. 69(1) ECSC on grounds of public policy and health). According to Art. 195 Euratom, the institutions of the Community, the Supply Agency, and the Joint Undertakings are to comply with the conditions of access to ores, source materials, and special fissile materials laid down in national rules for reasons of public policy or public health (for an interpretation of this provision, see Ruling 1/78 *Protection of Nuclear Materials* [1978] ECR 2151 at p. 2173).

Under the EC Treaty, the Member States may impose restrictions, justified on grounds of public policy, public security, or public health, on the free movement of goods (Art. 30, referring to the 'protection of health and life of humans, animals or plants'; *see under* **Free movement of goods**, section III.1); free movement of workers (Art. 39(3)); freedom of establishment (Art. 46(1)); freedom to provide services (Art. 46(1) in conjunction with Art. 55); and free movement of capital (Art. 58(1)(b), which mentions only public policy and public security, but not public health). Moreover, those grounds may be relied upon not only by Member States but also by individuals in order to justify limitations on the free movement of workers under agreements or other measures adopted by persons governed by private law (Case C-415/93 *Bosman* [1995] ECR I-4921 at p. I-5066; Case C-350/96 *Clean Car Autoservice* [1998] ECR I-2521 at pp. I-2545–6).

The ECJ has held that the above provisions, in particular Art. 46(1) in conjunction with Art. 55, permit Member States to restrict the freedom to provide medical and hospital services on grounds of public health, in so far as this is necessary for maintaining a high level of health protection, treatment capacity, or medical competence and a high-quality, balanced medical and hospital service open to all, provided that the measures taken do not exceed what is objectively necessary for those purposes and that the same result cannot be achieved by less restrictive rules (the principle of proportionality). However, those provisions do not allow the Member States to exclude the whole public health sector, as a sector of economic activity, from the application of the fundamental principle of the free movement of persons and services (Case C-158/96 *Kohll* [1998] ECR I-1931 at pp. I-1949–50; Case C-368/98 *Vanbraekel* [2001] ECR I-5363 at pp. I-5401–2;

Case C-157/99 *Geraets-Smits and Peerbooms* [2001] ECR I-5473 at p. I-5533; Case C-385/99 *Müller-Fauré and Van Riet* [2003] ECR I-4509, paras. 67–8; see also Case 131/85 *Gül* [1986] ECR 1573 at p. 1589. *See further under* **Freedom to provide services**, section V.3(*j*)). The Court also held that an Austrian law which restricted the exercise of the profession of 'Heilpraktiker'—lay health practitioner—to qualified doctors was justified on grounds of safeguarding public health (Case C-294/00 *Gräbner* [2002] ECR I-6515 at pp. I-6654–6; *see also under* **Freedom to provide services**, section V.3(*s*)).

The special measures that Member States may adopt under the EC Treaty on grounds of public health concerning the free movement and residence of Community nationals have been co-ordinated by Council Dir. 64/221 of 25 February 1964 (*OJ Sp. Edn.* 1963–4, p. 117). The directive lays down both substantive rules and procedural safeguards, which apply equally to measures adopted on grounds of public policy, public security, and public health (Art. 2(1)). Rather than laying down an exhaustive list of diseases and disabilities which might pose a threat to those general interests, the directive specifies in the Annex two groups of diseases: those that might endanger public health and those that might threaten public policy or public security (see also the fourth recital in the preamble). These are the only diseases and disabilities which may justify refusal to admit a Community national into a Member State or to issue a first residence permit to him. Diseases or disabilities occurring after a first residence permit has been issued do not justify refusal to renew the residence permit or expulsion from the national territory. New provisions or practices that are more restrictive than those in force at the date of notification of the directive may not be introduced by the Member States (Art. 4). The provisions of the directive are considered in detail under a separate entry (*see further under* **Public policy**).

See also **Freedom to provide services, Free movement of goods, Public policy, Public security.**

▶ **PUBLIC POLICY** One of the grounds on which the Member States may derogate from certain provisions of Community law (other, closely related grounds for derogations include public security, and public health). Thus, under Art. 96(1) Euratom, the Member States may impose limitations, on grounds of public policy, public security or public health, on the right of nationals of other Member States to take skilled employment in the field of nuclear energy (a similar derogation existed under Art. 69(1) ECSC on grounds of public policy and health). According to Art. 195 Euratom, the institutions of the Community, the Supply Agency and the Joint Undertakings are to comply with the conditions of access to ores, source materials, and special fissile materials laid down in national rules for reasons of public policy or public health (for an interpretation of this provision, see Ruling 1/78 *Protection of Nuclear Materials* [1978] ECR 2151 at p. 2173).

Under the EC Treaty, the Member States may impose restrictions, justified on grounds of public policy, public security, or public health, on the free movement of goods (Art. 30); free movement of workers (Art. 39(3)); freedom of establishment (Art. 46(1)); freedom to provide services (Art. 46(1) in conjunction with Art. 55); and free movement of capital (Art. 58(1)(b)). Moreover, those grounds may be relied upon not only by Member States but also by individuals in order to justify limitations on the free movement of workers under agreements or other measures adopted by persons governed by private law (Case C-415/93 *Bosman* [1995] ECR I-4921 at p. I-5066; Case C-350/96 *Clean Car Autoservice* [1998] ECR I-2521 at pp. I-2545–6).

This entry deals with public policy as a ground for restricting the free movement (entry and residence) of persons and of services under the EC Treaty (for public policy in the context of the free movement of capital and goods, *see under* **Free movement of capital**, section IV, **Free movement of goods**, section III.1. *See also* **Public health, Public security**).

I. The concept of public policy

The concept of public policy is not defined by Community law. In several cases, the ECJ has pointed out that by virtue of the reservations contained in Arts. 39(3), 46(1), and 55 EC, in principle the Member States continue to be free to determine the requirements of public policy in the light of their national needs. Since the particular circumstances justifying recourse to this concept may vary from one country to another and from one period to another, the national authorities must necessarily have an area of discretion in this matter within the limits imposed by the Treaty and secondary legislation. Nevertheless, the Court has also emphasized that where public policy is used as a justification for derogating from the fundamental principles of equal treatment and free movement of persons, it must be interpreted strictly. Its scope cannot be determined unilaterally by each Member State without being subject to control by the institutions of the Community. In particular, any appraisal as to whether national measures based on public policy are justified must have regard to all the rules of Community law that limit the discretionary powers of the Member States in this respect and protect the rights of the individuals who are subject to the restrictive measures (Case 41/74 *Van Duyn* [1974] ECR 1337 at p. 1350; Case 36/75 *Rutili* [1975] ECR 1219 at pp. 1231, 1235; Case 30/77 *Bouchereau* [1977] ECR 1999 at pp. 2013–14).

Since the rules of Community law include the general principles of law which, in turn, incorporate fundamental rights, any national measure which obstructs the exercise of one of the basic freedoms guaranteed by the Treaty must be assessed in the light of those general principles and fundamental rights. Any such restrictive measure may be justified on grounds of public policy only if it is compatible with the fundamental rights embodied in the European Convention on Human Rights and protected by Community law, such as freedom of expression (Case C-260/89 *ERT* [1991] ECR I-2925 at p. I-2964). Thus, ultimately, the power of the Member States to derogate from the provisions of the Treaty on grounds of public policy is subject to the observance of fundamental human rights. That power is limited by the general principle enshrined in various provisions of the European Convention on Human Rights (e.g. Arts. 8, 9, 10, 11), according to which only such restrictions in the public interest may be placed on the basic freedoms of the individual as are necessary for the protection of that interest 'in a democratic society' (Case 36/75 *Rutili*, above, at p. 1232). This is the principle of proportionality, which requires that derogating measures taken on grounds of public policy must not be disproportionate to the aim pursued: they must not go beyond what is objectively necessary in order to protect the interest in question (see Case 352/85 *Bond van Adverteerders* [1988] ECR 2085 at p. 2135; for other applications of this principle, see e.g. Case C-3/88 *Commission* v. *Italy* [1989] ECR 4035 at p. 4060; Case C-260/89 *ERT*, above, at p. I-2960; Case C-100/01 *Oteiza Olazabal* [2002] ECR I-10981, para. 43). It is for the national courts, in the first place, to ensure that such derogating national measures, whether legislative provisions or individual decisions taken in implementation of legislation, limiting the free movement of persons on grounds of public policy, are compatible with Community law (Case 36/75 *Rutili*, above, at pp. 1229–30).

It is clear from the foregoing that the derogations contained in Arts. 39(3) and 46(1) EC permit Member States to adopt, with regard to the nationals of other Member States and on grounds of public policy, measures that they cannot apply to their own nationals. Thus, for example, while Member States have no power to expel their own nationals from the national territory or to refuse them the right of entry and residence, they may adopt such measures in relation to the nationals of other Member States. Discriminatory treatment is thus allowed under Arts. 39(3) and 46(1); in fact such treatment on grounds of nationality is only allowed if it can be brought within the scope of those provisions (Case 15/69 *Ugliola* [1969] ECR 363 at pp. 368–9; Case 44/72 *Marsman* [1972] ECR 1243 at p. 1248, both referring to Art. 39(3); Case 352/85 *Bond van Adverteerders*, above, at pp. 2134–5; Case C-260/89 *ERT*, above, at p. I-2960, both referring to Art. 46(1) in conjunction with Art. 55. See also Case C-100/01 *Oteiza Olazabal*, above, para. 40 and the cases cited therein).

What is not permitted is arbitrary discrimination to the detriment of foreign nationals. Thus, in several cases the Court has emphasized that a national authority may rely on the concept of public policy in order to impose restrictions on the free movement of Community nationals only if their presence in the national territory would constitute 'a genuine and sufficiently serious threat to the requirements of public policy affecting one of the fundamental interests of society' (Case 30/77 *Bouchereau*, above, at p. 2014; see also Case 36/75 *Rutili*, above, at p. 1231). There must be a direct link between that threat, which must be current, and the discriminatory measure adopted to deal with it (Case C-466/98 *Commission* v. *United Kingdom* [2002] ECR I-9427, para. 57—'Open skies' case). Although Community law does not impose upon the Member States a uniform scale of values as regards public policy, the Court has pointed out that a conduct may not be considered to be of a 'sufficiently serious nature' to justify restrictions on the admission or residence of Community nationals where the same conduct, when attributable to the host State's own nationals, does not give rise to punitive measures or other genuine and effective measures designed to combat it (Cases 115/81 etc. *Adoui and Cornuaille* [1982] ECR 1665 at pp. 1707–8; Case 249/86 *Commission* v. *Germany* [1989] ECR 1263 at p. 1292; but see also Case 41/74 *Van Duyn*, below).

Moreover, the derogations in Arts. 39(3) and 46(1) must be construed not as a condition precedent to the acquisition of the right of entry and residence, but as affording the possibility of placing restrictions, in specific cases and where there is sufficient justification, on the exercise of a right derived directly from the Treaty. Accordingly, the public policy reservation may never justify administrative measures prescribing in a general way conditions and formalities other than those expressly provided for in the Community rules concerning the free movement of persons (Case 48/75 *Royer* [1976] ECR 497 at p. 512; Case 157/79 *Pieck* [1980] ECR 2171 at p. 2185; Case C-363/89 *Roux* [1991] ECR I-273 at p. I-294). Nor can the Member States rely on public policy, public security, or public health to exclude a whole economic sector or occupation from freedom of movement and thus from access to employment or self-employed activities, on the ground that its members are responsible for maintaining public order, safety, or health. Member States may invoke those grounds only to refuse access to their territory or residence there to persons whose presence would in itself constitute a danger for public policy, security, or health (Case 131/85 *Gül* [1986] ECR 1573 at p. 1589, concerning the public health sector; Case C-114/97 *Commission* v. *Spain* [1998] ECR I-6717 at p. I-6743, concerning the private security sector; Case C-47/02 *Anker* [2003] ECR I-10447, paras. 67–8, concerning the fishing sector and the occupation of master of fishing vessels; Case C-405/01 *Colegio de Oficiales de la Marina Mercante Española* [2003] ECR I-10391, paras. 48–9, concerning the merchant shipping sector and the occupations of master and chief mate in the merchant navy).

II. Directive 64/221

The special measures that Member States may adopt on grounds of public policy, public security, or public health concerning the entry and residence of Community nationals have been co-ordinated by Council Dir. 64/221 of 25 February 1964 (*OJ Sp. Edn.* 1963–4, p. 117). The aim of the directive is to protect Community nationals against any excessive exercise of the powers reserved to the authorities of the Member States (see Case 30/77 *Bouchereau*, above, at p. 2010). The directive lays down both substantive rules and procedural safeguards. The former determine the circumstances in which public policy and the other grounds may be relied on to restrict the free movement (entry and residence) of persons and to expel them from the national territory. The latter define the procedures to be followed by the Member States when invoking those grounds, and guarantee adequate legal remedies to foreign nationals against the decisions of the authorities. The directive thus sets out a number of limitations on the discretion enjoyed by the Member States in this area (see Case 48/75 *Royer*, above, at p. 518. See also the Commission's Communication to the Council and

Parliament of 19 July 1999, laying down guidelines for the correct interpretation and application of the directive in order to reduce disparities between the Member States in its implementation and to take account of the introduction of citizenship of the Union (COM(1999) 372)).

The directive applies to any national of a Member State who resides in or travels to another Member State either in order to pursue an activity as an employed or self-employed person, or as a recipient of services, and to his or her spouse and members of their family covered by the relevant regulations and directives (Art. 1). Thus, substantially identical provisions apply to workers, self-employed persons, and providers and recipients of services (ibid. at pp. 509–10). In addition, the scope of the directive has been extended to the following categories of persons and members of their families:

- workers exercising the right to remain in the territory of a Member State after having been employed in that State (Dir. 72/194, Art. 1, *OJ Sp. Edn.* 1972 (II), p. 474);
- self-employed persons exercising the right to remain in the territory of a Member State (Dir. 75/35, Art. 1, *OJ* 1975 L14/14);
- persons of independent means enjoying the right of residence in a Member State (Dir. 90/364, Art. 2(2), *OJ* 1990 L180/26);
- retired persons enjoying the right of residence in a Member State (Dir. 90/365, Art. 2(2), *OJ* 1990 L180/28);
- students enjoying the right of residence in a Member State (Dir. 93/96, Art. 2(2), *OJ* 1993 L317/59).

On 29 April 2004 the European Parliament and the Council adopted Dir. 2004/38 on the right of citizens of the Union and their family members to move and reside freely within the territory of the Member States (*OJ* 2004 L158/77). The purpose of the directive is to codify and review the existing Community instruments dealing separately with workers, self-employed persons, students, and other inactive persons, in order to simplify and strengthen the right of free movement and residence of all Union citizens (see the first four recitals in the preamble). The directive entered into force on 30 April 2004, and has to be implemented by the Member States by 30 April 2006. It will repeal and replace all of the above directives, and some others, from that date (Arts. 38, 40, 41. *See further under* **Right of entry and residence**, section VII).

III. Substantive rules

Dir. 64/221 applies to all measures concerning entry into their territory, issue or renewal of residence permits, or expulsion from their territory, taken by Member States on grounds of public policy, public security, or public health (Art. 2(1)). Such grounds may not be invoked to service economic ends (Art. 2(2); see also Case 352/85 *Bond van Adverteerders*, above, at p. 2135; Case C-17/92 *Distribuidores Cinematográficos* [1993] ECR I-2239 at p. I-2272) or to restrict the exercise of trade union rights (Case 36/75 *Rutili*, above, at pp. 1232, 1235).

Initially, the ECJ held that since the right of entry and residence is defined in the Treaty by reference to the whole territory of each Member State, prohibitions on residence on grounds of public policy could be imposed only in respect of the whole of the national territory. Partial prohibitions limited to certain areas of the territory might only be imposed on Community nationals in circumstances in which such measures might be applied to nationals of the host State (ibid. at pp. 1234–5). However, in Case C-100/01 *Oteiza Olazabal*, above, paras. 28–45, the Court ruled that neither Art. 39 EC nor the implementing secondary legislation preclude a Member State from imposing on a migrant worker administrative police measures limiting that worker's right of residence to a part of the national territory, provided, first, that such action is justified by reasons of public order or public security based on his individual conduct; secondly, that, by reason of their seriousness, those reasons would otherwise give rise to a measure banishing the migrant from the whole of the national territory; and thirdly, that the conduct involved entails, in the case of the host State's own nationals, punitive measures or other genuine and effective measures designed to combat it.

Art. 3(1) of the directive lays down the important rule that 'measures taken on grounds of public policy or of public security shall be based exclusively on the personal conduct of the individual concerned'. According to Art. 3(2), previous criminal convictions shall not in themselves constitute grounds for the taking of such measures. Both provisions have been held to produce direct effect in the sense of conferring on individuals rights which are enforceable in the national courts (see Case 41/74 *Van Duyn*, above, at p. 1349; Case 30/77 *Bouchereau*, above, at p. 2011), although the Court's case-law seems to indicate that the directive as a whole may produce such direct effect (see Case 36/75 *Rutili*, above, at pp. 1229–30. In Case 131/79 *Santillo* [1980] ECR 1585 at p. 1600, the Court held Art. 9 to be directly effective).

The term 'measure' in Art. 3(1) has been defined by the Court as any action which affects the right of persons covered by Community law to enter and reside freely in the Member States under the same conditions as the nationals of the host State. It thus includes not only provisions laid down by law, regulation, or administrative action, but also the actions of the judiciary, such as a recommendation for deportation made by a court to the executive authority, even if it has no binding effect. When making such a recommendation, the national court must take account of the provisions of the directive, including Art. 3 (Case 30/77 *Bouchereau*, above, at pp. 2011–12).

The reference in Art. 3(1) to the 'personal conduct' of the individual concerned indicates that any measure taken on grounds of public policy or public security must be justified on the basis of the individual circumstances of the person concerned and not on the basis of general considerations extraneous to the given case, such as the need to combat crime or prostitution. Thus, Art. 3(1) does not permit the adoption of measures, such as deportation, for the purpose of deterring other aliens, that is, for reasons of a 'general preventive nature' (Case 67/74 *Bonsignore* [1975] ECR 297 at

p. 307; Case 36/75 *Rutili*, above, at p. 1231; Cases 115/81 etc. *Adoui and Cornuaille*, above, at pp. 1708–9). Nevertheless, the mere failure to comply with the legal formalities concerning the entry, movement, and residence of aliens does not in itself constitute conduct threatening public policy and public security and cannot therefore by itself justify a measure ordering expulsion or temporary imprisonment for that purpose (Case 48/75 *Royer*, above, at pp. 513–15).

The ECJ has held that while past association with an organization cannot in itself constitute 'personal conduct' within the meaning of Art. 3(1), present association, which reflects participation in the activities of the organization and identification with its aims, may be considered a voluntary act and consequently part of personal conduct. Present association with an organization the activities of which are considered to be socially harmful may give rise to restrictive measures on grounds of public policy, even although those activities are not unlawful in the host State and no similar restrictions apply to the host State's own nationals (Case 41/74 *Van Duyn*, above, at pp. 1349–51, involving a Dutch national who was refused leave to enter the United Kingdom to take up employment with the 'Church of Scientology', the activities of which were considered to be socially harmful but not unlawful in the United Kingdom, and employment with which was not prohibited for British nationals. The ECJ held that such refusal was justified on grounds of public policy as the British authorities had taken administrative measures to counteract the activities of the organization).

Nevertheless, as seen above, a Member State may not impose restrictions on the free movement of Community nationals by reason of a conduct which, when attributable to its own nationals, does not at least give rise to repressive measures or other genuine and effective measures intended to combat such conduct (Cases 115/81 etc. *Adoui and Cornuaille*, above, at p. 1708).

It follows from Art. 3(2) that the mere existence of criminal convictions may not automatically constitute grounds for restrictive measures, such as deportation. As the ECJ has pointed out, previous criminal convictions can only be taken into account in so far as the circumstances which gave rise to them are evidence of personal conduct constituting a present threat to the requirements of public policy. Although, generally, a 'present threat' implies a propensity to act in the same way in the future, it is possible that past conduct alone may constitute such a threat to public policy. This question must be assessed by the national authorities and courts in the light of the circumstances of each individual case (Case 30/77 *Bouchereau*, above, at pp. 2012–13).

IV. Procedural safeguards

As regards procedural guarantees, Dir. 64/221 has created a double safeguard to protect the rights of persons falling within its scope of application. First, the person concerned must be officially notified not only of any decision to refuse the issue or renewal of a residence permit or to expel him from the territory of the host State (Art. 7), but also of the grounds of public policy, public security, or public health upon which such decision is based, unless this is contrary to the interests of the security of the host State (Art. 6). The notification of the grounds must be sufficiently detailed and precise to enable the person to take effective steps to prepare his defence. He must be able to comprehend the content and the effect of the decision, although it is not clear whether the notification must be in his mother tongue (see Cases 115/81 etc. *Adoui and Cornuaille*, above, at p. 1709, where the Court did not answer this question; see also Case 36/75 *Rutili*, above, at pp. 1232–3). Secondly, the person concerned must have 'adequate legal remedies' against the decision (third recital in the preamble to Dir. 64/221). Both safeguards must in fact be available to anyone against whom a restrictive measure has been taken (Case 36/75 *Rutili*, above, at p. 1233; Case 48/75 *Royer*, above, at p. 516).

The legal remedies referred to above are laid down in Arts. 8 and 9 of the directive. Art. 8 provides that the person concerned must have the same legal remedies in respect of any decision concerning entry, or refusing the issue or renewal of a residence permit, or ordering expulsion from the territory, as are available to the nationals of the host State in respect of acts of the administration. Where under national law different remedies are available in respect of acts of the administration generally and in respect of decisions concerning entry by nationals of the host State, Art. 8 is satisfied if nationals of other Member States enjoy the same remedies as those available against acts of the administration generally (Cases C-65/95 etc. *Shingara and Radiom* [1997] ECR I-3343 at p. I-3388).

While the 'legal remedies' referred to in Art. 8 mean remedies before a court of law, Art. 8 does not specify the courts from which such remedies may be sought. This depends on the judicial system of each Member State. If in a Member State remedies against acts of the administration may be sought from the ordinary courts, such remedies must be available to the persons covered by the directive. Thus, if in a Member State the administrative courts are not empowered to grant a stay of execution of an administrative decision or interim protective measures but such power is vested in the ordinary courts, that State is obliged to permit persons covered by the directive to apply to those courts on the same terms as nationals. However, this right depends on the organization of the courts and the division of their jurisdiction in the various Member States, since the only obligation imposed upon the Member States by Art. 8 is to grant to persons protected by Community law rights of appeal which are not less favourable, as regards form, procedure, and the powers of the courts, than those available to their own nationals against acts of the administration (see the cases cited below).

Although Art. 8 is silent on the question whether an appeal should have suspensory effect, the ECJ has held that the safeguards afforded by the directive would become illusory if the Member States could, by the immediate execution of a decision ordering expulsion, deprive the person concerned of the opportunity of effectively making use of the remedies guaranteed to him. Therefore, save in cases of urgency which have been properly justified, such a decision may not be executed before the party concerned is able to complete the formalities necessary to avail himself of the remedies provided for by Art. 8. However, the Court has added, it may not be inferred from Art. 8 that the Member States are obliged to permit a foreign national to remain in their territory for the duration of the proceedings initiated by him, although he must be able to obtain a fair hearing and to present his defence in full (Case 48/75 *Royer*, above, at pp. 515–17; Case 98/79 *Pecastaing* [1980] ECR 691 at pp. 711–14; Cases C-291/88 etc. *Dzodzi* [1990] ECR I-3763 at p. I-3798).

Art. 8, taken in itself, may not always be able to provide adequate remedies to persons covered by the directive. This is the case, in particular, in the following three situations. First, where there is no right of appeal to a court of law. Secondly, where such appeal may be only in respect of the legal validity of the decision. Thirdly, where the appeal cannot have suspensory effect. In order to mitigate the effect of these deficiencies, Art. 9 lays down complementary provisions the object of which is to ensure a minimum procedural safeguard for Community nationals. Art. 9(1) provides that in those three situations a decision refusing renewal of a residence permit or ordering the expulsion of the holder of a residence permit from the territory may not be taken by the administrative authority, save in cases of urgency, until an opinion has been obtained from a 'competent authority' of the host State before which the person concerned enjoys such rights of defence and of assistance or representation as the domestic law of that State provides for. This 'competent authority' must be different from that empowered to take the decision in question.

In the first situation, a complaint to a 'competent authority' is intended to compensate for the absence of any right of appeal to the courts. In the second situation, the purpose of the intervention of the 'competent authority' is to enable an exhaustive examination to be made of all the facts and circumstances, including the expediency of the proposed measure and the discretionary factors on which it is based, before the decision is definitely adopted. In the third situation, the purpose of the procedure is to permit the person concerned to request and to obtain, if appropriate, a stay of the execution of the proposed measure so as to compensate for the fact that the appeal to the courts does not have suspensory effect. It follows that, save in cases of urgency, the administrative authority may not take and execute a decision ordering expulsion until the opinion of the 'competent authority' has been obtained and notified to the person concerned. As soon as this has happened an expulsion order may be enforced immediately, subject to the right of that person to stay in the territory for the time necessary to avail himself of the remedies accorded to him under Art. 8 of the directive. The determination of the existence of urgency is a matter for the administrative authority. In cases of urgency which have been properly justified expulsion may be effected even before the competent authority has been able to give its opinion (see the cases cited below).

It thus follows that Art. 9 is not intended to confer upon the courts additional powers concerning suspension of the measures mentioned in the directive or to empower them to review the urgency of an expulsion order.

The performance of those duties by the national courts is governed by Art. 8, the scope and effectiveness of which may not be restricted by measures taken under Art. 9. Member States are therefore not required to make available to persons covered by the directive a right of appeal, prior to the execution of a decision refusing a residence permit or ordering expulsion, to a court empowered, under an urgency procedure, to adopt interim protective measures in connection with rights of residence (Case 48/75 *Royer*, above, at pp. 516–17; Case 98/79 *Pecastaing*, above, at pp. 714–15; Cases C-297/88 etc. *Dzodzi*, above, at pp. I-3799–801; Case C-175/94 *Gallagher* [1995] ECR I-4253 at pp. I-4276–8; see also the cases cited below).

The directive does not define the concept of the 'competent authority' referred to in Art. 9, nor does it specify how that authority is to be appointed, but leaves a margin of discretion to the Member States in this matter. The ECJ has held that the authority need not be a court or composed of members of the judiciary. Nor do its members have to be appointed for a specific period. The essential requirements are, first, that the authority must perform its duties in absolute independence and must not be directly or indirectly subject, in the exercise of its duties, to any control by the administrative authority empowered to take the measures provided for in the directive. Secondly, it must follow a procedure enabling the person concerned effectively to present his defence. Subject to these conditions, the competent authority may be appointed by the same administrative authority as takes the decision ordering expulsion (Case 131/79 *Santillo*, above, at p. 1601; Cases 115/81 etc. *Adoui and Cornuaille*, above, at p. 1710; Cases C-297/88 etc. *Dzodzi*, above, at pp. I-3799–800; Case C-175/94 *Gallagher*, above, at pp. I-4278–9).

In the United Kingdom, the criminal courts may be regarded as a competent authority, and a recommendation for deportation made by such courts at the time of conviction may constitute an opinion under Art. 9. However, the opinion must be sufficiently close in time to the decision ordering expulsion to ensure that there are no new factors to be taken into consideration, and both the administration and the person concerned should be in a position to take cognizance of the reasons that led the competent authority to give its opinion unless this is contrary to the interests of the security of the State. It follows that a lapse of time amounting to several years between the recommendation for deportation and the decision by the administration is liable to deprive the recommendation of its function as an opinion for the purposes of Art. 9. The social danger resulting from a foreigner's presence should be assessed at the time when the deportation order is made against him as the factors to be taken into account, particularly those concerning his conduct, are likely to change in the course of time (Case 131/79 *Santillo*, above, at pp. 1600–2). The procedure before the competent authority must not be less favourable to the person concerned than the procedure applicable before other national authorities of the same type. The opinion of the authority must be notified to that person, but there is no requirement that it should identify by name the members of the authority or indicate their professional status (Cases 115/81 etc. *Adoui and Cornuaille*, above, at p. 1711; Cases C-297/88 etc. *Dzodzi*, above, at p. I-3799; Case C-175/94 *Gallagher*, above, at p. I-4278).

According to Art. 9(2), any decision refusing the issue of a first residence permit or ordering expulsion of the foreign national before the issue of the permit must, where that person so requests, be referred for consideration to the competent authority. The foreign national is entitled to submit his defence in person, except where this would be contrary to the interests of national security. The matter may be brought before the authority by the person himself or by the authorities of the host State at his request. The Court has held that the provisions of Art. 9 must be interpreted broadly as regards the persons to whom they apply. Thus, a foreign national married to a national of a Member State has the right, under Art. 9(2), to refer to the competent authority a decision refusing to issue a first residence permit or ordering his expulsion before the issue of the permit even if he is not in possession of an identity document or even if, where requiring a visa, he has entered the territory of a Member State without one or has remained there after its expiry (Case C-459/99 *MRAX* [2002] ECR I-6591 at pp. I–6671–2).

The differences between Art. 9(1) and Art. 9(2) are, first, that Art. 9(1) covers the case of a Community national who is already lawfully residing within the territory of the host State (either because he already holds a residence permit or because under the law of the host State he is not required to hold one), while Art. 9(2) concerns decisions taken prior to the issue of a first residence permit. Secondly, under Art. 9(1) the opinion of the competent authority must be obtained before the decision is taken, whereas under Art. 9(2) the opinion is obtained after the decision has been taken and only at the request of the person concerned, if he has raised objections (Cases 115/81 etc. *Adoui and Cornuaille*, above, at p. 1711; Case C-175/94 *Gallagher*, above, at pp. I-4275–7). On the other hand, the similarities are, first, that the three situations mentioned in Art. 9(1) apply equally to Art. 9(2), and, secondly, that both Art. 9(1) and (2) apply to persons who are already physically present in the territory of the host Member State (Cases C-65/95 etc. *Shingara and Radiom*, above, at p. I-3390; Case C-357/98 *Yiadom* [2000] ECR I-9265 at pp. I-9298, I-9300).

While Art. 8 provides for legal remedies against 'any decision concerning entry', as well as against decisions refusing the issue or renewal of a residence permit or ordering expulsion, Art. 9 deals only with the last three situations but does not require any legal remedy in respect of decisions refusing entry to the national territory. A Community national who is the subject of such a decision is therefore granted, under Art. 8, only the same legal remedies as are available to the nationals of the host Member State in respect of acts of the administration, but is not entitled to the additional remedies referred to in Art. 9. The limited nature of the procedural safeguards granted to such an individual has been explained by the ECJ by the fact that, as a rule, such a person is not physically present in the host State and it is, therefore, materially impossible for him to submit his defence in person before the competent authority. Where, however, a Community national is temporarily admitted to a Member State pending the investigation of his case and is therefore physically present when a decision is made, a refusal of leave to enter the national territory on grounds of public policy, adopted after an interval of several months, cannot be classified as a 'decision concerning entry' within the meaning of Art. 8, but must be regarded as a decision falling within the scope of Art. 9 and thus entitling the individual to the procedural safeguards referred to therein (Case C-357/98 *Yiadom*, above, at pp. I-9299–301, concerning a Netherlands national of Ghanaian origin who was temporarily admitted to the United Kingdom and resided there for almost seven months before the decision refusing leave to enter was notified to her).

When a Community national who has been refused entry into another Member State for reasons of public policy or public security makes a fresh application after a reasonable time, he is entitled to a new decision which may be the subject of an appeal on the basis of Art. 8 and, where appropriate, Art. 9 of the directive (Cases C-65/95 etc. *Shingara and Radiom*, above, at p. I-3392). The ECJ has confirmed that the remedies contained in Arts. 8 and 9 fulfil the requirement of a 'fair hearing' set out in Art. 6 of the European Convention on Human Rights (Case 98/79 *Pecastaing*, above, at p. 716; Cases C-297/88 etc. *Dzodzi*, above, at p. I-3800).

See also **Expulsion, Freedom of establishment, Freedom to provide services, Free movement of capital, Free movement of goods, Free movement of persons, Public health, Public security, Residence permit, Right of entry and residence, Right to leave, Right to remain.**

Further reading 1. BOOKS: Barnard, *The Substantive Law of the EU. The Four Freedoms* (2004), ch. 14; Craig and de Búrca, *EU Law. Text, Cases, and Materials*, 3rd edn. (2003), ch. 19; Steiner, Woods, and Twigg-Flesner, *Textbook on EC Law*, 8th edn. (2003), ch. 17; Wyatt and Dashwood, *European Union Law*, 4th edn. (2000), ch. 14.

2. ARTICLES: Hall, 'European Convention on Human Rights and Public Policy Exceptions to the Free Movement of Workers under the EEC Treaty' (1991) *EL Rev.* 466; O'Keeffe, 'Practical Difficulties in the Application of Article 48 of the EEC Treaty' (1982) *CML Rev.* 35.

PUBLIC PROCUREMENT

I. The Treaty provisions

The EC Treaty does not specifically refer to public procurement as such. The right of contractors, suppliers, and service providers to be treated equally in the award of public contracts, without regard to their nationality or place of establishment, derives from fundamental principles enshrined in that Treaty, notably the right to equal treatment (Art. 12); the free movement of goods (Arts. 28 to 30); freedom to provide services (Arts. 49 to 56); and the principle of free and fair competition (Arts. 3(1)(g), 81, and 82). The directives that lay down the Community procurement regime reflect the principles set out in those provisions and must be interpreted in accordance with them. The procurement regime laid down in the directives is not exhaustive. Any contracts that do not come within their scope of application, as described below, are subject to the fundamental rules and principles of the EC Treaty and must be awarded accordingly (Case 45/87 *Commission* v. *Ireland* [1988] ECR 4929; Case C-324/98 *Telaustria and Telefonadress* [2000] ECR I-10745; Case C-59/00 *Vestergaard* [2001] ECR I-9505). This means, in effect, that in addition to the specific provisions of the EC Treaty and the directives, the award of contracts must comply with the general principles of equality of treatment at all stages of the procurement process (Case C-243/89 *Commission* v. *Denmark* [1993] ECR I-3353—'Storebælt' case; Case C-87/94 *Commission* v. *Belgium* [1996] ECR I-2043—'Walloon buses' case): transparency with respect to the decision to award a contract and the rules applicable to such award; proportionality with respect to the requirements imposed on tenderers; and mutual recognition of technical specifications and standards and such matters as the qualifications of tenderers.

II. The directives

The Community public procurement regime is set out in four directives. Three directives are applicable to the procurement of works, supplies, and services by State, regional, or local authorities or bodies governed by public law:

- Dir. 93/37 concerning the co-ordination of procedures for the award of public works contracts (*OJ* 1993 L199/54, the 'works directive');
- Dir. 93/36 co-ordinating procedures for the award of public supply contracts (*OJ* 1993 L199/1, the 'supplies directive');
- Dir. 92/50 relating to the co-ordination of procedures for the award of public services contracts (*OJ* 1992 L209/1, the 'services directive');
- A fourth directive deals with the procurement of works, supplies and services by the utilities: Dir. 93/38 on co-ordinating procurement procedures for entities operating in the water, energy, transport and telecommunications sectors (*OJ* 1993 L199/55, the 'utilities directive').

These four directives follow a common pattern, each being divided into six titles containing the following sets of rules:

(*i*) rules defining the scope of application of the directive from the point of view of the entities covered and the types of contract to which it applies;
(*ii*) rules prescribing contract award procedures;
(*iii*) rules on technical specifications;
(*iv*) advertising rules requiring notices to be drawn up in accordance with certain models set out in annexes to the directives and published in the *Official Journal of the European Communities*;
(*v*) common rules on participation comprising objective criteria for the qualitative selection of interested candidates and tenderers;
(*vi*) the criteria upon which contracts must be awarded.

Two further directives lay down the remedies which must be made available to contractors, suppliers, and service providers who have suffered damage as a result of the non-application or the mis-application to them of the Community procurement rules:

- Dir. 89/665 on the co-ordination of the laws, regulations and administrative provisions relating to the application of review procedures to the award of public supply and public works contracts (*OJ* 1989 L395/33, as amended by Dir. 92/50, the 'remedies directive');
- Dir. 92/13 co-ordinating the laws, regulations and administrative provisions relating to the application of Community rules on the procurement procedures of entities operating in the water, energy, transport and telecommunications sectors (*OJ* 1992 L76/14, the 'utilities remedies directive').

III. Legislative history

The development of the Community procurement regime, as set out in the directives, began more than thirty years ago with the adoption of the original works directive, Dir. 71/305 concerning the co-ordination of procedures for the award of public works contracts (*OJ* 1971 L185/5, *OJ Sp. Edn.* 1971(II), p. 682). The directive applied to all contracts for pecuniary consideration concluded in writing between a contractor and a State, regional or local authority, or other persons governed by public law. Contractors could be natural or legal persons, or consortia or both. No definition was given of what constituted a body governed by public law, but Art. 1(b) stated that the concept embraced those entities specified in Annex 1 to the directive. That Annex began by offering a general definition of what constituted, for the purposes of the directive, a body governed by public law but it then proceeded to list the entities conforming to this definition in each Member State. A reading of Art. 1(b) and Annex 1 leads to the conclusion that only the public bodies specified in Annex 1 were to be considered to be covered by the directive. The application of the original works directive was thus defined by reference to the status of the contracting authority without reference to its functions or activities. The value of the contracts covered by the directive was set at a minimum of €1 million. Numerous contracts were excluded from the scope of application of the directive, notably concessions, contracts awarded by utilities, and works subject to special security measures.

The procurement of supplies was first regulated on a Community level by Dir. 77/62 co-ordinating the procedures for the award of public supply contracts (*OJ* 1977 L131/1). The directive had its legal basis in Arts. 28 and 94 EC. It entered into force on 21 December 1978 although it was not properly implemented in many Member States for some considerable time after that date. The structure and content of the supplies directive strongly reflected that of the works directive. It applied to contracts for pecuniary consideration, having a given minimum value, concluded in writing between a supplier and a contracting authority for the supply of products. Such contracts could include siting and installation work. A contracting authority was defined in the same terms as those set out in the works directive. As with the works directive there were a number of contracts exempt from its application.

In spite of their clear provisions, in the years immediately following their adoption, the works and supplies directives had little impact upon the procurement patterns of public sector authorities in the Member States.

In 1974, a report presented to the Commission on the works directive noted that few contracts had been placed with entities situated outside the Member State of the contracting authority. The report concluded that 'in general the construction industry remains completely closed' (Clark and Charpentier, 'Les Achats Publics dans le Marche Commun', SEC(74) 4272).

Some ten years later the situation remained largely unchanged. In a report submitted by the Commission to the Council on the operation of the supplies directive it was concluded that:

> The impact of the public supply directives is in reality marginal . . . only 27% of all contracts awarded by central governments are subject to Community-wide competition ('Public Supply Contracts: Conclusions and Perspectives', COM(84) 717, at p. 12)

The report examined the scope of application of the supplies directive by the Member States concluding that it had been implemented in a haphazard manner, largely dictated by the level of regulation of public procurement on a national level. Member States that had specific legislation on public contracts transposed the directive clearly. The obligations of purchasing authorities were spelt out and the interests of potential suppliers were protected. Where public purchasing contracts were governed by administrative rules the situation was much more unsatisfactory. In those Member States where there was no systemic body of rules regulating public contracts, the works and supplies directives were simply sent to central and local authorities for information purposes. At the same time as the Commission was working on its report on the supplies directive, it was realized that in the case of high technology industries and, in particular, the telecommunications sector, the lack of Community-wide procurement market could be prejudicial to the development of the Community's technological base and the competitivity of Community industry.

IV. The White Paper on the internal market

In the White Paper entitled 'Completing the Internal Market' (COM(85) 210), the Commission proposed a two-fold course of action with respect to the opening up of the Community's public procurement market: the reinforcement of existing legislation and the extension of the procurement regime set out in that legislation to the hitherto largely excluded sectors of water, energy, transport, and telecommunications.

In the years following the publication of the White Paper, the Commission embarked upon an ambitious legislation programme. Beginning first with extensive amendments to the works and supplies directives (Dir. 88/295, *OJ*

1988 L127/1; Dir. 89/440 *OJ* 1989 L210/1), the Commission then proceeded to extend the procurement rules contained in those directives to the procurement of works and supplies by the utilities sectors (Dir. 90/531, *OJ* 1990 297/1), and finally into the domain of services (Dir. 92/50, *OJ* 1992 L209/1).

To ensure the efficacy of the public procurement regime, two directives on the remedies to be made available under national law for breach of the procurement rules were adopted in 1989 and 1992, respectively.

Consolidation of the works, supplies, and utilities directives took place in 1993. In 1996 the Commission published a Green Paper reviewing the application of the public procurement rules in the European Community (COM(96) 583).

A Communication of March 1998 set out the responses received to the Green Paper, which had largely been critical of the implementation of procurement legislation throughout the Community (COM(98) 143). The Communication concluded that legislative instruments governing procurement had to be simplified and adapted to the changing economic environment by facilitating electronic procurement and, in the case of complex contracts, introducing more scope for dialogue between contractors and tenderers. Two draft directives were proposed by the Commission to achieve these objectives in 2000. These directives were finally adopted by the European Parliament and the Council on 31 March 2004. Dir. 2004/17 (*OJ* 2004 L134/1) co-ordinating the procurement procedures of entities operating in the water, energy, transport, and postal services sectors will govern procurement by the utilities and reflects changes in the nature of utilities provision due in particular to the liberalization of those sectors. It will repeal Dir. 93/38. Dir. 2004/18 (*OJ* 2004 L134/114) on the co-ordination of procedures for the award of public works contracts, public supply contracts, and public services contracts will replace the current three directives on the procurement of works, supplies, and services, i.e. Dirs. 92/50, 93/36, and 93/37. Both directives have to be implemented by the Member States by 31 January 2006.

The directives have two main objectives: to simplify and clarify the existing legislation and to adapt it to modern procurement procedures, for example by facilitating electronic procurement and, in the case of complex contracts, by permitting dialogue between contracting authorities and tenderers.

V. Scope of application: general principles

The works, supplies, and services directives apply to all contracts awarded by a contracting authority of a given financial threshold for the procurement of works, supplies, or services. All types of contracts and invitations to tender appear to be covered by the directives (Case 194/88 R *Commission* v. *Italy* [1988] ECR 5647; Case C-399/98 *Ordine degli Architetti* [2001] ECR I-5409).

The contracts must be in writing and for consideration.

Contracting authorities are defined in each of the directives as the State, regional or local authorities, governed by public law, associations formed by one or several of such authorities, or bodies governed by public law. In Case 31/87 *Beentjes* [1988] ECR 4635, the ECJ held that the definition of contracting authorities within the works directive should be interpreted in functional terms:

. . . the term 'State' must be interpreted in functional terms. The aims of the directive, which is to ensure the effective attainment of freedom of establishment and freedom to provide services in respect of public works contracts, would be jeopardized if the provisions of the directive were to be held inapplicable solely because a public works contracts is awarded by a body which, although it was set up to carry out tasks entrusted to tit by legislation, it is not formally a part of the State administration (ibid. para. 11).

A body governed by public law is an entity closely dependent on the State, a local or regional authority, or another body governed by public law (Case C-44/96 *Mannesmann* [1998] ECR I-73; Case C-237/99 *Commission* v. *France* [2001] ECR I-939; Cases C-223/99 etc. *Agorà and Excelsior* [2001] ECR I-3605). Such close dependence may result in the State having an influence on the purchasing decisions of the entity in question.

The works, supplies, and services directives define 'a body governed by public law' in terms of three criteria:

Body governed by public law means any body:

- established for the specific purpose of meeting needs in the general interest, not having an industrial or commercial character and,
- having legal personality, and
- financed, for the most part, by the State or regional or local authorities to bodies governed by public law; or subject to management supervision by those bodies; or having an administrative, managerial or supervisory board. More than half of whose members are appointed by the State, regional or local authorities, or other bodies governed by public law.

These three conditions are cumulative (Case C-44/96 *Mannesmann*, above, para. 21).

The directives do not define what is meant by 'meeting needs in the general interest not having an industrial or commercial nature'. The following activities have been held by the ECJ to be in the general interest: the issuing of official documents such as passports, driving licences, and identity cards (*Mannesmann*, above); the collection and treatment of household refuse (Case C-360/96 *BFI Holding* [1998] ECR I-6821); the maintenance of national woods and of a forestry industry (Case C-306/97 *Connemara Machine Turf* [1998] ECR I-8761); the running of a university (Case C-380/98 *University of Cambridge* [2000] ECR I-8035); the provision of low rent housing (Case C-237/99 *Commission* v. *France* [2001] ECR I-939); the buying, selling, and leasing of property and the supply of property maintenance services by a town (Case C-18/01 *Korhonen* [2003] ECR I-5321); and the organization of exhibitions and fairs (Cases C-223/99 etc. *Agora and Excelsior*, above). From this case-law it would appear that needs in the general interest are those which are met otherwise than by the availability of goods or services in the market place or which for reasons associated with the general interest the State chooses to provide itself or over which provision it wishes to retain a decisive influence (Case C-360/96 *BFI Holding*, above). Recently the ECJ has held:

> if a body operates in normal market conditions, aims to make a profit, and bears the losses associated with the exercise of its activity, it is unlikely that the needs it aims to meet are not of an individual or commercial character (Case C-18/01 *Korhonen*, above, para. 51).

The third criterion is designed to ensure that contracting entities are not subject to any influence in their decision-making process by virtue of their dependence (either financial, managerial, or administrative) on the State, regional or local authorities, or other bodies governed by public law. Financed 'for the most part' has been held to mean financed by more than 50% (Case C-380/98 *University of Cambridge*, above).

'Management supervision' must be interpreted in a functional sense and turns on the question of whether the supervision in question give rise to influence over the contracting entity in relation to the award of the contract (Case C-237/99 *Commission* v. *France*, above).

VI. The works directive

The works directive applies to all public works contracts whose estimated value, net of VAT, is not less that €5 million (Art. 6).

Public works contracts are defined in Art. 1(a) as contracts for pecuniary interest concluded in writing between a contractor and a contracting authority and which have as their objective either the execution or both the design and execution of:

(*i*) a work defined in Art. 1(a) of the directive, that is the outcome of a building or civil engineering works taken as a whole which is sufficient of itself to fulfil a technical or economic function; or

(*ii*) a work corresponding to the requirements specified by the contracting authority; or

(*iii*) works related to one of the activities referred to in Annex II of the directive.

Member States are obliged to ensure a contracting authority complies with the works directive where such a contracting authority subsidizes directly by more than 50% of its value, any works contract. Thus, for example, although educational establishments may not be contracting authorities within the meaning of the works directive, their works contracts will be subject to the provisions of the directive if such works are subsidized by more than 50% of their value by an entity that is a contracting authority within the meaning of the directive. The term 'subsidize' is not defined in the directive, save that it extends only to direct subsidies in cash or in kind granted by a contracting authority for the execution of a works contract for which the recipient is not obliged to do anything in return.

Public works concession contracts having a value in excess €5 million are within the scope of the works directive.

A public works concession is defined as a public works contract the consideration for which consists either solely in the right to exploit the construction after completion or this right together with some payment (Art. 1(d) of Dir. 93/73).

Contracting authorities may require the concessionaire to award contracts of at least 30% of the total value of the work to be performed by third parties. If this is the case either the precise percentage in question must be specified in the concession contract or alternatively the contracting authority may require candidates to specify in their tenders the extent to which they intend to subcontract the work (Art. 3).

Only the works directive covers concessions. There is no similar provision in the services directive although, of course, services concessions are governed by the general EC Treaty rules (Case C-360/96 *BFI Holding*, above; Interpretative communication on concessions under Community law, *OJ* 2000 C121/2).

Lots. Where works are subdivided into several lots, each of which is the subject of a contract, the value of each lot must be taken into account when determining the value of the works to be carried out a whole. Where the aggregate value of all lots is €5 million or more, the directive applies to all lots.

Splitting. No work or contract for work may be split with the intention of avoiding the application of the works directive (Case 31/87 *Beentjes*, above). Where the value of a contract is calculated to include all the work necessary to make the project operational, i.e. finished and ready for intended use, it may be awarded in lots but this must be stated in the tender notice (Art. 6(4)).

VII. The supplies directive

The supplies directive applies to all public supply contracts that are defined as being contracts for pecuniary interest concluded in writing involving the purchase, lease, rental, or hire purchase with or without an option to buy, of products between a supplier and a contracting authority. The delivery of such products may include siting and installation operations (Art. 1(a)).

The directive only applies to contracts award by central government whose estimated value is €162,283. The corresponding figure for contracts awarded by other contracting entities subject to the directive, is €249,681 (*OJ* 2001 C332/03).

In the case of contracts for lease, rental, hire purchase of products, the basis calculating the estimated contract value is:

- in the case of fixed-term contracts where their term is twelve months or less, the total contract value for its duration, or where the term exceeds twelve months, its total value including the estimated residual value (Art. 5(2));

- in the case of contracts for an indefinite period or in cases where there is doubt as to the duration of contracts, the monthly value multiplied by 48 (Art. 5(2)).

The value of regular contracts or contracts which are to be renewed within a given time is to be established on the basis of:

- either the actual aggregation value of similar contracts concluded over the previous twelve-month period, or
- the estimates aggregate value during the twelve months following the first delivery or during the term of the contract where that is greater than twelve months.

The selection of valuation method must not be done with the intent of avoiding the application of the directive.

As with the procurement of works, no procurement may be split up with the intent of avoiding the application of the directive (Art. 5(b)). If several contracts of the same type are to be used for the procurement in question, the estimated value is the sum total of each contract (Art. 5(4)).

VIII. The services directive

The value threshold at which the services directive becomes applicable is the same as that of the supplies directive. A contract is to be valued by reference to the total remuneration to be paid to the service provider (Art. 7(2)). Contracts may not be split with a view to avoiding the operation of the directive.

In the case of contracts that do not specify the total price for the services to be provided, two methods are laid down for the calculation of their value for the purposes of determining whether the directive applies: one method is to be used in the case of fixed-term contracts, the other is to be applied in cases of contracts of indefinite duration. Where a contract is for a term not exceeding forty-eight months, the value of the contract is the total contract value for its duration. When a contract for indefinite duration or for a term exceeding forty-eight months, the monthly instalment due in respect of the services multiplied by 48 is to be taken as the contract value.

Where contracts are for the provision of regular services or may be renewed within a given time their contract value may be established on the basis of:

- either the actual aggregate cost of similar contracts for the same category of services awarded over the previous fiscal year or twelve-month period, adjusted, where possible for anticipated changes in volume or value over the twelve months following the initial contract; or
- the estimated aggregate cost during the twelve months following the service performed or during the term of the contract, where this is greater than twelve months (Art. 7(6)).

Where services are subdivided into lots, the value of each lot must be taken into account for the purpose of establishing whether the threshold laid down in the directive has been met.

The directive specifies a number of services and contracts which are exempt from its provisions (Art. 1(a)). Exempted services include contracts for the acquisition or rental of land, contracts for arbitration, or conciliation services, employment contracts, contracts which concern the essential interests of the security of the State, and public service contracts awarded by an entity, which is itself a contracting authority. Public works and public supply contracts are also excluded as are contracts awarded by the utilities.

Although the services directive applies to all contracts for services coming within its scope, it may not apply in the same way to them (Arts. 8 to 10). For the purposes of the application of the directive, services are divided into two categories generally known as priority services and non-priority service or residual services. Priority services are listed in Annex 1A to the directive; non-priority or residual services are listed in Annex 1B.

Priority services are subject to the full rigours of the directive. Residual services are only subject to the rules relating to technical specifications and standards. Where a contract envisages the provision of a number of services, some of which are priority and others residual, the nature of the contract is to be determined by the relative value of its components.

IX. The utilities directive

The utilities directive differs from the works, supplies, and services directives in a number of respects. Most importantly it allows the use of the negotiated procedure in awarding contract (contract award procedures are discussed below) and a system of qualification, that is the established of a list of qualified suppliers to whom contracts can be awarded. Provision is also made for the use of framework agreements, that is agreements which establish the terms under which a provider can enter into a works, supplies, or services contract or a series of them but which does not in itself award such a contract. Framework agreement are unique to the utilities directive.

The applicability of the utilities directive is determined by a complex series of considerations. As with the works, supplies, and services directives, an entity must be a public body and the contract to be awarded must fall above the threshold values specified. Additionally the awarding entity must provide one of the types of services specified in the directive. These criteria are cumulative: if only one is satisfied the directive does not apply. The use of a two-fold criterion is necessary in the case of procurement by the utilities in view of the mixed legal nature of the entities operating in the utilities sectors some of which are governed by public law, others by private law. In addition, some are fully open to competitive market forces (hence rendering the application of procurement regime superfluous) whilst others are protected from market forces.

Art. 2(2) of the utilities directive defines the relevant activities for the purposes of the directive as:

(a) the provision or operation of fixed networks intended to provide a service to the public in connection with the production, transport or distribution of:
  (i) drinking water; or
  (ii) electricity;
  (iii) gas or heat, or the supply of drinking water, electricity, gas or heat to such networks;
(b) the exploitation of a geographical area for the purpose of:
  (i) exploring for or extracting oil, gas or coal or other solid fuels, or
  (ii) the provision of airport, maritime or inland transport or other terminal facilities to carriers by air sea or inland waterway;
(c) the operation of networks providing a service to the public in the field of transport, by railway, automated systems, tramway, trolley bus or cable. As regards transport services, a network is considered to exist where the service is provided or is operating under conditions laid down by competent authorities, such as rules on the routes to be served, the capacity to be made available or the frequency of the service;
(d) the provision or operation of public telecommunications networks or the provision of one or more public communications services.

In addition to being engaged in the provision of one of the above-mentioned services the contracting entity must be:

(*i*) a public authority;
(*ii*) a public undertaking;
(*iii*) an entity constituted under public or private law that operates on the basis of special or exclusive rights granted by a competent authority of a Member State (Art. 2).

Special or exclusive rights are defined as:

rights deriving from authorizations granted by the competent authority of the Member State concerned by law, regulation or administrative action having as their result the reservation for one or more entities of the exploitation of one of the activities defined in para. 2 [of Art. 2].

In particular, a contracting entity is to be considered as enjoying special or exclusive rights where: (*i*) for the purpose of constructing networks or facilities referred to in the list of activities set out in Art. 2(2) it may take advantage of a procedure for the expropriation or the use of property or may place network equipment on, under or over a public highway; (*ii*) where an entity provides or operates a fixed network providing a service to the public that is connected with the production, transport, or distribution of drinking water, electricity or gas, or heat to a network, which is itself operated by an entity enjoying special or exclusive rights granted by the competent authority of the Member State concerned (Art. 2(3)).

The directive has a number of mandatory and optional exceptions.

The following sectors are excluded on a mandatory basis from the directive:

(*i*) air transport services;
(*ii*) shipping;
(*iii*) the operation of sea ferries;

(*iv*) bus transport services provided entities are free to provide such services in general or in a particular geographical area, under the same conditions as contracting authorities;
(*v*) the purchase of water supplies;
(*vi*) the supply of drinking water, electricity or gas to networks that provide a service to the public is not an activity within the scope of the directive and hence an entity operating such a network is not bound by the rules of the directive provided the conditions set out in the directive are fulfilled;
(*vii*) contracts for voice telephony, telex, and services;
(*viii*) contracts for the acquisition of land or buildings;
(*ix*) services awarded by utilities to a relevant affiliated undertaking or by a joint venture to a utility which is one of its members or to a relevant affiliated undertaking of a member utility.

Member States may ask the Commission to exempt activities connected with the exploitation of geographical areas for the purposes of exploiting oil, gas, or other solid fuels (Art. 3).

To come within the scope of the directive, the contract to be awarded must have an estimated value net of VAT, of not less than:

(*i*) €400,000 in the case of supply and services contracts including design contests awarded by entities operating in the water, energy, and transport sectors;
(*ii*) €600,000 in the case of supply and services contracts including design contests awarded by entities exercising activities in the telecommunications sector;
(*iii*) €5 million in the case of works contracts.

X. Contract award procedures

The directives provide for three types of contract award procedure: open, restricted, and negotiated. In the case of the open procedure all interested parties may submit tenders. A contracting authority simply advertises the contract to be awarded and whoever wishes submits a bid. Where the restricted procedure is used, only those contractors invited to submit bids may do so. In the case of the negotiated procedure, contracting authorities consult contractors of their choice and negotiate the terms of the contract with one or more of them.

Contractors who submit tenders either following an open procedure or as a result of being selected to participate in a restricted procedure are known as 'tenderers'. Contractors who seek an invitation to take part in a restricted or negotiated procedures are known as 'candidates'. Bidding for a contract to be awarded by the open procedure is done in a single stage: a contracting authority advertises the contract to be awarded and as many contractors as wish to tender can put in bids. The contract is then awarded to the bid which best satisfies the award criteria laid down by the contracting authority.

By contrast, the bid procedure in the case of a restricted or negotiated procedure falls into two distinct stages: the first is concerned with the selection of candidates; the second with the submission and examination of bids. The contracting authority invites candidates to participate in the award of a particular contract. Once the list of candidates is established, the contracting authority selects which contractors it will invite to submit tenders or to enter into negotiations.

A contracting authority is free to use the open or the restricted contract award procedure at its discretion. The use of the negotiated procedure is restricted to the circumstances set out in each of the directives (Art. 7(3) of the works and supplies directives; Art. 11(2) and (3) of the services directive). These include situations of urgency (e.g. natural catastrophe) where a contract needs to be awarded immediately or where there is little point in going through the procurement procedure because only one supplier is in a position to perform the contract due to its artistic or technical characteristics. In the case of the utilities directive, the negotiated procedure can be used as an alternative to the open or restricted procedure; its use is not constrained in the same way as is the case with procurement by non-utilities.

Each directive lays down a timeframe for the completion of each stage of the procurement process. This enables all interested bidders to formulate their bids effectively.

XI. Advertising requirements

In general, three types of notice are required to be published in the *Official Journal of the European Communities*: (*i*) a prior indicative notice; (*ii*) a call for competition; and (*iii*) a contract award notice. The form which the notices must take is set out in Dir. 2001/78 (*OJ* 2001 L285/1).

XII. Technical specifications

Technical specifications should define, in objective terms, the characteristics of the work, supplies, or services to be procured. Examples of technical specifications include quality, performance, safety or dimensions, packaging, marketing, and labelling. The directives lay down detailed rules as to how contracting authorities are to describe these requirements. As a general rule a functional description should be used. There is a strict prohibition on any reference to products of a specific make, source, or particular process especially any indication of trade marks, patents, or types since such descriptions could favour particular producers over others (Art. 8(6) of the supplies directive; Art. 10(6) of the works directive; Art. 14(6) of the services directive; Art. 18(5) of the utilities directive). Descriptions based on national products or standards are prohibited as being potentially discriminatory (Case 45/87 *Commission* v. *Ireland*, above).

Technical specifications should be defined, in the first place by reference to national standards implementing or by reference or European technical approvals or common technical specifications. A number of exceptions to the general rules exist. For example, there is no obligation to describe products by reference to European standards where to do so would oblige a contracting authority to acquire goods incompatible with equipment already in use or would entail disproportionate costs or disproportionate technical difficulties.

XIII. Selection and participation

The directives offers guidance to contracting authorities to assist in the selection of eligible bidders. These relate primarily to grounds on which bidders can be eliminated from the tendering process.

A contractor can be considered to be ineligible to tender for or to be awarded a contract in the following circumstances:

(*i*) if he is in a state of bankruptcy, insolvency, compulsory winding up, administration, receivership, or any other analogous state, or subject to relevant proceedings;
(*ii*) if he has been convicted of any criminal offence relating to business conduct;
(*iii*) if he has committed an act of grave misconduct in the course of business;
(*iv*) if he has not fulfilled obligation relating to the payment of taxes or social security contributions;
(*v*) if he is guilty of serious misreprestation in supply information;
(*vi*) if he has not registered on the professional or trade register of the relevant State in which he is established.

XIV. Economic and financial standing

Contracting authorities have the right to decide for themselves what standard of economic and financial standing they require (Cases 27/86 etc. *CEI and Bellini* [1987] ECR 3347). The directives set out a number of ways in which the appropriate financial and economic standing may be established:

(*i*) appropriate bankers statements;
(*ii*) statement of accounts;
(*iii*) statements of overall turnover and turnover over the past three years.

A contractor may rely on resources which are not its own but belong to others, provided that those resources are available to it, in order to prove technical, financial, or economic standing. In Case C-389/92 *Ballast Nedam I* [1994] ECR I-1289, the ECJ held that the contracting authority may admit in the tendering procedure a holding company which does not itself execute works but which intends to employ to the resources of a subsidiary. In Case C-5/97 *Ballast Nedam II* [1997] ECR I-7549, it was held that the contracting authority is obliged (not merely permitted) to take account references from the applicant's subsidiaries when assessing the suitability of the applicant in such cases.

XV. Award criteria

The directives provide for two award criteria:

(*i*) lowest price;
(*ii*) the most economically advantageous tender.

The criterion to be used must be specified in the published contract notice calling for tenders.

The most commonly used criterion is the 'most economically advantageous offer'. Examples of the criteria which may be used are quality, technical merit, aesthetic, and functional characteristics, technical assistance and after-sales services, delivery date, delivery period or period of completion, running costs, cost effectiveness, and price. The specific criteria to be used in the award of a contract must be published in the contract documents or contract notice, preferably in descending order of preference so that tenders can properly tailor their bids. Award criteria must be transparent in the sense that they must be readily intelligible to all reasonable informed and normally diligent tenderers. The award criteria must be applied in the same way throughout the procurement process and must be applies in an objective and uniform way to all tenders.

In determining the most economically advantageous tender the principle of non-discrimination must be observed. Any criterion that favours local tenderers and that is likely to make it more difficult for potential tenderers established in other Member State to be awarded the contract will constitute a restriction on freedom of movement of services. Furthermore no criterion can have the effect of giving a contracting authority unrestricted freedom of choice in selecting the winning tender (Case 31/87 *Beentjes*, above, para. 26).

Award criteria must bring some economic benefit to the awarding authority (Case C-380/98 *University of Cambridge*, above) and must be linked to the subject-matter of the contract or the manner in which it is to be performed.

The issue of whether public policy objectives such as the environment or social policy can be pursued through the public procurement process has been the subject of a number of cases before the ECJ. In *Beentjes*, the Court held that a criterion relating to the employment of the long-term unemployed was compatible with the works directive if it has no direct or indirect discriminatory effect on tenderers from other Member States. An additional specific condition of this kind must be mentioned in the contract notice. This principle was followed in Case C-225/98 *Commission* v. *France* [2000] ECR I-7445. Case C-513/99 *Concordia Bus Finland* [2002] ECR I-7213 arose out of a dispute concerning the award of a contract to the City of Helsinki for the operation of bus services in Helsinki. It was alleged by a disappointed tenderer that the procurement rules had been infringed in that additional points had been obtained at the award stage by bidders who proposed the use of buses with nitrate oxide emissions and noise levels below certain thresholds. Moreover, the transport company of the City of Helsinki, also bidding for the contract, was one of the few companies which owned buses powered by natural gas which fulfilled these requirements. The Court held that the criteria set out in the directives may be used to determine the most economically advantageous tender were not exhaustive. Non-economic factors such as environmental criteria may also be used but such criteria must be linked to the subject-matter of the contract, must be specified in the contract notice, and must be compatible with the other rules of EC law.

This case-law prompted the Commission to issue two interpretative communications on the issue (Commission interpretative communication on the Community law applicable to public procurement and the possibility of integrating environmental consideration into public procurement, COM(2001) 274; Commission interpretative communication on the Community law applicable to public procurement and the possibility of integrating social considerations into public procurement, COM(2001) 566).

XVI. Abnormally low bids

Abnormally low bids may not be automatically excluded from the award process on the basis of the application of mathematically formulae (Case 76/81 *Transporoute* [1982] ECR 417; Case 103/88 *Fratelli Costanzo* [1989] ECR 1839; Cases C-285/99 etc. *Lombardini* [2001] ECR I-9233). Before rejecting an abnormally low tender, a contracting authority must require the contractor in question to explain the individual components of his tender. The contracting authority must then verify those elements in the light of any information it has received from the supplier. Where tenders are rejected as being abnormally low a contracting authority must inform the Commission of its reasons for doing so (*Transporoute; Fratelli Costanzo*; Case C-295/89 *Donà Alfonso* [1991] ECR I-2967).

XVII. Enforcement and remedies

There are two directives laying down minimum remedies that must be made available to persons claiming to have suffered damage as a result of non-compliance with the procurement rules: Dir. 89/665 on the co-ordination of the laws, regulations and administrative provisions relating to the application of review procedures to the award of public supply and public works contracts rules (*OJ* 1989 L395/33, the 'remedies directive') and Dir. 92/13 co-ordinating the laws, regulations and administrative provisions relating to the Community rules on the procurement procedures of entities operating in the water, energy, transport and telecommunications sectors (*OJ* 1992 L76/14, the 'utilities remedies directive').

XVIII. The remedies directive

The remedies directive was extended by Dir. 92/50 to contract procedures governing the award of contracts for services (*OJ* 1992 L209/1). It requires Member States to adopt the measures necessary to ensure that, with respect to the works, supplies, and services directives, decision taken by contracting authorities may be reviewed effectively and rapidly on the grounds that such decisions have infringed Community law in the field of public procurement or national rules implementing them (Art. 2(1)). Member States must appoint a body responsible for reviewing procurement decisions. They are free to confer such powers upon any entity within their judicial or administrative system. Decisions of review bodies must be capable of effective enforcement (Art. 2(7)).

Any person having or having had an interest in obtaining a particular contract and who has been or risks being harmed may bring an action for review of the procurement process, but he must first inform the contracting authority of the alleged infringement and of his intention to seek review of its decision. It is to be hoped that contracting authorities which have inadvertently breached the Community rules will, at this stage, voluntarily take the steps necessary to cure any fault in their procedures or practices (Art. 1(3)).

Although the concept of 'interested person' is broadly defined, it seems to require that a person must have a direct interest in the contract award procedure which is the subject of the proceedings.

XIX. Procedures

The detailed rules under which the review procedures are to be made available to aggrieved persons have to be established by the Member States themselves but are subject to the general principle of equality of treatment and to the minimum standards specified in Art. 2 of the directive. Authorities entrusted with review procedures must be empowered to:

(*i*) take at the earliest opportunity and by way of interlocutory procedures, interim measures to correct the infringement and to prevent further damage, including measures to correct the alleged infringement and to prevent further damage, including measures to suspend or to ensure the suspension of the procedures to award a contract to the implementation of any decision relating to that award;

(*ii*) either to set aside or to ensure the setting aside of decision taken unlawfully, including the removal of discriminatory technical, economic, or financial specifications in the invitation to tender, the contract documents or any other document relating to the contract award procedures;

(*iii*) award damages to person harmed by the infringement.

No indication is given as to how damages are to be quantified nor are the conditions under which interim relief is to be granted. These are matters that are left to each Member State to organize in accordance with its own rules and practices.

Review procedures do not have an automatic suspensive effect on contract award procedures (Art. 2(3)). The effect of any review proceedings on any contract already concluded is a matter for national law (Art. 2(6)). Member States may provide that an award of damages can only be made after the decision that has allegedly caused loss has been set aside (Art. 2(5)). There is no right to interim relief: where interim measures are requested the responsible body must weigh up the consequences of such an order for all concerned, including the general public. Where the negative consequences of suspending a contract award procedure would exceed its benefits the review body may decline to make an order (Art. 2(4)).

XX. Appeals

Where bodies responsible for review procedures are not judicial in character, written reasons for the decisions must be given and those decisions must be reviewable by another independent entity that is a court or tribunal for the purposes of Art. 234 EC.

XXI. The corrective mechanism

Although the remedies directive is primarily concerned with the introduction of minimum standards of redress on a national level, Art. 3 thereof creates a new Community procedure commonly known as the 'corrective mechanism', the objective of which is to rectify any breach of the Community procurement rules before a contract is awarded. Where, before the award of a contract, the Commission believes that a clear and manifest infringement of the Community rule on public procurement has been committed during a contract award procedure (Art. 3(1)). In such an event the Commission must notify the Member State and the contracting authority concerned of the reasons that led it to conclude that a clear and manifest infringement has been committed and to request its correction. Within twenty-one days of the receipt of this notification the Member State concerned must notify the Commission either that the infringement in question has been corrected or offer a reasoned submission as to why no correction has been made or that the contract award procedure has been suspended.

XXII. The utilities remedies directive

Although the remedies directive and the utilities remedies directive have the same objective, there are significant differences between the two measures. The particular characteristics of the utilities and their organization within the different Member States require procedures additional to those provided for by the remedies directive, to be made available against contracting authorities operating in the utilities sector. Accordingly the range of remedies to be made available to aggrieved bidders by Member States is broader and more detailed. For example, payment of a sum of money of a level to be high enough to dissuade a contracting authority from committing or persisting in an infringement. Obviously, this must be set at a level that takes into account the size of the contract awarded and the scale of the awarding entity. Whilst there is no indication in the directive of what this sum might be, early drafts of the directive suggest that, in general the amount in question should not be less at than 1% of the value of the contract (COM(91) 158 at p. 31).

Proof of, and the fixing of the level of damages, are a matter for national law but where a claim for damages represents only the cost of preparing the bid or participating in the contract award procedure, the person making the claim is required to prove only three factors:

(*i*) an infringement of Community law in the field of procurement or national rules implementing that law; and

(*ii*) that he would have had a real chance of winning the contract in question; and (*iii*) as a consequence of the infringement the chance was adversely affected (Art. 2(7)).

The disappointed contractor is not required to prove that he would have won the contract but merely that an infringement had occurred and that infringement materially affected his right to a favorably opportunity to compete for that contract.

Further the directive in Art. 2(7) provides that a complainant who is seeking to recover tendering costs need not prove that he would have won the contract but merely that an infringement occurred and this affected his chances to compete for the contract. Whilst Art. 2(7) makes a claim for damages for bidding costs relatively easy, if a claimant want to claim more than his costs he is entitled to claim for recovery of lost profits. Damages for such loss involved complex issues which are to be resolved by the Member States in the context of their particular approaches to the quantification of economic loss (COM(90) 287, para. 16).

XXIII. Attestation

Chapter 2 of the utilities directive provides for a new type of remedy called 'attestation'. It has no counterpart in the remedies directive. The purpose of attestation is to provide an independent confirmation that the contracting authority, which has been attested, has taken account of its obligations under the utilities directive; taken steps to ensure that those rules and procedures were effectively applied within its organization; and has implemented its rules in such a way as to give supplier and contractors to secure a fair award of the contracts.

The directive lays down the essential requirements of the attestation system. Attestors must be independent of contracting authorities and must present their reports in writing to the contracting authorities.

XXIV. Conciliation

Chapter 4 of the utilities remedies directive provides for a conciliation procedure at a Community level to be made available to interested parties as a non-litigious method of dispute settlement but without prejudice to the rights of the parties to undertake review proceedings. There is no provision in the remedies directive for such a procedure.

See also **Freedom to provide services.**

Further reading Arrowsmith, *The Law of Public and Utilities Procurement* (1996, new edition due in June 2005); Diggins and Bennett, *EC Public Procurement* (2003; two-volume looseleaf updated regularly); Fernandez Martin, *The EC Public Procurement Rules* (1996).

► **PUBLIC SECURITY** One of the grounds on which the Member States may derogate from certain provisions of Community law (other, closely related grounds for derogations include public policy and public health). Thus, under Art. 96(1) Euratom, the Member States may impose limitations, on grounds of public policy, public security, or public health, on the right of the nationals of other Member States to take skilled employment in the field of nuclear energy.

Under the EC Treaty, the Member States may impose restrictions, justified on grounds of public policy, public security, or public health, on the free movement of goods (Art. 30); free movement of workers (Art. 39(3)); freedom of establishment (Art. 46(1)); freedom to provide services (Art. 46(1) in conjunction with Art. 55); and free movement of capital (Art. 58(1)(b)). Moreover, those grounds may be relied upon not only by Member States but also by individuals in order to justify limitations on the free movement of workers under agreements or other measures adopted by persons governed by private law (Case C-415/93 *Bosman* [1995] ECR I-4921 at p. I-5066; Case C-350/96 *Clean Car Autoservice* [1998] ECR I-2521 at pp. I-2545–6).

In addition to the above provisions, Art. 296 authorizes the Member States not to supply information the disclosure of which may be contrary to the essential interests of their security, and to take such measures as they consider necessary for the protection of essential security interests that are connected with the production of or trade in arms, munitions, and war material. Under Art. 297, Member States are permitted to take the necessary measures in the event of serious internal disturbances affecting the maintenance of law and order, in the event of war, serious international tension constituting a threat of war, or in order to carry out their obligations in connection with the maintenance of peace and international security. However, the Member States must consult each other with a view to taking together the steps needed to prevent the functioning of the common market being affected by such measures.

The concept of public security is not defined by Community law. The case-law of the ECJ shows that that concept does not have a single and specific meaning. Thus, it covers both the internal security of a Member State (see Art. 64(1) EC) and its external security (Case C-367/89 *Richardt* [1991] ECR I-4621 at p. I-4652; Case C-70/94 *Werner* [1995] ECR I-3189 at p. I-3227), as well as the interruption of supplies of essential commodities such as petroleum products which may threaten the very existence of a country (Case 72/83 *Campus Oil* [1984] ECR 2727 at p. 2751; all three cases concern the free movement of goods). Thus, the safeguarding of energy supplies in the event of a crisis falls within the ambit of public security (Case C-483/99 *Commission* v. *France* [2002] ECR I-4781 at p. I-4804; Case C-503/99 *Commission* v. *Belgium* [2002] ECR I-4809 at pp. I-4832–3; both cases concern the free movement of capital). So do police measures taken against a member of an armed and organized group whose activity constitutes a threat to public order (Case C-100/01 *Oteiza Olazabal* [2002] ECR I-10981, para. 35, concerning the free movement of persons). The concept of public security can also encompass situations in which public access to particular documents could obstruct the attempts of authorities to prevent criminal activities (Case T-174/95 *Svenska Journalistförbundet* v. *Council* [1998] ECR II-2289 at p. II-2326).

The Member States are, in principle, free to determine the requirements of public security in the light of their national needs. Nevertheless, being a derogation from the fundamental principle of free movement, the concept of public security must be interpreted strictly so that its scope cannot be determined unilaterally by each Member State without any control by the Community institutions. Thus, public security may be relied on only if there is a genuine and sufficiently serious threat to a fundamental interest of society, and the principle of proportionality must also be observed. This means that any derogation must remain within the limits of what is appropriate and necessary for achieving the desired objective. Moreover, the derogation must not serve purely economic ends and any person affected by a restrictive measure based on such derogation must have access to legal redress (Case C-54/99 *Église de Scientologie* [2000] ECR I-1335 at pp. I-1361–2; Case C-423/98 *Albore* [2000] ECR I-5965 at p. I-6002; Case C-483/99 *Commission* v. *France*, above, at p. I-4804; Case C-503/99 *Commission* v. *Belgium*, above, at p. I-4833; all of these cases concern the free movement of capital).

The ECJ has held that the provisions of the EC Treaty which allow derogations on grounds of public security (Arts. 30, 39(3), 46(1), 55, 58(1)(b), 64(1), 296, and 297) deal with exceptional and clearly defined cases. Because of their limited character, those Articles cannot be interpreted broadly. It is not possible to infer from them that there is inherent in the Treaty a general exception covering all measures taken for reasons of public security. If every provision of Community law were subject to a general exception, the Court has pointed out, regardless of the specific requirements laid down by the Treaty, this might prejudice the binding nature of Community law and its uniform application. Most of the derogations mentioned above concern only the free movement of goods, persons, services, and capital, and not the social provisions of the Treaty, including the principle of equal treatment of men and women. This principle is not subject to any general derogation on grounds of public security, even in relation to the organization of the armed forces, apart from the possible application of Art. 297, which concerns a wholly exceptional situation. The principle of equal treatment is governed entirely by the specific provisions of Dir. 76/207 (*OJ* 1976 L39/40) (Case 222/84 *Johnston* [1986] ECR 1651 at p. 1684; Case C-273/97 *Sirdar* [1999] ECR I-7403 at pp. I-7439–40; Case C-186/01 *Dory* [2003] ECR I-2479, paras. 29–36. *See further under* **Equal treatment**).

The special measures which Member States may adopt under the EC Treaty on grounds of public security concerning the free movement and residence of Community nationals have been co-ordinated by Council Dir. 64/221 of 25 February 1964 (*OJ Sp. Edn.* 1963–4, p. 117). The directive lays down both substantive rules and procedural safeguards, which apply equally to measures adopted on grounds of public policy, public security, and public health (Art. 2(1)). Its provisions are considered in detail under a separate entry (*see further under* **Public policy**. For public security in the context of the free movement of capital and goods, *see under* **Free movement of capital,** section IV, **Free movement of goods,** section III.1).

See also **Equal treatment, Free movement of capital, Free movement of goods, Public health, Public policy.**

Further reading: Peers, 'National Security and European Law' (1996) *YEL* 363.

► **PUBLIC SERVICE** Art. 39(4) EC provides that the rules laid down in Art. 39 concerning freedom of movement for workers within the Community and the prohibition of discrimination on grounds of nationality are not to apply to employment in the 'public service'. However, neither the Treaty itself nor any act of secondary legislation defines the concept of 'public service'. Nevertheless, in several cases the ECJ has established certain criteria for interpreting this concept, which may be summarized as follows.

First, being a derogation from the fundamental principles of free movement and non-discrimination, Art. 39(4) must be construed narrowly, in such a way as to limit its scope to what is strictly necessary for safeguarding the interests which it allows the Member States to protect (Case 66/85 *Lawrie-Blum* [1986] ECR 2121 at p. 2146; Case 225/85 *Commission* v. *Italy* [1987] ECR 2625 at p. 2638; see also Case 152/73 *Sotgiu* [1974] ECR 153 at p. 162).

Secondly, the concept of public service requires uniform interpretation and application throughout the Community (Case 149/79 *Commission* v. *Belgium* [1980] ECR 3881 at p. 3901).

Thirdly, the interpretation of that concept cannot be based on domestic law alone as this would restrict the effectiveness and scope of the rules of Community law relating to the free movement of workers and equality of treatment (ibid. at p. 3903; Case 307/84 *Commission* v. *France* [1986] ECR 1725 at pp. 1738–9).

Fourthly, the scope of the exception in Art. 39(4) cannot be determined by reference to the nature of the legal relationship between the employee and the employing administration, and therefore it is irrelevant whether a worker is engaged as a workman, a clerk, or an official and whether he is employed under public or private law. These legal designations can be varied at will by the Member States, which could thus unilaterally extend the number of posts covered by the exception. These designations cannot therefore provide a criterion for interpretation appropriate to Community law. Access to certain posts may not be limited by reason of the fact that in a given Member State persons appointed to such posts have the status of civil servants or are governed by staff regulations which provide for establishment (Case 152/75 *Sotgiu*, above, at p. 163; Case 307/84 *Commission* v. *France*, above, at p. 1738; Case 66/85 *Lawrie-Blum*, above, at p. 2146; Case 225/85 *Commission* v. *Italy*, above, at p. 2638).

Fifthly, while Art. 39(4) allows Member States to restrict access of foreign nationals to certain activities in the public service, once such nationals have been admitted to the public service, Art. 39(4) cannot justify discriminatory measures with regard to remuneration or other conditions of employment against them, or their exclusion from Community treatment in any other way (Case 152/73 *Sotgiu*, above, at p. 162; Case 225/85 *Commission* v. *Italy*, above, at p. 2639; Cases 389/87 etc. *Echternach and Moritz* [1989] ECR 723 at pp. 759–60; Case 33/88 *Allué I* [1989] ECR 1591 at p. 1609).

In the light of these considerations, the Court has adopted functional criteria for the definition of the concept of public service, based on the nature of the tasks (functions) and responsibilities inherent in the posts in question. Thus, the Court has said that the concept of public service covers:

> a series of posts which involve direct or indirect participation in the exercise of powers conferred by public law and duties designed to safeguard the general interests of the State or of other public authorities. Such posts in fact presume on the part of those occupying them the existence of a special relationship of allegiance to the State and reciprocity of rights and duties which form the foundation of the bond of nationality (Case 149/79 *Commission* v. *Belgium*, above, at p. 3900, interim judgment).

On the other hand, the Court has observed, Art. 39(4) does not apply to posts that, whilst coming under the State or other organizations governed by public law, still do not involve any association with the functions that are typical of the specific activities of the public service properly so called, such as posts entailing responsibilities of an economic and/or social nature. The extension of the Art. 39(4) exception to such posts, the Court has pointed out, would have the effect of removing a considerable number of posts from the scope of the principles set out in the Treaty and creating inequalities between Member States according to the different ways in which the State and certain sectors of economic life are organized (ibid. at pp. 3900–1; see also the cases cited below which in substance repeat the above definition).

Accordingly, in the final judgment given in Case 149/79 *Commission* v. *Belgium* [1982] ECR 1845 at pp. 1851–2, the Court held that, having regard to the tasks and responsibilities involved, posts described as head technical office supervisor, principal supervisor, works supervisor, stock controller, and night watchman with the municipality of Brussels and architect with the municipalities of Brussels and Auderghem fell within the scope of the exception contained in Art. 39(4). By contrast, the posts of shunters, loaders, drivers, plate-layers, and signalmen with the Belgian National Railways, office cleaners, painter's assistants, assistant furnishers, battery servicers, coil-winders, armature servicers, night watchmen, cleaners, canteen staff, and workshop hands with the National Local Railways, joiners, garden hands, hospital nurses, children's nurses, inspectors, crèche nurses, electricians, and plumbers with the municipalities of Brussels and Auderghem did not constitute employment in the public service.

Applying the 'very strict conditions' laid down in the above cases, in Case 225/85 *Commission* v. *Italy*, above, at p. 2639 the Court held that researchers working for the Italian National Research Council could not be regarded as being employed in the public service because they were not responsible for exercising powers conferred by public law or for safeguarding the general interests of the State. The Court said that only duties of management or of advising the State on scientific and technical questions could be described as employment in the public service, but those duties were not carried out by the researchers in question.

In Case C-47/02 *Anker* [2003] ECR I-10447, paras. 61–4, 69 and in Case C-405/01 *Colegio de Oficiales de la Marina Mercante Española* [2003] ECR I-10391, paras. 42–5, 50, the Court recognized that the powers conferred by German law on masters of fishing vessels flying the German flag and by Spanish law on masters and chief mates of merchant ships flying the Spanish flag, respectively, such as powers connected to the maintenance of safety, police powers, powers of investigation, coercion, and punishment, as well as certain auxiliary duties in respect of the registration of births, marriages, and deaths, constituted 'participation in the exercise of powers conferred by public law for the purposes of safeguarding the general interests of the flag State' within the meaning of the above definition. However, the Court held that this was in itself insufficient to justify recourse to the Art. 39(4) derogation. It was also necessary that such powers were in fact exercised on a regular basis by the holders of those posts and did not represent a very minor part of their activities. This was not the case here since the duty of representing the flag State was in practice exercised only occasionally and to an insignificant extent by the persons concerned. A reservation of those posts for German and Spanish nationals could not be justified on the basis of Art. 39(4).

Applying the above-cited definition, the Court has found that the following posts do not fall within the concept of public service:

- trainee teachers (Case 66/85 *Lawrie-Blum*, above, at p. 2147);
- foreign-language assistants at universities (Case 33/88 *Allué*, above, at p. 1610);
- secondary school teachers (Case C-4/91 *Bleis* [1991] ECR I-5627 at p. I-5641);
- contractual teachers and teaching assistants (Case C-195/98 *Österreichischer Gewerkschaftsbund* [2000] ECR I-10497 at p. I-10548);
- nurses in public hospitals (Case 307/84 *Commission* v. *France*, above, at p. 1739; see also Case 149/79 *Commission* v. *Belgium*, above, at pp. 1851–2, final judgment);
- managers in the hospital public service (Case C-285/01 *Burbaud* [2003] ECR I-8219, para. 40);
- specialist doctors (Case C-15/96 *Schöning-Kougebetopoulou* [1998] ECR I-47 at pp. I-65–6);
- private security guards and undertakings and, generally, employment by a private natural or legal person, whatever the duties of the employee (Case C-114/97 *Commission* v. *Spain* [1998] ECR I-6717 at p. I-6741; Case C-283/99 *Commission* v. *Italy* [2001] ECR I-4363 at pp. I-4386–7).

It may be noted that Art. 39(4) does not prohibit Member States from reserving for their own nationals entry to those posts within a career bracket that involve the exercise of powers conferred by public law or responsibilities for the safeguarding of the general interests of the State. Thus, nationals of other Member States may be excluded from promotion or transfer to certain posts, but this possibility must not have the effect of debarring them from the totality of posts in the public service, including those that do not involve such powers and responsibilities (Case 149/79 *Commission* v. *Belgium*, above, at p. 3904, interim judgment; Case 225/85 *Commission* v. *Italy*, above, at p. 2639).

In a Communication published in 1988, entitled 'Freedom of movement of workers and access to employment in the public service of the Member States' (*OJ* 1988 C72/2), the Commission set out proposals for action with a view to increasing access to certain posts in the public service that had been previously reserved for nationals of the host country. Relying upon the Court's case-law, the Communication states that the derogation in Art. 39(4) covers, in the first place, specific functions of the State and similar bodies such as the armed forces, the police and other forces for the maintenance of order, the judiciary, the tax authorities, and the diplomatic corps. It also covers posts in State Ministries, regional and local authorities and other similar bodies, central banks, and other public bodies, where the duties of the post involve the exercise of State authority, such as the preparation and implementation of legal acts, monitoring of their application and supervision of subordinate bodies.

On the other hand, according to the Communication, certain forms of public employment are for the most part too remote from the specific activities of the public service as defined by the Court to be covered in general by the Art. 39(4) exception. These include bodies responsible for administering commercial services (e.g. public transport, electricity and gas supply, airline and shipping companies, post and telecommunications, radio and television companies); public health care services; teaching in State educational institutions; and research for non-military purposes in public establishments. The Communication points out that each of these activities also exists in the private sector, to which Art. 39(4) does not apply, or may be exercised in the public sector without the imposition of the nationality requirement. It is in these sectors that the Commission would implement its action, requiring the Member States to open access to employment to workers who are nationals of other Member States.

The Commission's Communication and its subsequent implementation have been endorsed by the ECJ in several cases. Thus, in Case C-473/93 *Commission* v. *Luxembourg* [1996] ECR I-3207 at pp. I-3261–2, the Court agreed with the Commission that by maintaining the requirement of Luxembourg nationality for access to all civil servants' or public employees' posts in the public sectors of research, education, health, inland transport, posts, and telecommunications, and in the water, gas, and electricity distribution services, Luxembourg infringed Art. 39 of the Treaty (see also Case C-173/94 *Commission* v. *Belgium* [1996] ECR I-3265 at pp. I-3282–3; Case C-290/94 *Commission* v. *Greece* [1996] ECR I-3285 at pp. I-3328–9).

See also **Free movement of persons, Official authority.**

Q

QUANTITATIVE RESTRICTIONS Art. 28 EC prohibits quantitative restrictions on imports and measures of equivalent effect on imports between Member States, while Art. 29 EC prohibits the same restrictions when imposed on exports between Member States.

The Court of Justice has held that 'the prohibition on quantitative restrictions covers measures which amount to a total or partial restraint of, according to the circumstances, imports, exports or goods in transit' (Case 2/73 *Geddo* [1973] ECR 865 at p. 879). This concept thus covers total bans (Case 34/79 *Henn and Darby* [1979] ECR 3795 at p. 3812) as well as import and export quotas. Plainly, this concept is considerably narrower than the related concept of measures having an equivalent effect.

It is still a moot point whether an import ban is to be regarded as a quantitative restriction or a measure of equivalent effect, if it is matched by a ban on sales within the Member State concerned. In any case, nothing turns on this distinction.

Arts. 28 and 29 have direct effect (see Case 74/76 *Iannelli* [1977] ECR 577; Case 83/78 *Redmond* [1978] ECR 2347).

Art. 33 of the original EEC Treaty required quantitative restrictions on imports to be abolished by the end of 1969 at the latest, while the original Art. 35 made provision for liberalization to proceed more rapidly if economic circumstances permitted. Accordingly, by virtue Council Dec. 66/532 (*JO* 1966 165), the ban took effect in July 1966, save for agricultural products. As to quantitative restrictions on exports, the original Art. 34 required such measures to be abolished by the end of 1961.

In exceptional cases, quantitative restrictions may fall under the various safeguard clauses, particularly Art. 30 EC. In practice, however, it would seem that only total bans on imports or exports may be justified under the latter provision; in contrast, it would be hard to imagine that import or export quotas could ever be so justified.

See also **Free movement of goods, Goods, Measures having equivalent effect to quantitative restrictions, State commercial monopoly.**

Further reading Bermann, Goebel, Davey, and Fox, *Cases and Materials on European Union Law*, 2nd edn. (2002), ch. 13; Müller-Graff in *Kommentar zum EU-/EG-Vertrag*, 6th edn. (2003) vol. I, p. 970 and 769; Oliver, *Free Movement of Goods in the European Community*, 4th edn. (2003), ch. 5.

RESIDENCE DOCUMENT *see* **RESIDENCE PERMIT**

RESIDENCE PERMIT Document serving as proof that the holder is entitled under Community law to the right of residence in the territory of the issuing Member State. As Community law stands at present, the following categories of person are entitled to the right of residence and, consequently, to a residence permit, provided that they are nationals of a Member State (the nationality requirement does not apply to family members):

- workers employed in the host Member State and members of their families to whom Reg. 1612/68 applies (Dir. 68/360, Arts. 1 and 4(1) and (2), *OJ Sp. Edn.* 1968 (II), p. 485);
- workers remaining in the host Member State after having been employed there and members of their families as defined in Art. 10 of Reg. 1612/68 (Reg. 1251/70, Arts. 1 and 6, *OJ Sp. Edn.* 1970 (II), p. 402);
- persons established in the host Member State in order to pursue self-employed activities and members of their families (Dir. 73/148, Arts. 1(1) and 4(1), *OJ* 1973 L172/14); persons providing or receiving services in the host Member State whose stay there exceeds three months and members of their families are issued with a right of abode as proof of the right of residence (Arts. 1(1) and 4(2));
- persons remaining in the host Member State after having pursued self-employed activities there and members of their families (Dir. 75/34, Arts. 1 and 6(1), *OJ* 1975 L14/10);
- persons of independent means and members of their families (Dir. 90/364, Arts. 1 and 2(1), *OJ* 1990 L180/26);
- retired persons and members of their families (Dir. 90/365, Arts. 1 and 2(1), *OJ* 1990 L180/28);
- students and members of their families (Dir. 93/96, Arts. 1 and 2(1), *OJ* 1993 L317/59).

On 29 April 2004 the European Parliament and the Council adopted Dir. 2004/38 on the right of citizens of the Union and their family members to move and reside freely within the territory of the Member States (*OJ* 2004 L158/77). The purpose of the directive is to codify and review the existing Community instruments dealing separately with workers, self-employed persons, students, and other inactive persons, in order to simplify and strengthen the right of free movement and residence of all Union citizens (see the first four recitals in the preamble). The directive entered into force on 30 April 2004, and has to be implemented by the Member States by 30 April 2006. With effect from that date, it will repeal and replace Arts. 10 and 11 of Reg. 1612/68 (relating to workers' families) and all the above directives, as well as Dir. 64/221, referred to below (Arts. 38, 40, 41). Residence permits will be replaced by other documents (*see further under* **Right of entry and residence**, section VII).

It should be noted that although Dir. 73/148 applies both to Community nationals exercising freedom of establishment and to those exercising freedom to provide or receive services, in one respect it makes a distinction between the two categories. Persons who establish themselves in the host Member State in order to pursue activities as self-employed persons are to be granted the right of permanent residence and, as proof thereof, a residence permit. On the other hand, persons who provide or receive services in the host Member State are entitled to the right of residence only for the period during which the services are provided. If this period exceeds three months, they are to be issued with a right of abode as proof of the right of residence (second recital in the preamble and Art. 4(1) and (2)). Any national of a Member State who is not entitled to the right of permanent residence under Art. 4(1) but who is authorized by the host Member State to pursue an activity within its territory is to be granted a right of abode for the duration of the authorization (Art. 4(1)).

In several cases, the ECJ has made it clear that a residence permit does not as such give rise to the right of residence since this right is conferred directly by Community law on any person who is entitled to it, independently of the issue of a residence permit by the host State. Such a permit has a purely declaratory effect, its sole purpose being to prove the status of the holder under Community law. The grant of the right of residence and the issue of a residence permit as proof thereof, is not a discretionary measure on the part of the national authorities. The Member States are under an obligation to grant such a right and to issue such a permit to any person who provides proof, by means of the appropriate documents to be discussed below, that he belongs to one of the categories of beneficiaries listed above (Case 48/75 *Royer* [1976] ECR 497 at pp. 512–13; see also e.g. Case 249/86 *Commission* v. *Germany* [1989] ECR 1263 at pp. 1289–90). Proof of carrying on an economic activity is in itself sufficient, without there being any need to classify that activity as employment or self-employed activity, since Arts. 39 and 43 EC, on which the right of residence is based, afford the same legal protection (Case C-363/89 *Roux* [1991] ECR I-273 at p. I-293). The issue of documents by the host State other than a residence permit, such as registration certificates, which entail excessive burdens for the migrant, is not permitted (Case C-344/95 *Commission* v. *Belgium* [1997] ECR I-1035 at pp. I-1054–5).

Because the issue of a residence permit does not create the rights guaranteed by Community law, the lack of such a permit cannot affect the exercise of those rights. Thus, enjoyment of the right to education, entry and residence, and study finance granted by Community law to workers' children and students cannot be made conditional on the possession of a residence permit (Cases 389/87 etc. *Echternach and Moritz* [1989] ECR 723 at pp. 762–3 *per Curiam*, p. 752 *per* A.-G. Darmon; Case C-357/89 *Raulin* [1992] ECR I-1027 at pp. I-1065–7).

For the issue of a residence permit (the full title is : 'Residence Permit for a National of a Member State of the EC') or a right of abode, Member States may require only the production of the following documents:

- by a worker: the document with which he entered the territory of the host State, which may be either a valid identity card or a valid passport, and a confirmation of engagement from the employer or a certificate of employment (Art. 4(3)(a) and (b) of Dir. 68/360 in conjunction with Art. 3(1)). Thus, the right of residence, and therefore a residence permit, is accorded only to persons who are already in employment in the host State. Persons seeking employment are excluded (Case C-138/02 *Collins* [2004] ECR I-0000, paras. 41–4). An identity card which proves the holder's identity and nationality fulfils the above requirement even if it does not authorize the person concerned to leave the territory of the issuing Member State and even if it was issued before the accession of that State to the Communities. Moreover, the host State must accept either an identity card or a passport, regardless of the document with which the person entered its territory (Case C-376/89 *Giagounidis* [1991] ECR I-1069 at pp. I-1091–3). Member States may not impose any additional conditions for the issue of a residence permit, such as the prior registration with a particular social security scheme or compliance with national social security legislation (Case C-363/89 *Roux*, above, at pp. I-290–5);
- by the members of the worker's family: the document with which they entered the territory of the host State (identity card or passport); a document proving their relationship; and, in the case of dependent relatives referred to in Art. 10(1) and (2) of Reg. 1612/68, a document testifying that they are dependent on the worker or that they live under his roof (Art. 4(3)(c) to (e) of Dir. 68/360 in conjunction with Art. 3(1));
- by a self-employed person, a provider or recipient of services, and the members of their families: the identity card or passport with which they entered the territory of the host State and proof that they come within one of the classes of person covered by Dir. 73/148 (Art. 6 of Dir. 73/148 in conjunction with Arts. 1 and 4). Since the means of proof are not specified, any appropriate evidence is admissible and the host State is precluded from accepting only prior registration in a social security scheme as such evidence (Case C-363/89 *Roux*, above, at pp. I-291–2);
- by persons of independent means, retired persons, students, and the members of their families: a valid identity card or passport and proof that they meet the conditions laid down in the relevant directive (Art. 2(1) of Dirs. 90/364, 90/365, and 93/96, respectively. For the prescribed conditions, *see further under* **Right of entry and residence**, sections III to V).

In each of the above cases, a member of the family who is not a national of a Member State is issued with a residence document which has the same validity as the residence permit or right of abode issued to the person on whom he or she depends (Art. 4(4) of Dir. 68/360; Art. 4(3) of Dir. 73/148; Art. 2(1) of Dirs. 90/364, 90/365, and 93/96).

The ECJ has held that refusal of a residence permit based solely on the failure of the person concerned to comply with the above-mentioned legal formalities would impair the very substance of the right of residence and would be manifestly disproportionate to the gravity of the infringement. Therefore, Art. 4 of Dir. 68/360 and Art. 6 of Dir. 73/148 do not permit a Member State to refuse the issue of a residence permit to a third-country national who is able to furnish proof of his identity and of his marriage to a national of a Member State on the sole ground that he has entered the territory of the Member State concerned unlawfully (Case C-459/99 *MRAX* [2002] ECR I-6591 at pp. I-6664–5). Moreover, those provisions do not require that the document with which the person entered the territory of the host State must still be valid when produced to obtain a residence permit. Accordingly, where a third-country national requires a visa, issue of a residence permit to him cannot be made subject to the condition that his visa is still valid. A Member State may not refuse to issue a residence permit to such a national who is married to a national of a Member State and entered the territory of the first Member State lawfully, on the sole ground that his visa expired before he applied for a residence permit (ibid. p. I-6668).

In general, the residence permit must be valid throughout the territory of the issuing Member State for at least five years and must be automatically renewable. Renewal of the residence permit of family members cannot be made conditional on their living in appropriate housing (Case 249/86 *Commission* v. *Germany*, above, at pp. 1291, 1293). In the case of persons of independent means and retired persons, the host State may require revalidation of the permit at the end of the first two years of residence. In the case of students, the validity of the permit may be limited to the duration of the course of studies or to one year where the course lasts longer; in the latter event it must be renewable annually. Breaks in residence not exceeding six consecutive months and absence on military service may not affect the validity of the permit. The residence permit must be issued and renewed free of charge or on payment of an amount not exceeding the dues and taxes charged for the issue of identity cards to nationals (for an infringement of this rule by Belgium, see Case C-344/95 *Commission* v. *Belgium*, above, at p. I-1055).

The formalities and procedures for obtaining a residence permit are to be simplified as much as possible and their completion cannot hinder the immediate beginning of employment under a contract already concluded by the applicant. In any case, a decision to grant or to refuse a first residence permit must be taken within six months of the date of application. Pending the decision the applicant must be allowed to remain temporarily in the host State. The authorities of the latter may seek information from other Member States concerning any previous police record, although this should not be done routinely. The decision to refuse the issue or renewal of a residence permit must be officially notified to the applicant who must be allowed a period for leaving the host State. Save in cases of urgency, this period cannot be less than fifteen days if he has not yet been granted a permit, and one month in other cases.

A valid residence permit may not be withdrawn from a worker or from a self-employed person solely on the grounds that he is no longer in employment, either because he is temporarily incapable of work as a result of illness or accident or (in the case of a worker) because he is involuntarily unemployed. Nevertheless, this rule does not confer a right of residence on a person who was unemployed in the host State at the time when the Member State of which he is a national acceded to the Community (Case C-171/91 *Tsiotras* [1993] ECR I-2925 at pp. I-2957–8). Where the worker has been involuntarily unemployed in the host State for more than twelve consecutive months, the period of residence may be restricted to not less than twelve months when the residence permit is renewed for the first time (Arts. 5, 6(1) and (2), 7, 9(1) and (3) of Dir. 68/360; Arts. 4(1), 5, 7(1) and (3) of Dir. 73/148; Art. 6 of Reg. 1251/70; Art. 6 of Dir. 75/34; Art. 2(1) and (2) of Dirs. 90/364, 90/365, and 93/96; Arts. 5 and 7 of Dir. 64/221, *OJ Sp. Edn.* 1963–4, p. 117).

A residence permit need not be issued to workers pursuing an activity not expected to last for more than three months, to frontier workers and to seasonal workers employed for a period of less than three months. In the first case, the document with which the worker entered the host State and a statement by the employer on the expected duration of the employment is sufficient to cover his stay. In the second case, the frontier worker may be issued with a special permit valid for five years and automatically renewable. A frontier worker is defined as 'a worker who, while having his residence in the territory of a Member State to which he returns as a rule, each day or at least once a week, is employed in the territory of another Member State' (Art. 8(1)(b) of Dir. 68/360). In the third case, a contract of employment stamped by the competent authority of the host State is sufficient. Likewise, providers and recipients of services whose stay in the host State does not exceed three months need not have a right of abode; the identity card or passport with which they entered the territory is sufficient to cover their stay. In all of these situations, however, the host State may require the person concerned to report his presence to the authorities (Art. 8(1) and (2) of Dir. 68/360; Art. 4(2) of Dir. 73/148).

According to the ECJ, the purpose of this requirement is to enable the national authorities to have an exact knowledge of population movements affecting their territory. The Court has held that such a requirement is, in principle, compatible with the rules concerning freedom of movement for persons provided that the period within which the person must report his presence is reasonable. A period of three days from the date of arrival cannot be regarded as reasonable. Moreover, the penalties laid down for a failure to comply with the duty to report or with any other rules and formalities relating to the control of aliens, or for a failure to obtain a residence permit, must be comparable to those applied to minor offences committed by the nationals of the host State (e.g. fines). The authorities of the latter are certainly not entitled to impose a penalty so disproportionate to the gravity of the infringement that it becomes an obstacle to the free movement of persons. This would be especially the case if the penalty included imprisonment or deportation (Case 48/75 *Royer*, above, at pp. 513–14; Case 118/75 *Watson and Belmann* [1976] ECR 1185 at pp. 1198–9; Case 157/79 *Pieck*

[1980] ECR 2171 at p. 2187; Case C-265/88 *Messner* [1989] ECR 4209 at pp. 4223–5 *per Curiam*, pp. 4216–19 *per* A.-G. Mischo, concerning the three-day time limit for reporting). Nor may a Member State require anything going beyond the duty to report one's presence, such as an authorization or a residence permit, or impose a charge when a person reports his presence (Case C-344/95 *Commission* v. *Belgium*, above, at pp. I-1056–7).

Where a worker is employed in the host State for a period exceeding three months but not exceeding one year, either by an employer in the host State or by a person providing services there, he is entitled to a temporary residence permit the validity of which may be limited to the expected period of the employment. A temporary residence permit is to be issued also to a seasonal worker employed for a period of more than three months, which must be shown in his certificate of employment (Art. 6(3) of Dir. 68/360).

A person who has been refused entry into or expelled from the territory of a Member State for reasons of public policy or public security may reapply for a fresh residence permit and is entitled to a new decision. The ECJ has held that such an application, when submitted after a reasonable period has elapsed, must be examined by the competent authority in the host State, which must consider, in particular, whether there has been a material change in the circumstances which justified the initial decision. However, where expulsion has been validly ordered under Community law and continues to be in force, the person has, under Community law, no right of entry into the host State during the examination of his further application (Cases 115/81 etc. *Adoui and Cornuaille* [1982] ECR 1665 at p. 1709; Cases C-65/95 etc. *Shingara and Radiom* [1997] ECR I-3343 at p. I-3392).

A residence permit may be refused or, apart from cases of voluntary unemployment and prolonged absence exceeding six consecutive months, withdrawn only as a special measure justified on grounds of public policy, public security, or public health, and only subject to strict procedural safeguards laid down by Community law (see Dir. 64/221 and Art. 10 of Dir. 68/360; Art. 8 of Dir. 73/148; Art. 9 of Dir. 75/34; Art. 2(2) of Dirs. 90/364, 90/365, and 93/96. *See further under* **Public health, Public policy, Public security**).

The special residence permit provided for by Community law must be distinguished from the general residence permit prescribed by domestic law for aliens in general. The issue of the latter is within the discretion of the national authorities. A Member State may not therefore require from a person enjoying the protection of Community law that he should possess a general residence permit instead of or in addition to that provided for by Community law, nor may it impose penalties for a failure to possess such a general permit (Case 8/77 *Sagulo, Brenca and Bakhouche* [1977] ECR 1495 at pp. 1503–4; Case 157/79 *Pieck*, above, at p. 2186).

See also **Expulsion, Freedom of establishment, Freedom to provide services, Free movement of persons, Public health, Public policy, Public security, Right of entry and residence, Right to leave, Right to remain, Worker.**

▶ **RIGHT OF ABODE** *see* **RESIDENCE PERMIT**

▶ **RIGHT OF ENTRY AND RESIDENCE** Right of the nationals of the Member States to enter and reside in the territory of the other Member States for the purposes intended by Community law. Initially, the EC Treaty granted this right to Community nationals to enable them to exercise the various freedoms created by it, i.e. the freedom of movement for workers, freedom of establishment, and freedom to provide and receive services. Consequently, the right of entry and residence was a necessary corollary to and prerequisite for the enjoyment of those freedoms, and was restricted to persons who were the beneficiaries of the freedoms: to workers, self-employed persons, providers and recipients of services, and the members of their families. It could only be exercised for one purpose: to carry on an economic activity in the host Member State as envisaged by the relevant provisions of the Treaty (Arts. 39, 43, and 49). For a long time, Community law did not recognize a general right of entry and residence available to any Community national for any purpose. This position has, however, changed in two respects. First, the right of entry and residence has been extended by secondary legislation to certain categories of persons not involved in any economic activity, such as persons of independent means, retired persons, and students. Secondly, Art. 18(1) EC, inserted by the Treaty on European Union (TEU), now expressly recognizes the right of 'every citizen of the Union . . . to move and reside freely within the territory of the Member States'.

Nevertheless, as the ECJ has pointed out in a number of cases, while the right of entry and residence is conferred directly by the Treaty, it can, in practice, be exercised only in accordance with the provisions laid down in secondary legislation. Thus, the right is not unconditional but is subject to compliance with the relevant rules, including the exceptions (derogations) contained in the Treaty itself. Even Art. 18(1) EC, cited above, has not created a universal and unconditional right of entry and residence, but subjects that right to 'the limitations and conditions laid down in this Treaty and by the measures adopted to give it effect'. Since these conditions are currently set out in a different instrument in respect of each category of beneficiaries, it is appropriate to consider each category separately (see sections I to V below). It is also necessary to discuss briefly the position of citizens of the Union (see section VI below). Finally, mention must be made of the most recent legislation, which reviews and codifies in a single legislative act the existing instruments, repealing and replacing them in due course (see section VII below). (In general, see Case 48/75 *Royer* [1976] ECR 497 at pp. 512–13; Case 157/79 *Pieck* [1980] ECR 2171 at p. 2183; Cases 389/87 etc. *Echternach and Moritz* [1989] ECR 723 at p. 762; Case 249/86 *Commission* v. *Germany* [1989] ECR 1263 at pp. 1289–90; Case C-363/89 *Roux* [1991] ECR I-273 at pp. I-290, I-293; Case C-68/89 *Commission* v. *Netherlands* [1991] ECR I-2637 at p. I-2655; Case C-370/90 *Singh* [1992] ECR I-4265 at p. I-4293; Case C-356/98 *Kaba I* [2000] ECR I-2623 at pp. I-2676–7; Case C-413/99 *Baumbast and R* [2002] ECR I-7091, para. 85.)

I. Workers

In respect of workers, the relevant instrument is Council Dir. 68/360 of 15 October 1968 on the abolition of restrictions on movement and residence within the Community for workers of Member States and their families (*OJ Sp. Edn.* 1968 (II), p. 485). The purpose of the directive is to abolish all remaining restrictions on entry and residence to enable workers to exercise the rights and privileges accorded them by Reg. 1612/68 (*OJ Sp. Edn.* 1968 (II), p. 475), and in particular the right to move freely within the Community in order to pursue activities as employed persons. Thus, the rules applicable to residence are intended, as far as possible, to bring the position of workers from other Member States and members of their families into line with that of nationals (first and second recitals in the preamble). The directive must be interpreted in the light of these objectives (Case 157/79 *Pieck*, above, at pp. 2184–5).

Art. 1 of the directive requires the Member States to abolish restrictions on the movement and residence of workers who are nationals of the Member States and of 'members of their families to whom Reg. 1612/68 applies'. Art. 10(1) of Reg. 1612/68 grants the right 'to install themselves with a worker' to the following members of his family, irrespective of their nationality:

(*a*) his spouse and their descendants who are under the age of 21 years or are dependants;

(*b*) dependent relatives in the ascending line of the worker and his spouse.

In addition, Art. 10(2) of Reg. 1612/68 requires the Member States to 'facilitate' the admission of any member of the family not coming within the above categories if dependent on the worker or living under his roof in the country whence he comes, but without giving these persons a legal right of entry and residence. Nevertheless, in listing the persons who are entitled to the right of residence and hence to the issue of a residence permit, Art. 4(3)(e) of Dir. 68/360 refers not only to Art. 10(1) but also to Art. 10(2) of Reg. 1612/68, thereby implying that the persons mentioned there have a legal right as opposed to an entitlement dependent on the discretion of each Member State. Although this apparent discrepancy between the two instruments is yet to be resolved by the Court, the preferable view seems to be that the broader provisions of Art. 4(3)(e) should prevail over the strict wording of Art. 10(2).

As a result of Arts. 1 and 4 of Dir. 68/360, in conjunction with Art. 10 of Reg. 1612/68, Member States must grant the spouse and dependent relatives of a migrant worker a right of residence equivalent to that granted to the worker himself (Case C-370/90 *Singh*, above, at p. I-4293). However, Member States are not required to grant the spouse a more extensive right of residence than that conferred on the worker (Case C-356/98 *Kaba I*, above, at pp. I-2675–8, where the spouse of a migrant worker was seeking indefinite leave to remain in the United Kingdom. For this case, *see further under* **Free movement of persons**, section III.4(*a*); see also Case C-466/00 *Kaba II*

[2003] ECR I-2219). In order to qualify for that right, the members of a worker's family are not required to live permanently with the worker (Case 267/83 *Diatta* [1985] ECR 567 at p. 590).

Nevertheless, the members of the family may claim the right of entry and residence only if the worker himself has already exercised the right to freedom of movement within the Community, i.e. if he is or has been employed in a Member State other than that of which he is a national. Since the provisions of Community law on the free movement of persons cannot be applied to purely internal situations, a spouse or a dependent relative who is a national of a non-Member State is not entitled to enter and reside in the territory of a Member State solely in his or her capacity as a member of the family of a worker who is a national of that State but has never pursued an activity in another Member State as an employed or self-employed person (Cases 35/82 etc. *Morson and Jhanjan* [1982] ECR 3723 at pp. 3735–7; Cases C-297/88 etc. *Dzodzi* [1990] ECR I-3763 at pp. I-3791–2. However, for providers of services see section II below. As regards the free movement of workers and the members of their families in general, *see further under* **Free movement of persons**, section I).

The persons who are covered by Art. 1 must be allowed to enter the territory of Member States simply on production of a valid identity card or passport (Art. 3(1)). In several cases, the ECJ has interpreted this provision very strictly by saying that the production of one of these documents is the only precondition that the Member States may impose on the right of entry. Thus, so long as the person concerned actually pursues or seriously wishes to pursue in the host State an effective and genuine activity as an employed person, the motives that may have prompted him to do so are irrelevant as regards his right of entry and residence, and must not be taken into consideration (Case 53/81 *Levin* [1982] ECR 1035 at pp. 1051–2). At the time of crossing the frontier, a migrant may not be required, in addition to producing one of the documents mentioned, to provide evidence that he belongs to one of the categories of persons covered by the directive. It is only when a residence permit is issued that he may be asked to furnish proof of his right of residence. Therefore, he cannot be obliged, as a precondition for entry, to answer questions put by frontier officials regarding the purpose and duration of his journey and the financial means at his disposal (Case C-68/89 *Commission* v. *Netherlands*, above, at pp. I-2655–6).

Likewise, while migrants may be required to carry their residence or establishment permit at all times within the territory of the host State where the same obligation is imposed on local nationals in respect of their identity card, a requirement to produce the residence permit when entering the host State, in addition to the passport or identity card, would be contrary to Community law if enforced in a systematic, arbitrary, or unnecessarily restrictive manner. On the other hand, sporadic and unsystematic checks at the frontier are permitted, provided that they are not a precondition for entry (Case 321/87 *Commission* v. *Belgium* [1989] ECR 997 at pp. 1010–11. The considerations in this case and in the previous and following cases apply equally to self-employed persons, see section II below). Failure to possess a valid identity card, passport, or residence permit, or to produce it when required, may attract penalties, but these must be comparable to those imposed on nationals for similar offences, and must not be so severe as to cause an obstacle to the freedom of entry and residence (Case 8/77 *Sagulo, Brenca and Bakhouche* [1977] ECR 1495 at pp. 1505–6; Case C-24/97 *Commission* v. *Germany* [1998] ECR I-2133 at p. I-2145).

According to Art. 3(2), no entry visa or equivalent document may be required except from members of the family who are not nationals of a Member State. Such persons must be accorded every facility for obtaining any necessary visas (ibid.), which must be available free of charge (Art. 9(2)). This means that a visa must be issued without delay and, as far as possible, at the place of entry into national territory. In view of the importance which Community law attaches to the protection of family life, and in accordance with the principle of proportionality, a Member State may not send back at the border a third-country national who is married to a national of a Member State and attempts to enter its territory without being in possession of a valid identity card or passport or, if necessary, a visa, where he is able to prove his identity and the conjugal ties and there is no evidence to establish that he represents a risk to the requirements of public policy, public security or public health (Case C-459/99 *MRAX* [2002] ECR I-6591 at pp. I-6659–60).

The term 'entry visa or equivalent document' in Art. 3(2) is not restricted to a clearance issued before the migrant arrives at the frontier. It covers any formality for the purpose of granting leave to enter the territory of the host State which is coupled with a passport or identity card check at the frontier, whatever may be the place or time at which, and the form in which, that leave is granted. It thus includes an endorsement stamped on a passport at the time of arrival, which is consequently also contrary to Art. 3(2) (Case 157/79 *Pieck*, above, at pp. 2184–5).

Art. 4(1) provides that 'Member States shall grant the right of residence in their territory to the persons referred to in Article 1 who are able to produce the documents listed in para. 3'. These are the documents required for the issue of a residence permit, which is used as a proof of the right of residence (Art. 4(2); *see further under* **Residence permit**). The ECJ has held that Art. 4(1) entails an obligation for the Member States to grant the right of residence to any person falling within the categories set out in Art. 1 and who is able to prove this fact by means of the documents specified in Art. 4(3) (Case 48/75 *Royer*, above, at p. 513), even if the person has entered the national territory unlawfully (Case C-459/99 *MRAX*, above, at p. I-6665, dealing with a third-country national married to a Member State national).

According to Art. 4(3), the worker has to produce, in addition to the document with which he entered the host Member State's territory, a confirmation of engagement from the employer or a certificate of employment. From this requirement, the Court has concluded that the right of residence under the directive is accorded only to nationals of a Member State who are already in employment in the host State. Persons seeking employment are excluded. They can rely solely on the provisions of the directive concerning their movement within the Community, although they can derive a right of residence directly from Art. 39 EC itself (Case C-138/02 *Collins* [2004] ECR I-0000, paras. 36–44). This situation may be explained by the fact that Dir. 68/360 had been adopted before the Court interpreted Art. 39 to the effect that it grants a right of entry and residence also to persons who seek employment in another Member State (*see further under* **Free movement of persons**, section I.2(*a*)).

The right of residence must be granted for the whole of the national territory and normally for five years; it cannot be limited to a certain period determined by national law (Case 36/75 *Rutili* [1975] ECR 1219 at p. 1234; Case 157/79 *Pieck*, above, at p. 2185; see also Art. 6). It may, however, be restricted to six months in the case of a person who goes to another Member State in order to seek employment, unless he provides evidence that after the expiry of that period he is continuing to seek employment and that he has genuine chances of being engaged (Case C-292/89 *Antonissen* [1991] ECR I-745 at p. I-779). The persons covered by Art. 1 include the nationals of a 'new' Member State who were already employed in one of the 'old' Member States at the time of their country's accession to the Community (Case 9/88 *Lopes da Veiga* [1989] ECR 2989 at p. 3011 concerning the accession of Portugal), but do not include those nationals of a new Member State who were unemployed in an old Member State at the time of accession (Case C-171/91 *Tsiotras* [1993] ECR I-2925 at pp. I-2957–8 concerning the accession of Greece. For the provisions of the Act of Accession of 2003 regarding the free movement of workers, *see under* **Free movement of persons**, section I.2(*d*)).

II. Self-employed persons and providers and recipients of services

These persons are covered by Council Dir. 73/148 of 21 May 1973 on the abolition of restrictions on movement and residence within the Community for nationals of Member States with regard to establishment and the provision of services (*OJ* 1973 L172/14). The directive applies only to natural persons and its provisions cannot be applied by analogy to legal persons. It therefore confers no right on a company to transfer its central management and control to another Member State (Case 81/87 *Daily Mail* [1988] ECR 5483 at p. 5513). The directive is not applicable to the overseas countries and territories (OCTs), which are subject to special provisions (Cases C-100/89 etc. *Kaefer and Procacci* [1990] ECR I-4647 at p. I-4672; *see further under* **Freedom of establishment**, section I.1, and **Freedom to provide services**, section I.1).

Art. 1(1) of the directive requires the Member States to abolish restrictions on the movement and residence of the following categories of persons:

(*a*) nationals of a Member State who are established or who wish to establish themselves in another Member State in order to pursue activities as self-employed persons, or who wish to provide services in that State;

(*b*) nationals of Member States wishing to go to another Member State as recipients of services;

(*c*) the spouse and the children under 21 years of age of such nationals, irrespective of their nationality;

(*d*) the relatives in the ascending and descending lines of such nationals and of the spouse of such nationals, which relatives are dependent on them, irrespective of their nationality.

According to Art. 1(2), Member States are to 'favour' (but are not required to ensure) the admission of any other member of the family of a national listed under (*a*) or (*b*) above, or of the spouse of such national, if that member is dependent on the national concerned or was living under the same roof in the country of origin. In this respect, therefore, Dir. 73/148 is different from Dir. 68/360, which appears to grant the right of residence to this category of family members independently of the host State's discretion (see section I above).

It follows from Art. 1(1) that the directive applies only to nationals of Member States who leave their State of origin and move to another Member State in order to establish themselves or to provide or receive services there, and to the members of their families who move with them. The directive does not grant the right of residence to the family members of a provider of services in his Member State of origin. However, in Case C-60/00 *Carpenter* [2002] ECR I-6279 at pp. I-6318–22, the Court interpreted the provisions of the directive broadly, in the light of the fundamental right to respect for family life as guaranteed by Art. 8 of the European Convention on Human Rights. It held that where a Member State national provides services to recipients established in other Member States, the refusal by his Member State of origin to grant the right of entry and residence to his spouse who is a national of a third country constitutes an interference with his family life and is, therefore, detrimental to the conditions under which he exercises a fundamental freedom. Such a refusal is contrary to Art. 49 EC.

While the directive cannot be applied to purely internal situations, it does guarantee the right of entry and residence to the spouse, of whatever nationality, of a national of a Member State who has already exercised the right to freedom of movement by having gone to another Member State as a worker and who is returning, with his spouse, to his State of origin as a self-employed person. In such a situation, the spouse must enjoy at least the same rights as would be granted to him or her under Community law if his or her spouse entered and resided in the territory, not of his/her own country, but that of another Member State (Case C-370/90 *Singh*, above, at pp. I-4294–5).

Dir. 73/148 grants the spouse and dependent relatives only the right to enter and reside in the host State. However, Art. 11 of Reg. 1612/68, which generally applies to workers, entitles the spouse of a migrant self-employed person, and those of his children who are under the age of 21 years or dependent on him, to take up any activity as an employed person throughout the territory of the host State, even if they are not nationals of any Member State. Nevertheless, this provision does not expressly allow these family members to take up self-employed activity in that State. This is in strange contrast to the position of the spouse and dependent children of migrants not involved in any economic activity, such as persons of independent means, retired persons, and students, who are granted the right to take up any employed *or* self-employed activity anywhere in the host State, even if they are not nationals of a Member State (see sections III to V below). This creates discrimination against the members of the families of self-employed persons, particularly where they are third-country nationals. (If these family members are nationals of a Member State, then they may pursue activities as employed or self-employed persons in their own right, independently of Art. 11.) There seems to be no reason why this anomalous situation should be maintained, particularly as it disadvantages those who should be the primary beneficiaries of the right to free movement, namely, the economically active.

The persons who are covered by Art. 1(1) must be granted the right to enter the territory of Member States simply on production of a valid identity card or passport (Art. 3(1)). This is the only precondition that the Member States may impose on the right of entry. Once one of these documents is presented, the authorities are not entitled to dispute the nationality of the holder, nor to require proof that he belongs to one of the categories of persons covered by the directive. Such proof is only necessary for the purpose of issuing a residence permit (Case C-68/89 *Commission* v. *Netherlands*, above, at pp. I-2655–6; Case C-369/90 *Micheletti* [1992] ECR I-4239 at p. I-4263; see also Art. 6). In this respect, therefore, the same considerations apply as in the case of workers (see section I above). Similarly, no entry visa or equivalent document may be required except from members of the family who are not nationals of a Member State. Such persons must be afforded every facility for obtaining any necessary visas, which must be available free of charge (Arts. 3(2) and 7(2); see Case C-459/99 *MRAX*, above, at pp. I-6659–60, cited in section I).

While the directive applies both to Community nationals exercising freedom of establishment and to those exercising freedom to provide or receive services, in one respect it makes a distinction between the two categories. Persons who go to another Member State in order to establish themselves there as self-employed persons must be granted the right of permanent residence and, as proof thereof, a residence permit. On the other hand, persons who provide or receive services in another Member State are entitled to the right of residence only for the period during which the services are provided. If this period exceeds three months, they are to be issued with a right of abode as proof of the right of residence. The right of residence must be effective throughout the territory of the host Member State (second recital in the preamble and Arts. 4 and 5; for the requirements concerning the issue of a residence permit or right of abode, *see further under* **Residence permit**).

III. Persons of independent means

These persons are covered by Council Dir. 90/364 of 28 June 1990 on the right of residence (*OJ* 1990 L180/26). The directive was adopted to implement Art. 14 EC by ensuring freedom of movement and residence within the internal market for persons in general (see the second and third recitals in the preamble). Art. 1 requires the Member States to grant the right of residence to nationals of other Member States who do not enjoy this right under other provisions of Community law and to members of their families as defined below. The grant of the right is subject to two conditions. First, the persons and the members of their families must be covered by sickness insurance in respect of all risks in the host Member State. Secondly, they must have sufficient resources to avoid becoming a burden on the social assistance system of the host State during their period of residence. The resources are deemed sufficient where they are higher than the level of resources below which the host State may grant social assistance to its nationals or, where this is not applicable, higher than the level of the minimum social security pension paid by the host State. The Member States may not limit the types of proof used by the beneficiaries of the directive to show that they fulfil the above conditions (Case C-424/98 *Commission* v. *Italy* [2000] ECR I-4001 at pp. I-4030–1; this applies also to Dir. 90/365, see section IV below).

The ECJ has held that the conditions imposed by the directive must be applied in compliance with the limits imposed by Community law and in accordance with the general principles of that law, in particular, the principle of proportionality. Since the directive only requires that the beneficiaries of the right of residence must not become an 'unreasonable' burden on the public finances of the host Member State (fourth recital in the preamble), to refuse to allow a person to exercise that right on the sole ground that his sickness insurance does not cover emergency treatment in the host State would amount to a disproportionate interference with the exercise of the right of residence (Case C-413/99 *Baumbast and R*, above, paras. 87–94).

Family members to whom the right of residence must be extended include, irrespective of their nationality, the person's spouse and their descendants who are dependants, and dependent relatives in the ascending line of the person and his or her spouse. The spouse and the dependent children are entitled to take up any employed or self-employed activity anywhere within the host State, even if they are not nationals of a Member State (Art. 2(2)).

The right of residence is granted only for as long as the beneficiaries fulfil the two conditions mentioned above (Art. 3). It is evidenced by the issue of a residence permit (Art. 2(1), *see further under* **Residence permit**). The beneficiaries of the directive are covered by administrative arrangements similar to those applicable to workers under Dir. 68/360 (sixth recital and Art. 2(2); see section I above).

IV. Retired persons

These are covered by Council Dir. 90/365 of 28 June 1990 on the right of residence for employees and self-employed persons who have ceased their occupational activity (*OJ* 1990 L180/28). According to Art. 1 and the third recital, Member States are to grant the right of residence to nationals of other Member States who have been employees or self-employed persons and have ceased their occupational activity, even if they have never exercised their right to freedom of movement during their working life, and to members of their families defined in the same way as under Dir. 90/364 (see section III above). The grant of the right is subject to two conditions. First, the persons concerned must be recipients of an invalidity or early retirement pension or old-age benefits, or of a pension in respect of an industrial accident or disease of an amount sufficient to avoid becoming a burden on the social security system of the host State during their period of residence. Secondly, they must be covered by sickness insurance in respect of all risks in the host State. The resources are deemed sufficient in the same circumstances as under Dir. 90/364 (see section III above).

The spouse and the dependent children of the person concerned are entitled to take up any employed or self-employed activity anywhere within the host State, even if they are not nationals of a Member State (Art. 2(2)). The right of residence is granted only for as long as the beneficiaries fulfil the two conditions mentioned above (Art. 3). It is evidenced by the issue of a residence permit (Art. 2(1)). The beneficiaries of the directive are covered by administrative arrangements similar to those applicable to workers under Dir. 68/360 (seventh recital and Art. 2(2); see section I above).

V. Students

Students were first granted the right of residence by Dir. 90/366 of 28 June 1990 (*OJ* 1990 L180/30). However, in Case C-295/90 *Parliament* v. *Council* [1992] ECR I-4193 at pp. I-4235–6, the ECJ annulled this directive on the grounds that it was adopted on the wrong legal basis (Art. 308). The Court pointed out that the correct legal basis was Art. 12(2), under which the Council could adopt rules designed to prohibit discrimination where such rules were necessary to enable rights derived from Art. 12(1) to be exercised effectively. Since access to vocational training without discrimination, which implied a right of residence, was covered by Art. 12, the directive did not exceed the scope of Art. 12, and recourse to Art. 308 was not justified.

Dir. 90/366 was replaced by Council Dir. 93/96 of 29 October 1993 on the right of residence for students (*OJ* 1993 L317/59). The purpose of the directive is to guarantee access to vocational training anywhere in the Community in a non-discriminatory manner by facilitating the exercise of the right of residence by students for the duration of the course. In accordance with the case-law of the ECJ, such right of residence is implicit in, and is a corollary to, the right of admission to vocational training (third and fifth recitals; see also Case C-357/89 *Raulin* [1992] ECR I-1027 at pp. I-1065–7).

Art. 1 requires the Member States to recognize the right of residence for any student who is a national of a Member State and who does not enjoy that right under other provisions of Community law, and for the student's spouse and their dependent children, subject to three conditions. First, the student must assure the relevant national authority, by means of a declaration or by any other equivalent means, that he has sufficient resources to avoid becoming a burden on the social assistance system of the host Member State during his period of residence. Secondly, the student must be enrolled in a recognized educational establishment for the principal purpose of following a vocational training course. Thirdly, he must be covered by sickness insurance in respect of all risks in the host State.

The directive does not require resources of a specific amount, evidenced by specified documents, but gives the student a choice between a declaration and such alternative means as are at least equivalent. The Member States cannot impose stricter conditions (Case C-424/98 *Commission* v. *Italy*, above, at pp. I-4033–4; Case C-184/99 *Grzelczyk* [2001] ECR I-6193 at pp. I-6244–5). Nevertheless, a Member State may decide that a student who has recourse to social assistance no longer fulfils the conditions of the directive and may for that reason either withdraw his residence permit or not renew it. However, such measures may not be the automatic consequence of a student's recourse to social assistance. Although the right of residence exists for as long as the beneficiaries fulfil the above conditions (Art. 4), the directive only requires that they must not become an 'unreasonable' burden on the public finances of the host Member State (sixth recital in the preamble). The host State therefore must not deprive a student of his right of residence just because he encounters temporary financial difficulties or because his financial position has changed for reasons beyond his control, since he made his original declaration (*Grzelczyk*, above, at pp. I-6245–6).

The right of residence is restricted to the duration of the course of studies in question and must be evidenced by a residence permit (Art. 2(1); see also Case C-357/89 *Raulin*, above, at pp. I-1066–7, which makes it clear that possession of a residence permit cannot be a precondition for obtaining study finance). The spouse and the dependent children of the student are entitled to take up any employed or self-employed activity anywhere within the host State, even if they are not nationals of a Member State (Art. 2(2)). The directive does not establish any entitlement to the payment of maintenance grants by the host State to students benefiting from the right of residence (Art. 3; see also the seventh recital). On the other hand, the directive does not preclude the beneficiaries from receiving social security benefits (*Grzelczyk*, above, at p. I-6244).

The directive does not apply to students who enjoy the right of residence by virtue of the fact that they are or have been effectively engaged in economic activities or are members of the family of a migrant worker (tenth recital). The position of these students is governed by the rules of Community law relating to workers. Nor does the directive apply to students who follow a general (i.e. non-vocational) course. Those students are probably covered by Dir. 90/364 (for the status of students in general, *see further under* **Free movement of persons**, section II). The beneficiaries of the directive are covered by administrative arrangements similar to those applicable to workers under Dir. 68/360 (ninth recital and Art. 2(2); see section I above).

In the case of all five categories of beneficiaries, the right of entry and residence may be restricted only on grounds of public policy, public security, or public health in accordance with Dir. 64/221 (Art. 10 of Dir. 68/360; Art. 8 of Dir. 73/148; Art. 2(2) of Dir. 90/364, Dir. 90/365, and Dir. 93/96). In several cases, the ECJ has emphasized that this restriction must be regarded not as a condition precedent to the acquisition of the right of entry and residence but as providing the possibility, in individual cases where there is sufficient justification, of imposing restrictions on the exercise of a right derived directly from the Treaty. It does not therefore justify administrative measures requiring in a general way formalities at the frontier other than those laid down in the various directives, i.e. the simple production of a valid identity card or passport (see e.g. Case 157/79 *Pieck*, above, at p. 2185. *See further under* **Public health, Public policy, Public security**. For an assessment of the implementation of the three directives relating to non-economically active persons, see the Commission's Report to Parliament and the Council on the implementation of Council Directives 90/364, 90/365 and 93/96 on the right of residence, adopted on 17 March 1999, COM(1999) 127).

VI. Citizens of the Union

Art. 18(1) EC, inserted by the TEU, provides that:

> Every citizen of the Union shall have the right to move and reside freely within the territory of the Member States, subject to the limitations and conditions laid down in this Treaty and by the measures adopted to give it effect.

This Article therefore both confers the right of free movement and residence and subjects that right to limitations and conditions. Each element of the provision will be considered briefly in turn.

As regards the right of movement and residence, in Case C-413/99 *Baumbast and R*, above, paras. 81–3, the ECJ pointed out that although before the TEU entered into force that right had been subject to the condition that the beneficiary was carrying on an economic activity within the meaning of Arts. 39, 43, and 49 EC, this was no longer the case. Under Art. 17(1) EC, every national of a Member State is a citizen of the Union with the consequence that Union citizenship has become the fundamental status of Member State nationals. Moreover, the TEU does not require that citizens of the Union pursue a professional or trade activity in order to enjoy the rights attached to citizenship. The Court concluded that the right of movement and residence 'is conferred directly on every citizen of the Union by a clear and precise provision of the Treaty. *Purely as a national of a Member State, and consequently a citizen of the Union,* [*a person*] *therefore has the right to rely on Art. 18(1)*' (ibid. para. 84, emphasis added). Furthermore, the rights conferred by Art. 18(1) on individuals are enforceable by them before the national courts. In other words, Art. 18(1) has direct effect (ibid. para. 86).

As regards the limitations and conditions, those are not set out in a separate instrument applicable to citizens only, as in the case of the other categories of persons discussed earlier. It appears from the case-law of the Court that the 'limitations and conditions' to which Art. 18(1) refers are those which apply to the free movement of workers, self-employed persons, providers and recipients of services under Arts. 39 to 55 EC and the implementing legislation (Dirs. 68/360, 73/148, and 64/221 dealing with limitations on grounds of public policy, public security, and public health), and to the right of residence of economically inactive persons under the three residence directives (Dirs. 90/364, 90/365, and 93/96) (see sections I to V above). Nevertheless, those limitations and conditions, being derogations from a fundamental freedom, must be interpreted strictly and applied in accordance with the principle of proportionality (Case C-413/99 *Baumbast and R*, paras. 87–94, see section III above. For a more detailed discussion of the Court's case-law on the right of movement and residence of Union citizens, *see further under* **Free movement of persons**, section III.4(*b*)).

VII. Directive 2004/38

Directive 2004/38 of the European Parliament and of the Council on the right of citizens of the Union and their family members to move and reside freely within the territory of the Member States was adopted on 29 April 2004 and entered into force on 30 April 2004, on the day of its publication in the *Official Journal*, in accordance with Art. 41 (*OJ* 2004 L158/77). The directive has to be implemented by the Member States by 30 April 2006, from which date it will repeal and replace Arts. 10 and 11 of Reg. 1612/68 (relating to workers' families) and Dirs. 64/221, 68/360, 72/194, 73/148, 75/34, 75/35, 90/364, 90/365, and 93/96 (Arts. 38 and 40).

The main objective of the directive is to simplify and strengthen the right of free movement and residence of persons, which constitutes both an essential aspect of Union citizenship and one of the fundamental freedoms of the internal market. For this purpose, the directive codifies and reviews the existing Community instruments dealing separately with workers, self-employed persons, students, and other economically inactive persons (see sections I to V above), with a view to replacing this sector-by-sector, piecemeal approach by a single legislative act (see the first four recitals in the preamble). The directive retains many of the detailed rules of existing legislation and incorporates the relevant case-law of the Court of Justice. Since these are both covered in the various entries dealing with this subject-matter in this volume (see the cross-references at the end of this entry), the following summary highlights mainly those provisions of the directive which will introduce major changes in the law when the directive is implemented by the Member States.

1. Subjects covered. The directive covers three main subjects: the conditions governing the exercise of the right of free movement and residence by Union citizens and their family members; the right of permanent residence; and the limits placed on those rights on grounds of public policy, public security, or public health (Art. 1).

2. Beneficiaries. The directive applies to all Union citizens who move to or reside in a Member State other than that of which they are nationals ('host Member State'), and to their family members who accompany or join them (Art. 3(1)). Family members include, in addition to those defined in Art. 10 of Reg. 1612/68, the partner with whom the Union citizen has contracted a registered partnership if the host Member State treats registered partnerships as equivalent to marriage (Art. 2(2)(b)). In addition, the host Member

State is to facilitate entry and residence of other family members as defined in Art. 3(2).

3. Right of exit. Union citizens and their family members with a valid identity card or passport have the right to leave the territory of a Member State to travel to another Member State without any exit visa (Art. 4).

4. Right of entry. The directive makes a distinction between the right of entry and the right of residence. Member States are to grant Union citizens leave to enter their territory with a valid identity card or passport without any entry visa. Family members who are not nationals of a Member State must have a valid passport and an entry visa if required by Reg. 539/2001 or by national law. Possession of a valid residence card (see below) exempts such family members from the visa requirement (Art. 5).

5. Right of residence. The directive distinguishes between the right of residence (Chapter III) and the right of permanent residence (Chapter IV). Union citizens have the right of residence in the host Member State for a period of up to three months without any conditions or formalities other than the requirement to hold a valid identity card or passport. The same applies to family members in possession of a valid passport who are not nationals of a Member State, accompanying or joining the Union citizen (Art. 6).

All Union citizens have the right of residence in the host Member State for a period of longer than three months if they:

(*a*) are workers or self-employed persons; or
(*b*) have sufficient resources and comprehensive sickness insurance; or
(*c*) are students and have sufficient resources and comprehensive sickness insurance; or
(*d*) are family members accompanying or joining those listed above, even if they are not nationals of a Member State (Art. 7).

For periods of residence longer than three months, the host Member State may require Union citizens to register with the relevant authorities, in which case a registration certificate will be issued (this replaces the present residence permit) (Art. 8). However, to family members of a Union citizen who are not nationals of a Member State a residence card is to be issued, valid for five years (Arts. 9 to 11). Since the right of residence is conferred directly on Union citizens by the Treaty, it is not dependent upon their having fulfilled administrative procedures (eleventh recital in the preamble).

An important innovation of the directive is that, subject to certain conditions, family members retain the right of residence in the event of death or departure of the Union citizen from the host Member State, and in the event of divorce, annulment of marriage, or termination of registered partnership (Arts. 12 and 13). As long as the beneficiaries of the right of residence do not become an unreasonable burden on the social assistance system of the host Member State they cannot be expelled, except on the grounds mentioned below. An expulsion measure cannot be the automatic consequence of recourse to the social assistance system and may in no case be adopted against workers, self-employed persons, and job-seekers except on grounds of public policy or public security (Art. 14 and sixteenth recital in the preamble).

6. Right of permanent residence. Union citizens who have resided legally for a continuous period of five years in the host Member State have the right of permanent residence there. This right is not subject to the conditions applicable to the right of residence. The same applies also to family members who are not nationals of a Member State and have legally resided with the Union citizen in the host Member State for a continuous period of five years. Continuity of residence is not affected by certain events. Once acquired, the right of permanent residence is lost only through absence from the host Member State for a period exceeding two consecutive years (Art. 16). In certain situations, workers or self-employed persons and their family members acquire the right of permanent residence before completion of the five-year period (Art. 17). These situations correspond to those in which these persons already have the right to remain permanently in the host Member State after having been employed or self-employed there (*see further under* **Right to remain**). These constitute acquired rights, which should be maintained (see the nineteenth recital in the preamble). Eligible Union citizens are issued with a document certifying permanent residence (Art. 19), while eligible family members who are not nationals of a Member State are issued with a permanent residence card, which is renewable automatically every ten years (Art. 20). As the preamble explains, enjoyment of permanent residence in the host Member State strengthens the feeling of Union citizenship and is a key element in promoting social cohesion, which is one of the fundamental objectives of the Union (seventeenth recital).

7. Restrictions on the right of entry and residence on grounds of public policy, public security, or public health. While the directive incorporates some of the existing rules, as interpreted by the Court of Justice, in many respects it tightens the conditions and procedural safeguards subject to which Union citizens and their family members may be denied leave to enter or may be expelled. Thus, before taking an expulsion decision, the host Member State must take into account a number of factors, such as the length of the person's residence on its territory, his/her age, state of health, family and economic situation, social and cultural integration into the host State, and the extent of his/her links with the country of origin. Generally, the greater the degree of integration in the host Member State, the greater the degree of protection against expulsion should be. Union citizens or their family members who have the right of permanent residence may be expelled only on serious grounds of public policy or public security. Union citizens who have resided in the host Member State for the previous ten years or are minors may be expelled only on imperative grounds of public security (Art. 28, see also the twenty-fourth recital in the preamble). An application for lifting of the exclusion order may be submitted after a reasonable period, and in any event after three years (Art. 32). Restrictions on grounds of public health are limited to diseases with epidemic potential as defined by the World Health Organization and other infectious diseases if they are the subject of protection measures in the host State (Art. 29). The persons concerned must have access to effective judicial and administrative redress procedures (Art. 31). Member States are allowed to take the necessary measures against any abuse of rights or fraud, such as marriages of convenience (Art. 35). They may apply effective and proportionate sanctions against breaches of national rules adopted for the implementation of the directive (Art. 36).

See also **Expulsion, Freedom of establishment, Freedom to provide services, Free movement of persons, Public health, Public policy, Public security, Residence permit, Right to leave, Right to remain.**

Further reading: *See under* **Freedom of establishment, Freedom to provide services, Free movement of persons.**

▶ **RIGHT TO LEAVE** Right of the nationals of the Member States to leave the territory of their State of origin in order to pursue an economic activity in another Member Sate. The freedom of movement guaranteed by the EC Treaty would be rendered meaningless if the Member States could prohibit or hinder their nationals from leaving their territory in order to move to another Member State for the purposes recognized by Community law. As the ECJ has pointed out, 'provisions which preclude or deter a national of a Member State from leaving his country of origin in order to exercise his right to freedom of movement . . . constitute an obstacle to that freedom even if they apply without regard to the nationality of the workers concerned' (Case C-415/93 *Bosman* [1995] ECR I-4921 at p. I-5069, concerning the movement of workers; see also Case 81/87 *Daily Mail* [1988] ECR 5483 at p. 5510, where the Court first laid down this principle in the context of the right of establishment). Such provisions are incompatible with the Treaty (for examples of such prohibited provisions, *see further under* **Free movement of persons**, section I.2(*a*)).

Although the right to leave is derived directly from the Treaty, it is also expressly granted by secondary legislation to the various categories of persons who enjoy the right of entry and residence (of which it forms a natural corollary), that is to say, to:

- workers and members of their families (Art. 2 of Dir. 68/360, *OJ Sp. Edn.* 1968 (II), p. 485);
- self-employed persons and providers and recipients of services and members of their families (Art. 2 of Dir. 73/148, *OJ* 1973 L172/14);
- persons of independent means and members of their families (Art. 2(2) of Dir. 90/364, *OJ* 1990 L180/26);
- retired persons and member of their families (Art. 2(2) of Dir. 90/365, *OJ* 1990 L180/28);
- students and members of their families (Art. 2(2) of Dir. 93/96, *OJ* 1993 L317/59. For a definition of these various categories of persons, *see further under* **Right of entry and residence**).

It should be noted that all of the above directives and some others concerning the movement and residence of persons will be repealed and replaced as from 30 April 2006 by Dir. 2004/38 of the European Parliament and of the Council of 29 April 2004 on the right of citizens of the Union and their family members to move and reside freely within the territory of the Member States (*OJ* 2004 L158/77, Art. 38. For a discussion of this directive, *see further under* **Right of entry and residence**, section VII).

The right to leave is granted only to natural persons. In the present state of Community law, neither Arts. 43 and 48 of the EC Treaty nor Dir. 73/148 confer on a company incorporated under the legislation of a Member State and having its registered office there a right to transfer its central management and control and its central administration to another Member State (Case 81/87 *Daily Mail*, above, at pp. 5512–13; *see further under* **Freedom of establishment**, section V.1).

According to the directives, all the above beneficiaries must be able to exercise the right to leave simply on production of a valid identity card or passport, which must be issued or renewed by the Member States and which must state in particular the holder's nationality. The passport must be valid at least for all Member States and for countries through which the holder must pass when travelling between Member States. Where a passport is the only document on which the holder may lawfully leave the country, its period of validity must be not less than five years. No exit visa or equivalent document may be demanded from the beneficiaries. The Member States may derogate from the above provisions only on grounds of public policy, public security, or public health.

See also **Freedom of establishment, Freedom to provide services, Free movement of persons, Public health, Public policy, Public security, Right of entry and residence.**

► **RIGHT TO REMAIN** Right of the nationals of the Member States to remain in the territory of another Member State after having pursued therein activities as employed or self-employed persons. Such a right is seen as a corollary to the right of residence in that it enables the persons concerned to maintain their residence in the host State even after their working life has come to an end. It therefore furthers the attainment of freedom of movement for persons, which is one of the foundations of the European Community (see the preambles to the two instruments referred to below).

In the case of employed persons (workers), the right to remain is directly conferred by Art. 39(3)(d) EC, which has been implemented by Comm. Reg. 1251/70 of 29 June 1970 on the right of workers to remain in the territory of a Member State after having been employed in that State (*OJ Sp. Edn.* 1970 (II), p. 402). In the case of self-employed persons, Arts. 43 *et seq.* do not expressly provide for a similar right, but the right to remain has been established by Council Dir. 75/34 of 17 December 1974 concerning the right of nationals of a Member State to remain in the territory of another Member State after having pursued therein an activity in a self-employed capacity

(*OJ* 1975 L14/10), which was adopted under Art. 308 EC and is substantially identical to Reg. 1251/70. The two measures will be discussed together below. It should be noted that Dir. 75/34 and many others concerning the movement and residence of persons (although not Reg. 1251/70) will be repealed and replaced as from 30 April 2006 by Dir. 2004/38 of the European Parliament and of the Council of 29 April 2004 on the right of citizens of the Union and their family members to move and reside freely within the territory of the Member States (*OJ* 2004 L158/77, Art. 38. For a discussion of this directive, *see further under* **Right of entry and residence**, section VII).

According to Art. 1 of each measure, the right to remain is granted to nationals of a Member State who have worked as employed persons or have pursued activities as self-employed persons in the territory of another Member State and to members of their families, as defined in Art. 10 of Reg. 1612/68 (in the case of workers) or in Art. 1 of Dir. 73/148 (in the case of self-employed persons. For these definitions, *see further under* **Right of entry and residence**).

The right to remain permanently in the host State is subject to certain conditions that depend on the reasons which have led to the termination of employment or self-employed activity. In this respect, both the regulation and the directive make a clear distinction between retirement, the normal and foreseeable end of working life, and permanent incapacity to work, which leads to a premature and unforeseeable termination of activity. In the former case, the right to remain is granted to a worker or self-employed person who, at the time of termination of his activity, has reached the age laid down by the law of the host State for entitlement to an old-age pension and who has been employed or self-employed in that State for at least the previous twelve months and has resided there continuously for more than three years. Where the law of the host State does not grant the right to an old-age pension to certain categories of self-employed persons, the age requirement is satisfied when the beneficiary reaches 65 years of age (Art. 2(1)(a) of Reg. 1251/70 and of Dir. 75/34).

Where the termination of activity is due to permanent incapacity to work, the normal condition for acquiring the right to remain is continuous residence in the host State for more than two years. If, however, such incapacity is the result of an accident at work or an occupational disease entitling the person concerned to a pension that is payable in whole or in part by an institution of the host State, the condition regarding length of residence is waived (Art. 2(1)(b)). The incapacity must occur while the person is employed in the host State in the context of freedom of movement for workers under Community law, and not during a period of residence authorized solely under national law (Case C-171/91 *Tsiotras* [1993] ECR I-2925 at pp. I-2958–9).

The right to remain is also granted to persons who, after completing three years' continuous employment or self-employed activity and residence in the host State, pursue their activities in a third State, while retaining their residence in the former State, to which they return, as a rule, each day or at least once a week. Periods of employment or self-employed activity so completed in the third State are deemed to have been completed in the State of residence for the purposes of acquiring the right to remain there upon retirement or in the event of incapacity (Art. 2(1)(c)).

The above conditions as to length of residence and activity in the host State are waived if the spouse of the person concerned is a national of the host State or has lost that nationality as a result of the marriage (Art. 2(2)).

Once the worker or self-employed person has acquired the right to remain in the host State, the members of his family who are residing with him will be entitled to remain there permanently, even after his death. If, however, the person dies during his working life and before having acquired the right to remain, members of his family will be eligible to remain in the host State permanently only if the person, on the date of his decease, had resided continuously in that State for at least two years; or his death resulted from an accident at work or an occupational disease; or the surviving spouse is a national of the host State or lost that nationality by the marriage (Art. 3). The period of two years' continuous residence must immediately precede the person's death (Case C-257/00 *Givane* [2003] ECR I-345, para. 50). Since the provisions of Community law on the free movement of persons cannot be applied to purely internal situations, a spouse or a dependent relative who is a national of a non-Member State is not entitled to remain in the territory of a Member State solely in his or her capacity as a member of the family of a national of that State if the latter has never exercised freedom of movement under Community law (Cases C-297/88 etc. *Dzodzi* [1990] ECR I-3763 at pp. I-3791–2).

Continuity of residence may be proved by any means used in the host State. It is not affected by temporary absences not exceeding three months per year, nor by longer absences due to military service. Periods of involuntary unemployment or of inactivity due to circumstances beyond the control of the self-employed person, and periods of inactivity due to illness or accident, are to be considered as periods of employment or self-employed activity (Art. 4).

The beneficiaries may exercise the right to remain, without any particular formality, within two years from the time of becoming entitled to it. During this period, they may leave the territory of the host State without losing their right (Art. 5). They are entitled to a residence permit (Art. 6). They are also to enjoy the right to equality of treatment laid down in Reg. 1612/68 and in the various directives implementing freedom of establishment (Art. 7; see Case C-334/94 *Commission* v. *France* [1996] ECR I-1307 at p. I-1341). In several cases the ECJ has confirmed that the equality of treatment provided for in Art. 7(2) of Reg. 1612/68 in respect of social advantages applies to the benefit of a worker's dependent relatives who have chosen to remain in the host Member State, even if those advantages are only sought after the worker's death (Case 32/75 *Cristini* [1975] ECR 1085 at p. 1095; see also Case 261/83 *Castelli* [1984] ECR 3199 at p. 3213; Case 316/85 *Lebon* [1987] ECR 2811 at pp. 2835–7. *See further under* **Social advantage**).

The regulation and the directive are not to affect national provisions that are more favourable to nationals of other Member States. Member States are required to facilitate readmission of workers and self-employed persons who left their territories after a long period of permanent residence and activity there and who wish to return upon retirement or in the event of incapacity (Art. 8). Member States may derogate from the provisions of the regulation and directive only on grounds of public policy, public security, or public health, in accordance with Dir. 64/221 (Art. 9 of Dir. 75/34. The scope of Dir. 64/221 has been extended to workers and self-employed persons exercising the right to remain by Dirs. 72/194 and 75/35, respectively. *See further under* **Public health, Public policy, Public security**).

***See also* Freedom of establishment, Freedom to provide services, Free movement of persons, Public health, Public policy, Public security, Residence permit, Right of entry and residence, Right to leave, Social advantage.**

► SCHENGEN AGREEMENTS *see* FREE MOVEMENT OF PERSONS

S

► SEASONAL WORKER *see* RESIDENCE PERMIT *and* WORKER

► **SOCIAL ADVANTAGE** Art. 7(2) of Reg. 1612/68 on freedom of movement for workers within the Community (*OJ Sp. Edn.* 1968 (II), p. 475) provides that a worker who is a national of a Member State and is employed in the territory of another Member State ('migrant worker') is to enjoy the same 'social advantages' as the workers of the host State. The concept of 'social advantage' is not defined in the regulation. However, relying on the aim of the regulation, which is to achieve the free movement of workers and for this purpose to abolish all differences in treatment between national workers and migrant workers, in a long line of cases the ECJ has held that that concept cannot be interpreted restrictively. Thus, in Case 207/78 *Even* [1979] ECR 2019 at p. 2034, the Court gave an extremely broad definition, which it has used without change in all subsequent cases. According to that definition, the social advantages which the regulation extends to migrant workers are:

> all those which, whether or not linked to a contract of employment, are generally granted to national workers primarily because of their objective status as workers or by virtue of the mere fact of their residence on the national territory and the extension of which to workers who are nationals of other Member States therefore seems suitable to facilitate their mobility within the Community.

In order to enjoy a social advantage it is not necessary that a contract of employment should actually be in existence since migrant workers are guaranteed certain rights linked to the status of worker even when they are no longer in an employment relationship. A benefit the payment of which is dependent on the prior existence of an employment relationship that has come to an end may thus constitute a social advantage, since entitlement to that benefit is intrinsically linked to the recipient's objective status as worker. Generally, a Member State may not make payment of a social advantage dependent on the condition that the recipients be resident within its territory. Unless it is objectively justified and proportionate to its aim, such a residence condition amounts to prohibited indirect discrimination as it can be more easily met by national workers than by those from other Member States (Case C-57/96 *Meints* [1997] ECR I-6689 at pp. I-6719–21; see further below. *See also under* **Free movement of persons**, section I.4(*c*) and (*g*), and **Worker**).

Moreover, the Court has held that the principle of equal treatment laid down in Art. 7(2) is also intended to prevent discrimination against those members of the worker's family who, irrespective of their nationality, have the right to install themselves with the worker under Art. 10(1) of Reg. 1612/68 and who therefore fall within the class of beneficiaries of the regulation. These include the worker's spouse and their descendants who are under the age of 21 years or are dependants, and dependent relatives in the ascending line of the worker and his spouse. Once these persons have exercised the right to install themselves with the worker, they become the indirect beneficiaries of the equal treatment accorded to the migrant worker. As such, they are entitled to the same 'social advantages' as national workers and the members of their families, even after the death of the worker where they have remained in the territory of the host Member State in accordance with Reg. 1251/70 (*OJ Sp. Edn.* 1970 (II), p. 402). These family members may rely on Art. 7(2) even when they are dependent not on a migrant worker, but on a migrant self-employed person. Further, since Reg. 1612/68 has a general application, Art. 7(2) applies quite independently of Reg. 1408/71, as amended, dealing with social security for migrant workers (*OJ Sp. Edn.* 1971 (II), p. 416). Therefore, a social benefit may qualify as a 'social advantage' within the meaning of Art. 7(2) both where it is also covered by Reg. 1408/71 and where it is not (see the cases cited below).

By applying the above definition in a liberal manner, the Court has established that the following must be regarded as 'social advantages' under Art. 7(2) and must be granted to the migrant worker and the eligible members of his family under the same conditions as to national workers:

- fares reduction cards issued by a national railway authority to large families, which social advantage must be granted to the widow and children of a migrant worker, even if they only apply for it after the worker's death, if they remain in the host State (Case 32/75 *Cristini* [1975] ECR 1085 at pp. 1094–5);
- an allowance for handicapped adults (Case 63/76 *Inzirillo* [1976] ECR 2057 at pp. 2068–9; here the adult child of a migrant worker was held eligible because he was dependent upon his father. This allowance was also covered by Reg. 1408/71. See also Case C-310/91 *Schmid* [1993] ECR I-3011 at pp. I-3042–4 concerning disability benefits for adults);
- interest-free loans granted on childbirth by a credit institution, with financial assistance from the State, to families with a low income to stimulate the birthrate, even if they are granted on a discretionary basis and for reasons of demographic policy which is not, as such, within Community competence (Case 65/81 *Reina* [1982] ECR 33 at pp. 44–5);
- an old-age allowance that guarantees a minimum income to old people. The grant of such a social advantage to the migrant may not be made subject to the existence of a reciprocal agreement between the host State and the Member State of which the beneficiary is a national, nor to a condition requiring actual residence in the host State for a specified period if such a condition is not imposed on the nationals of that State (Case 261/83 *Castelli* [1984] ECR 3199 at pp. 3213–14; Case 157/84 *Frascogna I* [1985] ECR 1739 at pp. 1749–50; Case 256/86 *Frascogna II* [1987] ECR 3431 at pp. 3442–3; in each case the beneficiary was a dependent relative in the ascending line of a migrant worker. This allowance was not covered by Reg. 1408/71 as it was paid to old persons whether or not they were related to a worker);

- a social benefit guaranteeing a minimum means of subsistence in a general manner ('minimex'). The grant of such a benefit may not be made subject to the condition that the migrant worker and his family have resided in the host Member State for a certain period of time prior to the grant (Case 249/83 *Hoeckx* [1985] ECR 973 at pp. 988–9; this benefit was not covered by Reg. 1408/71 as it was granted to any person with inadequate means generally). In Case C-326/90 *Commission* v. *Belgium* [1992] ECR I-5517 at pp. I-5527–8, the Court held that by imposing such a residence requirement on migrants for the grant of allowances for handicapped persons, guaranteed income for elderly people and the above-mentioned 'minimex', Belgium infringed Art. 7(2) of Reg. 1612/68. Such a residence requirement, even if it is imposed irrespective of nationality, constitutes indirect discrimination contrary to Art. 7(2) (Case C-299/01 *Commission* v. *Luxembourg* [2002] ECR I-5899 at p. I-5914, involving guaranteed minimum income). Nor can entitlement to a social benefit, such as the 'minimex', be made conditional, in the case of nationals of other Member States, on their falling within the scope of Reg. 1612/68 (i.e. on their being workers or family members) when no such condition applies to the nationals of the host Member State (Case C-184/99 *Grzelczyk* [2001] ECR I-6193 at p. I-6246; for a discussion of this case, *see further under* **Free movement of persons**, sections II and III).

  Although a social benefit (such as the 'minimex' or the guaranteed income to old people or the 'tideover allowance' (see below)) must in principle be made available both to the migrant worker and to the members of his family, the latter qualify only indirectly for it, that is, only if the benefit may be regarded as a social advantage for the worker himself. That is not the case where the worker's descendants have reached the age of 21 and are no longer dependent on him since then the worker is no longer supporting them. Such descendants, if they are not workers themselves, are not entitled to equal treatment with regard to a social advantage (Case 316/85 *Lebon* [1987] ECR 2811 at pp. 2836–7; Case C-85/96 *Martinez Sala* [1998] ECR I-2691 at p. I-2719). Nor is a descendant so entitled if his father, who had been employed in a Member State (Germany), died before his country of origin (Spain) acceded to the Community and therefore never acquired the status of 'worker' within the meaning of Art. 39 EC and Reg. 1612/68 (Case C-131/96 *Mora Romero* [1997] ECR I-3659 at p. I-3682);
- special unemployment benefits, known as 'tideover allowances', provided for young people seeking their first employment after completing their studies or apprenticeships (Case 94/84 *Deak* [1985] ECR 1873 at pp. 1886–7; here the beneficiary was the dependent child of a migrant worker and was held eligible even although he was a national of a non-Member State; the benefit was not covered by Reg. 1408/71). The requirement that the applicant must have completed his studies in the Member State which grants the benefit (i.e. Belgium), even if it applies

without distinction as to nationality, constitutes indirect discrimination and is therefore contrary to Art. 39 EC and Art. 7(2) of Reg. 1612/68 (Case C-278/94 *Commission* v. *Belgium* [1996] ECR I-4307 at pp. I-4339–40, I-4343). Such a requirement is contrary to Community law even if it disadvantages the Member State's own nationals (Case C-224/98 *D'Hoop* [2002] ECR I-6191 at pp. I-6620, I-6224-5; for a discussion of this case, *see further under* **Free movement of persons**, sections II and III);

- the right to use his own language in (criminal) proceedings before the courts of the Member State in which the migrant resides, under the same conditions as national workers, even if that language is different from the one normally used in proceedings before the courts in question (Case 137/84 *Mutsch* [1985] ECR 2681 at p. 2696);
- the possibility for a migrant worker of obtaining permission for his unmarried companion to reside with him, where that companion is not a national of the host Member State, if that State grants the same advantage to its own nationals (Case 59/85 *Reed* [1986] ECR 1283 at pp. 1303–4);
- educational grants covering both registration and tuition fees and maintenance and training costs, subject to certain conditions, whether awarded to the migrant worker or to his dependent children. Those children can thus rely on Art. 7(2) in order to obtain study finance under the same conditions as are applicable to children of national workers (Case 39/86 *Lair* [1988] ECR 3161 at pp. 3195–201; Case 197/86 *Brown* [1988] ECR 3205 at pp. 3245–6; Case 235/87 *Matteucci* [1988] ECR 5589 at pp. 5611–12; Cases 389/87 etc. *Echternach and Moritz* [1989] ECR 723 at pp. 764–5; Case C-357/89 *Raulin* [1992] ECR I-1027 at pp. I-1061–2; Case C-3/90 *Bernini* [1992] ECR I-1071 at pp. I-1105–8). It follows that where national legislation does not impose any residence requirement on the children of national workers for the financing of their studies, such a requirement must be regarded as discriminatory and is prohibited if it is imposed on the children of workers who are nationals of other Member States. Moreover, dependent children may rely on Art. 7(2) not only where their parent (father or mother) is a migrant worker, but also where their parent is a migrant self-employed person (Case C-337/97 *Meeusen* [1999] ECR I-3289 at pp. I-3313–15, where a Belgian national residing in Belgium with her parents of Belgian nationality, one of whom was a self-employed person and the other a worker in the Netherlands, was entitled to a study grant in the Netherlands. *See further under* **Free movement of persons**, section II). Nevertheless, Art. 7(2) cannot be relied on, for the purposes of obtaining study finance, by a migrant worker who has ceased to work in the host Member State and returned to his Member State of origin, where his children also reside (Case C-33/99 *Fahmi and Esmoris Cerdeiro-Pinedo Amado* [2001] ECR I-2415 at pp. I-2472–4);

- the possibility of paying social security contributions at a lower rate (Case C-27/91 *Le Manoir* [1991] ECR I-5531 at p. I-5542);
- childbirth and maternity allowances (Case C-111/91 *Commission* v. *Luxembourg* [1993] ECR I-817 at pp. I-843–8; these allowances were also covered by Reg. 1408/71. The Court held that by imposing residence requirements for the grant of those allowances, Luxembourg infringed Art. 7(2) of Reg. 1612/68);
- a child-raising allowance that is automatically granted to persons fulfilling certain objective criteria (Case C-85/96 *Martinez Sala*, above, at p. I-2718; the allowance was covered both by Art. 7(2) and by Reg. 1408/71);
- special benefits for large families (Case C-185/96 *Commission* v. *Greece* [1998] ECR I-6601 at pp. I-6623–4);
- a funeral allowance (Case C-237/94 *O'Flynn* [1996] ECR I-2617 at p. I-2637);
- a benefit that takes the form of a single payment to agricultural workers whose contract of employment has been terminated as a result of the setting aside of land belonging to their former employer (Case C-57/96 *Meints*, above, at p. I-6719).

Art. 7(2) of Reg. 1612/68 applies not only where the migrant worker carries out his activities in another Member State, but also where, while employed by an undertaking established in another Member State, he is assigned to a temporary posting outside the Community (Case 237/83 *Prodest* [1984] ECR 3153 at pp. 3162–3, concerning the retention of affiliation to the general social security scheme of the host State during the temporary posting outside the Community).

On the other hand, Art. 7(2) does not apply to the following benefits, persons, or situations:

- benefits granted to certain categories of national workers for services rendered in wartime to their own country (Case 207/78 *Even*, above, at p. 2034, involving an early retirement pension without reduction);
- the continued payment by the employer of supplementary old-age and survivors' pension insurance contributions while a worker performs military service (Case C-315/94 *De Vos* [1996] ECR I-1417 at pp. I-1440–1);
- persons who move to another Member State in search of employment. Such persons qualify for equal treatment only as regards access to employment in accordance with Art. 39 EC and Arts. 2 and 5 of Reg. 1612/68, but not with regard to social and tax advantages under Art. 7(2) (Case 316/85 *Lebon*, above, at p. 2839). To qualify for social and tax advantages or unemployment benefits, a person must have already entered the employment market by exercising an effective and genuine occupational activity, which has conferred on him the status of 'worker'. By definition, that is not the case where people are seeking their first employment (Case C-278/94 *Commission* v. *Belgium*, above, at pp. I-4342–3; Case C-224/98 *D'Hoop*, above, at p. I-6220, both

cases dealing with tideover allowances in Belgium, see above; Case C-138/02 *Collins* [2004] ECR I-0000, paras. 30–3, 58, concerning job-seeker's allowance granted in the United Kingdom to people actively seeking employment). However, in *Collins* the Court felt it necessary to reinterpret this case-law in the light of the right to equal treatment enjoyed by citizens of the Union under Arts. 12 and 17 EC. The Court held that it was no longer possible to exclude from the scope of Art. 39(2) EC—which expresses the principle of equal treatment, guaranteed by Art. 12 EC—a benefit of a financial nature, such as a jobseeker's allowance, intended to facilitate access to employment in the labour market of a Member State (ibid. paras. 63–4). The Court recognized that it was legitimate for a Member State to subject the grant of such an allowance to the condition that a genuine link existed between the migrant seeking work and its employment market by imposing a residence requirement which was objectively justified and proportionate to the aim pursued (ibid. paras. 65–73. *See also under* **Free movement of persons**, section III.4(*a*));

- the non-Community spouse of a migrant worker where the non-Community spouse of a national worker is not entitled to the benefit in question, since in that case there is no social advantage for national workers (Case C-243/91 *Taghavi* [1992] ECR I-4401 at p. I-4418);
- situations which are purely internal to a Member State, that is, which have no factor linking them with any of the situations governed by Community law. Thus, a third-country national who is a member of the family of a worker having the nationality of a Member State cannot rely on Community law in order to claim social advantages granted to national workers and to migrant workers and to members of their families, when the worker of whose family he is a member has never exercised the right to freedom of movement within the Community (Case 147/87 *Zaoui* [1987] ECR 5511 at p. 5528; Case C-206/91 *Koua Poirrez* [1992] ECR I-6685 at p. I-6707).

See also **Free movement of persons, Social security, Worker.**

Further reading Ellis, 'Social Advantages: A New Lease of Life?' (2003) *CML Rev.* 639; O'Keeffe, 'Equal Rights for Migrants: The Concept of Social Advantages in Article 7(2), Regulation 1612/68' (1985) *YEL* 93. *See also under* **Free movement of persons.**

▶ **SOCIAL SECURITY** The Member States remain primarily responsible for the organization and administration of their social security systems. It is for them to decide who can contribute to the social security system, the range and level of benefits available under that system, and the conditions of entitlement to benefits (Case 238/82 *Duphar* [1984] ECR 523; Case C-70/95 *Sodemare* [1997] ECR I-3395) This competence is however subject to the Member States obligations under the EC Treaty. Thus in the organization and administration of social security benefits, Member States must respect, for example, the fundamental principle of equal treatment between nationals (Art. 12 EC) and the free movement of persons, goods, and services.

Although the concept of 'pay' in Art. 141 EC does not include State social systems, Dir. 79/7 on the progressive implementation of the principle of equal treatment for men and women in matters of social security (*OJ* 1979 L6/24), adopted on the basis of the general law-making powers set out in Art. 308 EC, applies the principle of equal treatment to such social security systems. In Case C-262/88 *Barber* [1990] ECR I-1889, the ECJ held that occupational social security systems were part of 'pay' and so came within the scope of Art. 141 EC. Prior to that judgment it had been widely believed that such systems were not part of pay and Dir. 86/378 on the implementation of the principle of equal treatment for men and women in occupational social security systems had been adopted making them subject to the principle of equal treatment (*OJ* 1986 L225/40). That directive was amended extensively following the judgment in *Barber* (see Dir. 96/97, *OJ* 1997 L46/20).

Although the Member States remain overwhelmingly responsible for social security systems, Art. 137 EC empowers the Community to 'support and complement' the activities of the Member States in the field of social security and social protection and the 'modernization' of social protection systems.

The following sections will set out the work of the Community in supporting and complementing Member States' social security systems and then proceed to discuss the Member States' obligations in the area of social security with respect to the free movement of goods and free provision of services. Most of the discussion will be concerned with the measures adopted to protect the social security rights of those exercising their right to free movement within the Community. It is in this area that the Community has been most active, enacting detailed legislation co-ordinating the social security system of the Member States which in turn has spawned a vast body of case-law.

I. Supporting and complementing national social security systems

In the case of social security and social protection the Council may adopt by means of directives, minimum requirements for 'gradual implementation' (Art. 137(2) EC). No directive has, as yet, been adopted pursuant to this provision.

Examples of the measures that the Commission has taken with respect to social security include the dissemination of information about national social security systems and the publication of reports on the modernization of social security systems. These reports, for the most part, discuss the prevailing levels of social protection, current common difficulties in ensuring adequate social protections, and the potential demands which will be placed on such systems (see 'Modernising and improving social protection in the European Union', COM(97) 102; 'A concerted strategy for modernising social protection', COM(99) 347; 'The future of health care and care for the elderly', COM(2001) 723).

II. Free movement of goods and services

The Member States are obliged to respect the letter and spirit of the EC Treaty with respect to the free movement of goods and services in the organization and administration of their social security systems. Thus in the field of medical care, insured persons must be given the right to go to another Member State and to purchase medical products and to receive medical care. This right includes the right to be reimbursed for such products and care by the social security institution with which they are insured. Moreover, if the financial equilibrium of a health care system so requires, the right to receive medical care in another Member State may be restricted (Case C-158/96 *Kohll* [1998] ECR I-1931, para. 41; Case C-157/99 *Geraets-Smit and Peerboom* [2001] ECR I-5473, para. 72; Case C-385/99 *Müller-Fauré and Van Riet* [2003] ECR I-4509).

The case-law of the European Court of Justice (ECJ) on the scope of claimants' rights and Member States' obligations with respect to medical care provided in a Member State, other than that of the social security regime to which the beneficiary is affiliated, can be summarized as follows:

(*i*) persons insured under the health-care system of a Member State have the right to obtain medical products (e.g. spectacles) in the territory of another Member States and to be reimbursed for those products at the rate prevailing in the Member State in which they are insured (Case C-120/95 *Decker* [1998] ECR I-1831). Prior authorization for the purchase of such products from the relevant health insurance fund is not required;

(*ii*) national rules that make the reimbursement of the cost of dental treatment provided in a Member State other than that in which the beneficiary is insured subject to prior authorization by the relevant social security institution are precluded by Arts. 49 and 50 EC (Case C-158/96 *Kohll*, above);

(*iii*) where reimbursement is sought for hospital treatment in a Member State other than that in which the beneficiary is insured, the responsible social security institution is entitled to require the seeking of an authorization for that treatment prior to its being carried out. The ECJ has laid down a number of principles which must govern the grant and refusal of authorization for treatment. The treatment in question must be regarded as 'normal' in the sense that it must be sufficiently recognizes in the professional circles concerned (Case C-157/99 *Geraerts-Smits and Peerboom*, above; Case C-385/99 *Muller-Faure and Van Riet*, above), the treatment must be necessary to the patient's condition and not capable of being provided without 'undue delay' within the health care system of the Member State in which the patient is insured (*Geraets-Smit and Peerbooms*, above, para. 103);

(*iv*) in the case of non-hospital treatment insured persons who go to another Member State and receive there medical treatment without having obtained the prior authorization of their health insurance fund, can claim reimbursement only within the limits of the cover provided under the social security system under which they are insured (*Müller-Fauré and Van Riet*, above, para. 98);

(*v*) a Member State that has a benefit in kind system under which treatment is provided but no cash exchanges hands can fix the amount of reimbursement to which patients who have received care in another Member State are entitled provided those amounts are based on objective, non-discriminatory and transparent criteria (*Müller-Fauré and Van Riet*, above, para. 107);

(*vi*) once a pensioner has registered with the competent social security institution of the Member State of his residence, it is that institution which is responsible for authorizing him to seek health care in another Member State (Case C-156/01 *Van der Duin* [2003] ECR I-7045).

III. Free movement of persons

The free movement of employed and self-employed persons within the Community requires the protection of the social security rights of those seeking to exercise the right of free movement. Such persons would be reluctant to exercise their right of free movement is they stood to lose social security rights acquired or in the process of being acquired under their home social security system. Employers would be reluctant to employ them if they ran the risk of being subject to social security contributions in more than one Member State. Employees themselves and the self-employed would likewise be dissuaded from seeking economic opportunities outside their home country if they were required to be affiliated to more than one social security system. To avoid these eventualities, the EC Treaty endowed the Community with powers to adopt such measures as were necessary to ensure that the social security rights of those who took advantage for the right to move, for economic purposes, throughout the Community were not prejudiced and further, that they and their employers were subject to the same social security obligations as nationals of the Member State in which they were exercising economic activity.

Art. 42 EC provides for the adoption by the Council:

> such measures in the field of social security as are necessary to provide freedom of movement for workers: to this end, it shall make arrangements to secure for migrant workers and their dependants:
>
> (a) aggregation, for the purposes of acquiring and retaining the right to benefit and of calculating the amount of benefit, of all periods taken into account under the laws of the several countries;
>
> (b) payment of benefits to persons resident in the territories of the Member States.

1. Legislative history. The social security regime required by Art. 42 EC to be set up in order to secure the free movement of workers was initially created, in the early days of the European Economic Community, under Reg. 3/58 (*JO* 1958 586) and Reg. 4/58 (*JO* 1958 597). These regulations were revised and amended extensively by Reg. 1408/71 (*OJ Sp. Edn.* 1971

(II), p. 416) and Reg. 574/72 (*OJ Sp. Edn.* 1972 (I), p. 159), henceforth referred to as the 'regulations'.

Changes in national social security systems, the accession of more States to the Community and the case-law of the European Court of Justice necessitated numerous amendments to these regulations.

Consolidated versions of both regulations were published in 1983, as Regs. 2003/83 and 2001/83 (*OJ* 1983 L230/6) and again in 1992 (*OJ* 1992 C325/1). Further consolidation and amendment took place in 1996 (Reg. 118/97, *OJ* 1997 L28/1). Since this consolidation exercise a further seven amendments to Reg. 1408/71 have been adopted (see *OJ* 1997 L176/1; *OJ* 1998 L168/1; *OJ* 1998 L209/1; *OJ* 1999 L38/1; *OJ* 1999 L164/1; *OJ* 2001 L187/1; *OJ* 2003 L124/1).

2. Current proposals. In 1998 the Commission published its proposals for a major reform of the legislation governing the social security rights of migrant workers (*OJ* 1999 C38/10). After much debate, political agreement was reached on the draft regulation in the Council on 1 December 2003, and Reg. 883/2004 on the co-ordination of social security systems was adopted on 29 April 2004 (*OJ* 2004 L166/1). The new regulation, which consolidates, updates, and simplifies the present complex mass of legislation, entered into force on the twentieth day after publication, and shall apply from the date of entry into force of the implementing regulation to be adopted later.

3. Direct effect. By virtue of Art. 42 EC, the regulations are directly applicable and as such, may be used by citizens and national authorities alike to enforce rights and obligations.

The regulations take precedence over national rules and practices and in case of an incompatibility between the two, the former must prevail. However, even if national measures are compatible with the regulations, this does not have the effect of removing those measures from the scope of provisions of the EC Treaty, for example the provisions on free movement of goods (Arts. 28 to 30) or those of freedom to supply and receive services (Arts. 49 to 55) (Case C-120/95 *Decker*, above; Case C-158/96 *Kohll*, above). Consequently, any provision in national law or the regulations which is incompatible with an EC Treaty provision is invalid.

IV. General principles

1. Basic principles. The fundamental objective of Art. 42 EC and the regulations is to safeguard the free movement of economically active persons throughout the Community. Those provisions must, therefore, be interpreted in the light of that objective. Any provision that is or is capable of being applied in a manner contrary to the principle of free movement is invalid. Moreover, in case of difficulties of interpretation, that meaning which accords with the objective of free movement takes precedence. The free movement of persons in turn rests upon the principle of equality of treatment between nationals and non-nationals. Community nationals who move from one Member State to another to engage in an economic activity either in an employed or self-employed capacity are required to be treated on an equal footing with nationals of the Member State in which they work.

2. Free movement. The pivotal role of the right of free movement in the protection of the social security rights of migrant workers and their families was first set out by the Court in 1975 in Case 7/75 *Fracas* [1975] ECR 679, where it was held that the handicapped child of an Italian national living and working in Belgium who fulfilled all the conditions for entitlement to a handicapped persons allowance must be granted that allowance when he reaches the age of majority, if he cannot by reason of his disability, take up employment even if that allowance was reserved to Belgian nationals:

If this were not the case, a worker anxious to ensure to his child the lasting enjoyment of the allowances necessitated by his conditions as a handicapped person would be induced not to remain in the Member State where he has established himself and has found his employment which would run counter to the objective sought to be attained by the principle of freedom of movement for workers within the Community (ibid. para. 20).

In Case C-228/88 *Bronzino* [1990] ECR I-531 and Case C-12/89 *Gatto* [1990] ECR I-557, the Court held that an Italian migrant workers employed and resident in Germany were entitled to an allowances for their dependent unemployed children resident in Italy even though under German law the allowances were required to be paid only to those young persons who resided in Germany:

The purpose of Article 73 is to prevent a Member State from being able to refuse to grant family benefits on account of the fact that a member of the worker's family resides in a Member State other than that providing the benefits. Such a refusal could deter Community workers from exercising their right to freedom of movement and would therefore constitute an obstacle to that movement (*Bronzino*, para. 12).

In Case C-406/93 *Reichling* [1994] ECR I-4061, the Court again stressed that the exercise of the right to free movement must not lead to any reduction in social security benefits:

The purpose of Article 42 is to facilitate freedom of movement for workers . . . The same objective is moreover pursued by Regulation 1408/71. That objective entails that migrant workers must not lose their right to social security benefits nor have the amount of those benefits reduced because they have exercised their right to free movement conferred on them by the Treaty. That situation may arise in a case such as that which is the subject of the main proceedings. It is common ground that if Mr Reichling has always worked and had completed all his periods of insurance in Belgium he would have received remuneration there and would not have been considered as a worker without remuneration. He would therefore have been entitled to an invalidity pension higher than that awarded him; At the time when he became incapacitated Mr Reichling was not in receipt of remuneration in Belgium but he was in receipt of remuneration in another Member State; That remuneration should have been taken into account by the competent Belgian institutions as if it had been remuneration received in Belgium . . . (ibid. paras. 22–6).

3. Equality of treatment. Art. 12 EC prohibits discrimination on the grounds of nationality (Case C-406/93 *Reichling*, above). Both direct and indirect discrimination are prohibited. Art. 3(1) of Reg. 1408/71 contains a specific expression of that general principle:

subject to the special provision of the regulation, persons resident in the territory of one of the Member States to whom this regulation applies shall be subject to the same obligations and enjoy the same benefits under the legislation of any Member State as nationals of that State.

Any derogation from the principle of equal treatment based on the provisions of Reg. 1408/71 must be objectively justified if the fundamental rule of non-discrimination laid down in Art. 3(1) is not to be deprived of meaning (Case C-308/93 *Cabanis-Issarte* [1996] ECR I-2097, para. 26; Case C-124/99 *Borawitz* [2000] ECR I-7293). Member States are responsible for determining who is and who is not a national of their respective countries.

Discrimination in social security can occur either directly by reference to nationality or indirectly, for example, through the application of a residency requirement, whereby mainly non-nationals are prejudiced. Thus, in Case 237/78 *Palermo* [1979] ECR 2645, the Court held that the grant of a non-contributory old-age pension could not be made dependent either on the nationality of the person concerned or on that of her children, provided that the nationality in issue was that of one of the Member States. Consequently a nationality requirement may be imposed on third-country nationals except where bilateral or multilateral agreement provide otherwise.

Both in the levying of contributions, other conditions of affiliation and entitlement to benefits, non-nationals must be treated on the same terms as nationals. It is legitimate for each Member State to lay down conditions creating the right or the obligation to become affiliated to a social security scheme or to a particular branch of such a scheme provided always that there is no discrimination in such conditions between national and non-nationals (Case 43/86 *De Rijke* [1987] ECR 3611).

In Case 33/88 *Allué I* [1989] ECR 1591, the Court found that Italian legislation which required foreign language university lecturers, who were predominantly non-Italian, to pay their own social security contributions whereas lecturers in other subjects had the greater part of their contributions paid by their employing university violated Art. 3 of Reg. 1408/71. Any system for the calculation of contributions must assimilate factors occurring in another Member State to those occurring on its territory. For example, contributions levied on trainee workers are required to be calculated in order to treat period of training completed under the educational system of another Member State in the same ways as those completed under its national educational system (Case C-27/91 *Le Manoir* [1991] ECR I-5531).

Exemptions of certain types of economic activity from the payment of contributions in one Member State must be available even if such economic activity is carried out on the territory of another Member State (Case 143/87 *Stanton* [1988] ECR 3877; Case C-204/90 *Bachmann* [1992] ECR I-249; Case C-300/90 *Commission* v. *Belgium* [1992] ECR I-305).

Employed and self-employed persons must have the right to receive the full range benefits under the social security system to which they are affiliated. For example, family benefits are required to be paid in respect of members of the family of an insured person who are resident in a Member

State other than that in which he is employer or self-employed on the same terms as if they were resident with him (Case 41/84 *Pinna* [1986] ECR 1). In Case C-124/99 *Borawitz*, above, the ECJ held that German legislation which fixed the amount of cash benefit that can be paid to a Community national resident in another Member State at a higher level than that required when the benefit was paid on the territory of the competent Member State contravened the principle of equal treatment in Art. 3(1). But if the administrative costs involved in exporting the benefit were higher than those which were incurred if the benefit was paid on national territory then a reduction in the level of benefit payable could be objectively justified provided it was proportionate to the administrative costs in question.

Conditions of entitlement to benefits that although apparently neutral, in the sense that they appear to have a similar effect on nationals and non-nationals alike, but which, in effect, prejudice non-nationals are incompatible with the principle of free movement (Case 41/84 *Pinna*, above). In Case C-277/99 *Kaske* [2002] ECR I-1261, the ECJ held that a provision in Austrian law which conferred on unemployed person who had spent fifteen years in Austria before their last employment abroad, benefited Austrians settled in Austria to the detriment of Austrian nationals who had exercised their right to free movement and of most nationals of other Member States. Consequently such a provision must be regarded as a restriction on the right to freedom of movement and as discriminatory on the grounds of nationality.

4. Co-ordination. The regulations do not aim to create a harmonized or uniform system of social security within the Community. They do not affect the substance of national social security systems save to extend their territorial application beyond national boundaries. Member States are free to organize their social security systems as they wish. In Case 29/88 *Schmitt* [1989] ECR 581, the Court held that Art. 42 EC and Reg. 1408/71 were not applicable for the purpose of determining the conditions of membership of a social security scheme whether compulsory or voluntary (see also Case 266/78 *Brunori* [1979] ECR 2705; Case 110/79 *Coonan* [1980] ECR 1445; Case 70/80 *Vigier* [1981] ECR 229). The Court said:

> it is for the legislature of each Member State to lay down the conditions creating the right or the obligation to become affiliated to a social security scheme or to a particular branch under such a scheme provided always that in this connection there is no discrimination between national of the host State and nationals of other Member States (*Coonan*, para. 12).

In Case C-33/99 *Fahmi and Esmoris Cerdeiro-Pinedo Amado* [2001] ECR I-2415, the Court held that a Member State was entitled to abolish an allowance for dependent children aged between 18 and 27 years pursuing studies provided that its abolition did not involve discrimination based on nationality.

Although neither Art. 42 EC nor the regulations affect with the substance of Member States social security systems, they link those systems together in such a way as to provide constant social security coverage for the employed, the self-employed, and their families wherever they move and for whatever reason within the territory of the European Community. Two processes are involved in the co-ordination of social security systems:

- aggregation and
- proraterization.

Aggregation enables an employed or self-employed person to gain title to benefit on one Member State on the basis of social security contributions made in another Member State. Contributions paid or periods of employed completed in several Member States can be added together to give title to benefit.

Proraterization is the process whereby the cost of providing benefits is divided out amongst the Member States in which the beneficiary has been insured. In this way each Member State bears the costs of providing the benefit in proportion to the contributions it has received for or on behalf of the beneficiary.

V. Scope of application: who is covered, for what, and where?

1. Persons covered. Art. 42 EC applies only to workers; no mention is made of the self-employed. Reg. 1408/71 initially applied only to workers but was extended to the self-employed by virtue of Reg. 1390/81 (*OJ* 1981 L143/1).

The scope of application of Reg. 1408/71 is defined in terms of national social security systems. The regulation applies to employed and self-employed persons, students and their families and survivors, who are, or have been, insured under the social security of a Member State.

Employed, self-employed persons, and students must be nationals of a Member State as must be their survivors. The nationality of members of the family is irrelevant. The regulation is also applicable to refugees and stateless persons who are resident in a Member State and to the members of their families and survivors (Art. 2).

Whether a person comes within the scope of the regulations is a matter to be determined largely by reference to the national social security scheme to which he is affiliated.

Art. 1(a) of Reg. 1408/71 provides that the following persons are deemed to be employed or self-employed for the purposes of the regulation:

- any person who is insured compulsorily or on an optional continued basis, for one or more of the contingencies covered by the branches of a social security scheme for employed or self-employed persons or by a special scheme for civil servants;
- any person who is compulsorily insured for one or more of the branches of social security dealt with in Reg. 1408/71 under a scheme for all residents or for the whole working population, if such a person:
  (*a*) can be identified as an employed or self-employed person by virtue of the manner in which the scheme is administered or financed; or

(*b*) who is insured for another contingency specified in Annex 1 under another scheme for employed or self-employed persons; or
(*c*) where the criteria in (*a*) and (*b*) cannot be satisfied, if he satisfies the criteria set out in Annex 1 to the regulation;

- any person who is compulsorily insured for several of the contingencies covered by the branches dealt with in Reg. 1408/71 under a standard social security scheme for the whole rural population in accordance with the criteria laid down in Annex 1;
- any person who is voluntarily insured for one or more of the contingencies covered by the branches of social security dealt with in Reg. 1408/71 under a social security scheme of a Member State for employed or self-employed persons or for all residents or for certain categories of residents:
  — if such person carried out an activity as an employed or self-employed person, or
  — if such a person has previously been compulsorily insured for the same contingency under a scheme for employed or self-employed person for the same Member State.

Annex 1 specifies in the case of some Member States (Denmark, France, Germany, Greece, Ireland, the Netherlands, and the United Kingdom), which persons are to be considered for the purposes of the regulation as employed or self-employed persons.

A student is defined as a person, other then an employed or self-employed person or a member of his family or a survivor, who studies or receives vocational training leading to a qualification officially recognized by the authorities of a Member State, and is insured under a general social security scheme or a special social security scheme applicable to students.

Whether a person is covered by Reg. 1408/71 is therefore a question of national law and the criterion is whether a person can be identified as an employed or self-employed person in the light of the social security system that is applicable to him. Occupational status is irrelevant, as is the question of how much time a claimant spends in economic activity (Case C-275/96 *Kuusijarvi* [1998] ECR I-3419; Case C-2/89 *Kits van Heijningen* [1990] ECR I-1755). As the Court has held:

> There is nothing in Article 1(a) or Article 2(1) of Regulation 1408/71 which permits certain categories of person to be excluded from the scope of the regulation on the basis of the amount of time they devote to their activities (*Kits van Heijningen*, para. 10).

In Case 84/77 *Tessier* [1978] ECR 7, the Court held that a French national who had worked as an au pair in the United Kingdom and at the same time had followed a part-time course of studies, could be covered by Reg. 1408/71 if she paid social security contributions as an employed person.

The source of remuneration or the means by which it is paid to the claimant is also not decisive. In Case 300/84 *Van Roosmalen* [1986] ECR 3097, a missionary priest who was supported by those who received the benefits of his services was held to be covered by the regulations:

it is not necessary that the self-employed person should receive remuneration as a direct reward for his activity. It is sufficient if he receives, in respect of that activity, income which permits him to meet all or some of his needs even if that income is supplies, as in this case, by third parties benefiting from the services of a missionary priest (ibid. para. 22).

Any person insured on a compulsory or optional basis under a general or special social security scheme even for only one of the risks covered by such a scheme is covered by the regulations (Case C-85/96 *Martinez Sala* [1998] ECR I-2691; Case C-71/93 *Van Poucke* [1994] ECR I-1101; Case C-275/96 *Kuusijarvi*, above).

Actual affiliation at the time of the materialization of the risk for which benefits are claimed is not necessary provided that the claimant had complied with all the substantive conditions necessary for affiliation even if he had not completed all the steps necessary for actual affiliation (Case 39/76 *Mouthaan* [1976] ECR 1901). Likewise, being economically active or the payment of contributions at the moment of claiming is not essential provided that the claimant has fulfilled the contribution conditions for the benefit in issue (Case 143/79 *Walsh* [1980] ECR 1639; Case C-275/96 *Kuusijarvi*, above).

2. **Frontier workers and seasonal workers** come within the scope of the regulations. Frontier workers are defined in Art. 1(b) of Reg. 1408/71 as persons who are employed or self-employed on the territory of one Member State and who reside in the territory of another Member State to which they return at least once a week. It follows that a worker who after transferring his residence to a Member State other than the State of employment, no longer returns to that State to pursue his occupation is not a frontier worker within the meaning of Art. 1(b) (Case 236/87 *Bergemann* [1988] ECR 5125).

Seasonal workers are those who go to a Member State other than the one of normal residence to do seasonal work for a period which does not exceed eight months (Art. 1(c) of Reg. 1408/71).

3. **Nationality.** The general rule is that employed persons, the self-employed, frontier workers, and seasonal workers and their survivors must hold the nationality of a Member State. The question of nationality is one for each Member State to determine. Where a person has dual nationality and one of those nationalities is that of a third country and the other that of a Member State, he must be considered to hold the nationality of a Member State (Case C-369/90 *Micheletti* [1992] ECR I-4239). The nationality of a claimant must be considered at the time he pursued the occupation to which his insurance contributions related: his nationality at the time of the claiming of benefits is irrelevant (Case 10/78 *Belbouab* [1978] ECR 1915; Case C-105/89 *Buhari* [1990] ECR I-4211, paras. 17–18).

4. **Nationals of third countries.** As from 20 June 2003, the regulations have been extended to nationals of third countries who have not already been

covered by the regulations solely on account of their nationality, i.e. persons who have been economically active in more than one Member State. The members of the families of such persons and their survivors are also brought within the scope of the regulations. Third-country nationals and their families must be legally resident in a Member State and in a situation that is not confined in all respects within a single Member State. Thus a third-country national who has lived and worked all his life in one Member State remains outside the scope of the regulations—movement is essential.

5. Members of the family. Art. 1(f) of Reg. 1408/71 defines what is meant by family members; the definition has been amended in recent years by Reg. 1290/97 (*OJ* 1997 L176/1) and Reg. 307/1999 (*OJ* 1999 L38/1) to take account of the case-law of the ECJ and the extension of Reg. 1408/71 to students.

A member of the family in general means any person defined or recognized as a member of the family or designated as a member of the household by the legislation under which benefits are provided. Where under that legislation a member of the family or a member of the household is a person living under the same roof as the employed, self-employed person, or student, this condition is considered to be satisfied if the person in question is mainly dependent on the employed, self-employed person, or student. Where the legislation of a Member State does not enable members of the family to be distinguished from the other persons to whom it applies, the term 'a member of the family' has the meaning given to it in Annex 1.

Where the benefits in issue are benefits for disabled person granted under the legislation of a Member State to all nationals of that State who fulfil the prescribed conditions, the term 'a member of the family' means at least the spouse of an employed or self-employed person or student and the children of such person who are either minors or dependent upon such a person.

In earlier years the ECJ adopted a fairly restrictive view of what constituted the social security rights of family members under the regulations. In Case 40/76 *Kermaschek* [1976] ECR 1669, the Court held that, while workers could claim benefits covered by the regulations in their own right, members of the family of a worker could only claim derived rights, acquired through their status as a member of the family but not in their own right. This ruling was adhered to for some further twenty years (see Case 157/84 *Frascogna* [1985] ECR 1739; Case 94/84 *Deak* [1985] ECR 1873; Case 147/87 *Zaoui* [1987] ECR 5511; Case C-243/91 *Taghavi* [1992] ECR I-4401; Case C-310/91 *Schmid* [1993] ECR I-3011). In Case C-308/93 *Cabanis-Issarte*, above, the Court took a different view. It found that the distinction between rights in person and derived rights:

> may undermine the fundamental Community law requirement that its rules should be applied uniformly, by making their applicability to individuals depend on whether the national law relating to the benefits in question treats the rights in person as derived rights, in the light of the specific features of the domestic social security scheme (ibid. para. 31).

Consequently, the Court concluded that in the light of the facts in the *Cabanis-Issarte* case the rule in *Kermaschek* should be limited to the factual circumstances in that case.

6. Survivors. Art. 1(g) of Reg. 1408/71 defines a survivor as:

any person defined or recognized as such by the legislation under which the benefits are granted: where, however, the said legislation regards as a survivor only a person which was living under the same roof as the deceased this condition shall be considered as satisfied if such a person was mainly dependent on the deceased.

7. Refugees. The concept refugee for the purposes of the regulation is to be interpreted in accordance with the provisions of the Convention on the Status of Refugees of 28 July 1951.

8. Stateless persons. Stateless persons are those considered to be such under Art. 1 of the Convention on the Status of Stateless Persons signed in New York on 28 September 1954, that is a person who is not considered a national by any State under the operation of its law.

Stateless persons and refugees must be resident in one of the Member State in order to benefit from the provisions of Reg. 1408/71.

9. Proposed amendments. The Commission has proposed two amendments to Reg. 1408/71, which would define the persons to whom the regulations are applicable. In 1998, it proposed amending Art. 2(1) as follows:

1. This regulation shall apply to employed and self-employed persons who are or have been subject to the legislation of one or more Member States as well as to the members of their families and survivors (*OJ* 1998 C6/6).

This amendment would have the effect of eliminating any national requirement for the employed and the self-employed so bringing them into line with other persons covered by the regulation who are not subject to any nationality requirement.

The Commission's subsequent proposal of 1998 (*OJ* 1999 C38/10) carries forward the idea of abandoning nationality requirements and at the same time broadens considerably the potential scope of application of the regulations:

This regulation shall apply to persons who are or have been subject to the social security legislation of one or more Member States as well as to members of their families and to their survivors.

This broad definition would sweep away the current provisions which set out certain groups of persons eligible to avail themselves of the provisions of the regulations but whose eligibility largely depends on how they are treated under their national social security systems. The proposed new definition would make the scope of Reg. 1408/71 far less dependent on national law (see further section III.2 above).

10. Benefits and schemes covered. The regulation applies to all legislation governing the classic branches of social security: sickness and maternity benefits, invalidity benefits, old-age benefits, survivors' benefits, benefits in respect of accidents at work and occupational diseases, death grants, unemployment benefit, and family benefits (Art. 4(1) of Reg. 1408/71).

The regulations apply to general and special social security schemes created under the legislation of a Member State. Legislation is defined in Art. 1(j) as:

statutes, regulations and other provisions and all other implementing measures, present or future, relating to the branches and schemes of social security covered by Article 4(1) and (2) or those special non-contributory benefits covered by Article 4(2a).

The term 'legislation' includes all provisions laid down by law, legislative, and administrative acts by the Member States and includes national measures applicable not only within the metropolitan territory of the Member States but also in territories with which the Member States have a special relationship. In Case 87/76 *Bozzone* [1977] ECR 687, the ECJ found that a Belgian Colonial Decree establishing a sickness and invalidity scheme for the benefit of colonial employees working in Belgian colonies in Africa constituted legislation within the meaning of Art. 1(j) of Reg. 1408/71.

Collective agreements are expressly excluded save where they serve to operate compulsory social security schemes and are administered by the same institutions in a Member State as administer the legislative social security systems of that State (Case C-253/90 *Commission* v. *Belgium* [1992] ECR I-531). In such a case, Reg. 1408/71 may be made applicable to them by the Member State in which they operate provided that Member State has made a declaration to that effect. That declaration will be published in the *Official Journal*. In the absence of a declaration, the regulation is not applicable to social security schemes which are constituted under collective agreements. As the ECJ has held:

The provisions of the above-mentioned French schemes relating to early retirement and supplementary pensions were introduced under agreements concluded by the competent authorities with trade or inter-trade bodies, trade union organizations or individual undertakings or under collective agreements concluded between both sides of industry and have not been made the subject of a declaration as specified in the second paragraph of Article 1(j) of Regulation 1408/71. It must therefore be declared that those schemes do not constitute legislation within the meaning of the first paragraph of Article 1(j) of Regulation 1408/71 (Case C-57/90 *Commission* v. *France* [1992] ECR I-75, paras. 19 and 20).

Occupational or private social insurance schemes are outside the scope of the regulations (Case 313/82 *Tiel Utrecht* [1984] ECR 1389; Case C-253/90 *Commission* v. *Belgium*, above).

Two types of benefit are expressly excluded from the scope of the regulation: benefits for victims of war and social and medical assistance.

11. Benefits for victims of war. Benefits for victims of war are not regarded as social security benefits even if they are administered by the competent social security institutions of a Member State since their purpose is to compensate for losses or injury caused by war. They are thus not linked to the exercise of any economic activity and the beneficiaries of such benefits are not identifiable as employed or self-employed persons. Examples of war benefits that the Court has held to be excluded from the scope of the regulations include an allowance payable under German law to compensate persons for injury or damage caused by racial persecution (Case 93/75 *Adlerblum* [1975] ECR 2147); provisions of the French social security code that granted certain privileges to ex-servicemen and former prisoners of war who claimed pension before the normal pension age (Case 9/78 *Gillard* [1978] ECR 1661); a Belgian law which gave Belgian workers who had fought in the allied forces between 10 May 1940 and 8 May 1945 and who were as a result incapacitated and unable to work, the right to an early retirement pension (Case 207/78 *Even* [1979] ECR 2019). By contrast, in Case 70/80 *Vigier*, above, the Court held that the German Reparation Law which allows the retroactive payment of contributions by victims of persecution during the last war was not a benefit for victims of war and therefore not excluded from the scope of Reg. 1408/71:

> It is clear from the papers in the case that although the Reparation Law has the appearance of a lex specialis it does not seek to establish an independent scheme of compensation. The provisions of the Reparation Law merely constitute rules supplementing or adjusting the general provisions in the field of social insurance (ibid. para. 14).

12. Special schemes for civil servants. Special social security schemes for civil servants were originally excluded from the scope of application of the regulations but were brought within them in 1998 (Reg. 1606/98, *OJ* 1998 L209). A special scheme for civil servants is defined as:

> any social security scheme which is different from the general social security scheme applicable to employed persons in the Member States concerned, and to which all, or certain categories of, civil servants or person treated as such are directly subject (Art. 1(j) of Reg. 1408/71).

13. Social and medical assistance. Social and medical assistance schemes are outside the scope of application of the regulation (Art. 4(4) of Reg. 1408/71). This exclusion has given rise to a considerable amount of case-law given the difficulties of differentiating between such schemes and social security schemes. When the system of co-ordination contained in the regulations was initially set up in 1958 social and medical assistance could be differentiated from social security by the fact that the latter were for the most part contributory benefits whereas the former were not, and whilst social security benefits were paid as of right to those who satisfied the conditions for entitlement, social and medical assistance was largely granted on the basis of proven need and on discretionary basis. Since then the distinction between social security and social assistance has become blurred as national social security systems move towards recognizing the basis right of citizens to social welfare benefits. This has led to the replacing of social assistance benefits by non-contributory social security benefits granted upon the fulfilment of objectively defined conditions. This changing nature of social welfare provision has over the years engendered a certain confusion as to the applicability of the regulations and hence, as mentioned above, a number of references for preliminary rulings to the European Court of Justice. The Court has laid down three criteria which must be fulfilled in order that a benefit may be classified as a social security benefit within the meaning of the regulations:

(*i*) the legislation under which the benefit is granted must place claimants in a legally defined position as a result of which he has an absolute right to benefit as opposed to a conditional right dependent upon the exercise of discretionary power in their favour;

(*ii*) the benefit must cover one of the risks enumerated in Art. 4(1) of Reg. 1408/71. A benefit that is general in nature, that is which grants as of right a minimum income to all citizens, will not fall within the scope the regulations;

(*iii*) the beneficiary must have been subject to the social security system of the State under whose legislation the benefit is claimed.

Provided a benefit (regardless of its characterization under national law) satisfies these criteria and covers one of the risks enumerated in Art. 4(1) of Reg. 1408/71, it is to be considered to be a social security benefit for the purposes of the regulations (Case 1/72 *Frilli* [1972] ECR 457; Case 187/73 *Callemeyn* [1974] ECR 553; Case 39/74 *Mazzier* [1974] ECR 1251; Case 7/75 *Fracas*, above; Case 63/76 *Inzirillo* [1976] ECR 2057; Case 24/74 *Biason* [1974] ECR 999; Case 139/82 *Pisicitello* [1983] ECR 1427; Case 249/83 *Hoeckx* [1985] ECR 973; Case 122/84 *Scrivner* [1985] ECR 1027; Cases 379/85 etc. *Giletti* [1987] ECR 955; Case C-356/89 *Newton* [1991] ECR I-3017; Cases C-245/94 etc. *Hoever and Zachow* [1996] ECR I-4895).

In order to take account of this case-law and the changing nature of social security schemes which now featured, Reg. 1408/71 was amended.

Art. 4(2a) now provides that the regulations applies to special non-contributory benefits where those benefits are provided under legislation or schemes other than those referred to under Art. 4(1) or excluded under Art. 4(4) where such benefits are intended:

(*a*) either to provide supplementary, substitute, or ancillary cover against the risks covered by the branches of social security covered by Reg. 1408/71; or

(*b*) solely as specific protection for the disabled.

A number of special non-contributory benefits referred to in Annex II of the regulation remain excluded from its scope.

14. Proposed amendments. In 1996 the Commission proposed amending Reg. 1408/71 to include pre-retirement benefits (*OJ* 1996 C62/5). Pre-retirement benefits are defined in the proposal as:

all cash benefits, other than an early retirement benefit provided to wholly unemployed workers from a specified age until the age at which they qualify for an old-age pension or an unreduced early retirement pension, the receipt of which is not conditional upon the person concerned being available to the employment services of the competent State.

The purpose of this amendment is to bring within the scope of the regulations those schemes that induce elderly person to leave the labour market by providing them with a guaranteed income until they reach normal retirement age. At present such schemes frequently have a residence clause as a conditional for entitlement.

15. Territory. Art. 42 EC and the regulations apply within the territory of the European Community. That territory is defined in Art. 299 EC. Art. 51 of the original EEC Treaty [now Art. 42 EC] and the regulations were expressly extended to the French overseas departments by a Council decision of 1971 (Council Dec. 71/238, *OJ* 1971/L149/1). Since the regulations do not apply to third countries, social security contributions paid or periods of insurance completed under the legislation of those countries do not have to be taken into account, by virtue of the regulations, by Member States in determining entitlement to benefit (Case 16/72 *Allgemeine Ortskrankenkasse Hamburg* [1972] ECR 1141). However, if the contributions were paid under the social security system of a Member State it matters not that they were paid in respect of employment in a non-member State: the essential criterion is whether contributions were paid under the legislation of Member State or territory that forms part of the territory of the European Community as defined in Art. 299 EC and not where the employment is carried out (Case 87/76 *Bozzone*, above; Case 300/84 *Van Roosmalen*, above). As the Court has stated:

Since the decisive criterion is the affiliation of an insured person to a social security scheme of a Member State, the fact that the insurance periods were completed under that scheme in non-member countries is unimportant (Cases 82/86 etc. *Laborero and Sabato* [1987] ECR 3401).

VI. The regulations and bilateral or multilateral social security treaties

1. Conventions over which Regulation 1408/71 takes precedence. The purpose of the regulations was to replace the plethora of social security treaties and other arrangements regulating the rights and obligations of migrant workers which existed between the different Member State with one single social security code. Accordingly, Art. 6 of Reg. 1408/71 provides that the provisions of any social security convention which binds two or more Member States exclusively are replaced by the regulation (Case 82/72 *Walder* [1973] ECR 599; Case C-475/93 *Thévenon* [1995] ECR I-3813). But this rule is inapplicable where it would result in the loss of social security benefits for those exercising the right to free movement under national law or national law combined with the provisions of an international social security conventions operating between two or more Member States (C-227/

89 *Ronfeldt* [1991] ECR I-323; Case C-113/96 *Rodriguez* [1998] ECR I-2461).

Where a convention binds two or more Member States and one or more non-member States, it is replaced where the issue in question involves two or more Member States only (Art. 6(b)).

Exceptionally, Art. 46(4), which concerns the calculation of pensions, provides that where the total of benefits due to a claimant by the competent social security institutions of two or more Member States under the provisions of a multilateral social security convention do not exceed the total which would be due from such Member States under Art. 46(i) and (ii), the claimant shall benefit from Art. 46. In other words, the claimant in such a case gets the greater of the two benefits.

The principle of precedence of Reg. 1408/71 does not mean that Member States cannot make bilateral or multilateral agreements between themselves, only that such arrangements must be compatible with the regulations. Such agreements must be notified to the President of the Council and will be published in the *Official Journal of the European Communities* (Art. 8).

2. Conventions which take precedence over Regulation 1408/71. Art. 7 of Reg. 1408/71 provides that Reg. 1408/71 does not affect obligations arising from:

(*i*) any Convention adopted by the International Labour Conference which, after ratification by two or more Member States, has entered into force;
(*ii*) the European Interim Agreements on social security of 11 December 1953 concluded between the Member States of the Council of Europe;
(*iii*) the Agreements of 27 July 1950 and 30 November 1979 concerning social security for Rhine boatmen;
(*iv*) the European Convention of 9 July 1956 concerning social security for workers in international transport;
(*v*) the Conventions listed in Annex III to Reg. 1408/71.

Claimants who have rights under any of the above-mentioned conventions and Reg. 1408/71 have the best of both worlds: they benefit from whichever provisions are most favourable to them. As the ECJ has stated:

> it must be concluded that in the framework of its field of application to persons and to matters covered, Regulation 1408/71 takes precedence over the European Interim Agreement on social security . . . in so far as it is more favourable for those entitled (Case 187/73 *Callemeyn*, above, para. 21).

This is again an application of the principle of free movement: no employed or self-employed person should be denied rights available to him whether those rights arise under national law or as a result of the application of an international convention, because he has exercised his right to free movement.

VII. Export of benefits

Art. 42 EC specifically provides for the export of benefits from one Member State to another. Art. 10 of Reg. 1408/71 reinforces the right of beneficiaries to receive benefits in their Member State of residence.

Art. 10(1) provides:

Save as otherwise provided in this regulation, invalidity, old-age or survivors cash benefits, pensions for accidents at work or occupational diseases and death grants acquired under the legislation of one or more Member States shall not be subject to any reduction, modification, suspension or withdrawal or confiscation by reason of the fact that the recipient resides in the territory of a Member State other than that in which the institution responsible for payment is situated.

Art. 10(1) applies to all benefits set out in Art. 4(1) of Reg. 1408/71 (Case 24/74 *Biason*, above; Case 139/82 *Piscitello*, above; Case C-356/89 *Newton*, above).

The purpose Art. 10(1) is to guarantee the right to free movement.

The aim of Arts. 39 to 41 would not be attained if, as a consequence of the exercise of the right to freedom of movement, workers were to lose the advantages in the field of social security guaranteed to them by the laws of a single Member State. As the Court has pointed out:

Consequently the purpose of Article 10(1) of Regulation 1408/71 concerning the waiving of residence clauses is to guarantee the person concerned his right to social security benefits even after taking up residence in a different Member State and to promote the freedom of movement of workers, by insulating those concerned from the harmful consequences which might result when they transfer their residence from one Member State to another (Case C-293/88 *Winter-Lutzins* [1990] ECR I-1623).

Art. 10(1) must be interpreted as meaning that a person may not be precluded from acquiring or retaining entitlement to social security benefits on the sole ground that he does not reside within the territory of the Member State in which the institution responsible for payment is situate (Cases 379/85 etc. *Gilleti*, above; Case C-236/88 *Commission* v. *France* [1990] ECR I-3163).

Increases in benefits awarded under national law must be paid to beneficiaries resident outside the competent Member State on the same basis as they are paid to those resident therein (Art. 11).

The export of benefits is guaranteed only to persons resident in a Member State. Exportability to third countries is a matter for national law. It follows therefore that Community law does not preclude national legislation that provides that a self-employed person's retirement pension is payable abroad only to beneficiaries residing in a non-member State pursuant to a reciprocity agreement (Case C-105/89 *Buhari*, above).

There is an exception to the general principle of exportability in the case of the special non-contributory cash benefits referred to in Art. 4(2a) that is benefits which provide supplementary, substitute, or ancillary cover against the risks specified in Art. 4(1) of the regulations or benefits whose sole purpose if the protection of the disabled. In the case of such benefits they are to be provided exclusively in the territory of the Member State in which the claimant resides. Such benefits must be listed in Annex IIa to the regulation. Those benefits are to be granted by and at the expense of the institution of the place of residence of the claimant (Art. 10a).

Both in Case C-20/96 *Snares* [1997] ECR I-6057 and in the subsequent Case C-297/96 *Partridge* [1998] ECR I-3467 the Court held Art. 10a to be applicable to a disability benefit payable under United Kingdom law which was listed in Annex IIa to the regulation. Consequently, there does not appear to be any possibility of challenging the applicability of Art. 10a once the benefit in issue is listed in Annex IIa:

> The fact that the Community legislature refers to legislation in Annex IIa to Regulation 1408/71 must be accepted as establishing that benefits granted pursuant to that legislation are special non-contributory benefits falling within the scope of Article 10a of Regulation 1408/71 (*Snares*, para. 30; *Partridge*, para. 31).

In *Snares* the Court rejected the contention that Art. 10a, in restricting exportability, was contrary to Art. 42 EC, ruling that the principle of exportability of benefit prevailed only in the absence of derogating provision adopted by the Community legislature. Art. 10(1) provides that the principle that residence clauses should be waived applies save as otherwise provided in this regulation and since Art. 10a limits the exportability of non-contributory benefits, it constitutes an exception to the general principle of exportability envisaged by Art. 10(1).

The Court was unmoved by the argument that Art. 10a could be invalidated where a claimant was not entitled to an invalidity benefit in his Member State of residence or only a benefit at a lower rate than that to which he would have been entitled in the competent Member State had he been resident there. It stated:

> . . . as regards special non-contributory benefits such as those in issue in the main proceedings, the Court has pointed out on numerous occasions that the principle of exportability of social security benefits applies as long as no derogating provisions have been adopted by the Community legislature.
>
> The Court has in the past accepted that the grant of benefits closely linked with the social environment may be made subject to a condition of residence in the State of the competent institution (*Snares*, paras. 41 and 42).

Where title to the non-contributory benefits is dependent upon the completion of periods of employment or self-employment or residence any such periods completed in the territory of any other Member State shall count as periods completed in the Member State of residence of the claimant. Where a disability or invalidity benefit is subject to the condition that the disability should be diagnosed for the first time in the territory of the Member State under whose legislation it is claimed, this condition is deemed to have been fulfilled where such a diagnosis is made for the first time in the territory of another Member State (Art. 10a(4)).

VIII. Applicable legislation

1. Introduction. Arts. 13 to 17 of Reg. 1408/71 set out the rules that determine to which social security system a person should be affiliated. As a general rule a person is required to be subject to one social security system only (Art. 13(1) of Reg. 1408/71; Case 102/76 *Perenboom* [1977] ECR 815; Case 60/85 *Luijtens* [1986] ECR 2365). That system is determined exclusively by the provisions of Reg. 1408/71 (Case 276/81 *Kuijpers* [1982] ECR 3027).

2. General rules. Employed persons and the self-employed are subject to the social security system of the Member State in which they carry out their economic activity regardless of where they are resident (Art. 13(2)(a) and (b) of Reg. 1408/71). A person who works part-time in the territory of a Member State is subject to the legislation of that Member State both on the days when he is employed and on those days when he is not (Case C-2/89 *Kits van Heijningen*, above).

A person employed on board a vessel flying the flag of a Member State is subject to the social security scheme of that Member State (Art. 13(2)(c) of Reg. 1408/71).

Civil servants and persons treated as such are subject to the legislation of the Member State to which their employer administration is subject (Art. 13(2)(d) of Reg. 1408/71).

Pensioners are not specifically mentioned in Art. 13 but their rights have been clarified by the European Court of Justice in Case C-140/88 *Noij* [1991] ECR I-387 and in Art. 17a adopted subject to the judgment of the ECJ in that case. In *Noij* the Court ruled that an employed person who has been employed on the territory of a Member State as a result of which he received a retirement pension, and who takes up residence in another Member State in which he does not carry out any economic activity may be required to become subject to the legislation of that State by virtue of his residence there. But he cannot be required to pay contributions to the social security system of his Member State of residence to cover benefits payable under the social security system of another Member State. Art. 17a of Reg. 1408/71, inserted subsequent to the *Noij* judgment, provides that the recipient of a pension due under the legislation of a Member State or of pension due under the legislation of several Member States who resides in the territory of another Member State may request to be exempt from the legislation of the latter State provided that he is not subject to that legislation because of the pursuit of an occupation.

A person to whom the legislation of a Member State ceases to become applicable, without the legislation of another Member State becoming applicable to him in accordance with the provisions of Reg. 1408/71, is subject to the legislation of the Member State in whose territory he resides (Art. 13(f) of Reg. 1408/71). This provision is designed to govern a situation where no legislation is applicable by virtue of the other provisions of Art. 13(2) or the provisions of Arts. 14b and 17. Art. 13(f) applies not only to those who have ceased definitively all occupational activity but also to persons who have merely ceased their occupational activity for whatever reason in a given Member State (Case C-275/96 *Kuusijarvi*, above).

3. Employed and self-employed persons working temporarily in another Member State. A person employed in the territory of a Member State by an undertaking to which he is normally attached who is posted by that undertaking to the territory of another Member State to perform work there for that undertaking continues to be subject to the legislation of the first Member State. A self-employed person who normally carries out his economic activity in the territory of one Member State and who goes to work temporarily in the territory of another Member State remains subject to the legislation of the first Member State. This general rule is subject to two provisos: (*i*) the anticipated duration of the work does not exceed twelve months, and (*ii*) he is not sent to replace another person who has completed his term of posting (Art. 14(1) of Reg. 1408/71). If the duration of the work to be done extends beyond the duration originally anticipated, owing to unforeseeable circumstances and exceeds twelve months, the legislation of the first Member State continues to apply until the completion of the work provided that the competent authority of the Member State in whose territory the person concerned is posted gives its consent. Such consent cannot be given for a period exceeding twelve months (Arts. 14(1)(b) and 14a(1) of Reg. 1408/71).

In order to take advantage of the above-mentioned provisions, an undertaking engaged in providing temporary personnel, which, from one Member State, makes workers available on a temporary basis to undertakings based in another Member State, must normally carry on its activities in the first State. An undertaking engaged in providing temporary personnel normally carries on its activities in the Member State in which it is established if it habitually carries on significant activities in that State (Case C-202/97 *Fitzwilliam Executive Search* [2000] ECR I-883).

The continued affiliation of an employed or self-employed person, working abroad temporarily, to his home social security scheme is evidenced by Form 101 issued by the competent authority in the Member State where work is normally carried out. As long as this form is not withdrawn by the issuing authority it remains valid. A Form 101 can be issued with retroactive effect (Case C-178/97 *Barry Banks* [2000] ECR I- 2005).

4. Persons normally employed or self-employed in the territory of two or more Member States. A person normally employed in the territory of two or more Member States is subject to the legislation of the Member State in which he resides, if he pursues his activity partly in that Member State or if he is attached to several undertakings or several employers who have their registered office or places of business in the territory of different Member States. If he does not reside in any of the Member States in whose territory he is pursuing his activities he is subject to the legislation of the Member State where the registered office or place of business of his employer is situate (Art. 14(2)(b) of Reg. 1408/71). A self-employed person who is normally self-employed in the territory of two or more Member States is subject to the legislation of the Member State in which he resides if he pursues any part of his activity in the territory of that Member State. If he does not pursue any activity in the territory of the Member State in which he resides he is subject to the legislation of the Member State in whose territory he pursues his main activity (Art. 14a(2) of Reg. 1408/71). Whether a person is employed or self-employed is a matter to be determined by reference to the social security system to which he is affiliated (Case C-221/95 *Hervein* [1997] ECR I-609; Case C-340/94 *De Jaeck* [1997] ECR I-461).

The regulation does not preclude the legislation of one of two Member States from insuring a person against only some of the risks covered by its social security scheme. Nor is a Member State obliged to take into account in calculating the contributions owed in respect of work carried out on its territory for part of the week the fact that a person is employed or self-employed elsewhere for the other part of the week (*De Jaeck*).

Persons who are members of the travelling or flying personnel of an undertaking that, for hire or reward or on its own account, operates international transport services for passengers or foods by rail, road, air, or inland waterway and has its registered office or place of business in the territory of a Member State shall be subject to the legislation of the latter State (Art. 14(2)(a) of Reg. 1408/71. There are a number of restrictions on this rule set out in Art. 14(2)(a)(i) and (ii)).

5. Mariners. A mariner who is normally employed by an undertaking or on board a vessel flying the flag of a Member State who is posted by that undertaking on board a vessel flying the flag of another Member State to perform work there for that undertaking shall continue to be subject to the legislation of the first Member State (Art. 14b(1) of Reg. 1408/71). A similar rule applies to a self-employed mariner normally working on a vessel flying the flag of a Member State and who performs work on his own account on a vessel flying the flag of another Member State (Art. 14b(2) of Reg. 1408/71). This rule is subject to the restrictions concerning the duration of the work on board the other vessels as applicable to employed and self-employed person working abroad temporarily set out in Art. 14(1).

6. Persons who are simultaneously employed in the territory of one Member State and self-employed in the territory of another. A person who is simultaneously employed in the territory of one Member State and self-employed in the territory of another Member State is subject, as a general rule, to the legislation of the Member State in the territory of which he is engaged in paid employment or, where he pursues such an activity in the territory of two or more Member States, to the legislation determined in accordance with Art. 14(2) or (3) of Reg. 1408/71 (Art. 14c).

Where persons are economically active in more than one Member State, the social security system to which they are subject governs all their economic activities regardless of where they are performed as if they were performed on the territory of that Member State (Art. 14d(1) of Reg. 1408/71).

7. Diplomats, consular staff, and auxiliary staff of the European Communities. The rules applicable to persons in these posts are set out in Art. 16 of Reg. 1408/71.

8. Alternative bilateral or multilateral arrangements. Two or more Member States can provide for exceptions to the rules in Arts. 13 to 16 of Reg. 1408/71.

IX. Claiming and calculation of benefits

1. General principles. There are a number of general principles governing the claiming and calculation of benefits set out in Arts. 9 to 12 of Reg. 1408/71 and Arts. 6 to 10 and 15 of Reg. 574/72. In addition to these general principles, there are a number of specific rules applicable to the different benefits covered by Reg. 1408/71 which will be set out below.

2. Claims procedure. Claims for benefit are made to the competent institution in the competent Member State. The competent institution may be that with which the claimant is insured, the institution in his place of resident or stay. Art. 1(o) of Reg. 1408/71 defines the possible competent institutions to which a claim may be made:

(*i*) the institution with which the person concerned is insured at the time of the application for the benefit;
(*ii*) the institution from which the person concerned is entitled or would be entitled to benefits if he or the members of his family were resident in the territory of the Member State in which the institution is situated;
(*iii*) the institution designated by the competent authority of the Member State concerned;
(*iv*) where the liability of an employer or an insurer is in issue, the body or authority of the Member State concerned.

The regulations may specify the precise institution to which a claim may be made; otherwise the matter is left up to each Member State.

3. Forms. Claims are made on forms designed by the Administrative Commission for the Social Security of Migrant Workers.

4. Language. Claims may be made in any Community language (Art. 84(4) of Reg. 1408/71; Case 55/77 *Reboulet* [1977] ECR 2327; Case 66/74 *Farrauto* [1975] ECR 157).

5. Aggregation. Art. 45(1) of Reg. 1408/71 sets out the general principle of aggregation: periods of insurance, periods of employment, or periods of residence (depending on what is the basis for entitlement to benefit) completed in more than one Member State may be added together to claim title to benefit. Such periods of insurance, employment, or residence must be treated as if they had been completed in the Member State in which benefit is claimed (Case 33/75 *Galati* [1975] ECR 1323).

Periods of insurance are defined in Art. 1(r) of Reg. 1408/71 as periods of contribution or periods of employment or self-employment as defined or recognized as periods of insurance by the legislation under which they were completed. It is for each Member State to determine what is a period of insurance for the purposes of claiming entitlement to benefit under its social security scheme (Case 70/80 *Vigier*, above; Case 43/86 *De Rijke*, above).

Periods of residence are those regarded as such by the legislation under which they were completed (Art. 1(s) of Reg. 1408/71).

Periods of employment are those treated as such under the legislation in which they were completed (Art. 1(r) of Reg. 1408/71; Case 2/72 *Murru* [1972] ECR 333; Case 126/77 *Frangiamore* [1978] ECR 725).

6. Overlapping insurance periods. As a general rule compulsory periods of insurance, periods of residence completed at the same point in time is not permissible (Art. 12(1) of Reg. 1408/71). There are a number of exceptions to this rule (Arts. 41, 43(2) and (3), 46, and 50 of Reg. 1408/71).

7. Overlapping benefits. National rules governing the reduction, suspension, or withdrawal of two or more benefits payable at the same time for the same risk may be applied even where one of those benefits was acquired under the law of another Member State (Art. 12(2) of Reg. 1408/71).

X. Sickness and maternity benefits

The rules relating to sickness and maternity benefits are largely concerned with situations where medical treatment is supplied outside the territory of the competent State. They are designed to ensure the provision of necessary medical services and equipment to insured persons outside the territory of the competent State whilst at the same time providing for equitable distribution of the cost of such treatment or equipment between the health care institutions of the providing Member State and those of the insurer Member State.

The relevant rules are set out in Arts. 18 to 36 of Reg. 1408/71 and Arts. 16 to 34 of Reg. 574/72.

1. Aggregation. Art. 18(1) of Reg. 1408/71 provides that account shall be taken by the competent institution for the purposes of establishing title to sickness and maternity benefits, of periods of insurance, employment, or residence completed under the legislation of any Member State as if they had been completed in the Member State of residence (Case C-482/93 *Klaus* [1995] ECR I-3551; Case 150/82 *Coppola* [1983] ECR 43).

2. Residence in a Member State other than the competent State. An employed or self-employed person who is resident in a Member State other than the competent State is entitled to the following benefits:

(*i*) benefits in kind provided by the social security institution of his place of residence on behalf of the competent institution in accordance with the provision of the legislation of the Member State of residence;

(*ii*) cash benefits provided by the competent institution in accordance with the legislation which it administers. Such benefits may actually be provided by the institutions of the Member State of residence by agreement with the competent Member State (Art. 19(1) of Reg. 1408/71).

These benefits are payable even if the claimant fell ill after having worked and been insured in the competent State but before taking work in the Member State of residence (Case C-215/90 *Twomey* [1992] ECR I-1823).

The concepts of 'benefits in kind' and 'cash benefits' are not defined in the regulations but the ECJ has given some guidance as to what they are. Cash benefits are those that are designed to compensate for loss of earnings during illness, while benefits in kind include prostheses and appliances or monies paid to the claimant to acquire the same (Case 61/65 *Vaassen* [1966] ECR 261; Case C-160/96 *Molenaar* [1998] ECR I-843).

Members of the family of employed or self-employed persons who reside in the Member State of residence but have no title to benefits in that Member State are entitled to benefits in kind and cash benefits from the competent institution according to the same rules as those applicable to employed and self-employed persons (Art. 19(2)). There is an exception to this rule. Where title to benefits in the Member State of residence of the members of the family is not dependent upon the payment of contributions or the completion of periods of employment, any benefits in kind provided by the Member State of residence are considered as having been provided by the Member State with which the employed or self-employed person is insured unless the spouse or person looking after the children who receive the benefits pursues a professional or trade activity in the territory of the Member State of residence. The objective of these rules is to ensure that the State which is receiving contribution for sickness and maternity benefits remains responsible for the cost of the provision of those benefits (Art. 19(2)).

3. Entitlement to benefits in a Member State other than the competent Member State or the Member State of residence. An employed or self-employed person who is entitled to sickness or maternity benefits under the legislation of the competent State, is entitled to receive benefits on the territory of another Member State any of the following circumstances:

(*i*) where his condition necessitates immediate benefits during a stay in the territory of another Member State;

(*ii*) where, having become entitled to benefits chargeable to the competent institution is authorized to return to the Member State where he resides or to transfer his residence to another Member State. Authorization may only be refused where it is established that the movement of the person concerned would be prejudicial to his state of health to the provision of medical treatment;.

(*iii*) where he is authorized by the competent institution to go to the territory of another Member State to receive treatment there appropriate to his condition. Authorization cannot be refused where the treatment in question is provided under the legislation of the Member State in which the claimant resides but he cannot be given that treatment within the time normally necessary in that Member State taking into account his current state of health and the probable course of the disease (Art. 22(1) and (2) of Reg. 1408/71).

In general, members of the family have the same rights to sickness and maternity benefits as employed or self-employed persons (Art. 22(3) of Reg. 1408/71).

Persons who are nationals of a Member State (even if they are not exercising an economic activity or pursuing studies) and who are insured under the legislation of a Member State and the members of their families residing with them are entitled to the benefits set out in (*i*) and (*iii*) above (Art. 22a of Reg. 1408/71).

Benefits in kind are provided by the institution of the place of stay on behalf of the competent institution. Whilst the benefits are provided in accordance with the legislation of the Member State of residence, the duration for which they are provided is governed by the law of the competent State. Cash benefits are provided by the competent institution in accordance with its rules but may be administered by the Member State of residence (Art. 22(i) of Reg. 1408/71).

Where a claimant wishes to travel to another Member State to purchase medical supplies or equipment there, or to receive medical treatment there (excluding hospital treatment), he is not obliged to obtain an authorization from the competent Member State, but without that authorization he is entitled only to the level of reimbursement for the goods or services provided to him which is prescribed by the law of the competent Member State. If, by contrast, he does obtain the authorization of the competent Member State to purchase medical supplies or obtain medical services pursuant to Art. 22 of Reg. 1408/71, as set out above, he will be entitled to the level of reimbursement prevailing in the Member State in which the goods or treatment were obtained (Case C-120/95 *Decker*, above; Case C-158/96 *Kohll*, above).

4. Exceptions. Some exceptions or variations to general rules applicable to employed, self-employed persons, and members of their families that are set out above are applicable to the unemployed and their families (Arts. 25 and 25a of Reg. 1408/71), pensioners and their families (Arts. 26 to 34 of Reg. 1408/71), frontier workers (Art. 20 of Reg. 1408/71), seasonal workers (Art. 18(2) of Reg. 1408/71), and students (Art. 34a of Reg. 1408/71).

5. Calculation of cash benefits. Where under the law of the competent State cash benefits are to be calculated on the basis of average or standard earnings or average or standard contributions, reference is to be made to earning or contributions made under that legislation (Art. 23 of Reg. 1408/71).

6. Major benefits in kind. Where the right of a claimant to a major appliance or other substantial benefit in kind has been recognized by the social security authorities of one Member State but the claimant subsequently becomes insured in another Member State, the cost of the benefit in kind remains the expense of the institution of the former Member State even though the claimant is no longer insured with it (Art. 24 of Reg. 1408/71).

As discussed above, Community citizens may be able to rely on Arts. 28 and 49 to 55 EC to receive medical products and medical care in a Member State other than that of the social security system to which they are insured and to be reimbursed for the cost of such products or treatment.

XI. Invalidity benefits

Arts. 37 to 43 of Reg. 1408/71 and Arts. 35 to 39 of Reg. 574/72 govern the award of invalidity benefits.

Invalidity benefits are classified into four categories: (*i*) those benefits which are not dependent upon the completion of insurance periods. Such benefits are specified in Annex VI, Part A and are known as Type A benefits; (*ii*) benefits to which title is dependent upon the completion or periods of insurance and residence; (*iii*) benefits that are awarded on the basis of insurance periods completed under a special scheme for those employed in a particular occupation; (*iv*) benefits to which title is gained as a result of contributions paid to a special scheme for self-employed persons. Such benefits are specified in Annex IV, Part B. Benefits falling into categories (*ii*), (*iii*), and (*iv*) are known as Type B benefits. Title to Type B benefits may depend upon aggregation of insurance periods or periods of employment and entitlement is to be calculated in the same way as entitlement to old-age and death pensions.

1. Benefits that are dependent upon the completion of insurance periods or periods of employment (Category ii). Where the social security legislation of a Member State makes entitlement to benefit subject to the completion of insurance periods or periods of employment, the competent institution of the Member States must take into account, where necessary, periods of insurance or of residence completed under the legislation of any other Member State regardless of whether those periods were completed under the legislation of any other Member State be it under a general scheme or under a special scheme and either as an employed or self-employed person (Art. 38 (1)). Such periods must be counted as if they had been completed under the legislation of the competent State.

2. Benefits that are dependent upon the completion of insurance periods in an occupation which is subject to a special scheme for employed persons (Category iii). Where the legislation of a Member State under which invalidity benefits are claimed makes the granting of benefits conditional upon the periods of insurance having been completed only in an occupation which is subject to a special scheme for employed persons or, where appropriate, in a specific employment, periods completed under the legislation of other Member States are to be taken into account only to the extent that they have been completed under an corresponding scheme or failing that in the same occupation or in the same employment. However if this aggregation exercise does not result in entitlement to benefit recourse may be had to contributions paid to the general social security scheme or under the general scheme applicable to manual or clerical workers (Art. 38(2)).

3. Benefits that are dependent upon the completion of insurance periods under an occupation subject to a special scheme for the self-employed (Category iv). If the legislation of a Member State makes the grant of invalidity benefits conditional upon periods of insurance having been completed only in an occupation subject to a special scheme for the self-employed, periods completed under the legislation of another Member State are to be taken into account only if completed under a corresponding scheme or failing that in the same occupation. As is the case with Category (ii) schemes, if the aggregation of contribution completed under special scheme or given occupation does not result in title to benefit then contributions completed under a general scheme or in a scheme applicable to manual or clerical workers may be taken into account (Art. 38 (3)).

4. Award of benefits. If, at the time the invalidity occurs title to invalidity benefits exists (taking into account period of insurance or employment completed in other Member States) under the legislation of the Member State to which the claimant was subject at that time, benefits are to be paid out by the competent institution of that State in accordance with its legislative provisions (Art. 39(1)). If no title exists under the legislation of the competent State, the claimant can receive benefits under the legislation of another Member State relying on the principle of aggregation where necessary.

In calculating benefit amounts account must be taken of family members resident outside the competent State (Art. 39(4)).

5. Calculation of benefits. Type B benefits are calculated in the same way as pensions.

XII. Pensions

1. Introduction. Some of the most complex provisions of Regs. 1408/71 and 574/71 concern the claiming and calculation of pensions. These provisions have been the subject of a considerable body of case-law of the European Court of Justice that has resulted in a major overhaul of the provisions of the regulations in 1992.

The relevant provisions governing pension rights are contained in Arts. 44 to 51 of Reg. 1408/71 and Arts. 35 to 39 of Reg. 574/72. These provisions are applicable to old-age and survivors' pensions and those invalidity pensions where the amount of benefit is dependent upon the completion of insurance periods. Pensions are frequently referred to as long-term benefits reflecting both the length of insurance periods required to gain title and the indefinite duration of the benefits themselves.

Only pensions paid under statutory social security schemes are covered by the regulations: private and occupational schemes are excluded.

2. Aggregation. The general rule of aggregation applies to the determination of pension entitlement. Title to benefit must be determined on the basis of all the contributions paid to all the social security scheme to which the claimant has been subject (Art. 44(2) of Reg. 1408/71). The purpose of this rule is to prevent the unjustified cumulation of pension entitlements. There are three exceptions to this general rule: (*i*) if a claimant requests that the pension to which he is entitled under the legislation of one Member State be postponed, the legislation of that Member State need not be taken into account in calculating the pension (Art. 44(2) of Reg. 1408/71); (*ii*) if the claimant does not satisfy the conditions for entitlement to a pension in one of the Member State in which he has been affiliated to a pension scheme, his insurance contributions paid or period of residence completed in that Member State may be ignored (Art. 49 of Reg. 1408/71); (*iii*) periods of insurance or residence of less than one year may be ignored in calculating a pension if no right to benefit is acquired by virtue of them. (Art. 48 of Reg. 1408/71).

Where entitlement is claimed to a pension under a general social security scheme (as opposed to a special social security scheme for those in a particular employment or occupation), all insurance contributions or periods of residence completed under the legislation of any Member State (regardless of whether they were completed under a general scheme or a special scheme) may be taken into consideration in determining entitlement (Art. 45(2) of Reg. 1408/71).Where a Member State makes the granting of benefit conditional upon periods of insurance having been completed only in an occupation which is subject to a special scheme for employed persons or, where appropriate, in specific employment only insurance contributions completed under a corresponding scheme in another Member State may be taken into account (Art. 45(3) of Reg. 1408/71).

3. Calculation of pensions. There are two methods for calculating pension entitlement. The first is applicable when the claimant is not entitled to a pension under the legislation of the Member State in which he has been insured or in which he has completed residence and is obliged therefore to aggregate contributions or periods of residence completed in other Member States. The second method of pension calculation applies where a claimant is entitled to a pension under the legislation of one Member State alone.

4. Entitlement to benefit on the basis of insurance periods completed in more than one Member State. Where pension entitlement under the law of a Member State can only be gained by aggregating contributions or periods of residence completed in another Member State two calculations need to be made by the competent authority.

The competent institution first calculates the amount of benefit to which the claimant would have been entitled had he completed all his periods of insurance or periods of residence under the legislation of that State. The sum that this calculation yields up is known as the 'theoretical amount'.

The competent institution then calculates the amount of pension pro rata to which the claimant is entitled on the basis of the contributions or period of residence completed under the legislation which it administers to the total of all the periods of insurance or residence completed before the date on which the pension was claimed. The claimant is entitled to the higher of these two amounts from each of the Member States in which he has been insured and in which he makes a claim. This right is without prejudice to any application of the provision concerning the reduction, suspension, or withdrawal provided for by the legislation under which benefit is due. The right of Member States to reduce, suspend, or withdraw benefit is subject to a number of restrictions set out in Art. 46a of Reg. 1408/71.

Arts. 47 and 48 set out a number of specific rules for the calculation of the theoretical amount and pro rata pensions. These include rules relating to the calculation of benefits based on average earnings or average contributions or standards earning or a fixed amount. Art. 48 provides for the possibility of ignoring periods of insurance or periods of residence of less than one year.

XIII. Accidents at work and occupational diseases

The rules relating to the payment of benefits for accidents at work and occupational diseases are set out in Arts. 52 to 63 of Reg. 1408/71 and Arts. 60 to 77 of Reg. 574/72.

Benefits for accidents at work and occupational diseases are awarded in accordance with the law of the competent Member State, that is the Member State in which the claimant was insured at the time at the accident occurred or the disease materialized. Under the social security laws of the Member States title to benefit for an accident at work or an occupational disease is not insurance based or dependent upon the completion of periods of employment or residence. There are consequently no rules relating to aggregation set out in the section of Reg. 1408/71 which deals with work-related accidents and diseases.

Where an accident at work occurs or a work-related disease is contracted outside the territory of the competent Member State, the claimant is entitled to benefits in kind in accordance with the law of the Member State of residence. The cost of these benefits is borne by the competent institution. Cash benefits are payable in accordance with the legislation of the competent Member State and provided by the competent institution (Art. 52 of Reg. 1408/71).

An employed or self-employed person who sustains an accident at work or an occupational disease and:

(*i*) who is staying in the territory of a Member State other than the competent State; or

(*ii*) who, after becoming entitled to benefits chargeable to the competent institution is authorized by that institution to return to the territory of the Member State where he is resident or to transfer his place of residence to the territory of another Member State; or

(*iii*) who is authorized (and authorization cannot be refused where the treatment in question cannot be given to the person concerned in the territory of the Member State where he resides) to go to the territory of another Member State in order to receive treatment appropriate to his condition (Art. 55 of Reg. 1408/71) is entitled to the following benefits:

- benefits in kind provided by the institution of the place of residence or stay in accordance with the legislation administered by it for the duration specified by the legislation of the competent State;
- cash benefits provided by the competent institution in accordance with the legislation which it administers (Art. 54 of Reg. 1408/71).

1. Accidents in the course of travel. An accident that occurs while travelling outside the territory of the competent State shall be deemed to have occurred in the territory of competent State (Art. 56 of Reg. 1408/71).

2. Exposure to risks in several Member States. Where a person who contracts an occupational disease, has, under the legislation of two or more Member States, pursued an activity which, by its nature, is likely to cause that disease, the benefits that he and his survivors may claim are to be awarded exclusively under the legislation of the last of these Member States whose conditions of entitlement are satisfied (Art. 57 of Reg. 1408/71).

3. Aggravation of an occupational disease for which benefit has been awarded. In the case of aggravation of an occupational disease in respect of which a claimant is already receiving benefit, under the legislation of a Member State the following rules apply:

(*i*) if the beneficiary has not, while in receipt of benefit, engaged in an occupation in another Member State which is likely to cause or aggravate the disease in question, the competent institution of the first Member State is bound to meet the costs of the benefit under the legislation it administers taking into account the aggravation (Art. 60(1)(a) of Reg. 1408/71);

(*ii*) if the beneficiary has, while in receipt of benefits, pursued an activity in another Member State the competent institution of the first Member State is bound only to pay the amount of benefit due without taking the aggravation into account. The competent institution of the second Member State must grant a supplement in respect of the aggravation (Art. 60(1)(b) of Reg. 1408/71).

XIV. Death grants

Arts. 64 to 66a of Reg. 1408/71 and of Reg. 574/72 set out the co-ordination rules relating to death grants.

A death grant is defined in Art. 1(v) of Reg. 1408/71 as a once-for-all payment in the event of death exclusive of lump sum benefits which are paid in lieu of a pension. The general rule relating to the aggregation of contribution periods prevails (Art. 64 of Reg. 1408/71). If an employed or self-employed person, a pensioner, or a student dies in the territory of a Member State other than the competent Member State that death is deemed to have occurred on the territory of that State (Art. 65(1) of Reg. 1408/71). The competent institution must award the death grant payable under the system which it administers, even if the beneficiary resides in a Member State other than the competent State (Art. 65(2) of Reg. 1408/71).

A death grant payable in respect of a pensioner or a member of his family who is resident in a Member State other than that responsible for the granting of sickness benefits in kind as determined by Art. 28 of Reg. 1408/71 falls to be paid out by the latter as if the pensioner or his family member had been resident in the territory of that State at the time of death (Art. 66 of Reg. 1408/71).

XV. Unemployment benefit

1. Introduction. The rules that govern the entitlement of the employed and the self-employed (in the few cases where unemployment benefit is payable to the self-employed) who exercise their right to free movement to unemployment benefit are set out in Arts. 67 to 71 and Annex VI of Reg. 1408/71, and Arts. 80 to 84 of Reg. 574/72. Although aggregation of contributions or periods of employment completed in a Member State other than the competent State is permitted, the possibility of exporting unemployment benefits from the competent Member State to the Member State of residence of the claimant is severely limited.

Unemployment benefits are not specifically defined in the regulations but they must logically be understood to refer to whatever benefits are paid under the social security system of the competent Member State to the unemployed. For example, the concept of unemployment benefits includes financial assistance for vocational training granted to persons in employment facing loss of their jobs (Case 375/85 *Campana* [1987] ECR 2387).

2. Aggregation. Art. 67 of Reg. 1408/71 sets out the general principle of aggregation, that is periods of insurance or periods of employment completed in one Member State must be taken into account when assessing entitlement to benefits under the legislation of another Member State.

Art. 67(3) creates an exception to this general principle. Unemployed persons subject to the legislation of a Member State where entitlement to benefit is conditional upon the completion of insurance periods or periods of employment are not entitled to benefits in that Member State on the basis of insurance periods or periods of employment completed in another Member State unless the claimant has completed periods of insurance or periods of employment immediately prior to claiming unemployment benefit (Case C-272/90 *Van Noorden* [1991] ECR I-2543). This exception to the general rule of aggregation is not applicable to frontier workers or to persons who, at the time of their last employment, were resident in a Member State other than the competent Member State and who make themselves available to the employment services of their Member State of residence (Art. 71(1)(a)(ii) and (b)(ii)).

3. Calculation of benefits. Where benefit is based upon amount of remuneration prior to unemployment, only the remuneration completed in the last employment in the competent State may be taken into consideration. There is an exception to this rule where a person has been employed in another Member State for less than four weeks prior to becoming unemployed (Art. 68(1)). Where the amount of benefit payable varies in accordance with the number of members of the family of the unemployed person, members of the family resident in the territory of another Member State must be taken into account as though they were resident in the territory of the competent State. However the latter provision does not apply, where, in the country of residence of the members of the family, another member of the family is entitled to unemployment benefit and members of the family are taken into consideration in calculating the level of benefit payable (Art. 68(2); Case C-66/92 *Acciardi* [1993] ECR I-4567).

4. Exportability of benefit. As a general rule the principle of equality of treatment requires that benefits should be enjoyed by claimants regardless of where they are residing within the Community. This rule is departed from in the case of unemployment benefit which requires the fulfilment of a number of conditions for the export of benefits and even where these are fulfilled, limits the period of time for which benefits can be exported to three months. The legality of this rule has been upheld by the ECJ (Cases 41/79 etc. *Testa* [1980] ECR 1979).

Where an unemployed person goes to another Member State to seek employment there, he must take the following steps to ensure that he retains his title to unemployment benefit whilst absent from the competent Member State (Art. 69(1)):

(*i*) he must register as a person seeking work in the competent Member State and be available for work for at least four weeks after becoming unemployed unless he is authorized by the competent social security authorities to leave the Member State before this time period has expired;

(*ii*) he must register as a person seeking work with the employment services of the Member State to which he goes within seven days of ceasing to be available to the employment services of the Member State which he has left.

If these conditions are fulfilled the unemployed person may continue to receive benefit for a period of three months from the date on which he ceased to be available to the employment services of the competent Member State unless of course his period of entitlement is less than three months in which case benefit cease to be exported on the date on which entitlement ceases (Art. 69(1)(c)). In exceptional cases the three-month period during which unemployment benefit may be exported may be extended (Case 139/78 *Coccioli* [1979] ECR 991). Benefit is paid by the institution of the Member State to which the claimant has gone to seek employment and is reimbursed to that institution by the competent Member State (Art. 70).

If a claimant returns to the competent State upon the expiry of the three-month period set out above, his title to unemployment benefit continues until expiry of the period of entitlement; if he does not return within the three-month period he loses all title to benefit (Art. 69(2)).

5. Proposed amendment. In 1996 the Commission proposed an amendment to Art. 69 of Reg. 1408/71, which has not yet been adopted (*OJ* 1996 C68/8). This amendment would broaden the provisions relating to unemployment benefits in a number of respects. Any person going to a Member State other than the competent Member State would be subject to the control of the relevant authorities in the Member State to which he goes (Art. 69a). Such a person would remain entitled to have unemployment benefit exported to him from the competent Member State for an initial period of three months, after which period of time, the competent State may continue to pay benefit under its legislation subject to two limitations: (*i*) the total duration of benefit under the legislation of the competent State may not exceed the period during which the unemployed person would have been entitled to benefit if during his last employment he had been subject to the legislation of the Member State in which he has gone to seek work; (*ii*) the amount of benefits to which the unemployed person continues to be entitled may not exceed the amount of benefits to which he would have been entitled if during his last employment he had been subject to the legislation of the Member State to which he has gone in search of work.

An unemployed person who returns to the competent State would continue to be entitled to benefits in accordance with the legislation of that State but the period during which he received benefits outside the competent State would be deducted from the period during which he continued to be entitled under the legislation of the competent State.

The possibility of going to another Member State and continuing to remain entitled to benefit under the legislation of the competent Member State will only be able to be invoked once between two periods of employment.

XVI. Family benefits and family allowances

The rules relating specifically to family allowances and family benefits are set out in Arts. 72 to 76 of Reg. 1408/71 and Arts. 85 to 86 of Reg. 574/72.

Family benefits are defined in Art. 1(u)(i) as all benefits in cash or in kind designed to meet family expenses excluding a number of special childbirth or adoption allowances referred to in Annex II. All benefits that are granted to families on the basis of the fulfilment of objective criteria relating for example to the size, income, and capital resources of the family fall within the scope of Reg. 1408/71 (Case C-78/91 *Hughes* [1992] ECR I-4839).

Family allowances are periodic cash benefits granted exclusively by reference to the number and, where appropriate, the age of members of the family.

1. Aggregation. The general principle of aggregation applies to claims for family benefits and family allowances: insurance periods, periods of employment and self-employment completed in one Member State must be taken into account in assessing entitlement to family benefits and family allowances in another Member State (Art. 72 of Reg. 1408/71).

2. Family members resident outside the territory of the competent State. Employed or self-employed persons, and those in receipt of unemployment benefit under the legislation of the competent State, who have family members residing in another Member State are entitled to the full range of family benefit and family allowances payable under the legislation of the competent State in respect of those family members (Arts. 73 and 74 of Reg. 1408/71; Case C-78/91 *Hughes*, above; Case 104/80 *Beeck* [1981] ECR 503). There are a number of exceptions to this rule specified in Annex VI to Reg. 1408/71.

Events occurring in the territory of a Member State other than the competent Member State must be taken into account by the competent Member State in assessing entitlement to benefit (Case C-228/88 *Bronzino*, above; Case C-12/89 *Gatto*, above).

3. Overlapping entitlement. Where family benefits are provided under the legislation of the Member State where the family members are residing, by reason of the carrying out of an economic activity from which entitlement to such benefits is derived, entitlement to family benefits under the legislation of another Member State is suspended up to the level of entitlement in the Member State of residence (Art. 76 of Reg. 1408/71; Case 104/84 *Kromhout* [1985] ECR 2205; Case 377/85 *Burchell* [1987] ECR 3329). Entitlement to benefit must actually exist in the Member State of residence for suspension to occur (Case 134/77 *Ragazzoni* [1978] ECR 963).

4. Provision of benefits. Family benefits are provided by the competent institution of the Member State in which entitlement arises. This institution applies its own rules for the provision of benefits regardless of the Member State of residence or stay of the person to whom benefits have to be paid. Payment can be made to the person actually, maintaining the family (Art. 75).

Special rules apply to benefits for dependent children of pensioners and orphans.

5. Pensioners. Those receiving pensions in respect of old age, invalidity, accidents at work, or occupational diseases are entitled to family allowances only (and not any other family benefits) in respect of their dependent children payable in accordance with the provisions of Art. 77(2). As a general rule family allowances for dependent children of pensioners are granted according to the legislation of the Member State under which the pension is granted.

6. Orphans. Benefits for orphans (regardless of their Member State of residence) family allowances, and supplements or special allowances for orphans and orphans' pensions except for those granted under insurance schemes for accidents at work and occupational diseases (Art. 78(1)). As a general rule, orphans' benefits are granted in accordance with the legislation of the Member State to which the deceased employed or self-employed person was subject. Special rules apply to the orphans of a deceased employed or self-employed persons who was subject to the legislation of one or more Member States (Art. 78(2)(b)).

The general principle of aggregation applies to the acquisition of title to family allowances by the dependent children of pensioners and orphans benefits.

XVII. The Administrative Commission and the Advisory Committee

The Administrative Commission on the Social Security for Migrant Workers was established by Art. 80 of Reg. 1408/71 (the Administrative

Commission). It is composed of a government representative from each Member State. Technical assistance is provided by the International Labour Office. A number of tasks are entrusted to the Administrative Commission under Art. 81 of Reg. 1408/71. These tasks are all designed to ensure the smooth administration of the regulations. The Administrative Commission issues decisions on various aspect of the regulations. In all some 120 decisions are currently applicable.

The Advisory Committee consists of ninety members comprising government representatives, representatives from the trade unions' and employers' organizations (Art. 82 of Reg. 1408/71). The Advisory Committee examines general questions or question of principle and problems arising out of the regulations. It formulates opinions for the Administrative Commission and on any proposals for amendments to them.

XVIII. Rights against third parties

Reg. 1408/71 gives the social security institutions of a Member State the right to recover the costs of benefits paid out by them in respect of injuries occurred in another Member State from third parties responsible for those injuries (Art. 93). It is, in effect, a fair and logical counterpart to the extension of the obligations of those institutions beyond the national territory (Case C-428/92 *Laererstandens Brandforsikring* [1994] ECR I-2259).

Art. 93(1) provides where a social security institution is responsible for benefits is, by virtue of the legislation that it administers subrogated to the rights which the recipient has against a third party, such subrogation must be recognized by each Member State. Where such an institution has direct rights against a third party such rights must be recognized by each Member State (Art. 93(2)).

XIX. Regulation 1612/68

Employed persons and their families can, in addition to Reg. 1408/71, rely upon Art. 7(2) of Reg. 1612/68 (*OJ Sp. Edn.* 1998 (II), p. 475) as amended by Reg. 312/76 (*OJ* 1976 L39/2) and Reg. 2434/92 (*OJ* 1992 L245/1). Art. 7(2) provides that a migrant worker has the right to 'enjoy the same social and tax advantages as national workers'. The ECJ has held that Art. 7(2) extends to workers' families (Case 32/75 *Fiorini* [1975] ECR 1085; Case 261/83 *Castelli* [1984] ECR 3199).

The term 'social and tax advantages' has been interpreted broadly by the ECJ to include social security and social assistance benefits (Case 63/76 *Inzirillo*, above; Case C-111/91 *Commission* v. *Luxembourg* [1993] ECR I-817; Case 94/84 *Deak*, above; Case 157/84 *Frascogna*, above; Case C-326/90 *Commission* v. *Belgium* [1992] ECR I-5517; Case C-310/91 *Schmid*, above).

Art. 7(2) entitles a worker and his family to enjoy social security and social assistance benefit in the territory of the Member State in which the worker is employed. It does not entail the right to have benefits exported to another Member State nor does it require that contributions to the social security system of another Member State be taken into account when assessing entitlement to benefits.

The concept of social advantage includes social assistance benefits of a kind excluded from the scope of application of Reg. 1408/71 (*see further under* **Social advantage**).

XX. Equality of treatment between men and women

Art. 141 EC requires equality of treatment between men and women in the matter of occupational social security systems (Case C-262/88 *Barber*, above). That principle is implemented by Dir. 86/378 on the implementation of the principle of equal treatment for men and women in occupational social security schemes (*OJ* 1986 L225/40, as amended by Dir. 96/97, *OJ* 1997 L46/20). Equality of treatment between men and women in State social security schemes is the subject of Dir. 79/7 on the principle of equal treatment for men and women in matters of social security (*OJ* 1979 L6/24) (*see further under* **Equal pay, Equal treatment**).

See also **Equal pay, Equal treatment, Freedom to provide services, Free movement of goods, Free movement of persons, Social advantage.**

Further reading 1. BOOKS: Van der Mei, *Free Movement of Persons within the European Community* (2003); Van Rapenbusch, *La securite sociale des personnes qui circulent a l'interieur de la CEE* (1991); Watson, *Social Security Law of the European Community* (1980).

2. ARTICLES: Cornelissen, 'The Principle of Territoriality and the Community Regulations on Social Security' (1996) *CML Rev.* 439; Kessler, 'L'exportation des prestations non-contributives de securite social' (2001) *Droit Social* 15.

► **STATE COMMERCIAL MONOPOLY** 'Any body through which a Member State, in law or in fact, either directly or indirectly supervises, determines or appreciably influences imports or exports between Member States' (Art. 31(1) EC [ex Art. 37(1) EEC]). The concept also includes monopolies delegated by the State to others (ibid.).

Art. 37 of the original EEC Treaty, which was amended by the Treaty of Amsterdam (ToA, see Art. 6, point 24) and renumbered Art. 31, required the Member States progressively to adjust any State monopolies of a commercial character so as to ensure that when the transitional period ended on 31 December 1969 no discrimination remained between their nationals regarding the conditions under which goods were procured and marketed. The timetable for the adjustment, which was to be harmonized with the abolition of quantitative restrictions, as well as the manner of adjustment, were to be laid down by the Commission in recommendations (Art. 37(3) and (6) EEC, deleted by the ToA). Following a number of recommendations, the Member States did carry out certain adjustments to their monopolies during the transitional period, but in most cases the complete elimination of all forms of discrimination covered by Art. 37 [now Art. 31] was not achieved by the end of 1969. The Commission has therefore continued its work of implementing Art. 37 [Art. 31] ever since, partly through recommendations and partly through infringement actions under Art. 226 EC. Following the successive enlargements of the Community, the acceding Member States were required to abolish all exclusive export rights and certain exclusive import rights and to adjust their State monopolies progressively by the dates laid down in the respective Acts of Accession. The existing Member States had equivalent obligations. The Commission was to make the necessary recommendations and supervise implementation.

The amended Art. 31(1) still requires Member States to adjust any State monopolies of a commercial character 'so as to ensure that no discrimination regarding the conditions under which goods are procured and marketed exists between nationals of Member States'. Under Art. 31(2), Member States are to refrain from introducing any new measure which is contrary to these principles or which restricts the scope of the Articles dealing with the prohibition of customs duties and quantitative restrictions.

Examples of State monopolies within the meaning of Art. 31 have included the French alcohol, manufactured tobacco, petroleum products, potash fertilizers, basic slag, matches, gunpowder and explosives monopolies; the Italian manufactured tobacco, lighters, flints, salt, cigarette paper, and matches monopolies; the German alcohol monopoly; the Belgian natural gas monopoly; the Greek petroleum products, matches, cigarette paper, potash fertilizers, and pharmaceutical monopolies; the Spanish oil and tobacco products monopolies; the Portuguese oil and alcohol monopolies; the Swedish and Finnish alcohol monopolies; and the Austrian alcohol, salt, and manufactured tobacco monopolies. Some of these have been abolished as a result of the Commission's efforts (see the relevant chapters in the Commission's annual *Report on Competition Policy* and the cases cited below).

State monopolies may exist for a number of different reasons, whether political, economic, or financial, such as the protection of national production, assurance of supplies, fiscal objectives, etc. Whatever their purpose, however, by virtue of their *exclusive import and marketing rights*, they are able to determine the limits and terms on which foreign products are admitted to the national market. They thus tend to have a discriminatory effect on the conditions of supply and marketing of goods to the detriment of foreign suppliers. For example, they may refuse to import at all, or may impose on imports quantitative restrictions or more onerous marketing conditions than those applied to national products, including discriminatory advertising conditions, etc. The purpose of granting *exclusive export rights* may be different, but the discriminatory effects are the same. Thus, the aim may be to supply the domestic market on a priority basis or to sell under different conditions on the domestic and foreign markets. The result is discrimination against nationals of other Member States who may wish to buy the products in question. The purpose of Art. 31 is precisely to ensure that products which are subject to a State monopoly of a commercial character are in the same position as any other products with regard to the free movement of goods under Arts. 28 and 29 EC (see 1st *Comp. Rep.* (1971), pp. 148–53; Case 20/64 *Albatros* [1965] ECR 29 at pp. 42 *et seq. per* A.-G. Gand).

In interpreting and applying Art. 31, in several cases the ECJ has started from the fact that Art. 31 appears in that part of the EC Treaty that deals with the free movement of goods, and in particular with the prohibition of quantitative restrictions between Member States (Part Three, Title I, Chapter 2). From this, the Court has drawn a number of important conclusions regarding the scope and effects of Art. 31 and its relationship with other provisions of the Treaty. These may be summarized as follows.

I. The scope of Article 31

1. Art. 31(1) does not prohibit the creation of State monopolies in general, but merely those 'of a commercial character', and then only in so far as they tend to introduce the discrimination referred to therein. To fall within this prohibition, the State monopolies and bodies in question must, first, have as their object transactions regarding a commercial product capable of being the subject of competition and trade between Member States, and secondly, play an effective part in such trade. Thus, in determining whether a monopoly or body falls within the scope of Art. 31, what matters is not the legal form nor the legal nature of the body under national public law, but the effective part played by it in trade between Member States (Case 6/64 *Costa* [1964] ECR 585 at p. 598 *per Curiam*, p. 611 *per* A.-G. Lagrange, dealing with the Italian National Electricity Board, ENEL). In that case, A.-G. Lagrange pointed out that while Art. 31 might apply to an industrial or commercial public service, it did not normally apply to one which was not involved in international trade, such as a public service for the production and distribution of electricity. While the ECJ left it to the national court to assess whether ENEL met the above criteria, the Commission interpreted this judgment as confirming that gas and electricity were to be treated as goods and were thus covered by Arts. 28 and 31 (see 21st *Comp. Rep.* (1991), p. 190, where the Commission pointed out that trade in gas and electricity in the Community had grown substantially over the years. See point 2 below). In Case 82/71 *SAIL* [1972] ECR 119 at p. 142, A.-G. Roemer thought that Art. 31 applied to Italian milk centres since milk could be the subject of international trade.

2. Dealing with the scope of Art. 31, in Case C-393/92 *Almelo* [1994] ECR I-1477 at p. I-1516, the Court pointed out that it follows both from the position that Art. 31 occupies in the chapter on the prohibition of quantitative restrictions and from the use of the words 'imports', 'exports', and 'products' that it covers trade in goods. At the same time, referring to its judgment in *Costa*, above, the Court expressly confirmed that electricity constituted 'goods' within the meaning of the Treaty, which might fall within the scope of Art. 31. Accordingly, Art. 31 applies to trade in goods and does not apply to a monopoly over the provision of services, even if such a monopoly enables the Member State concerned to direct a branch of the national economy, except in so far as such a monopoly contravenes the principle of the free movement of goods by discriminating against imported products to

the advantage of domestic products (Cases C-46/90 etc. *Lagauche* [1993] ECR I-5267 at p. I-5329). Thus, Art. 31 does not apply to broadcasts of any kind, including televised commercial advertising and broadcasts of films, etc. (Case 155/73 *Sacchi* [1974] ECR 409 at p. 428); to artificial insemination of cattle (Case 271/81 *Mialocq* [1983] ECR 2057 at pp. 2072–3); to external services for funerals (Case 30/87 *Bodson* [1988] ECR 2479 at p. 2511); and to any monopoly in the operation of games of chance or gambling (Case C-6/01 *Anomar* [2003] ECR I-8621, paras. 58–61).

3. For Art. 31 to apply there must exist a 'body' through which a Member State, in law or in fact, either directly or indirectly, supervises, determines, or appreciably influences imports or exports between Member States. The sole fact that a Member State subjects the import of certain goods or certain industrial or commercial operations to a compulsory licensing system does not create a State monopoly within the meaning of Art. 31, provided that any qualified person or undertaking is free to apply for and obtain the required licence (Case 161/82 *Commission* v. *France* [1983] ECR 2079 at pp. 2094–5 concerning the importation into France of semen intended for the artificial insemination of cattle; Case 118/86 *Nertsvoederfabriek Nederland* [1987] ECR 3883 at pp. 3906–7, concerning the operation of a rendering plant). Nor is a situation covered by Art. 31 where the influence on patterns of trade between Member States is the result of the conduct of undertakings to which the monopoly-holder has granted concessions to carry on certain activities, and not of the monopoly-holder itself (Case 30/87 *Bodson*, above, at pp. 2511–12). Art. 31 likewise does not apply to national legislation which reserves the exclusive right of retail sale of manufactured tobacco products to distributors to whom the State monopoly has issued a concession or authorization, but which does not allow the national authorities to intervene in the operation of tobacco outlets so as to control or influence the procurement choices of retailers, in order to ensure an outlet for the monopoly's tobacco products or to encourage or discourage certain types of imports from other Member States (Case C-387/93 *Banchero II* [1995] ECR I-4663 at p. I-4693, dealing with the Italian monopoly in manufactured tobacco products).

The concept of a 'body' that may hold and operate a monopoly is very widely defined. It may be (and very often is) the State itself, acting through organizations established for that purpose or through central, regional, or municipal authorities; territorial units of the State such as communes; but equally monopolies may be delegated to others, such as undertakings or groups of undertakings acting under the control and supervision of the State and operating either over the whole territory of the State or only in a part of it (Case 30/87 *Bodson*, above, at p. 2511, where a monopoly to provide external services for funerals was granted to French communes; Case 82/71 *SAIL*, above, at p. 143 *per* A.-G. Roemer, concerning Italian milk centres having an exclusive right of sale. They were run by associations governed by private law, but established and supervised by the public authorities).

4. Generally, an exclusive right conferred on the State to import and market a product will constitute a State monopoly within the meaning of

Art. 31. This is, however, not always so. In Case C-347/88 *Commission* v. *Greece* [1990] ECR I-4747 at pp. I-4786–8, the Commission argued that a Greek law which conferred on the State the exclusive right to import crude oil intended for refining was contrary to Art. 31(1) because it precluded any possibility of importation by traders other than the State. However, the same law also conferred on the State the monopoly to refine crude oil, which was not challenged by the Commission. In those circumstances, the Court held that the refining monopoly, which was quite lawful, already enabled the State to exercise full control over imports of crude oil intended for refining, making the possibility of importation by other traders wholly theoretical. Therefore, the fact that imports were effected exclusively by the State or under its control was inherent in the refining monopoly and was not the consequence of the exclusive right to import. The legality of the latter could not be called in question separately from that of the former (see also the opinion of A.-G. Tesauro, ibid. at p. I-4774). The same law also conferred on the Greek State the exclusive right to import and market a quantity of finished petroleum products corresponding to 65% of the requirements of the domestic market. The Court held that this right gave Greece enough power to exert an 'appreciable influence' on imports of those products for it to constitute a State monopoly of a commercial character within the meaning of Art. 31 (ibid. at p. I-4789).

5. The wide definition of a State monopoly in Art. 31(1) includes not only activities by which the State is involved directly in trade between Member States but also those whereby it acts '*de facto*' or 'indirectly', as well as activities by which the State merely 'influences' rather than 'supervises' or 'determines' such trade. From this the ECJ has concluded that 'the application of Article 31 is not limited to imports or exports which are directly subject to the monopoly but covers all measures which are connected with its existence and affect trade between Member States in certain products, whether or not subject to the monopoly. It is therefore possible that the introduction, after the entry into force of the Treaty, of an import duty on a product, a constituent part of which is subject to the monopoly, may amount to a "new measure" within the meaning of Article 31(2)' (Case 13/70 *Cinzano* [1970] ECR 1089 at pp. 1095–6 concerning the imposition of a charge on drinks with a wine base—*in casu* vermouths—imported from another Member State into Germany where domestic and imported ethyl alcohol was subject to a State monopoly but the drinks in question were not. The Court held that the charge fell within the scope of Art. 31, but see further section II.4(*a*) below). Moreover, Art. 31(1) is not concerned exclusively with quantitative restrictions but also prohibits charges which result in discrimination against imported products as compared with national products coming under the monopoly (Case 45/75 *Rewe* [1976] ECR 181 at pp. 198–9; Case 91/75 *Miritz* [1976] ECR 217 at pp. 229–30).

6. Since Art. 31 is intended to promote the free movement of goods within the Community and to maintain normal conditions of competition between the economies of Member States, it cannot be applied to products imported from third countries. Such imports are subject, not to the

provisions governing the internal market but to those relating to the common commercial policy. On the other hand, products originating in the overseas countries and territories (OCTs) associated with the EC must receive the same treatment on importation into the EC as products of Community origin as regards any discriminatory practices on the part of a State monopoly (Case 91/78 *Hansen II* [1979] ECR 935 at pp. 956–7).

7. As regards agricultural products, Art. 31(3) provides that if a State monopoly has rules which are designed to make it easier to dispose of such products or obtain for them the best return, steps should be taken in applying Art. 31 to ensure equivalent safeguards for the employment and standard of living of the producers concerned. In Case 91/75 *Miritz*, above, at p. 230 the German Government argued, relying on the relevant recommendation of the Commission, that Art. 31(3) constituted justification for a charge designed to ensure safeguards for the employment and standard of living of German producers of agricultural alcohol, which was imposed on imported alcoholic products (called the 'Preisausgleichsabgabe'—special equalization charge). The Government's reasoning was that the charge was the equivalent of the safeguards which the German producers had enjoyed by virtue of the German alcohol monopoly's exclusive right to import, which was abolished in accordance with Art. 31(1). However, the Court did not accept this argument. It held that Art. 31(1) laid down a specific and unconditional obligation to achieve results by the end of the transitional period to which Art. 31(3) could not be construed as providing for an exception. The purpose of this provision was to enable the national authorities, if necessary in co-operation with the Community institutions, to adopt certain measures designed to compensate for the effects of the adjustment of State monopolies, but these measures must themselves be compatible with Art. 31(1) and (2). Thus, Art. 31(3) could not be taken to derogate from the other provisions of Art. 31 (ibid. at pp. 230–1, see also section II.4(*c*) below).

II. The effects of Article 31

1. The objective of Article 31. The objective of Art. 31 has been described by the ECJ as follows:

> It is clear not only from the wording of Article 31 but also from the position which it occupies in the general scheme of the Treaty that the Article is designed to ensure compliance with the fundamental principle that goods should be able to move freely throughout the common market, in particular by requiring quantitative restrictions and measures having equivalent effect in trade between Member States to be abolished, and thereby to ensure maintenance of normal conditions of competition between the economies of Member States in the event that a given product is subject, in one or other of those States, to a national monopoly of a commercial character. . .
>
> The purpose of Article 31 of the Treaty is to reconcile the possibility for Member States to maintain certain monopolies of a commercial character as instruments for the pursuit of public interest aims with the requirements of the establishment and functioning of the common market. It aims at the elimination of obstacles to the free movement of goods, save, however, for restrictions on trade which are inherent in the existence of the monopolies in question.
>
> Thus, Article 31 requires that the organization and operation of the monopoly be

arranged so as to exclude any discrimination between nationals of Member States as regards conditions of supply and outlets, so that trade in goods from other Member States is not put at a disadvantage, in law or in fact, in relation to that in domestic goods and that competition between the economies of the Member States is not distorted (Case C-189/95 *Franzen* [1997] ECR I-5909 at pp. I-5967–8).

In that case, the Court examined the compatibility of the Swedish alcohol retail monopoly with Arts. 28 and 31. The Court accepted that in aiming to protect public health against the harm caused by alcohol, the monopoly pursued a public interest objective. The product selection system, sales network, and promotion method used by the monopoly were neither discriminatory nor apt to put imported beverages at a disadvantage. Overall, the Court found that the monopoly's exclusive right to retail alcoholic beverages was compatible with Art. 31. On the other hand, the system of wholesale import and distribution licences was contrary to Art. 28 (ibid. at pp. I-5968–77).

While Art. 31 does not require the total abolition of State commercial monopolies, it lays down two obligations. The first is that such monopolies must be adjusted in such a way as to ensure that no discrimination exists between nationals of the Member States regarding the conditions under which goods are procured and marketed (para. 1). The second is that no new measure must be introduced by the Member States which would be contrary to the above principles or would restrict the scope of the Articles dealing with the prohibition of customs duties and quantitative restrictions (the 'standstill' clause, para. 2).

From these provisions the ECJ has drawn the important conclusion that the effect of Art. 31(1) was that as from 31 December 1969, the end of the transitional period, every national commercial monopoly had to be adjusted so as to eliminate any exclusive right to import goods from other Member States. This time limit was laid down by the Treaty mandatorily and could not therefore be extended or varied by the institutions or the Member States (Case 59/75 *Manghera* [1976] ECR 91 at pp. 100–2, interpreting Art. 31(1) and the Council Res. of 21 April 1970 which required the abolition of the exclusive import and marketing rights of the French and Italian State monopolies by 1 January 1976 at the latest. See also Case 20/64 *Albatros*, above, at p. 35; Case 91/78 *Hansen II*, above, at p. 952; Case 78/82 *Commission* v. *Italy* [1983] ECR 1955 at pp. 1967–8; Case C-347/88 *Commission* v. *Greece*, above, at pp. I-4789–91, where the Court held that by maintaining in force the exclusive right of the State to import and market finished petroleum products, Greece was seeking to secure an outlet for the products of its public-sector refineries and thereby discriminated against exporters established in other Member States. This was contrary to Art. 31(1)).

2. The standstill provision. The concept of a 'new measure' that is prohibited by Art. 31(2) is closely linked to the definition of the activities constituting a State monopoly set out in Art. 31(1). Thus, the effect of Art. 31(2) was to prohibit in absolute terms, as from 1 January 1958, the date of the coming into force of the Treaty, any new monopolies or bodies in so far as they tended to introduce new cases of discrimination regarding the conditions under which goods were procured and marketed, as well as the use of the then existing monopolies to aggravate discrimination or to re-establish customs duties or quantitative restrictions in intra-Community trade (Case 6/64 *Costa*, above, at pp. 597–8; Case 13/70 *Cinzano*, above, at pp. 1095–6; Case 91/78 *Hansen II*, above, at p. 952).

3. Direct effect. Art. 31(1) and (2) produce direct effect in the sense of creating individual rights which the national courts must protect. The direct effect of Art. 31(1) commenced with the expiry of the transitional period on 31 December 1969 (Case 59/75 *Manghera*, above, at p. 101; Case 45/75 *Rewe*, above, at pp. 197–8); the direct effect of Art. 31(2) started immediately upon the Treaty coming into force on 1 January 1958 (Case 6/64 *Costa*, above, at pp. 597–8. See also Case 91/78 *Hansen II*, above, at pp. 955–6 dealing with the direct effect of Art. 31 as a whole).

4. Prohibition of discrimination. The requirement that the discrimination to which Art. 31(1) refers must be abolished is a strict one: it involves the elimination not only of actual but also of potential (possible) discrimination. Generally, where a State monopoly has an exclusive right of sale or an exclusive right to import, it is in a position to discriminate against goods from other countries even if it is not itself a producer (see the opinions of A.-G. Roemer in Case 82/71 *SAIL*, above, at pp. 143–4 and of A.-G. Warner in Case 59/75 *Manghera*, above, at pp. 107–8). As the Court has explained:

> the existence of exclusive import and export rights in a Member State gives rise to discrimination against exporters and importers established in other Member States, since that trade is carried on exclusively by the holder of those rights and all the economic operators in the other Member States are automatically excluded from direct imports and exports and deprived of the freedom to choose their customers or suppliers in the Member State in which the holder of those rights is established (Case C-158/94 *Commission* v. *Italy* [1997] ECR I-5789 at p. I-5803. See also the other three cases decided by the Court on the same day, brought by the Commission against the Netherlands, France, and Spain, concerning exclusive import and export rights for electricity. All four actions were dismissed).

It was this consideration which led the Court to the conclusion that Art. 31 required the elimination of any exclusive right to import (see point 1 above). To determine what does or does not constitute prohibited 'discrimination' within the meaning of Art. 31(1) has been the key issue in many of the cases brought before the Court concerning State commercial monopolies. The case-law of the Court on this point may be summarized as follows.

(*a*) Discrimination exists only where higher charges are imposed on imported products than on similar domestic products. There is therefore no discrimination when the imported product is subject to the same conditions as the domestic product covered by a State monopoly. Moreover, the extension to imported products of a charge which prior to the entry into force of the EEC Treaty was imposed only on similar domestic products subject to a monopoly does not amount to a customs duty or a charge having equivalent effect, and is therefore not prohibited by Art. 31(2), provided that such a new charge is imposed on the imported products only to the same extent as on domestic products affected by the monopoly (Case 13/30 *Cinzano*, above, at pp. 1096–7; see also section I.5 above).

(*b*) The concept of discrimination within the meaning of Art. 31(1) includes the extraction of a contribution to the State monopoly's own administrative costs from an imported product alone, but does not cover the imposition of identical taxation on an imported product and a similar domestic product, even if the charge imposed on the latter is, in part, allocated for the purposes of financing the monopoly, whilst the charge levied on the imported product is imposed for the benefit of the general budget of the State (Case 45/75 *Rewe*, above, at pp. 198–9 dealing with the German 'Monopolausgleichspitze'—surcharge on monopoly equalization duty—imposed on imported spirits and spirituous beverages).

(*c*) Since Art. 31(1) prohibits charges which result in discrimination against imported products as compared with national products coming under the monopoly (see section I.5 above), it prevents a Member State, after the end of the transitional period, from imposing a charge only on an imported product for the purpose of compensating for the difference between the selling price of that product in the country of origin and the higher price paid by the State monopoly to domestic producers of the same product (Case 91/75 *Miritz*, above, at pp. 229–31 dealing with the German 'Preisausgleichsabgabe'—special equalization charge—imposed on imported alcoholic products).

(*d*) Whether or not a domestic product is subject to a commercial monopoly, Art. 31 does not prohibit a Member State from imposing on that domestic product internal taxation in excess of that imposed on a similar imported product or, *a fortiori*, in excess of that imposed on a similar product in another Member State (Case 86/78 *Peureux I* [1979] ECR 897 at p. 914 dealing with certain aspects of the French alcohol monopoly).

(*e*) Art. 31(1) prohibits a State monopoly from marketing a domestic product (such as spirits) with the aid of public funds at an abnormally low resale price compared to the price, before tax, of products of comparable quality imported from another Member State. Such a practice is contrary to the equality of opportunity which must be accorded to imported products (Case 91/78 *Hansen II*, above, at pp. 954–5). The position is different, however, where the price reduction is not a measure peculiar to the monopoly but a purely commercial measure dictated by competition, and the State aid used has been duly notified to, and approved by, the Commission (Case 253/83 *Kupferberg* [1985] ECR 157 at pp. 185–6).

(*f*) A national provision prohibiting the distillation, for the purpose of producing alcohol reserved to a State monopoly, of raw materials imported from other Member States constitutes discrimination where the same prohibition does not apply to identical raw materials produced domestically. However, the fact alone that an obligation imposed on national producers of alcohol to deliver their production only to the State alcohol monopoly, and the corresponding obligation on the monopoly to buy such products at officially fixed prices, applies only to domestic alcohol cannot be regarded as discrimination nor as a quantitative restriction (Case 119/78 *Peureux II* [1979] ECR 975 at pp. 986–7 dealing with the French alcohol monopoly).

(g) The fixing by a State monopoly covering both the production and the distribution of manufactured tobacco products, of uniform trading margins for the retail trade that apply without distinction to domestic and imported products does not amount to discrimination. Such a scheme makes the granting of marketing premiums impossible as much for the national monopoly as for foreign producers and does not affect the freedom of producers to fix the retail prices of their products (Case 78/82 *Commission* v. *Italy*, above, at pp. 1968–70 dealing with the Italian tobacco monopoly). By contrast, the fixing by the State, within the framework of a national monopoly, of the retail selling prices of imported manufactured tobacco at a different level from that determined by the manufacturers or importers is contrary to Art. 31. In fact, such a measure constitutes an extension to imported tobacco of a prerogative typical of a national monopoly, which is bound adversely to affect the marketing of imported products (Case 90/82 *Commission* v. *France* [1983] ECR 2011 at pp. 2031–2 dealing with the French tobacco monopoly).

III. Article 31 and other Treaty provisions

The field of application of Art. 31 overlaps with that of certain other provisions of the Treaty, such as those relating to the free movement of goods (in particular, Arts. 25, 28, and 29), agriculture (Arts. 32 to 38), competition (Arts. 81 and 82), public undertakings (Art. 86), State aids (Arts. 87 and 88), and taxation (Art. 90). In several cases, the ECJ has been faced with the problem of defining the mutual relationship between Art. 31 on the one hand, and these other provisions, on the other. In Case 91/78 *Hansen II*, above, at p. 952, the Commission put forward the view that when State monopolies were adjusted at the end of the transitional period, the effectiveness of Art. 31 was exhausted and the field covered by it became governed by the general rules relating to the free movement of goods and non-discriminatory taxation. However, the Court did not share this view. It confirmed that 'Article 31 remains applicable wherever, even after the adjustment prescribed in the Treaty, the exercise by a State monopoly of its exclusive rights entails a discrimination or restriction prohibited by that Article' (ibid.; see also Case 90/82 *Commission* v. *France*, above, at p. 2027).

The general principles of delimitation adopted by the Court seem to be that where a case concerns an activity specifically connected with the exercise by a State monopoly of its exclusive right to purchase, make, and sell goods, Art. 31 may be applicable (Case 91/78 *Hansen II*, above, at p. 952). On the other hand, Art. 31 is irrelevant to national provisions which are unconnected with the exercise by a State monopoly of its exclusive rights and apply in a general manner to the production and marketing of goods, whether or not the goods in question are covered by the monopoly (Case 120/78 *Rewe* [1979] ECR 649 at p. 662—*Cassis de Dijon* case; Case 86/78 *Peureux I*, above, at p. 913; Case 119/78 *Peureux II*, above, at p. 986; Cases

C-78/90 etc. *Compagnie Commerciale de l'Ouest* [1992] ECR I-1847 at pp. I-1883–4). Applying these principles to the particular circumstances of individual cases before it, the Court has clarified the relationship between Art. 31 and the above-mentioned provisions as follows.

1. Customs duties and charges having equivalent effect (Article 25). Where the structure and character of a charge link it to the system of a national commercial monopoly, it must be assessed under Art. 31 and not under Art. 25 (Case 91/75 *Miritz*, above, at p. 229, dealing with the 'Preisausgleichsabgabe', a special equalization charge forming part of the adjustment of the German State monopoly in alcohol and imposed only on imported spirits and alcoholic products; see also section II.4(*c*) above).

2. Quantitative restrictions and measures having equivalent effect (Articles 28 and 29). National measures that do not concern the exercise by a public monopoly of its specific function, namely, its exclusive rights, but apply in a general manner to the production and marketing of goods, whether or not the latter are covered by the monopoly, must be examined solely under Art. 28 and not under Art. 31 (Case 120/78 *Rewe*, above, at p. 662, dealing with the German rules relating to the marketing of alcoholic beverages and fixing a minimum alcoholic strength). Likewise, the effect on intra-Community trade of national provisions which are separable from the operation of the monopoly although they have a bearing upon it, must be examined with reference to Art. 28 (Case C-189/95 *Franzen*, above, at p. I-5966). Nevertheless, it is possible for a measure or a set of measures adopted within the framework or in relation to a State monopoly, to be contrary to *both* Art. 28 *and* Art. 31 at the same time, namely, where it constitutes a quantitative restriction or a measure having equivalent effect within the meaning of Art. 28 *and* discrimination within the meaning of Art. 31(1) (see e.g. Case 119/78 *Peureux II*, above, at p. 987; Case 90/82 *Commission* v. *France*, above, at p. 2031; Case C-347/88 *Commission* v. *Greece*, above, at pp. I-4788–91; for the context, see sections II.4(*f*), II.4(*g*), I.4, and II.1 above, respectively).

3. Agriculture (Articles 32 to 38). It follows from Art. 32(2) that the provisions of the Treaty relating to the common agricultural policy have precedence, in case of any discrepancy, over the rules relating to the establishment of the common market, including Art. 31. Therefore, the specific provisions of a regulation setting up a common organization of the market cannot be derogated from by relying on Art. 31 (Case 83/78 *Redmond* [1978] ECR 2347 at p. 2368; Case 177/78 *McCarren* [1979] ECR 2161 at p. 2191, both concerning the common organization of the market in pig-meat).

4. Competition (Articles 81 and 82). A situation in which the effect on trade between Member States is the result of the conduct of undertakings to which the monopoly-holder has granted concessions to carry on the activity covered by the monopoly, and not of the monopoly-holder itself, is governed by Arts. 81 and 82 (and, possibly, by Art. 86), not by Art. 31 (Case 30/87 *Bodson*, above, at pp. 2511–12, concerning the provision of funeral services by French communes).

5. Revenue-producing monopolies (Article 86(2)). The relationship between Art. 31 and Art. 86(2) is determined by the rules relating to public undertakings.

6. State aids (Articles 87 and 88). The relationship between Art. 31 and Arts. 87 and 88 is determined by the rules relating to State aids.

7. Discriminatory taxation (Article 90). Art. 31 is a *lex specialis* in relation to Art. 90, which prohibits the imposition of discriminatory taxes on the products of other Member States. On this basis, in Case 45/75 *Rewe*, above, at p. 210, A.-G. Reischl suggested that a tax imposed in the context of the adjustment of a State commercial monopoly (*in casu* the so-called 'Monopolausgleich'—monopoly equalization duty) should be examined solely under Art. 31. However, the Court examined the tax under both Art. 90 and Art. 31, saying that 'the fact that a national measure complies with the requirements of Article 90 does not imply that it is valid in relation to other provisions of the Treaty, such as Article 31' (ibid. at p. 197). The Court concluded that both Art. 90 and Art. 31 are infringed if a charge imposed on an imported product is different from that imposed on a similar domestic product which is covered, directly or indirectly, by a State monopoly (ibid. at p. 199). Relying on this ruling, in Case 148/77 *Hansen I* [1978] ECR 1787 at pp. 1814, 1817, A.-G. Capotorti expressed the opinion that tax discrimination which is connected with the existence of a commercial monopoly must be appraised under both Art. 31 and Art. 90, which are jointly applicable. However, the Court found that the preferential tax arrangements at issue in the case before it could exist independently of any connection with a commercial monopoly, within the framework of legislation of a purely fiscal character. In those circumstances, the Court held it 'preferable' to examine the problem primarily from the point of view of the rule on taxation laid down in Art. 90 'because it is of a general nature', and not from that of Art. 31 'which is specific to arrangements for State monopolies' (ibid. at p. 1806). This approach was further justified, the Court said, by the fact that Art. 31 was based on the same principle as Art. 90, namely, the elimination of all discrimination in trade between Member States (ibid.). The Court followed this approach in Case 86/78 *Peureux I*, above, at p. 913, by confirming that after the end of the transitional period, Art. 31(1) no longer allowed derogations from the prohibition contained in Art. 90, which applied solely to the imposition of internal taxation on imported products as compared with national products, whether or not the latter came under a commercial monopoly. Art. 31 concerned only activities intrinsically connected with the specific business of a monopoly and was irrelevant to national provisions which had no connection with such specific business (ibid.).

See also **Charges having equivalent effect to customs duties, Free movement of goods, Goods, Measures having equivalent effect to quantitative restrictions, Quantitative restrictions, Taxation of goods.**

Further reading 1. BOOKS: Bellamy and Child, *European Community Law of Competition*, 5th edn. (2001), ch. 13; Oliver, *Free Movement of Goods in the European Community*, 4th edn. (2003), ch. 11.

2. ARTICLES: Burrows, 'State Monopolies' (1983) *YEL* 25; Oliver, 'Recent Case-Law on Article 37 EEC' (1980) *CML Rev.* 251; Ross, 'Article 37—Redundancy or Reinstatement' (1982) *EL Rev.* 281; Wooldridge, 'Some Recent Decisions Concerning the Ambit of Article 37 of the EEC Treaty' (1979/1) *LIEI* 105.

▶ **STUDENTS *see* FREE MOVEMENT OF PERSONS**

T

▶ **TAXATION OF GOODS (PROHIBITION OF DISCRIMINATION)** Rules intended to prevent tax discrimination in relation to movements of goods between Member States. The taxation of goods may not be used as a means of favouring domestic products, either by protecting them against imports or by providing disguised export subsidies. Arts. 90 and 91 EC prohibit such discrimination, and reflect the second paragraph of Art. III of the General Agreement on Tariffs and Trade (GATT). Art. 92 prohibits Member States from making border tax adjustments in respect of direct taxation unless permitted to do so by the Council.

I. Article 90

Art. 90 EC lays down a general prohibition on fiscal discrimination against products imported from other Member States. It is worded as follows:

> No Member State shall impose, directly or indirectly, on the products of other Member States any internal taxation of any kind in excess of that imposed directly or indirectly on similar domestic products.
>
> Furthermore, no Member State shall impose on the products of other Member States any internal taxation of such a nature as to afford indirect protection to other products.

The function of Art. 90 in the scheme of the Treaty is twofold: first of all, it complements the other provisions of the Treaty aimed at ensuring free movement of goods. Arts. 23 to 25 EC prohibit customs duties on imports and exports and charges having equivalent effect in trade between Member States. Arts. 28 to 30 prohibit quantitative restrictions and equivalent measures. As a third line of defence, Art. 90 precludes fiscal barriers to trade by forbidding protectionist internal taxation.

Arts. 90 to 92 are also intended to contribute to the achievement of the wider aims of the Treaty. Art. 90 is aimed at the establishment of a single market for goods and seeks to ensure free competition by placing all products of Member States on an equal footing from the tax point of view. Member States may not give domestic products an unfair competitive advantage by means of discriminatory taxation. Conversely, it allows Member States to ensure that foreign products bear as much tax as domestic products and thus do not derive an advantage from the fact that they may have been exported free of tax from their country of origin.

1. Direct effect. Art. 90 was one of the first articles of the Treaty to be held by the Court of Justice to have direct effect (Case 57/65 *Lütticke* [1966] ECR 205 at pp. 210–11). Coupled with the principle that Community law takes precedence over inconsistent provisions of national law, that means that individuals and companies who are charged tax contrary to the prohibition on discrimination can challenge the tax in the national courts.

Art. 90 is a superior rule of Community law with which any secondary legislation must comply. Consequently, national measures implementing the common VAT system—and the Community VAT directives themselves—remain subject to scrutiny under Art. 90 (Case 42/83 *Dansk Denkavit*

[1984] ECR 2649 at p. 2680; Case 15/81 *Schul I* [1982] ECR 1409 at pp. 1430–3).

2. The relationship between Article 90 and other articles of the Treaty. Art. 90 interacts and overlaps with a number of other Treaty articles: the most significant are Arts. 23 and 25, which prohibit customs duties and charges having equivalent effect in trade between Member States; Art. 28, which prohibits quantitative restrictions on imports and measures having equivalent effect; Art. 31, on State monopolies of a commercial character; and Arts. 87 and 88, which regulate State aid.

(*a*) ***Arts. 23 and 25 EC.*** Whereas Arts. 23 and 25 prohibit any pecuniary charge imposed on goods by reason of the fact that they cross a frontier, Art. 90 prohibits discriminatory internal taxation on products of other Member States.

Since importation may be a chargeable event in a system of internal taxation, it is not always easy to distinguish between internal taxation and customs duties. The distinction is stated in Case 24/68 *Commission* v. *Italy* [1969] ECR 193 at p. 201 (and is repeated frequently—see for example Case C-90/94 *Haahr Petroleum* [1997] ECR I-4085 at p. I-4150):

> Any pecuniary charge, however small and whatever its designation and mode of application, which is imposed unilaterally on domestic or foreign goods by reason of the fact that they cross a frontier, and which is not a customs duty in the strict sense, constitutes a charge having equivalent effect . . . even if it is not imposed for the benefit of the State, is not discriminatory or protective in effect and if the product on which the charge is imposed is not in competition with any domestic product.
>
> . . .
>
> It follows from Articles 90 *et seq.* that the concept of a charge having equivalent effect does not include taxation which is imposed in the same way within a State on similar or comparable domestic products, or at least falls, in the absence of such products, within the framework of general internal taxation, or which is intended to compensate for such internal taxation within the limits laid down by the Treaty.

Accordingly, financial charges forming part of a general system of internal taxation applied systematically to imports and domestic products according to the same criteria constitute internal taxation subject to Art. 90, even if they are charged on the occasion of importation (Case 7/67 *Wöhrmann* [1968] ECR 177 at p. 184). On the other hand, charges imposed on goods entering one region of a Member State constitute a charge equivalent in effect to a customs duty (Case C-163/90 *Legros* [1992] ECR I-4625—the *octroi de mer* charged on imports into the French overseas *départements*; Cases C-485/93 etc. *Simitzi* [1995] ECR I-2655—a tax on imports into the Dodecanese).

An internal tax is not to be regarded as a charge equivalent in effect to a customs duty simply because there is no similar domestic product (Case 20/67 *Kunstmühle Tivoli* [1968] ECR 199; Case 90/79 *Commission* v. *France* [1981] ECR 283 at p. 301; Case 193/85 *Co-Frutta* [1987] ECR 2085 at

p. 2108). It must be considered to be internal taxation if it is applied on the basis of objective criteria to whole classes of imports and domestic goods irrespective of their origin (see also Case 27/67 *Fink-Frucht* [1968] ECR 223; Case 31/67 *Stier* [1968] ECR 235; Case 78/76 *Steinike and Weinlig* [1977] ECR 595 at p. 613). Internal taxation is by definition fiscal in purpose, and there is no reason to place certain imports in a privileged position simply because there are no domestic products to be protected (for instance, the importation into northern countries of Mediterranean products such as citrus fruits).

However, where an internal charge applied to all products of a certain description is used to support activities that specifically benefit taxed domestic products, the charge represents a real tax burden for the import but is offset by benefits received in respect of the domestic product. If the charge imposed on the domestic product is made good in full, it must be regarded as a charge equivalent in effect to a customs duty, since in real terms only the import is taxed (Case 77/76 *Cucchi* [1977] ECR 987 and Case 105/76 *Interzuccheri* [1977] ECR 1029—a surcharge on sugar used to finance support measures for domestic growers and processors; this principle was first outlined in Case 77/72 *Capolongo* [1973] ECR 611). If, conversely, the charge on domestic products is only partly compensated for by benefits that their producers receive, then there is simply discriminatory taxation (Case 73/79 *Commission* v. *Italy* [1980] ECR 1533, and a series of more recent cases including Cases C-78/90 etc. *Compagnie Commerciale de l'Ouest* [1992] ECR I-1847 at p. I-1881; Case C-72/92 *Scharbatke* [1993] ECR I-5509 at p. I-5529; Case C-347/95 *UCAL* [1997] ECR I-4911 at p. I-4930). The same applies in relation to exports, if the benefits flow mainly to products destined for the domestic market (see Case C-234/99 *Nygård* [2002] ECR I-3657).

(*b*) ***Art. 28.*** Essentially, Art. 90 is concerned with fiscal barriers to trade, Art. 28 with non-fiscal barriers (Case C-383/01 *De Danske Bilimportører* [2003] ECR I-6065). In Case 74/76 *Iannelli* [1977] ECR 557 at p. 574, the Court stated that Art. 28 does not extend to obstacles to trade covered by other articles of the Treaty, so that it is necessary to have regard to the particular purpose of each provision and its distinct field of application. Different aspects of the same scheme may, however, fall under different provisions. For example, health inspections may be a barrier to trade outlawed by Art. 28; where such inspections are permissible under Art. 30, fees charged for them may constitute internal taxation to which Art. 90 applies (Case 35/76 *Simmenthal* [1976] ECR 1871; see also Case 50/85 *Schloh* [1986] ECR 1855—roadworthiness tests on imported cars).

(*c*) ***Art. 31.*** State monopolies of a commercial character are frequently financed by charges levied on the products concerned. The purpose of Art. 31 is to prevent the operations of State (or delegated) monopolies from resulting in discrimination against imports and exports. As the Court held in Case 45/75 *Rewe* [1976] ECR 181 at p. 198, that covers not only quantitative restrictions but all discrimination affecting the conditions under which goods are procured and marketed, including charges which result in discrimination against imports.

Often the result would be the same whichever provision were applied. In many cases where questions have been referred to the Court on both Art. 31 and Art. 90 the Court has preferred to focus on Art. 90. While both provisions are aimed at eliminating discrimination, Art. 90 is more general in scope, since Art. 31 is concerned only with matters 'intrinsically connected with the business of the monopoly' (Case 148/77 *Hansen I* [1978] ECR 1787 at p. 1806; Case 17/81 *Pabst & Richarz* [1982] ECR 1331 at p. 1349; Cases C-78/90 etc. *Compagnie Commerciale de l'Ouest*, above—a charge on petrol and other fuels held to be unconnected with a monopoly on the importation and marketing of petroleum products).

(*d*) ***Arts. 87 and 88.*** Art. 90 and the provisions of the Treaty on State aid are both directed at least in part towards ensuring equal conditions of competition for domestic industry and that in other Member States. Where the same measure has elements of both State aid and discriminatory taxation both sets of provisions must be complied with (see e.g. Case C-266/91 *CELBI* [1993] ECR I-4337—a charge on woodpulp used to finance activities in the interest of the domestic forest industry). Thus, where a tax charged on imports and domestic products alike is used to finance aid to domestic production it cannot be argued that the financing of aid can be challenged only under Art. 88 (Case 73/79 *Commission* v. *Italy*, above; Case C-234/99 *Nygård*, above). Discriminatory taxation is not exempted from Art. 90 simply because it forms part of an aid scheme and can therefore be challenged by other means. Furthermore, the discretion enjoyed by the Commission and the Council under Arts. 87 and 88 cannot be exercised in a manner contrary to Art. 90; the Commission cannot authorize discriminatory taxation as a form of aid (Cases 142/80 etc. *Essevi and Salengo* [1981] ECR 1413; Case C-204/97 *Portugal* v. *Commission* [2001] ECR I-3175). Equally, the fact that a Member State is authorized to grant aid does not mean that it is free to finance the aid in whatever way it pleases (see Case 105/76 *Interzuccheri*, above).

Conversely, the manner in which an aid scheme is financed must be taken into account in determining whether it 'affects trade between Member States' for the purposes of Art. 87. Aid financed by a charge which is contrary to Art. 90 is incompatible with the common market for the purposes of Art. 88(2) (Case 47/69 *France* v. *Commission* [1970] ECR 487).

3. The scope of Article 90

(*a*) ***Internal taxation.*** The meaning of 'internal' taxation may be seen from the discussion of the respective scopes of Art. 90 and the provisions on customs duties, above. As for the second element of the phrase, taxation for the purposes of Art. 90 includes not only taxes levied by central government but any fiscal or para-fiscal levy imposed by or with the authority of any level of government, including levies charged by or for quasi-official bodies and allocated to a specific purpose (see, for example, Case 74/76 *Iannelli*, above, a levy on paper products used to finance support measures for domestic industry; Case 222/82 *Lewis* [1983] ECR 4083, a levy on growers to finance the activities of a producers' organization).

(*b*) ***Taxes imposed directly or indirectly on products.*** Art. 90 is concerned with the taxation of things rather than persons, and only with taxes that affect products in a fairly immediate manner. It does not permit the taxation of imported products in order to offset the burden of direct taxation on domestic manufacturers. The expression 'imposed . . . indirectly on . . . products' captures taxation of raw materials and intermediate products but not of factors of production or, for example, stamp duties levied generally on businesses as such (see Case 45/64 *Commission* v. *Italy* [1965] ECR 857, an Art. 91 case). The definition given by the Court in Case 28/67 *Molkerei–Zentrale Westfalen* [1968] ECR 143 at p. 155, seems still to be valid:

> All taxation which is actually and specifically imposed on the domestic product at all earlier stages of its manufacture and marketing or which corresponds to the stage at which the product is imported from the other Member State, it being nevertheless understood that the effect of this taxation diminishes in proportion as the previous stages of manufacture and marketing become more remote and that this burden tends rapidly to become negligible.

Besides excise duties, turnover taxes (including VAT), consumption taxes, sales taxes, and the like, this includes fees for health inspections (Case 35/76 *Simmenthal*, above), registration fees for pharmaceutical products (Case 32/80 *Kortmann* [1981] ECR 251), and fees for roadworthiness tests on cars (Case 50/85 *Schloh*, above).

Art. 90 extends to taxes on the use of products rather than the products themselves, see Case 252/86 *Bergandi* [1988] ECR 1343 (tax on the use of amusement arcade machines); see also the cases on the French annual car registration tax (e.g. Case 112/84 *Humblot* [1985] ECR 1367). A tax on the carriage of goods by road or on the use of a port falls within the scope of Art. 90, since it has an immediate effect on the cost of domestic and imported products (Case 20/76 *Schöttle* [1977] ECR 247; Case C-90/94 *Haahr Petroleum*, above).

In most cases the distinction between products and, for example, services is clear. Savings deposits (and so, presumably, other financial 'products') fall under the provisions of the Treaty on freedom to provide services and the free movement of capital, and are not products for the purposes of Art. 90 (Case 267/86 *Van Eycke* [1988] ECR 4769). Electricity, on the other hand, is a product falling within the scope of Art. 90 (Case C-213/96 *Outukumpu* [1998] ECR I-1777).

The scope of Art. 90 may also be defined negatively in terms of the internal charges or expenses that cannot be offset by taxation of imports. Often these are additional non-fiscal burdens that are borne by domestic products, and the Court has held more generally that there can be no compensation between a tax applied to imports and a charge of a different nature imposed on the domestic product (Case 45/75 *Rewe*, above, at p. 195). There are various examples in the case-law. In Cases 2/62 etc.

Commission v. *Luxembourg and Belgium* [1962] ECR 425 ('Pain d'épices') the tax held illegal was intended to compensate for the extra financial burden on domestic producers resulting from the high support price for rye in Belgium and Luxembourg. In Case 4/81 *Andresen* [1981] ECR 2835 a charge on domestic products to cover the administrative costs of the German spirits monopoly was held not to justify a corresponding tax on imports. Monetary problems resulting from the rate of the green pound in Ireland could not be corrected by taxation of imports (Case 55/79 *Commission* v. *Ireland* [1980] ECR 481). Fees for the inspection of (live) domestic poultry cannot be offset by a charge for inspection of imported poultry meat (Case 314/82 *Commission* v. *Belgium* [1984] ECR 1543). A tax may not be imposed on imports to offset a difference in production costs (Case 323/87 *Commission* v. *Italy* [1989] ECR 2275).

Where a tax on imports is intended to offset a non-fiscal burden of that kind, the tax will most frequently be regarded as a charge equivalent in effect to a customs duty, contrary to Art. 25, but in some circumstances, where the tax is part of a scheme of taxation of a category of products, it may be held to be a discriminatory internal tax and thus contrary to Art. 90.

(*c*) ***Products of other Member States.*** Art. 90 is concerned with discriminatory taxation of products of other Member States; reverse discrimination is unobjectionable (Case 86/78 *Peureux I* [1979] ECR 897). For at least some purposes the Benelux countries are to be regarded as a single territory (Cases C-367/93 etc. *Roders* [1995] ECR I-2229). Art. 90 clearly applies to products imported from Community customs territory, as defined in Reg. 2913/92 of 12 October 1992 establishing the Community Customs Code (*OJ* 1992 L302/1). Art. 90 is not itself applicable to the overseas countries and territories referred to in Part Four of the Treaty, but the Court's judgment in Case 91/78 *Hansen II* [1979] ECR 935 treats the prohibition of tax discrimination contained in the Council legislation on the association of the overseas countries and territories with the European Community as effectively equivalent to Art. 90 (relations with these countries and territories are now governed by Council Dec. 2001/822, *OJ* 2001 L314/1).

Similar provisions in association agreements with non-member countries are interpreted in their respective contexts. Agreements on free trade pursue a less ambitious objective than the EC Treaty (the latter being aimed at the establishment of a single integrated market), so that the Court's interpretation of Art. 90 cannot simply be applied by analogy (Case 104/81 *Kupferberg* [1982] ECR 3641 at p. 3666—association agreement with Portugal; Case C-312/91 *Metalsa* [1993] ECR I-3751 at p. I-3774—association agreement with Austria; Case C-469/93 *Chiquita Italia* [1995] ECR I-4533 at p. I-4571—Fourth ACP–EEC Lomé Convention). Nevertheless, the Court has applied the Art. 90 case-law to an association agreement intended to prepare for the accession of the country in question (Case 17/81 *Pabst & Richarz*, above, at p. 1350, concerning the EEC–Greece Association Agreement). The same conclusion must follow in relation to the EEA Agreement: Art. 14 of the Agreement is identical in its wording to Art. 90, and the

Agreement itself is intended to create a broader single market (a 'homogenous European Economic Area' according to Art. 1).

While the wording of Art. 90 refers only to products *of* Member States, the Court has extended its application to goods in free circulation in a Member State, including those imported from outside the Community. In Case 193/85 *Co-Frutta*, above, at p. 2112 (importation of Colombian bananas from the Benelux to Italy) it held that the aim of Art. 90 is to ensure free movement of goods in normal conditions of competition by eliminating all forms of protection resulting from discriminatory internal taxation. Its role is to preclude any circumvention of the prohibitions of customs duties and of quantitative restrictions by means of fiscal measures; not to apply Art. 90 to products in free circulation would therefore be contrary to the spirit and system of the Treaty.

(*d*) ***Beneficiaries of Art. 90.*** Importers of products from other Member States may naturally rely on Art. 90 in order to challenge discriminatory taxation in the courts of the Member State of importation. Domestic manufacturers of products that are caught by higher rates of tax aimed at imports cannot rely on Art. 90; it applies only where there is some transnational element in the case (Case 68/79 *Just* [1980] ECR 501 at p. 519).

(*e*) ***Applicability to exports.*** The sections of the Treaty on customs duties and on quantitative restrictions include express prohibitions of restrictions on exports. Art. 90 refers solely to imports, and there is no corresponding provision prohibiting discrimination against exports. However, the Court has interpreted Art. 90 as equally prohibiting discrimination against exports (Case 142/77 *Larsen* [1978] ECR 1543; Case C-234/99 *Nygård*, above; Case C-355/00 *Freskot* [2003] ECR I-5263), on the ground that the Treaty seeks to ensure neutrality of internal taxation in relation to intra-Community trade generally.

4. The distinction between the first and second paragraphs of Article 90. The two paragraphs of Art. 90 cover what are presented as distinct situations. The first paragraph states that imports must not bear more tax than 'similar' domestic products. The second paragraph prohibits taxation of imports in such a way as to protect 'other' products (that is, products which are not similar but nevertheless compete to some degree, so that the level of taxation on one may favour the other). Together they cover what is in fact a continuum of competitive relationships, from effectively identical products at one extreme to products which are only marginally substitutable at the other. The essential question is whether the tax burden differs in such a way as to distort competition. Where two products are close substitutes, any difference in the burden of taxation will have a discriminatory or protective effect; the first paragraph of Art. 90 thus prohibits any such difference. For products in a more remote competitive relationship, the second paragraph lays down a broad prohibition of indirect protection (see, generally, Case 168/78 *Commission* v. *France* [1980] ECR 347; Case 169/78

Commission v. *Italy* [1980] ECR 385; Case 170/78 *Commission* v. *United Kingdom* [1980] ECR 417 (interlocutory judgment); and Case 171/78 *Commission* v. *Denmark* [1980] ECR 447, on the taxation of various types of alcoholic drink).

In many cases it is clear that there is discrimination or protection, so that the Court need not enter into the question which paragraph applies. In some cases involving ranges of different products, moreover, it has held that some of the products were similar but all were in competition with each other, so that Art. 90 as whole was applicable.

5. Article 90, first paragraph

(*a*) ***Similar products.*** Similarity must be determined on a single basis for the whole Community, not, for example, on the basis of national tax classifications. Although in some early cases it referred to tax or customs classifications, the Court normally examines the particular characteristics of the products and the needs or wishes of the consumer (an analogy may be drawn with the notion of substitutability of demand in competition law).

Many cases on this topic concern alcoholic drinks. Thus in Case 216/81 *Cogis* [1982] ECR 2701 (spirits distilled from grain or from grape) the Court held that the expression 'similar products' is a flexible one, covering products with similar characteristics that meet the same consumer needs, due regard being had to consumer habits in the Community as a whole (not consumer habits in the country in question, which may not be used to justify discriminatory taxation, see Case 170/78 *Commission* v. *United Kingdom*, above, and Case 319/81 *Commission* v. *Italy* [1983] ECR 601). In deciding whether products are similar it is necessary first to examine their objective characteristics, and then consider whether they can be used by consumers for the same purposes (see also Case 106/84 *Commission* v. *Denmark* [1986] ECR 833; Cases C-367/93 etc. *Roders*, above; Case C-265/99 *Commission* v. *France* [2001] ECR I-2305 (cars incorporating innovative technology)).

This apparently broad definition does not always bring together broad categories of products. In Case 184/85 *Commission* v. *Italy* [1987] ECR 2013 concerning a duty on bananas the Court held that bananas had different characteristics from other fruit and were therefore not similar (see Case 27/76 *United Brands* v. *Commission* [1978] ECR 207 for the same result in the context of Art. 82 EC; see also Case 104/81 *Kupferberg*, above (port and German liqueur wine not 'like products' under the EEC–Portugal Agreement because of differences in method of manufacture and characteristics)).

In the 1980 alcohol judgments (Case 168/78 *Commission* v. *France*, Case 169/78 *Commission* v. *Italy* and Case 171/78 *Commission* v. *Denmark*, above) the Court observed that all the spirits in question (whisky, brandy, rum, anise, akvavit, etc.) had common features but that some had distinct characteristics, stemming from the raw materials used, the manufacturing process, or added flavouring. It concluded that some at least of the drinks were similar and the others were clearly in competition with each other so as to come within the second paragraph of Art. 90, so that Art. 90 should be applied as a whole.

(b) Equal treatment. Art. 90 prohibits tax preference for domestic products. In order to comply with the first paragraph of Art. 90, the tax on imports need not necessarily be the same as that on domestic products, but the charge to tax may not be higher. Art. 90 is infringed if the tax on imports and domestic products is calculated in a different manner or according to different criteria so that—even if only in some cases—the domestic product bears less tax (Case 45/75 *Rewe*, above; Case C-68/96 *Grundig Italiana* [1998] ECR I-3775). It is no excuse to say that the imported product is cheaper than the similar domestic product, so that a higher level of tax merely places them on the same footing (Case C-345/93 *Nunes Tadeu* [1995] ECR I-479), or conversely that in any event the imported product is more expensive, so that a higher level of tax does not significantly alter the competitive relationship.

Discrimination can arise not only from a difference in the rate of tax, but also from differences in calculation methods, for example the basis of assessment (Case C-68/96 *Grundig Italiana*; Case C-228/98 *Dounias* [2000] ECR I-577 (costs included in the taxable value)) or the stage of processing at which tax is assessed (see Case 74/76 *Iannelli*, above (imported wallpaper taxed on a fixed proportion of the value of the finished product, domestic tax on raw paper); Case 77/69 *Commission* v. *Belgium* [1970] ECR 237 (sawn timber)). A flat-rate tax on imports may be discriminatory if domestic products are taxed according to their value or other characteristics (Case 16/69 *Commission* v. *Italy* [1969] ECR 377; Case C-213/96 *Outukumpu*, above (different means of generating electricity); see Case C-393/98 *Gomes Valente* [2001] ECR I-1327; Case C-101/00 *Siilin* [2002] ECR I-7487 (taxation of imported used cars which did not take full account of depreciation)).

More generally, equality is required in all aspects of taxation. The same exemptions and reductions must be available (Case 257/86 *Commission* v. *Italy* [1988] ECR 3249 (free samples of low value); Case 21/79 *Commission* v. *Italy* [1980] ECR 1 (regenerated waste oil)). The tax must be calculated in the same manner (Case 45/75 *Rewe*, above). Imports may not be taxed twice where domestic products would only be taxed once (Case 54/72 *FOR* [1973] ECR 193 (imported machinery taxed both on importation and on installation)). The possibility of deferred payment should be available in the same manner (Case 55/79 *Commission* v. *Ireland*, above; Case C-68/96 *Grundig Italiana*, above; but see Case 42/83 *Dansk Denkavit*, above, on differing payment periods under the common system of VAT).

The penalties imposed for breaches must be uniform, or at least not disproportionate (Case 299/86 *Drexl* [1988] ECR 1213; see also Case C-276/91 *Commission* v. *France* [1993] ECR I-4413).

The requirement of equal treatment under Art. 90 has striking effects in the common system of VAT. In Case 15/81 *Schul I*, above, (import VAT on a boat bought second-hand in another Member State), the Court held that the

VAT charged in the importing State must be reduced by the amount of residual VAT that was charged in the exporting country and not refunded on exportation. Calculation of the taxable amount and the residual amount of tax is discussed in Case 47/84 *Schul II* [1985] ECR 1491; see also the Commission notice on importation of used goods in such circumstances (*OJ* 1986 C13/2).

The *Schul* approach is possible only in relation to a common system of tax, since otherwise the tax paid in the exporting Member State is no concern of the importing country, and vice versa (see Case C-72/92 *Scharbatke*, above; Case C-234/99 *Nygård*, above).

Since Art. 90 is directed at equal treatment for imports and domestic products it follows that it is only the discriminatory aspect or part of a tax that is unlawful (Case C-90/94 *Haahr Petroleum*, above).

6. Article 90, second paragraph. The second paragraph of Art. 90 prohibits measures which discriminate against imports in favour of 'other products', an expression taken to mean products which are in competition, partially, indirectly, or potentially (Case 168/78 *Commission* v. *France*, above; Case 184/85 *Commission* v. *Italy*, above; Case 193/85 *Co-Frutta*, above). The products in question must have sufficient characteristics in common that they are an alternative choice for consumers in some circumstances (for example wine and beer, see Case 170/78 *Commission* v. *United Kingdom*). The examination of possible substitution cannot be restricted to existing consumer habits, and the tax system cannot be allowed to consolidate these habits, even in relation to what are perceived to be luxury items (final judgment in Case 170/78 *Commission* v. *United Kingdom* [1983] ECR 2265; Case 319/81 *Commission* v. *Italy*, above).

Indirect protection. Whereas the first paragraph of Art. 90 entails a simple comparison of the levels of tax, the second paragraph requires demonstration of the economic disadvantage caused by an additional tax burden. Direct statistical evidence of reduced demand for the imported product is generally regarded as inconclusive, since it cannot show what the position would have been in the absence of the difference in treatment (Case 216/81 *Cogis*, above; see also the opinions of A.-G. Reischl in Case 168/78 *France* and Case 170/78 *Commission* v. *United Kingdom* (interlocutory stage), above).

A protective effect has been inferred from the existence of a heavier burden of tax on the imported product. In order to identify discriminatory taxation it is necessary to have regard to the competitive relationship between products (see, for example, the opinion of A.-G. Lagrange in Case 13/63 *Italy* v. *Commission* [1963] ECR 165 at p. 190). For example, to apply the same tax by volume to beer and wine may discriminate against beer, since beer is typically less strong and is drunk in greater quantity. If wine is a typically domestic product and beer normally imported, the result will be protection of domestic wine producers.

It is necessary for that purpose to determine the proper basis of comparison, which is not always an easy task. A striking example is the final judgment in *Commission* v. *United Kingdom*, above, on the taxation of wine and beer. The parties referred variously to volume and alcoholic strength taken together, the average price of each drink, or volume alone, subject to a corrective factor of 1:1.5 to reflect the difference in consumption. The Court did not decide which approach was most appropriate, since on any criterion wine was subject to an additional tax burden affording protection to domestic beer production.

The difficulty of ascertaining the appropriate basis of comparison means that it is not easy to demonstrate a protective effect. In some cases the Court has been able simply to hold that the nature and structure of the tax system was clearly protective, having regard to the relationship of competition and substitution between products, inasmuch as domestic products generally fell within a favourable tax category while products which were mainly imported from other Member States were in an unfavourable category (see the 1980 alcohol judgments: Cases 168/78 *France*, 169/78 *Italy*, 170/78 *United Kingdom* (interlocutory) and 171/78 *Denmark*, above, and the cases on taxation of motor vehicles, beginning with Case 112/84 *Humblot*, above). More recently the Court has focused on the real effect: whereas the first paragraph of Art. 90 is based on a straightforward comparison of tax burdens, the second paragraph refers to the more general criterion of protection, so that it is necessary to examine the impact of taxation on competitive relationships and determine whether it has the effect of reducing demand for the imported product (Case 356/85 *Commission* v. *Belgium*, above (rates of VAT applicable to wine and beer); Cases C-367/93 etc. *Roders*, above).

7. Differentiated systems of taxation. Particular problems arise where a Member State has a progressive scale of taxation. National tax systems may, for social or economic reasons, provide low rates for certain categories of goods or producers, higher rates for others. Such schemes treat similar or competing products differently. In general the Court has considered that imports should be taxed according to the same criteria as domestic products. It is necessary to ensure, first, that those criteria can be applied to imports and, secondly, that they do not themselves place imports at a disadvantage. The scheme as a whole must be neutral as between imports and domestic products.

A Member State that chooses to grant special tax advantages for certain products must grant them without distinction to domestic products and imports alike, even where the advantages are granted for purely domestic social or economic reasons (Case 127/75 *Bobie Getränkevertrieb* [1976] ECR 1079 (low rate of tax on beer produced by small breweries); Case 148/77 *Hansen I*, above, and Case 26/80 *Schneider-Import* [1980] ECR 3469 (small distilleries)). Differentiated systems of taxation are permissible so long as they are based on objective criteria (for instance the raw material or the production method), they pursue legitimate social or economic objectives that are consistent with the Treaty and there is no direct or indirect discrimination or protection in favour of domestic products (Cases 142/80 etc. *Essevi and Salengo*, above; Case 200/85 *Commission* v. *Italy* [1986] ECR 3953; Case 196/85 *Commission* v. *France* [1987] ECR 1597 ('vins doux naturels'); Case 252/86 *Bergandi*, above; Case C-213/96 *Outukumpu*, above). Progressive taxation in particular is permissible.

The conditions of entitlement must be capable of being met by imports; criteria that reflect specifically national circumstances and thus favour national production are discriminatory in effect (see e.g. Case 319/81 *Commission* v. *Italy*, above (higher rate of tax for spirits protected by a denomination of origin, of which there were none in Italy)). The use of discriminatory criteria does not necessarily invalidate the scheme altogether. Where a scheme relies on some criteria which are truly general and others which imports cannot meet because of geographical considerations or the legislation applicable to their production in their country of origin, the latter may simply be ignored, so that imports which meet the general criteria are entitled to the tax advantage (Case 153/80 *Rumhaus Hansen* [1981] ECR 1165; Case 38/82 *Hansen III* [1983] ECR 1271).

Secondary criteria relating to supervision or verification of compliance may not exclude imports. The Member State may require proof that the conditions of entitlement have been fulfilled, but its evidentiary requirements may not be disproportionate. One option for a Member State which wishes to apply strict rules involving close supervision is to apply those rules only to domestic products and to apply a simpler criterion to imports. That is acceptable so long as the practical effect of the rules applied to imports is no less favourable than those applied to domestic products (Case 26/80 *Schneider-Import*, above). A Member State may legitimately require that imports be subject in the Member State of origin to controls equivalent to those applied in the importing State (Case 196/85 *Commission* v. *France*, above ('Vins doux naturels')). Conversely, if the criteria are such that verification is impossible in relation to imports, then the system as such is incompatible with Community law, for there is no way of avoiding discrimination (Case C-213/96 *Outukumpu*, above).

Where the differential tax is aimed not at favouring particular producers or products but at ensuring progressive taxation, it may be difficult to find neutral criteria. A Member State may impose a higher rate on luxuries, but it must not discriminate in doing so. The prestige which may attach to foreign products, and national habits of consumption, cannot in themselves justify a higher rate of taxation (Case 319/81 *Commission* v. *Italy*, above; Case 170/78 *Commission* v. *United Kingdom* (final judgment), above). That suggests that only products which would be regarded as luxury goods everywhere in the Community may be taxed more heavily.

In a progressive system, problems may arise where products at the higher end of the scale are not produced in the Member State concerned. The choice of criteria or the rate of tax may penalize imports and thus have a protective effect. A special annual road tax for cars with a power rating for tax purposes above that of the most powerful domestic cars has been considered discriminatory (Case 112/84 *Humblot*, above). The same reasoning applies to a road tax scheme that contains an abrupt increase in tax for cars with a rating above that of the most powerful domestic cars (Case 433/85 *Feldain* [1987] ECR 3521). Progressive taxation of powerful cars is legitimate, but the system must not favour domestic production (see, most recently, Case C-421/97 *Tarantik* [1999] ECR I-3633).

A system of differential taxation is discriminatory where an advantage is granted to a single product which represents the bulk of domestic production (Case 68/79 *Just*, above; Case 106/84 *Commission* v. *Denmark*, above) or where the scheme excludes certain imports (Case 319/81 *Commission* v. *Italy*, above; Case 278/83 *Commission* v. *Italy* [1985] ECR 2503). It may also offend against Art. 90 where an advantage is given to one domestic product among many (Case 277/83 *Commission* v. *Italy* [1985] ECR 2049 (tax advantage for Marsala wine)). There is no discrimination, on the other hand, where a significant proportion of domestic production falls into each category (Case 243/84 *Walker* [1986] ECR 875; Case 200/85 *Commission* v. *Italy*, above), and a system is not to be regarded as discriminatory solely because only imports fall into the most highly taxed category, although in the latter case the situation must be examined closely (Case 200/85 *Commission* v. *Italy*; Case C-132/88 *Commission* v. *Greece* [1990] ECR I-1567).

The difficulty of identifying discrimination in borderline cases is illustrated by Case 140/79 *Chemial* [1981] ECR 1 and Case 46/80 *Vinal* [1981] ECR 77. A special tax was imposed on denatured synthetic alcohol in order to guarantee an outlet for agricultural alcohol. The result was to make production of synthetic alcohol in Italy uneconomic, so that only imported alcohol was in fact taxed. In response to the argument that the tax discriminated against imports, the Court held that the tax was not discriminatory, since although it hampered imports it also prevented profitable domestic production.

II. Article 91

Art. 91 EC is the corollary to Art. 90; it prohibits the concealed subsidization of exports through the tax system:

> Where products are exported to the territory of any Member State, any repayment of internal taxation shall not exceed the internal taxation imposed on them whether directly or indirectly.

Like Art. 90, it assumes a destination system of taxation. Goods are normally taxed in the country where they are consumed, and it follows that they may be exported free of tax. It is necessary, however, to ensure that exporters are not covertly aided by the 'repayment' of more tax than they have paid. Art. 91 permits Member States to refund tax but does not compel them to do so, or to refund the full amount of tax paid (Case 27/74 *Demag* [1974] ECR 1037).

The scope of Art. 91—its place in the scheme of the Treaty, its purpose, and its relationship with other provisions of the Treaty—is essentially the same as Art. 90. It certainly has direct effect, as it lays down a clear and unconditional obligation for Member States.

The main issue that has been addressed in the very few decided cases on

Art. 91 is the identification of the amount of tax paid and its character as a tax imposed directly or indirectly on goods. Taxes such as registration, stamp and mortgage duties, licence and concession charges, taxes on vehicles, and advertising are not taxes on the exported products, and cannot be refunded under Art. 91 (Case 45/64 *Commission* v. *Italy*, above; second judgment [1969] ECR 433). While flat-rate refund systems are not forbidden, it is incumbent on the Member State to show that the refund is never more than the amount of tax actually paid (Case 45/64 *Commission* v. *Italy*; see also the Belgian and Luxembourg beer cases: Case C-152/89 *Commission* v. *Luxembourg* [1991] ECR I-3141 and Case C-153/89 *Commission* v. *Belgium* [1991] ECR I-3171).

III. Article 92

Arts. 90 and 91 are concerned with indirect taxation, imposed on products. However, direct taxes paid by producers have an impact on their costs, and where the relative importance of indirect and direct taxation differs from one country to another producers may be placed at a competitive disadvantage. Art. 92 thus provides for a possible derogation from Art. 91:

> In the case of charges other than turnover taxes, excise duties and other forms of indirect taxation, remissions and repayments in respect of exports to other Member States may not be granted and countervailing charges in respect of imports from Member States may not be imposed unless the measures contemplated have been previously approved by the Council acting by a qualified majority on a proposal from the Commission.

Member States may request the Commission to submit an appropriate proposal to the Council, which must then decide whether the proposed measure is justified. The exceptional nature of such a derogation is underlined by the fact that it may be granted only for a limited period. No proposal has ever been made pursuant to Art. 92.

See also **Charges having equivalent effect to customs duties, Direct taxation, Excise duties and similar taxes, State commercial monopoly, Tax harmonization, Value added tax.**

Further reading Beveridge and Riley, *European Community Taxation Law* (expected 2004); Communier, *Droit Fiscal Communautaire* (2001); Easson, *Taxation in the European Community* (1993); Farmer and Lyal, *EC Tax Law*, 2nd edn. (expected 2005); Commentaire Mégret, *Le Droit de la CEE*, 2nd edn. (1993), vol. 5; Terra and Wattel, *European Tax Law* (2002).

► **TAX DISCRIMINATION *see* DIRECT TAXATION, FREEDOM OF ESTABLISHMENT, FREEDOM TO PROVIDE SERVICES, *and* FREE MOVEMENT OF PERSONS**

► **TAX HARMONIZATION** The purpose of harmonization in tax matters is to remove tax barriers to the operation of the internal market, namely those barriers that distort competition, or hinder the free movement of goods, services, and capital. Tax harmonization involves the application of common tax laws in Member States. The Commission has commented on its policy regarding tax harmonization in Member States in the following terms:

> It is clear that there is no need for an across the board harmonization of Member States' tax systems. Provided that they respect Community rules, Member States are free to choose the tax systems that they consider most appropriate and according to their preferences (Tax policy in the European Union—Priorities for the years ahead, COM(2001) 260).

The extent of tax harmonization in the areas of indirect taxation and direct taxation are as follows:

1. Value added tax (VAT) is applied on a common basis in the EC. The legal basis for a common system of VAT is Art. 93 EC, which imposes an obligation on the Council to adopt provisions for the harmonization of turnover taxes to ensure the establishment and the functioning of the internal market. The principal harmonization directives relating to VAT are: Council Dir. 67/227 (*OJ Sp. Edn.*, 1967, p. 14) (known as the 'First Directive'), which provided for a common VAT system to be applied in Member States. The purpose of harmonization is revealed by the preamble to the First Directive, which states 'the main objective of the Treaty is to establish, within the framework of an economic union, a common market within which there is healthy competition and whose characteristics are similar to those of a domestic market' (first recital). The recitals go on to state that the achievement of such an objective presupposes the prior application in Member States of laws that will not distort competition, or hinder the free movement of goods (second recital). The recitals to the First Directive state that the laws did not then achieve the objective of the Treaty, and 'it is therefore in the interest of the common market to achieve such harmonization of legislation concerning turnover taxes as will eliminate, as far as possible, factors which may distort conditions of competition, whether at national or Community level' (third recital). Council Dir. 77/388 (*OJ* 1977 L145/1) (known as the 'Sixth Directive') provides the common basic rules for the application of VAT in Member States. The Sixth Directive has resulted in a partial alignment of VAT rates, however there remains diversity in the level of rates applied in Member States. Council Dir. 79/1072 (*OJ* 1979 L331/11) (known as the 'Eighth Directive') provides for the refund of VAT incurred by a taxable person in those Member States where they do not have a business establishment. Council Dir. 86/560 (*OJ* 1986 L326/40) (known as the 'Thirteenth Directive') requires Member States to refund VAT to taxable persons who are not established in the EU.

2. Indirect taxes, i.e. capital duty, imposed on raising capital for companies is harmonized by Council Dir. 69/335 (*OJ* 1969 L249/25), as amended by Council Dir. 85/303. The result of the directive is that capital duty imposed on capital raising transactions cannot exceed 1%, and can be abolished.

3. Direct taxes, such as corporation tax, income tax, and capital gains tax are not subject to any universal requirement under the EC Treaty to be

harmonized. Art. 94 EC imposes an obligation on the Council to issue directives for the 'approximation' of laws in Member States, which directly affect the establishment, or functioning of the common market. The EU 'harmonization' of business taxation has been confined to the following areas, which are concerned with specific aspects of either double taxation or cross-border economic activity between Member States: mergers and acquisitions (Council Dir. 90/434, *OJ* 1990 L225/1); dividend payments between parent and subsidiary (Council Dir. 90/435, *OJ* 1990 L225/6); interest and royalty payments between associated companies (Council Dir. 2003/49, *OJ* 2003 L157/49); interest payments to individuals and the exchange of information (Council Dir. 2003/48, *OJ* 2003 L157/38). Member States have also concluded an arbitration convention (Dir. 90/436, *OJ* 1990 L225/10) under Art. 293 EC to prevent the double taxation of profits adjusted between associated companies in different Member States.

See also **Direct taxation, Excise duties and similar taxes, Value added tax.**

Further reading 1. BOOKS: Farmer and Lyal, *EC Tax Law*, 2nd edn. (expected 2005); Terra and Wattel, *European Tax Law* (2002).

2. OFFICIAL PUBLICATIONS: European Commission, *Tax policy in the European Union—Priorities for the years ahead* (COM(2001) 260); id., *Taxation in the European Union* (SEC(96) 487); id., *A package to tackle harmful tax competition in the European Union* (COM(97) 564).

▶ **TEMPORARY RESIDENCE PERMIT *see* RESIDENCE PERMIT**

▶ **TOPOGRAPHIES OF SEMICONDUCTOR PRODUCTS *see* INTELLECTUAL PROPERTY RIGHTS**

▶ **TRADE MARK *see* INTELLECTUAL PROPERTY RIGHTS**

▶ **TRANSIT PROCEDURES *see* CUSTOMS PROCEDURES**

▶ **TRIPS AGREEMENT *see* INTELLECTUAL PROPERTY RIGHTS**

V

VALUE ADDED TAX (VAT) A common system of tax imposed in each Member State of the EC on the supply of goods and services. The amount of VAT is a fixed percentage, such as 17.5% in the United Kingdom or 20% in Italy, of the consideration given for the supply, which is known as the 'taxable amount'. The supplies subject to VAT are known as 'taxable transactions'. VAT is a tax borne by the final consumer in the supply of goods or services; and is an indirect form of taxation that is collected by certain suppliers, which is then paid to the national tax authority of a Member State. A supplier who is required to charge VAT is known as the 'taxable person'.

The legal basis for a common system of VAT is Art. 93 EC, which imposes an obligation on the Council to adopt provisions for the harmonization of turnover taxes to ensure the establishment and the functioning of the internal market. The Council is authorized, acting on a proposal from the Commission, and after consulting the European Parliament, to issue directives for the approximation of laws on turnover taxes (see Art. 94). Council Dec. 70/243 of 21 April 1970 on the replacement of financial contributions from Member States by the Communities' own resources (*OJ Sp. Edn.* 1970 (I), p. 224) provides that a percentage of national VAT revenues are paid to the EC to provide it with 'own resources'.

VAT was adopted in the EU by Council Dir. 67/227 of 11 April 1967 (*OJ Sp. Edn.* 1967, p. 14) (the 'First Council Directive') on the harmonization of legislation of Member States concerning turnover taxes, which provides that the principle of the common system of VAT 'involves the application to goods and services of a general tax on consumption exactly proportional to the price of the goods and services, whatever the number of transactions which take place in the production and distribution process before the stage at which tax is charged' (Art. 2). The principle of VAT requires that on each transaction the tax is calculated on the price of the goods or services at the applicable rate only after deduction of the amount of VAT borne directly by the various cost components; and that it is imposed up to and including the retail trade stage (Art. 2).

The common system of VAT entitles a taxable person who enters into taxable transactions to deduct the amount of VAT (known as 'input tax') incurred on goods or services in making such taxable transactions against the amount of VAT received (known as 'output tax') in entering into those taxable transactions (Arts. 17, 18(2)). This is the essence of VAT, namely the deduction of input VAT by all taxable persons except the final consumer.

An example of the application of VAT is as follows: X manufactures goods from raw materials (assume no cost is incurred), which are purchased by Y Ltd. for £100 for the purposes of sale to non-business customers. Z purchases a quantity of the goods for £500. X and Y Ltd are both taxable persons. The rate of VAT is 15%. The 'value added' on the goods by X is £100 (i.e. the value of the goods sold to Y Ltd), and by Y Ltd is £400 (i.e. the difference between £500 and £100). However, the supply of goods is subject to VAT, which must be accounted for in the following way in relation to the 'value added' at each stage of the supply process. The sale to Y Ltd. is subject to VAT of 15% with the result that Y Ltd must pay £115 to X, and £15 must be paid by X to the tax authority (i.e. 15% of £100). The sale by Y Ltd. to Z is subject to VAT of 15% with the result that Z must pay £575 to Y Ltd., and Y Ltd. must pay £60 to the tax authority (i.e. £75 (15% of £500) minus the VAT paid to Z of £15). In this way Z and Y Ltd. are only required to account to the tax authority for the amount of VAT that relates to the 'value added' by them at each stage of the supply chain. The tax authority obtains £75, which reflects £15 from Z, and £60 from Y Ltd.

A framework for the rules and principles on the application of VAT in Member States is laid down in Council Dir. 77/388 of 17 May 1977 (the 'Sixth Directive') on the harmonization of the laws of the Member States relating to turnover taxes, which provides for a common system of VAT (*OJ* 1977 L145/1). The Sixth Directive leaves a number of options and derogations to Member States. The principal implementing legislation in the United Kingdom is the Value Added Tax Act 1994, and the Value Added Tax Regulations 1995, SI 1995/2518. The provisions of the Sixth Directive are capable of having direct effect in Member States provided they are unconditional and sufficiently precise. In Case 8/81 *Becker* [1982] ECR 53, it was held that the finance exemption under Art. 13B(d) could be relied upon in Germany by a credit negotiator although the exemption had not been implemented in domestic legislation. The Sixth Directive permits the Council to authorize any Member State to introduce special measures for derogation from the provisions of the Sixth Directive for the purposes of simplifying the procedure for charging VAT, or to prevent certain types of VAT evasion or avoidance (Art. 27). Where measures are sought to simplify the charging of VAT the derogation cannot effect the amount of VAT due at the final consumption stage (Art. 27).

There are three distinct circumstances in which a charge to VAT arises in the EC, and these circumstances are explained in further detail in the following commentary. VAT is charged on supplies of goods and services made in a Member State in the course of business by a taxable person (see section I below), VAT is charged on the acquisition of goods and on services acquired from within the EC from another Member State (see section II below), and VAT is charged on the importation of goods and certain services into a Member State from outside the EC by a taxable person or a non-taxable person (see section III below). The supply of goods and services outside the EU are not subject to VAT (see section IV below). In certain circumstances VAT is refunded to a person located in another Member State, or outside the EC (see section V below).

For VAT purposes there are three categories of supply, namely taxable transactions, exempt transactions with a right of deduction for VAT (known as 'zero-rating' in the United Kingdom), and exempt transactions with no right of recovery of VAT. A taxable person who charges VAT on taxable transactions (i.e. taxable supplies of goods or services), known as 'output tax', made in the course of business is required to account for that amount to the tax authority in the supplier's Member State. In accounting for the amount of output tax, as illustrated in the example above, the taxable person is entitled to deduct the amount of VAT incurred on goods or services, known as 'input tax', in making his supplies. The right of deduction enables any VAT paid by a taxable person on inputs of goods or services related to transactions within the scope of VAT to be taken into account. Exempt supplies are those that are not subject to a VAT charge. Where a supplier makes exempt supplies there is no right to deduct the input tax incurred in making the exempt supplies. However, there are some exempt supplies with a right of deduction which are not subject to any VAT, but which entitle the taxable person to deduct the input tax incurred in making the supplies. Such taxable persons are entitled to repayment of the VAT incurred in making those supplies.

I. VAT on supplies within an EC Member State

The Sixth Directive requires VAT to be imposed on the supply of goods or services effected for consideration within a Member State by a taxable person (Art. 2). The most important rules and principles relating to supplies within an EC Member State are provided in the Sixth Directive, and are summarized as follows:

1. The person who is required to charge VAT on the supply of either goods or services, and pay the net amount to the national tax authority of the Member State in which that person is located is known as the 'taxable person' (Art. 21(1)). A person who is not a taxable person has no obligation to impose VAT and no right to claim any deduction for VAT paid. A 'taxable person' is any person who independently carries out in any place any 'economic activity', irrespective of the purpose or results of that activity (Art. 4(1)). Accordingly, a non-profit making organization can be subject to VAT. The term 'economic activity' is defined as 'all activities of producers, traders and persons supplying services including mining and agricultural activities and activities of the professions' (Art. 4(2)). The term also includes the exploitation of tangible or intangible property for the purpose of obtaining income therefrom on a continuing basis (Art. 4(2)). Not all persons who carry on an economic activity are required to register for VAT purposes. In the United Kingdom only persons with a minimum financial turnover of £58,000 (2004–5) in respect of taxable supplies are required to register for VAT purposes, and accordingly be treated as taxable persons (Value Added Tax Act 1994, s. 3(2), Sch. 1). Those persons below the financial threshold may seek a voluntary registration with the result that they become taxable persons. The advantage of such registration is that they are entitled to deduct VAT paid in making their business supplies. The Sixth Directive does not apply to all forms of economic activity. The ECJ held in Case 289/86 *Happy Family* [1988] ECR 3655, that supplies of prohibited drugs were not subject to VAT. Despite the wide definition of 'economic activity' not all activities will be within its ambit. In Case C-155/94 *Wellcome Trust* [1996] ECR I-3013, the ECJ held that the purchase and sale of shares as an investment by a charitable trust was not an economic activity. This was because the activity did not involve a commercial share dealing activity, and was not the acquisition of shares so as to secure involvement in the management of companies. The activity of the Wellcome Trust was managing an investment

portfolio in the same way as a private investor. The ECJ also held in Case C-60/90 *Polysar Investments Netherlands* [1991] ECR I-3111 that the mere acquisition and holding of shares by a holding company was not an economic activity. The reasoning of the ECJ was that the mere acquisition of holdings in other undertakings (in the absence of any direct or indirect involvement in the management) does not amount to the exploitation of property for the purpose of obtaining income therefrom on a continuing basis since any dividend derived from the holding was only as a result of ownership of the property.

The reference to a person 'independently' carrying on an economic activity does not include employees with the result that there is no obligation on employees to charge VAT on the services rendered to their employer (Art. 4(4)). The Sixth Directive provides that each Member State may treat as a single taxable person several independent persons who are established in a Member State who are 'closely bound to one another by financial, economic and organisational links' (Art. 4(4)). Accordingly, companies within the same group will usually qualify to be treated as a single taxable person, with the consequences that supplies made between members of the same group are not subject to VAT. Bodies that are governed by public law (such as regional and local government authorities) are not taxable persons, subject to certain reservations discussed below, in relation to the activities or transactions in which they engage as public authorities (Art. 4(5)). This exclusion in relation to public bodies applies even though they may collect dues, fees, contributions, or payments in connection with their activities. However, where the activities in which they engage as public authorities would lead to significant distortions of competition because of their treatment as non-taxable persons, then in such circumstances they will become taxable persons (Art. 4(5)). Public bodies are deemed to be taxable persons in relation to the activities specified in Annex D of the Sixth Directive. The Annex D activities include telecommunications, supply of water, gas, electricity, steam, port and airport services, passenger transport, travel agencies, and activities of public radio and television bodies of a commercial nature.

A taxable person is required to notify the tax authority of the Member State in which he is located of when his activity as a taxable person commences, changes, or ceases (Art. 22(1)(a)). A taxable person must comply with various obligations in the operation of VAT, such as keeping accounts of VAT for inspection by the tax authority, issue a VAT invoice in respect of goods or services which he has supplied to another taxable person or to a non-taxable person. A taxable person is required to submit a return by a deadline determined by Member States in relation to a specified tax period (Art. 22(4)(a)). In the United Kingdom a taxable person must file a VAT return each quarter. The return must set forth all the information needed to calculate the VAT that has become chargeable, and the VAT deductions to be made.

2. The time when VAT becomes chargeable is known as the 'chargeable event' (known as the 'time of supply' under domestic law), and in relation to goods this means when they are delivered, and in relation to services when they are performed (Art. 10(2)). Special rules apply in relation to successive

statements of account or payments, and continuous supplies which take place over a period of time (see Art. 10(2)). Where payment is made on account before goods are delivered by the taxable person, or the services are performed by the taxable person, VAT is chargeable on receipt of the payment, and on the amount received (Art. 10(2)). The Sixth Directive permits Member States to provide that VAT shall become chargeable by reference to different events, namely either no later than the issue of an invoice, or no later than the receipt of the price for the goods or services, or where an invoice is not issued, or is issued late, within a specified period from the date of the chargeable event (Art. 10(3)). It is the taxable person who is liable to make payment for the VAT to the relevant tax authority (Art. 21).

3. A 'supply of goods' is defined as meaning the transfer of the right to dispose of tangible property as owner (Art. 5(1)). The ECJ has interpreted this concept to mean that there will be a supply of goods even though legal title to the goods is not transferred under procedures prescribed by applicable national laws, provided that any transfer to a person has the effect of giving that person the power to dispose of property as if he were its owner (see Case C-320/88 *Shipping and Forwarding Enterprise Safe* [1990] ECR I-285).

The meaning of 'goods' is extended beyond the usual meaning of the word, since it is intended that VAT will apply to all economic activities. The Sixth Directive requires certain supplies to be treated as a supply of goods, whilst permitting at the discretion of Member States certain types of supply to be treated as a supply of goods. The Sixth Directive deems certain supplies to be a 'supply of goods', namely, the supply of electric current, gas, heat, refrigeration, a transfer in pursuance of the law of ownership of property against payment of compensation, transfer of goods pursuant to a contract of hire or sale of goods on deferred terms pursuant to which ownership will pass at the latest upon payment of the final instalment, transfer of goods pursuant to a contract under which commission is payable on purchase or sale (Art. 5(2), 5(4)(a) to (c)). Member States are permitted to treat the transfer of a totality of assets or part thereof (whether for consideration or not, or as a contribution to a company) as not being a supply of goods, and in consequence of which the recipient will be treated as the successor of the transferor (Art. 5(8)). Such a transfer of a totality of assets is usually referred to as 'the transfer of a going concern'. The effect of treating a supply in this way is that no VAT arises on the transfer. Where a taxable person applies goods that are business assets for either private use or of his staff, or makes a gift of such goods, or applies such goods for non-business purposes, and VAT has been deducted in respect of such goods, they will be treated as supplies made for consideration and so subject to VAT (Art. 5(6)). The reason for bringing personal consumption of goods within the scope of VAT is that the taxable person will have received a credit for the VAT incurred on their acquisition. In the absence of a rule recapturing VAT on the goods such a person's consumption would be supported by a subsidy with the result there would be a distortion in the market.

The giving of samples, or the making of gifts of small value for the purposes of a taxable person's business is not treated as a supply made for consideration (Art. 5(6)). Member States may treat as a supply of goods certain interests in immovable property, rights *in rem* giving the holder a right of use over immovable property, shares or interests equivalent to shares giving the holder thereof *de jure* or *de facto* rights of ownership or possession over immovable property or part thereof (Art. 5(3)). If Member States do not choose to treat such transactions as a supply of goods, they will be treated as a supply of services. Member States may also treat as a supply of goods the handing over of certain works of construction (Art. 5(5)). The following supplies of goods may also be treated by Member States as supplies made for consideration: (*a*) the application by a taxable person for business purposes of goods produced, constructed, extracted, processed, purchased, or imported in the course of his business where the VAT in respect of such goods had they been acquired from another taxable person would not be wholly deductible (i.e. this potential head of charge relates to self-constructed goods); (*b*) the application of goods by a taxable person for the purpose of a non-taxable transaction where the VAT on such goods became wholly or partly deductible upon their acquisition or upon their application in accordance with (*a*); (*c*) the retention of goods by a taxable person when he ceases to carry out a taxable economic activity where the VAT on such goods became wholly or partly deductible upon their acquisition or upon their application in accordance with (*a*) (Art. 5(7)).

4. A 'supply of services' is defined on a residual basis as meaning 'any transaction which does not constitute a supply of goods' as defined in Art. 5 of the Sixth Directive (Art. 6(1)). Transactions that may be included (without limitation) within the definition of a 'supply of services' are assignments of intangible property, obligations to refrain from an act or to tolerate an act or situation (i.e. negative events are covered), the performances of services in pursuance of an order made by or in the name of a public authority or in pursuance of the law (Art. 6(1)). A taxable person who acts in his own name on behalf of another person, and takes part in a supply of services is treated as having received and supplied those services himself (Art. 6(4)). As is the case for a supply of goods, Member States are permitted to treat the transfer of a totality of assets or part thereof (whether for consideration or not, or as a contribution to a company) as not being a supply of services, and in consequence of which the recipient will be treated as the successor of the transferor (Art. 6(5)). The effect is that such a transfer of a going concern is not subject to VAT.

The Sixth Directive provides that the following supplies will be treated as a supply of services for consideration, namely, the use of goods forming part of a business asset for the private use of the taxable person or of his staff, or more generally for non-business purposes where the VAT on such goods is wholly or partly deductible; and supplies of services carried out free of charge by a taxable person for his own private use or that of his staff, or more generally for non-business purposes (Art. 6(2)). The function of this rule is to prevent the non-business use of services being funded by a hidden subsidy, i.e. a taxable person obtaining a deduction for VAT on inputs, without being required to account for VAT on consumption. However, Member States are permitted to derogate from such treatment provided that such derogation does not lead to distortion of competition.

5. For a VAT charge to arise on a supply of goods or services in a Member State, the place of supply must be within that Member State. If the place of supply is in another Member State a charge to VAT will arise in that Member State, i.e. the country of destination of the supply. The rules for determining the place of supply of goods or services are designed to ensure that there is equal treatment in the application of VAT between Member States. The rules that have been adopted are those, which are designed to achieve the avoidance of double taxation between Member States, non-taxation of supplies and those that prevent economic distortion. A summary of the place of supply rules is provided in the following table.

Type and Method of Supply	Place of Supply	Sixth Directive
Goods		
• Goods dispatched or transported either by the supplier or by the person to whom they are supplied or by a third person	• Place where the goods are at the time when dispatch or transport to the person to whom they are supplied begins	Art. 8(1)(a)
• Goods installed or assembled, with or without a trial run, by or on behalf of the supplier	• Place of supply is deemed to be the place where the goods are installed or assembled	Art. 8(1)(a)
• Goods not dispatched or transported	• Place where the goods are when the supply takes place	Art. 8(1)(b)
• Goods supplied on board ships, aircraft or trains during the part of a transport of passengers effected in the EC	• At the point of the departure of the transport of passengers	Art. 8(1)(c)
Services		
• Supply of services [Default rule unless falling within one of the following classifications]	Place where supplier has: • Established his business, or • A fixed establishment from which the service is supplied, or • In the absence of the foregoing where the supplier has his permanent address or usually resides	Art. 9(1)
• Services connected with immovable property, including the services of estate agents and experts, and of services for preparing and co-ordinating construction works, such as the services of architects and of firms providing on-site supervision	• Place where the property is situated	Art. 9(2)(a)
• Transport services	• Place where transport takes place, having regard to the distances covered	Art. 9(2)(b)

Type and Method of Supply	Place of Supply	Sixth Directive
• Cultural, artistic, sporting, scientific, educational, entertainment, or similar activities, including the activities of the organizers of such activities, and where appropriate, supply of ancillary services	• Place where services are physically carried out	Art. 9(2)(c)
• Ancillary transport activities such as loading, handling, and similar activities	• Place where services are physically carried out	Art. 9(2)(c)
• Valuations of movable tangible property	• Place where services are physically carried out	Art. 9(2)(c)
• Work on movable tangible property	• Place where services are physically carried out	Art. 9(2)(c)
• Transfers and assignments of copyrights, patents, licences, trade marks, and similar rights	• When performed for customers established outside the EC, or for taxable persons established in the EC but not in the same country as the supplier, the place where the customer has established his business or has a fixed establishment to which the service is supplied, or in the absence of such a place, the place where he has his permanent address or usually resides	Art. 9(2)(e)
• Advertising services	• When performed for customers established outside the EC, or for taxable persons established in the EC but not in the same country as the supplier, the place where the customer has established his business or has a fixed establishment to which the service is supplied, or in the absence of such a place, the place where he has his permanent address or usually resides	Art. 9(2)(e)
• Services of consultants, engineers, consultancy bureaux, lawyers, accountants, and other similar services, as well as data processing and the supplying of information	• When performed for customers established outside the EC, or for taxable persons established in the EC but not in the same country as the supplier, the place where the customer has established his business or has a fixed establishment to which the service is supplied, or in the absence of such a place, the place where he has his permanent address or usually resides	Art. 9(2)(e)

Type and Method of Supply	Place of Supply	Sixth Directive
• Hiring out of movable tangible property with the exception of all forms of transport	• When performed for customers established outside the EC, or for taxable persons established in the EC but not in the same country as the supplier, the place where the customer has established his business or has a fixed establishment to which the service is supplied, or in the absence of such a place, the place where he has his permanent address or usually resides	Art. 9(2)(e)
• Obligations to refrain from pursuing or exercising, in whole or in part, a business activity or a right referred to in Art. 9(2)(e) of the Sixth Directive	• When performed for customers established outside the EC, or for taxable persons established in the EC but not in the same country as the supplier, the place where the customer has established his business or has a fixed establishment to which the service is supplied, or in the absence of such a place, the place where he has his permanent address or usually resides	Art. 9(2)(e)
• Banking, financial, and insurance transactions including reinsurance, with the exception of the hire of safes	• When performed for customers established outside the EC, or for taxable persons established in the EC but not in the same country as the supplier, the place where the customer has established his business or has a fixed establishment to which the service is supplied, or in the absence of such a place, the place where he has his permanent address or usually resides	Art. 9(2)(e)
• Supply of staff	• When performed for customers established outside the EC, or for taxable persons established in the EC but not in the same country as the supplier, the place where the customer has established his business or has a fixed establishment to which the service is supplied, or in the absence of such a place, the place where he has his permanent address or usually resides	Art. 9(2)(e)

Type and Method of Supply	Place of Supply	Sixth Directive
• Services of agents who act in the name and for the account of another, when they procure for their principal the services referred to in Art. 9(2)(e) of the Sixth Directive	• When performed for customers established outside the EC, or for taxable persons established in the EC but not in the same country as the supplier, the place where the customer has established his business or has a fixed establishment to which the service is supplied, or in the absence of such a place, the place where he has his permanent address or usually resides	Art. 9(2)(e)
• Telecommunications services. The Sixth Directive deems 'telecommunications services' to be 'services relating to the transmission, emission or reception of signals, writing, images and sounds or information of any nature by wire, radio, optical or other electromagnetic systems, including the related transfer or assignment of the right to use capacity for such transmission, emission or reception' (Art. 9(2)(e)). Telecommunications services also includes provision of access to global information networks (Art. 9(2)(e))	• When performed for customers established outside the EC, or for taxable persons established in the EC but not in the same country as the supplier, the place where the customer has established his business or has a fixed establishment to which the service is supplied, or in the absence of such a place, the place where he has his permanent address or usually resides	Art. 9(2)(e)
• Radio and television broadcasting services	• When performed for customers established outside the EC, or for taxable persons established in the EC but not in the same country as the supplier, the place where the customer has established his business or has a fixed establishment to which the service is supplied, or in the absence of such a place, the place where he has his permanent address or usually resides	Art. 9(2)(e)
• Electronically supplied services. 'Electronically supplied' services means those specified in Annex L to the Sixth Directive, which include web site supply, web-hosting, supply of images, text and information, supply of music, films and games, supply of distance learning	• When performed for customers established outside the EC, or for taxable persons established in the EC but not in the same country as the supplier, the place where the customer has established his business or has a fixed establishment to which the service is supplied, or in the absence of such a place, the place where he has his permanent address or usually resides	Art. 9(2)(e)(f)

Type and Method of Supply	Place of Supply	Sixth Directive
	• Where these services are performed for non-taxable persons who are established, have their permanent address or usually reside in a Member State, by a taxable person who has established his business or has a fixed establishment from which the service is supplied outside the EC, or in the absence of such a place of business or fixed establishment has his permanent address or usually resides outside the EC, the place of supply is the place where the non-taxable person is established, has his permanent address or usually resides	Art. 9(2)(e)(f)
• Services subject to Art. 9(2)(e) of the Sixth Directive and hiring out of forms of transport, but excluding electronically supplied services supplied to non-taxable persons	• The Directive permits Member States for the purposes of avoiding double taxation, non-taxation, or the distortion of competition to consider: — the place of supply, which would be situated within the territory of the country, as being situated outside the EC where the effective use and enjoyment of the services take place outside the EC; and — the place of supply, which would be situated outside the EC, as being within the territory of the country where the effective use and enjoyment of the services take place within the territory of the country	Art. 9(3)
• Telecommunication services, radio and television broadcasting services	• When performed for non-taxable persons who are established, have their permanent address or usually reside in a Member State, which are supplied by a taxable person who has established his business, or has a fixed establishment from which the service is supplied outside the EC, or has his permanent address or usually resides outside the EU, the place of supply, which would be situated outside the EC, is treated as being within the territory of the country where the effective use and enjoyment of the services take place within the territory of the country	Art. 9(4)

As illustrated in the table above, the concept of 'fixed establishment' is central to the operation of the place of supply rules. In Case 168/84 *Berkholz* [1985] ECR 2251, gaming machines were installed on ferries operating between Denmark and West Germany. The tax authority in Germany sought to apply VAT on the receipts derived from operating the gaming machines. The owner of the gaming machines employed individuals to maintain the machines and collect money from them, which was done on board the ferries. The operation of these machines earned the owner approximately 346,701.20 DEM, and VAT was assessed on the amount. The question arose as to whether the gaming machines were fixed establishments for the purposes of determining the place of supply of services. The ECJ held that a fixed establishment can be an installation (such as a gaming machine), but subject to the proviso that it permanently has both the human and technical resources for the provision of the services. The concept of 'fixed establishment' was also considered by the ECJ in Case C-190/95 *ARO Lease* [1997] ECR I-4383, which involved a company established in the Netherlands that carried on a car leasing business. Cars were leased to customers located in Belgium. The company accounted for VAT to the Netherlands' VAT authority in relation to the leasing transactions, but submitted a repayment claim on the basis that the place of supply was in Belgium. The company's repayment claim failed. The Netherlands' VAT authority refused the claim on the basis that the company did not have any staff or technical facilities in Belgium sufficient to constitute a 'fixed establishment'. The ECJ confirmed the decision of the Netherlands' VAT authority. The ECJ commented (at paras. 15 and 16) that in applying the place of supply rules to services, the primary point of reference must be where the supplier has established his business (i.e. the general rule in Art. 9(1)), unless reference to the main place of business does not lead to a rational result for tax purposes, or creates conflict with another Member State. An alternative place of supply, such as an establishment can only be regarded as an appropriate reference point if the establishment has the 'minimum degree of stability derived from the permanent presence of both the human and technical resources necessary for the provision of the services.' In addition, the alternative establishment must be able to supply the services on an independent basis.

The European Commission has adopted a proposal that would result in amending the provisions relating to supplies of services to taxable persons (COM(2003) 822, 2003/0329/CNS). The proposal is for a new general rule for services provided to taxable persons which would state that such services are supplied at the place where the customer is established. The proposal would maintain a number of exceptions to the general rule, which would be based on existing criteria.

6. The charge to VAT is in relation to the supply of goods or services 'effected for consideration' (Art. 2(1)). The term 'consideration' is not defined by the Sixth Directive. The requirement that consideration must be given for a VAT charge to arise means that many non-business activities are not within the scope of VAT, such as gifts made for personal reasons. The amount in respect of which VAT is applied is known as 'the taxable amount', and subject to the exceptions discussed below is 'everything which constitutes the consideration which has been or is to be obtained by the supplier from the purchaser, the customer or a third party for such supplies including subsidies directly linked to the price of such supplies' (Art. 11A(1)(a)). The

consideration referred to in Art. 11A(1)(a) is the value actually received in each case, i.e. the subjective value, and not a value estimated by objective criteria (Case C-317/94 *Elida Gibbs* [1996] ECR I-5339). In Case 154/80 *Coöperatieve Aardappelenbewaarplaats* [1981] ECR 445, the ECJ held that under the Second Directive the basis of assessment in relation to a service was everything that made up the consideration for the service, and that there must be a direct link between the service provided and the consideration received if the supply of a service was to be taxable. In Case 230/87 *Naturally Yours Cosmetics* [1988] ECR 6365, the ECJ confirmed the approach in *Coöperatieve Aardappelenbewaarplaats*, that such a direct link must exist between a supply and the consideration received for the purposes of the Sixth Directive. In Case C-16/93 *Tolsma* [1994] ECR I-743, the ECJ held that an individual who played a barrel organ on the public highway was not providing services 'for consideration'. This was because there was no legal link between the provider and recipient of the service; and there was no necessary link between the service and payments received from passers-by. For instance, they did not request music to be played for them, and the giving of money may have been motivated by other reasons.

There are exceptions to the general rule, which provide for specific amounts to be treated as the taxable amount as follows (Art. 11A(1)(b) to (d)):

(a) in respect of self-supplies of goods relating to private and non-business use, and internal supplies, the taxable amount is the purchase price of the goods or of similar goods or, in the absence of a purchase price, the cost price, determined at the time of supply;
(b) in respect of self-supplies of services relating to private and non-business use, the taxable amount is the full cost to the taxable person of providing the services.

The Sixth Directive specifically provides that the 'taxable amount' will include taxes, duties, levies (although excluding VAT), and incidental expenses, such as commission, packing, transport, insurance costs charged by the supplier (Art. 11A(2)). However, the term 'taxable amount' does not include price reductions by way of discount for early payment, or price discounts and rebates allowed to the customer and accounted for at the time of the supply, or amounts received by a taxable person from his purchaser or customer as repayment for expenses paid out in the name, and for the account of the purchaser or customer, and which are entered in the taxable person's books in a suspense account (Art. 11A(3)(a)(b)(c)). The Sixth Directive provides for the reduction of the 'taxable amount' on cancellation, refusal, or total or partial non-payment (although Member States may derogate in respect of a total or partial non-payment), or where the price is reduced after the supply takes place (Art. 11C(1)).

Special arrangements relating to determining the taxable amount apply to second-hand goods, works of art, collectors' items, and antiques as a result of Council Dir. 94/5 of 14 February 1994 (*OJ* 1994 L60/16), which supplements the common system of VAT, and amended the Sixth Directive. Consideration of such arrangements is beyond the scope of this commentary.

7. A supply of goods or services, depending on its classification under the Sixth Directive, may be subject to either a standard or reduced rate of VAT. Alternatively, the supply may be classified, as an exempt supply with the consequence that the supply is excluded from the scope of VAT. The purpose of exclusions is to limit the potential scope of the application of VAT with the consequence that by definition such supplies are not taxable transactions. The Sixth Directive as amended by Council Dir. 2001/41 (*OJ* 2001 L22/17 requires each Member State to set a standard rate of VAT on the supply of goods or services at a rate of not less than 15% (Art. 12(3)(a)). The VAT rate is a percentage of 'the taxable amount' (Art. 12(3)(a)). Member States are permitted to apply a reduced rate of VAT of not less than 5% in relation to the categories of supply specified in Annex H of the Sixth Directive, which include foodstuffs for human and animal consumption, water supplies, services supplied by or royalties due to writers, composers, and performing artists, and use of sporting facilities (Art. 12(3)(a)). The Sixth Directive permits Member States to apply a reduced rate of VAT to supplies of natural gas and electricity provided that the reduction will not result in a distortion of competition (Art. 12(3)(b)). In addition some Member States, such as the United Kingdom, allow the zero-rating of some supplies with the consequence that the taxable person is able to obtain a deduction for input VAT incurred in making the supply of such goods or services. Zero-rating (otherwise known as exemption with a right of deduction) is permitted by the Sixth Directive where such rates existed at 1 January 1991, and provided that the rates are 'in accordance with Community law' (Art. 28(2)(b)). The United Kingdom has an extensive list of supplies (subject to exclusions) that qualify for zero-rating, and include (see Value Added Tax Act 1994, Sch. 8): bank notes, books, clothing and footwear, construction of buildings, food, gold, imports and exports.

8. The Sixth Directive provides various categories of supply that are exempt from VAT without a right of deduction (i.e. no right to deduct input VAT). In the application of exemptions their ambit is strictly construed on the basis that they are an exception to the general rule that VAT is charged on all economic activity (Case 348/87 *Stichting Uitvoering Financiële Acties* [1989] ECR 1737).

The categories listed below are exempt on the basis that such supplies are in the public interest, although Member States are required to impose conditions for the purposes of preventing evasion, avoidance, or abuse (Art. 13A(1)):

(a) the supply by the public postal services of services other than passenger transport and telecommunications services, and the supply of goods incidental thereto;
(b) hospital and medical care and closely related activities undertaken by bodies governed by public law or, under social conditions comparable to those applicable to bodies governed by public law, by hospitals, centres for medical

treatment or diagnosis and other duly recognized establishments of a similar nature;

(c) the provision of medical care in the exercise of the medical and paramedical professions as defined by the Member State concerned;
(d) supplies of human organs, blood and milk;
(e) services supplied by dental technicians in their professional capacity and dental prostheses supplied by dentists and dental technicians;
(f) services supplied by independent groups of persons whose activities are exempt from or are not subject to value added tax, for the purpose of rendering their members the services directly necessary for the exercise of their activity, where these groups merely claim from their members exact reimbursement of their share of the joint expenses, provided that such exemption is not likely to produce distortion of competition;
(g) the supply of services and of goods closely linked to welfare and social security work, including those supplied by old people's homes, by bodies governed by public law or by other organizations recognized as charitable by the Member State concerned;
(h) the supply of services and of goods closely linked to the protection of children and young persons by bodies governed by public law or by other organizations recognized as charitable by the Member State concerned;
(i) children's or young people's education, school or university education, vocational training or retraining, including the supply of services and of goods closely related thereto, provided by bodies governed by public law having such as their aim or by other organizations defined by the Member State concerned as having similar objects;
(j) tuition given privately by teachers and covering school or university education;
(k) certain supplies of staff by religious or philosophical institutions for the purpose of sub-paragraphs (b), (g), (h) and (i) and with a view to spiritual welfare;
(l) supply of services and goods closely linked thereto for the benefit of their members in return for a subscription fixed in accordance with their rules by non-profit-making organizations with aims of a political, trade-union, religious, patriotic, philosophical, philanthropic or civic nature, provided that this exemption is not likely to cause distortion of competition;
(m) certain services closely linked to sport or physical education supplied by non-profit-making organizations to persons taking part in sport or physical education;
(n) certain cultural services and goods closely linked thereto supplied by bodies governed by public law or by other cultural bodies recognized by the Member State concerned;
(o) the supply of services and goods by organizations whose activities are exempt under the provisions of sub-paragraphs (b), (g), (h), (i), (l), (m) and (n) above in connection with fund-raising events organized exclusively for their own benefit provided that exemption is not likely to cause distortion of competition. Member states may introduce any necessary restrictions in particular as regards the number of events or the amount of receipts which give entitlement to exemption;
(p) the supply of transport services for sick or injured persons in vehicles specially designed for the purpose by duly authorized bodies;

(q) activities of public radio and television bodies other than those of a commercial nature.

The categories of supply referred to in (b), (g), (h), (i), (l), (m), and (n) above will not be granted exemption from VAT if it is not essential to the transactions exempted; and its basic purpose is to obtain additional income for the organization by carrying out transactions that are in direct competition with those of commercial enterprises liable to VAT (Art. 13(2)(b)).

Further exemptions, listed below, are provided in the Sixth Directive other than on the basis that they are in the public interest, although Member States are required as is the case for the public interest exemptions to impose conditions for the purposes of preventing evasion, avoidance, or abuse (Art. 13B):

(a) insurance and reinsurance transactions, including related services performed by insurance brokers and insurance agents;

(b) the leasing or letting of immovable property excluding:
  1. the provisions of accommodation, as defined in the laws of the Member States, in the hotel sector or in sectors with a similar function, including the provision of accommodation in holiday camps or on sites developed for use as camping sites;
  2. the letting of premises and sites for parking vehicles;
  3. lettings of permanently installed equipment and machinery;
  4. hire of safes.

  Member States may apply further exclusions to the scope of this exemption;

(c) supplies of goods used wholly for an activity exempted under this Article . . . when these goods have not given rise to the right to deduction, or of goods on the acquisition or production of which, by virtue of Article 17(6) [namely, expenditure which is not strictly business expenditure, such as that on luxuries, amusements or entertainment], value added tax did not become deductible;

(d) the following transactions:
  1. the granting and the negotiation of credit and the management of credit by the person granting it;
  2. the negotiation of or any dealings in credit guarantees or any other security for money and the management of credit guarantees by the person who is granting the credit;
  3. transaction, including negotiation, concerning deposit and current accounts, payments, transfers, debts, cheques and other negotiable instruments, but excluding debt collection and factoring;
  4. transactions, including negotiation, concerning currency, bank notes and coins used as legal tender, with the exception of collectors' items; 'collectors' items' shall be taken to mean gold, silver or other metal coins or bank notes which are not normally used as legal tender or coins of numismatic interest;
  5. transactions, including negotiation, excluding management and safekeeping, in shares, interests in companies or associations, debentures and other securities, excluding:
     — documents establishing title to goods,
     — the rights or securities [which are interests in immovable property, or rights of ownership or possession over immovable property];

6. management of special investment funds as defined by Member States;

(e) the supply at face value of postage stamps valid for use for postal services within the territory of the country, fiscal stamps, and other similar stamps;

(f) betting, lotteries and other forms of gambling, subject to conditions and limitations laid down by each Member State;

(g) the supply of buildings or parts thereof, and of the land on which they stand, other than [the supply before first occupation of buildings or parts of buildings and the land on which they stand];

(h) the supply of land which has not been built on other than building land [which is unimproved or improved land as defined by the Member State].

The Directive permits Member States to allow taxpayers a right of option for taxation in cases of: (*a*) letting and leasing of immovable property; (*b*) the transactions covered in (d), (g), and (h) above of this paragraph (Art. 13C).

9. The common system of VAT, as explained previously, entitles a taxable person who enters into taxable transactions to deduct the amount of VAT (known as 'input tax') incurred on goods or services in making such taxable transactions against the amount of VAT received (known as 'output tax') in entering into those taxable transactions (Arts. 17, 18(2)). This is the essence of VAT, namely the deduction of input VAT by all taxable persons except the final consumer. In Case 268/83 *Rompelman* [1985] ECR 655, paras. 15 to 19, the ECJ explained the basis of the right to deduct in the following terms: '. . . the deduction system is meant to relieve the trader entirely of the burden of the VAT payable or paid in the course of all his economic activities. The common system of value-added tax therefore ensures that all economic activities, whatever their purpose or results, provided that they are themselves subject to VAT, are taxed in a wholly neutral way.'

Specifically, provided the goods and services are used for the purposes of taxable transactions, the taxable person is entitled to deduct from the VAT that he is liable to pay to his National Tax Authority: (*a*) VAT due or paid within the territory of the country in respect of goods or services supplied or to be supplied to him by another taxable person; (*b*) VAT due or paid in respect of imported goods within the territory of the country; (*c*) VAT paid on the intra-Community acquisition of goods (Art. 17(2)). Member States are also required to grant a taxable person the right to the deduction or refund of VAT provided the goods and services are used for the purposes of, *inter alia*, (*a*) transactions relating to economic activities, carried out in another country, which would be deductible if they had been performed within the territory of the country; (*b*) transactions which are exempt with a right of deduction, such as the exports from the EC, goods subject to special exemption linked to international good traffic (e.g. goods placed under customs warehousing arrangements, and the supply of services relating to such supply of goods); and (*c*) exempt transactions relating to insurance, reinsurance, granting and negotiation of credit, when the customer is established outside the EC, or when those transactions are directly linked with goods to be exported to a country outside the EC (Art. 17(3)).

A taxable person is only entitled to recover input tax in relation to transactions that he is specifically entitled to recover for under the Sixth Directive. Accordingly, where goods and services are used by a taxable person for transactions in respect of which VAT is not deductible (i.e. an exempt transaction with no right of deduction) he will only be able to deduct the proportion that is attributable to the transactions for which such VAT can be deducted (Art. 17(5)). The Sixth Directive provides various methods of calculation for determining the relevant deductible proportion (see Art. 19). The net amount of VAT resulting from the foregoing computations is paid when the taxable person submits his VAT return (Art. 22(5)).

The right to deduct input tax is subject to a taxable person holding such evidence as is required by the Sixth Directive (Art. 18(1)). For example, a taxable person who seeks to exercise the right of deduction in relation to VAT paid in respect of goods or services supplied to him by another taxable person must hold an invoice which complies with, *inter alia*, the following formalities: date of issue, name and address of the taxable person and his customer, the VAT rate applied, and the VAT amount payable (Art. 22(3)).

If the amount of input tax exceeds the amount of VAT due then the amount of the excess may either be refunded to the taxable person, or carried forward to be set against any future liability (Art. 18(4)).

The right to deduct input tax in relation to 'capital goods' is sometimes subject to restrictions. 'Capital goods' are in essence items that represent capital expenditure. The restrictions require the input tax to be deducted over a period of years (i.e. similar to depreciation allowances on capital assets for corporation tax purposes). The Sixth Directive provides in relation to capital goods for input tax credits to be spread over five years, and the adjustment is limited to one fifth of the tax imposed on the goods (Art. 20(2)). In relation to immovable property the deduction can be extended to a period of up to twenty years (Art. 20(2)). Member States are permitted to disapply the rules.

II. Intra-Community trade

Intra-EC trade, i.e. that relating to the supply of goods or services to other Member States, is subject to different rules than supplies in a Member State.

1. Goods: acquisition of goods. The system of rules for the application of VAT to trade in goods between Member States were introduced by Council Dir. 91/680 of 16 December 1991 (*OJ* 1991 L376/1) the purpose being to supplement the common system of VAT with a view to the abolition of fiscal frontiers. The rules are transitional and will remain in their current form until the Council has decided on a definitive system. The main principles relating to the acquisition of goods is provided in the Sixth Directive as amended by Council Dir. 91/680, which are summarized as follows.

1. VAT is imposed in three circumstances on intra-Community acquisitions. First, VAT is imposed on the intra-Community acquisition of goods for consideration within a Member State by a taxable person, or by a non-taxable legal person where the vendor is a taxable person who is not covered by certain arrangements (Art. 28a(1)(a)). The term 'intra-Community acquisition of goods' is defined as the 'acquisition of the right to dispose as owner of movable tangible property dispatched or transported to the person acquiring the goods by or on behalf of the vendor or the person acquiring the goods to a Member State other than that from which the goods are dispatched or transported' (Art. 28a(3)). However, this VAT charge does not apply in certain circumstances, which include the intra-Community acquisition of goods not exceeding a specified threshold in Member States by a taxable person who carries out supplies in respect of which VAT is not deductible, or by a non-taxable legal person (Art. 28a(1a)(b)). The threshold must be at least the national currency equivalent of €10,000 (Art. 28a(1a)(b)). In these circumstances the VAT rules discussed in section I above will apply.

Second, VAT is imposed on intra-Community acquisitions of a new means of transport effected for consideration within a country by taxable persons or certain non-taxable legal persons (Art. 28a(1)(b)). Third, VAT is imposed on the intra-Community acquisition of goods which are subject to excise duties effected for consideration within the territory of the country by a taxable person or certain non-taxable legal persons (Art. 28a(1)(c)). The term 'intra-Community acquisition of goods' includes those transactions that would have been classified as a supply of goods if carried out within a Member State (Art. 28a(7)). The Sixth Directive deems the transfer by a taxable person of goods from his undertaking to another Member State to be effected for consideration, and accordingly within the rules relating to intra-Community acquisition of goods (Art. 28a(5)(b)).

2. VAT in relation to intra-Community acquisition of goods is chargeable on the fifteenth day of the month following that during which a 'chargeable event' occurs (Art. 28d(2)). The chargeable event is when the intra-Community acquisition of goods is effected, and for these purposes the acquisition is regarded as effected when the supply of similar goods is regarded as being effected within the territory of the Member State (Art. 28(d)(1)). If an invoice is issued before the fifteenth day the VAT will become chargeable at that stage (Art. 28d(3)). As is the case in relation to supplies within a Member State, VAT is charged by reference to a 'taxable amount' which is established on the basis of the same elements as those used to determine the taxable amount for the supply of the same goods within a Member State (Art. 28e(1)). The VAT rate applicable to the intra-Community acquisition of goods is that applied to the supply of like goods within the territory of a Member State (Art. 28e(4)).

3. A summary of the place of supply rules relating to the intra-Community acquisition of goods is provided in the following Table.

Intra-Community Acquisition of Goods		
Type of Supply	Place of Supply	Sixth Directive
• Intra-Community acquisition of goods	• Place where the goods are at the time when dispatch or transport to the person acquiring them ends	Art. 28b(1)
• Intra-Community acquisition of goods	• Without prejudice to the foregoing the place of the intra-Community acquisition of goods is deemed to be within the territory of the Member State that issued the VAT identification number under which the person acquiring the goods made the acquisition, unless the person acquiring the goods establishes that that acquisition has been subject to VAT in accordance with the first principle set out above	Art. 28b(2)

4. Provided the goods acquired are used for the purposes of taxable transactions, the taxable person is entitled to deduct from the VAT that he is liable to pay the amount of VAT due on the intra-Community acquisition of goods (Art. 17(2)(d)).

5. The Sixth Directive provides for the following exemptions from VAT in relation to intra-Community acquisitions of goods (Art. 28c(B)):

(*a*) the intra-Community acquisition of goods the supply of which by taxable persons would in all circumstances be exempt within the territory of the country;

(*b*) the intra-Community acquisition of goods the importation of which would in all circumstances be exempt under the exemptions relating to importation. In other words, the supply of goods in the Member State will be exempt if its importation would be exempt;

(*c*) the intra-Community acquisition of goods where the person acquiring the goods would in all circumstances be entitled to full reimbursement of the VAT due (i.e. because the taxable person is not established within the Member State where the VAT is incurred).

2. Goods: distance selling. Where intra-Community trade relates to the supply of goods that are not subject to the rules explained above, in the absence of any further provision the VAT rule would be that VAT is charged at the rate applicable in the Member State of dispatch, i.e. the Member State in which the purchase is made (Art. 8(1)(a) as discussed in section I above). This general rule is displaced by what are known as 'the distance sales' rules, the main principles of which are summarized as follows.

1. The general rule is that goods dispatched or transported from a Member State, either by the supplier or by the person to whom they are

supplied or by a third person, are deemed to be supplied at the place where the goods are at the time when dispatch or transport to the person to whom they are supplied begins (i.e. the country of origin) (Art. 8(1)(a)). Where the country of origin is the place of supply the taxable person will charge VAT in accordance with the prevailing rate in that Member State. However, the place of supply in relation to the supply of goods to: (*i*) taxable persons who are not entitled to deduct VAT, (*ii*) non-taxable legal persons in another Member State who are subject to the €10,000 threshold (as discussed above), and (*iii*) other non-taxable persons (i.e. private consumers) is charged to VAT in the place of destination (i.e. the place where the goods are when dispatch or transport to the purchaser ends) where the supply is of goods by or on behalf of the supplier (Art. 28b(B)(1)). However, the supply must be other than a new means of transport, and other than goods supplied after assembly or installation (Art. 28b(B)(1)).

Where the country of destination (i.e. country of consumption) is the place of supply under these rules the taxable person in the other Member State (i.e. country of origin) is required to register in the country of destination and charge VAT at the prevailing rate in the country of destination in respect of the supply of goods. However, the place of destination rule does not apply where the total value of the supplies (less VAT) does not in one calendar year exceed the equivalent in national currency of €100,000; and the total value (less VAT) of the supplies of goods in the previous calendar year did not exceed €100,000 (Art. 28b(B)(2)). The destination Member State is permitted to lower the threshold to the equivalent in national currency of €35,000 where that Member State believes the threshold of €100,000 'would lead to serious distortions of the conditions of competition.' (Art. 28b(B)(2)).

2. The Sixth Directive provides for the following exemptions from VAT in respect of the distance selling provisions (Art. 28c(A)):

(*a*) supplies of goods dispatched or transported by or on behalf of the vendor or the person acquiring the goods out of the territory but within the EC, effected for another taxable person or a non-taxable legal person acting as such in a Member State other than that of the departure of the dispatch or transport of the goods;

(*b*) supplies of new means of transport, dispatched or transported to the purchaser by or on behalf of the vendor or the purchaser out of the territory but within the EC, effected for taxable persons or certain non-taxable persons;

(*c*) the supply of goods subject to excise duty dispatched or transported to the purchaser, by the vendor, by the purchaser or on his behalf, outside the territory but inside the EC, effected for taxable persons or certain non-taxable persons.

3. Services. Where intra-Community trade relates to the supply of services to taxable persons, different rules apply than those relating to intra-Community services supplied to non-taxable persons. The main principles relating to the supply of services are provided in the Sixth Directive, which are summarized as follows.

1. Services supplied by a taxable person located in a Member State to a non-taxable person in another Member State are subject to VAT in accordance with the place of supply rules discussed in section I above. The place of supply will usually be where the supplier is located, with the result that VAT at the rate prevailing in the country of origin will be imposed on the supply.

2. The place of supply for the services listed below, as summarized in the table in section I, will be the place where the customer has established his business or has a fixed establishment to which the service is supplied or, in the absence of such a place, the place where he has his permanent address or usually resides (Art. 9(2)(e)).

- Transfers and assignments of copyrights, patents, licences, trade marks, and similar rights
- Advertising services
- Services of consultants, engineers, consultancy bureaux, lawyers, accountants, and other similar services, as well as data processing and the supplying of information
- Hiring out of movable tangible property with the exception of all forms of transport
- Obligations to refrain from pursuing or exercising, in whole or in part, a business activity or a right referred to in this list
- Banking, financial, and insurance transactions including reinsurance, with the exception of the hire of safes
- Supply of staff
- Services of agents who act in the name and for the account of another, when they procure for their principal the services referred to in this list
- Telecommunications services
- Radio and television broadcasting services

Where the services listed above are supplied by a taxable person located in a Member State to a taxable person in another Member State the supply will be subject to what are known as 'the reverse charge' rules with the consequence that the recipient will be deemed to make the supply, and will be required to account for VAT in respect of the services at the rate prevailing in the Member State (Art. 21(1)(b)). In other words, the effect of the 'reverse charge' is that the recipient is treated as making the supply to itself. The taxable person will then account to the tax authority for the amount of VAT due, as output tax, on that supply. If the person is able to claim the VAT as input tax, there will be no VAT payable to the tax authority arising out of the reverse charge since both amounts will be netted off against each other.

III. Goods and services received from outside the EC

The application of VAT to goods and services received from outside the EC is required to be imposed on a basis consistent to the VAT charge imposed on like goods and services supplied within the EC. This is because Member

States are subject to international obligations relating to non-discrimination under the General Agreement on Tariffs and Trade (GATT) 1994, which comprises the obligations contained in the GATT's text adopted in 1947. Art. III(2) of GATT 1947 provides:

> The products of the territory of any contracting party imported into the territory of any other contracting party shall not be subject, directly or indirectly, to internal taxes or other internal charges of any kind in excess of those applied, directly or indirectly, to like domestic products.

To ensure that Member States are not in breach of their international obligations the imposition of VAT on the importation of goods or services from outside the EC must not be in excess of that imposed on transactions within the EC.

1. Goods. 1. The Sixth Directive requires VAT to be imposed on the importation of goods by any person (i.e. including by a non-taxable person) (Art. 2). The VAT rate is the same as that applied to the supply of like goods within the Member State into which the goods are imported (Art. 12(5)). The concept of 'importation of goods' means the entry into the EC of goods in respect of which customs formalities have not been complied with and the duties have not been paid; and also includes the entry into the EC of goods from a 'third territory' (i.e. a non-EC territory) (Art. 7). VAT is chargeable at the time when the goods are imported (Art. 10(3)). However, where imported goods are placed under one of the arrangements, described below, upon entry into the EC the VAT becomes chargeable when the goods cease to be covered by the arrangements (Art. 10(3)). If the imported goods are subject to customs duties the tax will become chargeable at the time when the customs duties become chargeable (Art. 10(3)). A taxable person has the right to deduct from the amount of VAT which he is liable to pay, any VAT paid in respect of imported goods into the Member State (Art. 17(2)(b)). However, to exercise the right to deduct, the taxable person must hold an import document stating that he is the either the consignee or importer, and which specifies the amount of VAT due (Art. 18(1)(b)). In relation to import declarations and payment of VAT on imports the Sixth Directive requires Member States to lay down detailed rules (Art. 23).

2. The place of import within the EC is the Member State in which the goods enter into the EC (Art. 7(2)). However, the place of supply is altered where goods are placed under arrangements for temporary importation, and then in such circumstances the place of import is the Member State in which the goods cease to be covered by the arrangements (Art. 7(3)). The 'arrangements' are those where the supply of goods are intended to be (*a*) produced to customs, and where applicable placed in temporary storage, (*b*) placed in a free zone or in a free warehouse, (*c*) placed under customs warehousing arrangements or inward processing arrangements, (*d*) admitted into territorial waters: in order to be incorporated into drilling or production of platforms, or for the fuelling and provisioning of drilling or production platforms (Art. 16(1)(B)).

3. VAT is applied to the 'taxable amount', which is defined as 'the value for customs purposes, determined in accordance with the Community provisions in force' (Art. 11(B)(1)). The 'taxable amount' includes: taxes, duties, levies, and other charges due outside the importing Member State, plus those due by reason of importation, but excluding the VAT which is to be levied (Art. 11(B)(1)(a)). In addition, the amount includes incidental expenses (e.g. commission, packing, transport, insurance) incurred up to the first place of destination within the Member State into which the goods are first imported (Art. 11(B)(1)(b)). For importation purposes, the taxable amount must not include price reductions by way of discount for early payment; or price discounts and rebates allowed to the customer (Art. 11(B)(4)).

4. The Sixth Directive provides that the categories of supply listed below are exempt from VAT on imports, although Member States are required to impose conditions for the purposes of preventing evasion, avoidance, or abuse (Art. 14(1)):

(a) final importation of goods of which the supply by a taxable person would in all circumstances be exempted within the country;
(b) final importation of goods qualifying for exemption from customs duties other than as provided for in the Common Customs Tariff;
(c) reimportation by the person who exported them of goods in the state in which they were exported, where they qualify for exemption from customs duties or would qualify therefor if they were imported from a third country;
(d) importations of goods:
   — under diplomatic and consular arrangements, which qualify for exemption from customs duties,
   — by international organizations recognized as such by the public authorities of the host country, and by members of such organizations, within the limits and under the conditions laid down by the international conventions establishing the organizations or by headquarters agreements,
   — into the territory of Member States which are parties to the North Atlantic Treaty by the armed forces of other States which are parties to that Treaty for the use of such forces or the civilian staff accompanying them or for supplying their messes or canteens where such forces take part in the common defence effort;
(e) importation into ports by sea fishing undertakings of their catches, unprocessed or after undergoing preservation for marketing but before being supplied;
(f) the supply of services, in connection with the importation of goods where the value of such services is included in the taxable amount;
(g) importation of gold by Central Banks.

2. Services. Where the services listed below are supplied by a person outside the EC to a taxable person in a Member State the supply will be subject to what are known as 'the reverse-charge' rules with the consequence that the recipient will be deemed to make the supply, and will be required to account for VAT in respect of the services at the rate prevailing in the Member State (Art. 21(1)(b)). A person will become a taxable person where the supply deemed to be received under the 'reverse charge' is equal to, or more than the financial threshold for registration. The place of supply for the services listed below will be the place where the customer has established his business or has a fixed establishment to which the service is supplied or, in the absence of such a place, the place where he has his permanent address or usually resides (Art. 9(2)(e)).

- Transfers and assignments of copyrights, patents, licences, trade marks, and similar rights
- Advertising services
- Services of consultants, engineers, consultancy bureaux, lawyers, accountants, and other similar services, as well as data processing and the supplying of information
- Hiring out of movable tangible property with the exception of all forms of transport
- Obligations to refrain from pursuing or exercising, in whole or in part, a business activity or a right referred to in this list
- Banking, financial, and insurance transactions including reinsurance, with the exception of the hire of safes
- Supply of staff
- Services of agents who act in the name and for the account of another, when they procure for their principal the services referred to in this list
- Telecommunications services
- Radio and television broadcasting services.

3. Electronically supplied services received from outside the EU. 1. Prior to 1 July 2003 a non-EU supplier who supplied radio services, television services, or certain electronically supplied services was not required to account for VAT to any tax authority within the EU because under the Sixth Directive the place of supply was deemed to be outside the EU (Art. 9(1)). The recipient of service supplies received from such a non-EU supplier is only required to account for VAT if the supply is received for business purposes, and are within the scope of the reverse charge provisions as discussed above. By contrast a private consumer of such service supplies was not required to pay any VAT. In these circumstances the non-EU supplier had a competitive advantage over EU suppliers in respect of supplies to private consumers. Council Dir. 2002/38 of 7 May 2002 amended the Sixth Directive on a temporary basis for three years from 1 July 2003, which can then either be extended or revised, in relation to the place of supply as regards radio and television broadcasting services and certain electronically supplied services delivered by non-EU suppliers (*OJ* 2002 L337/41). The amendments seek to rectify the weakness of the Sixth Directive in respect of such services supplied from outside the EU by the imposition of an obligation on non-EU suppliers to charge VAT in respect of such supplies to EU private consumers. The effect of the amendments is to impose an extraterritorial tax obligation on persons with no physical presence in the EU. An illustrative list of 'electronically supplied services' subject to the amendments are specified in Annex L of the Sixth Directive as follows:

1. Web site supply, web-hosting, distance maintenance of programs and equipment.
2. Supply of software and updating thereof.
3. Supply of images, text and information, and making databases available.
4. Supply of music, films, and games, including games of chance and gambling games, and of political, cultural, artistic, sporting, scientific, and entertainment broadcasts and events.
5. Supply of distance teaching.

The amendments to the place of supply rules do not apply in the case where the supplier and his customer communicate via electronic mail, because such a form of communication is not regarded of itself as meaning that the service which is performed is an electronic service (Sixth Directive, Annex L). A non-EU supplier will be required to account for VAT at the rate applicable in the Member State where the non-business customer is resident. The rules apply to services such as digital products supplied online and to pay-per-view radio and television broadcasting. There is no obligation to register in respect of business-to-business transactions because of the operation of the reverse-charge mechanism.

2. The reason for the amendments is to combat the threat represented by non-EU suppliers who deliver services electronically to individual customers located in Member States of the EU free of any EU VAT (see the first three recitals). Prior to the amendment, the place of supply of services was deemed to be where the supplier is located. The amendment provides that the place where electronically supplied services are supplied when performed for non-taxable persons who are established, have their permanent address or usually reside in a Member State, by a taxable person who has established his business or has a fixed establishment from which the service is supplied outside the EC, or in the absence of such a place of business or fixed establishment, has his permanent address or usually resides outside the EC, the place of supply will be the place where the non-taxable person is established, has his permanent address or usually resides (Art. 9.2(f)). As a result of Council Dir. 2002/38 in relation to the supply of radio and television broadcasting services Member States are required to deem that supplies by taxable persons outside the EU performed for non-taxable persons established in the EU are made in the territory where the effective use and enjoyment of the services takes place (Art. 9(4)).

3. The Sixth Directive, as a result of amendments by Council Dir. 2002/38, makes provision for a special scheme for non-EU established taxable persons to comply with their obligations under the place of supply rules for electronically supplied services (Art. 26c). The scheme applies to a 'non-established taxable person', which is defined as meaning 'a taxable person who neither has established his business nor has a fixed establishment within the territory of the Community and who is not otherwise required to be identified . . .' (Art. 26c(a)). The non-established person is required to choose a Member State of the EU referred to under the scheme as the

'Member State of identification' for the purposes of notifying when his activity as a taxable person commences, ceases or changes (Art. 26c(B)(2)). The notification must be made electronically and contain the following details (Art. 26c(B)(2)):

- Name,
- postal address,
- electronic addresses, including web sites,
- national tax number, if any.

The non-established taxable person must include in the notification a statement that he is not otherwise identified for VAT purposes within the EU (Art. 26c(B)(2)). Upon notification the Member State of identification will then issue an identification number to the non-established person (Art. 26c(B)(3)). There are various circumstances in which a non-established taxable person can be removed from an identification register maintained under the scheme, such as where a person no longer supplies electronic services (Art. 26c(B)(4)). Under the scheme a non-established taxable person is required to submit by electronic means to the Member State of identification a VAT return for each calendar quarter irrespective of whether or not electronic services have been supplied (Art. 26c(B)(5)). The VAT return must be submitted within twenty days of the end of the reporting period to which the return relates, and must contain the following information (Art. 26c(B)(5)):

- the non-established taxable person's identification number;
- for each Member State in which the supply of electronically delivered services is deemed to take place (known as the 'Member State of consumption') the total value, less VAT, of supplies of electronic services for the relevant reporting period and the total amount of the corresponding VAT;
- the applicable VAT rates, and the total VAT due.

The VAT return must be made in euros, unless a Member State has not adopted the euro in which case it may require the return to be made in its national currency (Art. 26c(B)(6)). The VAT due is required to be paid on submission of the VAT return (Art. 26c(B)(7)). The non-established taxable person is required to keep records to enable the tax administration of the Member State of consumption to determine that the amount of VAT due is correct (Art. 26c(B)(9)). The records must be maintained for a period of ten years from the end of the year in which the transaction was carried out (Art. 26c(B)(9)).

In appropriate circumstances a non-established taxable person will be entitled to a refund of VAT incurred in making the supply of the services. The refund is made in accordance with Council Dir. 86/560 (the 'Thirteenth Directive') (Art. 26c(B)(8)). The Thirteenth Directive as discussed below relates to the harmonization of the laws of Member States relating to turnover taxes, and arrangements for the refund of VAT to taxable persons not established in the EC.

IV. Supplies of goods and services outside the EC

1. Goods. 1. The export of goods out of the EC is not subject to VAT. The Sixth Directive provides for various categories of supply of goods that are exempt from VAT, although Member States are required to impose conditions for the purposes of preventing evasion, avoidance, or abuse (Art. 15). The categories include:

(*a*) the supply of goods dispatched or transported to a destination outside the EC by or on behalf of the vendor;
(*b*) the supply of goods dispatched or transported to a destination outside the EC by or on behalf of the purchaser not established within a Member State;
(*c*) the supply of goods for the fuelling and provisioning of vessels used for navigation on the high seas and carrying passengers for reward or used for the purpose of commercial, industrial, or fishing activities;
(*d*) the supply, modification, repair, maintenance, chartering, and hiring of aircraft used by airlines operating for reward chiefly on international routes, and the supply, hiring, repair, and maintenance of equipment incorporated or used therein;
(*e*) supplies of goods and services under diplomatic and consular arrangements;
(*f*) supplies of gold to Central Banks.

2. A taxable person is entitled to a right of deduction in relation to VAT paid in respect of goods or services used for the purposes of transactions relating to the export of goods (Art. 17(3)(b)).

2. Services. 1. Where the supply of services is to a person outside the EC the place of supply rules will determine whether VAT is chargeable. If the place of supply is outside the EC no VAT is chargeable. The place of supply rules are summarized in the table shown in section I above.

2. A taxable person is entitled to a right of deduction in relation to VAT in respect of goods or services used for the purposes of transactions relating to insurance and reinsurance transactions, granting and negotiation of credit, the negotiation of or any dealings in credit guarantees, payments, transfers, debts, cheques, negotiation concerning currency, transactions in shares, interests in companies, and debentures, provided the customer is established outside the EC, or when such transactions are directly linked with goods to be exported to a country outside the EC (Art. 17(3)(c)).

V. Refund of VAT

1. Council Dir. 79/1072 of 6 December 1979 (the 'Eighth Directive') provides for arrangements relating to the refund of VAT to taxable persons not established in the territory of a Member State (*OJ* 1979 L331/11). If such a person were established in a Member State he would be required to account for VAT in accordance with that Member State's domestic law (see section I above). The Eighth Directive enables a taxable person in a Member State to obtain a refund in respect of VAT incurred in another Member State, which

the taxable person would not otherwise be able to obtain as an input tax deduction in his own Member State, for example, if the goods or services are also used in the Member State in which they are acquired. A Member State is required to refund to any 'taxable person who is not established in the territory of the country but who is established in another Member State' any VAT charged in respect of (*a*) services or movable property supplied to the taxable person by other taxable persons within that EC Member State, or (*b*) the importation of goods into that Member State, provided that such goods and services are used for the purposes of (*i*) transactions relating to economic activities carried out in another country which would be deductible if they had been performed within that country; (*ii*) transactions related to imports, exports, and international goods traffic; (*iii*) the provision of services in cases where the VAT on the supply is payable solely by the person to whom they are supplied (i.e. services subject to Art. 9(2)(e) and the reverse charge provisions: see table in section I above) (Art. 2). The term 'a taxable person not established in the territory of the country' means a person carrying out an economic activity within the meaning of the Sixth Directive, and who for the period to which the claim relates: 'has had in the Member State neither the seat of his economic activity, nor a fixed establishment from which business transactions are effected, nor if no such seat or fixed establishment exists, his domicile or normal place of residence, and who, during the same period, has supplied no goods or services deemed to have been supplied in that country [with the exception of transport services carried out in connection with the international carriage of goods, or services subject to Art. 9(2)(e) and the reverse charge provisions]' (Art. 1). To qualify for a refund it is necessary to submit an application, which complies with various formalities, to the tax authority in the relevant Member State (Arts. 3 and 4). However, a VAT refund is only available to the extent that a credit for such VAT would be allowed to a taxable person in the relevant Member State (Art. 5).

2. Council Dir. 86/560 of 17 November 1986 (the 'Thirteenth Directive') provides for arrangements relating to the refund of VAT to taxable persons not established in the EC (*OJ* 1986 L326/40). The term 'a taxable person not established in the territory of the [EC]' means a taxable person carrying out an economic activity within the meaning of the Sixth Directive, and who for the period to which the claim relates: 'has had in that territory neither his business nor a fixed establishment from which business transactions are effected, nor if no such business or fixed establishment exists, his permanent address or usual place of residence, and who, during the same period, has supplied no goods or services deemed to have been supplied in the [relevant] Member State' with the exception of transport services carried out in connection with the international carriage of goods, or services subject Art. 9(2)(e) and the reverse charge provisions (Art. 1(1)).

The Thirteenth Directive imposes an obligation on Member States to refund to any taxable person not established in the EC any VAT charged in respect of services rendered or movable property supplied to him in the territory or the country by other taxable persons or charged in respect of the importation of goods into the country, in so far as such goods and services are used for the purposes of (*i*) transactions relating to economic activities carried out in another country that would be deductible if they had been performed within that country; (*ii*) transactions related to imports, exports, and international goods traffic; (*iii*) the provision of services in cases where the VAT on the supply is payable solely by the person to whom they are supplied (i.e. services subject to Art. 9(2)(e) and the reverse charge provisions: see table in section I above) (Art. 2). Certain administrative arrangements must be complied with in order to qualify for a refund (Art. 3). The refund of VAT by a Member State cannot be granted under conditions more favourable than those applied to EC taxable persons (Art. 3).

***See also* Direct taxation, Excise duties and similar taxes, Tax harmonization.**

Further reading 1. BOOKS: Terra and Kajus, *Guide to European VAT Directives* (looseleaf); Farmer and Lyal, *EC Tax Law*, 2nd edn. (expected 2005); Terra and Wattel, *European Tax Law* (2002); De Voil, *Indirect Tax Service* (looseleaf).

2. OFFICIAL PUBLICATIONS: European Commission web site relating to VAT: http://europa.eu.int/comm/taxation–customs/taxation/vatindex–en.htm

European Commission, *Tax policy in the European Union—Priorities for the years ahead* (COM(2001) 260); id., *First report on the application of the common system of value added tax* (COM(1983) 426).

▶ **VOCATIONAL TRAINING *see* FREE MOVEMENT OF PERSONS**

W

WORKER One of three categories of persons for whom the original EEC Treaty and Title III of Part Three of the present EC Treaty guarantee freedom of movement within the Community (the other two categories being self-employed persons and persons providing or receiving services).

While Art. 39(1) EC expressly secures freedom of movement for 'workers', and Art. 1(1) of implementing Reg. 1612/68 (*OJ Sp. Edn.* 1968 (II), p. 475) refers to the right to take up an activity as an 'employed person', these concepts are not defined in primary or secondary Community law (except for the purposes of social security, see Art. 1(a) of Reg. 1408/71, *OJ Sp. Edn.* 1971 (II), p. 416, as amended; *see further under* **Social security**). In fact, the ECJ has pointed out that there is no single definition of worker in Community law: it varies according to the area in which the definition is to be applied. Thus, the definition of worker used in the context of Art. 39 EC and Reg. 1612/68 does not necessarily coincide with the definition applied in relation to Art. 42 EC and Reg. 1408/71 in the context of social security (Case C-85/96 *Martinez Sala* [1998] ECR I-2691 at p. I-2719). Even within Reg. 1612/68 itself, the concept of worker, as interpreted in the Court's case-law, is not used in a uniform manner. While in certain provisions of the regulation (Title II of Part I) this term covers only persons who have already entered the employment market in the host Member State, in other parts it covers persons who have not yet entered into an employment relationship in the host Member State but are looking for work there (Case C-138/02 *Collins* [2004] ECR I-0000, paras. 30–3; see further below).

Nevertheless, it is clear from the Court's case-law that the terms 'worker' and 'employed person' may not be defined by reference to the national laws of the Member States but have a specific Community meaning for the purposes of Art. 39. Otherwise, the Community rules on the free movement of workers would be ineffective as the meaning of those terms could be determined and modified unilaterally by national laws, without any control by the Community institutions. This could lead to the exclusion of certain categories of persons from the benefits and protection provided by Community law. The meaning and the scope of those concepts must therefore be defined in the light of the principles of the legal order of the Community. Moreover, since those concepts determine the field of application of one of the fundamental freedoms guaranteed by the Treaty, they may not be interpreted restrictively but must be given the broadest possible meaning (Case 75/63 *Hoekstra* [1964] ECR 177 at p. 184; Case 53/81 *Levin* [1982] ECR 1035 at pp. 1048–9; Case 139/85 *Kempf* [1986] ECR 1741 at pp. 1750–1; see also the cases cited below).

In accordance with these general considerations, the Court has stated that the concept of 'worker' or 'employed person' must be defined according to 'objective criteria which distinguish the employment relationship by reference to the rights and duties of the persons concerned'. The essential feature of an employment relationship is, the Court has said, that 'for a certain period of time a person performs services for and under the direction of another person in return for which he receives remuneration' (Case 66/85

Lawrie-Blum [1986] ECR 2121 at p. 2144). Thus, there are three criteria which must all be fulfilled for a person to be considered a worker: he must provide a service of some economic value; he must be under the direction of another person; and he must receive remuneration for the service provided (ibid.). Moreover, within the framework of the employment relationship thus defined, the worker must carry on an activity that is effective and genuine, to the exclusion of activities on such a small scale as to be regarded as purely marginal and ancillary. This is because the provisions of Title III of Part Three of the Treaty 'guarantee only the free movement of persons who pursue or are desirous of pursuing an economic activity' (Case 53/81 *Levin*, above, at p. 1050). Community law does not impose any additional conditions for a person to be classifiable as a worker, and the Member States cannot unilaterally add any (Case 197/86 *Brown* [1988] ECR 3205 at p. 3244).

Once the employment relationship has ended, the person concerned as a rule loses his status of worker, although that status may produce certain effects even after the termination of the contract of employment. Thus, workers are guaranteed certain rights linked to their status as such, even when they are no longer in an employment relationship (Case C-85/96 *Martinez Sala*, above, at p. I-2719; Case C-35/97 *Commission* v. *France* [1998] ECR I-5325 at p. I-5352).

By applying the various criteria of the above definition liberally, the Court has developed a broad Community concept of worker, thereby considerably extending the category of persons who are entitled to benefit from the right to free movement and related rights guaranteed by Art. 39 EC. Thus, the Court has confirmed that, provided that the essential elements of an employment relationship are present and that the work is effective and genuine, the concept of 'worker' includes the following persons:

- non-manual workers (Case 61/65 *Vaassen* [1966] ECR 261 at p. 276);
- permanent, temporary, frontier, and seasonal workers and workers who pursue their activities for the purpose of providing services (fourth recital in the preamble to Reg. 1612/68; Case C-106/91 *Ramrath* [1992] ECR I-3351 at p. I-3383; Case C-57/96 *Meints* [1997] ECR I-6689 at p. I-6721; Case C-35/97 *Commission* v. *France*, above, at p. I-5352. For the taxation of frontier workers, see Case C-336/96 *Gilly* [1998] ECR I-2793). The concepts of 'frontier worker' and 'seasonal worker' are defined, for the purposes of social security, in Art. 1(b) and (c) of Reg. 1408/71, respectively. In addition, Art. 8(1)(b) of Dir. 68/360 (*OJ Sp. Edn.* 1968 (II), p. 485) defines 'frontier worker' as 'a worker who, while having his residence in the territory of a Member State to which he returns as a rule, each day or at least once a week, is employed in the territory of another Member State';
- persons who have worked only for a short period (e.g. two and a half months in two and a half years) in the host Member State, the circumstances preceding and following the period of employment

being irrelevant (Case C-413/01 *Ninni-Orasche* [2003] ECR I-0000, paras. 25–32);

- part-time workers irrespective of the level of their remuneration and even if it is lower than the minimum means of subsistence, it being irrelevant whether they are satisfied with such low remuneration or wish to supplement it with other lawful income, again it being irrelevant whether the latter is derived from property, from the employment of a member of their family, or from financial assistance payable out of the public funds of the host Member State (Case 53/81 *Levin*, above, at pp. 1049–51; Case 139/85 *Kempf*, above, at pp. 1750–1);
- trainee teachers and students undergoing occupational or vocational training, even if they work only a small number of hours per week and consequently receive limited remuneration, provided that they have completed a sufficient number of hours in order to familiarize themselves with the work (Case 66/85 *Lawrie-Blum*, above, at pp. 2144–5; Case C-27/91 *Le Manoir* [1991] ECR I-5531 at p. I-5541; Case C-3/90 *Bernini* [1992] ECR I-1071 at pp. I-1104–5);
- workers employed under an 'on-call contract' usually involving a small amount of work per day or per week, although in assessing the effective and genuine nature of the activity in question, the national court may take account of the irregular nature and limited duration of the work actually performed and of the fact that the person must remain available to work if called upon to do so by the employer (Case C-357/89 *Raulin* [1992] ECR I-1027 at pp. I-1059–60);
- persons whose remuneration is calculated on a collective basis, e.g. fishermen who are paid a share of the proceeds of the sale of their catches (Case C-3/87 *Agegate* [1989] ECR 4459 at p. 4505);
- members of a religious community who work within and on behalf of the community in connection with its commercial activities and whose material needs, including pocket-money, are in return provided for by the community irrespective of the nature and the extent of the work (Case 196/87 *Steymann* [1988] ECR 6159 at pp. 6172–3);
- civil servants and other persons whose status is governed by public law, European Community law, or even public international law (e.g. EC officials, employees of an international organization, such as the European Space Agency, whose status is governed by international agreements), since the nature of the legal relationship between employee and employer, whether involving public law status or a private law contract, is immaterial (Case 66/85 *Lawrie-Blum*, above, at p. 2145; Cases 389/87 etc. *Echternach and Moritz* [1989] ECR 723 at pp. 759–60; Case C-71/93 *Van Poucke* [1994] ECR I-1101 at p. I-1117; Case C-411/98 *Ferlini* [2000] ECR I-8081 at pp. I-8139–40). Nevertheless, officials of the European Communities are subject to special rules in matters of taxation that distinguish them from other workers (Case C-209/01 *Schilling* [2003] ECR I-0000, paras. 28–9);

- persons pursuing economic activities partially or temporarily outside the territory of the Community, as well as persons permanently employed on board a ship flying the flag of another Member State, provided that in both situations the legal relationship of employment can be located within the territory of the Community or retains a sufficiently close link with it (Case 9/88 *Lopes da Veiga* [1989] ECR 2989 at pp. 3009–10);
- professional sportsmen employed by a sports club for remuneration under a contract of employment (Case C-176/96 *Lehtonen and Castors Braine* [2000] ECR I-2681 at pp. I-2731–2);
- persons seeking employment in another Member State (Case C-292/89 *Antonissen* [1991] ECR I-745 at p. I-777). However, such persons qualify as 'workers' only for the purposes of access to employment in accordance with Art. 39 EC and Arts. 2 and 5 of Reg. 1612/68, but not for the purposes of Title II of Part I of that regulation, which deals, *inter alia*, with social and tax advantages and covers only persons who have already entered the employment market in the host Member Sate (Case 316/85 *Lebon* [1987] ECR 2811 at p. 2839; Case C-278/94 *Commission* v. *Belgium* [1996] ECR I-4307 at pp. I-4342–3; Case C-138/02 *Collins*, above, paras. 30–3. *See further under* **Social advantage**).

On the other hand, the Court has held that the following persons do not qualify as 'workers' for the purposes of Community law:

- a person who, because of his drug addiction, is employed in a rehabilitation centre. Although the essential features of an employment relationship may be present (the person performs some work under the direction of another person in return for which he receives remuneration), the activity cannot be regarded as an effective and genuine economic activity since it constitutes merely a means of rehabilitation and reintegration and is adapted to the physical and mental capabilities of the person concerned who is unable to take up employment under normal conditions (Case 344/87 *Bettray* [1989] ECR 1621 at pp. 1645–6);
- the director of a company of which he is the sole shareholder. Since such a person is not carrying out his activity in the context of a relationship of sub-ordination, he is not a worker but a self-employed person within the meaning of Art. 43 (Case C-107/94 *Asscher* [1996] ECR I-3089 at p. I-3121). Nevertheless, the spouse of such a person who is employed by the same company may still qualify as a worker if she is acting in the context of a relationship of sub-ordination within the organization of the company (Case C-337/97 *Meeusen* [1999] ECR I-3289 at p. I-3311);
- a person who has stopped working and is not seeking employment (Case C-389/99 *Rundgren* [2001] ECR I-3731 at pp. I-3776–7). Although such a person continues to be entitled to certain advantages acquired during his former employment relationship (e.g. right to a

pension), he cannot acquire new rights having no links with his former occupation (Case C-43/99 *Leclere and Deaconescu* [2001] ECR I-4265 at pp. I-4314–15).

See also **Free movement of persons, Social advantage, Social security.**

Further reading: *See under* **Free movement of persons.**

► **WORLD TRADE ORGANIZATION (WTO)** ***see*** **COMMON CUSTOMS TARIFF, CUSTOMS UNION,** ***and*** **CUSTOMS VALUE**

INDEX

A

B

E

F

M

O

P

S

W

Printed and bound by CPI Group (UK) Ltd, Croydon, CR0 4YY